9/06

Frommer's®

India

2nd Edition

by Pippa de Bruyn, Niloufer Venkatraman
& Dr. Keith Bain

D0448489

Here's what the critics say about Frommer's:

"Amazingly easy to use. Very portable, very complete."
—*Booklist*

"Detailed, accurate, and easy-to-read information for all price ranges."
—*Glamour Magazine*

"Hotel information is close to encyclopedic."
—*Des Moines Sunday Register*

"Frommer's Guides have a way of giving you a real feel for a place."
—*Knight Ridder Newspapers*

WILEY

Wiley Publishing, Inc.

About the Authors

Pippa de Bruyn is an award-winning journalist, travel writer (author of *Frommer's South Africa*), and freelance editor. **Niloufer Venkatraman** has a doctoral degree in anthropology from Temple University in Philadelphia. She has traveled widely since the age of 9, and has always been as awed by other places and cultures as her own. A resident of her native Mumbai, she has worked as lecturer in sociology and anthropology, giving up the bureaucratic Indian academic scene in 2001 to turn her attention to working as a freelance writer and editor. **Dr. Keith Bain** has a doctoral degree in cinema. When he's not traveling the world in search of fantastic experiences, he spends his time writing and lecturing about film, media, theater, and contemporary culture.

Published by:

Wiley Publishing, Inc.

111 River St.
Hoboken, NJ 07030-5774

ISBN-13: 978-0-7645-9899-9
ISBN-10: 0-7645-9899-6

Editor: Alexis Lipsitz Flippin
Production Editor: Ian Skinnari
Cartographer: Andrew Murphy
Photo Editor: Richard Fox
Production by Wiley Indianapolis Composition Services

For information on our other products and services or to obtain technical support, please contact our Customer Care Department within the U.S. at 800/762-2974, outside the U.S. at 317/572-3993 or fax 317/572-4002.

Wiley also publishes its books in a variety of electronic formats. Some content that appears in print may not be available in electronic formats.

Manufactured in the United States of America

5   4   3   2   1

Contents

9 The Heart of India: Delhi, the Taj, Uttar Pradesh & Madhya Pradesh   285

10 Rajasthan: Land of Princes   371

11 Himachal Pradesh: On Top of the World   459

12 Uttaranchal: Sacred Source of the Ganges 502

13 Kolkata (Calcutta) & East India 520

Appendix: India in Depth 558

Index 581

List of Maps

Acknowledgments

Fact-checking for this update would not have been possible without many painstaking hours put in by **Munira Rampurawala.** Sincerest thanks also to several individuals who assisted and contributed to updating sections of this book in varying degrees; they are: **Abhishek Madhukar** (Kerala, Rajasthan, and Varanasi), **Munira Rampurawala** (Goa and Kumaon), **Jayati Vora** (dining and nightlife in Mumbai), **Yasmin Menon** (Chennai and Bangalore), and **André Morris** (Amritsar and Dharamsala).

An Invitation to the Reader

In researching this book, we discovered many wonderful places—hotels, restaurants, shops, and more. We're sure you'll find others. Please tell us about them, so we can share the information with your fellow travelers in upcoming editions. If you were disappointed with a recommendation, we'd love to know that, too. Please write to:

Frommer's India, 2nd Edition
Wiley Publishing, Inc. • 111 River St. • Hoboken, NJ 07030-5774

An Additional Note

Please be advised that travel information is subject to change at any time—and this is especially true of prices. We therefore suggest that you write or call ahead for confirmation when making your travel plans. The authors, editors, and publisher cannot be held responsible for the experiences of readers while traveling. Your safety is important to us, however, so we encourage you to stay alert and be aware of your surroundings. Keep a close eye on cameras, purses, and wallets, all favorite targets of thieves and pickpockets.

Frommer's Star Ratings, Icons & Abbreviations

Every hotel, restaurant, and attraction listing in this guide has been ranked for quality, value, service, amenities, and special features using a **star-rating system.** In country, state, and regional guides, we also rate towns and regions to help you narrow down your choices and budget your time accordingly. Hotels and restaurants are rated on a scale of zero (recommended) to three stars (exceptional). Attractions, shopping, nightlife, towns, and regions are rated according to the following scale: zero stars (recommended), one star (highly recommended), two stars (very highly recommended), and three stars (must-see).

In addition to the star-rating system, we also use **seven feature icons** that point you to the great deals, in-the-know advice, and unique experiences that separate travelers from tourists. Throughout the book, look for:

Finds	Special finds—those places only insiders know about
Fun Fact	Fun facts—details that make travelers more informed and their trips more fun
Kids	Best bets for kids and advice for the whole family
Moments	Special moments—those experiences that memories are made of
Overrated	Places or experiences not worth your time or money
Tips	Insider tips—great ways to save time and money
Value	Great values—where to get the best deals

The following **abbreviations** are used for credit cards:

AE	American Express	DISC	Discover	V	Visa
DC	Diners Club	MC	MasterCard		

Frommers.com

Now that you have the guidebook to a great trip, visit our website at **www.frommers.com** for travel information on more than 3,000 destinations. With features updated regularly, we give you instant access to the most current trip-planning information available. At Frommers.com, you'll also find the best prices on airfares, accommodations, and car rentals—and you can even book travel online through our travel booking partners. At Frommers.com, you'll also find the following:

- Online updates to our most popular guidebooks
- Vacation sweepstakes and contest giveaways
- Newsletter highlighting the hottest travel trends
- Online travel message boards with featured travel discussions

What's New in India

With a booming economy and greatly improved relations with neighboring Pakistan, India's overseas tourism sector saw a **20% growth** in 2004, finally crossing the 3-million-visitor mark. Indeed, if you're planning a repeat visit to India, you can't help but notice the changes wrought by the country's growing affluence, from massive billboards advertising the latest luxury goods and new (smooth!) state highways to the rapidly expanding choices in classy restaurants and chic hotels, aimed as much at the burgeoning domestic market as the overseas sector. But you will see little change on the urban street corners, where beggars still beseech you for handouts, or in rural areas, where grinding poverty continues to plague the vast majority of the population, and at principal tourist destinations, where touts try every trick to part you and your dollar. To this end we have added a few more tips on how to avoid becoming a victim in chapter 2 (and we've included more advice on how to avoid getting ripped off in each chapter). Chapter 2 also offers a range of brand-new tips and strategies to help ease your journey through India, including information on how to book a train ticket without problems, how to rent a chauffeured car, and how to hire the services of a travel agent if you need one (and India is one destination where you likely will benefit from a travel agent's expertise at some stage).

An interesting phenomenon further fueling India's current popularity is what is commonly referred to as **"medical tourism."** For the longest time this meant a week rejuvenating at one of Kerala's Ayurvedic refuges, but the term now includes travel to India in search of relatively low-cost, world-class medical treatment of visitors with heart conditions, cataracts, and orthopedic problems. You may have heard about the well-publicized case of 14-year-old U.K. resident Elliot Knott, who came to India in 2005 for complex spine surgery because the NHS had asked him to wait 17 weeks to see a consultant and 9 months for surgery! However, we figure that most of you are still coming to India simply to de-stress and revitalize yourselves physically and spiritually. To this end we have increased the amount of information in our section, "Discovering Spiritual India," in chapter 2. So whether you're looking to learn more about yoga or meditation or are ready to commit to an ashram, we've provided comprehensive suggestions (and cautions). Kerala, of course, remains the haven for **Ayurvedic treatments,** and never more so than now. **Eco-conscious tourism** is also emerging as a travel choice in the region, with retreats like **Friday's Place** and **Malabar House** making steps in this direction. We have also focused outside Kerala on accommodations that offer more than a bed; these include **Ranjit's Svaasa** in Amritsar, and an overview of the options in Bangalore, where you can choose between pampering in a super-luxury spa or detoxing in an organic healing treatment center.

Thankfully, the one area that has seen relatively little change in the last 2 years is **prices:** In spite of skyrocketing oil costs, levels of inflation in India remain—at least for now—relatively low. Although there has been an upward revision of hotel rates (and yes, a handful that actually doubled), hotel room rates have generally increased only marginally, with most mid-range and budget options barely adding a few hundred rupees. Combined with the introduction of a slew of low-cost airlines in the past few years, this will no doubt further ensure that India continues to be a highly affordable destination.

Of course, if watching your rupees is not a priority, you will be delighted to know that Aman Resorts, the first word in luxury lodging, has entered India's top-end fray with two new properties: **Aman-i-Khás** at Ranthambhore National Park, Rajasthan, is a stylish tented wilderness camp that operates from October to April; while **Amanbagh,** also in Rajasthan (within striking distance of the city of Jaipur), is a luxurious pink-sandstone resort in a fabulous oasis in the middle of the desert. Both bring Aman's style of sophisticated indulgence to the continuously expanding possibilities of upmarket accommodations in India.

But upmarket additions aren't all you'll find added to this second edition. Travelers on a budget will find new **mid-range and budget accommodations** in every chapter, while those who prefer a more personal immersion in the culture of your destination will enjoy the expanded **homestay** options, the best of which is **Tranquil** in northern Kerala. If it's tranquillity you're after, we've included several new boutique hotels in Goa. Although this small state is still the hippest on the subcontinent, it is at times unbearably busy, so places like **Presa di Goa, Panchavatti,** and **Casa Britona** offer a serene environment far from the madding crowds—perfect places in which to unwind, and great value too, of course. Having rejuvenated in paradise,

we recommend an extended trip to Karnataka: To this end we've added a section on the magnificent ruins of **Badami, Aihole,** and **Pattadakal** and a trip to **Bijapur**—all within striking distance of the more popular Hampi.

Moving north, we were saddened to find **Lake Pichola** in Udaipur still, at press time, bone-dry—the result of a prolonged drought and unbridled construction in the outlying catchment areas; our fingers are crossed in the hope that a really good monsoon will restore the lake's placid beauty. But the still-extant beauty of Udaipur's palaces and outlying rural excursions means that, the state of the lake aside, this remains one of the best destinations in northern India. Just make sure that your hotel choice isn't based on a lake view, unless, of course, you've ascertained that the hoped-for waters have returned.

If you simply must have your lakes filled with water, make time to explore the **Kumaon Himalayas** in Uttaranchal. Known as India's lake district, Kumaon is much more accessible from Delhi than Himachal Pradesh, and relatively untouched areas like Binsar and Naukuchiatal are perfect for a quiet sojourn, especially for those for whom time is a premium. This is why we've expanded the accommodations options here, almost all of which are away from the heavy tourist belts. New accommodations listed in the hills are often family-run and friendly, and offer guests intimate experiences in a homestay setting or on a well-run estate, with personalized hospitality, atmospheric experiences, and a chance to mingle with the Indian families who live in the hills.

India is a **culinary paradise.** This edition has seen a host of local writers researching new ways for visitors to experience all aspects of the cuisine—safely. We have provided literally dozens of new spots at which to sample the myriad cuisines of India, many of them alongside locals in unpretentious street outlets. Generally acknowledged as India's best city for dining, the chapter on **Mumbai** enjoys an expanded "Where to Dine" section in this guide. In spite of Mumbai's fantastic seaside location, places that exploit the lovely views are few in existence; here we explore the best opportunities for enjoying superb views of Mumbai's bay and harbor. We also offer a fully revised section detailing Mumbai's happening **nightlife,** with something to excite every kind of night owl. Nightlife segments in Delhi and Bangalore have also been expanded for party animals wanting to immerse yourselves in modern India. And new **shopping** options in Pondicherry, Chennai, Goa, and Mumbai may leave the shopaholics among you wishing for more baggage allowance. Furthermore, this edition includes **new maps** to assist you in exploring this fascinating country. Happy holidays.

1

The Best of India

India will humble, awe, frustrate, amaze, and intimidate you—all on the same day. Home to some of the world's most spectacular medieval structures and largest slums; sacred rivers and filth-strewn streets; deeply religious ritual and endless traffic jams; aristocratic tigers and low-caste untouchables; jewel-encrusted tombs and pavement-bound beggars; ancient traditions and modern-day scams—there is so much to take in. Whether you're here to soak up India's spirituality, chill out on the beaches, rejuvenate at an Ayurvedic spa, or live like a king in the land of princes, this chapter will help you experience the very best India has to offer.

1 Experiencing Spiritual India

Visiting temples that pulsate with devotion will evoke a sense of the sacred, but in India, where religion is such an integral part of daily life, spiritual experiences occur when you least expect them.

- **See Things As It Really Are** (Vipassana Centers throughout India): Maintaining a strict code of silence with no sensory stimulation for 10 days may sound like a self-induced hell, but after attending a 10-day Vipassana meditation course, most people claim transformation and find the mental training invaluable. And it costs nothing. See chapter 2.

- **Hop on a Motorbike and Head for the Drumbeat** (Goa): Once capital of the global beach party, Goa may be past its prime, but when rumors start that an event is in the making at a to-be-announced venue, keep your ear to the ground. Why? Because only in some deserted clearing near a golden Goan beach can you trance out with the nationals of the world, and find solace in the serenity of a rural villager's smile as she hands over cups of

soothing *chai* for the duration of the party. See chapter 5.

- **Worship the Sunrise as It Touches the Southernmost Tip** (Kanyakumari, Tamil Nadu): You can't help but be moved by a sense of the miraculous when a simple daily occurrence is venerated by thousands of pilgrims who plunge themselves into the turbulent swell, believing that the tri-oceanic waters at India's southernmost tip are holy, while others delight in the glorious spectacle as if it's a major Bollywood (the nickname for India's booming film industry) premiere. See chapter 6.

- **Lose All Sense of Reality in the City of Light** (Varanasi, Uttar Pradesh): Drifting at dawn on a boat on the Ganges along Varanasi's bathing *ghats* (steps leading down to the river), against a backdrop of 18th- and 19th-century temples and palaces, you will witness surreal sights—hundreds of pilgrims waist-deep in the Ganges cleansing their souls in its holy waters, while others pound laundry, meditate by staring into the sun, or limber up to wrestle. All the while, bodies burn on the sacred banks, thereby achieving *moksha*—liberation from the eternal cycle of rebirth. See chapter 9.

- **Purchase a Pushkar Passport** (Pushkar, Rajasthan): As you wander around the ghats of Pushkar, the beautifully serene temple town on the edge of the Thar Desert, you will almost certainly be approached by a Brahmin priest to offer *puja* (prayers) at the sacred lake. In exchange for a "donation," he will tie a red thread around your wrist—the "passport" you can brandish at the next priest who approaches. This is the commercial side of India's spirituality, and one you need to be aware of. See chapter 10.

- **Make a Wish at the Tomb of a Sufi Saint** (Ajmer, Rajasthan): The great Sufi saint Khwaja Moin-ud-Din Chisti was known as "the protector of the poor," and his tomb is said to possess the power to grant the wishes of all those who visit. His Dargah Sharif is the most sacred Islamic shrine in India, second in importance only to Mecca but frequented by Hindus and Muslims alike. The atmosphere of pure devotion is both ancient and surreal; some pray fervently, and others tie threads onto the latticework while supplicating the saint to fulfill their wish, while throughout these activities, the *qawwali* singers seated in front of the tomb repeat the same beautiful, haunting melodies that have been sung for centuries. See chapter 10.

- **Carry the Holy *Granth Sahib* to its Evening Resting Place** (Amritsar, Punjab): In Sikh temples, the *Granth Sahib*—Holy Book of the Sikhs—is an object of devotion in its own right, and nowhere is this more evocative than at the Golden Temple, the most tangibly spiritual destination in the country. In the evenings men line up to carry the precious *Granth Sahib* from its golden sanctuary at the center of the Amrit Sarovar (Pool of Nectar), crossing **Guru's Bridge,** which symbolizes the journey of the soul after death, to **Akal Takht,** where the Holy Book rests for the night. You can take part in this ceremony by joining the line that forms behind and ahead of the heavy palanquin. Being part of this ancient tradition is a deeply moving experience and indicative of the embracing atmosphere you'll find in Sikh temples throughout India. See chapter 11.

- **Look into the Eyes of the Dalai Lama** (Dharamsala, Himachal Pradesh): There's a good chance you'll meet the Dalai Lama in person if you visit Dharamsala, home to the exiled Tibetan government, which fled its homeland in 1959. Arranging a private audience isn't easy (unless you're Richard Gere), but if you attend one of his public appearances, you will—like everyone else in the audience—receive a personal blessing. And whatever your convictions, when you look into the eyes of His Holiness, you know you are in the presence of pure energy. See chapter 11.

- **Witness a Thousand Prayers Take Flight on the Wind** (Leh, Ladakh): Take the overland journey from Manali to Leh and enter the stark world of the Trans-Himalayas—a breathtakingly beautiful yet desolate lunarlike landscape, with arid peaks and ancient Buddhist monasteries perched on rocky crags. Here prayer flags flutter against an impossibly blue sky, sending their silent prayers to the heavens. See chapter 11.

2 The Best Temples, Monuments & Lost Cities

- **Cave Temples at Ajanta & Ellora** (Aurangabad, Maharashtra): Fashioned out of rock by little more than simple hand-held tools, the cave temples at Ajanta (created by Buddhist monks between the 2nd and 7th c.) and Ellora (a marriage of Buddhist, Hindu, and Jain temples, created between the 4th and 9th c.) are the finest examples of rock-cut architecture in India, and deserving of their World Heritage status. The zenith is **Kailashnath Temple,** effectively a mountain whittled down to a free-standing temple. See "Aurangabad & the Ellora and Ajanta Caves" in chapter 4.

- **Lord Gomateswara Monolith** (Sravanabelagola, Karnataka): One of the oldest (ca. A.D. 918) and most important Jain pilgrimage sites, this 18m (60-ft.) statue of the naked Lord Gomateswara—a representation of Bahubali, son of the first Jain *tirthankara,* said to have sought enlightenment by standing naked and motionless for an entire year—is the tallest monolithic statue on Earth. See "Exploring the Hoysala Heartland: Belur, Halebid & Sravanabelagola" in chapter 8.

- **Hampi** (Karnataka): Scattered among the Henri Moore–like boulders in the heart of Karnataka's rural interior, Hampi was once the royal seat of the powerful Vijayanagar kingdom, its size and wealth drawing comparisons with imperial Rome. Today, the city has crumbled away to a few starkly beautiful leftovers, but the remote setting couldn't be more romantic. See "Hampi & the Ruined City of Vijayanagar" in chapter 8.

- **The Temples of Mamallapuram** (Tamil Nadu): A visit to this once-thriving port city of the Pallava dynasty, who ruled much of South India between the 4th and 9th centuries A.D., is an essential stop on Tamil Nadu's temple tour. The earliest examples of monumental architecture in southern India (the celebrated **Arjuna's Penance** is the largest relief-carving on earth), these rock-cut shrines are best explored in the morning, leaving you time to unwind on the pleasant beach and dine on succulent seafood at village cafes for a song. See "Mamallapuram (Mahabalipurum)" in chapter 7.

- **Shri Meenakshi-Sundareshwarar Temple** (Madurai, Tamil Nadu): Alive with prayers, processions, garland-makers, and joyous devotees who celebrate the mythological romance between the beautiful three-breasted goddess and her mighty Lord Shiva, this colorful and lively complex of shrines, halls, and market stalls is almost Disneyesque, marked as it is by numerous entrance towers tangled with colorful stucco gods, demons, beasts, and mythological heroes. It truly embodies the spirit of Tamil Nadu's deeply embedded temple culture. See "Madurai" in chapter 7.

- **Taj Mahal** (Agra, Uttar Pradesh): Nothing can prepare you for the beauty of the Taj. The perfect symmetry, the ethereal luminescence, the wonderful proportions, the sheer scale—virtually impossible to imagine from staring at its oft-reproduced image—and the exquisite detailing make this bejeweled monument to love a justifiable wonder of the world. See "Agra" in chapter 9.

- **Fatehpur Sikri** (near Agra, Uttar Pradesh): From the intricacy of the glittering white marble screens that surround the *dargah* (tomb) of Salim Chisti, to Parcheesi Court, where the emperor played a ludo-like game using the ladies of his harem as live pieces, this magnificent ghost city—built almost entirely from red sandstone in 1571 and deserted only 14 years later—is a testament to the secular vision of Akbar, one of the great players in India's most dynamic dynasty. See "Agra" in chapter 9.

- **The Temples of Khajuraho** (Khajuraho, Madhya Pradesh): Built between the 10th and 12th centuries by the Chandela Rajputs, these World Heritage Site monuments are most famous for the erotic sculptures that writhe across the interiors and exteriors. But even the temple designs—their soaring *shikharas* (spires) serving as metaphoric "stairways to heaven"—are striking, and are considered the apotheosis of medieval Hindu architecture. See "Khajuraho" in chapter 9.

- **Mehrangarh Fort** (Jodhpur, Rajasthan): The impenetrable walls of this 15th-century edifice to Rajput valor rise seamlessly from the rocky outcrop on which they were built, literally dwarfing the labyrinthine city at its base; from its crenelated ramparts you enjoy postcard views of the "Blue City" below. In the distance is the grand silhouette of Umaid Bhawan Palace, heritage hotel and residence of the current Maharaja. Within the fort is one of the best palace museums in India. See "Jodhpur" in chapter 10.

- **Jain Temples of Rajasthan & Gujarat** (Ranakpur and Mount Abu, near Udaipur, Rajasthan, and Palitana, Gujarat): The Jains put all their devotional passion (and not inconsiderable wealth) into the creation of the most ornate marble temples; with exquisitely detailed relief carvings covering every inch, they are all jaw-droppingly beautiful. Make sure you visit at least one while you're in India, preferably either Ranakpur Temple or Dilwara Temple in Rajasthan. Or head for Palitana, in Gujarat, where 850 Jain temples and 1,000 shrines top sacred Mount Satrunjaya, "the hill that conquers enemies." See chapter 10.

- **Golden Temple** (Amritsar, Punjab): Arguably the greatest spiritual monument in India. The name derives from the central gold-plated Hari Mandir—the inner sanctuary featuring gold-plated copper cupolas and white marble walls inlaid with precious stones—which sits at the center of the "Pool of Nectar." Every day thousands of disciplined devotees pay their respects, touching their heads to the glistening marble floor while singing devotional songs continuously—a wonderful, welcoming, and humbling experience. See "The Golden Temple in Amritsar" in chapter 11.

- **Tabo** (Spiti Valley, Himachal Pradesh): This 1,005-year-old Buddhist complex houses magnificent frescoes and brilliant stucco and relief figures that recount ancient myths and celebrate the deities and demons that make up the Buddhist pantheon. You'll need a flashlight to adequately explore the dark, smoldering halls and shrines lit only by thin shafts of natural light, and brought to life by the resonant chants and ringing of bells by the monks and nuns who populate this sacred center of Tibetan Buddhism. See "Exploring Kinnaur & Spiti" in chapter 11.

- **The Sun Temple at Konark** (near Bhubaneswar, Orissa): An enormous war chariot carved from a massive chunk of rock during the 13th century, this masterpiece of Indian temple art is covered with detailed sculpted scenes, from the erotic to the mythological. Guarded by stone elephants and lions, the immense structure is seen as the gigantic chariot of the sun god emerging from the ocean, not far from Orissa's 500km (300-mile) beach. See "Orissa's Golden Temple Triangle" in chapter 13.

3 Unique Places to Stay

Not surprisingly, most of these are in Rajasthan, which has almost 80 heritage properties—castles, palaces, forts, and ornate *havelis* (traditional mansions), now hotels offering varying degrees of comfort.

- **Taj Mahal Hotel** (Mumbai): George Bernard Shaw famously claimed that after staying here, he no longer had any need to visit the real Taj Mahal in Agra. Built just over a century ago by an Indian industrialist, the Taj hosts the world's rich and famous and remains the most celebrated address in Mumbai. See p. 103.

- **Nilaya Hermitage** (Goa): Parisian fashion stylist Claudia Derain and her husband, Hari Ajwani, came to Goa on vacation and—like so many—never left. Together with Goan architect Dean D'Cruz, they've created an *Arabian Nights* fantasy, with only 12 "cosmic-themed" guest suites and gorgeously informal public spaces overlooking paddy fields and coconut-palm groves. Despite being 6km (4 miles) from the nearest beach, Nilaya is one of Goa's most perfect getaways. See p. 149.

- **Surya Samudra Beach Garden** (near Kovalam, Kerala): A small collection of traditional cottages on a terraced hillside overlooking the sea, with direct access to two picture-perfect beaches, Surya Samudra is quite simply the most Paradisiacal destination on the Malabar coast. Gazing over the Arabian Sea from your private deck (ask for a cottage near the beach), you will no doubt wish you'd spent your entire vacation here. See p. 203.

- **Tranquil Resorts** (Wyanad, Northern Kerala): Experiencing life on a 162-hectare (400-acre) working coffee and vanilla plantation at the edge of Wyanad National Park with hosts Victor and Ranjini Dey is like being at a grand coffee-planter's private house party where you are the guest of honor. This has got to be the warmest, most wonderful homestay in all of India. See p. 216.

- **Amarvilas** (Agra, Uttar Pradesh): If you've always dreamed of seeing the Taj Mahal, this is the place to celebrate that achievement. Built within the green belt that surrounds the monument, you can literally see the Taj from your bed, but you'll probably spend just as much time gazing at your immediate surroundings. With its huge reflecting pools, colonnaded courts, terraced lawns, inlaid murals, and pillowed pavilions, this palatial hotel is worth every cent. See p. 328.

- **Rajvilas** (near Jaipur, Rajasthan): This is arguably the best of the Oberoi's flagship Vilas properties. Built like a traditional fortified Rajasthani palace, Rajvilas may not have the history of an authentic heritage hotel, but it offers a level of comfort, luxury, and service other properties cannot match, enabling even the most world-weary guest (Bill Clinton loved it) to "live in the princely style of Rajasthan." See p. 390.

- **Aman-i-Khás** (Ranthambhore, Rajasthan): Located a stone's throw from India's most famous tiger sanctuary, the superb accommodations—huge temperature-controlled Mughal-style royal tents stylishly divided by cool white drapes—and impeccable service are distinctly Aman. At night, lanterns light your way to the giant flaming *uruli* (large metal vessel) around which guests gather to enjoy the night sky and the ethereal calm, broken only by the occasional call from the wilds. See p. 403.

- **Deogarh Mahal & Rawla Narlai** (Rural Rajasthan): An ornate 17th-century fort-palace with domed turrets and balconies, personally managed by the charming Thakur of Deogarh, Deogarh Mahal is one of the most authentic and best-value heritage hotels in Rajasthan, best visited on a road trip between Jaipur and Udaipur. Book the aptly named "Royal" suite, and it's not hard to feel that all you survey from your private balcony is yours. Rawla Narlai, the 17th-century hunting retreat of the Maharajah of Jodhpur, is another rural gem that will have you feeling like a royal guest—and it's the ideal stopover if you're traveling between Udaipur and Jodhpur. You'll stay for one night and wish you'd planned for three. See p. 439 and 440.

- **Lake Palace Hotel** (Udaipur, Rajasthan): Built on an island by the Maharana in 1740 as a cool summer retreat (swimming distance from his palace), this is perhaps the most romantic—certainly the most photographed—hotel in India. Whizzing across the waters to your private palace, you'll feel you've finally arrived—and if you've booked one of the heritage suites, you have. Floating like a beautiful white ship on the waters of Lake Pichola, the hotel offers good service, comfortable lodging, and picture-perfect 360-degree views—though it must be noted that a severe drought has currently left the palace somewhat grounded at press time. See p. 435.

- **Kankarwa** (Udaipur, Rajasthan): A short stroll from the City Palace, this ancient haveli right on the shores of Lake Pichola is the best budget heritage option in Rajasthan. Run by a family who have resided here for 200 years, rooms cost just Rs 1,200 to Rs 1,650 ($28–$38). Book room no.

204—a cool, whitewashed room with white bedding, perfectly offset by two touches of color: the blue waters of the lake reflected outside the *jarokha* (window seat), and a red lamp indoors. See p. 436.

- **Devi Garh** (near Udaipur, Rajasthan): If you're a modern-design enthusiast, this hotel will blow you away. An 18th-century Rajput palace-fort, its formidable exterior, towering over the tiny village at its base, remains unchanged. But step inside and you'll find a totally reinvented minimalist interior, with 14 floors transformed into 23 chic suites (with 18 more opening soon) that have clearly utilized the talents of the best young Indian designers—all of whom laid to rest the perception that design here reached its apotheosis with the Mughals. It's an unparalleled modern Indian masterpiece, and a destination in its own right. See p. 438.

- **Amanbagh** (Ajabgarh, Rajasthan): Fringed with date palms and mango and jamun trees, Aman's shimmering new pink-sandstone resort is the oasis you have always wanted to stumble upon while traversing the Thar Desert. Begin your day sipping ruby-red pomegranate juice on your private porch, then hike to ancient Somsagar Lake or explore the haunted ruins at Bhangarh. Or go nowhere but the pool pavilion on the edge of the palm-lined canal and listen to the joyful twittering of birds. See p. 389.

- **Killa Bhawan** (Jaisalmer, Rajasthan): Built entirely from yellow sandstone, **Sonar Qila (Golden Fort)** rises like a giant sandcastle from its desert surrounds—this is the world's only living medieval fort, inhabited by families who have been here for more than 8 centuries. Within the ramparts, Killa Bhawan is a charming seven-room guesthouse with rather basic facilities (only two rooms are en-suite) but lovely furnishings and stunning views, best enjoyed from the rooftop, which is comfortably furnished with mattresses and bolsters. See p. 453.

- **Gangeshwari Suite at The Glasshouse on the Ganges** (Garhwal, Uttaranchal): Just steps away from the raging Ganges River, this thoroughly inventive suite oozes style. The immaculately laid-out sleeping area has a four-poster canopy bed and antique furniture, while the alfresco bathroom features a tub carved into the rock, with greenery spilling down the walls. You can relax on your private balcony and watch India's holiest river gushing by, or head for a hammock strung between the mango, lychee, and citrus trees. See p. 507.

4 Most Memorable Moments

- **Sharing a Cup of *Chai* with a Perfect Stranger:** You will typically be asked to sit and share a cup of *chai* (tea) a dozen times a day, usually by merchants keen to keep you browsing. Although you may at first be nervous of what this may entail, don't hesitate to accept when you're feeling more comfortable, for while sipping the milky sweet brew (often flavored with ginger and cardamom), conversation will flow, and you might find yourself discussing anything from women's rights in India to the individualism that mars Western society.

- **Helping Lord Venkateshwara Repay His Debt to the God of Wealth** (Tirupati, Andhra Pradesh): Tirupati, the richest temple in India, is the most active religious pilgrimage destination on earth, drawing more than 10 million devoted pilgrims every year (more than either Jerusalem or Rome!) who line up for hours, even days, to see the diamond-decorated black stone idol Lord Venkateshwara (aka Vishnu) for just a few seconds. Afterward, you stare in disbelief as vast piles of cash and other contributions are counted by scores of clerks behind a wall of glass. See chapter 7.

- **Watching the Moon Rise from Pushkar Palace during the Pushkar Mela** (Pushkar, Rajasthan): The sunset is a spectacular sight on any given evening, but on the evening of the full moon during the Pushkar *mela*, hundreds of Hindu pilgrims, accompanied by temple bells and drums, wade into a sacred lake—believed to miraculously cleanse the soul—before lighting clay lamps and setting them afloat on its holy waters, the twinkling lights a surreal reflection of the desert night sky. If you're lucky enough to have bagged a room at Pushkar Palace, you can watch this ancient ritual from a deck chair on the terrace on the banks of the lake. See chapter 10.

- **Gawking & Being Gawked At** (Dungarpur, near Udaipur, Rajasthan): As a foreigner, you may attract uncomfortably long stares (particularly on public transport), but there are a few moments that you will recall with a wry smile, like the gimlet eye of the toothless old royal retainer as he watches your reaction to the explicit *Kama Sutra* paintings he will reveal hidden in a cupboard of Dungarpur's 13th-century Juna Mahal—one of the Rajasthan's undiscovered gems. See chapter 10.

- **Playing Chicken with a Tata Truck:** The rules of the road (which is almost always single-laned, potholed, and unmarked) are hard to understand, but it would seem that (after the cow, which is of course sacred) Tata trucks, all with HORN ON PLEASE written on their bumpers, rule the road, an assumption your hired driver is likely to test—and you will, more than once, find yourself involuntarily closing your eyes as destiny appears to race toward you, blaring its horn.

- **Meeting a Maharaja** (Rajasthan): India must be the only place in the world where you can, armed with a credit card, find yourself sleeping in a king's bed, having dined with the aristocrat whose forebears built, and quite often died for, the castle or palace walls that surround it. While most heritage properties are still owned by India's oldest monarchies, many of whom live there, only some (like Mandawa Castle and Deogarh Mahal in Rajasthan, and Nilambagh Palace in Gujarat) are personally managed by these urbane aristocrats. See chapter 10.

- **Unraveling the Intricacies of Hinduism** (Master Paying Guest House, Delhi): Staying here is not only the best-value deal in town, but the sophisticated, charming, and extremely knowledgeable Avnish Puri will take you on a "Hidden Delhi" tour, showing you a world not seen by many outsiders, during which he will unravel Hinduism's spiritual tenets in

a profoundly logical way—no mean feat! See chapter 9.

- **Being Blessed by an Elephant:** While you may expect to see an elephant in a national park, it's always a wonderful surprise when you see one ambling down a crowded street in urban Mumbai or Delhi. Outside Thirupparankundram Temple, near Madurai, the resident temple elephant waits patiently to bestow blessings on those willing to donate a rupee.

- **Setting a Candle Adrift on the Sacred Ganges** (Rishikesh, Uttaranchal): By day, Rishikesh is a spiritual Disneyland, where the commercial excesses of packaged meditation and two-for-one tantric yoga hang heavily about the concrete ashrams, bedecked with gaudy statues of Vishnu and Shiva. But at night, to the accompaniment of hypnotic prayers and harmonious singing, the town undergoes a magical transformation, when thousands of golden marigolds and devotional candles mounted on banana leaves are set adrift on the river, a gloriously simple spectacle that reminds all that this really is a spiritual retreat. See chapter 12.

5 Exploring Natural India

- **Watch Cows Sunbathing with Tourists on the Beach** (Goa): While there's plenty of marijuana doing the rounds in Goa, you don't have to smoke a thing to be amused by the mellow cows that wander onto the beach and chill out among the tanning tourists and hawkers. Chewing their cud while seemingly gazing out to sea, these cows really take the Goan motto, *"Sossegade"* ("Take it easy"), to heart. See chapter 5.

- **Ply the Backwaters on a *Kettuvallam*** (Alleppey & Kumarakom, Kerala): Aboard your private houseboat, you aimlessly drift past villages,

temples, and churches, watching as village children, unperturbed by your drifting presence, play at the water's edge, and elephants and water buffalo wade at will. Though the facilities might strike the well-heeled as basic, you're looked after by a private team (guide, cook, and pilot) who manage to be both discreetly invisible and at your beck and call. See chapter 6.

- **Quench Your Thirst with Fresh Coconut Water on a Tropical Island** (Lakshadweep): One of India's best-kept secrets, the 36 atolls and coral reefs that make up the remote union territory of Lakshadweep are rated among the best diving destinations in Asia. Only 10 of the islands are populated, almost exclusively by Malayalam-speaking Muslims who make their living from fishing and harvesting coconuts. These relaxed islanders are supremely welcoming, happily climbing a towering coconut tree to help you quench your thirst. See chapter 6.

- **Wake to Hear a Herd of Elephants Approaching** (Periyar Wildlife Sanctuary, Kerala): The best way to experience this park—famous for its herds of wild elephants—is on a trek with the privately run Periyar Tiger Trail. Accompanied by a naturalist and a game ranger armed with a rifle, you are taken farther into the tourist zone than any other operator is allowed to penetrate. What's more, you are looked after by a team of reformed poachers, who skillfully track and spot animals, carry all the gear, strike camp, cook, clean, and—most importantly—stand sentinel throughout the night when the danger of being trampled by elephants becomes a serious risk. See chapter 6.

- **Immortalize a Wild Tiger from the Back of an Elephant** (Bandhavgarh National Park, Madhya Pradesh): With the densest population of tigers of any park in India, you are practically guaranteed a sighting at this relatively low-key, remote part of Madhya Pradesh. But it's the approach that's so exciting—elephant *mahouts* set off at dawn to track the royal cats. As soon as they've spotted one, you rendezvous with your pachyderm, who then takes you within striking distance of this most royal of cats. The tiger—unperturbed by the presence of an elephant—will then strike a pose of utter indifference for your camera. See chapter 9.

- **Pick a Picture-Perfect Beach** (Goa, Kerala): India has some of the world's best beaches, most of them on the Malabar Coast. Easily accessed, **Asvem** (northern Goa) is an idyllic haven, while just south of Goa, **Morjim** has been drawing Olive Ridley turtles to its shores for centuries. Both beaches are off the well-beaten tourist track. **Palolem** (southern Goa), a gorgeous crescent of sand backed by coconut palms and a handful of laid-back shacks where you can feast on fresh fish and bottles of cold beer, is another of India's loveliest beaches. From here, time allowing, you should head over the border to beautiful and remote **Om** Beach (Gokam, Karnataka). In Kerala, the competition is equally stiff, but we award the picture-perfect prize to the beaches at **Marari** and **Surya Samudra** resorts. The absolute stunners, if you can get that far, are at **Bangaram** and **Agatti,** in Lakshadweep. See chapters 5 and 6.

- **Find Divinity in** *Devbhumi,* **"Land of the Gods"** (Spiti to Kinnaur, Himachal Pradesh): The stark, rust-colored, snowcapped slopes in the Indo-Tibetan regions of Kinnaur, Spiti, and Lahaul are the stuff adventurers' dreams are made of, offering sublime mountainscapes, flower-filled valleys, terrifying roads, atmospheric Tibetan Buddhist *gompas* (monasteries), and high-altitude villages that seem to cling to the mountainsides. The region is one of the most profoundly beautiful in the world, but the drive is not for the fainthearted. See chapter 11.

- **Get a Rush While Rafting Down the Zanskar** (Ladakh): White-water rafting on the Zanskar is not only exhilarating and challenging, but you pass through the most incredibly desolate, scenic gorges and stupendous cliffs. A full river journey takes at least 12 days round-trip from Leh, so this is only for the truly committed—though there are slightly tamer options closer to Leh. See chapter 11.

6 The Best Ayurvedic Pampering

- **Pousada Tauma** (Goa): Loved by top Indian director Mira Nair as well as jet-setting French designer Michéle Klein, this intimate 12-suite resort, fashioned entirely from distinctively Goan laterite stone, offers a small, exclusive Ayurvedic center—the ideal place to finish off a day spent on the beach, with a professional doctor, two excellent treatment rooms, and an exhaustive range of Ayurvedic packages. An excellent in-house restaurant offers tailor-made Ayurvedic meals. See p. 150.

- **The Marari Beach** (Alleppey, Kerala): Ayurveda is taken very seriously at this attractive beach resort in South India, not far from Kerala's tantalizing backwaters. The well-stocked Ayurvedic center is run by two physicians, who dispense sound medical advice as well as treatments, and your program is backed up with special Ayurvedic meals at the resort's restaurant. Or forgo the rules and just head for the beach, cocktail in hand. See p. 188.

- **Kumarakom Lake Resort** (Kumarakom, Kerala): The swankiest of Kumarakom's retreats, this has an extensive Ayurvedic spa—one of Kerala's most sophisticated, catering primarily to the well-heeled globetrotter—but there's more besides, like the exquisite, traditionally styled teak-and-rosewood houses with open-air garden bathrooms, a fabulous restaurant, and super-slick service. See p. 184.

- **Somatheeram** (Southern Kerala): This shabby-chic center, carved out of red sandy soil and perched on a terraced cliff overlooking a beach, is more hospital than hotel, but it has been inundated with awards for "Best Ayurvedic Center" (mostly from Kerala's Tourism Department). Ayurvedic therapy is the primary reason to book here, joining the many European "patients" who shuffle around in pastel dressing gowns, serene expressions on their tanned faces. See p. 202.

- **Poovar Island Resort** (Southern Kerala): It's the location as much as anything that sets this stylish resort apart. Set amid dense coconut groves and banana trees, this island resort is only accessible by boat, and you can elect to stay on a floating cottage built of Malaysian teak and coconut timber. There's not much to do but idle away your time watching fishermen from your private veranda or pool, and entrust yourself to the staff of the excellent bamboo-walled Ayurvedic center: two doctors and a handful of top-notch, no-nonsense masseurs. See p. 201.

- **Shalimar Spice Garden Resort** (Kerala): Not far from Periyar Tiger Reserve, this lovely inland resort occupies a 2.4-hectare (6-acre) plantation scented by exotic spices. Over and above the enchanting Euro-chic accommodations designed by Italian owner-architect Maria Angela Fernhof is an intimate Ayurvedic center drawing a regular European clientele. Built according to traditional specifications, with a stone floor, handmade brick walls, and an open fire for heating the medicated oils, the small space is always filled with the aroma of coconut oil. See p. 210.

- **Wildflower Hall, Mashobra** (near Shimla, Himachal Pradesh): The *pièce de résistance* at what once was the mountain retreat of Lord Kitchener and is today the most beautiful resort in the Himalayas is the spa—not only because the highly trained therapists offer the ultimate rubdown (Balinese, Thai, Swedish, Ayurvedic—and that's just for starters), but because it takes place while you stare out blissfully at snowcapped peaks and a magnificent deodar valley, swirling with mists. See p. 474.

- **Ananda-in-the-Himalayas** (near Rishikesh, Uttaranchal): The 1,951-sq.-m (21,000-sq.-ft.) Wellness Center at this destination spa resort, located high above the Ganges, is rated one of the best in the world. This reputation is well-earned—thanks not only to its ultra-efficient

team of therapists, masseuses, and yoga instructors, but also because you are totally pampered from the moment you wake (to a steaming cup of honey, lemon, and ginger) until you retire to a bath (where a pre-lit candle heats fragrant essential oils) and a bed (warmed by a hot-water bottle). See p. 507.

7 The Best Eating & Drinking Experiences

- **Bumping into a Bollywood Idol** (Mumbai): Nowhere in India is dining more rewarding than in Mumbai, where the streets are filled with literally thousands of restaurants representing every kind of Indian cuisine. But if it's star-gazing you're after, head for places like the **Olive Bar and Kitchen** restaurant in Bandra or **Enigma** nightclub in Juhu. Alternatively, hang out at **Leopold Café;** casting agents looking for foreigners to work as extras frequently scan the clientele at this favored travelers' hangout. See chapter 4.

- **Eating Alphonso Mangoes in Mumbai:** You may have eaten mangoes in Mexico, Thailand, or even other parts of India, but until you've had an Alphonso from Ratnagiri in rural Maharashtra, you'll be missing a sensory experience like no other. The king of mangoes has a succulent bright orange pulp, bewitching scent, and divine flavor. See chapter 4.

- **Dining with Ancient Delhi at Your Feet** (Delhi, Uttar Pradesh): Head for **Thai Wok,** the designer-chic rooftop restaurant with great views of ancient Qutb Minar—the sandstone Victory Tower built by Qutbuddin Aibak in 1193. Reached via an ancient elevator and a short set of stairs, the artful alfresco setting includes a walled area with cushioned seating under wind-blown canopies; reserve well ahead to

sit here. Seafood dishes are exceptional; try red snapper in chili-sour sauce, or prawns stir-fried with fresh green chilies and sweet basil. See p. 312.

- **Eating with Your Hands:** Though it may initially go against the grain, there's something immensely rewarding about digging into a delicious meal with your hands. Indians generally do, and—at least once—you should follow suit. Note that ideally you only use your right hand, and in the North, where the food is "drier," you are traditionally not supposed to dirty more than the first two digits; in the South you may use the whole hand. See the appendix, "India in Depth."

- **Sipping a Sweet Lassi:** A delicious drink of liquefied sweetened yogurt, this is almost a meal in a glass and should definitely be sampled (some of the best we've tried were in Amritsar, Goa, and Jaipur). Do, however, make sure that no water has been added (including ice), and beware the *bhang* lassi—spiced with marijuana, it can make the usually surreal scenes of India a little too out of this world.

- **Sitting Around a Bonfire under a Desert Sky** (Rajasthan): There's nothing quite like eating a superb meal around a raging campfire in the peace of the desert night. Camel and horseback safaris are run out of Shekhawati, Bikaner, Pushkar, and Jaisalmer. If you opt for the latter,

Royal Desert Safaris has a permanent tented camp with en-suite tents near Sam Dunes, run by Fort Rajwada, with food supplied by the team of chefs that cooks up a storm at Trio, Jaisalmer's best restaurant. See chapter 10.

- **Sampling *Bod-Jha,* Tibetan Butter Tea, with a Buddhist Lama** (Leh, Ladakh): Many people gag at the taste of butter tea, made with salt and—you guessed it—a good dollop of the clarified butter known as ghee. It's an acquired taste, but if you get the hang of it, sipping the buttery concoction with a friendly Buddhist monk when you visit one of the many monasteries tucked in the lunar landscapes around Leh is a truly memorable experience. See chapter 11.

8 The Best Savvy Traveler Tips

- **"You pay what you like":** This rather annoying response from guides, drivers, and rickshaw-*wallas* to the question "How much will it cost?" will no doubt end with at least one of you feeling very disappointed. Try to find out how much something should cost *before* you enter into this dialogue (we've tried to advise this wherever possible), and always negotiate the fare or rate upfront. (Note that "I come later" is another irritating response, this time after you decline service, and you will need to remain firm or prepare to go through the entire experience again.)

- **"Just look, no buy":** You will be urged to enter shops from all corners in both explicit and less obvious ways—your driver, guide, even the seemingly innocent bystander offering assistance, are almost all operating on the ubiquitous commission system, and whatever they make on the deal is added to the quoted price. Note that to avoid this kind of hassle, look for the fixed-rate shops or those that mark their wares with prices. But as is the case everywhere, do beware of closely named imitations of fixed-rate shops with good reputations—for example, Cottage Industries Exposition shops, often marked CIE, are seriously overpriced outlets that cash in on the fame (and closely related name) of the government-owned Central Cottage Industries Emporiums. The latter may not be the cheapest, but it offers good value, and you really can "just look, no buy."

- **"We look; we look":** This response from a rickshaw-*walla* or driver usually means that the person either doesn't know where you've asked him to take you, or you'll end up somewhere with a similar name but nothing else to recommend it (Hotel *Chandra,* for example, rather than Hotel *Chand*). Prebook your accommodations whenever you can, so that you don't have to deal with touts and hawkers when you arrive. And be aware that a hotel or guesthouse that is successful will often have a rival opening within the year with a confusingly similar name.

- **"So where are you from, good gentleman?"** (or more commonly, "Coming from?"): You will be asked this often, so prepare yourself. One of the possible reasons Indians kick-start conversations this way is that where you come from may in the past have indicated caste or social position; whatever the reason, engage in the opener—it's far preferable to living in a five-star hotel cocoon.

- **"Hashish, taxi, guide, young girls?":** In the well-traveled parts of India, you will be inundated with offers of assistance; again, the best response is to doggedly desist in what is essentially a game of endurance, and certainly ignore those unsolicited offers that are illicit—these can carry a hefty penalty, including a lengthy jail sentence.

- **"Cof-fay, chai; cof-fay, chai; cof-fay, chai?":** This incessant call given by the *chai-walla* wandering the corridors of your train will put to rest any romantic notions about the relaxation of train travel. Note that you will be most comfortable aboard the overnight **Rajdhanis** which connect all the major cities, while the best daytime trains are the **Shatabdis** (book Chair Class). Time allowing, you should definitely book a "toy train" to the hill stations of Shimla or Darjeeling—the latter approach is so spectacular it has been named a World Heritage Site.

- **"Yes, Madam"; "Yes, Sir":** You will hear this everywhere, usually from hawkers wanting to draw your attention and con artists wanting to strike up a conversation. Unfortunately, the only way to get rid of these irritants is to completely ignore them. In places like Varanasi, even saying "no" is perceived as a willingness to interact, and your pursuer will then continue to try to draw you into conversation. Just pretend you can't be bothered, and hopefully, in a little while, you won't.

- **"You wait, no problem":** Finally, we can't emphasize enough how important it is to simply relax and accept whatever's going on around you. Many Indians subscribe to the philosophy that life is destiny, and getting uptight or flying into a rage usually won't solve much. You'll have a far better vacation if you simply give in to the moment and enjoy the experience; after all, the only aspect you have control over is your response.

2

Planning Your Trip To India

Once the playing fields of only die-hard budget New Age travelers, India has in the past decade come into its own for top-end travelers who want to be pampered and rejuvenated as well as spiritually and culturally challenged. Given its vast size, the majority of India's top attractions are remarkably easy to get to, using a clever combination of internal flights or long-haul train journeys and chauffeur-driven cars (no sane traveler would self-drive). Hotels, particularly in the heritage category, offer excellent value-for-money in Western terms, and despite a number of potential health concerns, sensible travelers will enjoy their sojourn with little more than a brief tummy upset. It is, however, very important to plot out your itinerary and make reservations well in advance. Finally, though India has definite Third World elements—infrastructure and service levels leave much to be desired—you'll find almost everything you need here, particularly if you're armed with a credit card and *Frommer's India, 2nd edition*, of course.

1 The Regions in Brief

India is a vast country, roughly divided—for the purposes of this book—into North, East, and South.

The South (again, for the purposes of this book), accessed most conveniently via **Mumbai** (state capital of **Maharashtra**), refers to **Goa, Karnataka** (with an excursion to **Hyderabad,** capital of Andhra Pradesh), **Kerala,** and **Tamil Nadu.**

The North refers to **Rajasthan** (and its southern neighbor **Gujarat**); west of this area; **Delhi;** and **Uttar Pradesh;** with **Madhya Pradesh** in the center (only **Bodhgaya** in **Bihar** is covered in brief). Northeast of Delhi lie the largely unvisited states of **Haryana** and **Punjab** (with the exception of the Golden Temple at Amritsar, one of India's most wonderful attractions), and—moving even farther north—**Uttaranchal** and **Himachal Pradesh** (with references to Ladakh in **Jammu** and **Kashmir**) in the Himalayas.

The East refers to Jharkhand (not a tourist destination), West Bengal (centered around **Kolkata,** or Calcutta), **Orissa** (with top attraction Konark) and, moving north into the Himalayas again, **Sikkim.** Seven more states lie farther east (north and east of Bangladesh); their infrastructure is virtually nonexistent. Because travel in these areas is considered less than safe, they are not covered here.

The largest differences lie between the northern and southern regions. The former offers predominantly a plethora of medieval Mughal and Rajput architecture, ancient cities, deserts, camel safaris, heritage accommodations, tiger parks, Buddhism, and the snowcapped peaks of the Himalayas. The latter is rich with beautiful beaches, Ayurvedic spas, ancient Dravidian/Hindu temples, cosmopolitan colonial coastal towns, and a generally more laid-back atmosphere. We suggest that rather than try to cover both the North and the South, concentrate your energies on one. If you do decide to combine the two, stick to two states, or

India

you'll find yourself exhausted at the end of your vacation.

MUMBAI (BOMBAY) & MAHARASHTRA Teetering on the edge of the Arabian Sea, its heaving population barely contained by palm-fringed beaches, India's sexiest city is a vibrant, confident metropolis that's tangibly high on energy. The state capital of Maharashtra, this is home to many of the subcontinent's best restaurants and great hotels. It's also the ideal starting point for a tour northwest to **Gujarat,** or south along the Konkan railway to **Goa** and beyond. Whichever you choose, do plan for an eastward jaunt to the ancient rock-cut caves of **Ajanta** and **Ellora,** Maharashtra's startling World Heritage Sites.

GOA Nirvana for flower children since the late 1960s, Goa still attracts a cosmopolitan mix of youngsters who cruise from beach to beach, looking for action. But Goa is more than a party in paradise. A Portuguese colonial heritage has left an indelible mark on this tiny enclave (India's smallest state), from cuisine to architecture, with plenty to see. And if the crowded beaches and vibrant markets leave you gasping for solitude, you can still find the original Goan paradise on far-flung beaches or in quiet boutique hotels, reviewed in detail in this book.

KARNATAKA & KERALA Traveling south along India's west coast, you will pass through untouched Karnataka; it's possible you'll overnight in the hip city of **Bangalore.** From there you can head to **Hyderabad,** the 400-year-old capital of Andhra Pradesh, as famous for its food and minarets as for its burgeoning software industry; or south to **Mysore,** "City of Incense." Whatever you do, set aside time to explore the lost city of **Hampi,** arguably Karnataka's most evocative attraction, or to join the Jain pilgrimage to anoint the giant feet of **Lord Gomateswara,** said to be the largest monolith in the world. There's more

besides, but who can tarry long when Kerala, "God's own country," awaits? South India's top destination, particularly for the well-heeled traveler in search of pampering and relaxation, Kerala offers ancient backwaters plied by houseboats, herds of wild elephant, coconut-lined beaches and, of course, the ancient healing art of Ayurveda.

TAMIL NADU Occupying a long stretch of the eastern Indian Ocean coastline, India's southernmost state seems little touched by the cocktail of foreign influences that contributed to the cultural developments in the North. This is where you'll find India's most superb Dravidian temples, from **Mamallapuram** (7th c. A.D.) to the **Madurai temple complex** (16th c. A.D.). When you're all templed out, there's always **Pondicherry,** the former French coastal town where traditional Indian snack joints feature signs proclaiming MEALS READY—BIEN VENUE and loincloth-clad locals converse in flawless French.

DELHI, MADHYA & UTTAR PRADESH Entered through Delhi, capital of the largest democracy in the world, the central states of Madhya and Uttar Pradesh are the real heart of India, where great rulers battled for power over vast swaths of India, and where you'll find arguably the densest concentration of top attractions on the subcontinent. From the "seven cities" of Delhi, it's a short train or road journey to **Agra,** home to the Taj Mahal and other superb examples of medieval Mughal architecture. From there you can either head west to Rajasthan, or east—via the erotic temples of **Khajuraho,** considered the pinnacle of Hindu medieval architecture—to the ancient city of **Varanasi,** India's holiest pilgrimage site, where the faithful come to die on the banks of the sacred Ganges to achieve *moksha*—liberation from earthly life. To escape the well-beaten tourist track, head south to the vast plains of Madhya Pradesh, to **Bandhavgarh National Park,** one of the best places to see tigers in Asia.

RAJASTHAN & GUJARAT With crenelated forts and impregnable palaces that rise like giant fairy-tale sets above dusty sun-scorched plains and shimmering lakes, Rajasthan—literally "land of princes"—epitomizes the romance of India. Whether you choose to linger in the untainted medieval atmosphere of little towns like **Bundi,** browse the bumper-to-bumper shops in **Jaipur,** track tigers in **Ranthambhore,** overnight on the lake in the beautiful city of **Udaipur,** or explore the world's oldest living fort in **Jaisalmer,** you will want to see it all. South lies the less-traveled state of Gujarat, filled with hidden gems and lacking the touts and hawkers of more heavily traveled sites.

HIMACHAL PRADESH & LADAKH Bordered by Tibet to the east, Himachal Pradesh incorporates great topographic diversity, from vast, bleak tracts of the rust-colored high-altitude Trans-Himalayan desert to dense green deodar forests, apple orchards, and cultivated terraces. Together with **Ladakh** (known as "Little Tibet"), this is also where you'll find India's largest concentration of Buddhists, their atmospheric *gompas* (temples, including **Tabo,** the World Heritage Site in Spiti) a total contrast to the pageantry of Hindu temples. An easy—and highly recommended—detour to the region is via Amritsar to view the **Golden Temple,** arguably the most spiritual destination in India.

UTTARANCHAL Comprising the pre-Vedic territories of Garhwal and Kumaon, the mountains of the central Himalayan state of Uttaranchal are riven with ancient Hindu pilgrimage routes, and offer wonderful trekking routes. Non-hikers come here to practice yoga at **Rishikesh** on the banks of the holy river Ganges, or to take a road trip through the less-traveled parts of **Kumaon,** possibly ending their sojourn looking for tigers in **Corbett National Park,** which vies with Ranthambhore for accessibility from Delhi.

KOLKATA (CALCUTTA) & THE EAST Kolkata, the much-maligned capital of West Bengal, never fails to surprise the visitor with its beautiful albeit crumbling colonial architecture, sophisticated Bengali culture, and wonderful restaurants and hotels. From here you can either head north to the cooling breezes of West Bengal's hill station, **Darjeeling,** famous for its tea, and on to the Buddhist state of **Sikkim** (in many ways even more remote than Himachal Pradesh); or you can head south to Orissa to visit the monolithic **Sun Temple** at Konark, yet another of India's awesome array of World Heritage Sites.

2 Visitor Information

India's **Tourism Information Department** is going all out to seduce international visitors, and has fairly extensive representation around the globe. Access one of its **websites** (www.tourisminindia.com, www.tourindia.com, or www.incredibleindia.com) for general information, but be aware that some pages may be out of date or permanently under construction. The websites do offer links to all of India's regional tourism departments, some of which provide fantastic coverage of what's on offer.

Indian tourism offices may be found worldwide as follows. In the **U.S.:** 3550 Wilshire Blvd., Room 204, Los Angeles, CA 90010; ✆ **213/380-8855;** and Suite 1808, 1270 Avenue of the Americas, New York, NY 10020; ✆ **212/751-6840.** In the **U.K.:** 7 Cork St., London W1X 2LN; ✆ **71-437-3677.** In **Canada:** 60 Bloor St. (W), Suite 1003, Toronto, Ontario M4W 3B8; ✆ **416-962-3787.** In **Australia:** Level 2, Piccadilly, 210 Pitt St., Sydney, NWS 2000; ✆ **2-9264-4855.**

Tips Visa Savvy

Travelers to India can apply for a tourist visa from their nearest Indian Consulate or High Commission. This is valid for multiple entries for a minimum of 6 months from the date of issue. Given the nature of India's bureaucracy, the rules and fees for application change regularly, so it's best to check with your travel agent or with the relevant authority for the latest visa information. Accurately completed visa application forms must be accompanied by two passport-size photographs (on a light background) and the appropriate processing fee; apply well in advance to avoid unforeseeable delays. You won't be admitted to India unless your passport is valid for at least 6 months after your entry, and it should typically also be valid for at least 3 months beyond the period of your intended stay. Check for fee structure and more details at www.indianembassy.org.   In the U.S., the **Indian Embassy** is at 2107 Massachusetts Ave., Washington, DC 20008 (© **202-939-9861**); and there are consulates in Houston, New York, San Francisco, and Chicago. In the U.K., **India House** is in Aldwych, London WC2B 4NA (© **020-7240-1012;** www.hcilondon.net). If you're applying for a visa in a country where India does not have a representative, you are advised to make inquiries at the nearest British authority.

A **special permit** is required for foreigners wishing to visit the Lakshadweep Islands, as well as remote areas such as Sikkim and Ladakh. For Lakshadweep, your permit will be arranged when your accommodations are reserved. Permits for the other restricted regions can be obtained in India; specific details are given in the appropriate chapters. Carry a number of passport-size photographs and copies of the personal particulars and Indian visa pages of your passport in order to apply for these permits.

Websites   You can access up-to-the-minute news and stories through the websites of some of the country's largest English dailies, including **www.time sofindia.com**, **www.expressindia.com**, **www.hindustantimes.com**, and **www. thehinduonnet.com**. For up-to-date news and updates on Bollywood movies, visit **www.rediff.com** or **www.indiainfo.com**; for travel-related information and features, visit **www.outlooktraveller.com**. Travel Spirit International (**www.tsiindia.com**) has a wide range of links as well as easy access to sites where you can book reduced-price accommodations and travel.

3 Entry Requirements & Customs

ENTRY REQUIREMENTS

For information on how to get a passport, go to the "Fast Facts: India" section, later in this chapter. The websites listed there provide downloadable passport applications as well as the current fees for processing passport applications. For an up-to-date country-by-country listing of passport requirements around the world, go to the "Foreign Entry Requirement" Web page of the U.S. State Department at **http:// travel.state.gov**.

CUSTOMS

WHAT YOU CAN BRING INTO INDIA

You can bring as much foreign currency into India as you like; if you have over $10,000 in cash or traveler's checks, however, you should complete a declaration form. You may not import Indian currency into India. In addition to your personal effects, you are allowed 2 liters of alcohol, and 200 cigarettes or 50 cigars. (Know that foreign liquors and imported cigarettes are very heavily taxed and in some areas difficult to come by.) You may carry a cellphone, camera, and pair of binoculars, but officially you may have only five rolls of film. You must complete a special Tourist Baggage Re-Export Form if you are carrying valuables such as a laptop computer, video equipment, special camera gear, or jewelry. Although there is a strong possibility that you may encounter difficulties upon leaving if these forms are not completed, you'll discover a general malaise among Customs officials, who seldom hassle foreign visitors on international flights. Also, much of the bureaucratic heavy-handedness has eased in recent years, and there is less suspicion of foreign travelers.

WHAT YOU CAN TAKE HOME FROM INDIA

You may not export Indian currency. Exchange all notes at the airport before you depart. Note that airport money-changers frequently run out of certain currencies, so you might want to complete any exchange before you go to the airport. There is a restriction on the exportation of anything over 100 years old, particularly works of art and items of cultural significance. It is illegal to export animal or snake skins, ivory, *shatoosh* wool, or anything that has been produced using these materials. Generally, jewelry valued under Rs 10,000 ($218) may be exported, while gold jewelry valued up to Rs 2,000 ($44) is allowed.

Returning **U.S. citizens** who have been away for at least 48 hours are allowed to bring back, once every 30 days, $400 worth of merchandise duty-free. You'll be charged a flat rate of 4% duty on the next $1,000 worth of purchases. Be sure to have your receipts handy. On mailed gifts, the duty-free limit is $100. With some exceptions, you cannot bring fresh fruits and vegetables into the United States. For specifics on what you can bring back, download the invaluable free pamphlet *Know Before You Go!* online at **www.customs.gov**. (Click on "Travel," then on "Know Before You Go! Online Brochure.") Or contact the **U.S. Customs & Border Patrol Protection (CBP),** 1300 Pennsylvania Ave. NW, Washington, DC 20229 (© 877/287-8867), and request the pamphlet.

For a clear summary of **Canadian** rules, write for the booklet *I Declare,* issued by the **Canada Border Services Agency** (© 800/461-9999 in Canada, or call 204/983-3500; www.cbsa-asfc.gc.ca). Canada allows its citizens a C$750 exemption, and you're allowed to bring back, duty-free, one carton of cigarettes, one can of tobacco, 40 imperial ounces of liquor, and 50 cigars. In addition, you're allowed to mail gifts to Canada valued at less than C$60 a day, provided they're unsolicited and don't contain alcohol or tobacco (write on the package "Unsolicited gift, under $60 value"). You should declare all valuables on the Y-38 form before your departure from Canada, including serial numbers of valuables you already own, such as foreign cameras. *Note:* The $750 exemption can only be used once a year and only after an absence of 7 days.

Citizens of the U.K. returning from **a non-E.U. country** have a Customs allowance of: 200 cigarettes; 50 cigars; 250 grams of smoking tobacco; 2 liters of still table wine; 1 liter of spirits or strong liqueurs (over 22% volume); 2 liters of fortified wine, sparkling wine, or other liqueurs; 60cc (ml) of perfume; 250cc (ml) of toilet water; and £145 worth of all other goods, including gifts and souvenirs. People under 17 cannot have the tobacco or alcohol allowance. For more information, contact **HM Customs & Excise** at © **0845/010-9000** (from outside the U.K., 020/8929-0152), or consult their website at www.hmce.gov.uk.

The duty-free allowance in **Australia** is A$400 or, for those under 18, A$200. Citizens can bring in 250 cigarettes or 250 grams of loose tobacco, and 1,125 milliliters of alcohol. If you're returning with valuables you already own, such as foreign-made cameras, you should file Form B263. A helpful brochure available from Australian consulates or Customs offices is *Know Before You Go.* For more information, call the **Australian Customs Service** at © **1300/363-263,** or log on to www.customs.gov.au.

The duty-free allowance for **New Zealand** is NZ$700. Citizens over 17 can bring in 200 cigarettes, 50 cigars, or 250 grams of tobacco (or a mixture of all three if their combined weight doesn't exceed 250g); plus 4.5 liters of wine and beer, or 1.125 liters of liquor. New Zealand currency does not carry import or export restrictions. Fill out a certificate of export, listing the valuables you are taking out of the country; that way, you can bring them back without paying duty. Most questions are answered in a free pamphlet available at New Zealand consulates and Customs offices: *New Zealand Customs Guide for Travellers, Notice no. 4.* For more information, contact **New Zealand Customs,** The Customhouse, 1721 Whitmore St., Box 2218, Wellington (© **04/473-6099** or 0800/428-786; www.customs. govt.nz).

4 Money

CURRENCY

The Indian rupee (Rs) is available in denominations of Rs 1,000, Rs 500, Rs 100, Rs 50, Rs 20, Rs 10, and Rs 5 notes. You will occasionally come across Rs 1 or Rs 2 notes—treat them as souvenirs. Minted coins come in denominations of Rs 5, Rs 2, and Rs 1, as well as 50 and 25 paise. There are 100 paise in a rupee.

Note: Badly damaged or torn rupee notes (of which there are many) may be refused, particularly in larger cities, but less fuss is made over them in small towns. Check the change you are given and avoid accepting these.

EXCHANGE RATES

Exchange rates fluctuate dramatically. At press time, US$1 bought you around Rs 44 (43.9), and 1 euro equaled Rs 54, while £1 was worth around Rs 78. Bear in mind that a few dollars, pounds, or euros go a very long way in India. You will enjoy your vacation a whole lot more

if you don't sweat the small stuff: A difference of a couple of rupees will hardly show up on your bank statement. For up-to-the-minute **currency conversions,** log on to www.xe.com/ucc.

You cannot obtain Indian currency anywhere outside India, and you may not carry rupees beyond India's borders. You may have to exchange at least some money at the airport upon your arrival; change just enough to cover airport incidentals and transportation to your hotel, since the rate will be quite unfavorable.

Tip: India is one destination in which it is really worthwhile to arrange an airport transfer with your hotel so that you can avoid waiting in long lines at the airport money-changer, dealing with prepaid booths, or negotiating fees with drivers and touts. After a good night's rest, head to the nearest bank or ATM for a cash infusion.

Banks offer the best exchange rates, but they tend to be inefficient and the staff lethargic about tending to foreigners'

What Things Cost in India

This is a sampling of *average* prices you're likely to pay in India. Bear in mind that big cities generally have much higher prices than smaller towns, and that any place that attracts tourists inevitably attracts rip-off artists.

	Rupees	U.S. Dollar	British Pound
Luxury hotel room	Rs 3,500–Rs 30,000	$80–$690	£45–£383
Budget–moderate hotel room	Rs 150–Rs 4,500	$3.40–$102	£2–£57
Cup of tea from a stall	Rs 2–Rs 7	4¢–11¢	£0.025–£0.08
Cup of tea at a hotel	Rs 10–Rs 150	23¢–$3.40	£0.12–£2
Newspaper	Rs 3–Rs 5	6¢–10¢	£0.038–£0.7
Weekly magazine	Rs 15–Rs 25	35¢–55¢	£0.19–£0.3
Taxi for the day	Rs 600–Rs 2,000	$13.65–$46	£8–£25
1km by auto-rickshaw	Rs 8–Rs 12	15¢–30¢	£.10–£0.15
Meal at a local diner *(dhaba)*	Rs 30–Rs 100	65¢–$1.30	£.38–£1.28
Main course in a luxury restaurant	Rs 150–Rs 800	$3.40–$18.20	£2–£10

needs. You run the risk of being ripped off by using **unauthorized money-changers;** the most convenient option is to avail yourself of ATMs while you're in the big cities. Always ask for an encashment receipt when you change cash—you will need this when you use local currency to pay for major expenses (such as accommodations and transport, though you should use a credit card wherever possible). You will also be asked to produce this receipt when you re-exchange your rupees before you leave India.

ATMs (AUTOMATED TELLER MACHINES)

Getting cash from your checking account (or cash advances on your credit card) at

---

Tips The Battle of the Haggle

Sure, things are cheap to begin with and you may feel silly haggling over a few rupees, but keep in mind that if you're given a verbal quote for an unmarked item, it's probably (but not always) twice the realistic asking price. Use discretion though, because items that are priced ridiculously low to begin with are hardly worth reducing further—either you're being conned or you're being cruel. To haggle effectively, make a counter-offer under half price, and don't get emotional. Protests and adamant assertions ("This is less than it cost me to buy!") will follow. Stick to your guns and see what transpires; stop once you've reached a price you can live with. Remember that once the haggle is on, a challenge has been initiated, and it's fun to regard your opponent's act of salesmanship as an artistic endeavor. Let your guard slip, and he will empty your wallet. Take into account the disposition and situation of the merchant; you don't want to haggle a genuinely poor man into deeper poverty! And if you've been taken (and we all have), see it as a small contribution to a family that lives on a great deal less than you do.

> **_Tips_ Small Change**
>
> When you change money, ask for some small bills (a wad of Rs 10 and Rs 20s) for tipping or _baksheesh_ (see "Tipping" under "Fast Facts: India," later in this chapter). At smaller outlets and vendors, you'll also frequently be told that there is no change for your Rs 500 note. Keep your smaller bills separate from the larger ones, so that they're readily accessible and you'll be less of a target for theft.

an ATM is by far the easiest way to get money. These 24-hour machines are readily available in most Indian cities and larger towns and at large commercial banks such as Citibank, Standard Chartered, ABN Amro, and Hong Kong & Shanghai Bank. **Cirrus** (*©* **800/424-7747;** www.mastercard.com) and **PLUS** (*©* **800/843-7587;** www.visa.com) networks span the globe; call or check online for ATM locations at your destination. Be sure to find out your daily withdrawal limit before you depart. Also keep in mind that many banks impose a fee every time a card is used at a different bank's ATM, and that fee can be higher for international transactions (up to $5 or more). On top of this, the bank from which you withdraw cash likely charges its own fee. To find out what these international withdrawal fees are, ask your bank.

Keep in mind that credit card companies try to protect themselves from theft by limiting the funds you can withdraw outside your home country, so call your credit card company before you leave home. You should have no problem withdrawing Rs 10,000 (almost $200) at a time from an ATM (which goes a long way in India), although some may have slightly lower limits.

TRAVELER'S CHECKS

Traveler's checks are useful in that, unlike cash, they can be replaced if lost or stolen, but they are far less popular now that most cities have 24-hour ATMs that allow you to withdraw small amounts of cash as needed. If you want to avoid the high withdrawal fees most ATMS impose, you might be better off using traveler's checks—but know that you may not get the best exchange rate in the process. Keep a record of their serial numbers separate from your checks in the event that they are stolen or lost.

You can get traveler's checks at almost any bank. **American Express** offers denominations of $20, $50, $100, $500, and (for cardholders only) $1,000. You'll pay a service charge ranging from 1% to 4%. You can also get American Express traveler's checks over the phone by calling *©* **800/221-7282;** Amex gold and platinum cardholders who use this number are exempt from the 1% fee. American Automobile Association members can obtain checks without a fee at most AAA offices. **Visa** offers traveler's checks at Citibank locations nationwide, as well as at several other banks. The service charge ranges between 1.5% and 2%; checks come in denominations of $20, $50, $100, $500, and $1,000. Call *©* **800/732-1322** for information. **MasterCard** also offers traveler's checks; call *©* **800/223-9920** for a location near you.

CREDIT CARDS

Credit cards are a safe way to carry money, they provide a convenient record of all your expenses, and they generally offer good exchange rates. You can also withdraw cash advances from your credit card at banks or ATMs, provided you know your PIN (personal identification number). If you've forgotten your PIN or didn't even know you have one, call the phone number on the back of your credit card and ask the bank to send it to you. It usually takes 5 to 7 business days, though some banks will give you the number over the phone if you provide personal information. Your credit card company will likely charge a commission (1% or 2%) on every foreign purchase, but you'll still get the best deal with credit cards when you factor in things like ATM fees and traveler's check exchange rates. MasterCard and Visa are commonly accepted throughout India. American Express is accepted by most major hotels and restaurants; Diners Club has a much smaller following.

5 When to Go

Your choice of where and when to go will be determined primarily by the weather. India's vastness means that the climate varies greatly from region to region, and sometimes even from day to night, as in the desert regions. The Indian year features six seasons: spring, summer, the rainy season, early and late autumn, and winter, but effectively there are but three—summer, winter, and monsoon.

You'll be better off visiting during the **high-season winter** months (Nov–Mar), when most of the country experiences pleasant, moderate temperatures (still hot enough to luxuriate in the pool), though cities in the North get chillier days as snow falls in the Himalayas. As a rule, always be prepared for warm to hot days, with the possibility of cooler weather at night. (If this has you worrying about how to pack, remember that you can pick up the most wonderful throwaway cotton garments for next to nothing and a real Pashmina scarf in every color to ward off an unexpected chill.) As with all season-driven destinations, there is a downside to traveling during peak months: From December to January, for example, Goa swells to bursting point with foreigners and city folk who arrive for the sensational beaches and parties. Lodging rates often soar during these periods, so you may want to wait until the **shoulder season** (Sept, Oct, Mar, Apr), when there are fewer people and rates are very negotiable.

Summer (generally Apr–June) sees little traffic, and for good reason—the daytime heat, particularly in India's north-central regions, is debilitating, even for the locals. This is the time to plan your trip to the Himalayas instead, particularly to the Himachal Pradesh region. Ladakh, a magical region in the far north of the country, can only be visited July through September—the rest of the year it remains cut off by cold and snow.

The **monsoon** drenches much of the country between June and September, usually starting its season in Kerala. In Tamil Nadu and parts of Andhra Pradesh, a second monsoon hits around mid-October and runs through December. In Rajasthan, central India, and the northern plains, the rains typically arrive by July and fall until early September. Some of the regions are at their most beautiful during the monsoon, but it can be difficult to move around, and there is a higher risk of exposure to diseases like malaria. Flooding, power failures, and natural destruction are also not uncommon.

INDIA'S WEATHER MONTH BY MONTH

The following charts indicate the average maximum and minimum temperatures for each month of the year, as well as the average rainfall, in major tourist-destination cities and towns.

THE HIMALAYA
SHIMLA

	Jan	Feb	Mar	Apr	May	June	July	Aug	Sept	Oct	Nov	Dec
Temp (°F)	48/36	50/37	57/45	66/52	73/59	75/61	70/61	68/59	68/57	64/52	59/45	52/39
Temp (°C)	9/2	10/3	14/7	19/11	23/15	24/16	21/16	20/15	20/14	18/11	15/7	11/4
Rainfall (mm)	50	50	50	25	50	150	400	375	200	50	0	25

MAHARASHTRA
MUMBAI

	Jan	Feb	Mar	Apr	May	June	July	Aug	Sept	Oct	Nov	Dec
Temp (°F)	88/61	90/63	91/68	92/75	90/79	90/79	86/79	84/79	86/79	90/75	91/64	90/55
Temp (°C)	31/16	32/17	33/20	33/24	33/26	32/26	30/26	29/26	30/26	32/24	33/18	32/13
Rainfall (mm)	0	1	0	0	20	647	945	660	309	117	7	1

SOUTH INDIA
PANJIM, GOA

	Jan	Feb	Mar	Apr	May	June	July	Aug	Sept	Oct	Nov	Dec
Temp (°F)	88/70	90/63	90/68	91/75	91/81	88/75	84/73	84/75	84/75	88/75	91/73	91/70
Temp (°C)	31/21	32/17	32/20	33/24	33/27	31/24	29/23	29/24	29/24	31/24	33/23	33/21
Rainfall (mm)	2	0	4	17	18	580	892	341	277	122	20	37

COCHIN, KERALA

	Jan	Feb	Mar	Apr	May	June	July	Aug	Sept	Oct	Nov	Dec
Temp (°F)	88/73	88/75	88/79	88/79	88/79	84/75	82/75	82/75	82/75	84/75	86/75	86/73
Temp (°C)	31/23	31/24	31/26	31/26	31/26	29/24	28/24	28/24	28/24	29/24	30/24	30/23
Rainfall (mm)	9	34	50	139	364	756	572	386	235	333	184	37

MADURAI

	Jan	Feb	Mar	Apr	May	June	July	Aug	Sept	Oct	Nov	Dec
Temp (°F)	86/70	90/72	95/73	97/77	99/79	99/79	97/79	95/77	95/77	91/75	88/73	86/72
Temp (°C)	30/21	32/22	35/23	36/25	37/26	37/26	36/26	35/25	35/25	33/24	31/23	30/22
Rainfall (mm)	26	16	21	81	59	31	48	117	123	179	161	43

HYDERABAD

	Jan	Feb	Mar	Apr	May	June	July	Aug	Sept	Oct	Nov	Dec
Temp (°F)	86/59	90/63	88/73	100/75	102/81	95/75	88/73	86/72	86/72	88/68	84/68	84/55
Temp (°C)	30/15	32/17	31/23	38/24	39/27	35/24	31/23	30/22	30/22	31/20	29/20	29/13
Rainfall (mm)	8	10	14	30	28	110	140	133	163	63	28	8

DELHI, RAJASTHAN & CENTRAL INDIA
DELHI/AGRA

	Jan	Feb	Mar	Apr	May	June	July	Aug	Sept	Oct	Nov	Dec
Temp (°F)	70/45	75/50	86/59	97/70	106/81	104/84	95/81	93/79	93/77	95/66	84/54	73/46
Temp (°C)	21/7	24/10	30/15	36/21	41/27	40/29	35/27	34/26	34/25	35/19	29/12	23/8
Rainfall (mm)	25	22	17	7	8	65	211	173	150	31	1	5

JAIPUR

	Jan	Feb	Mar	Apr	May	June	July	Aug	Sept	Oct	Nov	Dec
Temp (°F)	72/46	77/52	88/59	99/70	106/79	102/81	93/79	90/75	91/73	91/64	84/54	75/48
Temp (°C)	22/8	25/11	31/15	37/21	41/26	39/27	34/26	32/24	33/23	33/18	29/12	24/9
Rainfall (mm)	14	8	9	4	10	54	193	239	90	19	3	4

EAST INDIA
KOLKATA

	Jan	Feb	Mar	Apr	May	June	July	Aug	Sept	Oct	Nov	Dec
Temp (°F)	79/54	84/59	93/68	97/75	97/79	93/79	90/79	90/79	90/79	88/75	84/64	81/55
Temp (°C)	26/12	29/15	34/20	36/24	36/26	34/26	32/26	32/26	32/26	31/24	29/18	27/13
Rainfall (mm)	13	22	30	50	135	263	320	318	253	134	29	4

EVENTS, HAPPENINGS & FESTIVALS

Indians love to celebrate, and there is no end to the list of festivals that are held in honor of the gods, gurus, and historical figures that make this such a spiritually saturated and colorful destination. Festivals usually coincide with the lunar calendar, with dates published only a year in advance, so check with the local tourism office about exact dates (some may move into another month). India has relatively few national holidays when attractions, government offices, and banks are closed: Republic Day, January 26; Independence Day, August 15; Gandhi's Birthday, October 2; and Christmas.

January/February

Basant Festival, countrywide. The onset of spring *(basant)* is marked by various celebrations. Citrus-colored clothes are worn, and there is a profusion of dancing and singing coupled with great dinner spreads and feasts to mark the season of agricultural plenty.

Holi, northern India. Celebrated predominantly in the North, this joyous Hindu festival is held during the full moon—expect to be bombarded with colored water and powder.

Desert Festival, Rajasthan. This festival takes place in Jaisalmer.

Muharram. Best experienced in the city of Lucknow, the 10-day Shi'ite festival commemorates the martyrdom of the grandson of the Prophet Mohammed; during a parade of religious fervor, penitents scourge themselves with whips—often with nails or blades attached.

March

Carnival, Goa. It may not be on quite the same level as celebrations in Rio, but the riot of colorful costumes and processions, as well as the exuberant dancing and music, make this an especially fun time to visit the tiny state and its beautiful beaches.

Ellora Festival of Classical Dance and Music, Maharashtran interior. This festival draws some of the country's top artists to the ancient caves at this World Heritage Site.

International Yoga Festival, Rishikesh. Spiritually inclined visitors head here to take classes with *Yogacharyas* from all over the world teaching a variety of yogic disciplines.

Khajuraho Dance Festival, Madhya Pradesh. Get a glimpse of all of India's great classical dance forms.

June/July

Rath Yatra, Puri. In Orissa's seaside temple town of Puri, this is one of the largest annual gatherings of humanity; thousands of devotees come together to help pull the Lord of the Universe and his two siblings through the streets on massive cars.

Hemis Tsechu, Ladakh. The town's most impressive monastic celebration happens on July 6 and 7, 2006, when the birthday of the founder of Tibetan Buddhism is celebrated with Lamaistic masked dances *(chaams),* chanting, and music at Hemis Monastery.

August/September

Nehru Cup Snake Boat Races, Alleppey. Kerala's backwaters come alive with these renowned snake boat races. Second Saturday of August.

Independence Day, countrywide. Indians unite to celebrate independence. August 15.

Ganesh Chhaturthi, countrywide. This 10-day celebration of Ganesha, the elephant-headed god, is popular across India, but Mumbai is arguably the best place to experience this vibrant event, celebrated with huge processions, fireworks, and the construction of special shrines. At the end of the festival, clay images of the god are immersed in the sea.

September/October

Kullu Dussehra. Head for the Kullu Valley in Himachal Pradesh, where you can join the crowds when idols of Hindu deities from around the region are brought together in a colorful Festival of the Gods. Similarly ecstatic

revelry occurs in Mysore (Karnataka) and Ahmedabad (Gujarat).

October/November

Diwali (Festival of Lights; also **Deepavali**), countrywide. This huge celebration among Hindu Indians is best experienced on the lawns of Umaid Bhawan Palace in Jodhpur, at a wonderful party hosted by the Maharajah (which hotel guests are invited to attend). Note, however, that just as Christmas has been exploited commercially in the West, Diwali has become a time of excessive noise, increased alcohol consumption, and all-night fireworks.

Mela **(Cattle Fair),** Pushkar, Rajasthan. The annual cattle fair in Pushkar, Rajasthan, is the biggest of its kind in Asia. Traders, pilgrims, and tourists from all over the world turn this tiny temple town into a huge tented city, with camel races, cattle auctions, huge bonfires, traditional dances, and the like.

December/January

Christmas, New Year, countrywide. Prepare for increased hotel prices as wealthy Indians celebrate both Christmas and New Year, often by taking the entire family on an extravagant vacation. New Year, in particular, may be marked by compulsory hidden extras such as special entertainment and celebratory meals. Christmas is celebrated with as much fervor, if not more, as it is in the West. City hotels take great advantage of the situation, while in certain areas, such as Goa, midnight Mass and other traditions are observed.

6 Travel Insurance

Check your existing insurance policies and credit card coverage before you buy travel insurance. You may already be covered for lost luggage, canceled tickets, or medical expenses. The cost of travel insurance varies widely, depending on the cost and length of your trip, your age, your health, and the type of trip you're taking.

TRIP-CANCELLATION INSURANCE
Trip-cancellation insurance helps you get your money back if you have to back out of a trip, if you have to go home early, or if your travel supplier goes bankrupt.

Allowed reasons for cancellation can range from sickness to natural disaster to the State Department declaring your destination unsafe for travel. (Insurers usually won't cover vague fears, though, as many travelers discovered when they tried to cancel their trips in Oct 2001 because they were wary of flying.) In this unstable world, trip-cancellation insurance is a good buy if you're getting tickets well in advance. Insurance policy details vary, so read the fine print and make sure that your airline or cruise line is on the list of carriers covered in case of **bankruptcy** (note that purchasing with a credit card is often a good insurance against the carrier going bankrupt, if you request the refund within 60 days of the bankruptcy). For information, contact one of the following insurers: **Access America** (© 866/807-3982; www.accessamerica.com); **Travel Guard International** (© 800/826-4919; www.travelguard.com); **Travel Insured International** (© 800/243-3174; www.travelinsured.com); and **Travelex Insurance Services** (© 888/457-4602; www.travelex-insurance.com).

MEDICAL INSURANCE Most health insurance policies cover you if you get sick away from home. However, do check, particularly if you're insured by an HMO. With the exception of certain HMOs and Medicare/Medicaid, your medical insurance should cover medical treatment and even hospital care overseas. However, most out-of-country hospitals make you pay your bills upfront, and send you a refund after you've returned home and filed the necessary paperwork. And in a worst-case scenario, there's the high cost of emergency evacuation. If you require additional medical insurance, try **MEDEX International** (© 410/453-6300; www.medexassist.com) or **Travel Assistance International** (© 800/821-2828; www.travelassistance.com). For general information on services, call the latter company's **Worldwide Assistance Services, Inc.,** at © 800/777-8710.

LOST-LUGGAGE INSURANCE On international flights (including U.S. portions of international trips), baggage is limited to approximately $9.07 per pound, up to approximately $635 per checked bag. If you plan to check items more valuable than the standard liability, see if your valuables are covered by your homeowner's policy, get baggage insurance as part of your comprehensive travel-insurance package, or buy Travel Guard's "BagTrak" product. Don't buy insurance at the airport—it's usually overpriced. Put any valuables or irreplaceable items in your carry-on luggage—many items (including books, money, and electronics) aren't covered by airline policies.

Tip: It's a good idea to arrive in India with as little luggage as possible—you can buy cheap clothes when you arrive and you don't have to worry about losing them or about laundry mishaps (which can happen even in India's five-star hotels).

7 Health & Safety

STAYING HEALTHY

Consult your doctor or local travel clinic concerning precautions against diseases that are prevalent in India. The following cautionary list may have you wondering whether travel is advisable at all. However, don't be alarmed: Millions of travelers leave India having suffered nothing more than an upset stomach—even this small inconvenience should settle within a few days, your system all the stronger for it.

VACCINATIONS You will almost certainly be advised to be vaccinated against **hepatitis A, cholera, tetanus,** and **typhoid;** also make sure your polio immunization is up to date. Longer-stay visitors should consider getting the hepatitis B and meningitis vaccinations as well. Note that travelers arriving from yellow fever–infected areas must have a yellow fever vaccination certificate.

MALARIA Most doctors will advise you to take a course of anti-malarial tablets, but as is the case elsewhere, the best prevention is not to get bitten. Malaria is a parasitic infection borne by the female Anopheles mosquito, and risks are greater in warm, wet areas (particularly during monsoon) and at night, when mosquitoes are at their most active. Cover all exposed skin with anti-mosquito creams (many effective creams are available in India) or sprays as evening approaches, and use repellent coils or electric plug-in mosquito repellents as a preventive measure at night, particularly in hotel rooms without air-conditioning. Note that some plug-in repellents can cause a mild sore throat, in which case stick with creams. Wear loose, floppy clothes that cover as much skin as possible, but remember that mosquitoes sometimes do bite through thin clothing, so you may need to apply repellent on your clothes as well. Note that many travelers on anti-malarial tablets suffer side effects including nausea, vomiting, and abdominal pain; ask your doctor to suggest an alternative anti-malarial that you can take if you end up having serious side effects (but bear in mind that chloroquine is not an effective anti-malarial for India).

TROPICAL ILLNESSES India's mosquitoes are also responsible for spreading untreatable dengue fever and virulent Japanese encephalitis. Again, the best advice it to avoid getting bitten in the first place (see above).

PACKING A FIRST-AID KIT Besides anti-diarrheal medication, of which the most important are rehydration salts (available all over India as ORS—oral rehydration salts), it may be worthwhile to carry a course of antibiotics (such as Ciprofloxacin) for **stomach-related illnesses.** It's also worthwhile to take an antiseptic cream, and possibly an antibacterial soap (though the type of soap used matters less than vigilance: Wash your hands regularly, particularly before eating). Pack **prescription medications** in your carry-on luggage in their original containers with pharmacy labels, so they'll make it through airport security. Also bring along copies of your prescriptions in case you lose your pills or run out (include the generic name; local pharmacists will be unfamiliar with brand names). Don't forget an extra pair of contact lenses or prescription glasses or an extra inhaler.

SEXUALLY TRANSMITTED DISEASES & BLOOD INFECTIONS Keep in mind that HIV and hepatitis B are transmitted not only through sexual contact, but by infected blood. This means that any procedure involving a used needle or a blade can be hazardous. Avoid getting tattoos or piercings, and steer clear of roadside barbers offering shaves. For haircuts and procedures such as manicures and pedicures, stick to salons in upmarket hotels. Take the usual precautions if you are about to engage in any sexual activities—AIDS numbers are not well publicized, but this is a huge and growing problem.

DIETARY RED FLAGS & TUMMY TROUBLES Many visitors to India fall victim to the ubiquitous "Delhi belly," an unfortunate reaction to unfamiliar rich and spicy foodstuffs that can overwhelm the system and cause symptoms ranging from slight discomfort and "the runs" to extreme cases of nausea, fever, and delirium. To avoid this, simply be sensible. Adjust slowly; move on to spicy foods in small doses. You should also be on your guard about *where* you eat; if you have any fears at all, stick to the upmarket restaurants, usually those in five-star hotels—but do venture out to those recommended in this guide. Remember that uncooked vegetables or fruit can be hazardous if washed in water that has not been boiled, so peel all your own fresh fruit and avoid salads. Unless you're in an upmarket hotel, don't eat fruit that has already been cut—any water on the knife or on the skin of the fruit is likely to seep into the flesh. Be wary of undercooked meats—they may harbor intestinal worms—and stay away from pork unless you're in a five-star hotel. (For more tips and guidelines, see the appendix: "India in Depth.")

The first thing to bear in mind when diarrhea or nausea strike is that your body is trying to cleanse itself, so only use an anti-diarrhea medication (like Imodium) if you are desperate—about to embark on a long train journey, for example. Ideally, you should plan a few days of rest and cut back on all food except plain basics (a diet of boiled rice and bananas is ideal), and drink plenty of boiled water (or black tea) or bottled water with rehydration salts. If your tummy trouble doesn't clear up after 3 to 4 days, consult a physician—you may be suffering from something more serious: a protozoa (amoeba or giardia) or a viral or bacterial infection.

WATER CONCERNS   More than anything else in India, it is the water that is likely to make you ill. For this reason, you should not only avoid untreated drinking water, but be on your guard against any food product that is washed with water or has had water added to it. When buying tea (or *chai*) on the streets, for example, check that the cup is washed with hot water and even ask to dry it yourself—carry a small cloth or napkins so that you can remove any and all water from anything that is going to go into your mouth. Use bottled water when you brush your teeth, and do not open your mouth in the shower. Do not have ice added to your drink unless you've been assured that it's purified. If you purchasing bottled water from roadside stalls, dodgy-looking shops, or small towns, check the seal on the cap and investigate the bottle for any signs of tampering. Also try to determine the age of the packaged water; if it looks like it's been sitting on the shelf for too long, give it a miss. The only exception to the bottled water rule may be if you are 100% sure the water has been boiled for 20 minutes. Even in very upmarket hotels and restaurants that purify their water in-house, it's advisable to stick to bottled water. Remember not to clean wounds, cuts, or sores with tap water. Instead, douse and cleanse any open wound with antiseptic solution, cover it with an adhesive bandage, and consult a doctor if it doesn't heal soon.

BUGS, BITES & OTHER WILDLIFE CONCERNS   Remote areas are alive with insects and creepy-crawlies, but the greatest risk is malaria (see above). Wear shoes when trekking or in wet areas; you can be contaminated from worm-infested soil or mud, which can also be a source of microbial, bacterial, or hookworm infection. Leeches are a common problem in the rainforest regions. Do not try to pull them off your skin; salt usually does the trick. It's possible to prevent this nasty experience by wearing special anti-leech "socks" and dousing your shoes with lime powder. You're more likely to be bitten by a rabid dog or monkey than by a snake, spider, centipede, or sea creature, but it does occur: Wear thick trousers and boots when hiking, tread carefully, keep your eyes peeled, and in the unlikely event that you are bitten, try to get a good look at the animal so that medical staff know what antivenin to use. And yes, get to a doctor or hospital as soon as possible. Animals are seldom treated as pets in India—as a general rule, steer clear of them, and should you be bitten, use antiseptic and consult a physician immediately.

Animal lovers beware: India will horrify you if you have a real soft spot for animals. You will feel particularly sickened by the "dancing bears" in North

India—sloth bears cruelly tethered and forced to perform for tourists—as well as severely malnourished dogs, feral cats, diseased pigs, and even cows, considered sacred, looking emaciated and chewing on plastic bags and cardboard for sustenance. If you can see someone to rant at, do, but for the most part you have to bear it.

SUN/ELEMENTS/EXTREME WEATHER EXPOSURE   Carry high-SPF sunscreen and use it liberally. It's also advisable to wear a hat or cap during the day, and try to avoid midday sun wherever possible. In the cities, pollution often cloaks the high-level exposure, so keep that hat on. Remember that in the high-altitude Himalayan regions, you can experience cold weather and chilly winds while being burnt to a cinder. During the monsoons, certain regions can become impossible to traverse because of flooding. Orissa, Tamil Nadu, and Andhra Pradesh are prone to cyclones in November and December. Keep abreast of conditions by following weather reports.

POLLUTION   Air pollution levels in many Indian cities are very high and contain high levels of suspended particulate matter. This is mostly from vehicles, but in places like Varanasi it is compounded by the use of diesel generators. The best thing to do is to always carry a cotton handkerchief with you to hold over your mouth and nose as a mask to breathe through until you are past the offending area. India is also plagued by noise pollution, and most visitors are usually shocked at how often drivers blare their horns. There's really nothing you can do other than accept that honking is usually a necessary precaution to avoid smashing into people, stray dogs, cattle, and all kinds of other obstacles (including cars).

WHAT TO DO IF YOU GET SICK IN INDIA

Don't panic. Medicines are widely and easily available in India. You can even describe your problem to your hotel concierge or receptionist and he or she will arrange for the necessary medication to be dropped off, doing away with possible translation problems. Pharmacies and chemists hand out pills and antibacterial medication upon request—even those that would require a prescription back home. (This is not always a good thing; if possible, consult a physician before resorting to over-the-counter drugs. Also beware of being given incomplete courses of antibiotics.) There are hospital listings for major cities in each chapter, but it's best to consult your hotel concierge regarding the best medical attention in town, particularly if you're in a more remote area. In fact, *do not solicit the assistance of anyone who is unknown to your hotel.* Well-documented scams operating in certain tourist destinations involve prolonging your illness in order to attract large payouts from your insurance company. If you or someone you are traveling with needs hospitalization, shell out for a private one, and if you're able to travel, head for the nearest big city. Advise your consulate and your medical insurance company as soon as possible.

In most cases, your existing health plan will provide the coverage you need. Double-check—you may want to buy **travel medical insurance** (see "Travel Insurance," above). Bring your insurance ID card with you when you travel and make sure you have the right local number to call for assistance.

The United States **Centers for Disease Control and Prevention** (© 877/394-8747; www.cdc.gov) provides up-to-date information on necessary vaccines and health hazards by region or country.

STAYING SAFE

Considering its poverty and population size, India enjoys an amazingly low incidence of violent crime, and the vast majority of visits to India tend to be trouble-free. That said, the usual rules apply—no wandering around back alleys at night, for example, no flashing of valuables or wads of cash. Foreign visitors may be targeted by corrupt cops looking to get a handsome bribe or payoff, so you'd best steer clear of any suspicious behavior such as purchasing illegal drugs. If you're caught, even with marijuana, there is a good chance that you could be thrown in prison. If you're involved in a car accident, have your hotel manager report the incident immediately. Avoid provocative debates and arguments where alcohol may be involved. Exercise caution during festivals and religious processions, where crowds are usually overwhelming and can become unruly.

TERRORISM & CIVIL UNREST

Avoid political demonstrations—these occasionally erupt into violence. Election rallies frequently turn bitter, and you don't want to be caught in the middle of an angry mob. In recent years, there have been incidents of terrorist bombings, kidnapping, and murder in various parts of India, particularly in the northernmost state of Jammu and Kashmir, where the terrorist organization Harakat Ul Mujahideen has issued a ban on Americans, including tourists. With the exception of the eastern district of Ladakh, avoid travel in this volatile and unsafe war-torn region, no matter what tour operators and tourist offices have to say; more than 284 terrorist attacks occurred in Kashmir in 2004 alone, and some 500 civilians have been killed by terrorists. Travelers should also exercise extreme caution when undertaking treks and travel to remote parts of Ladakh, where solo travelers are not permitted and can potentially be targeted by terrorist factions; in isolated cases, unaccompanied trekkers have been kidnapped or simply disappear. Trekkers in Himachal Pradesh should stay clear of any drug-related activity—the trade has begun to attract nasty criminal elements. Travel to the northeastern states of Assam, Manipur, Nagaland, Tripura, and Meghalaya remains risky due to sporadic incidents of ethnic insurgent violence. These areas—and Kashmir—have not been included in this guide.

Bomb blasts believed to be connected with the unrest in Jammu and Kashmir have also occurred in public places in other parts of the country. Incidents include two bomb blasts in Mumbai in August 2003 that left 52 Indians dead, and at the Indian Parliament in December 2001, while civil unrest between Hindus and Muslims plagued the state of Gujarat throughout 2002. The motive for several of these bomb blasts has yet to be established. Communal violence can occur without advance warning, but such incidents rarely involve foreigners, and thus far there have been no attacks directed against Americans or other foreigners. That said, the threat here—as anywhere in the world—should not be ignored completely: Exercise vigilance and caution if you find yourself near any government installations or tourist attractions that might be regarded as potential terrorist targets; read the local papers, heeding any relevant reports and travel advisories. Access up-to-the-minute travel warnings at **www.travel.state.gov**. U.S. citizens can also contact the U.S. Embassy or the nearest U.S. Consulate for more information about the current situation in areas you plan to visit.

CRIME   Yes, India is one of the safest destinations in the world when it comes to violent assault or threat, but petty crime, like pickpocketing, can be a problem. Apply common sense at all times. Don't carry wallets prominently; and keep a firm hand on purses (women have reported having their purse straps cut or purse bottoms slit). Don't wear flashy jewelry or carry around other valuables. Most hotels have in-room electronic safes where you should stash valuables, including

Surviving Scams & Con Artists

In India, scamming is an art form—and you, the tourist, a prime target. The best defense against the regular plague of touts and con men, who will try to tap into your supply of foreign currency by calling themselves "guides" or representatives of a local temple, is a combination of awareness, common sense, and fortitude. Scammers rely largely on **human psychology** to either win your confidence or tap into your irrational sense of guilt. Stick to your guns when you're approached by anyone offering to get you something "cheap," "quality," or "easy" by firmly declining. In fact, get used to shaking your head and saying "no" three to four times without losing your temper. If someone tells you upfront that they're not interested in your money, the warning bells should begin to sound. Remember: **Don't pay for services you have not requested.** And when you do ask for help, ask if there's going to be a demand for money at the end, and decide on a price upfront. Rude as it seems, often the only way to get rid of a persistent tout, beggar, or con artist is to **ignore them and pretend they don't exist.** If nothing works and you are being excessively harassed, try to find a policeman or other person of authority to help you. Here, then, is a guide to handling India's touts, hucksters, scam artists, and general wheeling and dealing.

- **Street touts** Touts operate under guises of initial friendship, wanting to practice their English or making promises of cheap accommodations or shopping. Often (but not always), the initial kindness turns sour when you don't comply with a suggestion that you buy something or check in at a crummy hotel. When browsing a street or market, you will be accosted by what appears to be the owner of the shop but is in fact one of a host of men to whom shopkeepers pay a commission to bring you inside. Since scam artists know that foreigners rely on hired transport, you also need to be particularly wary when considering car hire, taxis, guides, sightseeing tours, or travel agents.

- **"Official" unofficial operators** Even more annoying than the slippery-tongued con artists of the street are those who operate under the guise of perceived legitimacy by calling themselves "travel agents" or "tour operators"—and a sign saying "government-approved" often means anything but. Before purchasing anything, you need to know in advance what the going rate is, and preferably deal with someone who comes recommended by this book or a reputable operator recommended by your hotel.

- **Dealing with drivers** Taxi drivers are notorious for telling passengers that their hotel does not exist or has closed. Never allow yourself to be taken to a hotel or restaurant *unless it is the one you've asked to be taken to* (specified by *exact* name and address). Note that any successful establishment will soon have competition opening with a similar or almost identical name. Drivers also moonlight as restaurant and shop touts and receive a commission for getting you through the door. Taxi drivers often have meters that have been tampered with, or refuse to use fare-conversion charts issued by the city authority. Whenever you're suspicious about a driver's conduct, ask to be let out of the vehicle immediately, or seek the assistance of your hotel manager before paying the cab fare. When arriving at major airports and train stations, make use of **prepaid taxis** (the booths are clearly marked) whenever possible.

- **The commission system** Try to establish the commission fee upfront. It's not just street touts you need to be wary of, but even your rickshaw-*walla,* guide, or driver (hotels are surrounded by taxis that work on a commission basis). All are out to earn commission from the shops they suggest you visit. Then this gets added to the price you're quoted—as much as 50%.

- **Bargains** *Beware of unmarked wares*—this means the goods are priced according to the salesperson's projection of your ability to pay. Any deal that seems too good to be true, is. If this all sounds too tedious, head for the government shops, where goods are sold at fixed prices. (But again, beware of imitations, like Cottage Industries Exposition, often only marked "CIE," which are seriously overpriced outlets that cash in on the fame of the good-value government-owned Cottage Industries Emporiums.) Know that even though the real government-owned shops have prices that are not negotiable and are sometimes slightly higher than elsewhere, they are *not* a rip-off.

- **Creating needs** Another common scam to watch for is when you are suddenly offered a service that is judiciously timed just when you need it—often because a trickster has created the very conditions that create the need. One common Delhi scam is run by shoeshine boys who suddenly appear with their polishing equipment and point to your shoes which, when you look down, suddenly have poop on them. You can be sure that the source of the poop is almost certainly the little guy himself or his accomplice.

- **Getting the goods on precious goods** If you're shopping for **silk carpets,** ask the salesman to razor a small sample and light it with a match. Unlike wool, silk does not burn, it smolders. Tricksters will mix silk and wool—which is why you'll need to ask for a sample across the whole color range. And don't fall for anyone who tries to persuade you to purchase **precious stones** on the premise that you can resell them at a profit to a company they supposedly know back home (a Jaipur scam). Note that **gold** is imported and therefore hugely overpriced, so cheap gold jewelry is exactly that.

- **Scam doctors** Be wary when offered food or drink by a stranger. There have been isolated incidences of travelers being drugged or poisoned in order to rob them. Worse still, there are well-documented (though again isolated) accounts of these kinds of scammers in cahoots with doctors. Once you are ill, they will recommend a doctor, and your medical insurance company is contacted, and you're kept ill until a substantial medical bill has been run up.

passports and most of your cash. Be discreet about your money, and never take out large wads of cash in public; exercise modesty at all times. Solo travelers are at greater risk of becoming victims of crime; unless you're relatively streetwise, touring India alone may be more pain than pleasure. But know that it is as a victim of a scam that you are most at risk, which at least hurts nothing but your pocket and your pride; see "Surviving Scams & Con Artists," above.

8 Etiquette & Customs

As a rule of thumb, pay attention to what local people are doing, and try to blend in as much as possible.

APPROPRIATE ATTIRE In India, your attire will often signal your status, and casual dress will make it more difficult for you to elicit respect. Women should wear loose, cool clothing that covers up as much as possible. Exposed flesh suggests that you're too poor to dress properly, or that you're shameless about flaunting your body. Tight clothes are also considered shameless; the more you can disguise your shape, the better. Men should avoid shorts, which are considered bizarre. Women visiting public beaches should be as discreet as possible and avoid sunbathing on empty beaches. In mosques and Sikh *gurudwaras* you need to make sure your head is covered—a worthwhile purchase is a scarf you can keep in your bag at all times. In certain Hindu temples—particularly in South India—a man may be required to wear a *lungi* (a long piece of cloth worn like a kilt) and remove his shirt. Always check what others are wearing before venturing in, and approach slowly so that someone can intervene before you offend the sanctity of the holy sanctuary.

SHOES Shoes are never worn in places of worship—you are even required to remove your shoes when entering certain churches. It makes good sense to wear a pair of comfortable, cool, and cheap sandals, like flip-flops—they're easy to remove and unlikely to be stolen; leaving a pair of expensive shoes outside a temple or mosque is not a good idea. However, you can leave your footwear with an attendant outside for a (Rs 2–Rs 5/4¢–10¢) tip—and you will almost certainly get them back. Some museums and historical monuments may also require you to remove your shoes, and you should extend a similar courtesy when entering someone's home. In Sikh *gurudwaras* you are expected to wash your feet after removing your shoes.

TOUCHING Public physical contact between men and women is far less acceptable in India than in other parts of the world. Some Indians—particularly those who live in the larger cities and have traveled—understand that Western men and women may shake hands (or even kiss) as expressions of social friendship, but you should be cautious of casually touching an Indian woman in small towns and villages. Even the slightest touch can have a sexual connotation. Remember that it is not unusual to encounter someone who has never seen a foreign face; attempting to shake hands with such a person may prove overwhelming to him or her. When in doubt, fold your hands in front of you, bow your head slightly, and simply say "*Namaste*" (pronounced nah-mah-*stay*). Traditionally, Indian people use the left hand as part of their toilet routine. Consequently, the left hand is considered unclean, and you should only offer your right hand when greeting someone. Don't touch a religious object with your feet or left hand. If you wish to put your feet up in a train or other form of public transport, take your shoes off first. If you are booked on a higher berth and don't want to leave your expensive shoes at floor level, put them in a plastic bag and take them up to your berth with you. If you inadvertently touch/kick someone with your foot, it's customary to extend an apology. In fact you will notice that in some parts of India, if an Indian accidentally touches you with their foot, they will immediately follow that up with a hand gesture that first lightly brushes you with the tips of the fingers and then brings that hand up towards their chest or forehead. Even if nothing is said, this constitutes an apology.

AVOIDING OFFENSE Indians love to discuss all manner of subjects, and more educated individuals will readily get into wonderfully heated debates—which may be among your most memorable moments in India. Do exercise discretion, however, when trying to understand the enigma of India's overwhelming poverty and the caste system. Don't harshly judge or criticize things you don't understand fully; Indians can be quite passionate about their nation and will defend it unequivocally. Words are seldom enough to offend an Indian, but avoid strong swear words in the context of an argument or insult. And always be considerate and humble when entering a place of worship.

EATING & DRINKING When eating at someone's home, remember that it is not unusual for the woman to cook and spend the entire evening serving. Don't interfere with this custom, and don't try to lend a hand by venturing into the kitchen—especially if you're a man. Foreign women will generally be treated as "honorary men" and should dine at the table unless an alternative suggestion is made. Note that the above rules apply more in orthodox homes and to a much lesser degree in modern city homes, where in fact it is polite to offer help, even if the answer is negative. Use only your right hand when eating (unless knives

and forks are used), and follow the lead of your host when you're unsure. Don't be afraid to ask about the food, but you must be quite firm about not drinking water (unless it's bottled) and being mindful of salads and cut fruit (see above). Consider bringing your own bottled water with you.

MIND YOUR TEMPER When confronted with bureaucracy and IST (Indian "Stretchable" Time), maintain your cool. Schedules are bound to go awry and government offices are notoriously inefficient, so there's simply no point in losing your temper. You'd be well advised to adopt a similar attitude with wealthy and "important" Indian men who, as a matter of course, jump the line. Rather than fly into a rage, point out the lack of consideration firmly and earnestly or, better still, smile beatifically and practice a meditation technique.

PHOTOGRAPHY Photography at airports or military installations is strictly forbidden, as it is at all burning *ghats* (crematorium sites) in Varanasi. Note that carrying a camera to attractions throughout India will add significantly to your entry fee. In touristy areas don't be surprised if people offer to be photographed and then demand payment.

SAYING YES EVEN WHEN THE ANSWER IS NO When you ask for directions, people will often send you in the wrong direction rather than admit they don't know the way. Try not to ask questions that require a "Yes" or "No" answer, because you will almost always only hear "Yes." In other words, rather than ask, "Is this the way to the Gateway of India?" try, "Can you tell me the way to the Gateway of India?" If the person seems hesitant when giving you directions, verify that you are going the right way by asking someone else a few minutes down the road.

9 Specialized Travel Resources

TRAVELERS WITH DISABILITIES

Disabilities shouldn't stop anyone from traveling, but it must be noted that India—despite the fact that it has such a high population of people with disabilities—is not well geared for travelers with disabilities. Destinations are far from wheelchair friendly, and it is hard enough for an able-bodied person to negotiate the crowded, filth-strewn, and potholed streets, where cars, animals, and rickshaws drive at will. Access to historical monuments is also difficult (though you will have the small reward of free access). Certainly you would need to be accompanied by a traveler familiar with the destination, and you must carefully sift through the accommodations options, only a handful of which have facilities specifically geared to travelers with disabilities.

GAY & LESBIAN TRAVELERS

Homosexuality remains frowned upon in India, and the law actively outlaws sexual acts between men (although gay women do not attract this prejudicial legislation). On the other hand, Indian men are a great deal more affectionate with one another than they are with women in public, and you'll frequently see men walking hand-in-hand, arm-in-arm, and embracing, though this is said to be an act of "brotherliness" without any sexual connotation. Recent high-profile cases have brought the issue of gay and lesbian rights into the social and political sphere, and there is increased awareness in this regard. Nevertheless, discretion is probably best observed outside your hotel room (note that no one questions the same sex sharing a room).

A useful website is **www.gaybombay. org**, which offers information on gay venues in Mumbai. For more information and gay- and lesbian-friendly contacts nationwide, write to friend@gay bombay.org or **Bombay Dost** (105A Veena-Beena Shopping Centre, Bandra Station Rd., Bandra, Mumbai, 400 050); or to the **Gay Info Centre** (P.O. Box 1662 Secunderabad HPO 500 003, Andhra Pradesh).

SENIOR TRAVEL

India is not for the fainthearted, and this is definitely the one place senior travelers should utilize the services of a reliable agency and organization that targets the 50-plus market. **Elderhostel** (© 877/ **426-8056;** www.elderhostel.org) arranges study programs for those ages 55 and over (and a spouse or companion of any age) in India. Most courses last 15 to 21 days and include airfare, accommodations, meals, and tuition.

FAMILY TRAVEL

Just reading the list of inoculations and possible diseases in "Staying Safe" will probably make you think twice about taking your kids to India. But many do, and if the color and pageantry of India amaze adults, they will absolutely delight smaller eyes, opening them to the rich cultural texture of the world at large. What's more, children receive the most wonderful attention, and can do no wrong in Indian eyes—for instance, restaurants are a nightmare for those who don't like children, as kids are allowed to run roughshod and make as much noise as they want while parents look on benignly. All hotels are geared toward kids (Indian parents always travel with their children), and babysitting is generally available everywhere. On the downside of taking your family with you: the extreme heat, the likelihood of tummy trouble from the water (it's very hard to avoid ingesting a single molecule), and the unavailability of suitable foodstuffs outside the big cities.

WOMEN TRAVELERS

Foreign women will almost certainly experience India as sexist, but if you are confident, relaxed, and assertive, you are unlikely to experience any serious hassles. That said, traveling solo is only for the very brave and thick-skinned, unless of course you're traveling in comfort (using the accommodations selected in this book) and have hired a car and driver for the duration (using public transport is when you are at your most vulnerable). At best, you will experience being stared at intensely for an unbearable length of time, at worst you may be groped—some men are convinced that all Western women are loose and slutty. To a great extent, Western cinema and fashion trends have helped fuel the legend that women from abroad welcome these attentions, and you'd do well to take precautions, like wearing appropriate attire (see "Etiquette & Customs," above). On trains, on buses, and in other public places, you are best off ignoring advances or questions from suspicious-looking men. Another strategy that often helps single women travelers ward off unwanted male attention is to wear a ring and invent a husband; if you're approached, say that you are meeting your "husband" at the next station/destination. You should have little difficulty determining when a line of questioning is likely to lead to problems. In particular, steer clear of men who have been drinking alcohol. "Eve-teasing" (the word denoting unwanted attention and public harassment by men) is an offense in certain parts of India, and you are within your rights to report inappropriate advances or remarks to the police—the easiest response, however, is to loudly tell the offender off, and even strike him—you will almost certainly be supported by those around you. You may want to ask whether or not your hotel offers a special room for solo women travelers; these are now offered in a few upmarket hotels in the larger cities, and include special privacy/security features.

Note that women are excluded from entering certain religious sites and attractions (which we have pointed out wherever relevant), but this is unlikely to impact too strongly on your plans. Menstruating women are, technically, not entitled to enter Jain temples or mosques.

SINGLE TRAVELERS

Many people prefer traveling alone, and solo journeys in India certainly offer infinite opportunities to meet locals keen to make friends. You will be approached almost everywhere by people (almost always men) keen to strike up conversations (see the tips in "Surviving Scams & Con Artists" earlier in this chapter, to help you distinguish between a genuine encounter and a con game).

Indians are notoriously curious about visitors to their country, and their seemingly nosy line of questioning can spark a connection that will aid you throughout your trip. Besides opening conversations with lines like, "What is your good name?" or "So what is your line of service?" Indians may ask your marital status and family details because family is very important in India. The idea that someone would want to travel alone is alien to most. Don't be offended if questions seem too personal by your standards (such as your age or father's profession); you can always choose not to answer or give a vague reply.

This natural curiosity, together with the fact that a high proportion of Indians are remarkably fluent in English, means that you are more likely to engage in lively discussions with total strangers in India than almost anywhere else. Be as curious about their country as they are about yours, but voice any judgmental or critical questions in discreet terms.

Unfortunately, single travelers are always at an economic disadvantage. Single occupancy in guest rooms costs almost as much as double occupancy, and only a few hotels have specifically designated "single rooms." Avoid this disadvantage, of course, by agreeing to room with other single travelers.

10 Planning Your Trip Online

SURFING FOR AIRFARES

The "big three" online travel agencies, **Expedia.com, Travelocity.com,** and **Orbitz.com,** sell most of the air tickets bought on the Internet. (Canadian travelers should try Expedia.ca and Travelocity.ca; U.K. residents can go for Expedia.co.uk.) Each website has different business deals with the airlines and may offer different fares for the same flights, so shop around. Travelocity.com has a section devoted specifically to India, so you may want to begin your search there.

Also be sure to check **airline websites** for special offers. Plus you can often shave a few bucks off a fare by booking directly through the airline online.

SURFING FOR HOTELS

Most of the budget or moderate hotel recommendations do not have websites, and many hotel websites are poorly maintained, which means you may come across tariffs and information dating as far back as the previous decade. Smaller hotels change e-mail service providers almost as often as they change sheets. For basic information on about 3,000 listed hotels in India, the website for the **Federation of Hotel and Restaurant Associations of India** (www.fhrai.com) can be a useful if undiscriminating resource.

You'll also come up against a plethora of accommodations booking services that presume to be direct representatives of the hotel you're searching for, but that actually hike up the lowest available tariff considerably, which may leave you feeling ripped off before you even bed down. Always compare the website rate with the cheapest rate offered directly by the hotel before making a reservation. On the upside, several hotel networks offer unbelievable Internet discounts that simply can't be ignored.

For recommended hotel groups, websites, and essential lodging advice, see "Tips on Accommodations," later in this chapter.

Frommers.com: The Complete Travel Resource

For an excellent travel-planning resource, we highly recommend **Frommers.com** (www.frommers.com), voted Best Travel Site by *PC Magazine*. We're a little biased, of course, but we guarantee that you'll find the travel tips, reviews, monthly vacation giveaways, bookstore, and online-booking capabilities thoroughly indispensable. Among the special features are our popular **Destinations** section, where you'll get expert travel tips, hotel and dining recommendations, and advice on the sights to see for more than 3,500 destinations around the globe; the **Frommers.com Newsletter,** with the latest deals, travel trends, and money-saving secrets; our **Community** area featuring **Message Boards,** where Frommer's readers post queries and share advice (sometimes even our authors show up to answer questions); and our **Photo Center,** where you can post and share vacation tips. When your research is finished, the **Online Reservations System** (www.frommers.com/book_a_trip) takes you to Frommer's preferred online partners to book your vacation at an affordable price.

SURFING FOR RENTAL CARS

It is only occasionally possible and certainly not advisable to hire a self-drive car (without a driver) in India. Driving is the most dangerous activity you can undertake, with the rules of the road (which are usually in an awful state) totally incomprehensible to an outsider, and no sign of law enforcement. Besides, you won't save any money by self-driving—it is often more expensive than hiring a chauffeured car. To hire a car and driver, you're best off contacting the recommended operators or drivers listed in relevant "Getting Around" sections in each chapter; or deal directly with the local tourism office.

11 The 21st-Century Traveler

INTERNET ACCESS AWAY FROM HOME

Travelers have any number of ways to check e-mail and access the Internet on the road. Your laptop, PDA (personal digital assistant), or electronic organizer with modem gives you the most flexibility, but you run the risk of having it stolen or lost. Best to access your e-mail from cybercafes or your hotel. All big cities in India have a host of cybercafes.

Hotels Wi-Fi facilities or dataports (and well-equipped business centers) are available in all luxury city hotels in India (as well as in many hotels outside city limits). Note that the electric current is 220–240 volts AC, and that different socket and plug standards are used in different parts of the country. Although good hotels usually have multi-socket units, you should consider bringing a universal adaptor (if you're unsure, call your hotel in advance to find out what the options are). Note that power outages are regular, as are variations in voltage, so be prepared for any eventuality.

USING A CELLPHONE

The three letters that define much of the world's **wireless capabilities** are GSM (Global System for Mobiles), a big, seamless network that makes for easy cross-border cellphones. If your cellphone is on a GSM system and you have a world-capable (tri-band) phone such as many (but not all) Nokia, Sony Ericsson, Motorola, or Samsung models, you can make and receive calls across much of the globe. Just call your wireless operator and ask for "international roaming" to be activated on your account. Unfortunately, per-minute charges can be high—up to $5.

World-phone owners can bring down per-minute charges with a bit of trickery. Call your cellular operator and say you'll be going abroad for several months and want to "unlock" your phone to use it with a local provider. Usually, they'll oblige. Then, pick up a cheap, prepaid phone **SIM card** at a mobile phone store or at tens of thousands of shops throughout the length and breadth of India, and slip it into your phone. (Show your phone to the salesperson, as not all phones work on all networks.) You'll get a local phone number in your destination country, and much, much lower calling rates. Then you can refill your talk time by purchasing a prepaid refill when you need it. Note that if you don't have a compatible phone, you can buy a decent cellphone for Rs 3,000 to Rs 4,000 ($68–$90) in India—buy from an authorized dealer who will give you a receipt and warranty. Later, when you leave the country, you can usually sell the phone for half what you paid for it at a local vendor dealing in secondhand phones, found everywhere in Delhi and Mumbai. Alternatively, you can buy a **CDMA (Code Division Multiple Access) prepaid phone** in India. **Reliance India***Mobile* (www.reliance info.com) has the largest countrywide network, and you can pick up a low-end phone for Rs 3,000 ($68). Note, however, that some low-end phones have difficult-to-use software; the most user-friendly ones are usually Nokia models. Once you have this phone, you can prepay a balance, and refill it when necessary. Phone calls are charged at about Rs 2.50 (5¢) per minute within India and Rs 17 (40¢) per minute for international calls. The disadvantage of the CDMA is that once you are ready to go home, the phone has no value and has to be discarded.

Otherwise, you can rent a phone in India—but because of security reasons, mobile phone rental is currently not widely available in India; you'll need copies of your passport and go through other security checks, as well as make a hefty deposit. Most five-star hotels will rent a phone to you at a fairly high rate. If Delhi is your gateway, call Matrix (© 011/2680-0000) to rent a phone; in Mumbai call Colorama Centre (© 022/2204-0362), located in the Hilton Towers hotel. You'll pay about Rs 50 to Rs 150 ($1.15–$3.40) per day for the handset, Rs 2 to Rs 6 (4¢–12¢) per minute for calls within India, and Rs 22 (50¢) per minute for international calls.

12 Discovering Spiritual India

However you choose to spend your time in India, you are unlikely to return home unaffected by your sojourn here. Indeed, you are likely to find a moment of enlightenment in the most unexpected places, whether you're engaged in conversation with a shopkeeper over a cup of *chai* or people-watching on a suffocatingly crowded city street. But for generations visitors have come to India specifically seeking some sort of spiritual transformation, and the increasing plethora of first-rate accommodations and Western-style food options are making it easier than ever—and in some ways more difficult, by cocooning travelers from unvarnished India.

Basic **yoga** classes are conducted in many hotels all over the country, but those of you who want to stretch more than a few muscles can attend anything from 5-day to 5-month programs. Similarly with **meditation:** Various techniques and methods are taught around the country, but in order to truly gain an understanding of these, you should spend at least a week in study and practice. But the best way to experience and improve your skills in either or both of these disciplines—and possibly find true bliss or meaning in life through a spiritual leader—is to spend time at an **ashram,** where philosophical (or religious, depending on where you go) discourse accompanies a meditation and/or yoga program.

There are innumerable ashrams all over the country, some the domain of a dynamic **guru** (the teacher whose role it is to assist the spiritual awakening of devotees); while others (like the Vipassana centers; see below) are not driven by a single personality. In the following paragraphs we discuss where you can go to study and practice classic spiritual disciplines during your trip to India.

MEDITATION   One of India's most ancient meditation techniques is **Vipassana,** which translates as "seeing things as they really are." Taught at 10-day residential courses at many centers around the country, this program is not for the fickle—during the course of the program you must adhere to a strict code of conduct, such as consuming nothing after midday. For many, however, the hardest part of the course is the rule of absolute silence, in which you're not allowed to speak (or read) a word for the first 9 days. The lack of any form of entertainment or sensory stimulation as well is meant to assist true inner awakening. This is certainly one of the most authentic meditation programs you will find anywhere, and one not based on devotion to a single guru or charismatic personality. The course is also *absolutely free* with no charges for food and board. Check out **www.dhamma.org** for more details.

For meditation in the Tibetan Mahayana Buddhist tradition, **Tushita Meditation Centre** (www.tushita.info), a few kilometers north of Mcleodganj, offers short- and long-term programs for beginners as well as the experienced. Unlike Vipassana courses, which are more or less secular and nonsectarian, Tushita courses include teaching of Buddhist philosophy and religion as well as different meditation techniques.

If all this sounds too committed, *Sudarshan Kriya,* the revered Sri Sri Ravi Shankar's highly acclaimed breathing and meditation technique, can be learned through courses conducted by **The Art of Living Foundation** throughout India. This foundation, with a large yuppie following, is also well-known for stress-relief Ayurvedic medicine and other wellness programs. Students are not required to undergo any physical hardship, and courses are offered in large cities, after which you can return at night to the comfort of your five-star hotel room. For more information, see Bangalore in chapter 8 or visit **www.artofliving.org**.

YOGA For seriously dedicated yoga students willing to make a commitment of at least a month, the country has several well-known centers. Be aware, however, that at most of these places, room facilities are rather basic. The **Bihar School of Yoga** has an ashram on the banks of the Ganga in Munger, Bihar, where students come from around the world, usually for at least 4 months (www.yogavision.net). Requiring at least 1 month of dedicated practice is the hugely popular (and highly regarded) **Ashtanga Yoga Nilayam** in Mysore, where the fee of $600 for the first month (less for subsequent months) is heftier than most, and does not include room and board (see www.ayri.org). For yoga in the tradition of that most famous of Indian yoga gurus, **BKS Iyengar,** you can contact the regional center in Mumbai.

The courses at the Pune headquarters are only for long-term yoga experts and are booked up to 2 years in advance (www.bksiyengar.com). Less intensive, and more flexible for the traveler, is the **Himalayan Iyengar Yoga Centre** (www.hiyogacentre.com), located near Dharamsala (near Dharamkot). Run seasonally (closed during the monsoon season), this visitor-friendly organization has retreats in two locations: in Goa right on the sand dunes at Arambol Beach, and in Dharamsala, an hour's drive from the center.

ASHRAMS For those travelers intent on working on their dharma and karma, destinations like Varanasi (Uttar Pradesh), Bodhgaya (Bihar), Rishikesh, and Haridwar (both in Uttaranchal) have numerous centers, each providing some direction to an individuals' spiritual quest. In Rishikesh, the **Divine Life Society** welcomes daily visitors to its ashram on the banks of the Ganga; it professes to embrace the essential truth found in all the religions of the world. Chanting continues 24 hours a day (check the website www.divinelifesoity.org for details). In Bodhgaya, the **Root Institute** runs 6- to 12-day courses and retreats in Buddhist philosophy and spiritual awakening meant to bring peace and happiness to daily life. You can also attend 1-day workshops and take short courses on topics such as how to meditate, peaceful living and dying, and transforming problems into happiness. Accommodations are available at the institute.

You can also find programs offered by more well-known groups, such as **ISKCON** (Hare Krishna; www.iskcon.com), **Ramakrishna Mission** (www.sriramakrishna.org), and **Aurobindo Ashram** (www.sriaurobindoashram.org) in Pondicherry, as well as gurus with large, worldwide followings such as **Amritanandamayi** of Kerala (www.amritapuri.org).

Arguably the most upmarket ashram in India is **Osho International Resort** in the city of Pune (near Mumbai; www. osho.com). It's aimed at those who simply won't find their spirit unless they are surrounded by plenty of attentive red-robed staff and stylish design (with the requisite Barcelona chairs and 50 acres styled on the Japanese water garden concept, with "Zennis" courts, so pack a racquet). At Rs 2,750 ($63) per day, you can stay in the ashram at the Osho guesthouse, or you're welcome to find cheaper accommodations outside and attend the ashram activities throughout the day.

For a deeper, more authentic experience—spiritually and culturally—**Sri Ramanasramam** is 3 hours west of Chennai, in Tiruvannamalai, Tamil Nadu (www.ramana-maharshi.org). Rooms are small, basic, and cheap, but you will have to book 1 month in advance. Another fairly upmarket ashram, one with a strong following among Westerners, is run by the **Siddha Yoga** foundation at Ganeshpuri, also near Mumbai (www.siddha yoga.org). Note that this ashram does not encourage casual tourists dropping in; you have to be in touch with their programs to be allowed onto the beautiful walled estate.

A note of caution: Although all the yoga and meditation centers listed here

are legitimate, care should be taken before embarking on any spiritual journey in India. (If you don't believe us, read Gita Mehta's *Karma Cola* [Vintage Books], an acerbic and witty investigation into the way in which unscrupulous gurus market Indian spirituality to credulous Westerners in search of something more "enlightened.") There are some who feel that spiritual teaching should come free, while others argue that spiritualism is being packaged for Westerners in a way they can relate to, and performs basically the same function as a psychotherapist might in the West. Most importantly: Be aware that literally thousands of gurus and ashrams, "pseudo" or "real," are spread all over the country, some of whose principal aim is to part you from your money or, in worst-case scenarios, to sexually exploit you. Principally, be suspicious of two things: gurus who claim to have supernatural or magical "powers" or are "miracle workers," and those who ask for hefty donations. Check credentials and make your choice wisely. And having made your choice, feel free to leave instantly if you feel you are being taken advantage of or if events are crossing the line you consider rational or reasonable.

13 Getting There

BY PLANE

Most major airline carriers have flights to India. It's a good idea to shop around for fares or make use of a consolidator that hunts for the cheapest available seats on your travel dates.

From North America Count on spending between 18 and 22 hours traveling if you fly directly to India; you'll have to touch down at least once in Europe, the Gulf, or an Asian destination. With flights from the U.S. or Canada, the following airlines all offer service to India:

British Airways (© 800/247-9297; www.british-airways.com); **Virgin Atlantic** (© 800/821-5438; www.virgin-atlantic.com) via London; **Air-India** (© 800-223-7776; www.airindia.com); **KLM/Northwest** (© 800/447-4747; www.nwa.com); **Lufthansa** (© 800/645-3880 in the U.S., 800/563-5954 in Canada; www.lufthansa.com); and **Air France** (© 800/237-2747 in the U.S., 800/667-2747 in Canada; www.airfrance. com). **Air Canada** (© 888-712-7786) flies directly from Vancouver to Delhi with a touchdown in London. From other Canadian hubs, you'll fly to London or

Zurich, where you pick up the connecting flight to Delhi.

From the U.K.   Flights are usually cheaper if you're prepared to change to a connecting flight in continental Europe or in the Middle East; a number of European airlines (such as KLM and Alitalia) will get you there affordably if you don't mind a change of planes.

British Airways (© 0870-850-9-850; www.ba.com) has daily direct flights to both Delhi and Mumbai, and occasional direct flights to Kolkata and Chennai. **Air-India** (© 0208-745-1000 or 020/8560-9996; www.airindia.com) is the national carrier operating regular nonstop flights to Delhi and Mumbai. **Virgin Atlantic** (© 0870-574-7747) operates nonstop flights to Mumbai three times a week, while **British Midland** (© 0870-6070-222) offers them four times a week. India's best domestic carrier, **Jet Airways** (© 0870-9101-000; www.jetairways.com), has also recently introduced daily nonstop flights between London and Mumbai.

Emirates (© 0870/243-2222; www.emirates.com) flies to Mumbai, Delhi, and Cochin, via Dubai. **KLM UK** (© 0870/243-0541; www.klmuk.com) operates flights from all over Britain to Amsterdam, where you pick up your connection with **KLM Royal Dutch Airlines** (www.klm.com) to Delhi.

Lufthansa (www.lufthansa.co.uk) has flights to Delhi, Mumbai, Chennai, Bangalore, and Amritsar through Frankfurt.

From Australia & New Zealand   You can't fly directly to India from either Australia or New Zealand, and you will more than likely be offered a flight package that incorporates more than one airline. The majority of touchdowns and changeovers are in Malaysia, Thailand, and Singapore.

The following airlines offer service to India: **Singapore Airlines** (© 13-1011 in Australia; www.singaporeair.com); **Qantas** (© 13-1313 or 29-691-3636 in Australia, 0800/80-8767 or 09/375-8900 in New Zealand; www.qantas.com).

From South Africa: South African Airways (© 0861-359-722; www.flysaa.com) flies nonstop to Mumbai several times a week from Johannesburg.

INTERNATIONAL AIRPORTS

India has several international airports: **Mumbai, Delhi, Kolkata (Calcutta), Chennai, Trivandrum, Ahmedabad, Bangalore, Amritsar, and Cochin.** Mumbai (Bombay) receives the greatest amount of international traffic and is the best point of arrival for onward travel to Goa, South India, or Gujarat. Be warned, however, that Mumbai airport facilities are poor. Most Mumbai flights arrive late at night, so be wary of booking "immediate" onward domestic flights; you don't want to spend any significant amount of time waiting at the airport. Delhi's international airport—the principal starting point for journeys throughout North India, including the Himalayan regions and Rajasthan as well as east India—is substantially better. Only fly in to Kolkata (Calcutta) if you plan to explore east India exclusively.

14 Customized Tours for the Independent Traveler

PACKAGE TOURS   Before you start your search for the lowest airfare, consider booking your flight as part of a travel package. Package tours (not to be confused with escorted tours) are simply a way to buy the airfare, accommodations, and other elements of your trip (such as car rentals, airport transfers, and sometimes activities) at the same time and often at discounted prices—one-stop shopping that saves you money but allows for independent travel.

RECOMMENDED OPERATORS FOR CUSTOMIZED PACKAGE & ADVENTURE TOURS

If you're happy to pay good money for a very well-organized deluxe tailored tour, **Abercrombie & Kent** (www.abercrombie kent.com) are the masters, not only choosing the most expensive accommodations options, but the best (there is often a difference!). The company also specializes in putting together trekking trips and packages that tap into India's great wildlife resources—in comfort, of course. The only drawback is that always traveling in style can cocoon you from the raw experiences that make India such a memorable experience. For this, consider a tour that includes houseboat and private homestays in Kerala, Tamil Nadu, and Haryana on tours organized by **Colours of India** (www.colours-of-india.co.uk); the selection is very exciting. Another Indian stalwart is **Cox & Kings** (www.coxandkings.com) who, like Abercrombie & Kent, work hard to create a really relaxing top-end holiday (rather than the hard work that India can be), tailor-made to personal preferences. Another good upmarket agency, specializing in customized travel itineraries, is **Western & Oriental** (www.westernoriental.com).

A highly recommended option if you're traveling on a budget (or even if you have money to burn) is Raj Singh, proprietor of **Exotic Journeys,** who arranges tailor-made tours throughout India—you can literally contact him and tell him your area of interest and a daily limit, and he will come up with the goods (2 weeks in Rajasthan, Agra, Delhi: upwards of $50 per person per day including accommodations, entry fees, and private car and driver!). Contact him at exotic@del2.vsnl.net.in or at ✆ **011/2617-8685.**

A U.S.-based travel agency specializing in India is **United Fairfax Travel/Manaca Travel and Tours** (9864 Main St., Fairfax, VA; ✆ **703-591-3544;** vnegi@ufxtravel.com). Owned by Vinod Negi, this very professional outfit is able to plan a comprehensive itinerary and make all travel arrangements. Vinod is also extremely flexible; once you're on the road, any changes you want made are dealt with efficiently. Vinod deals directly with local agency India Travelite, located at 50H, Vandhna Building 11, Tolstoy Marg, New Delhi.

Another reliable local operator is **Sita World Travel** for both individually tailored and escorted tours (www.sitaindia.com). Goa-based **Odyssey Tours & Travels** is also a highly dependable agent that arranges individual and customized tours all over India; check them out at www.traveljadoo.com, or e-mail director Hans Tuinman at res@odyssey.co.in.

Audley Travel (www.audleytravel.com) is a recommended U.K.-based outfit. If you're specifically looking for an agent for trekking, try **Trans Indus Travel** (www.transindus.co.uk), although their itineraries are not limited to outdoor excursions. **Steppes East Ltd.** (www.steppeseast.co.uk) is another reputable option; they let you conveniently create your personal itinerary online. **Wilderness Travel** (www.wildernesstravel.com) specializes in Rajasthan camel safaris and elephant expeditions. Other Himalayan trekking outfits are **Mountain Travel/Sobek** (www.mtsobek.com), **Geographic Expeditions** (www.geoex.com), and **Adventure Center** (www.adventurecenter.com); the latter two also have general adventure expeditions.

15 Escorted Tours

Escorted tours are structured group tours with a group leader. The price usually includes everything from airfare to hotels, meals, tours, admission costs, and local transportation.

Many people (particularly those with limited mobility) derive a certain ease and security from escorted trips, and many tours let you see the maximum number of sights in the minimum amount of time with the least amount of hassle or worry. On the downside, an escorted tour often requires a big deposit upfront, and lodging and dining choices are predetermined. As part of a crowd of tourists, you'll get little opportunity for serendipitous interactions with locals. The tours can be jam-packed with activities, leaving little room for individual sightseeing, whim, or adventure—plus they often focus only on the heavily touristed sites, so you miss out on the lesser-known gems.

Before you invest in an escorted tour, ask about the **cancellation policy** and think strongly about purchasing trip-cancellation insurance, especially if the tour operator asks you to pay upfront. See the section on "Travel Insurance," earlier in this chapter. You'll also want to get a complete **schedule** of the trip to find out how much sightseeing is planned each day and whether enough time has been allotted for relaxing or for wandering solo. The **size** and **demographics** of the group are also important to know upfront. Generally, the smaller the group, the more flexible the itinerary, and the less time you'll spend waiting for people to get on and off the bus. Discuss what is included and excluded in the **price.** Also check the **accommodations choices** by looking up the reviews in a Frommer's guide (and do check rates to see if you're getting good value).

For small, high-end, exotic bird-watching tours of India, look no further than **Victor Emanuel Nature Tours** (www.ventbird.com), based in Austin, Texas; the tours are usually sold out as soon as they come online. Victor often includes the "Palace on Wheels," a weeklong journey through Rajasthan (including Agra) in a luxury train; for standard Palace on Wheels tours, see "Getting Around India," below. **Dagmar von Harryegg** is based in Australia but is passionate about India, particularly the desert states of Rajasthan and Gujarat, where she has developed an extensive network of contacts and friends, from elephant *mahouts* to reclusive princes. She offers personally tailored special-interest trips (anything from yoga or bird-watching to Bollywood and/or classical dance lessons) for a maximum of eight travelers—preferably friends, thereby ensuring a flexible timetable "cruising in wonderfully old-fashioned Ambassador limousines with overnight stays in off-the-beaten-track destinations." She also arranges large Hindi-style traditional weddings for couples looking for a really memorable nuptial celebration. Most trips take off in Delhi and can include a visit to the Taj Mahal. For information, contact Dagmar at dagmarvh@tpg.com.au.

For midrange and budget tours, U.K.-based **Imaginative Traveller** is popular for its escorted tours for a maximum group size of 15 (www.imaginative-traveller.com).

One of India's foremost tourism operators, **Sita World Travel** (called **SOTC** in some places) is represented throughout the length and breadth of India. Sita offers a wide range of tours to cover a range of budgets and interests. These include sightseeing trips and excursions to India's top attractions, as well as soft-adventure and special-interest tours that can really get you off the beaten track (www.e-holidaysindia.com).

Note that many of the recommended individual and adventure operators listed above offer escorted group tours.

16 Getting Around India

BY CAR

India's roads are statistically the most dangerous in the world; renting your own car and attempting to traverse the chaos that passes for traffic is simply suicidal. That said, having your own vehicle—and a driver who knows the roads, can read road signs when they're present, and can communicate with locals—is in many ways the best way to get around. You can set your own pace, without having to worry about making public-transport connections (a major headache taken care of), and you can see the sights and experience many of the attractions without feeling anxious (your driver will be a huge help in providing advice on customs and pricing), as well as experience off-the-beaten-track towns and rural scenes that give you the only sense of real India. And by American and European standards, the luxury of being chauffeured around the country—not necessarily in a high-end luxury vehicle, keep in mind—is ridiculously cheap. Certainly this is the way to go to concentrate on certain parts of India, such as Rajasthan, but it's not advisable as a way to cover long-distance journeys—aim to spend no more than 3 to 4 hours a day in the car (there will be, of course, exceptions). *Note:* Whatever you do, make sure your plan does not include traveling at night.

What kind of car?   Standard cars are often antique-looking and very romantic Ambassadors, tough cars despite their appearance, but sometimes unpredictable; don't rely on them for long out-of-town journeys—better perhaps to opt for a modern vehicle like the little Indica. A vehicle with off-road capabilities is essential in some of the more remote and hilly regions, including eastern Himachal Pradesh, Ladakh, Sikkim, and parts of Uttaranchal; it is also recommended for some of the awful road conditions in

Madhya Pradesh and Karnataka, for example, where there may be more potholes than patches of tarmac. Air-conditioned vehicles cost more but are always recommended because you may want to keep windows closed in order to shut out the endless traffic noise and pollution.

How much will it cost?   Charges for this sort of car hire vary considerably. Use a hotel rental service, and you stand the chance of forking out exorbitant fees—although the vehicle and quality of service will generally be top-notch. At the other end of the scale, you can walk up to a driver in the street, negotiate an excellent deal, and spend the rest of your vacation watching the tires being changed. It's always a good idea to start by contacting the Tourist Development Corporation in whatever state you wish to hire a car (contact details are in individual chapters). Their rates are usually reasonable and fixed; you'll be spared the battle of the haggle; and you won't have to live with the misery of being overcharged. We provide price indications in individual chapters, but a good way to estimate how much a vehicle should cost for a multiday run is to calculate three things: a) the approximate distance you will travel multiplied by the per-kilometer rate; b) an overnight charge of Rs 150 to Rs 300 ($3.45–$6.85) per night, plus state taxes, tolls, and across-state permits and fees; and c) the mileage for the car to return to its place of origin, even if it returns empty.

Each chapter lists travel agencies that can assist you with car rental, many with their own fleet of vehicles and drivers; if the price doesn't seem right, shop around. Finally, when it comes to tipping your driver, a fair amount is Rs 100 to Rs 150 ($2.30–$3.45) for each day he's been with you. If you feel you got exemplary service and want to give him more, however, by all means give him what you feel he deserves. If, on the other hand, you've had to tolerate a surly, uncooperative, and inefficient chauffeur, make sure you let the agency know, and reflect it in the tip as you see fit. *Tip:* Your car driver may sometimes drive you around for an hour in a new city rather than do the sensible thing and ask for directions. Remember, in most cities the best people to ask for directions are usually auto-rickshaw or taxi drivers, so insist that your driver ask one of them if you appear to be lost. If you are on foot, however, more often than not if you ask a rickshaw or cab driver for directions, he'll probably tell you your destination is "too far" and that you need to hire his services.

Bear in mind that if you are involved in an accident, it's best to get out of your vehicle and away from the scene without delay, inform your rental agency or hotel immediately, and have them inform local authorities. An accident involving the injury or death of a cow or person may result in a mob assault on all occupants of the offending vehicle as well as its incineration.

Taxis & Auto-rickshaws   These modes of transport are the ways to go within your chosen city or town. Auto-rickshaws are best for short journeys only, being slow, bumpy, and open-air—in other words, open to pollution. Always, always negotiate the rate upfront, having established the average going rate (unless the driver is using a "meter reading chart," in which case check it carefully, and make sure he is not using the night 11pm–5am chart, when charges are higher). We have tried to indicate these rates throughout, but given the potential escalation in fuel costs, it's best to ask about the going rate (your hotel or host should know) and figure out a fixed price for a given journey. To get from the station or airport to your hotel, use the prepaid taxi booths; remember to hand over your receipt only *after* reaching your destination. Be aware that in some cities it's a toss-up between forcing the driver to use his meter, only to be taken for a citywide spin, and agreeing to a slightly higher than normal price and being taken from A to B.

Remember: Carry your passport at all times—many of the borders between states have checkpoints where passports may be checked. Also always have with you at least one photocopy of your passport and visa and four to five passport-size photographs; you will need them for permits and other unforeseen bureaucratic paperwork, like getting a prepaid SIM card for a cellphone.

BY PLANE

Because train travel is time-consuming, amenities like clean toilets usually lacking, and roads generally appalling, the best way to cover distances is by air. The best airline by far is **Jet Airways** (www. jetairways.com), with its fleet of new planes, First-World service, and good connections (it's rapidly on track in its goal to link almost every significant destination in the country). If you have to use the state-run carrier, **Indian Airlines** (http://indian-airlines.nic.in), you will find that it leaves much to be desired in terms of reliability, cleanliness, and service, but it does get you where you want to go, with the subcontinent's most extensive network. Of the smaller carriers, **Air Sahara** (www.airsahara.net) is the best established and often offers excellent deals despite the fact that it doesn't cover all major destinations. Note that on these airlines, foreigners have to pay a dollar airfare that is higher than the regular rupee fare.

The recently launched **Kingfisher Airlines** (© 1600/180-0101; www.flyking fisher.com) operates with brand-new aircraft and a young cabin crew. At press time it was operating only between Mumbai, Delhi, Bangalore, and Goa, but its network was expanding fast.

Both Jet Airways and Indian Airlines offer special **unlimited travel programs** that allow multiple flights over a certain period of time. These cost $630 for 15 days, and $895 for 21 days; backtracking is not permitted. A similar package costing $320 on Jet Airways covers a week's worth of travel but only within particular regional zones, while Indian Airlines gives you seven flight coupons for $400, valid for 7 days (restrictions apply). Children under 12 pay half, while those under 2 pay only 10% of the dollar fare.

Passengers between ages 12 and 30 can receive a 25% **youth discount** on dollar fares; you are required to submit a copy of the main page of your passport when paying in order to qualify.

More recently, a slew of **low-cost airlines** have been launched, making air travel in India much cheaper and providing more options. Most importantly, these airlines have standard fares that anyone can buy, and foreigners don't have to pay a special higher dollar fare. You can certainly save money with these airlines—but don't expect top-notch service. Currently operating are **Air Deccan** (© **98925-77008** or 080/3900-8888; www.airdeccan.net) and **Spice Jet** (© **1600-180-3333;** www.spice jet.com), with several other no-frills outfits

likely to join the ranks by 2006. Look for names like **IndiGo, Air One, Indus Air, Magic Airlines,** and **Kerala Airways.**

India's **domestic and international check-in and preboarding procedure** may be one of the most rigorous in the world. Technically, check-in will start 180 minutes prior to international departure, and you need to produce a ticket before being allowed access to the airport building (if you plan to purchase your ticket inside the airport, speak to a security officer, who will escort you to the appropriate ticket counter). Arriving less than 60 minutes prior to domestic departure is *definitely* not recommended. Your checked baggage must be scanned and sealed before you report to the check-in counter. The list of dangerous items not permitted in your carry-on bags is fairly extensive; you will be asked to remove batteries from your camera, and these will be stowed by security until you reach your destination. Check-in closes 30 minutes prior to departure. After check-in, you should immediately head for the first security check, which will involve a body pat-down and a scan of your carry-on luggage. Boarding gates close 15 minutes prior to scheduled departure (although delays are fairly frequent), and

---

⌐Tips Winter Fog

In January, parts of northern India are often enveloped in thick fog at night and early in the morning, usually passing once the sun comes out. If you plan to take a road journey and visibility seems poor, ask your hotel concierge's advice before departing (and make sure your car has fog headlights). If necessary, make the wise decision to delay departure, even if your driver insists (and many do) that he has no problem driving in zero visibility. In Delhi the fog sometimes causes flight delays or cancellations; most airlines have a fog helpline during this time where you get updates on the status of your flight (check the dailies or use the general numbers we've supplied). Also note that most international flights leave India in the middle of the night so that they can arrive at European/North American destinations in daylight. If, because of the fog, your international flight cannot depart in time to arrive at your destination before the airport closes, your flight can be canceled or rerouted.

Tips Train Booking Simplified

Even though you will be told that there are no special lines or windows for foreigners who want to book train tickets, we assure you that this is not the case. More important, most trains have a quota of seats specifically for foreigners. This means that even if a train is completely booked up, as a foreigner you may be able to get a seat, unless other foreigners booking through the same service have already filled the seat quota. This is valuable information to keep in mind, because an agent cannot book a seat for you on this quota, nor can this be booked from the regular booking window; you must go personally to a **Foreign Tourist Rail Reservation Counter** (sometimes called Foreign Tourist Bureaus) with your passport, and pay either in foreign currency (cash or credit card) or show a currency encashment certificate or ATM receipt. The ticket costs exactly the same as the regular ticket (except for credit card surcharges). Train stations at the following Indian cities have a Foreign Tourist Rail Reservation Counter: Agra-Cantonment, Ahmedabad, Aurangabad, Bangalore, Chennai, New Delhi, Jaipur, Jodhpur, Kolkata, Mumbai, Secunderabad, Vadodara, Varanasi, and Vasco-Da-Gama (Goa). There's also a counter at the Delhi Tourism & Transport Development Corporation office at Indira Gandhi International Airport in the Arrivals lounge. In Mumbai, this office is tucked away next to the Government Tourist Office, on the first floor of the Western Railway Building, opposite Churchgate Station.

there will be second body and carry-on checks before you are permitted to board the plane. In some instances, you will be asked to identify your checked luggage on the tarmac. While frequent travelers may be irritated by these ungainly, time-consuming methods, others find the process provides peace of mind.

Tip: Always have your concierge (or yourself to be sure) reconfirm your flight at least 72 hours before departure to save yourself the frustration of arriving at the airport only to find that your name has been deleted from the computer.

BY TRAIN

India's rail network is the second largest in the world, and you can pretty much get anywhere in the country by train. That said, train journeys between major destinations can consume massive amounts of time (often more than car travel); and the network, tiers (one of the A/C, or air-conditioned classes may, for instance, be better than first class), and connections can be confusing. It's best to determine well in advance whether or not your destination is accessible from your point of origin and which tier is the most comfortable, and then factor in delays; some slow trains stop at every two-hut village along the way, and this can extend traveling time by hours. Generally, you should only consider long-distance train travel if you are assured of exotic scenery (like the **Konkan Railway,** which connects Mumbai with Goa, Karnataka, and Kerala, running along the Konkan coast); or if the journey is overnight (like Delhi to Varanasi) and you have reserved a **first-class air-conditioned sleeper** or **second-class air-conditioned sleeper** berth, preferably the two-tier variety. (Never book regular **second class,** which can be torturous, claustrophobic, and distressing if you are at all intimidated by crowds.) You will be particularly comfortable aboard the overnight **Rajdhani**— the superfast train connects Delhi to Mumbai for Rs 2,210 ($50) or to Kolkata (Howrah) for Rs 2,335 ($54) in the two-tier A/C (air-conditioned) class; it also connects Delhi with Chennai, Bangalore, Bhubaneswar, Thiruvananthapuram, Abu Road, Ahmedabad, and Ajmer. The best daytime travel train is the **Shatabdi;** these intercity trains have several routes between important tourist destinations (Delhi to Amritsar: Rs 635/$14; Mumbai to Madgaon (Goa): Rs 675/$15; Delhi to Jaipur: Rs 495/$11). Book a seat in the air-conditioned **Chair Car** class; small meals, tea, coffee, and bottled water are included in the ticket price, and seats are comfortable and clean.

For extensive railway information, log on to **www.indianrail.gov.in**, which shows routes, availability, and prices for all Indian trains. Purchasing tickets usually requires some advance planning, and it's a good idea to make all-important **ticket reservations** (particularly for overnight travel) before you leave for India, especially if you're coming during peak holiday season. Alternatively, you can make ticket reservations through your hotel or an agent (usually for a relatively small fee), or you can brave the possibility of long lines and silly form-filling at the train station; that said, check out "Train Booking Simplified," below, to see if the station you're heading to has a counter set up especially for foreigners. Not only is this an easy way to book your seat, it may be the only way to secure tickets when trains are completely full and agents can do nothing to assist.

Indian Railways Indrail Pass is a "discount" ticket for unlimited travel over a specific number of days (for example, air-conditioned chair car/first and second class: 7 days $135), but these still require reservations and are only likely to benefit travelers who expect to make two or more long-distance journeys in a short time.

In every chapter we have included telephone numbers for railway stations, but don't expect too much information from these, if indeed you are even able to get through.

Tip: To avoid unnecessary stress while traveling by train (particularly on overnight journeys), use a chain and padlock to secure your luggage and fasten it to some part of your berth or cabin. Be sensible,

The Romance of Rail: India's Special Train Journeys

India's most famous luxury train, **Palace on Wheels,** currently operates in Rajasthan, and has 14 opulently furnished en-suite saloons, a bar, and two restaurants (© U.S./Canada toll-free **1-888-INDIA-99**; www.palaceonwheels. net; $770 double per night). Over 7 days, the train travels from Delhi to Jaipur, Jaisalmer, Jodhpur, Sawai Madhopur (Ranthambhore), Chittaurgarh, Udaipur, Bharatpur, and Agra; and finishes its trip back in Delhi. Getting to the hill stations of Shimla (Himachal Pradesh), Darjeeling (West Bengal), and Ooty (Tamil Nadu) can be a scenic novelty if you don't mind spending long hours traveling in the atmospheric **"toy trains"** that chug their ways along narrow-gauge tracks to high altitudes by way of an endless series of hairpin loops—fabulous views are guaranteed. And then, of course, there is the **Konkan Railway,** which runs along the Malabar coast and has truly wonderful scenery almost every click-clack of the way.

and don't leave valuables lying around while you sleep.

BY BUS

Unless you are on a serious budget and traveling in India for months, we recommend you avoid all forms of bus travel. Often crammed full of commuters, state-operated buses are driven at blood-curdling speeds along dangerous and punishing roads. Numerous so-called deluxe or luxury buses, operated by private companies, often ply similarly dangerous routes overnight. You may be tempted to save time and money with this option, but be aware that safety is rarely a priority, and sleeping is almost impossible thanks to generally uncomfortable seating and/or noise. Regular stops at roadside truck stops along the way will have you arriving at your destination bleary-eyed and exhausted, wondering why you've opted for a holiday in hell. On some routes (such as Delhi–Jaipur or Cochin–Bangalore), the exception is the comfortable "Volvo" bus with good suspension. Another exception is the Manali-to-Leh route, where the Trans-Himalayan scenery is jaw-droppingly awesome, and an overnight stop in tents is part of the deal (see chapter 11).

Note: Buses in India do not have onboard toilets (thankfully, given the state of so many of these on trains), so stops are usually at grimy roadside *dhabas* (local diners) or just along the side of the road.

17 Tips on Accommodations

One of the best developments in the past decade has been the increase in **luxury boutique-type options** offering international standards of service and comfort, and flavored with Indian accents—like beautiful craftsmanship and ancient traditions (we're talking Ayurvedic masseurs on tap)—which means that the subcontinent is now a very desirable destination for the visitor wanting relaxation and pampering. A few independent hotels have sprung up, such as **Nilaya Hermitage** (Goa) and **Devi Garh** (outside Udaipur), and ultra-luxe **Amanresorts** have entered the fray with two new properties in Rajasthan, but the pace was first set by the **Vilas** properties, owned by India's very own, very fabulous **Oberoi** chain. Besides the Vilas properties (the best of which are **Amarvilas** in Agra, and **Rajvilas** in Jaipur, though some rate **Udaivilas** in Udaipur as their top choice), Oberoi runs some of the very best city hotels, as well as several spa resorts in key tourist destinations and a luxury backwater cruiser in Kerala. You will pay top dollar, but you can generally count on superb service and attention to detail. Best of all, you can often get great discounts on room rates by reserving in advance over the Internet (**www.oberoihotels.com**). Note that Oberoi also operates a tier of smaller, less opulent hotels under the **Trident Hilton** banner, aimed principally at business or family travelers.

India's other famous hotel chain is the **Taj Group** (**www.tajhotels.com**), with an enormous inventory of properties, particularly in South India, where Oberoi is largely absent. Quality varies somewhat (and service does not match that of the Oberoi group), but comfort is generally guaranteed, particularly in big cities and resort destinations—the best properties are the **Taj Mahal** in Mumbai and **Lake Palace Hotel** in Udaipur.

Tip: Be aware that any hovel will attach "palace" to its name in the hopes that this may attract more customers. This is often amusing if you're walking past, but disastrous if you're checking in.

HERITAGE HOTELS Staying in a medieval palace or fort is a unique and wonderful option among India's accommodations (particularly in Rajasthan), especially when your host is the aristocrat whose forebears built the palace or fort in which you're overnighting; the best are discussed in detail in relevant sections throughout this guide. Many were built centuries ago, so it's not surprising that heritage hotels are seldom the most luxurious option, with the possibilities of many stairs, dodgy plumbing, low ceilings, strange room layouts, and other eccentricities. Acting principally as marketing agencies for privately owned palaces, forts, and *havelis* (Indian mansions), as well as a number of small resorts around the country (primarily North India), two websites worth checking out are **www.indianheritagehotels.com** and **www.heritagehotels.com**.

Most heritage properties are individually owned, but a group that enjoys an excellent reputation for selecting and renovating these is **Neemrana;** check out **www.neemranahotels.com** to view their select collection of really lovely boutique heritage hotels, often located in off-the-beaten-track destinations; rates generally represent excellent value for these atmospheric gems.

BEST OF KERALA In Kerala, the **Casino** group of hotels (**www.cghearth. com**) is committed to investing in ecologically sound resorts that combine great comfort, friendly and professional service, unpretentious charm, and beautiful natural settings. Also based in Kerala, **TourIndia Holidays** (**www.tourindiakerala.com**) is run by entrepreneur Babu Varghese, who came up with the popular "backwater houseboat" concept. TourIndia Holidays also offers the best opportunity to overnight in a tent in the heart of the Periyar Reserve.

CITY HOTELS The biggest problem in big cities and popular tourist areas is that the good hotels are often priced way out of reach, while moderate options are thin on the ground. **Mid-range hotels** are substandard by Western standards,

though considerably cheaper. Wherever possible, we've provided budget options that are scrupulously clean and moderately comfortable. It's worth keeping an eye out for a new chain of budget hotels called **IndiOne;** launched by the Taj group and catering specially to the middling business market, these 100-room "Smart Basics" hotels offer accommodations priced at just Rs 950 ($22) for a double (limited number available). They won't have any of the opulence of the Taj hotels; in fact, rooms are small and rather plain in design, albeit comfortable and with all the amenities, including an ATM in the hotel. **IndiOne Hotels** (www. indionehotels.com) has already opened in Bangalore, and will soon be operating in Nashik, Mysore, Haridwar, Panjim, Bhubaneswar, Varanasi, Trivandrum, Jamshedpur, and Durgapur.

Most of the top-of-the-range city hotels are operated by major international chains, including many of the usual suspects: **Sheraton** (www.starwoodhotels. com), **Hyatt** (www.hyatt.com), **Radisson** (www.radisson.com), **Le Meridien** (www. lemeridien.com), **Nikko Hotels** (www. nikkohotels.com), and **Marriott** (www. marriott.com).

THE RATING SYSTEM India's hotel rating system refers to size and facilities on offer, not to the potential quality of your stay. Often the best hotels have no rating because they are heritage properties and—despite their overwhelming loveliness—don't conform to the norms laid down by India's tourism department.

Tip: One hotel chain to avoid is the so-called "five-star deluxe" government-operated **Ashok group.** Most of its properties have "five-star facilities" and an inventory of hundreds of rooms, but they are often decaying concrete blocks with disinterested staff. In fact, as a general rule of thumb, government-run properties are best avoided throughout the country.

Of Hotels & Taxes

Almost every hotel in India will quote a rate to which an additional uniform, countrywide value-added-tax (VAT) of 12.5% is added. This tax applies to all luxury hotels, restaurants, and bars. Some states such as Tamil Nadu add an astronomical 73.5% tax to your imported liquor bill. *Always* check whether the tax has been included in the rate you've been quoted and, if it hasn't, exactly how much it is.

BARGAINING In India, even hotel rates are up for a bit of hard-core bargaining. If you're thin-skinned, bargain online (many hotels offer Internet-only discounts); alternatively, show up and stay tough—when you hear the rate quoted, brazenly pretend to walk out; there's no shame in India in turning back and accepting the rate. You'll also be surprised to find that luxury hotels in cities can often be had at mid-range prices, simply because room occupancy is low. Always ask about daily specials, and call and check prices at hotels that may appear out of your reach because of high rack rates—you may actually get a room there for a song.

In remote areas, small towns and villages, and many places in Goa and the Himalayan foothills, you can find good (basic but clean) budget accommodations at unbelievable prices. The same cannot generally be said of the major cities, where a cheap, dingy hotel may expose you to bedbugs and despair; stick to the budget recommendations in this book.

Note: Prices in a number of the hotel listings throughout the book are stated in U.S. dollars or, increasingly, in euros—this is, in fact, the way hotels targeting foreign markets quote their rates.

Wherever you stay, you will be asked to fill out a foreign tourist information form, so have your passport ready in order to complete the details; the best hotels will fill out the form on your behalf so all you need do is sign. Also note that top-range hotels (usually the options listed that only quote their rates in dollars) require payment in foreign

currency; this is when a credit card is invaluable.

Tip: All over India, floors are marked and understood differently from many in the U.S. First floor is the floor above the ground level, second floor is the floor above that, and so on. The ground floor or lobby level is just that.

LANDING THE BEST ROOM

Somebody has to get the best room in the house. It might as well be you. Make sure your room has air-conditioning. Ask for a room with split air-conditioning (an air conditioner with a separate indoor and outdoor unit); it's far less noisy—and ugly—than a window air conditioner. If it doesn't, ask whether there is a ceiling fan or a water-cooling system. Ask about nonsmoking rooms, rooms with views (though many hotel staff don't understand this concept in India, so it's best to look around on arrival), showers or tubs (tubs in medium or budget category are usually old and stained, so don't shy away from shower-only options), and bed size. Ask for one of the most recently renovated or redecorated rooms—bathrooms in particular seem to suffer heavy wear and tear in India. If you aren't happy with your room when you arrive, say so and look around. If another room is available, most lodgings will be willing to accommodate you.

Tip: Indians often use the term "hotel" to refer to a restaurant or eating place, so don't be surprised if someone suggests you eat at a hotel down the road, and you arrive there to find a five-table shack.

FAST FACTS: India

American Express Report lost or stolen cards by calling ✆ **0124/28-1800** from anywhere in India; or call ✆ **98109-00800** (Delhi) or ✆ **98926-00800** (Mumbai). Individual branches are listed in the "Fast Facts" sections of individual cities.

Area Codes The international telephone access code for India is **91**. Area codes for principal cities and towns are listed in the "Fast Facts" sections in each chapter. All numbers listed in this guide include the local area code (which you would dial from another Indian town or city); this is separated from the actual telephone number by a forward slash (/).

Business Hours Banks are usually open weekdays from 10am to 2pm and Saturday from 10am to noon, though banks in larger cities have much longer hours. Most museums are closed Monday, and the Taj Mahal is closed on Friday. Hours of retail outlets vary depending on where you are, but many close on Sunday.

Cameras & Film You can purchase film just about anywhere in India, but it's best to buy it from high-traffic areas. Remember to store your film in transparent baggies, so if necessary you can remove it easily before you go through airport scanners (now often film-safe). Always place your loaded camcorder on the screening conveyor belt or have it hand-inspected. Be sure your batteries are charged, as you will probably be required to turn the device on to ensure that it's what it appears to be. **Film Safety for Traveling on Planes,** or **FSTOP** (✆ **888/301-2665**; www.f-stop.org), can provide additional tips for traveling with film and equipment.

Electricity 220–240 volts AC.

Embassies & Consulates Embassies of major English-speaking countries are listed in the "Fast Facts" section for Delhi; see chapter 9. For quick reference, here are some embassy numbers: **Australia** ✆ **011/5139-9900; Canada** ✆ **011/5178-2000; New Zealand** ✆ **011/2688-3170;** and the **U.K.** ✆ **011/2687-2161.** The U.S. State Department encourages American citizens visiting India to register at the **U.S. Embassy** in New Delhi (Shantipath, Chanakyapuri; ✆ **011/2419-8000;** fax 011/2419-0017; http://newdelhi.usembassy.gov) or at one of the U.S. consulates in India; a booklet entitled "Guidelines for American Travelers in India" is available. The U.S. Consulate General in Mumbai is located at Lincoln House, 78 Bhulabhai Desai Rd., 400 026 (✆ **022/2363-3611;** fax 022/2363-0350; http://mumbai.usconsulate.gov). The U.S. Consulate General in Kolkata is at 5/1 Ho Chi Minh Sarani, 700 071 (✆ **033/2282-3611;** fax 033/2282-2335; http://calcutta.usconsulate.gov). The U.S. Consulate General in Chennai is at 220 Anna Salai, Gemini Circle, 600 006 (✆ **044/2811-2000;** fax 044/2811-2027; http://chennai.usconsulate.gov).

Emergencies Refer to "Fast Facts" sections in individual chapters for police, ambulance, and emergency contact numbers.

Internet Access Although they're not always fantastic in terms of connection speed (or cleanliness), cybercafes are a roaring trade and usually cheap, albeit frustratingly slow. Keep an eye out for **Sify i way** (www.iway.com) and **Reliance Webworld** (www.relianceinfo.com) Internet centers, both offering much faster broadband connections than average stand-alone establishments. Sify, for instance, has some 2,500 Internet browsing centers around the country, half of which also offer Internet telephone services (about Rs 3/7¢ per minute for international calls). Log on to their websites to find a list of centers in a particular city. Avoid checking your e-mail in small towns; there's simply no point in spending hours behind a computer screen in Darjeeling trying to send a single message when you could be admiring Mount Everest. *Tip:* Business centers at luxury hotels charge exorbitant rates; there's often Internet connection for 10% of the cost just around the corner.

Language You shouldn't have to battle too much if you speak English with a clear accent. Don't assume, however, that everyone in India understands or speaks English. Also don't feel affronted when you run into locals who seem to smile in acknowledgement, only to reveal much later that they haven't the foggiest notion what you're talking about; they are simply trying to make you feel more at home. Hindi is widely spoken throughout North India, while all the states are divided linguistically. For example, Tamil is spoken in Tamil Nadu, Kannada in Karnataka, Telugu in Andhra Pradesh, Malayalam in Kerala, Gujarati in Gujarat, and Konkani in Goa; and there are literally hundreds of local dialects.

Liquor Laws Attitudes toward alcohol vary considerably. In Gujarat, prohibition is in force and liquor can only be obtained from the permit rooms of luxury hotels, a concession made principally for foreigners and out-of-state businesspeople. In most other non-Muslim areas, alcohol is freely available and exceedingly popular. In top hotels, you'll find a full range of imported liquor, available to those who can afford the extravagance. In most cities you will encounter "country liquor" bars and insalubrious liquor "dens"; and somewhere on your travels you may be offered local bootlegged stuff—all of which you're advised to stay clear of.

Lost & Found Be sure to contact your credit card companies the minute you discover that your wallet has been lost or stolen. Also file a report at the nearest police precinct, because your credit card company or insurer may require a police report number. Most credit card companies have an emergency number to call if your card is lost or stolen. They may be able to wire you a cash advance immediately or deliver an emergency credit card in a day or two. **Visa's** U.S. emergency number is ✆ **866/670-0955. American Express** cardholders and traveler's check holders should call ✆ **905/474-0870. MasterCard** holders should call ✆ **636/722-7111.** If you need emergency cash over the weekend, when all banks and American Express offices are closed, you can have money wired to you via **Western Union** (in India call ✆ **1-600-44-1851** or 1-600-111-911, or go to www.moneyintime.com; in the U.S. call ✆ **1-800/435-2226;** www.westernunion. com). You can **call all these numbers collect by using the access code 000-117** (see "Telephones: Toll-free numbers" below).

Mail Buy stamps for letters and postcards from your hotel, and have your concierge post them for you. International postage is extremely affordable (letter, Rs 15 first 20 grams), and the Indian postal service is generally efficient. However, sending a package or parcel abroad involves a tedious process of wrapping it in cloth and sealing it with string and wax (again, ask your concierge); you'll also have to complete a Customs declaration form. All this may cost you a great deal of time at the post office (9am–5pm). Also, bear in mind that surface mail runs the risk of spending months in the system, or of never arriving at all. You can spare yourself a great deal of torment by having a local or international courier company deliver important packages or by using registered mail.

Newspapers & Magazines Major English dailies include *The Hindu* (www.thehindu onnet.com), *The Indian Express* (www.expressindia.com), *The Times of India* (www.timesofindia.com), and *Hindustan Times* (www.hindustantimes.com), as well as Kolkata's *The Statesman* (www.thestatesman.net) and *The Telegraph* (www.telegraphindia.com). These make for interesting reading and will keep you up-to-date on local and international events. You may find that much of the writing assumes a great deal on your part, however. If you haven't been follow-ing certain stories for some time, the latest update may be impossible to fathom. For our money, *The Economic Times* provides the most news-intensive articles, written in a language that's less colorful but easier to follow. Each week you can pick up fresh issues of *The Week, India Today, Outlook,* and *Frontline* (which pro-vide quite venomous analyses of the nation's social, political, and economic situ-ations. These are available at newsstands and railway stations and not only help you pass travel time but add immensely to your understanding of India. If you're looking for general travel features, the monthly *Outlook Traveller* (www. outlooktraveller.com) features colorful articles from an Indian perspective.

Passports For residents of the **United States:** Whether you're applying in per-son or by mail, you can download passport applications from the U.S. State Department website at **http://travel.state.gov**. For general information, call the **National Passport Agency** (© **202/647-0518**). To find your regional passport office, either check the U.S. State Department website or call the **National Pass-port Information Center** (© **900/225-5674**); the fee is 55¢ per minute for auto-mated information and $1.50 per minute for operator-assisted calls.

For residents of **Canada:** Passport applications are available at travel agencies throughout Canada or from the central **Passport Office,** Department of Foreign Affairs and International Trade, Ottawa, ON K1A 0G3 (© **800/567-6868;** www. dfait-maeci.gc.ca/passport).

For residents of the **United Kingdom:** To pick up an application for a stan-dard 10-year passport (5-year passport for children under 16), visit your nearest passport office, major post office, or travel agency; or contact the **United King-dom Passport Service** at © **0870/521-0410;** www.ukpa.gov.uk.

For residents of **Ireland:** You can apply for a 10-year passport at the **Passport Office,** Setanta Centre, Molesworth Street, Dublin 2 (© **01/671-1633;** www.irlgov. ie/iveagh). Those under age 18 and over 65 must apply for a 3-year passport. You can also apply at 1A South Mall, Cork (© **021/272-525**) or at most main post offices.

For residents of **Australia:** You can pick up an application at your local post office or any branch of Passports Australia, but you must schedule an interview at the passport office to present your application materials. Call the **Australian**

Passport Information Service at © **131-232,** or visit the government website at www.passports.gov.au.

For residents of **New Zealand:** You can pick up a passport application at any New Zealand Passports Office or download it from their website. Contact the **Passports Office** at © **0800/225-050** in New Zealand or © 04/474-8100; or log on to www.passports.govt.nz.

Police Emergency and police contact numbers are listed in "Fast Facts" sections for major cities.

Restrooms Avoid public restrooms in India. Always carry toilet paper or tissues with you, since they're not always provided. Walk into five-star hotels to use their facilities even if you are not staying there.

Smoking Whatever curbs the government has tried to place on cigarette usage, there are no signs of society giving in to concerns about the hazards of smoking. Nearly every male in India seems to smoke something. An exception is Trivandrum City, where, at press time, smoking in restaurants and public places was banned (and enforced). Smoking is also forbidden on all trains, so if someone is smoking on your train, you are well within your rights to ask them to stop. Most luxury hotels have introduced nonsmoking rooms; if you don't smoke, request one when you book your reservation.

Taxes According to a new tax law, the luxury tax (VAT) on hotel accommodations, restaurants, and hotels is a flat 12.5%. Additional taxes on alcohol vary from state to state. Imported liquors attract a similarly disagreeable sin tax, making local brands far more attractive than their quality might suggest. In Tamil Nadu, for example, a whopping 73.5% tax is levied on imported liquor. Restaurant bills often include additional charges (such as a service tax) that usually account for between 10% and 15% of the total cost of your meal.

Telephones Phone numbers in India change at the drop of a hat, and businesses are slow in updating contact information, including websites.

To call India:
1. Dial the international access code: 011 (from the U.S. and Canada); 00 (from the U.K., Ireland, or New Zealand); or 0011 (from Australia).
2. Dial the country code: **91.**
3. Dial the city code (these are provided in the relevant chapters), omitting the first zero.
4. Dial the telephone number.

Note: To call a cellphone number in India, follow up to step 2 above and then dial the 10-digit cellphone number, which should begin with "9."

Making calls within India: Hotel telephone costs are exorbitant, even when you make a domestic long-distance call. All over India, you'll see illuminated yellow **ISD/STD** signs indicating a privately operated "International Subscriber Dialing" and "Standard Trunk Dialing" facility; these are very reasonably priced. Your call is monitored by a computer system, and you pay at the end of your session. Make sure you have the correct phone number with you—and check that the phone is in a quiet spot, or you run the risk of not hearing a word during your conversation. To call a mobile phone number that is not in the city in which you are based, dial "0" before the 10-digit number.

Making calls from cellphones: When making calls from cellphones, you'll need to punch in the full area code of the city and telephone number irrespective of where you are calling from. In other words, even if you are in Mumbai and want to call the city's Taj Mahal Hotel, you'd need to dial 022/5665-3366 from your cellphone. To call a cellphone number within a city, just dial the 10-digit cellphone number; to call a cellphone outside your city, add a "0" before the number.

To make international calls: Dial 00 and then the country code (U.S. or Canada 1, U.K. 44, Ireland 353, Australia 61, New Zealand 64). Next, dial the area code and number. For example, if you want to call the British Embassy in Washington, D.C., dial © **00-1-202-588-7800.**

For directory assistance: Dial **197** if you're looking for a local number within India, and dial **183** for long-distance numbers within India. Don't hold your breath for accurate or up-to-date assistance, and speak slowly and clearly. There's also every chance you won't be able to get through to the number at all, or that your question will not be correctly answered. In the "Fast Facts" sections for some cities you'll find listed numbers for private, talking Yellow Pages services; these are more helpful in giving up-to-date information.

For operator assistance: If the phone you're using is not an International Subscriber Dialing (ISD) facility, you'll need operator assistance and must dial **186.** Using an ISD facility without the need for an operator will save you a great deal of time. **Toll-free numbers:** To call a 1-800 number in the U.S. from India, first contact the international operator through the Direct Access service. For a call to the U.S., call © **000-117** (AT&T Direct Access), which gives you an AT&T operator, through whom you can make your **toll-free** or **collect call.** Note, however, that these Direct Access calls cannot be made from everywhere; to ensure you won't be charged for the call, check with your hotel before dialing.

Time Zone Despite India's vastness, the entire country operates according to the same time zone, 5½ hours ahead of Greenwich Mean Time. That's 9½ hours ahead of Eastern Standard Time (New York) or 10½ when daylight saving time comes into effect in the U.S. *Note:* You may find your sense of time threatened while you're in India; the rule of thumb is *don't panic.* Remember that there's no point in getting worked up about delayed trains and such. In fact, when you arrive on time or ahead of schedule, be thankful. Use "wasted time" to chat with locals.

Tipping Tipping in India is an industry unto itself, and it's a relief to find yourself in an environment like the Oberoi, where individual tipping is not encouraged, for this very reason. Money certainly speeds up most processes, and you're treated with a certain degree of dignity and respect the moment you produce a wad of cash—don't tip and you'll more than likely have to deal with a disgruntled and/or depressed porter/driver/guide. Bear in mind that many of the people who serve you are possibly living on the bread line, and your monetary contribution will be greatly appreciated; handing over an Rs 10 (25¢) or Rs 20 (45¢) note will hardly dent your pocket. Obviously it's not worthwhile to tip someone who hasn't eased your journey, but do reward those drivers, guides, and hotel staff who go out of their way to make your stay an enjoyable one. A driver or guide who's been with you an entire day will be most grateful for an extra Rs 100 to RS 150 ($2.30–$3.45).

Tipping is but one strain of India's all-pervasive *baksheesh* system, which is apparently an accepted means of distributing wealth to the lower echelons of society. As a foreigner, you will be regarded as wealthy, and your endless charity is almost expected by those who are less fortunate. It's therefore an excellent idea to always keep a stash of Rs 10 notes in an easy-to-access pocket, so that you can hand cash to the person who has just carried your bags or given you an unsolicited tour or looked after your shoes (the list is endless), and is now hanging around hopefully. Occasionally, someone will bluntly demand *baksheesh,* which is the same term that may be used by beggars, religious mendicants, and barefoot children looking for a handout. You are not obliged to pay anything, of course, but your conscience and irritation level will probably sway you either way. *Tip:* In Hindu temples, priests will happily encourage you to hand over huge sums of cash, often insisting that the money is for the poor. Be wary of such scams, and bear in mind that many temple officials have grown wealthy on charity intended for the poor.

3

Suggested India Itineraries

India is such a vast country and has so much to see that visitors are tempted to pack in as much as possible. Begin any trip to India with the knowledge that no matter how long your vacation, it will not be long enough. Knowing this can help you make the best of your time here and prevent you from planning a punishing schedule that will not only leave you thoroughly exhausted and overwhelmed, but with an uncomfortable feeling that you've rushed through most of what you did see.

Despite greatly improved accommodations and transportation options, India is still a challenging destination, and you should always be prepared to take in stride a delayed flight, slow check-in, or upset tummy on, say, a long-distance train. Set aside time to acclimatize and simply unwind—this is, after all, a holiday.

Ideally, you should use this book's "Best of" chapter to work out a route that covers those experiences or sights that really appeal to you, as the range of possible itineraries is endless; what we've suggested below is three rather full programs covering either North or South India over a **2-week period.** If possible, you should extend your holiday—2 weeks is not enough time to come to grips with India—and set aside more time for those destinations that sound most appealing to you. The fourth itinerary is for those who want to experience India at a languid, easy pace while still taking in key attractions—and there is no better place to do this than in southern India.

You could, of course, combine a trip to both the North and the South, but then you really should stick to one state (even one hotel!) in each area. For instance, you can arrive in Delhi, travel through Agra and then Jaipur, Bundi, and Udaipur, covering this region in 8 days, and then head south to Kerala. In Kerala, you can cover Cochin and Kumarakom (cruising the backwaters) and finish off with a couple of days south of Kovalam, before flying out of Bangalore or Mumbai.

None of the itineraries below includes a trip into any of the fabulous Himalayan regions covered in this book. If you do in fact extend your time in India, make your way from Delhi to the Golden Temple in Amritsar, and then explore the remote valleys of Kinnaur, Lahaul, and Spiti before heading into surreal Ladakh; alternatively, you can take a road trip from Delhi through the picturesque Kumaon in Uttaranchal, or take off from Kolkata to Darjeeling (book the famous toy train there) and Buddhist Sikkim. Though the Himalayas represent one geological phenomenon, these different regions offer varied and distinct environments and cultures that are in their own ways intriguing and breathtaking.

Whatever you finally decide to do, we highly recommend that you end your holiday in one of India's natural paradises, at least to recover from the sensual assault you'll experience exploring the crowded and often polluted urban areas. These oases include the beaches on the Malabar coast and Goa, the backwaters of

Kerala, the lunar landscapes and wooded hills of the Himalayas, and the wonderful hotels and resorts in Rajasthan.

Important: Should limited time force you to include only the most obvious stops in your itinerary, you will invariably only make contact with those locals who depend on you for a living, which regrettably could leave you with a frustrated sense that many of India's inhabitants are grasping, manipulative, or downright pushy. This is why it's so important to get off the beaten tourist track, and book at least one homestay in order to experience firsthand the warmth, hospitality, and generosity of the Indian people and their culture, which celebrates an ancient philosophy of the guest as god.

1 North India Highlights in 15 Days

Stunning Mughal architecture, heritage hotels, old palaces, forts, and colorful markets make North India an exciting experience that imparts a heady, sensory feeling in any visitor. No 2-week trip can exhaustively cover all the main sights, but this itinerary covers many of the most popular tourist attractions of northern India. It's a hectic schedule, so keep in mind that relaxation is required between sights, if only to catch your breath and dwell on what you've seen before leaping forward to the next equally striking sight.

Days ❶–❸: Delhi

You'll most likely arrive in Delhi in the wee hours of the morning. As a general rule, take it easy on Day 1 in India—the country takes serious acclimation. There's no better way to ease into your trip than to start your vacation at Delhi's finest hotel, **The Imperial.** Allow yourself a late morning on Day 2, and hire a car and driver for the day if you want to wander out for some slow-paced sightseeing. Take in central New Delhi's imperial architecture—beginning at **India Gate,** built to commemorate those who died in World War I. From there, set off on foot along **Rajpath** to the beautifully ornate gates of **Rashtrapati Bhavan,** official residence of the president of India. Then drive south to visit the 12th-century **Qutb Minar.** For a break, escape to **Lodi Gardens,** where lawns and golfing greens are studded with the crumbling 15th-century tombs of once-powerful dynasties. A short drive west brings you to the splendid medieval buildings of **Humayun's Tomb** and **Hazrat Nizamuddin Aulia.** Finally, stop off at **Dilli Haat** and check out the range of handicrafts and handmade goods sold by artisans from around India, before you return to The Imperial's **Spice Route** for dinner.

On Day 3, explore **Old Delhi (Shahjahanabad).** Must-sees include **Lal Qila (Red Fort)** and **Jama Masjid,** both built by Shah Jahan, the most prolific architect of the Mughal empire. You can also stop off at vibrant **Gauri Shankar Temple,** which has an 800-year-old lingam (a phallic symbol used in the worship of the Hindu god Shiva); **Sisganj Gurudwara,** an unassuming but atmospheric and welcoming Sikh temple that marks the spot where Guru Tegh Bahadur, the ninth Sikh guru, was beheaded by Aurangzeb; and **Sunehri** and **Fatehpuri masjids.** If you can handle the massive crowds, wander around **Chandni Chowk, Khari Baoli** (reputed to be Asia's biggest spice market), and jam-packed **Kinari Bazaar**—but keep a close watch on your belongings at all times.

Days ❹ & ❺: Varanasi–Khajuraho

Fly into Varanasi, a crumbling maze of a city that rises from the *ghats* (steps) on the western banks of the Ganges River.

Varanasi is in many ways quintessential India—it is one of the holiest of Indian pilgrimage sites, home of Shiva, where the devout come to wash away their sins. Many come here to die with the hope that they may achieve *moksha,* salvation of the soul from the cycle of birth, death, and rebirth. Take a **boat cruise** past the ghats at dawn; you can repeat this at sunset or, better still, head for **Dasashwamedh Ghat** to watch the **Ganga Fire Arti.** For 45 minutes, young Brahmin priests perform age-old prayer rituals with conch shells and burning braziers, accompanied by drummers, while children hawk candles for you to light and set adrift. Aside from these must-sees, you should set aside some time to wander the ancient lanes of the **Old City,** particularly those around **Kashi Vishwanath Temple.** When you feel the need for peace and solitude, hire a car and visit **Sarnath,** where Buddha first revealed his Eightfold Path to Nirvana; spend a few hours exploring the archaeological ruins and the modern Buddhist temple and monasteries. Overnight at **Ganga View Guesthouse** in Varanasi, a lovely, comfortable colonial lodge at the edge of the river. On the afternoon of Day 5, take a flight to Khajuraho. After you check in at your hotel, head off immediately to either the Eastern or Southern group of temples, with a guide from the Raja Café. The **Radisson Jass** is the best hotel in Khajuraho, though some of the options aren't too bad.

Day ❻: Khajuraho

Khajuraho is known the world over for its transgressive, taboo-breaking erotic sculptures, images that are almost as intimately associated with India as the Taj. But the temples also represent an outstanding synthesis of advanced architecture and refined sculpture. Try to enter as soon as the **Western Group** of temples opens (sunrise), not only for the light's quality, but to avoid the busloads of tourists who will arrive later. Take your time admiring the beautifully rendered friezes of gods, nymphs, animals, and energetically twisting bodies locked together in acts of hot-blooded passion. Cover the Western, Eastern, and Southern groups (unless you visited them the day before), ending your day at the 50-minute **sound-and-light show** held at 6:30pm, which provides a fascinating history of Khajuraho.

Day ❼: Orchha

From Khajuraho, drive to Orchha, the deserted royal citadel of Raja Rudra Pratap, on a rocky island on the Betwa River. This is one of India's most fabulous Mughal heritage sites and a wonderfully relaxing stop sandwiched between the intense huckster-heavy destinations of Varanasi/Khajuraho and Agra. Orchha, founded in 1531, was the capital of the Bundela kings until 1738. Today the weathered temples, palaces, and cenotaphs are the royal quarters of emerald parakeets and black-faced langurs, while traditional whitewashed, flat-roofed structures house the laid-back villagers. Besides the **palace complex,** three beautiful temples are worth seeking out, as well as 14 graceful *chhatris* (cenotaphs) commemorating the Orchha rulers, built upstream along the riverbank. Though all these can be covered in a day, get the most out of this surreally tranquil haven by spending the night at the **Orchha Resort.**

Days ❽ & ❾: Agra

Drive to Jhansi, and take an express train to Agra, home of the **Taj Mahal.** Besides the exquisite Taj, visit the city of **Fatehpur Sikri** and the tombs of **Itmad-ud-Daulah** and **Akbar,** as well as well-preserved **Agra Fort.** If you can afford it (and this one is worth saving up for), overnight at the Oberoi's luxurious **Amarvilas,** where your room will have a view of the Taj Mahal. Ideally, visit the Taj at dawn and spend the whole morning there. Built by Shah Jahan as an eternal symbol of his love for his favorite wife Mumtaz Mahal ("Jewel of the Palace"), the Taj has immortalized him as one of the great architectural patrons of the world. It's not only the perfect symmetry, the ethereal luminescence, the wonderful proportions, or the sheer scale that justifies it as a wonder of the world, but the exquisite detail covering every inch of marble.

Day ⑩: Jaipur

Drive to Jaipur, where you can explore the **City Palace** and **Amber Fort** in a day,

though you'll need a little more time if you want to go to **Samode Palace,** an hour's drive away. However, no amount of time is enough for shopping; Jaipur is a **bargain-hunter's** haven, where you will find gorgeous Rajasthani crafts for sale that are hard to resist. In Jaipur, overnight at **Rajvilas** or at any of the heritage properties reviewed, which cover a range of budgets.

Day ⑪: Pushkar

Late in the afternoon, drive from Jaipur to the temple town of **Pushkar,** stopping en route to view **Dargah Sharif,** the top attraction of **Ajmer** along the way. Get your "Pushkar Passport" as early as possible, which will then free you from further harassment by priests. Spend the night on the shores of Pushkar Lake, preferably at **Pushkar Palace.**

Day ⑫: Pushkar–Jodhpur

Start out early to explore Pushkar, a charming (if now touristy) town surrounding a sacred lake on the eastern edge of the Thar Desert. An important pilgrimage site for Hindus, it remains a hugely atmospheric place despite its popularity with foreign hippies. Browse the **street bazaar,** where you can pick up the most gorgeous throwaway gear, great secondhand books, and CDs at bargain prices. Pushkar can be explored entirely on foot—it will take you about 45 minutes to walk around the holy lake and its 52 ghats (stairs). From Pushkar, move on to Jodhpur, where you must set aside half a day to visit fabulous **Mehrangarh Fort and Museum,** arguably Rajasthan's most impressive fort, with sheer clifflike walls that soar above the city. Situated on another raised outcrop, with sprawling grounds creating an almost rural ambience, is **Umaid Bhawan Palace,** built by Maharaja Umaid Singh as a poverty-relief exercise to aid his drought-stricken subjects. Designed by Henry Lanchester, a great admirer of Lutyens (the man who designed New Delhi), it was started in 1929, took 3,000 laborers 13 years to complete, and remains one of the best examples of Indo-Saracenic Art Deco style. It is topped with a massive dome, beyond which the buildings are perfectly symmetrical. Stop off at **The Pillars** restaurant, from where you can enjoy a spellbinding view of the fort in the distance. Move on to **Rawla Narlai** or even (if you don't mind a detour) **Deogarh Mahal** to overnight.

Days ⑬ & ⑭: Udaipur

Enjoy the morning at Rawla Narlai or Deogarh Mahal, then head to Udaipur, stopping at the **Ranakpur temples** (and, if you've left early enough, Kumbhalgarh) en route. If the waters have returned to Lake Pichola, overnight at **Lake Palace** or any of the recommended accommodations that have a lake view. Time allowing, take a sunset cruise on the lake. If the lake is still dry, you're better of staying at **Devi Garh,** 45 minutes outside Udaipur. The following day, visit the **City Palace and Museum** in Udaipur. Prime attractions worth pursuing and doable in the time available are the temples at **Nathdwara** and **Eklingji.** Or spend the rest of the day lounging around the pool.

Day ⑮: Udaipur–Delhi

Enjoy a leisurely morning roaming Udaipur's lovely bazaars, or relax at the Devi Garh pool, before taking an afternoon flight back to Delhi. If you have space left in your baggage (fat chance!), stop for last-minute souvenirs and gifts before you board your flight home.

2 The Golden Triangle & Rajasthan Highlights

Though this itinerary includes Delhi, Agra, and Jaipur (the "Golden Triangle") and captures many of the essential Rajasthan sights, it does not include **Jaisalmer,** one of Rajasthan's most wonderful destinations, primarily because it's not very easy to get to. In a 2-week vacation that also takes in Delhi and Agra, it would be hard (but not impossible) to include Jaisalmer. Best to extend your stay in India by a few days if you want to cover this oldest "living" fortified city in Rajasthan. Located in the heart of the Thar Desert on India's far western border, Jaisalmer has breathtakingly beautiful sandstone mansions, though its main attraction, **Sonar Killa (Golden Fort),** is reason enough to travel this far west. Though not as impressive as Jodhpur's Mehrangarh

The Golden Triangle & Rajasthan Highlights

Fort, Jaisalmer has its unique charm as an inhabited medieval fort, and the tiny guesthouses that lie within its ramparts offer fabulous views. This is a place with no heavy traffic, minimal pollution, and a wonderful sense of timelessness. So if you do come to Jaisalmer, plan to spend 2 nights here, not least because it takes so long to get to.

Days ❶–❸: Delhi

After your long flight and no doubt middle-of-the-night arrival, have a car waiting for you and check in at Delhi's finest hotel, **The Imperial,** or at Delhi's best B&B, **Master Paying Guest House,** which will also arrange an airport transfer. (If you opt for the latter, you'll need to have booked well in advance.) When you feel you're ready to face the world, take in a few New Delhi sights, including **India Gate,** built to commemorate those who died in World War I. Walk from **Rajpath** to **Rashtrapati Bhavan,** where the president of India lives. After you cover the 12th-century **Qutb Minar** complex in South Delhi, grab a rooftop table at **Thai Wok** with a view of the complex, or at one of the recommended restaurants in the nearby suburb of Hauz Khas. After lunch, visit the garden tombs of **Humayun** and of **Hazrat Nizamuddin Aulia** (the saint Sheikh Nizamuddin Aulia), one of the holiest Muslim sites in India. Time allowing, stop off at **Rajghat,** the place where Gandhi was cremated in 1948. Of course if you're here to shop or want to browse, scrap these and head for **Dilli Haat,** a great place to check out the range of handicrafts you'll find on your travels through India. Pick one of Delhi's excellent restaurants for dinner.

Prepare yourself for the chaos of the crowded streets of 17th-century **Shahjahanabad,** or Old Delhi—just a few kilometers from Connaught Place, it feels a hundred years away, and the pungent smells from the ancient streets are a heady reminder that you are far from home. Still surrounded by crumbling city walls and three surviving gates, the vibrant, bustling Shahjahanabad, built over a period of 10 years by Emperor Shah Jahan, is very much a separate city—predominantly a labyrinth of tiny lanes crowded with rickshaws and lined with *havelis* (Indian "mansions"), their balustrades broken and once-ornate facades defaced with rusted signs and sprouting satellite dishes. Start with imposing **Lal Qila (Red Fort)** and **Jama Masjid,** India's largest mosque. If the crowds haven't left you exhausted, visit **Gauri Shankar Temple, Sisganj Gurudwara,** and **Sunehri** and **Fatehpuri masjids.** The city's lanes and back lanes are exciting to wander through, especially **Chandni Chowk, Khari Baoli** (the spice market), and **Kinari Bazaar**—but do hold tightly to your belongings.

Days ❹ & ❺: Shekhawati

Make an early start and drive to the Shekhawati region, the open-air art gallery of Rajasthan. Today there are some 30 "painted towns" in the region, but the most essential to include in a first-time itinerary are **Ramgarh, Nawalgarh, Fatehpur,** and **Mandawa.** Mandawa is a quaint town with a number of beautifully painted buildings; it is also centrally located and has the best accommodations in the area. Overnight at **Castle Mandawa** or, if you want to stay in a haveli, at **Mandawa Haveli.**

Days ❻ & ❼: Jaipur–Ranthambhore

Drive to the "Pink City" of Jaipur. If possible, book into the wonderful **Rajvilas** hotel, though Jaipur is one city that has a host of pleasant heritage options to suit every budget, and you may prefer the authenticity of a real heritage hotel. Explore the **City Palace,** including a visit to Hawa Mahal and Jantar Mantar, and then focus on sites farther afield: **Amber Fort,** first royal residence of the Maharajas of Kachchwaha, lies 11km (6¾ miles) north, while popular **Samode Palace** is an hour's drive away. Jaipur, famous for gems and jewelry, enamel and brassware, blue pottery, embroidered leather footwear, rugs, tie-and-dye cotton fabrics, hand-blocked prints, fine *Kota doria* saris, and ready-made linens and home furnishings, is a **shopper's paradise.** You could spend days bargain-hunting through the region's wonderful crafts, so be prepared to extend your stay by at least a day. If this is not possible, set off on the evening of Day 7 to **Ranthambhore National Park,** and overnight at **Sher Bagh, Aman-i-Khás,** or **Vanyavilas.**

Day ❽: Ranthambhore

Take an early-morning or afternoon game drive into the park. Set aside a few hours to visit **Ranthambhore Fort,** whose high, jagged escarpment has towered over the park's forests for nearly a thousand years. Go **tiger tracking;** the highlight of a trip here is spotting a tiger. Even if you don't see a tiger (and do be prepared for this eventuality), the physical beauty of the park is worth experiencing. Other species worth looking for include caracal (a wildcat), crocodile, *nilgai* (large antelope resembling cattle), *chital* (spotted deer), black buck (delicate buck with spiraling horns), *chinkara* (a dainty gazelle), and *sambar.* The park also holds leopards, wild boars, sloth bears, and rich birdlife. At night, unwind around a campfire and swap stories with other travelers, or discuss the fate of the highly endangered tiger.

Day ❾: Bundi

Drive to the tiny, off-the-beaten-track town of Bundi, where life goes on pretty much as it has for centuries. Approached through a gorge, the town is embraced by the hills of the Aravalli Range, topped by Taragarh Fort. Exploring Bundi's narrow streets, with its tiny cupboardlike shops

raised a meter or more above street level, is wonderful, with photo opportunities everywhere: old men beating copper pots into perfect shape; tailors working with beautiful fabrics on ancient Singers; huge mounds of orange, red, and yellow spices offset by fresh, colorful local vegetables; rickshaws carting women adorned in color-saturated saris; and temples blaring live music. Besides wandering the streets, visit **Garh Palace** and **Raniji-ki-Baori,** the state's most impressive step well. Bundi is also a great place to pick up miniature paintings. Overnight at charming **Haveli Braj Bhushanjee.**

Days ❿ & ⓫: Udaipur

Visit Udaipur's lovely bazaars and towering **City Palace and Museum.** If Lake Pichola has water, take a boat ride and overnight at either **Lake Palace** or one of the other accommodations with a lake view. Or spend the night at elegant **Devi Garh** just 26km (16 miles) from Udaipur. If the lake is dry, tarry no longer than a day, moving on the next day to one of the excursions outside Udaipur. Begin with the temples at **Nathdwara, Nagda,** and **Eklingji;** then move on to the awesome Jain temples at **Ranakpur** (a must on any itinerary), **Kumbhalgarh Wildlife Sanctuary,** and magnificent **Kumbhalgarh Fort.** Alternatively, consider another long, full-day trip to **Chittaurgarh,** site of the most legendary Mewar battles. Overnight on Day 11 at **Rawla Narlai** or **Deogarh Mahal,** from where you can head northwest for Jodhpur.

Day ⓬: Jodhpur–Delhi

Make an early start to drive to "the Blue City" of Jodhpur and explore fabulous **Mehrangarh Fort and Museum.** For many, this looming, 15th-century edifice to Rajput valor is still Rajasthan's most impressive fort, with walls that soar like sheer cliffs 122m (400 ft.) high—literally dwarfing the city at its base—and a proud history of never having fallen to its many invaders. Don't miss out on **Umaid Bhawan Palace,** once the largest private residence in the world—a vivid reminder of the decadence the Rajput rulers enjoyed during the British Raj. Then, catch a flight to Delhi, where you can relax after a rather long day.

Days ⓭ & ⓮: Agra

Drive to Agra to visit the jewel of India, the **Taj Mahal,** stopping en route at **Fatehpur Sikri.** Visit **Itmad-ud-Daulah's tomb** and **Agra Fort.** If you have the time, see beautiful **Jama Masjid,** built in 1648 by Jahanara Begum, Shah Jahan's favorite daughter. Overnight at the Oberoi's **Amarvilas,** a worthwhile splurge for your last night in India. Ideally, you can visit the **Taj** at dawn on Day 14 and spend as much time as you like there before you head back to Delhi for your flight out. If you get into Delhi before nightfall, you'll still have time to do last-minute shopping, as most shops are open till at least 7pm.

3 South India in 2 Weeks

South India is where the great Dravidian kingdoms were established, and anyone interested in ancient history and grand temples must visit Tamil Nadu or Karnataka. Here we've included only a few temples, but if you crave more, you'll find an exhaustive variety of exquisitely carved temples to explore. For natural beauty and rejuvenation, there are few places in India like Kerala, India's most verdant state, where we recommend you end your trip. This itinerary also takes you through its tea estates, backwaters, and wildlife parks.

Days ❶ & ❷: Bangalore

Fly straight into Bangalore. You'll probably arrive in the middle of the night, so spend the day relaxing or wandering through Karnataka's capital city and IT hub. At some point, take in **Bull Temple** on Bugle Hill. Built by the city's original architect, Kempe Gowda, this 16th-century black-granite statue of Nandi (Shiva's sacred bull "vehicle") literally dwarfs its "master," and is kept glistening by regular applications of coconut oil. Stay at either the ultra-modern **Park hotel** or the **Taj West End** for old-world charm. If you're on a budget, book a room at lovely **Villa Pottipati.** If you arrive in Mumbai instead, you can spend the day relaxing at one of the city's numerous luxury hotels or at a good-value option like Gordons. Set aside a few hours to wander around and acclimate yourself to India's most bustling metropolis.

Day ❸: Chennai–Mamallapuram

From Bangalore (or Mumbai), fly to Chennai (or take the train). You can either head straight down the coast to **Fisherman's Cove** resort (1 hr.) or take a detour to **Kanchipuram** 80km (50 miles) southwest of Chennai to visit the temples there before heading to Fisherman's Cove. If you prefer to be closer to Mamallapuram, book a room at **Temple Bay** resort instead. En route, stop along the scenic East Coast Highway at the cultural centers of **Cholamandalam** and **Dakshina Chitra** for local arts and crafts. At **Cholamandalam Artists' Village,** you can observe artists at work, while **Dakshina Chitra** is a heritage center showcasing different living styles from India's four southern states: Karnataka, Tamil Nadu, Kerala, and Andhra Pradesh.

Day ❹: Mamallapuram

Set out early and take in Mamallapuram's monolithic shrines and rock-cut cave temples, which lie scattered over a landscape heaped with boulders and rocky hillocks. Among these, the excellent **Shore Temple,** built to Lord Shiva, and the **Five Rathas,** a cluster of temples named for the five Pandava brothers of *Mahabharata* fame, are definitely worth seeking out. The celebrated **Arjuna's Penance** is the largest relief-carving on earth. When you've finished your tour, you can enjoy a great seafood meal at one of the numerous beach shacks or restaurants before continuing down the coast to the French colonial town of Pondicherry. Overnight at **Hotel de l'Orient.**

Days ❺ & ❻: Pondicherry

Besides hanging out in your antiques-filled colonial hotel or sauntering around the oceanfront **French Quarter,** you can visit **Auroville,** an interesting experiment in alternative living, also optimistically known as the City of Dawn; or you can join New Age travelers and visit the ashram

of **Sri Aurobindo.** While wandering the Quarter, you may want to take a look at the **Sacred Heart of Jesus (Eglise de Sacre Coeur de Jésus),** an 18th-century neo-Gothic Catholic church on South Boulevard; and at the **Church of Immaculate Conception** on Mission Street. At twilight, stroll to **Goubert Salai** (Beach Rd.), where you'll see the colonial **Hôtel de Ville** (now the Municipal Offices building) and a statue of Gandhi standing at the pier. On the evening of Day 6, drive to Chennai, from where you can take a flight to Madurai. Overnight at the **Taj Garden Retreat, Madurai.**

Day ❼: Madurai

Early in the morning, visit **Shri Meenakshi-Sundareshwarar Temple,** one of South

India's biggest, busiest pilgrimage sites. Garish stucco gods, demons, beasts, and heroes smother the various towers in a writhing, fascinating mass of symbolism, vividly painted a riot of bright colors. Near the inner gate, a temple elephant, daubed with eye shadow and blusher, earns her keep by accepting a few rupees in exchange for a blessing—bestowed with a light tap of her dexterous trunk. From here you can wander at will, finding your way at some stage to the **Thousand Pillar Museum,** housed in the impressive 16th-century Hall of a Thousand Pillars. This hall has 985 elegantly sculpted columns, including a set of "musical pillars" that produce the seven Carnatic musical notes when tapped. All around the complex of shrines and effigies, various *pujas* (prayers) and rituals are conducted. Once you're done exploring the site and have spent an hour or so wandering the lanes adjacent to the temple, drive to Munnar, sometimes referred to as Kerala's Scottish highlands. Overnight at **The Siena Village,** a 30-minute drive from Munnar town.

Day ❽: Munnar

Munnar is a collection of vast green tea estates first established by a Scotsman in the late 19th century. Besides enjoying the rolling mists and endless greenery, you can arrange a **tea factory visit** and a stopover at the **Tea Museum.** To get up close to some of the world's last Nilgiri tahr (a variety of mountain goat or ibex), visit nearby **Eravikulam National Park.** Existing only in the mountain grasslands of the Western ghats at altitudes above 2,000m (6,561 ft.), the tahr is as endangered as the tiger.

Day ❾: Periyar

Drive to **Periyar Wildlife Sanctuary,** originally the hunting grounds of the Maharajah of Travancore. The park covers 777 sq. km (8,364 sq. ft.) and is divided into core, buffer, and tourist zones. Although this is a tiger reserve, tiger sightings are rare,

particularly in the tourist zone, but the reserve is also home to the elephant, sloth bear, sambar, Indian bison or gaur, wild dog, leopard, spotted deer, Malabar flying squirrel, barking deer, and Nilgiri tahr, as well as some 260 species of birds. More than 2,000 species of flowering plants grow here, including at least 150 different kinds of orchids. Organize a **private boat launch** ride from where you can view animals coming to drink at the water's edge. You can also take one of the 3-hour **daily walks,** which give you the opportunity to admire the stunning flora of the region. To ensure you have a truly close-up encounter with an elephant, go on a 30-minute **elephant ride** in the park. Overnight at **Shalimar Spice Garden Resort.**

Day ❿: Kumarakom

Drive to the heart of Kerala's backwaters region to Kumarakom, which has by far the best accommodations. Idle away the hours on a backwaters cruise, indulge in Ayurvedic therapies, and laze under the tropical sun—that's about as busy as your day is likely to get. Overnight at the **Kumarakom Lake Resort.**

Day ⓫: Houseboat

Reset your watch to a rhythm of life that has remained relatively unchanged for centuries: Board a *kettuvallam,* one of the long, beautifully crafted cargo boats that ply the waterways. The houseboat experience allows you to aimlessly drift past villages, temples, and churches and be thoroughly exposed to the rural lifestyle of the backwaters. As you drift along, you can watch women, unperturbed by your presence, wash their long ebony tresses or pound away at laundry, while children play at the water's edge, men dive for mussels, and elephants and water buffalo wade at will. Although the onboard facilities might strike some as rather basic, you'll be spoiled rotten by your private team—a guide, a cook, and a pilot—who work hard to make your experience unique and exceptional.

Days ⓬ & ⓭: Cochin (Kochi)

Travel north to Cochin and settle into a hotel in **Fort Kochi** (we suggest either The Brunton Boatyard Hotel or the Malabar Residency), then explore Fort Kochi on foot. Start your tour at the harbor near Vasco da Gama Square, where you can watch the **Chinese fishing nets,** then visit **St. Francis Church** and **Santa Cruz Cathedral.** Stop to admire the facade of **Koder House**—built in 1808 by Jewish patriarch Samuel Koder, it's a good example of the hybrid Indo-European style that developed in Cochin. Also nearby is the **Pierce Leslie Bungalow,** a charming 19th-century mansion reflecting Portuguese and Dutch influences on local architecture. Take an auto-rickshaw to Mattancherry, where you should visit the **Dutch (Mattancherry) Palace** and **Paradesi Synagogue** before discovering the fragrant scents of Kerala's **spice warehouses.** Make time to visit a few of the antiques warehouses, where some real treasures are to be found. A **sunset cruise** around the harbor is another must; it's the best way to enjoy the most-photographed of Cochin's historic sights, the Chinese fishing nets that form wonderful silhouettes against a red- and orange-hued sky.

Day ⓮: Wyanad

From Cochin, take the early Cannanore Express train to Calicut, from where you can catch a taxi for the 2-hour journey to Sulthan Bathery in Wyanad. Without a doubt the best accommodations, **Tranquil Resorts** is a wonderful homestay on a 162-hectare (400-acre) coffee and vanilla plantation at the edge of Wyanad National Park. Visit tea, pepper, cardamom, coffee, banana, and coconut plantations, or take one of the many splendid walks on this scenic estate; alternatively, take a trip into the park or to Edakkal Caves. Either way, the hospitality of Victor and Ranjini Dey at this gorgeous planter's bungalow makes for an excellent end-of-trip sojourn.

Day ⓯: Wyanad–Calicut–Home

Hearts heavy with regret, you must now make your way back to Calicut to fly to either Mumbai or Bangalore to connect to your flight home. If you arrive in Mumbai, you will need to transfer from the domestic to the international airport. En route, you can stop off for dinner at one of the superb restaurants near the airport (Dum Pukht or Dakshin at the ITC Grand Maratha Sheraton; or Stax, the Italian restaurant at the Hyatt Regency, if you'd prefer a less spice-intense meal), before you catch the late-night flight home.

4 A Leisurely Southern Sojourn

South India is perfect for a slow-paced 2-week holiday that's more unhurried escape than hectic vacation filled with must-see sights. This itinerary does explore a few tourist sites, but mostly it's about relaxing and enjoying a few beautiful and varied environments. Kerala is the ideal place to unwind and indulge; this is, after all, where succumbing to therapeutic Ayurvedic massages and treatments is as mandatory as idling away an afternoon aboard a slowly drifting *kettuvallam,* or sipping coconut water under a tropical sun.

Days ❶ & ❷: Mumbai

Though Mumbai is India's busiest city, it's also a perfect place to begin an unhurried vacation. From the airport, head either to the **Taj Mahal Palace and Tower** (only a Heritage Wing room will do) or **The Oberoi;** enjoy the warm weather on a sun-bed by the pool, or make your way to the hotel spa for the pampering you deserve after that long journey. Alternatively, a stay at **Gordon House Hotel,** Colaba's sexiest lodging option, will suit party animals who appreciate the in-house nightclub. Mumbai doesn't have a wealth of historical attractions; it's a city you *experience* rather than sightsee, and sampling the restaurants' fare should be high on your must-do list. From your hotel you can also explore on foot the **Marine Drive/Chowpatty Beach** area, and if you're at all inspired by Gothic Victorian architecture, plan a jaunt through Mumbai's older districts. Stop off at the **Gateway of India,** from where it's a 15-minute walk north to Fort, passing the **Prince of Wales Museum** as well as a host of Raj-era Gothic architectural highlights. From the museum, continue to Flora Fountain and beyond to **Victoria Terminus Station.** Wander back to the **Fountain,** taking in the impressive **High Court** building and the **Rajabai Clock Tower,** which overlooks the Bombay University complex. Some of the best restaurants in Mumbai are in this general neighborhood, so take your pick. If you want to sample the coastal seafood for which Mumbai is famous, go no farther than **Mahesh Lunch Home** in Fort.

Days ❸ & ❹: Goa

Fly to Goa, old Portuguese colony and beach paradise. Take your pick of accommodations, from sprawling beachfront five-star hotels to small boutique hotels. If pampering is part of your plan, book into the **Pousada Tauma,** a gorgeous getaway and Ayurvedic retreat with a superb in-house restaurant. If you can drag yourself away from the beach and poolside, explore Old Goa; most sights are clustered together, so it can be covered in a few hours. These include **Arch of the Viceroys,** built in 1597 in commemoration of the arrival of Vasco da Gama in India; **Church of St. Cajetan,** modeled

after St. Peter's in Rome; and **Adil Shah's Gate,** a simple lintel supported by two black basalt columns. Southwest of St. Cajetan's are the highlights of Old Goa: splendid **Sé Cathedral,** said to be larger than any church in Portugal; and the **Basilica of Bom Jesus (Cathedral of the Good Jesus).** Nearby is the **Convent and Church of St. Francis of Assisi,** while up the hill are the ruins of the **Church of St. Augustine;** below are the **Church and Convent of Santa Monica** and the **Chapel of the Weeping Cross.**

Days ❺ & ❻: Hampi

Take the biweekly train from Goa to Hampi, endure an overnight bus ride, or fly to Bangalore the previous evening, from where you can get a convenient overnight train to Hospet. Check in at **Hampi's Boulders.** Spend your time leisurely exploring the ancient city, whose isolated ruins are scattered among impossibly balanced wind-smoothed boulders and immense stretches of verdant landscape. Highlights are fabulous **Virupaksha Temple** and **Vitthala Temple,** dedicated to an incarnation of Vishnu and one of the most spectacular of Hampi's monuments; also make sure to see the **royal enclosure,** which incorporates the ruined palaces where the Vijayanagara kings would have lived and held court. Not much survives, but you can still visit **Hazara Rama Temple** (where the royals went to worship), a small **stepped tank,** and **Mahanavami Dibba** (a platform where performances and entertainment were held). On the outskirts of the royal complex, you will see the *zenana* enclosure, marked by the two-story Indo-Saracenic pavilion, **Kamala (Lotus) Mahal** and, just outside the enclosure, the awesome **Elephant Stables.**

Days ❼ & ❽: Cochin (Kochi)

Take the train to Bangalore and from there fly to Cochin, where you should get a room in Fort Kochi (at either the Brunton Boatyard Hotel or the Malabar Residency). Fort

Kochi can be explored on foot. Visit **St. Francis Church** and **Santa Cruz Cathedral;** stop to gaze at the famous **Chinese fishing nets.** Drive to **Mattancherry Palace (Dutch Palace)** and **Paradesi Synagogue** before following your nose to the **spice warehouses.** Antiques lovers will be bowled over by Cochin's antiques warehouses full of real treasures. Take a **sunset cruise** around the harbor at dusk and end your day dining on a seafood platter at one of Cochin's wonderful restaurants.

Days ❾ & ❿: Kumarakom

Drive to Alleppey to experience Kerala's backwaters. Spend 2 nights at one of the wonderful homestays in the region (**Philipkutty's Farm** or **Emerald Isle**) or on a **houseboat;** alternatively, book into **Coconut Lagoon** or **Kumarakom Lake Resort.** If you opt for the houseboat experience, you bed aboard a *kettuvallam,* one of the long, beautifully crafted cargo boats that ply the waterways—a wonderful way to experience the rural lifestyle of the backwaters as you aimlessly drift past villages, temples, and churches. If the facilities strike you as too basic, and if you're not keen on a homestay either, spend the night at the intimate **Kayaloram Lake Resort** and take a sunset backwaters cruise instead.

Days ⓫–⓭: Kovalam & Beyond

Drive to **Trivandrum** and continue beyond it to the famous **Surya Samudra Beach Garden.** Spread over 8 hectares (20 acres) amid terraced gardens, Surya has such a glorious setting that as soon as you arrive you will wonder why you didn't come straight here in the first place. Accommodations are in the centuries-old carved wooden cottages transplanted from villages around Kerala. Much of your time here is best spent lazing by the infinity pool carved out of the rock bed or on one of the two beaches. Spend the rest of your time here enjoying Ayurvedic treatments and massages and figuring out how soon you can return. If you can bear to tear yourself away, take an early-morning excursion to sacred **Kanyakumari,** the southernmost tip of India, where three oceans meet and crowds worship the sunrise; or to **Padmanabhapuram Palace,** for several centuries the traditional home of Kerala's Travancore royal family. Alternatively, spend a night in the hills nearby at **Duke's Forest Lodge,** located on the edge of a river and rubber plantation near Pepara Sanctuary. Book a pool pavilion—each with its own plunge pool—and enjoy a secluded romantic getaway before heading back to Surya Samudra for your final night in India.

Day ⑭: Trivandrum–Home

Completely relaxed and rejuvenated, make your way back to Trivandrum, and from there fly to Mumbai or Bangalore for your international flight back home. If you arrive in Mumbai, where you will have many hours before your flight, enjoy dinner at one of the marvelous restaurants in Mumbai's suburbs, since the airport has no dining facilities.

4

Mumbai: City of Dreamers

Mumbai will bowl you over. Teetering on the edge of the Arabian Sea, its heaving population barely contained by palm-fringed beaches, India's commercial capital, formerly known as Bombay, is a vibrant, confident metropolis that's tangibly high in energy.

Originally home to Koli fisherfolk, the seven swampy islands that today comprise Mumbai originally commanded little significance. The largest of the islands was part of a dowry given by Portugal to England, which promptly took control of the six remaining islands and then leased the lot to the East India Company for a paltry £10. Massive land-reclamation projects followed, and by the 19th century all seven islands had been fused to form one narrow promontory and India's principal port.

Today the city continues to draw fortune-seekers from all over India. More than a hundred newcomers squeeze their way in every day, adding to the coffers of greedy slum lords and placing the city, which already has a population density four times greater than New York City's, on target for a population of 28 million by 2015.

A city with a dual identity, Mumbai is as flamboyantly materialistic as it is downright choked by squalor and social drudgery. The citizens of Mumbai pay almost 40% of India's taxes, yet half of its 18 million people are homeless. While the moneyed groovers and label-conscious shakers retire in luxury behind the security gates of their Malabar Hill man-

sions, emaciated survivors stumble home to cardboard shacks in congested shanty-towns or onto tiny patches of open pavement. At every intersection you are accosted by these destitute hopefuls, framed against a backdrop of Bollywood vanity boards and massive advertisements promoting provocative underwear and sleek mobile-phone technology. Feeding into this social schizophrenia are the one-dollar whores, half-naked fakirs, underworld gunmen, bearded *sadhus,* Bhangra VJs and, of course, movie moguls and cellphone-clutching starlets.

It's not just the economic disparities that are bewildering: Looking down from the Hanging Gardens on Malabar Hill, you see the assertively modern metropolis of Nariman Point—but just a little farther south, on Malabar Point, is the Banganga Tank, one of the city's holiest sites, where apartment blocks overlook pilgrims who come to cleanse their souls by bathing in its mossy waters. Twenty-first-century Mumbai is brassy and vital, yet it can also transport you to another epoch. It is, in this sense, a quintessentially Indian city, encapsulating the raw paradoxes of the entire subcontinent.

Your plane will almost certainly touch down in Mumbai—it's the most common point of arrival for visitors, and well connected to the rest of the country (including the UNESCO World Heritage Sites of Ajanta and Ellora, also located in Maharashtra, and described at the end of the chapter). If you're looking for peace and quiet in meditative surroundings,

Fun Fact **You Say Mumbai, I Say Bombay**

In 1995, Bombay, the name the British bestowed upon the city, was renamed in honor of the local incarnation of the Hindu goddess Parvati, "Mumba Devi." The city's name change (along with a host of others that harked back to its colonial past) was enforced by the ruling Shiv Sena, a Hindu fundamentalist party that eschews the presence of any other than the Marathi people, a glaring irony given that this is a city of immigrants—a cocktail influenced as much by the grand Gothic monuments left by the British as by the many cultures who've set up shop here. Although it's difficult to understand how goodwill can prevail in a city led by politicians bred on xenophobia, Mumbai's well-intentioned optimism and its social cosmopolitanism prevail, and many of Mumbai's English-speaking inhabitants still refer to it as Bombay.

move on as fast as jet lag and arrival times dictate. But if you want to experience modern India at its vibrant best, and dine at what are arguably some of the finest restaurants on the globe, tarry for at least 2 days. You may arrive appalled by the pitiful faces of the poor, shocked by the paradox of such wealth and poverty, and overcome by the heavy, heady stench and toxic pollution. But give India's dream factory a little time, and you'll discover it has a sexy, smoldering soul, and a head-spinning groove worth getting hip to.

1 Arrival & Orientation

ARRIVING

BY PLANE   Most Westerners experience moderate shock when they arrive at Mumbai's sprawling **Chhatrapati Shivaji International Airport** (© 022/2682-9000 or -9112), which wears its years of wear and tear with the indifference characteristic of much of India. The airport is located in Sahar, 30km (19 miles) north of the center (which is why it's often called Sahar Airport). Its flights usually arrive and depart between midnight and dawn, which can make finding your feet difficult. A **Government of India Tourist Office** (© 022/2682-9000, ext. 3253) at the airport should be open 24 hours but—as is the case in most of India's tourist offices—it's certainly not the best place to obtain advice; you'll find the contents of this book far more useful.

Because you will no doubt have to wait in line for foreign exchange (there is only one small booth), it is advisable that you arrange an **airport transfer** to meet you—important, too, because you will be accosted by a loud, expectant mass of touts and taxi drivers the minute you exit the terminal doors, all of whom need to be treated with a degree of caution. If you are expecting a pickup, don't get sidetracked or deterred from boarding the correct hotel shuttle—ignore strangers offering help.

Should you need to hire a taxi, make use of the reliable **prepaid taxi service** (© 022/2682-9922); a trip to a city-center hotel should cost from Rs 330 to Rs 400 ($8–$9) and an additional Rs 10 (25¢) per bag. (Expect to pay well over double these rates for a hotel airport transfer, but you'll also get a much better vehicle to travel in.) Because most international flights arrive late at night, traffic delays are usually not a problem, and you should be at your hotel within an hour even if you're staying downtown.

Note: **Auto-rickshaws** are banned from the city's center, so don't rely on these unless your hotel is located in the immediate vicinity of the airport.

DOMESTIC AIRPORT   If you are flying direct from Mumbai's international airport on to the next destination, note that you will have to transfer (there is a free bus; make sure you get on it) to the **Santa Cruz Domestic Airport** (© **022/2615-6500;** 4km/2½ miles from the international airport and 26km/16 miles north of the city). You will have to spend the rest of the night in a very uncomfortable airport seat. If you have arrived at Santa Cruz and plan to spend some time in Mumbai, you can catch a metered taxi from the airport, which should set you back about Rs 300 ($6.85) for a trip to a hotel in the city center. Since domestic flights are likely to arrive during the day, be prepared for a long, congested, frustrating journey into Mumbai.

BY TRAIN   If you are traveling from Central, South, or East India, you will no doubt arrive at "VT," Victoria Station (otherwise known as Chhatrapati Shivaji Terminus or CST). A taxi ride farther downtown, to Colaba, should take about 10 to 15 minutes. From the north, you'll arrive at Mumbai Central Station; from here you can either cross a footbridge to the local platform and catch another train to Churchgate Station, Colaba, or you can brave the traffic and take a taxi.

WHEN TO GO   Mumbai's humidity—even in the small hours of the morning—is felt instantly, and the sun shines year-round, except in the monsoon months. You always seem drenched in warm sweat, and the heat can be terribly cruel, making sightseeing far less agreeable than a tour of the city's wonderful restaurants and drinking holes. Winter (Nov–Feb) is still hot, although not so entirely unpleasant; the sultry sea air sets the tone for an adventure in exotic dining and an intoxicating jaunt through lively, Victorian-era streets that are constantly crammed with people. The only real relief from the heat comes for brief periods in December and January, and midyear, when the annual monsoon drenches the city with heavy, nonstop tropical rains.

CITY LAYOUT

Mumbai city lies on the western coast of India, on a thin peninsula that extends southward almost parallel to the mainland. At the southern end of this peninsula are Colaba and the adjoining Fort area, on the east of which lies Mumbai's deep, natural harbor and India's busiest port. West of Fort, hugging the Arabian Sea, is the popular promenade Marine Drive, which begins at the business district of Nariman Point and terminates at Chowpatty Beach and Malabar Hill. These are the focal nodes for tourists who, unlike the locals, often refer to the area as downtown. In fact, locals say they are going "into town," by which they mean they are going toward South Mumbai, the area stretching south from Mahim Creek to Colaba. South Mumbai is where most tourists choose to base themselves. It is the historic heart of the city, with attractions like the Gateway of India and the Prince of Wales Museum, and the widest selection of restaurants and accommodations. The South Mumbai neighborhoods are described in detail below, but to see where most Mumbaikars (or Bombayites) live, including the jet-set stars, it may be worthwhile to take a trip into one of the suburbs. Of these, the most interesting (and a good alternative to South Mumbai if you're staying just one night—it's a great deal closer to the airport) is Juhu. Extending northward of Churchgate is the Western Railway local train line, and moving north of Victoria Terminus (or CST; see below) is the Central Railway network. Together, these two suburban train systems transport over 6 million commuters each day.

Mumbai

DINING ◆
Britannia **13**
Dome **7**
Excellensea **12**
Gaylord Bake Shop **6**
Geoffrey's **4**
India Jones **3**
Kandahar **3**
Konkan Café **1**
Mahesh Lunch
  Home/Apoorva **11**
Moshe's **2**
Noorani **18**
Pearl of the Orient **9**
Pisces **16**
Swati Snacks **17**
Salt Water Grill **15**
Stadium/Mocha **10**
Thackers **14**
Tiffin **3**

ACCOMMODATIONS ■
Ambassador **9**
Chateau Windsor Hotel **8**
Hotel Marine Plaza **4**
InterContinental
  Marine Drive **7**
The Oberoi/Hilton Towers **3**
Sea Green Hotel **5**
Taj President **1**

83

NEIGHBORHOODS IN BRIEF

Colaba

Because of its proximity to most of Mumbai's landmarks and colonial buildings, this, the southern tip of Mumbai, is the real tourist hub. In many ways its location has contributed to Colaba's slightly seedy side, though certain areas have recently been rejuvenated. Many of the city's budget accommodations are situated along **Colaba Causeway,** punctuated by (at the northernmost end) the **Taj Mahal Hotel,** Mumbai's most famous, which is located opposite the **Gateway of India,** Mumbai's most famous marker, across from which you can see the oil rigs of Bombay High. **Apollo Bunder** refers to the area around the Gateway of India, though the easiest way to get there is to ask for directions to the Taj. Southwest of this is **Cuffe Parade,** an upmarket residential neighborhood, and farther south, the restricted navy Cantonment area.

If you travel west from Colaba to the other end of the narrow peninsula until you hit the sea, you'll arrive at **Nariman Point,** starting point of Marine Drive. Nariman Point was once Mumbai's most bustling business district but is now facing decline (though most airline offices and several foreign embassies are still situated here).

Fort

North from Colaba is the business neighborhood called Fort. By day the area comprising **Fort, Fountain, Ballard Estate,** and **VT** (or **CST**) **Station** is an extremely busy commercial district, but at night the neighborhood is rather forlorn, with many of the large parks *(maidans)* empty. A little beyond VT Station is **Crawford Market,** which leads to the heart of Mumbai's congested markets.

Just west of the Fort area is **Churchgate Station. Veer Nariman Road,** the street leading from Churchgate Station to Marine Drive, is lined with restaurants.

Marine Drive/Chowpatty Beach

Marine Drive stretches from Nariman Point in the south to Malabar Hill in the north. Edged by a broad promenade that follows the curve of the seafront, this is a very popular place to take a morning or evening walk. At night the streetlights along this drive accentuate the dramatic arch of the bay, giving it the name **Queen's Necklace,** though obviously this term is less frequently used these days. Marine Drive is a long arterial road that runs along the curve of Back Bay. This road ends at **Chowpatty Beach** and then climbs uphill toward the very expensive and prestigious neighborhood of Malabar Hill.

Malabar Hill/Breach Candy/ Peddar Road

Malabar Hill connects to Napean Sea Road and beyond to **Breach Candy, Kemps Corner,** and **Peddar Road**— all upmarket residential areas. Several hotels in this area and particularly along Kemps Corner are good options for tourists who want to avoid the heavily touristed parts of Colaba and Churchgate.

Central Mumbai

Central Mumbai extends beyond Crawford Market through **Mohammedali Road** and **Kalbadevi** to **Mumbai Central Station** and the fast-growing commercial areas of **Lower Parel.** The greatest developments are occurring around **Phoenix Mills,** where some of the erstwhile mill buildings have been converted into shopping complexes, restaurants, and gaming and entertainment spots. West from Mumbai Central Station are **Tardeo** and **Haji Ali,** where

Colaba

1/10 mile

100 metres

Rope Walk Lane

Hope St.

Subhash Chowk

Mahatma Gandhi Rd.

Dubash Marg (Kala Ghoda)

Prince of Wales Museum

SP Mukherji Chowk (Wellington Circle)

Madame Cama Rd.

Cooperage Marg

Regal Theatre

American Express

Shivaji Marg

Cottage Industries Emporium

Nathalai Parekh Marg

Rajkavi Gulshan Marg

(Woodhouse Rd.)

Tulloch Rd.

Nawroji F. Marg

Police Station

Ormiston Rd.

Mandlik Marg

Bus Depot

Barrow Rd.

Henry Rd.

Road

Walton Rd.

Mereweather

Shahid Bhagat Singh Marg (Colaba Causeway)

Garden Rd.

Arthur Bunder Rd.

Strand Rd.

Strand Cinema

P J Ramchandani Marg (Apollo Bunder)

Ormiston Rd.

Bombay Yacht Club

Launches to Elephanta

Gateway of India

Arabian Sea

New Delhi

India

MAHARASHTRA

Mumbai
Colaba

Bay of Bengal

you drive along yet another of Mumbai's bays.

Suburbs (Bandra & Juhu)

North of Mahim Creek extend Mumbai's vast suburbs, from where millions commute daily. First up, just across the creek, is Bandra which, along with Juhu and Andheri (West), just north of it, is where Bollywood stars live and hang out. Although it's not really on the tourist circuit, Bandra, being home to a sizeable portion of the city's elite, is packed with lively restaurants, steamy clubs, and trendy bars. At night young people gather along Carter Road and Turner Road to drink, smoke (cigarettes or dope), and chill out before making their way to favored clubs. The area around Juhu Beach is where many of the city's middle classes escape; crowded with a host of vendors flogging popular eats, ice cream, coconuts, and fresh fruit juice, it's worth a visit to soak up Mumbai's carnivalesque atmosphere rather than contemplate sunbathing on the beach, which is filthy, or venturing into the even dirtier seawater. It does, however, have some fine hotels, restaurants, and nightclubs—Enigma at Juhu's JW Marriott Hotel is one of Mumbai's most happening spots.

Just east of Juhu lie the city's two airports and a host of upmarket hotels. The area of **Andheri (East)** around the international airport has become a crowded (and rather polluted) commercial and residential neighborhood. Yet many business visitors prefer to stay in this part of town if their business lies here, to avoid the stressful commute. Farther north in the suburbs is **Goregaon,** home to Film City, where many Bollywood films are shot; past that is **Borivali,** where Mumbai's most popular theme park, EsselWorld, is situated. Beyond, the city goes on (and on), with little to tempt the visitor.

VISITOR INFORMATION

Technically, there are tourist information desks at both airports, and these should be open for all flight arrivals. Don't count on it, however, and don't expect a lot of help, other than being handed a brochure or booklet and given some bland details of available hotels. That said, an excellent source of visitor information is the comprehensive *City Info* booklet, published fortnightly (every 2 weeks) and available at tourist information offices as well as upmarket hotels and even certain pubs and restaurants. For the best listings of the city's current events and what's hip and happening, look no further than the fortnightly magazine *Time Out,* available at all newsstands. The main **Government of India Tourist Office** (123 Maharishi Karve Rd., Churchgate; ✆ 022/2207-4333 or -4334; Mon–Fri 8:30am–6pm, Sat 8:30am–2pm) is where to head for general tourist-related information, but if you're staying at one of the city's better hotels, your concierge will be a good source of information on sightseeing, performances, events, and activities.

FAST FACTS: Mumbai

Airlines Domestic airlines connect Mumbai to nearly every corner of the subcontinent. For the best service, try **Jet Airways,** Amarchand Mansion, Madame Cama Road (✆ 022/5698-6111). It's open Monday to Friday 9am to 7pm; Saturday 9am to 5:30pm; Sunday 9am to 1pm. Its **check-in/reservations desk** (✆ 022/5698-6111) is open round-the-clock. **Indian Airlines** (✆ 022/2202-3031 or -5654) is the state-owned carrier, while **Air Sahara** (© 022/3030-2020) flies to considerably fewer destinations. The slew of new low-cost airlines includes **Air Deccan** (© 9892577008 or 080/3900-8888), **Spice Jet** (©1600/180-3333), and **Kingfisher Airlines** (© 1600/180-0101).

Ambulance Dial **102.** You can also contact **Bacha's Nursing Home** (La Citadelle, New Marine Lines; © 022/2203-2977 or 022/2200-0963) or **Bombay Hospital** (12 New Marine Lines; © 022/2206-7676). Or try **Swati Ambulance** (© 022/2387-1215), which has 24-hour service.

American Express The office is at the Regal Cinema Building at the start of Colaba Causeway (© 022/2204-8291). Hours are Monday to Friday 9:30am to 6:30pm; Saturday 9:30am to 2:30pm.

Area Code The area code for **Mumbai** is **022.**

ATMs Undoubtedly the most convenient way to get local currency, ATMs are to be found throughout the city, many of them with 24-hour security guards. Your best bet for a quick transaction is to head for an ATM machine belonging to either UTI, HDFC, ICICI, or Standard Chartered banking system.

Bookstores **Crossword Bookstore** (Mohammedbhai Mansion, Kemps Corner, below flyover; © 022/2384-2001 through -2005) has a Western ambience and Mumbai's largest selection of books. Alternatively, stop at **Shankar's Bookstore** (© 022/2285-1887), a tiny stall just outside Café Mondegar, Colaba Causeway; or at **Strand Book Stall** (Sir PM Rd., Fort; © 022/2266-1994 or -1719), which offers books at great discounts. Inside the Taj Mahal Hotel is **Nalanda** (© 022/2287-1306), a good spot to shop for coffee-table books and travel-related selections.

Car Hires See "Getting Around," below.

Consulates **U.S.:** Lincoln House, 78 Bhulabhai Desai Rd., Breach Candy (© 022/2363-3611 or -3617); Monday to Friday 8:30am to 1pm and 2 to 5pm; closed second and fourth Fridays of the month. **U.K.:** 2nd floor, Maker Chambers IV, J. B. Marg, 521 Nariman Point (© 022/5650-2222); Monday to Thursday 8am to 4pm and Friday 8am to 1:30pm. **Australia:** Maker Chamber VI, Nariman Point (© 022/5669-2000); Monday to Friday 9am to 5pm. **Canada:** 41/42 Maker Chambers VI, Nariman Point (© 022/2287-6027); Monday to Thursday 9am to 5:30pm; Friday 9am to 3pm. **South Africa:** Gandhi Mansion, Altamount Road, near Kemp's Corner (© 022/2389-3725); Monday to Friday 8:30am to 4:30pm.

Currency Exchange **Thomas Cook India** is located in the Thomas Cook Building, Dr. D. Naoroji Road, Fort (© 022/2204-8556), and is open Monday to Saturday 9:30am to 7pm. Or head to the American Express Office (details above).

Directory Assistance The main directory inquiry number is © **197** (if you can get through). For talking Yellow Pages service or any other useful information, call the much more helpful **Just Dial Services** at © **022/2888-8888, Times Info-line** at © **022/2600-5555,** or **Ask Me** at © **022/2261-6666.**

Drugstores In South Mumbai, **Bombay Hospital Chemist** (© 022/2206-7676) is open 24 hours. Near Juhu, call **Empire Chemists** (© 022/2671-8970).

Emergencies See "Police," below.

Hospitals **Breach Candy Hospital,** 60 Warden Rd., Breach Candy (📞 **022/2363-3651,** 022/2367-1888, or 022/2367-2888), is open 24 hours and is one of the most advanced and reliable hospitals in Mumbai. **Bombay Hospital,** 12 New Marine Lines (📞 **022/2206-7676**), is more centrally located and has a 24-hour ambulance service.

Internet Access For a cheap (about Rs 30/70¢ per hour), reliable connection, pop into **Waghela,** 23-B Nowroji Furdunji Rd., Colaba (📞 **022/2204-8718**). Open daily 8:30am to midnight, it's just around the corner from Leopold's Café. For better broadband speeds, try **Amrut Cyberworld Cybercafé** near Churchgate Station (8 Prem Court, behind Samrat Hotel; 📞 **022/2284-0174**).

Newspapers & Magazines For the scoop on day-to-day city news, buy a copy of the local rag *Mid Day,* sold on street corners and at intersections from early in the morning. *The Indian Express* and *The Times of India* are both good national dailies that provide the lowdown on current and social events. *Time Out Mumbai* is a fortnightly (twice-monthly) magazine that has the best listings of events and happenings, as well as interesting city features.

Police Call 📞 **1090** for a general police emergency number. Local numbers are: Colaba 📞 022/2285-6817; Cuffe Parade 📞 022/2218-8009; Juhu 📞 022/2618-4308; Khar 📞 022/2649-6030; Malabar Hill 📞 022/2363-7571; Andheri 📞 022/2683-1562.

Post Office You'll find the **General Post Office** near Victoria Terminus, off Nagar Chowk (📞 **022/2262-4343** or -0956). It's open Monday to Saturday 9am to 6pm.

Restrooms Make full use of your bathroom facilities *before* you head out for a day of sightseeing. Use only restrooms in hotels and upmarket restaurants.

Taxis See "Getting Around," below.

Travel Agencies Contact IATA-affiliated **NAC Travels Pvt Ltd,** 412 Raheja Centre, Nariman Point (📞 **022/2202-8810;** nactravels@vsnl.net); or the reliable **Travel Corporation of India (TCI)** in the Chandermukhi Building, also at Nariman Point (📞 **022/2202-1881** or -7120).

2 Getting Around

Mumbai is a city on the go—but don't expect to get anywhere fast, because traffic is lousy at the best of times. Already, close to a million vehicles crowd the streets, and each week another 1,400 scooters and cars join the congestion caused by battered black-and-yellow taxis, Marutis, expensive sedans and SUVs, copies of leftover red double-decker Routemaster buses, and the occasional cow. You will certainly need to take a taxi to get around (or, if you're arriving from the airport, arrange a transfer with your hotel; see "Arriving," earlier in this chapter). If you're overnighting in the Colaba–Fort area, you will, for the most part, be able to get around on foot.

PUBLIC TRANSPORTATION

BY TAXI   Metered taxis (in which you don't bargain but pay a rate dependent on mileage predetermined by a structured fare card) are available everywhere (flag them down when you see the meter flag up), but note that you'll be riding in rather battered

Fiats from the 1960s. That said, Mumbai is one of the few places in India where using the meter is the norm—in fact, no local would go anywhere without a taxi driver using his meter. Typically, the taxi meters in Mumbai are mounted on the vehicle hoods, and taxi drivers are required to carry a conversion chart that tells passengers how much they owe, based on the original fare displayed on the ludicrously old-fashioned meters. Do not start the journey before checking to see if the driver is carrying the correct chart; these are sometimes tampered with, so vital information is missing—for example, the part of the chart informing you that the rates quoted are for nighttime travel, which are higher. If you're in any doubt, ask a policeman or your hotel doorman to decipher the fare for you, but in essence you can calculate how much you have to pay by multiplying what's on the meter by approximately Rs 14 (32¢); add on 25% if you are traveling between midnight and 5am, and Rs 5 to Rs 7 (10¢–15¢) per piece of sizeable luggage. Nothing more.

If you're looking for a vehicle for the day, you can strike a deal with a private taxi driver directly, but here you should negotiate the deal upfront—you should pay around Rs 700 to Rs 800 ($16–$18), plus a tip, for an 8-hour (or 80km/50-mile) stint. Note that it's worth shelling out extra for an air-conditioned cab—you're likely to spend long stretches waiting in traffic jams at overcrowded intersections. To rent an air-conditioned car and an English-speaking driver privately (which will cost a bit more but may remove the hassle of haggling), the following operators are recommended: **Cool Cabs** (52 Andheri; ℂ **022/2492-7006,** 022/2822-7006, or 022/ 2824-6216); **Car Hirers** (1403 Arcadia, Nariman Point; ℂ **022/2283-4689;** www. carhirers.com); **Euro Cars** (Suburban Service Station, 261 S.V. Rd., Bandra W.; ℂ **022/2655-2424;** www.eurocars-india.com); and **Ketan Travels Pvt. Ltd.** (R.T. Building, P.M. Rd., Vile Parle E.; ℂ **022/2614-0554;** www.ketancars.com). **Hertz** (ℂ **022/5570-2126;** mumbai@carzonrent.com) offers chauffeur-driven cars throughout the subcontinent.

Hiring a taxi through your hotel can get very pricey, but the fleet of cars maintained by some of the upmarket hotels is unlikely to be matched in quality by anyone in the city, and it may be convenient to have taxi charges added to your hotel bill. Do, however, remember to tip your driver directly.

BY TRAIN   Train travel in the city is strictly for the adventurous, but then again, joining the peak-hour commuters gives you the opportunity to see how the other half lives, as the tracks wend their ways through some of the city's most squalid slums. A first-class return ticket from Victoria Terminus to the suburb of Thane costs about Rs 210 ($5). Travel only during off-peak times and leave luggage and valuables in your hotel room.

Finding (and Losing) Your Way . . .

It soon becomes apparent that Mumbai is not a planned city but has mushroomed according to the needs, wisdom, and follies of its citizens and administrators. Street names in particular can be confusing to first-time visitors; street signs, when they exist, are often ignored—many people continue to use the old colonial names instead. Colaba Causeway, for example, is the colloquial name for Shahid Bhagat Singh Road; Breach Candy for Bhulabhai Desai Road; and Peddar Road for Deshmukh Marg. In times of confusion, refer to a landmark (or hotel); for example, if you're trying to find Veer Nariman Road and no one understands you, ask for Churchgate Station instead.

Tips Dealing with Beggars

When long-time BBC India Bureau Chief Mark Tully was asked: "How do you cope with the poverty of India?" he responded, "I don't have to; *they* do." As a first-time visitor, you will no doubt be struck first and foremost by the seemingly endless ordeal of the impoverished masses. Families of beggars will twist and weave their way around the cars at traffic lights, hopping and even crawling to your window with displays of open wounds, diseased sores, crushed limbs, and starving babies, their hollow eyes imploring you for a few life-saving rupees. Locals will tell you that these poverty performances are Mafia-style rackets, with protection money going to gangs, and sickly babies being passed around to gain more sympathy for their "parents." In the worst of these tales of horror, children are maimed to up the ante by making them appear more pathetic. The choice is stark: Either lower the window and risk having a sea of unwelcome faces descend on you, or stare ahead and ignore them. To salve your conscience, tip generously those who have made it onto the first rung of employment.

ORGANIZED TOURS & TRIPS

You will be offered tours of various descriptions by at least half the people you meet on the streets of Mumbai; everyone from your taxi driver to the man who asks you for the time will have a contact in the tourism industry who'll be more than happy to take you sightseeing. Use your discretion, watch your wallet, and remember that Mumbai's traffic makes it impossible to see everything in one day.

To arrange a legitimate tour of the city, set it up through your hotel, which should have access to the best guides (meaning those with the best English and best knowledge). Or contact **Maharashtra Tourist Development Corporation** (Madame Cama Rd., opposite L.I.C. Building; ✆ **022/2202-6713** or -7762) or any **Government of India Tourist Office** (123 Maharishi Karve Rd., Churchgate; ✆ **022/2203-3144;** Mon–Sat 10am–5pm).

Bear in mind that there's little point in seeing Mumbai only from the back seat of a chauffeur-driven taxi; leave time to explore the city on foot. If you're keen on architecture, a group of young architects conducts **Bombay Heritage Walks** on Sunday (✆ **022/2683-5856;** mid-Sept to May 5–6:30pm; by prior arrangement only; Rs 100/$2.30)—these tours take in various fascinating parts of the city.

Note: One of the best-organized trips in the city is the boat trip departing half-hourly from the Gateway to Elephanta Island (see "What to See & Do," below).

3 What to See & Do

Mumbai doesn't have the wealth of historical attractions of, say, Kolkata or Delhi. Rather, it is a city that revolves around its manic pace and the head-spin energy exuded by the millions of diverse people who have settled here. This is a city you *experience* rather than sightsee, and sampling from the fantastic restaurants described later in the chapter should be highest on your must-do list. That said, Mumbai does have a few attractions you should make time for; and be sure to set aside time to explore at least part of the **Colaba/Fort area,** described below, on foot—do this at the beginning of the day before the heat becomes suffocating. Another good area to explore on foot is the **Marine Drive/Chowpatty Beach stretch,** possibly after a boat trip to **Elephanta Island.** Finally, you may wish to visit **Malabar Hill,** also in the South Mumbai area and home to two top attractions (see below), as well as the **Hanging Gardens** (also known as Ferozeshah Mehta Gardens). Laid out in the early 1880s, the terraced park at the top of Malabar Hill covers (or "hangs over") the city's main water reservoir, but unfortunately it fails to live up to its spectacular-sounding name. The best reason to visit here is to wander over to **Kamala Nehru Park** (across the road from the Hanging Gardens), from where you have a great view of Nariman Point's skyscrapers and the sumptuous curve of Marine Drive.

EXPLORING COLABA & FORT

If you're at all inspired by Gothic Victorian architecture, then a jaunt through Mumbai's older districts is essential. Most tours kick off at the **Gateway of India** (see below), but a more authentic place to start, given Mumbai's origins, is **Sassoon Docks** ☆☆ (aka the Fisherman's Market; daily 4am–noon), which lies just south of the Gateway, off Shahid Bhagat Singh Marg (near Colaba Bus Station). Most of the delicious seafood dishes in the city's finest establishments start out here, where Koli women in rainbow-colored saris whip the shells off prawns while others gut and sort fish. Get here early (5am), when the boats return with their first catch, for the vibrant, communal spirit as baskets full of fish are moved around the dock through various stages of processing. It makes for absorbing viewing.

From here, catch a cab or walk to the Gateway, possibly stopping for a refresher at the Taj Mahal Hotel, situated directly opposite. From here it's a 15-minute walk north to Fort, Mumbai's cultural center, where you will find the superb **Prince of Wales Museum** (see below), nearby **Jehangir Art Gallery,** and the **National Gallery of Modern Art,** as well as a host of Raj-era Gothic architectural highlights. From the museum you can either head north along M. Gandhi Road to Flora Fountain, hub of downtown Mumbai, or travel southwest down the famous Colaba Causeway.

Surrounded by colonial buildings that testify to the solid architecture of a bygone era, **Flora Fountain** has, since 1960, had to compete for attention with a **Martyrs' Memorial** that honors those who died in the creation of the state of Maharashtra. As you head toward the fountain, take in the impressive **High Court** building (which overlooks the Oval Maidan, where aspiring cricketers practice their paces), the neo-classical **Army & Navy Building,** and the 78m (256-ft.) **Rajabai Clock Tower,** which towers over the Bombay University complex. East of the fountain lies **Horniman Circle,** where you will find the **Town Hall,** a regal colonnaded building with original parquet wood floors, wrought-iron loggias, spiral staircases, and marble statues of leaders associated with Mumbai's history. The major drawing card here is the **Asiatic Society Library,** which has a collection of around 800,000 valuable texts. You can join the seniors and students who fill the library's popular reading room to peruse local newspapers and check out the public book collection, but you'll need special permission if you're interested in looking at some of the priceless treasures.

Also facing Horniman Circle is the late-19th-century Gothic Venetian **Elphinstone Building** and, opposite it, on Veer Nariman Road, **St. Thomas' Cathedral,** thought to be the oldest colonial structure in Mumbai. (Note that if you head west along Veer Nariman Rd., known for its many good restaurants, you will come to Marine Dr.) St. Thomas' Cathedral is a stark contrast to the pink and blue neoclassical **Kenneth Eliyahoo Synagogue,** Mumbai's oldest and loveliest Sephardic synagogue, located off

Need a Break?

Besides the options listed under "Where to Dine," below, the following are pleasant places to pop in for a snack or drink if you don't feel like having a full meal. In the Colaba area are several superb spots. The recently opened **Indigo Deli** was created very much in the image of an upmarket New York delicatessen (© 022/5656-1010; open until midnight). It serves typically Western breakfasts from 7:30 to 10:30am, but buzzes all day long. The Indigo has a variety of imported cheeses, cold meats, and fresh breads—all of exceptional quality—which can be transformed into sandwiches of your choice. Prices are steep, especially the for wines, but you're also paying for the ambience. At the south end of the Causeway is **Theobroma,** a small bakery run by sisters Tina and Kainaz, who make you feel immediately at home. You can sit at one of the few tables and nibble on brownies (six varieties!), a chicken pesto sandwich, or one of the other innumerable desserts (Cusrow Baug, Shop no. 24, Colaba Causeway; © 022/5629-2929; sandwiches Rs 55–Rs 75/$1.15–$1.75; desserts Rs 15–Rs 55/35¢–$1.15). Across the street and toward the sea is **Café Basilico** (Sentinel House, Arthur Bunder Rd., next to Radio Club, Colaba; © 022/5634-5670 or -5671; sandwiches Rs 145–Rs 210/$3.40–$4.75; mains Rs 190–Rs 320/$4.50–$7), which does lip-smacking waffles, muffins, breads, cereals, and juices for breakfast, and sandwiches, pastas, and much more throughout the day. Sunday brunch here is a feast and great value at Rs 400 ($9.10). The cafe is also one of the few places in the city where you can get a bagel, though we can't vouch for its authenticity. At Cuffe Parade is **Moshe's** (Minoo Manor; © 022/2216-1226; breakfast Rs 85–Rs 175/$2–$4; sandwiches Rs 175–Rs 210/$4–$4.75; mains Rs 190–Rs 320/$4.50–$7), an upmarket restaurant that offers Middle Eastern fusion food (plus wine), sandwiches, snacks, good breakfasts, and a fairly decent bagel with cream cheese (Rs 45/$1). Avoid dinnertime, when it's crowded and unbelievably noisy. Moshe's also has a little cafe at Kemp's Corner inside the Crossword Bookstore. **Stadium** (© 022/2204-6819) is a cheap, unpretentious Irani restaurant outside Churchgate Station where you can sip *chai* or a cold drink while you contemplate your next move. Across the street (though you will have to walk all around to get there) is **Gaylords Bake Shop,** with fresh breads, croissants, and assorted bites available all day. **Geoffrey's** ☙ (© 022/2285-1212), at the Marine Plaza Hotel, is a cozy bar, with a somewhat overdone English-pub decor. More casual is **New York** (© 022/5608-4187) on Hughes Road—not to be mistaken for the **New Yorker** restaurant, also at Chowpatty nearby, where you can sip a beer anytime; it's one of the few places in the city with a jukebox. On Chowpatty, **Cream Centre** (see Marine Dr. and Chowpatty Beach in "Top Attractions: Downtown") serves good food, but it's not the kind of place you can linger. You *can* hang around almost endlessly at any of the numerous coffee shops that have opened all over the city. **Barista** and **Café Coffee Day** outlets are everywhere, but more atmospheric is **Mocha,** which also serves specialty coffees (and fruit-flavored hookahs outdoors) at its cafes at Churchgate (Nagin Mahal, Veer Nariman Rd.; © 022/5633-6070), Bandra (Hill Rd., near Holy Family Hospital; © 022/2643-3098), and Juhu (just across from the beach; © 022/2617-7524).

K. Dubash Marg, on Forbes Street. North of Flora Fountain, up Dr. Dadabhai Naoroji Road, is the Art Deco–style Parsi fire temple, **Watcha Agiary.** Built in 1881, it features carvings in a distinctly Assyrian style.

If you prefer shopping (albeit of a tourist-trap nature) to architecture, opt for the famous **Causeway** (now officially renamed **Shahid Bhagat Singh Marg,** though, thankfully, no one refers to it as such). Budget travelers have long been drawn to this vibrant street, but in recent years Colaba and its side streets have begun to slip into an increasingly urbane and upmarket second skin. Hip bars, swinging clubs, and tasteful restaurants are drawing the smart crowd. Anything and everything seems to be available from the hawkers on Colaba's sidewalks and back alleys, whether it's fruit, cheap cigarettes, currency, or hashish. Shop in exclusive boutiques or rummage through heaps of cheap trinkets sold on the sidewalks, where you can bargain for everything from imitation perfume to piles of cheap, tasteless T-shirts, all the while avoiding the advances of streetwise beggars and con artists sporting half-moon smiles and incongruous American accents.

Beyond the southernmost end of the Causeway (that's if you manage to get this far south before grabbing a taxi and heading for the peace of your hotel room!), in the restricted Navy Nagar area, you will see the neo-Gothic **Afghan Memorial Church of St. John the Evangelist.** Dating back to 1858, it memorializes those who fell in the First Afghan War—proof yet again of Mumbai's mosaic past.

TOP ATTRACTIONS: DOWNTOWN

Gateway of India & Taj Mahal Hotel ✶✶✶
Easily the most recognizable remnant of the British Raj, the Gateway was designed by George Wittet (also responsible for the Prince of Wales Museum). The Gujarati-inspired yellow basalt structure was supposed to commemorate the visit of King George V and Queen Mary, who arrived in 1911 to find a fake cardboard structure instead; the Gateway was eventually completed in 1924 and was the final departure point for the British when they left Indian soil in 1947. It is the most obvious starting point for any tour of Mumbai (and is where the boats to Elephanta are launched), and to this end it draws large numbers of visitors as well as hordes of locals keen to take money off unsuspecting foreigners. The area makes for a quick-fix introduction to Mumbai tout dynamics; expect to be offered everything from photographs of yourself posing here to hashish to young girls. Opposite the Gateway is an equestrian statue of Chhatrapati Shivaji, the Maratha hero who gives his name to several renamed Mumbai institutions.

More impressive—in beauty and size—is the hotel behind the Gateway, which in many ways symbolizes Mumbaikars' determined and enterprising attitudes. Inspired by its namesake in Agra, the **Taj Mahal Hotel** (see "Where to Stay," below) was built just over a century ago by an ambitious industrialist named Jamshedji Tata—according to legend, because he wanted to avenge the whites-only policy of Watson's, then the city's poshest hotel. Designed by a European architect who mailed the plans to India, it has been said that the hotel was mistakenly constructed back-to-front, so what was meant to be a fantastic sea-facing facade actually overlooks a side street— patently untrue, as you will see if you walk around the palatial edifice. What cannot be refuted is how much it dominates Colaba's waterfront, its six-story domed structure best viewed from an offshore boat. Alternatively, for a great view of the Gateway, head inside the Taj and make for the **Sea Lounge** or **Harbour Bar.**

Chhatrapati Shivaji Maharaj Marg. Gateway information: ✆ 022/2202-3585 or -6364. Half-hour harbor cruise Rs 40 (90¢) deluxe.

Elephanta Island Caves ✿✿✿   For a taste of Mumbai's early history and an opportunity to view the city's skyline from the water (not to mention escape from the tumult
of the streets), grab a ferry and head out to Elephanta Island, declared a UNESCO
World Heritage Site in 1987. The hour-long trip also provides a good introduction to
Hinduism; the guides on board describe the religious significance of what you're about
to see, though the origins of the Shiva temple caves—thought to date from the revival-
ist Hindu movement between A.D. 450 and 750—remain obscure.

Entry is via the main northern entrance to a massive hall supported by large pillars,
where the enormous Trimurti statue is housed. At 6.3m (18 ft.), the remarkable sculpture depicts Shiva in his three-headed aspect: as Creator (Vamadeva, facing right), Protector (Maheshmurti, the crowned face at the center), and Destroyer (Bhairadeva,
facing left, with serpents for hair). Left of the Trimurti is Shiva as both male and
female: Ardhanarishvara, an aspect suggesting the unity of all opposites. Other sculptures refer to specific actions of the god and events in Hindu mythology, but many
were damaged or destroyed by the Portuguese, who apparently used the Hindu gods
for target practice. It's practical to bring along a local guide (free) even though they
rarely speak very good English. Watch listings for music and dance performances.

Tip: Plan your trip so that you can witness sunset over the Mumbai skyline on your
return journey, then pop into the Taj Mahal Hotel for a post-culture cocktail. Note
that music and dance festival performances are held here every year in February.

9km (5½ miles) from Mumbai. Tickets and ferries from the Gateway of India. Admission Rs 250 ($5.70), Rs 25 (55¢)
camera, Rs 25 (55¢) video. Ferry ticket Rs 110 ($2.50). Boats depart from the Gateway of India every half-hour
Tues–Sun 9am–3:30pm.

Prince of Wales Museum ✿✿✿   Renamed Chhatrapati Shivaji Maharaj Vastu
Sangrahalaya, but thankfully also known by its colonial name, this is Mumbai's top
museum and arguably the best in India, providing an extensive and accessible introduction to Indian history and culture. The Indo-Saracenic building itself is rather
lovely, but it is the collection that is outstanding, not least because it is well laid out
(unlike the collections of most museums throughout the subcontinent) and aided by
a useful audioguide highlighting "Curator's Choice" exhibits. The central hall features
a "précis" of the collection, but don't stop there—from sculptures of Hindu deities to
beautiful temple art, Buddhist *thangkas* from Nepal and Tibet to gruesome Maratha
weaponry, there is much to see. Highlights are found on the first floor: Among them
are the spectacular collection of more than 2,000 miniature paintings representing
India's various schools of art (look for the portrait of Shah Jahan, creator of the Taj
Mahal), and the exhibit relating to the Indus Valley Civilization (which is remarkably
civilized considering that it dates from 3500 B.C.). Least impressive is the natural history section with its collection of stuffed animals.

Note: Art lovers may wish to include a visit to **Jehangir Art Gallery** (© 022/
2284-3989), located a little farther along M Gandhi Road, and open daily from 11am
to 7pm, free of charge. You can probably give the main exhibition halls on the ground
floor a miss—the exhibits there are fairly mediocre. Instead, head upstairs to **Gallery
Chemould** (© 022/2284-4356; daily 10:30am–6:30pm), a tiny, history-filled gallery
that often features some of India's best contemporary artists. For reviews of current art
exhibitions, consult *Time Out Mumbai* or "The Hot List," the entertainment supplement in the local rag *Mid Day.*

159/161 Mahatma Gandhi Rd., Fort. © 022/2284-4519. powm@vsnl.com. Rs 300 ($6.85), includes audioguide.
Tues–Sun 10:15am–5:45pm.

Victoria Terminus (Chhatrapati Shivaji Terminus) 𝒦𝒦𝒦   Also rechristened in

Mumbai's nationalist-inspired anti-Raj drive, but more often than not referred to as "VT," this baroque, cathedral-like building must rank as Mumbai's most marvelous Raj-era monument. India's very first steam engine left this station when it was completed in 1887; today at least a thousand trains leave every day, carrying some 2.5 million commuters in and out of the city. With its vaulted roofs, arches, Gothic spires, flying buttresses, gables crowned by neoclassical sculptures, stone carvings, and exquisite friezes, the terminus is an architectural gem, worth entering to see the massive ribbed Central Dome (topped by a statue of the torch-wielding "Progress") that caps an octagonal tower featuring beautiful stained-glass windows with colorful images of trains and floral patterns. But come, too, for the spectacle of the disparate people, from sari-clad beauties to half-naked fakirs, that makes up Mumbai. Get here just before lunch to watch the famous *dabba-wallas* stream out into the city: A vast network of *dabba-wallas* transfer some 200,000 cooked lunches, prepared by housewives for their office-bound husbands, and kept warm in identical *dabbas* (metal tiffin containers), through a unique sorting and multiple-relay distribution system; later in the afternoon these empty *dabbas* are returned to their home of origin. The success of this system (no one gets the wrong lunch) is proof of how well India works, despite its reputation for obstructive bureaucracy. In fact, following a study of this network, U.S. business magazine *Forbes* gave it a Six Sigma (99.99% accuracy) performance rating, which means that just one error occurs in six million transactions.

Dr. Dadabhai Naoroji Rd., Fort.

Marine Drive & Chowpatty Beach 𝒦𝒦𝒦   Marine Drive (renamed Netaji Sub-

hash Chandra Marg) follows the sweeping curve of sea that stretches north from Nariman Point's high-rise buildings to infamous Chowpatty Beach, located at the foot of Malabar Hill. It's the ultimate seaside promenade, where Mumbaikars come to escape the claustrophobia of central Mumbai, gratefully eyeing an endless horizon while strolling or jogging along the broad windswept promenade. In the evenings, casual, single-item snack stalls are set up for brisk trade. This is the city's ultimate sunset spot, when—having watched the orange globe sink into the Arabian Sea—you can witness the street lights transform Marine Drive into the aptly named Queen's Necklace, a choker-length of twinkling jewels adorning Back Bay. The scene is perhaps best enjoyed with cocktail in hand at one of Marine Drive's classier establishments: either the rooftop restaurant at the **InterContinental Marine Drive** or The Oberoi's **Bayview Bar,** which also offers jazz music and cigars.

Once the sun has set, catch a ride (or walk) north along Marine Drive to Chowpatty, Bombay's oldest seafront. Chowpatty is no longer the filth-ridden extravaganza its long-acquired reputation suggests (though it's still not in any state for sunbathing or swimming), and at night it assumes the demeanor of a colorful fair. Children of all ages flock to ride the ancient Ferris wheels and tacky merry-go-rounds, and fly-by-night astrologers, self-styled contortionists, snake charmers, and trained monkeys provide the flavor of the bazaar—and bizarre—especially on weekends. This is where locals love to consume the city's famous street snacks, especially *bhelpuri:* crisp puffed rice, vegetables, and fried lentil-flour noodles doused in a pungent chutney of chili, mint, and tamarind, then scooped up with a flat *puri* (puffy deep-fried bread). Chowpatty bhelpuri is renowned throughout India, sold here by the eponymous *bhelwallas,* who now ply their trade in Bhel Plaza, where other traditional treats like *kulfi* are on offer at dirt-cheap prices. *Tip:* It's inadvisable to eat here—unfortunately, flavor, not hygiene, enjoys top priority. After you've watched the multitudes gorging vast quantities of assorted snack foods, cross the street and get your own *chaat* at **Cream Centre** 🕮🕮 (25 Fulchand Niwas, Chowpatty Beach; 𝒞 022/2367-9222 or -9333; all credit cards accepted; noon–midnight). For close to half a century, this vegetarian snack place has been serving up delicious food—so good, in fact, that whenever you pass Chowpatty Beach in the evening, you'll see a queue of people waiting to get in. Alternatively, make a meal of the signature *channa bhatura* (spiced chickpeas and a large puri), a typical Punjabi dish that is made everywhere but rarely so well as here. When you're done, step out of the restaurant, turn left, and walk down to the end of the pavement to a hole-in-the-wall (but very hygienic) juice shop called **Bachelorr's** (yes, with two r's) for deliciously refreshing seasonal fresh fruit ice creams and juices—but do make sure you ask for your juice without ice, water, or masala.

To experience Mumbai at its most exuberant, head to Chowpatty Beach for the culmination of **Ganesh Chaturthi** 🕮🕮🕮, the city's biggest and most explosive celebration. Held in honor of the much-loved elephant-headed god (here called Ganpati), the 10-day festival culminates on the last day, when a jubilant procession is held and thousands of huge Ganpati idols are immersed in the sea. Ganesh Chaturthi is held in September; for exact dates contact the Government of India Tourist Office.

Jain Temple 🕮🕮   This is arguably the prettiest temple in Mumbai (indeed, Jain temples are generally the prettiest in India). If your itinerary does not include a visit to one elsewhere (the most famous being in Rajasthan), do make the time to visit Mumbai's. Members of the Jain community are known to be exceptionally adept in the world of business, and although they believe in self-restraint and aestheticism (orthodox Jains will not tread on an ant, and at their most extreme wear masks to

---

Moments Touching God

There were still hundreds of people streaming onto Chowpatty Beach for the finale on Monday, when idols of Ganpati are immersed in the sea. I had expected to see the shore where it normally is, but today it extended another quarter-mile—thousands of people were already in the water! Trucks with 6m-high (20-ft.) Ganesh idols lined up on the sand, awaiting their turn alongside families wanting to drop their small, lap-sized idols into the sea. Engulfed by teeming masses and deafened by the sound of singing devotees and driving drumbeats, Vanessa and I locked hands so that we wouldn't lose each other. As we navigated the crowds, one of the large Ganesh idols rocked forward off its flatbed, prompting a small stampede as people standing nearby tried to escape. Luckily, the men holding the ropes managed to steady and pull the giant idol upright. Hundreds of volunteers and security officials worked to maintain order, many thankfully eager to help two conspicuously foreign women—one official even held an entire line of men at bay. As he ushered us to a less crowded space, a giant Ganesh adorned with plastic grass and flowers passed en route to the shore. The security guard watched the two of us admiring the decorations and asked, "Would you like to touch God?" "Sure!" I exclaimed. As I reached over to touch Ganesh's feet, I wondered why every Monday couldn't include an intimate moment with the divine.

—Megan Neumeister, Indophile

Bollywood Celebrity: High-Octane Overdrive

It's inevitable that the world's biggest film industry (twice as many films are made here as in Hollywood) would produce a host of celebrities, but in India stars are worshipped with the fervor usually reserved for gods and goddesses. Sadly, the virtues associated with religious idols often don't apply to the stars themselves. In 2002, when one of Bollywood's high-octane celebrities, 37-year-old Salman Khan, got slam-drunk and skidded onto a sidewalk, killing a man who—like so many of Mumbai's citizens—lived on the pavement outside the laundry where he worked, it turned out to be one of the media events of the decade, with arresting officers ordering prints of the front-page photos of themselves "posing" with the superstar, and readers rallying behind the "unfair" treatment of their hero. Khan's stardom proved to be his "get-out-of-jail-quick" card; he spent a mere 17 days in prison, claiming it was his chauffeur who had been behind the wheel. Frankly, it will be a miracle if he is ever convicted.

avoid breathing in even tiny insects), they pour large sums into the construction and maintenance of their places of worship. Officially called **Babu Amichand Panalal Adishwarji Jain Temple,** this beautifully decorated and adorned temple has an entrance flanked by two stone elephants. The downstairs area houses an array of deities and saints, including an image of Ganesh that recalls historical links between Jainism and Hinduism.

Ridge Rd., Walkeshwar (Malabar Hill). ℂ 022/2369-2727. Daily 5am–9pm.

Mani Bhavan Gandhi Museum 𝓕𝓕   Mahatma Gandhi lived in this quaint Gujarati-style house from 1917 to 1934, and it was here in November 1921 that he conducted a 4-day fast in order to restore peace to the city. This quiet three-story home on a beautiful Laburnum tree-lined avenue now preserves the spirit of the man who selflessly put his nation before himself. There's a library of Gandhi-related works, as well as displays of photographs, posters, slogans, and other items that document and explain Gandhi's legendary life; dioramas depicting major events and turning points in his fight for the nation's freedom draw particular attention to his devotion to the poor. You can see Gandhi's old *charkha* (spinning wheel), which in many ways symbolized the struggle for independence, as it represented a return to roots and to sustainable home industry, where anyone can weave his or her own cloth. A visit to this tranquil spot makes a welcome change from the continuous hubbub of life in Mumbai—go up to the roof to really appreciate the relative stillness of the surrounding neighborhood.

19 Laburnam Rd., near Malabar Hill. ℂ 022/2380-5864. www.gandhi-manibhavan.org. Donations appreciated. Daily 10am–5:30pm.

Banganga Tank 𝓕𝓕   Here the paradox of traditional life coexisting with unbridled modernization is all too vivid. Near the edge of the Arabian Sea at the southern tip of Malabar Hill, several small, crumbling, stone-turreted temples and flower-garlanded shrines surround a rectangular pool of holy water in an area of looming modern-day skyscrapers and encroaching urbanization. Ritual bathers who come here believe the mossy waters have healing powers and originated from a natural spring created by an arrow shot by Rama (the hero of the *Ramayana*), who rested here while on a mission to rescue his beloved Sita from the demon king's abode in Lanka. The source of the spring is said to be an underground offshoot of the Ganga, and the waters are considered just as sacred as those of the great river itself. In the shadow of one of present-day Mumbai's most prosperous neighborhoods, Banganga continues to function as an out-of-time devotional hub, its tolling bells and mantra-chanting *pujaris* drawing devotees to worship the divine. If you're here in December, scour local newspapers for news of the open-air concerts held at the Banganga Festival.

Walkeshwar Rd., Malabar Hill.

TOP ATTRACTIONS OUTSIDE DOWNTOWN MUMBAI

Dhobi Ghat 🎯🎯 It's a fascinating spectacle, looking down on row upon row of open-air concrete wash pens, each fitted with its own flogging stone, while Bombay's *dhobis* (around 200 *dhobi* families work together here) relentlessly pound the dirt from the city's garments in a timeless tradition. Known as the world's largest outdoor laundry, Dhobi Ghat is where Mumbai's traditional washerfolk—or *dhobis*—provide a wonderful service, collecting dirty laundry, washing it, and returning it neatly pressed, all for a very small fee. Stubborn stains are removed by soaking garments in a boiling vat of caustic soda; drying takes place on long, brightly colored lines; and heavy wood-burning irons are used for pressing. At the very least, it's a great photo opportunity, though most locals think it rather amusing that their everyday work arouses such curiosity. (Note that there is another Dhobi Ghat off Capt. Prakash Petha Marg, Colaba, which may be more accessible.)

Dr. E. Moses Rd. (near Mahalakshmi Station).

MARKETS

Mumbai has more than 70 markets, and it's worthwhile to spend a couple of hours exploring at least one, not so much for the shopping (for that, see "Shopping," later in this chapter) as for the human spectacle of it all. Flowers are an intrinsic part of Indian culture, and **Bhuleshwar Wholesale Flower Market** 🎯🎯 (CP Tank Circle; dawn–noon) is the best place in the city to witness the Indian romance with color and fragrance. Note that according to Hindu beliefs, if you touch or sniff the flowers, you'll ruin them—so don't. **Chor Bazaar (Thieves' Market)** 🎯🎯 (Mutton St., off Sardar Vallabhbhai Patel Rd.; Sat–Thurs 11am–7pm) conjures up *Arabian Nights'* cloak-and-dagger intrigue and

---

Moments Bewitched by Alphonso

Along with the unbearable heat, summer brings forth crops of beauteous mangoes, dozens of varieties of which are available only in India. King of them all is unquestionably the Alphonso. You may have eaten mangoes in Mexico, Thailand, or even other parts of India, but until you've sucked on the succulent bright orange pulp of the Alphonso, with its bewitching scent and unimaginably divine flavor, you'll miss a sensory experience like no other. The best Alphonsos originate from Ratnagiri in rural Maharashtra. To make sure you're getting the real thing, ask your hotel to find you one, or explore the fruit section at Mumbai's Crawford Market. Prices start at Rs 1,000 ($23) a dozen in March and go down to Rs 160 ($3.45) a dozen when the season peaks in May; note that these mangoes often need to be kept a day or two to ripen before eating.

Moments **Catch a Bollywood Blockbuster**

You can't say you've properly done the biggest film-producing city on earth if you haven't gone to the cinema to catch a blockbuster, or tried to. Listings are found in daily newspapers, where you can also determine quality and even figure out the storyline by reading reviews written by contenders for the world's bitchiest critic; alternatively, ask your hotel concierge for recommendations. Of course, you can always get completely into the swing of things by picking up a copy of one of Bollywood's gossip magazines. *Filmfare* and *Stardust* not only fill you in on what's hot or what's not, but are crammed with glossy, airbrushed close-ups of silver-screen idols. Cinemas that also offer historic Art Deco appeal include once wonderful but now run-down **Eros Cinema** (opposite Churchgate Station; ✆ **022/2282-2335**); and lovely **Liberty Cinema** ✿✿ (✆ **022/2203-1196;** a short walk from Eros, near Bombay Hospital), where upper-stall tickets (the best in the house) still cost just Rs 60 ($1.35). Besides the Bollywood melodrama, you get to admire the wonderful Art Deco interiors, with majestic high ceilings, white cedar and teak paneling, '60s-style soda fountain, magnificent huge etched mirrors on the stairwells, mock fountains, and old movie posters.

---

visions of precious rings sold with the finger of the former owner still attached, but in reality this is a fun place to rummage through an extravagant assortment of antiques, fakes, and junk and get into the rhythm of that favorite Indian pastime: bargaining.

If you visit only one market, make it **Crawford Market** ✿✿✿ (Lokmanya Tilak Marg and Dr. Dadabhai Naoroji Rd.; Mon–Sat 11:30am–8pm), Mumbai's quintessential fresh-produce shopping experience, now officially known as **Mahatma Jyotiba Phule Market.** Dating back to the 1860s, it combines the traditional Indian bazaar experience with both Norman and Flemish architecture. (*Note:* Above the main entrance is a bas-relief frieze designed by Rudyard Kipling's father.) Admire the colorful pyramids of heavenly mangoes (see box on "Bewitched by Alphonso," above) and ripe bananas, but steer clear of the disturbing pet stalls.

Clothing is one of Mumbai's major exports, and at **Fashion Street** ✿ (Mahatma Gandhi Rd., across the road from Bombay Gymkhana), a motley collection of shops and stalls, you will pay a fraction of the prices asked in foreign stores. Much of what is here is surplus stock; other garments have been rejected by quality controllers. Start your haggling at under half the quoted price.

Taxi drivers get nervous when you tell them you want to visit **Zaveri Bazaar** ✿✿ (Sheik Memon St.; Mon–Sat 11am–7pm). You'll soon discover why. Shoppers and space-fillers shuffle and push their ways endlessly through narrow gaps in this cluttered, heaving market, and it's often impossible to inch forward by car—or even on foot. Behind the street stalls and milling masses, glittering jewels are sold from family shops. If the glitzy accessories don't fascinate you, perhaps you'll be drawn to packed **Mumbadevi Temple,** where the city's namesake deity is housed. Activity around the temple is chaotic, with devotees splurging to prove their devotion to the powerful goddess.

CRICKET

Although hockey is India's official national sport, cricket is by far the best-loved game, and even watching a group of schoolboys practicing in a field is an experience unto itself. Mumbaikars play the game with an enthusiasm that's quite intoxicating—almost as if it provides some measure of relief from the hardships of daily life. In cricket-crazy India, the stars of the game are worshipped as keenly as film stars and gods, and Indian spectators at international games have the ability to transform even the blandest match into an exciting event.

During the season (Oct–Mar), several matches are held each week at **Wankhede Stadium** (Churchgate), which is where Mumbai's big national and international games are hosted. Tickets are sold by the **Mumbai Cricket Association** (© 022/2281-9910 or 022/2281-2714), but it's worth asking your concierge to arrange good seats for you at a decent price (top-tier tickets can go for as much as $100 officially, and up to $300 on the black market). There's no doubt that watching a cricket match in an Indian stadium with tens of thousands of fans is one of the more fascinating experiences to be had in India, but if crowds make you nervous, watch the World Cup, Sharjah Cup, or any major cricketing event live at a local bar or lounge, with a few dozen cricket-crazy Indians to provide the spectacle.

4 Where to Stay

With greater supply than demand for rooms in Mumbai over the last few years, and the emergence of numerous five-star properties in the suburbs, rooms in downtown Mumbai can often be booked at good rates. Don't always go by a hotel's published tariff; ask about seasonal or daily discounts and cruise the Internet for bargains. It's not uncommon to find ridiculously cheap deals for rooms in hotels like the Taj President, available even during the popular winter season. That said, budget travelers should be prepared to spend more on lodging in Mumbai than in any other city on the subcontinent; standards at the low end can be difficult to stomach, so you're better off forking out a little more for a decent place to stay.

Marine Drive is a great option if you want a prime view of the Arabian Sea, but it's pricey. With a variety of options to suit every budget (top choice obviously being the Taj Mahal Hotel, reviewed below), Colaba-Fort is where most tourists end up. If you're on a really tight budget, a cheap, decent option worth noting is **Bentley's Hotel** (17 Oliver Rd., Colaba; © 022/2284-1474 or -1733; bentleyshotel@hotmail.com), which has old, threadbare accommodations with enough character and antique furniture to make it livable. You can get a room with wooden floors, a balcony, and an attached bathroom for under Rs 1,385 ($32); be warned that at least several days' advance reservation might be necessary. If you are literally overnighting and have no desire to spend time in Mumbai, a number of options are located close to the international airport, but no bargains here. A good compromise is Juhu, which has cheaper choices and a great nighttime atmosphere, and is only a 30-minute drive from the airport.

Note: The prices below are sometimes given in rupees, with U.S. dollar conversions; others are stated in U.S. dollars only, which is how many hotels targeting foreign markets quote their rates.

MARINE DRIVE

Within walking distance of the city's commercial center, Marine Drive is a great place to base yourself, not least for the sea views and sense of space these provide—offering a relief from the hustling, bustling streets that lie east. Expect to pay for the privilege, however. If your budget can't stretch to pay for the suggestions below, check out **Sea Green Hotel** (© 022/5633-6525 or 022/2282-2294; www.seagreenhotel.com) or the slightly better **South Sea Green** next door. The Sea Green is the best budget option on Marine Drive, where relatively large guest rooms with French doors (and flaking paint) open onto balconies overlooking Back Bay. It has a slightly seedy air, and furnishings are quite awful, but the attached shower-toilets are large and clean, and each room comes with TV, air-conditioning, and a minibar. You can bed down on your foam mattress for Rs 2,820 ($65) double.

VERY EXPENSIVE

Hotel Marine Plaza 𝒞𝒞 Any address along Marine Drive is highly sought after, and the blue-mirrored glass facade of this self-styled "fashionably small" upmarket establishment is no exception, though it's not in the same class as The Oberoi or Inter-Continental. Like the hotel, the marble lobby is small, its main stairway concealing a quaint lounge from which you can stare up at people swimming in the glass-bottom pool on the fifth floor. Most of the accommodations are suites, some of which are relatively well-priced but require neck-straining to get a look at the view; make sure to specify a room with a direct sea view. Besides swimming, the pool deck affords wonderful views over Back Bay and the entire Queen's Necklace strip. Like many other upscale hotels in Mumbai, Marine Plaza gets busy at weekends, especially on weekend nights and at Sunday lunch, when the popular **Bayview** and **Oriental Blossom** restaurants are filled with locals, and the bar, **Geoffrey's,** buzzes until 2am.

29 Marine Dr., Mumbai 400 020. ℭ 022/2285-1212. Fax 022/2282-8585. www.sarovarparkplaza.com. hmp@hotel marineplaza.com. 68 units. $275 superior double; $300 executive double, $400 deluxe suite, $575 special suite. AE, DC, MC, V. **Amenities:** 2 restaurants; pastry shop; bar; pool w/Jacuzzi; gym; business center; Wi-Fi enabled; 24-hr. room service; laundry; doctor-on-call. *In room:* A/C, TV, dataport, minibar, tea- and coffee-making facility, electronic safe.

InterContinental Marine Drive 𝒞𝒞𝒞 When it comes to views, few contenders can match those of the new InterContinental, which opened in 2003. Designed with business travelers in mind, yet relatively intimate (only 59 rooms), the hotel spared no expense in ensuring you a good night's sleep—there's even a "Pillow and Quilt Menu": Will it be a set of "air" pillows tonight or a mix of Korean and bamboo pillows? Satin or silk quilts? Beside the bed is your choice of oils for clarity of thought, stress relief, or peaceful sleep; in the bathroom are heavenly toiletries from Bvlgari. At a whopping 42 sq. m (450 sq. ft.), the rooms here must be largest in the city. (While all rooms offer some view of the sea, best are the "deluxe seafront.") All rooms come with 42-inch plasma TV and DVD player. Bathrooms are large, separated from the main room only by sliding doors (in the suite) or windows, creating a feeling of spaciousness. Although the in-house dining isn't exceptional, the rooftop **Dome** bar (see "Hot Spots with Views," below) is perfect for a romantic evening drink. Also pleasant is the lobby lounge with its leather sofas, where you can enjoy coffee, tea, and snacks; watch a humungous plasma TV; or peruse the interesting book collection.

InterContinental Marine Dr., 135 Marine Dr., Mumbai 400 020. ℭ 022/5639-9699. Fax 022/5639-9600. www. intercontinental.com. 59 units. $315 deluxe double, $350 deluxe bay-view double, $380 deluxe seafront double; $600 deluxe bay-view suite, $700 deluxe corner suite, $1,900–$2,300 presidential suite. AE, DC, MC, V. **Amenities:** 2 restaurants; 2 bars; health club; travel desk and car hire; tour guides, business center; currency exchange; 24-hr. room service; in-room massages and salon treatment; laundry and dry cleaning; DVD and CD library. *In room:* A/C, plasma TV, Wi-Fi, fax, DVD player, minibar, hair dryer, electronic safe, aromatherapy.

The Oberoi 𝒞𝒞𝒞 What do Bill Gates, Richard Gere, Michael Jackson, Rupert Murdoch, and the leaders or the heads of state of the United States, Russia, Greece, China, Indonesia, and Iceland have in common? Yes, they've all stayed at the best hotel on Marine Drive, and arguably the best in Mumbai. It's particularly from a service point of view that The Oberoi wins hands-down; touches like a personal butler on each floor summoned by the touch of an "Ask Jeeves" button, and genuflecting staff members who go out of their way to make you feel revered, are always welcome. And the genteel atmosphere is a relief—tranquil, sophisticated, and relaxed, this is where you want to retreat after spending a few hours out on the street. You can head for the top-rated **Banyan Tree spa,** or make a beeline for the azure pool where you can soak up the Mumbai sun next to a dramatic faux-rock waterfall. For those who can really splurge, choose the immaculate Kohinoor Suite, which covers 152 sq. m (1,634 sq. ft.) on a corner with smashing 270-degree views of Marine Drive and the bay. All accommodations are spacious, with tasteful decor, but the best rooms are the corner suites on each floor, which showcase Marine Drive almost as beautifully as the plush Kohinoor Suite but make a smaller dent in your wallet. If you can afford it, ask for the deluxe suite, which exudes pure luxury and comfort: In soothing pastel green and white hues, it offers a canopied four-poster bed, an eclectic collection on the bookshelf, a lavish bathroom with a lovely separate shower and tub, a telescope with which to survey the bay, and dramatic views of Queen's Necklace—a dazzling pre-dinner spectacle.

Note: If the rates at The Oberoi are a tad stiff for your budget, overnight instead in the adjoining **Hilton Towers** 🍴🍴 (owned and run by The Oberoi Hotels with a Hilton tie-in). No, a stay here is by no means as luxurious as what's on offer at its more exclusive neighbor (and rooms are smaller), but this is still an excellent hotel, offering good value—plus you'll have access to all the facilities next door. Rates vary daily and can be as low as $150 a night, including breakfast (www.hilton.com; © **022/5632-4343,** in the U.S. dial 800/HILTONS).

Nariman Point, Mumbai 400 021. © **022/5632-5757;** reservations 022/5632-6887. Fax 022/5632-4142. www.oberoi hotels.com. 333 units. $355 superior city-facing double, $375 premium bay-view double, $425 deluxe ocean-view double; $805 executive ocean-view suite, $1,080 deluxe ocean-view suite, $1,500–$2,280 presidential suite. Airport transfers and breakfast included. AE, DC, MC, V. **Amenities:** 3 restaurants; bar; an additional 3 restaurants and bar in adjoining Hilton Towers; pool; spa, salon, and health club; concierge; sightseeing, travel, and limousine service; business center; currency exchange; shopping arcade; bookshop; 24-hr. room service; laundry and dry cleaning; doctor-on-call; floor butler. *In room:* A/C, TV, fax machine, dataport, minibar, tea- and coffee-making facilities, hair dryer, electronic safe, scale. Sea-facing rooms and suites have DVD players; suites and deluxe rooms include CD players.

EXPENSIVE

Ambassador 🍴 Capped by the city's only revolving restaurant, this kitsch 1940s hotel welcomes you with a baroque-inspired marble lobby adorned with cheap cherub statues, giant decorative vases, and an eclectic, extravagant mix of furniture, all under a gold-painted molded ceiling dripping with chandeliers. If you want a sea view (and that's why you're on the Drive), opt for one of the "superior" guest rooms: Clean, neat, and functional, these occupy the second, third, and fourth floors; carpeted passages are decorated with Mughlai miniatures and the theme is red and white. The slightly cheaper "executive" rooms on the upper floors include some units with partial sea views: Ask for room no. 8, 9, or 10. On the plus side, executive rooms are reasonably sized and have a slightly less overwhelming white, cream, and blue decor; roomy white-and-gray marble bathrooms feature large tubs. Apart from the enthusiastic turbaned doorman and the dedicated restaurant staff, service here is unexceptional, with some irritating heel-dragging that's particularly evident behind the crowded reception counter.

Veer Nariman Rd., off Marine Dr., Churchgate 400 020. © **022/2204-1131.** Fax 022/2204-0004. www.ambassador india.com. 110 units. $150 executive double, $170 superior double, $225 premier double; $475 suite. $25 extra bed. No charge for children under 12 sharing parent's room. AE, DC, MC, V. **Amenities:** 3 restaurants; bar; travel assistance and car hires; business center; currency exchange; florist; 24-hr. room service; laundry and dry cleaning; doctor-on-call. *In room:* A/C, TV, bedside console, minibar, hair dryer on request, electronic safe.

INEXPENSIVE

Chateau Windsor Hotel *Value*   With clean, very basic rooms on the second, fourth, and fifth floors of an apartment block, this "hotel" is approached via an ancient elevator that may have you panicking before check-in. Don't. It may be unspectacular but it's cheap—perhaps the best accommodations in its price bracket—and you get to hang out with real Mumbaikars. Do specify that you want an air-conditioned room with attached bathroom; these units have small balconies, stone tile floors, and foam mattresses with clean white sheets and towels. The simple furnishings include an armless "sofa," a linoleum-topped table, and a small, narrow cupboard. Management is generally helpful. Although there is no restaurant, you can sit in the terrace garden and nosh, or get room service; you'll have few reasons to do this, however, given the neighborhood's large number of excellent restaurants. The kitchen is also available for you to do your own cooking—as long as it's vegetarian.

86 Veer Nariman Rd., Churchgate, Mumbai 400 020. ℂ **022/2204-4455.** Fax 022/2202-6459. www.chateauwindsor.com. info@ChateauWindsor.com. 55 units. Rs 1,590 ($35) small non-A/C double, Rs 1,890 ($43) standard non-A/C double, Rs 2,190 ($51) standard A/C double. Rs 300 ($6.85) extra person; Rs 150 ($3.40) children ages 3–12 sharing parent's room. AE, MC, V. **Amenities:** Travel assistance; free Internet access in lobby; 24-hr. room service; laundry; doctor-on-call. *In room:* A/C, TV, fridge (in some).

COLABA

With the city's densest concentration of sights, hotels, and restaurants (of which the best are reviewed below), Colaba is an ideal location. The Taj Mahal is here, as is the excellent-value Gordon House, a personal favorite.

VERY EXPENSIVE

The Taj Mahal Palace & Tower 𝄞𝄞𝄞   George Bernard Shaw famously claimed that after staying here, he no longer had any need to visit the original Taj Mahal in Agra. But seriously stiff competition from the nearby Oberoi and InterContinental (and even from so-called "suburban" hotels like the JW Marriott, Hyatt Regency, Grand Hyatt, and ITC Maratha Sheraton) has The Taj in the process of reinventing itself to keep its crown as *the* most celebrated address in Mumbai. As such, it is launching the brand-new **Jiva** spa and a number of new restaurants and watering holes (see "Top Attractions: Downtown," earlier in this chapter). Then again, the history here is tangible: Public areas are decorated with carefully chosen antiques and vintage artwork. Bombay's very first licensed drinking establishment, **Harbour Bar,** can be found here, as can the still trendy **Insomnia** nightclub (now open to all). If you do opt for The Taj Mahal Palace, you'll want to wallow in the luxurious old-world splendor of the Heritage Wing; individually themed high-ceilinged suites transport you to another era, when the likes of Somerset Maugham and Duke Ellington bedded down in the city's best hotel. For a view of the Gateway, book a Taj Club sea-view or luxury sea-view room, but if money is no object, nothing less than the Rajput Suite will do. As the crowning glory of one of India's most prominent hotel chains, The Taj Mahal Palace may well double as the nerve center for money-eyed mischief, but it remains a great blend of old-world charm and modern conveniences. That said, its reputation for service has in recent years been less than stellar, something we hope will be addressed along with the physical revamping of the hotel. Note that the hotel's looming Tower Wing is more business-oriented, and a bit of a letdown once you've explored the original parts of the hotel.

Hot Spots with Views

With the waters of the Arabian Sea lapping the entire length of the city on both its eastern and western flanks, Mumbai enjoys a fabulous seaside location, yet the city has relatively few nightspots with views worth mentioning. Most can be found in five-star establishments. With the dark blue horizon just beyond the terrace's glass railing and a star-studded sky above, **Dome** 𝕮𝕮 (𝒞 022/5639-9600; reservations recommended on weekends), on the rooftop of the InterContinental Marine Drive, commands the best vista. Sink into the inviting off-white sofas and overstuffed armchairs that surround scented candles and order a Caipiroska or a Mohito, or even a Long Island Iced Tea. Give the food a pass, although you may want to sample the mango gelato with champagne. Farther along Marine Drive at the Hotel Marine Plaza, **Bayview** 𝕮 (𝒞 022/2285-1212) is a 24-hour restaurant. Its drinks and buffets (Rs 250–Rs 450/$5.70–$10) are great value for money; avoid weekends when the place is packed with noisy families. Alternatively, get right on the beach and grab a hammock at **Salt Water Grill** (see full review later in this chapter) on Chowpatty (H2O Water Sports Complex; 𝒞 022/2368-5459). Drink in lovely views of the Arabian Sea along with heady cocktails. For an elegant evening, **Pearl of the Orient** 𝕮 (𝒞 022/2204-1131), the revolving restaurant atop the Ambassador Hotel, offers more lovely views of Mumbai and good service; the food is fairly satisfying and includes Korean barbecue, inauthentic Japanese, and a sprinkling of Thai and Chinese dishes.

On the opposite shore of Mumbai's southern tip, overlooking the harbor, you'll find another set of views, quite different but every bit as remarkable. For a refined setting with a splendid view of the Gateway, make your way

---

Apollo Bunder, Mumbai 400 001. 𝒞 **022/5665-3366.** Fax 022/5665-0300. www.tajhotels.com. mahal.mumbai@taj hotels.com. 565 units. Tower Wing doubles: $275 superior city-view, $295 superior sea-view, $315 deluxe city-view, $335 deluxe sea-view. Heritage Wing doubles: $355 luxury city/pool-view, $370 luxury sea-view, $375 luxury grande city/pool view, $405 luxury grande sea-view, $435 Taj Club city/pool-view, $465 Taj Club sea-view. Heritage suites: $600 junior, $800 executive, $1,200 luxury, $1,600 grand luxury, $2,300 presidential. (Taj Club and suites include limousine airport transfer, club floor check-in, breakfast, personal valet, buffet breakfast, high tea, business services, and cocktail hour.) AE, DC, MC, V. **Amenities:** 5 restaurants; pastry shop; 3 bars; nightclub; swimming pool; sports arrangements on request (golf, badminton, squash, billiards, tennis, table tennis); fitness center; concierge; travel desk; car hire; business center; currency exchange; shopping arcade; salon; wireless newspaper service; babysitting; laundry; doctor-on-call; valet service; personal valet service for Grand Luxe and Presidential Suite guests. *In room:* A/C, TV (plasma in some), fax machine on request, DVD player, MP3 stereo, 2-line speaker phones, dataport, minibar, hair dryer, electronic safe. Suites have in-built personal spa.

EXPENSIVE

Taj President 𝕮𝕮   It may not be the most beautiful or luxurious hotel in Mumbai, but this classy business property offers ultra-efficient service, excellent restaurants, and a convenient location in a smart neighborhood not too far from the maelstrom of busy Colaba. Shades of purple combine with marble, wood, and metal, and are playfully offset by elegant bonsai trees in a brand-new lobby that pays homage to the 1970s. Standard rooms are decently sized, with solid wooden furniture, brown-red carpets, to the **Harbour Bar** in the Taj, where martinis, champagne, and cigars are the order of the day. Also in the Taj is **Souk** (© **022/5665-3366**), the rooftop restaurant that pretentiously calls its food "Eastern Mediterranean"; the cuisine it serves is generally known elsewhere as Middle Eastern or West Asian. Best is the *mezze* buffet offering the usual suspects (hummus, salads, baba ganoush, tabbouleh, falafel, and assorted olives), as well as three interesting meat- or seafood-based salads, all accompanied by delicious, hot pita breads. Souk's location is great, but the tables near the window are placed in such a way that only one person at a table for two gets the harbor view. Go figure. If you bag a window table at **Sea Lounge** (© **022/5665-3366**), the Taj's renowned coffee shop, you can watch the boats float by while demanding more Earl Grey. Although you don't have to be a guest in the hotel to enjoy any of these Taj options, do note that your manner of dress (and perceived status) has a direct effect on how well you are treated.

Moving north of the city, you can take a break at **Vista,** the cafe at the Taj Land's End in Bandra; or at **Ming Yang,** the hotel's Szechuan Chinese eatery. Both afford diners fine views of the Arabian Sea and the Portuguese fort, if you can snag a table near the window (both © **022/5668-1234**). Farther north near Juhu Beach is a personal favorite, the low-key, reasonably priced seaside-veranda restaurant at **Citizen Hotel** (© **022/5693-2525**), which serves formulaic Indian and Continental fare in a tranquil setting that provides one of the best unobstructed views of the sea. An air-conditioned, glass-walled section also has good views.

and an emphasis on paisley fabrics. It's worth paying a little extra for a room on the Executive Floor, which has received an ultra-contemporary makeover by one of Bombay's leading designers; pale tones and modern works of art combine to make this, the 17th floor, quite different from the other, old-fashioned floors.

90 Cuffe Parade, Mumbai 400 005, Maharashtra. © 022/5665-0808. Fax 022/5665-0303. www.tajhotels.com. president.mumbai@tajhotels.com. 300 units. $220 standard city-facing double, $230 standard sea-facing double, $240 executive double; $300 executive suite. $20 extra bed. Executive rooms and suites include breakfast. Ask about daily discounts. AE, DC, MC, V. **Amenities:** 3 restaurants; pastry shop; bar; pool; fitness center (gym, steam, massage); concierge; travel desk; car hires; business center; currency exchange; shops; salon; 24-hr. room service; babysitting; laundry service; safe deposit lockers; doctor-on-call; Wi-Fi enabled. *In room:* A/C, TV (satellite), dataport, tea- and coffee-making facilities, hair dryer, scale. Fax machines in executive rooms and suites.

MODERATE

The Gordon House Hotel (((*Value*   Set among a rash of rather ordinary old-fashioned hotels, Colaba's sexiest lodging option and Mumbai's only boutique-style hotel is perfect for those raring to have a good time. Originally owned by Arthur Gordon, an early-20th-century trader who made his fortune in Bombay, and now the pride of Sanjay Narang, one of Mumbai's most high-profile restaurateurs, this trendy pad with its toothpaste-white interiors comes as a breath of fresh air, as does the slick, attentive service that starts with the super-fast check-in. There are three themed guest room floors: The Scandinavian level offers smart, contemporary rooms with parquet floors and sleek Ikea-style furniture, timber blinds, and large Euro-themed black-and-white photographs. Mediterranean rooms are equally charming, with bright blues and yellows, tiled floors, cane chairs, John Miller posters, and cool aqua-toned bathrooms. Rooms on the feminine Country Floor are strictly floral, patchwork, and pastel fans. Accommodations are small but well proportioned, with comfortable beds and extras like a stereo system with VCD (video compact disc, a media format popular in Asia that never really caught on in the West) and CD player so you can rent a movie or request complimentary music from the hotel's library. A selection of magazines, bowls of sweets, designer toiletries, free Internet access, and complimentary ironing are more thoughtful touches. The bathrooms may be tiny, but they offer great walk-in showers. Opulent and over the top, the one and only suite has been themed on the Sun King's palace at Versailles, complete with crystal chandeliers and lavish gilded furniture (and available at the price you'd pay for a regular room elsewhere). **All Stir Fry,** the pleasant do-it-yourself Asian restaurant, is quite good, but look for a new rooftop restaurant (serving Hyderabadi cuisine) to open in early 2006. Sadly, the place has one drawback: The nonstop thumping from the in-house nightclub **Polly Esther's,** which particularly affects rooms on the second floor.

5 Battery St., Apollo Bunder, Colaba, Mumbai 400 039. (℃) 022/2287-1122. Fax 022/2287-2026. www.ghhotel.com. sales@ghhotel.com. 29 units. Rs 6,000 ($137) double; Rs 10,000 ($230) Versailles Suite. Tariff includes American breakfast. AE, MC, V. **Amenities:** 2 restaurants; bar; nightclub; health club privileges; exercise equipment; concierge; travel, transport, and sightseeing arrangements; 24-hr. room service; laundry and dry cleaning; complimentary ironing; doctor-on-call; express check-out. *In room:* A/C, TV, CD and VCD player (CDs on request); bedside console, minibar, tea- and coffee-making facility, hair dryer, iron and ironing board on request, electronic safe.

INEXPENSIVE

Hotel Godwin   The facade of this nine-story budget hotel harks back to the 1930s and suggests a faded grandeur that is sadly not realized in most of the rooms. Because the range of accommodations varies a lot here, you should specifically request a centrally air-conditioned deluxe room that has been refurbished. Also insist that it's one of the eighth-floor units blessed with a view (distant as it is) of the Taj Mahal Hotel.

Note: Guest rooms at the Godwin's sister establishment, the **Garden Hotel** (℃ 022/ 2284-1476; gardenhotel@mail.com), immediately next door, are slightly cheaper but are cluttered and a bit grubby.

Jasmine Building, 41 Garden Rd., Colaba, Mumbai 400 039. (℃) 022/2287-2050. Fax 022/2287-1592. godwinht@ vsnl.in. 52 units. Rs 2,750 ($63) standard double, Rs 2,850 ($66) deluxe double; Rs 2,950 ($68) suite. AE, MC, V. **Amenities:** Restaurant; bar; currency exchange; 24-hr. room service; laundry; doctor-on-call. *In room:* A/C, TV, minibar, tea- and coffee-making facility on request, hair dryer on request.

Hotel Suba Palace ⚡   A friendly doorman sporting an elaborate moustache welcomes you politely to this small, rather nondescript hotel not far from the Gateway of India. Despite the side-street location and total absence of views, a full upgrade in 2001 rendered it bright and spotless, with renewed focus on service (such as 24-hr. room service—always useful). Accommodations are on the small side, and there are no bedside lamps, but the Suba will suit the traveler looking for a reasonably smart option (as opposed to character-filled, like Shelleys) that offers good value.

Near Gateway of India, Apollo Bunder, Mumbai 400 039. (℃) 022/2202-0636 or 022/22885444. Fax 022/22020812. www.hotelsubapalace.com. info@hotelsubapalace.com. 51 units. Rs 2,844 ($65) double, breakfast included. AE, MC, V. **Amenities:** Restaurant; travel assistance; foreign exchange; 24-hr. room service; laundry; doctor-on-call. *In room:* A/C, TV, hair dryer.

Shelleys ✦ *Value*   Ignore the gruff bloke at reception; for this type of money you won't find a better location (on the waterfront and near the Gateway) with the same degree of comfort, a fact that makes up for the lack of facilities. Shelleys has, for instance, no restaurant, but there is no shortage of options in the neighborhood. Try to book one of the six sea-facing rooms (preferably one of the two with tile floors, which look fresher); each features blue or green bedcovers and color-coordinated drapes over shallow bay windows, large dark wood cupboards, a desk, and—inexplicably—a big, fake orange-painted "oak" tree. The large, clean bathrooms have tubs and natural light, and there's even small dressing areas. Public sea-facing terraces with deep, black leatherette sofas catch the sea breeze and afford lovely views. Budget rates mean putting up with wall-attached air-conditioning units and ancient elevators, but many find the old-fashioned ambience very agreeable.

30 P.J. Ramchandani Marg (opposite Radio Club), Colaba, Mumbai 400 039. © 022/2284-0229 or 022/2284-0270. Fax 022/2284-0385. www.shelleyshotel.com. shelleyshotel@vsnl.com. 17 units. Rs 1,935 ($44) sea-facing double, Rs 1,622 ($40) non-sea-facing double. AE, DC, MC, V. **Amenities:** Tea-cum-waiting room; laundry. *In room:* A/C, TV, fridge.

JUHU & BANDRA

A 60- to 90-minute drive from the heavily touristed downtown area, the seaside suburb of Juhu attracts a predominantly local, moneyed crowd, and as such affords in many ways a truly genuine introduction to Mumbai. Juhu's relative proximity to the airport (it's a 30-min. drive) makes it the ideal stopover if you have no strong desire to engage with the historical side of the city, or if you need to recover from jet lag before moving on, but aren't keen to fork over the exorbitant rates demanded by the airport hotels.

VERY EXPENSIVE

JW Marriott Hotel ✦   Designed by the renowned architect Bill Bensley, the opulent JW is Juhu's most luxurious hotel and top choice if you choose a hotel by the quality of its in-house dining. **Lotus Café,** the sprawling 24-hour coffee shop at the bottom of the split-level lobby, is a popular hangout with the local trendy crowd, who enjoy its consistently good daily buffets; at **Mezzo Mezzo,** friendly chef Sebastiano Mastrangelo serves light, healthy dishes using locally available ingredients (which for Mumbai means an emphasis on seafood); and **BBC (Bombay Baking Company)** is quite simply the city's best bakery. Set over five floors, the guest rooms are comfortable, with modern, albeit rather predictable, decor and amenities; each has some kind of sea view, though most are side views. The best aspect of the hotel, aside from its dining, is the expansive tropical seaside garden, with torch-lit pathways, a lotus pond, and Indian sandstone sculptures crafted by artisans from Rajasthan. It's also got two wonderful pools, as well as a well-equipped fitness center and spa—definitely required after all the extra calories you're likely to consume at BBC while staying here.

Juhu Tara Rd., Juhu Beach, Mumbai 400 099. © 022/5693-3000. Fax 022/5693-3100. 358 units. $300 superior double, $340 executive double, $360 executive deluxe double; $600–$750 suite. All rates except superior double include breakfast and transfers. AE, DC, MC, V. **Amenities:** 4 restaurants; bakery and cafe; 2 bars; nightclub; 2 pools; kids' pool; fitness center/spa; personal trainer; game room and video games; concierge; business center; shopping arcade; 24-hr. room service; babysitting w/advance notice; laundry and dry cleaning; doctor-on-call. *In room:* A/C, TV, Web TV, dataport, minibar, tea- and coffee-making facility, hair dryer, iron and ironing board, electronic safe.

EXPENSIVE

Holiday Inn   Until the JW opened, this rather anonymous hotel was Juhu's best, no doubt because of its beachfront location and extensive facilities. The superior deluxe rooms feature pale-blue partially wallpapered walls and granite floors covered with carpets that match the curtains; beds are comfortable, if a little low. Costing just 10 euros more (and worth it) are the more spacious Club Select rooms on the sixth and seventh floors; these have a breezier feel, with bright blue carpets and bedcovers in pink, beige, and blue—guests here also have access to an exclusive lounge. Direct sea views are only available from the suites.

Balraj Sahani Marg, Juhu Beach, Mumbai 400 049. ℂ 022/5693-4444. Fax 022/5693-4455 or -4466. www.holiday innbombay.com. hib@holidayinnbombay.com. 191 units. 150€ ($186) standard double, 170€ ($210) superior deluxe double; 180€ ($224) Club Select, 300€ ($373) special suite, 350€ ($435) deluxe suite, 400€ ($497) superior deluxe suite, 550€ ($683) presidential suite. Rates include breakfast and airport transfers. AE, DC, MC, V. **Amenities:** 3 restaurants; pub; pool; health club; travel agency; car hires; shopping arcade; salon; 24-hr. room service; laundry and dry cleaning. *In room:* A/C, TV, bedside panel, minibar, tea- and coffee-making facility, hair dryer, safe, scale. Suites include stereo system and kitchenette w/microwave and fridge.

Taj Lands End 🕮🕮   Location, location, location! It may be away from the central tourist area of Colaba, but this hotel enjoys a lovely seaside setting in one of Mumbai's hippest suburbs. It originally opened in 1999 as the Regent, but in 2002 the Taj Group took it over and refurbished it, turning it into one of the city's finest hotels, with each and every guest room affording views of the Arabian Sea through palm trees. The lobby is done up in earth tones and has potted plants, huge metal pots, and sculptures of horses; the atrium, with its grand piano, hosts live music every evening. Plush and slightly over the top, the carpeted guest rooms feature wonderful, solid, king-size mattresses covered in soft, cool white linen. Pale pink or darker maroon walls are decorated with contemporary prints and watercolors, and the rooms feature quality embroidered fabrics and plenty of wood—only the slightly ruddy carpets could do with a makeover. If you don't mind shelling out the extra $85, get a Taj Club room on the 21st floor, which has wonderful wood floors, a personal butler, express check-in and -out, and a separate lounge area with complimentary French wine and exotic dry fruits. (Ask about special promotions and rates, which the hotel has been using to entice new visitors.)

Land's End, Bandstand, Bandra (West), Mumbai 400 050. ℂ 022/5668-1234. Fax 022/5699-4488. www.tajhotels. com. landsend.mumbai@tajhotels.com. 508 units. $305 superior double, $325 deluxe double, $355 luxury double; $390 Taj Club, $450 executive suite, $600 luxury suite, $1,000 grand luxury suite, $1,500 presidential suite. Taj Club rooms have complimentary breakfast, cocktail hour, high tea. AE, DC, MC, V. **Amenities:** 3 restaurants; bar; pool; spa; fitness center; concierge; travel desk; car hires; business center; currency exchange; bookshop; salon; 24-hr. room service; laundry and dry cleaning; doctor-on-call; butler on call; luxury and club lounge floors; Wi-Fi enabled. *In room:* A/C, TV, electronic bedside console, dataport, minibar, hair dryer, tea- and coffee-making facilities, electronic safe, scale, magnifying shaving mirror. Taj Club rooms have plasma TV.

MODERATE

Sun-n-Sand 🕮   This small, old-fashioned beachfront hotel was getting a much-needed overhaul at press time; however, the revamp includes an attempt to conserve water (making bathtubs now available only in the suites). Specify a sea-facing standard double room: Breakfast, cocktail hour, and airport transfers are included in the rate. Rooms have flatscreen TVs, and the hotel is Wi-Fi enabled. The luxury suites are done in various themes—"Suko Thai" has wooden floors, Thai rocking chair, figurines, lamps, flower-painted columns, and a pleasant circular seating area, while Galleria is apparently inspired by a contemporary art gallery, with mod lights, curved wall paneling, and a Jacuzzi bath and exercise area—but for the same rate you might as well be at the JW Marriott, which has infinitely better service and amenities. Service borders on the adequate, with staff a little too lethargic; this doesn't seem to matter much to yesteryear Bollywood stars frequenting the bar.

39 Juhu Beach, Mumbai 400 049. ℰ 022/5693-8888. Fax 022/2620-2170. www.sunnsandhotel.com. reservations@ sunnsandhotel.com. 120 units. $190 superior double, $ 210 superior sea-facing double, $230 executive double, $250 deluxe double; $300–$450 suite. Rates include buffet breakfast, airport transfers, and cocktail hours. AE, DC, MC, V. **Amenities:** 3 restaurants; bar; pool; health and fitness center; massage; Jacuzzi; travel desk; business center; shops; salon; babysitting; laundry; doctor on call; Wi-Fi enabled. *In room:* A/C, TV, dataport, minibar, tea- and coffee-making facility (in suites), hair dryer, electronic safe.

NEAR THE AIRPORT

The reasons for staying here are obvious, but with the exception of the Hyatt, it seems a pity to stay in these cocoons when The Taj Mahal and Oberoi beckon from Colaba. Note that cheaper airport options are less than salubrious. An airport choice you may come across, but one that's not in the same league as those described below, is the **Leela** (ℰ **022/5691-1234;** fax 022/5691-1212; www.theleela.com; leelarsv@theleela.com). A stalwart of Mumbai's hospitality industry (and favored by the Dalai Lama), the Leela has considerably lowered its rates since the competition heated up in the form of several new hotels ($265–$675 double; ask for daily discounts). Relative to new competitors like the Hyatt Regency, the Leela appears rather old-fashioned. Still, it's a good hotel, and you may want to check it out.

Hyatt Regency 🛦🛦🛦 *Value*   With all the dramatic design-intensive *joie de vivre* of a modern art gallery, this is the latest newcomer to vie for the tourist and businessman's buck, and we think it wins hands-down (especially if you can get a room at a particularly low rate—these change daily, so call or check out the online rates). Stacked glass walls, brilliant mood lighting, floating ebony ceiling effects, and Italian marble are offset by marigolds in tailored cube bouquets—and that's just the lobby. Sleek and stylish, guest rooms deliver great comfort. The ultra-contemporary design-conscious accommodations ignore typical hotel-room configurations, the dramatic interiors enhanced by the judicious use of space, imaginative lighting concepts, and elegant fittings. One entire wall is a mirror, floors are Malaysian teakwood, desks are swivel-top slabs of glass, and the televisions are flatscreen. White-marble bathrooms offer a choice between large rain showers or separate step-down bathtubs—a welcome treat after a long plane journey or a day in Mumbai. The **Club Prana spa** is a popular pre- and post-flight venue; while **Stax,** the newly revamped Coastal Italian restaurant, is a classy dining option if you're ever in the vicinity of the airport.

Sahar Airport Rd., Mumbai 400 099. ℰ 022/5696-1234. Fax 022/5696-1235. www.hyatt.com. 397 units. Rates on day-to-day basis. $212 standard double; $240 Regency Club. Rates include breakfast and airport transfers. Club rate includes use of private lounge, dedicated concierge, complimentary use of meeting room, all-day tea and coffee service, and evening cocktails and canapés. AE, DC, MC, V. **Amenities:** 3 restaurants; bar; pool; lighted tennis and squash courts; spa and fitness center; 24-hr. room service; laundry; doctor-on-call. *In room:* A/C, TV, dataport, minibar, tea- and coffee-making facility, electronic safe.

ITC Hotel Grand Maratha Sheraton & Towers 🛦🛦   Since its opening in 2001, the Grand Maratha has already been recognized with at least one award as the country's best hotel. An imposing pink-sandstone neoclassical building topped by a futuristic dome, the Sheraton recalls elements of India's rich architectural legacy: thick columns, imposing contours, arches, a cobbled entrance flanked by two wooden horses and, in the porte-cochere, a Goan-inspired coffered ceiling. Rooms don't disappoint: Beds are fabulously comfy, London-based interior designer Francesca Basu has captured the local love of bright colors, and the garden views in some rooms (ask for one) are lovely. The six different restaurants, all of excellent quality, are reason enough to stay here: Both **Dakshin,** offering the cuisines of South India; and **Dum**

Pukht, its specialties inherited from the *Nawabs* of Awadh, are good places to go, particularly if you haven't had (or won't have) a chance to sample these cuisines elsewhere in India.

Sahar, Mumbai 400 099. ℂ 022/2830-3030. Delhi reservations: ℂ 011/2614-1821. Fax 022/2830-3131. www.welcom group.com. 386 units. $350 Executive Club double, $400 Sheraton Towers double, $425 ITC One double. Daily discounts available. AE, DC, MC, V. **Amenities:** 6 restaurants; bar; pool; golf by arrangement; wellness center w/gym, steam, sauna, Jacuzzi, massage and spa treatments; concierge; travel and tour desk; car hires; business center; currency exchange; shops and boutiques; salon; 24-hr. room service; babysitting; laundry and valet service; doctor-on-call. *In room:* A/C, TV, minibar, tea- and coffee-making facility, hair dryer, electronic safe, scale. Sheraton Towers rooms include butler service. ITC One rooms include step machine, hand-held massager, massage chair, fax machine.

Le Royal Meridien ℛ   Wrapped in wall-to-wall marble and dripping with chandeliers, the small lobby of this lavish baroque-style hotel sports a winter garden off the atrium balconies and a wood-paneled cigar-and-brandy bar near the lobby; at night live jazz replaces the daytime piped harpsichord-inspired Western classical music and keeps the lobby abuzz. Ask for a corner room—these are larger. If it's views you're after, ask for a room on the first, second, or third floor. Royal Club rooms have wooden floors and include playfully eccentric touches like plastic ducks in the bathrooms and teddy bears on the canopied king-size poster beds; dark wooden chests with inlaid metalwork, beautiful glassware bedside lamps, and wall prints and photos reflecting local history create a strong sense of luxury. Standard rooms are less spacious but no less luxurious. Unfortunately, the in-house dining, particularly the at 24-hour **La Brasserie,** is rather disappointing, and all in all is a pricey option.

Sahar Airport Rd. ℂ 022/2838-0000. Fax 022/2838-0101. www.mumbai.lemeridien.com. lm@lrmmumbai.com. 171 units. Doubles include airport pickup. $315 standard double; $325 deluxe double; $360 Royal Club (includes airport drop and other club perks), $500 suite, minimum $500 (rate on request) presidential suite. AE, DC, MC, V. **Amenities:** 3 restaurants; 2 bars; pool; health club w/steam, sauna, and massage; business center; salon; doctor-on-call; library; florist; Wi-Fi enabled. *In room:* A/C, TV, fax machine, DVD player, minibar, tea- and coffee-making facility, electronic safe.

The Orchid ℛ   In a city this polluted, a stay at this multiple-award-winning eco-friendly hotel at least serves to relieve some tourist guilt. But that's not the only reason to stay here: Thankfully, the hotel's commitment to preserving the environment is combined with reasonably good taste and impressive service. Environment-friendly considerations include solar-powered terrace lights, wastewater treatment technology, in-room recycle bins, and a UV-treated chlorine-free swimming pool. You'll find plants in all the rooms (which are comfortable) and understated furniture made from Nuwud Medium Density Fibre "wood," the eco-conscious alternative to ripping down entire forests. Emphasizing the eco-theme, paintings and prints of orchids and flowers are found throughout the hotel, and the lobby features a six-story water curtain—recycled water, of course. The rooftop pool with its Mexican hacienda–style barbecue restaurant offers interesting views—particularly if you enjoy watching Mumbai's heavy air traffic come and go.

Adjacent Domestic Airport, Nehru Rd., Vile Parle (East), Mumbai 400 099. ℂ 022/2616-4040. Toll-free 1-600-22-5432. Fax 022/2616-4141. www.orchidhotel.com. info@orchidhotel.com. 245 units. $270 deluxe double; $285 executive suite, $310 Club Privé room, $325 Club Privé suite, $435 Orchid suite, $800 presidential suite. $40 extra bed. Children under 12 stay free in parent's room. AE, DC, MC, V. **Amenities:** 3 restaurants; bar; pool; fitness center; travel desk; airport transfers; business center; foreign exchange; gourmet shop; 24-hr. room service; laundry and dry cleaning; Wi-Fi enabled. *In room:* A/C, TV, minibar, tea- and coffee-making facilities, hair dryer, iron, scale, magnifying shaving mirror.

5 Where to Dine

Nowhere in India is dining more rewarding than in Mumbai. The city literally holds thousands of restaurants, and being a city of migrants, every kind of Indian cuisine is represented—though Konkan, or coastal food, is considered the local specialty. You can mingle with the city's crème de la crème at fine-dining or hip venues, or choose from a vast array of inexpensive eating places. Restaurants serving South Indian fast food (also called Udipi restaurants) can be found on every street, but if you sample only one, make it either **Madras Café** (𝒞 022/2401-4419; Tues–Sun) in Matunga or **A. Ramanayak Udipi Shri Krishna Boarding** 𝄐𝄐 (Main Market Building, 1st floor, near Matunga Railway Station; 𝒞 022/2414-2422). The latter's authentic Madras-style meal is served on a banana leaf (Rs 60/$1.35), and you eat with your hands. Other Indian cuisines you will come across everywhere are neighborhood kebab places (**Noorani** 𝄐; Haji Ali; 𝒞 022/2494-4753 or -3054, serves good kebabs and will even deliver to your South Mumbai hotel); restaurants specializing in local favorites like *pau bhaji* (mixed vegetables and bread); Irani restaurants serving fresh inexpensive breads and pastries; and Chinese restaurants offering "Indianized Chinese." Not surprisingly, vegetarians are particularly well catered for, even in specialty seafood restaurants.

Seafood Thrillers

Anyone with a penchant for seafood will love dining in Mumbai—whether it's Coastal, Konkani, Manglorean, or Malvani cuisine, you are in for a treat. Besides Mahesh Lunch Home and Trishna (see reviews below), you can try **Apoorva** 𝄐 (Brelvi Marg, near Horniman Circle; 𝒞 022/2287-0335 or 022/2288-1457), which has similar Manglorean fare, as does **Excellensea** 𝄐 (Mint Rd., near RBI; 𝒞 022/2261-8991). The latter is on the first floor above **Bharat Restaurant** 𝄐, a non-air-conditioned economy version of Excellensea serving the same food. Note that if you are in a Konkan restaurant, you may want to try the *soul kadi*, a slightly pungent coconut milk drink and a great appetizer. Also sample fresh *appams* and *neer dosas*—both these Southern breads make excellent accompaniments to your seafood. Closer to central Mumbai is **Pisces** 𝄐𝄐 (𝒞 022/2380-5886 or -4367), done up in the standard fish-themed decor but offering more variety in cooking styles. You haven't lived until you've tried the tamarind prawns (not on the menu; they can be requested)—these alone are worth the trip. Also try the *malai chingri* (a cashew nut–based coconut curry with prawns). Manohar Shetty, the owner of Pisces, believes patrons should know exactly what they are getting, so the uncooked fish, prawns, and crab are paraded before you before they are transformed into one of these delectable dishes. In the suburbs in Bandra, you'll get real value for money and atmosphere at **Soul Fry** 𝄐 (𝒞 022/2604-689), which makes great flaky stuffed grilled *rawas* (a local fish). Monday is karaoke night, and even if you can't sing to save your life, it's a great experience to watch extremely talented locals unabashedly take the mic and have the whole place rocking till at least 2am. Soul Fry is an extremely lively and friendly restaurant. On weekends, live music often accompanies the home-style Goan dishes.

Tip: Bear in mind that Mumbaikars usually venture out to eat late, around 9pm, so if you're intent on eating at a popular fine-dining restaurant and don't have a reservation, ask if you can arrive at 7:30pm.

COLABA (INCLUDING MARINE DR.) & FORT
EXPENSIVE

Henry Tham 🍴🍴 CHINESE   Dining at this exclusive eatery makes you feel like royalty, beginning with the red velvet throne-like chairs that extend several feet behind your head. Sleek black tables dip gently in the center and counterpoint the straight, modern lines of this chic restaurant, reflected in a larger-than-life mirror on the wall. Take your pick from three seven-course set menus: Emperor, Empress, or Princess (vegetarian), which change periodically. First to be delivered is *dim sum* (small bites), each with matching sauce. Next up is Silken Pillow Talk, superb miso soup with seaweed and squares of tofu. Then, if you ordered the Emperor set menu, you'll be served delicately steamed grouper (aubergine for the vegetarian option) with a hint of scallion, followed by shredded lamb that's been slow-cooked to perfection and topped with garlic cream, served in a martini glass. King prawn comes next, or grilled zucchini and broccoli florets, the latter with a strong wasabi mayonnaise. By the time the main course (unagi, tenderloin, or chicken, infused in Chinese rice wine, or the vegetarian counterpart of mixed mushrooms, sautéed snowpeas, and broccoli) arrives, you'll probably be sated, which is just as well— the finale, the fruit-based "tree of life," deserves full marks for presentation but is something of a letdown. Overall, this is a classy affair—perfect for a celebration dinner or a special treat. Note that the restaurant offers an a la carte menu (though it's not what Henry Tham is famous for) and a separate (much cheaper) lunchtime set menu.

Dhanraj Mahal, Apollo Bunder. © 022/2202-3186. Reservations essential. Dinner set menus Rs 925–Rs 1,625 ($21–$37); lunch set menus Rs 485–Rs 810 ($11–$19); a la carte main courses Rs 315–Rs 810 ($7–$19). AE, MC, V. Daily 12:30–3:30pm and 7:30pm–midnight.

India Jones 🍴🍴🍴 SOUTHEAST ASIAN   The menu, in the form of an old traveler's map and diary, is a treasure trove of exciting Asian dishes. Start by sharing an appetizer platter—among the superb array are fried prawns in egg noodles, chicken/shrimp siu mai, satay chicken, and cucumber salad with lime, mint, and basil, served with a selection of dips. Or two of you can share the platter of spring rolls from across Southeast Asia: Vietnamese rice-paper rolls, fried rice-paper rolls with crab, deep-fried mango and prawn rolls, bean-curd and chicken rolls—you name it, they roll it. But the hands-down favorite, certainly with locals who want to sample as much as possible of the extensive menu, is the "India Jones Grand Platter": an appetizer assortment; soup (*tom yam* or *tom kha*); and a platter of green chicken curry, wok-fried prawns, stir-fried sea bass with celery, barbecued pork with honey, wok-fried mixed vegetables in black-peppercorn sauce—and the list goes on. At Rs 2,700 ($62) for two, it's pricey, but it's a feast that will leave you bursting. For the not-so-ravenous, there's plenty more: the Wok Platter (also highly recommended), live seafood (try the grouper in soy-ginger broth), a separate dim sum menu, a *teppanyaki* counter—controlled by chef Sam Wong—and outstanding sushi, which is not even on the menu but is ordered all around. As expected of any Oberoi restaurant, the service and decor are exemplary.

Hilton Towers, Nariman Point. © 022/5632-4343. Main courses Rs 195–Rs 1,200 ($4.50–$25); platters Rs 395–Rs 1,350 ($9–$31) per head. AE, DC, MC, V. Daily 12:30–11:45pm.

Indigo ✿✿✿ INTERNATIONAL   Well-known restaurateur-chef Rahul Akerkar has created a restaurant that tops every food critic's A-list and has been listed by *Condé Nast Traveler* as one of the 60 best restaurants in the world. Credit for the tasteful understated elegance of this bi-level restaurant goes to co-owner Malini Akerkar; we recommend you sit upstairs in the open-air terrace section with its frangipani trees. Indigo's chic ambience is enhanced by the clientele: By 9:30pm the entire bar section is heaving with the city's Beautiful People. The international/fusion menu is not extensive, changing once a year, but specials are on offer, with something for every appetite. Start with the flavorful beet and coconut soup; or the herbed goat cheese, spinach, and grilled apples, drizzled with walnut vinaigrette. The lobster risotto is perfect, as is the seared tuna loin rubbed with cracked mustard seeds and served with sesame bok choy, oyster mushrooms, and a roast tomato drizzle. Also recommended is the chargrilled beef tenderloin with Gorgonzola, served with black-eyed-pea ragout, asparagus tips, and a tandoor-roasted onion. The Camembert soufflé was a bit too eggy for our taste. End the meal with the unique chocolate fondant with jalapeño peppers or the out-of-this-world cappuccino soufflé (not always on the menu, but ask for it anyway), made by pastry chef Suresh Kumar.

4 Mandlik House, Colaba, Mumbai 400 001. © **022/5636-8999** or 022/2202-3592. Reservations essential. Main courses Rs 325–Rs 735 ($7–$17). AE, DC, MC, V. Daily 12:30–3pm and 7:30–11:45pm.

Kandahar ✿✿✿ NORTHWEST FRONTIER   This classy, well-appointed restaurant, also located in The Oberoi, is a great place to sample the traditionally rich cuisine of the Northwest Frontier as well as lighter, home-style dishes. Kebabs are a specialty here, and the robust *Kabuli raan* (soft, fragrant, and utterly delicious, prepared a day in advance to enable the meat to stew in its own juices and assorted spices) in particular has long been hailed the best in the city. Home-style dishes include *dahiwali bhindi* (okra cooked in yogurt) and *lasuni palak* (delicately flavored garlicky spinach); the latter, especially, is a perfect complement to the heavier meat dishes. Mop up the butter-soaked, sinfully rich Kandahari or Kaali *dal* (black dal) with *pudina paratha* (mint bread) or *zaafraani naan* cooked with saffron and poppy seeds. One letdown was the *laal maas* (literally translated, "red meat"), a Rajasthani specialty, that didn't live up to its potential—it was smothered rather than spiced with clove. Skip ahead to dessert: The *malpua with rabri* (pancake topped with sweet, thickened milk and nuts) is excellent. Or ask for one of the homemade *kulfis* (ice creams). Wash it all down with a refreshing *shikanjvi*, a tall glass of lemonade with masala spices and a slice of lime. The meal is accompanied by live Indian classical instrumental music. (Note that Kandahar hosts regular food festivals; if you're around, don't miss one—you're sure to sample some unrivaled delights.)

The Oberoi, Nariman Point. © **022/5632-5757**. Average meal Rs 1,500 ($35) per person. AE, DC, MC, V. Daily 12:30–2:45pm and 7:30–11.30pm.

Khyber ✿✿ NORTH INDIAN   Khyber has been going strong for decades now, so much so that there is not even a sign outside to mark the restaurant, but its classic Mughlai cuisine and tender kebabs remain outstanding. Start with *kali mirch rawas* (fish seasoned in black pepper), firm yet meltingly good; or chicken *badami* (in rich almond sauce) and *paneer shashlik* (grilled Indian cottage cheese, spices, and vegetables). Follow these with Khyber *raan* (lamb) or mutton *chaap* Mughlai and piping-hot *naan* bread. To cleanse the palate (Mughlai cuisine is very rich), order the fresh seasonal fruit or the *ras malai*. Besides the great food, Khyber is an experience in royal dining: The opulent decor includes original paintings by some of India's most famous artists (the likes of M. F. Hussain and Anjolie Ela Menon). Seating is intimate and maximizes privacy—perfect for a romantic dinner (ask to be seated in the Anjolie Ela Menon Room). Recent experiences were marred by patchy service—you may have to remind your waiter of a request.

154 MG Rd., Kala Ghoda. ℂ 022/2267-3227 through -3229. Reservations usually required on weekends. Main courses Rs 230–Rs 280 ($5–$6.30); average meal Rs 600 ($14) per person. MC, V. Daily 12:30–3:30pm and 7:30–11:30pm.

Tiffin ☙☙☙ PACIFIC RIM/FUSION   The only way to do justice to Tiffin's impressive 89-item, all-day dining menu featuring food from China, Mexico, Japan, and Australia (along with some Indian) is to come back repeatedly. Eating is a celebration here, enhanced by presentation and a lively decor. We recommend the following: salad of palm hearts, fennel, thin slices of tart apple, and water chestnut; chargrilled lamb chops served with string beans and prosciutto chips; grilled basil chicken teamed with a zucchini risotto, flavored with just the right amount of Parmesan; or pork chops and apple tatin. You can also get a rigorously Japanese sushi and sashimi platter at the interactive sushi bar, where Filipino chef Francesco Balanquit takes orders. Don't miss pastry chef Manuel's house-special ice creams, which combine unusual flavors such as wasabi and caramelized brown sugar, green tea and candied ginger (refreshing), or rose and lychee (a local favorite). Wash it down with a fresh juice, though some of the "healthier" ones containing *amla* (Indian gooseberry) can run a tad sour; opt instead for the more sane apple, red beet, and celery blend.

The Oberoi, Nariman Point. ℂ 022/5632-5757. Main courses Rs 450–Rs 850 ($10–$19); champagne brunch Sun Rs 1,500 ($35). AE, MC, V. Daily 6.30am–11.30pm.

Trishna ☙☙☙ SEAFOOD   Another restaurant frequented by the who's who of Mumbai, Trishna, presided over by owner Ravi Anchan, is a seafood legend in Mumbai and is considered one of the best in the world. Butter pepper garlic king crab is Trishna's signature dish, but you'll also find jumbo pomfrets and tiger prawns (done in any style) cooked to perfection. Despite its reputation as a somewhat snobbish restaurant, Trishna isn't about ambience (the decor in fact is somewhat tacky and, yes, staff do have a reputation for snootiness)—everyone is here for the food. Recommended dishes include pomfret Hyderabadi—barbecued with black pepper, it's a true masterpiece; pomfret *hariyali* enveloped in green masala and baked in a tandoor; fish *sholay* kebab; Kolhapuri prawns (spicy, so order a drink); or squid expertly prepared with butter, pepper, and garlic. Don't expect to get in any night without a reservation, unless you're willing to arrive by 7pm and be out by 8pm.

Birla Mansion, Sai Baba Marg (next to Commerce House), Kala Ghoda, Fort. ℂ 022/2270-3213 or -3214. Reservations essential. Main courses Rs 140–Rs 780 ($3.40–$18) depending on fish size; crab/lobster Rs 500–Rs 1,050 ($11–$24). AE, DC, MC, V. Daily noon–3:30pm and 6pm–12:15am (from 7pm on weekends and holidays).

MODERATE/INEXPENSIVE

Now in its 28th year, **Delhi Darbar** (ℂ 022/2202-0235; daily 11:30am–midnight; average meal Rs 300/$6.80) is a Mumbai institution serving rather standard (and oily) Mughlai food. It has several branches in Mumbai, but we recommend only the one at Colaba. No one comes here for the ambience or service—most come for the tandoori dishes or the mutton or chicken *biryani*. Ignore the Chinese menu. No alcohol is served or allowed.

Tips   The Skinny on Street Food

Street food is something you should be careful about experimenting with any-where in India. The spots we recommend are not on the street; they serve sani-tized (yet authentic) versions of what is available on the street. One place where you can safely try street food while sipping chilled beer is **Vithal Bhelwala** *,* near the Excelsior Theatre, Fort (© 022/5631-7211 or -7212; daily 11am–11pm). You get to eat real Mumbai-style street food under very sanitary (if busy and noisy) conditions at **Swati Snacks** **, in Tardeo (© 022/5680-8405 or -8406; daily 11am–11pm). This is the best street food that's not actually on the street. Try the *sev puri, bhel, dahi batata puri* (Rs 41/90¢ each), or any of the numerous snack items topped with delicious sweet, sour, and spicy chutneys and sauces (ask for milder sauces if you prefer). Round out your meal with homemade fruit-flavored ice creams. Locals come here more for the traditional Gujarati dishes not found anywhere else. If you want to experiment, try the superb *peru nu shak* (spiced guava eaten with Indian bread) and *panki* (thin pancakes steamed in banana leaf). Come for a late lunch, or you will have to wait at least 15 min-utes for a table—a wait that's justly rewarded once you're inside.

Britannia ** Moments IRANI   This no-nonsense, no-frills, 90-year-old Irani (Per-sian) restaurant is the last of a dying breed of establishments once found on every cor-ner of South Mumbai. The environment is simple and functional, with little room for extras like presentation and ambience. Most people come here to consume one or more of three excellent dishes: Berry *pulao* (a version of the Iranian *zereshk polow*) is the outstanding signature dish, made with succulent spiced boneless mutton (or chicken), fragrant long-grain basmati rice, and tart barberries imported from Iran. *Patra ni machchi* is pomfret fish coated in chutney made with cilantro, coconut, and assorted spices; wrapped in a banana leaf; and steamed—always moist and flaky with flavors all the way down to the bone. The mutton *dhansak* is a combination of fra-grant brown rice and thick *dal* in which the meat has been cooked—a dense, hearty meal that tastes a million times better than it looks. (Vegetarians, though catered to, should give this restaurant a miss.)

Opposite New Customs House, Ballard Estate Fort. © 022/2261-5264. Berry *pulao* Rs 160–Rs 180 ($3.45–$12); dhansak or patra ni machchi Rs 150 ($3.40). AE, DC, MC, V. Lunch only Mon–Sat 11:30am–3:30pm.

Konkan Café ** KONKAN   Chef Ananda Solomon has earned an enviable rep-utation for his inspired specialties, garnered from up and down the Konkan coast and served with style. Although the menu is constantly reinvented, look for specialties like the red snapper cooked in a spicy tomato-onion sauce and baked in banana leaves; and the heavenly *sukha* mutton. You can also sample such Goan specialties as chicken *caf-real* (chicken marinated with chilies and spices and roasted or barbecued) or pomfret *recheado* (a hot and spicy masala) with *feni* (the Goan liquor distilled from coconuts or cashews). Savor the spectacular crab cakes with a fine bottle of wine from an exten-sive selection.

Taj President Hotel (see "Where to Stay," earlier in this chapter). © 022/5665-0808. Thali Rs 375 ($8.40) vegetar-ian, Rs 450 ($10) non-veg; a la carte Rs 600 ($14) per person. AE, DC, MC, V. Daily 12:30–2:45pm and 7–11:45pm.

Koyla 𝒢 INDIAN/HOOKAH BAR   Come here primarily for the leisurely ambience and setting: a candlelit terrace with Arabian music playing in the background. The restaurant is located on the rooftop of the Gulf Hotel in Colaba (torn down by the municipality in early 2005 for unregulated structures, but because it's owned by the son of a local politician, it was up and running again within months). The most popular item on the menu is not food, but the *sheesha* (hookah or pipe), with fruity flavors like green apple and strawberry. For just Rs 100 ($2.30), several friends can share a pipe that lasts about 20 to 30 minutes. The fairly regular fare might be worthwhile just to enjoy the cool evening breeze (rare in humid Mumbai) and partial view. Or come after dinner relax, sit back, and linger over a "mocktail" (no alcohol is served). The atmosphere is laid-back and no one will hustle you out—but service can be painfully slow. Reservations are recommended; even then, expect a wait. The Rs 100 ($2.30) per-person cover charge is redeemable against your bill.

Gulf Hotel, next to Radio Club, Colaba, Mumbai 400 005. ℂ **022/5636-9999.** Kebabs Rs 135–Rs 165 ($3–$3.70); Main courses average Rs 250 ($5.70). AE, DC,MC, V. Daily 8pm–2.30am.

Leopold Café 𝒢 CONTINENTAL/INDIAN/CHINESE   It's not uncommon to walk into this Colaba institution and not see a single Indian face around. Why it's such a hit with foreigners is a mystery, since the food is good but not exceptional, and the atmosphere can be noisy and rather smoky. All the same, it is consistent, and because it's one of those popular places where tourists like to share stories with other tourists over a beer, it deserves mention. It caters to Western tastes by providing items like cereals, eggs and toast, fish and chips, and club sandwiches side by side with chicken *biryani* and Indian-Chinese fare. The fresh fruit juices and *lassis* (yogurt drinks) are always a good bet if you're looking for a light pick-me-up during shopping forays on the causeway. And if you're keen to get the inside scoop on how Bollywood films are made, hang out here; casting agents looking for foreigners to work as extras on current productions frequently scan the clientele for able bodies at this favored travelers' hangout. *Tip:* Check your bill before you pay it to make sure it doesn't contain anything you didn't order.

Colaba Causeway, Mumbai 400 005. ℂ **022/2287-3362.** Lassis/juices/milkshakes Rs 50 ($1.15); Mughlai main courses Rs 95 ($2.15); Chinese main courses Rs 110 ($2.50). AE, DC, MC, V. Daily 8am–midnight.

Mahesh Lunch Home 𝒢𝒢𝒢 SEAFOOD   The ceiling may be too low and the tables too close together, but this Manglorean seafood restaurant should not be missed if you love fish—it's one of Mumbai's best restaurants, consistently dishing out pleasing specialties. Everything is incredibly fresh, but favorites include surmai fry, pomfret curry, and tandoori pomfret—all outstanding. The latter (listed as a starter, but you can order it as a main) is served flawlessly moist; eaten with butter *naan*, it provides the most heavenly gastronomic experience imaginable. Also try the scrumptious prawns Koliwada, crab tandoori, pomfret in green masala, or any of the fish curries or *gassis,* all first-rate. (Note that *gassi* refers to the thick, spicy, coconut-based Manglorean curry, while the "curries" on the menu are a thinner version of the same.) Mahesh also serves meat, chicken, and Chinese dishes, but only the misguided would come here and skip the sensational seafood.

8D Cowasji Patel St., off Pherozeshah Mehta Rd., Fort, Mumbai 400 001. ℂ **022/2287-0938** or 022/2202-3965. Fish fry/curry/gassi Rs 85–Rs 140 ($2–$3.20); jumbo pomfret/crab/lobster Rs 500–Rs 1,200 ($11–$28); other main courses Rs 200–Rs 325 ($4.55–$7.25). AE, DC, MC, V. Daily 11:30am–3:30pm and 6pm–midnight.

Samovar ✿✿INDIAN   This long, narrow restaurant inside Jehangir Art Gallery is another South Mumbai institution that has retained its charm and low prices in spite of its popularity. With quick, efficient service and a policy of not hurrying diners even if others are waiting, this is the perfect stopover after a day roaming the Prince of Wales museum and other local landmarks. Start with a delicious seasonal fruit juice— the guava juice is the best when it's in season. *Boti* rolls (spiced meat wrapped in chapatis) rival with *parathas* (fried breads with a great assortment of stuffings) to satiate the taste buds along with the yummy bean-sprout salad. A stop here is a must: This is as close to home cooking as you are likely to get on a short visit to Mumbai.

Jehangir Art Gallery, Kala Ghoda, Fort, Mumbai 400 023. ✆ 022/2284-8000. Average meal Rs 150 ($3.40). No credit cards. Mon–Sat 11am–7:30pm. Closed Sun.

BEYOND DOWNTOWN: CHOWPATTY TO WORLI

Copper Chimney ✿✿✿ KEBABS/MUGHLAI   For more than 23 years, Copper Chimney has delighted those looking for the perfect kebabs. To this end, two pages of the menu are dedicated to kebabs, from the popular *reshmi* kebab (chicken) to the *jhinga nisha* (prawn) and tandoori prawn kebabs. These tender, creamy, smoky-flavored, melt-in-your-mouth kebabs can be followed by traditional Dum Pukht specialties such as chicken *makhani* (butter chicken) or the even more exquisite Peshawari lamb. No matter what you pick, you will leave satisfied. There's also a daily buffet lunch, but don't be swayed by the variety—some of the best items on the menu (such as the unfailingly wonderful butter chicken) are not offered at the buffet. Note that although Copper Chimney branches are found all over the city, the one at Worli is the only one to patronize.

Dr. Annie Besant Rd., Worli, Mumbai 400 018. ✆ 022/2492-0505 or -5333. Mains Rs 135–Rs 180 ($3.05–$4); tiger prawns Rs 575 ($13). AE, DC, MC, V. daily noon–4pm and 6pm–midnight.

Salt Water Grill ✿✿ INTERNATIONAL   Alongside Chowpatty's watersports complex H2O, this newly opened restaurant sits on the edge of the beach, a few feet from breaking waves. Well-lit terra-cotta sculptures add to the serene atmosphere of this absolutely stunning location. Pick from a variety of seating options—hammocks, lounge chairs, sofas, or traditional tables—and wiggle your toes in the sand, enjoying the sea breeze. Ask for the bartender's special (hopefully it's the plum vodka—made in-house—with peach schnapps and cranberry juice), or try one of the fresh fruit cocktails. Restaurant manager Naveen Kotyankar, who also designed the bar menu and is the in-house alchemist, tries hard to move customers away from mundane cocktails; he made us a Watermelon Caipiroska, definitely one of the best drinks on offer. Unfortunately, things go rather downhill from here: We sampled several chicken and fish main courses, but found them all below average. In the works, however, are a sangria bar and a sundowner snack menu, as well as casual upper-level seating on beanbags and coconut-leaf beach-umbrella-sheltered sun beds.

H2O Water Sports Complex, next to Mafatlal Swimming Club, Marine Dr. ✆ 022/2368-5459. Main courses Rs 280–Rs 650 ($6.35–$15); cocktails Rs 275–Rs 400 ($6.30–$9.10). AE, MC, V. Daily 7pm–12:30am.

SUBURBS—BANDRA TO JUHU & NEAR THE AIRPORT

For prime people-watching, spend some time at **Prithvi Café** ✿✿ (✆ 022/2617-4118) in the Prithvi Theatre compound in Juhu. This pleasant, unpretentious cafe is where many of Mumbai's up-and-coming and/or struggling *artistes* come to nosh and discuss their art. The cafe serves great fresh *parathas* and a variety of teas and coffees over which you can linger undisturbed. If it's stargazing you're after, the restaurant that takes the prize is the **Olive Bar and Kitchen** ⚜ (Pali Hill Tourist Hotel, 14 Union Park Khar [W]; ✆ **022/2605-8228**), the trendiest restaurant in Bandra. This Mediterranean restaurant is expensive and the food inconsistent, but it's the place to see and be seen. At the other end of the spectrum is **Govinda** ⚜ (✆ **022/2620-0337**), at the Hare Krishna Temple in Juhu, where you can gorge from a 56-item all-vegetarian buffet (no onions or garlic, either). Everything is cooked in pure ghee (clarified butter), however, so expect the meal to be extremely heavy. Some great dining options are available in the numerous five-star hotels in the vicinity of the airport. **Dum Pukht** and **Dakshin** at the ITC Grand Maratha Sheraton are worth mentioning, as are **Stax** at the Hyatt Regency near the international airport, and **M Bar** at the Grand Hyatt, closer to the domestic airport.

MODERATE

Papa Päncho   PUNJABI   Done up in honor of the thousands of truck drivers who endlessly careen around the roads of India, this gorgeously atmospheric restaurant is a faux take on the ubiquitous roadside *dhaba* (roadside eatery). Outside, beautiful Mumbaikars sit or lie on traditional *manjis* (beds), often whiling away the entire afternoon; you can join them, or sit indoors at copper-covered tables. A recently added larger section allows you to imagine yourself escaping to the peace and quiet of a Punjabi village, with Phulkari embroidery and handicrafts displayed on the stucco walls and dangling from the ceiling, along with old Punjabi folk music albums. The kitchen churns out authentic home-style dishes, but with a health-conscious emphasis on less butter and cream, making the food lighter than you'd find in a real village. Ask the charming hostess-cum-co-owner, "Mamta" Sekhri, about any specials, and insist that she bring you at least one *chaat* (snack) to whet your appetite. *Papdi chaat* topped with yogurt is cool, fresh, and delicately spiced—simply wonderful.

Shop no. 12, Gaspar Enclave, Dr. Ambedkar Rd., near Rupee Bank, Bandra W. ✆ **022/2651-8732** or -8733. Main courses Rs 85–Rs 175 ($1.90–$3.95). MC, V. Daily 12:30pm–midnight.

EXPENSIVE

M Bar   GRILLHOUSE   This American-style, fine-dining grillhouse is a good place to kill a few hours before your domestic flight (the airport has no in-house dining options). Decor is a tad bland—in fact, more that of an executive-class airport lounge than a fine-dining restaurant—but the restaurant's focal point is its wine library, which stocks over 90 labels and 1,400 bottles in ceiling-to-floor glass display cases, as well as its menu of 40-odd martinis (in part what the M stands for). For starters, sample the smoked salmon served on a bed of wild rice with sour cream and garnished with finely chopped onions; or order the asparagus and sun-dried tomato salad with toasted pecans. Meats are grilled or barbecued, and come with a sauce of your choice; try the marinated boneless chicken with green-peppercorn sauce. In the dessert department, both the New York cheesecake and coffee mousse disappoint; skip them and opt for another delicious fruit-flavored martini.

Grand Hyatt Mumbai Hotel, off Western Express Hwy., Santa Cruz (E). ✆ **022/5676-1234**. Main courses Rs 250–Rs 320 ($5.70–$7.25) vegetarian, Rs 450–Rs 1,300 ($10–$30) non-vegetarian. AE, DC, MC, V. Daily 6pm (bar), dinner 7pm–midnight; Sun brunch 11am–4pm.

Saffron   INDIAN   The decor may be of the generic interior-decorating-magazine type, but if you like your kebabs, this is the place to come, with unlimited kebab platters on offer, served with a buttery dal cooked in a clay pot *(thikri ki makhni dal)*, a

My, what an inefficient way to fish.

Ring toss, good. Horseshoes, bad.

Faster! Faster! Faster!

We take care of the fiddly bits, from providing over 43,000 customer reviews of hotels, to helping you find our best fares, to giving you 24/7 customer service. So you can focus on the only thing that matters. Goofing off.

travelocity
You'll never roam alone.℠

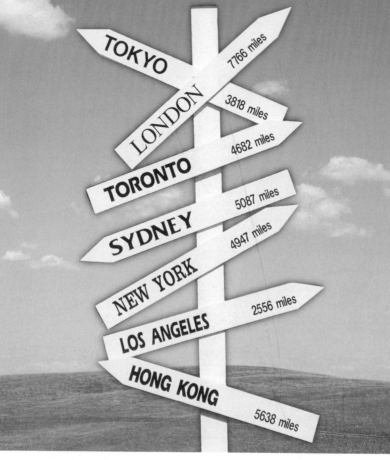

curry, and choice of flaky *naan* or *kulcha* (pita-like bread), salad, and dessert. Particularly spectacular is the pink salmon kebab, which is beautifully moist with just the right light touch of spices. The garlic butter *naan* is so good it hardly needs accompaniment. Chicken and mutton mains like *bhuna gosht* and *dum ki murg* are good, but we doubt you'll get beyond the kebab platters! **Warning:** The food is rich and heavy, so don't come here for a light meal. Service, like that at all the restaurants in this hotel, is exceptionally good. Some tables are a bit too close to each other; ask for corner seating.

JW Marriott, Juhu-Tara Rd. © 022/5693-3000. Kebab platters Rs 695–Rs 1,250 ($16–$29); mains Rs 395–Rs 595 ($9–$14). AE, DC, MC, V. Daily 7pm–midnight.

Stax ✶✶ ITALIAN/SEAFOOD   Very near the international airport, this is another good place to kill time if you're waiting for a flight (again, the airport has no in-house dining options). Focusing on food from the coastal provinces of Italy, it has a wonderful fresh seafood tank. Chef Giovanni Parrella produces great antipasti, from the basic *insalata caprese* to the Naples-style seafood salad with zucchini and peppers. Or order classic Sicilian seafood soup, so good you'll want to order a refill. Pasta-lovers should order the delicate Sardinian linguine with lobster, mint, and saffron sauce, though we favored the lamb shank, cooked Milanese style, with saffron risotto. Portions are large, so it may be difficult to eat both an Italian-style *primi* and a *secondi*, but that probably has more to do with the clientele than the chef. The decor here is modern and mostly pleasant, except for the large tacky Styrofoam shapes overhead. Tables are placed far enough from each other so that even when the restaurant is packed, you can enjoy a

---

The Thali: Gujarati & Rajasthani Cuisine at its Best

You can't leave this city without consuming at least one thali, the meal that really tests the size of your appetite! It works like this: Sit down, and in less than a minute you're expected to declare which thali you want—ordinary, special, and so on. Seconds later, a large, stainless-steel (or silver) plate *(thali)* arrives along with six to eight small bowls *(katoris)* resting on it. The waiters then fill every one of the multiple katoris as well as the rest of the plate with a large assortment of steaming-hot, spiced vegetables, savories, *dals,* beans, *rotis, puris,* and so on. To wash it down, you're served water and a glass of delicious, super-thin, cumin-flavored buttermilk *(chaas).* As you eat, your katoris will be topped up, so indicate what you want for seconds, thirds, fourths—a veritable onslaught that won't stop until you say so. Then it's a round of rice or *khichdi* (a mixture of rice and dal) and, in some restaurants, dessert. Not only are thalis a great value (you pay Rs 50–Rs 250/$1.15–$5.70), but they come pretty close to the home cooking of the country's Gujarati (or Rajasthani) population. A personal favorite is **Panchvati Gaurav** ✶✶ (© **022/2208-4877;** opposite Bombay Hospital, Marine Lines; Tues–Sun 11am–3pm and 7–10:30pm; Mon lunch only), where you'll pay Rs 105 to Rs 180 ($2.40–$4.10) for an excellent meal. Alternatively, try **Thackers** ✶✶ (© **022/2205-3641;** 116 Marine St., Marine Lines; daily 12:30–3pm and 7:30–11pm) for a Surat-style Gujarati meal served on silver plates at perhaps a more relaxed pace. **Chetna Restaurant and Bar** ✶ (© **022/2284-4968;** Fort; daily 12:30–3:30pm, 4:30–6:30pm [snacks only], and 7:30–11:30pm) has many options and even serves a diet thali (Chetna Lite)—but doesn't that miss the point?

private conversation and dinner. Service is exemplary, as is the wine selection, and the desserts are just divine, with the crowning glory definitely the heavenly hazelnut gelato.

Hyatt Regency, Sahar Airport Rd., Mumbai 400 099. ℂ 022/5696-1234. Main courses Rs 380–Rs 950 ($8.65–$22). AE, DC, MC, V. Daily 7pm–midnight.

Zenzi 🐒🐒 ECLECTIC   Overstuffed sofas scattered with plump cushions beckon as you enter this hip, warm-hued, lounge-bar-restaurant on Bandra's restaurant-happy Waterfield Road. Candles in *chai* glasses illuminate the glossy wood tables, and funky tunes foment a laid-back atmosphere. You can sit in the quieter restaurant area or at a table near the long bar that is filled with expats, upwardly mobile couples, and office workers. Better still, if the weather is fine, sit outside on the terrace. Fortunately, the great atmosphere comes with good food. Begin with Zenzi Dream, a salad with arugula, cherry tomatoes, and goat cheese doused in a honey-ginger dressing. Or start with the soft-shell crab roll, wrapped in roasted nori-sheet glass noodles. Main-course portions are large; we recommend the Zenzi Wok with neatly leaf-wrapped sliced lamb tenderloin. Drinks are also good but cost as much as a main course. In a place where the food looks as pretty as the decor, the art for sale on the walls can be a bit disconcerting—especially when said art includes a larger-than-life fetus being slashed with barbed wire. On varying nights, you may encounter live bands, DJs spinning modern tracks, or stand-up comedy acts adding perk to your meal.

183 Waterfield Rd., Bandra (W), Mumbai 400 050. ℂ 022/5643-0670. Fax 022/56490135. www.zenzi-india.com. Main courses Rs 200–Rs 480 ($4.55–$11). MC, V. Daily 11:30am–1am (separate menus for snacks, Sun brunch, lunch, drinks, wine, dinner, and specials).

6 Shopping

From internationally renowned haute couture to dirt-cheap one-season wonders, intricate jewelry and unique antiques to tawdry gifts and fabulous textiles, Mumbai is known as a shopper's paradise, and you'll find pretty much everything the country has to offer here. If you're shopping on the street or in the markets (see "Markets," earlier in this chapter), take your time, sift and sort, establish authenticity and, if necessary, don't be afraid to bargain hard. That said, bear in mind that (as elsewhere in India) a "bargain," particularly when it comes to jewelry and antiques, is probably a cheap bauble or reproduction—fakes are a dime a dozen, as are the con men who sell them. Besides the areas described below, you will find that the suburb of Bandra has become a local shopping haven, with Linking Road, Hill Road, and several other streets overflowing with shops and street stalls selling clothes, shoes, and everything else under the sun. In addition, Western-style multistory department stores like **Shopper's Stop** and **Globus** are filled with all kinds of garments and fashions. If you're shopping in Bandra, make time to visit the very upmarket **Frazer and Haws** store (Landmark Building, Pali Naka, Bandra; ℂ 022/5675-0200), which carries eclectic and funky silver objets d'art, including sleek idols of Indian gods and goddesses like Ganesha and Laxmi. Also in Bandra are **Fab India** (see below) and dozens of trendy jewelry stores.

CLOTHING, FABRICS & HOME TEXTILES
COLABA, FORT & MARINE DRIVE
Central Cottage Industries Emporium (behind Regal Cinema; ℂ 022/2202-6564 or -7537; daily 10am–7pm) is the large, government-owned, fixed-price shop aimed at tourists, with a reputation for carrying well-crafted items that offer relatively good value (not the cheapest stuff out there but you won't get ripped off). Established dur-

ing the 1950s in an attempt to sustain traditional handicrafts, the massive showroom is crammed full of everything and anything that's likely to remind you of India. At the very least, a visit here will give you an idea of what items should more or less cost. A better shopping experience, at least from a store and design point of view, is the **Bombay Store** (Sir P.M. Rd., Fort; ℂ **022/2288-5048,** -5049, or -5052; Mon–Sat 10:30am–7:30pm, Sun 10:30am–6:30pm), where you'll find every imaginable Indian handicraft and design, from bed linens and crockery to incense and aromatherapy oils. And if you're looking for another reason to book into the **Taj Mahal Hotel,** it's worth knowing that the in-house shops are stocked with sought-after international and Indian brands and products (particularly Pashmina shawls, from simple water Pashminas at around Rs 600/$14 to high-end quality ones for around Rs 6,000/$137), though obviously you pay a price for the convenience of location, and the shopping experience is relatively sterile. The same holds true for the in-house shop at the **Hilton Towers.**

Having created garments for Hillary Clinton, Demi Moore, and Liza Minneli, and earned the accolades "Crystal King" and "Czar of Embroidery," Azeem Khan is one of Mumbai's best-known designers. To find your very own slice of Indian haute couture, visit **Azeem Khan Couture** in Colaba (1 Usha Sadan; ℂ **022/2215-1028;** www.azeemkhan.com). **Ensemble** (Great Western Building, 130/132 Shahid Bhagat Singh Marg, Kala Ghoda/Fort; ℂ **022/2287-2882,** 022/2284-3227, or -5118) is an upmarket boutique where you will find the greatest variety of East-meets-West evening wear; prominent designers to look for here include Shahab Durazi, Tarun Tahiliani, Rajesh Pratap, Monisha Jaisingh, Tarana Rajpal, Abhishek Gupta, and Sunita Shankar. At **Indian Textiles** (Taj Mahal Hotel; ℂ **022/2202-8783** or 022/2204-9278), you'll find some of the best Benarasi woven silks and brocades in the country, sold by the yard, as well as authentic Pashmina shawls. Also look for hand-dyed silk stoles by **Jamnadas Khatri** (ℂ **022/2242-5711** or 022/2374-0947), made with vegetable dyes using the Rajasthani tie-and-dye technique. Hand-loomed products are found in abundance at fabulous **Fab India** (Jeroo Building, 137 M.G. Rd., Kala Ghoda; ℂ **022/2262-6539;** other outlets in Bandra).

If you've loved the furnishings at many of the Taj hotels around the country, make your way to **Zeba** in Colaba or Worli (Bhaveshwar, 148–B, Dr. Annie Besant Rd., Worli Naka; ℂ **022/2495-3711;** also at Royal Terrace, 58 Wodehouse Rd., Colaba; ℂ **022/2218-8797**) for extensive collections of highly desirable home textiles, accessories, carpets, and *dhurries* in great original styles. Zeba is owned by the young, flamboyant Krsna Mehta, whose outfit creates in-house designs for its textiles in cotton, silk, jute, and a range of graceful fabrics, using both earthy and vibrant colors. Zeba will custom-design any living space. **Yamini** (President House, Wodehouse Rd., Colaba; ℂ **022/2218-4143** or -4145; also in Bandra, ℂ **022/2643-7667**) stocks designer linen, tablecloths, bolsters, curtains, bed covers, napkins, and even lampshades. Mumbaikar Reva Sethi is the fashion designer responsible for the collection, and her designs have even been used on board the prime minister's private jet.

If quality is all that matters and price is not a concern, **Ravissant** (17A Cooperage Rd., New India Insurance Centre; ℂ **022/2287-3405**) has a selection of sterling-silver teapots, vases, photo frames, and assorted stylish collectibles that sport clean modern lines and hark back to the Deco period.

CHOWPATTY, PEDDER ROAD, NAPEAN SEA ROAD
Contemporary Arts and Crafts, in the residential neighborhood of Napean Sea Road (near Kemps Corner; ℂ **022/2363-1979;** Mon–Sat 10am–8pm, Sun 10am–7pm),

has tasteful and sometimes uncommon gifts from all over India. Famous Indian designer Ritu Kumar has several outlets specializing in silk and cotton designer-ethnic wear, much of it a blend of Western and Indian influences. **Ritu's Boutique** can be found on Warden Road (✆ **022/2367-8593** or -2947) as well as at Hilton Towers and Phoenix Mills. Another boutique that is a must-see for fashionistas is **Mélange** (33 Altamount Rd., Kemps Corner; ✆ **022/2385-4492** or 022/2386-9628), known for its ultra-feminine designer dresses made from delicate chiffon. If you don't plan to visit Jaipur, stop at the Mumbai branch of **Anokhi** (Rasik Nivas, Metro Motors Lane, off Hughes Rd.; ✆ **022/2368-5761**), for its East-meets-West garments, accessories, and housewares. Nearby is **Cottons** (✆ **022/2368-5950** or 022/2368-5987), also head-quartered in Jaipur, a boutique that sells both Indo-Western and ethnic Indian wear at more affordable rates.

India's most famous *dhurrie* designer is **Shyam Ahuja** (78 India House, Kemps Corner; ✆ **022/2386-7372;** also an outlet store in the far-out suburb of Thane), known for outstanding and expensive hand-woven products. Besides gorgeous home furnishings, table linen, bathrobes, and towels, you can purchase authentic Pashmina shawls here.

JEWELRY

Tribhovandas Bhimji Zaveri (241/43 Zaveri Bazaar; ✆ **022/2342-5001** or -5002), stretching over five separate floors, has a reputation for exceptional gold and diamond jewelry that dates back to 1865. It's very popular with Mumbai's wealthier crowd, so don't expect exceptionally good prices. **Gazdar** (Taj Mahal Hotel shopping arcade; ✆ **022/2202-3666**) has been selling Indian, Western, antique, and contemporary jewelry for more than 70 years; again, the prices go with the territory. Serious buyers looking for one-of-a-kind pieces should consider contacting master craftspeople **Viren Bhagat** (✆ **022/2361-1171** or -1172) or **Panna J. Jhaveri** (✆ **022/2369-0751**), both by appointment only. And prices aren't that ridiculous; you can pick up a pair of diamond earrings from Panna J. Jhaveri for under $100.

ANTIQUES, ART & FURNITURE

For real antique finds and colonial furniture, there's no place like **Chor Bazaar's Mutton Street** (see "Markets," earlier in this chapter; closed Fri), which is a wonderful place at which to browse and discover hidden treasures. You'll spot plenty of imitation antiques and faux products here, but these are usually pretty easy to identify. Store owners will often (but not always) tell you which are genuine items and which are reproductions. If, however, walking through dirty streets and sifting through dusty shops is not your cup of tea, head straight for the more established antiques stores in the city, some of the best of which are downtown in Colaba. **Natesan's Antiqarts** (✆ **022/2285-2700**), conveniently located at Jehangir Art Gallery, deals principally in stone, wood, and bronze items. Whether you pick up an ornate teak and sandalwood carving, a bronze piece created using the 4,500-year-old lost-wax process, or a refurbished antique, Natesan's will arrange shipment. Nearby **Phillips Antiques** (opposite Prince of Wales Museum, Colaba; ✆ **022/2202-0564** or 022/2282-0782; www.phillipsantiques.com) offers a similar service; besides four-poster beds, armchairs, writing tables, and hat stands, you'll find gorgeous porcelain and pottery, brass and silverware, and a range of marble items for the home, not to mention ornamental pieces, antiquarian maps, lithographs, engravings, old photographs, and lovely lamps. Filled with beautiful objects, **Heeramaneck** (Readymoney Building, Battery

---

ⓘ Tips Leaving Mumbai

The trip from central Mumbai to either of the airports can take far longer than expected—even outside peak traffic hours. Because most international flights are scheduled at similar, unusual hours, you will not be the only traveler racing to catch a plane. For international flights, you'll also need 3 hours at the airport to negotiate the endless security checks and long waits at passport control. If you're flying out after midnight, plan to leave the city at least 4 hours ahead of your flight. For daytime and earlier evening flights, you may want to add another hour to contend with the slow-moving traffic.

Adventurous travelers who've already spent some time in Mumbai can cut down on time spent in traffic by catching a train from Churchgate Station to Vile Parle (around Rs 80/$1.80 for a first-class ticket) and then taking an autorickshaw (also Rs 80/$1.80) or taxi to the airport.

St., Colaba; ⓒ **022/2202-1778** or 022/2285-6340) is another essential pit stop for antiques lovers. It has an especially good collection of Victorian and Indian silverware, including tea sets, candle stands, and cutlery.

7 Mumbai After Dark

BARS & CAFES

Join the backpackers and other Western tourists for a cold Kingfisher beer at **Leopold's Café** (ⓒ **022/2287-3362** or 022/2282-8185) on Colaba Causeway; or step into smoky, popular **Café Mondegar** or Mondy's (near Regal Cinema; ⓒ **022/2202-0591**), where the atmosphere is always lively and the jukebox fires up popular Western music. **Indus,** behind the Taj Mahal Hotel, is another bar/restaurant (ⓒ **022/2202-1661**) with recently revamped interiors that's become a popular local hangout—not only because it serves relatively inexpensive alcohol, but because the in-house DJ provides a pleasant change from the overdose of Hindi remixes you hear everywhere else. Nearby is the **Sports Bar** (ⓒ **022/5639-6681**), perfect for beer-quaffers who can get a huge pitcher of beer (3 liters) for just Rs 475 ($11), and where you can also play pool or shoot hoops. If rock 'n' roll is more your taste, head for **Tavern** (Hotel Fariyas; ⓒ **022/2204-2911**), farther down Colaba, where the jeans-and-T-shirt clique groove to classic rock and cheap drinks. Or grab a drink and request a song at popular but small **Ghetto** (ⓒ **022/2351-4725**) at Mahalaxmi, near Haji Ali. This is where you'll find collegians and after-workers rubbing shoulders with graying hippies who still salute Bob Marley and Jim Morrison; live bands are on tap some nights (entry free). If you're in the hip suburb of Bandra, you'll find a similar scene at **Toto's Garage** (Pali Naka; ⓒ **022/2600-5494**), where the main attraction, apart from the music, is the shell of a car hanging from the ceiling over patrons' heads.

For über-trendy, you can't beat **Indigo** (ⓒ **022/5636-8999** or 022/2202-3592; see "Where To Dine," earlier in this chapter). At Colaba's hippest joint, low tables with flickering candles light up the who's who of Mumbai as they sip fine wines and other drinks. Similarly chic but in Bandra is **Olive Bar and Kitchen** ⓕ (Pali Hill Tourist Hotel, 14 Union Park Khar [W]; ⓒ **022/2605-8228**), where celeb-spotting is the acknowledged pastime.

Hidden behind two massive glass doors, the **Library Bar** (© **022/5665-0808**) at the Taj President Hotel is a classy watering hole whose clientele consists of whiskey-swilling businesspeople and high rollers; check out the leather-bound books and live music (Tues–Sun) provided by a youthful Filipino duo. Despite the plush, sophisticated decor, the atmosphere is pleasantly laid-back. Vivacious Maria, the singer, is especially known for her ability to make the most crusty barfly dance. If your holy grail is a chic, exclusive lounge bar, nothing beats **Opium Den** at the Hilton Towers (© **022/5632-6320**), which attracts well-heeled 30-something locals, expats, and hotel guests. Not far away is **Geoffrey's** (Hotel Marine Plaza; © **022/2285-1212**), which is always packed, especially with its post-10pm happy hour. Around the corner from Geoffrey's is **Not Just Jazz By the Bay** (© **022/2282-0957**), which has live bands Wednesday to Saturday and karaoke Sunday through Tuesday.

If you're in Central Mumbai's new business districts, **Dublin** (© **022/2410-1010**) in the ITC Grand Central Sheraton and Towers, with its cool green walls, leather sofas, and stained-glass panels, is a good place for a quiet drink. For more options, see "Hot Spots with Views," earlier in this chapter.

MUSIC, THEATER & CINEMA

The best way to figure out what's going on in the city is to pick up a copy of *Time Out Mumbai,* the fortnightly (twice-monthly) magazine that has the most comprehensive Mumbai listings. "The Hot List" supplement in the daily tabloid *Mid Day* also carries extensive listings of live music events, stage productions, and film screenings. *The Times of India* features an extensive "Bombay Times" section that lists and advertises cultural activities, entertainment happenings, and movies.

Mumbai has numerous performance spaces, including its premier **National Centre for the Performing Arts** (Nariman Point; © **022/2283-3737**). The NCPA houses several stages, including the city's "first opera theater," Jamshed Bhabha Theatre, which saw its first operatic production in 2003. English dramas and lavish musical concerts are held in Tata Theatre; the aptly named Little Theatre features work of a more intimate scale. For offbeat drama, student work, and small-scale music and dance, the black-box Experimental Theatre, with its audience proximity, is the place to go. The NCPA may occasionally host special film events and festivals, but these are open only to members. Lunchtime concerts in the foyer of Tata Theatre are a pleasant new addition; the buffet (1–2pm) may be lackluster, but the accompanying live musicians are usually good.

Not far from Juhu Beach is one of Mumbai's best-known theaters, **Prithvi Theatre** (Janki-Kutir, Juhu-Church Rd.; © **022/2614-9546;** www.prithvitheatre.org), which is owned by Bollywood's founding family, the Kapoors. Prithvi has a small, intimate, and excellent performance space with great acoustics, and the aisles and steps are often crammed with enthusiasts. The country's best plays are staged here during an annual drama festival (Nov–Dec), and the garden cafe outside is popular with the city's culturati. Over the first weekend of every month (except June–Sept), free play readings and other performances are held in the gardens at **Horniman Circle** in the Fort area; contact Prithvi for details.

Both Indian and Western theater and music performances are staged in the main auditorium of **Nehru Centre** (Dr. Annie Besant Rd., near Mahalaxmi Race Course, Worli; © **022/2493-2667**). There's also a smaller stage for experimental work. Nehru Centre also houses **Nehru Science Museum** and a **Planetarium** (© **022/2492-0510**), with (not exceptional) shows Tuesday through Sunday at 3pm.

NIGHTCLUBS

You could spend your entire stay in Mumbai partying in fantastic clubs each night and recovering the following day in your hotel room—this is one Indian city that loves to party. Although Western music is popular and has the buff and the gorgeous strutting their stuff every night of the week, Mumbaikars (thankfully) have a deep passion for contemporary Hindi songs as well, and it's not unusual to spot young studs demonstrating the choreographed rhythms of *MTV India*'s latest local video, much to the delight of their female companions. There are literally dozens of nightspots in the city, the most attractive being in the five-star hotels. However, over the last 2 years the nightclub scene has shifted so far into the suburbs of Colaba, Bandra, and Juhu that even affluent South Mumbaikars who wouldn't normally venture to the 'burbs make a beeline for the happening clubs there. For the most up-to-date news on what's hot and what's not, talk to your concierge, because the nightclub scene changes rapidly.

Here's a list of some of the most popular nightspots in mid-2005—and the ones most likely to continue to stay in top gear. Entry fees differ depending on the night, and prices are often per (heterosexual) couple; usually this entitles you to coupons that can be exchanged for overpriced drinks of a stipulated value. Note that many nightclubs charge extra for males entering alone, while most don't allow "stag" entry at all, though foreigners may sometimes sidestep this rule. Closing times vary each night; there are "official" (currently 1:30am) and unofficial hours—which essentially means that most clubs stay open later than the time stipulated by law. The popularity of a club is sustained only if it can keep the cops out and stay open into the wee hours of the morning (five-star clubs can remain open until 3am, since they are inside private hotels). *Tip:* Take a page out of a hard-partying Mumbaikar's book and tank up at one of the city's watering holes before heading to a nightclub, where drink prices are usually exorbitant. In general, party-loving locals hit more than one nightclub/bar/lounge per evening throughout this island city; if you hook up with a group, you may want to join them. *Note:* If you crave Latin and ballroom dancing, including salsa, merengue, tango, jive, and the like, several spots in the city have Latin Ballroom Nights. Call **Starters & More** (© 022/2281-4124) at Churchgate (which also holds Jazz Nights the first Wed of the month) or **Trafalgar Chowk** (© 022/2645-9151) in Bandra for details.

Enigma 🏵🏵 This is one of Mumbai's hottest nightspots and a celeb-magnet. A 2004 face-lift gave it a circular central bar, a large dance floor, and a huge, colorful chandelier that shines almost as brightly as the Bollywood stars in attendance. Drinks are as expensive as the cover charge, but when well-known DJs Ryan Beck and Aqueel get behind the console, most don't really care. Music is very modern—a combination of commercial Western music and Bollywood. Enigma is invariably packed to the hilt with a long queue of people waiting outside, though hotel guests can jump the line. It's open Wednesday to Saturday only, and entry costs Rs 800 to Rs 1,500 ($18–$35) per couple, with coupons redeemable for drinks. JW Marriott, Juhu Tara Rd., Juhu Beach. © 022/5693-3000.

Hawaiian Shack 🏵🏵 This popular Bandra club turns from beer bar on slow weekdays to happening nightspot on weekends. A boat-shaped bar, waiters in colorful Hawaiian shirts and straw hats, mostly Western '80s music, and an extremely laidback atmosphere make this more popular than many of the more expensive clubs. Avoid Saturday night, when the dance floor is packed with swaying, sweaty bodies from bar to washroom. The music is dance-friendly, as is the crowd. and once your feet start tapping, it'll be hard to resist jumping into the melee. It opens at 7pm, 2 full

The Spirit of Mumbai: 944 Millimeters, But Not Out

On July 26, 2005, it was pouring in Mumbai, a typical day in monsoon season. Until 2pm, that is, when a sudden, massive downpour began. It was later learned that this downpour was caused by an offshore vortex that created a giant cloudburst, mostly over the north of the city. In a single day, 944 millimeters (37.2 in.) of rain was spilled on Mumbai, the highest rainfall level ever recorded anywhere in India in one day, and well above the annual rainfall of cities like Chicago. Within hours, millions of people were stranded getting home as streets were dangerously flooded and traffic came to a standstill. The city's lifeline, the dependable suburban train system that ferries some 6 million people each day, shut down, power outages occurred everywhere, cellphone networks failed, and phone lines were either dead or erratic. Those who could, began to walk home (some 10, 15, and up to 40km/25 miles away) through waist-deep, sometimes chest-deep water. But there were many who couldn't. Busloads of schoolchildren were stranded in floodwaters higher than their heads, with parents clueless about their whereabouts. In this catastrophic situation, the spirit of Mumbai came through, in hundreds of little incidents reported throughout the city. In Juhu an elderly couple went downstairs in pouring rain and arranged to evacuate 40 schoolchildren trapped in a flooded bus outside their building; they corralled the kids into their modest 93-sq.-m (1,000-sq.-ft.) flat upstairs. They rounded up a few cookies, laid sheets on the ground for the kids to spend the night, and tried all the while to contact

hours before most other clubs, with an entry fee of Rs 400 to Rs 600 ($9.10–$14) per couple. Hotel Real Palace, 16th Rd., Pali Village, Bandra W. ℂ 022/2605-8753.

Insomnia 𝒢𝒢   The crowd that comes to this hugely popular upmarket, multi-space club is here to see and be seen, and the decor is comparable to that of some of the most fashionable nightclubs in the world. It's also a fun place where guests can wangle free drinks, depending on the playful announcements: Women wearing more than two ear-studs get a Bacardi Breezer on the house; the guy who dances the longest on the bar wins a vodka—you get the picture. See if you fit the bill to cop a gratis entry: Some nights it's women, or bankers, or journalists who get in free—but hey, professional ID required. The entry fee of Rs 600 to Rs 1,000 ($14–$23) buys two to four drinks; entry is free for hotel guests. Taj Mahal Hotel, Apollo Bunder, Colaba. ℂ 022/5665-3366.

J49 𝒢𝒢   Named after its postal address—Juhu, zip code 400049—this suburban nightclub booms with Bollywood beats each Sunday. Bollywood Nights celebrate the end of the week with a party that starts just before midnight (though the club opens by 8:30pm, and attracts minor ramp and big-screen celebs). It's also one of the most reasonably priced places to get the local flavor: Weekend entry is only Rs 400 ($9.10) per couple; weeknights, Rs 200 ($4.55). Hotel Juhu Presidency, 148/B Juhu Tara Rd., Juhu. ℂ 022/2618-4546.

Polly Esther's 𝒢   Recently expanded, this Colaba nightclub (and rip-off from the American chain of nightclubs) attracts a mixed crowd, from teenyboppers to 40-somethings, with its mix of Bollywood, pop, and '80s music. The retro theme is echoed in posters of Michael Jackson and Madonna, managers with clown noses and multicolored frantic parents whose phones, like most in the city, were malfunctioning. Young men stood for all-night vigils around old open manholes in waist-deep water to forewarn people who might accidentally step in. People used old tires, construction equipment, huge rolls of cables, empty drums, and whatever they could find to rescue folk and give them shelter in their neighborhoods. Men and women cooked everything they had and stepped out of their homes to feed strangers trapped in unbelievable 40-hour traffic jams on highways all over the city. Strangers took strangers into their homes and fed and clothed them, vehicles that could move stopped to give pedestrians a ride, and some auto-rickshaw drivers ferried people short distances through the night without charging a rupee. Several men drowned rescuing others, and the death toll in the city eventually rose to nearly 1,000. During all this, there was no disaster management plan in place and no government announcement forthcoming; no politician even bothered to go on air to tell people what to do. Instead, private radio stations began airing messages between lost loved ones who could not reach each other. People communicated through radio jockeys who kept the announcements going nonstop, telling people what was going on, what to expect, what not to do, and how to stay safe. The disaster exposed the unique, never-say-die spirit of Mumbai, the can-do attitude that gets people up and going, to act when those who should be responsible and accountable fail to do so. On July 26, Mumbai showed itself as a community that put humanity first.

frizzy wigs, and a Polaroid man who'll take your picture for Rs 50 ($1.15). The club's spaciousness provides a welcome break from the cramped, smoky rooms found in other clubs around the city. Drinks are relatively reasonably priced, and the entry fee is Rs 600 to Rs 1,000 ($14–$23) per couple. Gordon House Hotel, Apollo Bunder, Colaba. © 022/2287-1122.

Ra ✯✯ In the gentrified Phoenix Mills Compound, three nightclubs sit cheek-by-jowl—**Lush,** popular with young adults; **Provogue Lounge,** store by day and club by night; and the latest entrant, **Ra.** Designed as an upmarket version of Lush, Ra plays the latest rage in loud music, from hip-hop to Hindi remixes. Entry is steep (Rs 1,000/$23 on Wed, Rs 1,500/$35 on Fri and Sat per couple), topped only by the drink prices (G&Ts cost Rs 450/$10). But judging by the numbers the bouncers turn away on weekends, nobody seems to mind. Phoenix Mills Complex, Lower Parel. © 022/5661-4343.

Vie Lounge and Bar ✯✯ Set in a bungalow at the edge of Juhu Beach, Vie has three spaces: a restaurant (average), an enclosed nightclub area, and the pièce de résistance—an open-air lounge overlooking the Arabian Sea. We recommend the outer area for its sea breeze and laid-back ambience. Inside it's louder (house and commercial music) and more like a traditional nightclub, with the DJ console nestled against the bar. Vie is open daily and earlier than most counterparts (8pm), but it is sometimes booked for a private party, so call ahead. Friday- and Saturday-night entrance fees are Rs 1,000 ($23) per couple; Wednesday is Ladies' Night, with free alcohol for women while men pay Rs 700 ($16); and the rest of the week, entry is free. 102 Juhu Tara Rd., diagonally opposite Maneckji Cooper High School, Juhu. © 022/2660-3003.

8 Aurangabad & the Ellora and Ajanta Caves

The ancient cave temples at Ellora and Ajanta are among the finest historical sites India has to offer, and a detour to this far-flung region of Maharashtra to view these World Heritage Sites is well worth the effort. You can cover both Ellora and Ajanta comfortably in 2 days, but for those who are truly pressed for time, it is possible to see both sets of caves in a single (long, tiring) day. To do this, you'll need a packed lunch from your hotel, and plenty of bottled water. Set out for Ajanta at about 7am, reaching the ticket office as it opens (recommended for the tranquillity of the experience, even if you're not trying to cover both in a day). Spend no more than 3 hours exploring Ajanta, before heading for Ellora; your driver should be aware of the detour along the Ajanta–Aurangabad road that will get you there much faster. The caves at Ellora are spread out, so don't drag your heels, and be sure not to miss the ultimate jaw-dropper, known as "Cave 16": the Kailashnath temple complex is more carved mountain than cave. The world's largest monolithic structure, it is twice the size of the Parthenon. Note that Ajanta is closed on Monday and Ellora on Tuesday.

ESSENTIALS

GETTING THERE   The quickest way to get here is to fly to Aurangabad's airport (in Chikalthana, Jalna Rd., just 10km/6¼ miles from the city center) with **Jet Airways** (© 022/2285-5788 in Mumbai, 0240/244-1770 in Aurangabad). The flight from Mumbai lasts 45 minutes to an hour and costs around $85. You can also try **Indian Airlines** (© 0240/248-5421 or -3392). For a cheaper and fairly comfortable journey, book an air-conditioned chair car seat (Rs 369/$8.45) on the **Tapovan Express** train that leaves Mumbai's VT/CST Station at 6:10am and reaches Aurangabad at 1:30pm. An alternative is the **Devagiri Express,** an overnight train that reaches Aurangabad at an inconvenient 4:10am (second-class air-conditioned sleeper berth Rs 731/$17).

VISITOR INFORMATION   You'll find a tourist information booth at the airport arrivals hall, where you can pick up brochures on Aurangabad, Ajanta, and Ellora. The **India Tourism Development Corporation (ITDC) office,** in the **MTDC Holiday Resort** (Station Rd., Aurangabad 431 001; © 0240/233-1143; www.maharashtra tourism.gov.in; daily 7am–1pm and 3–8pm), is where you can book government-operated guided tours to both sets of caves. You can also book a **private guide** for the caves here, although it'll work out cheaper to pick one up at the caves themselves.

GETTING AROUND   Taxis and **auto-rickshaws** are widely available in Aurangabad, and you'll be approached at the airport by the usual touts offering you a "good deal." Though the scamsters and touts here are far less aggressive or annoying than those you encounter farther north, always arrange the fare upfront; a taxi from the airport into the city should cost about Rs 200 ($4.55). **Classic Travel Related Services** (at the MTDC Holiday Resort; see above; © 0240/233-7788 or -5598; classic tours@vsnl.com) lives up to its name, and will arrange just about any type of transport for travel within Aurangabad and environs (count on around Rs 1,800/$40 for a full day with a car and driver; less if you're only going to Ellora), and beyond. All hotels have travel desks that will organize a car with a guide for any of the sights in the area.

AJANTA TRAVEL ADVISORY   The drive from Aurangabad to Ajanta takes between 2 and 3 hours, so you're advised to set off early in the day to avoid as much of the midday heat as possible. There are two ways of getting to the caves. Generally, visitors are dropped off in the public parking lot, several kilometers from the caves themselves; here you'll find stalls selling awful souvenirs, snacks, and tourist paraphernalia, and "guides" flogging their services. You'll also find green, eco-friendly buses that are the only vehicles allowed in the vicinity of the caves. Purchase a ticket and hop aboard for the short drive to the Ajanta ticket office.

A far more rigorous but rewarding alternative is to have your driver drop you at the "Viewpoint," reached via a turnoff some distance before the official parking facility. From here you can take in a panoramic view of the site across the river, then make your way down the rather difficult pathway (don't attempt this route if you're unsteady on your feet) and eventually to a footbridge that spans the Waghora River. Make for the ticket booth and proceed to the caves. Be sure to arrange to have your driver collect you from the parking lot when you're done.

ELLORA TRAVEL ADVISORY These caves are only 30km (19 miles) from Aurangabad, but you should rent a car and driver for the day for transfers between certain caves. Starting at **Cave 1,** visit as many of the principal caves as you have time for, until you reach **Cave 16,** where you should arrange for your driver to pick you up and then drive you to **Cave 21,** which is worth investigating. Having seen this cave, again have your driver take you to **Cave 29,** located alongside a waterfall, reachable via a rather dangerous pathway. Another short drive will take you to the **Jain Group** of temples, of which **Cave 32** is the best example.

Be warned that Ellora is enormously popular—especially during weekends and school vacations. Time your visit accordingly, or get here as soon as it opens, preferably not on a weekend. Ellora can be explored independently or with a guide (who may or may not understand English and who may sound like a recorded message); currently, the official rate is Rs 350 ($8) for the first 4 hours, or—if you're really enthusiastic—Rs 500 ($11) for up to 8 hours.

AURANGABAD

388km (240 miles) E of Mumbai; 30km (19 miles) SE of Ellora; 106km (66 miles) SW of Ajanta

Aurangabad takes its name from the last of the great Moghul emperors, the hard-edged Aurangzeb, who enacted an almost Shakespearean drama in the 17th century when he took control of the empire by murdering his siblings and imprisoning his father, Shah Jahan (see chapter 9), before leaving Delhi in 1693 to make this city his base. Today the sprawling city of Aurangabad is one of the fastest-growing industrial cities in India, and not a destination in its own right. However, time allowing, it has

---

Tips The Finest of Fabrics

Aurangabad is the only place in the world where *himroo* is still practiced, a millennia-old brocade-weaving craft that combines silk and cotton yarn into an almost satinlike fabric. Weavers spend around 2 to 3 months working on a single sari, even longer on more intricate and detailed designs. A custom-woven sari featuring a design based on one of the Ajanta murals takes a year to produce and costs about Rs 90,000 ($2,100)—which makes a beautiful himroo shawl with gold-plated silver thread for Rs 2,300 ($53) seem a real bargain. Head for **Paithani Silk Weaving Centre,** 54 P1 Town Center, behind Indian Airlines Booking Office, opposite M.G.M. College (© **0240/248-2811;** daily 11am–8pm).

a few attractions worth noting. Best known is **Bibi-ka-Maqbara,** the "Mini-Taj," a mausoleum built for Aurangzeb's empress by his son, Azam Shah, and a supposed replica of the more famous mausoleum built by his grandfather in Agra. Set amid large landscaped gardens and surrounded by high walls, it's primarily interesting from a historical point of view, lacking as it does the fine detail and white marble of its inspiration (the builders were forced to complete the project in stone and plaster because of financial constraints). Although you can't enter the tomb itself, an amble through the grounds (daily sunrise–10pm; admission Rs 100/$2.30) affords you the opportunity to compare this project with the original Agra masterpiece. If you follow the dirt road that leads past Bibi-ka-Maqbara up into the hills for some 2km (1¼ miles)—a stiff climb—you will come across the **Aurangabad Buddhist Caves** (Rs 100/$2.30), a series of nine man-made caves dating back to the 6th to 8th centuries. Similar to the Buddhist Caves at Ajanta (but not in the same class), they feature original painting fragments and offer spectacular views of the city and the landscape beyond.

On the way to Ellora is **Daulatabad Fort** (Rs 100/$2.30). Built by the Yadavas between the 10th and 11th centuries A.D., it comprises an elaborate system of maze-like tunnels that served as an ingenious defense system: Once intruders were holed up deep within the tunnels, guards would welcome them with flaming torches, hot oil, or burning coals, effectively grilling them alive.

A place largely untouched by tourism is **Lonar Crater**—created some 50,000 years ago when a meteorite careered into the basalt rock. It has a diameter of 1,800m (5,760 ft.), making it the largest crater in the world. Filling the bottom of the crater is water in which Ram and Sita are believed to have bathed while they were exiled from Ayodhya; temple ruins lie at the water's edge. Tranquil and remote, the crater is about 150km (93 miles) east of Aurangabad.

THE BUDDHIST CAVES OF AJANTA ✦✦✦

During the 2nd century B.C., a long, curving swath of rock at a sharp hairpin bend in the Waghora River was chosen as the site for one of the most significant chapters in the creative history of Buddhism. Buddhist monks spent the next 700 years carving out prayer halls for worship *(chaitya grihas)* and monasteries *(viharas)* using little more than simple hand-held tools, natural pigments, and oil lamps and natural light reflected off bits of metal or pools of water. They decorated the caves with sculptures and magnificent murals that depict the life of the Buddha as well as everyday life.

The caves were abandoned rather abruptly after almost 9 centuries of activity and were only rediscovered in 1819 (by a British cavalryman out terrorizing wild boars). Time has taken its toll on many of the murals, and modern-day restoration projects have even contributed to the near-ruin of some of the work. Despite this, the paintings continue to enthrall, and it's hard to imagine the patience and profound sense of spiritual duty and devotion that led to the creation of this, arguably the best Buddhist site in India.

It takes some time to explore all 29 caves (which are numbered from east to west), and the sensory overload can prove exhausting; try at least to see the eight described below. It's a good idea to make your way to the last cave, then view the caves in reverse numerical order—in this way you won't be running with the masses, and you won't have a long walk back to the exit when you're done.

Richly decorated with carved Buddha figures, **Cave 26** is a chaitya hall featuring a *stupa* (dome-shaped shrine) on which an image of the Master seated in a pavilion appears. In the left-hand wall is a huge carved figure of the reclining Buddha—a depiction of the *Mahaparinirvana,* his final salvation from the cycle of life and death. Beneath him, his disciples mourn his passing; above, celestial beings rejoice. Featuring the greatest profusion of well-preserved paintings is **Cave 17,** where maidens float overhead, accompanied by celestial musicians, and the doorway is adorned with Buddhas, female guardians, river goddesses, lotus petals, and scrollwork. One celebrated mural here depicts Prince Simhala's encounter with the man-eating ogresses of Ceylon, where he'd been shipwrecked.

Cave 16 has a rather lovely painting of Princess Sundari fainting upon hearing that her husband—the Buddha's half-brother, Nanda—has decided to become a monk. **Cave 10** is thought to be the oldest Ajanta temple, dating from around the 2nd century B.C. Dating to the 1st century B.C., **Cave 9** is one of the earliest chaitya grihas, and is renowned for the elegant arched windows carved into the facade that allow soft diffused light into the atmospheric prayer hall. A large stupa is found at the back of the prayer hall.

Cave 4 is incomplete, but its grandiose design makes it the largest of the Ajanta monasteries. Take a quick look, then head for **Cave 2.** The facade features images of Naga kings and their entourage. Inside the sanctum, a glorious mandala dominates the ceiling amid a profusion of beautiful floral designs, concentric circles, and abstract geometric designs with fantastic arrangements of flying figures, beasts, birds, flowers, and fruits. On the walls, well-preserved panels relate the birth of the Buddha.

Cave 1 is one of the finest and most popular of the viharas at Ajanta, especially renowned for the fantastic murals of two bodhisattvas (saintly beings destined to become the Buddha) that flank the doorway of the antechamber. To the right, holding a thunderbolt, is Avalokitesvara (or Vajrapani), the most significant bodhisattva in Mahayana Buddhism. To the left is bejeweled Padmapani, his eyes cast humbly downward, a water lily in his hand. Within the antechamber is a huge seated Buddha with the Wheel of Dharma (or life) beneath his throne—his hands are in the *Dharmachakra pravartana mudra,* the gesture that initiates the motion of the wheel. On the wall to the right of the Buddha is an image of the dark princess being offered lotuses by another damsel.

Last but not least, for a magnificent view of the entire Ajanta site and an idea of just why this particular spot was chosen, visit the viewing platforms on the opposite side of the river; the natural beauty of this horseshoe-shaped cliff is the perfect setting for a project so singularly inspired by spiritual fervor. It may even be the ideal starting point for your exploration.

Note: You will be required to remove your shoes before entering many of the caves, so take comfortable (and cheap) footwear that slips on and off easily.

Rs 250 ($5.70). Tues–Sun 9am–5:30pm; closed national holidays. No photography inside caves.

EXPLORING ELLORA ଈଈଈ

Ellora's 34 rock-sculpted temples, created sometime between the 4th and 9th centuries, were chiseled out of the hillside by Buddhists, Hindus, and Jains. A visit here allows for an excellent comparison of the stylistic features and narrative concerns of three distinct but compatible spiritual streams.

Of the 12 Buddhist cave-temples, carved between the 6th and 8th centuries, the largest is **Cave 5.** The "cave of the celestial carpenter, Vishwakarma" **(Cave 10),** is acknowledged to be most beautiful of the Buddhist group. A large ribbed, vaulted chamber, it houses a big figure of the Teaching Buddha, while smaller figures look down from panels above. The atmosphere here is chilling, a place for the suspension

Ambient Dining

For a pleasant lunch on the way back from Ellora, try **Ambience,** which belongs to the same group that owns the excellent Tandoor restaurant in Aurangabad (see review below). It's set in pleasant gardens 12km (7½ miles) outside the city, in the vicinity of Daulatabad Fort. The place is also a lovely, atmospheric venue for dinner. Contact Ranjit (© **0240/261-5995;** daily noon–midnight), or inquire at Tandoor.

---

of worldly realities and for complete focus on things divine. In the three-story *vihara* (monks' domicile) of **Cave 12,** note the monks' beds and pillows carved out of rock. **Cave 13** marks the first of those carved by the Hindus which, when viewed in combination, offer a wealth of dynamic, exuberant representations of the colorful Hindu pantheon: Shiva as Natraj performs the dance of creation in **Cave 14** (where he is also seen playing dice with his wife Parvati and piercing the blind demon Andhaka with a spear); and in **Cave 15,** the manifold avatars of Vishnu tell numerous tales while Shiva rides the divine chariot and prepares to destroy the palaces of the demons.

Created over 150 years by 800 artisans, **Kailashnath Temple (Cave 16)** is the zenith of rock-cut Deccan architecture, and Ellora's star attraction. A dazzling visualization of Mount Kailash, the mythical sacred abode of Shiva in the Tibetan Himalayas, it is unlike the other caves at Ellora, which were excavated into the hillside—it is effectively a mountain that has been whittled down to a free-standing temple, measuring 1,700 sq. m (18,299 sq. ft.). The intricacy of detail is remarkable; the temple basement, for example, consists of a row of mythical elephants carrying lotuses in their trunks as they appear to support the entire structure on their backs. Sculpted detail abounds in the temple and its excavated courtyard, with hardly an inch of wall space left unadorned—demons, dwarfs, deities, humans, celestial *asparas,* and animals occur in abundance. In the Nandi Pavilion facing the entrance is a beautiful carving of Laxshmi surrounded by adoring figures; seated in a pond, she is being bathed by attendant elephants carrying pots in their trunks. Also be on the lookout for *mithunas*—male and female figures in erotic situations.

Ellora: Caves free. Entry to Kailashnath Temple Rs 250 ($5.70), free for children under 15. No filming of interiors. Wed–Mon 9am–5:30pm.

WHERE TO STAY

If you want ultra-cheap and functional and intend to eat out, then by all means endure a night or two at the government-run **MTDC Holiday Resort** (Station Rd., Aurangabad 431 001; © **0240/233-1513**), which offers relatively clean rooms in a central location (near restaurants, the taxi hub, and travel agencies) but little else. Insist on an air-conditioned unit. Standard rooms are Rs 750 ($17) and family rooms are Rs 780 ($18).

The Ambassador Ajanta ⭐   Set amid lovely lawns with fountains and well-maintained flower beds, The Ambassador offers good facilities and a comfortable environment—ideal for relaxing after a hectic day of cave exploration. Moghul artworks fill the white-and-beige marble lobby, creating a pleasant atmosphere (if not as stylish as at the Taj), and the public spaces are decorated with statues and objets d'art that reflect the creative spirit of Ellora and Ajanta. The best units overlook the swimming pool

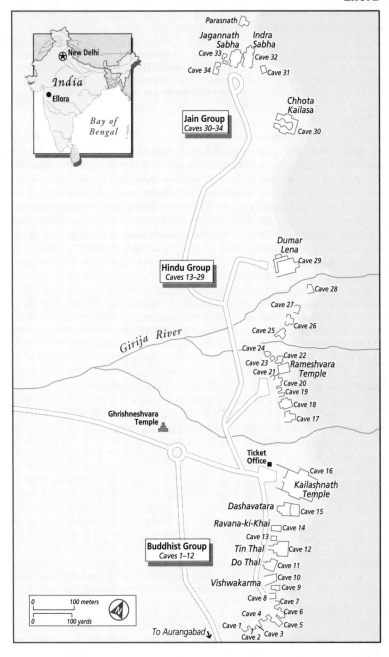

(ask for room nos. 201–204 or 220–225). Service here is personal and attentive but certainly not up to the standards set in larger cities.

Jalna Rd., CIDCO, Aurangabad. © **0240/248-5211**, -5212, -5213, or -5214. Fax 0240/248-4367. www.ambassador india.com. 92 units. $75 executive room double; $85 superior room double; $95 deluxe suite double. Ajanta and presidential suite tariffs on request. AE, DC, MC, V. **Amenities:** Restaurant; bar; pool; putting green; tennis court; badminton court; squash court; jogging track; health spa; travel assistance and car hires; business center; Internet access; currency exchange; shopping arcade; 24-hr. room service; babysitting on request; laundry and dry cleaning; doctoron-call. *In room:* A/C, TV, electronic bedside console, fridge, hair dryer, safe (except executive rooms), DVD player on request.

Quality Inn The Meadows ☆ (Kids)   Surrounded by 5.2 hectares (13 acres) of pleasant gardens, this small resort—built in 1996—is great if you'd rather stay out of town. Accommodations are in a variety of simple cottages, the size and level of privacy varying according to price. Deluxe cottages, while recently repainted, are quite basic, so opt for the superior category (ask for G1), with white marble flooring, stiff cane chairs, and tiled bathrooms with drench showers. There's plenty here to keep young children occupied (including rabbits) while you relax in a quiet corner after sightseeing under the Maharashtrian sun. Breakfast is served poolside, under large, umbrellalike canopies; exotic birds, wild parrots, and busy butterflies provide the entertainment. Service tends to be a tad amateurish when guest numbers are down, so you may need to exercise patience.

Gat no. 135 and 136, Village Mitmita, Mumbai-Nasik Hwy., Aurangabad 431 002. © **0240/267-7412**, -7413, or -7414. Fax 0240/267-7416. Reservations (Mumbai): © **022/5654-8361** or -8362. Fax 022/5635-0032. 48 units. Rs 2,900 ($66) deluxe cottage double, Rs 3,500 ($80) superior cottage double; Rs 5,500 ($126) 1-bedroom suite, Rs 8,500 ($194) 2-bedroom suite. Rs 600 ($14) extra bed. Rates include airport/station transfers and breakfast. AE, MC, V. **Amenities:** 2 restaurants; bar; pool; health club; skating rink; children's playground; currency exchange; 24-hr. room service; laundry and dry cleaning. *In room:* A/C, TV, minibar in suites, tea- and coffee-making facilities (except deluxe cottages), hair dryer and DVD player on request.

Taj Residency ☆☆   This is the best hotel in town, catering to Aurangabad's high society crowd as well as to business and leisure travelers. A brand-new wing with 24 deluxe rooms opened in 2005, so ask for a room there. Located away from the center, the tranquil retreat is surrounded by verdant gardens overlooked or accessed by guest rooms; ground-floor patios also have swings. Don't expect the type of ultra-luxurious decor you'll find in major city hotels (the mattresses are foam and the carpeting slightly tatty in places), but accommodations are reasonably spacious, with teak furniture, Mughal arch-shaped mirrors, and miniature paintings on the walls. Ask for one of the corner units (no. 201 or 221)—these have extra balcony space. Suites, which include all meals, are large and plush and have wonderful private terraces.

8-N-12 CIDCO, Aurangabad 431 003. © **0240/238-1106** through -1110. Fax 0240/238-1053. www.tajhotels.com. residency.aurangabad@tajhotels.com. 66 units. $75 standard double; $90 executive double, $100 deluxe double; $135 executive suite double. $180 deluxe suite. All rates except standard include breakfast and airport pick-up. AE, DC, MC, V. **Amenities:** Restaurant; bar; pool; fitness center; travel assistance and car hires; banqueting; business center; Internet access; currency exchange; 24-hr. room service; babysitting on request; laundry and dry cleaning; doctoron-call. *In room:* A/C, TV, minibar, tea- and coffee-making facilities (except in standard rooms), hair dryer.

WHERE TO DINE

Most foreign visitors end up at **Food Lovers** (Station Rd. E., MTDC Holiday Resort), a palace of kitsch done in bamboo and fish tanks, with a separate entrance for "Families, Foreigners and Non-drinking Gents." Backpackers swear by the food (the Chinese is actually better than the Indian), and prices are very reasonable. Our money's on Tandoor, however (see review below). Another spot worth noting is **Angeethi Restaurant & Bar** (Jalna Rd.; ✆ **0240/244-1988**; Rs 38–Rs 225/90¢–$5), one of Aurangabad's most popular restaurants, particularly with the business set. Try the Afghani chicken masala (pieces of boneless chicken cooked in a cashew-nut gravy), or the popular—and spicy—tandoori chicken masala. For something authentically Maharashtran, order chicken *kolahpuri* (not on the menu, but ask for it anyway), a spicy-hot chicken dish with a sharp chili, onion, and garlic base; if you can handle the sting, it's delicious. But if it's real authenticity you're looking for, head to the no-frills **Thaliwala's Bhoj** (Bhau Phatak Smruti Kamgar Bhavan, opposite Hotel Kartiki; ✆ **0240/235-9438**) and order a thali for a mere Rs 60 ($1.35). (See "The Thali: Gujarati & Rajasthani Cuisine at its Best," earlier in this chapter.) Waiters (who generally don't speak a syllable of English) will fill your platter with wonderful concoctions—mop it all up with savory, freshly prepared chapati.

Tandoor ☙☙☙ INDIAN/MUGHLAI/CHINESE   A large square door swings open to reveal this stylish eatery with walls of clay face-brick, tiled flooring, and a bold collection of Egyptian figures (King Tut's head emerges incongruously from the brickwork). Though a bit far from the main hotels, this hot favorite since 1988 is our choice for Aurangabad's best eating experience. It's greatly enhanced by wonderful service and welcoming management. You can spend ages pondering the extensive menu, or you can ask the manager, Mr. Hussain, for his choices. Okra *(bhindi)* is a house specialty. The fenugreek-leaves-flavored *kasturi kebab* (chicken) and *kabuli* tandoori chicken (marinated in creamy yogurt and flavored with ginger, garlic, turmeric, and white pepper) are both outstanding. If you're looking for a mild curry that's been delicately prepared to bring out the most subtle flavors, ask for chicken *korma*—the sauce is made from cashew nuts, poppy seeds, sweet-melon seeds, and white sesame seeds.

Shyam Chambers, Station Rd. ✆ **0240/232-8481**. Main courses Rs 45–Rs 360 ($1–$8.15). MC, V. Daily 11am–4pm and 6:30pm–last order.

5

Goa: Party in Paradise

Nirvana for dropouts, flower children, and New Age travelers since the late 1960s, Goa's hippie invasion peaked in the '70s, when Anjuna Beach became a rocking venue for party demons and naturalists who would sell their last piece of clothing at the local flea market for just enough cash to buy more dope and extend their stay. For many, Goa still conjures up images of all-night parties and tripping hippies sauntering along sun-soaked beaches. But there is more to this tiny western state than sea and sand, hippies and hedonists. A rich amalgam of Portuguese and Indian influences, its history alone has ensured that its persona is unlike any other in India. Arriving in 1498, the Portuguese stayed for almost 500 years (kicked out, finally, in 1961—the last Europeans to withdraw from the subcontinent), leaving an indelible impression on the local population and landscape. Goans still take a siesta every afternoon; many are Catholic, and you'll meet Portuguese-speaking Mirandas, D'Souzas, and Braganzas, their ancestors renamed by the colonial priests who converted them, often by force. Garden Hindu shrines stand cheek-by-jowl with holy crosses, and the local *vindaloo* (curry) is made with pork. Dotted among the palm groves and rice fields are dainty villas bearing European coats of arms and imposing mansions with wrought-iron gates—built not only for European gentry but for the Brahmins who, by converting, earned the right to own land.

Over the past 8 years Goa has become more hip than hippie, with well-heeled Indians frequenting the new rash of flashy international-style restaurants and design-conscious furniture and lifestyle stores at which they shop in order to adorn their ostentatious Goa mansions. Joining them every winter are the white-skinned package tourists, come to indulge in the rather commercialized trance culture, and Indian youngsters who cruise from beach to beach, legs wrapped around cheap motorbikes and credit cards tucked into their Diesel jeans.

Goa is very much "India Light," a cosmopolitan tourist-oriented place of five-star resorts and boutique guest houses, and in many ways this is the perfect introduction to a country that, elsewhere, can be very challenging indeed. Of course, when the crowds arrive, particularly over New Year's, Goa's beaches and markets are anything but tranquil. Sun beds and shacks line the most commercial beaches, and hawkers haggle ceaselessly with droves of fresh-off-the-charter-plane Europeans here to sample paradise at bargain prices while Mumbai and Bangalore puppies crowd the shoreline bars and restaurants. If it's action you're after, you will run into endless opportunities for all-night partying and reckless abandon, but Goa's true pleasures are found away from the crowds, on the more remote beaches to the far north and south, on the semi-private beaches adjoining expensive luxury resorts, or in the charming

Tips Mayhem in Paradise

Every year from December 23 to January 7, tens of thousands of world tourists, both domestic and foreign, descend on Goa, so if you plan to spend Christmas or New Year's here, expect to negotiate crowds everywhere, particularly along the bursting-to-the-seams Baga–Calangute stretch. You can avoid the crowds to some extent by confining yourself to your hotel or guesthouse, but all the popular bars and restaurants will be filled to capacity, with queues so long they can cause traffic jams. Besides, everything—particularly accommodations—will be extremely expensive at this time. Almost every hotel charges a separate end-of-year tariff, most with an accompanying surcharge for the in-house "festive party" (even if you don't plan to attend). If loud and raucous merriment is not your style, avoid Goa during this time; your money will go twice the distance here once the revelers have departed.

guesthouses located farther inland. Come for at least 3 days, and you may end up staying for a lifetime—as a number of very content expats from around the world have done. However you decide to play it, live the local motto—*"Sossegade"*: "Take it easy."

1 Arrival & Orientation

ESSENTIALS

GETTING THERE   By Air   The state capital is Panjim (also called Panaji), which is pretty much centrally located; **Dabolim Airport** lies 29km (18 miles) south. Many travelers to Goa arrive on charter flights as part of ever-popular package deals direct from the U.K. Or you can fly in from Mumbai (nine flights per day) or Delhi (two flights per day), as well as from Kolkata, Chennai, Cochin, Hyderabad, Bangalore, and Ahmedabad. The flight from Mumbai is a mere 40 minutes, and the best service is offered by **Jet Airways** (© **022/5698-6111** in Mumbai). A helpful government **tourist desk** (© **0832/251-2644**) is in the baggage-claim hall. If you have a hotel or resort reservation, a **courtesy bus or taxi** will probably be waiting for you. If not, use a **prepaid taxi** (see chapter 2) or bargain directly with a driver; the trip to Panjim should cost Rs 400 to Rs 500 ($9.10–$11). As is the case everywhere, prebook your accommodations, and don't fall for a tout's offer of "discount" lodgings.

By Train   Goa's three main jumping-off points are **Thivim** in the north (20km/12 miles inland from Vagator), **Karmali** (12km/7½ miles from Panjim), and **Madgaon** in the south (also known as Margao). If you're going straight to Palolem in the far south (almost on the border with Karnataka, where the fabulous Om Beach is) on a train bound/originating farther south, jump off at **Canacona.**

Several trains travel daily from Mumbai to Goa along the **Konkan Railway;** most of these take a good 10 to 13 hours, so it's best to book the overnight **Konkan Kanya Express,** which leaves Mumbai at 11pm and gets into Madgaon at 12:30pm. For a slightly quicker option, you'll need to get up early for the 5:30am **Mumbai-Madgaon Jan Shatabdi** (from Dadar Station; Thurs–Tues) that reaches Madgaon by 4pm. If you're traveling from the south, catch the 11am **Matsyaganda Express** from Mangalore to Madgaon (6½ hr.); the trip offers mesmerizing views along the Konkan coast.

Note that it's worthwhile to book your train reservation in your home country, especially if you plan on moving to Goa soon after your arrival in India or in peak season when trains between Mumbai and Goa are often fully booked.

By Bus   If you want to travel to Goa but all trains and flights are full, or if you want to save on airfare, your next-best option is a bus from Mumbai, Pune, Hyderabad, Bangalore, or Mangalore. Numerous overnight buses leave from Mumbai (near Metro Cinema–Fashion St.) every day at 7pm; try to book an air-conditioned bus. Preferably, this should be a sleeper, not advisable if you are traveling alone, as you will sleep beside a stranger; in this case, buy two tickets for Rs 800 to Rs 1,000 ($11–$23). Or you can opt for a semi-sleeper or "slumberette," a comfy 135-degree reclining seat for Rs 500 to Rs 800 ($11–$18), depending on the season and quality of the bus. Some companies provide blankets and bottled water. **Paulo Travels** (Mumbai: © 022/ 2643-3023 or -6764; Goa: © 0832/243-8531 through -8537) is a reliable private operator; all bookings are made at the small ticket booths near St. Xavier's College, Mumbai. If you are booking through other agents, make sure you ask for a Volvo bus (better suspension, more spacious seating) and that you get a confirmed ticket with your seat number. For the north Goa beaches, jump off at Mapusa; for the south, at Panjim. *Tip:* A single woman can request to have another woman seated beside her, though this may not always happen. Seats in the first few rows have more legroom.

VISITOR INFORMATION   For general information on the state, visit the **Government of Goa Department of Tourism office** in Panjim (Patto Tourist Home; © 0832/243-8750 through -8752; http://goatourism.nic.in; Mon–Fri 9:30am–1pm and 2–5:45pm). Branch offices are in **Mapusa** (in the shopping complex next to Mapusa Residency; © 0832/226-2390) and **Margao** (Margao Residency; © 0832/ 271-5204). There's also an information counter at the **Konkan Railway Station** in Madgaon (© 0832/270-2298).

GETTING AROUND   Note that it shouldn't take much longer than 4 hours to cruise the entire coastline, so everything in this chapter is within easy reach.

By Motorbike   Motorbikes are *trés* cool in Goa, and you'll encounter an endless barrage of young backpackers and old hippies zipping around Goa's roads on two-wheelers—*sans* helmets. At press time there was some talk of introducing a law that would make wearing helmets mandatory, so check if this has been enforced (certainly it's worth wearing one on the main highways and in the main cities). Renting a bike gives you absolute freedom to move from beach to beach, village shack to all-night party. Have your international two-wheeler driver's license handy (just in case; you'll rarely be asked for a license, and most visitors simply pay off the authorities if caught), and check the bike thoroughly before handing over any cash; bank on paying around Rs 300 ($6.80) a day (or Rs 200/$4.55 for gearless bikes—which are easy to use even if you've never ridden them before). Note that at these prices, these two-wheelers don't come with insurance, so if you seriously damage one, you must pay for the repairs. You can find motorbikes practically everywhere; in Panjim, try across the road from the post office. Riding on the back of someone else's motorbike is another popular way to get around; this can be both invigorating and terrifying. When someone stops to ask if you need a lift (and they will), negotiate a price in advance. And, if you don't like the pace or style of driving, say something immediately.

By Taxi & Auto-Rickshaw   Negotiate privately with one of the many taxi drivers found around tourist areas—including those near your hotel entranceway (you can get

Goa

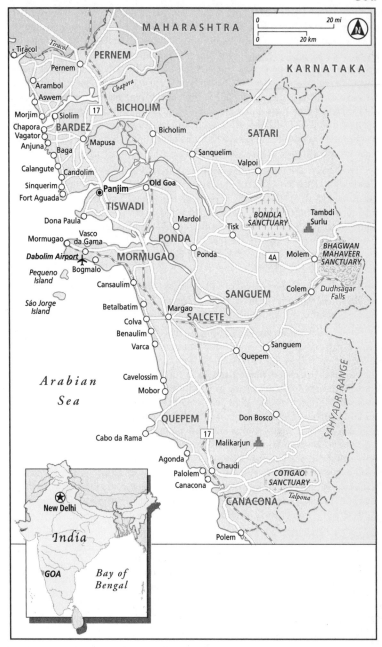

one through your hotel, of course, but at a five-star lodging the cost will almost double). Figure on spending Rs 600 to Rs 750 ($14–$17) for a 6-hour outing, but specify which locations you hope to cover, or agree to pay up to Rs 8 (15¢) per kilometer for a non-air-conditioned cab (80km minimum distance). Remember that if you need a one-way lift to a more remote region, you'll be asked to pay for the return journey. If you plan to take a day trip to a far-off beach, you're better off fixing a price for the day (Rs 1,800/$42 for a trip to Palolem from north Goa). Auto-rickshaws are considerably cheaper than taxis, but a great deal more uncomfortable. **Dalesh** is a reliable taxi driver (℅ **98221-02964**) who can be booked for the whole day or for a pickup or drop-off (Rs 500–Rs 800/$11–$18 for an airport ride from Calangute). *Note:* All rates vary according to demand and season.

By Car Goa is also perhaps the only place in India where you can hire self-drive cars (Rs 800–Rs 1,200/$18–$25 for the day for a basic model; souped-up open-air jeeps cost Rs 1,000–Rs 1,500/$23–$35) but, like many of the motorbike rental services, most of these outfits aren't registered or licensed to commercially rent out vehicles. Consequently, you may not be properly insured—you hire at your own risk; if you have an accident, you pay for the repairs. For better, fully insured cars with or without a chauffeur, call Dominic of **Velankini Car Rentals** (℅ **0832/248-9047,** 0832/309-0584, or 98221-01598).

By Bus Buses ply their ways up and down the state, stopping in a rather chaotic fashion whenever someone needs to get on or off. If you're in a hurry, try to catch an express bus; otherwise you could be in for an endless series of stop-starts.

By Boat Andy of **Marin Boat Trip** (stationed at Reggie's Café) will organize sea-going excursions anywhere in Goa. For trips to Terakol (Goa's northernmost point), he charges Rs 900 to Rs 1,000 ($21–$23) each, including refreshments, for a minimum of seven passengers. **Goan Bananas** (℅ **0832/227-6362** or -6739, at Calangute Beach) organizes dolphin-spotting trips as well as jet-skiing and parasailing. At Kenilworth Beach Resort in south Goa, **Sea Adventure** (Utorda; ℅ **98221-61712**) organizes bird-watching and a backwater cruise that takes in basking river crocodiles. The operation runs from late October until the end of April. For a more comfortable and luxurious cruise, book a trip on the 27-seater yacht *Solita* (immortalized in a song by India's most famous Goan rock musician, Remo). Choose among an early-morning dolphin-spotting cruise on the sea or an evening sunset cruise on the Mapusa and Mandovi rivers (Rs 1,000/$23 plus taxes). You can charter the boat (Rs 7,500/$171 per hour for 2-hr. minimum) for a romantic dinner cruise or party (**Odyssey Tours;** ℅ **0832/227-7124** or 98221-80826; www.traveljadoo.com).

TOURS & TRAVEL AGENTS

The **Goa Tourism Development Corporation** (Trionara Apartments, Dr. Alvares Costa Rd., Panjim; ℅ **0832/222-6515,** -4132, or -6728; www.goacom.com/goa tourism; daily 9:30am–5:30pm) has full-day tours of the north and the south aimed primarily at domestic tourists. For personalized adventure expeditions to any number of Goan destinations, try **Kennedy's Adventure Tours and Travels** (℅ **0832/227-6493,** -9381, -5076, or 98-2327-6520; kennedys@sancharnet.com).

   MGM International Travels has offices in both Panjim (Navelcar Trade Centre, opposite Azad Maidan; ℅ **0832/222-5150**) and Calangute (Simplex Chambers, Umtavaddo; ℅ **0832/227-6073**). Other reliable travel agents include **Trade Wings** (1st floor, Naik Building, opposite Don Bosco School, Panjim; ℅ **0832/243-2430**).

SCUBA DIVING   Barracuda Diving India (Goa Marriott Resort, Miramar, Panaji; ℭ **0832/246-3333,** ext. 6807, or 98221-82402; fax 0832/246-3300; www. barracudadiving.com; barracuda@vsnl.com) is a PADI-recognized dive center where you can rent equipment or take diving courses and get certified (from beginner to advanced levels). Venkatesh Charloo and Karen Gregory, both master diver-trainers, offer dive safaris south, in Karnataka, where visibility can reach up to 30m (100 ft.). Bookings can also be made through **Atlantis Water Sports** (see below).

WATERSPORTS   Most of the upmarket resorts offer a range of watersports facilities. Goa's best-established watersports company is **Atlantis Water Sports** (ℭ **0832/ 309-2909** or 98900-47272). Jet-skiing, parasailing, windsurfing, wakeboarding, scuba diving, and other ocean-going pastimes are available from a makeshift structure roughly halfway along the beach between Baga and Aguada (at the foot of Vila Goesa Rd., Cobra Vaddo, Calangute). Just outside the Taj Holiday Village is **Thunderwave,** a higher-priced watersports outfit that provides jet-skis and cruises for Taj guests, but is also open to the public.

FAST FACTS: Goa

Airlines Even the smallest hotels are able to make air travel arrangements for you, and usually charge a small fee to process tickets, which saves you the hassle of having to travel all the way to Panjim. **Jet Airways,** the best domestic airline, is open Monday to Saturday 9am to 6pm (Patto Plaza, near the Patto Tourist Hotel and the bus stand, Panjim; ℭ 0832/243-8792 or -7497).

Ambulance Dial ℭ **102,** or you can call the **Panjim City Round Table** (Panjim; ℭ 0832/222-7997). In Margao, call the local **Ambulance Trust** (ℭ 0832/273 1759). In Mapusa, call ℭ 0832/226-5119.

American Express Call **American Express** in Panjim (ℭ 0832/222-2945 or 0832/ 222-8557).

Area Code The area code for **Goa** is ℭ 0832.

ATMs Ask your hotel for the nearest ATM with credit card facilities. In Panjim. There's an ICICI ATM at the Sindur Business Centre on Swami Vivekananda Road. In Candolim there's an HDFC machine at Regal Villa (opposite SBI), and a UTI machine in the Dona Alcina Estate (also at the Brangaza Complex, opposite the Kadamba bus depot in Mapusa).

Banks & Currency Exchange For the best rates, you can exchange cash and traveler's checks at **Thomas Cook** in Panjim (8 Alcon Chambers, D. B. Marg; ℭ 0832/222-1312; Mon–Sat 9:30am–6pm; in winter, also Sun 10am–5pm). Another location is between Baga and Calangute, at the State Bank of India, in the Hotel Ofrill Building (ℭ 0832/227-5693).

Car Rentals Try **Sita World Travel** (101 Rizvi Chamber, Caetano Albuquerque Rd., Panjim; ℭ 0832/222-0476, -0477, -3134, -6477, or 0832/242-3552).

Drugstores Go to **Farmacia Salcete** in Panjim (18th June Rd.; ℭ 0832/222-5959; Mon–Sat 9am–7:30pm). **Walson and Walson Chemist** can be found on Calangute (ℭ 0832/227-6366; daily 8:30am–1:30pm and 3:30–9:30pm).

Emergencies In Panjim, dial ⓒ **102** for an ambulance, and ⓒ **101** in case of fire. See "Police," below.

Hospital **Dr. Bhandari Hospital** (ⓒ **0832/222-4966** or -5602) is in Panjim's Fontainhas area. For hospital emergencies in Margao, call **Margao Hospital** (ⓒ **0832/270-5664**). In Mapusa, **Vrindavan Hospital** (ⓒ **0832/225-0022** or 0832/225-0033) is reputed to be the best.

Internet Access High numbers of backpackers mean plenty of Internet facilities (Rs 25–Rs 80/55¢–$1.80 per hour), particularly in tourist areas. Wherever you are, ask or look out for **Sify i way** cybercafes (see "Fast Facts: India" in chapter 2). You can also try **Reliance Webworld** in Mapusa (ⓒ **0832/309-5011** or -5010).

Police Dial ⓒ **100**. **Panjim Police Headquarters** (ⓒ **0832/242-8400** or -3400) is on Malaca Road, at the western edge of Azad Maidan.

Post Office Panjim's **General Post Office** is at Patto Bridge and is open Monday to Friday 9:30am to 5:30pm.

GOA'S BEST BEACHES

Goa's reputation for having some of the world's best beaches is well-deserved, but inevitable commercialization has taken its toll, with the infamous **Baga-to-Calangute** area (north of Panjim) now part of a tourist-infested strip of sun loungers, backed by beach shacks serving beer, cocktails, and fresh seafood—the sort of packaged beach experience best avoided. A little north of Baga, **Anjuna** comes alive with parties and trance music during the winter, when full-moon festivals get the crowds howling. It also has a fabulous Wednesday market. Just north of Anjuna is lovely **Vagator** 🏵🏵, with Chapora Fort overlooked by stark red cliffs. But the real northern paradise starts at **Asvem** 🏵🏵🏵, which has somehow managed to remain off the beaten tourist road. A little north of Asvem, **Arambol** 🏵🏵🏵, seductively far away from the package-tour masses, is one of the last refuges of hard-core hippies. Though there are no private beaches in Goa, the southern beaches generally become the private domain of the five-star resorts fronting them, because of the sheer sizes of property they occupy. In the far south, gorgeous **Palolem** 🏵🏵🏵 has just one large resort close by (the InterContinental Grand, a few kilometers south in Cancona), and gets our vote for the best beach in Goa: Although it's become increasingly popular in the high season and is home to a sizable hippie community, it has yet to be overwhelmed by day-trippers. Just 7km (4 miles) north of Palolem, **Agonda** 🏵🏵🏵 is even more isolated and peaceful, while to the south, **Galgibaga** 🏵🏵🏵 is another remote haven with eucalyptus trees and empty stretches of sand. And then, of course, there's **Om** 🏵🏵🏵 Beach, just over the border, an hour into neighboring state of Karnataka, considered by many to be the best beach in India and one of the most beautiful in the world. However, the hippies have zeroed in on it, so don't expect seclusion.

2 Panjim (Panaji) & Old Goa

Located at the mouth of the Mandovi River, the state capital of Panjim (moved here from Old Goa in 1759) is a breezy, laid-back town that lends itself to easy exploration. The chief attraction is the wonderful colonial Portuguese architecture, particularly in the eastern neighborhoods of Fontainhas and Sao Tome, where the atmospheric cobbled streets are lined with old mansions and churches dating as far back as the mid-1700s—look for Fontainhas's **Chapel of St. Sebastian,** where the crucifix from Old Goa's "Palace of the Inquisition" is now kept. The figure of Christ on the crucifix here is unusual, with head upright and eyes wide open, unlike the usual figures who feature lowered head and eyes.

Dominating Panjim's town center is the imposing **Church of the Immaculate Conception,** built in the Portuguese baroque style in 1541. Nearer the water's edge is the **Secretariat;** an old palace of Adil Shah of Bijapur, this became the Portuguese viceroy's residence when the colonial administration moved here.

Wandering around Panjim on foot shouldn't take more than a few hours. If you're pushed for time, skip the walk and hop onto an auto-rickshaw or on the back of a bike to **Old Goa** (30 min. from Panjim), reviewed in detail below. From Old Goa, it's a short trip (and a great contrast) to view the popular Hindu temples that lie north of the dull town of Ponda, on National Highway 4. Very few Hindu temples dating back earlier than the 19th century still exist. (Affronted by the Hindus' "pagan" practices, the Portuguese tore them down.) **Sri Mangeshi Temple** was built specifically as a refuge for icons of deities smuggled from the coast during the violent years of the 16th-century Inquisition. A path lined with palm trees leads to a colorful entrance-way, behind which the tiled, steep-roofed temple exemplifies a fusion of Hindu and Christian architectural styles, hardly surprising considering that it was constructed by Goan craftsmen weaned on 200 years of Portuguese church-building. Walking distance from here (15 min. south) is the slightly less commercial (no temple "guides") **Sri Mahalsa Temple.**

EXPLORING OLD GOA ON FOOT ✿✿

The once-bustling Goan capital is said to have been the richest and most splendid city in Asia during the late 16th and early 17th centuries, before a spate of cholera and malaria epidemics forced a move in 1759. Today, this World Heritage Site is tepid testament to the splendor it once enjoyed. The tranquillity behind this well-preserved tourist site (barring the grubby stands selling refreshments and tacky souvenirs) belies the fact that it was built on plunder and forced conversions, though you'll see little evidence (like the basalt architraves) of the mass destruction of the Hindu temples initiated by fervent colonialists.

The entire area can easily be explored on foot because the most interesting buildings are clustered together. To the northwest is the **Arch of the Viceroys,** built in 1597 in commemoration of the arrival of Vasco da Gama in India. Nearby, the Corinthian-styled **Church of St. Cajetan** (1651) was built by Italian friars of the Theatine order,

---

Moments Carnival!

Each year in February, during the festivities leading up to Lent, the people of Goa get down for 3 days and nights of hedonistic revelry as King Momo commands them to party hard. Goa's most famous festival—a Latin-inspired extravaganza of drinking and dancing—traces its roots to ancient Roman and Grecian ritual feasts. Cities and towns come under the spell of colorful parades, dances, floats, balls, and bands, concluding with the red-and-black dance at Panjim's Club National.

Hindu Christians

In 1623 the pope agreed to tolerate converted Brahmin Catholics, who were then allowed to wear the marks of their Hindu caste. This extraordinary concession played its part in allowing Goa to ultimately adopt a practice of syncretism that embraced Hindus and Christians alike, though it drew its fair share of criticism from the more narrow-minded: The British adventurer Sir Richard Burton once noted that the "good" Hindus converted to Catholicism by the Portuguese were simply "bad" Christians.

who modeled it after St. Peter's in Rome. Under the church is a crypt in which embalmed Portuguese governors were kept before being shipped back to Lisbon—in 1992, three forgotten cadavers were removed. St. Cajetan's is a short walk down the lane from **Adil Shah's Gate,** a simple lintel supported by two black basalt columns.

Southwest of St. Cajetan's are the highlights of Old Goa: splendid **Sé Cathedral** ✴, which took nearly 80 years to build and is said to be larger than any church in Portugal; and the **Basilica of Bom Jesus (Cathedral of the Good Jesus)** ✴. The so-called Miraculous Cross, housed in a box in a chapel behind a decorative screen, was brought here from a Goan village after a vision of Christ was seen on it—apparently a single touch (there is a hole in the glass for just this purpose) will cure the sick. The surviving tower of the Sé's whitewashed Tuscan exterior houses the Golden Bell, whose tolling indicated commencement of the *auto da fés,* brutal public spectacles in which suspected heretics were tortured and burnt at the stake. Nearby, the **Convent and Church of St. Francis of Assisi** (now an unimpressive archaeological museum) has a floor of gravestones and coats of arms; note that the images of Mary and Christ are darker-skinned than usual.

Opposite the Sé, the **Basilica of Bom** was built between 1594 and 1605 as a resting place for the remains of the patron saint of Goa, Francis Xavier (one of the original seven founders of the Jesuit order and responsible for most of the 16th-c. conversions). The withered body of the venerated saint lies in a silver casket to the right of the altar, his corpse surprisingly well-preserved (although one arm is on display in Rome and a missing toe is believed to have been bitten off in 1634 by an overzealous devotee looking to take home her very own relic, during the first exposition of the body—now a decennial event).

Up the hill from the Basilica are the ruins of the **Church of St. Augustine;** below is the **Church and Convent of Santa Monica and Chapel of the Weeping Cross,** where a miraculous image of the crucified Christ is said to have once regularly bled, spoken, and opened its eyes.

Basilica de Bom Jesus: Mon–Sat 6am–6:30pm. Sé Cathedral: daily 7:30am–6pm. Archaeological Museum: daily 9am–12.30pm and 3–6.30pm; admission Rs 5 (10¢). Convent and Church of St. Francis of Assisi: Mon–Sat 7:30am–6:30pm. Church of St. Cajetan: daily 9am–5:30pm.

WHERE TO STAY & DINE

In the unlikely event that you will stay this close to the capital, two good options are reviewed below: The **Marriott** is an upmarket resort situated on the outskirts of the city (avoid **Cidade de Goa,** which is looking tired and is overpriced), while **Panjim Pousada, Panjim Inn,** and **Panjim People's,** situated in the heart of the Fontainhas neighborhood, have more character; Pousada is also very affordable.

Panjim is filled with shabby-looking "pure veg" *udipi* eating halls. If you're in the mood for an Indian snack or a quick cheap dish, aren't afraid to get your hands dirty, and feel like hanging with the locals, try one out; **Vihar** (31 Janeiro Rd.; ✆ 0832/ 222-5744) is a good option. Opposite the Church of Our Lady of Immaculate Conception, **George Restaurant** is convenient; if a really spicy chorizo-style sausage appeals to you, order Goan sausage. For more atmosphere, make a reservation at Luiz D'Souza's **Hospedaria Venite** ✧ (31st January Rd., Fontainhas; ✆ 0832/242-5537), a tiny upstairs restaurant in a 200-year-old building where you can sit on the balcony and order wonderful Goan specialties (or try the delicious shrimp salsa and stuffed crab).

Catering to a steady stream of tourists who are told that it's the best restaurant in town for North Indian cuisine, **Delhi Darbar** (M.G. Rd.; ✆ 0832/222-2544; 11am–4pm and 7–11pm) turns a heavy trade, but it's an unexciting experience. Instead, head across the Mandovi Bridge to Povorim where **O'Coquiero's** (near Water Tank; ✆ 0832/2417271) has been churning out traditional Goan food for decades (try the squid masala or chicken *cafreal*). For more on Goan food, see "The Unique Flavors of Goa," below.

Down the road from the **Goa Marriott Resort** (which, incidentally, has a marvelous seafood restaurant, **Simply Fish,** an outdoor venue overlooking the bay) is **Mum's Kitchen** (Martin's Building, D. B. Marg, Miramar; ✆ 98221-75559 or 3100873; daily noon–midnight). It has a laid-back Mediterranean atmosphere and does wonderful crab *xec-xec* (cooked in thick, spicy coconut gravy) and pomfret *recheado* (fish stuffed with hot spices and pan-fried). The owner, Rony Martins, not only invites you to examine his kitchen for standards of hygiene and his fish for freshness, he is on a mission to revive authentic Goan cuisine. He sources and adopts old "grandma" recipes and has started "A Cry of Goa": an exercise to save Goan cuisine, in which locals are invited to eat at his restaurant free or at nominal cost and provide constructive criticism/suggestions for improvement.

To sample traditional Goan sweets while wandering Fontainhas, pop into **Confeitaria 31 de Janueiro,** one of the oldest bakeries in the state (31 Janeiro Rd.; ✆ 0832/222-5791).

Goa Marriott Resort ✧   With its gorgeous rim-flow pool (and swim-up bar) situated as near as possible to the edge of riverside Miramar Beach, this stylish business hotel claims to have the only PADI-recognized diving center on the subcontinent. This is definitely the capital's smartest hotel, with great facilities and within convenient walking distance of Panjim. Guest rooms are tastefully furnished, if a little cramped. Each one has its own tiny balcony; however, be sure to book a sea-facing executive room. Airport transfers are included.

Miramar, Goa 403 001. ✆ 0832/246-3333. Fax 0832/246-3300. www.marriott.com. 165 units. Oct 15–Mar 31, excluding Dec 23–Jan 6: $210 executive garden-view double, $210 executive bay-view double, $190 bay-view double, $180 garden-view double; $300–$400 suite. AE, MC, V. **Amenities:** 3 restaurants; 3 bars; dance club; tennis courts; health club (including Ayurveda); squash; table tennis; watersports; dive center; tours and travel desk; vehicle rental with chauffeur and taxi hire; boutique; salon; room service; babysitting; laundry; house doctor; on-site astrologer. *In room:* A/C, TV, dataport, minibar, tea- and coffee-making facilities, hair dryer.

Panjim Inn, Panjim Pousada, and Panjim People's ✧   Situated in Panjim's historic Fontainhas district, these are the only authentically Goan guesthouses in Panjim. Retired engineer Ajit Sukhija and his son Jack provide warm Goan hospitality, regaling you with local history while proudly pointing out family photographs. The best option is the recently opened Panjim **People's**, a four-room heritage hotel (until

The Unique Flavors of Goa

If you don't know your *xacuti* from your *baboti,* here's a short guide: Chicken *cafreal* is chicken marinated in green herb and garlic marinade and then fried. *Vindaloo* is a curry usually made with pork and marinated in vinegar, garlic, chilies, and assorted spices. Prawn *Balchao* is a shrimp preserve made with spices and coconut *feni*. *Ambot-tik* is a hot curry soured with kokum berries and usually made with baby shark. The state's favorite fish, kingfish *(isvon) recheado,* is stuffed with chilies and spices blended in vinegar. *Xacuti* is a coconut-based masala; *baboti* is a sweet and spicy ground-beef dish. *Sorpote*—not for the fainthearted—is traditionally a spicy concoction of pork, offal, feni, vinegar, red chilies, and spices. *Bebinca* is the traditional layered dessert made with lots of eggs and coconut milk. Goa is famous for its cashew nuts available in many forms; get the roasted salted variety (great with any drink) from Zantye's or Kajuwala in Panjim. Speaking of which, *feni* is the deceptively light alcoholic spirit distilled from the cashew fruit (or coconut); try it, but be wary.

recently a prominent local school) with spacious rooms and modern bathrooms; ask for the room in which Ajit's mother's lovely rosewood four-poster bed is the centerpiece. There's nothing particularly luxurious about the restored colonial-era Hindu **Pousada,** but it offers a taste of Panjim's 19th-century upper-class lifestyle (along with hot water). The simple rooms are furnished with antiques (including four-poster beds) arranged around an empty courtyard. Windows and balconies look onto the back streets and backyards of Panjim's old "Latin Quarter." The Pousada's older Catholic sister, **Panjim Inn,** is located on an old family property dating back to 1880; as with the Pousada, rooms vary in size and price, so it's best to look around before deciding. You can also browse the latest offering, **Gallery Geetanjali,** which showcases up-and-coming artists.

Panjim Inn reception: E-212, 31st January/31 Janeiro Rd., Fontainhas. ℂ **0832/222-8136** or -6523. Fax 0832/222-8136 or -6523. 9 units. Rs 810–Rs 2,880 ($18.25–$66) double. **Panjim Pousada,** House no. 156, Circle no. 5, Cunha Gonsalves Rd., Fontainhas. www.panjiminn.com. panjiminn@sancharnet.in. 9 units. Rs 720–Rs 1,710 ($16–$40) double. Rs 270–Rs 360 ($6.15–$8.15) A/C charge; Rs 60–Rs 450 ($1.35–$10) extra person. **Panjim People's** (opposite Panjim Inn): 4 units. Rs 3,000–Rs 5,850 ($68–$133) double. Rs 450–Rs 900 ($10–$21) extra person. MC, V. **Amenities:** Restaurant; foreign exchange; room service; laundry; doctor-on-call. *In room:* A/C in all but 4 units.

3 North of Panjim

Goa's reputation as a hangout for hippies during the '60s and '70s was made on the northern beaches of **Calangute, Baga,** and **Anjuna.** Along with the relaxed lifestyle and good times came busloads of Indian men keen to observe free-spirited foreigners and, finally, a crackdown by local government. This forced fun-loving hippies to head to more remote tracts of coastline, leaving the door open for backpackers and package tourists. Thus were the north's most famous beaches transformed into tanning lots for the masses—even Anjuna has become an Ibiza-like experience—and today no card-carrying hippie would deign to set foot on the beach that stretches between Calangute and Baga (defined by resort-centered **Sinquerim** in the south to **Vagator** in the north). That said, you can't deny the beauty of the beaches (in south Vagator, **Ozran** Beach is peaceful and beautiful, with relaxed swimming in a bay at its southernmost end)—certainly this is where you'll want to be if you're here to party during the season. Baga is the smaller, slightly less-developed area of activity. Beach shacks like **Britto's** (Baga) and **Fisherman's Paradise** (Calangute) are crowded with beer-quaffing visitors recovering from the previous night's adventure at the legendary bar-cum-nightclub, **Tito's.** (Be warned that the "special lassis" served at some Goan beach shacks will dramatically increase your amusement at the cows sunbathing alongside the tourists on Baga Beach.)

For a sense of Goa's hippie origins, head for **Arambol,** Goa's most northerly beach (36km/22 miles northwest of Mapusa). It also offers better bodysurfing—the water's a little more turbulent. It draws quite a crowd during the season (you arrive through a lane crammed with stalls selling CDs and T-shirts, and laid-back restaurants playing competing brands of music), but the setting is nevertheless lovely, with a hill looming over a small freshwater lake fed by a spring. The farther north you walk, the more solitude you enjoy. Besides looking at beautiful bodies, you can spend hours watching the surf glide. Better still, head a little farther south from Arambol for **Asvem** Beach. For a bite to eat, the best shack (at the south end of Asvem) is white-curtained **La Plage** (*©* **98221-21712**), run by the same French trio who own Le Restaurant Français (see review later in this chapter). Feast on great steak or fish barbecued in a banana leaf, or just sip a cool mint lassi (daily 8.30am–sunset; closed May to mid-Nov). Just south of Asvem is the dark sand beach of **Morjim,** more popular with the Olive Ridley turtles that have been coming here for centuries than with either package tourists or hippies.

WHERE TO STAY

Naturally, Goa offers a wide range of accommodations, but the luxury resorts tend to offer the best proximity to secluded beaches. If you're design-conscious and keen on a "non-hotel" experience, Goa's best options by far are Nilaya Hermitage and Pousada Tauma, both reviewed below, or—if you're looking for something more mid-range—Presa di Goa, also reviewed below. If the beach is not a priority, we recommend these options for their tranquil surroundings. Another good choice is the two suites (Rs 1,000–Rs 2,000/$23–$46) at **Hotel Bougainvillea** (*©* **0832/227-3270** or -3271) at Anjuna (closed May–Oct); book the one with its own garden. Inherited by Betina Faria, it was built by her grandfather and is consequently also known as Grandpa's Inn. The small accommodations are quiet and cool; there's a lovely garden, swimming

---

Shopping in the Global Village Markets

Anjuna is the site of Goa's wonderful **Wednesday market** 𝒦𝒦, where a non-stop trance soundtrack sets the scene, and a thousand stalls sell everything from futuristic rave gear to hammocks that you can string up between two palm trees on the nearby beach. It's a wonderful place to meet people from all over the world as well as Rajasthanis, Gujaratis, Tibetans—even drought-impoverished Karnataka farmers with "fortune-telling" cows. It's a bit like London's Camden, but everyone's tanned and the weather's almost always wonderful. When the crowd gets too much, pull up a chair at **Mango Shade,** an outdoor family-run restaurant at the edge of the market. Come the weekend, Goa's global residents head for **Ingo's Saturday Night Bazaar,** where most of the spending seems to involve liquor and food. Scores of happy-go-lucky revelers dance and cruise, exchanging plans for the remainder of the evening.

pool, and old pool table. At Goa's very northernmost point is the rather remote enclave of Tiracol, where the owners of Nilaya Hermitage have restored seven rooms in their characteristic Euro-chic style. Although the views from **Hotel Tiracol Fort** (Querim, Pernem; ℂ **02366/22-7631;** nilaya@sancharnet.in; Rs 3,480/$80 standard, Rs 5,480/$125 suite) are outstanding and the food superb, you may find life a little dull (no pool, and the beach is a 3-min. ferry away) and isolated (90 min. from Baga). However, it's hard to beat if you want to *really* get away from it all.

Casa Britona ℱ   Far away from the crowds, this 17th-century Customs warehouse, located on the riverside in the fishing village of Charmanos, has been converted by owner Sheela Dhody and architect Dean D'Cruz (talk about a proven track record!) into a colonial-style boutique hotel. With just eight individually furnished rooms, you are ensured privacy, though sound travels fairly easily between rooms. Ask for a room on the first floor; these share a long veranda (with planter's chairs) overlooking the pool. Almost 40 minutes from the shore, this may not be the ideal location for beach-lovers, but you are assured of peace, excellent service from managers Sunny and Poppy, and a multitude of chirping birds as backdrop while you unwind on the lounge deck by the pool or on the wooden boardwalk on the Mandovi River. On the boardwalk are tables where you can be served a lovely dinner by candlelight.

Charmanos, Badem, Salvador-do-Mundo, Bardez. ℂ **0832/241-0962** or 98505-57665. Fax 0832/241-3389. www. casabritona.com. casabritona@sancharnet.in. 8 units. Apr 1–Sept 30, Octt 1–Nov 30, Dec 1–Dec 22, Dec 23–Jan 3, Jan 4–Jan 15, Jan 16–Jan 30, Feb 1–March 31: Rs 4,000/6,000/8,000/20,000/12,000/8,000/6000 ($91/$137/$182/$460/$274/$182/$137). Rates include breakfast and 2 laundry items. Taxes extra. No credit cards. **Amenities:** Restaurant; pool; fax and Internet; Ayurvedic treatment on request; complimentary airport transfers; car hire; 24-hr. room service; laundry; doctor-on-call; TV lounge. *In room:* A/C, hair dryer on request.

Fort Aguada Beach Resort & Hermitage ℱℱ   Situated on the short peninsula upon which the Portuguese built their defensive Fortress of Aguada, this resort complex (comprising the Beach Resort, Hermitage, and Taj Holiday Village) has one of the most spectacular locations in all of Goa, with picture-postcard views of the beach, which stretches all the way to Baga, 8km (5 miles) away. Behind the main Beach Resort block are 42 cottages tucked almost invisibly among groves of lantana, cashew, and bougainvillea bush; these are the best places to stay at the Beach Resort. Alternatively, for absolute privacy (ideal for groups or families), consider one of the 15 top-end Hermitage cottages, built as a retreat for delegates during the 1983 meeting of the Commonwealth heads of government. The cottages are set among terraced gardens of exotic orchids, bougainvilleas, cashew trees, jasmine, and Krishna ficus. Each villa has a separate living room; a dining area; one, two, or three bedrooms; two bathrooms; a *balcao* (balcony); and a private garden. Interiors are luxurious and include all modern amenities; request a villa near Sunset Point, where cocktails are served while the sun descends over the Arabian Sea. It's quite a stiff climb between the cottages and the hotel lobby (shared with the Beach Resort); courtesy vehicles are available for the short transfer. Also sharing the facilities offered by Fort Aguada Resort is Taj Holiday Village, fronted by Sinquerim Beach, with cottages and villas scattered among towering coconut trees and lush vegetation. Accommodations at this resort vary considerably, ranging from lavish sea-facing villas to less desirable suites in clustered or duplex cottages.

Sinquerim, Bardez, Goa 403 519. ℂ **0832/479123-136.** Fax 0832/479200. www.tajhotels.com. fortaguada.goa@ tajhotels.com. 130 units. Sept 1–Dec 22, Jan 8–Aug 31, Dec 23–27, Dec 28–Jan 5: $180–$345 superior double, $205–$370 superior sea-view double, $215–$380 cottage garden-view double, $300–$465 suite. Hermitage villas (Sept 1–Dec 22, Jan 8–Aug 31, Dec 23–27, Dec 28–Jan 5): $275–$440 1-bedroom garden-view, $300–$465 1-bedroom sea-view, $500–$665 2-bedroom sea-view, $900–$1,065 3-bedroom sea-view. Taj Holiday Village doubles

(Sept 1–Dec 22, Jan 8–Aug 31, Dec 23–27, Dec 28–Jan 5): $155–$380 standard, $805–$405 superior, $190–$415 cottage garden-view, $235–$460 villa, $215–$440 cottage sea-view villa, $225–$450 deluxe cottage sea-view. Ask about multiday or monsoon specials that may include transfers, food, and other conveniences. AE, DC, MC, V. **Amenities:** 3 restaurants; 2 bars; pool; tennis; volleyball; squash; badminton; billiards; table tennis; adventure activities (trekking, rock climbing, rappelling); cycling; watersports; fitness center; spa; activity center; airport transfers; currency exchange; shop; salon; room service; babysitting; laundry; house doctor. *In room:* A/C, TV, minibar, tea- and coffee-making facilities, hair dryer, safe.

Nilaya Hermitage 🗲🗲🗲   From the moment you arrive, you know you're going to be very comfortable indeed. Ex-Parisian fashion stylist Claudia Derain and her Indian husband, Hari Ajwani, started this exclusive hillside resort when they fell in love with Goa during a vacation from Europe. Together with Goan architect Dean D'Cruz, they have created something out of *Arabian Nights,* with 12 cosmic-themed guest suites featuring vibrant colors, terrazzo flooring, and minimalist decor. Giant mosquito nets hang from a high-beamed ceilings, and sweeping archways lead off to open-plan bathrooms with views of the tropical garden. Like a chic harem, the split-level, saffron-colored "Music Room" is where guests unwind on sprawling mattresses, or meditate while soothing music plays beneath a high blue-domed ceiling. Overlooking paddy fields and coconut palm groves, the setting is romantic and classy, and despite being 6km (4 miles) from the nearest beach, Nilaya is one of Goa's most perfect getaways, as its extensive celebrity guest list (Kate Moss, Peter Lindbergh, Phillippe Starck) indicates. Do also look into **Hotel Tiracol Fort,** their new venture overlooking the sea at Goa's northernmost point.

Arpora Bhati, Goa 403 518. ℂ **0832/227-6793,** -6794, -5187, or -5188. Fax 0832/227-6792. www.nilayahermitage. com. 12 units. 140€ ($175) double low season; 280€ ($348) double high season; 450€ ($560) double Dec 20–Jan 10. Rates include breakfast, dinner, and airport transfers. MC, V. **Amenities:** Restaurant; breakfast area; bar; cultural performances; pool; tennis court; Ayurvedic center; spa; travel assistance; room service; laundry; doctor-on-call; meditation room. *In room:* Some have A/C; TV and DVD players can be arranged.

Panchavatti 🗲🗲 *finds*   If you're looking for a little peace and quiet in a soul-stirring setting and don't care too much for phones, air conditioners, bathtubs, and the like, then Isla (Loulou) Van Damme's place is the ultimate refuge from the overwhelming frenzy of India. Most people come to Goa for the beaches, but Loulou's guesthouse (also her home), with its stunning location on a hill on Corjuem Island, is where you come to put your feet up and relax, take a dip or yoga instruction, or contemplate life. With thoughtful landscaping and innate good taste, this charming Belgian woman, who provides simple, spacious rooms and Western-style set meals, has created an extraordinary getaway. Tariff includes three meals (and soft drinks)—and they are meals to die for, served on the large open colonnaded balcony that overlooks the valley. In Loulou's inimitable style, there are no latches or locks on any of the doors—even the bathrooms are curtained off from the bedrooms with only thin cotton saris. Book one of the four rooms that open onto the large balcony (the rest overlook a central courtyard and garden). A music room is stacked with CDs and a small collection of nonfiction books. The pool is fabulously placed—on the edge of a hill. When you want to experience the beach, however, you'll have to hire a taxi for the 30-minute schlep there.

Collomuddi, Corjuem Island, Aldonna, Bardez, Goa 403 508. ℂ **98225-80632.** islapolak@hotmail.com. 7 units. Doubles Rs 7,000 ($160); includes all meals. No credit cards. Closed except for yoga workshops June to mid-Oct. **Amenities:** Pool; music room; travel assistance; limited room service; yoga and meditation; Ayurvedic massage; babysitting; laundry. *In room:* Fan, electronic safe, iron and hair dryer on request.

Pousada Tauma 🐠🐠🐠   This is Goa's top Ayurvedic retreat (a professional doctor presides over two excellent treatment rooms), and even though it's located in the heart of a bustling tourist center (a 10-min. walk from popular Calangute Beach), it is sheltered from the high-season madness by thick, verdant vegetation. Neville Proenca, the charming owner-manager, takes a hands-on approach—a far cry from the package-mentality tourism that's swept through the state. Working with award-winning architect Dean D'Cruz (who also created Nilaya), it took Neville 3½ years to create his retreat, fashioned entirely out of distinctively Goan laterite stone and set around a pool with cascading water. Each suite has its own balcony, overlooking either the garden or pool, and is themed with eccentric pieces (a cradle-turned-table; dentist chair-turned-recliner). The stylish bathrooms are done in shattered tile mosaics. Pousada is the perfect getaway for artists and sophisticated socialites—filmmaker Mira Nair stayed in the Mountain Suite after filming *Monsoon Wedding,* while French designer Michéle Klein enjoys the deluxe Castle Suite, a fairy-tale tower with two living rooms off a single bedroom. In addition to its Goan menu, the excellent **Copper Bowl Restaurant** offers Ayurvedic meals.

Porba Vaddo, Calangute, Bardez. ✆ **0832/227-9061.** Fax 0832/227-9064. www.pousada-tauma.com. 12 units. 130€–370€ ($162–$460) standard suite, 140€–420€ ($175–$525) superior suite, 170€–495€ ($210–$620) deluxe suite. Off season (June 1–Sept 30) 130€–170€ ($162–$210). Rates include breakfast. MC, V. No children. **Amenities:** Restaurant; bar; pool; gym; Ayurvedic center; travel services, airport transfers; room service (until 11pm); Internet access. *In room:* A/C, TV, minibar, hair dryer on request.

Presa di Goa 🐠🐠 *Value*   Luxembourg native Edouard Spaeck and his adopted Goan son Judas (with wife, Cynthia) have turned this country house in Nagoa into a cool retreat, with friendly staff and good service. Unless you want a room close to the pool, book one of the value-for-money junior suites upstairs, which have their own balconies. Rooms, each named after a flower (we recommend Crossandra), are cozy and tastefully furnished with well-restored antiques that include four-poster beds, sofas, desks, and wardrobes or chests of drawers; the simple bathrooms contain bathtubs. Unfortunately, the closest beach is overrun Calangute, though frankly, it's hard to believe this quiet place is just 10 minutes away (complimentary drop-offs 9–11am, pickups 4–7pm). If you want to head to a better beach, ask the hotel to arrange a taxi. The poolside restaurant, **Turkish Grill,** serves the only Turkish food in Goa. Recommended dishes are the vegetarian starters, followed by Anatolian beef stew cooked in red-wine sauce and served with a glass of *ayran,* the Turkish national drink (much like a salty lassi with herbs).

353/1 Arais Wado, Nagoa, Calangute, Bardez. ✆ **0832/240-9067.** Fax 0832/240-9070. www.presadigoa.com. reservation@presadigoa.com. 7 units. Apr 1–Dec 19, Dec 20–Jan 10, Jan 11–Mar 31: 30€/120€/66€ ($37/$148/$80) standard double; 50€/180€/98€ ($62/$224/$123) junior suite; 10€/20€/20€ ($12/$25/$25) extra bed. Children under 6 stay free in parent's room. Children 6–12 pay 50% of extra bed rate. Half-board supplement 10€ ($12) per person, full-board supplement 17€ ($20) per person. 7€ ($8.70) A/C surcharge in summer. Rates include breakfast, taxes, airport transfers, service charges, and daily beach transfers. Ask about special rates for stays of 1 week or more. MC, V. **Amenities:** Restaurant; bar; wine cellar; pool; Ayurvedic treatment on request; airport transfers; car and motorbike hire; 24-hr. room service; laundry; doctor-on-call. *In room:* A/C, TV, hair dryer on request.

Siolim House 🐠   Leafy Siolim village (30 min. from the busy market town of Mapusa—delightfully far from the madding crowd) is where you will find the 300-year-old former residence of a governor of Macau, which has been wonderfully restored by London-based investment banker Varun Sood (who, incidentally, designed the wrought-iron furniture mixed in with the antiques). Located around an open courtyard with a lovely blue-tiled fountain, spacious guest rooms feature whitewashed walls with hand-painted friezes, solid wood-beamed ceilings, decorative terra-cotta tile floors, mother-of-pearl windowpanes, and wonderful open-plan showers. Too bad the new manager is far from eager to expedite bookings, being obsessive about screening guests to get just the "right kind"—in essence, he lacks traditional Goan hospitality. Meals are prepared according to personal requests, so let your imagination wander.

Waddi (opposite Wadi Chapel), Siolim, Bardez. ℂ 0832/227-2138. Fax 0832/27-2941. www.siolimhouse.com. info@siolim.com. 7 units. 58€ ($73) standard suite, 72€ ($88) superior suite. Children under 12 say free in parent's room but not always welcome. Rates include breakfast. 25% extra during peak season (Dec 19–Jan 10). MC, V. **Amenities:** Restaurant; pool; bicycles; airport transfers; car and motorbike hire; room service; Ayurvedic massage; babysitting; laundry; doctor-on-call; Internet access; TV lounge; library.

WHERE TO DINE

Beach-shack dining is one of the essential Goa experiences—sipping *feni* while you feast on grilled tiger prawns or masala shark at unbelievable prices is a must. With at least 200 licensed seasonal shacks between Candolim and Baga, you certainly won't go hungry, but with names like Lover's Corner, Fawlty Towers, and Goan Waves, don't expect culinary magic. And if you don't like the look of the kitchen (ask where the dishes are washed), opt for Britto's (at Calangute, reviewed below) or one of the following.

Also at Calangute, **Souza Lobo**'s seafood enjoys a legendary reputation, and deservedly so. Reserve a table on the beachfront patio and order the tandoor kingfish and crab-stuffed *papad,* or the expensive but excellent grilled lobster or tiger prawns (ℂ **0832/228-1234** or 0832/227-6463; reservations taken before 8pm; after that, wait in line). While in Baga, check out **Casa Portuguesa** (Baga Beach; ℂ **0832/227-7024;** closed Mon and May–Oct), set in a charming old bungalow near the beach; the chicken *cafreal* is highly recommended. Or stop at **Fiesta** (7/35 Saunta Vaddo; ℂ **0832/227-9894**) just for the ambience (and decent pizzas but slow service) or a pick from their dessert menu. It's perched on the sand dunes near Tito's and run by Yellow and Maneck Contractor.

A number of good restaurants can also be found **along the stretch of road between Arpora Hill and Baga Creek,** leading inland from Baga Beach. When Indian spices begin to take their toll, **Lila Café** (Baga River)—Goa's number-one breakfast and lunch cafe (and apparently where Gregory Peck, David Niven, and Roger Moore hung out when filming *Sea of Wolves*)—is the perfect place (with views of paddy fields and coconut groves) to enjoy a decent breakfast: muesli and cereals, along with a selection of breads and croissants served with a variety of toppings. The fresh salads are also good, as is the catch of the day and the goulash with spaetzle. Famous **J & A's Little Italy** 𝒜𝒜 (ℂ **0832/228-2364** or 98231-39488; closed end of Apr to mid-Oct) is where Jamshed and Ayesha Madon serve fantastic pastas, wood-fired pizzas, and amazing organic salads in a great alfresco setting. During peak season there's always a long wait (well worth it), so do make reservations. The *regalo di mare* (prawns and squid in a tomato vinaigrette dressing served with pesto crostini) and *crespelle coi gamberi* (crepes stuffed with seafood) are personal favorites. Or try the delicious steaks or the perfect *al dente* pastas tossed in heavenly sauces. Nearby, in an unusual orange house near the Baga River, is **Moon Crest Restaurant** (ℂ **0832/2275790;** closed May–Oct), a popular hangout where hip locals enjoy the casual atmosphere and the friendly vibe conjured up by the personable host, David Gonzalves. You can sit outside on long-backed wooden chairs, and on Thursday a live jazz band entertains you.

Choices range from chateaubriand to chicken stuffed with crabmeat, but it's the seafood that you simply must try; the crusty fried prawns are superb.

After Eight 🐸🐸🐸 EUROPEAN   It's definitely worth tracking down this difficult-to-find restaurant (located between Calangute and Candolim near the Sarkar ice factory), for it's one of Goa's best. Owned by the gracious Leo D'Souza and superchef Soumyen Chakraborty (both spent years at Taj hotels), this alfresco restaurant is set on the lawns of Leo's house. You can watch your meal being cooked in the glass-fronted kitchen, and discuss how you liked it afterward, when the chef visits every table. Begin with the best Camembert soufflé east of France, and move on to the delectable *"Ocean's Fantasy"* seafood platter, or the chargrilled filet steak with blue cheese sauce, both marvelous. Finally, whether you have room for dessert or not, we must recommend the chocolate mousse with orange Curaçao or the unbelievably light and delicious orange soufflé. Service is top-notch.

1/274B Gaura Vaddo, Calangute, Bardez. © **0832/227-9757** or 92261-88288. Reservations essential. Main courses Rs 230–Rs 895 ($5.25–$20). AE, MC, V. Daily 6:30–11:30pm.

Banyan Tree 🐸🐸🐸 THAI   Each year since 1988, a different Thai chef is imported from Thailand to spruce up the menu and add a personal touch. Set back from the main road behind a 320-year-old banyan tree within the gardens of the Taj Holiday Village, this upmarket Asian eatery is proud of its herb garden, where essential Thai ingredients like lemon grass, *kha* (Siamese) ginger, pandanus leaves, *kachai* (a peppery ginger), and bird chilies are grown. Start with spicy *talle tom yam* seafood soup, a hot-and-sour concoction of mushrooms, calamari, chili, and ginger (not for the faint-hearted); or try the very tangy *som tham* papaya salad, which comes with a peanut sauce. This being Goa, the seafood creations are a must; try the tasty *poo gathi*—a curry-sauce infusion of river crabmeat that's spicy yet flavorful—or the rather pricey (not always on the menu, so ask) *choo chi goong mangkon* (diced lobster in a *makrut* [lime]-infused red-curry sauce). If you've overdone the chili and spice, spoil yourself with refreshing *tab tim grob*—water chestnuts soaked in rose syrup and dusted with tapioca flour—with or without coconut-flavored ice cream.

Taj Holiday Village, Sinquerim, Bardez. © **0832/564-5858**. Main courses Rs 215–Rs 975 ($4.75–$22). AE, DC, MC, V. Daily 12:30–2:45pm and 7:30–10:45pm.

Bean Me Up 🐸 *Kids* ORGANIC/VEGETARIAN   Two years ago Lisa Camps decided to open this wholesome, clean organic-food restaurant at Vagator, as an alternative to the predominantly non-vegetarian food available all over Goa. Meat-lovers won't miss anything once they sample Lisa's tofu lasagna or one of the daily house specials. But most delicious are the huge salads Lisa promises are the "safest in Goa." Expect soya in almost everything at this "Soya Station," including tofu ice cream and tofu cheesecake. If all this sounds too over-the-top healthy and New Age for you, you can sip on the unusual but tasty drinks and juices while you watch a movie (Thurs) or a dance performance or live Spanish band (Sun). Kids are well taken care of in the kids' corner, with its comfy floor mattresses and cushions, reading and coloring books and—yes, 'fraid so—a TV playing Cartoon Network.

House no. 1639/2 Deul Vaddo, Anjuna-Vagator, Bardez. © **0832/227-3479**. Reservations suggested for dinner during peak season. Main courses Rs 60–Rs 150 ($1.35–$3.40). MC, V. Sun–Fri noon–4pm and 7–11pm.

Britto's *Moments* GOAN BEACH SHACK   At this terrific food stop, you can sit in the beach shack or in the restaurant section. Cajie Britto, the owner-chef, dishes out a wicked pork vindaloo and excellent prawn curry, their tastiness corroborated by the number of locals who come here. If something less spicy is more your style, dig into the seafood platter or a juicy steak, and round it off with the Alpine chocolate mousse. And to quench your thirst, there are always bottles of chilled Kings beer available. A live one-man band plays on Monday night, karaoke is offered on Thursday, and a barbecue is held on both nights (make a reservation in peak season).

Calangute Beach. ℂ 0832/227-7331 or 0832/227-6291. Main courses Rs 60–Rs 190 ($1.35–$4.30). MC. Daily 8.30am–midnight. Closed June 21–Aug 10.

Copper Bowl ✦✦✦ GOAN/ECLECTIC It's not just the setting that makes dining here so pleasurable, it's the food, which is sensational. Graciously served from quaint copper pots, the typically Goan dishes are exquisite; try coconut-based chicken *xacuti* (pronounced cha-*cooty*) or fragrant prawn *balchao*, a mouthwatering combination of crispy prawns, aromatic spices, chili, onion, and prawn powder. If your taste leans more toward non-spicy cuisine, try the seafood in coconut-milk soup, followed by the "Seafood Treasure"—baby lobster, prawns, and two kinds of fish served in a banana leaf. Guests at the Pousada are even allowed to take over the kitchen and prepare their own specialties, but nothing will be served unless it's fresh.

Pousada Tauma, Porba Vaddo, Calangute. ℂ 0832/227-9061. Main courses Rs 300–Rs 1,400 ($6.85–$33). MC, V. Dining all day, but reservations essential if you're not a resident.

Le Restaurant Français ✦✦✦ FRENCH/FUSION Lit by the moon, the stars, and a number of old chandeliers dangling from the branches of surrounding trees, this charming slice of Gaul shares the same magical garden venue as the daytime eatery, **Milky Way,** where Janis Joplin and The Beatles once hung out. Those erstwhile pop stars would have loved the elegantly laid-back atmosphere that fun-loving accidental restaurateurs Morgan, Florence, and Serge brought with them from the Continent. The menu (beautifully handwritten by Florence in French, with lively English translations) features imaginatively innovative dishes concocted by Morgan, who likes to "escape" (read: "experiment"), so dishes change regularly, along with the decor. Musttries include the baby calamari stuffed with a ratatouille of prawns, and the filet of sardines on phyllo pastry with mint coulis. This is also the only place in Goa where rabbit is served, and the fresh (nonfrozen) beef is specially flown in from Bangalore. Be sure to leave space for the addictive chocolate cake, whose recipe Morgan once used as *baksheesh* at airport Customs.

Baga Rd., Calangute. ℂ 98/2212-1712. frenchfoodindia@hotmail.com. Main courses Rs 260–Rs 690 ($5.75–$15). No credit cards. Dec 10–Apr 28, Tues—Fri 7:30pm–late.

SHOPPING

Besides the vibrant markets (see "Shopping in the Global Village Markets" box, earlier in this chapter), Calangute has a variety of options worth checking out. **Casa Goa** is a stylish boutique featuring designer wear by celebrated Goan designer Wendell Rodricks, as well as local artwork, silk drapes, and a variety of antiques (Khobra Vaddo, Baga Rd.; ℂ 0832/228-1048). Then take a look at **Leela Art Palace** nearby; with any luck, proprietor Ravi will be in. You might find yourself agreeing to accompany him on an exotic journey into some of the country's remotest regions, where he regularly treks to source tribal art. Also in Calangute, **Subodh Kerkar Art Gallery,** run by Goa's well-known watercolorist, showcases contemporary Indian art including ceramics, hand-painted chests, and Rajasthani sculptures (Gauro Vaddo; ℂ 0832/ 227-6017). Each Tuesday (6:45–8pm; Rs 300/$6.85), an interesting classical dance and music performance is held at the gallery.

Psychedelic Journeys

Rave parties are now almost as synonymous with Goa as hippie culture. If you want to attend one of the winter rave parties, held around full moon, you have to ask around at shacks (at little Vagator, Anjuna, or Arambol). Location is often kept secret until late in the evening to avoid harassment from cops, and is disclosed only few hours before the party starts. These underground dance and music parties usually start at 11pm and go on till at least 8am; sometimes they carry on for 3 to 4 days, as the party moves from one location to another. Various intoxicants are freely available and consumed, and local women set up stalls outside selling *chai* and snacks. DJs play techno/psychedelic/trance music (or psy-trance); ravers often dress up in old-fashioned costumes and wear rave belts and colorful clothes, all part of setting the mood for their psychedelic journey. Regulars insist that these are not just massive techno freak-outs where everybody is "tripping," but a mystical, devotional experience akin to a spiritual encounter.

Located in a 200-year-old Portuguese mansion, **Sangolda** is the lifestyle boutique venture by the dynamic duo behind the boutique hotel Nilaya Hermitage; here you can shop for unusual home accessories and furniture sourced from all over India—from rattan loungers from Kerala to Rajasthani chests. Attached is a gallery-cum-coffee-shop (Chogm Rd., Sangolda; © **0832/240-9309** or -9310). Also in Sangolda is **Monsoon Heritage,** a contemporary design studio created by internationally renowned designers Yahel Chirinian and Doris Zacheres (recently selected as one of the 23 most happening designers in the world by *UrbanO* magazine), who pair huge discarded tropical trees with mirrors and glass to create exclusive design pieces for the (very) rich and famous. You'll find their showrooms in Paris and Santa Monica, but their main base (and inspiration) is Goa (276/1 Livrament Vaddo, Sangolda; © **0832/240-9800;** www.monsoonheritage.com).

For authentic Goan souvenirs, proceed to **Velha Goa Galleria** (© **0832/242-6628**) in Fountainhas, Panjim, for *azulejos,* attractive Portuguese-style hand-painted tiles and ceramics. They will also pack these delicate items carefully so that they survive the journey home. Also in Panjim, the government-run **Craft Complex** (© **0832/222-6448**) stocks basic handicrafts from all over Goa.

Fashionistas will be pleased with **Wendell Rodricks Design Space** in Altinho, Panjim (© **0832/223-8177**). Wendell believes in affordable designer wear, and his store has everything from evening gowns to casual wear. And then there's **Sosa's,** a trendy fashion store stocking couture by Goan designer Savio Jon as well as other young and rising designers (E-245 Rua de Ourem; © **0832/222-8063**). Not far from Panjim on Ribander Road, **Camelot** (© **0832/244-4503;** closed Apr–Sept) is an über-chic store housed in an old villa on the Mandovi River. Surrounded by walls painted gold, fuchsia, and royal blue, you can shop for designer clothing as well as exquisite silks, objets d'art, linen, and furniture.

WHERE'S THE PARTY?

Your best bet for finding a good party is to hang out around whatever appears to be the most popular beach shack of the season, and chat up the locals (but be wary of getting lifts to unknown venues with strangers). Other excellent spots for picking up the scent of out-of-the-way parties are **Ingo's Saturday Night Bazaar,** Anjuna's **Wednesday Market,** or ever-popular **Tito's** (© 0832/275028)—still the most happening nightclub in Goa (closed off season). This local institution has been going for years and attracts anyone and everyone who's up for a party. For a less rocking atmosphere accompanied by fairly good food, check out **Kamaki** (© 98232-76520), a lounge bar up the road from Tito's that's open 24 hours; or hang out at **Mambo's,** an open-air pub where DJs Ajit and Yuri spin 1980s rock music (but no trance). For a cooler, more fashionable night out, try **Congo Lounge** (Souza Vaddo; © 0832/564-4226)—its pink and jungle-green decor forms a great backdrop for the designer-wear-clad patrons.

4 South of Panjim

Compared with the beach playgrounds of north Goa, the south is more about solitude and stretches of virgin sand (with the north only a short ride away). For the most part, you'll be sunning yourself on whatever beach is slap-bang in front of your resort hotel—each with its own idyllic setting, these stretches of largely untouched beaches are paradise. If you're on a tighter budget or want a bit more atmosphere, head farther south to picturesque **Palolem** ✦✦✦. Remote and tranquil (yet only 40km/25 miles from Madgaon), this is one of Goa's most beautiful stretches of coastline, a gorgeous sandy crescent cove lined with coconut palms and a few shacks and stalls. Although it's becoming increasingly popular over the high season, it remains free of sun beds, day-trippers, and large resorts, with accommodations limited to thatched tree houses or wooden houses on stilts. At sunset, Palolem becomes a natural meditation spot; the sun disappearing slowly behind the beach's northernmost promontory casts a shadow over local fishing boats, swimmers, joggers, and cavorting dogs, as the rusticated bars come to life with pleasant lounge music. Just 7km (4½ miles) north of Palolem, **Agonda** is even more isolated and peaceful, while to the south, **Galgibaga** is another remote haven with eucalyptus trees and empty stretches of sand.

Getting There   From Panjim you can travel directly to your beachfront resort by taxi or motorbike (the latter should take no more than 2–3 hr.), possibly stopping off for a swim at **Bogmalo.** One of the quietest of south Goa's popular beaches, it has quaint shacks (as well as a number of ugly concrete buildings), fishing boats, and a view of two small islands some distance out to sea—ask about trips to the islands at the **Watersports Goa** shack, which also has equipment for activities like windsurfing and water-skiing. Farther south, you can stop for lunch at **Martin's Corner** (© 0832/288-0061 or -0413; 11am–3pm and 6:30–11pm; follow the back road between Majorda and Colva to Betalbatim), where Martin Pereira's widow, Carafina, runs the kitchen with an iron fist. She began cooking wonderful dishes for this family restaurant back in 1994, when it opened with only two tables. Now Martin's sons operate a successful and extremely popular courtyard establishment, surrounded by mango, coconut, and jackfruit groves. Order snapper *recheado,* butter-garlic prawns, or pomfret *caldin* made with a coconut milk curry. Carafina makes a mean homemade masala, prepared according to a secret family recipe with fresh Goan spices.

Alternatively, consider a meandering trip via the Goan interior, traveling past Ponda to the Bhagwan Mahaveer Sanctuary to view Goa's oldest Hindu temple, **Mahadeva Temple** in Tambdi Surla, and the 600m-high (190-ft.) **Dudhsagar (Sea of Milk) Falls.** Constructed from slabs of black basalt, the 11th-century Mahadeva Temple is one of the few to have survived the Portuguese, thanks largely to its distance from the coast (some 75km/46 miles from Panjim). To reach the falls, you will need a jeep, so either set off with one from the outset (see "Arrival & Orientation," earlier in this chapter), or hire one in nearby Collem. Take lunch (look out for greedy monkeys) and a bathing suit for a swim in the deep, icy pool surrounded by rocks and wild greenery. There is no reason to stop in Goa's second city, **Madgaon (Margao),** which has little more to offer than a stroll through the sprawling spice-scented town market—a maze of covered stalls selling everything from garlands of flowers and peeled prawns to sacks bursting with turmeric, chilies, and tamarind—but two worthwhile house museums are nearby. In Loutolim (10km/6¼ miles north of Margao), you can tour the Araujo Alvares family home, **Casa Araujo Alvares** (arrangements through Loutolim's Ancestral Goa Museum; ℂ **0832/277-7034;** daily 9am–1pm and 2–6pm), while 13km (8 miles) west lies the old Portuguese village of Chandor and impressive **Casa de Braganza** ℱ, Goa's largest residence. The two-story facade of this Indo-Portuguese mansion—which practically takes up an entire street—features 28 balconies fronted by a lush, narrow garden. The land-owning Braganzas rose to prominence during the 17th century and today are divided into two clans, the Pereira-Braganzas and the Menezes-Braganzas, who occupy separate wings of the house. The large, high-ceilinged rooms (including a 250-year-old library) are filled with original antiques, rosewood four-poster beds, mosaic floors, and Belgian glass chandeliers. Sun-lit galleries and parlors are filled with bric-a-brac, and French windows open onto an interior garden. You can arrange (℃ **0832/278-4201**) to have a private tour conducted by Mrs Braganza; concentrate on the west wing, which is in the best condition.

WHERE TO STAY & DINE

South Goa has more five-star resorts than north Goa, and the number is added to annually (raising the hackles of eco-watchdogs). The upmarket newcomer farthest south is humongous **InterContinental The Grand Resort,** which sprawls over 34 hectares (85 acres) and an exclusive stretch of beach; its 255 luxurious suites are

Om Beach: Escape to Paradise

Often cited as the top beach in India and one of the best in the world, Paradisiacal **Om Beach** ℱℱℱ lies south in Gokarna, an hour across the border into Karnataka. Black rocks divide the superb white sand into three interconnected bays that more or less resemble the Sanskrit "om" symbol, the invocation that created the universe. Infrastructure here remains practically nonexistent, but new shacks and small "guesthouses" emerge every season. Alternatively, tranquil **Devbagh Beach Resort** (℃ **08382/22-1603,** 080/2559-7021, -7024, or -7025; www.junglelodges.com) in Karwar, slightly north of Gokarna, makes for a pleasant getaway. Guests stay in log cabins on stilts among groves of casuarina trees—spend your days snorkeling (through **General Thimayya National Academy of Adventures;** ℃ **080/221-0454**), visiting outlying islands, beachcombing, or lazing in your hammock.

currently being offered at good rates (from $200). At the other end, closest to Panjim, with the biggest pool in Goa, is the **Park Hyatt Goa Resort and Spa** (© 0832/272-1234; www.goa.park.hyatt.com; from $300)—spread over 18 hectares (45 acres) on the virgin beach of Arrossim. Midway down the south coast are **Radisson White Sands Resort** (© 0832/272-7272; from $250) at Varca Beach; and **Taj Exotica** at Benaulim (see review below). Note that all of these resorts are very child-friendly, often with separate pools and activities, and babysitters are always available.

The beach of Palolem is one of the last areas of south Goa free of resorts; here you'll have to venture back to nature at one of many budget options, or cozy up at the wonderful **Bhakti Kutir** eco-resort, reviewed below. Even if you've just come for the day, dine at **Aahar,** where you're served inexpensive, delicious organic health food under a giant cloth draped from the surrounding trees—try the dal and red spinach, served with organic rice, coconut chutney, and fresh, nutty hummus; or sunflower seed and *moong* (mung) bean-sprout salad with steamed spinach, toasted nuts and seeds, and tofu, served with homemade whole-wheat rice-bread. The stir-fried bean, paprika, and mushroom salad is also good. The fish curry is light and not too spicy, made with coconut gravy, and is delicious mopped up with the wheatgrass chapati.

Bhakti Kutir ✸ Ꮩᵃˡᵘᵉ Ꮶⁱᵈˢ   This is by far Palolem's most atmospheric and comfortable option, though don't expect any real luxury. It's the brainchild of Panta Ferrao, a Goan lawyer who (aided by his German wife, Ute) dropped out to start an ecologically sensitive resort that would empower local people with skills and provide comfortable accommodations in a fantastic location. Bhakti Kutir offers a selection of mud-plastered bamboo "cottages" made entirely from natural materials, with en-suite ablution facilities—squat toilets (organic, of course) and bucket showers. Windows are ingeniously crafted from seashells, while the cushions, fabrics, beds, and even mattresses (some comfortable, others hard) are all made by locals. Try to book room no. 6, which is built on different levels; no. 8, a double-story unit with an upstairs balcony; or the "stone house" (built with Panta's German in-laws in mind) with more traditionally Western facilities (like a toilet). Come prepared for mosquitoes, dark pathways, and plenty of back-to-nature experiences. Set a short distance from the beach, the resort features a health-conscious, mostly vegetarian restaurant (fresh seafood is the exception), a bar serving beer and wine, and an assortment of esoteric activities like Ayurvedic treatments, yoga, and meditation. Workshops and cooking classes are held for those wishing to extend their knowledge of local culture. They've recently added an alternative school to keep the kids happy and busy. It's very popular, so reserve well in advance.

Palolem. © **0832/264-3469** or -3472. bhaktikutir@yahoo.com. 22 units. Jan 15–Dec 15 Rs 3,000 ($68) stone house, Rs 1,200–Rs 1,500 ($28–$35) cabana, Rs 2,500–Rs 2,800 ($58–$64) 2-bedroom cabana. Ask for off-season discounts; rates are flexible (higher Dec 15–Jan 15). No credit cards. **Amenities:** Restaurant; bar; amphitheater; pool table; airport transfers; Ayurvedic and healing center, massage, yoga, meditation, mud baths, cooling baths; boutique; babysitting; laundry; kitchen; tailor; school. *In room:* Mosquito net.

InterContinental The Grand ✸✸✸   Just when we thought you couldn't go any farther south, the mother of all luxurious Goa resorts opens at Canacona Beach, south of Palolem. Its first plus, over other five-star resorts, is its long, exclusive beachfront, followed by its (*very* Grand) architecture—an impressive two-level yellow baroque-Portuguese *quinta* is topped with a red-tile roof. Interiors flaunt classic mahogany furniture, patterned terrazzo flooring, and old-fashioned ceiling fans. And then, of course, there are all the trappings of a luxurious resort, including a **Champneys spa**

with an exhaustive list of revitalization treatments. As at The Leela, however, you will need a golf cart to take you to the beach or pool, or just about anywhere. Ask for one of the lovely, spacious, sea-facing suites that also overlook the expansive golf course. Numerous restaurants offer a variety of cuisines: most interesting is **Sea BQ,** the open-air restaurant where your meal is cooked on a Japanese barbecue grill on your table. The resort also owns a three-bedroom yacht, *Blue Diamond,* which is rented out to guests. On the downside, The Grand is a 2-hour traipse to Panjim, which means you'll spend half your day traveling if you want to venture out.

Raj Baga, Canacona, Goa 403 702. © **0832/264-4777.** Fax 0832/264-4711. www.thegrandhotels.net. 255 units. $200–$375 garden-view suite; $250–$425 sea-view suite; $350–$750 luxury suite; $1,000–$2,200 presidential suite. $40 extra bed. Taxes extra. AE, MC, V. **Amenities:** 4 restaurants; 2 bars; pool; children's pool; 18-hole golf course; tennis courts; squash courts; jogging tracks; health club; table tennis; billiards; spa; yoga; watersports; children's activity center; travel desk; airport transfers; business center; conference room; salon; 24-hr. room service; laundry; dry cleaning; doctor-on-call; valet. *In room:* A/C, TV, dataport, Wi-Fi enabled, minibar, tea- and coffee-making facilities, hair dryer, weighing scale, safe.

The Leela ✸✸   Spectacularly positioned at the edge of the bleached-white sands of a near-private stretch of beach with scattered coconut palms, the resort—fashioned after the palaces of the great 14th-century Hindu kingdom of Vijayanagar—straddles the slender Mobor peninsula where the Sal River flows into the sea. Most of the accommodations are in an expansive "pavilion," all with views overlooking the lagoon—an unfortunate use of the superb location. No doubt you'd much rather face the Arabian Sea (as you can at most rooms at the Taj Exotica and InterContinental).

Cavelossim, Mobor, Goa 403 731. © **0832/287-1234.** Fax 0832/287-1352. www.ghmhotels.com. 152 units. Apr 1–Sept 30, Oct 1–Dec 27, Dec 28–Jan 2: $165/$320/$420 pavilion double; $275/$495/$715 lagoon suite; $330/$540/$880 lagoon deluxe suite; $605/$1,155/$1,980 royal villa; $1,595/$2,200/$3,300 presidential villa. AE, MC, V. **Amenities:** 4 restaurants; 4 bars; casino; pool; children's pool; 12-hole golf course; tennis courts; health club; Ayurvedic spa; watersports; yoga; children's activity center; travel desk; airport transfers; shopping arcade; salon; 24-hr. room service; babysitting; laundry; dry cleaning; doctor-on-call; valet. *In room:* A/C, TV, VCR, hi-fi with DVD player, dataport, tea- and coffee-making facilities, hair dryer, iron on request, electronic safe.

Taj Exotica Goa ✸✸   Packing much the same punch as The Leela, this resort features lovely surrounds (23 hectares/56 acres of landscaped gardens with 36 varieties of hibiscus trees), great accommodations, warm service, and a kick-ass beach that might as well be private. It's not as expensive as The Leela (it may look cheaper during the monsoon season, but most of the year you're looking at about $100 to $150 more for a comparable room), and even the cheapest "deluxe" guest rooms are spacious, with large picture windows and private patios or balconies. Ask for one on the ground floor—these are accessed via their own garden areas. The private villas are ideal if you don't want to be in the main block, which looks something like a large Portuguese hacienda—specify a sea-facing room for a sea view (the cheaper villas have garden views). The sunset pool villas have all been recently upgraded and have private plunge pools—plus, the main pool is large and inviting. Another good reason to book here is **Alegria,** where the most delicious home-cooked Goan, Portuguese, and Hindu Goan Saraswat meals are prepared. Mainstay dishes include *komdeche lomin* (gently spiced grilled chicken), *sungtachi koddi* (prawns in a fragrant gravy of coconut milk and mild spices), *galinha cafreal* (chicken in garlic, fresh coriander, and ginger), and authentic Goan *sorpotel* (a spicy pork stew). Upstairs, **Miguel Arcanjo** makes some of the best pizzas in Goa.

Calwaddo, Benaulim, Salcete, Goa 403 716. © **0832/277-1234.** Fax 0832/277-1515. www.tajhotels.com. exotica. goa@tajhotels.com. 140 units. Sept 1–Dec 22, Jan 5–Oct 31, Dec 22–Jan 5: $270/$330/$445 garden-facing villa double, $295/$355/$470 deluxe sea-facing double, $370/$430/$545 luxury double; $320/$380/$495 sea-facing villa, $445/$505/$620 sunset pool villa, $700/$760/$1,100 luxury suite. $20 extra bed. Mandatory $115 per person Christmas Eve dinner and $250 New Year's Eve dinner. AE, MC, V. **Amenities:** 5 restaurants; 4 bars; pool with Jacuzzi; kids' pool; 9-hole pitch and putt golf course; 2 tennis courts; fitness center, Ayurvedic spa, yoga, aerobics; beach volleyball; jogging track; table tennis; pool tables; watersports; children's activity center; concierge; currency exchange; travel desk, car rental; complimentary airport transfers; helipad; shopping arcade; salon; 24-hr. room service; babysitting; doctor-on-call. *In room:* A/C, TV, minibar, tea- and coffee-making facilities, hair dryer, safe.

6

God's Own Country: Kerala & Lakshadweep

The god who made Kerala, according to a popular Malayali saying, had a green thumb. Indeed, India's most verdant state—rated by *National Geographic Traveler* as one of the world's 50 must-see destinations—is a paradisiacal landscape of palm-lined beaches, steamy jungles, plantation-covered hills, and tropical rivers and lakes. Visitors come here primarily to unwind and indulge; this is, after all, where succumbing to a therapeutic Ayurvedic massage is as mandatory as idling away an afternoon aboard a slowly drifting *kettuvallam,* or sipping coconut water under a tropical sun before taking in a wonderfully ritualized Kathakali dance. Eastward, the spice-scented Cardamom Hills and wild elephants of Periyar beckon, while a short flight west takes you to the little-known but sublime tropical reefs of the Lakshadweep islands. All of which make Kerala not just a must-see on your India itinerary, but a major destination in its own right.

A thin strip on the southwest coastline, sandwiched between the Lakshadweep Sea and the forested Western Ghats that define its border with Tamil Nadu to the east, Kerala covers a mere 1.3% of the country's total land area, yet its rich resources have long attracted visitors from across the oceans—it is in fact here that the first seafarers set foot on Indian soil. Legend has it that King Solomon's ships traded off the Malabar coast between 972 and 932 B.C., followed by the Phoenicians, Romans, Christians, Arabs, and Chinese, all of whom came to stock up on Malabar's monkeys, tigers, parrots, timber and, of course, the abundance of spices that were literally worth their weight in gold. Seafarers not only brought trade but built synagogues and churches in the emerging port cities, while an entirely Muslim population set up shop on the islands of Lakshadweep. Despite its religious cosmopolitanism (many locals will tell you they subscribe to both Hinduism and Christianity), Kerala's Hindu tradition is deeply engrained in daily life. Most temples do not permit non-Hindus to enter, but almost every month brings magnificent temple processions involving chanting devotees and squadrons of elephants adorned in flamboyant caparisons.

Contemporary Kerala was created in 1956 from the former princely states of Travancore, Kochi, and Malabar. Largely ruled by benevolent Maharajas who introduced social reforms emphasizing the provision of education and basic services, Kerala remains one of the most progressive, literate, and educated states in post-independence India. In 1957, it became the first place in the world to democratically elect a Communist government, and the first Indian state to introduce a family-planning program. Despite its high population density, Keralites have the country's highest life expectancy and the lowest infant mortality rates. Kerala is considered one of the cleanest and most peaceful parts of India,

Ayurveda: Kerala's Healing Balm

An ancient healing tradition that draws on 3,000 years of Vedic culture, Ayurveda is the subcontinent's traditional science of "life, vitality, health, and longevity" or, to tap into a more contemporary buzzphrase, "the science of well-being." Kerala has long been considered the home of Ayurveda, no doubt due to the abundance of herbal and medicinal plants that thrive in its tropical environment. You will find therapists, physicians, and commercial Ayurvedic shops selling roots, herbs, and bark throughout the state.

Renowned for its curative and rejuvenating powers (and a gift from no other than Lord Brahma), Ayurveda works on your physical, mental, and emotional well-being by rectifying any imbalances in the three *doshas*— *vata* (air), *pitta* (fire), and *kapha* (water)—that are believed to make up the human constitution. In fact, in one ancient tome on Ayurveda, the *Caraka Samhita,* it is stated that the mind, body, and soul are like a tripod, and that the world's continued existence relies on their combination.

It takes 5½ years of training to qualify as an Ayurvedic doctor, who is then able to prescribe the herbal remedies and related therapies. While much of what is practiced in Ayurvedic medicine has similarities to Western medical practice (the first 3 years of training in anatomy are basically the same), the most significant difference lies in the area of pharmacology, since Ayurvedic medicines are all natural. Some may scoff, but no one can deny the sheer pleasure of the treatments—Ayurveda will suit those skeptics who merely seek the ultimate in pampering, whether you opt for a soothing facial treatment, in which the face is massaged and steamed with herbal oils, or for an energizing full body massage performed with hands and feet (and often by several masseuses simultaneously). Skeptics take note: To truly experience the strange bliss and resultant high of Ayurveda, book a *sirodhara* treatment, wherein 5 to 6 liters of warm herbal oil (selected according to the body constitution) are poured steadily onto your "third eye" (the forehead) for the better part of an hour while (or after which) you are massaged—this is said to retard the aging process (by arresting the degeneration of cells) and to relieve the body of all stress.

No matter which balm you choose, you'll find that the well-practiced masseuses of Kerala will treat your body like a temple; for them, the massage or treatment is a spiritual exercise. Of course, it helps to know that your body is being worshipped when you're lying there in your birthday suit (note that in strict accordance with Indian piety, you will be assigned a same-sex therapist). Whatever its purported virtues and pleasures, Ayurveda lures thousands of Westerners to Kerala, which in turn sustains a thriving industry that puts food on the table for many people. For our selection of the best Ayurvedic resorts, see chapter 1.

a claim substantiated by its prosperity—the state remains a major source of India's bananas, rubber, coconuts, cashews, and ginger. While much of Kerala retains an untouched charm, this prosperity has a downside: A highly educated population has meant that many are unwilling to do menial jobs, creating extensive unemployment. Others head for the Gulf to seek their fortunes, returning with sufficient cash to tear down the traditional carved wood dwellings that so greatly characterize the region and replace them with "modern" status symbols. Many of these traditional homes have been bought and reassembled at top-notch resorts like Coconut Lagoon and Surya Samudra, a practice vilified as exploitative by Kerala native Arundhati Roy in her Booker Prize–winning *The God of Small Things*. Others applaud their preservation. For visitors, a stay in these *tharavadu* cottages is one of the most charming aspects of a trip to Kerala.

If you're interested in ancient history and grand temples, you should include a visit to neighboring Tamil Nadu or Karnataka, but if all you need is rejuvenation, head straight for Fort Cochin, then south to cruise the backwaters and wash up on some of the world's most beautiful beaches. "God's Own Country" is one tourist slogan that really does deliver.

1 Cochin (Kochi)

1,080km (670 miles) S of Mumbai

Cochin is not the capital of Kerala, but it is its most charming city, blessed with its own international airport and a relatively good infrastructure, making it the ideal gateway to the state. This has been the case since 1341, the year nature carved out Cochin's harbor with a massive flood. As a result, Cochin became the first port of call for Arabs, Chinese and, finally, European sea merchants, who sailed for barter into what came to be known as the "Queen of the Arabian Sea."

Lured by the promise of pepper, the Portuguese under Vasco da Gama arrived in 1500, and the Franciscan friars who accompanied the explorer Pedro Alvarez Cabral established a church and set about converting the locals. By 1553, the Maharaja of Cochin had granted permission for the construction of the first European fort in India, and what had been an obscure fishing hamlet became India's first European settlement. In 1663, Cochin fell to the Dutch, and then to the British in 1795. Each of these foreign influences left their mark, resulting in a distinctly Indo-European culture, most evident in the architecture.

Today, Cochin (or Kochi, as it has been renamed) comprises three distinct areas. Down at heel, but wonderfully atmospheric, the historic districts of Mattancherry and Fort Cochin lie on one of two peninsular arms that shield the Kochi harbor—this is where you should try to find accommodations and spend most of your time. Opposite it, on the mainland that creates the eastern peninsula, lies modern Ernakulam. Between the two are the islands, well connected to the mainland by bridges.

Fort Cochin, the oldest European settlement in India, retains an old-world charm. Its battlements no longer stand, but the combination of Portuguese, Dutch, Jewish, British, and local influences is evident in the tiled, steep-roofed bungalows that line its quaint streets, and it's home to the oldest synagogue in the Commonwealth. Plan to spend at least 2 nights in Cochin, enjoying its charming atmosphere and low-key sights at a lazy, relaxed pace. Take in a Kathakali performance, dig into the delectable seafood, enjoy a romantic sunset cruise around the harbor and, if you're at all interested in bargains in antiques, get ready to wade through stores packed with unexpected curiosities.

Kerala

Kasargode
Bekkal

KARNATAKA

17

Parassinikadavu
Kannur
(Cannanore)
Azhikode
Tellicherry
Mananthavady
Badagara
Kalpetta
Vythiri

UPPER & LOWER
WYANAD WILDLIFE
SANCTUARY

Sulthan
Bathery

Kozhikode
(Calicut)

KERALA

Mannarkkad

*Lakshadweep
Sea*

Ponnani
Shoranur
Palakkad
47

**TAMIL
NADU**

Guruvayur
Trissur

Irinjalakuda
Kodungallur
Angamali
Malayattur
Alwaye
Kaladi
Ernakulam
Thripunitra
Kochi
(Cochin)
Vaikom
Idukki

ERAVIKULAM
NATIONAL
PARK
Munnar

Periyar

CARDAMOM
HILLS

THE
BACKWATERS

Kottayam
Pirmed
Thekaddi

Kumarakom
Alappuzha
(Alleppey)
Sabarimala

PERIYAR
WILDLIFE
SANCTUARY

Kayamkulam
Aranmula
Karunagapalli

Achankovil

47

Kollam
(Quilon)

AGASTYA
HILLS

Varkala
**Thiruvananthapuram
(Trivandrum)**
Neyyar Dam
Kovalam
Somatheeram
Vizhinjam
47

Map inset

100 mi
100 km

N

New Delhi

India

Bay of
Bengal

KERALA

Lakshadweep inset

Cherbaniani Reef

Byramgore Reef

Amindivi Islands
Kadmat Is.
Bangaram Is.
Andrott Is.
Agatti Is.
Kavaratti Is.

Cannanore Islands
Kalpeni Is.
Suheli Is.

*Lakshadweep
Sea*

Minicoy Is.

Cochin (Kochi)

Bolgatty Island

Mulavukadu Rd.

16 Ferry Station

ERNAKULAM

Goods Station

Chitoor Rd.

Spices Board

Edapally Rd.

Kaloor-Kadavanthara Rd.

Banerji Road

Lissy Hospital Road

Stock Exchange

Veekshanam Rd.

Marine Drive

Shanmugham Rd.

Broadway

Market Rd.

Prabhu Rd.

Pullepaddy Rd.

Katrikadavu Rd.

Jews St.

M. G. Road

Gopalaprabhu Rd.

KSRTC Central Bus Station

Convent Rd.

Ammankovil Rd.

17

Mullassery Canal Rd.

Saleem Rajan Rd.

Main Ferry Station

ℹ️

T. D. Road

Hospital Rd.

Shiva Temple

Fore Shore Rd.

GANDHI NAGAR

Single Lane Rd.

Marat Rd.

M. G. Road

Warriom Rd.

Sahodaran Ayyappan Road

18 →

WDI 14th Cross Rd.

PANIMPILLY COLONY

Cochin Shipyard

Old Thevara Rd.

Air India

Panampilly Ave.

Alappat Rd.

K. P. Vallon Road

Willingdon Island

Bristow Rd.

15

M. G. Road

Kizhavana Rd.

ESSENTIALS

VISITOR INFORMATION   Kerala has perhaps the best tourism bureaus in India, and Cochin is no exception. In Ernakulam and on Willingdon Island, you will find the helpful **Kerala Tourism Development Corporation** (**KTDC,** Shanmugham Rd., Ernakulam; ℂ **0484/235-3234;** Willingdon Island branch near Taj Malabar Hotel; both daily 8am–7pm). The best one-stop place for info is probably the privately run **Tourist Desk Information Counter** (℃ **0484/237-1761;** daily 8am–6pm), located at Ernakulam's Main Boat Jetty. Be sure to pick up *Hello Cochin,* a bimonthly free booklet filled with useful contacts and information. If you're traveling farther afield and need general information, visit the **Government of India Tourist Office** (near the Taj Malabar, Willingdon Island; ℂ **0484/266-8352;** Mon–Fri 9am–5:30pm, Sat 9am–1pm). A **Tourism Information Counter** (℃ **0484/261-0113,** ext. 2105) at the airport is usually open for all arrivals.

GETTING THERE & AWAY   By Air   Kochi International Airport (℃ **0484/ 261-0115** or -0116) is one of India's best. It's located alongside National Highway 47, in Nedumbassery, which is 42km (26 miles) from the historic heart of Fort Cochin. There are flights to and from Mumbai, Delhi, Chennai, Goa, Lakshadweep, Kozhikode, Tiruchirappalli, Thiruvananthapuram, and Bangalore; international flights are mostly through the Middle East, with flights also arriving from Singapore, the Maldives, and Sri Lanka.

A prepaid taxi service into the city is available at the airport; transfers to Fort Cochin cost about Rs 590 ($13) plus Rs 10 (25¢) per piece of luggage. **Kerala Adventures** (29/1027A Vyttila; ℂ **98470-35627** or 93888-17544; touch@keralaadventures. com) operates a taxi service between the city and the airport (Rs 650/$14.80); e-mail them your arrival plans, and a taxi will be waiting for you, or look for them when you exit.

By Train   Cochin is well connected by rail to almost every part of India. Some of the journeys can be long and grueling, however, so check on times, or opt for train travel only within Kerala. Departing from Delhi, the biweekly (Tues and Sat) **Trivandrum Rajdhani** makes its way to Calicut, Cochin, and Trivandrum; this is one of the best connections in Kerala—some of the journey is very scenic but it's a punishing 48 hours if you start from Delhi.

Cochin has three principal railway stations: **Ernakulam Town Station** (℃ **0484/ 239-0920** or -5198), **Ernakulam Junction** (℃ **1364**), and Willingdon Island's **Cochin Harbour Railway Station** (℃ **0484/266-6050**); ask your hotel which is best to disembark from. The **computerized reservations office** is at the Junction Railway Station (Mon–Sat 8am–2pm and 2:15–8pm; Sun 8am–2pm).

By Road   Traveling around Kerala with a rented car and driver can be wonderful and exhilarating; there's plenty of natural beauty worth taking in. Compared with roads in other parts of India, Kerala's roads are in good shape. North of Cochin, coast-hugging National Highway 17 passes through Calicut and runs all the way to Mangalore in Karnataka. Traveling south between Cochin and the capital Trivandrum (6 hr.), National Highway 47 has been resurfaced in recent years, and the highway really spreads out for the popular segment between Cochin and the backwater town of Alleppey. For journeys between Tamil Nadu and Kerala, you can expect long but beautiful stretches along National Highway 47, which traverses hairpin mountain passes. Private and state buses connect Cochin with many cities and towns throughout South India; these provide something bordering on a theme-park experience, however, and have a reputation for thrill-ride speeds.

GETTING AROUND   By Taxi & Auto-Rickshaw   Speak to your hotel management about the most up-to-date rates. For the most part, it's best to negotiate a mutually agreeable fare before starting off; auto-rickshaws should charge around Rs 8 (20¢) for the first kilometer, with the rate dropping to Rs 4 (10¢) for each additional kilometer. For longer journeys, you'll be asked to pay for the return trip. Many auto-rickshaws will refuse to travel between Ernakulam and Fort Cochin; some drivers even pretend they've never heard of it. Taxicabs are reasonable, charging around double the auto-rickshaw rates: A one-way trip between Fort Cochin and Ernakulam should cost in the region of Rs 175 ($4).

Note that the New Mattancherry Bridge between Fort Cochin and Willingdon, built in 2001, charges a Rs 10 (25¢) toll for cars, jeeps, and vans.

By Ferry   The ferry is a quick, convenient, and cheap way to get between any of Kochi's main areas and to travel to any of the islands. Ernakulam's two most important jetties are the **Main Jetty** off Fore Shore Road, for services to Willingdon Island (about 15 min.), Fort Cochin (about 30 min.), and Vypeen; and **High Court Jetty** off Shanmugham Road, from where you can get to Bolgatty Island. Ferry services begin at 6am and continue until 9:30pm; fares are nominal.

GUIDED TOURS & TRAVEL AGENTS   Kerala Tourism Development Corporation (**KTDC,** Shanmugham Rd., Ernakulam; ✆ **0484/235-3234**) and the privately run **Tourist Desk** (Main Boat Jetty, Ernakulam; ✆ **0484/237-1761**) offer half-day boat cruises of Cochin as well as daily tours and longer *kettuvallam* houseboat cruises of the backwaters near Cochin. **Sita Travels** (Tharakan Building, M.G. Rd., Ravipuram, Ernakulam; ✆ **0484/236-3801** or 0484/237-4122; cok@sitaindia.com) is useful for private tours of the entire state; they can also help with booking arrangements. You can also tailor splendid packages to destinations all over Kerala through **Cox & Kings** (www.coxandkings.co.uk). The same company can arrange tours by train or with car and driver, as well as trips of varying duration on Kerala's famous backwater houseboats. Babu John of **Kerala Adventures** (✆ **98470-35627** or 93888-17544; fax 0484/230-7544; touch@keralaadventures.com) is a reliable local agent who has a fleet of vehicles for rent. He can customize itineraries and is well-versed in the needs of foreign clients, with all services provided at going rates. If you're the kind who doesn't plan ahead, you can even call Babu from the airport, request a pickup, and ask to be shown a few hotels in your preferred price range before deciding where to stay. The **Kerala Tourism Development Corporation Limited (KTDC)** offers a wide range of tours and packages to suit different budgets, but be aware that most of these will include accommodations at state-run hotels, which are of varying standards, usually on the poor side. For details and bookings, contact their central reservations in Trivandrum, the capital (Mascot Sq.; ✆ **0471/231-6736;** fax 0471/233-4780; www.ktdc.com; ktdc@vsnl.com; Mon–Sat 8am–6pm, Sun and public holidays 10am–4pm).

Contact **TourIndia Holidays** (31/670 Narayani Nivas, Sahodaran Ayyappan Rd., Vyttila, Kochi; ✆ **0484/238-9862;** fax 0484/238-9029; tourindia@asianetindia.com) for trekking in Periyar; they also arrange houseboat trips.

WHEN TO GO   The best time to visit Kerala is between mid-October and April, with December and January the most pleasant months, though many resorts charge

Homestays in Kerala

A homestay, in which you board with a local household, is a great way to immerse yourself in real Indian culture and hospitality. It is highly recommended as an alternative or addition to the one-size-fits-all hotel experience. Kerala has a number of homestay options, including the sublime **Tranquil Resorts** (see "In & Around Wyanad," later in the chapter), our favorite in all of India, as well as homestays in Periyar Wildlife Sanctuary and Kottayam and the backwaters. Check them out on **www.homestayskerala.com**, or call the agency **Homestay Kerala** at ✆ **0484/231-0324.**

accordingly, some even doubling their rates. The backwaters are best visited from mid-November to February, when the muggy heat and mosquitoes are less bothersome. From about August to May, caparisoned elephants take to the streets in spectacular festivals; by far the biggest festival is the Pooram Temple festival, which takes place in April/May in Thrissur (Trichur), 74km (46 miles) north of Cochin. Contact the tourist offices in Cochin (through whom you can reach almost any of the festivals) for exact dates.

FAST FACTS: Cochin

Airlines For the **Jet Airways city office** (Elmar Sq., M.G. Rd., Ravipuram, Ernakulam), call ✆ **0484/229-3231;** for the **airport counter,** call ✆ **0484/261-0037.** The **Indian Airlines city office** (Durbar Hall Rd., Ernakulam; ✆ **0484/237-1141**) is open Monday to Saturday 10am to 4:30pm; or call the **airport counter** at ✆ **0484/261-0101** or 0484/261-0041.

Ambulance Dial **101.**

Area Code The area code for **Cochin** is ✆ **0484.**

ATMs This is always the best way to get instant cash in Indian cities. Cochin now has several ATMs at which you can use your Visa or MasterCard, if it has been encoded in your home country.

Banks See "Currency Exchange," below.

Bookstores Both branches of **Idiom Books** are wonderful for a wide variety of books on India, its culture, and its literature. In Fort Cochin, the store is at the corner of Bastion and Quirose streets (✆ **0484/221-7075;** Mon–Sat 9am–9pm, Sun 9am–6pm). In Mattancherry, it's opposite the Boat Jetty on Jew Street (✆ **0484/222-5604;** daily 10am–6pm).

Car Hires & Taxis On average, you can expect to pay Rs 8 to Rs 10 (20¢–23¢) per kilometer for a car and driver. More expensive cars include air-conditioning, which will prove invaluable in Kerala's sultry climate. Also count on paying an overnight fee for each stopover. The **Government of India Tourist Office** (near Taj Malabar Hotel, Willingdon Island; ✆ **0484/266-8352;** Mon–Fri 9am–5:30pm, Sat 9am–1pm) has a fleet of vehicles. Also try: **Sita Travels** (Tharakan Building, M.G. Rd., Ernakulam; ✆ **0484/237-4122**) and **Kerala Adventures** (see "Guided Tours & Travel Agents," above).

Currency Exchange Your best option is **Thomas Cook** (M.G. Rd., Ernakulam; ℭ **0484/237-1337**; Mon–Sat 9:30am–6pm), which also has a branch at the airport (ℭ **0484/261-0052** or -0032). **Canara Bank** in Fort Cochin (Kunnumpuram Junction, Amaravathy Rd.; ℭ **0484/221-5467**; Mon–Fri 10am–2pm and 2:30–3:30pm, Sat 10am–noon) can exchange traveler's checks and give cash advances against your credit card. Also try **Standard Chartered** (M.G. Rd., Ernakulam; Mon–Fri 9:30am–4:30pm, Sat till 1pm).

Drugstores **Medilab** (Doraiswamy Iyer Rd., Ernakulam; ℭ **0484/236-8963**) is open around the clock.

Emergencies For fires and other emergencies, including medical services, call ℭ **101.**

Hospitals In Ernakulam, head for **Medical Trust Hospital** (M.G. Rd.; ℭ **0484/ 235-8001**) or **Lissy Hospital** (Lissy Junction; ℭ **0484/240-2668**). If you have a medical emergency in Fort Cochin, your hotel should be able to organize good medical assistance.

Internet Access Cochin has plenty of Internet cafes. These generally charge more than any of the options in Ernakulam. **Call'n'Fax/Shop'n'Save** (Princess St.; ℭ **0484/221-5438**; Mon–Sat 8am–10pm, Sun 9am–10pm) charges Rs 40 (90¢) per hour.

Police Dial ℭ **100.**

Post Office In Ernakulam, use the **General Post Office** on Hospital Road. The **Kochi Head Post Office is** in Fort Cochin (behind St. Francis Church).

Website Visit **www.keralatourism.org** for up-to-date information.

WHAT TO SEE & DO

Lazy and laid-back, Fort Cochin offers a tranquillity that is in complete contrast to the heaving city experience of Ernakulam, which is ultimately missable. Comprising **Mattancherry** and **Jew Town,** Fort Cochin has a historic atmosphere—it is, after all, a town where 14 different languages are spoken, and tumbled-down mansions line narrow ancient lanes. Near the water's edge, old warehouses (or *godowns*) are filled with the state's treasured cash crops—pepper, tea, Ayurvedic herbs, whole ginger, and betel nuts—being dried, sorted, and prepared for direct sale or auction. The area is wonderful for historic walks, particularly into Jew Town, which hosts a community that dates back to the 1st century A.D. and was augmented during the 16th century when the Inquisition brought a fresh wave of Jewish immigrants here. Today only a handful of aging "white Jewish" families remain in Cochin, but their residential quarter retains a charming ambience, with cobbled streets and fascinating antiques shops and spice markets.

Man-made **Willingdon Island,** a short ferry ride or bridge journey away, was created in the 20th century by large-scale dredging. There are several good hotels here, but the island is primarily concerned with naval and commercial port activity and is not worth visiting unless you're based here. **Bolgatty Island,** reached by ferry, is of no interest other than the rather lovely palace, which has been converted into a government-run hotel.

EXPLORING FORT COCHIN ON FOOT

Start your tour at the harbor near Vasco da Gama Square, where you can watch fishermen hoisting their catch from the cantilevered **Chinese fishing nets** that line the shore, then head along Church Road to **St. Francis Church.** Keep going toward Parade Road (near the Malabar House Residency; see "Where to Stay," below), making a left onto **Peter Celli Street** to explore a few local shops before you drift down Bastion Street, in the direction of **Santa Cruz Cathedral.** Then head back toward Princess Street, where you can see **Koder House.** Built in 1808 by Jewish patriarch Samuel Koder, this is a good example of the hybrid Indo-European style that developed in Cochin. It's still occupied, so you'll have to appreciate it from the sidewalk. On the same road, the **Pierce Leslie Bungalow** is a charming 19th-century mansion reflecting Portuguese and Dutch influences on local architecture. Take a break at **Kashi Art Café** (Burgher St.; ✆ **0484/221-5769**), where the food and service are uninspired but the contemporary art and vibrant atmosphere provide a colorful contrast to the historic surroundings. Afterwards, catch an auto-rickshaw to Mattancherry, where you should visit **Mattancherry (Dutch) Palace** and **Paradesi Synagogue** (see below) before discovering the fragrant scents of Kerala's **spice warehouses.** Make time to visit a few of the antiques warehouses, and don't be put off by the layers of dust and grime—there are some real treasures to be found. End your day full circle with a **sunset cruise** ✿✿✿ around the harbor; this is the best way to enjoy the most-photographed of Cochin's historic sights, the Chinese fishing nets that form wonderful silhouettes against a red- and orange-hued sky.

Chinese Fishing Nets ✿✿

Said to have been introduced by traders from the court of Kublai Khan, these cantilevered nets, set up on teak and bamboo poles, are physical remnants of Fort Cochin's ancient trade with the Far East. Fishermen work the nets all day long, lowering them into the water and then hauling them up using a remarkably efficient pulley system. The best place to watch them at work is from **Vasco da Gama Square** or from a boat at sunset. Nearby, the Indo-European **Bastion Bungalow** (now the official residence of the Sub Collector) dates back to 1667; built on the site of the old Dutch Fort's Stromberg Bastion, it is believed to stand above a network of secret tunnels.

Vasco da Gama Sq. is on the water's edge along River Rd.

Mattancherry Palace ✿✿

Also known as the Dutch Palace, this large two-story 16th-century building was actually built by the Portuguese, who gave it to the Raja of Cochin as thanks for trading rights and favors granted to them. When the Dutch claimed Cochin in 1663, they took control of the palace and gave it a makeover. The large two-story building with its sloping roofs and pale walls is now a shadow of what it must have once been. Part of it is open to visitors, and displays include a collection of coronation robes, palanquins, and royal family portraits, but the real reason to visit is to view the bedroom chamber, where vibrant murals, executed in vivid red, green, and yellow ocher, are truly exquisite. Particularly notable are erotic scenes of the divine lover, Krishna, surrounded by enraptured female figures. Vishnu, Shiva, and various Hindu deities fill the large walls, their eyes wide and bodies full. These are among the first examples of a school of painting specific to Kerala.

Palace Rd., Mattancherry. Admission Rs 2 (5¢). No photography. Sat–Thurs 10am–5pm.

Paradesi Synagogue ✿✿✿

Cochin's first Jewish settlers arrived from Yemen and Babylon as early as A.D. 52; this—the oldest synagogue in the Commonwealth—was originally built 1,500 years later. Set in a corner of Jew Town and rather hemmed in by other buildings, with only the 18th-century clock tower visible from the outside, it must be entered before you can view its most interesting feature: the beautiful blue-and-white Cantonese ceramic floor tiles—each individual tile hand-painted, so no two are alike. Above, glorious Belgian chandeliers dangle from the ceiling. At one end of the hall, old Torah scrolls are kept behind the gilded doors of the holy tabernacle.

At press time, only a handful of Jews were living in Cochin, though they uphold the traditions of their ancestors, and the synagogue is moving testament to the effects of the Diaspora. The number remaining are not enough to form a *minyan* (the number of men needed to sustain a synagogue), so Jews from outlying areas travel to Cochin to worship in this historic Judaic monument. The synagogue elders are understandably concerned about tourist numbers, and numerous signs warn that NO ONE IS ALLOWED UPSTAIRS, NO ONE IS ALLOWED INSIDE THE PULPIT, and NO ONE IS ALLOWED TO TOUCH ANYTHING.

Jew Town Rd., Mattancherry. Admission Rs 2 (5¢). No video. Sun–Thurs 10am–noon and 3–5pm; closed for Jewish holidays.

St. Francis Church ✿   India's earliest European church was originally constructed in wood, but this was replaced by a stone structure in 1546. It was also originally Roman Catholic, but under the British it became Anglican. Vasco da Gama was originally buried here when he died in Cochin on Christmas Eve, 1524; although his body was later moved to Lisbon, he is still memorialized here with a tombstone. Having passed through the hands of Franciscan friars, Dutch Protestants, and Anglicans, the presiding Church of South India continues to hold its services here every morning at 8am. Note that, as at Hindu temples and Muslim mosques, you are required to remove your shoes before entering.

Church St., Fort Cochin. Mon–Sat 9:30am–5pm; Sun 9:30am–noon.

Santa Cruz Basilica ✿   Pope Paul IV elevated this Portuguese church to a cathedral in 1558, but the original building was destroyed by the British in 1795. A new building was commissioned on the same site in 1887; it was declared a basilica in 1984 by Pope John Paul II. The basilica's interiors are worth a look, especially the

---

Black Gold

In Kerala, pepper is still referred to as *karuthu ponnu,* or "black gold," and represents the backbone of the state's international spice trade. Although the furious trade around spices has subsided considerably these days, the sorting houses, warehouses, and auction houses from which these valuable products find their way to the rest of the world still operate in much the same way they have for centuries (though given the current crises surrounding many of the traditional cash crops, there is a possibility that these side-street sights will not be around forever). Ask your guide or auto-rickshaw driver to take you to the ginger, black pepper, betel nut, and Ayurvedic medicine warehouses, reminiscent of Salman Rushdie's *The Moor's Last Sigh;* or head for the **Kochi International Pepper Exchange** (Jew Town Rd., Mattancherry), which you can visit from Monday to Saturday (10am–5pm) to see Kerala's black gold being furiously sold off to the highest bidder. Call ✆ **0484/222-4263** to organize a pass.

caryatids and exquisite stained glass. If the basilica is closed, ask the priest, who lives in the same complex, if he will open it for you.

Parade Rd. and K. B. Jacob Rd., near Bastion St., Fort Cochin. www.sanatcruzbasilica.org. Mon–Sat 9:30am–5pm; Sun morning Mass only.

WHERE TO STAY

The best area to stay is Fort Cochin. Alternatively, opt for Willingdon Island or Vypeen Island, just across the bay. Ernakulam is a busy, rather ugly city but it does have more affordable accommodations, and Fort Cochin is then a short, pleasant ferry journey away. *A general note of caution:* If you plan to be in Cochin in December or January, be sure to book well in advance.

If you don't mind being far from the ambience of Fort Cochin and the harbor, a truly upscale option is the new **Le Meridien** (NH 47 Bypass, Kundannur Junction, Kochi 682 304; ✆ **0484/270-5777** or -5451; from $175). Guests have access to a superb range of resort facilities and services, including a top-rated Ayurvedic spa—check it out on www.cochin.lemeridien.com. If, on the other hand, you want a budget to mid-range option, and everything in Fort Cochin is full, consider a stay on Vypeen Island, where you can get quality Ayurvedic massages at laid-back **Cherai Beach Resorts** ✯, 30km (18 miles) north of Cochin by road, or 15km (9⅓ miles) from the Vypeen jetty. Offering both beach and backwaters, this is a good option for those in search of a little relaxation. Ask for a heritage cottage with an open-air bathroom and patio on stilts overlooking the backwaters. Although the newer rooms are sleeker, they lack the charm of the heritage cottages, with their bamboo and canework. The resort is simple, but the Ayurvedic rejuvenation massages are excellent, and you get decent Kerala food. Staff are helpful and friendly. The rate offers very good value (✆ **0484/ 248-1818** or 0484/241-6949; www.cheraibeachresorts.com; Rs 1,000–Rs 4,000/ $23–$90).

Note: The prices below are sometimes given in rupees, with U.S. dollar conversions. But a number of others are given in U.S. dollars only or in euros with U.S. dollar conversions—which is how hotels targeting foreign markets quote their rates.

FORT COCHIN

If you're on a tight budget, consider **Spencer's Tourist Home** (Parade Rd.; ✆ **0484/ 221-5049;** spencerhomestay@rediffmail.com), which has rooms with attached bathrooms for Rs 400 to Rs 1,000 ($9.10–$23). Located in a lovely 300-year-old house with a shared sitting room and a garden, its guest rooms are spotlessly clean and spacious, and the beds are comfortable.

The Brunton Boatyard Hotel ✯✯✯   Situated at the water's edge on the site of a bustling boatyard, this is considered by most to be Fort Cochin's most elegant hotel. A smart whitewashed colonial warehouse-style building with sloping tiled roofs, deep verandas, and terra-cotta floors set around a large open grassy courtyard, Brunton certainly captures the gracious ambience of a bygone era. An open-plan lobby—decked out with a billiards table, antique furniture, and overhead fans—spills into spacious passages that lead to the guest rooms, all of which overlook the busy harbor. Each room has its own balcony from which to enjoy views of the fishing boats and ferries that cruise between the islands; those on the second floor are better for views. Original and reproduction antiques include typical Kerala four-poster beds, high enough off the ground to make the footstools a necessity. A sunset cruise from the hotel's own jetty is a great way to kick off the evening. The only possible drawback to staying here is the hotel's proximity to the boatyard—you are literally berthed steps away from the very active waterways, though others may argue that the low-level soundtrack lends an air of authenticity.

Near Aspinwall, Calvathy, Fort Cochin. ✆ **0484/221-5461,** -5462, -5463, -5464, –5465, or 0484/221-5557. Fax 0484/221-5562. bruntonboatyard@cghearth.com. www.cghearth.com. 26 units. $260–$280 sea-facing double; $360–$410 deluxe suite. $40 extra person. Rates include breakfast. AE, DC, MC, V. **Amenities:** 2 restaurants; bar; tea lounge; pool; Ayurvedic center; sunset cruise; boat rental; car hire; business facilities; shop; room service; laundry; doctor-on-call. *In room:* A/C, TV, minibar, hair dryer, scale, electronic safe. Suites include personal butler, kitchenette.

Fort Heritage ✿

This small heritage hotel, built by the Dutch East India Company in 1668, features huge, airy, simple guest rooms. The rooms have teak ceilings and floors and both traditional and antique furniture, as well as attached bathrooms and modern amenities. Ask for an upstairs room, preferably with air-conditioning and a private balcony. There are two double suites in a newer building, but avoid these— they lack atmosphere and are rather dowdy. After a full day of sightseeing, you can return for a wonderful Ayurvedic massage and steam bath. Or relax in the lovely upstairs lounge, where there's a romantic swing and chaise longue in which you can curl up with a book from the small library. Fresh, local seafood is served in the **Heritage Zone** restaurant. Service is patchy, but the rates are great.

1/283 Napier St., Elphinstone Rd., Fort Cochin. ✆ **0484/221-5333,** -6901, or -5455. Fax 0484/221-5333. www.fortheritage.com. 12 units. $59 heritage double; $85 deluxe suite. $10 extra bed. Rates include breakfast and taxes. AE, DC, MC, V. **Amenities:** Restaurant; steam; Internet access; houseboat hire; travel assistance; sightseeing arrangements; car hire; Ayurvedic massage; laundry; doctor-on-call. *In room:* A/C, TV.

The Fort House ✿ *Value*

The best features of this small budget hotel are undoubtedly its location right on the waterfront—it even has a private jetty and a boat—and its homey, laid-back atmosphere, centered around a garden with pleasant outdoor seating. You can request to dine on the jetty, or sit there all day watching the world go by. Standard veranda rooms are clean and basic, and beds have mosquito nets; bamboo rooms are more atmospheric and, in typical traditional Kerala style, dimly lit. There's a pleasant cafe, but you are welcome to buy your own fish and vegetables and ask that the cook prepare them—or even try your hand at experimenting with owner Nova Thomas's Portuguese-inspired recipes. Local guides and sightseeing can be arranged, and an in-house tailor can whip up casual clothing in a matter of hours at incredibly low prices. Though it has no pool, Fort House has an arrangement with Malabar House that allows guests to swim there for a Rs 200 ($4.55) fee. Bottom line: What Fort House lacks in amenities and heritage, it makes up for in price.

2/6 A, Calvathy Rd., Cochin 682 001. ✆ **0484/221-7103** or 989/519-6236. www.forthousecochin.com. fort_hs@yahoo.com. 9 units. Rs 1,400–Rs 1,800 ($32–$43) A/C double, Rs 950–Rs 1,200 ($22–$27) non-A/C double. Rates include breakfast. No credit cards. **Amenities:** Restaurant; travel desk; boat rental; room service; babysitting on request; laundry and dry cleaning; doctor-on-call. *In room:* A/C (2 rooms only).

Malabar House Residency ✿✿✿ *Value*

Bright, vibrant colors infuse this 18th-century mansion with a contemporary edge, creating a boutique hotel that is charmingly arty without being pretentious. Conceived, converted, and run by Joerg Drechsel and his Basque wife, Txuku, Malabar House is a chunky white colonial British bungalow at the edge of the Parade Maidan, a grassy expanse for schoolboy cricketers and frolicking goats. Its *tharavadu*-style sloping terra-cotta roof is typically Keralan, while the tropical inner courtyard (trees, potted shrubs, and stone pathways) features a lovely plunge pool, wooden foldaway chairs, a small open-air theater area, and a covered restaurant. Rooms feature waxed black Kadapa stone floors offset by bright red or yellow walls and, in some rooms, a hint of turquoise. Each contains a selection of paintings, sculptures, and period furniture reflecting the cultural heritage of Kerala, while the beds, solid in every sense, are made from carved teak and rosewood. Discarded pillars from traditional 18th-century Tamil Nadu houses up the atmosphere ante and dramatically enhance the use of space in the generous suites. Five of the (marginally more) expensive guest suites have private roof gardens—these are the best on offer in the main house; alternatively, book room no. 4. Best of all, book a room in the **Trinity** annex just across the street, with its own plunge pool and sun deck—it's worth every penny, with tasteful designs and probably the best bathrooms in Cochin (large, open-air, beautifully painted, with sunken zinc shower, plants, flowers, and a *shivalingam,* a carved stone phallic symbol). Although you don't have views of the harbor, this hotel is better value than Brunton and scores high on privacy, class, and tranquillity. And if this doesn't convert you, it was also the first operation in India to be certified by Green Globe, the global environmental certification program for travel and tourism.

1/268, 1/269 Parade Rd., Fort Cochin 682 001. ℂ **0484/221-6666.** Fax 0484/221-7777. www.malabarhouse.com. 17 units. 110€–210€ ($136–$260) deluxe double; 175€–325€ ($217–$404) Malabar suite; 145€–275€ ($180–$343) roof garden suite. 25€ ($31) extra bed. Rates include breakfast. AE, MC, V. **Amenities:** Restaurant; pool; Ayurvedic spa; bicycles; boat rental; airline bookings; travel desk; car hire; currency exchange; boutique; 24-hr. room service; babysitting (with prior notice); laundry; doctor-on-call; tailor. *In room:* A/C, TV, mosquito net.

The Old Courtyard ⭐   This pleasant, intimate heritage hotel, located in the heart of Fort Cochin's quiet back streets, is well maintained, and accommodations are generally well priced. Each of the eight guest rooms in the 200-year-old Portuguese mansion is different, but all have wooden floors and high beamed ceilings, and most are furnished largely with antique furniture. The rooms are located in wings that lead off a central cobblestone courtyard, which has its own working well. Adjacent to the courtyard is a semi-enclosed restaurant serving a wide range of cuisines; traditional dances are performed here during the season. Premium rooms and suites have lovely original Portuguese four-poster beds and large, clean bathrooms (the cheapest room is strictly for bargain-hunters). A good option if you're looking for a heritage atmosphere, but service is a drawback.

1/371–372 Princess St., Fort Cochin 682 001. ℂ **0484/221-6302.** www.oldcourtyard.com. 8 units. Rs 2,000 ($46) regular non-A/C double, Rs 3,000 ($68) superior non-A/C double, Rs 3,500 ($80) premium non-A/C double, Rs 4,000 ($91) superior A/C double, Rs 4,500 ($103) premium A/C double; Rs 4,500 ($103) suite. Rs 500–Rs 750 ($12–$17) extra bed. Children under 12 free in parent's room. MC, V. **Amenities:** Restaurant; cultural performances; travel assistance; airport transfers; currency exchange; laundry; doctor-on-call; small book collection.

WILLINGDON ISLAND

A good option if those hotels below or in Fort Cochin are full is Willingdon's **Casino Hotel** (ℂ **0484/266-8221** or -8421; www.cghearth.com; from $90 double, rate includes breakfast). The name may set off alarm bells, suggesting as it does Las Vegas–style showgirls, but the atmosphere of this 1950s hotel is decidedly tame. The Casino has good facilities, staff are hospitable, and accommodations, though nothing to write home about, are clean, relatively spacious, and convenient—the nearest jetty for the harbor ferry to either Fort Cochin or Ernakulam is just over 1km (a half-mile) away.

Taj Malabar ⭐⭐   A hostel built for those traveling by steamship from England is today the Heritage Wing of Willingdon's only waterfront hotel, an elegant property that includes a more contemporary (and less desirable) pagoda-style low-rise Tower Wing. The generously proportioned Heritage Wing rooms feature wood floors,

period-style furniture, and assorted knickknacks—make sure to book one with a view of the channel. The chic Ayurvedic center in the Tamara spa occupies its own traditional-style building overlooking the gorgeous rim-flow pool. Enjoy sunset drinks on the pool deck or on one of the hotel's daily harbor cruises. Or—for those who prefer privacy—book *Cinnamon Coast,* the private yacht available for hire. Note that the Taj Malabar has two excellent restaurants (see "Where to Dine," below).

Willingdon Island, Cochin 682 009. ⓒ 0484/266-6811 or -8010. Fax 0484/266-8297. www.tajhotels.com. malabar. cochin@tajhotels.com. 96 units. Tower Wing: $180 superior double, $205 superior sea-view double, $230 deluxe sunset-view double; $325 executive suite. Heritage Wing: $180 superior double, $230 superior sea-view double; $375 deluxe suite. AE, MC, V. **Amenities:** 4 restaurants; bar; pool; gym; Jacuzzi; Ayurvedic center; travel desk; sightseeing; car hire; boat rental; business center; Wi-Fi enabled; currency exchange; salon; florist; 24-hr. room service; babysitting; laundry; doctor-on-call; valet service. *In room:* A/C, TV, minibar, tea- and coffee-making facility, hair dryer, electronic safe.

Trident Hilton Cochin ⓡ   This upmarket business hotel is quiet, tasteful, and replete with modern conveniences. Conceived by a Thai architect, the design blends Kerala and Thai elements, and the hotel has the ambience of a large villa. Accommodations surround a pleasant courtyard where you can swim in the pool and dine alfresco. Traditional artifacts and ornaments have been used to capture the ethos of Kerala; wooden cooking implements and earthenware pots converted into lamps adorn the walls, while the entrance is dominated by a giant *uruli* cooking pot mounted on old black-and-gold snake-boat prows. The modestly sized guest rooms have wooden floors and blue-and-beige decor and furnishings; bathrooms are small with marble surfaces.

Bristow Rd., Willingdon Island, Cochin 682 003, Kerala. ⓒ 0484/266-9595 or -6816. Fax 0484/266-9393. www. trident-hilton.com. cochin@trident-hilton.com. 85 units. $160 superior double; $265 suite. Ask for daily rates. AE, DC, MC, V. **Amenities:** 2 restaurants; bar; pool; gym; travel desk; sightseeing; car hire; business center; Wi-Fi enabled; currency exchange; gift shop; book shop; salon; 24-hr. room service; babysitting; laundry valet service. *In room:* A/C, TV, dataport, minibar, tea- and coffee-making facility, hair dryer, electronic safe.

ERNAKULAM

If you can't get a room at Fort Cochin or Willingdon Island, the following Ernakulam options are worth considering, but do note that all these are far from the main sights. **Avenue Regent** (39/2026 Mahatma Gandhi Rd.; ⓒ 0484/237-7977 or -7688; www. avenueregent.com; from Rs 2,900/$66 double) is a spruce six-floor business hotel located on a busy, noisy main road. Guest rooms are fairly large, with dull Western-style decor, potted palm trees, an abundance of floral fabric, and rather soft mattresses. Note that the same owners have opened the smart new **Avenue Center Hotel** in an attractive white neo-colonial building (Panampilly Ave., Panampilly Nagar, Ernakulam; ⓒ 0484/231-5301 or -5302; fax 0484/231-5304; www.avenuecenter.com), where doubles are Rs 1,600 ($37) and up. **The Woods Manor** (Woodlands Junction, Mahatma Gandhi Rd.; ⓒ 0484/238-2055 through -2059; www.thewoodsmanor. com; Rs 2,277–Rs 3,440/$52–$78 double, includes breakfast) is another neat, clean hotel. Set in the center of Ernakulam on a busy street, it has no views (but a great rooftop pool). The sixth-floor "Kerala" guest rooms are centrally air-conditioned. Beds have firm mattresses; the smallish attached bathrooms have small tubs. The hotel is well-located for the railway station and has a 24-hour check-out policy. The **Grand** (Mahatma Gandhi Rd., Ernakulam 682 011; ⓒ 0484/238-2061 or 0484/236-6833; www.grandhotelkerala.com; Rs 1,600–Rs 2,800/$37–$64 double) is Ernakulam's oldest hotel, but ongoing renovations (begun in 1998) have slowly brought improvements. Deluxe rooms have balconies and large black marble bathrooms. Popular with locals, the Grandeura Bar gets busy in the evenings.

Taj Residency $\mathcal{R}$ If you are going to stay in Ernakulam for business reasons, this luxury business hotel, which sits right on the harbor's edge and has its own jetty, is by far the best option. At press time the hotel was being given a major overhaul for a brighter, trendier look, but you should still make sure to book a harbor-view room. Also overlooking Cochin's busy port is the popular **Bubble Café,** a cheerful eatery on a glass-enclosed terrace with tables arranged around a brightly tiled fountain mosaic; or come around sunset and order a drink at the **Harbour View** bar.

Marine Dr., Ernakulam, Cochin 682 011. © **0484/237-1471.** Fax 0484/236-5161. www.tajhotels.com. residency.ernakulam@tajhotels.com. 108 units. $120 standard double, $130 harbor-facing double, $135 sea-facing double; $145 residency (includes breakfast), $200 junior suite (includes breakfast). $20 extra bed. AE, DC, MC, V. **Amenities:** 2 restaurants; patisserie; bar; fitness center; boat rental; sunset cruises; travel desk; car hire; business center; currency exchange; shops; florist; 24-hr. room service; babysitting; laundry; dry cleaning; doctor-on-call. *In room:* A/C, TV, mini-bar, tea- and coffee-making facilities.

BOLGATTY ISLAND

Bolgatty Palace $\mathcal{R}$ Built in 1744 by a Dutch trader and later used as the British Residency, this government-run hotel occupies 6 hectares (15 acres) of the southern tip of Bolgatty Island. Accessible only by ferry, the setting here is quite lovely, if a little inconvenient for sightseeing and exploring. Most guest rooms are situated in the Kerala courtyard–style Nalukettu Wing, pleasantly refurbished to blend well with the original palace. Accommodations are spacious, with high ceilings, wood furniture, bathtubs, and balconies with sea views. Rather pretentiously named after Dutch master painters—Vermeer, van Gogh, Rembrandt, and others—the massive suites in the original palace mansion have dark teak ceiling beams, reproduction period furniture, large beds, and thick drapery; bathrooms are enormous and have bidets, tubs, and separate glass-enclosed showers. Avoid the "honeymoon cottages" on stilts at the water's edge; these show signs of damp and disrepair. Kathakali performances, presented by the Bolgatty Performing Arts Centre, are held each night.

Bolgatty Island, Mulavukadu, Kochi 682 504, Kerala. © **0484/275-0500** or -0600. Fax 0484/275-0457. bolgatty@vsnl.com. www.ktdc.com. 26 units. Rs 2,700–Rs 3,450 ($62–$78) waterfront cottage double, Rs 3,000–Rs 4,250 ($68–$97) deluxe double; Rs 4,000–Rs 5,250 ($91–$120) executive suite, Rs 5,500–Rs 7,250 ($126–$165) palace suite. Rates include breakfast and dinner. AE, DC, MC, V. **Amenities:** Restaurant; beer parlor; pool; golf course; indoor recreation room; Ayurvedic center; travel assistance; backwater cruise; speedboat; conferencing; board room; currency exchange; limited room service. *In room:* A/C, TV, hair dryer on request.

WHERE TO DINE

Kochi's best eating establishments are located in the hotels at Fort Cochin and Willingdon. Seafood, always fresh and wonderful, is generally what you should order. Have protection against mosquitoes ready, particularly in outdoor restaurants, where nighttime attacks can be incessant.

Fort Cochin $\mathcal{RRR}$ SEAFOOD   Considered one of the state's best seafood restaurants, this casual catch-of-the-day semi-alfresco pad is something of a Kerala institution. The atmosphere is charmingly rustic: The excellent food is prepared at an open grill adjacent to a large waist-level fish tank filled with Chinese carp. Tables are set around a huge banyan tree and under light shades made from Chinese fishing baskets. Choose from a range of freshly caught seafood displayed on a cart that makes its way from table to table, and decide how you would like it prepared—grilled whole with heaps of spices, or delicately sliced with subtle herbs; the obliging maitre d' will help you make up your mind. The popular mixed-seafood platter is a selection of grilled fish, tiger prawns, and other shellfish. Call ahead after 4pm to hear what's on the evening cart.

A Traditional Keralite Feast

Don't pass up the opportunity to enjoy a traditional *sadhya* feast while in Kerala. This multicourse festive-occasion feast, served on a plantain leaf, will give you a very good overview of the state's cuisine. Expect rice and ghee (unclarified butter), served with various stews and curries with names like *sambar, rasam, kootu, pacchadi, appalam,* and *payasam,* all of which will be heaped endlessly upon your *ela* (leaf). Seafood in Kerala is exquisite and plentiful. A popular dish is *meen moilee,* a delicate fish curry tempered with fresh coconut milk. Coconut is a staple used in many dishes: *Avial* is a mixed-vegetable curry prepared with coconut, cumin, and turmeric; and *aadu olathiyathu* is a coconut-based curry made with cubes of fried mutton. A steamed rice pancake known as *appam* is very popular and is served with stew.

Casino Hotel, K.P.K. Menon Rd., Willingdon Island. © 0484/266-8221 or -8421. Prices determined on the day and by weight. Mixed-seafood platter Rs 875 ($20). AE, DC, MC, V. Daily 7–11:45pm.

The History & Terrace Grill ✸✸✸ KERALITE   The Terrace Grill, the alfresco section of the superb upstairs restaurant at Brunton Boatyard, serves only seafood platters with assorted lobster, tiger prawns, scampi, shrimp, squid, and catch of the day. Inside, The History serves seafood platters but also has seven cyclical menus that rotate through the week, depending on guest preferences. Most of the recipes are local, many borrowed from the kitchens of Cochin families. Depending on which day of the week you go, you could start with mildly spiced and steamed tiger prawns served with mango chutney, followed by *meen pollichathu*—fish marinated with shallots and spices, wrapped in a banana leaf, and grilled. Another lovely fish dish is *chuttulli meen,* marinated according to a local Jewish recipe in pearl onions and green spices. *Kuttanadan konju* is a delicious, slightly sour curry of king prawns cooked in fenugreek, kokum berries, and coconut milk. If you've had your fill of seafood, try *tharavupiralan,* tender duck cooked in onion and tomato and finished with coconut milk, which is not overly spicy. Another specialty is *Chuttirachi,* chunks of lamb cooked in a mixture of shallots and spices; it was first prepared by Jew Town's Hallugua family.

The Brunton Boatyard Hotel, 1/498 Fort Cochin, Kochi 682 001. © 0484/221-5461 through -0465. Main courses Rs 275–Rs 450 ($6.25–$10). AE, DC, MC, V. Daily 7:30–10:30pm.

Malabar Junction ✸✸ MALABAR-MEDITERRANEAN FUSION   Cochin's Malabar House Residency is the setting for this fine, sophisticated alfresco restaurant where guests sit in a small area covered by a ceiling of traditional Kerala woodwork, watching (at night) a performance on the adjacent stage. Start off with crispy fried prawns tempura, then have fish curry Malabar, which is rather mild for local tastes (if you prefer it spicy, say so). Chef Suresh also makes good seafood salads and pastas as well as a delicious tuna tartare.

Malabar House Residency, 1/268–1/269 Parade Rd., Fort Cochin. © 0484/221-6666. Menu changes regularly, but expect to pay Rs 250–Rs 550 ($5.70–$13) for a main course, Rs 850 ($19) for a seafood platter. AE, DC, MC, V. Daily 7–10:30am, noon–3pm, and 7–10:30pm.

Rice Boat ✸✸✸ KERALITE/SEAFOOD   One of *the* places to dine in India, Rice Boat is a small specialty restaurant where guests sit in, well, a rice boat. It's an excellent place to indulge in fresh seafood, including prawns, lobster, and crab. Find out what the catch of the day is, and have the chef add a touch of Kerala with a spicy, coconut-based gravy. Or get the mixed seafood grill and at least one traditional curry; we recommend the delectable Alleppey prawn curry. Lobster fans should order the amazing lobster *olathiyathu* (but note that it costs a whopping Rs 2,000/$46 per kilo). Whatever you order, leave room for one of the house-specialty spice ice creams; the Black Pepper Gelato is not to be missed.

Taj Malabar, Willingdon Island. © 0484/266-6811 or -8010. Average prices Rs 275–Rs 1,200 ($6.20–$28). AE, DC, MC, V. Daily 7:30–11:30pm.

Thai Pavilion ✦ THAI   Dishes here not only taste wonderful, they look fabulous, too. *Kai haw bai toey* is a starter of marinated chicken pieces wrapped in pandanus (a type of pine) leaves and deep-fried. Vegetarians should try *man jian*—potatoes flavored with ginger, mushroom, pimento, and a light soy sauce—or *fok thong kapprao*, a delightful combination of pumpkin, basil, and chilies. Here, the spiciness of traditional Thai red curry *(gaeng phad)* is toned down with coconut milk and fragrant lemon grass; served in a small earthenware bowl, it is prepared with your choice of meat, vegetables, or seafood. There's a number of stir-fried prawn dishes, each prepared with a delicate blend of spices and herbs—try *koong phad kapprao*, a hot combination of garlic, chili, and Thai basil leaves.

Taj Malabar, Willingdon Island. © 0484/266-6811 or -8010. Main courses Rs 150–Rs 750 ($3.40–$17). AE, DC, MC, V. Daily 12:30–2:45pm and 7:30–11:30pm.

SHOPPING

Ernakulam has scores of shops trading in Indian artifacts and treasures. However, you'll have far more fun exploring the antiques dealerships in Mattancherry and Jew Town, most of which are jam-packed with weird, wonderful, and genuine pieces from Kerala's multifangled past.

Cinnamon ✦✦✦   Don't be fooled by the gallery-like ambience; the lovely furniture and fashions available here are entirely homegrown. Find fishing nets made into pillowcases, vintage prints of Hindu deities, silk caftans, and designer tunics ideal for the Indian heat. This new addition, a branch of Bangalore's trendy store, is Cochin's most fashionable outlet. 1/658 Ridsdale Rd. © 0484/221-7124.

Crafters   In the heart of historic Mattancherry's Jew Town, Crafters is an antiques fetishist's dream come true. A huge selection of antiques ranging from religious curiosities to that perfect doorway are displayed in three different outlets and piled up in massive warehouses that will leave your jaw hanging open. After you've had a really good poke around, you can have your purchase shipped abroad. VI/141, Jew Town. © 0484/222-3346, -7652, or 0484/221-2210. www.craftersantique.com.

Galleria Synagogue Art Gallery   Local artists are well represented at this Jew Town art gallery, where you can purchase works by some of Cochin's most celebrated artists. 6/8 Jew Town. © 0484/222-2544 or -1458. www.galleriasynagogue.com.

COCHIN AFTER DARK

When the sun starts to sink, you should be on a harbor cruise or watching the boats from either the **Taj Malabar** on Willingdon Island or the **Taj Residency** in Ernakulam—both sit more or less at the water's edge and offer different venues for cocktails. After this, a Kathakali or Kalaripayattu demonstration (see below) can easily fill the gap before a fine seafood dinner.

Kathakali & Kalaripayattu: Kerala's Colorful Art Forms

A stay in Cochin affords you the opportunity to sample Kerala's best-known classical art form—Kathakali, a performance style that delves into the world of demons, deities, soldiers, sages, and satyrs, taken from Indian epics such as the *Mahabharata*. Combining various theatrical and performance elements, it is said to have developed during the 16th century under the auspices of the Raja of Kottaraka, and today the best Kathakali school is in Kalamandalam, founded by a poet named Vallathol Narayan Menon in 1930. Here, students undergo a rigorous training program that lasts 6 years and includes massage techniques, extensive make-up training, and knowledge of the precise and subtle finger, body, and eye movements that constitute the language and grand emotions of Kathakali. There is also a host of instruments that may be mastered, as no performance is without musical accompaniment. So striking are the costumes, make-up, and jewelry associated with this form of dance-theater, that the image of the elaborately adorned, heavily made-up, and almost mask-like face of the Kathakali performer has become the state's most recognizable icon. Performers employ exaggerated facial expressions (only enhanced by the make-up—bright paint applied thickly to the face) and a highly technical set of symbolic hand gestures (known as *mudras*). Vocalists and musicians help set the mood, utilizing the *chengila* (gong), *elathalam* (small cymbals), and *chenda* and *maddalam* (drums). Traditionally, Kathakali performances are held for entire nights, often as part of festival events. In Cochin, however, a number of Kathakali groups stage short extracts of the longer pieces specifically for tourist consumption. Kerala is also renowned for its unique martial arts form: the supremely acrobatic Kalaripayattu, believed to be the oldest defense-combat system in the world. Apparently discovered in ancient times by traveling Buddhist monks who needed to protect themselves against marauding bandits, Kalaripayattu is believed to predate more recognizable forms, like kung-fu, that emerged farther east. For demonstrations of Kathakali and Kalaripayattu, see recommendations below.

KATHAKALI PERFORMANCES

In Fort Cochin, **Kerala Kathakali** ✦✦✦ (River Rd.; ℂ **0484/221-5827**) hosts the best Kathakali demonstration in the city (see "Kathakali & Kalaripayattu: Kerala's Colorful Art Forms," above). This rustic, atmospheric "theater" also hosts occasional cultural events showcasing diverse dance forms and Karnatic music (the classical music of southern India). Performances are held daily from 6:30 to 8pm, with make-up demonstrations from 5pm; admission is Rs 100 ($2.30). Note that alongside the theater is **Old Port Restaurant** (ℂ **0484/221-5341**), a good venue for pre- or post-show meals; fresh fish dishes and various Keralite specialties are served right near the water's edge (bring mosquito repellent for both the show and the restaurant). If you're interested in attending a proper all-night Kathakali performance at a temple, speak to one of the organizers at Kerala Kathakali; some of their top performers are often involved in authentic rituals.

Other Kathakali venues worth noting are Fort Cochin's (air-conditioned) **Cochin Cultural Centre** (CC 2/10–A, near Seagull Hotel, Calvetty Rd.; ℂ **0484/221-6911**), which has daily shows from 6:30pm, but get there by 5:30pm to watch the artists putting on their elaborate make-up. Music, dance, and other performances are sometimes held at **Draavidia Art and Performance Gallery** (1/2002 YMCA Rd., Fort Cochin).

KALARIPAYATTU PERFORMANCES

While there are a number of dedicated training schools *(kalaris)* where Kerala's traditional martial arts form, Kalaripayattu, is taught for its intended purpose, it is usually performed in a staged environment for tourists. **Shiva Shakti Kalari Kshetram** (Kaloor, Ernakulam; ☎ **98952-90635** or 0484/253-9453) holds daily demonstrations of Kalaripayattu; the institute also provides training and Ayurvedic massage based on principles derived from the art of Kalari.

2 The Backwaters

Alleppey is 1,150km (713 miles) SE of Mumbai

Kerala's backwaters comprise a web of waterways that forms a natural inland transport network stretching from **Cochin,** the northern gateway, to **Kollam** (or Quilon), the backwaters' southernmost town. At its heart is Vembanad Lake, on the shores of which lie the top-notch resorts of **Kumarakom** and nearby Bird Sanctuary. Inland, just 12km (7½ miles) east of Kumarakom, is **Kottayam,** the bustling town described by Arundhati Roy in her Booker Prize–winning *The God of Small Things.* Located at the foot of the Western Ghats, it has two historically significant (but ultimately missable) early Syrian Christian churches.

Kumarakom has by far the best accommodations, but unless you're a keen birder, there's not a great deal to do here. Idle away the hours on a houseboat cruise, indulge in Ayurvedic therapies, and laze under the tropical sun—that's about as busy as your day is likely to get. Between November and March, the local **Bird Sanctuary** becomes home to numerous migratory flocks, many of which fly in from Siberia. Regularly seen here are little cormorants, darters (or snake birds), night herons, golden-backed woodpeckers, tree pies, and crow pheasants. Given its exclusivity and sublime setting, Kumarakom does not offer accommodations for budget-oriented travelers; for that you'll need to look farther south to **Alleppey** (or Alappuzha), also the focal point of backwater cruises.

Snake Boat Races

Every year Kerala's backwater canals host the world's largest team sport, when scores of streamlined *chundan vallams,* the ram-snouted boats commonly known as snake boats, are propelled across the waters at impressive speeds, cheered on by an exuberant audience. Typically, snake boats are manned by four helmsmen, 25 singers, and up to 100 oarsmen rowing in unison to the terrific rhythm of the *vanchipattu,* or "song of the boatman." The oldest and most popular event is the **Champakulam Moolam Boat Race,** held in monsoon-soaked July, but the most famous water battle is undoubtedly the **Nehru Trophy Boat Race,** held on the second Saturday of August on the Punnamada backwaters of Alleppey in conjunction with Kerala's important *Onam* harvest festival. Tickets for the event, which features at least 16 competing *chundan vallams* and attracts thousands of excited supporters, are available from the **District Tourism Promotion Council office** (see "Visitor Information," below).

Home to the coir (fibers made from coconut husks) industry, Alleppey once bore the nickname "Venice of the East" because of its famed palm-fringed canal network, the intricate byways and narrow streams that allow boats to transport huge bales of coconut fibers. Of the many **snake boat races** (see "Snake Boat Races," below) that take place in the backwaters throughout the year, Alleppey's Nehru Trophy event is the most significant. If you're keen to witness the event, it may be useful to find accommodations close to town.

The entire backwaters region is a tranquil paradise, and sustains a delightfully laid-back way of life that has endured for centuries—perfect for sultry, languid, do-nothing houseboat adventures that take you into the heart of Kerala country life. Besides booking into one of the resorts recommended below, a trip on a specially converted *kettuvallam* is a must (see "Hiring a Houseboat," below).

ESSENTIALS

VISITOR INFORMATION   The authority responsible for dishing out information to visitors is the **District Tourism Promotion Council,** which has various offices in the different backwaters towns. In **Alleppey,** it's on Boat Jetty Road (*©* **0477/225-3308;** daily 9:30am–5pm). In **Kollam,** there are tourism centers at the bus stand and at the railway station. In **Kottayam,** you can contact the **District Tourism Office** (*©* **0481/256-0479;** Mon–Fri 10am–5pm). If your main interest is houseboats, contact TourIndia Holidays (see "Hiring a Houseboat," below).

GETTING THERE   By Road   Taxis are easily available in all major towns and cities. From Cochin a taxi should cost about Rs 600 ($14) and get you to Kottayam in about 1½ hours.

By Air   For the northern backwater towns, the nearest airport is at Cochin (Kochi); to save time you'll probably want to head down the 76km (47-mile) road by car to Kottayam (for Kumarakom) or Alleppey (for a backwater cruise). For Kollam, located at the backwaters' southern end, Thiruvananthapuram Airport is 66km (40 miles) away.

By Train   Though there are railheads in Kottayam (for Kumarakom), Alleppey, and Kollam, your best bet is to get to Trivandrum or Cochin and then head out by road.

GETTING AROUND   By Water-Taxi & Ferry   Kottayam, Alleppey, and Kollam are all connected by ferries that ply the route daily. State Water Transport Department ferries between Alleppey and Kottayam depart from the tourist boat jetty near the bus station. Ferries between Alleppey and Kollam take 8 hours, departing from both the Alleppey and Kollam boat jetties at 10:30am and arriving in Kollam/Alleppey around 6:30pm.

GUIDED TOURS & CRUISES   Alleppey's helpful **District Tourism Promotion Council** (Boat Jetty, Alleppey; *©* **0477/225-3308**) has a daily backwater cruise to Kuttanad and back. The 3-hour trip departs at 10am and costs Rs 100 ($2.30). DTPC also offers private cruises for Rs 200 ($4.55) per hour; a cruise to Kumarakom takes 7 hours. See "Hiring a Houseboat," below, for guided overnight trips on traditional houseboats. Alternatively, any of the accommodations listed below can organize backwaters cruises or speedboat trips for you.

CRUISING THE BACKWATERS

Reset your watch to a rhythm of life that has gone unchanged for centuries by boarding a *kettuvallam,* the long, beautifully crafted cargo boats that ply the waterways with cargo (if you don't mind being referred to as such). An engineering feat, a *kettuvallam*

Cruising Kerala on the World's Smallest Luxury Liner

Leave it to Oberoi to take the traditional backwater cruise to new heights with the **MV** *Vrinda*—not exactly a liner, but the ultimate in luxury on Kerala's backwaters, and very Agatha Christie. After all, only on board the MV *Vrinda* can you find yourself watching life along the river from a comfy rattan chair on the breezy upper-deck lounge, or from your plush settee in the air-conditioned dining room while staff keep a watchful eye out for a raised finger. On the first night, you dock at Lake Vembanad for dinner (a thoroughly elegant affair accompanied by local entertainment), then bed down in one of only eight smart cabins, each decked out with luxuries like TV and DVD, en-suite showers, and lovely king-size beds. The following day, the boat makes its way to Lake Pamba, where you can climb aboard a small rice boat to explore the narrower backwaters. Three nights later you wend your way back to Cochin. Typical of the Oberoi, food is outstanding and you are treated like royalty—perfect if you prefer to see Kerala in a somewhat sanitized manner and sans its blemishes. The package costs $1,900 all-inclusive for 4 nights (3 on the cruiser, 1 at the Trident Hilton Cochin). For reservations, call the Oberoi at © **1600/11-2030** (www.oberoihotels.com).

is made from lengths of ironwood, anjili, or jackwood, and not a single nail is used in the construction—it's joined together with thick coir ropes. The boat is then sealed with fish oil and coated with a black caustic resin produced by boiling cashew kernels.

Today, numerous houseboat operators work out of the Alleppey area, but the original concept of turning cargo boats into tourist cruise vessels was the brainchild of Babu Varghese of TourIndia, an outfit that remains the top operator in the backwaters, with excellent guides and innovative boat designs that are upgraded annually. Varghese transformed the *kettuvallam* into a livable houseboat by expanding the original size to include two or three rooms, a flush toilet, a functioning shower, and a small viewing or sunbathing platform. Bamboo scaffolding is constructed over the hull, and a thatched roof of plaited palm leaves and walls of bamboo matting are added to create a rustic but very comfortable floating dwelling. With designs that owe some allegiance to the Chinese junk but that more closely resemble a small Sydney Opera House, these beautiful crafts may be propelled by pole (if you're in no particular hurry) or by a small, quiet motor.

The houseboat experience allows you to aimlessly drift past villages, temples, and churches and be thoroughly exposed to the rural lifestyle of the backwaters. As if you're on the very large set of a reality TV show, you can watch as women, unperturbed by your drifting presence, wash their long ebony tresses or pound away at laundry; children play at the water's edge and men dive for mussels; and elephants and water buffalo wade at will. Fishermen suavely holding umbrellas above their heads suddenly drift by, their nets at the ready, while floating vendors using single-log canoes and other modest craft deliver commodities such as rice and coir fiber. On the shore, toddy tappers whisk up palm trees (note that you can ask to stop at a village to buy unforeseen necessities like beer or coconut toddy); see "Toddy Tappers," below. And when the sun sets, the sky lights up in magnificent shades of orange and red. Gliding past the rural communities that cling to the banks is without a doubt one of the most relaxing and romantic ways to witness a timeless lifestyle, where people rely on impossibly tiny tracts of land to cultivate subsistence crops and keep a few animals, using slender jackfruit wood canoes to get around, deliver goods, and do a spot of fishing.

Kettuvallam houseboats are available at various levels of luxury, and may be rented for short trips or for sleep-in journeys of several days. Try to spend at least one night on board, since the major attractions are watching the setting sun and witnessing the lakeside activities of households at dawn and dusk. A great plan is to have a houseboat collect you from one resort (we suggest Coconut Lagoon or Kumarakom) and drop you off at your next destination (say, Kayaloram Lake Resort or—if your budget won't stretch that far—Keraleeyam Lake Resort).

While the general idea is to wind your way aimlessly through the waterways, one of the most popular stop-off points for visitors is **Mata Amritanandamayi Ashram** (© **0476/289-6179** or -6278), home of a female guru endearingly known as the Hugging Mother. Another possible stop is **Champakulam,** where 500-year-old **St. Mary's Church** shows definite traces of Hindu influence, from a small statue of Christ assuming a pose typical of Krishna, to the custom of leaving one's footwear outside.

HIRING A HOUSEBOAT

TourIndia Holidays ⭒⭒⭒ has a number of houseboats in a range of designs and accommodations to suit your requirements. These feature solar-panel power and heating, bio-toilets, and an average cruising speed of 8 to 10km (5–6 miles) per hour. Although the facilities might strike some as rather basic, you'll be spoiled rotten by your private team—a guide, a cook, and a pilot—who work hard to make your experience unique and exceptional (and discreetly manage to leave you to experience the backwaters in peace). Meals are authentic Kerala fare—served on a plantain leaf and eaten with your fingers. Bring your own drinks if you want something other than mineral water. And if you're curious about Kerala cuisine, you're welcome to observe proceedings in the tiny kitchen at the rear end of the boat. For reservations, contact TourIndia at Post Box no. 163, Mahatma Gandhi Road, Trivandrum 695 001; © **0471/233-0437** or -1507; fax 0471/233-1407; www.tourindiakerala.com.

Other reliable houseboat operators are **Spice Coast Cruises** ⭒⭒⭒ (House Boats, Puthenangadi, Alleppey; © **0484/266-8221** or 0478/258-2615; spicecoastcruise@ cghearth.com), run by the excellent Kerala-based Casino Hotel group; and **Soma Houseboats** (Nehru Trophy Finishing Point, Thathampally P.O., Alleppey; © **0477/ 226-8101;** reservations: Chowara P.O., Trivandrum 695 501; © **0471/226-8101;** www.somahouseboats.com). Expect to pay between $150 and $250 per night for a one-bedroom houseboat. For the ultimate in luxury, see "Cruising Kerala on the World's Smallest Luxury Liner," above.

Toddy Tappers

For generations, agile young village men have been clambering up coconut palms to tap into the sweet sap known as toddy, or *kallu*. Like their fathers and their fathers' fathers, these "toddy tappers" have made a good living over the years harvesting the sap to drink right away (sweet and refreshing, but definitely an acquired taste) or to ferment into an alcoholic drink. The morning's toddy is already a heady tipple by evening—by the next day, it's prodigiously potent.

WHERE TO STAY ON LAND
KUMARAKOM

Coconut Lagoon ✪✪✪ *Kids*   If private alfresco showers and hammocks rather than room service and television are your idea of bliss, then this is your kind of lakeside idyll (and was for Paul McCartney). Comprising reassembled wooden *tharavads* (traditional Kerala houses) set among coconut trees, hibiscus flowers, and specially grafted orchids, and boasting quite splendid views of Lake Vembanad and the Kavanar River, it's not surprising that this family-friendly resort is one of the most popular in Kerala. Most accommodations are in the traditional *tharavads*—choose between duplex-style mansions (nos. 201–204 have views of the lake) or simpler heritage bungalows (nos. 219–221, 223, and 225–228 face the river). Some of the homes here date back to the early 1700s, and each historic teak, anjili, or jackfruit building has been reassembled according to ancient carpentry rules known as *thachu shashtra*. The emphasis here is on providing an authentic Kerala feel and having as little impact as possible on the natural environment. Indeed, much of the resort's rustic charm lies in its simplicity; guest rooms are uncluttered and furnished with traditional Kerala cane and teak pieces, and have neither TVs nor (less satisfactorily) room service. Rooms were recently refurbished, and if the hotel is not too busy, ask if you can look around and pick yours. Better still, splurge on a pool cottage, which (you guessed it) has its own private pool and is situated right at the river's edge.

Kumarakom, Kottayam, Kerala. Contact c/o Casino Hotel, Willingdon Island, Cochin 682 003, Kerala. ☎ **0481/252-5834** through -5836. Fax 0481/252-4495. www.cghearth.com. coconutlagoon@cghearth.com. 50 units. $173–$200 bungalow; $220–$245 mansion; $350–$410 pool villa. $40 extra person. Rates include breakfast. AE, DC, MC, V. **Amenities:** 2 restaurants; bar; traditional performances; pool (cottages also have private pools); Ayurvedic center; houseboat; boat shuttle service; sunset cruise; hamper service; butterfly garden; village walks; bird-sanctuary visits; cooking demonstrations; shop; 48-hr. external laundry service. *In room:* A/C, minibar, tea- and coffee-making facility.

Kumarakom Lake Resort ✪✪✪   Situated on the edge of Vembanad Lake, in a remote, tranquil location, this is the swankiest and best of Kumarakom's backwater resorts. Like so many, it comprises exquisite *tharavadu*-style carved teak and rosewood houses with curved terra-cotta tiled roofs, many of them reassembled originals salvaged from Kerala villages. The interiors are decidedly more luxurious than those of their neighbors, however, with exquisite antiques and lovely examples of temple mural art. Each room has a beautiful, private small garden into which an open-to-the-air sunken bathtub and granite-floored drench showers have been installed. The cheaper lake-facing cottages offer the best value for money—they have a truly authentic heritage feel and are perfect for enjoying the setting sun (standard villas face a canal that reaches all the way to the lobby). In the resort's newest section, a second meandering freshwater pool snakes its way past the private balconies of luxurious cottages—which means you can swim around the property directly from your back door (which may

---

Mohiniattam: The Dance of the Enchantress

Mohiniattam is another classical dance form, and one of the few performed by a woman. Dressed in white and gold, with her hair gathered and adorned with jasmine, the dancer performs graceful, gliding movements together with elaborate *mudras* and exaggerated facial expressions. Any resort promising evening shows that showcase the region's performance arts (like Coconut Lagoon and Spice Village) will include at least one act of Mohiniattam.

Dining-Room Murder

The beautiful dining room at the Coconut Lagoon is apparently part of the house where the awful murder in Arundhati Roy's *The God of Small Things* actually occurred. The acclaimed writer has been very critical of the removal and reassembly of Kerala's traditional homes in what she calls "theme park" resorts, but resort owners argue that they have saved these historic properties from certain destruction. (The dining room at the Coconut Lagoon is not haunted, by the way, and the food is good.)

compromise your privacy, however, because others can choose to do the same). Should you fancy a night or two on the lake, the resort has two of its own fully equipped houseboats. The resort is also home to an excellent restaurant and an extensive Ayurvedic spa—one of Kerala's best, offering a wide range of treatments. And if that isn't enough to persuade you, staff are wonderfully efficient and go all out to make you feel like royalty.

Kumarakom N., Kottayam 686 566. © 0481/252-4900, -4501, -5020, or -5021. Fax 0481/252-4987 or toll-free 1 600 425 5030. www.klresort.com. klresort@vsnl.com. 50 units plus 3 houseboats. $195–$250 heritage garden-view villa, $225-300 heritage lake-view and meandering pool villa, $300–$375 meandering pool duplex villa. $50–$125 extra bed. Rates include breakfast. Tariffs increase Dec 10–Jan 10, plus Christmas/New Year's dinner supplements. AE, DC, MC, V. **Amenities:** 3 restaurants; 2 pools; gymnasium; Jacuzzi; Ayurvedic center; yoga; billiards; table tennis; children's play area; activity room; travel desk; sightseeing; business center; currency exchange; curio shop; salon; 24-hr. room service; babysitting; laundry; computer rentals. *In room:* A/C, TV, minibar, tea- and coffee-making facilities, hair dryer, electronic safe.

Taj Garden Retreat, Kumarakom 🏵🏵

This charming resort sits around the edges of a lagoon linked to Vembanad Lake by a narrow channel, just moments away from Kumarakom Bird Sanctuary. It's in much the same price range as the buzzier Coconut Lagoon, but the advantage here is near-absolute peace and privacy. Built in the late 1800s, Baker Bungalow was home to four generations of the Baker missionary family before the Taj group converted it into a tranquil resort. Lake-facing guest cottages (nos. 7–17 have the best views) have spacious bedrooms and small private patios that look directly onto the resort's private lagoon—even the lovely bathrooms have views, albeit of a tiny paved courtyard decorated with tall, narrow clay pots. For a few dollars more, the four cottages situated at the pool have slightly bigger bedrooms; ask for no. 18, since it overlooks the length of the lake. If it's colonial history you want, reserve one of the five massive rooms in the original Baker Bungalow. Furnished with antiques, these, too, have their own romantic atmosphere. Alternatively, you can stay in one of two air-conditioned, permanently moored houseboats, each with two roomy bedrooms, bathroom with tub, and attached private deck. The resort organizes romantic dinner cruises with music and entertainment on a *kettuvallam.*

1/404, Kumarakom, Kottayam 686 563. © 0481/252-4377, 0481/252-5711, or -5712 through -5716. Fax 0481/252-4371. www.tajhotels.com. retreat.kumarakom@tajhotels.com. 28 units. $160 standard lake-view and houseboat double, $200 cottage lake-view double, $225 deluxe lake- and pool-view double; $400 luxury villa with private pool. AE, DC, MC, V. **Amenities:** Restaurant; bar; pool; Ayurvedic center; fitness center; bicycle rentals; backwater cruises; watersports (wind sailing, water skiing); boating (speedboats, kayaking, canoeing, rowboats, water skis, water scooters); fishing; bird-watching; cultural performances; indoor games; travel desk; business center; currency exchange; florist; 24-hr. room service; laundry; doctor-on-call. *In room:* A/C, TV, minibar, hair dryer (all except standard).

KOTTAYAM

Lake Village Heritage Resort ☆   This is far from the best lagoon resort, but the rates aren't bad (they include all meals), and if you get the room choice right, you can literally fish from your balcony. The resort is set amid banana trees and manicured lawns, and its best accommodations are (predictably) in a series of reconstructed traditional Kerala mansions that have been converted to include indoor/outdoor bathrooms—book no. 104 or 105 for the balconies that project over the river, or no. 117 or 118, which create the impression of being surrounded by water. Cottages are on two levels, with bedrooms on the upper floors; room interiors are a little dark and uninspiring. An open-air Kerala cuisine eatery, cultural performances at the *mandapam,* boat rides in *chundan vallams,* and an Ayurvedic center make up for views of the adjoining Windsor "Castle" Hotel—this is, incidentally, where you have to check in, and guests have access to all the Windsor Castle facilities. *Note:* Don't confuse Lake Village Heritage Resort with the super-kitschy and awful **Vembanad Lake Resort** next door.

Kottayam 686 039. © **0481/236-3637** or -3638. Fax 0481/236-3738. www.thewindsorcastle.net. 47 units including 7 cottages. $115–$165 double. $12 extra bed. Rates include all meals. AE, MC, V. **Amenities:** 2 restaurants; pastry shop; bar; 2 pools; Ayurvedic center; car hire; boat rental (house, row, and pedal); boat jetty; currency exchange; salon; 24-hr. room service; doctor-on-call. *In room:* A/C, TV, minibar.

Philipkutty's Farm ☆☆ *(Kids* *(Value*   This is a real gem, ideal for those who find the whole resort experience a little pretentious. Here you get to experience first-hand the hospitality of a local farming family, albeit in the privacy of your very own waterfront cottage, surrounded by 18 hectares (45 acres) that include banana, mango, nutmeg, coconut, and pepper plantations. The first cottage was designed by Karl Damschen, a Swiss architect who combined traditional Keralite design—open-plan living, carved wooden doors, and a veranda—with personal touches. The breezy, homey cottages, named after flowers growing in the courtyard, are filled with antiques, and the en-suite bathrooms are modern; we recommend you book Ashokam or Mandheerama (these are more spacious). Hosts Vinod and Anu Mathew treat guests as part of the family yet provide privacy (they stay in a separate house) and time to soak up the tranquillity. Vinod's mother and Anu are the kitchen genies, preparing three marvelous feasts a day, and you're welcome to watch them cooking in the kitchen. Ask for your breakfast to be served in the pleasant open-air pavilion. The only real drawback is that there's no pool, but some guests venture into the waters of Vembanad Lake. As it is, you're taken on informative excursions of the plantations and get to enjoy a free backwater cruise on a canoe. Children are warmly welcomed.

Pallivathukal, Ambika Market P.O., Vechoor, Kottayam. © **04829/27-6529,** -6530, or 98950-75130. www.philipkuttys farm.com. 5 units. Rs 7,900 ($180) double. Rs 1,000 ($23) children 5–12; Rs 2,000 ($46) children over 12. Rates include all meals, tea and coffee, sunset cruise, and farm excursions. 20% discount June–Sept. Credit cards for overseas bank deposits only. **Amenities:** Dining facilities.

IN & AROUND ALLEPPEY (ALAPPUZHA)

Emerald Isle ☆☆ *(Value*   Yet another backwater treasure, this 150-year-old heritage villa, located between the Pamba River and Vembanad Lake, is ideal for travelers looking for an authentic Kerala backwater homestay experience that still provides privacy. The magic begins when a boatman picks you up in a dugout canoe from "Landing Point" (next to Nazareth church), and rows you to the Job family home. There you are welcomed with filter coffee, tea, coconut water, or toddy. The home is sparklingly clean and has a glorious old-world charm—history-lovers will enjoy the 250-year-old property deed etched in palm leaves, newspaper cuttings from 1909, and even the ancient cooking pot–turned–coffee table in the living room; others might opt to do nothing but sink into in the inviting wicker chairs. The en-suite guest rooms have ancestral carved teakwood furniture; ask for one of the two with great open-air bathrooms. (Only one room is air-conditioned, but the attached bathroom is small.) Freshly prepared meals are eaten with the family, but you pick what's on the menu: Choose among chicken curry and *appams* (lace pancakes), *karimeen pollichathu* (pearl spot fish), *avoli* fry, *neimeen* curry, egg roasts, or catch of the day. The place is filled with history, which the Jobs are happy to share; they can also provide information on local culture, cuisine (you're invited into the kitchen), or anything that raises your curiosity. In addition, the Jobs will organize boat cruises, backwater trips, fishing, walks through paddy and coconut plantations, and village tours. Beautifully maintained, this retreat has 3 hectares (7 acres) of plantations and gardens and is a wonderful way to experience a Kerala that's a world away from the posher but sometimes sterile five-star accommodations.

Kanjooparambil-Manimalathara, Chathurthiakary P.O, Alleppey 688 511. ℂ **0477/270-3899,** 0477/309-0577, or 94470-77555. www.emeraldislekerala.com. info@emeraldislekerala.com. 4 units. Rs 2,800 ($64) deluxe double, Rs 3,500 ($80) A/C double. Rates include boat transfers and all meals. AE, MC, V. **Amenities:** Boat cruises; massage; free cooking classes; fishing, toddy tapping.

Kayaloram Lake Resort ๓๓๓   A scenic 15-minute boat ride from Alleppey's jetty brings you to one of the best resorts the backwaters have to offer: Kayaloram is a relatively intimate and very private lakeside resort, with watery views that seem to stretch forever (or at the very least to distant Kumarakom and Kollam). Guest rooms are in four transplanted and remodeled 75-year-old *tharavads* with wraparound teak verandas and intricately patterned gables. Rooms are uncluttered and feature the de rigueur high-beamed ceilings, bamboo blinds, coir carpets, terra-cotta tiled floors, and paneled walls of dark jackfruit wood. Outdoor bathrooms with open-air showers are glorious. The best views are from room nos. 2, 3, and 5, which face the lake, less than 10m (30 ft.) away, and allow you to watch the prawn fishermen's lights twinkling on the lake at night. During the day, the continuously changing spectacle of passing boats, canoes, and *chundan vallams* (snake boats) is equally magical. In keeping with the personalized service, individual lunch and dinner orders are taken a few hours in advance (Ayurvedic cuisine is available) to ensure that tastes, needs, and moods are adequately met. Complimentary sunset backwater cruises are also on offer; alternatively, the resort will organize longer backwater trips for you, and you will be picked up from the lawn outside your room. The manager is fond of taking guests on walking tours through some of the backwater villages located near the resort. The Ayurvedic treatments, while not extensive, are considered some of the best in India.

Punnamada, Alleppey 688 006. ℂ **0477/226-2931,** 0477/223-2040, or -1573. Fax 0477/225-2918. www.kayaloram. com. kayaloram@vsnl.com or kayaloram@satyam.net.in. 12 units. $95–$118 pool-facing double, $118–$147 lake-facing double. Rates include 2 transfers and breakfast. Meals are $7 each. AE, MC, V. **Amenities:** Restaurant; beer available; pool; Ayurvedic treatments; doctor-on-call. *In room:* A/C.

Keraleeyam Lake Resort ๓ *Value*   This 70-year-old Kerala home is one of the best-value deals on the backwaters, and unbeatable if you want to experience the heritage atmosphere of the top-notch resorts at budget rates. Set on the water's edge, it includes five rooms and nine cottages. The guest rooms in *tharavad* houses feature high-beamed ceilings, wooden shutters, and small doorways with traditional thick wooden *saksha* locks. Each cottage (without air-conditioning, but naturally cooled by the thatch roofs) has a direct lake view with a private balcony, a personal coconut palm, and an open-to-the-sky shower in a lovely indoor-outdoor bathroom. Air-conditioned cottages, while made entirely of teak, have very standard bathrooms and shared balcony. Pleasures include backwater cruises and a visit to a living village, as well as Ayurvedic massage facilities.

Thathampally, Alappuzha 688 006. ⓒ 0477/223-1468 or -6950. Fax 0477/225-1068. www.keraleeyam.com. 5 units, 9 cottages. $25 A/C double; $40 A/C cottage, $30 non-A/C cottage. Child under 12 sharing parent's room $5. Food tariff of $13 includes all meals. MC, V. **Amenities:** Restaurant; Ayurvedic center; tours and sightseeing; boat cruises; canoeing; elephant rides; fortune teller; limited room service. *In room:* Some have A/C.

The Marari Beach 🅰🅰🅰 (Kids   This is without a doubt one of the best beach resorts in Kerala (if not India), with a superb beachfront location. It's also a good choice if you have neither the time nor the inclination to travel farther south to the better-known beach resorts. That said, it's a pretty mellow, down-to-earth place (in other words, not in the same class as the heritage-soaked Surya Samudra or the Poovar Island resort, the best beachfront resorts south of Trivandrum). The Marari Beach features comfortable and spacious (but relatively basic) stand-alone thatched cottages, spread over 15 hectares (36 acres) of lawns and pathways enveloped by coconut groves. The best rooms are nos. 19 and 20, as these are conveniently located near the beach, bar, restaurants, and pool. Marari's laid-back charms are complemented by its eco-friendly undertakings, which include a water-recycling plant, an organic vegetable garden, rainwater harvesting, and a solar-heated hot-water project. The extensive Ayurvedic center is considered one of Kerala's best, serviced by two dedicated doctors and backed up by therapists and special dietary options from the restaurant. But the best aspect is the resort's *au naturelle* setting, with a 25km (15-mile) beach shared only with fellow guests, local fishermen, and a Laurel-and-Hardy duo who serve as the resort's lifeguards.

Mararikulam, Alleppey 688 549, Kerala. ⓒ **0478/286-3801** through -3809. Fax 0478/286-3810. 58 units. www. cghearth.com. $200–$220 garden villa, $350–$410 pool villa, $410–$465 deluxe pool villa. $40 extra bed. Rates include breakfast. AE, DC, MC, V. **Amenities:** 2 restaurants; bar; pool; 2 tennis courts; volleyball; badminton; bicycles; Ayurvedic center; car hire; currency exchange; shop; laundry; doctor-on-call. *In room:* A/C, minibar, tea- and coffee-making facility, safe.

Privacy 🅰🅰   A secluded bungalow with two en-suite rooms and a central dining/reception room situated at the edge of Vembanad Lake, this lodging option certainly lives up to its name, with the bungalow only rented out to one party at a time (though you only pay for the room you occupy). It's gorgeous, too, with the original workshop-cum-shack converted into a private resort by a Cochin-based architect; interiors were designed by owner Joerg Drechsel (owner of super-stylish Malabar House), who incorporated local skills and elements with his personal take on Kerala style. Polished black oxide flooring contrasts with blue and mustard-yellow fabrics in the bedrooms; latticed walls, large mirrors framed in teakwood, antiques, and traditional masks complete the picture. On the porch, wooden rocking chairs with extendable leg-rests invite hours of relaxation. The front door is just steps from the lake, where *kettuvallams* idle and birds swoop down to catch fish. Completing the idyll, guests enjoy the personal attention of a dedicated chef and housekeeper. Privacy may make you feel a million miles from anywhere, but it's only 45km (28 miles) from Cochin and 15km (9⅓ miles) from the backwater-access town of Alleppey.

Reservations through Malabar House Residency, 1/268–1/269 Parade Rd., Fort Cochin 682 001. ⓒ **0484/221-6666.** Fax 0484/221-7777. www.malabarhouse.com. 250€ ($310) suite; 180€ ($224) cottage. 25€ extra bed. Rates include breakfast. Cottage rented to 1 party at a time. Extra bed 20€ ($25). MC, V. *In room:* TV, fax machine, kitchenette w/tea- and coffee-making facility.

KOLLAM
1,220km (756 miles) S of Mumbai

There is no reason to spend any time in what is the official southern point of Kerala's backwaters, but two accommodations on the outskirts of town are worth considering, particularly if you plan to head north in a houseboat to Alleppey or beyond. Budget travelers can get a taste of history in a British mansion that's been converted into the **Tourist Bungalow,** which functions primarily as a Government Guest House (Tourist Bungalow Rd.; ✆ **0474/274-3620**). Located a short distance out of town, the mansion isn't in the best shape, with neglected antiques and aging facilities, but the guest rooms (with attached bathrooms) have a faded grandeur and cost less than Rs 220 to Rs 440 ($5–$10) per night. A better option, not least because it's on the water, is the rather pompously named **Aquaserene,** a quiet resort with a number of facilities (Ayurvedic center, room service, guided tours) set on a promontory almost entirely bordered by water. A network of canals and concrete pathways links the collection of cottages with various parts of the resort, and coconut palms and watery rockeries set a tropical mood. The Lake Heritage Villas are duplex guest rooms in red-tile-roof *tharavad*-style cottages that make use of restored teak pieces and feature indoor-outdoor bathrooms. The upstairs bedroom has a balcony with cane chairs to take in the lovely watery views. Only eight have double beds, so book one of these in advance. Doubles cost $90 to $125, meals $4 to $9. Contact the resort at ✆ **0474/251-2410** or check it out at www.aquasereneindia.com.

3 Thiruvananthapuram (Trivandrum) & Varkala
1,200km (756 miles) S of Mumbai

"Thiruvananthapuram" (City of the Sacred Serpent) is the mouthful of a name given to Kerala's seaside state capital, but thankfully almost everyone calls it Trivandrum. Although the city has some interesting museums and a temple that's of great significance to Hindus (and off-limits to non-Hindus), the only reason to find yourself here is to utilize the city's excellent transport connections and head for the beautiful beaches that lie north, at Varkala, or south, to Kovalam and beyond. While Varkala has certainly been "discovered," it's a more laid-back alternative to Kovalam, which—no doubt due to its proximity to Trivandrum (a mere 10–20-min. drive south)—has been a popular seaside vacation spot for more than 70 years, and as a result has become overcommercialized and saturated with tourist-hungry businesses. If you're looking for Kerala's most stunning, upmarket seaside options, many with more-or-less private beaches, you'll have to travel farther south of Kovalam (see "From Kovalam to the Tip of India," later in this chapter).

ESSENTIALS
VISITOR INFORMATION   As the state capital, Trivandrum has plenty of outlets for tourist information. There are two **Tourist Information Counters** at the airport; one is run by the Government of India (✆ **0471/250-2298**) and the other by the Government of Kerala (✆ **0471/250-1085;** daily 10am–5pm, closed a flexible hour for lunch); the latter also has counters at the Central Bus Station in Thampanoor (✆ **0471/232-7224**) and at the Railway Station (✆ **0471/233-4470**), both of which are open daily from 8am to 8pm. Kerala's **Department of Tourism** operates a 24-hour

toll-free information line (✆ 1 600 425-4747). Also providing tourist information is **Kerala Tourism** (Park View, Museum Rd., opposite the museum complex; ✆ 0471/232-1132; daily 10am–5pm). For local tour information, go to the **Kerala Tourism Development Corporation** or KTDC (at Hotel Chaithram, adjacent to Central Bus Station in Thampanoor; ✆ 0471/233-0031; daily 6:30am–9:30pm).

In Kovalam, visit the **Tourist Facilitation Centre** (✆ 0471/248-0085; Mon–Sat 10am–1pm and 1:30–5pm) at the ITDC Compound. Besides giving information, the center assists with tour bookings, car hires, boat rides, and lodging. Consider any government-owned accommodations carefully.

GETTING THERE & AWAY   By Road   As mentioned earlier, Kerala is ideal for exploration with a hired car and driver; roads are relatively good, and the countryside is spectacular. See "Guided Tours," below. Trivandrum is connected by principal roads and highways with all parts of the country. Super Deluxe bus services are operated by **Kerala State Road Transport Corporation** (✆ 0471/232-3886 or 0471/246-3497 for the Central Bus Station in Thampanoor; ✆ 0471/246-3029 for the City Bus Stand in Fort). Private operators run so-called deluxe coaches to more distant towns and cities in South India, but note that most overnight buses stop regularly, making sleep impossible. More recently, a few private operators have introduced overnight (Volvo) buses between the major cities in the South. An overnight bus from Bangalore to Kochi (or vice versa), for instance, takes 10 to 11 hours and costs Rs 600 ($14). Though the journey is long, it's relatively comfortable; buses are air-conditioned, have reclining seats, usually provide blankets, and stop only two or three times for toilet/food breaks.

By Air   Trivandrum is connected by air to Delhi, Mumbai, Kochi, Chennai, Bangalore, Hyderabad, and Tiruchirapali. The **international airport** (✆ 0471/250-1424 for international flight information) is served by **Jet Airways, Air-India,** and **Indian Airlines** (for details, see "Airlines" under "Fast Facts: Trivandrum," below). There are also international flights from various Asian cities, including Dubai, Abu Dhabi, and nearby Malé in the Maldives. The airport is 6km (3¾ miles) from the city center, and you can pick up a prepaid taxi for the journey into town (Rs 200/$4.55) or directly to Kovalam (Rs 450/$10).

By Train   There are regular trains between Trivandrum and other important destinations in Kerala, including Cochin (under 4 hr.), Alleppey (3½ hr.), Kollam (1½ hr.), and Varkala (1 hr.). If you're coming from Chennai in Tamil Nadu, the overnight **Trivandrum Mail** is convenient. Trains also reach India's southernmost point, Kanyakumari; the journey takes around 2½ hours.

Thiruvananthapuram Central Railway Station is just east of M.G. Road, on Station Road; for general railway inquiries, call ✆ 131. For reservations, call ✆ 132 or 0471/232-3066, or you can access the **Interactive Voice Response** service by calling ✆ 1361.

GETTING AROUND   By Taxi & Auto-Rickshaw   Metered rickshaws charge upwards of Rs 8 (20¢) for the first kilometer, Rs 4 (10¢) for each kilometer thereafter, but you'll more than likely find yourself haggling over a predetermined price, particularly in the resort areas around Kovalam. For auto-rickshaw trips between Trivandrum and Kovalam, expect to pay Rs 120 ($2.75). Between the airport and Kovalam, taxis charge around Rs 450 ($10) one-way. From Kovalam north to Varkala, taxis should charge Rs 900 ($21). To hire a car and driver, see "Guided Tours," below.

By Motorcycle & Scooter   You can rent an Enfield or Honda on a daily basis from **Kerala Adventures** (✆ **0471/231-0796**) in Trivandrum. Expect to pay between Rs 250 and Rs 350 ($5.70–$8) per day.

GUIDED TOURS   KTDC (Hotel Chaithram, adjacent Central Bus Station, Thampanoor; ✆ **0471/233-0031;** Mon–Sat 6:30am–9:30pm) organizes sightseeing tours in and around the city. These are cheap (Rs 130/$2.95 full day) but are aimed primarily at domestic tourists, so they are not recommended. A far better option is to hire a private car and driver and plan a personalized trip. Arrange this through your hotel, or contact **Sita World Travel** (G-2, P.R.S. Court, Ambujavilasam Rd., off G.P.O. Junction; ✆ **0471/247-0921** or 0471/257-3180; fax 0471/246-0173; trv@ sitaindia.com).

FAST FACTS: Trivandrum

Airlines As ever, your best option is **Jet Airways** (Akshaya Towers, Sasthaman-galam; ✆ **0471/272-1018** or -8864); you can also contact Jet at the airport (✆ **0471/250-0710** or 0471/250-0860). Options are **Indian Airlines** (Mascot Sq., M.G. Rd.; ✆ **140,** 141, or 0471/231-8288; airport location ✆ **142,** 143, or 0471/ 250-1537); and **Air-India** (Vellayambalam; ✆ **0471/231-0310;** airport location ✆ **0471/250-1426**).

Area Code The area code for **Trivandrum** is **0471.**

ATMs Numerous ATMs in Trivandrum accept Visa and MasterCard; there are no such facilities south of the capital.

Banks You can exchange currency and traveler's checks at **Canara Bank** (Spencer Junction, M.G. Rd.; ✆ **0471/233-1536;** Mon–Fri 10am–2pm and 2:30–3:30pm, Sat 10am–noon); you can also get cash advances against certain credit cards. Currency exchanges only can be made at **Central Bank of India** (Hotel Chaithram lobby, Central Station Rd.; ✆ **0471/233-0359;** Mon–Fri 10am–2pm, Sat 10am–noon).

Car Hire See "Guided Tours," above.

Currency Exchange Most hotels will exchange your dollars, pounds, or euros. Also see "Banks," above.

Drugstores Try **Darsana Medicals** (Station Rd.; ✆ **0471/233-1398;** daily 8am–9:30pm).

Emergencies For fires and other emergencies, including medical services, call ✆ **101.**

Hospitals You'll get good care at **Sree Uthradon Thirunal Hospital** (Pattom; ✆ **0471/244-6220**), which is privately run. Also try **Cosmopolitan Hospital** (Maurinja Palayam, Trivandrum; ✆ **0471/244-8182**).

Internet Access Expect to pay around Rs 20 to Rs 40 (45¢–90¢) per hour. Look for the signs for **Sify i way** or **Reliance Webworld**—these Internet centers usu-ally provide faster connections than most. In Trivandrum you can visit **Multidata** (3rd floor, Kottarathil Buildings, Newblock, behind Bank of Baroda, Parayam; ✆ **0471/232-1082**) or **Orbit Cybercafé** (Vasantham Chambers, S.S. Coil Rd.; daily 9:30am–10pm).

Police Dial ℂ 100. Thampanoor Police Station (ℂ 0471/233-1843) is on Station Road. For road accidents, call the police **help line** at ℂ 9846/100-100.

Post Office The **General Post Office** (ℂ 0471/247-3071; Mon–Sat 8am–7pm, Sun 10am–4pm) is along M.G. Road.

Travel Agents IATA-affiliated **Altima Tours & Travels** (Corporation Golden Jubilee Building, opposite SMV High School, M.G. Rd., Trivandrum 1; ℂ 0471/ 246-3569 or 047/247-1212; susan_rajendran@hotmail.com) is reliable. So is **Kerala Adventures,** a recommended agent that will provide a variety of travel-related services from car hire to hotel bookings (C1, Future House, Temple Rd., Sasthamangalam; ℂ 0471/231-9548, -0796, or 98470-65548; comvoyge@vsnl. net).

Visa Extensions Contact the **Office of the Commissioner of Police** (ℂ 0471/ 232-0579 or 0471/232-0380).

WHAT TO SEE & DO IN TRIVANDRUM

Trivandrum, to put it bluntly, is a dump, but it has a number of interesting buildings, including the stately **Secretariat and Legislative Assembly,** situated along Mahatma Gandhi Road, which is the main boulevard and center of activity through town. M.G. Road runs more or less north to south and links the two most significant areas of tourist interest: the **Museum Complex,** to the north of the city; and the Fort area, which houses **Sree Padmanabhaswamy Temple** and **Puthen Malika Palace Museum,** to the south. It is possible to walk from one area to the other (about 45 min.), and there are numerous shops en route. Alternatively, auto-rickshaws continuously buzz along the road's length, and you will have no trouble catching a ride from one area to the other. Aside from the attractions reviewed below, **Chacha Nehru Children's Museum** is sure to draw parents traveling with children with its collection of nearly 2,000 dolls.

Shri Padmanabhaswamy Temple 𝄐   This Dravidian-style Vishnu temple, said to be the largest in Kerala, may be off-limits to non-Hindus, but the "temple guides" manage to target foreigners with great ease, leading them to the obligatory spots from which to photograph the seven-story-high entrance tower, or *goparum*, which is pretty much all that can be viewed from the outside. The temple is believed to have come into existence on the first day of the Kaliyuga era (3102 B.C.)—legend has it that the temple "materialized" after a sage prayed to Vishnu asking him to appear in a form that he could comprehend with his limited human vision—but the greater part of the complex was built during the 18th century. The temple is fronted by a massive tank, where devotees take ritual dips. Alongside a promenade are stalls selling ritual items, religious souvenirs, and flowers for use inside the temple.

Fort, Trivandrum. ℂ 0471/245-0233. Closed to non-Hindus. 4am–noon and 5–7:30pm.

Puthenmalika (Kuthiramalika) Palace Museum 𝄐𝄐   A secret, private passage is believed to connect Padmanabhaswamy Temple with this Travancore-style palace, built in the early 18th century by the social reformer Maharajah Swathi Thirunal Balarama Varma, a poet and distinguished musician. Known as the Horse Palace because of the 122 carved horse brackets that buttress the exterior walls, the buildings include elaborate carvings, among them two extravagant thrones—one made from

25 elephant tusks, another made entirely from Bohemian crystal. Visitors are also allowed into the Maharaja's music room, from where you get the same view of the temple that was apparently a source of inspiration to the erstwhile ruler. Despite the value of much of the collection, the buildings are in need of renovation; the beauty of the carved teakwood ceilings and collected objets d'art are sometimes disguised by insufficient lighting and neglectful curatorship. You'll be taken around by an "official" guide—obviously he'll require a small tip.

100m (328 ft.) from the temple, Fort. (C) 0471/247-3952. Entrance Rs 20 (45¢) adult, Rs 10 (25¢) children. Tues–Sun 8:30am–1pm and 3–5:30pm.

Museum Complex (★ Mercifully, the remainder of Trivandrum's cultural sites are clustered in a huge formal public garden at the northern end of the city. **Napier Museum** occupies an early Indo-Saracenic building, created in 1880 in honor of the then-governor of Madras, Lord Napier. This priceless collection includes excellent 12th-century Chola bronzes, wood carvings, stone idols, and fascinating musical instruments, while more unique pieces include a temple chariot, a 400-year-old clock, and a royal cot made from herbal wood. Fine-art enthusiasts should visit **Sri Chitra Art Gallery,** which holds an assortment of miniature paintings from the Rajput, Moghul, and Tanjore schools, as well as more exotic works from Japan, China, Bali, and Tibet. One of the country's foremost artists, Raja Ravi Varma (1848–1905), whose well-known oil paintings explore Hindu mythological themes, is represented here. **K.C.S. Paniker Gallery** is a wholly unnecessary diversion, as is the **Natural History Museum** (unless you want to see stuffed animals and dolls in traditional costumes)—the anthropological exhibit at Kolkata's Indian Museum is far superior. And

A Cultural Rendezvous

Backed by UNESCO, **Vijnana Kala Vedi Cultural Centre** charitable trust was founded in 1977 by a French artist named Louba Schild, who has been living in Kerala since the late 1960s. The center endeavors to preserve traditional Keralite arts and crafts, and to nurture the potential of young artists. The center also runs programs concerned with teaching such diverse cultural traditions as Ayurvedic medicine, local architecture, languages like Sanskrit, Indian cooking, and mural painting, as well as training in classical performance styles such as Mohiniattam, Bharatanatyam, and Karnatic vocal music. Around 200 foreign artists, researchers, and cultural tourists attend the center to learn about local arts and culture, and you are invited to enroll in short- or long-term programs. Vijnana Kala Vedi is situated 3 hours from both Trivandrum and Kochi; the center will gladly make all arrangements for pickups from either airport. Six of the guest rooms have en-suite Western-style bathrooms, but hot water must be ordered by the bucket. Accommodations are simple but lovely, with ceiling fans and mosquito nets. The traditional Keralite meals are strictly vegetarian. For more information, contact **Vijnana Kala Vedi Cultural Centre** (Tharayil Mukku, Aranmula 689 533; (C) **0468/221-4483,** -3308, or 0468/231-0451; www.vijnana kalavedi.org). All-inclusive tariff per person for the first week $200, with a 10% discount for the second week; $630 1-month stay. A maximum of 3 nights costs $32 per night per person; for accommodations only for a maximum of 1 week, $15 per person per night.

stay away from the **zoo,** particularly if you're an animal lover—like most zoos in India, it lacks the funding to build bigger, more humane habitats for its animals.

Museum Rd. Purchase tickets for all museums at the ticket booth. Admission Rs 6 (5¢). Thurs–Sun and Tues 10am–4:45pm; Wed 1:30–4:45pm.

ARTS & ENTERTAINMENT

Shree Karthika Thirunal Theatre (alongside Lucia Continental Hotel; ✆ 0471/ 247-1335), in Trivandrum's Fort district, holds regular classical dance-theater performances (mostly Karnatic, but also Hindustani) throughout the year. The theater has its own company but hosts outside groups showcasing various genres, including Kathakali, Mohiniattam, and Bharatanatyam.

You can observe **Kalaripayattu** martial arts classes, and even arrange special performances or lecture demonstrations, through **C.V.N. Kalari Sangham** (Fort, Trivandrum; ✆ **0471/247-4182;** fax 0471/245-8996; www.cvnkalarikerala.com). Established in 1956, this institution has represented India at numerous international festivals.

NORTH OF TRIVANDRUM: THE RED CLIFFS OF VARKALA

A 55km (34-mile) drive north of Trivandrum (an hour by train), the seaside resort of Varkala draws numerous Hindu pilgrims who come to worship in the 2,000-year-old **Sri Janardhana Swami Temple** and ritualistically cleanse themselves in the mineral spring waters that gush from Varkala's ruby-red laterite cliffs. The cliffs overlook the rather aptly named "Beach of Redemption." Varkala attracts scores of backpackers searching for an untouched beach paradise—and several years ago, they might have found just that. Today, hawkers and shack-dwellers have drifted in and set up shop along the tops of the cliffs; the coconut palms have been replaced by cheap guesthouses and open-air cafes; and children flog cheap jewelry, yards of cloth, and back-to-nature hippie gear.

Nonetheless, being a holy beach, the sand at the base of the cliffs stays relatively free of human pollution—it's neither a convenient public ablution facility nor a waste-dumping ground. Instead, devotees of Vishnu attend to earnest *puja* sessions, offering banana leaves piled with boiled rice and brightly colored marigolds to be carried away by the ocean. Usually, the sand is soft and lovely, and you can find a quiet cove for sunbathing without the crowds that are inescapable in Kovalam. In fact, you can find relative peace and calm if you restrict your beach activities to the morning; by lunchtime the gawkers (female bathers are advised to be discreet), hawkers, and dread-locked Europeans start to file in, and it's time to venture back to the pool—with any luck, at the Taj Garden Retreat.

Other activities for visitors here include Kathakali demonstrations, elephant rides, village tours, and backwater trips. You can also take a pleasant evening walk (or auto-rickshaw ride) to the cliffs to visit Sunset Point. If you don't want to walk back, keep the rickshaw for your return trip (round-trip Rs 30–Rs 40/70¢–90¢; more if you want to go farther up the cliff).

WHERE TO STAY & DINE
TRIVANDRAM

Walk up the spiraling incline of **Maveli Coffee House** (between the Tourist Reception Centre and KSRTC bus stand; daily 7:30am–10pm), if only to be able to say afterwards that you've dined in one of the world's oddest restaurants. Located diagonally opposite the railway station, this unique coffeehouse was designed by Laurie Baker, an English architect who now lives in Kerala, and resembles a squat ocher-

---

Warning: Banana Chips Are Addictive

Although tourists are normally advised to stay off street food, there's one kind of street snack you can sample without a problem in Trivandrum. Banana chips are a Keralite's favorite snack, and you'll see *thattu kadas,* temporary food trolleys (particularly at night), with men slicing and frying bananas in coconut oil right on the street, almost all over Kerala. Buy them piping-hot and lightly salted—they're even more scrumptious than potato chips. Good spots to buy these fresh are near the British Library, or at a small shop in Kaithamukku (about 3km/2 miles west of the central train station), where A. Kannan has been frying some of the best banana chips in Kerala for close to 15 years. Note that banana chips come in myriad flavors depending on the variety of banana used. Those made with ripe bananas are slightly sweet, but we suggest you go for the thinly sliced variety. Be warned, however: They are seriously addictive.

---

colored version of Pisa's leaning tower. It's a favorite hangout for the locals, and an interesting spot in which to spend some time rubbing shoulders with the groundlings and businesspeople who come here for their *idlis, dosas,* and *chai* or coffee (you can purchase beans here, too). If you're exploring the Secretariat, head across the road to **Arul Jyothi** (Mahatma Gandhi Rd.; daily 6:30am–10pm). The capital's civil servants pile in here at lunchtime, when there's much ordering of *thalis* (platters featuring Indian breads and various curries and chutneys) and wonderful *masala dosas.* **Tip:** If you're keen to browse newspapers from back home, stop at the British Library nearby; it has a good collection of magazines and international dailies that you can peruse for no charge (just show your passport to enter).

For more salubrious surrounds (not to mention delicious Malabar fish curry and melt-in-your-mouth chicken masala), the smart **Regency Restaurant** at the South Park Hotel is the place to be (Spencer Junction, Mahatma Gandhi Rd.; © **0471/233-3333;** daily 12:30–3pm and 7:30–10:30pm).

There is little reason not to head south before nightfall, but if you really must stay in the city, **Muthoot Plaza** is Trivandrum's swankiest hotel (© **0471/233-7733;** www.sarovarparkplaza.com; $95–$250 double). A seven-story steel-and-glass hangout for foreign visitors and businesspeople who come to the state capital to pay *baksheesh* to various government representatives, Muthoot is functional, with good service and a convenient location, but it has no pool (though staff can arrange access to one). If you need a daily dip (and the best in-house restaurant), the **South Park** (© **0471/233-3333;** www.thesouthpark.com; Rs 3,000–Rs 8,000/$68–$182 double, including breakfast) is another good choice; the guest rooms benefited from a much-needed refurbishment in 2002, but they are still not as nice as those at the Muthoot. If you're looking for something slightly cheaper, the recently renovated **Hotel Saj Lucia** (© **0471/246-3443;** www.sajlucia.com; doubles from Rs 2,550/$59) is within strolling distance of Padmanabhaswamy Temple and the Palace Museum, two of the city's more interesting sights.

Budget travelers (or those who'd rather save your cash for the gorgeous resorts that lie south) should head for **Ariya Nivaas Hotel** (© **0471/233-0789;** www.ariyanivaas. com), an office-block-style hotel that offers good, clean lodging conveniently located near the Central Railway Station. Deluxe doubles go for Rs 1,000 ($23), and rooms without air-conditioning cost as little as Rs 600 ($14). Staff are friendly and can help with travel arrangements. The hotel has a decent restaurant and a useful 24-hour checkout policy. It's often full, so book in advance. A more pleasant budget option (certainly from an aesthetic point of view) is **Wild Palms Guest House,** where the welcoming Pereiras rent out six rooms in their lovely residence. Overlooking a typical city street in a residential area, Wild Palms (a misnomer, though it does have a small garden) is away from the noisy city, yet close enough to easily access important sights. Rooms are spacious and clean (each suite has its own balcony overlooking the street), and food is home-cooked (© **0471/247-1175;** from Rs 845/$19). This is a good choice if you're looking for a quiet place, but you may find it boring if you're alone and prefer to interact with others; note that it's often booked up in peak season.

Tip: A new law has made smoking in all restaurants and public spaces (like railway stations) in Trivandrum a fineable offence, so if you must puff, make sure you head out of town first.

VARKALA
Taj Garden Retreat, Varkala ⊛   Neatly set on the slopes of Varkala's red cliffs and overlooking a beautiful length of coastline, the Garden Retreat is hemmed in by verdant paddy fields and dense groves of coconut palms. Despite the fact that the hotel is showing its age and is in need of renovation, this is still the best address in town, definitely where you'll want to head when the crowds get irritating. But it is certainly not in the same class as some of the resorts that lie south of Kovalam—while the building is inspired by elements of traditional Keralite architecture, it's essentially a modern concrete hotel with pretty pastel interiors. Reserve a sea-facing superior room. Units aren't particularly large, but they are comfortable, with great views. Alternatively, you can head for the lobby's **Sunset Bar**—the view over the kidney-shaped pool toward the terraced paddy fields and the ocean below is intoxicating. *Note:* Although the beach is just a short distance away, some of the pathways leading down from the hotel toward the sand can be treacherous.

Janardhana Puram, Varkala 695 141. © **0470/260-3000.** Fax 0470/260-2296. www.tajhotels.com. retreat.varkala@ tajhotels.com. 30 units. $125 standard double, $135 superior sea-view double; $160 executive suite sea-view. $35 extra bed. Rates include breakfast and 1 other meal. AE, DC, MC, V. **Amenities:** Restaurant; 2 bars; cultural performances on request; pool with swim-up bar; children's wading pool; tennis; badminton; volleyball; fitness center with gymnasium, Jacuzzi, steam; Ayurvedic center; children's garden; indoor games; travel desk; car-hire service; backwater cruise; village tour; meeting room; currency exchange; 24-hr. room service; laundry; doctor-on-call; small library. *In room:* A/C, TV, minibar, hair dryer on request.

4 From Kovalam to the Tip of India
1,216km (754 miles) S of Mumbai

A mere 16km (10 miles) south of Trivandrum, Kovalam has been a haunt for beach tourism since the 1930s, but its fame as a coastal idyll has wrought the inevitable. Discovered by hippies and then by charter tour groups, it is now a swinging holiday resort, its once-virgin charm plundered by low-rise concrete hotels that have all but totally replaced the coconut palm groves. Even so, Kovalam's three crescent-shaped sandy beaches, flanked by rocky promontories, remain quite impressive. You can watch fishermen ply the waters in catamarans (derived from the local word *kattu-maram*) as they have for centuries, at night assisted by the red-and-white lighthouse that beams from Kovalam's southernmost beach.

Lighthouse Beach is, in fact, where you'll find the bulk of cheap hotels, restaurants, and bars, with fishing-net-strewn Hawa Beach and less-crowded Samudra

Beach lying to the north. After the rigors of India's crowded cities and comfort-free public transport, budget travelers are lured by the easy, comfortable (and high) life offered here, often staying until money (or good weather) runs out. You can rent umbrellas and watersports equipment along the beach, or hop aboard a fishing boat for a cruise out to sea. Stalls sell colorful fabrics, pseudo-ethnic hippie trinkets, and fresh fruit, fish, and coconut water; music wafts from shack-style cafes, and unofficial bars survive strict liquor laws by serving beer in ceramic mugs and teapots. (Party animals note, however: The vibe at Kovalam is still far tamer than Goa's.)

Immediately south of Kovalam is **Vizhinjam Beach,** the site of the erstwhile capital of southern Kerala's first dynastic rulers and, between the 8th and 13th centuries, a major natural port for local kingdoms. Now a poor fishing hamlet of thatched huts overlooked by a pink mosque, Vizhinjam is an interesting contrast to the tourist hub-bub of Kovalam; swimming here, however, is dangerous, no doubt the reason for its relatively untouched atmosphere. A number of shrines are found in Vizhinjam, including a rock-cut cave enclosing a shrine with a sculpture of Dakshinamurthy; the outer wall of the cave includes a half-complete relief depicting Lord Shiva and his consort, Parvathi.

Farther south, the Ayurvedic resorts that can still lay claim to the beach idyll that put Kovalam on the map dot the coast (see "Where To Stay & Dine," below). Visitors staying at any of these should seriously consider a day trip that takes in **Padmanabhapuram Palace** (see review below), on the way to **Kanyakumari,** India's southernmost tip, where you can enjoy one of the most interesting cultural experiences on the subcontinent (see box below).

From the terraced viewing area, you will see two rock islands, one of which is the site of the **Swami Vivekananda Rock Memorial** (8am–4pm; Rs 10/25¢ daily *darshan* or viewing of a deity). You can reach it by half-hourly ferry (Rs 20/45¢ round-trip). The memorial commemorates a Hindu guru and social reformer's meditative sojourn on the island in 1892. Several bookstores selling spiritual tomes are found on the island, but the best experience is to be had in the **Dhyana Mandapam,** a room where absolute silence is maintained so that pilgrims can meditate before a golden *om* symbol; children may not enter. A set of **Parvati's footprints** is enshrined in a temple built for it on the island. On the adjacent rocky island, a massive sculpture of the celebrated ancient Tamil poet-savant **Thiruvalluvar** stands 40m (133 ft.) high, punctuating the horizon like some bizarre homage to New York's Statue of Liberty.

The only attraction in the town itself is famous **Kumari Amman Temple** ✿ (daily 4:30am–noon and 4:30–8:30pm), dedicated to Kanyakumari, a virgin goddess. Devotees enter the temple through the north gate, making their way around various corridors and bridges before viewing the deity, here depicted as a young girl doing penance with a rosary in her right hand. It's said that her sparkling nose jewel—seen glowing from some distance away—was installed by Parasurama (Lord Rama, an avatar of Vishnu) himself. Non-Hindus wishing to enter the temple must remove shoes, and men must remove shirts and wear a *dhoti* (although a *lungi* passes; purchase one before you leave Kovalam). A willing temple priest will lead you on a very brisk (queue-jumping) tour of the temple, ending with the obligatory suggestion that a donation would be quite acceptable.

If, for some reason, you get trapped in this ramshackle pilgrim-choked town, head for **Hotel Maadhini** (East Car St.; ✆ 04652/24-6857 or -6787; www.hotelmaadhini. com), where you will be woken pre-dawn with tea and an urgent suggestion to watch

(Moments Watching the Sun Rise from the Subcontinent's Southernmost Tip

Just 87km (54 miles) southeast of Trivandrum, across the border with Tamil Nadu, **Kanyakumari** (also known as Cape Comorin) is not only India's southernmost tip but the much-venerated confluence of the Arabian Sea, the Bay of Bengal, and the Indian Ocean. **Watching the sun rise from the subcontinent's southernmost point** ʞʞ is an age-old ritual that attracts thousands of Indian pilgrims each morning. They plunge themselves into the turbulent swell, believing that the tri-oceanic waters are holy. Others revel in the glorious spectacle as though it were a major Bollywood premiere. Nature's daily show here becomes something akin to a miniature festival, with excited pilgrims besieged by *chai-*, coffee-, and souvenir-*wallas* selling everything from kitschy crafts (how else to describe conch shells with plastic flower bouquets glued to the top?) to ancient postcards and outdated booklets. But it's all part of the experience, which is quite wonderful; you can't help but be moved by the mass of people who gaze on a natural daily occurrence with such childlike wonder, effectively bestowing upon the event the spiritual significance that draws the crowds in the first place.

To get here, you need to arrange for an early-morning wake-up call and have your hotel organize a taxi. You should reach Kanyakumari at least half an hour before sunrise in order to take in the mounting excitement as the crowds prepare to greet the new day. (*Note:* **Kanyakumari sunsets,** which are obviously more convenient to reach, also draw a crowd but are only visible mid-Oct to mid-Mar and are not quite as atmospheric, except perhaps for *chaitra purnima,* the full-moon evening in Apr when the sunset and moonrise can be viewed simultaneously along the horizon.)

the rising sun from your balcony. Double rooms, with carpets, attached bathrooms, and hot water cost between Rs 750 and Rs 1,350 ($17–$31).

En route back towards Kerala, you can buy cheap, delicious palm fruits from children on the roadside and visit the fantastic palace in the town of **Padmanabhapuram,** capital of Travancore until 1790 (see below).

Padmanabhapuram Palace ʞʞʞ   Although technically in Tamil Nadu (but a mere 55km/34 miles south of Trivandrum), this gorgeous palace—one of the finest examples of secular architecture in India—was for several centuries the traditional home of Kerala's Travancore royal family. It's still well-maintained, and a meditation room features two lamps that have burned since its construction, tended by two dutiful women. Built over a number of generations during the 17th and 18th centuries, the palace exemplifies the aesthetic and functional appeal of Kerala's distinctive architectural style: sloping tiled roofs; elaborate slatted balconies; cool, polished floors; and slanting walls and wooden shutters—all effectively designed to counter the intense sunlight and heat. The private living quarters of the royal family are a maze of open corridors and pillared verandas; outside, small garden areas feature open courtyards where the sunlight can be enjoyed. Note that the king's chamber is furnished with a bed made from 64 different types of medicated wood and has its own beautifully decorated prayer room.

Padmanabhapuram is located 55km (34 miles) south of Trivandrum. Admission Rs 10 (25¢) adults, Rs 5 (10¢) children. Rs 25 (55¢) camera, Rs 100 ($2.30) video, Rs 20 (45¢) parking. Tues–Sun 9am–4pm. Ticket office closed 1–2pm. Visitors must be accompanied by a guide and must remove footwear at the entrance.

WHERE TO STAY & DINE

Backpackers head for the budget hotels on the fringes of Kovalam's beaches which, during peak season (Dec and Jan), are overrun by tourists and relentless hawkers. Most lodging is less pleasant than cheap, and you're likely to be at the constant mercy of blaring music from the beach and its sprawl of cafes. Note that these cafes are fine for a snack, but each should be judged according to the number of customers. The rule of thumb is: If it's empty, the food has been standing around too long. Your safest bet for a proper meal in Kovalam is the restaurant at **Hotel Rockholm** (Lighthouse Rd.; ℭ **0471/248-0306**), where you can dine on a terrace with ocean views; fresh seafood is always available, and it's carefully prepared. Also, even if you haven't opted to stay at the beautiful Surya Samudra resort (see below), it's worthwhile to dine at **Octopus.** Seafood is the order of the day: tiger prawns fried in ginger garlic, shark or barracuda steak grilled with ginger and chili, a wholesome tuna salad made with freshly caught fish, or perfectly fried mussels—all delivered daily by the local fishermen. Vegetarians are well catered to—try the green papaya curry or red spinach prepared in a coconut sauce—and there is also a selection of Western dishes, including a rather good spaetzle (the restaurant, after all, was once German-owned).

If you want to overnight close to Kovalam's tourist beach action, head for one of the establishments at Samudra Beach, like the government-run **KTDC Samudra** (G.V. Raja Rd., Kovalam 695 527; ℭ **0471/248-0089,** 0471/248-1412, or -1413; fax 0471/248-0242; www.ktdc.com; doubles from Rs 3,400/$78, including breakfast). It's sterile but enjoys a remarkable setting, perched close to the beach with fine views, a swimming pool, and Ayurvedic masseurs. The best-situated of all the hotels in Kovalam itself is sprawling **Leela Kovalam Beach** 𝒶𝒶𝒶, once the ITDC's run-down Kovalam Ashok Beach Resort and briefly Le Meridien (ℭ **0471/248-0101;** fax 0471/248-1522; www.theleela.com). Certainly if you're looking for the most stunning views over the Lakshadweep Sea with five-star resort-style amenities, this is the place to check into. Following a Rs 500 million makeover, 88 rooms were available by July 2005; by early 2006 (when another Rs 200 million will have been spent), the exclusive Sea View Wing will open. At press time promotional discounts were being offered, but in general, rooms start at around $240; make sure you book one of the

---

Tips Don't Flaunt It

Women should take care not to flaunt their bodies on Kovalam's beaches. Stories abound of women being harassed, and it is not uncommon for even teenage boys to boldly grab the breasts of Western bathers. Some argue that it's because some Western women consort with local men, and their "shameless" displays of affection create the impression that all foreign women are brazen hussies, keen to be had by virile Indian men. In short: Unless you're on a resort beach, where you'll be watched over by a "lifeguard," cover up, or make sure you have male accompaniment when bathing.

sea-view rooms with a balcony that's just meters away from the waves. Not as great on location, but an equal when it comes to amenities (and a great deal less crowded), the Taj's **Green Cove Resort & Spa** offers just 57 rooms spread over 10 acres of tropically landscaped gardens on the Kovalam cliffside. Cottages have traditional Kerala-style thatched roofs and are hidden among palm trees—maintaining privacy from the outside, but still offering good views. Make sure to ask for a superior sea-view room at $170—a mere $20 more than a standard room, and you're guaranteed spectacular views. Both of the Taj's restaurants, **Chemmeen,** an alfresco space specializing in Kerala cuisine, and **Curries,** serve good Indian food. The resort also has a beautiful **Jiva** spa, but reports of the services within haven't been good (© **0471/248-7733;** fax 0471/248-7744; www.tajhotels.com).

The resorts reviewed below have been chosen because they are situated away from mainstream Kovalam and offer peace, tranquillity, and charm, as well as some of the world's most pristine stretches of coastline.

Bethsaida Hermitage   Ten kilometers (6 miles) south of Kovalam, this collection of thatched bamboo and stone beach cottages was conceived of by a local priest who wanted to start an eco-friendly endeavor that could be used to aid a local orphanage. Set on a semi-private beach, amid 8 hectares (20 acres) of coconut palms, this is truly a back-to-nature experience, with very simple, clean accommodations (coconut-wood bed, table chair, and overhead fan) in a variety of configurations. Reserve one of the most recently built rooms, which are spacious, close to the beach, and have bamboo-walled open-to-the-sky bathrooms. Hot water is at the mercy of an occasionally moody electrical system, and you need to bring your own toiletries. Don't arrive expecting luxury (for that, go next door to Surya Samudra; see below); this is the place to indulge your inner hippie—red-and-yellow tie-dyed fabrics are used extensively, and there are even several "cave" rooms, but these can be rather claustrophobic. Tranquillity is the order of the day, and you'll feel good knowing that your room's rate (slightly overpriced, considering) will contribute to the welfare of some 2,500 children.

Pullinkudi, Mulloor, Kovalam Beach, Thiruvananthapuram 695 521. © 0471/248-1554. Fax 0471/248-1554. www.bethsaida-c.org. 46 units. 28 units. 46€ ($56) cave room; 70€ ($87) cottage; 100€ ($124) traditional *tharavad* with bay view. Rates include breakfast. 15% discount May–July. Credit cards for deposits only. Minimum 7-night stay over the Christmas and New Year's period. **Amenities:** Restaurant; indoor games; travel desk; airport transfers; Ayurvedic massage; prayer hall; meditation center.

Friday's Place ✦ (*Finds*)   Four wooden cottages on stilts, on a jetty in the wilderness extending straight out into the Neyyar backwaters near Poovar, comprise this small eco-lodge—the ideal destination for the nature lover who isn't afraid of the occasional palm mouse nibbling at the roof. Designed by owners Mark and Sujeewa Reynolds (who personally run the retreat), the cottages are outfitted with palm-leaf roofs to ensure that they are cool even on warm days, and each has a lovely veranda with hammock—just the place to admire the glorious birdlife at your door. The cottages are solar-powered and sport an eco-friendly sewage system—rooms lack an attached toilet, but the common bathroom is spacious, with a central copper-floor shower area. There's no pool, but the canals on the property are often filled and are good places for a dip. An experienced boatman will take you gliding down the backwaters in search of flora and fauna. Amid all this green wilderness, you would expect to encounter tons of mosquitoes, but we didn't see any, and the Reynolds assured us this was always the case. The retreat has no road access; you have to either walk 10 minutes through the palm garden or take a boat from the Poovar town wharf or the Poovar Island Resort jetty. Note that the resort is open November through April, serves vegetarian meals only, and has an inflexible minimum 3-night-stay policy.

Poovar Island, Poovar. Reservations via e-mail: letschill@fridaysplace.biz. In the U.K., © 44(0)1428 741510. Check website www.kukimedia.com/fridaysplace for more information and updated India telephone numbers. 3 units. £85 ($156) double per day. Rate includes all meals, complimentary sundown drinks, arrival taxi from Trivandrum airport, and boat connection. Minimum 3-night stay. No credit cards. *In room:* Veranda, fan.

Lagoona Davina ஃஃ Converted into a charming, laid-back sanctuary by English owner Davina Taylor Phillips, this charming little retreat is popular with visitors who don't like to pack their own suitcases. Send Davina your clothing sizes, and she'll have comfortable handmade cotton garments waiting in your room upon your arrival, along with personally chosen eco-friendly Ayurvedic toiletries. Guest rooms are small but lovely, each with a canopied four-poster bed covered in hand-loomed linen and mosquito net, freshly cut flowers, and bright yellow walls. Guests in the main house or in one of the Maharaja rooms also enjoy the services of a personal room attendant, who will pick you up at the airport if necessary. Various Ayurvedic treatments are available. You can relax after a stint on the beach in the tiny swimming pool near the edge of the lagoon. For solo female travelers, Davina arranges for someone to discreetly keep watch while you're lying on the beach.

Pachalloor 695 527. © 0471/238-0049 or -4857. Fax 0471/246-2935. www.lagoonadavina.com. 6 units, 1 cottage. Nov–Apr/May–Oct: $137/$84 main guesthouse sea-view double, $137/$50 Maharaja Room without sea-view double, $84/$50 cottage room double. 20% supplement for Christmas and New Year's. MC, V. Credit card payments made in India incur 5% service charge. **Amenities:** Restaurant; pool; cultural programs; boating; backwater excursions; library with indoor games; travel assistance; car hire; boutique; Ayurvedic massage, yoga, meditation, and Reiki; tailoring.

Nikki's Nest ஃஃ This is another resort set away from the tourist crowds and overlooking a secluded beach; it's as good as Davina's but service here is more professional, with the Baileys always on hand to ensure personalized assistance. Accommodations are in roomy thatch-roofed cottages (reserve an air-conditioning unit here) or in three restored traditional wooden Kerala houses. No matter which guest cottage you choose, you'll enjoy first-rate views of the ocean and beach below, thanks to the resort's elevated location on a small hill. A number of Ayurvedic treatments are on offer, or you can spend hours at the restaurant, which has equally spectacular views and heavenly fresh fruit juices. Located in the small village of Chowara, within verdant gardens and a collection of orchids, Nikki's Nest is virtually unknown to local taxi drivers but is located 12km (7½ miles) south of Trivandrum and a half-hour from the airport. Note that the Baileys also run **Duke's Forest Lodge,** situated at the edge of a river and rubber plantation near the Pepara Sanctuary some 50km (31 miles) away. This is a wonderfully untouched area, perfect for a romantic, secluded getaway, with each pool pavilion cabin boasting a private plunge pool on the ground floor and a room with standard amenities on the floor above ($50–$125 depending on season, including breakfast).

Azhimala Shiva Temple Rd., Pulinkudi, Chowara, S. Kovalam, Thiruvananthapuram 695 501. © 0471/226-8821, -8822, or 0471/226-7822. Fax 0471/226-7182. www.nikkisnest.com. nest@sancharnet.in. 20 units. $100–$170 nest double, $70–$135 big Kerala house double, $65–$125 deluxe double, $50–$85 non-A/C double. Add 20% per extra person. Rates include breakfast. AE, DC, MC, V. **Amenities:** Restaurant; pool; cultural programs; Ayurvedic spa; airport and railway transfers; currency exchange; travel desk; fax; Internet; shop; room service; laundry; doctor-on-call.

Poovar Island Resort ஃஃஃ Kerala's southernmost resort, at the border between Kerala and Tamil Nadu on a remote stretch of river lagoon, is a tranquil, Paradisiacal place of granite rock walkways and rubber-tree footbridges, sloping red-tiled roofs, and chocolate-brown villas. Add to this some of the best service, best food, and best

Ayurvedic treatments in all of Kerala—and the fact that the resort is visited only by fishermen (the only way to reach this island retreat is by boat)—and you see why this understated boutique resort is providing Samudra with some stiff competition. Catch the hotel water-taxi from the resort's mainland jetty, and you land in a hammock-lounging, pool-lazing, chill-out zone for weary travelers. Taking advantage of its island setting, Poovar has floating Malaysian teakwood cottages with elephant-grass roofs moored to jetties on the waters of the gorgeous Neyyar River not far from the estuary where it meets the Arabian Sea. Landlubbers can get cozy in quaint, rustic cottages (a little bigger than those moored at the jetty) with flecked-chocolate exteriors covered with a mixture of sandy soil, hay, and coal tar, and capped by Kerala-style tiled roofs. Interiors have blond-hued wood furniture; textured fabrics in cool orange, lime, yellow, and blue; and gorgeous bedside Tiffin lamps; antiques are thrown in for local flavor. Idle away your time watching fishermen from your private veranda or from the sunken bar at the large and lovely cross-shaped pool; or consign yourself to the excellent bamboo-walled Ayurvedic center, staffed by two doctors and a handful of top-notch no-nonsense masseurs. Expect outstanding service in every department. On the negative side, bathrooms are tiny, the floating cottages have only showers, and sometimes there's a problem with smells from the loo. Note, too, that the sea here is rough, so it's not a great place for ocean swimming.

K.P. 7/911, Poruthiyoor, Kulathoor Panchayat, Pozhiyoor P.O. Trivandrum 695 513, Kerala. (*) **0471/221-2068,** -2069, or -2073. Fax 0471/221-2092. www.nivalink.com/poovar. poovarisland@sify.com. 4 units (28 on land, 16 floating). 80€–130€ ($100–$161) superior double (includes all meals); 120€–150€ ($149–$186) floating cottage, 150€–225€ ($186–$280) deluxe floating villa. All rates include boat transfers and breakfast. Special rates for Christmas and New Year's. AE, MC, V. **Amenities:** 2 restaurants (1 floating, dinner only); bar; cake and pastry service; packed-meal service; cultural performances; pool; boating (kayaks, paddleboats); fishing trips; bird-watching; backwater cruises; Ayurvedic center; sightseeing and tours; car hire; currency exchange; shop; room service (on land only); babysitting; laundry; doctor-on-call; small library; photographer (with prior notice). *In room:* A/C, TV (on land and in deluxe floating cottages), tea- and coffee-making facility (in floating cottages).

Somatheeram 🦋 Dalí would have loved this shabby-chic "Ayurvedic hospital" carved out of red sandy soil and perched on a terraced cliff overlooking a beach. Somatheeram has been inundated with awards for "Best Ayurvedic Centre," and that is the primary reason to book here: Massages and treatments are provided in a hygienic environment by an experienced, professional staff who offer serious Ayurvedic rejuvenation rather than luxurious pampering. That said, European "patients" shuffle around in pastel dressing gowns with serene expressions on their golden-tanned faces; you'll swear everyone is recovering from a particularly blissful enema. Some accommodations are in traditional wooden Kerala houses, which have the standard shaded verandas and hand-carved pillars and are comfortable but not luxurious. Opt for an ordinary *nalukettu* room in one of these four-bedroom *tharavadu* houses, and ask for one with a good view of the ocean below. Substantially cheaper, the cottages are very basic round thatched structures built of stone or brick. For travelers on a tight budget, the adjacent sister resort, **Manaltheeram** ((*) **0471/248-1610;** www.manaltheeram. com) has sea-view thatched villas for 101€ ($125) during the peak season, and is also where the shared pool is located.

Chowara P.O. 695 501. (*) **0471/226-8610.** Fax 0471/248-0600. www.somatheeram.com. somatheeram@vsnl.com. 59 units. $105–$227 deluxe suite; $62–$136 Kerala house; $51–$101 ordinary Kerala house; $31–$80 special cottage; $19–$59 ordinary cottage. 20% extra per person sharing. AE, DC, MC, V. **Amenities:** Restaurant; Internet cafe; cultural performances; beach guards; boating; yoga and meditation; indoor games; travel and tour assistance; car hire; currency exchange; gift shop; 24-hr. room service; laundry; tailor; doctor-on-call (Ayurvedic hospital). *In room:* Fridge in deluxe units.

Surya Samudra Beach Garden ✿✿✿   Named for the sun and the sea, this is Kerala's most famous resort (at least for those who subscribe to *Condé Nast Traveler* or who have flipped through the picture-perfect *Hip Hotels*), and deservedly so. The small collection of authentic traditional cottages sits on a terraced hillside overlooking the sea, with access to two gorgeous beaches. The original "Octagon cottage suite" was built as a private getaway during the 1970s by Klaus Schleusener, a German professor working in Madras. Alarmed at how centuries-old carved wooden cottages from villages around Kerala were being torn down to make way for modern homes, Schleusener was the first person to come up with the inspired idea of transplanting them into an environment aimed at well-heeled tourists with impeccable taste. Spread over 8 hectares (20 acres) amid terraced gardens of hibiscus trees, coconut palms, and various indigenous palms, and interspersed with rustic pathways, Surya is not as slick (or coolly detached) as a five-star hotel, but the atmosphere is so romantic and the setting so glorious that you could easily spend your entire holiday here. Start the day with a yogic salutation to the sun, then spend it lazing by the infinity pool carved out of the rock bed; end it being lulled into dreamland by the sound of the ocean. You have a variety of accommodations to choose from, most with antique beds, beamed ceilings, heavy rosewood shutters, planter's chairs, peaceful verandas, and fans whirring lazily overhead. Without a doubt, the best options are the sea-facing rooms and suites, which have private patios and picture-frame windows looking onto the Arabian Sea, where villagers put their catamarans to work. The small beach cottages are good value for budget-conscious travelers who want a view. You can be picky and find incidental faults such as loose toilet seats, the presence of an insect or lizard, and other housekeeping oversights, but the luxury of unfettered tranquillity more than makes up for these. The hotel is relatively accessible: It's 40 minutes from Trivandrum airport, and a 90-minute walk along the beach to Kovalam.

Pulinkudi, Mullar P.O. Thiruvananthapuram 695 521. ✆ **0471/226-7333.** Fax 0471/226-7124. www.suryasamudra. com. 21 units. 140€–330€ ($174–$410) sea-front double, 180€–390€ ($224–$485) sea-front deluxe double; 180€–390€ ($224–$485) small beach cottage, 100€–270€ ($124–$335) private cottage, 160€–360€ ($200–$447) garden bungalow, 70€–125€ ($87–$155) heritage home. Dec 31 rates 360€–520€ ($448–$646). Children under 6 stay free if no extra bed required; extra bed 20% more. All rates include breakfast. Dec 31 rate includes complimentary drink, gala buffet dinner, and entertainment programs. MC, V. **Amenities:** Restaurant; pool; beach lifeguard; boating; Ayurvedic spa; tour arrangements; foreign exchange; shop; room service; babysitting (by prior booking); doctor-on-call; small library; personal butler and valet (20€/$25 per day). *In room:* Minibar, tea- and coffee-making facility. A/C in garden rooms.

Travancore Heritage ✿   Massive billboards along the highway south of Trivandrum announce this popular resort on Kerala's southern coast. Set on 3 hectares (7 acres) of land, amid tamarind and jackfruit trees and coconut palms, Travancore Heritage is separated from the beach by 152 steps; all but two guest rooms have views of the ocean. This is the place to come if you prefer your heritage faux. With sloping red-tile roofs, wooden walls and floors, high-pitched ceilings, and covered pillared verandas, structures recall the traditional style of the region; the main building is modeled on the royal palace at Edapally and features some wonderful reproductions and charming views from its upstairs balcony. Guest rooms are furnished with high wood-frame beds, old wicker-backed planter's chairs, and blinds made from gilded white *lungi* material. Views from the premium rooms, two of which have tubs rather than showers, are quite a bit better than those from their standard counterparts. Staff are helpful and friendly. There's a fine Ayurvedic center.

Chowara P.O., Trivandrum 695 501. ⓒ 0471/226-7828 or -7832. Fax 0471/226-7201. www.thetravancoreheritage. com. travancoreheritage@vsnl.net. 65 units. $70–$125 heritage home double, $75–$150 heritage premium double; $180–$245 pool mansion. $30 extra bed. AE, MC, V. **Amenities:** Restaurant; cultural performances; pool and kids' pool; beach volleyball; Ayurveda center; Jacuzzi; indoor games; travel, car hire, and tour assistance; currency exchange; room service; doctor-on-call; library. *In room:* A/C, TV, coffee-making facility.

5 Lakshadweep

Between 200km (124 miles) and 450km (279 miles) W of Kerala's coast

Ask any globe-trotting island-hopper if the globe holds any undiscovered gems, and Lakshadweep will be the among the first names to crop up. One of India's best-kept secrets, the 36 atolls and coral reefs making up the remote Union Territory of Lakshadweep (or Laccadives) are an extension of the better-known Maldives island group, where booming tourism has spawned a plethora of luxury resorts. Only three Lakshadweep islands—Agatti, Kadmat, and Bangaram—are open to foreign tourists, and the Indian government employs a strictly enforced entry-permit system. All the islands are "owned" by the indigenous people, and land is unavailable for purchase by non-natives—even a man marrying a local woman may not buy land here.

Ten islands in the archipelago are populated, almost exclusively by Malayalam-speaking Sunni Muslims who make their living from fishing and harvesting coconuts. Only Minicoy Island, which is closest to the nearby Maldives, shares aspects of its neighbor's culture, including a Maldivian dialect known as Mahl.

Being Muslim, the islands are officially dry, and alcohol is only available on Bangaram, which is technically uninhabited; avoid carrying any liquor with you. You are strongly advised to bring insect repellent since the mosquitoes become alarmingly active once the sun descends.

ESSENTIALS

PERMITS   No foreigner may visit the islands without prebooked accommodations. Visitors intending to stay at the Bangaram Island Resort can have all permit arrangements made through the **Casino Hotel Group central reservations** (Casino Hotel, Willingdon Island, Cochin 682 003; ⓒ **0484/266-8221;** fax 0484/266-8001; casino@vsnl.com). Foreigners must supply the hotel with your name, address, place and date of birth, passport number, place of issue, date of issue, and expiration date. Permits usually take 2 full working days to be processed. The Casino Hotel Group will also happily book your flight to and from Kochi for you.

To make your own permit arrangements (a laborious process), contact the **Society for Nature, Tourism and Sports (SPORTS)** run by Lakshadweep Tourism (ⓒ **0484/ 266-8387**) in Kochi. Or contact their Delhi office (ⓒ **011/2338-6807**).

VISITOR INFORMATION   See "Permits," above. For details about Lakshadweep, contact the Assistant Manager, SPORTS, Lakshadweep Administrative Office, Willingdon Island, Kochi; ⓒ **0484/266-8387** (10am–1pm and 2–5pm; closed Sun and 2nd Sat of the month).

GETTING THERE   Unless you fancy a time-munching trip from Cochin by ship (14–20 hr.), the only way to get to Bangaram is on one of Indian Airways' costly flights ($360 round-trip at press time) from Cochin. You arrive at the tiny airfield on Agatti (Agathi) Island, after which you'll be detained by some bothersome paperwork.

After this you'll be met by a resort representative, who'll usher you to a waiting boat anchored near the shore not far from the airport for a memorable 90-minute journey to nearby Bangaram Island. During the monsoon season (May 15–Sept 15), a heli-copter is used instead of a boat. Transfers cost $110 per person.

DIVING THE REEFS

Experienced divers rank the reefs of Lakshadweep among the best diving destinations in Asia, particularly the coral islands of Bangaram, Tinakara, Pirelli 1, and Pirelli 2. Bangaram Island Resort hosts **Lacadives,** a small dive center that is the first and only CMAS (an international underwater-sports federation) dive organization in India, with its headquarters on the island of Kadmat. Lacadives offers diving courses, rents out equipment, and conducts two dives a day (9:30am and 2:30pm). If you're not a qualified diver, you can rent a mask and go on one of the resort's snorkeling trips to a nearby wreck where an assortment of marine fauna will have you begging for more. The resort can organize big-game fishing with local boats, but anglers should bring their own equipment. For details, contact the **Lacadives Diving Centre,** Bangaram Island Resort, Bangaram (www.lacadives.com; lacadives@hotmail.com; in Kochi: Lak-shmi Niwas, 43/2051, K. Colony, Kadavanthra P.O., Kochi 682 020, ✆ **93886-19494,** fax 0484220-6766; in Mumbai: E-20, Everest Building, Tardeo Rd., Mumbai 400 034, ✆ **022/5662-7381** or -7382, fax 022/5666-9241).

WHERE TO STAY

Besides **Bangaram Island Resort** (see below), the only good option is **Agatti Island Beach Resort** ❀, on Agatti. Accommodations are in simple, spacious cottages with lagoon-facing porches and attached bathrooms (✆ **04894/24-2436** or 0484/236-2232; doubles $155 without A/C and $275 with A/C, including all meals, transfers, and kayaking). Unlike Bangaram, Agatti Island is home to 7,000 people, but it offers fantastic untouched white-sand beaches, aquamarine lagoons, and opportunities to explore (including PADI courses).

Bangaram Island Resort ❀❀❀   Lodging options are limited, so thank heavens for the Casino Hotel Group's keen appreciation of this unique environment. Bor-rowed from the pages of an old-style holiday brochure, this peaceful 50-hectare (123-acre) island is all silver beaches and towering coconut palms—no newspapers, television, minibars, or even air-conditioning get in the way of experiencing the island's beauty. Eco-consciously designed so as to all but disappear into the surround-ings, the modest 17-year-old resort is quite basic, with emphasis on the captivating setting rather than fussy luxuries. Guest cottages, arranged in a row a short distance back from the beach, are spartan and clean: palm-frond thatch-covered huts with sim-ple cane furniture, mesh screen windows, and private porches from which to admire the ocean. Cottages have electricity and running water (which is not heated but is never cold; it's taken straight from the ground, so although it's safe for showering, it has a detectably high salinity level and a slight sulphuric smell). The atmosphere here is so removed from workaday worries that you'll find no excuses not to recline in your hammock and stare into the magnificent cobalt waters. On the other hand, you could discover a new addiction: diving, which is a major draw. On foot (take shoes for coral-covered stretches), you can skirt the entire island in about an hour; en route you will discover a host of stunning milky-white beaches to call your own. Wandering around the island, you can also venture inland where, among the trees, you'll find the huts of the Lakshadweep locals who come to the island from time to time to harvest their coconuts. There's an Ayurvedic massage center for those days when sunbathing gets too stressful, and early risers can salute the rising sun with yoga on the helipad at

6:30am. The buffet meals are served outdoors so long as weather permits, but the best spot to be in the evenings is at the circular bar near the water's edge where, among other things, barman Joseph mixes a mean Bangaram Binge—a feisty blend of dark Indian rum and coconut milk, completed with one of his signature palm frond swizzle sticks.

Bangaram Island, Lakshadweep. Reservations: Casino Hotel, Willingdon Island, Cochin 682 003. © 0484/266-8221. Fax 0484/266-8001. www.casinogroupkerala.com or www.cghearth.com. casino@vsnl.com. 29 cottages. $290–$350 standard double, $120 off season; $525–$580 2-bed deluxe double, $225 off-season. (May 1–Sept 30 off season.) $30–$120 extra person. Rates include all meals. Boat transfers $30 per person. AE, DC, MC, V. **Amenities:** Restaurant; bar; Ayurvedic center; yoga; boat transfers; dive center; deep-sea fishing; island trips; kayaks; catamarans.

6 The Cardamom Hills & Periyar Wildlife Sanctuary

190km (118 miles) E of Kochi

Each year, around half a million travelers make their way up into the Cardamom Hills, where the crisp, cool air is redolent with the scents of spices, and soaring mountains give way to tea plantations and dense jungle. Most people head straight to Thekaddy to explore Periyar Wildlife Sanctuary, the stomping grounds for large herds of wild elephants. Periyar is one of India's largest and most popular reserves, and the site of one of the best-organized trek experiences in India. The best times to visit are late spring and summer (Dec–Apr), when streams and watering holes dry up and herds of wildlife come from the depths of the jungle to drink and bathe in Periyar Lake.

Another worthwhile destination in the Cardamom Hills, particularly if you're overlanding from Madurai in Tamil Nadu, is the region around **Munnar,** a 3-hour drive north of Thekkady. At a much greater altitude than Periyar, Munnar is a collection of vast green-tea estates first established by a Scotsman in the late 19th century—it's hardly surprising, then, that the area is sometimes referred to as Kerala's Scottish highlands. In the days of the Raj, it became a popular "hill station"—a place to escape from the summer heat in the plains. Today the landscape—for the most part—retains a classic hill station atmosphere. Watched over by Mount Anamudi, South India's highest peak, Munnar's primary attractions are its gorgeous views of rolling hills covered with tea and cardamom plantations, and the cool climate—great for leisurely walks and cycle-tours (not to mention a close encounter with the endangered Nilgiri tahr, a variety of mountain goat).

ESSENTIALS

VISITOR INFORMATION   All Periyar Wildlife Sanctuary inquiries should be made through the **Divisional Forest Office,** Thekkady (© 04869/22-2027; Mon–Sat 10am–5pm, closed second Sat of the month); entry to the park (Rs 150/$3.40) is between 6am and 6pm. Easiest by far is to ask your hotel to make arrangements; all the resorts will book and transfer you to the KTDC-arranged excursions (see "Exploring Periyar Wildlife Sanctuary," below). The **Idukki District Tourism Information Office** (© 04869/22-2620) is located in Kumily, the nearest village to the park, but it has very erratic opening hours.

In Munnar, the **Tourist Information Centre** (© 04865/23-1516; Mon–Sat 9am–7pm; www.munnartourism.com) in Old Munnar is good for arranging wildlife tours and local sightseeing excursions.

GETTING THERE   From Cochin   Periyar is a 4-hour drive east of Cochin, a fairly long but enjoyable drive that traverses mountain roads ascending 900m (3,000 ft.)

Finding Serenity on the Way to Periyar

En route from Cochin (110km/68 miles) to Periyar (90km/55 miles), and a mere 30km (19 miles) from Kottayam, **Serenity** ⚐⚐ is a lavishly converted 1920s bungalow on Kanam Estate, in the heart of a rubber plantation. It has a choice of six guest rooms, all with high wood-beam ceilings, generous windows, polished floors, cane chairs, and outlandish traditional masks mounted on display stands. Reservations are made through the Malabar House Residency in Cochin (1/268, 1/269 Parade Rd., Fort Cochin 682 001; ✆ **0484/221-6666;** fax 0484/221-7777; www.malabarhouse.com; info@malabarhouse.com).

---

above sea level. Munnar is a 2- to 3-hour drive north of Periyar (100km/62 miles), and another beautiful drive; you'll pass tea plantations and spice-growing embankments and drive through lovely sections of forest, quite different from Kerala's coastal region. See "Fast Facts: Cochin," earlier in this chapter, for information on car hires.

From Madurai, Tamil Nadu The drive from Madurai to Munnar (or you can bypass Munnar and go directly to Periyar) is also stunning, traversing many a mountain pass and scenic countryside. The drive from Madurai to Periyar should take about 4 hours (145km/90 miles). *Note:* Traveling by bus is arduous and time-consuming, at worst hair-raising, but if you want to save money, this is the way to go.

GETTING AROUND You can pick up a ride on a rickshaw or taxi almost anywhere in **Kumily,** near Periyar, where hordes of vehicles wait at the bus stand. Overcharging foreigners is common; try to ascertain from your hotel what the going rate for a particular route is, and bargain upfront. Taxicabs and auto-rickshaws are readily available in and around **Munnar,** or you can arrange a car and driver through your hotel.

EXPLORING PERIYAR WILDLIFE SANCTUARY

Originally the hunting grounds of the Maharajah of Travancore, Periyar Wildlife Sanctuary was declared a wildlife reserve in 1933. In 1979 it became a Project Tiger Reserve—India's homegrown initiative to protect the big cats' dwindling numbers. Today Periyar covers 777 sq. km (191,979 acres), and is divided into core, buffer, and tourist zones. Although tiger sightings are rare, particularly in the tourist zone, the reserve is home to elephants, sloth bears, sambar, Indian bison or gaur, wild dogs, leopards, spotted deer, Malabar flying squirrels, barking deer, Nilgiri tahr, and some 260 species of birds. It contains over 2,000 species of flowering plants, including at least 150 different kinds of orchid.

The best way to experience Periyar is with the privately run Periyar Tiger Trail (see below); other than this, all access to the park is arranged through the KTDC. These excursions are cheap, making them popular with exuberant domestic tourists who tend to be noisy, which somewhat inhibits the serenity of the experience. Most opt for the 2-hour **boat cruise** on Periyar Lake (Rs 110/$2.50 top deck; Rs 55/$1.15 lower), from where you can view animals coming to drink at the water's edge. Unfortunately, you're more likely to experience nonstop din from children (and their parents) who refuse to obey pleas for silence, preferring to rove around the boat and camcord each other. Boats depart at 7:30am, 9:30am, 11:30am, 2pm, and 4pm. A better option: Ask about the **private boat launches,** also offered by KTDC (✆ **04869/22-2023);**

these cost around Rs 4,400 ($100) and take a maximum of 12 passengers. Also recommended are the **daily walks;** these 3-hour treks depart at 7am, 11am, and 2pm, and provide you with the opportunity to admire some of the stunning flora of the region. And to ensure you have a truly close-up encounter with a pachyderm, you can mount one on a 30-minute **elephant ride** in the park (Rs 30/70¢; departing every 30 min. 11am–1pm and 2–4:30pm). Check **www.periyartigerreserve.org** for details on these and other adventures such as bamboo rafting, jungle patrol, and the park's own Periyar Tiger Trail.

Note: Whatever activities you have in mind, you're better off making all your arrangements through your hotel. Avoid any unsolicited offers from "guides" promising to take you on walks or tours into the reserve; this will only waste your time and test your patience.

Periyar Tiger Trail ⭐⭐⭐ *Moments*   By far the most exciting and tranquil way to experience the park (and one of the best in India) is an exclusive 2- or 3-day "Periyar Tiger Trail" organized by **TourIndia Holidays** (the same company that innovated the backwaters houseboat scene). Armed with anti-leech footwear and a sleeping bag (supplied), and accompanied by a naturalist and a game ranger armed with a rifle, you are taken farther into the tourist zone than any other operator is allowed to penetrate. What's more, you are led and looked after by a team of reformed poachers (sandalwood, cinnamon bark, and bison being their loot of choice) who know the terrain and the wildlife better than anyone. They skillfully track and spot animals, carry all the gear, strike camp, cook, clean, and—most important—stand sentinel throughout the night when the danger of being trampled by elephants becomes a serious risk. They also now play an essential role in catching poachers who remain active in the reserve.

You'll almost certainly come across elephants, wild pigs, sambar, black monkeys, wild dogs, and bison, and when you're not trekking to your next campsite, you'll be relaxing under forest cover or alongside a lake tributary. Meals are wholesome, authentic Kerala vegetarian fare: sweet *chai* and pleasant snack lunches served on silver trays with the grass for a tablecloth and a beetle symphony as background. Ablutions are performed in the great outdoors. If you have any special interests, such as ornithology, TourIndia will make arrangements to have a specialist guide you. *Note:* These exceptional hiking expeditions are limited to five visitors at a time, and only 20 participants

---

Tips **Alternatives to Spotting Elephants in Periyar**

You can pick up a range of spices from a massive number of shops lining the streets of Kumily, the nearest town to Periyar. The best option is to head straight for **Kerala Spices Centre** (Thekkady Rd.), where the chatty owner will offer to take you on a complimentary 4-to-5km (2½–3-mile) tour of the various plantations (transport not included, of course). He also sells nuts and delicious cardamom tea, and he's more than likely to invite you to join him for a cuppa *chai* prepared by his wife in their home around the back. Just down the road from Spice Village and Cardamom County, daily **Kathakali** performances are held at the **Mudra Kathakali Centre** (Thekkady Rd.; ℂ **94471-57636;** Rs 125/$2.85). Shows feature graduates of the Kalamandalam school. Show times (usually at 7pm, but get there by 6:30pm to watch the performers put on their elaborate make-up) change with the seasons, so call ahead.

are accepted per week, so book early, particularly in peak (winter) season. The trek starts at 8am, so you will have to stay in Thekkady the previous night.

Reservations: Post Box no. 163, Mahatma Gandhi Rd., Trivandrum 695 001. © 0471/233-0437 or -1507. Fax 0471/ 233-1407. www.tourindiakerala.com. tourindia@vsnl.com. 3-day, 2-night expedition with 20km (12 miles) of hiking and all gear, food, guides, and forest officer; $300 per person for 2 people sharing. Up to 5 people can be accommodated, in which case the cost is around $150 per person. Individual interests are catered to and special packages can be devised.

EXPLORING MUNNAR: HOME OF TEA & TAHRS

Munnar township is itself rather unpleasant and increasingly clogged by impulsive development; thankfully, the region's real attractions lie on its outskirts and have so far withstood the onslaught of tourist exploitation.

With plantations spread out as far as the eye can see, watching the mists creep over the valleys and come to rest like a blanket on the jade-colored hills is almost as refreshing as luxuriating in the cool climate—a welcome relief before you descend to the tropical Kerala coast or to sultry Madurai in neighboring Tamil Nadu.

Almost all the plantations are owned by the powerful Tata company, the same mighty conglomerate that produces India's buses, Sumo four-by-fours, and the Taj hotel chain. **Tea factory visits** can be arranged either through your hotel or by contacting Tata's regional office (© **04865/23-0561** through -0565), through which you can also visit the **Tea Museum** and the tea factory's processing unit (Rs 50/$1.15; Tues–Sun 10am–4pm). To get up close to some of the world's last Nilgiri tahr (a variety of mountain goat or ibex), visit nearby **Eravikulam National Park.** Existing only in the mountain grasslands of the Western Ghats at altitudes above 2,000m (6,400 ft.), the tahr is as endangered as the tiger, with fewer than 2,000 left. Of course, sighting what is basically a goat, no matter how rare, may not be as exhilarating as spotting a tiger, but your chances are far higher—in fact the tahrs have grown so used to visitors that you can get within a few yards of them. Enter the park at the Rajamala entrance, 15km (9⅓ miles) from Munnar, where you can buy tickets at the park office (© **04865/23-1587;** daily 8am–5pm; entry Rs 50/$1.15, light vehicles Rs 10/25¢). Avoid the usual noisy crowds by arriving early.

WHERE TO STAY & DINE
IN & AROUND PERIYAR

With the exception of the atmospheric KTDC Lake Palace, which is inside the park, visitors to Periyar are limited to accommodations that lie within a few minutes of each other along Thekkady Road (which links nearby Kumily with the park gate). Of these, Shalimar Spice Garden Resort (see below), located just off Thekkady Road, is by far your best bet. Even if you don't stay at the resort, it's worth booking a table at **Falling Leaf,** the excellent in-house restaurant. Superb Kerala cuisine is served the traditional way (on banana leaves), but the restaurant is well known for its Italian dishes—a hallmark of previous owner Maria Fernhof. The **Periyar Room,** the air-conditioned indoor-outdoor restaurant at the Taj Garden Retreat (see below), is another popular option and recommended for a romantic evening.

Cardamom County   You wouldn't say so from the dull lobby, but this hotel has some good suites with fine views into the Periyar sanctuary. Small cottages with tiled roofs and average-size rooms are terraced against a hill that slopes sharply up from the very public (and often noisy) kidney-shaped pool; bored waiters from the adjacent restaurant pass the time ogling the guests as they sunbathe. Units have high ceilings,

Once in a Blue Bloom

If you plan to visit to India's southern highlands in 2006, you may be lucky enough to glimpse the next blooming of the rare and exotic **Neelakurunji plant.** Its violet blossoms transform the hillsides around Munnar for 1 month— every 12 years. A pleasant 34km (21-mile) trip from Munnar, Top Station (the highest point on the Munnar–Kodaikanal road, from where you enjoy panoramic views of the surrounding plains and hills) is the place to witness this natural spectacle.

fans, and uninspiring black wooden furniture on red terra-cotta floor tiles. Those located higher up the steep hillside (nos. 305–314) offer superb views. Ask for room no. 303 or 304 (or even 317)—these have private balconies.

Thekkady Rd., Thekkady 685 536. © **04869/22-4501** or -4502. Fax 0486/22-2807. www.cardamomcounty.com. 44 units. $70–$110 Periyar cottage; $80–$140 county cottage; $140–$180 suite. Rates include breakfast. AE, DC, MC, V. **Amenities:** Restaurant; pool; health club; Ayurvedic center; indoor game room; tours; currency exchange; small shop; room service (6am–10pm); babysitting on request. In room: A/C, TV, minibar, and tea-and coffee-making facilities in some.

KTDC Lake Palace   The major draw of this old-fashioned stone, wood, and tile-roofed retreat—the former game lodge of the Maharajah of Travancore—is the gorgeous setting, best enjoyed from the wraparound veranda from which you're likely to spot a variety of game. In fact, the sense of wonderful remoteness kicks in when you take the 15-minute boat ride across Periyar Lake to reach the forested peninsula, inhabited only by hotel staff, a handful of fellow guests, and wild animals. The six "deluxe" guest suites are rather simple and forlorn, however: A few pieces of antique teak furniture (including four-poster twin or double beds), faux tiger-skin upholstery, and fake ivory tusks, tastelessly framing the dressing table mirrors, set the tone. Ask for a room on the east side, where the views are best. While some recent refurbishments have revealed old teak flooring, the old worn mattresses remain unchanged, and there is no air-conditioning. That aside, it's great not to have to travel to start your exploration— arrange for a predawn wakeup call and guide to take you into the jungle on foot.

Inside Periyar Wildlife Sanctuary. Reservations: Aranya Nivas and Lake Palace, Thekkady 685 536. © **04869/22-2024.** Fax 04869/22-2282. www.ktdc.com. aranyanivas@vsnl.com. 6 units. Rs 5,000–Rs 10,000 ($114–$228) double. Rs 1,900 ($43) extra person. Rates include all meals and boating. AE, DC, MC, V. **Amenities:** Restaurant; beer available; Ayurvedic treatments; travel assistance; boat cruises; car hire; currency exchange; laundry; doctor-on-call. In room: TV, minibar.

Shalimar Spice Garden Resort   In the off-the-map "village" of Murikkady, just 4km (2½ miles) from Thekkady, this pristine resort, situated on a 2.4-hectare (6-acre) plantation of palms, hardwood, fruit, coffee, and fragrant spices, offers the most enchanting accommodations in the region. Designed by the former owner and Italian architect Maria Angela Fernhof (since sold to the folks from Surya Samudra), it combines her idea of minimalist Euro-chic design with beautiful antique Kerala furniture and objets d'art from around the subcontinent, and works hard to retain the benefit of light in a dense forest setting. Scattered over a landscaped terraced hillock behind the lobby (situated in a 300-year-old traditional *pathayam,* or granary), granite and pebble pathways lead you to the thatch-roofed guest rooms and cottages. Enter through their teak and rosewood doorways to cool interiors filled with antique furniture and carefully chosen ornaments. Cottages feature whitewashed walls and pale terra-cotta tile floors, crystal stained glass, and breezy loggias; the en-suite bathrooms all have windows letting in natural light. The "rooms" are simpler and smaller than the cottages but no less elegant; instead of bathtubs, they feature drench showers. Shalimar's small Ayurvedic center draws a regular European clientele; it's built according to ancient traditions with a stone floor, handmade brick walls, and an open fire for heating the medicated oils. Up the terraced hill, along garden pathways decorated with stone bowls once used for grinding spices, the lilac-blue granite-bordered pool sits in a sun-drenched clearing. Outside and in, the scents of cinnamon, tea, pepper, cardamom, jasmine, guava, orange, gooseberry, mulberry, tapioca, passion fruit, and tamarind fill the air.

Murikkady P.O. 685 535. ℂ 04869/22-2132 or -3232. Fax 04869/22-3022. www.shalimarkerala.com. shalimar_resort@vsnl.com. 15 units. 70€–120€ ($87–$149) double. 80€–150€ ($99–$186) cottage. Extra bed is 20% of room rate. Children under 6 free without extra bed. Rates include breakfast. Add 15€ ($19) for each meal. Payment is required 30 days in advance. MC, V. **Amenities:** Restaurant; pool; Ayurvedic center; yoga; boat rides; birdwatching; sightseeing; trekking; taxi rental; currency exchange; laundry; doctor-on-call; valet/butler on request.

Spice Village 🏵🏵 (Kids)
Alive with fragrant spices and lush greenery, this "rustic village" resort has not only hosted its fair share of celebs but serves as a template for unpretentious yet quality holiday accommodations. Spread over a huge area around a network of pathways and intersections (if you're averse to walking, choose a low-numbered room, as these are closer to the public areas), the whitewashed bungalow cottages are all topped with thatch—a swell of thick elephant grass that plunges to the ground in an exaggerated curve, almost swallowing the red-tiled veranda; interiors are spacious but simply furnished. The well-priced and very private deluxe guest units are recommended; each has direct access to a private patio and garden, separate shower cubicle in the bathroom, and even a kitchenette. From the moment you arrive, when you're welcomed with a mint-lime soda and the delicate smell of incense, staff are eager to please: Guided plantation tours, Periyar excursions, Ayurvedic spa treatments, and various culturally flavored activities make up the to-do list. Nature lovers may be interested in visiting the resort's Wildlife Resource Center.

Thekkady-Kumily Rd., Thekkady 685 536. ℂ 04869/22-2314 through -2316. www.cghearth.com. 52 units. $85–$150 standard villa, $160–$210 deluxe villa. Rates include breakfast. AE, DC, MC, V. **Amenities:** Restaurant; bar; cultural performances; pool; tennis; badminton; recreation room; Ayurvedic spa; nature center; wildlife excursions; cooking demonstrations; plantation visits; shop; limited room service; doctor-on-call.

Taj Garden Retreat, Thekkady 🏵🏵
The delightful guest villas at this lush resort are mounted on 3.3m (11-ft.) stilts affording sweeping vistas of the verdant plantation-filled hills and valleys below. For the best views, try to book room no. 302, 501, or 601. The thatched-roofed guest rooms all feature high, pitched ceilings and private viewing decks; they're spacious and smartly furnished, with plenty of wood and attractive floral prints in natural fabrics. The gardens are also lovely, with indigenous trees as well as a number of exotic plants and flowers; during the season a naturalist is often on-site to talk you through the botany. The multi-cuisine restaurant here is the only real fine-dining establishment in the vicinity.

Amalambika Rd., Via Kumily, Thekkady, Idukki District, Kerala 685 536. ℂ 04869/22-2401 through -2406. Fax 04869/22-2106. www.tajhotels.com. retreat.thekkady@tajhotels.com. 32 units. $145 double. $20 extra bed. AE, DC, MC, V. **Amenities:** Restaurant; bar; banquet hall; pool; badminton; Ayurvedic center; forest treks; boat safaris; plantation visits; game viewing; activity room; tree house for kids; travel assistance; car hire; currency exchange; babysitting by request; doctor-on-call; nature library. *In room:* TV, minibar, tea- and coffee-making facility.

AROUND MUNNAR

For real Raj nostalgia, head for the **High Range Club** (© **04865/23-0253**), which has tennis courts, a golf course, and a billiards table guarded by looming animal trophies. It's popular with local tourists, so book well in advance; double rooms cost between Rs 1,150 and Rs 2,300 ($26–$53). Another option is **Eastend Edassery** (Temple Rd.; © **04865/23-0451;** www.edasserygroup.com), which has clean, pleasant guest rooms and several garden cottages. Rates range from Rs 1,950 ($44) for a deluxe cottage to Rs 2,200 ($50) for a large duplex suite. For a less personal experience, **Tea County Hill Resort** (Munnar 685 612; © **0471/231-8976** reservations or 04865/23-0460; fax 0486/23-0970; www.ktdc.com; ktdc@vsnl.com; from Rs 4,000/$91) is one of the better government-run hotel-resorts in India. The property occupies a sprawling, lovely estate atop a low-lying hill. Deluxe guest rooms are clean and comfortable, with small dressing rooms, tubs in the bathrooms, tiled floors, and small balconies with picturesque views. Plenty of guest facilities keep you distracted, including a very slick beer parlor with colonial ambience, and an elegant restaurant; order the Malabari fish curry or tandoori chicken.

Club Mahindra Lakeview ℛ *(Kids)*   Located smack in the middle of Tata's Tea Estates, 22km (14 miles) from Munnar, Club Mahindra Lakeview's guest rooms live up to the name, with lovely views of the lake below. A great spot to watch the mists swirl over the tea-plant-covered slopes below, this pleasant resort is aimed at wealthy Indian families. Choose to stay in either the main building, with its sophisticated, colonial country-club flavor (planters' chairs, four-poster beds, and faux fireplaces), or in the more down-to-earth home-away-from-home apartments, which come with basic cooking facilities. A team of people are at the ready to keep the kids busy while you relax in the Tea Room, sampling local varieties. Or opt for one of the formidable assortment of activities—from meditative yoga to rappelling on a rock-face. In the glass-fronted restaurant, Chef Debraj Bhaumik dishes out authentic Bengali cuisine, as well as a variety of other choices. Club Mahindra is often booked up with timeshare participants, so advance reservations are recommended. Note that as they do everywhere else, room rates soar over the Christmas/New Year's period.

Chinnakanal Village, Munnar 685 618. © **0486/24-9224,** -9226, -9228, -9290, or -9291. Fax 0486/284-9227. www.clubmahindra.com. reservations@clubmahindra.com. 104 units. $90–$125 standard double; $115–$140 superior double; $150–$215 suite; $150–$225 1-bedroom cottage; $200–$300 2-bedroom cottage. $25–$30 extra bed. AE, DC, MC, V. **Amenities:** Restaurant; yoga; boating; camping; adventure activities; children's activity center; travel and tour assistance; plantation tours; provisions shop; salon; 24-hr. room service; laundry; doctor-on-call. *In room:* A/C, TV.

The Siena Village ℛℛ *(Value)*   It's a striking half-hour drive from scruffy Munnar town to this interesting resort in what feels like genuine hill country. Accommodations are spread around a wide expanse of neatly trimmed lawns and a central open-air pavilion where barbecue dinners are held with a campfire and entertaining cultural performances. Split-level deluxe guest rooms are homey; these have downstairs living rooms with working fireplaces, treated wooden floors, and private balconies with lovely dam views. Ask for one with an upstairs bedroom. Bathrooms are smallish and don't have tubs. The **Peppermill Restaurant,** which only opens for breakfast (included in the room rates) and lunch, has a small upstairs section from where you can enjoy lovely views. A playground and activity center help keep younger visitors occupied.

Chinnakanal Village, Munnar 685 618. © **04868/24-9261.** www.sienavillage.com. 28 units. Rs 2,500 ($57) standard double; Rs 4,450 ($101) suite. Rs 600 ($13.65) extra person. Children under 5 free in parent's room. Rates include breakfast. Add Rs 1,200 ($28) for all meals. MC, V. **Amenities:** Restaurant; alcohol available; indoor games;

travel desk, sightseeing assistance; plantation tours; car hire, conferencing; shop; laundry; doctor-on-call. *In room:* TV. Deluxe guest rooms have fireplaces.

Windermere Estate ✦ Just outside Munnar on a 24-hectare (60-acre) estate, this intimate undertaking includes a stone farmhouse and two-unit Coffee Cottages. Warm service makes visitors feel like the personal guests of owner Dr. Simon, an ophthalmic surgeon. Accommodations are bright and clean, with wooden ceilings and floors and dark cane furniture; opt for one of the cottages, which are spacious with large bathrooms. The surrounding landscape is exceptionally good for scenic early-morning walks, organized daily, and you can try your luck fishing in one of several nearby streams. Food is fresh Kerala cuisine, with meats sourced from local farms.

P.O. Box 21, Pothamedu, Munnar 685 612. © **04865/23-0512.** Fax 04865/23-0978. Reservations: c/o Molly Simon, Trikkakara, Kochi 682 021. © **0484/242-5237.** Fax 0484/242-7575. www.windermeremunnar.com. info@windermunnar.com. 15 units. $125 farmhouse double, $155 garden double; $195 cottage. May–June off season 25% discount. Rates include breakfast and lunch or dinner. Payment in advance at Kochi. No credit cards. **Amenities:** Dining room; fishing; trekking; doctor-on-call; TV in lounge.

7 Malabar: Northern Kerala

Even though northern Kerala's history as a major spice-trade destination is well documented, it remains relatively untouched by tourism. This is largely because of the 8-hour drive it takes to get here from Kerala's better-favored beaches and backwaters. Nevertheless, this can be a wonderful region to explore if you are looking to get far away from the tourist crowds, and have time to spare. Certainly if you're traveling overland, from Goa or Karnataka to Kerala, it makes excellent sense to spend a day or two exploring this undervalued part of the subcontinent, particularly the **Wyanad Hills,** which remains one of India's last true wilderness areas.

ESSENTIALS

VISITOR INFORMATION In Calicut, a **Kerala Tourism information booth** (© **0495/270-2606;** daily 10am–1pm and 2–5pm) is located at the railway station. In Kannur, inquire at the **Kannur District Tourism Promotion Council** (Taluka Office Campus; © **0497/270-6336;** Mon–Sat 10am–5pm, closed Sun and second Sat of the month).

GETTING THERE   By Road   Kannur and Calicut are both on National Highway 17, which gets tricky in places as you head farther north. To get from Calicut to Vythiri in the Wyanad mountain ranges, take the Calicut–Bangalore highway.

By Air   There are regular flight connections to **Karipur Airport** (© **0495/271-2630** or -1314)—located 25km (16 miles) south of Calicut—with Mumbai, Chennai, and Coimbatore, and less frequent connections with Goa. Taxicabs into the city are expensive, costing Rs 500 ($11) non-air-conditioned and Rs 750 ($17) air-conditioned.

By Train   Calicut is an important jumping-off point for trains running up and down the coast of Kerala; there are daily trains from Mumbai and Delhi. Daytime journeys are wonderful if you're keen on enjoying fantastic views. Dial © **133** or 0495/270-1234 for inquiries at the **Calicut Railway Station,** or © **0495/270-3822** for reservations.

GETTING AROUND   By Taxi & Auto-Rickshaw   Auto-rickshaws are fine for short trips in Calicut and Kannur, but for longer journeys you will have to hire a car and driver.

CALICUT & THE WYANAD RAINFOREST
Calicut is 146km (90 miles) NW of Kochi

Archaeological evidence suggests that civilizations inhabited the fertile forests of the Wyanad around 3 millennia ago. Today pockets of tribal populations still practice ancient rituals and eke out a simple existence in harmony with nature, but the wonderfully temperate climate and almost permanently sodden soil has also meant that the region supports a sprawling network of coffee, cardamom, pepper, and rubber plantations, stretching over the undulating hills in every direction.

Malabar trade, which is still largely focused on spices and textiles, once centered on the teeming coastal town of **Calicut,** the unofficial capital of the North. Today this is one of India's cleanest cities, and incidentally where the term *calico* (white, unbleached cotton) originated. Vasco da Gama was first welcomed here in 1498; at the nearby village of Kappad, a commemorative plaque memorializes the spot where the Portuguese explorer is said to have landed. Now also known as Kozhikode, the city is of marginal interest to travelers, being more of a go-between point for journeys farther south or north, or inland to Kerala's highest rainfall region, the **Wyanad Hills** ＲＲＲ. One of India's last true wildernesses, the hills are home to **Tranquil Resorts,** wonderful homestay accommodations surrounded by a 160-hectare (400-acre) working coffee plantation (see below).

KANNUR
92km (57 miles) NW of Calicut; 266km (165 miles) N of Kochi

Kannur is a pretty coastal town predominantly inhabited by what is locally known as the Malabar Muslim. Unlike North India, where Islam was more often than not established through violent conquest, here it arrived initially through trade, and grew through love; Arab sailors coming to Malabar in search of precious spices married local women, establishing the Mappila (or Malabar Muslim) community, which in turn developed its own Arabi-Malayalam songs and poems and the "Mappila Pattu." This oral record of the unique history of the broad-minded Calicut rulers stands in stark contrast, for instance, with that of the intolerant Portuguese tyrants.

Tourism in this northerly region of Kerala is only recently coming into its own, which has distinct advantages if you're looking to get away from the crowds. It also means that infrastructure remains scant. Don't be put off, especially if you are traveling by road between Karnataka and destinations in south Kerala.

If you're looking to find a safe, practically untouched sunbathing and swimming spot, head for **Muzhapilangad Beach,** 15km (9 miles) south of Kannur, where you'll probably have much of the 4km (2½-mile) sandy stretch all to yourself. Closer to the

---

Not Quite Kung-Fu Fighting
While in Calicut you can watch students perform Kerala's spectacularly acrobatic, high-flying martial art form, Kalaripayattu (see the sidebar "Kathakali & Kalaripayattu: Kerala's Colorful Art Forms," earlier in this chapter) at **C.V.N. Kalari Nadakkavu** (E. Nadakkavu, Nadakkavu P.O., Kozhikode 673 011; ℂ **0495/ 276-9114** or -8214; www.cvnkalarikerala.com; cvnkalari@sify.com). The school holds open classes 6 to 8:30am and 4 to 6:30pm—with prior notice, foreigners with some martial arts training are allowed to join these. Ayurvedic treatments are given during the day.

Placating the Gods with *Theyyams*

Peculiar to the tribal region of northern Malabar, this ritual dance form evolved as a means of placating ancient village gods and ancestors. Combining temple ritual, rustic ballads, and folk art, *theyyams* are essentially representations of the collective consciousness of the village. Heavily made-up men with masks, elaborate costumes, spectacular jewelry, and often 2m-high (6-ft.) headgear essentially become oracle-like incarnations or manifestations of the godhead or of a valorous ancestor. The ceremony begins with a song of praise, performed in honor of the presiding deity; this is followed by a dance strongly influenced by Kalaripayattu, the traditional Kerala martial art thought to predate the better-known Far Eastern forms like kung fu. *Theyyams* traditionally last an entire day and include a great deal of music, singing, and lighting of torches—oil lamps are ceremoniously brandished as shields and swords. *Theyyams* are usually held between December and April. To ensure your chances of seeing a performance, visit **Sri Muthappan Temple** at Parassini Kadavu, 18km (11 miles) from Kannur, which has early-morning and evening performances throughout the year.

---

city, which the Europeans called Cannanore, the Portuguese built imposing **Fort St. Angelo** (daily 8am–6pm; no admission fee), a monumental laterite edifice from which visitors can view the fishing harbor below. Seventy kilometers (43 miles) north of Kannur lies **Bekal,** Kerala's largest fort, thought to date back to the mid–17th century, though there is no accurate account of its construction. **Bekal Fort** (© 0467/ 227-2900 or -2007) is open to visitors daily between 9am and 5pm; admission is $2.

WHERE TO STAY
CALICUT

A number of cheap hotels lie along Calicut's beachfront. Built as the Malabar English Club in 1890, the **Beach Hotel** (Beach Rd., Calicut 673 032; © 0495/276-2055 through -2057; fax 0495/236-5363; www.beachheritage.com) retains an air of history (it's where the likes of Somerset Maugham and Jawaharlal Nehru chose to stay), and the food is good (though service is a bit slow). You can get a beach-facing suite for Rs 1,400 ($33) or a simpler room for Rs 1,200 ($28), both air-conditioned. Slightly more expensive, but still relatively good value, **Fortune Park Hotel** (© 0495/276-8888; www.fortunecalicut.com; Rs 1,900–Rs 2,500/$43–$57 double) is a pleasant low-rise hotel with central air-conditioning and clean and comfortable rooms with small balconies. A range of amenities includes a swimming pool on the third floor and a popular restaurant with live Indian music. If you want a double bed, reserve a Fortune Room. The hotel is on a noisy main road, so ask for a room on a higher floor.

Taj Residency, Calicut ✦✦   With the opening of its swanky Ayurvedic treatment center in 1999, this luxury business-oriented hotel, the best in Calicut, is steadily drawing more leisure and health travelers. Guest rooms are carpeted and feature dark redwood furniture offset by dark green upholstery and pale curtains and bedcovers; a small sitting area under wooden ceiling beams adds space and character. The lobby is bright and welcoming, with wood-paneled pillars, cast-iron chandeliers, and wood-beam pitched ceilings. The sloping red terra-cotta tiled roof echoes the architecture of the region. If you do go for an Ayurvedic rejuvenation program, you can be assured of professional service. All treatments are made in consultation with the resident astrologer.

P.T. Usha Rd., Kozhikode 673 032. © **0495/276-5354.** Fax 0495/276-6448. www.tajhotels.com. residency.calicut@ tajhotels.com. 74 units. $80 standard double, $90 residency double (includes breakfast and happy hour); $110 executive suite (includes breakfast). AE, DC, MC, V. **Amenities:** 2 restaurants; bar; pool; kids' pool; health club; Ayurvedic center; travel assistance; car hire; business center; currency exchange; shopping arcade; 24-hr. room service; laundry, dry cleaning; doctor-on-call. *In room:* A/C, TV, safe.

IN & AROUND WYANAD

It takes about 2 hours to drive the 90km (56 miles) from the coastal city of Calicut to Vythiri, the nearest village to many of Wyanad's resorts, the best of which is **Tranquil Resorts** (reviewed below). Note that Green Magic Nature Resort, once considered "the best tree-house experience in Asia," is now run-down and not recommended. Besides Tranquil, you may want to check out **Vythiri Resort** ✦ (Vythiri, Lakkidi P.O., Wyanad 673 576; © **04936/25-5366;** fax 04936/25-5368; www.vythiriresort.com), not least for its excellent Serena spa with Ayurvedic facilities. Doubles cost between $68 and $80 for a tribal hut (avoid) and $80 to $110 for a cottage (recommended); all meals are included. This resort is extremely popular with large family and tour groups, however, especially in the summer, so if you're looking for a little more peace and quiet, head instead to **Edakkal Hermitage** ✦ (© **04936/22-1860**), located near the Edakkal Caves, which feature wall carvings dating from the Neolithic Age. Cottages have good views. The resort organizes unusual and rather romantic candlelit dinners in a cave. Book a cottage (Rs 3,300/$75) rather than the unconvincing tree house (Green Magic Nature Resort has a lot to answer for!).

Tranquil Resorts ✦✦✦   This is the way to experience life on a 160-hectare (400-acre) working coffee and vanilla plantation, located at the edge of the Wyanad National Park, thanks to the warm hospitality of Victor and Ranjini Dey. Situated in a 70-year-old planter's bungalow with rosewood floors, accommodations are aptly named Coffee, Cloves, and Cardamom, and are individually and tastefully designed, some with a glass-ceiling bath area that allows natural light to stream in. If you've always dreamed of sleeping in a tree house with the sights and sounds of a rainforest canopy, then Victor's latest project, a gorgeous tree villa 40m (128 ft.) aboveground and spread across three bright Flame of the Forest trees, is it. You get a personal balcony and deck with cane chairs and table, TV, and telephone. The elegantly designed bathroom comes with flush toilet and shower. Do bear in mind, however, that this is a forest, so insects may be the accompaniment to your sundowner on the deck in the evenings, though the villa itself has been secured with window nets. The Deys, both fine raconteurs, are very good about arranging tours of tea, pepper, cardamom, coffee, banana, and coconut plantations as well as a variety of walks on the estate, all clearly signposted, taking you through fabulous scenery. You can also see the workings of the estate, explore local sights, or take a trip into the park or to Edakkal caves. The staff cook wonderful meals with guest preferences in mind. The resort has a pool and an Ayurvedic Wing.

Kuppamudi Coffee Estate, Kolagapara P.O., Sultan Bathery, Wyanad 673 591. © **04936/22-0244.** Fax 04936/22-2358. www.tranquilresorts.com. homestay@vsnl.com. Reservations: TravelsKerala, Karimpatta Rd., opposite Medical Trust Hospital, Pallimukku, Kochi 682 016. © **0484/238-1038.** Fax 0484/236-4485. info@travelkerala.com. 6 units. $275 deluxe double; $330 Tree Villa. Rates include all meals, some sightseeing, and taxes. AE, MC, V (credit cards taken for room only; all other charges require cash payment). **Amenities:** Restaurant; pool; Ayurvedic treatments; plantation tours; sightseeing; laundry. *In room:* TV.

NEAR KANNUR

The best place to overnight in this northernmost part of Kerala is a family-run guest-house called **Ayisha Manzil** 🐾🐾 in Thalassery, which enjoys a majestic position atop a cliff with a terrace overlooking the sea. Built by an East India Company tradesman in 1862, this lovely two-story mansion was bought by a family of Muslim spice traders in 1900. Today, it is still run by the Moosas, and combines modern facilities with sumptu-ous wooden antiques and unique family heirlooms. The guesthouse has a pool and a dining room where traditional Keralite and Malabari dishes are served. The six en-suite guest rooms differ in size and layout; upstairs accommodations are more private. Each room has either one or two double beds. Doubles, including all meals and beach trans-fers, cost around $175. If you want to drink anything more than beer, you must bring your own alcohol. If it's a thoroughly unusual dining experience you're after, ask if you can be served breakfast on "the island"; if not, settle for breakfast on the beach instead. Nearby excursions include outings to Thalassery's fruit markets, and a tour through the property's original cinnamon plantation, apparently the largest in Asia. Ayisha Manzil (Court Rd., Thalassery 670 101; ✆ **0490/234-1590;** ayishamanzil@rediffmail.com) is 80km (50 miles) from Calicut's airport, and Thalassery (or Tellicherry) is served by trains from Calicut as well as Bangalore and Chennai. Transfers are easily organized.

7

Tamil Nadu: The Temple Tour

If your idea of India is one of ancient temples thick with incense and chanting masses worshipping dimly lit deities covered with vermilion paste and crushed marigolds, then Tamil Nadu is where your mental images will be replaced by vivid memories. Occupying a long stretch of the Bay of Bengal coastline known as the Coromandel Coast, India's southernmost state is dominated by a rich cultural and religious heritage that touches every aspect of life. For many, this is the Hindu heartland—home to one of India's oldest civilizations, the Dravidians, who pretty much escaped the Mughal influence that permeated so much of the cultural development in the North. Ruled predominantly by the powerful Chola, Pallava, and Pandyan dynasties, Dravidian culture flourished for more than a thousand years, developing a unique political and social hierarchy. In spite of globalization and the political dominance of the North, Tamil Nadu has retained its fervent nationalist sensibility—an almost zealous pride in Tamil language and literature and in its delicious and varied cuisines.

Thanks to heavy summer downpours, Tamil Nadu is green and lush—particularly in the Cauvery Delta toward the west, where the great Dravidian kingdoms were established and some of the finest temples built, like the 11th-century **Brihadeshvara Temple,** situated in Thanjavur, the Chola capital for 400 years. By contrast, **Chennai** (or Madras, as many still refer to it), the capital established by the British in the 17th century, exudes no such appeal. It's primarily of

interest as a gateway to some of the region's best attractions, like nearby **Kanchipuram,** one of the seven sacred cities of India, and **Sri Venkateshvara Temple** (in Tirupati, just over the border in Andhra Pradesh), said to be the wealthiest temple in the world. There, devotees line up for hours—even days—to hand over an annual 1.5 billion rupees to help Vishnu settle his debt with the God of Wealth. Just 2 hours south of Chennai lies the seaside village of **Mamallapuram,** where, right near the water's edge, the Pallavas built the earliest examples of monumental architecture in southern India during the 5th and 9th centuries. From here it's a relaxing 2½-hour drive farther south to charming **Pondicherry,** a former French coastal colony. Although the French officially left years ago, Pondicherry's Gallic spirit is still very much alive—traditional Indian snack joints feature signs proclaiming MEALS READY; BIEN VENUE; locals clad in *lungis* (traditional Indian clothing) converse in French; and gorgeous antiques-filled Indo-French colonial mansions have been restored as hotels—the kind of "temple" that will appeal to the lazy hedonist in you. Having caught your breath in the wide boulevards of Pondicherry, you can either travel to Tiruchirappalli, exploring the holy temple town of **Srirangam** and nearby **Thanjavur,** or head to **Sri Meenakshi-Sundareshwar Temple** at Madurai. A place of intense spiritual activity, this temple is where 15,000 pilgrims gather daily to celebrate the divine union of the goddess Meenakshi

Tsunami Aftermath

On December 26, 2004, an earthquake measuring 9.0 on the Richter scale occurred off Indonesia's coast, triggering the tsunami that sped across the Indian Ocean, destroying everything in its path. The Andaman Islands and Tamil Nadu were the worst-affected Indian states, with an estimated loss of 8,000 lives. In Tamil Nadu, the districts of Nagapattinam and Cuddalore suffered most; Chennai's Marina Beach and Kanyakumari were also hit, but suffered minimal damage—in fact, the Coromandel Coast's tourist sites remained more or less undamaged, and new discoveries were made at Mamallapuram when the wall of water receded (see below). At press time, an internationally coordinated high-tech tsunami early-warning system, to be shared by 27 countries around the Indian Ocean, was being put in place; at the same time, India was developing an indigenous warning system to be instated by early 2007.

(Parvati) and her eternal lover, Sundareshwar (Shiva)—one of the most evocative experiences in all of India.

Note: **Kanyakumari,** the venerated southernmost tip of Tamil Nadu, is discussed in chapter 6.

1 Chennai

Chennai is neither ancient nor lovely. Formerly called Madras, the capital of Tamil Nadu is a teeming, sprawling, bustling industrial metropolis established on the site of a fishing village in 1639 as the first British settlement in India. Today it is often choked by pollution, acrid smells—and people. The city is only marginally fascinating—it's a strange mix of British Raj–era monuments, Portuguese churches, Hindu temples, and one of the longest urban beaches on earth. Most travelers arrive here simply because it's a transport hub and soon leave, discouraged by the intense heat, polluted air, and fever-pitch crowds. One of its big attractions—**Kanchipuram,** city of "a thousand temples"—is a day excursion away, while the region's most celebrated tourist attraction lies 2 hours south at **Mamallapuram,** a spectacular World Heritage Site, where you'd do well to overnight.

ESSENTIALS

GETTING THERE & AWAY   By Air   Jet Airways has daily flights to Chennai's international **Meenambakkam Airport** (*©* **044/2256-1818**) from all major destinations in India; and both Madurai and Tiruchirappalli can be reached by flights from here. Anna International Terminal and Kamaraj Domestic Terminal are situated about 12km (7½ miles) from the center. The 30-minute taxi ride from the airport to downtown (Mount Rd.) Chennai should cost Rs 250 ($5.70).

By Train   Chennai has two major railway stations. **Chennai Central** (Georgetown) connects Chennai with most major destinations around India, while **Egmore** is the point of arrival and departure for trains within Tamil Nadu or Kerala. Some trains from within the state now also pull in at **Tambaram** Station, an hour from Chennai. You can get recorded train information by dialing the computerized *©* **1361** (remember to have your train number). To plan train travel, we suggest you go online to **www.indianrail. gov.in** or **www.southernrailway.org**. Or book your train at your hotel, at a travel agency (see below), or at the Rajaji Bhavan Complex (ground floor) in Besant Nagar.

Fun Fact **Rule of the Screen Gods**

It's not just temple gods who are worshipped here—much as in California, screen gods are adored by the local population, enough to elect them to the highest political office: in fact, the majority of Tami Nadu's leaders have kick-started their careers on the big screen. Across the state, you'll see massive billboards featuring the swollen face of **Jayalalitha,** a controversial actress-turned-politician who has been in and out of political power for 14 years but is currently Tamil Nadu's incorrigible chief minister. Kicked out of office on corruption charges in 2001, she jumped back in to reclaim her position, tossing her successor in jail. Once again declaring herself the voice of the people, she immediately set to work initiating a piece of state legislation to prevent the conversion of Hindus to other religions—a bill that no doubt earned her great favor with the powerful Brahmins who control the temples that so deeply influence the lives of the ordinary people.

By Road   You may not realize it by glancing at a map, but Tamil Nadu is a fairly massive chunk of India, and it will take over 15 hours to drive from Chennai to Kanyakumari in the far southwest of the state. Nevertheless, getting around is best done from the relative comfort of a rented car, with a driver who knows the way to the best temples, and who knows when and how to avoid peak traffic. The drive between Chennai and Bangalore, in Karnataka, should take around 8 hours along National Highway 4 (though you're better off taking the Shatabdi Express train for this journey). If you're moving on to Mamallapuram (about 2 hr. from Chennai), take the East Coast Road. Regular buses are available for travel to almost any point in the state, Bangalore, and Tirupati; contact the **State Express Transport Corporation Bus Stand** (© **044/2479-4707;** daily 7am–9pm).

VISITOR INFORMATION   For general tourist information, contact **India-tourism** (© **1913**). Staff at the Indiatourism offices (154 Anna Salai; © **044/2846-0285** or -1459; fax 044/2846-0193; indtour@vsnl.com; Mon–Fri 9am–6pm, Sat 9am–1pm), across the road from Spencer's, are busy but attentive. *Hallo! Madras* is a highly recommended monthly booklet with detailed information (Rs 10/25¢). City-Info's useful *Chennai This Fortnight* is another comprehensive visitors' guide; it highlights hotels, restaurants, and shopping options, and has listings for just about everything, from suggested walks to entertainment events. *Salaam Chennai* (Rs 25/55¢) is another similar publication released every 2 months. *Glance* is a tourist information booklet distributed four times a year; it covers both Chennai and Pondicherry.

ORIENTATION & NEIGHBORHOODS   Extending westward from the Bay of Bengal, Chennai is quite unwieldy. Linking the north and south of the city is Anna Salai, which starts out as G.S.T. Road (or Mount Rd.) near the airport in the southwest, and terminates at Fort St. George in George Town in the northeast. Two major rivers snake their way through the city—the Cooum River in the north, and the Adyar River several kilometers south. Between these, the most popular section of Marina Beach stretches between the sea and the city's busiest districts, where you'll find most

Tamil Nadu

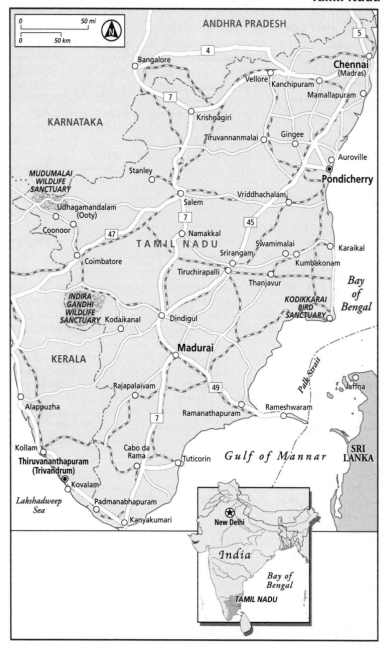

Tips Heritage Walks

Mylapore Times conducts two interesting heritage walks on Sundays from July to March. The **Mylapore–Santhome Walk** covers the ancient temples and churches and heritage houses of Chennai's old neighborhoods, the predominantly Hindu Mylapore, and the adjoining Christian Santhome. The walk starts at 6:45am; some sections are traveled by van. The fee is Rs 150 ($35). The **Fort St. George Walk** covers the 370-year-old fort, continues through old British offices and residences, St. Mary's Church, and army barracks, and ends at the Fort Museum. The walk starts at 7:30am and costs Rs 100 ($2.30). Each walk takes 3 hours (other months by special request); call Vasantha (© 044/2498-2244).

---

of its hotels and a number of attractions. George Town lies just north of the Cooum's confluence with the Bay of Bengal. Southwest of George Town (around the Cooum River), Egmore and Triplicane form the heart of the commercial city. Farther south, the neighborhoods of San Thome and Mylapore are where you'll find the most significant religious monuments—**San Thome Cathedral** and **Kapaleshvara Temple.**

GETTING AROUND   By Taxi & Auto-Rickshaw   Chennai is a large, sprawling city, and its many sights are spread out and quite impossible to cover on foot. Auto-rickshaw drivers in this city are particularly adept at squeezing impossible fares out of foreign visitors—you would be well-warned to always fix a price upfront. Unlike other large cities, Chennai does not have taxis cruising the streets or idling at taxi stands. If you want a taxi, you will have to phone for one—for short distances, this is hardly worth the long wait or cost. For longer rides, **call taxis** are a good option and run by fairly reliable meters that start at a base fare of Rs 15 (35¢). You can also negotiate flat rates, but always check whether there is a minimum charge. Some taxi companies ask for a minimum of Rs 30 (70¢); once the meter crosses that amount, the indicated fare applies. After 9pm, fares are surcharged anything from 25% more to double. Try **Bharat Call Taxi** (© 044/2814-2233) or **Chennai Call Taxi** (© 044/2561-0355). In "Fast Facts: Chennai" below, see "Taxis" for more call-taxi options, and "Car Rentals" for longer (1 or more days) excursions.

GUIDED TOURS & TRAVEL AGENTS   You can sign up for a range of tours of the city and the entire state at **Tamil Nadu Tourism** (4 E.V.R. Rd., opposite Central Railway Station, Park Town; © 044/2538-2916 or 044/2538-4356; fax 044/2536-1385; www.tamilnadutourism.org). Again, most of these tours are geared toward domestic tourists. We recommend that you approach a private operator instead, such as **Sita World Travel** (© 044/2825-2943 or 044/2827-0985; www.sitaindia.com; maa@sita india.com); **Travel House** (© 044/2811-6090 or 044/28111206; fax 044/2811-1206; www.travelhouseindia.com); or **Madura Travel Service** (© 044/2819-2002 or 044/ 2819-3858; fax 044/2819-1813; india@maduratravel.com; www.maduratravel.com).

FAST FACTS: Chennai

Airlines Phone numbers you may need are: **Jet Airways** (© **044/2841-4141,** 044/ **2858-7910, -7920,** or airport **044/2256-1818**); **Indian Airlines** (© **141;** reservations

044/2345-3305 or -3366, airport 044/2256-1971); and **Air Sahara** (① **044/5208-7070,** airport 044/2256-0909, inquiries 044/2256-1300).

Ambulance Dial ① **94440-78878.**

American Express Second Phase, 501 Spencer Plaza, Anna Salai; ① **044/2849-2582.** Open Monday to Friday 9:30am to 6:30pm; Saturday 9:30am to 2:30pm.

Area Code The area code for **Chennai** is **044.**

ATMs **UTI, ICICI,** and **IDBI** banks have numerous ATMs around the city; ask your hotel concierge about a machine near you. There's an **HSBC** ATM in Spencer Plaza.

Banks & Currency Exchange **Thomas Cook:** Eldorado Building, 112 Nungambakkam High Rd. (① **044/2827-2610);** Ceebros Centre, 45 Monteith Rd. (① **044/2855-3276** or -4600); 20 Rajaji Rd., George Town (① **044/2534-2374** or 044/2533-0105). Open Monday to Saturday 9am to 6pm.

Bookstores **Landmark** (3 Nungambakkam High Rd./M.G. Rd.; ① **044/2827-9637** or 044/2823-7438; open Mon–Sat 9am–9pm, Sun 10:30am–9pm) is Chennai's largest and most popular bookstore, carrying books, music, quality stationery, and other items. **Higginbothams** (116 Anna Salai; ① **044/2256-0586;** daily 9am–7:30pm) has a massive selection of books and Indian music.

Car Rentals **Europcar** (① **044/2852-0946** or -6090) and **Welcome Tours and Travels** (① **044/2846-0614** or -0908) both have a wide range of vehicles for rent at reasonable rates. Other car-rental companies include **Aviation Express** (① **044/2256-1013,** -0252, or 044/2435-0195) and **Bala Service** (① **044/2822-4444).**

Drugstore Located on the second floor of Spencer Plaza (769 Anna Salai) is **Health & Glow** (① **044/ 5205-6013;** Mon–Sat 9am–8pm, Sun 11am–7pm).

Embassies & Consulates **United Kingdom:** 24 Anderson Rd.; ① **044/52192151;** Monday to Friday 8:30am to 4pm. **United States:** 220 Anna Salai; ① **044/2811-2000;** Monday to Friday 8:15am to 5pm. **Canada:** No 18 Yafa Towers, Khader Nawaz Khan Road, Nungambakkam; ① **044/2833-0887;** Monday to Thursday 8:30am to 5:30pm, Friday 8:30am to 1pm. **New Zealand:** "Maithri," 32 Cathedral Rd.; ① **044/2811-2472/3;** Monday to Friday 8am to 4:45pm, Saturday 8 to 11:45am.

Emergencies Call **Apollo Hospital** at ① **044/2829-3333** or -0200.

Hospitals **Apollo Hospital** (21 Greams Lane, off Greams Rd.; ① **044/2829-3333** or -0200) offers the city's top service and also has a good round-the-clock pharmacy.

Police For emergencies, dial ① **100.** For traffic police, dial ① **103.**

Post Office Although the **General Post Office** (Rajaji Salai; ① **044**) is in George Town, you're best off making use of the **Head Post Office** on Anna Salai (① **044/2852-1892** or 044/2851-8668). Its hours are daily 10am to 8:30pm.

Taxis For call-taxi services worth recommending, see "Getting Around," above. Additional call-taxi services include **Fast Track** (① **044/2473-2020**) and **Rent-a-Benz** (① **044/2822-4444**). Generally, these services charge a minimum of Rs 30 (70¢) for the first 3km, and Rs 8 (20¢) per kilometer after that. Drivers also expect a tip (optional, of course) of about Rs 10 (25¢) per hour.

WHAT TO SEE & DO

Unfortunately, the city's monuments are very spread out, and getting around can be nightmarish; select a few choice attractions and get an air-conditioned taxi for the day. Presuming you've already spent the night in Chennai, get a predawn start by taking in the early-morning activities along the 12km (7½-mile) **Marina Beach;** you can watch fishing boats being launched (around 6am). If you'd rather sleep in, save the beach for dusk, when it becomes a colorful pageant of boys playing cricket, families strolling, vendors flogging souvenirs, and food carts offering fast-food snacks. The world's second-longest city beach, it has recently been completely cleaned up; the best area is in the vicinity of Triplicane, along Kamaraj Road.

The 8th-century **Parthasarathy Temple** (off Triplicane High Rd., west of South Beach Rd.; daily 7am–noon and 4–8pm) is near the main drag of Marina Beach; dedicated to Krishna, it is believed to be Chennai's oldest temple. South lies Mylapore's **Basilica of San Thome** (San Thome High Rd., Mylapore; daily 6am–6pm), where the so-called final resting place of Thomas the Apostle has become a neon-lit attraction. Legend has it that St. Thomas, one of Christ's disciples, was martyred at St. Thomas Mount (see below) after spending the final years of his life preaching on a nearby beach. Stained-glass windows recount the saint's tale, and wooden panels depict Christ's final days on earth. The interior is also decked with bits of tinsel and neon-pink polystyrene hearts dangling from the ceiling; other modern kitsch additions include a relief-sculpted crucifix with a neon orange border and a halo of fairy lights.

Near the basilica is **Kapaleshvara Temple** ☆☆ (off Kutchery Rd. and Chitrukullan N. St., Mylapore; daily 6am–12:30pm and 4–8:30pm), a classic example of Dravidian architecture, where thronging devotees will give you an idea of what Tamil Nadu's devout worship is all about. The temple is marked by a 36m (120-ft.) *goparum* (gateway) tower adorned with detailed figures and inscriptions dating back to A.D. 1250. The place really comes alive during the Arupathumoovar Festival, 10 days in March.

Built by the Portuguese, nearby **Luz Church** (Luz Church Rd., Mylapore) is the oldest church in Chennai. If it's peace and quiet that appeal to you, visit the 16th-century **Church of our Lady of Expectations (Senhora da Expectação),** atop **St. Thomas Mount.** Built in 1523 by the Portuguese, the little church provides fine views over the city and is serenely removed from the city's nonstop commotion. Alternatively, spend some time roaming the gardens of the **Theosophical Society,** a sprawling 270-acre campus of rambling pathways and countless trees (do make time to view the Adayar Banyan tree, said to be 400 years old). The society's headquarters are the Huddlestone mansion, built in 1776, where relief imagery and quotations representing various faiths are on display (E. Adyar; ✆ **044/2491-3528,** -7198, or -2904; daily 9am–4:30pm).

Chennai's **Government Museum** ☆ (Pantheon Rd.; ✆ **044/2819-3238;** admission to Pantheon Complex Rs 250/$5.70; Sat–Thurs 9:30am–5pm) is considered one of the finest receptacles of bronze sculpture in the country; visit if you're keen on museums or need to escape from the sun. One of the buildings in this complex is the beautifully renovated **Museum Theatre,** where you can perhaps catch a dance or a music performance. While in Egmore, pop into **St. Andrew's Kirk** (off Periyar E.V.R. High Rd., northeast of Egmore Station, Egmore; ✆ **044/2561-2608;** daily 9am–5pm)—inspired by London's St. Martin-in-the-Fields, St. Andrew's steeple rises 50m (160 ft.) into the air; you can climb this to reach a small balcony for a good city view. To experience grand architectural heritage, set aside a few hours to visit **Fort St.**

George ☙☙ (Kamaraj Rd.)—the first bastion of British power in India, constructed in 1640. The cluster of gray and white colonial buildings with pillared neoclassical facades now houses the Tamil Nadu State Legislature and the Secretariat. Visit its **Fort Museum** (© 044/2567-1127; Sat–Thurs 10am–5pm; admission Rs 100/$2.30; still camera without flash allowed with permission from tourist office) to see the collection of portraiture, oil paintings, sketches, and etchings that reveal the nature of colonial life in early Madras. In the compound is Asia's oldest existing Anglican church, **St. Mary's** (daily 9:30am–5pm), incidentally where Yale University's founder, Gov. Elihu Yale, was married. The church has numerous 17th- and 18th-century gravestones—look for the Latin memorial to Mrs. Elizabeth Baker (1652), believed to be the oldest British inscription in India.

Just north of the fort is the red-sandstone **High Court** (Mon–Sat 10am–5pm), built in the mid–19th century in the Indo-Saracenic style, and still in use today. Guided tours of the building take in the various courtrooms, many which are remarkably decorated. Busy **George Town,** bounded by Rajaji Salai and N.S.C Bose Road, was once known as "Black Town," a racist appellation for a settlement occupied by East India Company textile workers who came from Andhra Pradesh in the mid-1600s (the name "Chennai," incidentally, is derived from the name given to the area by the dyers and weavers who lived here: Chennapatnam). Today, George Town is a bustling collection of streets that should be explored on foot—not a good idea in the middle of the day.

DAY TRIP TO THE SACRED CITY OF KANCHIPURAM ☙☙☙

All of Kanchipuram's roads lead to *goparums,* the unmistakable temple gateways that tower over you as you prepare to enter the sacred shrines. This 2,000-year-old city of "a thousand temples"—also called Kanchi—features on many travel itineraries, and is best seen as a day trip out of Chennai. With a rich heritage, it's famous as a seat of both Shaivaite and Vaishnavite devotion and for exquisite silk saris. It was here that the Dravidian style really had its roots, and the sheer profusion of temples makes this an ideal place to get a feel for how South Indian temple architecture has developed over the centuries. The oldest structure in town is **Kailasnath Temple** (Putleri St.; 1.5km/¾ mile out of the town center; daily 6am–12:30pm and 4–8:30pm), entered via a small gateway. Built by the same Pallava king responsible for Mamallapuram's Shore Temple, Kailasnath shows signs of evolution from its seaside forebear; it's also less overwhelming than many of the more grandiose Tamil temples.

The 57m (180-ft.) white *goparum* marking the entrance to the 9th-century Shaivite **Ekambareswara Temple** (Puthupalayam St.; 6am–12:30pm and 4–8pm; non-Hindus not allowed in sanctum) was added as late as the 16th century. Through a passageway, visitors enter a courtyard and the "thousand-pillared" hall (though the number of pillars has dwindled significantly over the years). Within the temple, a mango tree believed to be 2,500 years old apparently yields four different varieties of the fruit. Legend has it that it was here Shiva and Parvati were married, and that Parvati fashioned a lingam (phallic symbol) of earth, one of the five sacred Hindu elements. As a test of her devotion, Shiva sent a flood through the town that destroyed everything in its path except the lingam, which she protected from the deluge with her body. Be on the lookout for touts who will aggressively try to get a donation out of you at this temple.

Dedicated to the *Shakti* cult, which celebrates creation's female aspect, the 14th-century **Kamakshi Amman Temple** (Mangadu; daily 6am–12:30pm and 4–8:30pm) was built by the Cholas. Apparently, the tank there is so sacred that demons sent to

Silk Route

In general, visitors are drawn to Kanchipuram for two main reasons: its famed temple and its silk. The city is famous for producing the most exquisite hand-loomed silk saris in the world—called *Kanjeevarams,* the bridalwear of choice that become coveted heirlooms. A single *Kanjeevaram* sari costs anything from Rs 2,500 to Rs 100,000 ($57–$2,285), and can—depending on the intricacy of the pattern (often taken from temple carvings) and vividness of the colors (*zari,* or gold thread, is often interwoven with the silk)—take from 10 days to a month to weave. Of course, you don't have to wear a sari to covet the silk; plenty of haute couture designers have discovered its beauty, and any fashionista worth her salt is in the know about Kanchipuram silk.

bathe were cleansed of their malevolent ways. Other worthwhile temples include **Vaikunta Perumal Temple** and **Varadaraja Temple,** both of which are dedicated to Vishnu.

Note that Kanchi's temples close from 12:30 until 4pm, which means that you'll need to head out rather early or—better still—arrive in time for evening *puja* (prayer). However, traffic into and out of Chennai can get hellish during peak hours. If you're hot and hungry, head for the air-conditioned room at the vegetarian restaurant in **Hotel Saravana Bhavan** (504 Gandhi Rd.; © 04112/22-2505; 6am–10:30pm), where you can feast on reasonably priced South Indian *dosas* (savory pancakes) or order a *thali* (multicourse platter).

Kanchipuram is 80km (50 miles) southwest of Chennai. Ask about guided tours of the temple town at the tourist office. Otherwise, guides can be picked up around Kailasnath Temple for around Rs 250 to Rs 300 ($4.55–$6.85); ask to see certification.

WHERE TO STAY

Given the generally insalubrious conditions of much of Chennai city, you're best off forking over some cash for a decent hotel, of which Chennai has a large inventory, providing reliable comfort and standardized service. Best of all, head down the coast to **Fisherman's Cove** resort, which is right on the beach, a mere 50 minutes' drive (28 km/17 miles) from Chennai airport and about 20km (12 miles) from Tamil Nadu's top temple destination (see Mamallapuram's lodging reviews, later in this section).

Should you decide to spend the night in town, **The Park** (reviewed below; don't confuse it with the **ITC Park Sheraton and Towers** on TTK Rd.), which blew the lid off Tamil Nadu's hospitality industry when it opened in 2002, is *the* place to be for fans of innovative contemporary design, with great night-life options. If, on the other hand, you prefer old-world charm and a place with some history, the lovely, laid-back **Taj Connemara** is your best bet (again, reviewed below). If for some reason these choices are unavailable, options include the **Taj Coromandel** (www.tajhotels.com; from $225) and two **Sheratons** (www.welcomgroup.com)—of the latter we recommend the smart **ITC Chola Sheraton** ⟨★★⟩ ($185). In a similar price range, but nearer the airport, the **Radisson GRT** (www.radisson.com) was offering great discounts at press time (doubles at $100, including breakfast and transfers). Even closer to the airport is the recently upgraded **Trident Hilton,** where you can get a courtyard- or pool-facing room for $170 (© 044/2234-4747; www.trident-hilton.com). *Note:* Many of the city's upmarket hotels offer significant discounts on published rates depending on the season and occupancy; ask about options. Also ask hotels about courtesy airport shuttle/transfers.

For travelers on a budget, prospects are limited. Your best option is the **YWCA International Guest House** (1086 EVR Periyar Salai, behind Egmore Station; ✆ **044/ 2532-4234;** fax 044/2532-4263; ywcaigh@indiainfo.com; doubles from Rs 786/$18), which has clean accommodations with en-suite bathrooms and Western toilets. It has a restaurant, and the staff are friendly and helpful. Chennai's only other recommendable budget option is **Nilgiris Nest** (58 Radhakrishna Salai, Mylapore; ✆ **044/2811-5111** or -5222), where standard doubles with breakfast go for Rs 1,800 ($41).

The Park 🖈🖈🖈 Even the most jaded visitor to one of India's dullest cities will be bowled over by this modish Chennai hotel, a dazzling contemporary space that could easily occupy the pages of *Wallpaper*. Guest rooms are a fabulous blend of comfort, style, and functionalism—for a mere $10 more, opt for a luxury room. Guest rooms follow the same contemporary-chic design of the public areas, making up for the lack of views with thoughtful, artistic touches, and the beds are tremendously comfortable. If you don't get a room here, be sure to pop in for a bite or a drink—this is where you'll find the best nightlife options in the city: the **Leather Bar** and **Pasha,** a nightclub (see below). The fabulous 24-hour eatery off the lobby, **Six-O-One (601),** is recommended as much for its contemporary design as for its unusual, varied menu—order mezze platters and seafood tapas to share, or opt for the fabulous seared fish kebab, prepared in the tandoor oven and served with a garlic sauce. The Park's other popular dining options include **Lotus,** a popular Thai restaurant; and **Aqua,** a cool cafe where the outdoor seating, on *diwans* (Indian recliner sofas) near the pool, is terrific.

601 Anna Salai, Chennai 600 006. ✆ **044/5214-4000.** Fax 044/5214-4100. www.theparkhotels.com. fo.che@thepark hotels.com. 214 units. $205 deluxe double; $215 luxury double; $225–$700 suite. Rates include buffet breakfast. AE, DC, MC, V. **Amenities:** 3 restaurants; bar; nightclub; health club; gym; spa; travel assistance; car hire; secretarial services; currency exchange; 24-hr. room service; laundry; doctor-on-call. *In room:* A/C, TV, minibar, tea- and coffee-making facilities, hair dryer, electronic safe.

Ramada Raj Park A turbaned doorman greets you at the entrance to the marble-and-chandelier lobby of this well-priced business hotel. Conveniently located and efficiently managed, this is one of Chennai's best moderately priced options, but it has no pool. Executive guest units are done in elegant albeit slightly old-fashioned decor, with comfortable beds, writing desks, and bathtubs. Deluxe guest rooms come with all the modern conveniences but are a little smaller, with an Indian-meets-faux-rococo flavor. Suites are plush, but not overstated, with two of everything and elegant high-backed sofas, armchairs, and a chaise longue in the sitting room.

180 T.T.K. Rd., Alwarpet, Chennai 600 018. ✆ **044/2498-7777,** 044/2499-3738, or 044/2467-0002. Fax 044/2499-0749. www.rajpark.com. reservation@rajpark.com. 87 units. $70 deluxe double; $80 executive double; $113 suite. $15 extra bed. 25% tax. Rates include breakfast. AE, DC, MC, V. **Amenities:** Restaurant; bar; car hire; shop; 24-hr. room service; laundry; doctor-on-call. *In room:* A/C, TV, dataport, minibar, tea- and coffee-making facilities (executive and suites only), hair dryer.

A Taxing State of Affairs

With the introduction of a uniform countrywide value-added-tax (VAT) in mid-2005, the tax you pay in luxury hotels across the country is 12.5%. However, Tamil Nadu still levies a hefty 73.5% surcharge on imported liquor.

Taj Connemara *ⱩⱩⱩ*   Book a heritage room at Chennai's oldest five-star hotel (it's been around since 1891) for colonial splendor and old-world charm right in the heart of Chennai. Although the exterior is very unprepossessing, when you enter you are transported into another era, with gracious public spaces, wide corridors, and high-ceilinged rooms, all tastefully decorated with wooden engravings, temple sculptures, and luxury fabrics. Add an attentive staff and the best restaurant in town, and you have a recipe for total comfort. Though all categories of rooms have top amenities (but no views to speak of), and the deluxe rooms have recently been revamped, they are very much hotel rooms. Our pick is without a doubt one of the striking heritage rooms, the largest in the city, with antique furniture, rich drapes, and soft furnishings in shades of gold and brown; the luxurious setting is fit for a king—even the room's ceiling fan rotates both ways, letting you decide which way the breeze should blow.

Binny Rd., Chennai 600 002. ℭ **044/5500-0555.** Fax 044/5500-0000. www.tajhotels.com. Connemara.chennai@taj hotels.com. 150 units. $180 superior double, $195 deluxe garden-facing double, $205 deluxe pool-facing double, $240 heritage double; $300–$500 suite. AE, DC, MC, V. **Amenities:** 2 restaurants; bar; 24-hr. coffee shop; pool; health club; travel desk; business center; currency exchange; salon; room service; laundry; doctor-on-call. *In room:* A/C, TV, dataport, minibar, tea- and coffee-making facilities, hair dryer, ironing equipment.

WHERE TO DINE

If you've overdosed on *tandoori* chicken, kebabs, and other North Indian heavies, Chennai is a great place to discover the unique and varied flavors of South India, particularly the cuisine of the Chettinad, best sampled at **Raintree,** the beautiful alfresco restaurant at the Taj Connemara (reviewed below). For reasonably priced but excellent Chettinad fare while you're sightseeing in Mylapore, stop at **Anjappar** (Nungambakkam; ℭ **044/2821-7200;** also other city locations), especially for the rabbit or quail. Or make your way to the superb **Kaaraikudi** *ⱩⱩ* (Radhakrishna Salai; ℭ **044/2491-0900;** other city locations as well), where the grilled stuffed pomfret or the special chicken pepper fry with *appams* are personal favorites. Both places also have great *thalis* (multicourse platters) for Rs 150 ($35). Note, however, that the ambience and service lack the finesse of more upmarket establishments. For lunch on the run, walk into any one of **Saravana Bhavan**'s 17 restaurants (ℭ **044/2811-5977**) for a delicious, authentic South Indian vegetarian meal. Order the special Tamil Nadu thali, an assortment of 23 items for just Rs 85 ($1.90), served in fairly basic surroundings. If that much food seems overwhelming, order a mini-tiffin (an assortment of tasty breakfast items) and a traditional South Indian coffee.

You'll also find many of the world's tastes represented in the city. Besides trying the classy **601** at The Park (see above), head for **Bella Ciao** (4 Shree Krishna Enclave, off Water Land Dr., Kottivakkam Beach; ℭ **044/2451-1130**), where Ciro Cattaneo serves authentic pizzas and pastas at a pleasant outdoor venue near the beach. For healthy dining in stylish surroundings, head for **Citrus** (Savera Hotel, Radhakrishna Salai, Mylapore; ℭ **044/2811-4700**), where fruit- and vegetable-based dishes and light cuts of meat and fish are cooked in unsaturated oil or low-fat dressing. **Hip Asia** *Ⱪ* (ℭ **044/5500-0000**), the Taj Connemara's brand-new restaurant, is another hot spot for a meal that's not so heavy on the gastric system. Here chefs twirl knives and jars at the Japanese *teppanyaki* counter. Delicate Vietnamese and Thai (avoid the Malay) dishes are superbly crafted, especially the starters, and served in a trendy setting that transforms itself from a lunch to dinner space.

Chennai also has several shop-and-unwind stops worth considering. **Moca Café,** better known by the store's name, Amethyst (Jeypore Colony, Gopalapuram;

© 044/5835-1627), is set in a delightful old colonial bungalow where you can choose to sit indoors or outdoors under the shade of huge, century-old trees. Kiran Rao, the cafe/shop owner, serves organic gourmet coffee and great cakes. Upstairs you'll find designer clothing in Western designs and Indian fabrics. Some evenings, performances or book or poetry readings are on offer. **Chamiers** (Chamiers Rd., across from ITC Park Sheraton; © **044/5203-0734**), situated in a charming bungalow, offers food similar to that at the Moca Café, juices, and fresh salads served in the shade of an almond tree. It's attached to Anokhi, the leading Jaipur design store (see chapter 10), where you can buy Western-style clothes designed in traditional India hand-block print fabric.

Annalakshmi 𝄞𝄞𝄞 INDIAN VEGETARIAN   Chennai's most famous vegetarian establishment is jam-packed with Indian artifacts and objets d'art. Unusually enough, it is administered by volunteers. It was founded in 1995 by an Indian guru named Swami Shantanand, and the food is prepared by local mothers, grandmothers, and devotees of the guru, with proceeds going to various charitable projects. Today it has outlets in Singapore, Perth, and Kuala Lumpur. Various set menus provide a good introduction to the different tastes of Indian cuisine; there are separate menus for lunch and dinner, and an entire menu is devoted to juices. From the a la carte selection, try French beans coconut curry or potato Chettinad. In season, try the herbal wine known as ambrosia *aroghya paan,* said to have Ayurvedic healing properties, or the date-and-honey milkshake. Another unusual drink is the *keshria chandan* sherbet (Rs 140/$3.25), a drink flavored with saffron, sandalwood paste, and other spices— beyond exotic.

804 Anna Salai. © **044/2852-5109** or 044/5214-1210. Reservations essential. Main courses Rs 180–Rs 600 ($4.10–$14); set menus Rs 350–Rs 2,000 ($8–$46). AE, DC, MC, V. Tues–Sun noon–2:45pm and 7:30–9:45pm.

Benjarong 𝄞𝄞𝄞 THAI   Popular with Chennai's international diplomats, Benjarong (the name refers to the hand-painted gold porcelain used in Royal Thai households) is the city's best Thai restaurant. You're welcomed with a ginger-flavored drink—a delicately refreshing concoction to whet the appetite—and with a selection of taste-size treats called *mein kam,* wrapped in leaves. The spicy *tom yam* soup is possibly the best you'll get outside Bangkok, made using *goong* (prawn brains) and tempered with ginger. Signature dishes include chargrilled duck *(ped yang)* done to perfection; also wonderful is spicy *gai pahd bai graprou,* ground chicken tossed with chilies and hot basil. If you're up for something simpler, green curry prawn is a standout favorite, as is the chicken wrapped in banana leaf; or go for fish delicately flavored with tamarind. Top off the evening with *tub tim siam* (water chestnut in chilled coconut milk), jackfruit custard (in summer), or *sankaya fathong* (coconut-pumpkin custard) and ice cream.

146 T.T.K. Rd., Alwarpet. © **044/2432-2640**. Reservations essential on weekends. Main courses Rs 98–Rs 298 ($2.25–$6.80). AE, DC, MC, V. Daily 12:15–3pm and 7:15–11:30pm.

Raintree 𝄞𝄞𝄞 CHETTINAD   It was in this fabulous outdoor restaurant—the best restaurant in the state, and one of the best in India—that Chettinad cuisine first came out of the Chettiar family kitchen and into the commercial arena. At the entrance, a pair of Brahmin women skillfully prepare savory South Indian vegetable starters. Other women, dressed in beautiful saris, string together jasmine blooms, which female guests are invited to wear in their hair. Nearby is a stage for nightly classical dance and music programs, where the best seats are beneath fairy lights and the massive rain trees that give the place its name. After sipping a welcome drink—a wide-brimmed copper goblet of *vasantha neer,* honey-sweetened tender coconut water, delicately flavored with mint leaves—you can't go wrong with *kozhi Chettinad,* boneless chicken in an authentic Chettinad sauce, best had with *appams* (rice flour pancakes); or try the *karaikudi kari* (lamb chops). For the really adventurous, *moolai melagu* is tender lamb brain cooked in a peppery masala. Order rice flavored with tamarind as an accompaniment. End with the delicious coconut dessert, *elaneer payasam.* Weekend buffets are good value; savor six vegetarian and six nonvegetarian dishes and an assortment of eight desserts.

Taj Connemara, Binny Rd. (C) 044/5500-0000. Reservations essential in winter season. Main courses Rs 140–Rs 525 ($3.25–$12); weekend buffet Rs 550 ($13). AE, DC, MC, V. Daily 7:30pm–midnight.

CHENNAI AFTER DARK

If there's one place you need to grab a drink, it's Chennai, and the best place to do so is the **Leather Bar** ✿✿✿ ((C) **044/5214-4000**), at The Park hotel. Go not just for the beautiful leather floor and suede-covered walls or the gorgeous clientele, but for the super-hip tunes belting from the orbital DJ booth, transporting you far away from Chennai's heat and hectic crowds. Afterwards, saunter over to The Park's new nightclub, **Pasha** ((C) **044/5214-4000**), a crowded, happening place to see and be seen—it warrants a visit if only for its completely over-the-top decor. Alternatively, head for **Distil** ((C) **044/5500-0000**) at the Taj Connemara: The newest bar in town, it has an energetic buzz (you can hear foot-tapping music down the hallway) and fresh fruit cocktails; try the lychee vodka or the watermelon martini, created by Distil's celebrity bartender/sommelier Nick Hawkins from the U.K. For a more subdued evening imbibing Spanish tapas and exotic cocktails, go to **Zaras Tapas** (74 Cathedral Rd.; (C) **044/28111462**), another stage on Chennai's happening beat.

SHOPPING

Chennai has some good shopping options if you're looking for a gift or souvenir to take home. For top-quality leather goods, head to **Hidesign** (Ispahani Center, 123/124 Nungambakkam High Rd.; (C) **044/2833-2111** or 044/5214-149). For housewares, handicrafts, and antique furniture, visit **Kalpa Druma** (71 Cathedral Rd.; (C) **044/2811-7652** or -1695). The famous **Fabindia** (Ilford House, 3 Woods

---

Temple Flashdance

Occupying 40 hectares (99 acres), Kalakshetra ("the Temple of Art") is a school for traditional music and dance that has produced some of the country's most revered modern-day dancers. It was set up in 1936 by Rukmani Devi Arundale, a follower of Annie Besant (who co-founded the Theosophical Society). Devi studied ballet under Russia's great ballerina Anna Pavlova; back in Madras, she studied *dasi attam* (also known as *Bharatnatyam*), a classic dance form traditionally restricted to temple dancers. She later set up the International Centre for the Arts, specifically concerned with reviving *dasi attam.* Visitors interested in observing day classes are welcome, and performances are staged in the school's auditorium. Visit **www.kalakshetra.net** for current events and the dates of the annual art festival (Thiruvanmiyur, E. Coast Rd., 29km/18 miles south of Chennai; (C) **044/2491-1169** or -1836).

Rd.; (✆ **044/2851-0395** or 044/5202-7015) is where you can pick up cotton garments, *kurtas* (tunics), and ethnic furnishings and linens. Go to the Taj Coromandel's **Khazana Shop** (37 M.G. Rd.; (✆ **044/5500-2012** or -2827), for silks, saris, and various objets d'art in an upmarket, luxurious environment. Across the road from the Coromandel, **Cottage Industries Emporium** (672 Anna Salai; (✆ **044/2433-0809** or -0898) is the fixed-price government emporium with a virtual monopoly on package tourist shoppers. Farther up the road is **Poompuhar** (818 Anna Salai [Mount Rd.], near Higginbothams), which has a better selection of Tamil Nadu art pieces. **The Design Store** on C. P. Ramaswamy Rd. ((✆ **044/2499-7157**) is a fine option for trendy, quality home decor with an ethnic touch. **Cane & Bamboo** (21 Marshalls Rd., Egmore; (✆ **044/2852-8672**) sells attractive curios, trays, bowls, spoons, lamps, and other handicrafts made of different species of wood sourced from all over India, and is managed by the knowledgeable Mrs. Thangam Philip, who can tell you about the different artifacts she stocks. **Anokhi** and **Amethyst** (see "Where to Dine," above) are both excellent for lovely Western-style clothing and other souvenir handicrafts made with Indian fabrics and design elements. Even if you have absolutely no intention of buying a silk sari, you must visit **Nalli Chinnasami Chetty** 𝒜𝒜 (9 Nageswaran Rd., T. Nagar, near Panagal Park; (✆ **044/2434-4115;** www.nallisilk.com), a Chennai institution, where you can't help but fall in love with the exquisite silks.

THE WORLD'S WEALTHIEST TEMPLE: A SIDE TRIP TO TIRUPATI IN ANDHRA PRADESH 𝒜𝒜

Situated on a peak of the Tirumalai Hills, overlooking Tirupati (just across the Tamil Nadu border into Andhra Pradesh), is the most active religious pilgrimage destination on earth, drawing more than 10 million devoted pilgrims every year—apparently, more than either Jerusalem or Rome. The richest in all India, and potentially the wealthiest single temple or church on earth, Dravidian-style **Sri Venkateshvara Temple** is said to be the heart of Hindu piety, but in many ways it appears to exist expressly for the collection of wealth connected to a legendary loan: Lord Venkateshwara, the living form of Vishnu, apparently borrowed an enormous amount of money from the God of Wealth in order to secure a dowry for his bride. Devotees donate generously in order to help their god settle his debt—the loan must be repaid in full, with interest, before the end of this epoch. Annual donations of jewelry, cash, and gold (along with sales of *laddus* or sweets and donated human hair) total around 1.5 billion rupees. Much of this goes to the temple kitchens that prepare meals, free accommodations for pilgrims, and various charitable hospitals and schools.

The inner shrine is presided over by a diamond-ornamented 2m (6-ft.) black idol that stands at the end of a narrow passage. Pilgrims queue for hours, sometimes days, excitedly preparing for *darshan*—the extraordinarily brief moment when you're all but pushed past the god by guards to ensure that the sanctum doesn't become clogged with devotees, many of whom succumb to the moment by falling to the ground. Waiting amid the mass of anxious, highly charged pilgrims, you'll get a good sense of the religious fervor of the Hindu faith. By the time you reach the moment of *darshan,* thousands of excited, expectant worshippers will be behind you, chanting Vishnu's name. Once out of the inner shrine (one of the few in South India that non-Hindus can enter), you'll make your way past a massive fish-tank-like enclosure, where temple clerks count the day's takings—possibly the most cash you're ever likely to see in one place.

Tips **Jumping the Queue**

Wealthier pilgrims can now make use of a computerized virtual queue system that streamlines the *darshan* experience. Pilgrims buy an arm band imprinted with their *darshan* time, shaving hours—even days—off their wait in line. Foreign visitors should bring their passports and appeal to the Assistant Executive Officer or A.E.O. (ask one of the temple police for directions) for a special *darshan* ticket, which costs anywhere from Rs 200 to Rs 3,500 ($4.55–$79) depending on the kind of speedy access you request (you will also be fingerprinted and photographed at this stage; ask your hotel if you need to book this a day in advance). Paid for at a special counter, it cuts waiting time to around 2 hours. Note that men must wear long pants or *lungis.* Prior to entering the queue, you'll be asked to sign allegiance to the god. Avoid taking part if you suffer from claustrophobia, since you'll still have to spend an hour or two within cagelike passages designed to prevent line-jumping. Temple activities commence at 3am with a wake-up call to the idol *(suprabhatham)* and continue until 12:45am the following morning.

Note: As you're waiting in line, you'll see many shaven heads—it's common practice for believers to have their heads tonsured before going before the deity as a devotional sacrifice. As a result, a lucrative human hair business contributes significantly to the temple coffers—Far East and Italian wig manufacturers are major consumers of world-renowned Tirumalai hair, shorn by a fleet of barbers permanently in the service of the temple.

ESSENTIALS   The easiest ways to get here are by train from Chennai (or Hyderabad, Bangalore, or Mumbai); or by one of **Indian Airlines'** (© **0877/228-3992**) four weekly flights to and from Hyderabad (taxis into town should cost around Rs 200/$4.55). To overnight, make sure to prebook a room at the dependable **ITC Fortune Kences** (© **0877/225-5855;** www.fortuneparkhotels.com; doubles Rs 1,500–Rs 1,800/$35–$41), which is located in the heart of the town and draws the more well-off devotees. Service is good and the hotel is comfortable (but not luxurious). It provides every amenity you'd require on a trip to Tirupati, including two restaurants and *two* bars.

2 Mamallapuram (Mahabalipurum) ★★★

51km (31 miles) S of Chennai

A visit to this once-thriving port city of the Pallavas, a dynasty that ruled much of South India between the 4th and 9th centuries A.D., is an excellent introduction to South Indian temple architecture. Established by Mamalla, "the Great Wrestler," the tourist town of Mamallapuram attracts thousands to view the earliest examples of monumental architecture in southern India—incredible rock-cut shrines that celebrate Hinduism's sacred pantheon and legends. Even today, the sounds of sculptors chipping away at blocks of stone—creating carvings for temples, hotel foyers, and tourists—echo through the streets, a reminder of the sort of devoted craftsmanship that must have possessed the original masons who created the World Heritage monuments of Mamallapuram. It's possible to survey the best monuments in a morning, provided you get an early start (ideally, long before domestic tourists arrive en masse around mid-morning). This leaves you time to unwind on the pleasant beach and dine on succulent seafood at a village cafe (for a song). But if you don't plan on hanging around, you can move on to Pondicherry after lunch and be sipping Gallic cocktails before sundown.

If, on the other hand, you are returning to Chennai via the scenic East Coast Highway, you may want to schedule a stop at the cultural centers of **Cholamandalam** and **Dakshina Chitra.** At **Cholamandalam Artists' Village** (Injambakkam, 13 km/8 miles south of Chennai; ✆ **044/2449-0092;** daily 9am–7pm), artists live, work, and exhibit their paintings, sculpture, graphic arts, and batik, and an open-air theater hosts regular dance performances. **Dakshina Chitra** is a heritage center showcasing different living styles from India's four southern states: Karnataka, Tamil Nadu, Kerala, and Andhra Pradesh. You can also observe weavers, potters, and traditional puppeteers at work, a good way to get in-depth knowledge of local arts and culture before they completely erode. Informative guided tours of the reconstructed heritage village are available for Rs 500 ($11; Muttukadu, East Coast Rd., 30km/18 miles south of Chennai; ✆ **044/2491-8943** or 044/2446-2435; entry Rs 175/$4; Wed–Mon 10am–6pm).

ESSENTIALS

GETTING THERE & AWAY   Mamallapuram is 2 hours south of Chennai, on the East Coast Highway (though you may want to schedule a stop; see above). Buses from Chennai arrive and depart every half-hour from the suburban Koyambedu bus stand (state-owned buses at Mofussil and private buses at Omni stand). Prepaid tourist taxis from downtown Chennai cost Rs 500 to Rs 600 ($11–$14), or Rs 400 ($9.10) from the Koyambedu bus stand, but may not include the Rs 50 ($1.15) toll (see "Fast Facts: Chennai," earlier in this chapter). Pondicherry is 2½ hours away by road; a taxi here should cost around Rs 1,200 to Rs 1,300 ($28–$30).

VISITOR INFORMATION   The **Government of Tamil Nadu Tourist Office** (Kovalam Rd.; ✆ **04114/242-232;** Mon–Fri 10am–5:45pm) can supply you with limited information and a map of Tamil Nadu or booklets on the town. You can also rent a **camping site** with Western toilet facilities (Rs 200/$4.55 per night), 2km (1¼ miles) from Mamallapuram, or a simple **cottage** with a sea view (Rs 550/$13).

GETTING AROUND   All of the town's attractions can be reached on foot, or you can rent a bicycle or catch an auto-rickshaw.

GUIDES & TOURS   **Hi-Tours** (123 East Raja St.; ✆ **04114/244-3260** or 04114/243-360; Mon–Sat 9am–6pm; also open Sun June–Sept and Jan–Mar; www.hitours.com) runs a smooth operation and will in fact customize a tour of the entire state for you, organizing flights, train tickets, taxis, and hotels at decent rates. **Guides** are available at the entrances to Panch Rathas and Shore Temple; they charge around Rs 250 to Rs 350 ($5.70–$8).

EXPLORING THE SHRINES & TEMPLES

Mamallapuram's monolithic shrines and rock-cut cave temples lie scattered over a landscape heaped with boulders and rocky hillocks. Among these, the excellent **Shore Temple,** built to Lord Shiva, and the **Five Rathas,** a cluster of temples named for the five Pandava brothers of *Mahabharata* fame, are definitely worth seeking out. The celebrated **Arjuna's Penance** is the largest relief-carving on earth—try to see these as early in the day as possible, before busloads of noisy holiday-makers descend. Also try to view **Mahishamardini Mandapa** (and give the nearby government-run Sculpture Museum a miss). If you feel the need to visit an active temple, head for **Talasayana Perumal Temple,** dedicated to Vishnu. It stands on the site of an original 9th-century Pallava temple but was rebuilt during the 14th century by the Vijayanagar King Parang Kusan, who feared that the sea would eventually erode Shore Temple. Half-hour *puja* (prayer) sessions are conducted daily at 9am, 11:30am, and 7:30pm. About 4km (2½ miles) north of Mamallapuram, **Tiger Cave** (Covelong Rd.) is the site of an 8th-century shrine to the tiger-loving goddess Durga. It's thought that the shallow cave, with its sculpted *yalis* (mythical beasts) framing the entrance, might have been used for open-air performances. Seventeen kilometers (11 miles) west of Mamallapuram, in the Kanchipuram district, **Tirukkazhukundram,** named for the holy kites (eagle-type birds) that make their home here, are popular with pilgrims who come to witness the Brahmin priests feeding the two birds of prey at midday. *Note:* Herpetologists and beleaguered parents may wish to make a pilgrimage of a very different kind: Set up by the famous herpetologist Romulus Whitaker, **Crocodile Bank** (15km/9 miles north of Mamallapuram; Rs 20/45¢; Wed–Mon 9am–5:30pm) is an extremely successful breeding and research center that currently sustains around 2,500 crocodiles, including 14 of the world's 26 species.

Arjuna's Penance   Opposite Talasayana Perumal Temple, the world's largest bas-relief is commonly referred to as "The Descent of the Ganges," depicting the sacred penance performed by one of the Pandava brothers. Standing on one leg, the meditative Arjuna contemplates Shiva—a painful reparation performed while lively representations of the gods, celestial nymphs, elephants, monkeys, and other creatures look on. A naturally occurring cleft down the rock is said to represent the Ganges, a symbol that comes to life during the rainy season when water flows into a tank below. Just a few meters away, to the left of Arjuna's Penance, is **Krishna Mandapam**, another bas-relief, carved in the mid–7th century; this one depicts Krishna using his divine strength to lift a mountain to protect people from imminent floods. The duality of the god's nature is expressed in carvings of him going about more mundane activities, including flirting with his milkmaids. Near Arjuna's Penance, to the north, is the huge spherical boulder known as **Krishna's Butter Ball,** balancing on a hillside.
W. Raja St.

Mahishasuramardini Cave   A lighthouse tops the hill where you'll find a number of superb rock-cut shrines—seek out **Mahishasuramardini Mandapa,** remarkable for the two impressive friezes at each end of its long veranda. In the panel to the right, Durga, the terrifying mother of the universe, is seated astride her lion *vahana* wielding an assortment of weapons. She is in the process of destroying the buffalo-headed demon, Mahisha, who disturbs the delicate balance of life. At the opposite end of the veranda, Vishnu is depicted sleeping peacefully on his serpent bed, the sea of eternity; gathered around him, the gods appeal to him to continue the creation. Also atop the hill, **Adivaraha Mandap** features various sculpted figures and mythical scenes, including one large panel of Vishnu as a gigantic boar.
W. Raja St.

Panch Pandava Rathas   The initial sight of these five *(panch)* monolithic stone shrines, set in a sandy fenced-off clearing, is dramatic, even though the structures themselves—named for the five brother-heroes of the *Mahabharata* and resembling

Lost City: The Temple Discovered Post-Tsunami

When the December 2004 tsunami hit Mamallapuram, it thankfully caused no damage. In fact, when the powerful wall of water began to recede, it uncovered ancient rock sculptures of lions, elephants, and peacocks—all fairly common motifs used to decorate walls and temples during the Pallava period in the 7th and 8th centuries. Could this be the remains of a once thriving city, submerged below the sea when the shoreline changed? Perhaps. Archaeologists working off the coast after the tsunami have already uncovered the remains of a massive collapsed temple, built entirely of granite blocks, renewing speculation that Mamallapuram was a part of the legendary Seven Pagodas, written of in the diaries of European travelers, and that six temples remain submerged in the ocean.

temple chariots *(rathas)*—are incomplete. The ancient sculpting techniques are astonishing: Carved out of single pieces of rock from the top down, these shrines reveal perfect, precise planning. The dome-shaped *shikhara* (tower finial) found on some of the temples became the template for later South Indian temples, successful experiments that were further refined and enlarged.

E. Raja St., 1km (a half-mile) south of Arjuna's Penance. Tickets available from ASI booth at the entrance. Single ticket for both Five Rathas and Shore Temple costs Rs 250 ($5.70). Daily 6:30am–5:30pm. Approved guides can be hired at the entrance.

Shore Temple ᏏᏏᏏ   Perched at the edge of a sandy beach on the Bay of Bengal, where it has been subjected to centuries of battering by salt water and oceanic winds, this early-8th-century stone temple is considered one of the oldest temples in South India, and a forerunner of the Dravidian style. Its two carved towers inspired a style that spread throughout the region and to more distant Asian shores. Vishnu is found reclining inside one shrine, while two others are dedicated to Shiva. A low boundary wall topped by rock-cut Nandi bulls surrounds the temple, and a veritable pride of lions rear their heads from the base of the pillars.

Northeast of the Panch Pandava Rathas, at the beach. Tickets available from ASI booth at the entrance. A single ticket for entrance to both the Five Rathas and the Shore Temple costs Rs 250 ($5.70). Daily 6:30am–5:30pm. Approved guides can be hired at the entrance.

WHERE TO STAY

If you want to be closer to Mamallapuram's temples, you have two good seafront options. **Temple Bay** is a wonderfully situated, chalet-style resort with good amenities (pool, travel desk, salon) and a view of the Shore Temple from the restaurant (avoid the canteen-style coffee shop, however). Its best accommodations are the cottages overlooking the ocean with private patios; these have air-conditioning, TV, and minibars (✆ **04114/242-251,** -2252, -2253, or -2254; mail@grttemplebay.com; www.grttemplebay.com; doubles Rs 5,000/$114). Located just 3km (2 miles) from Mamallapuram (near Tiger Caves), **Ideal Beach Resort** is a little more run-down but fairly well managed, with a range of standard amenities. The best thing about it is its location, right on the beach. Ask for an upstairs unit with an ocean view (✆ **04114/ 242-240;** www.idealresort.com; doubles Rs 1,700–Rs 5,000/$39–$114).

Taj Fisherman's Cove ᏏᏏᏏ   Built on the site of a 17th-century Dutch fort, this bright, breezy, beachfront resort is set on 8.8 manicured hectares (25 acres) with a labyrinth of tidy, shrub-lined pathways. It's a great refuge, within easy striking distance of both Chennai and Mamallapuram. Most guest rooms are in the main hotel block (those with sea views have expansive floor-to-ceiling windows). The shell-shaped cottages closer to the beach are delightful, with bamboo-enclosed alfresco showers; private hammocks; bright interiors in shades of orange, yellow, and green; and breezy patios with beautiful Chettinad swings. Those cottages facing the sea directly (nos. C4–C14) are the best spots from which to admire the surf. Larger luxury sea-facing cottages are also available; each one has a totally private garden with palm trees supporting your own hammock and cane-strung rockers on a covered porch. Interiors are a little more formal and old-fashioned, but also more spacious, with high-pitched ceilings and an indoor bathroom that has a separate tub and shower. When you're not out exploring ancient temples, you can try out the huge number of activities on offer, laze around a pool with a sunken swim-up bar, stroll along the beach to the nearby village of Kovalam (also known as Covelong; not to be mistaken for its more famous namesake in Kerala), peruse the menu at the thatched beachside **Bay View Point,** or dine on Mediterranean fare at the new **Upper Deck** (a lovely dinner location). At press time, plans were underway to open the Taj's new signature **Jiva** spa.

Covelong Beach, Kanchipuram District, Chennai 603 112. © 04114/27-2304 through -06. Fax 04114/27-2303. www.tajhotels.com. fishcove.Chennai@tajhotels.com. 50 units; 38 cottages. $160 standard double, $170 standard sea-view double; $195 cottage garden-view double; $220 sea-view cottage; $245 sea-view villa with private garden. $20 extra bed. Supplements: $60–$120 room (Dec 23–Jan 5); $70–$115 Christmas/New Year's. AE, MC, V. **Amenities:** 3 restaurants; 2 bars; pool; kids' pool; tennis; health club; beach volleyball; badminton; bicycles; children's activity center; indoor games; concierge; travel desk; catamaran trips; fishing excursions; ecology tours; car hire; currency exchange; shopping arcade; 24-hr. room service; Ayurvedic massage center; babysitting; doctor-on-call; library. *In room:* A/C, TV, minibar, tea- and coffee-making facilities, hair dryer.

WHERE TO DINE

Seafood, not surprisingly, is popular and abundant; it's also amazingly affordable, with the most expensive item being lobster at Rs 1,350 ($31) per kilogram (2.2 lbs.). *Note:* None of the following take credit cards. **Sea Shore** (Fisherman Colony, Mamallapuram Beach) is the cleanest of the shack-style restaurants situated directly on the beach, and it opens first thing in the morning. It has a great view of the Shore Temple; sit in the upstairs section, which has even better views. Tables are covered with simple Indian throws and chairs are plastic, but the seafood is fit for a king. Have your choice of fresh lobster, tiger prawns, calamari, tuna, or shark—all washed down with an ice-cold Kingfisher beer or delicious lassi. Another recommended shack-style beach restaurant with a view of the Shore Temple, **Luna Magica** (© **04114/24-2521**) is where Chef Rajindran has been pulling in customers since 1992. Also check out **Gazebo** on East Raja Street (© **04114/24-2525**), a relaxed, fan-cooled, all-day restaurant with Indian-print throws over the tables and brown rattan chairs; Bob Marley and classical Indian tunes set the mood. Freshly caught lobster is available grilled, boiled, braised (country-style), or Thermidor-style. If you tire of affordable seafood, the usual Indian suspects are on offer: *palak paneer,* vegetable *jalfrezi,* and Madras-style chicken curry.

3 Pondicherry ✮✮✮

189km (117 miles) S of Chennai

Pondicherry's ancient history dates back to the Vedic era; the Romans traded here 2 millennia ago, and the Portuguese arrived in 1521. Dutch and Danish traders followed, but it was the French—who purchased the town in the late 17th century, only relinquishing their hold in 1954—who left the most enduring legacy. Now a Union Territory, with its own local government, this seaside colony retains its French élan, tempered by South Indian warmth, making it one of India's most relaxing destinations. Besides hanging out in your antiques-filled colonial hotel or sauntering around the oceanfront **French Quarter** (where you'll see old men in thick-rimmed spectacles under the apparent illusion that they're in a Parisian *arrondissement*), you can visit **Auroville,** an interesting experiment in alternative living, also optimistically known as the City of Dawn; or you can join the New Age travelers here to visit the ashram of **Sri Aurobindo.** Ashramic allure and Aurovillian aura aside, Pondy (as it is affectionately called) is the type of charming seaside town where you arrive for a quick overnighter and end up staying; like Goa, it has a number of expats to prove it. And, yes, it's far friendlier than Bordeaux.

ESSENTIALS

GETTING THERE & AWAY   Pondicherry is best reached by road from Chennai, a 4-hour drive, mostly along a two-lane highway. To get here by train, you must first travel to Villuparam (1 hr. away) on the Chennai–Rameswaram line, and then switch to one of the four daily passenger trains to Pondicherry. Inquire at the **railway station** (South Blvd.; ⓒ **0413/233-6684**) about outbound trains.

VISITOR INFORMATION   Pondicherry's **Tourism Information Centre** (40 Goubert Ave.; ⓒ **0413/233-9497** or -4575; fax 0413/235-8389; daily 9am–5pm; http://tourism.pon.nic.in) can help you with maps, brochures, and tour bookings. Available in bookstores, *The Guide—Pondicherry* costs Rs 30 (70¢) and carries extensive local listings.

GETTING AROUND   **By Taxi & Auto-Rickshaw**   Auto-rickshaws prowl the streets in some areas, actively soliciting fares. Overcharging is rife, but if you've got several kilometers to cover, it may be worthwhile to hire one for a couple of extra rupees to avoid walking in the sun.

By Bicycle   By Indian standards, the streets and sidewalks of Pondicherry are immaculate and ideal for exploration by bike. You can rent a bike (Rs 5/10¢ per hour; Rs 20–Rs 40/45¢–90¢ per day) from Le Café on Beach Road, or from the Pondicherry Tourism Information Centre (see above). Ask about hiring the services of a guide who can cycle along with you.

By Boat   Offshore cruises are available through the **Tourism Information Counter** (40 Goubert Ave.; ⓒ **0413/233-8643**), where you can charter a boat for Rs 1,200 ($27.50) an hour.

GUIDED TOURS   Guided tours and sightseeing trips can be arranged through Pondicherry Tourism (see above). The **Indian National Trust for Art & Cultural Heritage** (INTACH, 14 Labourdonnais S.; ⓒ **0413/222-5991** or -7324; www.intach.org; ashokpan@yahoo.com) conducts 90-minute guided heritage walks for Rs 700 ($16) for fewer than five people; Rs 1,000 ($23) for 5 to 10 people.

WHAT TO SEE & DO

Pondicherry's tree-lined French Quarter is one of India's most prepossessing neighborhoods, and a real contrast to the area across the "Grand Canal" aqueduct that the French used to refer to as "black town"—a more typically Tamil neighborhood, with tiny shops lining crowded streets. If you want to unwind, stick to the French Quarter (or "white town"), with its wide boulevards, uncluttered roads, bilingual signs, stately government buildings, and gorgeous residential villas. Besides taking a few strolls, the only other attractions—and really, this is one place you will feel entirely guilt-free simply lazing on your hotel terrace for the duration of your stay—are **Aurobindo Ashram,** and a trip to **Auroville,** the City of Dawn.

While wandering the Quarter, you may want to take a look at the **Sacred Heart of Jesus (Eglise de Sacre Coeur de Jésus),** an 18th-century neo-Gothic Catholic church on South Boulevard. The facade of the **Church of Immaculate Conception** (Mission St.) has an air of pageantry enhanced by colorful banners (it's also interesting to note that many Christian devotees remove their shoes before entering). Dedicated to Ganesha, the elephant-headed god, **Sri Manakula Vinayagar Temple** is off a side street so popular that it's cordoned off during the early-evening hours; a temple elephant marks the entrance. For a quick glimpse of local historic memorabilia and collectibles, visit the **Pondicherry Museum** (49 Rue St. Louis; © **0413/233-6203;** Tues–Sun 9:45am–5:15pm), housed in a 17th-century colonial mansion once occupied by the French administrator. The museum features a collection of carriages and carts, stone sculptures, and a formidable bronze gallery. Along the same road, which runs along the northern end of a square known as **Government Place,** is **Raj Nivas,** the late-18th-century mansion occupied by Pondicherry's lieutenant governor.

At twilight, head for **Goubert Salai** (Beach Rd.). The most interesting sights along the promenade (aside from the locals enjoying themselves) include the colonial **Hôtel de Ville** (now the Municipal Offices building) and the 4m (12-ft.) statue of Gandhi standing at the pier. Cultural events, art exhibitions, and film screenings are conducted regularly by Pondicherry's **Alliance Française** (© **0413/233-8146;** fax 0413/233-4351; afpondy@satyam.net.in; Mon–Fri 8:30am–12:30pm and 2:30–6pm; temporary 3-month membership Rs 150/$3.40); contact this active organization for information regarding specific events.

SCIENCE FICTION IN THE CITY OF DAWN 👭

The **Auroville** project began in 1964, conceived by Sri Aurobindo's French-born disciple, Mirra Alfassa—"The Mother" (see "Looking for a Higher Level of Consciousness?" above). She spoke of a place on earth that could not be claimed or owned by any nation, one where all humanity could live freely and in peace—a city that would ultimately become a living embodiment of human unity. Largely designed by French architect Roger Anger, Auroville drew a motley global group, and was inaugurated in 1968 when soils from around the world were symbolically placed in an urn along with the Auroville Charter.

At its spiritual and physical heart is the futuristic spherical structure known as **Matrimandir** (Mon–Sat 10am–noon and 2–4pm; Sun 10am–noon), a place dedicated to the universal mother—a symbolic space devoted to the "divine creatrix." An ongoing project, the structure is a flattened dome spanning 36m (115 ft.) in diameter, surrounded by gardens, an amphitheater covered with red Agra stone, and meditation rooms. As development continues, glistening gold discs are fixed to the outer surface of the dome, enhancing the structure's sci-fi image. The white marble chamber of the dome houses the "Inner Room," which contains a crystal that reflects the sun's rays and produces a concentrated light that is used for enhanced meditation. Visitors who obtain passes can have a brief peek at this chamber between 4 and 5pm each day, and it's possible to stay for meditation until 6pm. Radiating from the Mandir and its gardens, the city is architecturally conceived along the lines of a galaxy, evolving organically within certain parameters. The original design planned accommodations for

Looking for a Higher Level of Consciousness?

Located in the heart of Pondicherry, **Aurobindo Ashram** ⚘ draws a global mix of ardent devotees and ordinary people searching for peace or looking to improve their meditation skills. Aurobindo Ghose, a politically active British-educated Bengali who sought asylum from the British in this small French enclave, took to meditation and yoga while developing theories of enlightenment that integrated his personal spirituality with the tenets of modern science. He also met Mirra Alfassa here, an artist on a similar spiritual quest; she became his soul mate, earning her the appellation "The Mother." Founded as a place to foster evolution to a higher level of spiritual consciousness, the ashram opened in 1926. With a significant following and numerous published titles to his credit, Aurobindo died in 1950. Today, those who share his vision of a better world place flowers and other gestures of remembrance upon the memorial chambers *(samadhis)* of Sri Aurobindo and The Mother, which lie one above the other in the center of the peaceful main courtyard beneath a frangipani tree. For more information, contact the ashram (Rue de la Marine; ✆ **0413/223-3649**; daily 8am–noon and 2–6pm; free admission; no children under 3).

50,000 residents but there currently are about 1,500, all committed to being "willing servitors of the Divine Consciousness." Auroville is far more than a place for devotional meditation; it's an experiment in self-sufficient living that takes both nature and culture into account. Its architectural innovation and utopian idealism make this a place of interest for anyone with a penchant for the unusual, the ethereal, or the novel.

Auroville is 8km (5 miles) north of Pondicherry. Auto-rickshaws charge around Rs 200 ($4.55) for the round-trip. Pondy's tourist office also organizes tours. Stop at the Tourist Information Centre first, where you can pick up brochures, shop, snack, and watch a video presentation. ✆ **0413/262-2239**. Fax 0413/262-2239. www.auroville.org. Daily 9am–1pm and 2–5:30pm.

WHERE TO STAY

If you're looking for very affordable lodging in the heart of the French Quarter, **Satsanga** restaurant (see "Where to Dine," below) has four clean, simple, air-conditioned rooms costing Rs 750 ($17).

Hotel de l'Orient ⚘⚘⚘ *(Value*   Tamil and Cajun spices scent the air of this award-winning heritage hotel (Pondicherry's best)—a 1760s manor house located in the heart of the French Quarter. The hotel has been beautifully restored, and captures the period grandeur of a colonial nobleman's mansion. Each of the 10 original guest rooms—set around an inner courtyard shaded by citrus and neem trees—is themed and named for a former French colony (a renovation of the adjacent bungalow has produced a new wing with four new rooms, done in the same colonial style, but not as charming as the original manor house rooms). Comfortable and airy, with shuttered windows, high ceilings (some original wood ceiling beams), private patios, and tall French doors, the rooms are elegantly attired in pinks, yellows, and cool emerald. Most of the furniture pieces are French colonial antiques. Bathrooms are very chic, though small (only some have tubs, so specify if you want one). Casimbazaar (no. 6) is the best of the standard rooms, but it's worthwhile to pay the extra $20 for an executive suite; these have original four-poster beds and private drawing rooms with Pondicheriennes (local planter's chairs). Avoid staying in Masulipatam on the ground floor—it can get noisy. Accommodations overlook the courtyard restaurant, **Carte Blanche,** where local "Creole" cuisine, a blend of South Indian and French, is served. A second, air-conditioned dining room is inside, where you can avoid mosquitoes. You can enjoy serene views of Pondicherry from the rooftop courtyard.

17 Rue Romain Rolland, Pondicherry 605 001. ✆ **0413/234-3067.** Fax 0413/222-7829. www.neemranahotels.com. orient1804@satyam.net.in. Delhi reservations: Neemrana Hotels Private Ltd., A–58 Nizamuddin E., New Delhi 110 013. ✆ **011/2435-6145** or -8962. Fax 011/2435-1112. sales@neemranahotels.com. 14 units. Rs 2,000 ($46) non-A/C double; Rs 2,500 ($57) standard suite, Rs 3,500 ($80) executive suite, Rs 4,300 ($98) luxury suite. AE, MC, V. **Amenities:** Restaurant; gift shop, laundry. *In room:* A/C, TV (executive suites only), tea- and coffee-making facilities, hair dryer on request.

Hotel de Pondichery ⋌⋌

You may have trouble deciding which of the individually styled guest rooms—designed by the talented Vasanthi Manet—in this beautifully restored Indo-French colonial mansion is your favorite, though "Mahe de Labourdonnais" is arguably the finest of the double rooms. All the high-ceilinged guest rooms are *trés* chic, blending Indian and colonial accents with wood-frame beds covered with crisp white sheets and satin bedcovers. Bathrooms (with drench showers) are bright and cheerful. The small hotel has a number of handsome public sitting areas with planter's chairs and smart cane sofas covered with bright pink cushions; fans whir overhead. From a facilities point of view, the hotel offers little besides great dining, but staff try hard, and rates are very reasonable.

38 Dumas St., Pondicherry 605 001. ✆ **0413/222-7409.** Fax 0413/233-0057. hotel_de_pondichery@yahoo.com. www.hoteldepondichery.com. 10 units. Rs 1,600–Rs 2,450 ($37–$56) double. Rs 300 ($6.85) extra bed. AE, DC, MC, V. **Amenities:** 3 restaurants; 24-hr. room service; tours; travel assistance; currency exchange; babysitting; laundry; doctor-on-call. *In room:* A/C.

Le Dupleix ⋌⋌

Contemporary chic meets heritage in this latest addition to Pondicherry's boutique hotels. Owner Deepak Kapur (creator of the posh leather brand Hidesign) restored and modernized this 18th-century French colonial villa (originally built for the mayor of Pondicherry), blending Old World and *au courant* with ease. Every room in this urbane hotel is unique, each with fashionable bathroom, mezzanine section for the kids (or for TV viewing without disturbing your companion), four-poster bed, and louvered wooden shutters. The public spaces have lovely touches—on the terrace, old-fashioned gas lamps hang from trees, a large traditional swing hangs in the hallway, and everywhere you'll find plenty of ornate woodwork (salvaged by Kapur when the house belonging to French governor of yore Marquis Joseph Francois Dupleix was demolished). A granite waterfall by French sculptor Francois Weil is reflected in the glass staircase landings, and walls are covered in a special Chettinad plaster—a mixture of egg white, powdered sea shells, and yogurt. Open-air dining is at the **Governor Lounge,** where Pondicherry-French and Indian fusion cuisine are served and where presentation is as important as flavor.

5 Rue De La Caserne, Pondicherry 605 00. ✆ **0413/2226-999.** Fax 0413/233-5278. ledupleix@sarovarparkplaza. com. www.sarovarparkplaza.com. 9 units. Rs 2,500 ($57) superior double, Rs 3,500 ($80) deluxe double, Rs 4,500 ($102) luxury double. MC, V. **Amenities:** Restaurant; bar; 24-hr. room service; safe deposit locker; travel desk; airport transfers. *In room:* A/C, TV, dataport, minibar, tea- and coffee-making facilities, hair dryer, safe.

Villa Helena ⋌⋌ *Value*

Owned by Roselyne Guitry, a perfumer from Burgundy who has lived in Bangkok, Delhi, and now Pondicherry, this guesthouse started out as a place in which Roselyne could keep her gorgeous collection of antiques and traditional furniture. A natural decorator, she claims the place was "thrown together," and operates her delightful villa as a nonprofit hobby and an opportunity to meet people from around the world. A communal porch with gracious arches and pillars, where you can relax in planters' chairs, is a plus, while the guest rooms (which have lovely high ceilings that extend into the shower-only bathrooms) feature an eclectic blend of classical and colonial knickknacks picked up by Roselyne from all over Asia. Upstairs is an enormous suite, which is more like an apartment: In addition to a large bedroom with its own terrace, it has two living rooms (one of which features a desk that's large enough to double as a dining table) and a sofa that doubles as a bed. The beds here are the best in town—proper thick-pile mattresses. Roselyne has recently opened another guesthouse called **Helena 2** (13 Lal Bahadur Shastri St.), similarly stylish but with a more inherently Indian flavor.

14 Suffren St., Pondicherry 605 001. © 0413/222-6789, -7075, or 98430-69443. Fax 0413/222-7087. villahelena@ satyam.net.in. 4 units each. Rs 1,500 ($35) standard double; Rs 2,500 ($57) suite. Coffee and soft drinks on demand. No credit cards. **Amenities:** Dining facility; sightseeing and travel assistance; 24-hr. room service; laundry. *In room:* A/C, TV (in suites).

WHERE TO DINE

When it comes to the best fusion food in town, it's a bit of a toss-up between The Bistro/Indochine, reviewed below, and the classy Hotel de l'Orient's **Carte Blanche** (see above). If you opt for the latter's leafy courtyard (residents get first option), make sure you order a dish involving fish—caught locally, it's so fresh it almost moves. **Satsanga** (30 Labourdonnais St.; © **0413/222-5867;** noon–2:30pm and 6–11pm) is a relaxing all-day eatery operated by an expat from the south of France who has been in Pondy for 33 years and who now resides in Auroville. If you're a carnivore, opt for the green-pepper filet *(filet au poivre vert)* or the fish *Provençale*— not always on the menu, but worth asking for anyway. If you're in Auroville in the afternoon, drop by the **Auroville Boulangerie** or grab a simple but tasty meal at their **Solar Kitchen** (you'll need an Auroville day pass, currently Rs 60/$1.35, to eat there).

The Bistro/Indochine FRENCH/ECLECTIC CAFE   These two restaurants at the atmospheric Hotel de Pondicherry share the same menu and venue; The Bistro transforms into the more exotic-sounding Indochine in the evenings. Set beneath a thatched roof, the venue has roll-down blinds, cane furniture, and green plastic seats for the spillover; fans work to kept customers cool, and potted plants add to the court-yard-cafe atmosphere. The menu is eclectic, with pizzas, hamburgers, savory pancakes, and great salads on offer. Pondicherry beef *paupiettes* and prawns a la Normandy are house faves. Also at Hotel de Pondicherry, the upstairs restaurant, **Le Club** , prides itself on serving authentic traditional French cuisine, using only the finest French herbs, cream, and butter. The menu offers chateaubriand *a la béarnaise,* chicken with mustard sauce, crab with saffron sauce, shallow fried prawns with basil and cream, and squid prepared with mustard and egg yolk.

Good Food to Go

If you miss some of the comforts of home, you'll delight in **Church Gate** (198 Mission St.; © **0413/34-9146;** Mon–Sat 9am–1pm and 4–9pm, Sun 9am–1pm). A grocery store billing itself "The Complete Shop," this is where you'll find imported food, pastries, fresh local fruit, and toiletries. It's an ideal place to stock up for a day trip or picnic or to get something wholesome for your minibar.

Hotel de Pondicherry, 38 Rue Dumas St. ⓒ 0413/222-7409. Breakfast Rs 115–Rs 195 ($2.60–$4.40); continental brunch Rs 200 ($4.55); main courses Rs 115–Rs 225 ($2.60–$5.10). Le Club main courses Rs 175–Rs 325 ($4–$7.35). AE, DC, MC, V. All day; Le Club only daily 7–11pm.

Rendezvous Café ⭐⭐ FRENCH/ITALIAN/INDIAN/CHINESE Vincent, the owner of this popular cafe, started out as a sailor cooking meals for ship's crews. One day he visited this century-old Indo-French restaurant and became violently ill. Instead of complaining, he decided to buy the restaurant and tap into its potential. With a shabby colonial-chic atmosphere, the restaurant derives much of its charm from the relaxed setting, with a large thatched-roof area upstairs. It stocks cigars, imported beers, and Scotch, especially for the European expats and diplomats who hang out here. Seafood is a specialty; have the lobster either in a rich garlic-butter sauce, or mildly spiced and grilled in the tandoor. Alternatively, try traditional Pondicherry prawn curry served with steamed white rice. The pork is bred by Jesuit priests in Kodaikanal; try the pork vindaloo or the more conventional roast pork, arguably the best in town.

30 Rue Suffren. ⓒ 0413/233-9132. Main courses Rs 120–Rs 400 ($2.75–$9.10). AE, DC, MC, V. Wed–Mon 9:30am–3:30pm and 6:30–11:30pm.

SHOPPING
Auromirayan (95 Canteen St.; ⓒ 0413/233-9351; Mon–Sat 9:30am–1pm and 4:30–8:30pm; cash only) is the factory shop for leather goods (shoes, handbags, belts) produced in Auroville. The tiny **Boutique Auroshree** (18 Jawaharlal Nehru St.; ⓒ 0413/222-2117) sells clothes and handicrafts from all over India; it has a small selection of silver jewelry, paintings, and handcrafted bronze, brass, and sandalwood items. **La Boutique d'Auroville** ⭐ (J. N. St.; ⓒ 0413/262-2150) sells everything from Auroville, from lovely pottery and handmade paper to original garments. **Curio Centre** (40 Roman Rolland St.; ⓒ 0413/222-5676) has a selection of objets d'art as well as indigenous and colonial antique furniture. Next door is **Art Colony** (32 Romain Rolland St.; ⓒ 0413/233-2395), with mostly antiques (as well as some reproduction furniture), wood carvings, and handicrafts. Auroville's outlet, **Kalki** ⭐⭐ (132 Mission St.; ⓒ 0413/233-9166), is where you browse for hand-painted silk clothing, perfumed candles, incense, oils, leatherware, ceramics, jewelry, and hand-made paper items to the accompaniment of artsy, esoteric music. Across the road is **Casablanca** (165 Mission St.; ⓒ 0413/222-6495 or 0413/233-6495), one of South India's funkiest department stores, with top international brands spread over three floors; there's even a fast-food cafe with Internet browsing. **Splendour** (16 Goubert Ave.; ⓒ 0413/233-6398) sells goods exclusively produced by the Aurobindo Society. Besides toys, belts, bags, and incense, you can pick up a wide range of books on the Society and Sri Aurobindo. **Focus** bookstore (ⓒ 0413/234-5513; Mission St.; closed Sun), next to the Church of Immaculate Conception, has hundreds of books on Indian culture and religion.

4 Tiruchirappalli & Thanjavur (Tanjore)

Tiruchirappalli is 325km (200 miles) SW of Chennai; Thanjavur is 55km (34 miles) E of Tiruchirappalli

Tiruchirappalli, or "the City of the Three-Headed Demon," sprawls at the foot of colossal **Rock Fort,** where the Vijayanagar empire built its once-impregnable citadel when they wrested power from the Cholas in the 10th century. The Vijayanagars and their successors, the Nayaks of Madurai, started work on one of South India's largest and most impressive temple towns, **Srirangam,** on an island created by the Cauvery and one of its tributaries, just beyond Tiruchirappalli.

During the bitter Carnatic wars, French and British forces battled for control of the city, both keen to establish control of the looming hilltop fortress. Today a number of neo-Gothic Christian monuments remain as evidence of the British influence during the 18th and 19th centuries, when a Cantonment was established here and when much of the present-day city was built.

Almost directly east of Tiruchirappalli (or Trichy, as it's thankfully known), **Thanjavur** (also known as Tanjore) was the capital of the Chola empire—which included present-day Kerala, Sri Lanka, and parts of Indonesia. Its 11th-century **Brihadeshvara Temple** is a World Heritage monument and, together with Mamallapuram and Madurai, an important stop on Tamil Nadu's temple route.

ESSENTIALS

GETTING THERE & AWAY You can fly to Trichy from Chennai (Tues, Thurs, Sat, and Sun) or from Trivandrum in Kerala (Mon, Wed, Fri, and Sun). The airport is 8km (5 miles) from the city. Chennai is 7 hours away by road; slightly quicker by train—several daily trains (3 hr.) connect Trichy with Madurai. To get to Thanjavur from Trichy, either hire a car or travel by train for the 1-hour journey. From Pondicherry, the fastest way to get to Trichy is by hired car; alternatively, check the current train schedule.

ORIENTATION Trichy's hotels are situated in the British-built Cantonment, separated from the busy industrial and bazaar neighborhood where Rock Fort is situated. Srirangam is a few kilometers north of Rock Fort.

VISITOR INFORMATION Mr. Janarthanam at Trichy's **Government of Tamil Nadu Tourism Department** (1 Williams Rd., Cantonment; 🕐 **0431/246-0136;** Mon–Fri 10am–5:45pm) can supply you with information, maps, and brochures. **Thanjavur's tourist office** (Hotel Tamil Nadu Complex Jawan Bhavan; 🕐 **04362/ 230-984;** Mon–Fri 10am–5:45pm) provides good information on local sights and can help you with transport.

GETTING AROUND It may be worthwhile to hire a car and driver through your hotel or the tourist information center. You can even manage to see all the major attractions in a single, exhausting day.

WHAT TO SEE & DO
TIRUCHIRAPPALLI

Spend anywhere from a half- to a full day here, devoting the majority of your time to the atmospheric temple town of **Srirangam.** In the evening, climb the steps to the summit of **Rock Fort** in time to witness the sun setting over the city (entrance at China Bazaar; Rs 1/2¢, Rs 10/25¢ camera, Rs 50/$1.15 video camera; daily 6am–8pm). This is also the time you're likely to encounter the greatest number of devotees coming to worship at the Shiva temple (off-limits to non-Hindus) and paying tribute to the elephant-headed god, Ganesh, at his summit shrine. Little of the old fortification has survived (though some inscriptions date back to the 3rd c. B.C.), but you may be interested to know that at 3,800 million years old, the rock itself is said to be one of the oldest on Earth, predating the Himalayan range by around a million years. Alongside Rock Fort is the huge **Teppakulam Tank,** and across from this, **Our Lady of Lourdes Church,** built in 1840.

Tips A Recommended Guide

In the tourist information center at the front entrance of Brihadeshvara Temple, you should be able to locate **K. T. Raja,** who has been working as a guide for more than a quarter of a century. He'll not only show you local temples, he'll arrange trips to outlying temple towns. Guide fees are about Rs 500 ($11.40) per day.

Srirangam ✱✱✱   Just 7km (4 miles) beyond Trichy, the vibrant, ancient holy town of Srirangam—one of India's biggest temple complexes—is the site of sprawling **Sri Ranganathaswamy Temple,** whose seven concentric boundary walls *(prakarams)* enclose 240 hectares (600 acres) devoted to the Hindu faith. Within the temple walls, a web of lanes lined with houses, shops, and businesses is also enclosed, making for fascinating exploration of what feels like a heaving medieval village. Dedicated to Vishnu (worshiped here as Ranganatha), the town sees almost nonstop feverish and colorful activity, with communal gatherings and festivals held throughout the year. The original 10th-century temple was destroyed by a Delhi sultan, but reconstruction began in the late 14th century. Ongoing expansion by Trichy's successive rulers culminated in the late 20th century, with the elaborately carved and brightly painted **Rajagopuram,** not only the largest of the 21 *goparums* (tower gateways) that surround the immense complex, but said to be the largest in Asia, soaring to a height of 72m (230 ft.). The most important shrines are within the inner four boundary walls, entered via a high gateway where smaller shrines mark the point beyond which lower-caste Hindus could not venture. Within this enclosure, you'll find a temple to the goddess Ranganayaki, as well as the **thousand-pillared hall,** which dates back to the Chola period. Arguably the most impressive of all is nearby **Seshagirirayar Mandapa,** where the pillars are decorated with stone carvings of rearing horses mounted by warriors. For a memorable view of the entire complex, make sure to purchase a ticket (Rs 10/25¢) to climb to the rooftop.

7km (4 miles) north of Trichy on an island on the River Cauvery. Free admission. Rs 50 ($1.15) still camera, Rs 100 ($2.30) video camera. No photography allowed inside the sanctum.

THANJAVUR

Brihadeshvara Temple ✱✱✱   This granite temple, a World Heritage Site built by the Chola kings a thousand years ago, is today very much alive with devotees. Standing in a vast courtyard, surrounded by a number of subsidiary shrines, the temple was built—no doubt at great expense—by the Chola Rajaraja I for the worship of Shiva. Pyramidal in shape, the monumental tower or *vimana* over the inner sanctum rises almost 70m (224 ft.) and is visible for miles around. It's capped by an octagonal cupola carved from a single block of granite that was hauled into place along a ramp that is said to have been 6km (4 miles) long. Within the sanctum is a 4m (13-ft.) lingam; facing the sanctum, a colossal 25-ton Nandi monolith, carved from solid granite, dominates the courtyard. Numerous extant inscriptions on the molded plinth describe the enormous wealth of the temple (much of it booty from Rajaraja's successful campaigns), as well as the copious acts of ritual and celebration that took place here. In its heyday, an enormous staff was maintained to attend to the temple's varied activities; these included everything from administration to procuring dancing girls.

West of Thanjavur bus stand. Visitors can make prior arrangements for entry to the sanctum and the upper floors of the temple by contacting the local tourist office. Daily 6am–noon and 3.30–8:30pm.

Thanjavur Palace Complex & Art Gallery 𝕽𝕽   Built as the home of the Nayak rulers, the 16th-century **Royal Palace** has fallen into a state of minor ruin but is home to the impressive **Rajaraja Museum** and **Art Gallery** (daily 10am–1pm and 2–5pm; admission Rs 15/35¢), which houses an eclectic collection of stone and bronze idols, mostly from the Chola period. Within the palace, you should also climb the narrow and tricky steps of the **arsenal tower** for fantastic views of the complex and the entire city, including Brihadeshvara Temple. Inside 17th-century **Durbar Hall,** built by the Marathas, who ruled after the Nayaks, are 11th-century statues of Vishnu and Parvathi, exhibited in Washington, D.C., in 1865. Near the museum is **Saraswati Mahal Library,** which houses a collection of rare books—including Sanskrit works and 18,623 palm-leaf manuscripts—assembled by the Maratha ruler Serfoji II, who ruled until 1832 and was known as a great patron of the arts. The attached **Museum** has highlights from the collection, including some detailed drawings of Chinese torture and punishment techniques. Give both the **Sadar Mahal Palace** and its **Royal Museum** a miss.

E. Main Rd. For information about Thanjavur Art Gallery, contact the Art Gallery Society (© 04362/239-823). Free admission. Rs 30 (70¢) camera. Daily 9am–1pm and 3–6pm.

WHERE TO STAY & DINE

You may end up spending the night in both Trichy and Thanjavur—a pity, because neither has exciting accommodations. But a stay may be hard to avoid—onward travel in either direction takes 2 hours, so you'd need to move at quite a pace, and Tamil Nadu's heat will inevitably slow you down.

TIRUCHIRAPALLI

Hotel Sangam Tiruchirappalli   Popular with tour groups, this friendly 30-year-old hotel benefits considerably from its location a short distance out of the city center, so it offers less noise and polluted congestion and a greater sense of space, enhanced by decent lawns. Marble and plaid are primary motifs, and linoleum surfaces are popular here. The large guest rooms are adequately furnished and immaculately clean. Ask for a room overlooking the swimming pool (these have even numbers). The restaurant, **Chembian,** where Chef Madi prepares some interesting dishes, is also agreeable—try the *kozhi milaau,* fragrant chicken flavored with ginger and tamarind.

Collector's Office Rd., Tiruchirappalli 620 001. © 0431/241-4700 or -4480. Fax 0431/241-5779. www.hotelsangam. com. 54 units. Rs 2,300 ($53) double; Rs 4,260 ($98) suite. AE, DC, MC, V. **Amenities:** 2 restaurants; bar; pool; health club; travel counter; shopping arcade; 24-hr. room service; laundry and dry cleaning; doctor-on-call. *In room:* A/C, TV, minibar (in some rooms), hair dryer on request.

Jenneys Residency   The lobby of this well-equipped five-floor business hotel is decked out in white marble, with large reflective pillars in a sort of fantasy of temple architecture. The centrally air-conditioned guest units are comfortable enough, with standard Western comforts that include fair-size bathrooms and tubs. They offer great value but tend to pick up noise from the busy main road outside. Some of the rooms offer excellent views of Rock Fort. The theme bar **Wild West** is very popular with locals—especially on weekends.

3/14 McDonald's Rd., Tiruchirappalli 620 001. © 0431/241-4414. Fax 0431/246-1451. jenneys@satyam.net.in. 86 units. $55 standard double; $75 executive suite, $100 luxury suite. $10 extra bed. Rates include breakfast. AE, DC,

MC, V. **Amenities:** 2 restaurants; bar; pool; health club; travel desk; currency exchange; florist; shopping arcade; salon; 24-hr. room service; Ayurvedic massage; laundry; doctor-on-call; valet. *In room:* A/C, TV, minibar.

THANJAVUR

The best hotel in town, **Hotel Sangam Thanjavur** (© 04362/239-451 or -452; www.hotelsangam.com; Rs 2,100/$48 double) benefits greatly from its quiet location on Trichy Road, away from the town center. Fronted by neat gardens, it has comfortable guest rooms (A/C, TV, minibar) and a good range of amenities (room service; pool; health club), and the staff is very helpful. The restaurant, **Thillana,** is one of India's rare small-town restaurants where your server not only manages to make convincing recommendations, but the food (rather spicy) actually meets your expectations—order chicken Chettinad, a Tamil favorite that explodes with tangy flavor, or vegetables sautéed in spicy Chettinad masala (avoid the Chinese and Continental dishes on offer).

For Thanjavur's best bargain, book into the **Ideal River View Resort,** cottage-style apartments clustered on the banks of a branch of the Cauvery River. Situated 7km (4 miles) out of town, the resort enjoys a remote setting amid paddy fields and wild vegetation. Each air-conditioned guest room has a balcony facing the Vennar River. With doubles at Rs 2,000 ($46) and an impressive range of amenities, including a pool, boating, riding, tennis, fortune-tellers, and Ayurvedic massage (© **04362/250-533** or -0633; www.idealresort.com), this is good value.

If, however, you have the time and energy, endure the 2-hour drive north of Thanjavur to overnight at the little village of **Tranquebar** (Tarangambadi in Tamil). Long forgotten, this coastal spot was a major 17th-century trading post for the Danes. Reserve a room at **Bungalow on the Beach** 👫, a Neemrana group "non-hotel" opened at the end of 2004 (© **04364/28-8065;** reservations only through Delhi office 011/2435-6145, -8962, or 011/51825001; sales@neemranahotels.com; www. neemranahotels.com; first-rate deluxe suite Rs 5,000/$114). Located in a 300-year-old building that used to house the British Collector, it has been wonderfully restored and furnished with classic period furniture. For those looking for atmospheric accommodations that are laid-back and have a fantastic location on the beach, this is definitely worth the 2-hour diversion. While you're in Tranquebar, take a leisurely morning to roam **Dansborg Fort,** with its interesting museum, and the ruins and churches of **King Street** and **Queen Street,** all very quiet and rather nontouristy; or take a stroll about this typical fishing village and along its beach.

5 Madurai 👫👫👫

498km (308 miles) SW of Chennai; 160km (99 miles) W of Trichy

Located on the banks of the Vaigai River, Madurai—apparently named for the nectar that flowed from Shiva's hair as a blessing for the new city (*madhuram* is the Tamil word for sweetness)—was built by the Pandyan king Kulasekara. It was the capital of a kingdom that ruled much of South India during the 4th century B.C., and that conducted trade as far afield as Greece and Rome.

Madurai also became a center for the great festivals of poetry and writing—the **Tamil Sangams**—that were being held more than 2 millennia ago. Through the millennia, various dynasties have battled over the city. The Vijayanagars built much of the temple during their reign, which lasted until the 16th century, when the Nayaks came to power, who in turn ruled until the arrival of the British in 1736. Today Madurai is also Tamil Nadu's second-largest city, an ugly industrial sprawl plagued by pollution and traffic jams and other ills characteristic of unchecked development. But modern Madurai still embodies the spirit of Tamil Nadu's deeply embedded temple culture, and labyrinthine **Meenakshi Temple**—celebrating the love of the Meenakshi goddess and her groom, Sundareswarar (the "Handsome God"), an avatar of Lord Shiva—is easily our first choice among Tamil Nadu's temple destinations.

ESSENTIALS

GETTING THERE & AWAY Daily flights connect Madurai to Chennai or Mumbai. The **airport** is 12km (7½ miles) south of the city center. Contact **Indian Airlines** (© **0452/269-0333** or 0452/234-1234 at the airport; Mon–Sat 10am–5pm). For information about **Jet Airways'** daily flights, call © **0452/269-0771** through -0774. Trains from all over southern India pull in at **Madurai Junction Railway Station** (W. Veli St.; © **0452/274-3131**). The journey from Chennai is 10 hours; from Bangalore, it's 11 hours. From Pondicherry it's 6 hours by car or train; best to overnight at Trichy.

VISITOR INFORMATION Staff at the **Government of Tamil Nadu Tourist Office** (W. Veli St., next to the Tamil Nadu Hotel; © **0452/233-4757;** www.maduraicity.com; Mon–Sat 10am–5:45pm) provides maps, advice on government-sponsored hotels and shops, and recommendations on guides. As elsewhere, beware of fake "official guides" you meet on the streets.

GETTING AROUND Auto-rickshaw drivers tend to have a field day with foreign visitors; establish a flat rate before heading off.

FESTIVAL If you're in town for the **Chittrai Festival** (Apr–May), when Meenakshi's marriage to Sundareswarar is celebrated, you're in for a treat—the town attains a fever-pitch radiance.

WHAT TO SEE & DO

The principal reason to visit Madurai—for you as well as for tens of thousands of Hindu pilgrims—is to experience the ecstatic spiritual life of **Meenakshi Temple;** what little else there is to see and do in town will pale in comparison. Legend recalls that Meenakshi began life as a glorious princess, born of fire with three breasts and eyes like a fish. As she grew older, she overpowered all the gods with her impossible beauty until she encountered Shiva, who transformed her heart to ghee (butter) and married her. While sitting inside the temple itself can provide hours of entertainment and an appreciation of Tamil Nadu's vivid spirituality (as well as a sense of its religious commerce), the streets immediately near the great temple are full of character, and are best experienced by wandering around. Not far from the temple, **Tirumalai Nayak Mahal** (Palace Rd.; © **0452/233-2945;** daily 9am–5pm; admission Rs 50/$1.15) is a 17-century Indo-Saracenic palace built by Tirumalai Nayak and later restored to some extent by Madras governor Lord Napier (it is currently under further renovation). Not all that much of the palace remains except for the large pillared courtyard known as the "Heavenly Pavilion," where a nightly *son et lumière* show (English narration 6:45pm; Rs 10/25¢) sheds light on Madurai's history.

It was in Madurai in 1921 that Mahatma Gandhi historically exchanged his *kurta* and *dhoti* wardrobe for the loincloth, typically worn by the poor. Today the bloodstained *khadi* loincloth he wore when he was assassinated is encased in a glass shrine at **Gandhi Memorial Museum,** which chronicles India's history leading up to independence

(Tamukkam, 5km/3 miles east of the city center; © **0452/253/1060;** www.madurai. com/gandhi.htm; daily 10am–1pm and 2–5:45pm; free admission). Avoid the adjacent **Government Museum,** where visitors experience two million years of history in 30 seconds as they whiz past a 9th-century Vishnu statue, 12th-century Pandyan works, undated Chola statues, and a stuffed polar bear.

If you haven't tired of temples yet, **Thirupparankundram Temple** (free admission), 8km (5 miles) from Madurai, makes for a pleasant outing, particularly on Friday, when women with marriage or family troubles place candles or occasionally sit on the temple floor and create *rangoli* patterns on the ground, using colored powders and flowers, as offerings to Durga. Nearby, **Owayat,** the 40-year-old temple elephant, shuffles and waits to bestow blessings on those willing to donate a rupee, gracefully accepted in a cupped trunk.

Shri Meenakshi-Sundareshwarar Temple ✦✦✦

One of South India's biggest, busiest pilgrimage sites (around 15,000 pilgrims each day; 10,000 more on Fri), this sprawling temple, always undergoing renovation and repairs, is a place of intense spiritual activity almost unparalleled in India. A high wall surrounds the complex, and 12 looming *goparums* (pyramidal gateways) mark the various entrances. Garish stucco gods, demons, beasts, and heroes smother these towers in a writhing, fascinating mass of symbolism, vividly painted in a riot of bright Disneyesque colors. Traditionally, entrance to the complex is through the eastern **Ashta Shakti Mandapa,** a hall of pillars graced by sculptural representations of the goddess Shakti in her many aspects. Adjacent to this, **Meenakshi Nayaka Mandapa** is where pilgrims purchase all manner of devotional paraphernalia and holy souvenirs. Near the inner gate, a temple elephant, daubed with eye shadow and blusher, earns her keep by accepting a few rupees' donation in exchange for a blessing—bestowed with a light tap of her dexterous trunk. From here you can wander at will, finding your way at some stage to the impressive 16th-century Hall of a Thousand Pillars. This hall (or museum as it is also referred to) has 985 elegantly sculpted columns, including a set of "musical pillars" that produce the seven Carnatic musical notes when tapped (a ticket officer will gladly demonstrate in exchange for a tip).

All around the complex of shrines and effigies, various *pujas* (prayers) and rituals are conducted, some under the guiding hand of a bare-chested Brahmin priest, others as spontaneous expressions of personal, elated devotion. Against one stone image of buxom Meenakshi, devotees actually throw balls of ghee—a ritual prayer tossed at her to keep her cool, her heart apparently having turned to butter when she met Shiva. On other statues, layer upon layer of ghee and oil have turned surfaces smooth and black; they are stained by years of turmeric and vermilion powder sprinkled and daubed on them by believers seeking blessings and hope.

At the heart of the complex are the **sanctums** of the goddess Meenakshi (Parvati) and of Sundareshvara (Shiva). What often eludes visitors to the heaving temple at Madurai is the city's deeply imbedded cult of fertility; behind the reverence and severity of worship, the Meenakshi Temple is a celebration of the divine union of the eternal lovers, represented symbolically at the end of the day when they are ceremoniously carried (a ritual you can observe until they enter the inner sanctum, which is off-limits to non-Hindus) and brought together for an evening of celestial fornication. This is the time to head for the stairs around the great tank, where devotees gather to chat and relax at the end of the day.

Bounded by N., E., S., and W. Chitrai sts. ℂ **0452/234-4360**. www.maduraimeenakshi.org. Daily 4am–12:30pm and 4–9:30pm. Free admission. No entrance to main sanctum for non-Hindus. Deposit shoes outside entrance. Thousand Pillar Museum: Adults Rs 2 (4¢), children under 12 Rs 1 (2¢). Daily 7am–8pm.

WHERE TO STAY

Taj Garden Retreat, Madurai 🎔🎔   Situated on a hillock known as Pasumalai, and blessed with sprawling tree-filled grounds, this colonial-style hotel—without a doubt your best option in Madurai—offers panoramic views of the Temple City. Arrived at by a long driveway (a sign en route warns of PEACOCKS CROSSING), this was the original residence of Sir William Harvey. The main building, built in 1891, is decorated with hunting trophies and includes a well-stocked colonial-style bar. Accommodations are spread over five different blocks; opt for the spacious deluxe rooms that are housed in the original colonial buildings and offer fantastic views from wide bay windows (book room no. 21 or 22) and shared balconies. Superior rooms are no less comfortable, offering either pool or garden views. Among the hotel's offerings (2-hr. notice required) is palmist Mr. Mani, who has looked into the futures of nearly 25,000 people with "almost accuracy"!

40 T.P.K. Rd., Pasumalai, Madurai 625 004. ℂ **0452/237-1601**. Fax 0452/237-1636. www.tajhotels.com. 63 units. $115 standard double, $140 superior double, $155 deluxe double. $20 extra bed. Taxes extra. AE, DC, MC, V. **Amenities:** 2 restaurants; bar; pool; tennis court; badminton court; jogging track; Ayurvedic center; nursery; travel desk; car hire; 24-hr. room service; babysitting; laundry; dry cleaning; doctor-on-call; pharmacy service; palmist. *In room:* A/C, TV, minibar, hair dryer. Deluxe rooms have tea- and coffee-making facilities.

WHERE TO DINE

The city has a fair number of scruffy dining halls that are well attended by locals—and for good reason. *Thali* (multicourse) meals served in these dime-a-dozen joints are delicious and extremely economical. But if the idea of eating with your fingers makes you uncomfortable, head for the classy all-day restaurant at **Taj Garden Retreat, Madurai** (see above). Or head for the pleasant **Surya Rooftop Restaurant** 🎔 (110 W. Permal Maistry St.; ℂ **0452/234-3151;** daily 4pm–midnight; Rs 35–Rs 100/80¢–$2.30). Situated on the fairy-lights-adorned rooftop of the 1970s-style Supreme Hotel, Surya opens in time for an early sundowner session, making it a popular place from which to admire the setting sun on Meenakshi Temple. Of the food, a personal favorite is Hyderabadi vegetable balls, great with *tawa paratha,* a soft tandoori bread. Portions are generous and neatly served.

8

Karnataka & Hyderabad: Kingdoms of the South

Sixteenth-century visitors to the royal courts of present-day Karnataka returned to Europe with stupendous tales of wealth—cities overflowing with jewels, and streets littered with diamonds. Over the centuries, the lush green state that occupies a vast chunk of India's southwestern seaboard and much of the Deccan plateau saw numerous kingdoms rise and fall, powerful dynasties that left legacies of impressive palaces and monumental cities that now lie scattered throughout the interior, some of them well off the beaten track, but worth the effort and time it takes to seek them out.

The post-independence state of Karnataka, unified in 1950 on the basis of common language, is predominantly made up of the once-princely state of Mysore and the Berar territories of the Nizam of Hyderabad's kingdom. Once one of the richest cities in India, Hyderabad is now the vibrant capital of neighboring Andhra Pradesh, and a possible excursion from Bangalore, state capital of Karnataka. **Bangalore,** in many ways the

---

Tips **Planning Your Tour**

Most travelers head directly for **Bangalore,** Karnataka's capital, using it as a base to fly to **Hyderabad,** capital of Andhra Pradesh (discussed at the end of the chapter), or as a base from which to catch an overnight train to and from the "lost city" of **Hampi,** which lies 320km (198 miles) north. (Note that more adventurous travelers, usually backpackers, catch a bus from Goa and head straight here.) Remote and serene, Hampi is good for a few relaxing days—at least 3 if you intend to explore the under-visited **temples of the Chalukyas,** which lie north of Hampi. The second principal destination in Karnataka is **Mysore,** again usually reached from Bangalore. If you're in Tamil Nadu or Kerala, it's also possible to drive directly to Mysore, passing **Rajiv Gandhi National Park,** or to approach it from the coastal city of **Mangalore,** connected to Goa and Kerala via the Konkan railway. Spend at least a day in Mysore before spending the next day or two visiting the beautifully decorated **11th-century temples** at Belur and Halebid, and the nearby **Jain monolithic statue** at Sravanabelgola. Karnataka also has a few stunning **beaches,** just south of the Goan border, but unless you can make do with limited facilities, save your sunbathing for Goa and Kerala.

country's most "Western" city, is today famous for its energetic nightlife and highly evolved computer and technology industries. Although it offers little by way of sightseeing attractions, it's a great place to relax; you can shop by day and explore the bars and clubs at night before taking an overnight train to explore the ghost city of **Hampi.** This great medieval Hindu capital of the south is said to have once rivaled Rome in size and wealth. The ruins of the 14th-century Vijayanagar kingdom are set in a boulder-strewn landscape that proves fascinating in its own right—deservedly Karnataka's most famous attraction.

Karnataka's other primary destination is **Mysore,** the famous "City of Incense," where vibrant markets are perfumed with the scents of jasmine, musk, sandalwood, and frangipani. Ruled by India's most enlightened Maharajas, Mysore is home to some 17 palaces, of which **Amba Vilas** is arguably India's most opulent. Just a few hours south of Mysore is **Rajiv Gandhi National Park,** home to herds of wild elephant and the more elusive Bengal tiger. Northward lie the **"Jewel Box" temples** built by the mighty Hoysala warriors in the cities of Belur and Hal, best reached via Sravanabelgola, home to one of the oldest and most important Jain pilgrimage sites in India: an 18m (60-ft.) statue of the naked **Lord Gomateswara,** said to be the tallest monolithic statue on Earth and one of the most spiritually satisfying destinations in India.

1 Bangalore

If you've been in India a while, the capital of Karnataka will probably feel like a long, soothing break from endless commotion. The first city in India to get electricity, Bangalore continues, in many ways, to blaze the trail in terms of the country's quest for a modern identity. Once known as the Garden City (and less encouragingly as Pensioner's Paradise), the country's most pristine city evolved significantly when the high-tech revolution arrived and Bangalore suddenly found itself at the center of the nation's massive computer hardware and software industries. Its cosmopolitan spirit fueled as much by its lively bar and cafe culture as by the influx of international businesspeople, India's high-tech hub has a high-energy buzz, yet it's tangibly calmer and cleaner than most other places in the country, with far and away the best climate of any Indian city—no doubt the reason the majority of upwardly mobile Indians rank it the number-one city in which to live.

Unless you go in for cafe society, you won't find very many attractions. The city's real appeal is its zesty contemporary Indian lifestyle and its usefulness as a base for getting to the extraordinary temples and ruins of the Deccan interior and the vibrant cities of Hyderabad and Mysore.

ESSENTIALS

GETTING THERE & MOVING ON   By Air   Bangalore's airport (8km/5 miles from M.G. Rd.) is the busiest in South India, connected to most of the major cities in India (including Hyderabad). Several international flights to the Far East, Europe, and the U.S. fly out of the airport as well. To get to your hotel from the airport, it's best to use a taxi (about Rs 150–Rs 300/$3.40–$6.85) from the prepaid counter.

By Train   As a major transport hub, Bangalore is reached by a significant number of rail connections. Journeys from North Indian cities, however, are extremely time-consuming; the fastest connection with Delhi takes 35 hours, while Mumbai is 24 hours away. From Chennai (Tamil Nadu), take the 5-hour Shatabdi Express. To get to

Mysore, catch the 2-hour Shatabdi Express (departs Wed–Mon at 11am). For Hyderabad, catch the comfortable overnight Rajdhani Express (departs four times a week at 6:45pm). Bangalore City and Bangalore Cantonment are the two railway stations; the latter is a bit closer to the main downtown area.

By Road   For the greatest amount of freedom, you should hire a car and driver, particularly if you plan to get off the beaten track.

VISITOR INFORMATION   Karnataka State Tourism Development Corporation (KSTDC) information counters are found at the railway station (© **080/2287-0068;** daily 6:30am–9:30pm) and at the airport (© **080/2522- 0501;** 24 hr). **Karnataka Tourism** (Khanija Bhavan, Race Course Rd.; © **080/2235-2901** through -2903; Mon–Sat 10:30am–5:30pm, closed Sun and second Sat of the month; www.kstdc.nic.in) is reliable for sightseeing information rather than info on accommodations and dining; ask for a copy of *Bangalore This Fortnight.* The **Government of India Tourist Office** is at the KSFC Building, 48 Church St. (© **080/2558-5417;** Mon–Fri 9:30am–6pm, Sat 9am–1pm), where you can pick up a copy of the free quarterly guide *City Info.*

GETTING AROUND   By Auto-Rickshaw & Taxi   Insist that auto-rickshaw drivers use their meters. Generally, the first kilometer will cost Rs 10 (25¢); each kilometer after that costs Rs 5 (10¢). After 10pm, drivers will try to make you pay double; pay no more than 50% above the recorded fare. You won't find taxis that you can just hail off the street, but metered **"call taxis"** are available almost all over the city; see our recommendation in "Fast Facts: Bangalore," below; or ask your hotel for a reputable number (expect to pay minimum fare of Rs 35/80¢ for 4km/2½ miles, Rs 9/20¢ each additional kilometer, plus extra for waiting and luggage).

With Car & Driver   Plan on spending in the region of Rs 150 ($3.40) per hour, or Rs 400 ($9.10) for a 4-hour tour, which will include 40km (25 miles) of free mileage. To hire a car and driver, try **Hertz** (© **080/2532-5404;** Raheja Plaza, Commissariat Rd.), which operates around-the-clock.

GUIDED TOURS & TRAVEL AGENTS   KSTDC (address above; © **080/2235-2901**) conducts sightseeing tours around the state. **Sita Travels** (1 St. Mark's Rd.; © **080/2558-8892**) and **Marco Polo Tours** (2 Janardhan Towers, Residency Rd.; © **080/5122-1222**) are reliable all-rounders. **Cosmopole Travels** (© **080/2228-1591**) is useful for event-related destinations such as the Nrityagram Dance Village.

FAST FACTS: Bangalore

Airlines **Jet Airways:** © 080/2555-0856 or airport 080/2522-1929. **Indian Airlines:** © 080/2297-8406 through -8408 (airport) or 080/2522 6233.

Area Code The area code for **Bangalore** is **080.**

ATMs Visit the shop-intensive vicinity of M.G. Road.

Bookstores **Strand Book Stall** is at S113-114 Manipal Centre, Dickenson Road (© 080/2558-0000). **Higginbothams** is at 68 M.G. Rd. (© 080/2558- 6574). **Sankar's Book Stall** is at 15/2 Museum Rd. (© 080/2558-6867). The huge **Landmark** bookstore can be found at Forum Mall in Koramangala, far from downtown Bangalore.

Car Rentals **Gullivers Tours & Travels** is at B2-SPL Habitat, no. 138, Gangadhara Chetty Rd.; ((℃) **080/2558-0108** or -3213).

Currency Exchange Exchange cash or get credit card advances from **Wall Street Finances** (3 House of Lords, St. Mark's Rd.; ℃ **080/2227-1812;** Mon–Fri 9:30am–6pm, Sat 9:30am–5pm) or from **Standard Chartered** (Raheja Towers, 26 M.G. Rd.; Mon–Fri 10:30am–5pm, Sat 10:30am–1:30pm). Alternatively, you can go to **Thomas Cook** (55 M.G. Rd.; ℃ **080/2558-1337** or 2559-4168; Mon–Sat 9:30am–6pm).

Directory Assistance The number ℃ **080/2222-2222** operates much like a talking Yellow Pages service, where you get free updated telephone numbers and addresses for various city establishments.

Drugstores Twenty-four-hour chemists include **Khoday's Pharma** (214 Westminster, Cunningham Rd.; ℃ **080/5698-7386** or 080/2222-4306; other branches 080/2226-8677 and 080/2227-3111) and **Mallya Hospital** (Vittal Mallya Rd., south of Cubbon Park; ℃ **080/2227-7979**).

Emergencies Dial ℃ **100** for police emergencies.

Hospital Both **Manipal Hospital** (98 Rustum Bagh, Airport Rd.; ℃ **080/2526-8901** or -6447) and **St. John's Medical College and Hospital** (Sarjapur Rd.; ℃ **080/2553-0724** or -2411) are decent options.

Internet Access Cybercafes abound in this IT-savvy city (see "Cafe Society," below). You'll find a **Sify i way** on Residency Rd. (℃ **080-5112-4226;** www.iway. com) and a **Reliance Webworld** on M.G. Rd (℃ **080/3061-3080;** www.reliance info.com); outlets of both are found all over the city.

Police Contact **Cubbon Park Station** at ℃ 080/2294-2591, -2087, or 100.

Post Office As always, your best bet for sending mail is through your hotel. The **GPO** (℃ **080/2286-6772** or 080/2289-2036; Mon–Sat 10am–6pm, Sun 10:30am–1pm) is architecturally interesting. It's located at the intersection of Raj Bhavan and Ambedkar Road.

Railway For inquiries, dial ℃ **131** or 132.

Taxis Call **Gopinath Radio Call Taxi** (℃ **080/2360-5555** or 2856-5000; 24 hr.).

WHAT TO SEE & DO

Although it was ruled by various dynasties, Bangalore's chief historical sights date back to the 18th-century reign of Hyder Ali and his son Tipu Sultan, "the Lion of Mysore," who put up the most spirited resistance to British imperialism. But more than anything, Bangalore is about experiencing an Indian city that brims with bars, restaurants, clubs, and positive energy—a great place for walking, window-shopping and, at night, letting your hair down. The Garden City also has lovely parks, some of which date back over 2 centuries, of which the botanical gardens at **Lal Bagh** are the most impressive.

Set off early for Bugle Hill, site of the **Bull Temple** (sanctum timings daily 7:30am–11:30am and 4:30–8:30pm). Built by the city's original architect, Kempe Gowda, this 16th-century black-granite statue of Nandi (Shiva's sacred bull) literally dwarfs his "master," and is kept glistening by regular applications of coconut oil.

Cafe Society

Caffeine is a popular fix in a city where socializing is the favored pastime of a money-wielding cosmopolitan crowd. Get yours at **Java City** (24/1 Lavelle Rd.; ✆ 080/5112-0647; daily 11:30am–11:30pm; Wi-Fi enabled), where you can also indulge in a slice of rum-and-chocolate cake (other branches are at 47 Church St. and 13 Cunningham Rd.). Or head for cool **Cinnamon Barista** (11 Walton Rd., off Lavelle Rd.), attached to the highly recommended Cinnamon boutique. You can also surf the Internet while getting your caffeine rush at **Café Coffee Day,** Bangalore's first cybercafe (13 Brigade Rd.; ✆ 080/3090-2967; daily 8am–10:30pm; Rs 70/$1.60 for 1 hr. and two coffees). For something with less of a Starbucks feel and a larger menu, **Nilgiris Café** (171 Brigade Rd.; ✆ 080/2558-8401; daily 8am–10:30pm) is a welcome choice. Situated in the heart of Bangalore's busy shopping area, this simple, clean cafe serves great iced or Ceylon teas and cappuccinos at half the prices of other cafes.

Nearby is a Ganesha temple (Sri Dodda Ganapathi), which houses an enormous statue of the elephant-headed deity made of 100 kilos of rank-smelling butter. Apparently this idol is remade every 4 years, and the butter distributed to devotees as *prasad* (blessed food).

Picnicking with the family and cricketing with the boys are popular pastimes in **Cubbon Park** (Cantonment), laid out in 1864 by the Mysore engineer, Richard Sankey. Today many visitors come to view the lovely buildings that surround the park as well as to visit the **Government Museum and Venkatappa Art Gallery** (✆ 080/2286-4483; Tues–Sun 10am–5pm; Rs 4/8¢), which focuses on sculpture. It contains works from Khajuraho, Bihar, and Madhya Pradesh dating back to the 10th century, Buddhist figures from the 4th- and 5th-century Gandhara school, and Hoysala carvings from Belur, Halebid, and Hampi—not that these are really a match for the real thing, seen on location. While in the vicinity, take a walk or drive past **Vidhana Vidhi** to admire its Greco colonial–style buildings, including India's largest state headquarters, **Vidhana Soudha,** Karnataka's State Legislature and Secretariat building (no entry allowed), to marvel at what is termed "neo-Dravidian" architecture. Its blend of styles from across India is capped by one of India's most recognizable symbols—the four-headed gold lion of Ashoka, India's celebrated early Buddhist king. Over the entrance, a gleaming gold-lettered sign bears the somewhat optimistic slogan GOVERNMENT WORK IS GOD'S WORK. Across the road from the Vidhana Soudha, fringing Cubbon Park, is Karnataka's two-story High Court building, or **Attara Kacheri,** an attractive design with red bricks and monumental Corinthian columns.

If it's a real garden you're after, head straight for the botanical gardens at **Lal Bagh** (daily 9am–6pm; Rs 2/4¢), conceived and laid out by Sultan Hyder Ali in 1760. His son, Tipu, expanded the gardens further, planting exotic plants from Persia, Kabul, Turkey, and Mauritius (tropical and subtropical species) over 96 hectares (240 acres). Highlights include the Lawn Clock and the British-built glasshouse, structurally based on London's Crystal Palace. After visiting the gardens, be sure to pop in for a meal at *the* Bangalore lunch institution, **Mavalli Tiffin Rooms** (see "Where to Dine," below), a short distance from the entrance.

Tipu Sultan's Summer Palace (daily 9am–5pm; Rs 2/4¢), built toward the end of the 18th century entirely from timber, is a relic in a city committed more to progress

Karnataka

Breathe Away Anxiety & Stress with India's Hottest New Age Guru

Sri Sri Ravi Shankar, once a disciple of Maharishi Mahesh Yogi (renowned spiritual guide of the Beatles), is the subcontinent's hottest New Age guru— many consider "The Art of Living," his nonsectarian philosophy of enjoying life for the moment, the perfect spiritual currency for our material times. His main ashram lies on 24 hectares (60 acres) of lush green hillside in south Bangalore, where every evening thousands of the city's well-heeled gather for the evening lecture and *satsang* (devotional singing). The articulate Sri Sri's appeal lies in the fact that he does not emphasize incarnations or abstinences, but encourages his disciples to enjoy the present without guilt while also encouraging them to contribute towards humanitarian and environmental concerns. His adherents—predominantly from India's growing urban elite, but also hugely popular on foreign shores (San Franciscans have a real penchant for his teachings)—can go about their hectic lives and remain relatively apolitical yet feel good about not discarding all sense of religion and tradition.

A philosophy of convenience, some say, but even his fiercest detractors admit the value of *sudarshan kriya,* an ancient breathing technique taught when you attend the "Art of Living" course. The 30-minute-a-day practice is said to encourage the flow of oxygen to the whole body, ostensibly discouraging the storage of toxins and thus helping release anxiety, frustration, depression, and anger, leaving you with a genuine sense of calm and well-being.

To attend an evening session or a 14-hour Art of Living course spread over several days, call ahead (**(** 080/2843-2273, -2274, or -2832; 21st Km, Kanakapura Main Rd., Udayapura, Bangalore 560 082; www.artofliving.org).

than to preservation. It has a somewhat sophomoric exhibition with extensive text about Tipu's life and military conquests as well as those of his father, Hyder Ali Khan. Next door is an enormously active 17th-century temple, built by the Wodeyar kings; and just north are the ruins of **Bangalore Fort,** largely destroyed during the Anglo-Mysore War.

WHERE TO STAY

Bangalore has a huge range of excellent top-quality hotels, of which our personal favorites are **The Park hotel** for its contemporary über-slick styling and in-house nightlife, and the **Taj West End Hotel** for its heritage atmosphere (both reviewed below). You may want to compare online rates with the following hotel rates, which offer the same top-end luxury and amenities. As you'll find elsewhere in India, many of the lodgings in Bangalore quote their rates in dollars or euros.

ITC Hotel Windsor Sheraton & Towers, popular with Bollywood's elite and high-profile businesspeople and politicians (including Tony Blair), retains the look and character of a neoclassical English country house; ask for a room in the Manor Block (**(** **080/2226-9898;** fax 080/2226-4941; www.welcomgroup.com). The

Oberoi (37/39 M.G. Rd.; ✆ 080/2558-5858; www.oberoihotels.com; doubles from $335) is another excellent hotel, set amid gardens with lovely views over the lawns and the swimming pool. Standard units are not quite as large or as elegant as those at the Windsor Sheraton, but they're spacious enough and luxuriously decorated with floral fabrics and antique finishes; ask for a room on an upper floor for better views. But for over-the-top opulence, **Leela Palace Kempinski**—judged by *Forbes Magazine* one of the world's best new business hotels in 2001 and garnering CNN's Ultimate Service Award for the second year in a row in 2004—is the hands-down winner. A baroque rendition of contemporary Indo-Saracenic architecture, looming large in pale pink, it offers enormous "conservatory" rooms with private balconies and, along with all the modern conveniences, elegant four-poster beds, rococo gold-gilt lamps, and silk duvet covers. Deluxe rooms are also very spacious and styled in the same manner (23 Airport Rd.; ✆ **080/2521-1234;** www.theleela.com; doubles: $380 deluxe, $400 conservatory, including breakfast). In the (comparatively) moderate price range, opt for the Taj-run **Gateway Hotel on Residency Road;** its best accommodations are the recently refurbished "executive" guest rooms. Ask for an even-numbered, pool-facing room on the fourth floor (✆ **080/5660-4545;** www.tajhotels.com; doubles from $195). Much cheaper, but perfectly serviceable, **St. Mark's** is a small, neat business hotel (✆ **080/2227-9090;** www.stmarkshotel.com) with doubles from Rs 4,400 ($100); alternatively, **Ivory Towers** (✆ **080/2558-9333;** Rs 3,300/$75) has 12 spotless suites with great views (ask for one with a balcony) and all amenities (including Wi-Fi). Its restaurant, Ebony, is reviewed below. Perched on the 12th and 13th floors of Barton Centre, gob-smack on busy M.G. Road, Ivory Towers is conveniently located if you want to be downtown. But our top budget recommendation is the charming **Villa Pottipati** (reviewed below).

The Park ⚘⚘⚘   Themed around Bangalore's reputation as India's information-technology city and its historic connection with silk production, this compact boutique hotel features top-class interiors by Tina Ellis (of London-based Conran). In the lobby—dominated by a gigantic silk curtain—rough, smooth, and suede textures are offset with brushed metal and a row of large white orbs of light. The white-marble reception counter is topped by orange Apple laptops—behind the counter, staff wear pale gray jackets over white T-shirts. The four floors are styled around a palette of strong chromatic elements that refer to the Indian landscape; pale lime and iris purple suggest the mountains, while a desert oasis is alluded to with ultramarine and saffron. Guest rooms are on the small side and don't have great views (ask for a pool-facing room), but they are beautifully finished—oak flooring, designer rugs, black-and-white photographs of Bangalore, oak-and-leather director's chairs, and minimalist metal-framed four-poster beds. Bathrooms are great, with large rain showers that adjust to give you a water massage. Rooms on the desert-themed Residence Floor come with a host of additional services, including airport transfers, late checkout, sparkling wine on arrival, head and shoulder massage, Internet access, in-room fax and laptop on request, DVD player, and access to the elegant private lounge, where breakfast and all-day tea and coffee are served.

14/7 M.G. Rd., Bangalore 560 001. ✆ 080/2559-4666. Fax 080/2559-4029. www.theparkhotels.com. resv.blr@the parkhotels.com. 109 units. $225 deluxe double, $250 deluxe balcony double, $260 deluxe terrace double, $275 luxury double; $325 Residence Floor; $375–$400 suite. All rates include breakfast and one-way transfer. AE, DC, MC, V. **Amenities:** 3 restaurants; lounge bar; pool; health spa; indoor games; travel services; sightseeing; business center; currency exchange; gift shop; 24-hr. room service; babysitting; laundry; theater; doctor-on-call; valet; library. *In room:* A/C, TV, Wi-Fi enabled, minibar.

Taj West End Hotel ★★★ A member of The Leading Hotels of the World, West End dates back to 1887, when it was a 10-room Victorian boardinghouse. Today the luxury hotel retains its old-world charm while providing guests with modern conveniences. The stately lobby features a central atrium with skylight, dark walnut paneling, teakwood fluting on the walls, lots of plants, plush sofas, and a grand piano. It opens onto **Mynt,** the hotel's 24-hour coffee shop serving Mediterranean, Italian, and Indian food at separate counters, each with a chef who interacts with guests. Accommodations are spread over more than 9 hectares (22 acres) of gardens with wonderful old banyan trees—thankfully, a buggy whisks you to your room after check-in. Rooms comprise various pitched-roof-veranda blocks and more recent structures modeled on similar colonial architecture; each has a private balcony overlooking the extensive gardens. Try to book in the Heritage Wing, which has four-poster beds and old-Bangalore-theme lithographs. "Superior" rooms are by comparison rather ordinary, but the private balcony with lovely views is a consolation. If you value your space, fork out the extra cash for an executive suite; these are massive, warm-toned, carpeted spaces with long balconies and high arched ceilings. Bathrooms are large, with separate tub and shower, and a walk-in dressing room.

Race Course Rd., Bangalore 560 001. ✆ 080/5660-5660. Fax 080/5660-5700 or 080/2220-4575. www.tajhotels. com. 129 units. $285 superior double, $350 luxury double (includes one-way airport transfer); $405 Taj Club; $430–$550 suite. $20 extra bed. Taj Club rooms and suites include breakfast and airport transfers. AE, DC, MC, V. **Amenities:** 3 restaurants; 2 bars; 2 tennis courts; golf and riding on request; fitness center; travel assistance; car hire; currency exchange; shopping arcade; salon; 24-hr. room service; babysitting; laundry and dry cleaning; doctor-on-call. *In room:* A/C, TV (some wall-mounted plasma), minibar, hair dryer. Taj Club units: fax machines on request, DVD players, personal butlers.

Villa Pottipati ★★★ *Value* Surrounded by mango, jackfruit, avocado, jacaranda, and gulmohar trees, heady *shivalinga* blossoms at the entrance, this is the most authentic and reasonably priced heritage experience you can have in the heart of this city of steel, glass, and concrete. Time has stood still in this stately villa of red cement floors, teakwood beams, and high ceilings, furnished with teak and rosewood antique furniture and beautiful artifacts. Pottipati gets its name from a village in Andhra Pradesh, from where the Reddy family (who own this property, now managed by the Neemrana group) came 121 years ago. Service is personal and exceptional, with the kind of attention guests probably enjoyed a century ago. But you won't have to forgo any modern amenities, and at press time a new pool was being built. Dining is indoors, surrounded by teak and bronze, or outdoors under a canopy of mango trees; everything, from the calamari starter to the Goan prawn vindaloo, is delicious. As at all Neemrana properties, each guest room is different. No matter which room you stay in, do ask for a tour of unoccupied others, named after traditional South Indian saris. The Venkatagiri Suite, with a stunning turquoise-blue Venkatagiri sari covering the bed, offers incredible value, with a living room, a private dressing area, an area for kids, two large wardrobes, a bathroom with a large bathtub, and a veranda. The Rajadurga Suite rewards early birds with spectacular sunrise views. The fabulous Kanchipuram Suite has a private pillared balcony, an anteroom for kids, an old-fashioned lime-green bathroom, and a quaint antique gramophone.

142, 8th Cross, 4th Main Rd., Malleswaram, Bangalore 560 003. ✆ 080/2336-0777 or 080/5128-0832 through - 0834. Fax 080/5128-0835. www.neemranahotels.com. 8 units. Rs 2,500–Rs 4,000 ($57–$91) double. Rates include bed tea, evening tea, and breakfast. Taxes extra. AE, DC, MC, V. **Amenities:** Dining room; restaurant; bar; concierge; travel desk; car hire; currency exchange; laundry and dry cleaning; doctor-on-call. *In room:* A/C, TV, Wi-Fi enabled, hair dryer, safe.

WHERE TO DINE

With Bangalore's IT boom, the number of professionals with disposable cash has risen exponentially—leading in turn to an explosion of options on the dining scene. Though many of the best restaurants are located in hotels, there are countless other eating places to suit every mood. As in Tamil Nadu, you can get a good, clean, wholesome vegetarian *tiffin* ("light meal"—pronounced *tea*-pun) all over Bangalore. Most famous of all is **MTR** (reviewed below); but equally good for its Tamil Iyengar food is **Kadambam** (112 C South Block, Manipal Centre, Dickenson Rd.; other branches as well). Gold-framed pictures of deities line the wall, the simple open kitchen is spotless, the food is cheap and delicious, and the filter coffee—if, that is, you've developed a taste for sweetened South Indian filter coffee—is simply extraordinary. For authentic Karnataka cuisine, **Halli Mane** (no. 14, 3rd Cross Rd., off Sampige Rd., Malleswaram; ℂ **080/2346-9797**) is Bangalore's busiest restaurant. Its tiled roof, basic furnishings, and stainless-steel crockery evoke the ambience of a typical rural home. Pure vegetarian, dirt-cheap thalis (Rs 10/25¢) or buffet meals (Rs 50/$1.15) are served here without fuss. Chat with the friendly manager, Mr. Ramnath, who will assist you in selecting just the right dishes for your palate. For affordable, nonvegetarian coastal Karnataka cuisine, **Unicorn** (94/3 Infantry Rd.; ℂ **0802559-1670**) is great. The menu changes every week but expect fish, coconut milk, and lots of flavor.

In the big hotels, besides **Karavalli,** reviewed below, the following are worth a mention: For North and South Indian cuisine, **Jamavar** at Leela Palace Kempinski (ℂ **080/2521-1234**) is one of Bangalore's class acts, with arguably the best tandoor dishes in town. For specialty South Indian cuisine, there's no better place than **Dakshin** (ℂ **080/2226-9898**), the upmarket restaurant at the Hotel Windsor Sheraton, with a menu that represents the best of all four southern states. It's hard to know what to order from their extensive menu (Rs 300–Rs 800/$6.85–$18), so go with the maitre d's recommendation or get a thali (the seafood thali, Rs 1,000/$23, is fab). If your system needs a break from spicy cuisine, **i-t.ALIA** (reviewed below) is Bangalore's most stylish Italian restaurant; it's situated in The Park hotel. If you want to get out of the hotel atmosphere, head for **Sunny's** (Vittal Mallaya Rd.; ℂ **080/2224-3642**), with its spacious outdoor and indoor seating and lounge bar. The eclectic menu is a reflection of Bangalore's growing sophistication. Favorites here include baked brie with toasted almonds; stir-fried calamari with basil and garlic; angel-hair pasta with fresh chunky tomatoes and extra-virgin olive oil; and the flavorful, slightly spiced lamb lasagna, served piping hot. Even better is **Shiok** (Indiranagar; ℂ **080/5116-1800;** www.shiokfood. com), a fine-dining restaurant run by owner-chef Madhu Menon, who has traveled extensively in the Far East to study different styles of cooking. Thai, Malay, Indonesian, and Singaporean dishes are on offer, with more than 60% of the ingredients flown in from overseas: lemon-grass chili prawns (Rs 250/$5.70), spiced fish grilled in banana leaves (Rs 150/$3.40), and Buddha's Feast (Rs 110/$2.50) are all recommended.

Art 🦋🦋 ECLECTIC/FUSION   Pretentious as the name sounds, this is one of Bangalore's hippest restaurants, done out in bright shades of yellow and orange. Chef Ramdeo Das really does prepare each dish as though it were a work of art. A standout entree is "Birds in Flight," a seafood combo comprising prawns prepared in olive oil and lemon juice, and fresh fish stuffed with smoked salmon, served on a bed of spinach and broccoli and topped with a creamy basil sauce. Cheaper, quick meals are also available.

Cosmo Village, Magrath Rd. ⓒ 080/5112-7373 or -7474. Main courses Rs 170–Rs 350 ($3.90–$8); seafood platter Rs 750 ($17). AE, DC, MC, V. Daily noon–3:15pm and 7–11pm.

Blue Ginger ⁂ VIETNAMESE   Lush tropical foliage, a lotus pond, and the scent of frangipani in bloom set the mood for Taj West End's newest—and India's first—Vietnamese restaurant. The decor is Vietnamese-chic: water-hyacinth fiber and dark silks; leather ottomans and natural stone tables; silk lanterns and flaming torches. You can watch the chefs at work in their open kitchen. The hands-down favorite starter is the crunchy raw mango salad, followed by the coconut-based Vietnamese *caris* (curry) served in a clay pot, and accompanied not by rice but a baguette. For a lighter meal, we recommend the perfectly done braised fish with pepper and garlic or the stir-fried chicken with lemon grass and chili (vegetarians can order the crisp stir-fried greens with garlic). End with sweet sticky rice and mung bean in banana leaves, the mung bean ice cream, or the fresh fruit ice creams in seasonal flavors.

Taj West End. ⓒ 080/5660-5660. Main courses Rs 405–Rs 872 ($9.15–$20). AE, MC, DC, V. Daily 12:30–3pm and 7:30–11:45pm.

Ebony ⍟ ECLECTIC INDIAN   Here's an unexpected treat on the rooftop of a lurid city-center building. After the unpromising elevator ride up, you can dine alfresco and enjoy the best city views in Bangalore. Try mutton *pulao*, based on a Parsi recipe; it's made with tender meat and potatoes steeped in Persian spices (cinnamon, cardamom, and rose petals), then layered with saffron-flavored rice before being cooked with an onion-based gravy. Another fantastic meat dish is Manan's pepper mutton; this comes from the temple town of Kumbakonam (Tamil Nadu), where Manan is the owner of a small eatery. The mutton is cooked in a paste made from roasted pepper, coriander seeds, and Indian spices. If you'd prefer to avoid meat, try *paneer kairi dopiaza*, made from *paneer*, green mangoes, and fresh coriander; have it with garlic *naan* (bread). Thai food is served daily with a live cooking counter on Thursday and Friday (reserve ahead).

13th Floor, Ivory Tower Hotel, Barton Centre, 84 M.G. Rd. ⓒ 080/2558-9333 or -5164. Main courses Rs 175–Rs 335 ($1.70–$7.60). AE, DC, MC, V. Daily noon–3pm and 7:30–11:15pm.

i-t.ALIA ⁂ ITALIAN/INTERNATIONAL   Chef Abhijit Saha's brand-new menu may have items that are a mouthful to pronounce, but once you taste them, you will be left speechless. Flavor gets top priority here, but for this globe-trotting chef, creative presentation is equally important. Begin with the light and gentle-on-the-palate lettuce and asparagus soup and the *insalata di mela verde, noci arrostite sedano e gorgonzola*, a green apple and rocket lettuce salad with walnuts and Gorgonzola dressing—divine. Whether you pick a simple tapenade-stuffed potato gnocchi or the *gamberoni grigliati conpatate arrosto, carciofi e pomodoro* (king prawns with artichokes, roasted potatoes, and tomato), you will be served a platter as beautiful as it is delicious. Even the humble pizza is not so humble in this restaurant.

The Park hotel, 14/7 M.G. Rd., Bangalore 560 001. ⓒ 080/2559-4666. Main courses lunch Rs 400–Rs 625 ($9.10–$14), dinner Rs 275–Rs 1,100 ($6.30–$25). AE, DC, MC, V. Daily noon–2:45pm and 7–11:45pm.

Karavalli ⁂ INDIAN   For more than a decade, this indoor-outdoor restaurant has been wowing guests and winning awards. Sit in the open-air courtyard under the huge canopy of a raintree on wrought-iron garden chairs, or inside, in what resembles a Mangalorean home, with high ceilings, antique furniture, and walls adorned with old seafarer maps and a grandfather clock. For seafood lovers, Karavalli is a godsend, with Goan baby lobster, Mangalorean black pomfret, and pearlspot caught off the shores

Swinging in the Hip City of Bangalore

Spend at least an hour schmoozing on beanbags at The Park hotel's **i-BAR** 🎔🎔🎔—one of Bangalore's most happening spots—or dancing to house and trance on the small dance floor, where DJ Sasha mixes up a swinging party (Rs 500/$11 entry). Alternatively, head for **13th Floor** 🎔🎔 (Ivory Tower Hotel; M.G. Rd.; 7–11pm), a sexy 120-seater rooftop cocktail lounge where you get a large dose of the Bangalore skyline while you sip on cocktails named after weapons. **Liquor Café** 🎔🎔 is a groovy lounge bar on the covered rooftop of a building that houses several smart restaurants (including Art—see "Where to Dine," above); it attracts a hip young crowd who come for the funky, laid-back acid lounge music (Cosmo Village, Magrath Rd.; 🕿 080/2509-1160 or 080/5112-7373; daily 7–11pm).

Named for the Greek god of sleep, **Hypnos** 🎔 is a cocktail lounge that does anything but, even in the Moroccan Square, where you can smoke *shishas* (hookahs) filled with apple, strawberry, or grape tobacco while tucking into Lebanese and Mediterranean fusion cuisine (Gem Plaza, Infantry Rd.; 🕿 080/5111-3361 through -3364; Rs 500/$11 entry fee). Single men are technically unwelcome at **1912—The Living Room** 🎔 (previously **180 proof**), where the Mafioso-style management ensures that the industrial-chic atmosphere is enhanced by the highest-profile Bangalorean crowd. Housed in a lovely stone building that looks like a historic monument, this is probably *the* place in Bangalore to strut your stuff on the dance floor: Three locally based DJs run the show with a blend of rock, hip-hop, and from 8:30pm on, trance music, occasionally joined by record-spinners from Mumbai, San Francisco, and the U.K. (40 St. Marks Rd.; 🕿 080/2299-7290; daily 7–11:30pm). **Insomnia** 🎔 (Rs 400/$9.10 per couple, Rs 600/$14 single males on Fri and Sat; other days free entry) is a pleasant split-level club with a bar upstairs and a cozy DJ-operated dance floor below (Le Meridien, 🕿 080/2226-2233). Also in Le Meridien is **F-Bar and Lounge,** a franchise of the Fashion TV bar chain, with screens beaming Fashion TV while fashionistas nibble Japanese and Korean starters or dance to the music of DJ Jasmeet; the bar occasionally hosts live fashion shows. Another see-and-be-seen nightclub is **Spinn,** located in a 1940s Art Deco bungalow (80 3rd Cross, Residency Rd.; 🕿 080/2558-1555) where hip-hop, funk, and house music rule. **NASA** (1/A Church St.; 🕿 080/2558-6512) is worth a giggle: Staff are decked out in pilot outfits, and the interior is like the inside of a sci-fi space module; the bar is called the "Fuel Tank" and the loo is known as the "Humanoid Disposal" area. It's good for an afternoon pint, but happy hours draw massive crowds. For loud rock music and a crowd that likes to sing along, **Purple Haze** (M.G. Rd., near Richmond Circle; 🕿 080/2221-3758) is one of Bangalore's more popular nightclubs. The Oberoi Hotel's smart **Polo Club** combines deep leather sofas with the ubiquitous TV sports entertainment. Cigar aficionados should head for the **Jockey Club** (🕿 080/5660-4444) at the Taj Residency, popular with expats; while **Dublin,** the watering hole at the ITC Windsor Sheraton (🕿 080/2226-9898), serves up—yep, you guessed right—an Irish pub vibe.

of Cochin in Kerala. The west coast also provides fresh *bekti*, shrimp, tiger prawns, scampi, squid, sear, sole, and ladyfish, while the varying cuisines of India's southern coastal regions provide inspiration for dishes originally found in home kitchens. Chef Thimmaiah, who has been here since 1990, drums up sensational starters like the Coorg fried chicken, which you can follow with dry Malabar-style tiger prawns or Kane fry (ladyfish). If you've any room left for the main course, try the Alleppey fish curry or the Karavalli mutton curry with *appams* (savory rice-batter pancakes).

Taj Gateway Hotel, 66 Residency Rd. ℂ 080/5660-4545. Main courses Rs 115–Rs 800 ($2.65–$18.20); lunch thali Rs 410–Rs 485 ($9.30–$11.10). AE, DC, MC, V. Daily 12:30–3:30pm and 7:30–11:45pm.

Koshy's Restaurant and the Jewel Box ✸ *Moments* INDIAN/CONTINENTAL
Easily the most popular eating and meeting place on M.G. Road, this 50-year-old restaurant has changed little over the years. Food is varied, but it's more or less beside the point; you come here for the energetic buzz—it's a favorite gathering spot and has a distinct local flavor, attracting the coffeehouse intellectual and budding artist alike. You won't be bothered at all if you prefer to linger endlessly over a beer (Rs 100/$2.30) and your book. Those who would rather steer clear of the action can sit in the quieter, but rather bland, air-conditioned section, the Jewel Box.

39 St. Mark's Rd., Bangalore 560 001. ℂ 080/2221-3793 or -5030. Average meal Rs 350 ($8). AE, DC, MC, V. Daily noon–3pm and 7–11pm.

Rejuvenation City: Tip-Top Spas

Prompted by the emergence of an overstressed, well-heeled workforce, Bangalore has a number of well-known luxury and medical spas. Besides **The Spa** at Leela Palace Kempinski (ℂ 080/2521-1234) in the city, two luxury spas lie about an hour outside Bangalore. **The Golden Palms Spa** (ℂ 080/2371-2222), owned by Bollywood director Sanjay Khan, is part of an upmarket resort that not only provides routine spa treatments, but is the spot for discreet cosmetic surgery and anti-aging treatments. **Angsana Oasis Spa and Resort** (ℂ 080/2846-8893; www.angsana.com) offers spa packages from 205€ ($255) double for 2 nights (includes accommodations, breakfasts, and one traditional Thai massage). The attitude toward pampering is more laid-back. Neither of these spas will restrict your diet or ban smoking or alcohol; in contrast, **Soukya International Holistic Health Centre** (in Whitefield, 30 min. from Bangalore; ℂ 080/2794-5001 through -5004; www.soukya.com) is a medical spa that focuses on therapeutic and complementary therapies. Run by Dr Isaac Mathai, his nutritionist wife Suja, and a battery of experts, this is a nonsmoking, alcohol- and meat-free spa where everything is low fat, low salt, low spice, and organic. The focus is on individually created "holistic wellness programs" (from Hawaiian hot stone to specialized Ayurvedic treatments) that strengthen the body's immune system, including those belonging to some rather famous people, like Fergie, Princess of York; Archbishop Desmond Tutu; and healthy-living guru Andrew Weil. Rates start at Rs 6,300 ($144) per day—this includes accommodations, meals, and medical evaluation and assessment but not treatments.

Mavalli Tiffin Rooms (MTR) ☆☆ *Moments* SOUTH INDIAN VEGETARIAN
Possibly *the* essential Bangalore eating experience, this is an excellent spot to sample the
chaos of a traditional "tiffin" room, where scores of locals rush in for the Indian version
of fast food, served since 1924 with attitude and gusto from shiny silver buckets by
notoriously surly waiters in white. If you're here during lunch, order a thali and eat with
your fingers from a silver tray onto which various authentic South Indian concoctions
are heaped and continuously replenished. You sit in rather indecorous surroundings
(the current venue was built in 1949, and hasn't changed at all in over 40 years) on
brown plastic chairs at marble-top tables with orange steel legs; grab a table upstairs.
Adjacent, the **MTR Store** sells a wide range of South Indian treats and delicacies,
including popular sweets (like *badam halwa* and *ladu*) and ready-to-eat savories.
14 Lal Bagh Rd. ℂ 080/2222-0022. Typical meal Rs 75 ($1.70); individual items Rs 5–Rs 20 (10¢–45¢). No credit
cards. Tues–Sun 6:30am–noon, 12:30–2:30pm, and 7:30–9pm.

SHOPPING
You'll find the city's major shopping centers along and around **M.G. Road, Commercial Street,** and **Brigade Road.** M.G. Road is where you'll find the fixed-price tourist-
orientated (no bargains or bargaining) **Cauvery Arts and Crafts Emporium, Central
Cottage Industries Emporium,** and **Karnataka State Silk Industries Emporium.**
Fabulous silks and home textiles, as well as contemporary silverware from Neemrana
and traditional silver jewelry from Amrapali and Jaipur, are some of the highlights
available in **Shop Ananya,** located next to the Hotel Sarovar at 9/1 Dhondusa
Annexe, Richmond Circle (ℂ **080/2299-8922**). For antiques and other collectibles
in bronze, stone, teak, and silver, call on **Natesan's Antiqarts** (76 M.G. Rd.; ℂ **080/
2558-8344** or -7427). Pick up beautiful ethnic home accessories, rugs, and other gifts
at **The Bombay Store** (99 EGK Prestige, M.G. Rd.; ℂ **080/2532-0014** or -0015).
With four levels of saris and *salwar kameez* (for women) and *sherwanis* (for men), and
a nonstop clientele, you can understand why staff at **Deepam Silk International**
insist that there is "nowhere else in the whole world" better to shop for silk garments
(67 Bluemoon Complex, M.G. Rd.; ℂ **080/2558-8760**).

Cinnamon ☆☆   Some of India's top designers are represented in this cool, stylish
boutique, which often hosts small exhibitions. Abraham and Thakore, considered the
country's top design duo, have a range here, and this is the only place in India outside
Jaipur that you'll find clothing by Brigette Singh. Bangalorean designer Jason
Cheriyan refuses to sell his work anywhere else. Hours are Monday to Saturday
10:30am to 8pm, Sunday noon to 8pm. 11 Walton Rd., off Lavelle Rd. ℂ **080/2222-9794.**

CULTURAL ACTIVITIES
Check the local dailies for information about cultural events. Besides art exhibitions
and traditional dance and music performances, Bangalore draws major international
artists, including pop and rock stars.

The violin-shaped auditorium known as **Chowdaiah Memorial Hall** (Gayathri
Devi Park Extension, Vyalikaval; ℂ **080/2344-5810**) hosts regular classical music
performances, as well as film, dance, and drama. Plays are regularly staged at
Rabindra Kalakshetra (Jayachamarachendra Rd.; ℂ **080/2224-1325** or 080/2664-
6158), where you can also catch occasional art exhibitions. Numerous art galleries
around the city host contemporary Indian art and other exhibitions. **Venkatappa Art
Gallery,** attached to the Government Museum (Kasturba Rd.; ℂ **080/2286-4483;**

Tues–Sun 10am–5pm; Rs 10/25¢), displays more than 600 paintings year-round. **Chitrakala Parishat** (Art Complex, Kumara Krupa Rd.; © **080/2226-1816**) has a varied collection of traditional paintings, leather puppets, and artifacts from all over Karnataka. Visit its various art studios and gallery spaces, the open-air theater, and (in particular) the Roerich and Kejriwal galleries. For high-end art, check out **Gallerie Zen** (121 Dickenson Rd.; © **080/2559-8793** or 080/2558-1577; www.zenmrl.net; by appointment only).

Nrityagram Dance Village (along the Bangalore-Pune Hwy., 35km/22 miles from Bangalore) is a renowned center for Indian dance training. Performances feature students as well as established artists. Organized tours of the facility include lecture-demonstrations designed to introduce you to Indian culture, life philosophy, and both *kathak* and *odissi* dance forms (© **080/2846-6313;** Sept–May, Tues–Sat 10am–5:30pm, dance classes 10:30am–1pm; tours Rs 20/45¢ per person, advance bookings essential). A through-the-night dance and music festival is held in February; it attracts almost 30,000 spectators, so decent seating is at a premium.

2 Mysore ⚑⚑⚑

140km (87 miles) SW of Bangalore; 473km (293 miles) N of Chennai; 1,177km (730 miles) SE of Mumbai

A city of palatial buildings and tree-lined boulevards, laid-back Mysore is possessed of a quaint charm, a dignified hangover from the days when it was the capital of a rich princely state. It remains a popular destination for travelers, particularly for its **Maharajah's Palace.** Built over a period of 15 years at the turn of the 20th century at a cost of over Rs 4 million, this astonishing Indo-Saracenic palace is testament to the affluence of one of India's notably wealthy ruling families. During the 10-day **Dussehra Festival,** held here during the first half of October, the entire city is dressed up in show-off style; each night **Mysore Palace** is lit up by 80,000 bulbs, and on the final evening of festivities, the Maharajah himself leads one of the country's most spectacular processions through the city streets. But Mysore is also an ideal base from which to explore the temples known as the **"Jewel Boxes"** of Hoysala architecture, which lie some 3 hours north, as well as the nearby Jain pilgrimage site at **Sravanabelgola.**

ESSENTIALS

GETTING THERE & AWAY   Trains from Bangalore (3 hr.) and Hassan (for Hoysala heartland; 2–3 hr.) pull in regularly at the **railway station** (© **131** or 0821/ 242-2103), situated at the intersection of Jhansi Laxmi Bai Road and Irwin Road. For Rajiv Gandhi National Park, your best option is to hire a car.

VISITOR INFORMATION   For information, visit the **Karnataka Tourist Office** (Mayura Yatri Niwas, JLB Rd., near railway station; © **0821/242-3652;** daily 7am–9pm).

GETTING AROUND   Negotiate **taxi** prices in advance, or hire a vehicle for the day. **Auto-rickshaws** are cheap and plentiful; you can either insist that the driver use his meter or fix a price upfront; the latter is likely to get you to your destination quicker (see chapter 2).

GUIDED TOURS & TRAVEL AGENTS   Operating since 1976, **Seagull Travels** (8 Best Western Ramanashree Hotel Complex, Bangalore–Niligiri Rd.; © **0821/ 252-9732,** -0535, or 0821/243-5095; fax 0821/252-0549; www.seagulltravels.com; daily 9:30am–8:30pm) handles a wide range of travel needs, including ticketing, taxi arrangements, and individually packaged tours (although prices can fluctuate arbitrarily). Seagull is Mysore's only agent for the government's popular Jungle Lodges and Resorts, including the popular Kabini River Lodge (see below). Another local travel agent is **Skyway International Travels** (no. 3704/4, Jansi Laxmibai Rd.; ℭ **0821/ 244-4444;** fax 0821/242-6000; skyway@vsnl.com; www.skywaytour.com). Don't pay for any taxi or vehicle without first checking its condition. You can organize a car through your hotel travel desk, but it's likely to be more expensive.

WHAT TO SEE & DO

Besides Mysore's most famous palace, the Maharajah's Palace, and Keshava Temple, you might want to visit **Jagan Mohan Palace** (west of Mysore Palace, Dewan's Rd.; daily 8:30am–5pm; Rs 10/25¢), which once served as the royal auditorium. The building now exhibits South India's oddest assortment of kitsch memorabilia from the massive private collection of the Wodeyars. Southeast of downtown (3km/2 miles away), **Chamundi Hill** is where you can join throngs of huffing-puffing pilgrims, some of who recite or read Hindu verses along the way. Stop first at the **Shiva Temple,** where devotees meander around the statue in a clockwise direction while a friendly priest dishes out sacred water and dollops of vermilion paste. The summit of the hill is very active with pilgrims come to pay their respects to Durga. You can buy a *darshan* ticket from the computerized ticketing booth and join the queue for a peek at the deity inside **Sri Chamundeswari Temple** (3:30–6:30pm); or you can wander around the hilltop exploring smaller temples, many of which serve as bases for bright-robed grinning *sadhus* (holy persons) wanting to sell you a private photo opportunity.

Finally, no trip to Mysore is complete without getting lost in the dizzying scents of jasmine, musk, sandalwood, frangipani, and incense as you wander through the city's vibrant **market.** Mysore is also famous for its silk and sandalwood oil, and you can witness the production of both by taking a side trip to Vidyaranyapuram, 15 minutes away. For an escorted tour of the **Government Silk Weaving Factory,** call ℭ **0821/ 248-1803** (daily 11:30am–2:30pm); the **Government Sandal Oil Factory** is right next door (daily 11:30am–4pm).

Maharajah's Palace (Amba Vilas) ⟮⟮⟮ Generally considered *the* palace in South India, this was designed by Henry Irving at the turn of the 20th century; 15 years of nonstop construction produced a fabulous domed, arched, colonnaded, and turreted structure with lavish interiors—teak ceilings, carved marble handrails, gilded pillared halls, ivory deities, rococo lamp stands, Italian crystal chandeliers, stained-glass windows, miles of white marble floors, and ceilings made from stained glass brought all the way from Glasgow. You'll be hard-pressed to find an undecorated section of wall or ceiling; frescoes, paintings, statues, and delicate relief carvings recall religious as well as secular scenes, including glorious state processions. Within the inner courtyards, growling stone felines guard stairways, while elsewhere, elaborately carved rosewood doors mark the entrances of yet more splendid halls and chambers. Paintings by Raja Ravi Varma, golden chariots, gilt-framed mirrors, stately family portraits (including a wax sculpture of the Maharajah), and all manner of ornate fantasy objects add to the spectacle of abundant wealth. Overlooking the parade grounds, brought to life during the **Dussehra Festival** (Sept or Oct), a terraced grandstand pavilion is covered by a heavily decorated and frescoed ceiling, while huge, decaying chandeliers dangle precariously over the seating.

Don't bother to purchase an additional ticket for the disappointing **Maharajah's Residential Palace,** where a sad display of items gathers dust.

Ramvilas Rd., Mizra Rd., and Purandara Rd. ℂ **0821/242-2620.** Admission: Amber Vilas Rs 20 (45¢); Residential Palace Rs 20 (45¢). Daily 10:30am–5:30pm.

Keshava Temple ✹✹✹ Situated 38km (25 miles) from Mysore in the small village of Somnathpur, this is perhaps the best-preserved and most complete Hoysala monument in existence. Also referred to as Chennakeshava Temple, this beautiful religious monument is presided over by Vijayanarayana, one of the 24 incarnations of Vishnu. Built as early as 1268, it is constructed entirely of soapstone and rests on a raised plinth; typical of Hoysala temples, it has a star-shaped ground plan and exquisitely sculpted interiors. It's really worth exploring in detail; you may have to urge or bribe the caretaker to crank up the generator so that you have enough light to properly observe the three shrines in the temple. Somnathpur is serene and remote, and the lawns around the monument are ideal for picnicking—ask your hotel for a packed lunch.

Somnathpur is 38km (24 miles) east of Mysore. Admission Rs 100 ($2.30). Daily 8am–5:30pm.

WHERE TO STAY

Mysore has plenty of very basic places to stay; walk around Gandhi Square and you can take your pick. **Hotel Dasaprakash,** the local institution, is recommended. It has clean, modest rooms with running hot water 5 to 10am (ℂ **0821/244-2444;** from Rs 355/$8 double). If you're after a taste of history, stay a bit out of the main town at **Lalitha Mahal Palace Hotel** (T. Narsipur Rd.; ℂ **0821/247-0470** through -0476). Built in 1921 by the Maharajah of Mysore to accommodate the visiting Viceroy, this huge, three-level heritage property is a testament to faded extravagance. Sadly, the magnificent building is badly in need of upkeep, and service leaves much to be desired. The public areas are lavish and lovely, though, with marble stairways, molded plasterwork, quaint seating alcoves, chunky pillars, and majestic stained-glass ceiling domes. Modern amenities have not kept pace with the high prices of the rooms, but even so, the suites are enchanting, with four-poster beds and French windows that open onto verandas. You'll need to fork out the dough for a Victorian-styled suite ($230–$750) in the original palace building, but don't bother staying in a standard room ($160) situated in a wing added in 1980.

The Green Hotel ✹✹ This award-winning hotel began as Chittaranjan Palace, built in the 1920s by Wodeyar IV as a retreat for his three sisters. Today it looks and feels pretty much how you would imagine the home of a royal family in decline would look, with lots of character. The hotel is owned by a charity that employs disadvantaged people on good wages and, true to its name, tries to be environmentally conscious. The palace proper has a motley assortment of antique furniture and colorful memorabilia that rivals other tourist distractions in town. Light filters through stained-glass windows, and the large, open public spaces are swathed in teak and brimming with old-world charm, despite the incessant noise from the main road alongside. This erstwhile princesses' retreat also offers interesting lodging options. Choose one of the seven guest rooms in the original palace: The Princess's Room is enormous, with antique furniture, blue Indian throws, and sheer curtains over narrow slit windows. For added color, try the Deluxe Bollywood Room, where the antique wooden headboards are decorated with brightly colored renditions of old Bollywood starlets on painted glass. Though all rooms are garden-facing, guest rooms in the New Wing (built when the palace became a film studio), while offering value, lack the historical flavor of the palace.

Chittaranjan Palace, 2270 Vinoba Rd., Jayalamipuram, Mysore 570 012. © **0821/525-5001**, -5002, or -5003. Fax 0821/251-6139. www.greenhotelindia.com. 31 units. New Wing: Rs 1,650—Rs 2,450 ($38–$55) double. Palace Rooms: Rs 3,950 ($90) Marigold, Rs 2,500 ($57) Writer, Rs 2,500 ($57) Small Bollywood. Palace suites: Rs 4,750 ($108) Maharani Suite, Rs 4,250 ($97) regular suite. Rs 575 ($13) extra bed. Rates include breakfast. MC, V. **Amenities:** Restaurant; bar; volleyball; croquet; boule; indoor games; travel services; green auto-rickshaw service; room service on request; laundry; doctor-on-call; library; TV room; Internet facilities in lounge.

WHERE TO DINE

Visitors with a sweet tooth will get a kick out of the local specialty, Mysore *pak (mysurpa)*, made from gram flour and liters of ghee (clarified butter). You'll find a number of outlets at Devaraja Market. Try the famous **Guru Sweet Mart** (Sayaji Rao Rd.) for your sugar rush. Hotel Dasaprakash's canteenlike restaurant **Akshaya** (Gandhi Sq.; © **0821/244-2444**) serves simple, hygienic vegetarian fare, typical of the region, and a sumptuous thali that costs just Rs 45 ($1).

Lalitha Mahal Palace Hotel Restaurant ✆ ECLECTIC   Once the ballroom of the Maharajah's sumptuous guesthouse, the glorious baroque hall has an immensely high ceiling with domed skylights made of Belgian glass. Hindustani music, performed live at lunch and dinner, fills this pillared palatial space. Come here for a poke around the royal facilities, but don't expect too much from the food: Even though you're eating off delicate decorative china and silver thali platters, the cheap cutlery gives the game away. Thalis are enjoyable, however, and quite filling. Also worth trying are the Mangalore fish curry and *lassoni malai tikka,* chicken in a garlic-flavored masala prepared in the tandoor oven, and best enjoyed with *naan* or *roti.* If you're more interested in a snack, the menu includes items such as Maharajah club sandwiches and hamburgers.

Lalitha Mahal Palace Hotel, T. Narsipur Rd. © **0821/247-0470** through -0476. Reservations recommended. Main courses Rs 100–Rs 550 ($2.30–$13). AE, DC, MC, V. Daily 12:30–2:45pm and 8–11pm.

Le Olive Garden ✆ *Finds* NORTH INDIAN/ECLECTIC   At this restaurant, situated in a peaceful neighborhood away from central Mysore, you dine alfresco in a leafy garden with geese and wind chimes for company. Arranged on landscaped terracing, the dining area is surrounded by water and reached by tiny bridges. Most of the dishes are Indian, with a good range of kebabs on offer, but you can also order Chinese or choose from a small selection of Continental dishes. Although it's not on the menu, ask for *rogan gosht,* made with slightly fatty mutton and cooked in rich masala gravy made with cashew nuts.

Chamappaji Rd., opposite Horse Park, Nazarbad. © **0821/244-8762**. Main courses Rs 60–Rs 250 ($1.35–$5.70). MC, V. Daily 11:30am–3:30pm and 7–11:30pm.

VISITING RAJIV GANDHI NATIONAL PARK

Originally the private property of the Maharajah of Mysore, Karnataka's most popular elephant hangout became a national park in 1955, 3 years after the princely state of Mysore was absorbed into post-colonial India. Situated 95km (59 miles) southwest of Mysore, and spread over 511 sq. km (195 sq. miles) filled with teak, rosewood, sandal, and silver oak trees, Rajiv Gandhi National Park is also generously populated by *dhole* (wild dogs), *gaur* (Indian bison), antelope, sloth bears, panthers, otters, crocodiles, cobras, pythons, falcons, eagles, and great Indian horned owls. Keep an eye peeled for tiny *muntjac* deer; they stand only .6m (2 ft.) tall and are crowned by finger-length antlers. The big draw, of course, are the tigers (between 60 and 65 tigers reside here), but sightings are subject to a great deal of luck—although when Goldie Hawn came here to shoot a documentary, she apparently spotted several. Ms. Hawn stayed at the popular **Kabini River Lodge,** the most practical place to be if you want to have access to the park without any organizational fuss. A charmingly rustic retreat some 6 hours by car from Bangalore (3 hr. from Mysore), Kabini is spread over 22 hectares (55 acres), incorporating lush forest and largely untamed vegetation, just the way a "jungle resort" should. Its centerpiece is the Maharajah's original 18th-century hunting lodge. Accommodations with the best positions are the river-facing cottages. Expect small bathrooms, dated green sofas, and lumpy mattresses covered with charming Indian throws. Eyeball the skies for birds like hoopoes and drongos, tale part in a program of wildlife safaris, try a brief coracle (boat) trip, go for an elephant ride, and—of course—partake of the meals and tea laid out for you according to a precise schedule. The lodge was set up by Col. John Felix Wakefield, who at 90 still takes his meals on the terrace overlooking the river. A tiger hunter in his youth, now a celebrated sanctuary-tourism reformer, Wakefield can be a lively source of information about the region. Book a room at Kabini well in advance, and plan to arrive there at least an hour before the afternoon safari, which begins at 4:30pm (© **08228/26-4402** through -4405; head office in Bangalore © 080/2559-7021, -7024, or -7025; www. junglelodges.com; standard package 2 days, 1 night per person, $110; includes all meals, safaris, park entrance, and elephant and boat rides). For companies that offer the services of a car and driver for the 3-hour drive, see "Guided Tours & Travel Agents" under Mysore "Essentials," above.

3 Exploring the Hoysala Heartland: Belur, Halebid & Sravanabelagola

Halebid is 220km (136 miles) W of Bangalore; Belur is 14km (9 miles) SW of Halebid

The Hoysalas were a race of warriors who found time to allow their art to flourish despite regular military campaigns. What remains of this once-powerful dynasty are beautiful temples, usually commissioned to commemorate their victories or covenants made with their gods. Situated at the edge of the Western Ghats, the existing temples of the once-powerful cities of **Belur** and **Halebid** are often referred to as the "Jewel Boxes" of Hoysala architecture, and are comparable with the religious monuments of Khajuraho (in Madhya Pradesh) and Konark (in Orissa). The artists who created these compact, assiduously sculpted temples demonstrated enormous regard for the rules of proportion, and went to extreme lengths to ensure absolute spatial precision. Exterior temple walls are invariably covered in detailed sculpted decoration, while inside you will discover hand-lathe-turned filigreed pillars and figures with moveable jewelry, also carved from stone. The gods paraded at these temples are over 8 centuries old, yet continue to impress with the vigor with which they carry out their superhuman duties, slaying demons and moving mountains, while celestial maidens admire their reflections in eternally reflecting mirrors.

In quite a different vein, the living pilgrimage center at **Sravanabelagola** is where you will find the world's tallest monolithic sculpture. The statue of Gomateswara, a naked ascetic saint, is the object of one of the biggest Jain pilgrimages in the country—lacking any decoration whatsoever, yet awesome in its sheer grandeur.

To see these highlights of Karnataka's religious heritage, you have to veer off the main drag a little. Fortunately, if you're pressed for time, it is possible to cover all three destinations with ease in a single day. Most visitors base their exploration of this region out of the dusty, dull town of Hassan, but the coffee-growing town of Chikmagalur, 25km (15 miles) from Belur, offers far more glowing surroundings, highlighted by the pleasant accommodations of a **Taj Garden Retreat.**

ESSENTIALS
GETTING THERE & AROUND
The most convenient way to see the Hoysala sights is to hire a car and driver in Mysore or even Bangalore. A more affordable option is to catch a train from Mysore to Hassan (3 hr. away), from where you can pick up a taxi for a full day of sightseeing. Hassan can also be reached overland from Mangalore (see "Traveling Via Mangalore," below). If you need to hire a vehicle in Hassan, we recommend **Mr. Altaf** (© **94482-56479;** or ask the manager at Hotel Southern Star to give him a call), who offers excellent rates. Also ask for **Abdul Rafiek,** an affable driver with masterful control over his ancient Ambassador. Extraordinarily, Abdul even uses his indicators.

VISITOR INFORMATION
Visit the friendly **Regional Tourist Office** (Vartha Bhavan, B. M. Rd.; © **08172/ 268862;** 10am–5:30pm, closed Sun and 2nd Sat of the month) if you need to stock up on brochures. You can also deepen your knowledge at Hotel Mayura Velapuri's **Belur Tourist Information Centre** (Temple Rd.; © **08177/22-2209; daily** 9:30am–6:30pm). In Halebid, there's a **Tourist Help Desk** (Mon–Sat 10am–5:30pm) at Hoysalesvara Temple. You can pick up ASI-certified **guides** outside each of the two main temples in Belur and Halebid.

BELUR
Now a sleepy hamlet, Belur was the capital of the Hoysala kings at the height of their reign. The magnificent soapstone **Temple of Lord Channakeshava** 𝕶𝕶𝕶 (daily sunrise–sunset; free admission), built over a period of 103 years, was commissioned to commemorate the victory of Vishnuvardhana over the Cholas from Tamil Nadu; apparently, it was so admired by Belur's iconoclastic Muslim invaders that they decided to leave it intact.

Built on a star-shaped plan, the temple stands on a raised platform within a courtyard surrounded by an outer wall. After you survey the courtyard, approach the temple by climbing the short flight of steps. Despite its compact scale, the profusion of carved decoration is spectacular, the multicornered shape of the temple allowing maximum space for sculptures of Vishnu and a vast retinue of Hindu images. Covering the flat-roofed building are detailed representations of myriad themes—ranging from erotica to religious mythology, everyday events to episodes from the *Ramayana*— arranged in bands that wrap the entire exterior in delightful compositions. The temple itself is borne by almost 650 stone elephants. Don't miss the various bracket figures, which are considered the highlight of Hoysala workmanship. Use a torch to study the temple interior, at the center of which is a pillar adorned with smaller versions of the temple's 10,000 sculpted images. Belur is a living temple, and a silverplated image of Vishnu within the inner sanctum is still worshipped; *puja* (prayer) is performed at 9am and 7pm each day, and the inner sanctums are closed between 1 and 3pm and 5 and 6pm.

HALEBID
Once known as Dwara Samudra, "the gateway to the sea," Halebid usurped Belur's position as the Hoysalan capital in the 12th century. Unfortunately, when the

Muslim invaders arrived, Halebid failed to escape their wrath. Appropriately, its current name means "old city," as it consists of only a dusty road and some well-crafted temples amid a lush landscape with the Western Ghats as a distant backdrop. Exquisitely sculpted Hoysalesvara **Temple** ☆☆☆ (sunrise–sunset; free admission; shoe-check Rs 1/2¢) is the largest of the Hoysala temples. Hoysalesvara actually consists of two distinct temples resting upon a star-shaped platform, both dedicated to Shiva. It has more complex and detailed carvings than those at Belur. You can discover the 20,000-odd sculptures in and around the temple on your own, or enlist the services of a **guide** (who will approach you as you arrive at the monument; expect to pay around Rs 150/$3.40, but do include a tip). You can visit the on-site **Archaeological Museum** (Sat–Thurs 10am–5pm; Rs 2/4¢) to see more stone statues of Hindu gods, gathered from Halebid and its immediate environs. If you want more of the same, without the touristy vibe, head for **Kedareshvara Temple,** 300m (960 ft.) away and marked by its serene location.

Also in Halebid are several **Jain Bastis** that allude to the religious tolerance of the Hoysala kings, who extended patronage to other faiths. Although lacking the immense carved decoration of the Hindu monuments, **Parswanathasamy Temple** (daily sunrise–sunset; free admission) enjoys a lovely lakeside location.

SRAVANABELAGOLA

For members of the peace-loving, nonviolent Jain faith, this is one of the oldest and most important pilgrimage centers, famous for its colossal 18m (60-ft.) statue of Lord Gomateswara, said to be the tallest monolithic statue on earth, reached by climbing the 635 steps that lead to the hill's summit. Naked and imposing, the statue is a symbolic representation of worldly renunciation.

Commissioned in A.D. 981, the **Statue of Gomateswara** is a representation of Bahubali. Son of the first Jain Tirthankara, Bahubali renounced his kingdom and sought enlightenment by standing naked and motionless for an entire year while contemplating the meaning of life. Seen in detail on the legs of the statue, the creepers and plants twisting their way up his body are symbolic of his motionless mission of spiritual discovery. A special celebration is held here every 12 years, when the giant monolith is bathed with bucketfuls of milk and honey and other condiments. The next ceremony takes place in 2017.

WHERE TO STAY & DINE

Accommodations close to the temples are limited and hardly the stuff of kings. You'll find a number of government-run hotels in both Belur and Halebid; these have restaurants of questionable quality and extremely basic rooms. In Halebid, the tourism department's **Hotel Mayura Shanthala** (Temple Rd.; ☏ 08177/27-3224; doubles Rs 210–Rs 275/$4.75–$6.25) is within striking distance of a number of temples. Belur's **Hotel Mayura Velapuri** (☏ 08177/222-209; doubles Rs 312/$7) is located just outside the temple entrance. Better to opt for **Hotel Southern Star Hassan** (☏ 08172/25-1816 or -1817; www.ushashriramhotels.com; doubles from Rs 1,495/$45), a relatively new and welcome addition to Hassan's otherwise dismal accommodations scene. It offers pleasant service (including sightseeing advice) and safe dining. It's certainly not luxury level, but guest rooms are comfortable and clean. Views from odd-numbered rooms are of a less built-up part of the town.

Taj Garden Retreat, Chikmagalur   Located just outside the small coffee-growing town of Chikmagalur, this hillside retreat—originally built as a government rest

Tips Traveling Via Mangalore

Once a seaport of some significance, Mangalore is an important center for the processing and export of Karnataka's spices, coffee, and cashews. It is known as the *bidi* cigarette capital of the world. (The bidi, effectively a roll of dried tobacco leaf, is also known as the "pauper's puff." Apparently 90 people die every hour in India from tobacco-related cancer.) Its greatest significance for travelers is that it makes a convenient pit stop on the section of the Konkan Railway that runs between Goa and Kerala, and provides road access to Belur, Halebid, and Sravanabelgola, as well as Mysore. **Taj Manjarun** (© **0824/566-0420;** www.tajhotels.com; doubles from $65) is the best hotel in Mangalore. Accommodations are comfortable, if not particularly luxurious. Suite no. 401 ($120) has the best views, taking in the river and the ocean. Staff will arrange trips to the beach and local temples, as well as tours of a cashew-nut factory or tours to see how Mangalore's famous red-clay roof tiles are made.

house—is comfortable and idyllically remote, with sloping red-tile roofs echoing the style of the local colonial Malnad plantation homes. Reserve one of the cottages (only $10 more); these have high-pitched ceilings, polished floors, two double beds, and large balconies with scenic views. (Reserve no. 119 for an especially large balcony.) The attached bathrooms are spacious but have showers only. Visits to nearby coffee plantations set off Monday to Saturday at 3:30pm. Taj has also opened a new Ayurvedic massage center, so you can kick back and allow yourself to be stroked into good health.

K. M. Rd., opposite Pavitravana Jyothinagar Post, Chikmagalur. © **08262/220202** or -220404. Fax 08262/220222. www.tajhotels.com. 29 units. $80 standard double; $90 standard pool-view double; $100 cottage. $20 extra bed. AE, DC, MC, V. **Amenities:** Restaurant; bar; pool; pool table; table tennis; cycling; travel assistance; car hire; currency exchange; fax service; room service 7:30am–10:30pm; laundry; doctor-on-call. *In room:* A/C, TV, minibar, tea- and coffee-making facilities.

4 Hampi & the Ruined City of Vijayanagar ✦✦✦

Hampi is 460km (285 miles) NW of Bangalore; 13km (8 miles) E of Hospet

The surreal, boulder-strewn landscape of Karnataka's hinterland is the backdrop to the largest complex of ruins in India. Hampi, capital of one of India's most formidable empires, the powerful Vijayanagara—whose rule stretched from the Arabian Sea to the Indian Ocean—was home to a population of half a million, and protected by more than a million soldiers. Set in a vast valley sprawling from the banks of the Tungabhadra River, the splendid "City of Victory"—where even the king's horses were adorned in jewels—is now a ghost city with numerous temples, fortification ramparts, stables, royal apartments, and palaces, popular with determined sightseers and trance and rave party disciples. Long popular with Bollywood as a shooting location, Hampi is also where scenes from the 2005 Jackie Chan thriller *The Myth* were shot. Hampi may be a little difficult to get to, but this remoteness is to a large extent its charm. You can easily enjoy 2 or 3 days in this serene atmosphere, particularly if you've booked at

Hampi's Boulders (see "Where to Stay," below), a comfortable resort within striking distance of the ruins.

ESSENTIALS

GETTING THERE   The overnight **Hampi Express** leaves Bangalore daily at 10:05pm, arriving in unremarkable Hospet, the nearest town, at 7:40am. From Hyderabad, the Rayalseema Express departs at 5:25pm and arrives early the following morning, at 5:10am. Hampi is 15km (9 miles) away. Taxis charge around Rs 300 ($6.85) for the one-way trip; be sure to negotiate. Hampi is also connected to Goa by an overnight bus service.

VISITOR INFORMATION   If you reserve lodging at **Hampi's Boulders** (see "Where to Stay," below), you'll have no better source of information than your host, Bobby. In Hampi Bazaar, the unusually helpful staff at the government-run **tourist office** (© **08394/241-339;** daily 8am–1:30pm Apr–May; daily 10am–1:30pm and 2:15–5:30pm June–Mar) can provide information and organize coach bookings (not recommended) and English-speaking guides. At Hotel Malligi (see "Where to Stay," below), you can hire an **audioguide,** featuring Bollywood voices, for around Rs 50 ($1.15). In Hampi, you can pick up information and guides from the **information office** (© **08394/241-339**) on Bazaar Street.

GETTING AROUND   By Taxi & Auto-Rickshaw   Hampi's ruins cover 39 sq. km (15 sq. miles), and should be explored on wheels. Bicycles (for rent in Hampi Bazaar) are fine for the energetic, but only in winter. Taxis (around Rs 800/$18 for a full day, without air-conditioning) or even auto-rickshaws (count on Rs 350–Rs 400/$8–$9.10) are better if you'd rather not deal with maps, heat, and dirt tracks. Do, however, get out on foot whenever you can.

EXPLORING THE RUINED CITY OF VIJAYANAGARA

For anyone with dreams of Indiana Jones–style adventuring, the Hampi ruins provide the perfect setting—an ancient city with isolated ruins scattered among impossibly balanced wind-smoothed boulders and immense stretches of verdant landscape. Various excavations have uncovered evidence to suggest that Vijayanagara was occupied as long ago as the 3rd-century-B.C. Mauryan era. During early medieval times, armies were regularly dispatched to the Deccan by the Delhi Sultanate as part of its campaign to establish an empire that would encompass the whole of India. During one such campaign in the early 14th century, the invading forces captured Harihara and Bukka, two princes of Warangal, and took them to Delhi, where they fell in with the Sultanate. This allegiance eventually saw Harihara being crowned king of the region that is today known as Hampi. In celebration, Harihara lay the foundations of Vijayanagara, his new capital, on the southern banks of the Tungabhadra. His brother, Bukka, succeeded him 20 years later and ensured widespread support by issuing an edict that granted all religions equal protection. The monarchs who followed extended patronage to all manner of artists, poets, philosophers, and academics, effectively making Vijayanagara a center of learning that, in its grandeur, captivated visitors from as far away as Arabia, Portugal, and Italy.

The kingdom reached its zenith during the reign of Krishna Deva Raya (1509–29), when international trade flourished under progressive commercial practices and foreign trade agreements. Early accounts of the city tell of its massive fortifications, broad boulevards, grand gateways, efficient irrigation systems, and splendid civic amenities.

The kingdom of Vijayanagara fell in 1565 when five allied Deccan sultans laid siege to the city, which they then apparently ransacked—their soldiers looting, killing, and destroying at will.

While some of the individual ruins can only be visited upon purchase of a ticket, most of Hampi is a veritable free-for-all, with tame security in the form of a handful of guards at the major monuments. This means that you can mix and match your itinerary as you see fit, moving between the different locations in a taxi or—if you're up for it—on a bicycle. Pick up information or engage the services of an official guide from the government tourist office in Hampi. You can see Hampi's highlights in a morning if you set out early enough. However, it's spread over a vast area, and exploring can be quite exhausting, particularly in the midday heat—don't overdo it, or even the most impressive monuments begin to look like more of the same.

Hampi Bazaar is a broad, dusty boulevard lined with stalls and restaurants. It leads to the entrance of **Virupaksha Temple** ✸✸✸ , which predates the Vijayanagara kingdom yet remains a center of living Hindu faith (even though Hindu idols have been removed from the surrounding temples). Virupaksha's towering *goparum* is lavishly sculpted and rises several stories; within its courtyards, monkeys and children careen around ancient pillars, while a sad-faced temple elephant takes tips for much-rehearsed blessings granted with her trunk. In the far right corner of the complex, tucked within a chamber, look for the shadow of the main *goparum,* which falls—miraculously, it would seem—as an inverted image on the temple wall, created by light passing through a small window. South of Virupaksha Temple is a temple housing a massive **Shiva lingam** (phallic symbol) standing in a pool of water. Carved from a single rock, the lingam is adjacent to a fantastic **monolithic statue of Narasimha** ✸✸ , the man-lion avatar of Vishnu. Although partially damaged, the one-piece carving dating to the first half of the 16th century is one of the finest sculptures at Hampi.

Some distance from the bazaar, on a high elevation, is spectacular **Vitthala Temple** ✸✸✸ , dedicated to an incarnation of Vishnu, and one of the most fabulous and famous of Hampi's monuments. One of Hinduism's most enduring images, an ornate **stone chariot** ✸✸✸ , is found here. With solid stone wheels that can turn on their axles, the chariot faces a shaded dance hall where ancient musical dramas were once played out and from where you can now enjoy panoramic views of Vijayanagara. The pillars of the temple are commonly referred to as "musical pillars," each one producing a different note when tapped.

Nearby, the **King's Balance** was once a scale-like instrument used to measure out grain or even gold against the weight of the king. The weighed item was then given to the priests (or to the poor, depending on your guide's story).

The **royal enclosure** ✸ incorporates the ruined palaces where the Vijayanagara kings would have lived and held court. Not much survives, but you can still visit **Hazara Rama Temple,** where the royals went to worship, a small **stepped tank,** and **Mahanavami Dibba,** a platform where performances and entertainments were held. On the outskirts of the royal complex, you need to buy a ticket to see the zenana enclosure, where the two-story Indo-Saracenic pavilion known as **Kamala (Lotus) Mahal** ✸✸ features massive pillars, delicately punctuated arches, and fine stucco ornamentation; its unusual design blends elements of Muslim and Hindu architecture. Within the same enclosure are quarters believed to have been used by Hampi's Amazonian female guards, described by several Portuguese travelers. Just outside the enclosure are the superb **Elephant Stables** ✸✸✸ .

13km (8 miles) east of Hospet, Belary District. Guides can be hired through the government tourist office in Hampi Bazaar for Rs 300 ($6.85) half-day and Rs 500 ($11) full day. Entrance to Virupaksha Temple Rs 2 (4¢); 6am–12:30pm and 2–8pm. Entrance to both Lotus Mahal and Elephant Stables $5.

WHERE TO STAY

Hampi's Boulders 🐾🐾 The name says it all: This resort, established and run by the enterprising proprietor Bobby Vallabhchandra and his cousin Vikram, is set in and among the enormous natural boulders that define Karnataka's splendid landscape. Private, remote, and immersed in nature, Boulders resides alongside the Tungabhadra River on a 16-hectare (40-acre) spread, amid bamboo trees, coconut groves, mango trees, coffee plantations, and the namesake rocks. It's a mere 6km (4 miles) from Hampi, reached by crossing the river in a coracle (small boat) after a pleasant half-hour walk. Nearby, in the 4,800-hectare (12,000-acre) animal sanctuary, you can spot wolves, wild dogs, panthers, hyenas, foxes, jackals, sloth bears, and crocodiles. Accommodations in the Executive Cottage are top-notch; living rock boulders bulge through the walls, and the entire structure feels like a miniature castle (where, in the huge bathroom, the "throne" allows the occupant to gaze onto the river). There's also a gorgeous veranda and a rooftop viewing-platform. Guest cottages are pleasantly furnished, with attached bathrooms and private patios; the floors are marble and the ambience and furniture simple, but they're still far better than anything else near Hampi, and the setting is unmatched. Meals are served in a semi-exposed circular granite-walled thatched-roof dining area where there's no menu, but five-course meals are whipped up according to your mood.

Narayanpet, Bandi Harlapur–P.O., Via Munirabad-R-S, Koppal District and TQ. 🕾 08539/265939, 0934/260-2245, or 94480-34202. 11 units. Rs 2,500–Rs 3,500 ($57–$80) standard non-A/C double, Rs 3,500–Rs 4,500 ($80–$112) standard A/C double, Rs 9,000 ($205) executive double. No credit cards. **Amenities:** Restaurant; pool; play area; guided tours and safaris; fishing; beach volleyball; river rafting; birding; shop; laundry; doctor-on-call.

Hotel Malligi *Value* Long-standing base for visitors to Hampi, this campus of guest rooms, restaurants, and modest tourist facilities began as a small retiring house for medical reps supplying Hospet's first pharmacy, and today offers a wide range of accommodations. The complex, which at press time was being expanded to include 40 new rooms, is something of a regional institution and, most importantly, has a pool, essential after a grueling day of sightseeing under the pounding sun. Guest rooms are generally comfortable—those in the "super luxury" category are clean, with tiled floors, wood-paneled walls, and '80s fittings and furniture in shades of brown. At just $5 more, executive suites are far more attractive, in shades of gray and blue, with large bathrooms with tubs and private balconies. Bollywood stars shooting films in the area, however, book only the Honeymoon Suite, where a ceiling mirror hovers over the circular bed. Budget rooms are ridiculously cheap, considering the amenities offered by the hotel, though they don't offer much in the way of comfort or taste.

6/143 J. N. Rd., P. B. no. 1, Hospet 583 201. 🕾 08394/228-101. Fax 08394/227-038. malligihome@hotmail.com. 140 units. Rs 300–Rs 500 ($6.85–$11) non-A/C budget double, Rs 2,000 ($46) super luxury double; Rs 2,250 ($52) executive suite, Rs 2,500 ($57) honeymoon suite. AE, MC, V. **Amenities:** 2 restaurants; bar; pool; pool table; children's play area; travel desk; car hire; limited business facilities; banqueting, conferencing; currency exchange; salon; gift shop; bookshop; room service 6am–10pm; massage; laundry. *In room:* A/C, TV, minibar (in most rooms).

WHERE TO DINE

Mango Tree VEGETARIAN Although the food here is unremarkable, the rustic setting is undeniably welcoming. You sit under an enormous mango tree with a swing, in the backyard of a local family home, surrounded by boulders, acres of greenery, and kingfishers darting through the air. In front of you, the Tungabhadra River glides by. There's no electricity; you dine sitting on the ground on straw mats at low portable tables set at terraced levels, while the proprietor, Krishna, and his family wait on you. Order a Mango Tree special thali served on a banana leaf; finish with a cup of *chai* and a pancake, and quench your thirst with a banana coconut lassi.

400m (1,280 ft.) downriver from the main Virupaksha temple tank (walk through the banana grove to get there), Hampi. ☎ 94487-65213. Meals under Rs 150 ($3.40). No credit cards. Daily 7am–9:30pm.

Waves MULTI-CUISINE   Generous portions and plenty of cold beer (not freely found in Hampi) make this a popular if anonymous place to get a wholesome meal while you're in the Hampi area. It's on a covered terrace overlooking Hotel Malligi's pool and is open all day—which makes it a convenient spot to grab breakfast before you set out for the ruins. Stick to the Indian dishes, and be prepared for an invasion of mosquitoes once the sun goes down.

Hotel Malligi, 6/143 J. N. Rd. P. B. no. 1, Hospet. ☎ 08394/228101. Most mains Rs 50–Rs 150 ($1.15–$3.40). AE, MC, V. Daily 6am–midnight.

5 Side Trip to Northern Karnataka ✶✶✶

If you'd like to get off the principal tourist beat and discover the Deccan's architectural treasures in less-chartered territory, set aside a few more days to explore the splendid remains of the erstwhile **Chalukyan Empire** and—tucked within one of the state's northernmost corners—the Muslim city of **Bijapur,** filled with mosques, minarets, mausoleums, and palace ruins.

The easiest way to get to these sites is to rent a car and driver in Hospet (get one through Hotel Malligi; Rs 6–Rs 8/12¢–18¢ per kilometer, plus Rs 150/$3.40 per night out), and drive to Badami, stopping at Aihole and Pattadakal either on your way in or out. It is quite possible to spend a long day traveling from Hospet or Hampi to all three Chalukya sites, including a stop at **Mahakuteshwara** and **Mallikajuna temples** en route. After that you can either proceed to Bijapur, or return to Hampi before nightfall. If you prefer something a little less hectic, however, overnight in Badami, and then continue your journey the following day. The best accommodations choice is **Hotel Badami Court** (☎ 08357/220-230 through -0233; reservations in Bangalore 080/2529-5451 or -5452). It's located 2km (1¼ miles) from the town center and has a pool and decent air-conditioned rooms with TVs and bathtubs (ask for one of the garden-facing rooms, which are quieter) for around $62 (including breakfast).

BADAMI, AIHOLE & PATTADAKAL

Around 4 hours by car from Hospet, the remote, modest town of **Badami** was established around A.D. 543 when it became the capital of the Chalukyas, one of the most powerful of the Deccan dynasties. Today its most significant attraction is the complex of **cave temples** ✶✶✶ (daily sunrise–sunset; $5) carved into the imposing horseshoe-shaped red-sandstone cliff that once formed a natural fortification at the southern end of the town. Enter the pillared interiors and you'll discover elaborate symbolic and mystical carvings of the highest quality (not to mention a few scampering monkeys). It's worth hiring the services of a guide (around Rs 150/$3.40 for up to 3 hr.) to gain some understanding of the symbolism. Also worth exploring are the **Bhutanatha temples,** built over 4 centuries at a picturesque location at the edge of the Agasty-atirtha water tank; and atop the hill, 7th-century **Malegitti Shivalya Temple,** unusually decorated with dwarfs, geese, and various geometric patterns. Time allowing, stop at the **Archaeological Museum** (© **08357/22-0157**; Sat–Thurs 10am–5pm; Rs 2/4¢) to see well-preserved sculpted panels depicting the life of Krishna, and the **Lajja Gauri** sculpture, an extraordinary fertility cult symbol. Less than 30km (19 miles) from Badami, en route to Aihole, is the small settlement of **Pattadakal** and its UNESCO World Heritage–listed **temple complex** ✦✦✦ (daily sunrise–sunset; $10), where Chalukyan temple architecture reached its zenith in the 7th and 8th centuries. Some, like Papanatha Temple built around A.D. 680, are in the northern Indo-Aryan style, while others, like the main Virupaksha Temple built 80 years later, are in the South Indian Dravidian architectural style, with tiered pyramidal rather than conical roofs. A dance festival is held at Pattadakal each January. (Note that if you're pressed for time, the Pattadakal stop can be skipped.)

About 17km (11 miles) away, the riverbank village of **Aihole** ✦✦✦ is strewn with some 70 abandoned temples, built between A.D. 450 and 650 as architectural experiments by the early Chalukyan kings. Historians theorize that these obsessive rulers had a guild of architects, artists, and artisans working for them, and the variety of styles, including the Gupta (northern), incipient Dravidian, and elements of Buddhist architecture, reflect the various stages in the development of Chalukyan architecture. The chief attraction among these, fashioned along the lines of a Buddhist *chaitya* (prayer hall), is **Durga Temple** ✦✦✦ , with its magnificent circular colonnaded veranda studded with stunning sculptures and intricate carving. Contrast this with the Jain **Meguti Temple** ✦✦ situated atop a nearby hill—with an inscription putting its construction at A.D. 634, this was perhaps the last temple to be built in Aihole.

The interiors aren't lighted, so you should carry a flashlight—the detailing is well worth studying. In some temples, you'll discover images of fierce Chalukyan warriors in action, while elsewhere, amorous couples engage in a different sort of action. Admission to the main complex of temples is free; entrance to Durga Temple is $2. Hours are daily sunrise to sunset.

BIJAPUR

The walled city of **Bijapur,** in the far north of Karnataka, is often referred to as the "Agra of the South" because of its profusion of Muslim architecture. First founded during the reign of the Chalukyan dynasty, between the 10th and 11th centuries, Bijapur passed into Muslim rule and later into the hands of the Bahamani kings. When these rulers fell into decline, the city was taken over by its governor, Yusuf Adil Khan, the founder of the Adil Shahi dynasty, who established rule over the Deccan during the 16th and 17th centuries, with Bijapur as their capital. Muslim mausoleums, mosques, palaces, pavilions, and *burkha*-clad women will remind you that this is a city unlike any other in Karnataka. Head to the very helpful local **tourism office** (Station Rd.; © **08352/250-359**; daily 8am–1:30pm Apr–May, daily 10am–1:30pm and 2:15–5:30pm June–Mar) to hire a guide and get assistance with sightseeing. Monuments are open from sunrise to sunset and entry is free except where listed. Within the fortified **Citadel** in the city center lie the remains of royal structures, including **Anand Mahal** (pleasure palace), and **Saat Manzil.** Outside Saat Manzil is beautiful **Jal Mandir,** or water pavilion, now dry, so you can admire its carvings and porticos. Not far away (near the tourist office) is incomplete **Bara Kaman** ("12 Arches"), the roofless tomb of Ali Adil Shah II—a wonderful piece of architecture comprising 12 arches—surrounded by a garden.

Outside the Citadel's walls, near the edge of the city, is **Ibrahim Rouza** ✦✦✦ , the gorgeously proportioned and heavily decorated mausoleum of Ibrahim Adil Shah II and his wife, Taj Sultana (admission $2; daily 6am–6pm; leave shoes outside). Ignore the garbage dump near the entrance and admire what is considered the most beautiful Muslim structure in the Deccan, featuring richly engraved walls and inscribed ornamental stone windows. Move on to **Gol Gumbaz** ✦✦✦, the world's second-largest dome (after St. Peter's in Rome), atop the mausoleum of 17th-century sultan Muhammad Adil Shah (Mahatma Gandhi Rd.; admission $5, video cameras 50¢; leave shoes outside; daily 6am–6pm). Renowned for its remarkable engineering and stereophonic acoustics, the Gol Gumbaz can get noisy as visitors test the echo effect created by the massive dome—multiple distinct echoes are said to be produced for each sound uttered in the whispering gallery upstairs. Most visitors don't bother to whisper, however, which may leave you with an experience akin to an auditory hallucination. As is the case with the Taj, try to arrive as soon as the gates open for the most atmospheric visit. It's worth scaling the 115 steps to reach the dome's terrace for the excellent views of the formal gardens and tombs.

Jami Masjid (free admission; daily 6am–6pm), close to Gol Gumbaz, is the city's other major attraction. Also incomplete, this is the largest mosque in the region, dating back to A.D. 1576, when Ali Adil Shah I reigned. Consisting of a large dome and gorgeous white arcaded bays, this impressive mosque is spread over some 10,000 sq. m (107,639 sq. ft.).

WHERE TO STAY & DINE IN BIJAPUR

Hotel Madhuvan International   Bijapur's top business hotel doesn't offer the luxuries you might expect in cities catering to substantial numbers of Western visitors. Accommodations are comfortable enough, however, and some rooms have views of Gol Gumbaz. All bathrooms have tubs. You can organize your sightseeing through the hotel, and take meals in the relaxing garden restaurant (which serves only vegetarian food, by the way).

Station Rd., Bijapur 586 104. ✆ **08352/25-5571** through -5573. Fax 08352/25-6201. hotelmadhuvanint@yahoo.com. 36 units. $38 non-A/C double, $48 A/C double. Rates include breakfast. MC, V. **Amenities:** Restaurant; sightseeing; limited room service; laundry; doctor-on-call. *In room:* TV.

6 Hyderabad

490km (304 miles) N of Bangalore

One of the largest and wealthiest of India's former princely states, Hyderabad built its fortune on the trade of pearls, gold, steel, fabric and, above all, diamonds, which some believe remain hidden beneath the foundations of **Golconda Fort,** precursor to the city some 10km (6¼ miles) away. Once the most famous diamond mining area in the world, Golconda was where the 108-carat Koh-i-Noor diamond (not to mention the Orloff, Regent, and Hope diamonds) was excavated. It was in fact Golconda's legendary wealth that attracted the attention of the voracious Mughal emperor Aurangzeb, and with the aid of an inside agent he captured the fortress in 1678. Aurangzeb's invasion marked the temporary decline of the city, but when the Mughal empire began to fade, the enterprising local viceroy, Asaf Jah I, promptly proclaimed himself *Nizam* (ruler) and established independent rule over the Deccan state. Under the notoriously opulent Nizams of the Asaf Jahi dynasty, their power cemented by an alliance forged in 1798 with the British East India Company, Hyderabad again became a major influence, and even contributed to the British military campaigns against the recalcitrant Tipu Sultan of Mysore.

Fun Fact **Rich Man, Poor Man**

The Nizams of Hyderabad may have been ousted from power two generations ago, but their decadent tastes have only now been curtailed. Mukkaram Jah, grandson of the seventh and last Nizam of Hyderabad, is said to have inherited the richest fortune in the world when his grandfather died in 1967. Thirty-eight years later, he lives in Turkey, all but bankrupt, his wealth—once said to have been worth around $750 million—squandered by a lavish lifestyle (including four expensive divorces) or stuck in banks around the world pending the settlement of innumerable legal disputes and claims from hundreds of family members (real and fake) determined to get their pound of flesh.

Hyderabad is more than 400 years old, but today the state capital of Andhra Pradesh is as famous for its burgeoning information technology and biotech research industries as it is for its minarets. Like Bangalore, this is one of India's fastest-growing cities (with a projected population of 7.5 million by 2015), but unlike most Indian cities, Hyderabad is actually getting greener and cleaner. A substantial part of the city is the suburb of **Cyberabad,** where Microsoft and Oracle are but two major players in the development known as Hi-Tech City, responsible for the city's economic upswing.

Despite its newfound attractiveness as a business destination, the city remains steeped in history, and you're just as likely to share the road with camels and bullock carts, and haggle alongside Muslim women covered from head to toe in black *burkhas,* as you are to converse with cellphone-wielding yuppies. There may not be much by way of specific sights to see in Hyderabad, but it's a pleasantly manageable city with a vibrant culture, excellent-value luxury hotels, and a heavenly cuisine—perhaps the most enduring legacy of the decadent tastes and patronage of the cultured *Nizams* who first put the city on the map.

ESSENTIALS

GETTING THERE & AWAY   Hyderabad is pretty much slap-bang in the middle of very little else, so you're best off flying in, not least because you're unlikely to spend much time in Hyderabad proper (unless you plan to shop endlessly for pearls and eat yourself stupid). There are daily 2-hour flights from Delhi and 1-hour flights from Bangalore, Mumbai, Chennai, Kolkata, and Tirupati. **Begumpet Airport** (off Sardar Patel Rd.; ✆ **140** for Indian Airlines inquiries, 142 for recorded flight information) is 8km (5 miles) north of the city; a taxi into town should cost Rs 150 ($3.40). **Trains** to and from Bangalore, Tirupati, Chennai, and Mumbai take at least 14 hours; book an overnight journey several days in advance. There are two main stations: Nampally (also known as Hyderabad Station) and Secunderabad, with most longer-distance trains arriving at the latter. Call ✆ **1345** for specific information about outbound services.

VISITOR INFORMATION   For the lowdown on sights, tours, and events, visit **Andhra Pradesh Travel & Tourism Development Corporation** (✆ **040/2345-3036** or -0444; daily 7am–9pm), on the corner where Secretariat Road becomes Tank Bund. Avoid **Andhra Pradesh Tourism** right next door; the stench that hangs in the air from the fish market nearby competes with the staff's incompetence. The railway stations also have information counters. *Channel 6* (Rs 15/35¢) is a monthly booklet listing a wealth of information about the twin cities of Hyderabad and Secunderabad.

Hyderabad CityInfo (Rs 30/70¢) appears every 2 weeks and provides extensive information about hotels, restaurants, and current events. *Primetime Prism* (monthly; Rs 10/25¢) is filled with useful information about destinations all over the state.

GETTING AROUND Hyderabad—actually comprising the twin cities of Hyderabad and Secunderabad—is spread over a vast area, and its few sights are scattered, so you're best off renting a car and driver for a half- or full day. See **SOTC** (details below) for 24-hour car-hire service; or call **Cosy Cabs** (Karan Apartments, Begumpet; ✆ **040/2776-2023**). Note that the Old City is best explored on foot.

GUIDED TOURS & TRAVEL AGENTS The **Andhra Pradesh Travel & Tourism Development Corporation** (see "Visitor information," above) runs full-day guided tours of the city (Rs 190/$4.25) and 3-day trips to Tirupati (Rs 1,050/$24 including a night's accommodations). **SOTC** (3-5-874 Hyderguda Rd.; ✆ **040/2323-3628** or -3629; Mon–Fri 10am–6pm, Sat 9:30am–1:30pm) can make all your travel, sightseeing, and car-hire arrangements. For alternate quotes, call **Mercury Travels** (✆ **040/5520-2200**).

WHAT TO SEE & DO

To see Hyderabad in a day, first drive to **Qutb Shahi Tombs,** where Hyderabad's dynastic rulers are buried. Standing at the center of its own garden, Sultan Muhammed Quli Qutb Shah's tomb is considered the most impressive. Built around the same time as his tomb, the mortuary bath **(Hamaam)**—where the dead were washed before being laid to rest—lies at the center of the enclosure. From here, consider walking to **Golconda Fort;** have your driver show you the route, which is about 2km (1¼ miles) and takes you through lively villages where you may even be invited in for a cup of *chai* and a chat. Allow at least an hour to explore the ruins of the historic citadel, arranging for your driver to pick you up at the entrance. Next, head to **Charminar,** a four-sided archway with soaring minarets. It was laid out by Mohammad Quli Qutb Shahi as the centerpiece of a great new city when Golconda's disease epidemics forced him to move his seat to the banks of the Musi River. Explore the Old City quarter on foot, heading westward into **Laad Bazaar** ⋆⋆⋆, where double-story houses with tiny wooden shutters line narrow lanes. Wandering through these perpetually congested narrow lanes, you'll encounter numerous *burkha*-wearing women scanning the stalls for bargains, and you're likely to score a deal on anything from old saris, pearls, *bidri* (surface ornamentation) work, and silver and gold jewelry, to paper kites, henna, turmeric, and cheap china. *Lac* bangles, made from shellac encrusted with shiny, colorful stones, are a Hyderabadi specialty that you'll find in huge quantities here. It's also where the people of Hyderabad go to buy traditional bridal wear, or *Khopdia Joda,* consisting of a *kurta* pajama, *choli,* and *ghunghat.*

When you've had your fill of the Old City, the interiors of **Salar Jung Museum** are a cool diversion, filled with an unprecedented assortment of kitschy collectibles and works of art (see below). Also interesting for antiques-lovers is **Purani Haveli,** near the Salar Jung Museum, where several *Nizams* were born and lived. When Nawab Mir Mehboob Ali Khan, the sixth *Nizam,* lived here, he had a 73m-long (240-ft.) wooden chamber built with 150 huge cupboards (probably the world's largest walk-in closet), to stock his extensive collection of fine clothing and shoes (also called Nizam Jubilee Pavilion; daily 10am–6pm; Rs 40/90¢).

India's second-largest mosque, **Mecca Masjid** (Kishan Prasad Rd., near Charminar), is said to have been built with a few bricks brought from Mecca, and attracts thousands of worshippers during *Namaaz,* Friday prayers. It's off-limits to non-Muslims during prayers, but visitors are welcome at other times. Leave your shoes with an attendant before making your way through a long room that houses the tombs of the Nizams of the Asaf Jahi dynasty. Non-Muslims cannot enter the prayer hall but can view proceedings through a screen. In Gulzar Hauz is **Jami Masjid,** Hyderabad's oldest functioning mosque, dating back to 1597.

Round off the day by watching the sun set over Cyberabad from white-marble **Birla Mandir** ✦ (Kalabahad Hill; daily 6am–noon and 3–9pm; free admission). Commissioned by the Birlas, India's foremost industrial magnates, the main temple is dedicated to Lord Venkateshwara, and is pleasantly free of greedy "guides" and the like.

Golconda Fort ✦✦ Sitting at an elevated height on the outskirts of Hyderabad, Golconda—seat of the Qutb Shahis—was once a magnificent citadel and center of the world diamond trade. The fort took 62 years to build, and when it fell to Aurangzeb in 1687, he tore the place apart looking for diamonds and gold. Left to the birds of prey that circle high above the once-daunting battlements, Golconda would have become a tranquil retreat were it not for its popularity with visitors, who noisily explore the ramparts of Hyderabad's most illustrious attraction. That's why it's best if you visit it as soon as it opens, or around twilight (when it's far cooler and the dimming evening sky sheds a mysterious aura over the stone ruins).

Enclosing the graffiti-smeared remains of bazaars, homes, fields, barracks, armories, mosques, camel stables, Turkish baths, and water reservoirs, the battlements incorporate 87 bastions and extend some 5km (3 miles) in circumference. Four of the original eight gates are still in use; present-day visitors enter via the **Bala Hissar gate**—large teakwood doors with metal spikes designed to withstand charging elephants. Guides can assist by demonstrating the tremendous acoustics of the structure—a clap here is heard clearly when you are at the fort's highest point, 1km (½ mile) away; this was once an invaluable security-cum-intercom system. The Royal Palace complex comprises buildings constructed by the Qutb Shahi kings during different periods. Most are decorated with floral designs, glazed tilework on the walls, and cut-plaster decorations indicative of the Qutb Shahi style. Sadly, where royalty once went about their daily lives, rats, bats, garbage, grime, and tourists have taken over. At the top of the fort is the **Baradari,** reached by three stone stairways. As you make your way up, look along the walls for the remains of limestone pipes once part of a sophisticated plumbing system that used Persian wheels to carry water up the hill, so that it could be piped in for bathing, flushing cistern systems, and keeping the palace cool. The climb to the top is worth it for the excellent views alone.

The fort hosts an extremely popular **sound-and-light show** that recounts the history of Golconda using the illuminated ruins as a backdrop. There are performances

---

⟨Tips Getting a Guide

You'll be confronted by many would-be guides at the entrance to the Golconda Fort—ask around for **M. D. Rathmath** or **Shaikh Rajiv.** Both have a good grasp of English. The going rate is Rs 300 ($6.85) for 2 to 3 hours. At the end of the day, the guides gather on the lawn outside the fort entrance, near the ticket booth; join them if you're interested in learning more about Hyderabad culture.

Asthmatics Say "A-aah!"

One of the world's largest alternative medicinal gatherings takes place annually at **Nampally Exhibition Grounds** in Hyderabad, usually on June 7 or 8. Just as the monsoon sets in and brings with it all sorts of seasonal respiratory illnesses, hundreds of thousands of asthmatics from all over India flock to the city to receive an unusual cure administered orally by the Bathini Goud brothers. A special herbal medicine is stuffed into the mouth of a 2- or 3-inch *murrel* (sardine). The fish is then slipped into the patient's mouth, who swallows the slithering creature alive (the Gouds claim that the wriggling fish increases the efficacy of the medicine because it clears the patient's throat). The result: For more than 162 years, countless people have reported relief from a variety of respiratory-type disorders. Said to have been given to an ancestor of the present-day Gouds by a Hindu holy man back in 1845, the secret formula has been passed down through the generations and administered free of charge in accordance with the saint's wishes. Visit **www.fish-medicine.org** for more information.

in English each night; but be warned that power failures can disrupt the performance—and be sure to take insect repellent.

Situated 6km (4 miles) west of the city. ✆ **040/2351-3984.** Admission Rs 100 ($2.30). Daily 7am–6pm. English sound-and-light show: Mar–Oct daily 7–8pm; Nov–Feb daily 6:30–7:30pm. Admission Rs 40 (90¢). Tickets available 30 min. before the show; line up early.

Salar Jung Museum ✫✫✫   Marketed as the world's largest private collection of art, artifacts, and antiques, this eclectic assortment of more than 30,000 different exhibits was assembled by Salar Jung III, who served as prime minister *(wazir)* to the Nizam of Hyderabad. It's a truly fascinating collection—particularly the textiles and fine art section, which includes a fine collection of Indian miniature paintings demonstrating the evolution of styles and the differences between Rajput, Deccan, Pahari, and Mughal paintings, though the displays are somewhat disorganized. One of the most valuable pieces must be a 9th-century edition of the *Koran*, written in beautiful Kufic script. The weaponry collection includes a diamond-encrusted sword used ceremonially by the Salar Jungs, as well as pieces used by Mughal emperors. There's something to be said for the sheer profusion of design objects, ranging from boxes studded with precious gems and vessels blown from Indo-Persian glass to a chair made of solid ivory, a gift from Louis XV to Tipu Sultan. In one room, large crowds are drawn to a famous musical clock with a toy watchman who emerges from behind a door every hour in time to beat a melodious gong. Give yourself at least 90 minutes to explore.

C. L. Badari, Malakpet. ✆ **040/2452-3211.** Admission Rs 150 ($3.40). Sat–Thurs 10am–5pm, 4:15pm last entry. Cameras not allowed.

WHERE TO STAY

At press time, exquisite **Falaknuma Palace** (Tank Bund Rd.), a work of astonishing architectural opulence that has hosted the likes of King George V, was in the process of being converted into a heritage hotel by the Taj hotel group. This is likely to be the best place to stay in Hyderabad when it is ready at the end of 2006; visit www.taj hotels.com for ongoing developments.

A good budget option is **Green Park**. Catering primarily to business travelers, Green Park may not rank particularly high in terms of luxury and sophistication, but it's clean, comfortable, and convenient to the nearby airport. Ask for a garden-facing guest room (© **040/2375-7575;** www.hotelgreenpark.com; doubles from Rs 3,615/$81, breakfast included).

ITC Hotel Kakatiya Sheraton & Towers ✿✿✿   Not as opulently over-the-top as
Taj Krishna, this fully Wi-Fi–enabled hotel is billed as the best business hotel in town. Public spaces are smartly dressed in a vibrant and culturally evocative assortment of objets d'art typical of the region—decorative silver *bidri* pieces, detailed frescoes, and elegant furniture finished in rich fabrics. Guest rooms are wonderfully spacious; even the cheapest corporate rooms are large and attractively finished (twins only). The best views are of Hussain Sagar Lake, the city, and the pool (book a room with a number ending in 01, 03, or 05 for the least obstructed view). The atmosphere here is one of down-to-earth sophistication. Staff are friendly and helpful, if not always on the ball.

Begumpet, Hyderabad 500 016. © 040/2340-0132. Fax 040/2340-1045. www.welcomgroup.com. 189 units. $200 executive club double (includes breakfast and happy hour); $275 Sheraton Tower; $375–$900 suite. Tower rooms and suites include breakfast, airport transfer, and happy hour. AE, MC, V. **Amenities:** 4 restaurants; 2 bars; tea pavilion; patisserie; pool with Jacuzzi; tie-up with army golf course; health club; concierge; travel desk; currency exchange; Wi-Fi enabled; shopping arcade; florist; salon; room service; laundry; dry cleaning; doctor. *In room:* A/C, TV, minibar, tea-and coffee-making facilities, weighing scales in some rooms.

Taj Krishna ✿✿✿   Situated in the upmarket suburb of Banjara Hills, Hyderabad's
most luxurious hotel is fashioned to emulate the opulence and (sometimes high-kitsch) style of an Indian palace; guests have included the late Lady Di, the Dalai Lama, and Kofi Anan. Between its sumptuous arches, *zardozi* (embroidered) panels, and mother-of-pearl inlaid marble pillars, its lobby is packed full of Belgian chandeliers, ornately engraved mirrors, rococo marble statues, Asian vases, an original French gold-encrusted ornamental grandfather clock, and a fountain spouting water into a dark marble koi pond. The best guest rooms are those on the two Taj Club floors, which have beautiful wooden floors, embroidered sheer curtains, and large bathrooms; club benefits include breakfast, cocktails, and airport pickup. Book an even-numbered room facing the lake and the acre-long pool area. Note that if you opt for a cheaper room, you'll be more comfortable at the Sheraton. Krishna has some of the city's most exclusive restaurants (see "Where to Dine," below), its best nightlife option, and proximity to shopping outlets. The Krishna is very popular, which can tax the general efficiency of staff and elevators when occupancy is up.

Rd. no. 1, Banjara Hills, Hyderabad 500 034. © 040/5566-2323 or 040/2339-1313. Fax 040/5566-1313. www.taj hotels.com. 261 units. $225 deluxe double; $330 Taj Club (includes breakfast and airport transfers); $350 executive suite, $450 deluxe suite, $600 luxury suite, $900 presidential suite. $30 extra bed. AE, MC, V. **Amenities:** 3 restaurants; bar; tea lounge; nightclub; pool; clay tennis court; squash, badminton, golf, and sightseeing by arrangement; health club; concierge; travel desk; car hire; limousine service; currency exchange; salon; florist service; bookshop; pearl shop; 24-hr. room service; laundry; dry cleaning; doctor-on-call; library. *In room:* A/C, TV, dataport; minibar, tea-and coffee-making facilities, iron on request.

Viceroy ✿ (Value   This smart business hotel has a reputation for good value and fine
service. Offering prime views of the lake from some of its guest rooms, this hotel is marked by unfussy design—as the name implies, decor pays homage to the days of the Raj, with paintings of English lords and ladies throughout. Premier Club rooms are

partially lake-facing; at night, when Hussain Sagar is lit up, the view is quite lovely. Guest rooms are laid out for business convenience so they're no-nonsense though, strangely enough, dressed in shades of pink, with brown carpets.

Tank Bund Rd., Hyderabad 500 080. (C) 040/2753-8383. Fax 040/2753-8797. www.viceroyhotels.com. 178 units. $160 executive double; $185 premier club (includes privileges); $135–$160 suite. $15 extra bed. Rates include breakfast. AE, DC, MC, V. **Amenities:** 4 restaurants; bar; pool; health club; concierge; currency exchange; Internet lounge; shops; pearl shop; salon; 24-hr. room service; laundry; doctor. *In room:* A/C, TV, dataport, hair dryer. Also minibar and tea- and coffee-making facilities in Premier Club rooms.

WHERE TO DINE

In Hyderabad, food is as important as life itself, a world-view no doubt inherited from the *Nizams,* who reveled in culinary intemperance. Hyderabad is known for its *dum*-style cooking (with its origins in Lucknow): the practice of sealing the pot or dish and gently simmering its ingredients over a slow fire, thereby increasing the absorption of aromatic spices. Lavishly decorated in vibrant blues and distinctively Hyderabadi objets d'art, **Dum Pukht** ✰✰✰ (ITC Kakatiya Sheraton & Towers; (C) **040/2340-1032;** Rs 325–Rs 950/$7.40–$22) is the city's most celebrated upmarket restaurant, and known for its *dum*-style dishes. (*Dum Pukht* literally means cooking by locking in steam.) Try the chef's *kareli ki nahari,* mutton shanks cooked in their own juices and marrow, tinged with cardamom and saffron. Melt-in-the-mouth *kakori* kebabs prepared from finely minced mutton, green papaya, cloves, and cinnamon are skewered, chargrilled, and eaten with *sheermal,* saffron-and-milk-infused flaky bread.

One of the best examples of *dum*-style cooking is *biryani,* Hyderabad's most time-honored dish, best made with marinated mutton which, together with basmati rice and spices, is prepared in a sealed pot for an aromatic result. Available practically anywhere, it's best enjoyed with a spicy *mirch ka salan* (chili curry) and yogurt salad. **Azizia,** adjacent the Nampally railway station, is said to be the home of *biryani,* and its chefs claim to be descended from the *Nizams'* master chefs. Though it's pretty tough to get a bad *biryani* in Hyderabad, some restaurants, or so the locals say, are just a notch above the rest. Try **Paradise** (Paradise Circle, M.G. Rd.) or **Café Bahar** in Himayatnagar. Finish your meal with Hyderabad's famous desserts: *khubani ka meetha* (apricots and cream) or *double ka meetha* (bread pudding with cashews and almonds). Another place that serves authentic *biryani,* among other delights, is **Firdaus** ✰✰✰ (Taj Krishna, Rd. no. 1, Banjara Hills; (C) **040/2339-2323;** Rs 225–Rs 955/$5.10–$22). At this large, elegant restaurant, waiters serve dishes prepared by the young, enigmatic Chef Sumeet Sood; try the *shaane raan,* tender lamb steak marinated in assorted spices and tandoor grilled. But really, all the meals are fit for a *Nizam,* especially enjoyed against a backdrop of live *ghazal* music.

To sample the regional delights in a value-packed buffet, head for the Viceroy hotel's **Patio** coffee shop (see "Where to Stay," above) on Sunday night, when a great-value Hyderabadi *Shahi-Dastarkhan* ("Royal Dining Experience") is laid out. You can sample Chef Tarun's authentic *nehari* soup (trotter soup—strong, pungent, and powerful, this is possibly an acquired taste); flavorful *biryani;* and rich *haleem,* made with lamb, lentils, and cracked wheat, slow-cooked to a sticky-smooth consistency—in truth, somewhat akin to mashed mince.

But Hyderabad is not just the haven of regal Muslim fare. You will find toned-down versions of other Andhra cuisines at several city restaurants. If you're keen to sample regional Andhra cuisine without forever losing your sense of taste (it's intensely fiery), take a table at **Chutney's** ((C) **040/2335-8484;** Shilpa Arcade Rd. no. 3, Banjara

Hills), to sample their *pesarattu* (spiced mung bean flour pancake) eaten with *allam pachadi* (ginger pickle). Better still, make your way to the first floor and take your pick of a huge variety of vegetarian dishes at their reasonably priced all-you-can-eat daily buffet spread (Rs 135/$3.10).

SHOPPING

Pearls are a major draw in Hyderabad, but do be careful: There are a lot of fakes out there. **Kedarnathji Motiwale** (near Bata, Pathergatti; © **040/5571-2345** or 040/ 2456-6667; www.kedarnathji.com) has been supplying pearls and jewelry since 1908; **Meena Jewellers** (Babukhan Estate; © **040/2323-1073** or -7170) is also recommended, particularly if you're after exotic-looking pieces typical of Indian bridal wear. Catering to the wealthy is **Krishna Pearls & Jewellers** (www.krishnapearls.com), with branches in several of the upmarket hotels, including Taj Krishna (© **040/ 2339-5015**), Taj Residency (© **040/5556-4822**), and the ITC Kakatiya Sheraton & Towers (© **040/2340-0811** or 040/5556-4844). Besides high-quality Hyderabadi pearls, these jewelers also design and manufacture gold jewelry and various traditional handicrafts.

For high-quality traditional Indian garments, visit **Kalanjali,** a Hyderabadi institution, with four floors of air-conditioned shopping under one roof (opposite Public Gardens, 5-10-194 Hill Fort Rd., Saifabad; © **040/2323-1147** or 040/2329-7196/7). And to absorb the scents and colors of one of India's most evocative bazaars, spend some time in **Laad Bazaar** 🌟🌟 near Charminar (see "What to See & Do," above).

9

The Heart of India:
Delhi, the Taj, Uttar Pradesh
& Madhya Pradesh

The capital of India, Delhi, and its neighboring state, Uttar Pradesh, compose the geographical and historical heart of India, with ancient cities and awesome monuments that make for definite inclusion in the itineraries of most first-time visitors to the subcontinent.

With comfortable accommodations and a host of interesting sights, Delhi is a good place to acclimatize. But the main reason most visitors touch down here is its proximity to some of North India's most impressive sights, like the **Golden Temple** at Amritsar, one of the most spiritual destinations in India (see chapter 11); **Jaipur,** capital of Rajasthan, "land of princes" (see chapter 10); and **Agra.** The Mughal capital of Agra is famed for the timeless beauty of its monuments, of which the **Taj Mahal** is the most famous, but it is in the city of **Varanasi** that time has indeed stood still. Believed to be the oldest living city in the world, Varanasi is the holiest destination in Hindu India, where true believers come to die in order to achieve *moksha*—the final liberation of the soul from the continuous rebirth cycle of Hindu life. Rising like a densely populated crust from the banks of the Ganges, the city is saturated with a sense of the sacred, but while the experience is almost mind-altering, the crowds and filth you may encounter in the city's tiny medieval lanes are not for the fainthearted. For those travelers who prefer to keep the chaos of India at arm's length, it's better perhaps to head for **Lucknow,** the state capital, where space and serenity prevail, and where the decadence and good taste of the ruling *Nawabs* (Shiite Muslim rulers or landowners) live on in the rich cuisine and majestic *imambaras* (tombs).

South of Uttar Pradesh sprawls **Madhya Pradesh,** a vast landlocked state that contains some of the loveliest untouched vistas on the subcontinent. The most famous sights here are the deserted palaces of **Orchha** and the erotic shrines of **Khajuraho**—both easily included as side trips between Delhi or Agra and Varanasi. Deeper south, which sees a great deal less tourist traffic, lie **Sanchi,** one of the finest Buddhist *stupa* (commemorative cairn) complexes in Asia; and **Mandu,** an exotic Mughal stronghold. To the east lies **Bandhavgarh National Park,** with the densest concentration of tigers in India. These excursions will suit those keen to escape the hassle of more tourist-orientated destinations, but they take careful planning to reach; details are provided throughout the chapter.

1 Delhi

200km (124 miles) NW of Agra; 261km (324 miles) NE of Jaipur; 604km (375 miles) NE of Jodhpur

The capital of the world's largest democracy has a truly fascinating history, but with a population of 14 million sprawling over some 1,500 sq. km (585 sq. miles), and plagued by the subcontinent's highest levels of pollution, growth, and poverty, Delhi's delights are not immediately apparent. Even Delhiites, the majority of whom have been born elsewhere, seldom show pride in the city they now call home, bemoaning its drab mixture of civil servants, aspiring politicians, and avaricious businesspeople; the ever-expanding slums and "unauthorized" colonies; the relatively high levels of crime; and the general demise of traditional ways. Yet Delhi is in many ways the essence of modern India, with its startling paradox of old and new, foreign and familiar. And it remains the best starting point for exploring North India, not only because of its excellent transport connections and relatively sophisticated infrastructure, but because the history of Delhi, one of the oldest cities in the world, is essentially the history of India (see "A Tale of Seven Cities," below).

The city is littered with crumbling tombs and ruins, most of which are not even on the tourist map. They—like the elephant trundling alongside a traffic-logged road, where handwritten posters for CUSTOM CONFISCATED GOODS SOLD HERE vie with glossy fashion billboards—are just part of the strange fabric of Delhi. It doesn't have the vibrancy of Mumbai or the atmosphere of Kolkata, but in one day you can go from marveling at the sheer grace of the soaring **Qutb Minar Tower,** built in 1199 by the Turkish Slave King Qutb-ud-din Aibak to celebrate his victory over the Hindu Rajputs, to gawking at that 1920s British imperialist masterpiece, palatial **Rashtrapati Bhavan.** You can wander through the sculptural **Jantar Mantar,** a huge, open-air astronomy observatory built in 1725 by Jai Singh, creator and ruler of Jaipur, to the still-sacred atmosphere surrounding the **tomb of the 14th-century Sufi saint,** Sheikh Nizamuddin Aulia, or the **16th-century garden tomb of Mughal Emperor Humayun,** precursor to the Taj. Or, after the chaos of exploring the crowded streets of 17th-century **Shahjahanabad,** Delhi's oldest living city, you can escape to **Rajghat,** the park where Mahatma Gandhi was cremated in 1948; or to **Lodi Gardens,** where lawns and golfing greens are studded with the crumbling 15th-century tombs of once-powerful dynasties. And still you haven't covered the half of it. . . . But despite its host

The Plight of the Delhi Beggars

Some 50,000 people live on Delhi's pavements or squalid open lots. These squatters are predominantly from rural areas, many of them forced to move off their ancestral lands to make way for a network of dams that are being constructed across North India despite fierce opposition. Oblivious to the blatant injustice these people have suffered, Delhi's municipal authorities passed a law in September 2002 that makes it an offense to give money to beggars at traffic lights, in part because "it portrays an adverse picture of our country." Begging has in fact been illegal since the 1959 Beggars Act, and those arrested have to bribe the police to avoid spending up to 3 years in jail, but this is the first time the *actual act of giving* has been penalized. As local human-rights lawyers argue, the authorities are effectively criminalizing poverty. And if you deny the desperate right to beg, they are left with one alternative. Crime.

The Heart of India: Delhi, Uttar Pradesh & Madhya Pradesh

Delhi

WEST PATEL NAGAR

Guru Govind Singh Marg

Camp Cinema Rd.

Arya Samaj Rd.

EAST PATEL NAGAR

Patel Rd.

Sadhu Vaswani Marg

Shankar Rd.

Farm Rd.

Hillside Rd.

NEW RAJENDRA NAGAR

Todapur Rd.

BUDDHA JAYANTI PARK

POLO GROUND

Upper Ridge Rd.

Sardar Patel Marg

CHANAKYAPURI

Satya

Ring Rd.

MOTI BAGH

Benito Juarez Marg

Rao Tularem Rd.

A Tale of Seven Cities

Chosen by the strategically astute invaders who attacked from the north, east, and west, Delhi was not only the gateway to the fertile Gangetic plains and watered by its own Yamuna River, but it enjoyed some protection from the west by the Aravalli Mountains that cross latter-day Rajasthan, and by the Himalayas to the north. Despite this, waves of invaders resulted in the creation—and more often than not destruction—of at least seven distinct cities. The earliest accounts and archaeological finds date back to 1000 B.C., when—according to the *Mahabharata* epic, most revered of Hindu religious texts—the Pandavas and their cousins the Kauravas battled for the city of **Indraprastha,** thought to be located under the present ruins of Purana Qila, citadel of the sixth capital. But the earliest existing ruins date back to A.D. 736, when the Tomara Rajputs, one of the self-anointed warrior clans to which Rajasthan gave birth, built the fortress **Lal Kot,** around which grew **Qila Rai Pithora,** today known as the first city of Delhi. In 1180 the Tomaras were ousted by the Chauhan Rajputs, who were in turn forced back to Rajasthan by the Slave King Qutb-ud-din Aibak, a Turkish general. He built the **Qutb Complex** in 1199, which today remains one of the most interesting sights in the city (see "The Top Attractions," later in this chapter). Aibak served under the Afghani Muhammad Ghori until Ghori's assassination in 1206. Aibak took over the Indian spoils of war, founding the Delhi Sultanate, which was to rule over Delhi and the surrounding region for almost 2 centuries. In 1303, the Delhi Sultan Ala-ud-din Khilji built the second city, **Siri,** near present-day Hauz Khas. Then the Tughluqs built **Tughlaqabad,** 8km (5 miles) east of the Qutb complex, but this was deserted in 1321 and little remains today of what is now referred to as the third city. After a brief sojourn in latter-day Maharashtra, the Tughluqs moved the city again in 1327, this time between Lal Kot and Siri, and named this fourth city **Jahanpanah.** A mere 27 years later it was moved again, this time some distance north to an eminently sensible position next to the Yamuna River. Named **Ferozabad,** this sprawling fifth city was, according to legend, one of the richest in the world. But how the mighty do fall or, according to the Persian prophecy, "Whoever builds a new city in Delhi will lose it." Timur drove the Tughluqs out of Delhi, and while his successors, the Sayyids and Lodis, did not build brand-new cities, their tombs are found scattered in the appropriately named **Lodi Gardens.** Their defeat by the Mughal Babur signaled the end of Sultanate rule and the start of the Mughal empire, one of the world's greatest medieval dynasties, who were to rule over the region for more than 200 years.

It was Babur who first moved the capital to nearby Agra, but his son **Humayun** chose to return to Delhi in 1534, only to be forced into exile by the advancing army of the Afghan Sher Shah, who took possession of **Purana Qila** (literally "old fort") in 1540, rebuilt this sixth city, and renamed the citadel **Shergarh.** Fifteen years later, Humayun finally ousted the Afghan, only to die an ignominious death a year later, falling down his library steps—his tomb, which can be seen from the southern gate of Purana Qila, remains one of Delhi's top attractions.

Humayun's son, Akbar—generally revered for his religious tolerance and diplomacy—again chose to move the capital back to Agra. Only after Akbar's grandson, Shah Jahan, built the Taj Mahal for his wife, did Delhi again become the capital in 1638. Shah Jahan, the greatest architect of the Mughal dynasty, rebuilt an entirely new city, using materials from the ruins of Ferozabad (and, it is said, leaving the corpses of criminals to settle in the foundations). Not known for his humility, he named it **Shahjahanabad.** Shahjahanabad is still very much inhabited, and is today usually referred to as "Old Delhi," home to many of the city's top attractions. After Shah Jahan was viciously deposed by his son, Aurangzeb (see "The Life & Times of the Mughal Emperors," later in this chapter), Mughal power began to wane, and with it the importance of Delhi. It was only with the advent of British power that Delhi again played a pivotal role in the affairs of India. After the "Indian Mutiny" (or "The First War of Independence," depending on who's talking), a direct result of the racist and exploitative policies of the British East India Company, India was annexed by Britain as its colony in 1858, and Delhi was declared the capital of the Raj in 1911. The last (at least for the time being) of Delhi's cities to be built, **New Delhi** took shape between 1911 and 1933. Designed by the British imperialist architects Lutyens and Baker, the New Delhi's major buildings have a simple, almost brutal classicism and are considered the finest artifacts of the British empire, their sheer scale symbolizing its fascist ideals. But again Delhi was lost to her rulers, and in 1947 India's first democratically elected prime minister was sworn into power. The bungalows of New Delhi became home to Indian masters. Ever a city of paradoxes, Delhi's jubilation was tinged with tragedy, for this was also for many the demise of ancient Delhi: With the division ("Partition") of the subcontinent into India and Pakistan, bloody street battles between Hindu and Muslim broke out, leading to the wide-scale immigration of Delhi's urbane Muslim population to Pakistan, and to an even bigger, reverse influx of Punjabis from what is now Pakistan. Primarily farmers, but with a reputation for hard work and business acumen, the Punjabi immigrants effectively doubled the population of Delhi and forever changed its image of itself as a birthplace of civilization. As William Dalrymple describes it in *City of Djinns,* Delhi—"grandest of grand old aristocratic dowagers"— had become "a nouveau-riche heiress: all show and vulgarity and conspicuous consumption." But if one thing is constant, it is Delhi's ability to reconstitute herself—who knows what she will grow into next?

of attractions, unless you're staying in one of its top hotels (of which The Imperial is almost a destination in its own right), Delhi is not a very relaxing destination, and it is as famous for its pollution (it was rated the fourth-most-polluted city in the world through the 1990s) as it is for its sights. Unless you're a history buff or here on business, spend as much time as you need to recover from jet lag, choosing to view only a few of its many attractions (the best of which are listed below), and then move on. The rest of India, with its awesome array of experiences and beauty, awaits you.

ESSENTIALS

VISITOR INFORMATION To pick up a free map of Delhi or to get up-to-date information on sights, city tours, and taxi/rickshaw prices, head for the **Government of India Tourist Office** at 88 Janpath (near Connaught Place; ✆ 011/2332-0005 or -0008; Mon–Fri 9am–6pm, Sat 9am–2pm). You will also find Government of India Tourist offices at both airports (open 24 hr.). Do not confuse these with so-called "government authorized" tourist offices, which are not authorized by anyone and are very adept at fleecing the unsuspecting. You will find these fakes particularly along Janpath and at the New Delhi railway station; make sure you seek assistance only at 88 Janpath or from one of the recommended tour operators (see below). Note that the Government of India Tourist Office can supply information but will not make bookings. If you intend to travel anywhere during your sojourn in India by train, you may choose to make all your reservations in Delhi (though these are just as easily available in other big cities). You can make bookings at the helpful Indian Railways Counter at the airport. Alternatively, for information, visit the **Delhi Tourism and Transport Development Corporation** (DTTDC; Bombay Life Building, Middle Circle; ✆ 011/2331-5322; Mon–Sat 9:30am–6pm), or see "Getting There: By Train," below.

GETTING THERE **By Air** Most major international airlines operate in what is one of the best-connected cities in south Asia. Delhi has separate domestic and international airports that lie 8km (5 miles) apart; a free hourly shuttle bus runs between them. Note that the domestic airport has two terminals, 1A and 1B, also connected by free shuttle bus (1A is for Indian Airlines; check which one you need to be at when leaving). **Indira Gandhi International Airport** (✆ 011/2569-6021 or 011/2565-2011) lies 20km (12 miles) southwest of Connaught Place (the city center), 25 to 50 minutes away. The cheapest way (but one to be avoided) to get into town is to catch a State Transport bus (Rs 50/$1.15 plus luggage fee), but if you've just crossed time zones you'll want to opt for a taxi. If you've just arrived in India, it's also not worthwhile to hire a rickshaw; they may be cheaper than taxis, but they're very slow and bound to be uncomfortable if you're burdened with luggage—plus, you will almost certainly be pressured into handing over more money even if the price has been discussed upfront. Choosing, let alone negotiating with, a taxi driver is likely to make your head spin, so it's best to book a taxi at the official **prepaid taxi kiosk** (just outside the arrivals hall; ask for directions, and don't be sidelined). It offers fixed rates, with Rs 10 (25¢) for each piece of luggage, but expect to pay between Rs 195 and Rs 300 ($4.50–$6.85) into the center of town (25% more after 11pm). Better still, ask your hotel to arrange the transfer, though this will more than likely double the price. Note that you can change money at the international airport at the State Bank of India or Thomas Cook counters (both 24 hr.), but you can't draw money on your credit card.

By Train Of the five stations, most trains arrive at either **New Delhi Station,** a 10-minute walk from Connaught Place, or at **Old Delhi Station** in Shahjahanabad.

(Note that if you're traveling on to Agra, you may need to catch the passenger train that leaves from **Nizamuddin Station,** south of Connaught Place.) For rail inquiries and reservations, call ℂ **131** from 8am to 8pm. All stations are well-serviced by taxis and auto-rickshaws. Again, negotiate the fare upfront—expect to pay Rs 50 ($1.15) to Connaught Place; Rs 60 ($1.35) to Shahjahanabad/Old Delhi. Note that if you plan to travel elsewhere in India by train, you don't necessarily need to prebook all your train trips in Delhi (see chapter 2 for details on train travel). It's easiest to do this with a recommended travel agent like **Sadhana Travel** (ℂ **011/2646-5312** or 98100-58471), which also does air travel and tour itineraries; or work with a travel agent attached to your hotel. Keep in mind that on some trains a small quota of seats is set aside for foreign travelers. A travel agent cannot book these seats; you will need to go to the station to a special counter to book them (again, see chapter 2).

GETTING AROUND   Delhi finally has a subway, but this can get overcrowded and claustrophobic, and women traveling alone will get unwelcome attention. As is the case elsewhere, subways also provide no sense of the city layout or passing sights. The best way to get around is still in Delhi's black-and-yellow taxis or, for short distances, auto-rickshaws (run on eco-friendly CNG—compressed natural gas), but be sure to agree on the price upfront. For instance, traveling from Connaught Place to Red Fort shouldn't cost more than Rs 75 ($1.70) by auto-rickshaw, Rs 120 ($2.80) by taxi. If you feel you're being overcharged, accuse the driver of cheating, threaten to report him, and warn him that under Section 420 of the Indian Penal Code he could be imprisoned (not yet in force, but it should put the fear in him!); to complain, dial ℂ **96044-00400.** If the idea of having to haggle like this turns your stomach, **Dial-a-Cab** (ℂ **1929**) offers a convenient, albeit more expensive, alternative, with a fleet of air-conditioned cars outfitted with working meters (Rs 15/35¢ per kilometer, 25% extra 11pm–5am). If you'd prefer to hire a car and driver for a half- or full day, arrange this through your hotel or, for the best possible rate and reliable drivers, through the tourist office at 88 Janpath. You can also contact the charming **Rinku** (see "Guided Tours," below). If you plan to tour North India by car, setting off from Delhi, contact **Greaves Travels India** (ℂ **011/2437-3523** or -2426), a reputable operator with good drivers.

Note: It is inadvisable to travel anywhere during rush hour—you will almost certainly find yourself in a traffic jam in one of the most polluted cities in the world.

GUIDED TOURS   You can book an air-conditioned bus tour of New Delhi (daily 8am–1pm) and/or Old Delhi (daily 2–5:30pm) at the tourist office at 88 Janpath. (See "Visitor Information," above.) Expect to pay about Rs 200 ($4.55) for one tour, Rs 300 ($6.85) for both. Slightly cheaper tours are offered by the DTTDC (see "Visitor Information," above). Both also offer long-distance tours that include trips to Agra, Jaipur, and Rishikesh, but we definitely recommend you opt for a private operator like **TCI** (C-35 Connaught Place; ℂ **011/2341-5367** or 011/2341-6167). Their tours are more personal, cost Rs 750 ($17) per person (monument entry not included), cover all the main sights and lunch at Chor Bizarre, and require a minimum of only two people. If you want to create your own half- or full-day tour from the attractions listed below, contact **Rinku** (ℂ **011/2535-6278** or 98111-94983; rinku_dhall@yahoo.co.in or sanjeevjoney@rediffmail.com). Rinku is not, strictly speaking, a guide (he cannot, for instance, give you a detailed history of an attraction), but he knows his city forwards and backwards and can advise you on when you should hire a guide (usually available at every entrance) and how much it should cost, or when you need to remove your shoes or cover your shoulders, and whether you can include that last sight before the rush hour takes over. Rinku drives around with a friend in a non-air-conditioned van (Rs 800–Rs 1,000/$18–$23 for a full day), but if you'd like him to arrange more salubrious transportation, give him advance warning (Note that like all taxi drivers/guides in India, Rinku will try to take you to a travel agent or shop from whom he will make a commission, but unlike most, he won't press you further if you decline.) For an excellent introduction to Hinduism, as well as visits to some of the lesser-known sights in Old Delhi, book into **Master Paying Guest House** (see "Where to Stay," later in this chapter)—the erudite proprietor gives one of the best tours we've had in India, and runs one of the best-value guesthouses, too. For very comfortable customized tours of the city and farther afield, contact **Navigator Holidays** or **Banyan Tours and Travel** (see "Fast Facts: Delhi," below), or that U.K.-based stalwart in Indian travel, **Cox & Kings** (see chapter 2). Another company worth highlighting is **Exotic Journeys**—all you need to do is supply proprietor Raj Singh with your budget (as low as $50 per day, including car, driver, and accommodations, or higher, of course), number of days, and area of interest, and he will customize an excellent trip, kicking off with 2 days of sightseeing in Delhi. Contact him at exotic@del2.vsnl.net.in or at ✆ **011/2617-8685.**

FAST FACTS: Delhi

Airlines Most international airline offices are located on Janpath, Connaught Place, and Barakhamba Road. The best domestic airline, **Jet Airways,** is located at Jetair House, 13 Community Centre Yusuf Sarai (✆ **011/5164-1515,** booking offices 011/5164-1414). **Indian Airlines** is located at Safdarjung Airport (✆ **011/ 2462-2220**) and is open 24 hours; for general inquiries call ✆ **1407.** Other airlines: **Air Sahara** (✆ **011/3030-2020** or 011/2335-9801); **Kingfisher Airlines** (✆ **1600/180-0101**); **Spice Jet** (✆ **1600/180-3333** or 987/180-3333).

Ambulance For an ambulance call **East West Rescue** at ✆ **011/2469-9229,** -0429, or -3738.

American Express The office is located at A-Block Connaught Place (✆ **011/ 2332-6129** or 011/2330-8035).

Area Code The area code for **Delhi** is **011.**

ATMs There are hundreds of ATMs in the city; ask your hotel which is the closest. Alternatively, head for Connaught Place, where (among others) HSBC, Standard Chartered, and Citibank ATMs offer 24-hour cash machines that take Visa and MasterCard.

Banks Hours are normally Monday to Friday 10am to 2pm, Saturday 10am to noon, though many banks are also open 9am to 5pm. It's quickest to use 24-hour ATMs. See "ATMs," above.

Bookstores The best are in Khan Market—try **Bahri & Sons** (✆ **011/2469-4610**), **The Bookshop** (✆ **011/2469-7102**), or **Full Circle** (✆ **011/2465-5641**). If you're looking for something downtown, **Bookworm** (29 B-Block Connaught Place; ✆ **011/2332-2260**) is excellent, and will often obtain a book you want within 24 hours even if it's not in stock.

Car Hires See "Getting Around," above. For upmarket cars and other travel arrangements, a recommended operator is **Banyan Tours and Travels** (www. banyantours.com; banyan.delhi@vsnl.com; check website for latest numbers). Another operator to try is **Navigator Holidays** (L-5 2nd floor, Radiant Limo, Lajpat Nagar II; ✆ **011/5172-5020**).

Currency Exchange The international airport has 24-hour currency exchange but no facilities to let you draw money on your credit cards, so bring foreign notes or traveler's checks if you intend to catch a taxi from here. Thomas Cook is located at the airport (open 24/7) and at The Imperial hotel (Mon–Sat; see "Where to Stay," later in this chapter). See above for American Express. For cash withdrawals or exchange, see "ATMs" and "Banks," above.

Directory Assistance **Times Infoline** (✆ **011/5168-6868**) and **Ask Me Services** (✆ **011/2222-2222**) provide free and usually accurate information on restaurants, hotels, movie theaters, or other services (much like talking Yellow Pages).

Doctors & Dentists Most hotels listed here have doctors on call. The hotels are also your best bet for finding a reputable dentist.

Drugstores There are numerous 24-hour drugstores throughout the city. Best to ask your hotel to arrange a delivery or pickup.

Embassies & Consulates **U.S.:** Shanti Path, Chanakyapuri (✆ **011/2419-8000;** Mon–Fri 8:30am–1pm and 2–5:30pm). **U.K:** Shanti Path, Chanakyapuri (✆ **011/ 2687-2161;** Mon–Fri 9am–1pm and 2–4pm). **Australia:** 1/50-G Shanti Path, Chanakyapuri (✆ **011/5139-9900;** Mon–Fri 8:30am–1pm and 2–5pm). **Canada:** 7/8 Shanti Path Chanakyapuri (✆ **011/5178-2000**). **New Zealand:** 50-N Nyaya Marg (✆ **011/2688-3170** or 011/2687-6260).

Emergencies For police call ✆ **100**; for local stations ask your hotel or call the Government of India Tourist Office. See "Ambulance," above. For complaints about taxi or auto-rickshaw drivers, dial ✆ **96044-00400.**

Hospitals **All India Institute of Medicinal Sciences** (✆ **011/2658-8500**), on Ansari Nagar, has a 24-hour trauma unit. Alternatively, head for **Ram Manohar Lohia Hospital** (Baba Khadak Singh Marg; ✆ **011/2336-1014** or -5933). Farther afield is **Indraprastha Apollo Hospital,** on the Delhi–Mathura Road (✆ **011/ 2692-5858** or -5801), both with 24-hour emergency service.

Internet Access Numerous outlets are located all over the city and charge Rs 20 to Rs 50 (45¢–$1.15) per hour.

Mobile Phones You can buy prepaid cellphone cards almost anywhere in Delhi (see chapter 2). If you want to rent a cellphone, call **Matrix** at ✆ **011/2680-0000;** they promise to deliver a phone to you within 2 hours. Rental cellphones cost Rs 100 to Rs 150 ($2.30–$3.40) per day. Calls are charged at Rs 2 (4¢) local, Rs 6 (12¢) national, and Rs 22 (50¢) international/minute.

Newspapers & Magazines Indian Express, Hindustan Times, and *The Times of India* are good national dailies that provide the lowdown on (largely) the political scene. *Outlook* and *India Today* are weekly news magazines that cover a range of issues; of the two, *Outlook* is more populist and interesting to read. *First City* is a monthly magazine recommended for its comprehensive reviews and listings. *Delhi Diary* is a city guide published weekly, and *The Delhi City*

Complete Guide and Magazine (Rs 20/45¢) is published every 2 weeks; both are available at hotels and other tourist locations and are good sources of events listings. You can also check out the latter's website at www.thedelhicity.com. *Outlook Traveller* (www.outlooktraveller.com) is a top-quality locally produced travel magazine.

Police See "Emergencies," above.

Post Office Try the P.O. at Parliament St. (© 011/2336-4111) or the **GPO** at Gol Khana, 5 minutes from Connaught Place. But best to ask your hotel to post items.

Restrooms *Avoid.*

Safety Delhi, like the rest of India, is relatively safe, though the city has seen an increase in crime. It's unwise for women to travel alone at night.

Taxis See "Getting Around," above.

Weather Delhi's summers are notoriously unbearable; October/November to February are the best times to go.

THE TOP ATTRACTIONS

India's capital has more sights than any other city in India, but they are concentrated in three distinct areas—Old Delhi, New Delhi, and South Delhi (known as the **Qutb Minar Complex**)—which can be tackled as separate tours or grouped together. Most organized tours spend a half-day covering the top attractions in New Delhi, and another half-day exploring the 17th-century capital, Shahjahanabad. Commonly referred to as "Old Delhi," Shahjahanabad lies a mere 5km (3 miles) north of centrally located Connaught Place, the commercial heart of New Delhi, but it feels a hundred years away (400 to be exact). If you do only one sightseeing excursion, make it here, for this is most authentically India, where imposing **Lal Qila (Red Fort)** and **Jama Masjid,** India's largest mosque, pay testament to the vision and power of Shah Jahan, and the chaos and pungent smells from the overcrowded and ancient streets are a heady reminder that you are far from home. Surrounding and immediately south of Connaught Place is New Delhi, built by British imperialist architects Baker and Lutyens. Its primary attractions are the architectural gems centered around **Rajpath** and **Rashtrapati Bhavan,** official residence of the president of India. Of Delhi's remaining cities, all of which are today deserted and in ruins, only the 12th-century **Qutb Minar,** a World Heritage Site monument built in Delhi's first city and surprisingly intact, is definitely worth inclusion in your itinerary. (*Note:* Most museums in Delhi close Mon.)

SHAHJAHANABAD (OLD DELHI) ✿✿✿

Still surrounded by crumbling city walls and three surviving gates, the vibrant, bustling Shahjahanabad, built over a period of 10 years by Emperor Shah Jahan, is very much a separate city—predominantly a labyrinth of tiny lanes crowded with rickshaws, and lined with 17th-century *havelis* (Indian mansions), their balustrades broken and once-ornate facades defaced with rusted signs and sprouting satellite dishes. Old Delhi is inhabited by a predominantly Muslim population whose lives revolve around work and the local mosque, much as it was a century ago.

The best way to explore the area is to catch a taxi or auto-rickshaw to Red Fort (see below), then set off in a cycle-rickshaw (Rs 50–Rs 80/$1.15–$1.80 per hour), or on foot if it's too congested. Head down the principal street, **Chandni Chowk,** which leads from the main entrance to Red Fort. Along this busy commercial street are mosques, a church, and a number of temples. First up, opposite the fort, is **Digambar Jain Temple,** the oldest Jain temple in Delhi and surprisingly simple compared with other Jain temples, which are renowned for the intricacy of their carvings. Attached is a **bird hospital,** which smells less charming than it sounds. If you're pressed for time, skip these and proceed to vibrant **Gauri Shankar Temple** (look for the mounds of marigolds, sold to worshippers as they enter), which has an 800-year-old lingam. Or stop at **Sisganj Gurudwara,** an unassuming but superbly atmospheric and welcoming Sikh temple, which marks the spot where Guru Tegh Bahadur, the ninth Sikh guru, was beheaded by the fundamentalist Aurangzeb (Shah Jahan's intolerant son). You will be expected to hand over your shoes at a super-efficient kiosk and wash your hands and feet at the cheap taps plumbed right at the temple entrance; on the way out you may be offered food—politely decline (it's rich with ghee, clarified butter). Then, either turn left into Kinari Bazaar (see below) or head the length of Chandni Chowk to **Fatehpuri Masjid,** designed by one of Shah Jahan's wives. Take a detour to the right into Church Mission Marg and then left into **Khari Baoli**—reputed to be Asia's biggest spice market—the colors, textures, and aromas that literally spill out into the street are worth the side trip, but be careful with your belongings in these packed streets. Then double back down Chandni Chowk, turn right into jam-packed **Kinari Bazaar,** and stop to admire the cheap gold (we're talking mostly tinsel) and silver trinkets and accessories. Or keep going until the right turn into **Dariba Kalan,** "the jewelers' lane," where you can bargain hard for gorgeous baubles. Go south down Dariba Kalan to reach **Jama Masjid,** India's largest mosque, keeping an eye out on the right for the tall spire of **Shiv Temple.** Having explored Jama Masjid (see below), you can head west down **Chawri Bazaar** for brass and copper icons and other souvenirs, then up Nai Sarak (which specializes in the most magnificent stationery, some bound into diaries). Or head south to **Churiwali Galli,** the "lane of bangle-sellers," and make a final stop at **Karim's** to sample the authentic Mughlai cooking that has kept patrons coming back for over 100 years. A little farther along is **Sunehri Masjid,** recognizable by its three gilt domes from where the Persian invader Nadir Shah enjoyed a bird's-eye view as his men massacred some 3,000 of Shahjahanabad's citizens in 1739.

This done, you've pretty much covered Shahjahanabad's top attractions by rickshaw. A few more sights of interest within the old city walls may attract the die-hard tourist. Pretty **Zinat-ul Masjid (Daryaganj),** or "Cloud Mosque," built in 1710 by one of Aurangzeb's daughters, lies south, but doesn't see as much traffic as nearby **Rajghat** (Mahatma Gandhi Rd.; daily sunrise–sunset; leave shoes outside with attendant; Rs 5/10¢ tip), where Mahatma Gandhi, "Father of the Nation," was cremated. There's not much to see besides the black granite plinth inscribed with his last words, "Hé Ram!" ("Oh God!"), but it's worth getting here at 5pm on Friday (the day of the week he was assassinated), when devotees gather to sing melancholic *bhajans.* Nearby, **Gandhi Memorial Museum** (© 011/2331-1793; Tues–Sun 9:30am–5:30pm) documents his life and last rites, which must have been immensely moving. Also within the old city walls is **Feroze Shah Kotla (Bahadur Shah Zafar Marg),** the ruins of the palace of the fifth city, Ferozabad. The principal attraction here is the pristine polished sandstone pillar from the 3rd century B.C. that rises from the palace's crumbling remains. One of many pillars left by the Mauryan emperor Ashoka throughout North India, it was moved from the Punjab and erected here in 1356. North of Red Fort is **St. James Church** (Lothian Rd. near Kashmiri Gate; daily 8am–noon and 2–5pm). Consecrated in 1836, Delhi's oldest church was built by Col. James Skinner—the son of a Scotsman and his Rajput wife, who became one of Delhi's most flamboyant 19th-century characters—to repay a promise made during battle.

Lal Qila (Red Fort) 🏛️🏛️ Built by Shah Jahan, the most prolific architect and builder of the Mughal empire, Lal Qila must have been a very modern departure from labyrinthine Agra Fort (which is older but a great deal better preserved and atmospheric). It was the seat of Mughal power from 1639 to 1857. Named after the red sandstone used in its construction, Red Fort covers an area of almost 2km (1 mile). Visitors enter via three-story **Lahore Gate,** one of six impressive gateways. You'll pass through **Chatta Chowk,** which has quaint shops selling cheap souvenirs (some rather nice handbags). You'll arrive at **Naqqar Khana,** where the emperor's musicians used to play. From here you look up into **Diwan-I-Am,** the 60-pillared "hall of public audience," from where Emperor Shah Jahan used to listen to his subjects' queries and complaints as he sat cross-legged upon the beautifully carved throne (an age-old custom that his nasty son, Aurangzeb, discontinued). Behind this lie **Rang Mahal,** the royal quarters of the wives and mistresses, and **Mumtaz Mahal,** probably used by a favored wife or by Princess Jahanara, who evoked such envy in her sister's heart (see "Agra" introduction, later in this chapter). Next up are **Khas Mahal,** which housed the emperor's personal quarters (he would greet his subjects across the Yamuna River from the balcony); gilded **Diwan-I-Khas,** where the emperor would hold court with his inner circle from the famous jewel-encrusted Peacock Throne (taken by Persian invader Nadir Shah in 1739 and still in Iran); and finally the **Hamams,** or royal baths, whose fountains of rose-scented water would give modern-day spas a run for their money. In front of the hamams is **Moti Masjid,** built by Aurangzeb exclusively for his own use—a far cry from the huge Jama Masjid his father built to celebrate the faith together with thousands of his subjects.

A few examples of beautiful carving, inlay, and gilding remain, particularly in Diwan-I-Khas, but after so many years of successive plunder it takes some contemplation (and a guide) to imagine just how plush and glorious the palaces and gardens must have been in their heyday; they were ruined when the British ripped up the gardens and built their ugly barracks (the fort is incidentally still a military stronghold, with much of it off-limits). Consider hiring a guide at the entrance, but negotiate the fee upfront and don't expect much by way of dialogue (guides often speak English by rote and don't understand queries); do expect to be hassled for more money. If you're staying in an upmarket hotel, arrange a guide through the concierge.

Chandni Chowk. ☏ 011/2327-7705. Rs 100 ($2.30) entry, Rs 100–Rs 150 ($2.30–$3.40) guide. Tues–Sun sunrise–sunset. Evening light show 7:30pm Nov–Jan, 8:30pm Feb–Apr, 9pm May–Aug; Rs 50 ($1.15).

Jama Masjid 🏛️🏛️ Commissioned by Shah Jahan in 1656, this mosque took 5,000 laborers 6 years to complete and is still the largest in Asia, accommodating up to 25,000 worshippers during holy festivals such as Id. Sadly, non-Muslims are not allowed in during prayers, but photographs (sold elsewhere) of the thousands of supplicant worshippers provide some idea of the atmosphere as you wander the huge expanse within. The central pool is for washing hands, face, and feet; to the west (facing Mecca) is the main prayer hall with the traditional *mihrab* for the prayer leader.

You can ascend to the top of the southern minaret to enjoy fantastic views from Old Delhi to the distinctly different rooftops and high-rises of New Delhi—the climb is pretty stiff, but worth it. *Note:* If your knees or shoulders are bare, you'll have to rent a scarf or *lungi* (sarong or cloth) at the entrance to cover up.

Off Netaji Subhash Marg. Entry free; Rs 20 (45¢) for minaret rooftop viewing, Rs 150 ($3.40) camera or video. Daily 8:30am–12:15pm and 1:45 to half-hour before sunset; opens at 7am in summer. Closed during prayers 12:15–1:45pm. Shoes to be removed outside; Rs 2 (4¢).

NEW DELHI

Almost all of New Delhi's attractions lie south of **Connaught Place,** which you will no doubt visit to make onward bookings, get cash, eat, or shop. Built on concentric circles surrounding a central park, the retail heart of New Delhi was designed by Robert Tor Russell in the late 1920s. With its deep colonnaded verandas, gleaming banks, and host of burger joints and pizzerias, it's a far cry from Chandni Chowk but is still quite chaotic, crawling with touts and hucksters whose aim is to part you from your money as quickly and seductively as possible. From here, the closest attraction well worth visiting (unless you're moving on to Jaipur) is **Jantar Mantar** ★ (daily sunrise–sunset), which lies on Sansad Marg, on the way to Rashtrapati Bhavan. It's one of five open-air observatories built in the 18th century by Maharaja Jai Singh II, the eccentric genius who built Jaipur. The sculptural qualities of the huge instruments he designed are worth a visit alone, but note that Jantar Mantar in Jaipur, built by the same king, is both bigger and better preserved (see chapter 10).

The easiest way to take in central New Delhi's imperial architecture—for many the chief attraction—is to drive to **India Gate,** built to commemorate those who died in World War I. There an eternal flame burns in memory of those who gave their lives in the 1971 Indo-Pakistan war, their names inscribed on the memorial. Set off on foot west along **Rajpath** (the 3.2km/2-mile boulevard once known as King's Way) to the beautifully ornate gates of **Rashtrapati Bhavan,** flanked by the two almost identical **Secretariat buildings.** Having covered the architectural attractions of New Delhi, you can double back to **The National Museum** (see below) or catch a ride to the **National Gallery of Modern Art,** which lies near India Gate (Jaipur House; ☎ 011/2338-2835; Tues–Sun 10am–5pm; Rs 150/$3.40). Farther west lies **The Crafts Museum** (see below). Although the National Gallery is one of India's largest museums of modern art, it's pretty staid fare and unlikely to thrill those used to such Western shrines as London's Tate Modern or New York's Museum of Modern Art.

Other museums you may consider in the area include **Gandhi Smriti** ★ (Tees January Marg; ☎ 011/2301-2843; daily 10am–5pm). The colonial bungalow where Gandhi stayed when he was in Delhi, and where he was assassinated, it's more atmospheric than the museum near Raj Ghat in Old Delhi. **Nehru Memorial Museum and Library** (Teen Murti Marg; ☎ 011/2301-6734; Tues–Sun 9:30am–5pm; free admission) was the grand home of India's own "Kennedy clan": Nehru was India's first prime minister, a role his daughter and grandson, Indira and Rajiv respectively, were also to play before both were assassinated. Those interested in contemporary Indian history may wish to visit **Indira Gandhi Memorial Museum** (1 Safdarjung Rd.; ☎ 011/2301-0094; Tues–Sun 9:30am–4:45pm; free admission). A huge force in post-independence India (see "India Past to Present," in the appendix), Indira Gandhi was murdered here by her Sikh bodyguards. Among the displays (which provide a real sense of the woman) is her blood-soaked sari, as well as the clothes worn by her son Rajiv when he was killed in 1991.

The best temples to visit in central New Delhi are **Lakshmi Narayan Mandir** *⚜* (west of Connaught Place, on Mandir Marg; leave cameras and cellphones at counter outside), an ornate yet contemporary Hindu temple built by the wealthy industrialist B. D. Birla in 1938; and **Bangla Sahib Gurudwara** *⚜⚜* (off Ashoka Rd.), Delhi's principal Sikh temple. If you aren't heading north to the Golden Temple at Amritsar (see chapter 11 for more on Sikhism), a visit to the *gurudwara* is highly recommended, if only to experience the warm and welcoming atmosphere that seems to pervade all Sikh places of worship—evident in details like the efficient shoe deposit, a scarf to cover your head (both free), genuinely devoted guides who expect no recompense (available at the entrance), devotional hymns (sung constantly sunrise–9pm), free food (served three times daily), and *prasad* (communion) offered as you leave—be warned that it's very oily and you won't give offense if you decline. The *gurudwara* is certainly an interesting contrast to Lakshmi Narayan Mandir; a visit to one of the first Hindu temples to open its doors to all castes (including "outcasts" like the foreign Britishers) makes you feel very much like a tourist, whereas the more embracing atmosphere of the *gurudwaras* has you feeling rather humbled.

If all this sightseeing has you beat, you can retreat to **Lodi Gardens** (5km/3 miles south of Connaught Place), where green lawns surround the crumbling tombs of the 15th-century Sayyid and Lodi dynasties—the tombs are not well-preserved, but the green, shaded oasis may suffice as a break from the hectic traffic or shopping at nearby Khan Market (though I'd opt for a hotel pool). The 18th-century **Safdarjang's Tomb** lies just south of Lodi Gardens, but more impressive by far is **Humayun's Tomb** (a short rickshaw ride west) and, across the street, **Hazrat Nizamuddin Aulia** (both discussed below).

Finally, for the special-interest traveler, you can view India's largest collection of rare stamps free of charge at the **National Philatelic Museum,** located at the post office at Dak Bhavan (Sansad Marg; enter at back of post office; Mon–Fri 9:30am–4:30pm, closed 12:30–2:30pm).

New Delhi's Imperial Architecture *⚜⚜⚜*   Nehru wrote that "New Delhi is the visible symbol of British power, with all its ostentation and wasteful extravagance," but no one with any design interest fails to be impressed by the sheer scale and beauty of these buildings and the subtle blending of Indian influence on an otherwise stripped-down Western classicism—a far cry from the ornate Indo-Saracenic style so deplored by chief architect Sir Edwin Lutyens. Lutyens, known for his racist views, in fact despised all Indian architecture (he conveniently convinced himself that the Taj was actually the work of an Italian designer), but he was forced to include some "native" elements in his designs. Clearly, at first glance the Lutyens buildings of Central Delhi are symbols of imperial power intended to utterly dwarf and humble the individual, yet the Indian influences, such as the neo-Buddhist dome, tiny helmetlike *chattris* (cenotaphs), and filigree stonework, add a great deal to their stately beauty. Once the home of the viceroy of India, **Rashtrapati Bhavan** is today the official residence of the president of India and is closed to the public (though the Mughal Gardens, which are among the best in India, are open to the public in Feb). Note the slender column near the entrance gates, donated by the Maharaja of Jaipur. The two Secretariat buildings, designed by Sir Herbert Baker, show a similar subtle blend of colonial and Mughal influences and today house the Ministry of Home Affairs and the Home and Finance ministries. Northeast, at the end of Sansad Marg, is Sansad Bhavan (Parliament House), also designed by Baker, from where the country is managed (or not, as Booker

Prize–winner Arundhati Roy argues so succinctly in *The Algebra of Injustice*—a recommended but somewhat depressing read). Take a drive around the roads that lie just south of here (Krishna Menon Marg, for instance) to view the lovely bungalows, also designed by Lutyens, that line the tree-lined avenues.

The National Museum 𝕉𝕉   Okay, so this museum boasts 150,000 pieces covering some 5 millennia, but it is frustratingly hard for the layperson to traverse these hallowed corridors, some of which lie boarded up and empty, and all of which have displays with little or no information. That said, you can still find gems, like the **12th-century statue** of the cosmic dance of Lord Shiva (South Indian bronzes), which is almost an Indian archetype; and the truly wonderful collection of **miniature paintings**—this is one area (second floor) where you could easily spend a few hours. And if you have any interest in history, the sheer antiquity of many of the pieces will amaze you—here lies the country's finest collection of Indus Valley relics (ca. 2700 B.C.), as well as those garnered from central Asia's "Silk Route," but again very little is displayed in an accessible manner. This means that it takes time and effort (and preferably a guide) to appreciate the wealth of history that lies throughout the 30-odd galleries spread over three floors. If your visit coincides with one of the free tours offered, join in for a bit.

Corner of Janpath and Rajpath. ℂ **011/2301-9272.** Rs 150 ($3.40). Tues–Sun 10am–5pm. Free tours 10:30am–5pm.

The Crafts Museum 𝕉   If you plan to shop for crafts in India, this serves as an excellent introduction to what's out there, though when it comes to the antiques, like the 200-year-old life-size Bhuta figures from Karnataka or the Charrake bowls from Kerala, picking up anything nearly as beautiful is akin to winning a lottery. Some 20,000 artifacts—some more art than craft—are housed in five separate galleries, showcasing the creativity that has thrived here for centuries, not to mention the numerous ways in which it's expressed, depending on where you travel. The **Crafts Museum Shop** is also worth your time, at the very least to again familiarize yourself with the best crafts and textiles.

Bhairon Marg. ℂ **011/2337-1887.** Free admission. Tues–Sun 10am–5pm. Closed July–Sept.

Humayun's Tomb 𝕉𝕉𝕉   This tomb, built for the second Mughal emperor, launched a great Mughal architectural legacy—even the Taj, which was built by Humayun's great-grandson, was inspired by it. Though the Taj's beauty (and the money spent) eclipsed this magnificent example of a garden tomb, it's well worth a visit, even if your intention is to visit its progeny. Paid for by Humayun's "senior" wife, Haji Begum, and designed by the Persian (Iranian) architect Mirak Mirza Ghiyas, it's another grand testimony to love. Set in peaceful surrounds, the tomb features an artful combination of red sandstone and white marble, which plays with the wonderful symmetry and scale used by the makers of the Mughal empire. Though it doesn't have the fine detailing of the Taj, aspects such as the intricately carved stone trellis windows are lovely. If you're traveling on to Agra, it is interesting to see how the Mughals' prolonged stay in India started to influence design elements (the Persian finial that mounts the central marble dome was, for instance, later supplanted by the lotus). There are a number of outlying tombs, and if you want to do more than simply wander through the beautifully restored gardens and walkways and marvel at the sheer generosity of scale, this is again one place where the services of a guide are worthwhile. Hire one through your hotel or the central tourism office.

Lodi and Mathura Rd. ℂ **011/2435-5275.** Rs 250 ($5.70), Rs 25 (55¢) camera. Daily sunrise–sunset.

Hazrat Nizamuddin Aulia 🕉 Originally built in 1325, but added to during the following 2 centuries, the tomb of the saint Sheikh Nizamuddin Aulia (along with a few prominent others, including the favorite daughter of Shah Jahan) is one of the holiest Muslim pilgrimages in India. It is certainly one of Delhi's most fascinating attractions, not least because the only way to get here is to traverse the tiny, narrow medieval lanes of old Nizamuddin on foot. The entire experience will transport you back even further than a foray into Shahjahanabad. This is not for the fainthearted (or perhaps the recently arrived), however—the lanes are claustrophobic, you will be hassled by hawkers (perhaps best to purchase some flowers as sign of your good intentions upfront), and the smells are almost as assaulting as the hawkers who bar your way. Once there, you may be pressured into making a heftier donation (Rs 50/$1.15 is fair) than is necessary. This would in fact be a three-star attraction if it weren't for the sense that outsiders are not really welcome (though many have reported otherwise)—note that the main structure is a mosque, Jam-at Khana Masjid, and is closed to women. Best to dress decorously (women should consider covering their heads), pick up some flowers along the way, get here on a Thursday evening when *qawwals* gather to sing the most spiritually evocative devotional songs, take a seat, and soak up the medieval atmosphere.

Nizamuddin (6km/4 miles) south of Connaught Place. Donation expected.

SOUTH DELHI

Delhi's sprawling suburbs keep expanding southward, impervious of the remnants of the ancient cities they surround. Die-hard historians may feel impelled to visit the ruins of **Siri** (the second city), **Tughlaqabad** (the third) and **Jahanpanah** (the fourth), but the principal attraction here is the **Qutb Complex** (see below), built in the area that comprised the first city of Delhi. Located in Mehrauli Archaeological Park, it has a number of historic sites centered around the Dargah of Qutb Sahib, as well as a number of cafes and boutiques frequented by Delhi's well-heeled.

Nearby is **Hauz Khas** on the Delhi–Mehrauli road. Once a village, Haus Khas is now a gentrified upmarket suburb known more for its glossy boutiques and restaurants than for its 14th-century reservoir and ruins, including the tomb of Feroze Shah Tughlaq (Rs 100/$2.30). Rail enthusiasts shouldn't miss **The National Railway Museum** (📞 011/2688-1816; Tues–Sun 9:30am–1:30pm and 2:30–5pm; closes at 7pm Apr–Sept; Rs 10/25¢), said to be one of the world's most impressive—hardly surprising given India's huge network. It is situated southwest of Lodi Gardens, on Chanakyapuri. If you've traveled this far south, you may want to head a little east to the **Bahá'i House of Worship**, or "Lotus Temple," where 27 huge and beautiful marble "petals" create the lotus-shaped dome. Often likened to a mini-version of the Sydney Opera House, this contemporary temple invites people of all faiths for worship. It's sometimes described as a modern counterpoint to the Taj, but unlike the Taj, it's more photogenic than it appears in real life, with a lack of detailing and a drab interior (Bahapur, Kalkaji; 📞 011/2644-4029; Tues–Sun: 9am–7pm Apr–Oct, 9:30am–5:30pm Nov–Mar).

Qutb Complex 🕉🕉🕉 Originally built by Qutbuddin Aibak, first of the Delhi Sultanates who were to rule for some 4 centuries, the complex surrounds Qutb Minar, the sandstone Victory Tower that he started in 1193. The Minar was added to by his successor, Iltutmish (whose tomb lies in one corner); and the topmost stories, reaching 70m (234 ft.), were built in 1368 by Feroze Shah Tughlag. It is remarkably well preserved, and photographs don't really do the tower justice—not in scale, nor in the detail of its carving. The surrounding buildings show some of the earliest Islamic construction techniques used in India, as well as the first mingling of Islamic and Hindu decorative styles—Koranic texts are inscribed in the Minar and Alai Darwaza (old gateway to the complex), while Hindu motifs embellish the pillars of Quwwat-ul-Islam ("Might of Islam") mosque. The iron pillar in the courtyard dates back to the 4th century.

15km (9½ miles) south of Connaught Place on Aurobindo Marg, near Mehrauli. Rs 250 ($5.70), Rs 25 (55¢) camera. Daily sunrise–sunset.

WHERE TO STAY

The capital draws countless diplomats and businesspeople, which in turn has led to a thriving (and relatively pricey) five-star accommodations sector, with little innovation in the guesthouse or B&B areas (the big exception being the **Master Paying Guest House,** reviewed later in this chapter, which is the best place by far to stay if you're watching your rupees). As a result, you'll probably need to dig a little deeper in your pockets if you want a certain level of luxury—not a bad idea if this is your first stop in India. Although a five-star hotel may serve as a gentle introduction to India, most are a bland reproduction of what you can expect anywhere in the world, and some are downright hideous despite the hefty price tags. This is why we added a sidebar of all five-star properties we didn't include in our top picks, "Five-Star Hotels That Didn't Make the Grade," below (useful if they're part of a package you're buying). With so much parity in the top-end market, our hands-down recommendation is **The Imperial,** a classy hotel with an authentic colonial old-world atmosphere, friendly staff, superb restaurants, and the most central location (it's walking distance to Connaught Place). More of a brand, but still the ultimate in luxury, **The Oberoi** has the most lavishly cozy rooms of all the top-end hotels in Delhi, but you'll shell out for the privilege. It's worth checking the going rate at **Hyatt Regency,** which is not as conveniently located as either of these but operates specials throughout the year—you can often stay here for as little as $100 per night. Alternatively, check out **Oberoi Maidens,** Delhi's oldest hotel and one of the best-value options in Delhi. To decide among these, check out the full reviews below, and their websites. If you favor the trend toward intimate boutique-style hotels, **The Manor** 🏵🏵 (✆ **011/2692-5151;** www.themanordelhi.com; from $175) is a small luxury hotel that has been featured in a number of design books and magazines like *Tatler* and *Condé Nast Traveler.* Located in Friends Colony, a smart residential quarter in the southwestern part of New Delhi (in other words, not walking distance to anywhere), it has a fabulous chef and offers top-notch service, gracious lawns with pool, and an intimate atmosphere (18 rooms total). It is really one of the most elegant (all muted colors) and contemporary (a great mix of materials like silk, terrazzo, onyx, and granite) options in Delhi, and service in particular has improved even more since Amanresorts (whose clients stay here en route to Rajasthan) began operational assistance. Check it out yourself.

Note that if you're literally in transit, the **Radisson** 🏵 (National Highway 8, New Delhi 110 037; ✆ **011/2677-9191;** fax 011/2677-9090; www.radisson.com) is your best bet near the airport. It's perched on the edge of a major highway, but guest rooms (from $225) are large and sumptuous, with contemporary furnishings and king-size beds. Ask for a pool- or garden-facing unit.

Note: The prices below are sometimes given in rupees, with U.S. dollar conversions; others are stated in U.S. dollars only, which is how many hotels targeting foreign markets quote their rates.

Five-Star Hotels That Didn't Make the Grade

A stone's throw from Rajpath, but looming like a large glass-faced office block, is **Le Meridien** (Windsor Place, New Delhi 110 001; ℂ 011/2371-0101; www.lemeridien-newdelhi.com; doubles from $180). Endless holiday promotions and photo booths create a mall-like ambience, and even though the humongous chandelier in the lobby tries to create a more regal atmosphere, capsule elevators with twinkling lights go up and down the dark, casino-like atrium all day long—giving it a rather cramped and confused feel. Accommodations are comfortable enough, but as a place to relax and feel pampered, the hotel is a bit of a letdown. With its large room inventory and numerous food outlets, the **Grand Inter-Continental** (Barakhamba Ave., Connaught Place, New Delhi 110 001; ℂ 011/2341-1001; www. bharathotels.com; from $300 double) feels a bit like a small indoor city, offering practically everything you need so you never have to step outside, but the ambience is staid and the accommodations tasteless. **The Metropolitan Hotel Nikko CEN** (Bangla Sahib Rd., New Delhi 110 001; ℂ 011/2334-2000; $220), a member of the Japanese hotel chain, has a refined atmosphere, with a wildly eclectic mix of baroque furnishings and decorative elements. Unfortunately, the only real highlights here are the very chi-chi spa and authentic Japanese restaurant. Guest rooms are small and cluttered, with pastel-pink walls and ornate two-poster beds. The Taj Group has two five-star options in the city—and of the two, the **Taj Mahal Hotel** (see below) is far preferable. Slightly cheaper, the **Taj Palace Hotel** 𝒜 (2 Sadar Patel Marg, Diplomatic Enclave, New Delhi 110 021; ℂ 011/2611-0202; www.tajhotels.com; doubles from $235) pulsates with the energy of Delhi's bourgeoisie; at night it becomes a haven for see-and-be-seen weddings and gigantic corporate functions. The Western-style deluxe guest rooms are large and overlook the pool. Unfortunately, all the high-end social functions seem to have had a negative impact on service (this hotel has the longest checkout line in Delhi). Right next door is the **ITC Maurya Sheraton Hotel and Towers** 𝒜𝒜 (Diplomatic Enclave, New Delhi 110 021; ℂ 011/2611-2233; www.welcomgroup.com; from $300 double). Its location in the diplomatic sector and the expensive rooms are major drawbacks. On the positive side, it has two excellent Indian specialty restaurants. The other so-called five-star option in this neighborhood is the government-run **Ashok,** but it's tired and poorly managed, so definitely avoid this one.

Even farther south is the **Inter-Continental Eros** 𝒜 (Nehru Place, New Delhi 110 019; ℂ 011/5122-3344; www.newdelhi.intercontinental.com), which is a little more intimate than many of its competitors, with comfortable rooms and top-notch fittings and amenities (the best rooms have views of the Bahai Lotus Temple). It offers good value in the five-star category—doubles from only $180. **Marriott WelcomHotel** 𝒜 (District Centre, Saket, New Delhi 110 017; ℂ 011/5266-1122; newdelhi.marriott@welcomgroup.com) has rather small guest rooms priced at $210. You could do better elsewhere, particularly since the double-glazed bedroom windows fail to completely block out noise. If you do stay here, ask for a room on an upper floor.

NEW DELHI
Very Expensive
Claridges With nearly half a century behind it, this smart hotel—in a smart residential neighborhood, convenient to many Central Delhi sights—retains its authentic old-fashioned charm and period elegance but can't quite compete with The Imperial. A renovation in 2004 hardly justifies the corresponding steep jump (over 100%) in price. The cheapest accommodations are smart but slightly cramped. By contrast, the more expensive club suites are enormous; nos. 128 and 228 face the centrally located pool. Decor varies in style and color, but most rooms are carpeted and have some antique furniture and large bathrooms with tubs; those adjacent to the pool have marble floors and rugs (sacrificing historical ambience for a more contemporary look). It may not offer quite the same sophisticated luxury as the city's over-represented Western chains, but the Victorian aesthetic lingers, and you'll find friendly service and more than adequate amenities here. **Dhaba** is the hotel's Punjabi restaurant, done up like a roadside truck stop; it serves a refined, hygienic version of the simple, tasty food found along North India's busy highways.

12 Aurangzeb Rd., New Delhi 110 011. ℂ 011/2301-0211. Fax 011/2301-0625. info@claridges.com. www.claridges. com. 162 units. $265 deluxe double; $300 Claridges Room; $375 club suite, $600 deluxe suite, $750 luxury suite. $30 extra bed. Children under 12 stay free in parent's room. Check online for discounts. AE, DC, MC, V. **Amenities:** 4 restaurants; bar; patisserie; pool; health club; gym; sauna; steam; travel agency, car hire; business center; currency exchange; Wi-Fi enabled; shopping arcade; salon; 24-hr. room service; babysitting; laundry; dry cleaning; doctor-on-call. *In room:* A/C, TV, minibar, hair dryer, iron on request, electronic safe, scale, magnifying mirror.

The Imperial This gracious establishment (built in 1931) is the best hotel in Delhi—certainly for anyone wanting something a little more atmospheric than any chain, no matter how luxurious, can hope to offer. Only at The Imperial can you recover from your jet lag in luxury while experiencing something of the elegance of colonial-era Delhi—without even setting foot out of the lobby. It's also incredibly convenient (only a short stroll to Connaught Place) yet tranquil (it has one of the deepest, largest pools in Delhi). It's comfortable as well, having undergone a major renovation that left the Raj-era atmosphere untouched but loaded with every amenity you'd expect from a five-star hotel. Spacious guest rooms (no need for a suite; opt for an Imperial or Heritage Room) with wonderfully high ceilings are furnished in colonial-era elegance. However, it is the public areas, like the double-volume colonnaded veranda and grand 1911 bar, that are a sheer delight—huge, elegant (it's a word that tends to crop up whenever you try to describe The Imperial), and everywhere a showcase of Delhi's imperial past. A huge collection of original art adorns every corridor (a veritable museum of 18th- and 19th-century art, which you can explore with the resident curator). Silver-service breakfasts are among the best in the world. This quiet, dignified hotel is not only the perfect place to acclimatize, but we believe it ranks among the top city destinations in the world. Inevitably, prices have risen, but it's worth every penny.

1 Janpath, New Delhi 110 001. ℂ 011/2334-1234. Fax 011/2334-2255. www.theimperialindia.com. 232 units. $375 Imperial double, $500 Heritage double; $550–$3,900 suite. AE, DC, MC, V. **Amenities:** 5 restaurants; 2 bars; pool; fitness center; concierge; travel desk; car hire; Thomas Cook currency exchange; Wi-Fi enabled; bookshop; salon; 24-hr. room service; babysitting; laundry; dry cleaning; doctor-on-call; valet; art gallery. *In room:* A/C, TV, dataport, fax machine (on request), minibar, tea- and coffee-making facilities or butler service, hair dryer, electronic safe, scale, DVD player (all except Imperial Rooms).

The Oberoi If you like being treated with the reverence of a celebrity, this is the place to stay—just ask Harrison Ford, Mick Jagger, Nelson Mandela, and Salman

Rushdie. Even if you're not a star, staff are trained to genuflect—a typical characteristic of all the Oberoi hotels. Service aside, the hotel's location—east of the Lodi Gardens (near Humayun's Tomb) and surrounded by the green oasis of Delhi's golf course—makes for tranquillity. Its sophisticated elegance is also very relaxing—after a morning's sightseeing somewhere like Shahjahanabad, it's a great retreat. The carpeted guest rooms are richly textured, with upholstered carved wood furniture and bright pink scatter cushions offset with pale floral and paisley fabrics; walls feature artworks illustrating the rich variety of Indian culture. Bathrooms aren't huge but are impeccably decked out with top-notch fittings. The higher up your room, the better the view; odd-numbered rooms have views of Humayun's Tomb. The massive deluxe suites have private balconies, timber floors with rugs, large bathrooms with Jacuzzi tubs and bidets, cabinets with decorative inlay, and two-poster beds; executive suites are similarly lovely but more compact and not quite as lavish. Guest rooms on the top four floors not only have the benefit of excellent views, but also DVD players, complimentary breakfast, and free airport transfers.

Dr. Zakir Hussain Marg, New Delhi 110 003. © **011/2436-3030.** Fax 011/2436-0484. www.oberoihotels.com. reservations@oberoidel.com. 300 units. $350 premium double, $425 deluxe double; $650 executive suite, $900 deluxe suite, $1,400–$1,800 Presidential-Curzon. Rates include breakfast. Deluxe rooms onward include airport transfers. AE, DC, MC, V. **Amenities:** 4 restaurants; bar; patisserie; pool; health club; spa; concierge; travel desk, car hire; limousine service; shopping arcade; bookshop; salon; 24-hr. room service; Wi-Fi enabled; babysitting; laundry; dry cleaning; doctor-on-call; valet. *In room:* A/C, TV, dataport, fax machines (except 1st floor), minibar, tea- and coffee-making facilities or butler service, hair dryer, electronic safe, scale, magnifying mirror. Deluxe rooms and suites have DVD player.

Taj Mahal Hotel   This opulent, slightly brash hotel is not quite so massively over-the-top or overwhelming as its older sister, the Taj Palace Hotel, but it does have an exciting atmosphere and a range of superefficient amenities. Its major drawing card, however, is the high esteem in which it is held locally—this is one of the best places to watch the Delhi glitterati at play and work. Capped by *zardozi* domes, the carefully decorated lobby sees a variety of beautiful models and high-powered execs swishing in and out the front door. Despite wonderful service and every amenity you could wish for, guest rooms are unexceptional. You can splurge on a luxurious room on the Taj Club floor, where you'll enjoy a dedicated check-in after being fetched from the airport in a limousine, but at this price you may as well consider The Oberoi. A good-value alternative is to book at the Taj Group's Ambassador (see below) and hang out here (it has a great pool and restaurants) during the day.

Number One Mansingh Rd., New Delhi 110 011. © **011/2302-6162.** Fax 011/2302-6070. www.tajhotels.com. mahal.delhi@tajhotels.com. 296 units. $275 superior double, $300 deluxe double; $380 Taj Club (includes breakfast, limousine airport transfers, valet, and cocktail hour); $800–$5,000 suite. AE, DC, MC, V. **Amenities:** 5 restaurants; bar; pool; health center; concierge; travel desk; car hire; shopping arcade; bookshop; salon; currency exchange; florist; 24-hr. room service; babysitting; doctor-on-call. *In room:* A/C, TV, fax machine (all except superior), Wi-Fi enabled, minibar, tea- and coffee-making facilities, electronic safe.

Expensive

The Ambassador Hotel   Not far from Lodi Gardens and Humayun's Tomb, this hotel—operating since 1945—has an old-fashioned edge, with plenty of wood paneling and understated luxury. It's not particularly elegant, and standard guest rooms are small and cluttered, but it does provide good value. Our recommendation is to book a superior guest room (only $10 more), where French doors open onto private balconies. The bathrooms are large and enjoy natural light. Also pretty good value ($180) is the suite-size executive room, where a sliding door divides the bedroom from the comfortably furnished sitting room; sadly, the original Victorian fireplaces are now used for potted plants. Guests are entitled to make use of the extensive facilities offered by the flagship Taj Mahal hotel. The **Yellow Brick Road** coffee shop is bright and laid-back, with an open-kitchen concept and an ode-to-early-20th-century Americana decor. Less opulent and grandiose than some of the other upmarket hotels in town, this is a comfortable alternative with less formal but pleasant service.

Sujan Singh Park, Cornwallis Rd., New Delhi 110 003. ℂ **011/2463-2600.** Fax 011/2463-2252. www.tajhotels.com. ambassador.delhi@tajhotels.com. 88 units. $155 standard double; $165 superior double; $180 executive double; $200 deluxe suite. AE, DC, MC, V. **Amenities:** 2 restaurants; restaurant-bar; travel desk; currency exchange; bookshop; shopping arcade; salon; 24-hr. room service; Wi-Fi enabled; babysitting; doctor-on-call; access to Taj Mahal hotel facilities. *In room:* A/C, TV, minibar, tea- and coffee-making facilities, scale (except standard), iron and hair dryer on request.

The Hans Plaza Staff at this small hotel, conveniently located near Connaught Place, are wonderfully friendly and enthusiastic, which is a major draw. Filled with the strains of Indian classical music, the lobby is very 1980s, which is when the hotel was built. The deluxe guest rooms vary quite a bit: Ask for one on the 16th floor and you'll enjoy double beds with firm, comfortable mattresses and comfortable sofas, all in bronze-toned fabrics—very, neat, clean, and unexceptional; ask for one on the 18th floor, and you'll have a pleasant room with larger windows, but not the same good bed or furniture. The rooftop restaurant and bar afford grand views of the city.

15 Barakhamba Rd., Connaught Place, New Delhi. ℂ **011/2331-6861** through -6870. Fax 011/2331-4830. www. hanshotels.com. 67 units. Rs 5,000 ($114) superior double; Rs 6,000 ($137) executive suite, Rs 6,500 ($148) deluxe suite. Rates include breakfast. Some rates include transfer(s). AE, DC, MC, V. **Amenities:** Restaurant; bar; currency exchange; 24-hr. room service; babysitting; laundry; dry cleaning; doctor-on-call. *In room:* A/C, TV, dataport, minibar, hair dryer, iron on request, electronic safe, magnifying mirror, scale, tea- and coffee-making facilities (except superior room).

The Park ⚛ The pretty Park may be small, but its aspirations are high. A member of Small Luxury Hotels of the World, it fancies itself a boutique hotel, but with 224 rooms, it's a tad big for the category. That said, the accommodations, while not particularly spacious, do a good job of differentiating themselves from the look-alike luxury hotel rooms found elsewhere in town. Shades of yellow and orange create a warm ambience. Although the bathrooms are small, they feature tubs and elegant chrome fittings. Because of the curved shape of the hotel, guest rooms vary in size: The largest are near the elevators and at the corners of each floor—try to reserve no. 209, 309 or 409, or 211, 311, or 411. More expensive deluxe rooms occupy two separate floors of the "Residence" and are even more aesthetically pleasing, with smart furniture, in-room VCD (Video Compact Disc) players and Internet access, remote-controlled curtains, a bedside electronic console, and wonderful spring mattresses. Bathrooms have separate walk-in showers and Jacuzzi jets in the tub. For indulgences, there's a full spa; and **Agni**, the new bar designed by London's Conran & Partners, is worth popping into, not least for its funky decor. This is probably our favorite hotel in its price range.

15 Parliament St., New Delhi 110 001. ℂ **011/2374-3000.** Fax 011/2373-4400. resv.del@theparkhotels.com. 224 units. $225 luxury double; $250 club double; $275–$325 suite. $25 extra bed. Deluxe doubles and suites include airport transfers, breakfast, and happy hour. AE, DC, MC, V. **Amenities:** 2 restaurants; bar; pool; health club; gym; sauna; steam; travel desk; confectionery shop; gift shop; salon; 24-hr. room service; massage; babysitting; laundry; doctor-on-call. *In room:* A/C, TV, dataport, minibar, hair dryer, electronic safe. Residence rooms and suites include VCD player, personal hi-fi, computer on request. Suites have a fax machine.

Moderate

There is nothing exceptional in this price category, and what is good is often booked. Of the recommended options, two are located in the pleasant Sunder Nagar neighborhood, not far from Humayun's Tomb. The 50-room **Jukaso Inn** (49–50 Sunder Nagar; ℂ 011/2435-0308, -0309, or -2137; fax 011/2435-4402) has the most amenities (restaurant, room service, travel assistance). Public areas have gleaming white marble floors, but the best place to be is on the yellow painted terrace with its potted plants, tiny fountain, and wooden seats. The windowless basement rooms may be cheaper but aren't recommended; the best choice here is the suite, for which you will have to cough up Rs 5,000 ($114). Alternatively, ask for no. 208 or 209; each of these units has timber floors, a set of double beds, and a tub in the bathroom. Also in Sunder Nagar, located across the way from an open park, **La Sagrita Tourist Home** (14 Sunder Nagar; ℂ 011/2435-8572; www.lasagrita.com; Rs 2,490–Rs 3,090/$55–$70) is the most peaceful of the lodgings in the area, and the best value in its price bracket. Its major advantage is the generous amount of natural light that filters into some of the guest rooms. Specifically request room no. 203, which is large, with two double beds and plenty of window space. There's no restaurant, but the private garden makes a decent escape. If you'd rather be in Connaught Place, **Nirula's Hotel** (L-Block Connaught Circus, New Delhi 110 001; ℂ 011/5151-7070 through -7077; www.nirulas.com), a small two-story hotel linked to a swath of restaurants downstairs, is your best option. The tiny lobby is a sort of inner-city tribute to *Fawlty Towers* but without the sense of humor; accommodations are similarly uninspiring. Nevertheless, you are in the heart of India's capital, in an air-conditioned room with a TV, minibar, king-size bed (ask for room no. 202 or 205), and en-suite shower, for Rs 4,000 ($91). Much better value, however, is to choose Master Paying Guest House (below).

Inexpensive

Master Paying Guest House 🌟🌟 *Value*   Staying here is quite simply your best opportunity to discover what "real" Delhiites are all about: sophisticated, charming, and extremely knowledgeable. Filled with warmth and good taste, the guesthouse is owned and run by Avnish and Urvashi Puri. It's their energy and creative panache that make this a satisfying experience, as amenities are pretty basic. The four modest guest rooms occupy the two floors above their home; two of the rooms are located on the rooftop terrace. All rooms share two sets of immaculately clean bathroom facilities (showers only). You'll find comfortable beds, writing tables, and a carefully sourced objet d'art in each room, while the entire house is decorated with sculpted gods, handicrafts, and artworks. There's an aqua purification system, so you'll shower in cleaner water than the bottled stuff you drink, and an emergency inverter deals with Delhi's unpredictable electricity supply. Hot-water bottles and heaters are provided in winter, and there's air-conditioning when it gets warm. Home-cooked meals are prepared from fresh market ingredients and served in a small dining room—simply order by ringing a bell and jotting down your request. Meals are also served on the rooftop terrace; you'll find a scented garden nook as well as a meditation room cluttered with images of gurus and gods, and enthusiasts can enjoy an early-morning yoga session. The guesthouse is 4km (2½ miles) from Connaught Place, but Avnish offers a wonderful "Hidden Delhi" experiential tour through the city, showing you a world never seen by most visitors to Delhi, and he'll unravel Hinduism's spiritual origins in a profoundly logical way. Reserve in advance, and arrange for a pickup if you want to avoid haggling with taxi drivers at the airport; Avnish will also assist with onward transfers. The only drawback (for some) is that you feel more like a guest in someone's house than in a hotel, but again, this is the whole idea, and a very gentle introduction to India.

R-500 New Rajinder Nagar, New Delhi 110 060. © 011/2574-1089 or 011/2585-0914. www.master-guesthouse. com. 4 units. Rs 1,000 ($23) double. No credit cards. **Amenities:** Dining room; yoga; meditation; Reiki; transport assistance; airport transfers; sightseeing; excursions; laundry; hospital nearby; Internet access. *In room:* A/C, heater, electronic safe.

SOUTH DELHI

Hyatt Regency 🎖🎖🎖   Interesting design, unusual layout, and wonderful contemporary guest rooms mark this as one of the city's best hotels, and—depending on the day—certainly a winner when it comes to value. The lobby bears a faint resemblance to a Hindu temple, with mirrored panels and vaulted ceilings over rug-covered marble floors; accommodations have parquet wood floors and queen-size beds with lovely white duvets and thick mattresses. Pool-facing rooms are often only $20 more and are a much better size, while the "bay rooms" are even larger and not only have sleek designer furniture, but also gorgeous bathrooms with glass basins, large walk-in showers, and tubs. Hyatt Regency features the city's most authentic Italian restaurant (don't miss the pizzas here) and the famous **Djinns** pub (see "Delhi After Dark," later in this chapter). Expect fabulous service in all departments.

Bhikaji Cama Place, Ring Rd., New Delhi 110 066. © 011/2679-1234. Fax 011/2679-1122. www.delhi.hyatt.com. 508 units. From $218 double, but check website for current specials, as rates change daily. AE, DC, MC, V. **Amenities:** 4 restaurants; bar; nightclub; patisserie; pool; 2 tennis courts; fitness club; travel desk; currency exchange; shopping arcade; 24-hr. room service; babysitting; laundry; dry cleaning; doctor-on-call. *In room:* A/C, TV, dataport, minibar, tea-and coffee-making facilities, iron.

NORTH DELHI

Oberoi Maidens 🎖🎖 *Value*   This Georgian gem is a little out of the center of Delhi, but it has more character and charm than competitors charging twice its tariff. Delhi's oldest hotel, it retains much of its grand ambience, hinting at what it might have been like when Lutyens stayed here while supervising the development of the Raj Bhavan. Stained-glass windows, thick columns, stately arches, and deep corridors open to huge rooms on one side and small sunlit balconies on the other, all recalling a bygone style. Accommodations have been recently renovated and are carpeted, have high ceilings, and are done in elegant textiles. Room no. 105 is a particularly good option, with a second, smaller bedroom, and a large bathroom. It receives plenty of natural light, whereas some units have small windows. Lovely grounds, with plenty of established trees and bushes, and a period kidney-shaped pool, add further serenity, only disrupted when parties and weddings are hosted here (it's an understandably popular venue for wealthy families).

7 Sham Nath Marg, Delhi 110 054. © 011/2397-5464. Central reservations © 1 600 11 7070. Fax 011/2389-0595. www.maidenshotel.com. 56 units. $150 superior double; $180 executive suite, $225 deluxe suite. Check online for good off-season discounts. AE, DC, MC, V. **Amenities:** 2 restaurants; bar; pool; 2 tennis courts; travel assistance; car hire; currency exchange; 24-hr. room service; babysitting; laundry; doctor-on-call. *In room:* A/C, TV, minibar, hair dryer and iron on request.

WHERE TO DINE

Delhi doesn't enjoy the same reputation for its dining scene as Mumbai, but it's becoming increasingly lively as Delhi's smart, design-conscious elite steps out to see and be seen. That said, an irritating trend (at least for voyeurs) among the moneyed crowd is to eat at "members only" restaurants. The most popular of these very hip joints is **Oriental Octopus** (Habitat World, India Habitat Centre, Lodhi Rd.; © 011/2468-2222 or 5122-0000, ext. 2512), where you dine at curved, meandering tables shared by gorgeous designer-clad Delhiites—a million miles from the streets of Shahjahanabad. See if your concierge can arrange a reservation, or find a member and tag along. The food isn't bad either—start with Singaporean steamed spring rolls, and move on to Malaysian black-pepper prawns tossed in garlic and crushed pepper. It also has an interesting buffet spread for Rs 225 ($5.10). The smart set tend to hang out in the top hotel restaurants as well. Make every effort to dine at The Imperial's **Spice Route** (reviewed below); or book a table at **TK's Oriental Grill** (in the Hyatt) for great *teppanyaki* grills and the best salmon sashimi in town. If you're too nervous to dive headlong into the region's heavily spiced cuisine, the Hyatt is also where you'll find the best pizzas in town, at **La Piazza** ✸✸ (Bhikaji Cama Place, Ring Rd.; ✆ 011/2679-1234). Chef Mitele Sbardellini from Milan dishes out authentic Italian cuisine; plus an extensive wine list includes superb vintages from around the world, though the prices may have you gagging into your glass. Alternatively, for a more home-style Italian experience, there's **Flavors,** reviewed below.

VERY EXPENSIVE

Bukhara ✸✸✸ NORTHWEST FRONTIER   Staff at this international culinary flagship are immensely proud of the fact that Bill Clinton apparently chose to stay at the Maurya Sheraton "because of our restaurant," and report that when Putin was in town, he wanted to dine here three times a day. Hardly surprising then, that *Restaurant Magazine* rated Bukhara as one of the 50 best restaurants (and best Asian restaurant) in the world in 2004. It's a cozy venue, with stone walls and cushion-covered stools at mock log-top tables. In a busy display kitchen where meat and vegetables hang from swordlike kebab spears, chefs slave to produce delicacies from a menu that hasn't changed in over 25 years. The best way to experience Bukhara's internationally celebrated cuisine is to order an assorted kebab platter (there's even one named in Clinton's honor). Follow that up with any of Bukhara's classic lamb *(raan)* dishes, best savored with thin butter *naans.* Finish off with a traditional rice-based *phirni* pudding or one of their amazing *kulfis* (ice cream).

ITC Maurya Sheraton Hotel, Diplomatic Enclave. ✆ 011/2611-2233. Reservations 12:30–1:30pm and 7–8pm only. Main courses Rs 300–Rs 1,195 ($6.85–$27). AE, DC, MC, V. Daily 12:30–2:45pm and 7–11:45pm.

Haveli ✸✸✸ NORTH INDIAN   Besides the fact that Haveli's food is exceptional, it's almost worth a visit just to admire the sumptuous decor. One wall showcases fine floral frescoes and decorative reliefs, while the ceiling is adorned with carved wooden haveli eaves, gilt tiles, and Belgian chandeliers. In the evenings, musical and cultural performances are staged on a raised marble platform under a beautiful canopy. A great way to get a taste for North Indian cuisine is to order a Maharaja thali, a silver platter filled with tandoori prawns, masala chicken, spicy lamb, mixed vegetable curry, and heavenly black *dal,* a lentil specialty that's cooked for up to 20 hours over hot charcoal. Try the signature *murgh dhanya,* a mild chicken curry flavored with cilantro. (Note that the Taj Mahal Hotel also has a very good Chinese restaurant, **House of Ming;** it's not in the same class as Taipan in The Oberoi, but it's definitely easier on your wallet.)

Taj Mahal Hotel, Number One Mansingh Rd. ✆ 011/2302-6162. Main courses Rs 305–Rs 795 ($7–$18); thalis Rs 895–Rs 995 ($20–$22). AE, DC, MC, V. Daily 12:30–2:45pm and 7:30–11:45pm.

Masala Art ✸✸ CONTEMPORARY INDIAN   Artistic rendering of classic Indian cuisine is all the rage in the country's upscale city restaurants, and Masala Art makes a very conscious attempt to dazzle. The chefs turn cooking into performance art, putting on engaging food demonstrations at mealtimes; spectators eat whatever delicacies are produced. Of the daily a la carte specials, look for *achari jhinga* (prawns flavored with raw mango), and *galouti* kebabs prepared with finely minced lamb and 126 different herbs. If you're up for sharing a small feast, order *khushk raan,* a whole leg of lamb pot-roasted in a secret, heavenly marinade. Order homemade puffy *phulka* bread, made from ground wheat, on the side, and be sure to have a glass of fresh sugarcane juice or *bhune jeere ki chaas,* buttermilk seasoned with roasted cumin. End with *cheena payesh,* soft cottage cheese dumplings in reduced milk, topped with pistachios.

Taj Palace Hotel, 2 Sadar Patel Marg, Diplomatic Enclave. ✆ 011/2611-0202. Main courses Rs 325–Rs 950 ($7.35–$22). Food shows Rs 1,375 ($32) seafood, Rs 1,175 ($27) vegetarian or meat. AE, DC, MC, V. Daily 12:30–2:45pm and 7:30–11:45pm.

Orient Express ★★ FRENCH   You're best off dressing up for a meal in this posh replica of a Pullman Orient Express train carriage; look anything less than debonair and you're likely to be ignored. Enjoy pre-boarding drinks on the "platform," as the bar area is called, and scan the humidor for an expensive cigar. Your four-course journey is inspired by the countries through which the Orient Express passes on its Paris-to-Istanbul run, and is likely to include items such as Camembert soufflé with paprika sauce, pan-seared reef cod with raw papaya salad, and the extremely popular oven-roasted New Zealand rack of lamb, encrusted with herbs and almonds and served with lamb jus. Fish is flown in fresh daily—from France. Although the menu changes three or four times a year, one item will never be replaced: the sinful but wonderful warm chocolate pudding with a liquid chocolate center.

Taj Palace Hotel, 2 Sadar Patel Marg, Diplomatic Enclave. ✆ 011/2611-0202. Reservations essential. Children under 17 not allowed for dinner. 4-course meal Rs 2,395 ($55); 3-course meal Rs 2,095 ($48). AE, DC, MC, V. Daily 12:30–2:30pm and 6:30–11:30pm.

The Spice Route ★★★ ASIAN   It was voted one of the top 10 restaurants in the world by *Condé Nast Traveler,* and it certainly lives up to its promise with a vast menu that makes the mouth water at the variety of flavors and ingredients. The decor alone is worth a visit—every nook and cranny is hand-painted by temple artists flown in from Kerala, and antique beams, pillars, and ceilings are all imbued with meaning. The restaurant took 9 years to complete, and is divided into nine sections, each representing an aspect of the "journey of life"—for instance, the Wealth section is embellished with 24-karat gold leaf, whereas the Ancestral section has replicas of panels from Thai temples. If the evening is balmy, sit in the tranquil courtyard and be prepared to be blown away by the food—the best *tom kha kai* ever (the classic Thai soup, made with spicy chicken and coconut milk, flavored with lemon grass and kafir leaves) and mouthwatering *chemeen thoren* (Kerala-style prawns, stir-fried with coconut, curry leaves, and black tamarind, and flavored with mustard seeds). *Kung nang phad khing* is stir-fried lobster with ginger and Thai black mushrooms, and *malu miris* is composed of vegetables, coral mushrooms, and water chestnuts cooked in a Sri Lankan curry. As indicated by the name, the menu takes you on a complex culinary journey, from the Malabar Coast to Sri Lanka, Malaysia to Indonesia, Thailand to Vietnam. And although the lobster and the like are pretty pricey, you won't regret ordering them. There are plenty of other dishes in the Rs 400-to-Rs 600 ($9.10–$14) range. Service is superb—smart, discreet, and helpful.

The Imperial, 1 Janpath. ✆ 011/2334-1234. Main courses Rs 400–Rs 950 ($9.10–$22). AE, DC, MC, V. Daily 12:30–2:45pm and 7–11:45pm.

The Taipan ★★★ CHINESE   Singaporean chef Thian serves up amazing dim sum at this popular Chinese restaurant, arguably the best in town. Steamed and served in special bamboo baskets, Chinese dim sum are tiny dumplings filled with an assort-ment of tasty morsels; they draw a dedicated following, and it's quite possible to fill up on these starters without even moving on to the main courses. And, at lunchtime, when you can enjoy the fantastic view over Delhi Golf Course, an assorted platter of dim sum is ideal for a tasty midday meal that won't leave you feeling stuffed for the rest of the day. If you're up for a complete meal, don't miss the fantastic Peking duck or the chef's special, chicken tapering chili (sliced chicken and whole long tapering chilies, flavored with a light soya sauce). The chicken is not half as pungent as it sounds, unless you eat the whole chilies.

The Oberoi, Dr. Zakir Hussain Marg. ② **011/2436-3030**. Reservations recommended, essential on the weekend. Main courses Rs 350–Rs 1,600 ($8–$37); average veg dish Rs 400 ($9.10); non-veg dish Rs 550 ($13). AE, DC, MC, V. Daily 12:30–2:45pm and 7:30–11:45pm.

EXPENSIVE

Thai Wok 🎇🎇🎇 THAI   This is one of the best ways to enjoy Delhi, which is prob-ably why Delhi's smart crowd loves this designer-chic rooftop restaurant, with views of the Qutb Minar. Reached via an ancient elevator and a short set of stairs, the art-ful alfresco setting includes a bright-orange walled area with cushioned seating, wall torches, wind-blown pagodas, and white curtains that enhance an airy feel; reserve well ahead to sit here. The affable host will make plenty of recommendations; find out if the wonderful pork spareribs, marinated in Thai herbs and topped with a honey and garlic sauce, are on offer. Seafood dishes are exceptional; try red snapper in chili-sour sauce, prawns stir-fried with fresh green chilies and sweet basil, or deep-fried filet of sole tossed in chopped garlic and freshly crushed black pepper. Vegetarians will love the super-light batter-fried vegetables and outstanding green curry. Try one of the delightfully decadent cocktails or peruse the extensive wine list with vintages from France, Italy, Spain, Australia, Chile, New Zealand, and California—all at hefty prices, of course.

1091/1 Ambavata Complex, Mehrauli. ② **011/2664-4289**. Reservations highly recommended; essential on week-ends. Main courses Rs 195–Rs 400 ($4.50–$9.10). AE, MC, V. Noon–11:30pm. Snacks only, 3:30–7pm.

Turquoise Cottage 🎇 THAI/CHINESE   Another option (like Thai Wok) if you're in the Qutb Minar area, this smart Asian restaurant has turquoise walls, dark stone floors with turquoise tiles, wrought-iron furniture, contemporary chandeliers, and a fish tank or two. Start with an assortment of dim sum dumplings (mouthful-size por-tions of minced seafood, chicken, meat, or vegetables wrapped in handmade wontons and steamed). Then move on to a barbecue platter; it comes with spareribs, satay chicken, filet of sole, and prawns. Other interesting dishes include black-pepper crab, spicy basil prawns, crispy shredded lamb, stuffed squid, and pork chops prepared with fragrant lemon grass. After you've eaten, join the young, hip crowd in the bar down-stairs for some super-size vodka shots.

81/3 Adhchini, Sri Aurobindo Marg. ② **011/2685-3896** or 011/5168-1288. Reservations essential Wed, Fri, and Sat. Main courses Rs 85–Rs 500 ($2–$11). AE, DC, MC, V. Daily 12:30–3pm and 7:30–11:30pm.

MODERATE

Sagar is one of Delhi's favorite restaurant chains, serving reliable vegetarian South Indian food at reasonable prices till 11pm. Have one of the South Indian thali platters (Rs 72/$1.60), and eat with your hands. End your meal with Madrasi filter coffee, or you can start your day the same way—the restaurant opens at 8am, which is the best time for traditional *idli* (South India's favorite breakfast dumplings) and chutney. You'll find a good outlet at 18 Defence Colony Market (© **011/2433-3110** or 5565-0961); Defence Colony is about 10 minutes from India Gate. A popular lunchtime venue is **Basil and Thyme** ☞ (Santushti Shopping Complex, New Wellington Camp; © **011/2467-3322**), where you can taste playful experiments with healthy Continental fare from the kitchen of 82-year-old Bhickoo Maneckshaw. The day's special and other healthy selections rarely fail to please, and the fabulous homemade cheesecakes and ice creams should be declared illegal. Reserve ahead.

Chor Bizarre ☞☞ NORTH INDIAN/KASHMIRI   A fantasy of kitsch twisted into a unique and wonderful space that is more irreverent museum than diner, this is one restaurant that truly lives up to its name. Its name a pun on *chor bazaar,* which literally means "thieves' market," Chor Bizarre is packed with fascinating odds and ends, mismatched settings, out-of-place furnishings, and reassembled bits and pieces (matchboxes, coins, chessboards, antique combs, ivory sandals, jewelry, chandeliers, a jukebox . . .), innovatively displayed to create one of India's most visually dynamic restaurants (a branch of which is now also open in London). One table was previously a Maharaja's bed, while a 1927 vintage Fiat has become the buffet-carrying "*Chaat* mobile." Start with deep-fried lotus roots, prepared Kashmiri-style, and move on to *kakori kebab,* lamb marinated in 36 different spices and grilled in a tandoor. Cardamom-flavored lamb meatballs *(goshtaba)* are another delicious Kashmiri specialty, slow-cooked over an open flame. Alternatively, if you're up for a feast, try the Kashmiri *taramis* (thali), filled with treats and served from a traditional royal platter. Ask about walking tours that combine lunch with sights in Old Delhi.

Hotel Broadway, 4/15 A Asaf Ali Rd. (central New Delhi). © 011/2327-3821. Main courses Rs 290–Rs 395 ($6.75–$9); thalis Rs 245–Rs 345 ($5.65–$7.90); Rs 595 ($14) walking tour and set menu lunch. AE, DC, MC, V. Daily noon–3:30pm and 7:30–11:30pm.

Fa Yian ☞ *Finds* CHINESE   Judging by the exterior and the neighborhood, this might at first seem the type of place you don't want to be at night. But grit your teeth and venture inside—the brainchild of Gregory Kuok, this is the most authentic Chinese restaurant in Delhi, and the well-established menu has been tried and tested by some of the city's fussiest diners for well over a decade. Steamed wheat dumplings, filled with prawns, chicken, or vegetables and served with a garlic soya dip, are what gave Fa Yian its excellent reputation. The dumplings are prepared, along with the homemade noodles, fresh each day. Try these as a starter, followed by honey chicken, pepper-salt jumbo prawns, or the Fa Yian hot pot, which is prepared at the table according to your taste. Fish, brought in from Mumbai and steamed with a delicate hint of ginger, is lovely. Covering two levels, the ambience is relaxed and simple; ask for a table upstairs. Service is friendly and casual.

A Block, 25/5 Middle Circle, Connaught Place. © 011/2332-3237 or 011/5151-6788. Main courses Rs 135–Rs 165 ($3.05–$3.75); prawns Rs 465 ($11). AE, DC, MC, V. Daily noon–3pm and 7–11pm.

Flavors ☞☞ HOME-STYLE ITALIAN   Genuine home-style Italian cooking is the hallmark of Delhi's favorite Italian restaurant. Italian owner-chef Tarsilo Nataloni began this as an ice-cream shop and soon expanded to an extensive menu. Unless it's a blistering summer day and you prefer the air-conditioned section, grab a seat at a pretty wrought-iron table on the veranda. Order a wonderfully refreshing pink ginger fizz to sip on while you decide on what to eat. You could snack on panini made with ciabatta and imported cheese and meats, or get a delicious Greek salad followed by one of the perfect wood-fired oven pizzas (try the unusual pizza peri-peri). Flavors serves consistently good food, so go ahead and order any of the risottos or the fresh homemade pastas—you won't be disappointed. Pleasant young college students wait tables here (a rarity in India), and are eager to chat if you care for interaction; if not, this is a perfect spot for a relaxed evening after an exhausting day navigating Delhi's streets (about 10 min. drive south from India Gate; 10 min. drive east of Lodi Gardens). Advance booking is recommended on weekend evenings.

Moolchand Flyover Complex, Defence Colony, New Delhi. ⒸⒸ 011/2464-5644. Reservations recommended; necessary on weekends. Most main courses Rs 300–Rs 350 ($6.85–$8). AE, MC, V. Daily 11am–midnight.

Park Balluchi ⒶⒶⒶ MUGHLAI/AFHGHANI A regular winner of India's Tourism Award for the country's best restaurant, Park Balluchi enjoys a magical setting on the grounds of Delhi's leafy Deer Park, in Hauz Khas. Turbaned waiters in waistcoats and long shirts serve an extensive range of kebabs and spicy tandoor items. For some light drama, order Afghani-style *murgh-potli* (tandoori chicken): chicken breast stuffed with minced mutton and served over a flaming sword. The specialty at Balluchi is the *dohra kebab,* a unique combination of two meats. Vegetarians should order *mewa paneer tukra,* Indian cottage cheese stuffed with raisins, sultanas, walnuts, and other nuts; preparation of this dish takes at least 12 hours. Be sure to get a side order of *peshawri naan,* bread cooked in the tandoor oven with poppy seeds and coriander leaves. As you eat, you will likely catch a glimpse of scampering rabbits or strutting peacocks, making this an ideal lunch venue.

Deer Park, Hauz Khas Village. Ⓒ **011/2685-9369.** Reservations for dinner and weekends essential. Main courses Rs 180–Rs 530 ($4.10–$12). AE, MC, V. Daily noon–11:45pm.

Punjabi By Nature Ⓐ PUNJABI You'll know from the many Sikh families that eat here that this is one of Delhi's best-regarded Punjabi restaurants, with two floors for diners and a pub upstairs, all a mere 10 minutes' drive west of Haus Khas Village (or 15 min. from Safdarjung's tomb, the Hyatt Regency, or the Santushi Shopping Complex). On the first floor is a display kitchen where you can watch tandoori items and desserts being made; ask for a table here, where it's more atmospheric. Try tandoori trout, flown in from the icy streams of Himachal Pradesh, or masala quail *(bataear masaledar).* Lobster is brought fresh from Mumbai and cooked to perfection in the tandoor oven. Vegetarians can look forward to tandoori broccoli, prepared in a mustard marinade; or *sarson ka saag,* fresh mustard greens served with homemade cornmeal bread. Try the house specialty, a "gol gappa" shot: a tiny *puri* (fried puffed bread) filled with vodka, which you pop into your mouth whole.

11 Basant Lok, Vasant Vihar. Ⓒ **011/5151-6665** through -6669. Main courses Rs 225–Rs 495 ($5.10–$11); prawns Rs 495 ($11); lobster Rs 750 ($17). AE, DC, MC, V. Daily 12:30–3:30pm and 7:30–11:30pm.

The Rampur Kitchen ⒶⒶ NORTH INDIAN Named for a former princely capital in Uttar Pradesh, this bright, yellow-walled restaurant is a fantastic place for meat-eaters, and ideal if you've been browsing the Khan Market. It's intimate and extremely clean, with modern artworks depicting scenes from Delhi life. The Muslim food here is rich—the chefs don't exactly hold back on the ghee. Try *seekh kebab Rampuri,* tasty mutton kebabs that are generously spiced, mixed with boiled egg whites, and grilled over charcoal. *Gosht nahari* is a delicious mutton dish prepared in thick, spicy onion gravy and cooked overnight on a slow fire. Another delicacy is *haleem,* made from a thick mutton paste mixed with spices and pulses and garnished with chilies and ginger; order tasty *kulcha* bread as an accompaniment. Alcohol is not available.

8A Khan Market. (© 011/2460-3366 or 98682-60361. Reservations recommended. Main courses Rs 130–Rs 250 ($3–$5.70). DC, MC, V. Daily noon–3:30pm and 7–11pm.

INEXPENSIVE

With the explosion of Starbucks-style cafes all over the capital, few stand out for their distinctiveness. **Café Turtle** *ℱℱ*, perched above Full Circle Books and Music Store in Khan Market, is one lovely exception (© 011/2465-5641). Sit on the roof terrace surrounded by the tops of beautiful trees and sip fresh coffee or fragrant teas. Little disturbs your calm, as soft jazz plays in the background—unless, that is, you want a culinary adventure; if so, come here on a Saturday afternoon to sample something new, different, and off-the-menu. **United Coffee House** *ℱ* began 5 decades ago as a coffeehouse; now it's also a multi-cuisine restaurant. Fresh brews are brought to your table in a French press. Interesting Art Deco interiors, good Indian food, and happy hours that extend from late afternoon to 8pm make this a favorite with locals and travelers alike. You'll need to make a reservation for dinner (E-15, Inner Circle, Connaught Place; © 011/2341 or -6075). If on a meander through Hauz Khas you crave an inexpensive North Indian meal, stop at **Baujee ka dhaba** (18 Hauz Khas Village; © 011/2652-5511). Brightly painted *Madhubani* murals cover the walls of this restaurant, which has been outfitted to resemble a *dhaba* (a highway food stop). Even though the place has a thatched ceiling, hand-painted pots, and bamboo lampshades, it's far from a real *dhaba*, however. It might have captured the essence as far as the setting goes, but the food is distinctively Mughlai and Punjabi fare, rich and heavy, but unquestionably well-made and delicious. Get the ever-popular *shammi* kebab or *dum pukht* chicken. Or just nibble on assorted kebabs while you enjoy a reasonably priced chilled beer.

Karim Restaurant *ℱ* MUGHLAI   In the heart of Old Delhi, not far from the Jama Masjid, this legendary eatery dates back to 1913, when it was opened by a chef who hailed from a family of royal cooks who served, among other guests, the great Mughal emperor, Akbar. Come here for the food, and don't be put off by the informal setting; this is the genuine thing. It's primarily a meat-eaters' hangout, and the real princely treats are mutton *burra* kebabs. The butter-cooked chicken *(makhani murgh)* is also wonderful, as is the *badshahi badam pasanda,* mutton cooked with blended almonds and yogurt and fragrant spices. If you're really adventurous, you can also sample exotic fare such as spiced goat trotters, or the advance-order *bakra* feast—lamb stuffed with chicken, rice, eggs, and dried fruit, a meal made for a dozen people.

16 Jama Masjid, Matiya Mahal, opposite Hotel Bombay Orient. (© 011/2326-4981 or -9880. www.karimhoteldelhi. com. Main courses Rs 51–Rs 180 ($1.15–$4.10); *bakra* Rs 3,800 ($86). No credit cards. Daily 7am–midnight.

Naivedyam *ℱℱ* SOUTH INDIAN VEGETARIAN   Delhi has three branches of this fantastic little South Indian restaurant; the one in Hauz Khas is the original, atmospherically decorated with mirror-framed Tanjore paintings and pillars that have been beautifully carved and embossed. Soothing temple music fills the subtly lit interior. You start your meal with a spicy peppery lentil soup, called *rasam,* which is drunk as a curative and is something of an acquired taste. *Thalis,* or multicourse platters, are served at meal times, and are a good way to sample a variety of tastes from the South. Alternatively, you can choose from a whole range of *dosas* (akin to a pancake). Try *tangam paper masala dosa;* it's a paper-thin pancake made from rice and lentil flour. The ingredients may sound ridiculously simple, but *dosas* easily become addictive. On the side you'll be served chutney made from ground coconut and green chilies, and *sambar*, a souplike concoction of lentils, tamarind, and vegetables. Tea and coffee are served in the style typical of the South, but there's no alcohol. You'll recognize the restaurant by the stone Nandi bull statue that faces the front entrance.

1 Hauz Khas Village. © **011/2696-0426**. Main courses Rs 45–Rs 75 ($1–$1.70); thali Rs 90 ($2.05). AE, DC, MC, V. Daily 11am–11pm.

SHOPPING

The Delhi shopping experience is every bit as exciting as that found in Mumbai and Jaipur, but the sprawling size of the city makes it difficult to cover all in one day— best to concentrate on one area at a time. And if this is your first port of call, try not to load your luggage too early with stuff to take home. It is a good idea, however, to pop into Dilli Haat (reviewed below) to get a perspective of the range of regional arts and crafts and approximate prices. If something here really captures your heart, by all means get it and have it shipped home, for it may not be available when you return. Note that most shops (and markets) are open from 10am to 7pm and are closed on Sunday, unless mentioned otherwise. Besides the areas described below, you can spend an entire day covering the old city of Shahjahanabad (see "The Top Attractions," earlier in this chapter). Finally, keep in mind that the recommended shops that follow are only a fraction of what's out there; if you know what you're looking for, it's best to inquire at both your hotel and the Janpath tourist office for alternatives.

Connaught Place   If you want to get an idea of what lies ahead on your travels, you should definitely visit **Central Cottage Industries Emporium** on Janpath (across from The Imperial hotel, near Connaught Place), a huge, multistory complex brimming with quality goods from Pashminas to bronzes, from all over India (© **011/ 2335-8863**). *Tip:* If you've hired a car and driver for the day, note that this is the only spot in the area you will find parking, so it's best to visit here first and have the car wait for you while you browse the rest of Connaught Place. You can then visit a few of the 22 **State Government Emporiums** that line Baba Kharak Singh Marg; some recommended options are Himachal for blankets and shawls in particular (© **011/ 2336-3087**); Tamil Nadu ("Poompuhar") for sandalwood objects (© **011/2336- 3913**); Uttar Pradesh ("Gangotri") for the stone-inlay work made famous by the Taj, as well as copper/brasswork and leather goods (© **011/2336-4723**); **Kashmir Emporium** for superb carpets; and Orissa (Utkalika) for fabrics and traditional paintings (the latter off the beaten tourist track). If you're not moving on to Rajasthan, don't miss visiting both this and **Gurjari Emporium.** Both Cottage Industries Emporium and State Government Emporiums have fixed prices, so you are spared the incessant haggling you'll have to master elsewhere. Diagonally opposite Cottage Industries, also on Janpath, is the **Tibetan Market,** where it is said you will pick up a better selection of items (from antique locks to silver jewelry) at better prices than you will anywhere in Tibet. Having walked its length, you will find yourself in Connaught Place, the retail heart of imperial Delhi, where hundreds of outlets vie for your rupees. Visit **Benaras Silk House** for saris and the most beautiful fabrics on earth (N-13 Connaught Place, opposite Scindia House; © **011/2331-4751**). Then go to **Handloom House** to compare selection and prices (9A Connaught Place; © **011/2332-3057**). Head to **Jain Super Store** (172 Palika Bazaar, Gate 6; © **011/2332-1031;** www.jain perfumers.com) for perfumes, incense, and teas; it also has a store at 17 M. M. Janpath called **Arihant Fragrances,** which sells lovely silver jewelry alongside fabulous scented products. Stop at **Shaw Brothers** (Shop 8, Palika Bazaar; © **011/2332-9080**

or 011/2331-6573) for pure, high-quality Kashmiri shawls and elegant Pashminas—even if you don't buy, this is pretty much a must-see. For beautiful (and expensive) gemstones, gold jewelry, and bridal wear, try **Bholanath** (L-23 Connaught Circus) or nearby **Kapur di Hatti** (L-16), which also has Kundan jewelry.

Khan Market & Sunder Nagar Market   Khan Market is good for books, music, and DVDs. Sunder Nagar is considered the best market to trawl for authentic antiques, interesting secondhand goods, and unique artworks; it has a few good permanent stalls such as **Natesans** (13 Sunder Nagar Market; © 011/2435-9320), renowned for the quality of its artifacts and antiques (though these can be pricey). Browse **Anokhi** (32 Khan Market; © 011/2460-3423), patronized by expats and locals alike for its highly fashionable blend of Western- and Eastern-style clothing (see "Jaipur: Shopping" in chapter 10 for full review of the Anokhi headquarters), or its store at 9 Khan Market for lovely furnishings.

South Delhi   Seek out **Ravissant** (© 011/2683-7278; www.cest-ravissant.com) in New Friends Colony for beautiful contemporary pewter and silver houseware items (or visit the outlet conveniently located in The Oberoi hotel lobby). **Santushti Shopping Complex** is an upscale collection of shops (predominantly boutiques) housed in landscaped gardens 15 minutes from the center. Visit **Lotus Eaters** (© 011/2688-2264) to pick up a pretty jewelry item.

Even farther south (convenient to visit after viewing Qutb Minar) is trendy Hauz Khas Village, set against a 12th-century backdrop; and, slightly southeast (40 min. from the center), Greater Kailash—the latter shopping area (divided into M and N blocks) is the least atmospheric but has a large variety of shops in an upmarket atmosphere. Hauz Khas is the place to seek out designer boutique outlets, like Ritu Kumar (E-4; © 011/2656-8986 or -8097). Or head straight for Ogaan (H–2 Hauz Khas; © 011/2696-7595)—the formalwear version of Anokhi, it's perfect for unusual Indo-West and contemporary Indian designer clothing (it stocks a number of well-known labels). Hauz Khas also has a number of fine restaurants. (See "Where to Dine," above). **Tandon's** (4 Aurobindo Place; © 011/2696-6552) has high-quality Lucknow "Chikan" embroidered linen and clothing. For wonderful tailor-made garments, make your way to **Kavita & Vanita Sawhney** (B-78 Greater Kailash I; © 011/2646-4633). The most famous shop in N Block is **Fabindia** (see review below), specializing in stylish ethnic Indian homewear and clothing for all ages.

Dilli Haat ✿✿   This open area imitates a *haat* (rural marketplace), where 200 little stalls form a permanent open-air arts-and-crafts market. It's a unique shopping experience, and the most authentic and affordable in Delhi. Dilli Haat offers you the opportunity to buy directly from rural artisans and craftspeople who are allotted space rotationally for 2 weeks, making this a great place to browse the variety of crafts from all over India, whether you are traveling farther afield or not. From Bihar's *Madhubani* art to silver jewelry and furniture, as well as unusual gifts and souvenirs or colorful linens and other furnishings, the range is exhausting, the prices excellent. If you are in Delhi in early December, be sure to check out the **Master Crafts Fair** (normally held Dec 1–15), where award-winning artists and craftspeople display and sell their work. Numerous food stalls serve food from all over India, but the hygiene is questionable. Daily 10am to 10:30pm. Aurobindo Marg, opposite INA Market. New Delhi 110 023. © 011/2611-9055. Entry Rs10.

Fabindia ✿✿   If you've coveted Indian ethnic-chic at stores like the Conran Shop in London or New York, here's your chance to buy the fabrics and crafts at one-tenth the price. Fabindia sources its products from more than 7,500 craftspeople and artisans around India. Their distinctive use of handloom weaving techniques, natural dyes, and both vivid and earthy colors have made their products both fashionable and desirable. Do bear in mind that these fabrics usually require gentle hand washing and drip-drying. Also, sizing and quality are inconsistent, so it's best to try on any item of clothing before you buy. There are branch stores all over India as well as in Rome and Dubai. N Block Market and Greater Kailash Part I: daily 10am to 7pm. Khan Market store: Monday to Saturday 10am to 7pm. 13, 14, 15, (garments) and 5, 7, 9 (furnishings) N-Block Market, and Greater Kailash Part I. ✆ 011/2621-2183 through -2185. Fabindia Craft Store, Central Hall, Khan Market. www.fabindia.com. ✆ 011/5175-7141.

DELHI AFTER DARK

For current events and entertainment, pick up a copy of *The Delhi City Guide,* the weekly *Delhi Diary,* or the monthly *First City.*

Music, Dance & Film A worthwhile daily event is **Dances of India,** held at the Parsi Anjuman Hall, Bahadur, Shah Zafar Marg (✆ **011/2323-1228** or -8615). One of the most interesting (though touristy) evening shows in Delhi is the sound-and-light show held at **Red Fort;** most hotels will arrange tickets (Rs 150/$3.40). Call the **India Habitat Centre** (Lodhi Rd.; ✆ **011/2468-2222**) for information on theater, film festivals, and other cultural events held almost nightly. Nearby is **India International Centre** (✆ **011/2461-9431**), which also hosts a variety of cultural performances and film screenings (mostly in the cooler months of the year), as does **Siri Fort's auditorium** (Khelgaon Marg; ✆ **011/2649-3370**) in South Delhi. Entry to most events is free.

Bars & Pubs Cultural attractions aside, Delhi is in many ways most interesting at nighttime, when the "conspicuous consumers" to whom William Dalrymple refers in his *City of Djinns* head out and schmooze—to this end, **Djinns** (Bhikaiji Cama Place, Ring Rd.; ✆ **011/2679-1234**), named after Dalrymple's book, is worth a look. Located in the Hyatt Regency, the legendary pub attracts a mixed crowd, though rarely the hard-partying kind—a group in some ways as varied as the kitsch collectibles that deck the bar, everything from a red London telephone booth to a 1988 Iron Maiden concert poster (with Kiss, David Lee Roth, and Guns 'n' Roses supporting!). Like Djinns, **Dublin** is a very popular pub that also has a dance floor, though that's not the primary attraction (ITC Maurya Sheraton Hotel, Diplomatic Enclave; ✆ **011/2611-2233**). It has the largest selection of single malts in Delhi, and with its Irish theme decor fancies itself Delhi's most exclusive club. Which is why it's a members- and hotel-guests-only bar. If you want to enter, however, it's easy enough: Wait at the door and *just ask*—a member will happily sign you in. Wednesday night is media night, where hacks from all over the city congregate, while on Friday and Saturday DJ Sunny spins popular commercial music—a mix of fast-paced rhythms from hip-hop to '90s rock and even London bhangra.

For a more genteel and upmarket atmosphere, head to **Rick's** (1 Mansingh Rd.; ✆ **011/2302-6162**) at the Taj Mahal Hotel, where you can sip some of the best cocktails in Delhi while watching the city's fashionable set unwind. A DJ (Wed–Sat) plays retro music from 10:30pm onwards. Far more formal, and perhaps a tad demure, is **Club Bar** (The Oberoi, Dr. Zakir Hussain Marg; ✆ **011/2436-3030**); relaxed and spacious, and good for cigar smokers, it's the sort of place where you find yourself discussing business deals. **1911 Bar** in The Imperial (✆ **011/2334-1234**), with its horseshoe-shaped bar, quilted leather Montana chairs, vintage portraits, and stained-glass roof, is an elegant place to enjoy an evening drink; despite the TV stuck on sports channels, it attracts a discriminating clientele that includes expats, celebs, and political bigwigs. Another popular watering hole and lounge is **Q'Ba** (E 42-43 Connaught Place; ✆ **011/5151-2888**). It features a funky island bar on the lower level and dining upstairs—a good place to hang out with travel companions and swap stories. After 8:30pm the DJ plays commercial music.

Buzz ✮ (17 Community Centre, P.V.R. Saket; ✆ **011/2653-3000**) is another design-conscious restaurant/pub located in one of South Delhi's popular entertainment centers. where the cellphone generation gathers to watch Hollywood blockbusters. The crowd is young and self-consciously hip, and the modish decor includes glowing lava-orange wall panels, Roman blinds, contemporary orange chairs, and a glass bar filled with thousands of back-lit marbles. Expect funky lounge music at lunch and even funkier waiters. After 8:30pm a DJ comes on with commercial music; overpriced snacks and starters are available as side orders to precocious-sounding cocktails. Above Buzz is **T'zers** (✆ **011/2660-1510**, -1, or -2), where cocktails are sipped in the presence of trite new beats, while the toned, designer-wear crowd is perched on soft red cushions on metal-framed chairs. Smooth waiters cruise around in bright red shirts, serving a loud urban crowd.

Nightclubs   Delhi has its fair share of nightclubs, though most play standard commercial music. **The Other Side** ✮✮, downstairs at Turquoise Cottage (81/3 Adhchini, Sri Aurobindo Marg; ✆ **011/2685-396**), is not one of those, and draws a vibrant crowd. It has exposed brick walls decorated with an assortment of Western-inspired obsessions; one nook is dedicated to vintage cars, another is filled with Rolling Stones album covers, and still another is decorated with saddles. With its black walls and pink lights, **Decibel** (Hotel Samrat, Kautilya Marg; ✆ **011/2467-5293** or -5294) in Chanakyapuri is a trendy nightclub with a large dance floor that draws a jet-setting crowd. DJ Alex spins commercial music while night owls drink excellent cocktails and dance away the calories. If you want to party into the wee hours (5am), make your way to **Elevate** (Centre Stage Mall, 5th Floor, Noida ✆ **0120/251-3904**), a spacious three-story club that plays a variety of sounds including commercial, R&B, and electronic music, with some trance/psychedelic stuff thrown in for good measure. The club regularly has an international DJ playing the latest world trends.

Note: Bars and nightclubs in Delhi can be extremely popular for months, or even years, and then suddenly and inexplicably the crowds stop coming. All the establishments listed above have been popular for a significant period of time and are unlikely to turn into has-beens by the time you get there, but fads and trends guide people's movements, so it's best to ask around once you're there.

2 Agra

200km (124 miles) SE of Delhi; 60km (37 miles) E of Bharatpur, Rajasthan; 120km (75 miles) N of Gwalior

Agra is invariably included on every first-time visitor's itinerary, for who visits India without visiting the Taj? Home to three generations of one of the most dynamic dynasties in the medieval world, their talent and wealth immortalized in stone and marble, Agra is home to the finest examples of Mughal architecture in India, of which the Taj is simply the most famous. The beauty of these buildings will bowl you over, but knowing something of the history that played itself out on these stages (akin to reading a Shakespearean drama) makes the entire Agra experience come alive.

To soak up this fascinating history in the walls and rooms that resonated to Mughal voices, you should ideally set aside 2 full days here and hire the services of a good guide. And, if your budget can stretch that far, there's only one place to stay: the palatial **Amarvilas,** where every room has a view of the Taj.

ESSENTIALS

VISITOR INFORMATION   The **Government of India Tourist Office** is at 191 The Mall (© **0562/222-6378;** goitoagr@sancharnet.in; Mon–Fri 9am–5:30pm, Sat 9am–2pm). A 24-hour **Tourism Reception Centre** is at Agra Cantonment Railway Station (© **0562/242-1204**). Not as much on the ball, the state **U.P. Tourism Bureau** is at 64 Taj Rd. (© **0562/222-6431;** Mon–Sat 10am–5pm; closed second Sat of the month).

GETTING THERE & AWAY   By Road   Agra lies less than 4 hours away, on a good double-carriage highway from Delhi. Many operators in Delhi offer bus tours to Agra; see "Visitor Information" in the Delhi section, earlier in this chapter. If you don't mind being part of a bus tour, a good option is to take a day trip from Delhi with **TCI** (see "Guided Tours" below); alternatively, hire a car and driver. Should you need to stop for refreshments, the **Country Inn** at Kosi, 99km (61 miles) from Delhi, is a good bet.

By Air   At press time, operations of all flights to and from Agra were suspended. Both Jet Airways and Indian Airlines say they have plans to resume flights by 2006.

By Train   The **Bhopal Shatabdi** leaves New Delhi at 6am daily, arriving at Agra Cantonment Railway Station (2km/1 mile from downtown) at 8am; it returns to Delhi at 11:05pm. Alternatively, you can catch the **Taj Express,** which leaves Delhi's Nizamuddin Station at 7:15am, returning to Delhi at 10:05pm. **Agra Cantonment Railway Station** (inquiries © **131** or 133, reservations 0562/242-0998) has prepaid taxi/auto-rickshaw hire (Rs 50–Rs 120/$1.15–$2.80) at Platform 1; this is also where you can book a city sightseeing tour. Trains from Rajasthan pull in at the Agra Fort Station. (If you're arriving from elsewhere, avoid the inconveniently located Agra City Station.)

GETTING AROUND   By Taxi & Auto-Rickshaw   As is the case everywhere in India, make sure you negotiate your taxi or auto-rickshaw rate upfront (or use the prepaid facility). Hiring an air-conditioned car for 4 hours should run you Rs 600 to Rs 800 ($14–$18), a full day Rs 1,250 to Rs 1,750 ($29–$40), depending on how far you want to go. Unless you're traveling to Fatehpur Sikri, an auto-rickshaw should suffice. **Islam** is a reliable auto-rickshaw-*walla* originally from Nepal; if you'd like to hire his services for a day, or for the duration of your stay in Agra, he can be contacted at © **0562/223-4061,** preferably a day before your planned arrival (after 9pm); during the day he bases himself at the STD booth outside Hotel Jaypee. In an attempt to cut down on the air pollution that threatens the Taj, motorized transport is not allowed in the Taj Sanctuary area (2km/1-mile radius); walk or hire a cycle-rickshaw.

GUIDED TOURS   U.P. State Tourism Development Corporation (Tourist Bungalow, Raja-ki-Mandi; © **0562/285-1720** or -0120) operates city tours that cover all the major sights. The tour usually starts at 10am, costs Rs 1,350 ($31), and covers the Taj, Agra Fort, and Fatehpur Sikri and includes all entrance fees, a guide, and transport by an air-conditioned bus. A minimum of eight people are required for the tour. A recommended private tour operator from Delhi is **TCI** (C-35, Connaught Place;

Agra

ACCOMMODATIONS ■

Amarvilas Hotel **11**

Hotel Agra Ashok **2**

Hotel Clarks Shiraz **4**

Hotel Sheela **12**

Jaypee Palace Hotel **7**

Mansingh Palace **8**

Taj View Hotel **5**

Trident Hilton Agra **6**

Welcomhotel
    Mughal Sheraton **10**

DINING ◆

Esphahan **11**

Dasprakash **1**

Jhankar **5**

Mughal Room **4**

Peshawari **10**

Pizza Hut **9**

Zorba The Buddha **3**

ⓘ Information
✉ Post Office

The Life & Times of the Mughal Emperors

Babur, the first Mughal emperor—inspired by the Persians' belief that a cultured leader should re-create the Islamic ideal of a "garden of paradise" here on earth—built three gardens on the banks of the Yamuna. But Agra only took shape as a city under his grandson, Akbar, the third Mughal emperor. Son of the poet-astronomer-philosopher Humayun (whose tomb is in Delhi, described earlier in this chapter), Akbar moved the capital here in 1566. While Akbar was as versatile as his father, he was also a better statesman, revered for his religious tolerance and relatively understated lifestyle. He took the throne at age 13 and ruled for almost 50 years, during which time he consolidated the Mughal empire and wooed the Hindu "underlings" by abolishing taxes, banning the slaughter of cows, promoting Hindu warriors within his army, and taking a Rajput princess as his bride, who bore him a son, Jahangir. In gratitude for the appearance of an heir, Akbar built a brand-new city, **Fatehpur Sikri**, which lies 40km (25 miles) southwest and is today one of Agra's top attractions.

The grandeur of this statement of gratitude indicates that Akbar must have, at least at first, been a very indulgent father, though his joy must later have been tinged with disappointment, for at an age when he himself was ruling India, Jahangir (who was to be his only surviving son) was relishing his reputation as a womanizer and acquiring a deep affection for alcohol, opium, painting, and poetry. When Jahangir fell in love with **Nur Jahan,** his "light of the world," who was at the time married, Akbar opposed the alliance. But after her husband died (under mysterious circumstances, it must be said), Jahangir promised to give up "the pleasures of the world," so Akbar gave his consent. Jahangir had a coin minted in her honor, and when he was crowned emperor in Agra Fort in 1628, it was in fact the strong-willed and ambitious Nur Jahan who ruled the empire from behind the *jalis*

© 011/2341-5367 or -6167; tajtour_del@tci.co.in). The TCI bus departs Delhi at 7am and returns by 10pm, covering Agra Fort and the Taj; it costs Rs 1,500 ($35), including sightseeing, lunch at Hotel Taj View, snacks, and other conveniences (you pay your own entry fees at monuments). Traveling around with a tour group is, however, far from the ideal way to experience the mystery and magical allure of the Taj or Fatehpur Sikri. To book one of the best guides in Agra (one of the best, in fact, in India), contact the intelligent and knowledgeable **Rajiv Rajawat** before you even get to India, to ensure he is available on the days you'd like to use his services (Rs 750–Rs 1,000/$17–$23 per day). Rajiv's mobile number is © **98370-23601;** or contact him at rajivrajawat@yahoo.com. (Also see Taj Mahal, below.)

WHAT TO SEE & DO

Agra is today a large industrial city with a woeful infrastructure, but sightseeing is quite manageable given that there are five major attractions and very little else to keep you here. Ideally, you will see the **Taj** at dawn, then visit **Itmad-ud-Daulah's Tomb** and **Agra Fort,** and move on to **Fatehpur Sikri** the following dawn. Besides those (screens) for 16 years. She also built a magnificent garden tomb, another of Agra's top attractions and affectionately referred to as the "mini-Taj", for her father. By the time Jahangir died in 1644, reputedly a drunkard, Akbar must have been turning in his tomb (yet another of Agra's top attractions).

It was Jahangir's third son, **Shah Jahan** (not incidentally born of Nur Jahan), who came to power—apparently after murdering his two elder brothers, their two children, and two male cousins. Known as the "architect" of the dynasty, the fifth Mughal emperor began renovating the Agra Fort at age 16, but achieved the apotheosis of Mughal design when he built the Taj Mahal for his beloved **Mumtaz** (the niece of Nur Jahan). Bored, he moved the capital to Delhi when he was 47, building an entirely new city from scratch, designing modern geometric palaces (including a separate royal apartment for his favored daughter, Jahanara Begum) and beautiful gardens within the new Red Fort. But he was to pay a bitter price for the favoritism he showed Jahanara and his son, **Dara Shikoh.** His pious third son, **Aurangzeb,** aided by **Roshanara Begum** (Jahanara's embittered younger sister), seized the throne by betraying and/or murdering most of their siblings. Aurangzeb, the last of the great Mughal emperors, became the most repressive ruler North India had yet seen, destroying Hindu temples and images throughout the region and banning the playing of music or any other form of indulgent pleasure. Known as much for his cruelty as his ambition, Aurangzeb allegedly poisoned his ally Roshanara when he caught her in an illicit liaison in her quarters at the Red Fort. Having imprisoned his father in Agra Fort, Aurangzeb sent him a platter upon which he garnished the head of his favorite son, Dara. According to legend he instructed his servant to present it with the words, "Your son sends you this to let you see that he does not forget you."

sights listed below, you may also want to make time to visit beautiful **Jama Masjid,** built in 1648 by Jahanara Begum, Shah Jahan's favorite daughter, who clearly inherited some of his aesthetic sensibilities. It is in the heart of the medieval part of Agra, best approached by cycle- or auto-rickshaw; you can stop along the way to bargain for jewelry, fabrics, or carpets. The other sight worth swinging by is **Dayal Bagh Temple**—begun 95 years ago, it is still under construction and is being built by the progeny of the laborers who built the Taj. The families guard their traditional craft techniques like gold, passing them on only to the sons in the family. Other minor attractions are ill-kept and a disappointment after viewing those reviewed below. Note that Bharatpur, where Keoladeo Ghana National Park lies (see chapter 10), is only 54km (34 miles) from Agra, with a stop at Fatehpur Sikri along the way.

Taj Mahal 𝆺𝅥𝆹𝅥𝆹𝅥   You expect to be disappointed when coming face to face with an icon that is almost an archetype, but nothing can really prepare you for the beauty of the Taj Mahal. Built by Shah Jahan as an eternal symbol of his love for his favorite wife, whom he called Mumtaz Mahal ("Jewel of the Palace"), it has immortalized him forever as one of the great architectural patrons of the world. It's not just the perfect symmetry, the ethereal luminescence, the wonderful proportions, or the sheer scale (which is virtually impossible to imagine from staring at its oft-reproduced image), but the exquisite detailing covering every inch of marble that justifies it as a wonder of the world. What appears from afar to be perfectly proportioned white marble magnificence is in fact a massive bejeweled box, with *pietra dura* adorning the interior and exterior—said by some to be an Italian technique imported to Agra by Jahangir, but more likely to be a craft originating in Persia. These intricately carved floral bouquets are inlaid with precious stones: agate, jasper, malachite, turquoise, tiger's eye, lapis lazuli, coral, carnelian—every stone known to man, as well as different shades of marble, slate, and sandstone. Beautiful calligraphy, inlaid with black marble, is carefully increased in size as the eye moves higher, creating an optical illusion of perfectly balanced typography, with the letters the same size from whichever angle you look. Carved relief work, again usually of flowers, which symbolized paradise on earth for the Mughals, decorates much of the interior, while the delicacy of the filigree screens that surround the ceno-taph, carved out of a single piece of marble, is simply astounding. The tomb is flanked by two mosques—one is a prerequisite, but the other is a "dummy" built only in the interests of symmetry; both buildings are worthy of examination in their own right. At the center of it all lies Mumtaz Mahal's cenotaph with the words HELP US OH LORD TO BEAR WHAT WE CANNOT BEAR; Shah Jahan's cenotaph was added later.

Work started in 1641, and the structure took 20,000 laborers 22 years to com-plete—legend has it that Shah Jahan cut off the hands of the architect (Persian-born Ustad Ahmad Lahori) and his laborers to ensure that they would never build another, but there is little to substantiate this sensational story.

The Taj changes color depending on the time of day, and many recommend that you witness this by visiting in the morning and evening; however, your ticket is valid for one entry only. Eat a hearty breakfast before you head out (no food is allowed past security), and stay the day, or come in the early morning.

Note: The Taj is closed on Friday. Your Taj ticket also entitles you to a small dis-count at the other four major attractions (Agra Fort, Itmad-ud-Daulah, Sikandra, and Fatehpur Sikri), so keep it on hand and show it when paying to enter the others.

Finally, to understand the symbolism of the Taj, as well as what has been lost since Shah Jahan's day (such as the plunder of the pearl-encrusted silks that covered Mum-taz's cenotaph), it's definitely worth hiring the services of a good (read: official) guide, arranged through your hotel. Besides **Rajiv Rajawat** (see above), we recommend the services of **Sudhir Agarwal** (© **98371-42946** or 0562/260-2441; Rs 680/$15 for the day), who is fluent in both English and German.

Tips Be the First to Arrive

Get to the Taj entrance at dawn, before it opens, then rush—run if you must—straight to the cenotaph chamber (remember to remove your shoes before ascending the marble steps). If you manage to get there first, you will hear what might aptly be described as "the sound of infinity"—the vibration cre-ated by air moving through the huge ventilated dome. As soon as the first vis-itor walks in, jabbering away, it reverberates throughout the room, and the sacred moment is lost until closing time again.

Taj by Moonlight

When a full moon rises in the Agra night, you can experience the Taj differently—shimmering, ethereal, and thankfully in virtual silence. Since early 2005, the Taj has been open for night viewing for 5 days each lunar cycle: the full moon night and the 2 nights before and after. Do note, however, that you are not allowed inside the actual monument, and that viewing is strictly from a designated distance. If one of these 5 days is a Friday, the Taj remains closed. Tickets cost Rs 750 ($17), and entry (8pm–midnight) is limited to eight groups of 50 each, who are escorted from the Taj shilpgram (parking area) and given 30 minutes to look around. The best viewing time is around 10pm. At press time, the Taj night viewing wasn't very popular, making it easy to book on the spot and enjoy the quiet beauty in relative peace. Obviously, this lack of enthusiasm is due to the limited access, and the situation could change, especially if rules are relaxed to make this a more romantic and less bureaucratic experience.

Taj Ganj. ℂ 0562/233-0498. Rs 750 ($17), children under 15 free; Rs 50 ($1.15) video, but you're only allowed to use it till the first entrance and platform from where you see the Taj. Sat–Thurs 6am–7pm. Only water, camera, film, batteries, medicines, and other similar essentials (but not food!) are allowed. No food, sharp objects, cellphones, tripods, or electronics—if you have any of these items, you can leave them at reception.

Agra Fort 👁👁👁   Built by Akbar (or rather, by his 4,000 workmen) on the west bank of the Yamuna, Agra Fort first took shape between 1565 and 1573, but each successive emperor was to add his imprint, and today the towering red-sandstone ramparts house a variety of palace apartments, representing the different building styles of Akbar and his grandson Shah Jahan. Akbar's son, Jahangir, installed a **"chain of justice"** (1605) by which any of his subjects could call on him, which provides some insight into the ruling qualities of the man many dismiss as a drunkard. Entrance is through impressive **Amar Singh Gate.** On your right-hand side you pass **Jahangiri Mahal,** the palace that housed the women of the court, dating to Akbar's reign (ca. 1570). In front is a stone pool with steps both inside and outside—legend says it was filled with rose petals during Nur Jahan's time, so that she could bathe in their scent. Much of the exterior (the jutting *jarokhas,* for example, and the domed *chattris*) and almost the entire interior were clearly built by Hindu workmen, who used Hindu building styles and decorative motifs—indicative of Akbar's all-embracing religious tolerance. Adjacent, facing **Anguri Bagh (Grape Garden,** where flowing water, flower beds, hidden lamps, and hanging jewels would have transformed it into a fantasy garden), is **Khas Mahal** (1636), built overlooking the cooling breezes of the Yamuna. You are now entering Shah Jahan's palaces, immediately recognizable by the extensive use of white marble. Historians also point out that here—unlike in Akbar's buildings, which feature straightforward Hindu elements next to Islamic—a subtle blend of Hindu and Persian elements resulted in a totally new style, referred to as the "Mughal style," with its classical purity. The Khas Mahal is flanked by two **Golden Pavilions** (a reference to the fact that they were once gilded): the bedrooms of the princesses Jahanara and Roshanara, before the latter plotted the downfall of her father and sister. On the left is **Mussaman Burj,** an octagonal tower open to the cooling breezes, which may have been the emperor's bedroom. Romantic accounts would have us believe that Shah Jahan, imprisoned by his son in this room, would gaze at the Taj Mahal until his death of a broken heart in 1666. However, evidence points to death by a massive dose of opium, complicated by the prolonged use of aphrodisiacs. Near the tower are the mirrored **Sheesh Mahal** and **Mina Masjid (Gem Mosque)**; adjacent is **Diwan-i-Khas (Hall of Private Audience; 1637)**, its marble columns inlaid with semi-precious stones in *pietra dura* floral patterns. In front of Diwan-i-Khas are two **thrones** (from where the emperor watched elephant fights below); facing these is **Machchhi Bhavan (Fish House)**, once filled with the sounds of trickling water. Beyond lies **Diwan-i-Am (Hall of Public Audience)**, the arcaded hall where the emperor would listen to the complaints of his subjects, seated on the Peacock Throne (see Lal Qila [Red Fort], in Delhi, earlier in this chapter). Note the insensitive placement of the tomb of John Russell Colvin, who died here during the Mutiny and was laid to rest in front of Diwan-I-Am. The ugly barracks to the north are also 19th-century British additions. From here on, most of the buildings (except for **Nagina Masjid,** the private mosque of the ladies of the court) are closed to the public, being at press time structurally unsound. (*Note:* A sound-and-light-show is held each evening at 7pm—when the machinery is working, that is.)

Note: Avoid Fri, when the Taj is closed and entry is half-price for Indian visitors, making the place unpleasantly crowded. Yamuna Kinara Rd. Rs 300 ($6.85). Rs 50 ($1.15) discount with Taj ticket. Keep ticket until visit is over. Daily sunrise–sunset. *Son-et-lumiere* (sound-and-light show) Rs 75 ($1.70).

Itmad-ud-Daulah's Tomb ⭐⭐⭐   Described as a mini-Taj, this is the tomb of Mirza Ghiyath Beg, who served under Akbar and fathered Nur Jahan, the powerful wife of Jahangir who helped promote her father to his position as Lord of the Treasury and enshrined him here in this "bejeweled marble box"—proof of her powerful hold on the purse strings. Also built of translucent white marble, it was the most innovative building of 17th-century India, and marked the transition from the heavy red sandstone so favored by previous Mughal emperors. It no doubt inspired Shah Jahan with its beautiful symmetry and detailing; the *pietra duras* are as delicate as embroidery, and the dense gilding and paintwork feature typical Persian motifs, such as the wine-vase and the dish and cup, much favored by Jahangir at the time. The scale may be far less grand than that of the Taj, but the polychrome geometric ornamentation is more obviously decorative, and given the beauty of the proportions and the intricacy of its inlays and mosaics, it's amazing how little traffic this tomb sees relative to the Taj. It definitely warrants a short visit, if only to get a sense of how almost generic opulence was to the Mughal court.

Eastern Bank of Yamuna (30 min. from Taj). Rs 110 ($2.50). Admission for Indians is half-price on Fri, which can make it crowded. Daily sunrise–sunset.

Sikandra (Akbar's Tomb) ⭐⭐   Someone once described the rise and fall of the Mughal empire as rulers who started "as titans and finished as jewelers." To this end, Akbar's tomb is a less-elegant version of the bejeweled tombs of his great-granddaughter (or his daughter-in-law's father), yet more ornate than that of his father Humayun (see "Delhi: The Top Attractions"). That said, the perfect symmetry is typical of Persian architecture, and the scale is huge; the gateway alone, featuring more than 20 panels inlaid with intricate geometric patterning, will stop you in your tracks. Geometric patterning in fact dominates, with relatively few floral designs, as befits the last "titan" ruler. It's not surprising to hear that the tomb is believed to have been designed by Akbar; the detailing reflects the altogether more restrained lifestyle and masculine personality of this great ruler.

8km (5 miles) from Agra on NH 2. ☎ 0562/264-1230. Rs 110 ($2.50), Rs 25 (55¢) video. Admission for Indians is half-price on Fri, which can make it crowded. Daily sunrise–sunset.

Fatehpur Sikri

Fatehpur Sikri ★★★   Built from scratch in 1571 by Akbar in honor of the Sufi saint Salim Chisti, who had predicted the birth of a son (see "The Dargah Sharif & Other Ajmer Gems" in chapter 10), this grand ghost city is carved entirely from red sandstone. It was only inhabited for 14 years, after which—some say because of water shortages—it was totally abandoned. It's a bizarre experience to wander through these magnificent, architecturally fascinating sandstone arches, courtyards, and buildings. (Try to get here right when it opens, the only time it's peaceful.) The buildings combine a fine sense of proportion—indicative of Akbar's Persian ancestry—with strong Hindu and Jain design elements, indicative again of his embracing attitude to the conquered and their faiths. Upon entering, you will see **Diwan-i-Khas,** thought to be a debating chamber, on the right. Facing it is **Ankh Michali,** thought to be the treasury, which has mythical Hindu creatures carved on its stone struts. To the left is large **Parcheesi Court,** where Parcheesi (from which games such as backgammon and ludo were subsequently derived) was played with live pieces: the ladies of the harem. It is said that Akbar learned much about the personalities of his court and enemies by watching how they played, won, and lost. Surrounding the court are, from the left, **Diwan-i-Am,** a large pavilion where public hearings were held; the **Turkish Sultana's House,** an ornate sandstone pavilion; and **Abdar Khana,** where drinking water and fruit were apparently stored. Walk between the two latter buildings to enter **Akbar's**

private quarters. Facing **Anoop Talao**—the four-quartered pool—are the rooms in which he slept (note the ventilating shaft near his built-in bed) and his personal library with shelves carved into the walls. Also overlooking Parcheesi Court is **Panch Mahal,** the tallest pavilion, where Akbar's wives could watch the games and enjoy the breeze without being seen. Behind Panch Mahal are the female quarters, including **Maryam's House** and the **Haram Sara Complex.** The harem leads to **Jodha Bai's Palace,** a large courtyard surrounded by pavilions—note the green glazed roof tiles. To the east is **Birbal's House,** a two-story pavilion noted for its carvings; beyond lie the **servants' cells.** From here you exit to visit **Jama Masjid,** a mosque even more spectacular than the larger one Akbar's grandson built in Delhi. Set like a glittering pearl amid the towering red-sandstone bastions, punctuated by a grand gateway, is the white marble **dargah** (tomb) of Salim Chisti, which has some of the most beautiful carved screens in India. It attracts pilgrims from all over India, particularly (given the good fortune he brought Akbar) the childless, who make wishes while tying cotton threads onto the screens that surround the tomb.

Again, the services of a good guide are indispensable to a visit here (don't bother hiring one of the "official" guides at the entrance, however).

37km (23 miles) west of Agra. No phone. Rs 485 ($11). Admission for Indians half-price Fri, which can make it crowded. Daily sunrise–sunset.

WHERE TO STAY

Given that it is one of the most-visited tourist destinations in the world, Agra's accommodations are a real disappointment, no doubt a case of resting on the Taj's laurels. The big exception is **Amarvilas,** which—even if it means scrimping elsewhere—is worth every cent, not least for its proximity to the Taj and the views. Within the moderate price category, all located south and southwest (known as the Cantonment) of the Taj, there is incredible price parity; of these only the **Trident Hilton** offers good value. The best budget option, conveniently located within Tajganj (where the Taj is located), is the **Hotel Sheela,** reviewed below.

VERY EXPENSIVE

Amarvilas 🏩🏩🏩 *Value*   Given the rather dire alternatives, it is really worth splurging on this extraordinary hotel, which—despite the fact that it's not cheap—offers value, because it is located just 600m (1,900 ft.) from the Taj, of which every room has a beautiful view. Here you can literally sip a cappuccino in your king-size bed at dawn, watching the subtle color variations the monument undergoes as the sun rises; or you can order a cocktail on your private balcony at sunset, admiring the ethereal marble silhouette as staff light the burners that line the hotel's grand stepped terraces that lead down to the central pool. The lobby, bar, and lounge all offer the same surreal views of the Taj, but even those public spaces that don't offer a feast for the eye are lovely, with large reflecting pools, colonnaded courts, terraced lawns, and pillowed pavilions. By day some of the exteriors look a little bland and in need of the detailing featured in the interior, but at night it's a pure *Arabian Nights* fantasy, when burning braziers provide a wonderful contrast to the fountains and trickling streams. The rooms, which are compact but extremely luxurious, are pure Vilas (see the Rajvilas review under "Jaipur" in chapter 10), showcasing the best-quality Indian craftsmanship available but with every modern amenity, including a walk-in cupboard and marble bathroom with separate tub and shower. The only difference between the deluxe (standard) and superior is that the latter has a small balcony (recommended!). The in-house spa also has views of the Taj—lying there, gazing at the dreamlike monument, you might just have to ask the masseuse to pinch you. Without a doubt it's the best hotel in town, yet service isn't always smooth; this may irritate the well-traveled, though staff will go out of their way to make up for any problems. Note also that blaring temple music from town is ever-present when the windows are open, but with an open mind this can add to the charm.

Taj East Gate Rd., Taj Nagari Scheme, Agra 282 001. ℂ 0562/223-1515. Fax 0562/223-1516. www.oberoihotels. com. 102 units. $530 deluxe double, $560 deluxe double with terrace; $1,025–$1,700 suite. AE, DC, MC, V. **Amenities:** 2 restaurants; lounge; bar; cultural performances/entertainers (Oct–Mar); pool; fitness center; Banyan Tree spa; travel services; salon; room service; laundry; doctor-on-call; golf cart drop-off at Taj. *In room:* A/C, TV/DVD, minibar, hair dryer, personal butler.

EXPENSIVE

Jaypee Palace Hotel ℛ   This huge hotel and convention center at the edge of town is a bit overpriced, but ask about seasonal discounts. The red-sandstone buildings have a formal look, more reminiscent of a modern library or museum than a palace, but it's wonderfully quiet (at least at press time; a huge tour group could change this). The hotel is set on 10-hectare (25-acre) grounds with well-tended gardens, lovely walkways, fountains, and pergolas—you can even take a camel ride through the grounds. Fresh flowers breathe life into the large, carpeted guest rooms, which have comfortable beds with firm mattresses (specify that you want a double bed when you book—only a few are available), upholstered sofas, and well-considered work areas designed for businesspeople. Rooms are relatively tasteful, dressed in shades of blue and mushroom; deluxe rooms have balconies, while executive rooms are much bigger but lack the balconies. Agra's largest health club is situated here, where you can enjoy a yoga session or aromatherapy treatment. Guests receive coupons worth Rs 500 ($11) to play at Leisure Mall, which offers a bowling alley, virtual reality games, and other kinds of entertainment you never came to Agra for.

Fatehabad Rd., Agra 282 003. ℂ 0562/233-0800. Fax 0562/233-0850. www.jaypeehotels.com. 350 units. $170 standard double, $190 executive double; $260 junior suite. Ask about discounts. AE, DC, MC, V. **Amenities:** 4 restaurants; tea lounge; bar; disco; pool; putting greens; tennis; squash; jogging track; bowling alley; billiards; health club; aerobics; spa; children's play areas; virtual reality games; travel and transport counter; airport transfers; helipad; currency exchange; florist; salon; 24-hr. room service; babysitting; laundry; doctor-on-call. *In room:* A/C, TV, minibar, tea- and coffee-making facilities, hair dryer. Executive rooms have electronic safe.

Taj-View Hotel ℛ   Within 1km (a half-mile) of the Taj, this is a comfortable albeit unexceptional option. Although little can be done to change the exterior, which looks like a 1970s apartment block, recent renovations have spruced up the guest rooms. You pay at least $25 extra for a Taj-facing room, which has a view so distant that it's probably better value to book a city-facing room (but request one on an upper floor). With extensive landscaped lawns and a quiet, relaxing marble pool with its own swim-up bar, this is a fair place to come home to after the rush of sightseeing. It's more competitively priced than the brash Sheraton, but not as good value as the Trident.

Fatehabad Rd., Taj Ganj, Agra 282 001. ℂ 0562/223-2400 through -2418. Fax 0562/223-2420. www.tajhotels.com. 100 units. $120 superior city- or pool-facing double, $145 superior Taj-facing double, $160 deluxe Taj-facing double; $275 historical suite. AE, DC, MC, V. **Amenities:** 2 restaurants; coffee shop; seasonal poolside barbecue; bar; cultural performances by arrangement; pool; putting green; tennis court; health club with sauna, steam, Jacuzzi; fitness center; currency exchange; shops; travel services; car rental; airport transfers; sightseeing; 24-hr. room service; massage; babysitting; laundry; doctor-on-call; astrologer. *In room:* A/C, TV, minibar.

Welcomhotel Mughal Sheraton 🎐 *(Kids)* Before Amarvilas, this was billed the best lodging in town, but despite its awards for design (it's supposed to emulate the palatial residence of a Mughal king but looks tawdry in comparison to Amarvilas), this hotel has a rather frenetic ambience: The classical music that is constantly piped through the vast marble lobby is drowned out by the ever-present buzz of people who gather to drink, chat, and wait for sightseeing buses to depart, and your room may end up being the only place to relax. Given the high traffic, personal service is often elusive. Guest rooms are large, but those in the lowest price category—the so-called "Chamber of Kings"—are slightly cluttered. You'll have to fork out a little more ($35) for the better-designed Chamber of Emperors rooms, and $50 more for the Taj-facing guest rooms, which, given the distant views, are overpriced. On the plus side, the hotel offers sprawling gardens, relative proximity to the Taj, and an endless list of facilities. And, with a children's amusement park and an army of nannies, it's aimed at the top end of the domestic family market.

194 Fatehabad Rd., Taj Ganj, Agra 282 001. ⓒ **0562/233-1701** through -1723. Fax 0562/233-1730. www.welcom group.com. 289 units. $160 Chamber of Kings double, $195 Chamber of Emperors double, $210 Taj-facing Mughal chambers exclusive double; $350–$700 suite. AE, DC, MC, V. **Amenities:** 5 restaurants; bar; nightclub; cultural performances; entertainers; pool; 2 tennis courts; croquet; badminton; boating; miniature golf; billiards; jogging track; health club; sauna; children's amusement park; travel services; Wi-Fi enabled; currency exchange; bank; shopping arcade; salon; 24-hr. room service; babysitting; doctor-on-call; astrologer. *In room:* A/C, TV, minibar. Chamber of Emperors rooms have hair dryers, tea- and coffee-making facilities.

MODERATE

If for some the Trident Hilton Agra doesn't suit or is full, three more options are clean and relatively comfortable, though all show their age. The previously government-run **Hotel Agra Ashok** has neat and fairly spacious guest rooms and a number of amenities such as an in-house restaurant, 24-hour room service, a pool, a travel desk, and laundry (ⓒ **0562/236-1230** through -1232; moonagra@yahoo.com; doubles from $76). Styled as a faux fortress-palace, **Mansingh Palace** has similar amenities (ⓒ **0562/233-1771;** www.mansinghhotels.com; doubles from Rs 3,200/$73). Despite the unpromising lobby, guest rooms are unexpectedly pleasant, far roomier, and attractive than those at **Hotel Clarks Shiraz,** which is very tired-looking even though it has similar amenities and is less than 3km (2 miles) away from the Taj. The large lawns are the most attractive feature of this white-concrete edifice. Guest rooms are small, and extremely dull and dated with cheap touches like the TV remote chained to the bedside table. A few of the rooms (top floor) have Taj views; those with odd numbers on the top floor of the main wing are best (ⓒ **0562/222-6121** or -6132; www.hotelclarksshiraz.com; doubles from $95).

Trident Hilton Agra 🎐🎐 *(Value)* Another desperate attempt to emulate Agra's architectural heritage, this hotel uses the same red sandstone favored by the Mughal kings, but that's where the similarity ends. It is a tranquil option, though, with cool, neat, public spaces and service that is generally a great deal slicker than elsewhere in Agra—not surprising given that it's an Oberoi-managed hotel (which recently merged with the Hilton group). Guest rooms, which are decently proportioned, have clay tile floors with rugs and are coordinated in shades of tan and green—hardly the height of elegance, but soothing enough. Attached bathrooms feature tubs and green marble floors. Accommodations are arranged around a lovely central garden, with manicured lawns, trimmed hedges, and a swimming pool. As is the case elsewhere, a variety of cultural performances are held at night, including dancing, singing, and pottery demonstrations. Check online for daily price variations: You can sometimes get a superior room at a bargain rate.

Taj Nagri Scheme, Fatehabad Rd., Agra 282 001. ☎ **0562/233-1818** through -1826. Fax 0562/233-1827. www.trident-hilton.com. 138 units. Rates vary daily; $50–$160 superior or premium garden-view double. $20 extra bed. Children under 12 free in parent's room. Rates include breakfast. AE, DC, MC, V. **Amenities:** Restaurant; bar; pool; table tennis; travel agent; airport transfers; bookstore; jewelry store; salon; 24-hr. room service; babysitting; laundry; doctor-on-call. *In room:* A/C, TV, dataport, minibar, tea- and coffee-making facilities, electronic safe.

INEXPENSIVE

Hotel Sheela *Value* 　 As far as budget lodging goes in the immediate vicinity of the Taj Mahal, you won't do better than this peaceful complex of neat, cream-walled buildings with a pleasant garden courtyard filled with bougainvillea, parrots, peacocks, and squirrels. Aimed at the budget traveler, accommodations are very spartan, with patterned vinyl flooring and wallpaper designed like faux miniature brickwork. Beds are firm but have thin mattresses. The en-suite tiled bathrooms are clean and have towels; hot water is available in winter. Guest rooms have fans and mosquito screens over the windows, and some rooms have air coolers for summer. The manager, Manish Bansal, can help with sightseeing endeavors, guides, and organizing a taxi. During the winter season, you are advised to reserve in advance or risk ending up in one of the nearby hovels. Alternatively, you can ask about **Sheela Inn,** the hotel's new property, which is priced a little higher but has better in-room facilities (like TV and telephone) and is about half a kilometer away from the Taj complex.

East Gate, Taj Ganj, Agra 282 001. ☎ **0562/233-1194** or -3074. 22 units. Rs 200–Rs 400 ($4.55–$9.10) double. No credit cards. **Amenities:** Restaurant; taxi hire; sightseeing assistance. *In room:* Air cooler (some rooms).

WHERE TO DINE

As is the case with accommodations, dining (and nightlife) options are limited in Agra, and you may as well dine in your hotel. But if you're "slumming" elsewhere and have cash to burn, **Esphahan** (reviewed below) is definitely worth a splurge. At the other end of the scale, you can get a satisfying, reasonably priced meal at **Zorba the Buddha** (E13 Shopping Arcade, Gopi Chand Shivare Rd., Sadar Bazaar), which serves excellent, nongreasy vegetarian food. This tiny eatery is extremely hygienic, reason enough to go. Go early to get a good table and order the light spinach *parathas,* any of the Indian fare, or even a salad—all quite tasty, if a trifle bland. Vegetarians (or others avoiding meat) have another option: **Dasaprakash** (☎ **0562/236-3535**), located in the Meher Theatre Complex at 1 Gwalior Rd., is the city's best-known South Indian restaurant. Regular fare includes *sada dosa* (plain rice and lentil pancakes), *masala dosa* (pancake with potato stuffing), *uttappams* (thicker pancakes), and *idlis* (steamed dumplings), all served with coconut chutney and *sambar* (spiced dal). No alcohol is served. Those craving American-style pizza can take a break at **Pizza Hut** (Fatehabad Rd., next to Amar Yatri Niwas hotel), which besides the usual chain fare also serves beer. At some point, you will hear of **Only** restaurant on Taj Road, mentioned in every guidebook on the planet, but we find it avoidable.

Good upmarket dining options in the big hotels include **Jhankar** in the Taj View, **Peshawri** in the Mughal Sheraton, or **Mughal Room** in the Clarks Shiraz, where live *ghazals* (poetry readings) add to the experience.

Note: To add to Agra's repertoire of scams, new horror stories doing the rounds involve unsuspecting diners being taken for a ride by unscrupulous restaurateurs working in tandem with rickshaw-*wallas* and so-called doctors. ***Bottom line:*** Be careful where you eat, and if you feel ill, don't rely on the restaurateur to call a "doctor"; insist on being taken back to your hotel.

Chiman Lal Puri Wallah *(Moments* NORTH INDIAN   Raja Babu is the proprietor of this fifth-generation family eatery, where mountains of cheap, satisfying *puri* (deep-fried puffed bread) and vegetable curry are served in a grubby two-level corner shop not far from Agra's Jama Masjid. Using the fingers of your right hand, mop up the vegetable curry with the *puris,* adding the mint chutney and curd to taste. You'll be offered more *puris* and *subji* (the curry, or stew) until you flatly refuse to eat anything more; then comes saffron-flavored *kheer,* a traditional rice pudding. The "menu" does not change. Ever. Simple, yet exceptionally tasty, this is a real Indian dining experience.

Chimman Chauraha. ⓒ **0562/236-7430.** Meals around Rs 30 (70¢). No credit cards. Daily 7am–11pm.

Esphahan *(Moments* INDIAN   Even if you aren't staying at Amarvilas, you should dine at this Indian specialty restaurant—not only are the cuisine, service, and live Indian music superb, but arriving at the flame-lit latter-day palace is one of Agra's most memorable moments. (When you reserve, ask to have your predinner cocktail on the veranda so you can watch the sunset hues color the Taj and the magnificent pool area below.) Start with *tandoori phool,* stuffed cauliflower in a Kashmiri cumin marinade; or Sunhera *jheenga,* tiger prawns marinated in citrus yogurt; or the succulent chicken *tikka.* But you have so much more to choose from. The Bharwaan *gucchi* (stuffed Kashmiri morels in saffron gravy) is recommended, as is the *tarkari biryani,* in which garden-fresh vegetables and basmati rice are cooked in a terra-cotta pot. All dishes are served with *dal,* seasonal vegetables, and a choice of Indian bread. It makes for a memorable evening out, and the perfect place to celebrate seeing the Taj.

Amarvilas, Taj East Gate End. ⓒ **0562/223-1515.** Reservations essential. Rs 475–Rs 1,195 ($11–$28). AE, MC, V. Daily 7–10:30pm.

SHOPPING

Agra is famous for its marble and softstone inlay, as well as *zardori*-embroidered fabrics, leather goods, brassware, carpets, and jewelry. However, it's hard work dealing with what is probably the worst concentration of touts and scamsters in all India, so if you can, avoid shopping here. Don't be fooled by Cottage Industries Exposition, which is not a branch of the similarly named government-owned (Emporium) shops in other parts of the country. This one is overpriced, and whatever is sold here can quite easily be obtained in Delhi at half the price. If you absolutely must buy something to remind you of your visit here, **Subhash Emporium** (18/1 Gwalior Rd.; ⓒ **0562/222-5828**) sells good-quality inlay work, souvenirs, and other gifts. Or make your way to one of the *official* government emporiums for reasonably priced sources of local handicrafts.

3 Varanasi (Benaras)

320km (198 miles) SE of Lucknow; 765km (474 miles) SE of Delhi

A crumbling maze of a city that rises from the *ghats* (steps) on the western banks of the Ganges, Varanasi is in many senses the quintessential India. With an ancient history—Mark Twain famously described it as "older than history, older than tradition, older even than legend, and looks twice as old as all of them put together"—it is also one of the most sacred cities in the world today. Kashi, or "City of Light, where the eternal light of Shiva intersects the earth," as Varanasi is seen by devotees, is the holiest of

Varanasi

ACCOMMODATIONS ■
Ganga View
  Guesthouse **3**
Palace on Ganges **4**
Radisson Hotel Varanasi **1**
Shiva Ganges View **5**
Taj Ganges **2**

DINING ◆
Bread of Life Bakery **6**
Keshari Restaurant **8**
Sindhi Restaurant **7**

Indian pilgrimages, home of Shiva, where the devout come to wash away their sins. It is also one of the holiest *tirthas* (literally a "crossing" or sacred place where mortals can cross over to the divine, or the gods and goddesses come to bathe on Earth), where many return to die in the hope that they may achieve *moksha,* the salvation of the soul from the cycle of birth, death, and rebirth.

Named after the confluence of two rivers, Varuna and Asi, the city is centered on the ghats that line the waterfront, each honoring Shiva in the form of a *linga*—the rounded phallic-like shaft of stone found on every ghat. Cruise the waterfront at dawn and you will witness the most surreal scenes, when devotees come to bathe, meditate, and perform ancient rituals to greet the sun. Or even come at sunset, when *pundits* (priests) at Dasashwamedh Ghat perform *arti* (prayer ritual) with complicated fire rituals, and pilgrims light candles to float along the sacred waters.

Earliest accounts of the city go back 8,000 years, and "the city of learning and burning," as it is affectionately referred to, has attracted pilgrims from time immemorial, not all of them Hindu—even Buddha visited here in 500 B.C. after he achieved enlightenment, sharing his wisdom at nearby Sarnath. Successive raids by Muslim invaders (the last of whom was the Mughal emperor Aurangzeb) led to the destruction of many of the original Hindu temples, which means that most of the buildings here date back no further than the 18th century. Yet the sense of ancient history is almost palpable. Getting lost in the impossibly cramped labyrinth, you are crowded by pilgrims purchasing flowers for *puja* (offering, or prayer), grieving relatives bearing corpses, chanting priests sounding gongs, and sacred cows rooting in the rubbish—an experience you will never forget.

ESSENTIALS

VISITOR INFORMATION   The **Government of India Tourist Office** is located at 15B The Mall, Cantonment (✆ **0542/250-1784**; Mon–Fri 9am–5pm, Sat 9am–2pm). A satellite information counter is open during flight arrivals. The **U. P. Tourist Office** is on Parade Kothi (✆ **0542/220-6638**; Mon–Sat 10am–5pm); a satellite counter is at the railway station (✆ **0542/250-6670**; daily 9am–7pm).

GETTING THERE   By Road   Unless you have a lot of time on your hands, driving to Varanasi means spending too much time on a bumpy road with no interesting stops.

By Air   The airport is 23km (14 miles) from the Cantonment (Cantt.) area, where the most comfortable hotels are located, and 30km (18 miles) from the riverfront. Best to fly in with **Jet Airways** (reservations ✆ **0542/250-6444** or -6555, airport 0542/262-2795 or -2796). The flight from Delhi via Khajuraho lasts 75 minutes. **Indian Airlines** (reservations ✆ **0542/250-2527** or -2529, airport 0542/262-2090) flies in from Agra (though flights are currently suspended, so do confirm first), Delhi, Lucknow, and Mumbai. **Air Sahara** (central ✆ **0542/250-7871** through -7873, airport ✆ 0542/262-2547) connects the city with Delhi, Kolkata, and Bangalore. A taxi should run you Rs 300 ($6.85) to the Cantonment; the airport shuttle charges Rs 40 (90¢), but you may be in for a lengthy wait while it fills up with passengers.

By Train   Varanasi is conveniently reached by overnight train from Delhi; the Swatantra Express and Shiv Ganga Express take 12 to 13 hours. It is also connected with a host of other cities and towns. For inquiries, call ✆ **1331**; for Varanasi Cantonment reservations, call ✆ **0542/250-4131** or -4031. Prepaid taxis are available from the station. (Note that Mughal Sarai is 17km/11 miles out of town, so arrange to get off at Varanasi Cantonment. However, if you must, the reservations number for Mughal Sarai is ✆ **05412/25-5703**.)

GETTING AROUND   By Auto-Rickshaw & Cycle-Rickshaw   The narrow lanes and extremely crowded streets of the Old City and the lanes in and around Godaulia (also Gowdalia) are penetrable only by two-wheelers and extremely determined cycle-rickshaws. These are also useful—if sometimes bone-jarring—ways of getting from your hotel to the area near the ghats and other attractions. Once at (or near) the ghats, set off on foot. Note that most cycle-rickshaws don't have functioning brakes; their technique of stopping is to merely roll into the cycle-rickshaw in front; hold on and try not to be alarmed.

Bear in mind that Varanasi is a city of transport tricksters, and you have little chance of escaping at least one rickshaw-related con job. Ask your hotel what the current going rate is for any trip in either an auto- or cycle-rickshaw, and bargain for the correct fare. Be further warned that rickshaw-*wallas* will readily agree to take you somewhere without having the faintest idea where it is. Once you've been onboard for several minutes, you will suddenly be asked where you want to go and, more likely than not, you will end up at a shop where the driver expects to make a commission off your purchase. To avoid falling into this annoying and time-wasting trap, ensure that the driver can repeat the name of your destination (or the nearest prominent landmark), in recognizable English. In addition, avoid the shopping scam by using a bit of trickery yourself. To begin with, never use the word "shopping" with a *rickshaw-walla*. If you're heading to the shopping area in Godaulia, ask to be taken to Dasashwamedh Ghat, as if you plan to go there for a stroll. When you're almost there, you'll pass the Old City shopping area and Godaulia; stop your rickshaw and get off before you reach the ghats, or get to the ghats and take the 5-minute walk back into the market. To hire a car and driver to tour the surrounds, expect to pay at least Rs 600 ($14) for a half-day or Rs 1,100 ($25) for a full day.

GUIDED TOURS   At press time, the city offered no organized tours. We highly recommend that you explore the area with a personal guide, if only to know which temples you can enter or which street food to sample, and to avoid getting lost or conned. One of Varanasi's best guides is **Ajit Kumar Yadav** (© **0542/258-1052** or 94152-25994; ajitsashay@yahoo.com; book him in advance), an official, government-approved guide; he's often engaged for group tours during peak season. Ajit is perfect for those looking for an understanding of the city that goes beyond its history, covering religious rituals and mythological stories as well. His knowledge of Hinduism and Buddhism (for Sarnath) is unmatched, and most importantly, he never asks if you want to shop, unless you express a keen interest. **Dhananjay (Deejay) Singh** is another government-approved guide who is a font of knowledge and an absolutely charming host; contact him at © **98390-58228.** (Explore the Old City on foot or by boat, then arrange a car.) Alternatively, you can arrange both guide and car through your hotel, or contact the **Tourist Office** (see "Visitor Information," above) to arrange for an approved guide and vehicle (© **0542/250-1784**). To hire a boat (with oarsman), head for Dasashwamedh; the price should be around Rs 100 ($2.30) per hour.

FESTIVALS   Varanasi is in many ways like a huge trippy trance party that started centuries ago and has kept on going, its revelers refusing to discard their costumes and come down to earth. So there's no real reason to time your visit with a festival—on the contrary, any increase in numbers is worth avoiding. That said, the huge **Dev Deepavali (Diwali)** festival is by all accounts a spectacle, held during the full moon in October/November. Almost every ghat and building is covered by glowing earthen lamps, and the river is aglitter with floating candles (but with about 100,000 pilgrims about, you may never even get to the river). Other auspicious occasions are **Mahashivratri** (Jan/Feb), **Holi** (Mar/Apr), **Ganga Dashehra** (May/June), and **Sri Krishna Janmashtami** (Sept/Nov).

WHAT TO SEE & DO

If you do only one thing in Varanasi, take a **boat cruise** past the ghats at dawn (see below); you can repeat this at sunset or, better still, head for **Dasashwamedh Ghat** to watch the **Ganga Fire Arti.** For 45 minutes, young Brahmin priests perform age-old prayer rituals with conch shells and burning braziers accompanied by drummers, while children hawk candles for you to light and set adrift. Aside from these two must-sees,

Moments **Up in Flames**

You need a pretty strong constitution to hang around Varanasi's burning ghats (**Harish Chandra** or **Manikarnika** ghats) and watch a human corpse, wrapped in little more than a sheet, being cremated in public view. Bodies are burned around the clock at these famous open-air cremation sites, which draw a constant crowd of grievers, curious pilgrims, bug-eyed travelers, and confused cows. Only Varanasi's "Untouchables" are allowed to touch the bodies or perform the cremation. After bathing the body one last time in the holy Ganges, they place it on wood piles, where it is covered with more logs (ask your guide about the kinds of wood—teak, sandalwood, and so on—used and their significance) before being doused in a flammable paste, or ghee, and lightly coated with incense powder (the latter used to disguise the smell of burning flesh), after which a male relative, usually the son (female relatives of the deceased, even wives and daughters, rarely if ever visit the cremation grounds), lights the pyre. No photography is allowed, and you are expected to treat the mourners with the respect their grief deserves. Avoid touts offering to show you a cremation up close and personal; not only do many drug addicts trying to part tourists from their cash hang around these areas, but gawking at an unknown person's funeral pyre from close quarters is considered fairly offensive. To get a quiet glimpse of a cremation ritual from a respectable distance, without causing any offense, take a boat ride down to Manikarnika Ghat.

you should set aside some time to wander the ancient lanes of the **Old City,** particularly those centered around **Kashi Vishwanath Temple** (see below)—but a few hours of picking your way past cow pats amid the incessant din of clanging temple gongs, not to mention striking out to view the 24-hour cremations at **Manikarnika Ghat,** are likely to have you craving peace and solitude. Hire a car and visit **Sarnath,** where Buddha first revealed his Eightfold Path to Nirvana, and where you can spend a few hours exploring the archaeological ruins, visit a modern Buddhist temple, and admire the beautiful Indo-Greek and Mathura styles of Buddhist art and sculpture at the museum. Alternatively, stay in Varanasi to explore the fascinating collection in the **Bharat Kala Bhavan Museum** at Benaras Hindu University. Both experiences are enriched by having a good guide with you.

Ramnagar Fort (Rs 12/30¢; Oct–Mar daily 8am–noon and 2–6 pm, Apr–Sept daily 10am–5pm), the palace of the former Maharaja of Varanasi, is billed as another worthwhile attraction. Although the actual palace is beautiful in a run-down sort of way, and the location (the only Varanasi site on the east bank of the river) is lovely, the museum is filled with dusty, moth-eaten, decaying exhibits, such as the once-ornate *howdas* (elephant seats) that transported the royal family—fascinating in a way to see such beauty so discarded. Do stop for a glance at the palace's grand Durbar Hall, though it's hard to see through the filthy windows. The lack of care says much about the dedication of the current young Maharaja. Although he is said to involve himself in local tourism, his name certainly does not enjoy the reverence that the Maharajas of Rajasthan still evoke. That said, at press time, some renovations were underway, so do check for improvements. Last but not least of Varanasi's fascinating sights, **Bharat Mata,** or **Mother India Temple** (located just north of the Old City) is worth highlighting, if only because it is the incarnation of the spoken Hindu belief that the very land of India is sacred (ironic, given the pollution). Pilgrims walk around a large relief map of the subcontinent before Partition, featuring all its holy *tirthas,* mountains, and rivers.

Varanasi has produced some of India's most talented musicians (the great Ravi Shankar was born here; if you're unfamiliar with his genius, purchase without delay the CD *Chants of India,* produced by George Harrison—highly recommended). Ask your hotel what performances are being hosted while you are in town, or head for the **International Music Centre** in Ganesh Mahal on Wednesday and Saturday (check with your hotel for exact dates and times) for live Indian classical music performances by up-and-coming artists. **Naach Ghar** (Bungalow no. 25, Cantonment, near SSP Residence; ✆ **93354-93084**) is another place that puts on a dance performance almost every evening around 7:15 for Rs 500 ($11) per head.

If you'd like to learn to play the **tabla** (set of two small drums) in Varanasi, which is renowned for its tabla merchants, head for **Triveni Music Centre** (D24/38 Pandey Ghat) and ask for Nandlal. Nandlal and his father also stage regular concerts at Triveni. An imitation of the Triveni Music Centre, called Triveny Musical House, can be found at Shivala behind the Bread of Life Bakery. Here **Neeraj** (✆ **94153-53668;** 8am–6:30pm) can give you a crash course in a few Indian musical instruments (tabla, flute, sarangi, sitar, and violin) for Rs 100 ($2.30) an hour; he's not bad if you're just trying to get the feel of things and aren't too serious about the experience.

Yoga schools and teachers are a dime a dozen in Varanasi; even your hotel will likely have a morning yoga session you can join. If you're keen on learning some serious yoga or the philosophy behind it, however, contact **Dr. Vagisa Shastri** at his residence behind the Bread of Life Bakery (Vagyoga Chetanapitham, B 3/131A, Shivala) between 7 and 9am. He charges Rs 450 ($10) for a 3-hour session and expects students to be disciplined, interested listeners.

Note: If you take a cycle-rickshaw for the evening *arti* ceremony, you will encounter terrible pollution. Additionally, because the supply of electricity to Varanasi is erratic, most hotels and restaurants use diesel generators. Unfortunately, their exhaust pipes are often at face level, spewing diesel fumes into Varanasi's narrow streets as you walk or cycle by. Carry a cotton handkerchief/scarf with you, cover your nose and mouth with it, and breathe through the cotton to make your way through an otherwise suffocating environment.

CRUISING THE GHATS ✸✸✸

Drifting along the Ganges, admiring the densely textured backdrop of 18th- and 19th-century temples and palaces that line the 84-odd bathing ghats, you will be confronted with one of the most spiritually uplifting or downright weird tableaus on the entire crazy subcontinent: Down below, waist-deep pilgrims raise their arms in supplication, priests meditate by staring directly into the rising sun or are frozen in complicated yoga positions, wrestlers limber up, and disinterested onlookers toss live rats from the towering walls of the Old City, among other assorted goings-on. Note that you'll need to get here between 4:30am and 6am (check sunrise times with your hotel, as well as the time it takes to get to the ghats), so plan an early wake-up call. You should be able to hire a boat anywhere along the ghats, but most people either catch one from **Assi Ghat,** the southernmost ghat, or—particularly if you're staying in the Cantonment area—from **Dasashwamedh** (meaning "10-horse-sacrifice," referring to an ancient sacrifice performed by Brahma). Situated roughly halfway, this is the most accessible and popular ghat and is always crawling with pilgrims, hawkers, and priests surveying the scene from under bamboo umbrellas. Boats here operate at a fixed rate (at press time) of Rs 100 ($2.30) per hour. The following descriptions of the 100-odd ghats assume that you will leave from here; note that it's worth traveling both north and south. You can do another trip in the evening as the sun is setting, but don't travel too far—no boating is allowed after sunset (except at the time of *arti*, when you can sail up to Manikarnika Ghat—see "Up in Flames," above).

Heading North from Dasashwamedh Ghat   From here, you pass **Man Mandir Ghat** which, along with the beautiful palace that overlooks it, was built by the Maharaja Man Singh of Amber in 1600. Jai Singh, who built the Jantar Mantars, converted the palace into an observatory in 1710. Hours are 7am to 5:30pm; entrance costs Rs 100 ($2.30). Next is **Mir Ghat,** where the New Vishwanath Temple, Vishalakshi shrine, and Dharma Kupa (where the Lord of Death relinquished his hold over those who die in Varanasi), are found. North lies **Lalita Ghat,** with its distinctive Nepalese Temple, and beyond it is the "burning" **Manikarnika Ghat,** the principal and favored *smashan ghat* (cremation ground) of Varanasi, where you can see funeral-pyre flames burning 24 hours, tended by the *doms,* or "Untouchables"—touching the dead is considered polluting to all but these low castes. Boats are requested to keep their distance as a sign of respect. On this ghat is the venerated **Manikarnika Kund,** the world's first *tirtha,* said to have been dug out by Vishnu, whose sweat filled it as he created the world as ordered by Shiva. Some say that Shiva shivered in delight when he saw what Vishnu had created, dropping an earring into the pool; others say that it was the earring of Sati, Shiva's dead wife, hence the name Manikarnika: "jeweled earring." Between the Kund and the ghat is what is supposed to be Vishnu's footprint. Adjacent is **Scindia Ghat,** with its distinctive, half-submerged Shiva temple, toppled by weight; then **Ram Ghat** and **Panchganga Ghat** (said to be empowered by the five mythical streams that flow here into the Ganges), and one of the five *tirthas* at which pilgrims perform rituals. Behind the ghat glowers **Alamgir Mosque,** built by Aurangzeb on a Hindu temple he destroyed; note also the almost submerged cells where the Kashi pundits (priests) are freeze-framed in meditation poses. Proceed from here to **Gai, Trilochana,** and **Raj** ghats, but it's best (if you still want to proceed south) to turn back at Panchganga (or explore the north banks further on foot).

Heading South   Passing **Chaumsathi Ghat,** where the temple houses images of Kali and Durga; and **Dhobi Ghat,** alive with the sound of laundry workers rhythmically beating clothing that have been "cleansed" by the Ganges, you come to **Kedara Ghat,** notable for its red-and-white-striped South Indian–style temple. Farther south lie **Harishchandra Ghat,** Varanasi's second cremation ghat (though less popular because it also houses an electric crematorium); and **Tulsi Ghat,** named in honor of Goswami Tulsidas, a revered Hindu poet. Nearby is **Lolark Kund,** where childless women come to bathe and pray for progeny. The final stop (or the first, if your accommodations make a south-north journey more convenient) is **Assi Ghat,** a simple clay bank situated at the confluence of the Ganga and Assi rivers. From here you can walk to **Durga Temple,** which lies farther west from the ghat. *Note:* If you want to walk from Assi Ghat to Dasashwamedh, the trip will take a leisurely 60 to 90 minutes. Although the best time to walk or cruise the river is at sunrise or before sunset, you may wish to see the river in a completely different and relatively quiet "avatar," in which case take a late-afternoon stroll down the ghats in winter.

Fun Fact **The Polluted Elixir of Life**

According to religious belief, the Ganges is *amrita,* elixir of life, "cleanser of sin," "eternal womb," and "purifier of souls." Even from a scientific point of view, the river once had an almost miraculous ability to purify itself—up to 100 years ago, microbes such as cholera could not survive in these sacred waters. Sadly, the Ganges is today one of the most polluted rivers in the world. This is mostly due to the chemical toxins dumped by industrial factories that line the river, but Varanasi's ancient sewers and a population with equally ancient atti-tudes toward waste disposal (including the dumping of an annual estimated 45,000 uncremated corpses) are problems the Uttar Pradesh Water Board strug-gles to overcome. Several eco-groups like the Sankat Mochan Foundation at Tulsi Ghat are working to alleviate the environmental degradation of the Ganges, but as you will find abundantly clear within an hour of being in Varanasi, much more needs to be done.

Kashi Vishwanath Temple Of the more than 2,000 temples in Varanasi, the most important is Kashi Vishwanath Temple, or "Golden Temple," dedicated to Lord Shiva, the presiding deity of the city. Because of repeated destruction by the invading sultans and later by Aurangzeb, the current Vishwanath is a relatively modern building: It was built in 1777 by the Maharani of Indore, and the *shikhara* (spire) and ceilings were plated with 820 kilograms (1,808 lb.) of gold, a gift from the Maharaja Ranjit Singh, in 1839. Five major *aartis* are held daily, but the temple is always abuzz with worshippers. Sadly, non-Hindus may not enter, but by taking a stroll through the Vishwanath Galli (pronounced *gul*-ley, meaning lane) that runs the length of it, you can get a glimpse of the interior, which exudes pungent smells and constant noise. For a small donation, you can also climb to one of the second floors or rooftops of the shops that line the lane and get a good view. Note that adjacent is **Gyanvapi Mosque,** built by Aurangzeb on a Hindu temple site and heavily guarded to ensure that no trouble erupts. Ironically, this is also the starting point for many pilgrims on their quest to visit all the *tirthas* in a rit-ual journey, accompanied by a priest who keeps reciting the *sankalpa,* or "declaration of intent." Nearby is **Annapurna Temple,** dedicated to Shakti.

Vishwanath Galli. Temple is closed to non-Hindus; compound is accessible. No cameras or cellphones allowed within the Galli and temple compound.

Bharat Kala Bhavan Museum As is so often the case in India, this museum suffers from poor curatorship, with exhibits—which are marvelous—haphazardly dis-played and poorly labeled. You may even have trouble persuading the guards to turn on all the lights and show you the rooms behind the screen—hence the need for a good guide. The miniature-painting collection is superb, as are many of the Hindu and Buddhist sculptures and Mughal artifacts, though again, without a guide there is no way to know, for instance, that the otherwise nondescript coin behind the glass was minted by the Mughal emperor Akbar—and in keeping with his legendary religious tolerance, it has a Hindu symbol printed on one side and an Islamic on the other. Set aside 2 hours to explore.

Benaras Hindu University. Admission Rs 40 (90¢); still camera free, video not allowed. July–Apr Mon–Sat 11am–4pm. May–June closes at 12:30pm.

Sarnath ⚐   After gaining enlightenment, this is where Buddha gave his first sermon some 2,500 years ago, and continued to return with followers. For many centuries after this, it was renowned as a Buddhist center of learning, housing some 3,000 monks, but successive Muslim invasions and later lootings destroyed the monasteries and much of the art. Today it still attracts many pilgrims, but—unless you're very familiar with Buddha's personal history or are an archaeologist—the site itself is nowhere near as inspiring as his teachings. The most impressive sight is **Dhamekh Stupa,** if only for its sheer age. Built around A.D. 500, with a massive girth, it still towers 31m (102 ft.) into the air and is said to mark the very spot where Buddha revealed his Eightfold Path leading to nirvana. The ruins of **Dharmarajika Stupa** lie immediately north of the entrance. Beyond is the **Ashokan Pillar**—the stupa is said to have been one of 28 built by Ashoka, the 3rd-century-B.C. Mauryan king and bloodthirsty warrior who was to become one of the most passionate converts to Buddhism. Beyond these are the ruins of monasteries. Across the road from the entrance to the main site is **Sarnath Archaeological Museum,** where you can view the four-headed lion that once topped the Ashoka Pillar. The lion, with the wheel beneath representing Buddha's "wheel of dharma," is today a national emblem for India, found on all currency notes and official government documents. East of the Dhamek Stupa is **Mulagandha Kuti** (temple), which houses an image of Buddha (ironically enough, against his wishes, images of Buddha abounded after his death). The walls contain frescoes pertaining to his life history—a good crash course for the novice if accompanied by a guide.

Sarnath is 10km (6¼ miles) north of Varanasi. Admission Rs 100 ($2.30). Daily 9am–5pm. Museum Sat–Thurs 10am–5pm; Rs 2 (4¢); cameras not allowed (lockers provided). Mulagandha Kuti 4–11:30am and 1:30–8pm. Daily chanting: Nov–Feb 6pm, Mar–May 6:30pm, June–Oct 7pm. Rs 5 (10¢) for use of still camera, Rs 30 (70¢) video.

WHERE TO STAY

In a general sense, you have two options: You can stay in one of the waterfront lodgings, most of which (with the exception of the two reviewed below) are very basic; or you can spend the night in the relative peace and comfort of the Cantonment area, where the most "luxurious" options are. Still, other than those reviewed below, the Cantonment hotels are all looking very frayed if not downright decaying. And the downside of staying in the Cantonment is that you feel very cut off from the real Varanasi, and require an earlier morning wake-up call to get to the ghats; for the sunset *arti,* when the streets are often jammed, it may take 30 minutes to get there, and you'll walk the last part. These issues can be solved by staying in a hotel on the Ganges, but this also means you have no chance of unwinding at a pool, eating meat, or drinking alcohol—still, if you manage to bag a river-facing room, you will have the serenity of a waterfront view, with the surreal experience of Varanasi on your doorstep. Besides the options listed below, **Shiva Ganges View** (B-14/24, Mansarovar Ghat, near Andhra Ashram; ℂ **0542/245-0063** or 94153-01249; Rs 1,500–2,400/$35–$55) has a pleasant, airy, colonial charm and affable owners, and only six rooms. *Note:* Staying in one of the budget hotels away from the ghats is not advisable unless you're used to budget traveling; many have no windows, and the noise is incessant.

CANTONMENT

Radisson Hotel Varanasi   One of only two of Varanasi's so-called top-end hotels, this is relatively new, which gives it a bit of an edge on the dated Taj Ganges (see below). Guest rooms are large and comfortable (the thick mattresses are the best in town), with thick drapes and chocolate-brown furniture offset by brushed orange

walls. The green marble bathrooms—also the best in town—are moderately proportioned, with green marble floors and gleaming fittings. There's also a full spa and a
smallish pool with wooden deck chairs and its own bar; breakfasts are served in the
bright sunflower-themed coffee shop. The free railway station transfer is very convenient if you're arriving by overnight train from Delhi. The drawback of this otherwise
good chain hotel? None of the rooms have views worth mentioning.

The Mall, Cantonment, Varanasi 221 002. ℂ **0542/250-1515.** Fax 0542/250-1516. www.radisson.com.
radvar@sify.com. 117 units. High season (Oct–Apr): $130 superior double, $165 suite. Low season: $100–$120. Rates
include breakfast and railway transfers. $20 extra bed. AE, DC, MC, V. **Amenities:** 2 restaurants; bar; pool; travel desk;
foreign exchange; 24-hr. room service; babysitting; doctor-on-call. *In room:* A/C, TV, dataport, minibar, tea- and coffee-making facilities, hair dryer, iron and ironing board.

Taj Ganges   Before the Radisson opened, Taj Ganges was undisputedly the best
hotel away from the ghats, but this had more to do with the pathetic competition than
any superior features. Within an ugly 1970s monolith, rooms are small and look a little tired; the exceptions are the top-end suites (book no. 527, which occupies a top
corner and is very spacious and gracious, albeit old-fashioned). What distinguishes
this old five-star stalwart are service and the vast array of amenities, as well as a real
passion for the region; the hotel hires the best guides in the city, shopping tips are
excellent, and the travel desk will arrange tours as far afield as Bodhgaya. It also has
huge, sprawling grounds, a great pool, and two of the best restaurants in town (this
does not mean that the meal will be the best you have in India, however). If you don't
mind attracting a lot of attention, the Taj Ganges offers an unusual Ganges boat tour:
A beautiful old horse-drawn carriage, once belonging to the Maharajas, clip-clops
through the old city to the ghats in style, after which you board the most luxurious
boat on the Ganges, with a mattressed rooftop on which you recline in comfort while
watching the surreal scenes drift by. You can also take a carriage ride through the 16-
hectare (40-acre) hotel property, which include a genuine mini-palace in a state of
some disrepair. Sadly, nothing has yet come of long-term plans to turn **Nadesar
Palace** into luxurious suites.

Nadesar Palace, Varanasi 221 002. ℂ **0542/250-3001** through -3019. Fax 0542/220-4898. www.tajhotels.com. 130
units. $140 standard double, $150 superior large double; $190–$225 suite. $20 extra person. AE, MC, V. **Amenities:**
2 restaurants; bar; pool; tennis; health club; badminton; table tennis; yoga; indoor games; travel desk; 24-hr. room
service; massage; laundry; doctor-on-call; astrologer. *In room:* A/C, TV, dataport (soon to be Wi-Fi enabled), minibar,
tea-and coffee-making facilities, electronic safe.

WATERFRONT

Ganga View Guesthouse ✦✦ *Value*   You're required to remove your shoes upon
entering this lovely colonial lodge at the edge of the Ganges, and it's an appropriate gesture of respect given the effort that has turned this budget guesthouse—the best on the
Ganges—into such a comfortable haven. In fact, it's so popular with certain repeat
guests (many of them artists and musicians) that you'd do well to book your room up
to a year in advance. The gorgeous, simple guest rooms feature marble floors and
French doors that open onto enclosed corridors filled with ornamental columns,
charming bric-a-brac, antique furniture, and animal trophies. Straw mats and colorful
Indian throws add character to the tiny bedrooms. Book a rooftop room if you want
air-conditioning (and specify clearly). There is no formal dining area, but room service
is available. A delightful covered courtyard is stuffed full of portraits, religious artifacts,
memorabilia, objets d'art, and books. Upstairs, an open-air terrace packed with potted
plants and stylish cane furniture has excellent views of activity at the ghats.

B1/163 Assi Ghat, Varanasi 221 006. ℂ **0542/231-3218.** Fax 0542/236-9695. 12 units. Rs 2,500 ($57) A/C double, Rs 1,500 ($35) non-A/C double. No credit cards. **Amenities:** Musical performances; taxi and sightseeing arrangements; room service; laundry. *In room:* Some with A/C.

Palace on Ganges ⟨★⟩   It's no palace, but for the waterfront this is a reasonably smart option. Guest rooms are small but lovely, with marble floors and rugs, king-size beds with hard foam mattresses, and the best amenities on the Ganges. Walls are decorated with artworks reflecting aspects of Indian heritage sites, and each room is a tribute to a different regional style. Bathrooms, which have only showers, are done in colorful tiles. The heritage theme is carried throughout, with polished brown marble stairways, dark wood paneling, and intricately carved period furniture featuring inlaid decorative tiles. Although its location overlooking the Ganges is one of the selling points of the hotel, you aren't guaranteed a room with a view of the river (do request one, though longer stays enjoy first dibs), and views from the rooftop terrace restaurant (Jain food only) include an unpleasant garbage dump at the water's edge.

B-1/158 Assighat, Varanasi 221 001. ℂ **0542/231-5050,** -4304, or -4305. Fax 0542/220-4898 or 054/231-4306. www.palaceonganges.com. info@palaceonganges.com. 28 units. Rs 3,140 ($71) double, off-season (May–July) Rs 2,000 ($46) double; includes tax. AE, MC, V. **Amenities:** Restaurant; travel desk; car hire; 24-hr. room service; laundry; doctor-on-call. *In room:* A/C, TV, minibar.

WHERE TO DINE

Varanasi's best and smartest restaurant is **Varuna** (ℂ **0542/250-3001**), in the Taj Ganges hotel, which features a vast menu of Indian specialties (illustrated with chilies to indicate those that are super-strength), a comfortable air-conditioned interior, and helpful service. For the works, served on a traditional Varanasi silver platter, order the Satvik Thali (Rs 425/$9.65). That said, this is very much a hotel restaurant, and you may not be in the Cantonment area at lunchtime. The Taj's **Chowk** restaurant does dinner buffet spreads that are popular with foreign tour groups, and at Rs 400 ($9.10) the buffets offer very good value. For an authentic and hygienic Varanasi meal while you're exploring the Old City, head for one of the restaurants below.

Bread of Life Bakery & Restaurant ⟨★⟩ BAKERY/INTERNATIONAL CAFE This restaurant was established by James and Monika Hetherington, an American interior designer and a German flight attendant. The decor is a tad sterile (white vinyl-top tables), but the windows and small roadside terrace overlook an interesting street. You can enjoy wholesome Western dishes and freshly baked breads and muffins knowing that you are making a positive contribution—all profits from the bakery, and the silk shop above (which incidentally has a good selection of scarves and linen made by local weavers), go to local charities, including the Mother Teresa Hospice. Daily specials include steaming-hot vegetable moussaka, chickpea goulash, ratatouille, and warm Portuguese salad. Satisfy your sweet tooth with a generous helping of authentic German Black Forest cake. Hot dishes take a while to arrive, so you can be certain that everything is freshly prepared and, in a city known for food-related mishaps, that hygiene is a priority. Thick and fruity, the banana lassi is particularly good.

B3/445 Shivala, Varanasi 221 001. ℂ **0542/227-5012.** www.bolbar.com. Main courses Rs 50–Rs 180 ($1.15–$3.10); daily specials around Rs 80 ($1.80). No credit cards. Daily 9am–9pm.

The Keshari Restaurant ⟨*Value*⟩ INDIAN   A stern-looking, bespectacled clerk sits counting cash at the entrance of this busy, cramped restaurant (ideal if you're exploring the Old City) hidden away down a near-impossible-to-find back street. Inside, fans hover overhead and an ancient cooling system blasts away while waiters dash

Mindless Necrophagy or Road to Salvation?

Of all the *sadhus* (ascetics) and holy men you will see in Varanasi, perhaps the hardest to understand without brutal judgment are the Aghori sects and their bizarre rituals. You may spot the occasional aghori at a *smashan ghat* (cremation ground) in Varanasi, usually with matted hair and no clothing, or just covered in white ash, or at most wearing a funeral shroud. The skull he carries is his cranial eating and drinking bowl. Aghoris roam the cremation grounds, where they may smear themselves with the ash from the pyres and/or meditate sitting atop a corpse. It is alleged that as a once-in-a-lifetime act they sometimes also eat a piece of a corpse's flesh. While their rituals are extremely radical and even abhorrent to most, it's interesting to understand what underlies this bizarre behavior. Aghoris believe that acting contrary to the accepted norms and taboos of Brahmin ritual and belief is the necessary path to enlightenment. As a result, they eat meat, drink alcohol, and smoke intoxicants. By seeking to reverse all values entrenched within mainstream Hinduism, they choose to embrace all that a Brahmin considers impure. Close contact with the dead, they believe, is a way of focusing on their single-minded quest to live with reality. The funeral pyre is thus for the Aghoris a continual reminder that everyone has to die, and their obsession with death an attempt to live in intimate awareness of it.

---

between tables packed with locals, pilgrims, and bewildered foreigners. There's a huge selection of Indian, Chinese, and Continental dishes, all vegetarian, but we recommend you stick to the Indian fare, which includes *biryanis, pulao,* and a selection of breads. Try a thali; have the huge Keshari Thali if you're particularly ravenous. The Keshari special *dosa* (pancake) is filled with creamy *paneer* and cashew nuts. Lassis are all fantastic. To get here, head down the lane opposite the La-Ra Hotel.

Off Dasashwamedh Rd., near Godaulia crossing. ✆ 0542/240-1472. Main courses Rs 30–Rs 65 (70¢–$1.45); thali Rs 100 ($2.30). No credit cards. Daily 9am–10:30pm.

Sindhi Restaurant *(Value* INDIAN   The decor at this legendary eatery hasn't changed much since it first opened its doors in 1954. For more than 50 years, the same family has been operating a friendly, welcoming, and very popular eatery with comfortable brown *faux*-leather seats and plastic-topped wooden tables lined up in expectation of a brisk day's trade. Order a very filling special *thali* (multicourse platter), which includes chapati or *naan* bread, rice, two different vegetables, *dab bara, dal,* a *papad,* and something sweet to top it off. Among the other tasty vegetable dishes, the *dal makhani,* or *chole paneer,* a lively concoction made from chickpeas and *paneer* (cheese), are personal favorites.

Next to Lalitha Cinema, Kashinath Biswas Rd., Bhelupura, Lalitha. ✆ 0542/239-0313. Main courses Rs 15–Rs 50 (35¢–$1.15). No credit cards. Daily 8am–midnight.

SHOPPING

Varanasi is famous above all for its silk—every Indian bride wants a Benarasi silk sari in her trousseau, and around 3,000 kilograms (6,614 lb.) of silk are consumed by the weaving units daily. Wander through the Old City, or ask at your hotel or the tourist office for recommended wholesalers. **Silk Ways** (✆ 0542/221-0791), near Chhave

Mahal Cinema, has the most gossamer-like scarves, among other things. Or head for one of these two recommended sari shops in Chowk: **Narayan Das Jagdish Das** (© **0542/240-0561** or -0593) or **Ushnak Mal Mool Chand** (© **0542/227-6253**). You can also try **Kabir Sarees** in Madanpura (© **0542/240-1971**) or **Banarsi Saree. com** in Rathyatra (Varanasi © **0542/236-1464** or -1465).

4 Lucknow

497km (308 miles) SE of Delhi

Situated on the banks of the Gomti River, Lucknow, capital of Uttar Pradesh, has a relatively calm disposition, its urbane gentility and relative absence of beggars and touts a welcome change from the heady assault that so marks the experience in more popular North Indian cities. Lucknavis are in fact given to a peculiar strain of pomposity that seems entirely out of place in the 21st century—locals call out to you in *pukka* high-falutin' English "Good evening" at three in the afternoon, and a firm "How are you, gentleman?" is popular among locals keen to demonstrate their eloquent English, no matter how limited it really is.

Lucknow owes its sense of pride and heritage to the cultured Avadh *Nawabs:* A minor dynasty founded by the Persian aristocrat *Nawab* Saadat Khan Burhan-ul-Mulk, the *Nawabs* ruled the independent state of Avadh (or Oudh, as the British called it), which grew in splendor—so much so that by the middle of the 18th century (coinciding with the decline of Delhi), Lucknow was India's largest and most prosperous city, filled with grandiose palaces, gilded cupolas, and pleasure gardens. It was to retain this reputation for almost a century—in 1850 a correspondent for *The Times* of London favorably compared Lucknow with Rome, Athens, and Constantinople. While the *Nawabs* were known as men of refinement and taste, fond of poetry and courtly dance, they had some decadent predilections, highlighted by the last *Nawab's* weakness for *muta,* temporary marriages that often lasted a single night.

When the British summarily unseated the last *Nawab* and annexed Avadh in 1856, it helped spark the notorious Mutiny, known in India as the First War of Independence, during which 2,000 people were killed on the grounds of Lucknow's Residency. Much of Lucknow's former glory was further dissipated when, after Partition in 1947, the city's cultured elite emigrated en masse to Pakistan. Now the capital of a state plagued with corruption, Lucknow continues to draw the spotlight for the various political intrigues played out here by the state government.

ESSENTIALS

VISITOR INFORMATION There's a **U. P. Tourism Reception Counter** (© **0522/263-6173**) at Charbagh Station. The **U. P. Tourism Regional Office** (© **0522/263-8105;** Mon–Sat 10am–5pm, closed Sun and second Sat of the month) is at 10 Station Rd.; best to browse www.lucknowonline.com before your visit. The 24-hour **emergency help line** number is © **99355-667788.**

GETTING THERE By car, the trip from Delhi takes roughly 10 hours, by bus 12 hours; far better to fly. Lucknow's **Amausi Airport** is 14km (9 miles) from the town center (Rs 150–Rs 250/$3.40–$5.70 for a prepaid taxi into town). Lucknow is served by all the main domestic airlines. Flights from Delhi take an hour. Other connected cities include Mumbai, Kolkata, Chennai, Bangalore, Hyderabad, Ahmedabad, and Varanasi. The **Lucknow Mail** leaves Delhi at 10pm and arrives in Lucknow at 7am the following day. Alternatively, enjoy the scenery by catching the **Lucknow Shatabdi** at 6:15am; the train pulls in at Lucknow's **Charbagh Station** at 12:30pm.

GETTING AROUND   By Taxi & Auto-Rickshaw   You can see just about every-thing Lucknow has to offer in half a day. Hire an auto-rickshaw or a taxi with a driver for the duration; be sure to settle the price in advance.

GUIDED TOURS & TRAVEL AGENTS   One of the most reputable travel agents in Lucknow is **Tornos House** (✆ **0522/239-6965** or -9472; info@tornosindia.com; tornos@stayam.net.in), which supplies transport and keen guides (Rs 350/$8 half-day; Rs 500/$11 full day) who can take you to little-known places of interest. This is quite easily the best tour of Lucknow available, and from an extremely tourist-friendly company. Or for around Rs 125 ($2.85), you can join the **U. P. Tourism** bus tour of Lucknow, taking in the city's most popular sights, including the Residency, the three Imambaras, the Clock Tower, the Picture Gallery, and the Martyr's Memorial. **Sita World Travel/SOTC** (Rana Pratap Marg; ✆ **0522/220-9611**) is a consistently reli-able national travel agent.

FESTIVALS   Rooted in Shia Muslim traditions, Lucknow enjoys some unique cus-toms, the most significant of which is **Muharram,** a festival that commemorates the martyrdom of Imam Hussein, the Prophet's grandson. Whereas in other parts of the world, Muharram lasts between 10 and 12 days, in Lucknow it extends over 2 months and 8 days. During this time, people gather in the Shia *imambaras* in the presence of *taziyas* (replicas of the tombs of the martyrs), and it's not uncommon to see men flag-ellating themselves with knives and chains as symbolic acts of their need to be forgiven for being unable to help defend the martyr.

THINGS TO SEE & DO

You can easily see Lucknow's significant sights in a morning. At the top of the list is the **Bara (Great) Imambara** (see below). Your ticket also provides access to the nearby **Chhota (Little) Imambara** ✿, which contains the tombs of its creator, Mohammed Ali Shah, and his mother. Built in 1837, it features opulent and ornate interiors with colorful stucco walls, gilt-edged mirrors, a golden domed silver pulpit *(mimbar),* and chandeliers that are lit during Muharram. In between the two Imambaras is the **Husainabad Clock Tower,** and near it is the **Picture Gallery,** where life-size portraits of the *Nawabs* of Oudh are housed. Don't miss the portrait of Nawab Wajid Ali hid-den behind a curtain, allegedly because a British lady fainted after seeing the last *Nawab's* strategically exposed nipple.

La Martinière College ✿✿, a lovely stone mansion off Kalidas Marg, is one of the architectural highlights of Lucknow, and although it's not really open to visitors, you can admire the facade of the 17th-century home of Claude Martin, major general of the East India Company, and wander around the grounds. Huge stone lions with gap-ing jaws stand upon the mansion gables, and it's said that fires were lit in their mouths to illuminate the glaring eyes of these beasts in order to scare off the wild animals of the surrounding swamps.

Although **The Residency** (M.G. Rd.; Rs 105/$2.40; Tues–Sun 7am–5:30pm) is billed as one of the city's top attractions, the ruins here hold little appeal unless you're intimate with their history. The home of the British Resident appointed to look into the affairs of the Oudh, where more than 2,000 British residents and Indians loyal to the Raj died during the Mutiny, it bears the scars of fierce bombardment. The sprawl-ing complex of burnt-out, skeletal buildings is in pretty much the same state as the day the siege ended. Feel free to skip this, and head for the bazaars where you can experience Lucknow's colorful daily life. In the predominantly Shiite Muslim area of the Chowk, women in black *burkas* go about their daily shopping, while merchants in white prayer caps operate their businesses in premises downstairs from their family homes, protected from the sun by wooden shutters and *jalis* (screens).

Lucknow is famous for *attar,* the scented oils used to make perfumes. Used by Muslim men and women, the oils are made from a magnificent variety of flowers and fruits; some fragrances are created to smell like the earth during monsoon rains. Chowk Bazaar is filled with attar shops; to purchase a sample, visit **Izhar Ahmad & Sons,** or the granddaddy of them all, **Azam Ali-Alam Ali Industry,** which has been producing attars for centuries. Lucknow is also famous for delicate *chikankaari* embroidery, now a major industry. Wander around the shops of Aminabad and you'll definitely see some fabric or *kurtas* worth buying.

Try to take lunch at either branch of the famous **Tunday Kababi** (see "Where to Dine," below), which serves cheap, delicious bazaar food.

Bara Imambara ✨✨   Built in 1784, Lucknow's most significant monument is a large edifice of grandiose proportions, built of *lakhauri* bricks plastered with lime and decorated with molding. The Great Imambara houses what is said to be the largest vaulted hall in the world. The hall's interior is kept cool by massive hollow walls that also help lighten the load of the structure, completely unsupported by pillars or beams. Dripping with Belgian chandeliers and other ornate embellishments, the hall is where the *taziyas* (paper shrines representing the graves of Imam Hussain and the martyrs of Karbala) are kept when not being carried through the streets of the city each year during the solemn month of Muharram. Visitors to the Bara Imambara enter through **Rumi Darwaza,** an 18m (60-ft.) tower that stands like a sentinel overlooking the city's grand monuments. For a truly atmospheric experience with fabulous views of the complex and of the surrounding neighborhood, head upstairs to the attic's labyrinthine maze called the *bulbulya;* just above this is a flat roof where you can relax and observe the city. Adjacent the Bara Imambara, **Asafi Mosque** is off-limits to non-Muslims. Across from it is an atmospheric step well, or *bauli.* (The Bada Imambara is best appreciated with a good guide; see guided tours above.)

Hussainabad. Admission Rs 300 ($6.85), combined entry for all sites. Sat–Thurs 7am–7pm; closed during Muharram.

WHERE TO STAY

Besides the two hotels reviewed, the only option worth mentioning is **Clarks Avadh** (8 M.G. Rd.; ✆ **0522/261-6500;** doubles from Rs 4,500/$102). It's considerably

---

⌈Fun Fact⌋ Aristocrats at Work

The Bara Imambara was built not out of necessity, but to help its starving citizens during the onset of a terrible famine. Even noble and aristocratic Lucknavis, too proud to beg, worked on the project—though only at night to avoid being recognized. The following day masons and qualified artisans worked on the construction, usually after first tearing down the abysmal work done by the gentry. Those who helped in building were paid wages and given free food, and the community kitchen that was set up is said to have spawned the famous *dum pukht* style of cooking.

cheaper and better located than the luxurious Taj Residency, but you'll find better value at La Place Park Inn (see below). Accommodations are adequate (TV, A/C) but tasteless (room nos. 10–16, on the upper level, are the best), there is no pool, and the hotel is run by what appears to be a squadron of permanently grouchy managers. That said, the in-house restaurant, **Falaknuma** (reviewed below), serves excellent Lucknowi cuisine.

La Place Park Inn 🅡 *Value*   Conveniently situated near the city center, this smart business hotel with a neoclassical facade may not have fantastic views or any real sense of history, but it offers comfortable, quiet, and spacious accommodations. Elegant and uncluttered, the deluxe guest rooms have creamy marble floors, smart sofas, and good, firm mattresses. Bathrooms are also a decent size, and the second-floor deluxe and executive rooms have tubs. If you don't mind the extra dollars, the executive rooms are fabulously large, with plenty of cupboard space, separate sitting areas, and wonderful king-size beds. Stylish, but hardly ostentatious, La Place features a reliable restaurant and public areas punctuated with watercolors and color lithographs illustrating Lucknow's past. The inn has no pool, but businesspeople will be pleased to know that the entire hotel is Wi-Fi enabled.

6 Shahnajaf Rd., Lucknow 226 001. © **0522/262-0220**, 0522/228-2201, -2202, -2203, or -2204. Fax 0522/262-0522. lppi@sarovarparkplaza.com. www.parkinnlucknow.com. 50 units. Rs 3,600 ($82) deluxe double, Rs 4,500 ($102) executive double; Rs 6,500 ($148) executive suite. AE, DC, MC, V. **Amenities:** 2 restaurants; 2 bars; business center; airport transfers; currency exchange; 24-hr. room service; laundry; dry cleaning; doctor-on-call. *In room:* A/C, TV, minibar, hair dryer on request.

Taj Residency Lucknow 🅡🅡   Grandiose yet charming, this white neo-colonial-style building, set in vast landscaped gardens, is by far Lucknow's loveliest option. With its palatial white marble lobby and elegant architectural flourishes, it was originally conceived as a leisure hotel and is now aimed at business travelers and politicians. Accommodations are excellent; standard rooms have high ceilings and plush furniture, and bathrooms have tubs and are scented with potpourri and hibiscus flowers. Choose a ground-floor deluxe room (garden- or pool-facing) for heaps of space, a king-size four-poster bed, and a private balcony. There's a great swimming pool from where you can admire the hotel's arched and colonnaded rear facade.

Gomti Nagar, Lucknow 226 010. © **0522/239-3939**, -1201, -1202, or 1203. Fax 0522/239-2282 or -2465. www.taj hotels.com. 110 units. $155 standard double, $175 executive double, $215 deluxe double; $300 suite. $20 extra bed. All rates except standard include breakfast. AE, DC, MC, V. **Amenities:** 2 restaurants; bar; pool; fitness center (gymnasium, steam bath, Jacuzzi, massage); travel desk; sightseeing; guide service; car hire; business center; currency exchange; salon; 24-hr. room service; babysitting; laundry; dry cleaning; doctor-on-call. *In room:* A/C, TV, minibar, tea-and coffee-making facilities, hair dryer.

WHERE TO DINE

Gastronomically sophisticated, the *Nawabs* of Lucknow considered the skillful preparation of food an art form. Their kitchens *(bawarchi khana)* took pride of place in the royal courts, and it's a matter of legend that Nawab Salar Jung paid his *rakabdar* (gourmet cook) an exorbitant (at the time) Rs 1,200 ($28) per month. Today Lucknow is known for Avadhi cuisine with its rich, spicy meat dishes, the most famous of which is *nihari* (meat stew). Melt-in-the-mouth kebabs, *biryanis,* and tandoori chicken items are particularly favored, and cream, saffron, raisins, cashews, and almonds are all commonly used. A popular dessert is the royal bread-and-reduced-milk pudding, *shahi tukda.* The influence of the *Nawabs* lives on not only in the city's two top hotel restaurants, but also in the bazaars at Chowk and Aminabad, where the busier stalls are excellent for traditional no-frills food. For a plate of truly outstanding takeout *biryani*, stop off at the street-food stall of Mohammed Idris, opposite the Patanala Police booth at the Firangi Mahal bridge. **Rahim** (at Akbari gate) is Lucknow's favorite *nanfu* (specialized *roti* or bread-maker); dab up *nehari* with his amazing *kulchas* (flaky pan bread), and finish with *sheermal* (milk bread)—soft, buttery, and sweet.

Falaknuma 🅐🅐 LUCKNOWI   On the ninth floor of the Clarks Hotel, Falaknuma—a popular choice with local diners—offers excellent views of the city, so be sure to grab a table near a window. Live Indian music is performed every night except Tuesday. It offers a good variety of mouthwatering Lucknowi specialties; if you've never had *kakori kebab*, made with minced lamb and mixed Indian spices, try it here with *roomali roti*. Also excellent is Avadhi *murgh korma*, spring chicken cooked in golden gravy that's rich and spicy. The host, Mr. Srivastava, has been keeping guests satisfied for over a decade.

Clarks Avadh, 8 Mahatma Gandhi Marg. 🕐 0522/261-6500 through -6509. Main courses Rs 175–Rs 350 ($4–$8). AE, DC, MC, V. Daily 1–3:15pm and 8–11:30pm.

Oudhyana 🅐🅐🅐 LUCKNOWI/INDIAN   For years celebrity Avadhi cuisine chef Gulam Rasool ran this fine dining establishment, and even though he doesn't preside over their kitchen anymore, he's left behind a tradition of exemplary cooking. Start with a soothing *thandai* (a chilled blend of chopped almonds, cashew nuts, and pistachios blended with milk and a dash of pepper), and then move on to a kebab platter while sampling rich saffron-flavored bread *(sheermal)*, fresh from the tandoor. Favorites include *galawat ke kebab* (pan-fried medallions of minced lamb), *kakori kebab* (minced lamb blended with saffron, rose petals, and cardamom), *nihari* (thick mutton curry), and *murgh tikka "mirza hasnoo"* (chicken marinated in yogurt, flavored with saffron, and chargrilled with exotic spices). Vegetarians should definitely get the *dilkhush kofta* (made with *paneer* and dry fruits). Leave room for *shahi tukda*, a traditional Lucknowi dessert—deep-fried bread soaked in sweetened milk and saffron-flavored *rabri*, and finished with pistachios and almonds.

Taj Residency, Gomti Nagar. 🕐 0522/239-3939. Reservations recommended for dining 8–9pm. Main courses Rs 140–Rs 475 ($3.35–$11). AE, DC, MC, V. Daily 12:30–3pm and 7:30–11:15pm.

Tunday Kababi 🅐🅐 *(Moments)* LUCKNOWI KEBABS   More than a century old, this Muslim family-run establishment is named for an ancestor with a physical disability *(tunday)*, and it remains a very popular bazaar-based hot spot. This place is a relatively hygienic version of the original Tunday Kababi (beef-only stall) at Akbari Gate is often referred to as "grandson of Tunday." At both places chefs work over huge metallic woks and grills. While it is true that Tunday's mutton kebabs and tandoori chicken have represented the city at international food festivals, there's a significant difference in the quality of ingredients being used here, where a plate of kebabs sets you back a mere Rs 16 to Rs 20 (35¢–45¢).

Naaz Cinema Rd., Aminabad. Kebabs Rs 8–Rs 20 (20¢–45¢); half-tandoori chicken Rs 50 ($1.15). No credit cards. Daily 11am–11pm.

5 Khajuraho 🅐🅐🅐

600km (372 miles) SE of Delhi; 415km (257 miles) SW of Varanasi; 395km (245 miles) SE of Agra

Legend has it that when the Moon God saw the young maiden Hemavati bathing in a river, her beauty was such that he descended to Earth to engage in a passionate affair.

Fun Fact **India's Ancient Sex Manual**

Khajuraho's shops are filled with an endless variety of versions of the *Kama Sutra*, an ancient avatar of modern-day do-it-yourself sex manuals. With information about everything from "increasing the size of the male organ" to the benefits of "slaps and screams" and "bites and scratches," the ancient treatise on sensory pleasures—recorded by the scribe Vatsyayana from oral accounts sometime between the 1st and 6th century A.D.—remains the most famous Indian text in the world. The first English translation was published in 1883 by the Victorian adventurer Richard Burton, who adapted the text in order to dodge charges of obscenity; among other confusing details, he used the Sanskrit words *lingam* and *yoni* to denote the sexual organs.

Before his return to the celestial realm, he swore she would bear a son who would one day erect a great temple to celebrate the beauty of their divine love. Thus the founder of the mighty Chandela dynasty, a robust clan of the warrior Rajputs, was born, and between A.D. 900 and 1100, the Chandela kings—who settled in remote Khajuraho, where they were clearly unhindered by the usual distractions of fighting off invading forces—built not 1 but 85 temples, almost all of them featuring exquisite sculptures of men and women joyfully engaging in the most intimate and erotic acts. The Chandelas held sway here until the start of the 13th century, when the Sultans of Delhi increased their hold over vast swaths of central North India. By the end of the 15th century, the temples were abandoned, hidden deep within thick jungle, until their accidental discovery by a British military adventurer in 1838. By this time, 7 centuries after the political decline of their Chandela creators, only 22 of the original 85 temples remained. Today these UNESCO World Heritage Site monuments are famous for their transgressive, taboo-breaking erotic sculptures, images that are almost as intimately associated with India as the Taj. But the temples also represent an outstanding synthesis of advanced architecture and refined sculpture, and their beauty means that a trip here should definitely be included in your North India itinerary, particularly if you plan to fly from Agra or Delhi to Varanasi.

ESSENTIALS

GETTING THERE & AWAY   By Air   It's most convenient to fly in from Delhi (or Agra if flights have resumed) and fly on to Varanasi the following day. During the high season (winter), daily Jet Airways flights, which are usually pretty full of package tour groups, do exactly this. Khajuraho's airport is 3km (2 miles) from the town center; a taxi should cost Rs 150 ($3.40), an auto-rickshaw Rs 50 to Rs 60 ($1.15–$1.35).

By Train & Road   We cannot sufficiently emphasize the appalling state of the roads in Madhya Pradesh. Avoid lengthy road travel, ensure sufficient stops, and don't travel at night. If you must, rent the services of a sturdy 4WD and driver, and check that your vehicle has at least one spare wheel. If you're traveling by train from Delhi, Mumbai, or Chennai, you will disembark at Jhansi (175km/108 miles from Khajuraho). From New Delhi, catch the Bhopal Shatabdi, which leaves the capital's Nizamuddin Station at 6am and pulls in at Jhansi at 10:40am. From here, MPSRTC runs a bus service from Jhansi to Khajuraho, scheduled to meet the train from Delhi (Rs 85–Rs 90/$1.90–$2.05—not recommended), or you can catch a taxi (Rs 1,500/$35) to Khajuraho (4 hr.). You can also rent a car and driver for a few days if you have plans to see more of the region—note that Orchha (20km/12 miles from Jhansi) is definitely worth a stop en route to Khajuraho (Orchha is discussed later in the chapter). If you're traveling from Mumbai, Kolkata, or Varanasi, you will arrive at Satna, which is 117km (72 miles) or 3 hours from town.

VISITOR INFORMATION M. P. Tourism (© 07686/274-051; Mon–Sat 10am–5pm, closed Sun and second and third Sat of the month; mptkhaj@sancharnet. in) is in the Chandela Cultural Centre, Khajuraho. The more helpful **Government of India tourism office** (© 07686/27-2347; Mon–Fri 9:30am–6pm) is located opposite the Western Group of Temples. Note that the state tourism website, **www.mp tourism.com**, as well as the unrelated **www.khajuraho-temples.com**, are both excellent sources

GETTING AROUND **By Taxi, Auto-Rickshaw & Cycle-Rickshaw** You will be flooded with offers to take you from Khajuraho's airport to your accommodations; in return, touts and drivers expect you to use their services for the duration of your stay, and will even continue to lurk outside your hotel. Make it clear that yours is a one-time fare, and stick to cycle-rickshaws and walking for the duration of your stay (average cost Rs 15/35¢ per kilometer; or Rs 120/$2.75 for a half-day trip including a stop at the Southern Group). To visit the Panna temples, expect to pay Rs 1,000 ($23) for a taxi.

GUIDES Guides charge Rs 350 ($8) for a group of one to five people for 6 hours. You can hire the services of a guide at **Raja Café** (opposite the Western Group of temples; see below). Alternatively, the MPSTDC offers a "Walkman Tour"—an audioguide tour purchased at the M. P. Tourism counter at the entrance to the Western Group; this costs Rs 50 ($1.15), but do check that everything is in working order before you set out. Be warned that most guides in Khajuraho are just plain dreadful. They may be fine for pointing out details you might otherwise miss, but they regularly spout fundamentalist nonsense and provide the most unbelievable explanations for why erotica was carved on these temples (one classic explanation is that the scenes were created to tell people what *"not* to do"). An exception to the normal drivel is **Samson George** (ask for him at Raja Café), a light-hearted guy who provides savvy historical information, with explanations that separate fact from legend.

FESTIVALS The **Khajuraho Dance Festival** 🏵🏵 is held between February 25 and March 2, when the temples are transformed into a magical backdrop for India's top classical dancers, who perform traditional Odissi, Kuchipudi, and Bharatnatyam dance forms, as well as contemporary Indian dance styles. For up-to-date information, visit **www.khajuraho-temples.com**. *Tip:* Hotels get packed during this time, so you may need to book months ahead.

EXPLORING KHAJURAHO'S TEMPLES

Known for the profusion of sculptural embellishments on both exterior and interior walls, Khajuraho's temples are also recognizable for the exaggerated vertical sweep in the majority of the temples, with a series of *shikharas* (spires) that grow successively higher. Serving as both metaphoric and literal "stairways to heaven," these shikharas are believed to be a visual echo of the soaring Himalayan mountains, abode of Lord Shiva. Most of the sculpted temples are elevated on large plinths (often also shared by four smaller corner shrines), and follow the same five-part design. After admiring the

Khajuraho

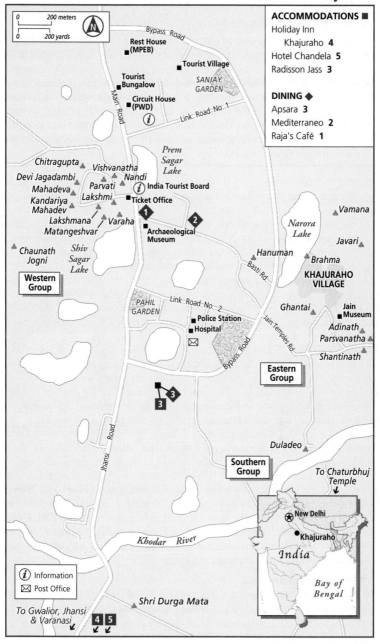

Tips Services Unlimited

As you wend your way around town, older teenage boys will try to "adopt" you by starting up polite conversations—a pattern you will quickly recognize— before getting down to the business of offering their services for a range of possible needs: tour guides, transport, bicycle hire, shopping assistance, advice, or a tour of the local village school. All are money-making enterprises of which you should be wary. On the other hand, there is little harm in enjoying the company and charm of a local host; best to make it very clear that you have no intention of parting with your money, and leave it to your new friend to decide whether or not to stick around.

---

raised entrance area, you will enter a colonnaded hall that leads to a smaller vestibule and then an inner courtyard, around which is an enclosed sanctum. You can circum-navigate the sanctum (move around the temple in a clockwise direction, in the man-ner of the ritual *pradakshina,* with your right shoulder nearest the temple building) to view the beautifully rendered friezes of gods, nymphs, animals, and energetically twist-ing bodies locked together in acts of hot-blooded passion.

Originally spread across a large open area, unprotected by walls, the temples—most of them built from sandstone lugged on bullock carts from the banks of the River Ken 30km (19 miles) away—are today roughly divided into three sections according to geo-graphic location: the Western, Eastern, and Southern groups. The most spectacular— and those most obviously dripping with erotic sculpture—are within the Western Group. The Eastern Group is located near the old village, and the Southern Group, which is the most missable, lies south of this. As none of the temples outside the West-ern Group are likely to evoke quite the same delighted reaction, see these first if you're pushed for time or tired; they're also conveniently located near the majority of hotels. Try to enter as soon as they open (sunrise), not only for the quality of light but to avoid the busloads of tourists who will almost certainly detract from the experience.

You can cover the Western Group in 2 hours. The baritone voice of Amitabh Bachchan, arguably India's most popular screen icon, narrates the fascinating history of Khajuraho for the 50-minute **sound-and-light show** held here each night at 6:30pm (an hour later in summer). Try to time your visit to the Eastern Group for about 3 or 4pm, so you can enjoy the sunset while you return either to the Western Group or to the imminently more peaceful Chaturbhuj Temple in the Southern Group. To save time and get the most out of the experience, an official guide—hired through the Raja Café, tourist office, or your hotel—is highly recommended; avoid all unofficial touts and guides. Note that you can rent an audioguide, which is useful if you don't want to be accompanied by a guide.

WESTERN GROUP ***

As you make your way around the complex in a clockwise direction, the first impor-tant structure you'll encounter is **Lakshmana Temple** ***, one of the three largest in Khajuraho. Built in commemoration of military victory and temporal power, it is thought to be one of the earliest Chandela temples, completed around A.D. 954, yet relatively intact. The structure is as high as it is long, and its raised platform is, like the entire temple, heavily decorated with a variety of sculptures that allude to the pleasures, pastimes, lifestyle, desires, and conquests of the Chandela dynasty. Here you will witness an astonishing diversity of scenes: horse-mounted hunters pursuing their prey, musicians providing lively entertainment for the court, couples drunk on love and liquor, female attendants fanning their king, elephants engaged in playful battle, soldiers on the march and, of course, amorous couples keeping themselves occupied in the most literal of pleasures. Higher up, above bands of images of Shiva and Vishnu, are the voluptuous depictions of women engaged in worldly activity while draped in little more than jewelry and gossamer-like garments.

Inside the temple, covered with more depictions of gorgeous women and deities in their various avatars and incarnations, light pours in through high balconies on each side of the structure, and shadows are cast seductively over the imaginatively carved walls. The main shrine was built to house the three-headed image of Vishnu-Vaikuntha, which features one human head and the head of two of Vishnu's avatars (incarnations), a lion and a boar.

Opposite the temple are two smaller structures, **Devi Mandap** and **Varaha Mandap** ⊛. The latter is an open sandstone pavilion on a high platform with 14 pillars supporting a high pyramidal roof with a flat ceiling carved with lovely lotus designs. A large stone sculpture of Varaha, the incarnation of Vishnu as the Boar, dominates the space. Varaha's polished monolithic body is carved with hundreds of tiny Brahmanical gods and goddesses.

At the northeastern end of the Western Group complex, a number of magnificent temples are found in close proximity to one another. Thought to have been built between A.D. 1017 and 1029, elegantly proportioned **Kandariya Mahadev Temple** ⊛⊛⊛ is considered the finest temple in Khajuraho, with 872 statues adorning the interior and exterior. Within niches around the temple are images of Ganesh and the seven mother goddesses or *Sapta Matrikas*. Again, among the sculptures of Shiva and the other deities is a profusion of female figures engaged in daily activities made lovely by the sheer exuberance of the sculptural technique: A woman stretches, another plays with a ball, another admires her reflection in a mirror. You won't have to search too hard to find fascinating erotic panels; kissing, caressing couples are depicted with their bodies entwined in blissful union.

To enter the temple building, you pass through the beautiful entrance *toran;* sculpted from a single piece of stone, this is a floral garland that stems from the mouths of *makaras,* ever-watchful mythical crocodiles, and is carried across the doorway by flying nymphs. Within the temple chambers, the walls are covered with exquisite carvings and sculptures: Don't forget to look upward to appreciate the sculpted flower and leaf motifs of the ceilings. There's a Shiva lingam deep within the *garbha griha,* or "womb chamber"; devotees today place flowers on and around the lingam.

Next to Kandariya Mahadev Temple is small **Mahadev Shrine,** which features a sculpted figure of what is thought to be the emblem of the Chandela dynasty, a raging lion fighting with a kneeling figure. Alongside it is **Devi Jagadambi Temple** ⊛⊛— note the graceful woman who stands half-naked as she interrupts her bath, possibly to catch a glimpse of Shiva's wedding procession. The southern wall includes a panel with a woman climbing up her lover's stout, standing body so that she can kiss him passionately. Although originally dedicated to Vishnu, the temple now houses a large image of Devi Jagadambi, the goddess of the universe, also known as Kali, one of the avatars of Shiva's divine consort. In both this and nearby **Chitragupta Temple** ⊛, images of Parvati and Shiva in the throes of amorous passion are symbolic of the "cosmic union that makes the world go round." Chitragupta, which was poorly renovated by the Maharaja of Chattarpur, is dedicated to Surya, the sun god; the relief carving around the entrance is the temple's highlight. Within the temple is the figure of Surya riding his sun chariot across the eternal sky.

Back near the entrance of the complex stands the **Temple of Vishvanatha** ⍟, built in A.D. 1002 by King Dhanga, and notable for three female figures that decorate the building. One maiden plays the flute, her back sensuously exposed to the viewer, another cradles a baby, and the third has a parrot seated on her wrist. Opposite the main entrance of the temple is **Nandi Pavilion** (or *mandap*), in which one of the largest figures of Shiva's companion, Nandi the bull, can be found, sculpted from a single piece of stone.

Outside the walls of the Western Group complex, but right alongside the Lakshman Temple, is the still-functioning **Matangeshvar Temple.** It is here that the annual Maha-Shivratri Festival culminates when the Shiva-Parvati marriage ceremony is accompanied by latter-day wedding rituals, lasting through the entire night in a fantastic collaboration of myth and reality.

Across the road from the entrance to the Western Group is the **Archaeological Museum,** with its modest selection of sculptures collected from various Khajuraho sites. The advantage of spending a few minutes here is that you get to see close-up details of carved figures that usually occur high up on the temple *shikharas.*

Main Rd., opposite the State Bank of India. Admission Rs 250 ($5.70). Daily 6:30am–sunset. English-language sound-and-light show Mar–June 7:30pm, Sept–Oct 7pm, Nov–Feb 6:30pm; Rs 250 ($5.70). Archaeological Museum Sat–Thurs 10am–5pm; Rs 5 (10¢). No photography in the museum.

EASTERN GROUP

The Eastern Group comprises both Hindu and Jain temples. The entrance to the Jain **Shantinath Temple** is guarded by a pair of mythical lions; inside, you are confronted by esoteric charts detailing some of the finer points of Jain philosophy. Photographs of important sculptures and Jain architecture line some of the walls, while the individual shrine entrances are carved with amorous, non-erotic couples and other figures. The main shrine contains a large sculpted image of a naked saint. Throughout the temple, devotees place grains of rice and nuts as tributes at the feet of the various saints.

Parsvanatha Temple ⍟ dates to the middle of the 10th century A.D. and is the finest and best preserved of Khajuraho's old Jain temples. Since Jainism promotes an ascetic doctrine, there are no erotic images here, but the sculptural decoration is rich nonetheless. In a large panel at the right side of the entrance are images of meditating and naked Jain saints *(tirthankaras),* while the temple exterior is covered in decorative sculptures of voluptuous maidens, embracing couples, and solo male figures representing various Hindu deities. This is a strong indication that the temple—which recalls the temples of the Western Group—was perhaps originally Hindu. In the same complex, **Adinath Temple** has been modified and reconstructed with plastered masonry and even concrete.

Moving north to the Hindu temples, you will pass **Ghantai Temple;** built in A.D. 1148, it is named for the pretty sculpted bells that adorn its pillars. Passing between Javari Temple and the granite and sandstone "Brahma" Temple (more likely to be dedicated to Shiva given the presence of a lingam), you come to the northernmost of the Eastern Group temples, the Hindu **Vamana Temple,** built between A.D. 1050 and 1075. Vamana is the short, plump, dwarf incarnation of Vishnu. The entrance to the inner sanctum of this temple is decorated with small erotic relief panels; within the sanctum you will see Vishnu in many forms, including the Buddha, believed to be one of his incarnations.

SOUTHERN GROUP

One of the last temples to be built, **Duladeo Temple** dates back to the 12th century A.D. but has been subjected to later restoration. Standing on the banks of Khuddar Stream, facing east, the temple is dedicated to Shiva. Elaborately crowned and ornamented *apsaras,* flying *vidyadharas,* crocodile-mounted *ashtavasu* figures, and sculptures of over-ornamented and stereotypically endowed characters in relatively shallow relief decorate the interior. As at Parshvanath Temple, the walls of Duladeo feature a narrow band of sculptures that depict the celestial garland carriers and musicians in attendance at the wedding of Shiva and Parvati.

The unexceptional **Chaturbhuj Temple,** 3km (2 miles) south of Duladeo, sees very little traffic but has a remarkable sculpture of Vishnu and is a peaceful place at the best of times, not least at sunset. Nearby excavations continue to unearth new temple complexes, as Khajuraho keeps revealing more hidden gems.

EXCURSIONS

Panna National Park ⌅ A mere 27km (17 miles) from Khajuraho, Panna covers 542 sq. km (211 sq. miles) of dry deciduous forests, fed by the Ken River—jungles of teak, Indian ebony, and flame-of-the-forest trees alternate with wide-open grassy plains in what were once the hunting grounds of several royal families. Although Panna has as few as 25 tigers, sightings have begun to escalate in recent years, so this is a good place to visit if you're unlikely to make it to any other tiger reserve. You're certainly likely to encounter *nilgai,* Indian gazelle, sambar, and four-horned antelope; sightings are dramatically improved if you take a relaxing elephant safari. Adjacent to the park is the ancient town of Panna, home to the largest diamond mines in Asia.

27km (17 miles) from Khajuraho. ✆ 07732/25-2135. Bookings through Forest Department, located at the park entrance. Park fees: Rs 500 ($11) admission; Rs 150 ($3.40) vehicle entry; Rs 100 ($2.30) guide; Rs 40 (90¢) still camera; Rs 300 ($6.85) video camera; Rs 600 ($14) elephant rides. Daily 6:30–10:30am and 3–5pm. Closed July–Sept.

WHERE TO STAY

If you're simply overnighting, it's best to stay in the village, from where you can walk to the majority of temples—the Radisson Jass is your best bet here. For those who want a more romantic, earthy experience and a visit to Panna National Park, Ken River Lodge is the place to be. Be warned that at present there is no fabulous lodging option to be found here, though in the pipeline (for the longest time) is the proposed creation of Khajuraho's first heritage accommodations, at the hitherto deserted 19th-century **Rajgarh Palace.** Situated some 25km (15 miles) from the village, at the foot of the Manijagarh Hills, this beautiful palace has exceptional views, and the end result is likely to be spectacular. You can get updated information about developments from the local tourism bureau.

IN KHAJURAHO

There are a few self-billed "luxury" options situated along Khajuraho's main road; if they're not included below, it's because they really aren't worth it. A large strip of hotels and guesthouses is dedicated to backpackers; rooms vary considerably. Budget travelers should head for **Hotel Surya** (Jain Temple Rd.; ✆ **07686/27-4145**), where Rs 600 to Rs 800 ($14–$18) buys you a clean, spartan room with an air conditioner and attached drench shower (ask for a room with a balcony, from where you can watch early risers practice yoga in the garden).

Holiday Inn Khajuraho   Ask for one of the newer guest rooms, which are spacious and cheerful, with marble floors, furniture with wooden inlay designs, pale yellow and gold curtains, matching bedcovers, and brass lamps; bathrooms are in marble and tile and have tubs and old-fashioned faucets. The hotel has a good range of amenities, and traditional Bundelkund buffet meals are sometimes served around the pool. In the evenings, catch classical music performances or Rajasthani puppet shows. Though this hotel is as unexceptional as the Hotel Chandela, you can get real value here when you check for online or seasonal specials.

Airport Rd., Khajuraho 471 606. ℂ **07686/27-2301** through -2303. Fax 07686/27-2304. www.ichotelsgroup.com. 84 units. $75 standard double; $120 suite. Taxes extra. Check online for 14-day advance purchase and other discounts. AE, DC, MC, V. **Amenities:** Restaurant; bar; pool; nightclub; tennis court; jogging track; health club with sauna; concierge; travel desk; safety deposit box; currency exchange; salon; room service; washer-dryer (self-laundry) facilities; doctor-on-call. *In room:* A/C, TV; some w/minibar, hair dryer, iron and ironing board.

Hotel Chandela   Located a mere kilometer from Khajuraho's main temple complex, this pleasant low-rise Taj hotel hardly represents innovative design, but nevertheless has peaceful gardens and comfortable accommodations, the best of which are around the rectangular pool. Guest rooms are dull and tired—a potted plant and prints reflecting India's artistic heritage pass for decor—but they are clean. Ask for a room on the ground floor; these open directly onto the pool mezzanine with its lawns and palms. The staff is friendly and helpful, but don't expect snappy big-city efficiency.

Airport Rd., Khajuraho 471 606. ℂ **07686/27-2355** through -2364. Fax 07686/27-2365/6. chandela.khajuraho@ tajhotels.com. www.tajhotels.com. 94 units. $85 standard double; $115 suite, $165 terrace suite. $20 extra person. 10% tax extra. Ask about off-season discounts. AE, DC, MC, V. **Amenities:** 2 restaurants; bar; pool; mini-golf; tennis court; fitness center; pool table; badminton; table tennis; darts; indoor games; archery; travel desk; salon; book shop; room service; laundry; doctor-on-call. *In room:* A/C, TV, minibar, hair dryer.

Radisson Jass ⋆⋆ ⟨Value⟩   The service and atmosphere make the Jass—which has a bizarrely futuristic appearance from the outside—the best Khajuraho has to offer. Bright white marble-floored public spaces are decorated with attractive Indian artworks, and you can spend some time wandering through the passages studying the collection of large Mughal paintings. After Radisson took over management, extensive renovations were undertaken throughout 2005, with new "super deluxe" rooms now available and a few new amenities added. (Strangely, at press time the hotel was still not on the Radisson website.) All guest rooms, now done in off-white hues, are fairly spacious and have balconies and either garden, pool, or mountain views; those overlooking the pool on the first floor (reached via a twisting marble staircase with an impressive chandelier hanging from a domed ceiling) are best. In the new wing, rooms have minibars and balconies with mountain views. The low-key atmosphere is enhanced by friendly, helpful staff.

By-Pass Rd., Khajuraho 471 606. ℂ **07686/27-2344.** Fax 07686/27-2345. tjokjr@sancharnet.in. 90 units. $90 super deluxe double; $120 suite. AE, DC, MC, V. **Amenities:** Restaurant; pool; tennis court; health club; billiards room; travel assistance; sightseeing; guides; car hire; airport transfers; currency exchange; shopping arcade; 24-hr. room service; babysitting with prior notice; laundry; doctor-on-call. *In room:* A/C, TV, minibar, safe, hair dryer, tea- and coffee-making facilities, iron and ironing board; suites have kitchenette with fridge.

OUTSIDE KHAJURAHO

Ken River Lodge ⋆⋆ ⟨Kids⟩ ⟨Value⟩   A short distance from the entrance to Panna National Park (about 30 min. from Khajuraho), this resort (comprising 10 tents and

10 cottages) is located right on the river and has a great deal more charm than its pricier counterparts in town. Three kilometers (2 miles) off the main road, it's an ideal hideaway in a gorgeous forest setting, where fishing enthusiasts can cast a line and hope for one of India's famous fighting *mahseer.* Accommodations are in 10 cottage rooms or in 10 army-style tents with an attached concrete bathroom (shower only). The main bedroom (only some of which have water coolers), has coir mat flooring, small rugs, and two large single beds (no doubles) with thin mattresses covered with Indian-style throws. Each tent also has a small private "porch." Tent no. 6 is the most secluded, while no. 1 is nearest the dining area and bar. The cottages are similarly furnished, but their concrete walls keep out the sounds of the forest, resulting in less of a wilderness feel. Meals are taken on a large *machaan,* a wood-and-mud platform built into a series of trees alongside the river. A thatched roof, tribal-design moldings, and a treetop observation deck contribute to the resort's immense appeal. If this isn't good enough, private romantic dinners can be arranged on a tiny private island in the middle of the river.

Village Madla, District Panna 488 001. ℂ **07732/27-5235.** In Delhi contact Manav Khanduja (ℂ 98100-24711). www.kenriverlodge.com. wildlifer@vsnl.net. 20 units. Rs 3,600 ($82) per couple, all meals included; Rs 9,000 ($205) per couple includes all meals and 2 all-inclusive safaris to Panna National Park; elephant rides extra. No credit cards. **Amenities:** Restaurant; bar; boating; fishing; tours and safaris; room service only in exceptional circumstances; laundry; doctor-on-call. *In room:* Water coolers (some units).

WHERE TO DINE

If you're down with a case of culinary homesickness, Khajuraho is awash with eateries proclaiming to serve "authentic" Italian dishes. Of these, **Mediterraneo** (Jain Temple Rd., opposite Surya Hotel; ℂ **07686/272-246;** no credit cards), an alfresco rooftop restaurant, is your best bet. Gigantic letters along the side of the building exclaim MEDITERRANEO CHEF TRAINED IN ROME, and although this is certainly not true, Rama, the owner, is from Rome, and the menu does offer a range of Italian favorites, including pizza (when available), pasta, and chicken dishes prepared with "Italian herbs." Across the road from the Western Group entrance is **Raja Swiss Café and Restaurant** (ℂ **07686/27-2307;** no credit cards). Run by a Swiss woman for the past 25 years, it has a sheltered rooftop terrace and a slate courtyard under a magnificent peepul tree. Come here after exploring the Western Group and sit upstairs; the food is unremarkable Indian and Western fare, but you can enjoy good views of the site you just visited. Chicken Basquaise is quite good, as is the caprese salad and *melanzane alla parmigiana* (aubergine baked with cheese and fresh tomato sauce). Be warned: The service is often slow and the place is popular with large groups.

Apsara ☆☆ ECLECTIC/NORTH INDIAN This smart and reliable restaurant at the Radisson Jass is the best place in town, particularly for North Indian cuisine (though a range of other dishes is also available). With lovely views of the gardens and pool, the atmosphere is quite soothing, enhanced by the charming maitre d'. At press time the restaurant was completing a renovation, but we were promised that all of the recommended Indian options will remain on the menu: mulligatawny soup flavored with curry leaves; fish marinated in mustard-flavored yogurt and cooked in a clay oven; Kashmiri *dum aloo* (potatoes stuffed with *paneer* and nuts in a saffron-flavored curry); *seekh kebab* (skewered minced lamb flavored with mint and carefully cooked over a charcoal flame); and spinach-and-cottage-cheese dumplings. If you want only a light bite, the sandwiches are outstanding. Don't miss out on the coffee mousse

---

Head Case?

Not sure who you are or where you're headed? **Shastri Di** is an aura and fore-head analyst who will help you "know thyself better," for a minimum fee of Rs 200 ($4.55). He can be contacted through the Mediterraneo restaurant (see above).

---

flavored with Tia Maria. If making the right choice is hard, opt for the sumptuous lunch or dinner buffet spreads.

Radisson Jass, Khajuraho. ℂ 07686/27-2344. Main courses Rs 140–Rs 550 ($3.35–$13); buffet Rs 450 ($10) lunch, Rs 550 ($13) dinner. AE, DC, MC, V. Daily noon–2pm and 7–10pm.

SHOPPING

Khajuraho can be a nightmare. In contrast with the tranquil village atmosphere, hawkers and touts ooze from every corner and have record-setting persistence. You'll no doubt develop a gut-wrenching dislike for the overstretched shopping areas in and around the main square, where everyone seems to demand that you step into yet another handicrafts shop to "just look, no buy." Do not enter any shop in Khajuraho with anyone other than fellow travelers. If you make a purchase on your own, you'll save yourself around 20%, which is the standard commission, borne by you, demanded by "agents" (taxi drivers, guides, or someone who has "befriended" you) for their "service" of bringing foreign business to local stores.

Amid all the hard-sell look-alike shops is one shining light. **Artist** (Surya Hotel Complex, Jain Temple Rd.; ℂ **07686/27-4496;** daily 9:30am–1:30pm and 3–10pm) is an appropriately named outlet for Pichhwai and Mughal paintings rendered by Dilip Singh and his two brothers, whose late father was a recipient of a National Award for Art many years back. The Singh brothers' paintings vary in subject, size, and quality, but the selection includes something to suit everyone's pocket. Miniatures start at a mere Rs 10 (25¢), and the most expensive paintings sell for up to Rs 13,000 ($300). Besides exquisite paintings on silk, fabric, and paper, you can also buy clever foldaway chairs, tables, and ornamental pieces at prices so low they'll make your head spin. If you want quality original art that reflects Mughal culture and history (and eroticism), be sure to spend some time in either of the two Artist outlets in Khajuraho. You can also commission a work if there's something in particular that you want to take home with you.

---

6 Orchha ⭐⭐⭐

440km (273 miles) SE of Delhi; 238km (148 miles) S of Agra; 120km (75 miles) SE of Gwalior

Located on a rocky island on the Betwa River, the deserted royal citadel of Raja Rudra Pratap is one of India's most fabulous Mughal heritage sites, yet Orchha (literally "hidden place") is mercifully free of development, making this a wonderfully relaxing stop. Founded in 1531, it was the capital of the Bundela kings until 1738. Today the weathered temples, palaces, and cenotaphs are the royal quarters of emerald parakeets and black-faced langurs, while traditional whitewashed, flat-roofed structures house the laid-back villagers. Besides the palace complex, three beautiful temples are worth seeking out, as well as 14 graceful *chhatris* (cenotaphs) commemorating the Orchha rulers, built upstream along the riverbank. Most of these sights can be covered in a day excursion on the way to Khajuraho, but to get the most out of this surreally tranquil haven, spend at least 1 night here.

ESSENTIALS

VISITOR INFORMATION   There is no official tourism bureau. The **MPTDC Sheesh Mahal** (✆ 07680/25-2624) acts as an informal tourism office (see "Where to Stay," below). They will arrange day trips and transfers.

GETTING THERE   The best way to get to Orchha is to catch a train to Jhansi, where trains from Delhi, Mumbai, or Chennai pull in, carrying visitors on their way to Khajuraho (see "Khajuraho: Getting There & Away," earlier in this chapter). You can catch an auto-rickshaw from Jhansi to Orchha (20km/12 miles) for about Rs 150 ($3.40). Alternatively, with time on your hands, you can hire a car and driver and travel by road from Agra, overnighting at Gwalior (see "The Gems of Gwalior," below).

EXPLORING ORCHHA'S FORGOTTEN MONUMENTS

The monuments of Orchha are fairly spread out, but close enough to be explored entirely on foot. You can spend a quick-paced morning poking through the ruins in which you're most interested, or take your time and spread your explorations over an entire day. A few of the sights require a ticket, which you can purchase from a booth at the front of the Raj Mahal (daily 9am–5pm); the Rs 30 (70¢) ticket provides access to all the main monuments.

Visible as you enter the village, Orchha's fortified palace complex is approached by a multi-arched medieval bridge. Once over the bridge, you'll first encounter the earliest of the palaces, **Raj Mahal** ⚐, built during the 16th century by the deeply religious Raja Madhukar Shah, who befriended the Mughal Emperor Akbar, an alliance that was to serve the rulers of Orchha well. Look for the bold, colorful murals on walls and ceilings, and climb to the uppermost levels of the palace for a more complete view of the entire complex. A pathway leads to the two-story **Rai Praveen Mahal;** according to legend, it was built in the mid–17th century for a concubine who the then-ruling Raja loved to watch dance. Surrounded by lovely lawns, the palace includes a ground-level hall where performances were once held, and naturally cooled subterranean apartments. Deemed Orchha's finest palace, with delicate *chhatris* (dome-shaped cenotaphs) and ornate stone *jalis* (screens) along its outer walls, **Jahangir Mahal** ⚐⚐ is distinguished by its domed pavilions, fortified bastions, and ornamental gateway flanked by stone elephants holding bells in their trunk, perhaps to announce the entry of the man in whose honor the palace was built: Emperor Jahangir, Akbar's son (see "The Life & Times of the Mughal Emperors," earlier in the chapter). He is said to have promised to visit, but accounts vary as to whether he actually arrived. The sandstone exterior bears the remains of beautiful turquoise- and lapis lazuli–tiled embellishments, while interior walls are decorated with lovely carvings. **Sheesh Mahal,** now a hotel, is a section of the palace complex built by a local king as a country getaway some time after Orchha's decline. If you wander along the paths heading away from the palace complex (to your left after you cross the bridge), you'll encounter the ruins of a number of small, atmospheric temples amid fields belonging to local farmers.

With both Persian and Rajput architectural influences, seven-story **Chaturbhuj Mandir** ⚐ looms hauntingly over Orchha village. Reached by a steep flight of steps, the 16th-century temple consists of an expansive vaulted assembly hall with impressive spires; make your way up the narrow spiral staircases for lovely views from the temple roof. Never used, the temple was supposed to have housed an image of Lord

The Gems of Gwalior

If you've chosen to travel by rail or road from Agra, 118km (73 miles) north, to Khajuraho via Orchha, 120km (75 miles) south, set aside a day to explore Gwalior's fine sights. To see them all necessitates an overnight stay in the palace that is part of the attraction and one of the best heritage properties in central India.

Looming over the three cities of modern Gwalior—Lashkar, Morar, and Gwalior—its 3km-long (2-mile) thick walls built atop steep cliff surfaces, **Gwalior Fort** ☞ (daily 8am–6pm; Rs 100/$2.30 entrance allows you into most sites, Rs 25/55¢ camera, Rs 75/$1.70 video) is believed to date back to the 3rd century A.D. The oldest surviving Hindu fort in the Bundelkund, it changed hands repeatedly and was admired by all who invaded it—even the first Mughal emperor, Babur, who admired very little else of India, famously described it as "the pearl among the fortresses of Hind" (though he still allowed his army to desecrate the Jain rock-cut sculptures, viewed as you approach the Urwahi Gate). Within the ancient walls are a number of palaces, temples, step wells, and underground pools (best to hire a taxi, available at the entrance), but its most significant structure is the monumental **Man Mandir Palace,** built by Raja Man Singh of the Tomara dynasty in the 15th century. Ornamented with a variety of glazed tile patterns, this is considered one of the finest examples of pre-Mughal Hindu palace architecture in India. Now housing a rather good **Archaeological Museum** (Tues–Sun 10am–5pm), **Gujari Mahal** was also built by Man Singh, this time for his favorite wife, a queen of the Gujjar tribe; he famously fell in love with her after he witnessed her courageously separate two warring buffaloes.

The oldest temple in the fort is **Teli-ka Mandir,** or **Temple of the Caste of Oil Sellers,** dating back to the 9th century. Built in the South Indian, or Dravidian, style, it was originally dedicated to Vishnu before apparently being used as a soda factory by the British when they occupied the fort in the 1800s. Just north of here is a large pool of water known as **Suraj Kund.** It was here that a divine hermit named Gwalipa, for whom the fort is named, is believed to have cured the fort's founder, King Suraj Sen, of leprosy. Other notable temples are late-11th-century **Sas Mandir (Temple of the Mother-in-law)** and **Bahu Mandir (Temple of the Daughter-in-law),** which form an elegant pair.

The last rulers of Gwalior were the Scindia clan, and during the British era the Scindia Maharaja, Jiyaji Rao, was known to be one of the most decadent of the Rajput rulers. In 1875 he built the over-the-top 19th-century **Jai Vilas**

Rama brought from Ayodhya by the wife of Orchha's king. Upon arriving, she found the temple incomplete, so she temporarily installed the deity in her palace. When Chaturbhuj was finally completed, the god refused to be moved, so the queen's palace became **Ram Raja Mandir** (daily 8am–noon and 8–10pm), today one of Orchha's main attractions for Hindus, despite its secular architecture.

Palace ⊛ for the express purpose of impressing the Prince of Wales. He filled it with treasures imported from Europe; in the Durbar Hall are the world's heaviest chandeliers, each weighing 3½ tons, which hang over the largest handmade carpet in Asia. In the dining room you can see the electric silver-and-crystal toy train the Maharaja used to dispense drinks and cigars around the massive dinner table—apparently refusing to stop the train in front of those he disliked. Jai Vilas Palace (② **0751/232-1101;** Thurs–Tues 10am–5pm; Rs 200/$4.55) is still occupied by his descendants.

Gwalior's has a long-standing tradition of musical excellence and innovation, and to this end **Sarod Ghar** ⊛ traces and showcases this legacy in the beautiful sandstone home of the Bagnash family. You might inquire about the **musical recitals** occasionally held in the museum's marble courtyard (② **0751/242-5607;** www.sarod.com; entry free; Tues–Sun 10:30am–4pm). Or find out whether musicians are performing at the simple white memorial **Tomb of Miyan Tansen.** One of India's greatest musicians, Miyan Tansen was considered one of the *navratna* (nine gems) of Mughal Emperor Akbar's court. For recital information, contact **M. P. State Tourism DC** (② **0751/ 234-0370;** mptgwalior@sancharnet.in; open 24 hr.).

The best place to overnight is the Taj's luxurious **Usha Kiran Palace Hotel** ⊛⊛ (② **0751/244-4000;** www.tajhotels.com), located right next door to the Jai Vilas Palace. Scindia royalty once resided here, and this handsome heritage hotel, extensively renovated in 2005, retains an evocative old-world atmosphere. Most accommodations (with A/C, TV, minibar) are arranged around a courtyard with a decorative fountain and are tastefully furnished, with high ceilings, pleasant sitting areas, and furniture that once belonged to the Maharaja. A stay here is definitely a taste of luxury (deluxe accommodations $170; check for online and seasonal discounts). The hotel offers guests several royal experiences, including a bathing ritual *(Mangal snana)* where you soak in a tub infused with rich traditional ingredients while live musicians play to you from behind a curtain. You can also get other forms of exceptional pampering at the hotel's Jiva spa. Around the hotel building, you'll discover broad passages, 51 differently designed sandstone trellises, ornate chandeliers, and an upstairs terrace affording views of Jai Vilas Palace and Gwalior Fort, ideal as a sundowner venue. If you do spend the night, you might want to watch the 45-minute sound-and-light show (Rs 150/$3.40; tickets available at the fort; closed July–Sept 15) held at the fortress each night at 7:30pm October through March and 8:30pm April through June.

Behind Ram Raja Mandir is a paved path that leads to **Lakshminarayan Mandir** ⊛⊛, atop a low hill less than 1km (a half-mile) from the village. The walk takes you past lovely flat-roofed houses that line part of the pathway. The 17th-century temple features interesting murals depicting military battles and religious myths. Although it's usually open to ticket-holders between 9am and 5pm, the temple is sometimes locked up, with no trace of the attendant.

After you explore the village and its trinket-filled stores, don't miss the 14 sandstone *chhatris,* or cenotaphs, alongside the Betwa River. Built as memorials to expired rulers of the Bundelkhand, they celebrate old alliances, combining elements of Mughal architecture, such as the arches, and Hindu temple design, such as the *shikharas* (spires).

WHERE TO STAY

Orchha is small but popular, with few decent lodging options, so be sure to book well in advance, particularly in winter when tour groups can arrive en masse. The best room in Orchha is the **Royal Suite** *&&* in the **Sheesh Mahal Hotel,** which was renovated in 2004 (© **07680/25-2624** or 011/2336-6528; www.mptourism.com; Rs 3,990/$90). An enormous room, with a domed ceiling over an assortment of paintings, cabinets, and fascinating Raj-era relics, the suite has its own dining area and a wonderful terrace with magical views. Even the bathroom is huge, with a marble tub and polished stone flooring. Despite the recent refurbishment, the rest of the hotel's guest rooms are quite ordinary and, like most government-run establishments, the place is poorly managed and the second-rate food is only to be consumed if you have no option. Despite these shortcomings, the Sheesh Mahal—no doubt due to its heritage status—is usually booked up days in advance.

The Orchha Resort *&* Orchha's smartest hotel enjoys a good location on the banks of the Betwa River near the cenotaphs. Popular with European tour groups, the resort is built in attractive pink sandstone and includes 11 deluxe tents (pitched Oct–Apr 15) arranged around the tennis court; these really are the best value. They're comfortably furnished and include all the regular amenities as well as en-suite toilets and showers and a small porch from where you have an incredible, close-up view of several impressive cenotaphs. Guest rooms in the main building are more expensive; they have marble floors, smallish bathrooms with tubs, and good-quality fabrics in shades of green and cream. Do beware of the slippery area around the pool when you go for a post-sightseeing dip. Owned by Jains, the restaurant is strictly vegetarian, but the food is fresh and appetizing.

Kanchanaghat, Orchha, Tikamgarh District 472 246. © **07680/25-2677** or -2678. Fax 07680/25-2677. Reservations: Oswal Motels and Resorts, A-17 Shopping Arcade, Sadar Bazaar, Agra 282 001. © 0562/222-5712. Fax 0562/222-5711. 45 units. Rs 2,500 ($57) tent double, Rs 3,500 ($80) double. AE, MC, V. **Amenities:** Restaurant; pool; tennis court; health club; sauna; table tennis; gift shop; 24-hr. room service; massage room; babysitting; laundry; doctor-on-call. *In room:* A/C, TV, minibar.

7 Bandhavgarh National Park *&&&*

237km (147 miles) S of Khajuraho

Known as "Kipling Country," despite the fact that the writer never set foot here, the nature reserves of Madhya Pradesh are archetypal India, with vast tracts of jungle, open grassy plains and, of course, tigers. Bandhavgarh National Park occupies 437 sq. km (168 sq. miles), making it a great deal smaller than its more famous cousin, Kahna National Park. But despite its relatively diminutive size, the park is home to some 50 to 70 tigers, the highest density of tigers in any park on Earth, and your chances of sighting one are as high as at Ranthambhore, in Rajasthan. Once the personal hunting grounds of local Maharajas who almost wiped out the tiger population, Bandhavgarh continues to experience problems with wayward poachers, usually suppliers for China's lucrative traditional medicine industry. But, as locals will assure you, your chances of seeing a wild tiger (those at Ranthambhore are almost tame) are still

Fun Fact **The White Tiger of Rewa**

The last elusive white tiger ever to roam free was a Bandhavgarh cub that was snared by Martand Singh, who bred the animal in captivity in order to exploit his deviant genes and so produce a new "genus"—the "White Tiger of Rewa." Today, the only places you'll see white tigers are zoos.

unmatched anywhere else in India. Best of all, you will approach your predator on elephant-back, giving the entire experience a totally unreal air.

Besides the sought-after tiger, the sanctuary is home to spotted deer, *sambar, nilgai* antelope, barking deer, shy *chinkara* (Indian gazelle), and wild boar; leopards and sloth bears are far more elusive. The varied topography includes dramatic cliffs that proved a natural location for the 14th-century **Bandhavgarh Fort.** If you give enough notice, you can arrange to visit the reserve's rock-cut caves, with inscriptions dating as far back as the 2nd century B.C.

ESSENTIALS

VISITOR INFORMATION Entry to Bandhavgarh is via the tiny village of Tala, where a number of lodges and resorts, a handful of *dhabas* (snack shacks), and several souvenir stalls are the only distractions from park activities. Try to get any information you require in advance. Contact **M. P. Tourism** at the White Tiger Forest Lodge at Bandhavgarh (℃ **07627/26-5308**) or the **Project Tiger Field Director** in Umaria (℃ **07653/22-2214;** fdbtr@rediffmail.com). You can also contact **M. P. Tourism** in Delhi (12 Janpath Hotel, Janpath Rd.; ℃ **011/3959-9000;** fax 011/2334-7264; www.mptourism.com) or in Mumbai (45 World Trade Centre, Cuffe Parade, Colaba; ℃ **022/2218-7603**).

GETTING THERE By Road Set aside an entire day for road journeys from destinations within Madhya Pradesh; surfaces are terrible at best, consisting of little more than endless potholes linked by clusters of asphalt and islands of sand. The nearest town of tourist interest is Khajuraho—what should be about a 5-hour journey takes around 10 hours.

By Air If you can afford it, take advantage of the helicopter trips from Delhi offered by several of the upmarket resorts in Bandhavgarh. If you decide to catch a commercial flight, Jabalpur is the nearest airport. It is situated 165km (102 miles) away; the 4-hour onward taxi trip will cost upward of Rs 3,200 ($73).

By Train Umaria, 45 minutes from Tala, is the nearest railhead. The best train from Delhi is the **Kalinga Utkal Express,** which leaves Nizamuddin Station at 12:50pm and arrives in Umaria the following day at 6:15am, a little too late for early entry to the park. Taxi rides to Tala cost around Rs 700 ($16). Other nearby railheads include Katni and Jabalpur.

WHEN TO GO The park opens as early as October (depending on the monsoon situation), but sightings are best February through June, when the heat forces more animals to search for water. Although the park attracts smaller crowds than Corbett and Ranthambhore, you should avoid Bandhavgarh the week before and after the Diwali, Holi, and New Year's holidays, when the park may be filled with queue-jumping VIPs and noisy families.

ORGANIZING YOUR BANDHAVGARH SAFARI

Regarding entry fees and permits, the best plan is to book accommodations that include *everything;* the resorts and lodges we've reviewed below will take care of all your safari arrangements. Get to the park first thing in the morning, when you will join the line of open-top jeeps and other 4WDs waiting at the entrance for the daily rush, which starts promptly at dawn. If you've hired a vehicle and driver privately, you will have to pay a small fee for the services of a park guide who will accompany you; this and other charges for entry permits, cameras, and such are all paid at the park entrance. Jeep safaris can cover a relatively large area within the park, but most sightings occur as a result of information shared among the various drivers and guides. Elephant-mounted *mahouts* head out early to search for tigers; once they locate them, the mahouts wait at the nearest road until safari jeeps begin to congregate and word spreads, ensuring the arrival of other vehicle-driven visitors. Rs 600 ($14) buys you an elephant-back ride for an unnervingly close-up view of the tigers, usually encountered minding their own business deep within the sal forest. You then have around 5 minutes to capture the elusive cat on film before your elephant returns to the road to pick up new passengers.

With any luck, your guide will be as interested in showing you the terrain, which is rugged and beautiful, as he is in finding your tiger. He may point out other species such as the *chital,* blue bull antelope, and *sambar;* and the many bird species such as spotted black kites, crested serpent eagles, storks, ibises, hornbills, white-eyed buzzards, black vultures, golden-backed woodpeckers, kingfishers, and dove parakeets. If all else fails, there are plenty of black-faced langur monkeys and rhesus macaques to keep you amused.

Tip: During the afternoon, the park offers more-substantial elephant safaris that are as much relaxing as they are a good opportunity to see more tigers in the wild, this time without feeling like you're part of a tourist conveyor belt.

Park entrance is at Tala. Park fees: Rs 500 ($11) admission; Rs 150 ($3.40) vehicle entry; Rs 100 ($2.30) guide; Rs 40 (90¢) camera; Rs 300 ($6.85) video; Rs 600 ($14) elephant ride per person. Daily 6:15–10am and 3–6pm.

WHERE TO STAY

Note that rates quoted here are "Jungle Plan" packages, which include all meals and two safaris into the park as well as all entrance, guide, and vehicle fees, and that all are situated within striking distance of the entrance. Besides the originally vaunted Bandhavgarh Jungle Lodge (see below), there are now two more options to consider. Located on the park's southern edge, 15 minutes from Tala gate, **Camp Mewar on Ketkiya** ⽊ (✆ 07627/26-5395 or 94141-59797; www.campmewar.com; $240 jungle plan; Oct 15–Apr 15) is the most recent and most luxurious option to arrive in the area. This 4-hectare (10-acre) property is not only quite enchanting, but at present represents the best value. "Tents" are really stone houses with a canvas canopy providing a tented feel; Aodhis (cottages in the design of hunting towers of old) are also quite lovely. Both have attached marble bathrooms with bathtubs, bidets, and other resort trimmings.

For a more homey atmosphere (but, strangely enough, heftier price tag), book a tent at **Churhat Kothi** ⽊, owned by the family who ran the now-closed Bandhavgarh Jungle Camp for 25 years (✆ 0124/506-8852 or 0124/235-3697; www.churhat kothi.com; Rs 20,800/$464). Not far from the park entrance, tent lodgings are attractive and comfortable; the main lodge is also tastefully furnished and has a fireplace and charming veranda overlooking a watering hole—a bonus for wildlife enthusiasts who get to interact with four resident naturalists.

Stalwart **Bandhavgarh Jungle Lodge** ⚜ remains a good option, situated in a garden of medicinal plants, fruit trees, and colorful flowers. Opt for one of the charming village-style mud-and-dung walled huts (wall-to-wall rugs; firm, comfortable beds; screened windows; and basic but clean attached bathrooms with showers) rather than the concrete cottages, which are less atmospheric but have tiled bathrooms with tubs. At night, all you have for company are the sounds of the jungle and a hot-water bottle tucked under white linen and a thick quilt. Service is pleasant and personal (there is also a resident naturalist), and the emphasis on the environment means that solar power is used for cooking and for hot water. Conversation in the lovely *boma*-style dining hall, serving adequate Anglo-Indian cuisine, usually revolves around tiger sightings and poaching (✆ **011/2626-6650** through -6655; www.welcomheritage. com; $310 double including all meals, taxes, and jungle excursions). The Disneyesque **Royal Tiger Resort** (✆ **011/2335-3247** or 07627/65374; www.royaltigerresort.com; $240–$300)—entered via a fortress-style gate with huge spiked doors flanked by a spear-wielding sentry guard—has the most amenities (pool, private lake, massage), and 16 large luxury tents, but taste is, regrettably, absent.

8 Bhopal & Sanchi

Bhopal is 744km (461 miles) S of Delhi; Sanchi is 46km (28 miles) NE of Bhopal

Despite its exciting marketplaces, grand old mosques, and lovely palaces, the capital of Madhya Pradesh is perhaps best known as site of the world's worst urban industrial disaster (see box below). But most foreign visitors find themselves in Bhopal in order to visit nearby Sanchi, a UNESCO World Heritage Site, and one of the most impressive Buddhist monuments in Asia. Architecturally unique and far from the beaten tourist track, the monuments and surrounding ruins are tranquil, free of hawkers and touts, and a worthwhile diversion from the more frequented destinations of Varanasi, Agra, Khajuraho, and Delhi.

If Bhopal's few monuments, its market, and the glorious Buddhist monuments at Sanchi leave you with time on your hands, head for the caves of **Bhimbetka,** where red-and-black prehistoric drawings recall the antics of ancient dancers and hunters, sticklike in the company of tigers and charging bulls.

ESSENTIALS

VISITOR INFORMATION For extensive information about any destination in Madhya Pradesh, as well as transport options, contact the extremely helpful Yogesh Argal at **Madhya Pradesh State Tourism Development Corporation** (**MPSTDC;** 4th Floor, Gangorti Complex, TT Nagar; ✆ **0755/277-8383;** info@mptourism.com). The website, **www.mptourism.com**, is also excellent. Sanchi is 46km (28 miles) from Bhopal, less than 2 hours by road. Regular train services from Bhopal pass through Sanchi.

GETTING THERE & AWAY As the state capital, Bhopal is well connected by air with numerous cities (including Delhi, Mumbai, Gwalior, and Indore). Bhopal is also on a main railway line, and frequent **trains** connect the city with Delhi, Agra, Gwalior, Jhansi (for Orchha), Mumbai, and Hyderabad.

GETTING AROUND Taxis and auto-rickshaws are common and easy to flag down.

The Bhopal Gas Tragedy

On the night of December 2, 1984, a tank at the Union Carbide pesticide manufacturing plant near Bhopal ruptured, leaking highly poisonous methyl isocyanate gas into the atmosphere. By the time it had dissipated, 1,600 people were dead—but final estimates are as high as 20,000. A claim of $6 billion in compensation was initially demanded by the government, but it settled out of court for $470 million. Adding insult to injury, the money, paid to the government, took 7 years and many more deaths before even a fraction of it reached the victims. Almost 2 decades later, survivors continue to protest the haphazard and inadequate manner in which the families of the victims were compensated. Evidence suggests that the continuing effects of the gas disaster may have affected as many as 300,000 people afflicted with various cancers and birth defects. Effigies of the Union Carbide bosses are regularly burned at memorial protests (failing to reach more than the evening news), and many victims continue to go without aid or recourse from the law. Meanwhile, Union Carbide, having abandoned the factory, has started up elsewhere as Eveready Industries India Ltd.

GUIDED TOURS Mrs. Rekha Chopra, of **Radiant Travels** (243/B, 1st Floor, Krishna Palace, M. P. Nagar, Zone I; ℂ **0755/273-8540** or 0755/254-0560), is not only an experienced tour guide, but introduces visitors to basic Indian cuisine with vegetarian meals at her home.

WHAT TO SEE & DO IN BHOPAL

No one spends much time in Bhopal itself, but the "City of Lakes" is not without its charms, and a handful of sights are worth setting time aside for. Note that most places are closed on Monday, and on Friday mosques are off-limits, unless you're Muslim.

A visit to the **Chowk (Bazaar),** in the heart of the Old City, can be a wonderful way to gain insight into the daily lives of Bhopal's warm, friendly citizens. Its ramshackle streets are lined with old havelis and atmospheric stalls; it's impossible not to get involved in the village vibe, where shopping, hard-core haggling, and gossiping occupy one's time. Shop around for embroidered velvet cushions, *tussar* silk, silver jewelry, and intricate beadwork. While you're in the Chowk, visit lovely **Jama Masjid** (built in 1837, it features gold-spiked minarets, distinguishing it from the "Pearl Mosque") or **Moti Masjid,** farther south. Sporting three large white Mughal domes and two soaring minarets, **Taj-ul-Masjid** ⌘, one of India's largest mosques, was started at the end of the 19th century by Bhopal's eighth ruler, the great queen Shah Jahan Begum, but was only completed in the 1970s.

Designed by the preeminent Indian architect, Charles Correa, the breezy, modern **Bharat Bhavan** ⌘⌘ (Shamla Hills; ℂ **0755/266-0353;** Tues–Sun: Feb–Oct, 2–8pm and Nov–Jan, 1–7pm; Rs 10/25¢, Fri free), overlooking Upper Lake, is one of the best cultural centers in the country, showcasing some wonderful contemporary and tribal art exhibitions.

If you're set on seeing a white tiger, **Van Vihar National Park** is the place to do it. Zoo conditions here are better than elsewhere in India, but it's still a depressing place to see a wild animal (Zoo Rd.; daily 7–11am and 3–5:30pm; Rs 100/$2.30, vehicle entry Rs 30/70¢; carnivores are fed around 4pm).

EXPLORING THE BUDDHIST COMPLEX AT SANCHI 🌾🌾🌾

Now a deserted site resembling an *X-Files* set, the monuments of Sanchi have not only survived despite nearly 2,000 years of neglect, but the stupa at Sanchi is considered India's finest and most evocative example of ancient Buddhist architecture. The Mauryan emperor Ashoka—famous for converting to Buddhism during a personal spiritual crisis after massacring thousands during his military campaigns in Orissa—was responsible for laying the foundations in the 3rd century B.C. Set upon a squat hill affording lovely views of the surrounding countryside, the complex of *stupas* (fat, domelike monuments housing Buddhist relics), monasteries, and temples probably owes its location as much to the serenity of the site as it does to its proximity to the once-prosperous city of Vidisha, where Ashoka's devoted Buddhist wife, Mahadevi, lived. Located at the confluence of the Bes and the Betwa rivers and two important trade routes, the Buddhist complex elicited the patronage of Vidisha's wealthy merchant communities. Even during the invasions of the Hun, life at Sanchi appears to have gone undisturbed, and is believed to have continued until the 13th century A.D., when a resurgence of Hinduism and an increasingly militant Islamic movement led to a decline of Buddhism in India. The site was deserted for more than 500 years before its rediscovery—again by a British military adventurer-type—in 1818. Today, aside from the attractive complex of ruins, Sanchi is little more than a railway station, a few guesthouses, snack stands, a museum, a restaurant, and a shop.

During the excavation that has taken place over the last century, the ruins of around 55 temples, pillars, monasteries, stupas, and other structures have been unearthed. It appears that Sanchi is unique in that its monuments cover the gamut of Buddhist architectural structures—dating from the 3rd century B.C. to the 12th century A.D.

The star attraction is Ashoka's large hemispherical stupa, which rises from the ground like a massive stone-carved alien craft. Around the middle of the 2nd century B.C., a balustrade was erected around the stupa, and the mound was covered in stone by the rulers of the Sunga dynasty. Facing the cardinal directions and contributing to the mystical appearance of the main stupa are the four intricately carved gateways, erected around 25 B.C. under the later Satvahana rulers. These striking entranceways feature finely detailed panels depicting incidents from the life of the Buddha and tales from the *Jatakas*. At that time, the current depiction of the Buddha in human form had not yet emerged, and instead he is symbolically depicted as a bodhi tree, lotus, wheel, pair of feet, or stupa.

The Sanchi monasteries consist of a central courtyard surrounded by cells that served as the sleeping quarters for the nuns or monks. Of these, the best is **Monastery 51,** which was first excavated in the 19th century.

WHERE TO STAY & DINE

Jehan Numa Palace 🌾🌾 *Value*   Built in 1890 as a royal guesthouse, this handsome low-rise white colonial-era building is fronted by attractive lawns with fountains, hedges, and colorful bougainvilleas. The two original heritage suites (ask specifically for either "Bourbon" or "Goddard") are very swish, with huge bedrooms, poster-beds, Regency furniture, spacious bathrooms with separate tubs and showers, and private patios. Executive guest rooms are off verandas around a fountain courtyard; these are large, with French doors and high ceilings. Standard rooms, in a new wing, are best avoided, as are the "cottage rooms." Colored with natural vegetable dyes, the eco-friendly linens are handmade by a local cottage industry, and walls are decorated with local handicrafts. Service is excellent. Facilities include the state's largest pool and a fitness center offering Ayurvedic massage.

157 Shamla Hill, Bhopal 462 013. ℂ **0755/266-1100.** Fax 0755/266-1720. www.hoteljehanumapalace.com. 82 units. Rs 2,800 ($64) cottage double, Rs 3,999 ($91) standard double, Rs 4,350 ($99) executive double, Rs 4,999 ($114) Imperial Room double; Rs 5,299 ($121) suite, Rs 6,699 ($153) Heritage Suite. Rs 500 ($11.40) extra bed. Rates include arrival transfer and breakfast. AE, DC, MC, V. **Amenities:** 3 restaurants; bar; club-cum-pub; garden barbecue; patisserie; pool; mini-golf; tennis court; jogging track; horseback riding; health club; gym; massage; Jacuzzi; sauna; steam; table tennis; pool table; concierge; barber shop; 24-hr. room service; massage; laundry; doctor-on-call. *In room:* A/C, TV, dataport, minibar. Suites and Imperial Rooms have tea- and coffee-making facilities, hair dryer.

9 The Fortress City of Mandu ⟨★⟨★⟨★

90km (56 miles) from Indore

Built at a cool height of over 600m (2,000 ft.) on the southwestern edge of the Malwa Plateau, with sweeping views of the Nimar Plains below, Mandu was once the largest fortified city on earth, and playpen to some of central India's most powerful rulers. Initially christened by the Malwa sultans as the "City of Joy," the medieval capital inspired its rulers to celebrate the most pleasurable of pastimes—one of Mandu's most famous palaces was built solely to house some 15,000 concubines, and it is said that the Mughal emperor Humayun was so mesmerized by Mandu's sanguine beauty that he developed an opium habit during his stay here. Today the exotic ghost city—still one of the most atmospheric destinations in India—draws but a handful of tourists, which makes the excursion here all the more rewarding. It's just 2 hours away from the industrial hub of Indore, yet Mandu, even more so than Orchha, is rural India at its best: a place of enduring beauty, both natural and man-made, with panoramic views. It's the perfect antidote to the well-traveled North India circuits. You can visit Mandu as a rather long day trip out of Indore, but for those willing to sacrifice luxury for serenity, it's worth spending a night or two here to revel in silence, fresh air, and wide-open space.

ESSENTIALS

GETTING THERE & AWAY   To visit Mandu, you have to travel via Indore, which is connected to important regional centers by daily flights and regular train services. The airport (ℂ **0731/262-1782** or -0758) is 8km (5 miles) out of the center. The train trip from Bhopal lasts 6 hours; the **Intercity Express** from Delhi takes 13 hours; and the **Avantika Express** from Mumbai takes 15 hours. Unless you plan to get to Mandu by bus (a long, tiring, but very cheap journey), hire a taxi; a recommended operator is **President Travels** (Hotel President, 163 R.N.T. Rd., Indore; ℂ **0731/ 252-8866**). Arrange a pick-up at the airport/station, and drive straight to Mandu (Rs 1,100/$25 non-A/C car; Rs 1,500–Rs 2,000/$35–$46 A/C car). M. P. Tourism (see below) also arranges cars.

VISITOR INFORMATION   **Madhya Pradesh Tourism** has an office at the Tourist Bungalow in Indore (ℂ **0731/252-8653** or -1717; mptourismind@sancharnet.in; 10am–5pm, closed Sun and second and third Sat of the month). In Mandu, ask the manager at **MPSTDC Tourist Cottages** (ℂ **07292/26-3235**) for assistance.

GETTING AROUND   Indore has plenty of **taxis** and **auto-rickshaws;** ask the driver to use his meter. In Mandu, you can hire a **bicycle,** or ride on the back of a **motorcycle** with a local guide as your driver.

EXPLORING MANDU

After passing through the narrow gates of the fortress and continuing for some distance, you'll arrive in "downtown" Mandu (a collection of shops and stalls in the vicinity of the **Central Group** of monuments). As soon as you emerge from your car or bus, you'll be approached by a local guide, who will offer his services with a nervous but easygoing disposition. Even if your guide—and there are only a couple in Mandu—is not a certified expert, this is one place where it can be fun to have someone show you around and enrich your experience with a version of history that overdoes the myth, romance, and fantasy of the place. However, do agree on a price upfront and establish that he speaks passable English. The fee should be Rs 200 to Rs 400 ($4.55–$9.10) depending on guide and hours. All monuments are open from 8am to 6pm.

If you don't plan to spend the night in Mandu, start your tour immediately with 15th-century **Jama Masjid** *.*. Said to have been inspired by the mosque in Damascus, this colossal colonnaded structure bears some Hindu influences, such as the carvings of lotus flowers and decorative bells. Adjacent the mosque is the **mausoleum of Hoshang Shah,** the first white marble tomb in India, said to have inspired those in Agra; it's ultimately missable. The **Royal Enclave** ** (Rs 100/$2.30; daily 8am–6pm) is dominated by enormous **Jahaz Mahal,** commonly known as the "ship palace." Built between two artificial lakes, it certainly was intended to be the ultimate stone pleasure cruiser, where the sultan Ghiyas Shah kept his 15,000 courtesans and an additional 1,000 Amazonians from Turkey and Abyssinia to guard them. Behind the ship palace is **Hindola Mahal;** its oddly sloping buttress walls have given it the nickname "Swing Palace."

Mandu's main road stretches southward, through open fields dotted with ruins and a few village houses, and continues into the **Rewa Kund** group of monuments, where the passionate romance between Maharaja Baz Bahadur, the last independent sultan of Malwa, and the beautiful Hindu shepherdess, Rupmati, is preserved in striking stone constructions. Apparently smitten by Rupmati's glorious singing voice, Baz built the **Rupmati Pavilion** ** (Rs 100/$2.30) so that she could see her village in the Narmada Valley below, but things went awry when the Mughal emperor Akbar came to hear of her legendary beauty and voice and wanted to take her home as a souvenir. After a fierce battle in which Baz was defeated, his beloved committed suicide. The view from the pavilion, which stands on the edge of a sheer precipice rising 365m (1,168 ft.) from the valley floor, is still sublime. On the way back from the pavilion, stop at **Baz Bahadur's Palace** (Rs 100/$2.30), where the acoustics enjoyed by the musically inclined king remain quite astonishing, even if some of the restoration work is a bit ham-fisted.

WHERE TO STAY & DINE

If the budget lodgings at Mandu are too basic, Indore has a number of fine business-orientated hotels where you'll find comfort and extensive facilities. The best of these is the **Fortune Landmark Hotel** (© **0731/25-5770;** www.fortuneparkhotels.com; doubles from $65). The amenities and comforts here match those of any smart city hotel, and the surrounding lawns and gardens are lovely.

Hotel Rupmati Close to the village bazaar on the edge of a cliff with fantastic views, this is the most impressive of Mandu's small selection of spartan hotels. Guest rooms are in a long stone building. Each large, white-walled unit has a thin, rock-hard mattress with white linen and a blanket; there's a small balcony. Attention has been paid to the lawns, and the cleanliness and tranquillity of the place make up for the budget facilities.

If you can't get in here, you'll have to try **MPSTDC Tourist Cottages,** situated on the bank of Mandu's largest lake, the Sagar Talab (© **07292/26-3235;** www.mp tourism.com; A/C rooms from Rs 1,490/$34).

Mandu 454 010. © **07292/26-3270** or -3279. Reservations in Indore: © 0731/270-2055. 12 units. Rs 880 ($20) A/C double, Rs 605 ($14) non-A/C double. No credit cards. **Amenities:** Restaurant; children's play area; room service 7am–10:30pm. *In room:* 8 units have A/C, TV.

Rajasthan: Land of Princes

For many, Rajasthan is the very essence of India, with crenelated forts and impregnable palaces that rise like giant fairy-tale sets above dusty sun-scorched plains and shimmering lakes. India's second-largest state—similar in size to France—is largely covered by the ever-encroaching Thar Desert, but despite its aridity, Rajasthan was once remarkably prosperous: Traders from as far afield as Persia and China had to cross its dry plains to reach the southern ports of Gujarat, something the warrior princes of Rajasthan were quick to capitalize on. Today the principal attraction of Rajasthan—the post-independence name for Rajputana, literally "land of princes"—is the large variety of forts and palaces its aristocrats built throughout the centuries, making it one of the most popular destinations in India. But Rajasthan offers so much more than desert castles and culture—from tracking down tigers in the Ranthambhore jungle (incidentally, the best place to spot wild tigers in Asia) to gaping at the world's most intricately carved marble temples on historic Mount Abu. Peopled by proud turbaned men and delicately boned women in saris of dazzling colors, the "land of princes" is rich with possibilities, and offers easy road access to the less-traveled state of Gujarat, discussed at the end of this chapter.

You could plan to spend your entire trip to India in Rajasthan, which is within easy striking distance of Delhi (and the Taj) by train, plane, or road. Certainly you'll need at least a week to take in the major destinations, of which the lake city of Udaipur and the desert fort of Jaisalmer—the only fort in the world still inhabited by villagers—are top highlights. Also vying for your time is the "blue city" of Jodhpur, which has the state's most impressive and best-preserved fort as well as the largest palace in India; the tiny town of Pushkar, built around a sacred lake and host to the biggest camel *mela* (fair) in Asia; the painted *havelis* (historic homes or mansions) of the Shekhawati region, referred to as India's open-air gallery; the tiny Keoladeo "Ghana" National Park, which boasts the largest concentration and variety of bird life in Asia; the untainted, almost medieval atmosphere of little towns like Bundi; and the bumper-to-bumper shops and bazaars in Jaipur (the state and retail capitals of Rajasthan). Shopping, in fact, is another of the state's chief attractions: Because of the liberal patronage of the wealthy Rajput princes, skilled artisans from all over the East settled here to adorn the aristocrats and their palaces. Today these same skills are on sale to the world's designers and travelers, and no one—from die-hard bargain-hunters to chi-chi fashionistas—leaves Rajasthan empty-handed. The question is how to choose from an unbelievable array of textiles, jewelry, paintings, handbags, rugs, pottery, diaries—even kitchen utensils—and then how to fit them into your bulging suitcase.

But perhaps the best reason to visit Rajasthan is to experience its unusual hotels: The state has almost 80 heritage properties—castles, palaces, forts, and ornate havelis—many of which are still

Land of Thirst: Rajasthan Today

Still very much a traditional, feudal society, the country's second-largest state is also one of its poorest. Although official estimates indicate that poverty is on the decrease, sheer numbers rather than percentages paint a more depressing picture—more than one million city-dwellers live in slums. Some 400,000 have no regular access to pure drinking water, and 330,000 have no access to proper toilet facilities. The plight of Rajasthan's people has in recent years been exacerbated by the worst drought in living memory—years of little rain have resulted in the widespread deaths of livestock and the decimation of crops. Many blame the government for undermining traditional ways of coping with drought: Widespread irrigation schemes have made farmers rely on taps and tanks rather than take a frugal approach to water. Regardless, the fact remains that—even with the prayed-for return of rain—it will be difficult for the rural sector to fully recover.

home to India's oldest monarchies. This must be the only place in the world where, armed with a credit card, you can find yourself sleeping in a king's bed, having earlier dined with the aristocrat whose forebears built and quite often died for the castle walls that surround it. Known for their valor and honor, and later for their decadence (see "Once Were Warriors: The History of the Rajput," below), the Rajputs are superb hosts, and it is almost possible to believe that you, too, are of aristocratic blood, as a turbaned aide awaits your every wish while you marvel at the starry night from the bastion of your castle. Long live the king (and queen), for you are it.

1 Planning Your Trip to Rajasthan

Rajasthan has so much to see, with long travel distances between top sites, that a trip here requires careful planning (particularly if you're going to hire a car and driver, which is the best way to tour the state). The following overview can help you plan your itinerary.

The three biggest cities in Rajasthan, all with airports, are **Jaipur,** the "Pink City"; **Jodhpur,** the "Blue City"; and **Udaipur,** the "White City." All are worthwhile destinations, not least because they offer easy access to great excursions. The tiny **Jaisalmer,** or "Golden City," is the most awkward to reach, and although some find it the highlight of their Rajasthan trip, others feel it isn't worth the schlep it takes to get there.

For most, the entry point is the state capital of Jaipur, near the eastern border, which is the third point (the others being nearby Delhi and Agra/Taj) of the much-traveled **Golden Triangle.** Should you choose to start your trip here, you are in fact well positioned to visit some of Rajasthan's top sites: Only a few hours from the city is **Ranthambhore National Park**—where you have your best chance of spotting a wild tiger—and Bharatpur's **Keoladeo National Park,** a must-see for birders, and virtually on the way from Agra. Jaipur is also within driving distance of **Bundi,** an untouched, off-the-beaten-track rural town that lies some hours away by train or car,

Rajasthan

Once Were Warriors: The History of the Rajput

Rajasthan's history is inextricably entwined with that of its self-proclaimed aristocracy: a warrior clan, calling themselves *Rajputs,* that emerged sometime during the 6th and 7th centuries. Given that no one too low in the social hierarchy could take the profession (like bearing arms) of a higher caste, this new clan, comprising both indigenous people and foreign invaders such as the Huns, held a special "rebirth" ceremony—purifying themselves with fire—at Mount Abu, where they assigned themselves a mythical descent from the sun and the moon. In calling themselves Rajputs (a corruption of the word *Raj Putra,* "sons of princes"), they officially segregated themselves from the rest of society. Proud and bloodthirsty, yet with a strict code of honor, they were to dominate the history of the region right up until independence, and are still treated with deference by their mostly loyal subjects.

The Rajputs offered their subjects protection in return for revenue, and together formed a kind of loose kinship in which each leader was entitled to unequal shares within the territory of his clan. The term they used for this collective sharing of power was "brotherhood," but predictably the clan did not remain a homogenous unit, and bitter internecine wars were fought. Besides these ongoing internal battles, the Hindu Rajputs had to defend their territory from repeated invasions by the Mughals and Marathas, but given the Rajputs' ferocity and unconquerable spirit, the most skillful invasion came in the form of diplomacy, when the great Mughal emperor Akbar married Jodhabai, daughter of Raja Bihar Mal, ruler of the Kachchwaha Rajputs (Jaipur region), who then bore him his first son, Jahangir.

Jahangir was to become the next Mughal emperor, and the bond between Mughal and Rajput was cemented when he in turn married another Kachchwaha princess (his mother's niece). A period of tremendous prosperity for the Kachchwaha clan followed, as their military prowess helped the Mughals conquer large swaths of India in return for booty. But many of the Rajput clans—particularly those of Mewar (in the Udaipur region)—were dismayed by what they saw as a capitulation to Mughal imperialism. In the end it was English diplomacy that truly tamed the maharajas. Rather than waste money and men going to war with the Rajput kings, the English offered them a treaty. This gave "the Britishers" control of Rajputana, but in return the empire recognized the royal status of the Rajputs and allowed them to keep the majority of the taxes extorted from their subjects and the many travelers who still plied the trade routes in the Thar Desert.

as well as nearby **Ajmer,** gateway to the sacred lake of **Pushkar** and site of the state's most famous camel fair.

Other than its proximity to these sites, however, as well as the excellent rail and flight connections to the rest of India, the only good reason to dally in Jaipur itself is to indulge in some retail therapy (or stay at Rajvilas, one of India's best hotels). Most

This resulted in a period of unprecedented decadence for the Rajputs, who now spent their days hunting for tigers, playing polo, and flying to Europe to stock up on the latest Cartier jewels and Belgian crystal. Legends abound of their spectacular hedonism, but perhaps the most famous surround the Maharaja Jai Singh of Alwar (north of Jaipur), who wore black silk gloves when he shook hands with the English king and reputedly used elderly women and children as tiger bait. When Jai Singh visited the showrooms of Rolls-Royce in London, he was affronted when the salesman implied that he couldn't afford to purchase one of the sleek new models—he promptly purchased 10, shipped them home, tore their roofs off, and used them to collect garbage. The English tolerated his bizarre behavior until, after being thrown from his horse during a polo match, he doused the animal with fuel and set it alight. Having ignored previous reports of child molestation, the horse-loving British finally acted with outrage and exiled him from the state.

Above all, the Rajput maharajas expressed their newfound wealth and decadence by embarking on a frenzied building spree, spending vast fortunes on gilding and furnishing new palaces and forts. The building period reached its peak in Jodhpur, with the completion of the Umaid Bhawan Palace in the 1930s, at the time the largest private residence in the world.

When the imperialists were finally forced to withdraw, the "special relationship" that existed between the Rajputs and the British was honored for another 3 decades—they were allowed to keep their titles and enjoyed a large government-funded "pension," but their loyalty to the British, even during the bloody 1857 uprisings, was to cost them in the long run.

In 1972 Prime Minister Indira Gandhi—sensibly, but no doubt in a bid to win popular votes—stripped the Rajputs of both stipends and titles. This left the former aristocracy almost destitute, unable to maintain either their lifestyles or their sprawling properties.

While many sold their properties and retired to live in middle-class comfort in Delhi or Mumbai, still others started opening their doors to paying guests like Jackie Kennedy and members of the English aristocracy, who came to recapture the romance of Raj-era India. By the dawn of a new millennium, these once-proud warriors had become first-rate hoteliers, offering people from all walks of life the opportunity to experience the princely lifestyle of Rajasthan.

visitors planning to travel farther by car circle Rajasthan in a counterclockwise direction, starting off in Jaipur and traveling the rather circuitous route west to Jodhpur (with a sojourn in Pushkar—a highly recommended option, particularly for younger travelers); then, from Jodhpur, you make the 5½- to 6-hour drive west to Jaisalmer for a few nights before you return to Jodhpur. An alternative route to Jaisalmer, which means you don't have to travel both to and from Jodhpur, is to travel from Delhi through the Shekhawati region to Bikaner, and from there on to Jaisalmer, before you travel east again to Jodhpur. (The other alternative is to skip Jaisalmer altogether, and if you're short on time this is what you may have to do, but we think it's a must-see city.) From Jodhpur you then travel south to Udaipur and, finally, head back north to Jaipur, stopping en route at one of many lovely palace hotels (or at Amanbagh) for a most relaxing end to your journey.

For someone with limited time (say, only enough to visit one of Rajasthan's cities), it's far better to fly direct to Udaipur—with great lodging options in all price brackets, this is arguably Rajasthan's most attractive city (though the recent drought has had a severe impact on the beauty of the City of so-called Lakes; do check the status of the lakes before planning your entire trip around it). From Udaipur you can take a wonderful (but long) day trip to **Kumbhalgarh Reserve** to take in Ranakpur's exquisitely carved **Jain temples** and impressive **Kumbhalgarh Fort** before overnighting at **Devi Garh,** one of India's top hotels. Alternatively, you can head east from Udaipur to Bundi, via the historic fort of **Chittaurgarh,** and then move on to **Ranthambhore National Park.** Or take the short trip directly south to the relatively undiscovered **palaces of Dungarpur,** or head out west to **Mount Abu,** the state's only hill station and sacred pilgrimage of the Jains, who come to visit the famous **Dilwara Temples.** Jodhpur and its majestic **Mehrangarh Fort** lie only 5 hours north of Udaipur by road, and you can break up the trip by overnighting at one of the recommended heritage properties along the way.

The state's other must-see city is Jaisalmer, which is rather inconveniently situated on the far-flung western outreaches of Rajasthan's Thar Desert. To get there, you have to either set off from Jodhpur, or travel via the less-than-spectacular desert town of Bikaner—both routes involve a lot of driving (Jodhpur is a 5½- to 6-hr. drive away; Bikaner a 6- to 7-hr. drive). You can opt to travel from Jodhpur to Jaisalmer by overnight train, but make sure to get a berth in the air-conditioned compartment of the Delhi–Jaisalmer Express (even though the desert nights can be bitterly cold, this is your most comfortable option) and carry a warm blanket.

You can fly between Rajasthan's major cities and hire a vehicle and driver from one of the recommended operators for the duration of your stay in each region, but the long-term hire of a car and driver is highly recommended—this is really the best way to tour Rajasthan because it means you can travel at your own pace, avoid public transport (or the daily grind of haggling with taxis), and get right off the beaten track. That said, Rajasthan's potholed roads make for slow going, drivers have unknown rules (but clearly the big trucks and cows rule, no matter what the circumstances), and traveling by night is only for the suicidal—even day trips will have you closing your eyes in supplication to some higher being.

Many operators are not keen to provide a breakdown of pricing, leaving you with the distinct feeling that you are being ripped off. To avoid this, get a per-kilometer rate for the specific kind of car you wish to hire, and the overnight supplement for the driver. Establish a ballpark per-kilometer rate from the **RTDC Transport Unit**—their rates are usually slightly higher than those offered by private operators, so it's worth going there first for a quote. The RTDC in Jaipur owns a number of vehicles or will contract out specific requests for vehicles; call them at © **0141/220-0778** (or write to cro@rajasthantourism.gov.in or rtdcpr@sancharnet.in). At press time, an air-conditioned car and driver in Jaipur cost about Rs 1,380 ($32) for 80km (50 miles) for 12 hours per day, and Rs 255 ($5.75) for every hour after that. For out-of-town trips, expect to pay Rs 6 to Rs 8 (11¢–22¢) per kilometer plus Rs 150 ($3.40) per night out.

A romantic way to go—but certainly not the fastest—is in an air-conditioned Ambassador, India's quaint homegrown brand of sedans, which provides you with a real sense of being in another world, not to mention another era.

2 Jaipur

259km (160 miles) SW of Delhi; 232km (144 miles) W of Agra

After independence, Jaipur became the administrative and commercial capital of what was known as Rajputana, a suitable conclusion to the dreams of its founder Maharaja Sawai Jai Singh II, a man famed for his talents as a politician, mathematician, and astronomer. At age 13 he ascended the throne of the Kachchwaha Rajputs, a clan that had enjoyed tremendous prosperity and power as a result of their canny alliance, dating back to Humayun's reign, with the Mughal emperors. It was in fact the emperor Aurangzeb, a fanatically pious Muslim, who—despite the fact that Jai Singh was a Hindu prince—named him Sawai, meaning "one and a quarter," for his larger-than-life intellect and wit. Having proved his prowess as a military tactician for Aurangzeb, increasing the emperor's royal coffers substantially, Jai Singh felt it safe to move his capital from the claustrophobic hills surrounding Amber to a dry lake in the valley below.

Begun in 1727 and completed in just 8 years, Jaipur was the first city in India to enjoy rigorous town planning according to the principles laid down in "Shilpa Shastra," an ancient Indian treatise on architecture. The city is protected by high walls, with wide, straight avenues that divide it into nine sectors (apparently reflecting the nine divisions of the universe, resembling the Indian horoscope), each named after the commodity and caste who lived and practiced their specific skills here—the order and space was at the time a total revolution in Indian cities. Although these market names still provide some clue as to what was once found in the otherwise rather uniform rows of shops that line the streets, the overall significance of these historic divisions is today lost to the traveler on foot trying to negotiate the chaos of the filth-strewn streets and pushy traders.

Despite the romantic nickname the "Pink City," Jaipur is not one of Rajasthan's most attractive cities, which is why, after taking in the centrally located City Palace (where the principal sights are located), it's probably wise to concentrate on sites farther afield: **Amber Fort,** first royal residence of the Maharajas of Kachchwaha, lies 11km (7 miles) north; and popular **Samode Palace** is an hour's drive away. But if the heat has you beat and the very thought of traipsing through another fort or durbar hall leaves you feeling exhausted, check out the shopping recommendations. A central repository for the region's wonderful crafts, Jaipur is famous for its gems and jewelry, enamel- and brassware, blue pottery, embroidered leather footwear, rugs, tie-and-dye cotton fabrics, hand-blocked prints, fine *Kota doria* saris, and ready-made linens and home furnishings.

ESSENTIALS

VISITOR INFO   The **Rajasthan Tourist Development Corporation (RTDC)** information bureau is located on Platform 1 at the Jaipur Railway Station (© **0141/ 220-3531;** open 24 hr.). There's a **tourist help desk** at Hotel Swagatam (behind Sadar Thana; © **0141/220-2586** or -0595; Mon–Sat 10am–5pm; closed second Sat of every month). Call the **24-hour help line,** © **1364,** for information or assistance in an emergency. The main office of the tourist commissioner is located at the **RTDC**

Jaipur

SITARAMPURA

Nahargarh
Fort

INDRAPURI

SHASTRINAGAR

Nirwan Marg

Vidyadhar Nagar Marg

Tulsi Marg

1

2

PURANI
BASTI

BANI
PARK

Marg

Chandpol
Gate

Chandpol Bazaar

Waterworks Road

Sawai Jai Singh Hwy

Shiva Marg

Kantichandra Marg

Kabir Marg

Central Bus
Station

Station Rd.

5

Sansar Chandra Marg

TOPKHANADESH

RTDC Central
Reservations
Office

i

6

7

Ajmeri
Gate

Jaipur
Train
Station

i

M. I. Road

Ganpati
Plaza

✉

Mirza Ismail Road

9

10

11

← To Ajmer

Sanjay Marg

Ajmer Rd.

Raj Mandir
Cinema

Ashok Marg

GOPALWARI

Jacob Rd.

ASHOK
NAGAR

Bhagwandas Marg

Mahavir Rd.

Sawai Ram Singh Rd.

4

Ajmer Rd.

NANDRAMPURA

Sadar Patel Marg

Prithviraj Marg

Statue
Circle

13

New Delhi

Jaipur

Bajaj Marg

Tilak Marg

Sawai Mansingh
Hospital

India

12

Anokhi

Bhagwandas Marg

RAMBAGH

Narain
Singh
Circle

i

Bay of
Bengal

Bhawani Singh Marg

GOLF &
POLO CLUB

14

14

Sawai Ram Singh Rd.

15

Bais Godam
Train Station

Ambedkar
Circle

SAWAI
MANSINGH
STADIUM

Rambagh
Circle

Narain Singh Rd.

BHOJPURA

To Airport
↓

0   1/2 mi
0   1 km

Fun Fact Why Pink?

Jaipur is known as the Pink City, a rather idealized description of the terra-cotta-colored lime plaster that coats the old part of the city's walls, buildings, and temples. The reasons for painting the town pink are unknown, but various theories have been tossed about, from using pink to cut down glare, to Jai Singh II's apparent devotion to Lord Shiva (whose favorite color is reputedly terra cotta). Others believe Singh wanted to imitate the color of the sandstone used in the forts and palaces of his Mughal emperor-friends. The most popular reason (spread no doubt by "Britishers" during the Raj era) is that pink is the traditional color of hospitality, and the city was freshly painted and paved with pink gravel to warmly welcome Edward VII for his visit here in 1876. The city is painted pink once every 10 years by the Municipal Corporation, and in 2000 the painting was timed for a state visit, this time by former U.S. president Bill Clinton. A few streets became off-limits to cars, but this is not the case anymore, and cars and rickshaws crowd areas such as Bapu Bazaar, which otherwise is one of the better places to browse. If you are being driven around, especially at peak hour, it will take you a very long time to get to your destination.

Tourist Hotel (Gangaur; ☏ **0141/511-0591** or -0596; same hours as station office; mainly for emergencies or problems) on M.I. Road, the main thoroughfare in Jaipur. For predeparture planning, check out the RTDC's website at www.rajasthantourism.gov.in, or contact them at secretary@rajasthantourism.gov.in. You'll find the less helpful **Government of India Tourist Office** at the Khasa Kothi hotel (☏ **0141/237-2200;** Mon–Fri 9am–6pm, Sat 9am–2pm).

To find out about any events or festivals or current arts and entertainment listings, pick up a copy of the daily *Hindustan Times* or the *Jaipur Vision* (Rs 20/45¢).

GETTING THERE

BY AIR   Both **Jet Airways** (☏ **0141/511-2222** through -2225 and **Indian Airlines** (☏ **0141/274-3500** or -3324) connect the city with Delhi (40 min.), Jodhpur (45 min.), Udaipur (1hr., 40 min.), Mumbai (directly 1 hr., 30 min.; hopper 4 hr., 20 min.), and Kolkata (1 hr., 55 min). **Sanganer Airport** lies 15 minutes south of the center of town; most hotels are 30 minutes away. A taxi ride costs around Rs 300 ($6.85); an auto-rickshaw ride costs Rs 150 to Rs 200 ($3.40–$4.55).

BY TRAIN   The Jaipur Railway Station is located west of the Old City (reservations Mon–Sat 8am–2pm and 2:15–8pm, Sun 8am–2pm). You can reach Jaipur by train from just about anywhere. The Ajmer Shatabdi connects Jaipur with Delhi in 4½ hours; from Agra the train takes about 5 hours. Dial ☏ **131** for railway inquiries, ☏ **0141/220-4531** for recorded arrival and departure information, and ☏ **135** for reservations. Reservations for foreign tourists are made at counter 8. To book a ticket, your easiest option is to get your hotel or a travel agent to do it for you. Either will charge a service fee of Rs 50 to Rs 100 ($1.15–$2.30) per passenger, well worth the bother of doing it yourself. You will be inundated with offers from rickshaw-*wallas* upon your arrival at Jaipur Station—to avoid this, go to the prepaid auto-rickshaw counter.

BY BUS   Buses arrive at the Inter-State Bus Terminal (also called Sindhi Camp bus stand) on Station Road. For information, call ☏ **0141/511-6043** for regular buses; or

☏ **0141/511-6031** or 0141/220-5790 for deluxe buses. Regular Goldline and Silver-line buses for Delhi (Rs 430/$10, plus luggage fee) will drop you off at Bikaner House, near India Gate. These comfortable, air-conditioned Volvo buses offer at least 12 departures a day (blankets and bottled water provided).

BY CAR   As is the case everywhere, you will need to hire a driver with your car. The Jaipur–Delhi National Highway no. 8 has been improved and transformed into a dual carriage road that should get you between the two cities in 4 hours. The single-road highway between Agra and Jaipur through Fatehpur Sikri and Bharatpur is in good condition, too. There's not much you can do about the driving habits of other drivers, but you can certainly say something if you feel yours is driving rashly.

GETTING AROUND

The best way to get around the crowded city center is on foot or by rickshaw. A rickshaw should set you back Rs 50 ($1.15) per hour—always discuss the fare upfront before you get into the rickshaw. You can hire a basic air-conditioned car and driver for use within the city for approximately 4 hours (40km/25 miles) at Rs 550 ($13); 8 hours (80km/50 miles) at Rs 1,000 ($23). Arya Niwas (see "Where to Stay," later in this chapter) offers a 3-hour round-trip to Amber for Rs 400 ($9.10). If you take the car up the hill, the cost will be Rs 500 ($11). If your intention is to hire a car and driver to tour Rajasthan at your own pace, contact **RTDC Transport Unit** (☏ **0141/220-0778**). For more information on hiring a car and driver from elsewhere, see chapter 2. **Rajasthan Travel** (☏ **0141/236-5408**) at Ganpati Plaza on M.I. Road rents non-air-conditioned cars at Rs 400 ($9.10) for 4 hours. **K. K. Holidays and Vacations** (105 Neelkanth, 1 Bhawani Singh Rd., opposite Nehru Sehkar Bhawan; ☏ **0141/510-6820**, -2241, or -2245) is a reliable travel agency that charges the standard going rate for hiring a car (local or outstation) and has a fleet of vehicles to suit all budgets and needs. Mahender Singh, the director, and his GM, I. V. Singh, are not only helpful but Internet-savvy and can pre-book all your car and hotel arrangements if you e-mail them in advance (kkholidays@tantramail.com).

GUIDED TOURS   You may be in for a frustrating time if you hire guides, registered or not, who hang around outside attractions—many have their English commentary down pat but more often than not can't engage in dialogue. One of the most respected guides in the city is **Jaimini Shastri** (☏ **93145-09684;** shastri_guide@yahoo.co.in; Rs 500/$11 for the day), who is well-versed in the city's history, culture, and arts and crafts. He can give you the best guided tour of Jantar Mantar, speaking at length on astronomy, astrology, and the observatory. Book him well in advance. Alternatively, organize a guide through your hotel, or contact **Rajasthan Travel** (☏ **0141/236-5408**) or **Sita World Travel** (☏ **0141/237-3996** or 0141/510-2020). Expect to pay about at least Rs 400 ($9.10) for 4 hours. If you don't mind groups (and the guide may, once again, have limited knowledge of English), **RTDC** (☏ **0141/231-5714**) offers several tours. A packed half-day (5-hr.) tour, departing 8am, 11:30am, and 1:30pm, covers Hawa Mahal, Amer Palace and Fort, Jal Mahal, the Gaitor Maharaja Cenotaphs, the City Palace and Museum, Jantar Mantar, the Central Museum, and Jawahar Kala Kendra. The 8am tour (Rs 100/$2.30) is advisable. The full-day tour (9am–6pm) includes all of the above as well as the Nahargarh and Jaigarh forts and Birla Planetarium; it costs Rs 150 ($3.40). Tours depart from the information bureau on platform 1, Jaipur Station.

(Moments Sunset over Jaipur

See the pink city at its rosiest from Nahargarh Fort (or "Tiger Fort") when the sun sinks behind the Aravalli Hills. Then—as night falls—watch the city skyline turn into the twinkling jewels for which it is famed. The view is always a winner, but during the festival of Diwali in November, when firecrackers explode above the city, it's one you will never forget. The fort (Rs 5/10¢) itself is largely in ruins, but the great vantage point alone is worth the trip. An RTDC-run cafe serves drinks and snacks.

CITY LAYOUT

The major attractions and best bazaars lie within the walls of the Old City. Just south of the wall lies **Mirza Ismail (M.I.) Road**—running west to east, this major thoroughfare is where most of the primary retail outlets and a few good restaurants are located, and divides the city between the old (north) and new (south). The Old City is clearly distinguishable by its pink walls and ramparts, and the new by its modern shops. Station Road, Sansar Chandra Marg, and Bhagwan Das Marg all intersect M.I. Road. Along these you will find all the services you need, from travel agents and money-changers to ATMs, restaurants, and Internet cafes. Farther south (but still within walking distance), diagonally opposite both Ajmeri Gate and New Gate of the Old City, lie Albert Hall and the Museum of Indology.

FESTIVALS

As is the case everywhere in India, Jaipur seems to celebrate something new every month, but the following are worth noting: In February during the **Harvest Festival (Basant Panchami)** the city celebrates a Kite Festival, when hundreds of colorful kites sail the blue Jaipur sky, especially around the City Palace area; there's also a competition and display. In March, when Holi celebrants throughout the country splash color on anything that moves, Jaipur celebrates an **Elephant Festival.** The massive pachyderms—dressed to the nines and decorated with paint—march through the city's streets to the City Palace, accompanied by loud drumbeats and chanting. The event sees a tug-of-war between the elephants and their *mahouts* (elephant trainers/caretakers), as well as men playing polo—on elephant-back, of course. Make sure you book accommodations in advance during this period.

The following month (Apr) is **Gangaur,** when the women of Rajasthan pray to the goddess Parvati (also known as Gangaur) for the longevity of their husbands or for husbands fair and kind. This culminates in a procession to Gangaur Temple by the symbolic Siva, accompanied by elephants, to take his bride home. **Teej** (July–Aug) sees Rajasthan's always colorfully clad women dressed in full regalia to celebrate the onset of the monsoon, while **Diwali (Festival of Lights),** the Hindu New Year, is celebrated throughout India in November.

Tip: Although all festivals are meant to be fun celebrations, a few unruly young men may try to ruin it with their aggressive behavior, especially during Holi and Diwali. Ask your hotel where it is advisable to go, and make sure you have your own transport if you are going to watch the festivities; single women travelers are advised to go with a male companion.

FAST FACTS: Jaipur

American Express Located on M.I. Road (✆ **0141/237-0117** or -0119) near Ganpati Plaza, the office is open daily 9am to 6pm.

Area Code For Jaipur, the area code is **0141.**

Banks You'll find several banks and ATMS on M.I. Road. The **Thomas Cook** office for foreign exchange is at Jaipur Tower ✆ **0141/236-0940** (Mon–Sat 9:30am–6pm). There's a Citibank ATM next to the General Post Office, HDFC Bank ATM on Ashok Marg, ICICI Bank ATM in Ganpati Plaza, and others within the Old City.

Climate Summers have a mean maximum temperature of 104°F (40°C) and a minimum of 75°F (26°C), while winters range between a mean maximum of 70°F (22°C) and minimum of 48°F (8°C). The best weather occurs October through February.

Directory Assistance For telephone numbers call ✆ **197.** The number ✆ **0141/274-4447** is a privately operated general information number (talking Yellow Pages) that you can call for directory inquiries or information on shopping, restaurants, and the like.

Emergencies Ambulance ✆ **102;** fire ✆ **101;** police ✆ **100.**

Hospitals **Santokba Durlabji Memorial Hospital** (✆ **0141/256-6251** to -57) is located on Bhawani Singh Marg.

Newspapers & Books You can pick up an amazing selection of newspapers, magazines, and books (considering its inconspicuous location and minute size) from **Books Corner** on M.I. Road, including *Jaipur Vision* and *Trains at a Glance.*

Police **Sindhi Camp Police Station** can be reached at ✆ **0141/220-6201.**

Post Office The GPO (✆ **0141/236-8740**) is on M.I. Road (Mon–Sat 10am–6pm).

Tourist Help Desk Calll the **24-hour tourist help desk** (✆ **1364**) if you want to report a theft or register a tourism-related complaint. If you can't get through, you can call the help desk's Delhi office at ✆ **0/98115-73315.**

WHAT TO SEE & DO

The principal attraction of the Old City of Jaipur is its **City Palace** (see below), nearby **Jantar Mantar** (also described below), and much-photographed **Hawa Mahal (Palace of Wind).** Built by Sawai Pratap Singh in 1799, Hawa Mahal (daily 9:30am–6pm; Rs 5/10¢ entry, Rs 30/70¢ camera) is principally a five-story facade of 593 latticed-stone screened windows, behind which the ladies of the palace could view the city without being seen. You can walk along the corridors that line the windows, which are mostly one room thick, but the building's principal attraction is the facade, which can be viewed from street level (entrance from Tripolia Bazaar, Police HQ lane). Also within the city complex, opposite Chandra Mahal, is **Govindji Temple** (daily 5–11am and 6–8pm), the most famous in the city and dedicated to Lord Krishna, Jai Singh II's favorite deity. The Krishna image was brought here from Brindavan in the late 17th century; devotees are allowed only a glimpse of it seven times a day.

In the new part of the city lies **Ram Niwas Bagh,** the city garden, which houses a depressing zoo and aviary. At the heart of the garden lies Albert Hall, which houses the **Central Museum** (✆ **0141/257-0099;** daily 10am–4:30pm; Rs 35/75¢; cameras not allowed). Designed by the prolific architect and past master of the hybrid Indo-Saracenic style of architecture, Swinton Jacob, this is of principal interest from an architectural point of view, and a slow turn around the building in a car will suffice for many. That's not to say that the exhibits are devoid of interest—the eclectic collection covers a wide range from musical instruments to bottled organs, and the tiny terra-cotta figures demonstrating myriad yoga positions are worth a look. A short drive due south lies the even stranger **Museum of Indology** (✆ **0141/260-7455;** daily 9am–6pm; Rs 40/90¢, Rs 100/$2.30 camera, Rs 500/$11 video), where an incredible selection of objects—all collected in one lifetime by the writer Acharya Vyakul—has been crammed into countless dusty display cases in every nook and cranny of his house. The collection is as eclectic as they come, including a map of India painted on a grain of rice, misprinted rupees, a 180-million-year-old fossil, a letter written by Jai Singh, and the Gayatri Mantra written on a single strand of hair. It's a great shame more money is not available to edit and present this collection professionally.

On M.I. Road, near the Panch Batti intersection (where you'll see a **statue of Sawai Jai Singh II**) is **Raj Mandir** (✆ **0141/237-9372** or 0141/236-4438)—one of the most over-the-top cinemas in the country. This is the place to watch a Bollywood blockbuster, though you will need to book tickets in advance to avoid waiting in line for hours. If the film is a new release, book a day in advance (daily 10am–2pm and 3–6pm). If you don't fancy sitting through 3 hours of Hindi melodrama, request that the doorman let you in for a sneak peak; he may oblige for a Rs 20 (45¢) tip if the hall isn't packed. Or arrive a few hours before the film, purchase your ticket, and kill time over a coffee and a pastry across the street at Barista, while you browse books on Rajasthani art and architecture, magazines, and bestsellers. Or you can visit the McDonald's next door—if only to people-watch a typical middle-class family or young collegians enjoying their Maharaja Macs and other uniquely Indian McDonald's fare.

The most disappointing attraction in the city is **Jawahar Kala Kendra.** Designed by the Indian architect Charles Correa in 1993, it has enjoyed exposure as a great example of contemporary Indian design and is celebrated as a center for the arts, with large exhibition spaces and studios for artists. Although the architecture may impress some, it is now all but empty of artists, and the exhibition spaces contain little more than a few broken chairs and the mattress of a homeless student—which may pass for art in the minds of the Turner Prize judges, but looks very much like a failed project.

CITY ESCAPES If the populous nature of Jaipur gets to be too much, take a trip to **Amber Fort** (see below), which can be covered in a few hours. Do bear in mind, however, that even here the crush of people can be exhausting, particularly over weekends; try to get here as soon as it opens. Time allowing, you may want to include a visit to **Jaigarh Fort** (daily 9am–4:30pm; Rs 30/70¢; City Palace entry ticket includes Jaigarh), whose walls snake high above Amber, creating a crenelated horizon. Built for defense purposes by Sawai Jai Singh II, it has a number of buildings, gardens, and reservoirs as well as the world's largest cannon on wheels and the only surviving medieval cannon foundry, but its principal attraction is the panoramic view across Amber.

On the way to Amber you'll see the turnoff for the imposing hilltop fort of **Nahargarh** (see "Sunset over Jaipur," above). Just below it is **Gaitor** (free entry; Rs 10/25¢ camera), a walled garden that houses the marble *chhatris*—erected over cremation platforms—of the Kachchwaha rulers. Needless to say, the most impressive one belongs to Jai Singh II. Farther along Amber Road you will see **Jal Mahal,** a lake palace originally built by Sawai Pratap Singh in 1799, who spent much of his childhood at Udaipur's Lake Palace. Sadly, Man Sagar Lake is dry from the protracted drought, stripping it of much of its romance. If it's romance you're after, take a leisurely drive to **Samode Palace** (see "Where to Stay," below; lunch Rs 500/$11) where, after touring Diwan-i-Khas and Diwan-i-Am, you can enjoy tea in the lovely courtyard, where bold sparrows will attempt to nibble your biscuits. Or—even better—book a table at **Rajvilas** for dinner (see "Where to Dine," later in this chapter).

East of Jaipur (8km/5 miles), on the road to Agra, you will find relative peace and fresh air at **Sisodia Rani Gardens** (© 0141/268-0494; daily 8am–6pm; Rs 5/10¢). Constructed by the Kachchwaha kings during the 18th and 19th centuries, it comprises terraced gardens with painted pavilions, the largest being **Sisodia Rani Ka Bagh,** built by the ever-prolific Jai Singh II for his Sisodia queen in yet another clever alliance—this time with the Rajputs from the Udaipur region. Her small palace—the perfect retreat for royal intrigue—has been featured in a number of Bollywood movies. Behind the gardens, a flight of stairs leads to a temple dedicated to Hanuman, the monkey god—hundreds of monkeys descend here at 4pm when the priests feed them. A little farther along the Agra road is pretty **Galta,** a gorge filled with sacred *kunds* (natural pools or reservoirs), all fed by pure spring water that falls from a rock resembling a carved cow's mouth, and surrounded by temples.

TOP ATTRACTIONS

City Palace (& Maharaja Sawai Man Singh II Museum) 🦚🦚🦚   The former
ruling family still lives in seven-story Chandra Mahal (Moon Palace) built by Sawai Jai Singh II, but the outer and inner courtyards have been converted into a museum. The first courtyard is where you'll find **Mubarak Mahal (Welcome Palace),** a "reception center" constructed by Maharaja Sawai Madho Singh II, grandfather of the present maharaja. Mubarak houses the textiles and costume section, where regal costumes provide insight into the tremendous wealth and status that the family enjoyed, as well as the extraordinarily high level of craftsmanship available to them over the centuries. These include embroidery so fine it looks like printwork, some of the best *bandhani odhnis* (tie-dye scarves/veils) to come out of Sanganer, Kashmiri shawls, gossamer muslin from Bangladesh, and silk saris from Varanasi. The **Armoury,** with a selection of exquisitely crafted yet truly vicious-looking daggers and swords, is housed in the adjacent palace—if Mughal history, with all its valor and intrigue, has caught your imagination, ask one of the attendants to point out the items belonging to the emperors Akbar, Jahangir, and Shah Jahan. The next courtyard reveals the raised **Diwan-i-Khas (Hall of Private Audience),** built in sandstone and marble. Look for the sun emblems decorating the walls—like most Rajput princes, the Kachchwaha clan belonged to the warrior caste, who traced their origins back to the sun (see "Once Were Warriors: The History of the Rajput," earlier in this chapter). To the west is **Pritam Niwas Chowk (Peacock Courtyard),** with its four beautifully painted doorways—from here you can search for signs of life from the royal residence that towers above. Move on to **Diwan-i-Am (Hall of Public Audience),** which houses a simply fantastic collection of miniature paintings, carpets, manuscripts, and photographs—look for the self-portraits of eccentric Ram Singh II, who found expression for his vanity in a passion for photography. The Friends of the Museum section sells lovely art and crafts; it's a good place to pick up a quality miniature painting or Kundan jewelry. Trying to see everything is time-consuming, but for many this is the real highlight of their visit to Jaipur.

Fun Fact I'll Take My Ganges Water to Go, Thanks

Inside Diwan-i-Khas are two huge silver urns, each weighing 345 kilograms (760 lb.). According to the *Guinness Book of Records,* these are the largest silver objects in the world. The Maharaja Sawai Madho Singh II, a devout Hindu, had these made before attending the coronation of King Edward VII in England to ensure that he had a constant supply of Ganges water to drink and to purify himself from extended contact with the "outcastes."

Chokri Shahad, Old City. Entrance through Atish Gate or Nakkar Gate. Get here as soon as it opens. © 0141/ 260-8055. Admission Rs 180 ($4); still camera free, Rs 200 ($4.55) video. Daily 9:30am–4:30pm.

Jantar Mantar Living proof of the genius of Sawai Jai Singh, this medieval observatory (built 1728–34) is the largest of its kind in the world, and the best preserved of Jai Singh's five observatories. Whether or not you understand how the instruments are read, the sheer sculptural shapes of the stone and marble objects and the monumental sizes of many (like the 23m-high/74-ft. Samrat Yantra, which forecasts crop prospects based on "the declination and hour of the heavenly bodies") are worth the trip and make for great photographs. The observatory looks more like a modern art exhibition or sci-fi set—hard to believe these instruments were constructed in the 18th century and remain functional. Some are still used to forecast how hot the summer will be, when the monsoon will arrive, and how long it will last. There are 18 instruments in all, erected between 1728 and 1734 by Sawai Jai Singh—many of his own invention. Try to get here before the sun gets too hot. You can hire a guide at the gate for Rs 150 ($3.40), but you'll do far better booking **Jaimini Shastri** (see "Guided Tours," earlier in this chapter); be sure to book him well in advance. *Tip:* If you want to see how the instruments work, avoid coming on an overcast day—almost all the instruments require sunlight to function.
Follow signs from city palace. Rs 10 (25¢), Rs 50 ($1.15) still camera, Rs 100 ($2.30) video. Daily 9am–4:30pm.

Amber (or Amer) Fort Amber was the capital of the Kachchwahas from 1037 to 1727, when Sawai Jai Singh II moved the capital to Jaipur. The approach is through a narrow pass, and the fort, an imposing edifice that grew over a period of 2 centuries, is naturally fortified by the Aravalli Hills, making it an ideal stronghold. It's a stiff 20-minute climb to **Suraj Pol (Sun Gate),** beyond which lies a beautiful complex of palaces, halls, pavilions, gardens, and temples. Either travel by car or pretend you are of royal blood and ascend on elephant-back (Rs 450/$10) for one to four riders; if you want to take pictures of the elephants, they pose for you for Rs 25 to Rs 50 (55¢–$1.15). After entering Jaleb Chowk through Suraj Pol (more elephants take riders for a turn around the courtyard), dismount and take the flight of stairs up through **Singh Pol (Lion Gate)** to **Diwan-i-Am (Hall of Public Audience),** a raised platform with 27 colonnades. Opposite you'll see the ornately carved silver doors leading to **Shila Devi Temple,** which contains an image of the goddess Kali, the appropriate family deity for the warring Rajput Kachchwaha. Massive, three-story, intricately decorated **Ganesh Pol (Elephant Gate)** leads to the private apartments of the royal family, built around a Mughal-style garden courtyard. **Sheesh Mahal (Mirror Palace)**—covered in mirror mosaics and colored glass—would have been the private quarters of the maharaja and his maharani, literally transformed into a glittering jewel box in flickering candlelight. Above is **Jas Mandir,** a hall of private audience, with floral glass inlays and alabaster relief work. Opposite, across the garden, is **Sukh Mahal (Pleasure Palace)**—note the perforations in the marble walls and channels where water was piped to cool the rooms. South lies the oldest part, the **Palace of Man Singh I.** If you want to explore the old town and its many temples, exit through Chand Pol, opposite Suraj Pol. *Note:* As is the case elsewhere, the press of bodies and noise levels can seriously detract from the experience—try to get here at 9am to avoid the heat and crowds and, if possible, avoid visiting on weekends.

Amber, 11km (7 miles) north of Jaipur. ℂ 0141/253-0293. Rs 50 ($1.15), Rs 75 ($1.65) with camera (if you want to pay for your camera after you have bought your entry ticket, you will still pay Rs 75/$1.65), Rs 150 ($3.40) video. Free lockers to store cameras. Daily 9am–4:30pm.

Anokhi Museum 𝒢𝒢 While you are in the Amber Fort area, take time to stop at this recently opened little gem. You may be told the museum doesn't exist, but persist by asking for Biharji Temple and looking for a pink haveli nearby. Anokhi began as an arts-and-crafts movement 30 years ago, and in this beautifully designed museum you can admire the textile traditions the movement has helped preserve. Each room is dedicated to a different style of fabric printing, displayed in glass cases along with artisans' implements. End your visit with a cuppa tea at the pleasant cafe and a stop at the expensive but exquisite museum shop (see shopping section later in this chapter).

Anokhi Haveli, Kheri Gate, Amber. ℂ 0141/253-0226 or 0141/275-0861. Rs 30 (55¢), Rs 50 ($1.15) still camera. Tues–Sat 10:30am–5pm; Sun 11am–4:30pm. Closed Mon and during major local and national holidays.

WHERE TO STAY

Jaipur has a plethora of places to stay, from standard Holiday Inns to the usual backpacker hostels. But no one in their right mind comes to Rajasthan to overnight in a bland room in some nondescript hotel chain when you could be sleeping in the very room where a maharaja seduced his maharani, or in the royal apartments of the family guests—hence our focus on heritage hotels. The following reviews represent the best in the city, in a variety of price categories. The exception to this is Rajvilas, which not only imitates the heritage property concept, but improves upon it.

You may come across a few heritage properties that did not make the selection, such as the **Jai Mahal Palace** (ℂ 0141/222-3636; www.tajhotels.com; $200 double). The hotel is architecturally splendid, with buildings dating back to 1745, but it's neither as grand as Taj Rambagh nor as romantic and authentic as Samode or Alsisar havelis (which also offer much better value for your money). The shabby-chic **Raj Mahal Palace** (ℂ 0141/510-5666) is a 14-room mansion that in its heyday (when Man Singh II and his beautiful wife, Gayatri Devi, moved here from Rambagh) hosted the likes of Jackie Kennedy and Princess Diana. It still has a gracious feel (not to mention the biggest hotel rooms in India), but is badly in need of refurbishment. If you're into nostalgia, check it out on www.royalfamilyjaipur.com, then book room no. 107, where the maharaja hosted Mrs. Kennedy. This is also the best place to bring kids, with its huge family suites, large grounds, and a pool; rates are from Rs 2,200 to Rs 2,500 ($50–$57) for a double, Rs 4,000 ($91) for a suite (taxes extra). Sadly, a similar air of decay hangs over **Bissau Palace** (ℂ 0141/230-4371 or -4391; www.bissau palace.com; Rs 1,500–Rs 1,800/$35–$41 A/C room). Built by the Rawal (Duke) of Bissau, with original buildings dating back to 1787, it offers much the same facilities as the cheaper Diggi Palace, with the advantage of a small pool. **Raj Palace** (ℂ 0141/ 263-4077 or -4078; www.rajpalace.com; $225–$275) is the most recent heritage conversion, but frankly, it's overpriced and just too kitschy for our taste.

Budget travelers looking for a lively atmosphere may want to check out **Arya Niwas** (© **0141/237-2456;** www.aryaniwas.com; tarun@aryaniwas.com; from Rs 600/ $13.65). This is not a heritage hotel, but it is incredibly popular with a wide array of international travelers, many of whom appear to spend a great deal of time sitting in the wicker chairs that line the deep veranda overlooking a small patch of lawn. It's efficiently run, with good-value tours and car hires, and the canteen-style dining hall has a great reputation (it serves only vegetarian food and no alcohol). If you need assistance organizing local trips, ask the extremely helpful Mr. Rajan at the front desk. The building and rooms at Arya Niwas have a very institutional feel, however—unlike the similarly priced, more laid-back Diggi Palace (see below). Another budget option worth considering is **Jas Vilas,** the large 1950s family home of the gracious Rathore family that has been converted into a 10-room hotel staffed by affable hosts Mahendra, Lily, and Kapil. It's an excellent option if you're looking for warmth, quiet, and a homey feel (and tub baths) but still want to be close to the heart of Jaipur. The hotel has verandas on every floor, though our favorite outdoor space is the cozy poolside wrought-iron seating (C-9 Sawai Jai Singh Hwy.; © **041/220-4638** or -4902; www. jasvilas.com; Rs 1,500/$35).

Note: The prices below are sometimes given in rupees, with U.S. dollar conversions; others are in U.S. dollars only (or in euros with U.S. dollar conversions), which is how hotels targeting foreign markets quote their rates.

Alsisar Haveli ⟨⟨⟨ (Value)

This is the most elegant heritage property in its price category in Jaipur, offering excellent value for money, and in slightly better condition than Narain Niwas. Built in 1892 and still owned by the Kachchwaha clan of Rajputs, it has all the traditional elements of Rajput architecture—scalloped arches and pretty cupolas, painted ceilings and colored glass windows, and a maze of corridors and stairs around and through inner courtyards. Rooms vary in size, but all are furnished with antiques and the block-printed fabrics typical of the region, and most have a padded alcove area for lounging. The only drawback is that some of the mattresses are a tad soft, and only some bathrooms have tubs. All bathrooms have recently been renovated, however. You can take tea around the pool, or retreat to the tables on the lawn for total peace. The lounge is beautifully furnished, but it is the dining hall that sets the place apart: Unlike the oppressive rooms so typical of heritage properties (like the much-vaunted Samode Haveli), Alsisar's is filled with light, thanks to the floor-to-ceiling glass walls and spotless white tablecloths. The food is good, albeit not particularly memorable; breakfast will run you Rs 200 ($4.55), while lunch and dinner (both buffets) costs Rs 330 ($7.50) plus taxes.

Sansar Chandra Rd., Jaipur 302 001. © 0141/236-8290 or -4685. Fax 0141/236-4652. www.alsisar.com. 37 units. Rs 2,750 ($63) double; Rs 3,300 ($75) suite. AE, DC, MC, V. **Amenities:** Restaurant; bar; pool; laundry. *In room:* A/C, TV, minibar, hair dryer.

Diggi Palace ⟨⟨ (Value)

This to our mind is the best budget option in Jaipur, where you get the opportunity to overnight in a 200-year-old heritage property for a fraction of the rate charged by Alsisar Haveli and Narain Niwas (though service and facilities are correspondingly not in the same class). Architecturally, the building reflects traditional Rajput style. Rooms, which vary in size, all feature cool, clean white tiles and whitewashed walls; some have antique furniture offset with bright block-printed fabrics. Book an air-conditioned room to beat the heat—they're also larger and still a steal at Rs 1,000 ($23). If you want your own veranda, ask for one of the larger rooms, particularly those overlooking the garden, which go for Rs 2,000 ($46); the small suite opposite room no. 202 is also a good pick. The "palace"—it would be more honest to describe it as a haveli—is within walking distance of Ram Niwas Gardens and the Central Museum. The drawbacks of this backpacker haven are that it's invariably full, it's a long walk from the Old City, and it has no pool, but the leafy, well-established gardens are a wonderful respite, filled with bird song. The open-air, first-floor veranda is where meals are served; dinner costs about Rs 150 ($3.40).

Shivaji Marg, C-scheme, Sawai Ram Singh Hwy., Jaipur 302 004. ⓒ **0141/237-3091**, 0141/236-6120, or 0141/236-6196. Fax 0141/230-359. diggihtl@datainfosys.net. 40 units. Rs 600 ($14) air-cooled double, Rs 1,000–Rs 2,000 ($23–$46) A/C double. No credit cards. **Amenities:** Dining hall; laundry; Internet facilities (Rs 45/$1 per hour); STD booth. *In room:* TV in some, A/C in some.

Narain Niwas Palace ✿   Like Alsisar, Narain Niwas provides you with an opportunity to live in a heritage property for relatively little money (though Alsisar currently has the edge in terms of atmosphere and service). Built in 1928 by Gen. Amar Singh, Thakur of Kanota and then commander of the Jaipur State forces, Narain Niwas was

---

Transcendent Treat

For its inspired location alone, **Amanbagh** ✿✿✿, the fabulous Amanresorts' newest property in India, deserves three stars. Date palms and mango and jamun trees dominate this truly exotic natural oasis in the Thar Desert, adjacent to Sariska National Park, near Alwar (142km/88 miles northeast of Jaipur). If you can afford it, get one of the pool pavilions facing the canal, thick with vegetation, that flows along the periphery (a terrace pavilion is next best, but ask for one facing the canal rather than the pool), and begin your day sipping ruby-red pomegranate juice on the porch while listening to the sweet twittering of birds. Designed by the architect Ed Tuttle, Amanbagh is an inspired take on local architecture, and is made almost entirely of pink sandstone by local stonemasons. Interiors exude sophisticated indulgence—glass doors in both the main room and bathroom open out onto the private pool area complete with sun beds and a sunken marble dining table atop a sandstone pedestal. A central green bathtub carved out of a single piece of *Kesariya* green marble dominates the humongous bath chamber—the same marble lines your private pool, which is cooled in summer and heated in winter. If you can bear to leave the premises, you can take picnics into the countryside, hike to ancient Somsagar Lake, explore the haunted ruins at Bhangarh, or visit the archaeological sites in the Paranagar area. Amanbagh's charming manager, Sally Baughen, and her staff provide the highest standards of service, so typical of Aman, while guest-relations-in-charge Vipul Rawal adds the local philosophy of "*atithi devo bhavo*" ("guest is God") to make your stay the most gratifying ever. Make this your final treat before you head home, and take peace with you.

Rates are $900 pool pavilion, $700 terrace haveli, $600 garden haveli, $550 courtyard haveli, and include Jaipur transfers. For reservations call ⓒ **65/6887-3337** in Singapore 24/7; fax 65/6887-3338; or go to www.aman resorts.com.

originally a country residence to which the *Thakur* would retreat from the walled city. The 3-hectare (7-acre) property remains an oasis, but the city now surrounds it. Since opening as a heritage hotel in 1978, it has been featured in glossy design publications like Taschen's *Indian Interiors*. Not surprisingly, staying in a room like the much-photographed suite no. 36, with its high ceilings, four-poster antique bed, fresco-painted walls and ceilings, and Raj-era chandelier, is like overnighting in a museum. (Sadly, the off-camera bathroom is very disappointing—with no tub and in serious need of a face-lift.) Standard room nos. 51 to 57 are worth booking; individually furnished with antique beds and chairs, these feature pretty frescoes and block-print fabrics and are close to the pool, opening onto a particularly lush part of the garden—an essential balm after tackling Jaipur's streets. Buffet-style meals are taken on the lawns or in the dining hall which, like the antiques-filled lounge, features scalloped arches decorated with frescoes, and colored-glass windows and baubles.

Kanota Bagh, Narain Sing Rd., Jaipur 302 004. ⓒ **0141/256-1291** or -3448. Fax 0141/256-1045. 31 units. Rs 3,000 ($68) double; Rs 3,700 ($84) suite. Taxes extra. AE, DC, MC, V. **Amenities:** Dining hall; bar; pool; travel desk; car hires; laundry. *In room:* A/C, TV in some, minibar, hair dryer.

Rajvilas ✪✪✪   Rajvilas is one of those luxury hotels that is a destination in its own right. It has won awards every year since it opened in December 1997 (including *Tatler*'s "Hotel of the Year," *Gourmet*'s "Most Exotic Resort in the World," and *Condé Nast Traveler*'s "Readers Travel Award") and is arguably the best of the Oberoi's flagship Vilas properties—this is, after all, where Bill Clinton stayed during his state visit to India and where Mr. Oberoi himself chose to celebrate his daughter's marriage. With a budget of $20 million, no expense was spared in showcasing the fine craftsmanship typical of the region to create and decorate what is ostensibly a traditional fortified Rajasthani palace—and though it may not have the history of an original heritage hotel, it more than makes up for this with a level of comfort and luxury that true heritage properties simply cannot match. Set amid 13 hectares (32 acres) of orchards, formal gardens, and decorative pools, accommodations are separate from the main fort (which houses the public spaces) in clusters of rooms—between four and six around each central courtyard—and a few luxury tents, all comfortably decorated with a tasteful blend of colonial and Rajasthani influences. The discreet yet attentive staff will not let you lift a finger, enabling even the most demanding guest to relish "living in the princely style of Rajasthan." The restaurant serves excellent food, with a wide range of Eastern and Western options. Even the Oberoi (Banyan Tree) spa, offering every conceivable treatment, is an award-winner. The only drawback (aside from the top-scale prices) is that you feel totally disconnected from Jaipur; but then again, for many this is an excellent reason to book here.

Goner Rd., Jaipur 303 012. ⓒ **800/5-OBEROI** toll-free in the U.S. and Canada, or 0141/268-0101. Fax 0141/268-0202. www.oberoihotels.com. 71 units. $530 deluxe double; $630 luxury tent, $1,325 royal tent; $1,800 villa, $3,000 royal villa. AE, DC, MC, V. **Amenities:** Restaurant; library/bar; pool (villas have private pools); mini-golf; tennis courts; croquet; gymnasium; health and beauty spa; elephant safari; horse riding; concierge; complimentary airport transfers; helipad; 24-hr. room service; laundry and dry cleaning. *In room:* A/C, TV, DVD player (complimentary access to music and films), minibar, hair dryer, electronic safe, scale.

Samode Haveli ✪✪   Ever since Samode Haveli made it into that glossy tome to style, *Hip Hotels: Budget,* and was selected by the author, Herbert Ypma, as one of his top 10 hotels in the world, it has enjoyed unprecedented popularity. One of the few accommodations within the old walled city (the nearby Raj Palace is not in the same class), this 200-year-old city mansion oozes authenticity, with higgledy-piggledy rooms of various sizes furnished in typical Rajasthani antiques and featuring pillars and cusped arches painted with traditional motifs, tiny colored-glass windows, marble floors, and deep alcoves for lounging. The best rooms are those housed in the *zenana* (traditionally the part of the house where women were secluded), particularly the Sheesh Mahal Suite, in which every inch of wall and ceiling is covered in tiny glass mirrors or delicately executed miniature paintings—the effect in candlelight is not dissimilar to the celebrated Sheesh Mahal at Amber Fort (though it's worth mentioning that some find the extra-low ceilings and numerous pillars claustrophobic). For all its romance and gracious atmosphere, this is no honeymooners' delight—only two rooms (nos. 114 and 115) have double beds. The main drawbacks here are the dining hall which, despite being beautifully decorated, feels gloomy and oppressive (particularly during the day), serves mediocre food, and has extremely patchy service. That said, the recently constructed pool area, with adjoining spa, is a very welcome addition, and the location is unbeatable.

Samode Haveli, Ganga Pol, Jaipur 302 992. © 0141/263-2407, -2370, or -1942. Fax 0141/263-1397. www.samode. com. reservations@samode.com. 22 units. Oct 1–Apr 31/May 1–Sept 30: 143€/80€ ($178/$100) standard double; 168€/100€ ($224/$124) deluxe suite, 207€/155€ ($257/$192) Sheesh Mahal or Haveli suite. 52€/40€ ($64/$50) extra bed. AE, DC, MC, V. **Amenities:** Dining hall; bar; pool; fitness center; steam room; airport transfers; massage; laundry. *In room:* A/C, TV, minibar, hair dryer.

Taj Rambagh Palace 🏵🏵🏵 If you're hell-bent on experiencing the blue blood of heritage properties, Rambagh Palace is both the largest (19 hectares/47 acres) and most elegant option in Jaipur; its origins date back to 1835. Converted into a hotel in 1957, it is today a favorite of Bollywood stars and worth visiting for a drink or dinner even if you're not staying here. Of the three room categories, the standards (which the Taj calls "superior") are disappointing—particularly those located in the new wing, where badly lit carpeted corridors run past an endless number of rooms with low ceilings and tacky hotel furniture. Then again, you probably won't spend a great deal of time in your room; you'll be too busy luxuriating in the gracious, beautiful palace buildings (which, incidentally, house one of Rajasthan's classiest bars, the **Polo**); or you'll be strolling the sweeping lawns. To feel as if you're actually living in a palace apartment, however, opt for a luxury room (no. 317 is just fabulous)—old-fashioned in a colonial rather than Rajasthani sense, elegant and spacious, they really are worth the extra $80. Dining at the swish **Suvarna Mahal** is a grand affair (see review below). Certainly the hotel has every amenity you could wish for (except an outdoor pool), but you sense that a certain complacency has crept in—even the best heritage hotel in Jaipur can't rest on its laurels forever.

Sawani Sing Rd., Jaipur 302 005. © 0141/221-1919. Fax 0141/238-5098. www.tajhotels.com. rambagh.jaipur@ tajhotels.com. 90 units. $320–$340 superior double, $400–$420 luxury double; $600–$625 historical suite, $1,000–$1,200 royal suite, $1,500–$1,700 grand royal suite. Taxes extra. Check online for special rates and discounts. AE, DC, MC, V. **Amenities:** 2 restaurants; bar; indoor pool; tennis; badminton and squash courts; health club; croquet; travel desk and car hires; concierge; business center; room service; laundry; camel rides; astrologer; henna. *In room:* A/C, TV, minibar, hair dryer.

AROUND JAIPUR

Samode Palace 🏵🏵 An hour's drive (45km/28 miles) from Jaipur, 400-year-old Samode Palace is popular, pretty, and very commercialized. Once an exclusive retreat for those in the know, it was put on the map by its starring role in the 1984 mini-series *The Far Pavilions,* resulting in some touristy additions like the new wing with its charmless low-ceilinged rooms, most of which overlook a parking lot. The original palace suites are beautiful, however: huge, with loads of natural light and furnished with a mix of antiques and contemporary pieces. Bathrooms need renovating but are adequate. Best value-for-money option is one of the rooms overlooking the lovely pool area (nos. 207, 216, 308, and 405 are a few)—ask for one with a balcony. Many visitors use this as a relaxing retreat from Jaipur, whose major attractions can be covered in a day trip, and it's also a good stepping-stone into the Shekhawati. However, the palace is far more commercial than, say, Deogarh Mahal (a 280km/174-mile drive from Jaipur), and there's not much to see or do here besides wander around the town to meet the tourist-savvy locals or shop for block-print fabrics and bangles (though Dukaan, the crafts shop located inside the palace, stocks a pretty good selection of jewelry and trinkets). An interesting and good-value alternative to the palace lies 10 minutes away, at **Samode Bagh,** a large garden established by the royal family, where the current owners have pitched 50 delightful en-suite tents. The tent walls feature beautiful Mughal-inspired patterns and are attractively furnished with carpets, standing lamps, and pretty wooden beds and chairs. The Bagh has its own pool and tennis courts, and all in all is an extremely peaceful getaway. Though the tents are situated a little too close to each other, the tent area is seldom full. You will, of course, need your own car and driver, because, sadly (as at all Samode properties), service is at best unpredictable.

Samode, Jaipur 303 806. ℭ 01423-24-0023. Reservations through Samode Haveli, Ganga Pol, Jaipur 302 992. ℭ **0141/263-2407,** -2370, or -1068. Fax 0141/263-1397. www.samode.com. 35 units (Palace); 50 units (Bagh). Oct 1–Apr 3/May 1–Sept 30: **Samode Palace** 195€/110€ ($4.50/2.50) deluxe double; 233€/145€ ($5.20/3.40) deluxe suite, 430€/350€ ($9.80/$8) Royal Suite. 65€/50€ ($1.50/1.15) extra bed. **Samode Bagh** 98€/75€ ($2.25/$1.70) double. Extra bed 46€/35€ ($1/75¢). All rates include breakfast and taxes; Royal Suite at Samode Palace includes dinner as well. AE, DC, MC, V. **Amenities:** Restaurant; bar; pool; tennis; gym; table tennis; camel safari; 24-hr. room service massage; laundry. *In room:* A/C, TV, minibar, tea- and coffee-making facilities, hair dryer, scale.

WHERE TO DINE

All the hotels reviewed above have dining halls or restaurants that usually serve buffets featuring mediocre to good North Indian food and mediocre to inedible "Continental" options. If you're spending more than one night or looking for somewhere local to lunch, check out the following. Note that you'll find the largest concentration of restaurants along M.I. Road, which is also the main shopping drag outside the Old City. If you're feeling peckish or thirsty during a visit to the City Palace, take a table in the courtyard at the **Palace Cafe,** inside the palace walls near the Jaleb Chowk entrance (Mon–Fri 9am–6pm, Sat–Sun 9–11am). It's a serene place with outdoor seating and an air-conditioned interior where historic photographs line the walls. Order a cold beer or a refreshing pot of tea and some cucumber sandwiches.

Mediterraneo, located on the roof of the slightly seedy Hotel Vijeet Palace (Sansar Chandra Rd.; ℭ **0141/237-8009** or -0562; Rs 135–Rs 195/$3.05–$4.50), just beyond Arya Niwas, does decent, reasonably priced Indo-Italian food and serves chilled beer; it's a good place to unwind after a hot day of sightseeing. **Indiana** (J2-34, Mahaveer Marg, behind Jai Club; ℭ **0141/236-2061** or -2062; Rs 130–Rs 300/$4–$6.85) is often packed with groups of tourists, but for good reason: The Indian fare is good, food and alcohol are reasonably priced, and a complimentary open-air folk dance show is held every evening. If you're headed for Johari Bazaar to shop, make sure you stop at **LMB (Laxmi Misthan Bhandar)** 🌴🌴 (ℭ 0141/256-5844; Rs 50–Rs 215/$1.15–$4.85). Anyone with even half a sweet tooth shouldn't miss stepping out of the madness of the bazaar into this cool oasis—even if it's just to salivate over the huge selection of sweets beautifully (and hygienically) displayed behind glass counters in the sweet *(mithai)* shop section. Sample the *paneer ghewar* (honeycomblike dessert soaked in sugary syrup)—

claimed to be the best in India. Beyond the takeout area lies the large air-conditioned restaurant. Perhaps renovated by a set designer with a love for the flamboyant 1980s, it remains strictly vegetarian, and no onion or garlic (believed to inflame the senses) are used in food preparation. No meat or alcohol are allowed on the premises. If you arrive between 4 and 7pm, you will be served only snacks. Try the freshly prepared *samosas* or potato and cashew-nut *tikkis,* and wash them down with the most delicious *lassis* (yogurt drinks) in Jaipur or exotic pomegranate juice. For an authentic meal, we recommend the Rajasthani *thali* (multicourse platter; Rs 215/$4.90), which begins with a tangy *papad mangori* soup and comes with traditional *ker sangri* (capers and desert beans), Rajasthani *kadhi* (dumplings in a yogurt sauce), five different vegetables, and three kinds of bread. Their legendary *paneer ghewar* rounds off the meal.

Chanakya Garden 🎯 *Value* NORTH INDIAN/VEGETARIAN   Chanakya recently moved to a new location (and adopted a new suffix), but it's as crammed as it always was with Jaipur businesspeople and Indian families relishing *koftas* (dumplings) and thalis from the extensive vegetarian-only menu. The *koftas* are particularly recommended: choose between the standard *malai kofta* (potato and *paneer* dumplings in a creamy, spicy sauce) or the *hariyali kofta* (vegetable dumplings served in a spinach sauce). To sample a bit of almost everything on the menu, order the Chanakya Special Thali—at Rs 160 ($3.70), it's the most expensive item on the menu, but it's big enough to share. Choose from 10 options on the bread menu—the restaurant enjoys a deservedly high reputation for the stuffed *paratha,* ideal as a starter or with *kofta.* Be warned, however, that this (like just about everything on offer) is rich—cooked and coated with pure ghee (clarified butter). Continental choices are best avoided. Waiters speak English, and service is excellent. No alcohol is served.

Ajmer Rd. (beyond DCM). 📞 **0141/235-7047** or 0141/309-7842. Main courses Rs 50–Rs 160 ($1.15–$3.70). MC, V. Daily noon–10:45pm; tandoor is closed 3–7pm.

Niros 🎯🎯 NORTH INDIAN/CHINESE   The name is the only inauthentic aspect of this very professionally run restaurant, where the constant traffic includes large extended Indian families, visiting Bollywood celebs, and foreign travelers drawn by its reputation. Well-situated on the shopping route, Niros does good Chinese as well as typical Rajasthani meat and vegetarian dishes. Plus, if your stomach is starting to curdle from the traditional (and liberal) use of ghee as a cooking medium, you'll be happy to know that Niros's chefs use only refined soybean oil. House specialties include *laal maas* (mutton cooked in a spicy red gravy) and *reshmi* kebab (mutton marinated in traditional spices and chargrilled). The *korma* dishes are all prepared in a deliciously creamy cashew-nut-based sauce, while the ever-popular chicken *tikka masala* is spicier than usual. Waiters speak English, and service is good.

M.I. Rd. 📞 **0141/237-4493.** www.nirosindia.com. Rs 70–Rs 320 ($1.60–$7.30). MC, V. Daily 10am–11pm.

Surya Mahal 🎯🎯🎯 INDIAN FUSION/CONTINENTAL   The courtyard adjoining the Surya Mahal restaurant is the most romantic place to have dinner in Jaipur. Lit by huge burning braziers, the courtyard features a raised platform where beautiful Rajasthani women give a short performance of their traditional dance (Sept 15–Mar only). Service is superb, as is the food—this is one place where the "Continental" cuisine, created by Chef Andrew Whiffen from Barbados, is as good as the Indian. Specialty Indian dishes include the kebab platter (any of the tandoor dishes are highly recommended) and traditional *thali* (multicourse platters). The *murgh malai tikka,* chicken marinated in yogurt and cream and cooked in the clay tandoor, is delicious,

---

Tips Lassi Heaven

Across the road from Niros is Lassiwalla, favored by the locals as *the* place to experience a *lassi* (cold yogurt drink). Not only is the lassi (salty or sweet; sadly, no banana) exquisitely creamy, but the price includes the large terra-cotta mug it's served in—to be kept as a memento or (as the locals do) thrown away after use. Imitators have sprung up next door, so make sure you go to the right one; the original *lassi-walla* has a board that says KISHAN LAL GOVIND NARAIN AGARWAL. He serves nothing but lassis and is usually sold out by 4pm. The current owner is Ashok Agarwal (*©* **0141/237-6892**), grandson of Govind Narain, who started the stall decades ago.

---

as is the seafood Kerala curry—prawns simmered in a mild coconut sauce and spiced with curry leaves, mustard seeds, and tamarind; mutton dishes, generally speaking, are less successful. All Indian dishes are served with dal, curried vegetables, steamed rice, Indian bread (choose from a variety), and chutneys. If you don't feel like eating Indian, try the pan-seared snapper; the penne with roast peppers, zucchini, cherry tomatoes, and basil oil; or the fettuccine with grilled chicken and basil pesto—all comparatively bland, but balm for a sensitive stomach.

Rajvilas (see "Where to Stay," above). Reservations essential. Rs 500–Rs 1,050 ($11–$24). AE, DC, MC, V. Daily noon–3pm and 7–10:30pm.

Suvarna Mahal *⊛* NORTH INDIAN/CHINESE/CONTINENTAL   The main reason to dine here is not the food—which is ultimately forgettable—but the grand colonial atmosphere of the room. Having had a drink at the elegant Polo bar, or grabbed a seat on the deep veranda that overlooks the lawns where a puppet show and/or Rajasthani dancers offer predinner entertainment, you are subsequently shown through enormous doors to a well-dressed table in a soaring double-volume space. Lit by four alabaster lamps, a wonderfully opulent, old-fashioned atmosphere is enhanced by huge gilded mirrors, walls covered in rich gold fabric, and an Italian Renaissance ceiling. It's a pity, then, that service is complacent: Not all the waiters are competent or have a good grasp of the menu (or of English), so insist on speaking to the maitre d'— we fully appreciated his recommendation of *hariyali murg tikka* (chicken marinated in spicy coriander-flavored marinade and cooked over charcoal), after having ordered a very bland *palak paneer.* We've had good reports about the *maas ke sule* (mutton marinated in Rajasthani spices and *kachri,* a local berry) and the *laal maas* (mutton in a red masala). Chinese and Continental food items are offered as well. (**Note:** As this book was going to press, we heard that the restaurant was undergoing renovation; we hope it is of a restorative rather than transformative nature, and that staff training is part of the plan.)

Taj Rambagh Palace (see "Where to Stay," above). *©* **0141/221-1919.** Rs 500–Rs 1,200 ($11–$28). AE, DC, V. Daily 7–11pm.

SHOPPING

Only Mumbai or Delhi comes close to offering the array of goods found here, and foreign buyers for wholesale and retail outlets descend in droves to stock up on textiles, rugs, pottery, jewelry, shoes, miniature paintings, and ready-made clothing and housewares. It's a cornucopia here, and the pressure to buy is immense—not least because everyone seems to be a tout for someone (see "Understanding the Commission System," below). Finding your way around the Old City is relatively easy—the divisions based on what is produced still hold true, though you'll find much more besides. Following are a few rough guidelines.

For jewelry and gems, head for **Johari Bazaar** in the Old City—the gem center of Jaipur (look for Bhuramal Rajmal Surana). While you're there, pick up a cool pair of *jootis* (traditional camel-hide sandals) at **Shivam Nagara Palace** (Shop 11, Johari Bazaar; ☎ 0141/257-1468). Alternatively, wander through **Chameliwala Market,** beyond Zarawar Singh Gate, on Amber Road, particularly if you're in search of silver, tribal, or ornamental jewelry. **Silver Mountain** (☎ 0141/237-7399) and **Maneeka** (☎ 0141/237-5913), both located at Chameliwala Market, are recommended.

Numerous factories and showrooms run the length of Amber Road, including those specializing in hand-blocked prints and antiques. And if you're looking to take home some of Jaipur's famous blue pottery, Amber Road is also where you'll find the largest concentration of outlets: **Jaipur Blue Pottery Art Centre** (near Jain Mandir, Amber Rd.; ☎ 0141/263-5375) is a reliable place to pick up items like blue pottery vases, trays, coasters, and wall plates.

The cutting, polishing, and selling of gems and the making of silver jewelry take place in the predominantly Muslim area of Pahar Ganj in the Surajpol Bazaar. Jewelry designers from all over the world continue to nurture the superlative gem-cutting and -setting skills of these craftspeople, but here, as in Johari Bazaar, be aware that bargains are hard to come by—more often than not, you really do get what you pay for. If you're knowledgeable enough, shop for gems and jewelry in the bazaars, but for most, a trip to the shops listed below is recommended. Fabric is another must-buy, as the finest quality silk, chiffon, and cotton are transformed through traditional block printing and tie-and-dye techniques into intricately patterned fabrics with vibrant contrasts and colors. The finest tie-dye process is known as *bandhani* (literally "to tie"): Tiny circles are made by tying the cloth with thread in a detailed design; the cloth is often sold with the thread still tied on (to be removed before first use) and is traditionally worn unironed, showing off the crinkly circles. **Bapu Bazaar** (around the corner from Johari Bazaar; closed Sun) is where you can bargain for a wide range of textiles and ready-made garments, as well as traditional camel-leather shoes *(jootis)* and bangles of glass and lacquer; it's also by far the most pleasant shopping street because it's pedestrianized. If you're looking for great inexpensive gifts, take a look at the tiny workshops producing beautiful bangles in **Maniharon Ka Rasta,** an alley off Tripolia Bazaar (closed Sun).

For block-print fabrics, a trip to Sanganer, a village 16km (10 miles) south of Jaipur, is a must—here printing takes place in the courtyard of almost every house. Famous as the birthplace of blockwork (and home to the largest handmade-paper industry in India), this is where you'll find the most refined block-print work in the world. Visit **Shilpi Handicrafts** (☎ 0141/273-1106) or **Sakshi** (☎ 0141/273-1862) for fabrics, and **Salim's** (☎ 0141/273-0222) for a range of handmade paper you'll be loathe to write on! Also visit **Anokhi** (reviewed below) for lovely block-print garments. One of the most reliable shops for knickknacks is **Neelam Handicrafts** at the Arya Niwas (☎ 0141/237-2456 or 0141/510-6010). This little shop stocks maps, postcards, and books on India as well as some music CDs. It also has a small collection of silver jewelry, Indian teas, handmade paper, and souvenirs—all good quality and sold at a fixed marked price (a rarity in Jaipur); incidentally, they are half the price quoted at most other city shops.

Tips Understanding the Commission System

Like everywhere in India, your rickshaw-*walla,* guide, or driver—even the well-spoken gentleman who strikes up a conversation, then offers to show you around (or wants "to practice his English")—are without fail out to earn commission from the shops they suggest you stop at, and this gets added to the price you're quoted. Even on foot you will be accosted by who appears to be the owner of the shop but is in fact one of a host of men paid by shopkeepers if they bring you inside—"to look, no buy, madam." It's an irritation you simply have to get used to, but try to establish upfront how much the commission is. Also, be aware of credit card fraud—unscrupulous traders will run off extra dockets, then forge your signature: Best not to let your credit card out of sight. And don't fall for anyone who tries to persuade you to purchase precious stones on the premise that you can sell them at a profit to a company they supposedly know of back home.

BLUE POTTERY

Kripal Singh Shekhawat ✸✸✸   If you want to make sure you're purchasing top-quality blue glazed pottery, make an appointment to view the work of Jaipur's most famous ceramist, Kripal Singh, often credited with reviving this dying art. Made from ground blue quartz stone, glass, borax, and clay, and utilizing traditional designs, his work is nothing short of exquisite. B-18A Shiv Marg (near Jaipur Inn), Bani Park. ✆ 0141/220-1127.

BOOKS

Books Corner ✸   You could easily miss this corner shop, but even though it's tiny, it's chockablock with magazines and books. If you're looking for more information on India, coffee-table books on Rajasthan, or just a good paperback read, this has the best selection around, at the fairest prices. M.I. Rd. ✆ 0141/236-6323.

CLOTHING & HOUSEWARES

Anokhi ✸✸✸   This company was created in the 1960s by a British designer who had items made here for export to the U.K. and elsewhere. The combination of Eastern and Western influences has resulted in elegant and flattering designs that have become hugely popular around the world. Anokhi is part of a growing design movement that taps into the skills of local craftspeople and gives those crafts a modern twist. Hand-blocked prints, hand-woven fabrics, and natural dyes are the hallmark of Anokhi's products, which include gorgeous garments for men, women, and children, and a wide range of feminine home furnishings—anything from duvet and cushion covers to napkins. Prices are significantly higher than those in the bazaars, but the quality of design is in another league. 2 Tilak Marg, C-Scheme. ✆ 0141/222-9247. www.anokhi.com.

JEWELRY

Amrapali ✸✸   In 1980, two young entrepreneurs, Rajesh Ajmera and Rajiv Arora, saw a gap in the market and started adapting traditional jewelry styles to appeal to a broader international market. Conveniently situated near Panch Batti and the city gate that leads into Jauhri Bazaar, Amrapali is famous for its tribal silver jewelry, but the gold showroom also contains some rare examples of kundan jewelry, a technique in which each gem is set by pressing fine strips of highly purified gold around it. Depending on how much you spend, you may be able to negotiate a discount. M.I. Rd. ℭ **0141/237-7940** or 0141/236-2768.

K. S. Durlabhji, Emerald House ✦   When a new emerald mine was discovered in Rhodesia (now Zimbabwe) in the 1920s, Mr. M. S. Durlabhji got on the very next boat and traveled south. Once there, he took one look at the deep-green quality of the emeralds and purchased the entire consignment, then continued to purchase every stone until the mine ran dry. Today his son Yogendra has a collection of emerald jewelry that makes jewelers across the world green with envy, and their buyers include a who's who of the world's top jewelers: Van Cleef, Harry Winston, Tiffany, Cartier, and Boucheron, to name a few. Subhash Marg, C-Scheme. ℭ **0141/237-2318** or -6044.

Gem Palace ✦✦✦   When the maharajas of Rajasthan were suddenly deprived of their privy purses in 1972, many were forced to sell off the family jewels. Gem Palace, whose owners had been serving their needs for four generations, was a discreet place to do so. Today you can admire these priceless items, now owned by the Kasliwals and displayed in this beautiful store, along with antiques from the Mughal period. You can also view the craftspeople here creating new pieces, destined for the necks, wrists, and fingers of the privileged all over the world; its celebrity customers have included Princess Diana, Bill Clinton, and Paul McCartney. Arguably the best and most exclusive jewelry shop in Jaipur, but not the place to pick up a bargain. M.I. Rd. ℭ **0141/236-3061** or 0141/237-4175. www.gempalacejaipur.com.

PASHMINAS

New Gandhi Handloom Coop ✦✦ *Value*   This tiny store is stuffed with a selection of Pashminas of varying quality—the cheapest cost Rs 100 ($2.30) and are available in just about every color under the sun, though at that price you're hardly getting much of the real Pashmina wool in it. The extremely helpful Kashmiri gentleman will of course tempt you to spend a great deal more on one of his pure Pashminas—prices aren't going to be any lower, even in Kashmir. Johari Bazaar, Old City.

3 The National Parks

The two most famous parks in Rajasthan, both within easy striking distance of Jaipur, are **Bharatpur-Keoladeo Ghana National Park,** a 2,600-hectare (6,400-acre) tract of land that attracts the largest concentration and variety of birdlife in Asia; and **Ranthambhore National Park,** which enjoys an enviable reputation as the one area where you are virtually guaranteed to see a tiger. Also relatively close to Jaipur (110km/68 miles; 2 hr.) is **Sariska National Park** where, sadly, tigers no longer roam (see "Wanted: Tigers," below), though the presence of a new luxury resort, Amanbagh, is cause for celebration (see the box "Transcendent Treat," under "Where to Stay," earlier in this chapter). The Sariska Palace Hotel, an aspiring luxury hotel built by the Machiavellian Maharaja Jay Singh of Alwar (see "Once Were Warriors: The History of the Rajput," earlier in this chapter), is a rather lovely French-Indo concoction (if you like your buildings to resemble over-the-top confections) furnished with many original pieces (rotting trophies included). Reports of service have been less than satisfactory, and it's really only worthwhile to pop in for tea if you're in the area. By contrast, Ranthambhore is far more beautiful and has two excellent accommodations as well as a fascinating conservation history.

BHARATPUR/KEOLADEO GHANA NATIONAL PARK

Referred to as the Eastern Gateway to Rajasthan, Bharatpur lies almost exactly halfway between Delhi (152km/94 miles) and Jaipur (176km/109 miles), and is a mere 55km (34 miles) from the Taj Mahal. The town itself holds no fascination, but a few kilometers south on National Highway 11 is Keoladeo "Ghana" National Park. Recognized by UNESCO as a World Heritage Site, the park is definitely worth visiting if you're a keen birder, but it's not a must-see for people who don't know the difference between a lark and a peacock.

A natural depression of land that was initially flooded by Maharaja Suraj Mal in 1726, the park abounds in large tracts of wetlands (covering more than a third of the terrain) as well as wood, scrub, and grasslands, a combination that attracts a large number of migratory birds that fly thousands of miles to find sanctuary here. It was not always so—for centuries, the area was the Maharaja of Bharatpur's private hunting reserve, and in 1902 it was inaugurated by Lord Curzon as an official duck-shoot reserve (some 20 species of duck are found here). In the most shameful incident in the park's history, Lord Linlithgow, then Viceroy of India, shot 4,273 birds in one day—the inscription of his record can still be read on a pillar near Keoladeo Temple. Thankfully, the park became a sanctuary in 1956 and was ultimately upgraded to national park status in 1982.

Today the park supports more than 375 bird species, including a large variety of herons, kingfishers, pelicans, storks, and ducks. It is the only known wintering region of the rare and endangered Siberian crane, which flies 8,050km (5,000 miles) to get here. The numbers are indeed staggering, and birds will fill your vision throughout your visit—particularly during the winter months (Oct–Feb), when the resident bird

Wanted: Tigers

On October 10, 2003, Chinese Customs officials apprehended a truck on the road to Lhasa. Wrapped in Delhi newspapers were the skins of 581 leopards, 778 otters, and 31 tigers—the latter representing 1% of the entire estimated tiger population of India. While wildlife non-governmental organizations (NGOs) like the Wildlife Protection Society of India have persistently highlighted the high level of organized wildlife crime and its inevitable effect on the tiger population, these facts were always denied by local authorities, who invariably reported increased tiger populations. But poaching remains rampant, with tigers in particular danger because of the Chinese belief that ingesting their crushed bones imbues potency. This was proven in February 2005, when journalist Jay Mazoomdaar blew the whistle on the complete disappearance of all tigers from the Sariska Sanctuary during the monsoon of 2004. The ensuing public outcry led to the formation of several high-level committees that attempted to get to the truth about tiger numbers. After a nationwide manhunt, kingpin wildlife butcher Sansar Chand—allegedly responsible for the poaching of at least 100 tigers—was arrested in Delhi on July 1, 2005. But unless sterner measures are instituted, conservationists and environmentalists remain skeptical of the continued survival of India's endangered tigers.

population swells to over half a million. The park is also home to 13 snake species (including the oft-spotted python); six species of large herbivores; and mongoose, civet, and otter. Although a dead tiger was discovered here in June 2005, Bharatpur is not regarded as a tiger sanctuary, and you sense that the signs urging caution are there to inject a sense of romance and wildness into what is otherwise a very tame experience. In fact, it is hard to understand how a World Heritage Site that attracts more than a million visitors a year can be so undervalued by those administering it—at dawn scores of people (as well as a few illegal vehicles) take the main road through the park as a shortcut into Bharatpur, feral cattle blithely grazing the grasslands transform the scene into one of ordinary farmland, the loud *khudu-khudu* of generators pumping water disturb the peace in many areas, and a general lack of facilities and tawdry appearance leave a lot to be desired, though the drought has no doubt exacerbated the situation over the past few years.

Tip: If you are staying in the area for a couple of days, an excursion well worth considering is to the architecturally beautiful **Deeg Palaces** (daily 8am–sunset; free), 30km (18 miles) northwest of Bharatpur, particularly in August during the 3-day Monsoon Festival, when the 500-odd fountains are turned on.

ESSENTIALS
VISITOR INFORMATION The **wildlife office** is located at the main gate on National Highway 11 (© 05644/22-2777). Entry is Rs 200 ($4.55) per person, Rs 200 ($4.55) per video camera. To really get into the excitement of birding, you should purchase a copy of Salim Ali's *The Book of Indian Birds* (OUP India) or *Collins Handguide to Birds of the Sub-Continent* and start ticking off those sightings!

GETTING THERE Bharatpur is a 4½-hour drive from Delhi; it's 55km (34 miles) west of Agra and 175km (108 miles) east of Jaipur. If you travel by train from Delhi, it will take 2½ hours by the convenient Kota Janshatabdi; it takes a little over 2 hours for this train to link you with Sawai Madhopur (Ranthambhore National Park). From Agra, the Marudhar Express gets you here in just 55 minutes.

GETTING AROUND You can set off on foot or rent your own bicycle near the entrance to the park (Rs 25/55¢ per hour; some rental shops ask that you leave your passport or a deposit of no more than Rs 500/$11), but roads aren't great and you will often find yourself on foot, actually burdened by the bike, especially if you try to traverse the dirt tracks. You can explore certain areas by boat (Rs 25/55¢), though if there is another drought, these will be out of operation. The best way to get around the park is with a cycle- or horse-rickshaw (Rs 50–Rs 70/$1.15–$1.60 per hour); many of the rickshaw-*wallas* have spent years trundling visitors around and now have a good knowledge of the birdlife as well as keen eyesight (though a less than satisfactory command of English). If you want them to double as guides, they will expect a tip (Rs 50–Rs 100/$1.15–$2.30), depending on how long you use them. Official guides (Rs 75/$1.65) carrying binoculars are also available at the entrance to the park; in a rather unwieldy arrangement, they travel alongside on their bicycles. Note that the park opens at 6am and closes by 5pm in winter or 6pm in summer.

WHERE TO STAY & DINE
The government-run **Hotel Bharatpur Ashok** or Forest Lodge (© 05644/22-2722 or -2760; itdchba@sancaharnet.in; Rs 2,799/$64 double) is the only option inside the park. The 17 rooms are clean but charmless, there is no pool, and you have to pay an entry fee every time you enter the park. On the plus side, it does have a lovely

bougainvillea-lined terrace—though you'll have to contend with monkeys should you choose to eat here (and you don't have to travel far to find the very reason you've come in the first place!). It's overpriced, however, which is why our money is on the far more charming **Laxmi Vilas Palace** (see below), a 15- to 20-minute drive away. If you're on a tighter budget, **Hotel Sunbird** (© 05644/22-5701 or -1533; www.hotelsunbird. com; $18–$24 double, including breakfast) and **Birder's Inn** (© 05644/22-7346 or in Delhi 011/2683-1792; www.birdersinn.com; Rs 1,425/$95 double including breakfast) are both located on National Highway 11 (which can be noisy) and within walking distance of the gates. Both offer pretty basic, but scrupulously clean, en-suite accommodations, with Birder's Inn set farther back from the road and owned by avid birder Tirath Singh.

Laxmi Vilas Palace ⊀   This is not a palace in any sense of the word, but an extremely pretty and ornately decorated double-story heritage hotel, originally built in 1899 for the Maharaja of Bharatpur's younger brother and still owned by members of the royal family, who live in a separate wing. It's not luxurious, but the rooms—ringing a central courtyard—are charming, some decorated in original Rajasthani antiques, with the best featuring small double doors leading onto the narrow balcony that circumambulates the exterior. Room no. 203 is a good bargain, a deluxe (the standard category) with a great pastoral view of the mustard fields. Suites are, as always, more spacious. My personal favorite is room no. 301, the "penthouse suite," which is hardly ever rented out because it has no air-conditioning. It's the only room on the rooftop, affording you wonderful privacy, with five double doors, three of which open onto a small private balcony overlooking the fields behind the house. Areas of the hotel look a tad run-down, but the original frescoes are undergoing lengthy restoration, and there is a lovely pool. Service is friendly. Food is of the tasty home-cooked variety—the dinner buffet offers the usual mix of North Indian and bland Continental. Grab a table in the inner courtyard rather than the more claustrophobic dining hall; it's also a good place for a snack. Masala cheese toast (Rs 70/$1.60) and vegetable *pakora* (Rs 50/$1.15) ordered at the pool took a long time to arrive but were well worth the wait. The hotel jeep can take you to the park or on any other excursions.

Kakaji Ki Kothi, Bharatpur 321 001 (2.5km/1½ miles from town; 55km/34 miles from Agra). © 05644/22-3523 or 05644/23-1199. Fax 05644/22-5259. www.laxmivilas.com. reservations@laxmivilas.com. 25 units. Rs 3,000 ($68) double; Rs 4,000 ($137) suite. Meals Rs 350 ($8) dinner; Rs 300 ($6.85) lunch; Rs 200 ($4.55) breakfast. AE, MC, V. **Amenities:** Dining hall; pool; kids' pool; Jacuzzi; car rental/transfers; travel desk; jeep safari; currency exchange; limited room service; laundry; doctor-on-call. *In room:* A/C, TV.

RANTHAMBHORE NATIONAL PARK

Ranthambhore—for many decades the hunting preserve of the princes of Jaipur—covers a mere 40,000 hectares (98,800 acres) but offers a fascinating combination of crumbling monuments, living temples, wild beauty, and your best chance to spot a wild tiger. Set within a high, jagged escarpment, **Ranthambhore Fort** (save a few hours for a visit) has towered over the park's forests for nearly a thousand years and has witnessed many a bloody combat—even the Mughal emperor Akbar fought a battle for supremacy here in the 16th century. Inside the fort (open dawn–dusk at no cost) lie a number of ruined palaces, step wells, and a celebrated Ganesha temple visited every year in September by two million pilgrims who come to worship during the Lord Ganesha's birthday. But it is the forests that lie shimmering in the gorges below, scattered with more ancient crumbling monuments, that attract the foreign pilgrims, who come during the winter months to catch a glimpse of the mighty Bengal tiger.

Sightings are recorded fairly regularly—it is said that between 75% and 95% of all the photographs ever taken of a tiger in the wild have been taken in Ranthambhore. This has meant that the 26-odd tigers living here have become totally habituated to human observation and are almost entirely indifferent to the sight and sound of vehicles and flashing light bulbs.

The success of the park is due in no small measure to the efforts of Fateh Singh Rathore. A member of the princely family of Jodhpur, Rathore was made field director of Ranthambhore in 1972, the year tiger hunting was banned in India. Almost single-handedly, Rathore mapped and built the park's roads and persuaded 12 entire villages to move voluntarily, having arranged financial compensation and constructed new villages with modern facilities that included schools, wells, and electricity. He also used a powerful spiritual argument: It is the tiger that always accompanies the goddess and demon-slayer Durga (who embodies the power of good over evil), so it therefore deserves protection; however, its survival remains forever compromised in a habitat shared with humans (see "Wanted: Tigers" above).

Under Rathore's protection, the Ranthambhore tiger population increased from 13 to 40, and his dedicated study and photography of the subjects brought much of the tiger's beauty and plight into the international spotlight. But at no small cost— Rathore was awarded the WWF International Valour Award after a mob of villagers, angry at no longer having access to their ancestral lands for grazing and hunting, attacked him, shattering his kneecaps and fracturing his skull. On his release from the hospital, Rathore simply returned to the village and challenged them to do it again.

After a brief scare in the early 1990s, when poaching (apparently by the park's own wardens) almost halved the resident tiger population, numbers stabilized by the year 2000. Today, people like Rathore and Valmik Thapar, one of India's foremost campaigners for the protection of the tiger, are once again fighting a crucial battle against widespread poaching; they argue that the authorities set up for the protection of the reserve are doing little. They have been proven right; in mid-2005 an independent committee appointed to carry out a tiger census discovered that numbers in Ranthambhore had dwindled from 40 to 26, in spite of the presence of several new cubs.

If you're keen on understanding the tiger politics of the region, you will no doubt find yourself engaged in intense discussion at Sher Bagh and Ranthambhore Bagh, both good accommodations. Fateh Singh's daughter-in-law manages Sher Bagh, while his son Goverdhan, a doctor, runs the nearby charitable hospital for the welfare of local people; it's one of the best-run rural hospitals in India. They also run an excellent rural school (visitors are welcome to visit both the school and hospital)—all this based on the philosophy that unless one develops solutions in concert with local people, it won't be possible to save the tiger for posterity. With an estimated 90,000 humans and almost a million livestock living within a 5km (3-mile) radius of the park, the pressure on this island of wilderness remains immense, but its popularity and the efforts of many wildlife supporters will hopefully stand it in good stead.

While tiger sightings are relatively common, don't expect the experience to be necessarily a romantic one. It can be ruined by the presence of other vehicles, particularly the open-topped 20-seater Canters buses with whooping kids on board. Only a limited number of vehicles are allowed at any sighting, but this regulation is not always respected, hence the designation of different routes (see "Getting Around," below) to keep number densities spread throughout the park. Even if you don't spot a tiger (and do be prepared for this eventuality), the sheer physical beauty of the park is worth experiencing—from lotus-filled lakes and dense jungle to craggy, boulder-strewn cliffs

---

Fun Fact **True Tiger Tidbits**

Much like the human fingerprint, every tiger's pug markings are totally unique. Unlike most cats, they have round pupils and are adept swimmers. When a tiger sticks its tongue out, curls its lips, and closes its eyes slightly (as if snarling), it's actually checking for scents in the air. This action, called the "Flehmen Response," is the tiger analyzing smells using sensory receptors in the roof of its mouth. Tigers are immensely powerful—strong enough to kill and drag an animal heavier than itself—and can eat over 30 kilograms (66 lb.) of meat in a single night. Females make better hunters, while the males are notoriously lazy—even when it comes to sex. When a female is in heat and makes a mating call, the male will often hide until the female seeks him out and foists herself upon him. Cubs are born blind; it takes 1 to 2 weeks before they can see. By the time hunting was banned in the 1970s, only 2,000 tigers were left out of an estimated population of 50,000 in the 19th century. Today some 6,000 survive throughout the world, of which between 2,000 and 3,000 are found in India.

---

and golden grasslands. Other species worth looking for include caracal (a wildcat), crocodile, *nilgai* (large antelope resembling cattle), *chital* (spotted deer), black buck (delicate buck with spiraling horns), *chinkara* (a dainty gazelle), and *sambar* (their distinctive barking call often warns of the presence of a tiger nearby). The park also has leopards (notoriously shy), wild boars, and sloth bears, and is rich in birdlife—over 400 resident and migrant species.

ESSENTIALS

VISITOR INFORMATION Unlike at Bharatpur, traffic and numbers are closely regulated. For general information, call the **Sawai Madhopur Tourist Centre** (Sawai Madhopur Railway Station; ℂ **07462/22-0808;** Mon–Sat 10am–1pm and 2–5pm). For game-drive bookings in a jeep (avoid the Canters buses), call the **Project Tiger office** (ℂ **07462/22-0223;** Mon–Sat 5–7am and noon–2pm for advance booking). Only 18 jeeps are allowed into the park at each drive, and these are booked 2 months in advance. If you have no alternative, Canters buses can be booked a day in advance at the tourist reception center at RTDC's Hotel Vinayak (Rs 225/$5.10 per person; Rs 200/$4.55 video; daily 4–5pm). If you book with any of the accommodations recommended below, they will arrange all this for you (they also enjoy unofficial priority access to the park). Please note, however, that you must let your host know when and how often you would like to go on a game drive as soon as possible—these officially need to be booked 60 days in advance. The price of a seat in a jeep varies depending on where you stay (see below). For a wonderful introduction to the park, ask your host to find a copy of *The Ultimate Ranthambhore Guide* (Rs 175/$4) by Sheena Sippy and Sanjna Kapoor, also sold at the park's gate. *Tip:* Although the park's seven routes are assigned randomly, and you are normally not allowed to choose which route you would like to go on, you *can* request that your host either try to have at least one game drive near a body of water in the park or in an area where a tiger was spotted the day before. The best time to visit the park is between November and April (Jan–Apr is best for tiger sightings). The park closes during the monsoon season (July–Sept).

GETTING THERE The nearest airport is Jaipur's, which lies 180km (112 miles) away; it is just under a 4-hour drive away. Alternatively, the sprawling village of Sawai

Madhopur (10km/6¼ miles from the park gates) is well connected by rail to Jaipur (just over 2 hr.) and to Jodhpur (8 hr.), and is on the main line between Delhi (5½ hr.) and Mumbai. All accommodations listed will arrange pick-ups from the station.

GETTING AROUND   A limited number of visitors are allowed entry into the park, hence the need to book your place in a jeep well in advance. There are two game drives: The early-morning (Mar–June 6:30–9:30am; Oct–Feb 7–10am) is often preferable to the afternoon drive (Mar–June 3:30–6:30pm; Oct–Feb 2:30–5:30pm), given that temperatures can make for muggy afternoons. However, you should pack something warm because it can get cold both early in the morning and once darkness approaches.

Routes (which drivers are pretty much forced to stick to) and guides are randomly allotted, which means you may be on a tight budget yet find yourself in a jeep with an excellent guide, watching a tiger bathe in the lotus lake that fronts the beautiful 250-year-old Jogi Mahal, while a hapless guest paying top dollar for the same trip trundles around with a monosyllabic guide with halitosis. At press time, there was talk of an overhaul of tourist entry procedures and rules; check with your host.

WHERE TO STAY & DINE

Almost all the best options are on Ranthambhore Road, which flanks the park. If you're on a real budget you may want to consider the government-run **Castle Jhoomar Baori** (© 07462/22-0495), a former hunting lodge with a great location (the only choice inside the park) but—as is the case with all RTDC hotels—service is complacent, fittings ancient, and facilities almost nonexistent.

If you're watching your dollar, a good-value option is the tastefully rustic **Ranthambhore Bagh** (© 07462/22-1728, reservations in Delhi © 011/2691-4417 or 011/2683/1792; www.ranthambhorebagh.com), where you can book luxury tents for $80 (including all meals; $65 per game drive by jeep). Located 5km (3 miles) from the park gate, accommodations here are simple but comfortable, and the fixed-menu buffet meals are often served outdoors. Frequented by photographers and conservationists, this is a good place to meet wildlife enthusiasts and discuss the future of tigers and wildlife in general.

Aman-i-Khás *፟፟፟*   This is surely the most stylish tented wilderness accommodations in all India. Unlike Vanyavilas, it lacks peripheral constructed walls, which gives it the ambience of the true outdoors, with its own small watering hole where you can watch for visiting animals. Each of the spacious air-conditioned (or heated) white tents, located a sensible distance away from each other, features typical Aman touches of discreet luxury, with spaces stylishly divided by cool white drapes. Sip a cocktail as you relax on the cowhide and teak chairs (with footstools, of course) or on the *charpais* (traditional woven bed) on your patio; browse glossy coffee-table books on India, wildlife, or Rajasthan in the library-cum-lounge; or get pampered silly with an Aman Raj massage in the spa tent. Each room is assigned a batman who is superbly efficient yet completely invisible unless you need him—screen windows open and close, beds are turned in, bathrobes replaced, all quite magically. Food is simply superb—fresh organic produce from the garden enhances refreshingly delicate flavors. At night, lanterns light the path from your room to the outdoor lounge, where a giant *uruli* (traditional bronze bowl) forms the central fireplace, and guests gather to enjoy the night sky, the ethereal calm, and the occasional call from the wild. Our main gripe? For this price, there should be a pool.

Ranthambhore Rd. (just beyond Sher Bagh), Sawai Madhopur. ☏ 07462/25-2052 or -2224. Fax 07462/25-2178. For reservations, contact: Amanresorts Central Sales and Reservations Office in Singapore (24/7) ☏ 65/6887-3337. Fax 65/6887-3338. reservations@amanresorts.com. www.amanresorts.com. 10 units. Oct–Apr only. $700–$750 tent; minimum 2 (preferably 3) nights' stay required, arriving Mon or Thurs. $75 board per person per day. Transfers extra. Game drives $35 minimum per person. AE, MC, DC, V. **Amenities:** Dining tent; library/lounge; spa tent; outdoor lounge w/fireplace; room service; laundry; safety deposit box. In room: A/C or heating, cooler w/drinks, CD Walkman on request.

Sawai Madhopur Lodge ☆   Built as a hunting lodge by Maharaja Sawai Man Singh II in the 1930s, the original two-story main house is still very attractive, with a deep veranda (furnished with comfortable Deco cane suites) that swoops in a semicircle overlooking the lawns and outbuildings where many of the standard and superior rooms are located. Given that you could be at Sher Bagh for less money (their rate includes meals), only the seriously unadventurous who prefer to sleep surrounded by mortar (and air-conditioning) should consider staying here—it is just a 20-minute drive to the park gates, but feels far away from the wilderness. Standard rooms look like a million other hotel rooms; superiors are simply slightly bigger. Tents are available, but they look neither warm nor inviting. The best rooms are the large, old-fashioned suites that are located in the original lodge and have lovely views of the property. Alternatively, ask for a room that leads onto the garden close to the pool. The lodge certainly has an old-world charm, but aspects like the pitiful stuffed tiger that guards the pool room, his seams split and claws rotting, and the green-algae tint of the pool, point to poor management. Lunch and dinner buffets will run you $12 and $15 respectively.

Ranthambhore National Park Rd., Sawai Madhopur. ☏ **07462/22-0541** or -0247. Fax 07462/22-0718. www.tajhotels. com. 38 units. $200–$220 tent double; $200–$240 standard double; $240–$260 suite. Game drives Rs 1,500 ($35) minimum for 2 people (less if you share a jeep). AE, MC, DC, V. **Amenities:** Dining hall; pool; tennis; croquet; pool table; bicycles; excursions; currency exchange; business center; limited room service; massage; laundry; doctor-on-call. In room: A/C, TV, minibar, tea- and coffee-making facilities, hair dryer.

Sher Bagh ☆☆ Value   If you're looking for a safari experience in India, this intimate camp is a great choice (though unlike its African counterpart, it's not situated in a reserve, but is as close to the park as you are likely to get). The irrepressible and charming owner, Jaisal Singh, is a superb host when he is around, and a member of what could be described as Ranthambhore royalty. (He is Fateh Singh Rathore's godchild and practically grew up in the park between bouts of polo playing and hobnobbing with the rich and famous.) Accommodations comprise a semicircle of comfortable tents (originally designed for the Maharaja of Jodhpur's hunting expeditions), each with an en-suite bathroom (no bathtubs; satisfying showers, but the hot water sometimes runs out). Tents are a little too close together and hot during the day, but there are a number of places to relax (the coolest is the first-floor bar/lounge area, which enjoys a breeze and has a great selection of books). Sadly, Sher Bagh has no pool. Tents are not air-conditioned but have fans. Meals are a welcome relief from standard North Indian fare; a full breakfast is served after the morning game drive followed by a light lunch (pesto pasta and salad, perhaps; almost all ingredients are grown on the farm). Cucumber sandwiches and delicious *chai* (tea) are served immediately after the afternoon game drive, followed by a lavish buffet dinner. At night, when the lanterns and torches are lit, the camp really comes into its own. Engaging in idle chatter while imbibing G&Ts, your feet in the sand and stars above, makes this one of the most relaxing experiences in North India.

Ranthambhore Rd. ☏ **07462/25-2120.** Bookings through 58–59 Regal Building, Parliament St., New Delhi 110 001. Fax 011/2334-5429. www.sherbagh.com. 12 units. $275 double including all meals, transfers, and taxes. $20 per person per game drive includes everything but video camera fee. No credit cards. **Amenities:** Dining tent; bar; complimentary station transfer; excursions; limited room service; laundry.

Vanyavilas ఈఈఈ   Set on 8 hectares (20 acres) of landscaped gardens, this still has the edge on the new Aman property (never underestimate the lure of a pool). The tent rooms are not as safari-like as those at Aman-i-Khas, and the overall outdoor setting not quite as back-to-nature, but they are nevertheless gorgeous, featuring huge canvas roofs shot through with gold sparkles, teak floors, solid walls hung with artwork, opulent Indo-colonial furnishings, and all the modern conveniences you could possibly need. Bathrooms are the sizes of most hotel rooms and have free-standing claw-foot tubs, fabulous showers, and doors leading out to private terraces with comfortable day beds on which to rest after plundering the well-stocked minibars. With each generous tent surrounded by a small walled garden, the property does sprawl somewhat, forcing a rather long walk to the pool or restaurant (you can, of course, call for a golf cart) and, unlike Sher Bagh and Aman-i-Khas, the well-manicured surroundings give you little sense of being on the edge of a wilderness. But the superb service, great dining (either in the restaurant or adjacent courtyard), excellent spa, and sheer opulence of the public spaces more than make up for this. Best of all is the opportunity to sit in on one of the regular lectures given by Fateh Singh Rathore, the man who put Ranthambhore on the map, not to mention the bliss of a sparkling pool.

Ranthambhore Rd., Sawai Madhopur 322 001. ℂ 800/6-OBEROI in the U.S., 07462/22-3999, or toll-free 1600/11-2030. www.oberoihotels.com. 25 units. $630 double. Game drive minimum Rs 2,600 ($60) for 2 (less if you share a jeep). AE, MC, V. **Amenities:** Restaurant; pool; library bar; gym; spa; billiards room; observation tower; elephant safaris; chauffeur-driven cars; complimentary station transfer; business center; salon; Internet; laundry. *In room:* A/C, TV, DVD, CD music system (including selection of CDs and DVDs), dataport, minibar, tea- and coffee-making facilities, hair dryer, safe.

SHOPPING

Find the time to visit **Dastkar Craft Centre** (near Sher Bagh, off Ranthambhore Rd.), which has a selection of pottery, textiles, and ready-made garments produced by the women in the area. Much of it is mediocre, but a few gems can be found at ridiculously low prices. Spending a few rupees here also helps alleviate the overwhelming poverty in the area. **Anokhi,** the famous Jaipur designer-ethnicwear outfitter, has a store in Ranthambhore as well. They offer a free pick-up (and drop-off) from your hotel (ℂ **07462/22-3206** or -2216), even if you don't buy anything. If you do, you contribute toward preserving the tiger's habitat.

4 Bundi

368km (228 miles) S of Jaipur; 438km (272 miles) SW of Agra

If you see only one off-the-beaten-track town in Rajasthan, the small town of Bundi, established in 1241, should be your first choice. It's worth a visit not just for the architectural magnificence of the palace that clings to the cliff above; the town's lack of modernization and abundance of temples, cenotaphs, and step wells; or even its renowned school of miniature paintings (arguably the best-value paintings in Rajasthan); it's the lack of hustling, which comes as a truly welcome relief. Approached through a gorge, the town is protected by the embracing hills of the Aravalli Hills, topped by Taragarh Fort, and life here goes on pretty much as it has for centuries. Because the population is in no way dependent on tourism, you are either greeted with real affection or total indifference. There's absolutely no sales pressure— a refreshing change after the constant barrage of "Please come see," and "Special price for you" that follows you everywhere in the cities and more popular towns.

Exploring Bundi's narrow streets, with tiny cupboardlike shops raised a meter or more above street level to avoid the monsoon floods, feels like seeing the real India.

Followed by giggling children trying to touch your hand or clothes, you will pass old men beating copper pots into perfect shape; tailors working with beautiful fabrics on ancient Singers; huge mounds of orange, red, and yellow spices offset by purple aubergines, red tomatoes, and green peppers; rickshaws carting women adorned in saris of saturated colors; and temples blaring live music—fresh and natural images that will have you grabbing your camera every 2 minutes. Besides wandering the streets, you can walk to a number of attractions, of which **Garh Palace** ✶✶✶ (described by Rudyard Kipling as "the work of goblins" and one of the few examples of pure Rajput style) and **Raniji-ki-Baori** ✶✶✶ (the state's most impressive step well) are not to be missed. Raniji-ki-Baori, which lies in a small park in the center of town, dates back to the 17th century and features ornately carved gates, pillars, and friezes. Garh Palace's exterior is astounding, but sadly, much of the interior is falling apart; entry is now restricted to the arcaded **Chitra Shala,** which is decorated with many of the fine murals in the miniature style the town is famous for (free entry; dawn–dusk). Given prior notice, the owner of Haveli Braj Bhushanjee can arrange for you to view palace sections currently closed to the public. Chitra Shala alone is worth the steep walk up to the imposing gates, as are the views of the town—much of it painted the same blue seen in the more famous "blue city" of Jodhpur. For an even better vantage point, keep ascending the rough path that leads up to Taragarh (not necessarily to the top), for a great sense of peace (you're unlikely to encounter anyone, bar the Hanuman langur monkeys and a lone goat herder) and superb photo ops of the town.

Sights farther afield, like **Sukh Mahal,** a summer palace where Kipling wrote *Kim,* are best explored with Haveli Braj Bhushanjee's picnic and sightseeing tour.

ESSENTIALS

VISITOR INFORMATION The **Tourist Information Bureau** (© 0747/244-3697; Mon–Sat 10am–5pm, closed second Sat of the month and Sun) is located at Circuit House, but the owners of the Haveli Braj Bhushanjee heritage hotel (see below) are a mine of information, supplying you with maps, arranging transport, and ready with advice on anything from how much to pay for a rickshaw to opening hours.

GETTING THERE Kota is 130km (80 miles) by road from Sawai Madhopur and 155km (96 miles) from Chittaurgarh, so you can either visit it after you see Ranthambhore and/or Jaipur, or combine it with a trip from Udaipur via Chittaurgarh. To get to Bundi, you have to travel through the industrialized town of Kota. If you have arrived by train (Kota is well connected to the rest of the state, including the main Delhi-to-Mumbai line, Jaipur, Sawai Madhopur, and Chittaurgarh), you will then have to catch a bus, jeep, or taxi to Bundi. A taxi to Bundi will run you Rs 600 ($14); a jeep costs Rs 500 ($11). Kota, which dates back to the 12th century, has a number of impressive monuments (particularly the Palace Fort), but it is only worth stopping at if you have arrived too late to catch a taxi to Bundi. If this is the case, recommended overnight options are **Brijraj Bhawan Palace** (© 0744/245-0529); and Welcomgroup's **Umed Bhawan Palace** (© 0744/232-5262), where doubles go for $55.

GETTING AROUND You can get around the town on foot with ease. Should you tire, auto-rickshaws traverse the narrow lanes. If you book into Haveli Braj Bhushanjee, the proprietor will arrange all your transport at very reasonable prices—yet another reason the hotel is so highly recommended. Expect to pay around Rs 1,200 ($28) for an air-conditioned taxi for the day.

WHERE TO STAY & DINE

Haveli Braj Bhushanjee 🏵🏵   This is without a doubt the best place to stay in Bundi, and—despite the small size of the rooms and basic facilities—one of the most authentic heritage properties in India. Situated on a narrow lane inside the walled city, just below the palace, it also happens to be one of the most professionally run guesthouses in India, managed by the discreetly proud Braj Bhushanjee brothers (four of whose ancestors were prime ministers of Bundi State in the 19th c.). Many of the walls are covered with exceptional-quality murals, again typical of the Bundi school of miniature painting, and though each room (like those in so many other guesthouses) is traditionally decorated, the choice of objects, fabrics, and carpets (all sourced from Bundi and surroundings) shows a great deal of thought and innate flair. All the rooms are beautiful (though those overlooking the lane are a tad noisy at times) and feature en-suite "shower rooms"— small, but freshly whitewashed and gleaming. No alcohol is served—you can bring your own, however—and meat is definitely not permitted on the premises. Though garlic and onion are rarely used in the cooking, dining is of exceptional quality. Rather than choosing from a menu, you are served a selection of simple, flavorful, home-cooked dishes (Rs 300/$6.85), either in the Darikhana, where images of ancestors glower and large colored glass baubles hang from the ceiling, or on the terrace, from where you have a picture-perfect view of the illuminated palace at night. The brothers are a wealth of information about the area and can arrange wonderful sightseeing tours on request (they will, for instance, pack a picnic and carry it up to the fort for you). They also have an excellent (and extensive) collection of miniature paintings and other tribal and traditional crafts for sale—you may pay a little more than you would if you purchased directly from the artist (see "Shopping," below), but be assured that the brothers know the difference between a pretty souvenir and a real investment. At press time, six new rooms and a swimming pool were being added to the property, the latter certain to draw visitors into staying for more than a day.

Below Fort, opposite Ayurvedic Hospital, Bundi 323 001. ℂ **0747/244-2322** or 0747/244-2509. Fax 0747/244-2142. www.kiplingsbundi.com. 30 units. Rs 1,500 ($35) small double, Rs 1,850 ($42) standard double, Rs 2,450 ($55) palace-view double. AE, MC, V. **Amenities:** Dining hall; 24-hr. room service; laundry. *In room:* A/C, TV, hair dryer on request.

SHOPPING

If you want to take home a few miniature paintings (and you do—the style is exquisite and the prices laughably cheap), Bundi is one of the best places to do so. If the vast selection at Haveli Braj Bhushanjee doesn't suffice, the charming **Gopal Soni** has a little shop near the haveli where he paints beautiful miniatures (mostly copies of those in Chitra Shala) on anything from paper and silk to fingernails! They make a delightful souvenir or gift (prices start from Rs 50/$1.15); plus, for a mere Rs 25 (55¢)

For the Pleasures of the Raj

Traveling to and from Kota and Bundi, you will see fields of wheat, castor beans (from which castor oil is made)—and opium poppy. An ancient crop grown for the pleasures of Rajput kings and queens and Mughal emperors, the poppy is today ostensibly grown for the pharmaceutical industry. However, much of it makes its way into the hands of the Mumbai Mafia, and addiction in the area is reported to be rife.

---

per fingernail, you can adorn your hands with miniature elephants, peacocks, or tigers. Call ✆ **0747/244-7297**(daily 8am–noon and 1–8pm Aug–Apr; 9am–noon and 4–7pm May–July).

5 Shekhawati

200km (125 miles) SW of Delhi; 160km (100 miles) NW of Jaipur

Shekhawati, known as the open-air art gallery of Rajasthan, lies in the roughly triangular area between Delhi, Jaipur, and Bikaner, and encompasses the districts of Jhunjhunu, Sikar, and Churu. Its largely semi-desert, wide-open (uninhabited) spaces offer a peaceful respite from the cities. But the primary drawing card is its remarkable art collection—unusual for the unique painting styles and for the fact that the exhibition space consists of the exterior and interior walls of literally hundreds of havelis, temples, cenotaphs, wells, and forts in the region. The trend for decorating walls in this way was imported from the courts of Amber and Jaipur, where the Rajput princes in turn were inspired by the Mughal emperors' patronage of the miniature-mural artform. The Shekhawati's patronage was funded by duties imposed on merchandise carried across that section of the Spice Route that traversed their region (cleverly, the local barons here ensured that their duties were lower than those of the house of Jaipur, thereby diverting trade), or by raids across the borders, but patronage truly flourished during the British Raj, a period when the Shekhawati merchants, renowned for their business acumen, moved to the ports of Calcutta, Madras, and Bombay to capitalize on the growing trade in these new centers. There they made small fortunes and celebrated their wealth by adorning their mansions—an age-old urge, but the result here is a great deal more interesting than anything Martha Stewart might have suggested.

The demand was such that skilled artists could not paint fast enough. Even local masons tried their hand, injecting a wonderful naiveté into many of the paintings. Subject matters vary tremendously, from mythological stories and epics such as the *Ramayana* and *Mahabharata* to local legends of battles and hunts; but perhaps the most amusing are copies of British photographs featuring hot-air balloons, trains, and cars—objects most of the painters had never set their eyes on but faithfully rendered according to the descriptions and prints supplied by their employers.

Today there are some 30 "painted towns" in the region, but the most essential to include in a first-time itinerary are **Ramgarh** (the town with the most painted buildings), **Nawalgarh** (second in number, but with a superior selection, some better preserved than Ramgarh's, particularly the restored Anandi Lal Poddar Haveli), **Fatehpur** (together with Jhunjhunu, this is Shekhawati's oldest town, featuring murals that predate any others in the region as well as the **Haveli Française;** see box below), and **Mandawa** (a quaint town with a number of beautiful painted buildings, and centrally located with the best accommodations in the area).

Armed with a good map (see "Visitor Information," below) and a car, it is relatively easy to explore the surrounds on your own—not least because of the usual army of small kids eager to accompany you and point out the relevant sights. But to know more about the history of the buildings, the artisans, and the area, you may wish to hire the services of a guide through the hotels listed below. Most of the buildings are still inhabited and are accessible for a small fee (Rs 10–Rs 20/25¢–45 ¢ per haveli to the caretaker or watchman); negotiating payment (and whether you should offer to pay at all) is where a guide comes in handy. (Remember that, as is the case in all temples, you may need to *remove your shoes* to enter the inhabited havelis; ask before you

Cantering through the Indian Outback

A great way to experience the real Rajasthan is with **Royal Riding Holidays,** an outfit based at Roop Niwas Palace in Nawalgarh, Shekhawati. You can choose between a variety of 2- to 4-day camel safaris or 3- to 8-day horse safaris on predominantly Marwari horses, the traditional battle horses of Rajputana. Routes, led by expert guides, cover semi-desert terrain, forests, salt lake, marshes, and flat grasslands, and include visits to local villages and passing nomads. Evening and lunch breaks feature folk music and, on request, anything from a resident masseuse and turban-tying lessons to a lecture on the caste system or local wildlife. Although the purebred Indian horses are well schooled, they are spirited, and you should try to spend a few days before the safari choosing and getting to know your steed (there is no cost for these pre-safari rides). Riders need to be competent and fit as well—the routes cover 25 to 40km (16–25 miles) per day in 4 to 5 hours. Tented camps consist of colorful Asian-style tents with chairs, beds with white sheets and linen, blankets, mosquito nets, hot-water bottles, and a full floor covering. Lighting in tents is by kerosene lamps. Toilet and bath tents are one-piece units. Each bath tent has a wooden floor, towels, looking-glass mirrors, a wash basin, and hangers for clothes. Each toilet tent contains a wooden/metal commode with a pit. Hot water for baths is provided in buckets in both the morning and evening. The cost is between $150 and $225 per person per day, including full board. Contact **Royal Riding Holidays** or **Roop Niwas Palace** (© 01594/22-2008 or -4152; www.royalridingholidays.com).

enter.) Although the region evokes real passion in some and has resulted in a number of excellent books, it must be said that many of the murals are mere shadows of their former selves, either defaced by human indifference—posters and graffiti mar many of the walls—or faded by the increased water supply to the region, the rise in the water table creating damper conditions. Including this area in your itinerary can be tricky as well, unless you are intent on traveling the long haul through Bikaner to Jaisalmer, or journeying directly from Delhi and then moving on to Jaipur or vice versa, both of which mean many hours spent on the road.

Note: If you've missed out on a camel safari elsewhere in Rajasthan, Shekhawati is a good place to try it out; camel rides lasting 1 to 2 hours cost Rs 300 ($6.85) per person; overnight safaris cost Rs 3,000 ($68) for two. For a reliable operator, contact **Dinesh Dhabhai,** the owner of Mandawa Haveli (© 98291-93798; see below), who incidentally is also an extremely useful and helpful source for local travel information and advice.

ESSENTIALS

VISITOR INFORMATION   Jhunjhunu has a tourist office (© 015945-23-2909; Mon–Sat 10am–5pm; closed Sun and second Sat of the month), but you'll have more success finding information and arranging a guide through your hotel. Ilay Cooper's illustrated *The Painted Towns of Shekhawati* (Mapin Guides) is still the original bible, with a concise history of the region as well as a breakdown of towns, easy-to-follow maps, and listings of all the sites worth visiting. You can purchase a copy at Books Corner in Jaipur, at Mandawa Castle, or at Desert Resort. Another book worth considering is *Shekhawati: Rajasthan's Painted Homes* by Pankaj Rakesh and Karoki Lewis (Lustre Press Roli Books).

Tip: Traditionally dressed local women often approach tourists to have their picture taken and then demand a tip of Rs 10 to Rs 20 (25¢–45¢) a head. If you don't want to encourage this, ignore them as they follow you around town. Another popular local scam is children asking for a donation for their school—a ploy that will most likely fall apart if you ask to be taken to the school to receive an official receipt.

GETTING THERE Public transport is relatively limited, so the easiest way to explore the area is to hire a car and driver in Jaipur, stop at a few towns along the way, and overnight at Mandawa or Nawalgarh. Or you could take a 2-day detour to Mandawa en route from Delhi to Jaipur (driving time Delhi–Mandawa 7 hr.; Mandawa–Jaipur 4 hr.) or vice versa.

GETTING AROUND Again, you will need a car and driver to go from town to town with ease. Once there, it is relatively easy to explore each area on foot with a guide or by following Ilay Cooper's maps in *The Painted Towns of Shekhawati*.

A suggested driving tour: Travel from Jaipur (or Samode Palace) to Sikar, stopping to look at the *havelis* (historic homes or mansions of wealthy merchants) in Nawalgarh. Have lunch at Roop Niwas, then set off for Mandawa and overnight there. The following day, visit Fatehpur (see "Haveli Française," below) and Lachhmangarh before heading south to Sikar and back down to Jaipur or onward to Delhi.

WHERE TO STAY & DINE

If you're traveling here directly from Delhi, a highly recommended overnight stop is **Neemrana Fort-Palace** (reviewed below). Situated a few hours from Delhi on the eastern outskirts of Shekhawati, it is considered one of the best fort conversions in the country. Once in the Shekhawati region, the three properties described below are your best bets, providing you with both central location and comfort (it's worth mentioning that Dundlod Castle, another well-known heritage property in the area, has fallen into disrepute, with very few rooms operating, none of them in savory condition). Another option worth mentioning if you're looking to save money and live in one of

Haveli Française

In 1999 French artist Nadine Le Prince bought a haveli in Fatehpur and, with the help of Dinesh Dhabhai of Mandawa Haveli, spent the next year locating the right artisans, paints, and methods of restoring it. Now called **Haveli Nadine** (though locals call it *angrez ki haveli*—Englishwoman's haveli), it's been converted into a cultural center that's aimed at bringing together the art of Rajasthani with that of foreign artists, and preserving the art forms of Shekhawati. When rain and humidity damaged her newly restored haveli in 2003, Nadine waited for the walls to dry up, and began restoration work in earnest again. Serious art lovers should make an effort to stop here, particularly when an exhibition is on; you can discover Rajasthan through paintings or sculptures not available in any of the normal tourist centers. Either way, touring this gorgeous, painstakingly restored haveli is one way you can visualize what this region's art might have looked like in its heyday (Rs 100/$2.30 entry).

the original Shekhawati havelis is **Mandawa Haveli.** Carefully restored, with its frescoes in excellent condition, the 115-year-old haveli has some good rooms, several with newly renovated bathrooms (ask for the Nilesh Room on the first floor; suites are also good bargains). You're looking at more than Rs 2,160 ($50) double for these (© **01592/ 22-3088** or 98291-93798; hotelmandawahaveli@yahoo.com; other doubles from Rs 1,550/$37). Dungar Singh, the friendly manager, organizes superb candle-lit dinners on the rooftop for Rs 300 ($6.85). Alternatively, **Hotel Heritage Mandawa** (© **0159/ 22-3742** or -3743; www.hotelheritagemandawa.com; Rs 1,300–Rs 2,000/$30–$46) offers similar facilities and has wonderfully hospitable owners.

Castle Mandawa 🏰🏰   The castle, well situated to explore the region, is one of the most authentic heritage properties in Rajasthan, not least because of the presence of urbane host Kesri Singh, who was one of the first to start converting the rooms of his 16th-century castle into a hotel in the late 1970s. A thoroughly gregarious and charming host, he usually (assuming he's in residence) invites guests to share a drink with him on one of the turreted battlements that tower above the town roofs before he ushers you to a table on a large roof terrace under the stars. If the hotel is hosting a group, a special fire dance is given by one of the castle's oldest retainers, during which guests help themselves to a tasty buffet. Given the age of the property, its conversion to modern hotel has been remarkably sensitive, maintaining much of the original feel of the castle (no doubt to the approval of the Mandawa ancestors, whose portraits decorate many of the walls) without sacrificing comfort. (Bear in mind that this cannot be said of the most recently added wing, which features boring, uniformly sized rooms with none of the authentic charm of the original castle.) If you have a poor sense of direction, the journey from the veranda bar to your room can be challenging, but really, getting lost and clambering up and down the narrow staircases is half the fun. Rooms vary hugely in size, and some have special features like built-in swings and alcoves furnished with bolster cushions. Nos. 304 and 313 are particularly lovely rooms; no. 215 is smaller (standard) but also a good choice. For more luxury, pick the Peacock Suite (no. 401), which has a marble water fountain; or no. 303, the Tower Suite. Both are located in the castle turrets. The hotel has a few small drawbacks: Situated in the middle of town, it makes for a strangely urban experience—the town's blaring temple music ceases to charm when it's turned on at the crack of dawn—and the hotel has no gardens or pool to relax in after a day's heavy sightseeing.

Mandawa, Jhunjhunu District, Shekhawati 333 704, Rajasthan. Jaipur reservations © **0141/237-1194** or -4112. Fax 0141/237-2084 or 0141/510-6082. reservation@castlemandawa.com. www.castlemandawa.com. 70 units. Rs 2,650 ($61) standard double, Rs 4,400 ($100) deluxe double; Rs 6,000–Rs 10,000 ($151–$228) suite. AE, MC, V. **Amenities:** Dining; veranda bar; badminton; table tennis; camel/horse/jeep safaris; heritage walk; Ayurvedic massage; laundry; doctor-on-call. *In room:* A/C, minibar (suites only), hair dryer (on request).

Desert Resort 🏰🏰   Situated in the semi-arid Shekhawati Desert and built in the style of a Rajasthani village, this is arguably Shekhawati's most peaceful option, which is no doubt why—together with its unusual architecture—it's featured in the glossy coffee-table tome *Hip Hotels: Escape.* Ethnic accommodations consist primarily of circular mud-thatch huts, their organic shapes charmingly decorated with tribal motifs—stark white on dark brown—making features of even the air-conditioning units. Beds are covered in pretty embroidered linen traditional in the area—in fact, almost everything in each hut has been sourced from the Shekhawati. The rustic charm is endearing, though some may find the hard mud beds and thin mattresses a bit uncomfortable; if you do, ask the hotel for an extra mattress and they'll gladly provide one. Our recommendation is to book the suite right next to the pool—it makes no overtures to the tribal theme, being squared off and comfortably furnished with a mix of colonial-era antiques, and it's huge, with some great desert views, even from the bathroom. And you'll be hard-pressed to leave the pool, which is filled with fresh spring water, wonderfully soft and a fabulous temperature (lounge chairs and fresh towels provided). Meals are similar to those served at Castle Mandawa (buffet dinner with entertainment Rs 600/$14), also under the stars, but this time on the manicured lawns; or request seating at the pool. At press time there were plans to add a spa and cafe; check to see if these have been completed.

Mandawa, Jhunjhunu District, Shekhawati 333 704, Rajasthan. Jaipur reservations: ⓒ **0141/237-1194** or -4112. Fax 0141/237-2084 or 0141/510-6082. www.mandawahotels.com. reservation@castlemandawa.com. 60 units. Rs 2,650 ($61) standard double; Rs 4,400 ($100) deluxe cottage; Rs 6,600–Rs 10,000 ($151–$228) suite. AE, MC, V. **Amenities:** Restaurant; bar; pool; badminton; table tennis; croquet; card room; snooker; camel/horse/jeep safaris; Ayurvedic massage; laundry. *In room:* A/C, minibar (suites only), hair dryer (on request).

Neemrana Fort-Palace 🏰🏰 Since it first opened 13 years ago, Neemrana Fort has become the flagship of the highly regarded Neemrana Group (check out their website; you can almost plan your entire trip around their atmospheric heritage properties). Purchased by historians Aman Nath and Francis Wacziarg, who spotted the ruined fort while researching a book on Rajasthan, it has been sensitively and painstakingly rebuilt into what is billed a "non-hotel." Almost every room has an arresting view, though no two are alike and not all will please you, so do ask for a description before paying. For instance, Lehsuniya Mahal is windowless, Geru Mahal has just a short wall separating living and bathing space, only a few rooms have double beds, and others have tiny bathing spaces; getting to the most far-off rooms (usually with private terraces) may require some fitness. Among the standard rooms, Jalaj Mahal (Lotus Palace) is quiet and located near a pretty lotus pond, while the Chandra Mahal suite, formerly a court room, is spacious and cool and once roomed Kate Winslet; Deva Mahal is a huge apartment conveniently located near the pool. Service, while not five-star, is well-intended. Buffet meals are served in the courtyard and adjoining hall; stick to the Indian food and avoid the French restaurant, which doesn't cut the mustard. An evening sipping a drink while watching the sunset or under the stars at any of the lovely outdoor spaces will no doubt be one of the highlights of your Rajasthan trip. An enchanting destination, Neemrana is likely to inspire contemplation and creativity, and is highly recommended.

Village Neemrana, District Alwar, Rajasthan 301 705. ⓒ **01494/24-6006** through -6008. Reservations, Delhi only, ⓒ 011/2435-6145, -8962, or 011/5182-5001. Fax 011/2435-1112. www.neemranahotels.com. 46 units. Rs 1,500–Rs 6,000 ($35–$137) double; Rs 4,000–Rs 8,000 ($91–$182) suite. Rs 300 ($6.85) extra bed. Rates include bed tea and evening tea. AE, DC, MC, V. **Amenities:** Restaurants and multiple dining areas; bar; cultural programs; pool; Jacuzzi; spa; yoga; indoor game room; TV lounge; concierge; travel desk; Ayurvedic massage; library. *In room:* A/C (most rooms), tea-and coffee-making facilities (some suites).

Roop Niwas Palace 🏰 An unlikely choice if you're looking for a bit of action, the Roop Niwas "palace" is situated on the outskirts of Nawalgarh, the town that boasts the largest number of painted havelis in Shekhawati. The hotel doesn't see even half as much traffic as the Mandawa properties, and as a result has a slightly desolate air. The rural atmosphere and gracious Indo-colonial architecture are still rather charming, and even though the surrounding gardens have gone to seed, they attract strutting peacocks—all very evocative of a decadent era that no longer exists, or certainly not in this town. Rooms are clean and furnished with colonial and Rajput pieces, all with ensuite bathrooms (none with tubs). Although the pool is currently empty, horse lovers will find the stables, with 80 steeds, a wonderful drawing card. This is a good option if you're after real peace and quiet (though if your budget can stretch that far, Desert Resort is a better bet). An in-house guide is available.

Nawalgarh, District Jhunjhunu, Rajasthan. ✆ **01594/22-2008** or -4152. Fax 01594/22-3388. 36 units. Rs 1,700 ($39) standard double, Rs 2,100 ($48) deluxe double; Rs 3,000 ($68) suite. AE. **Amenities:** Dining hall; billiards; horse and camel safaris; laundry. In room: A/C (in some standard and all deluxe rooms).

SHOPPING

Outside some havelis, caretakers sell Rajasthani puppets and postcards. You can see artisans and craftspeople at work in their shops in Mandawa, along Sonthaliya Gate and the bazaar. Lac bangles in bright natural colors make pretty gifts (Rs 10–Rs 50/25¢–$1.15 each); if you find the sizes too small, have a pair custom-made while you wait. Another good buy is the camel-leather Rajasthani shoes *(jootis)*, once a symbol of royalty.

6 Pushkar

288km (180 miles) W of Jaipur

On the eastern edge of the vast Thar Desert, with a beautiful backdrop in the embracing arms of the Aravalli Hills, Pushkar is one of the most sacred—and atmospheric—towns in India. Legend has it that the holy lake at its center was created when Brahma dropped the petals of a lotus flower *(pushpa)* from his hand *(kar)*. The tiny temple town that sprung up on the lake shores remains an important pilgrimage site for Hindus, its population swollen in recent years by the hippies who came for a few days and never left—a sore point for visitors who remember its untouched charm, but happily a matter of indifference to the first-time visitor. Their presence has transformed the sleepy desert town into a semi-permanent trance party, however, with *bhang* (marijuana) lassis imbibed at the myriad tiny eateries, falafels on every menu, long-bearded rabbis on bicycles, and world music pumping from speakers that line the street bazaar that runs along the lake's northern edge. This street bazaar is the center of all activity in Pushkar and incidentally one of the best shopping experiences in Rajasthan, where you can pick up the most gorgeous throwaway gear, great secondhand books, and a huge selection of CDs at bargain prices.

Pushkar is somewhat of a mini-Varanasi, only more charming—it really is possible to explore the town entirely on foot, and outside the annual camel *mela* (fair) it doesn't have the same claustrophobic crowds you find at Varanasi. It takes about 45 minutes to walk around the holy lake and its 52 ghats. Built to represent each of the Rajput Maharajas who constructed their "holiday homes" on its banks, ghats are broad sets of stairs from where Hindus pilgrims take ritual baths to cleanse their souls. Note that you will need a "Pushkar Passport" to perambulate without harassment (see "Passport to Pushkar: Saying Your Prayers," below), that shoes need to be removed 9m (30 ft.) from the holy lake (bring cheap flip-flops if you're worried about losing them), and that photography of bathers is prohibited.

Surrounding the lake and encroaching on the hills that enhance the town's wonderful sense of remoteness are some 500 temples, of which the one dedicated to Brahma, said to be 2,000 years old, is the most famous, not least because it's one of only a handful in India dedicated to the Hindu Lord of Creation. The doors to the enshrined deity are shut between 1:30 and 3pm, but you can wander around the temple courtyard during these hours. The other two worth noting (but a stiff 50-min. climb to reach) are dedicated to his consorts: It is said that Brahma was cursed by his first wife, Savitri, when he briefly took up with another woman, Gayatri—to this day, the temple of Savitri sits sulking on a hill overlooking the temple town, while across the lake, on another hill, no doubt nervous of retribution, the Gayatri Temple keeps a lookout. Ideally, Savitri should be visited at sunset, while a visit to Gayatri should coincide with the beautiful sunrise. *Note:* The Vishnu temple, encountered as you enter town, is the only temple off-limits to non-Hindus, but photography is permitted from outside the temple gates.

Unless you're expecting authentic untouched India, Pushkar is a delight to visit any time of the year, with its laid-back, almost European atmosphere offset by the unique aromas of India and tons of tiny shops, temples, Brahmin eateries, and operators offering camel- and horseback safaris into the surrounding desert (about Rs 100/ $2.30 per hour, Rs 350/$8 full day). But the town is most famous for its annual *mela*—the largest camel fair in Asia. Attracting an estimated 200,000 rural traders, red-turbaned Rabari and Bhil tribal folk, pilgrims, and tourists, the *mela* stretches tiny Pushkar into sprawling villages of temporary campsites—interspersed with food stalls and open-air theaters—created solely to house, feed, and entertain the swollen population that flocks to the specially built amphitheater on the outskirts of the town to watch the races and attend the auctions. Like most desert destinations, however, it is at night that the atmosphere takes on an unreal intimacy, as pilgrims and tourists get to know each other around the many campfires, and Rajasthani dancers and traditional folk singers create a timeless backdrop. The Pushkar *mela* takes place in the Hindu month of Kartik, over the waxing and waning of the full moon that occurs in late October or in November.

On the evening of the full *mela* moon, as the desert sun sets behind the low-slung hills (a spectacular sight at the best of times), temple bells and drums call the devout to *puja,* and hundreds of pilgrims wade into the lake—believed to miraculously cleanse the soul—before lighting clay lamps and setting them afloat on its holy waters, the twinkling lights a surreal reflection of the desert night sky. If you're lucky enough to have booked a room at Pushkar Palace, you can watch this ancient ritual from a deck chair on the terrace (it can be quite a scramble to get a view from the ghats themselves)—a wonderful sight and one of those mystic moments that make a trip to India among the most memorable of your life.

ESSENTIALS
VISITOR INFORMATION Pushkar doesn't have its own tourist office. The rather useless **RTDC office** is located at the very mediocre RTDC Hotel Sarovar (© **0145/ 277-2040**), and is open daily from 9am to 5pm.

GETTING THERE Pushkar lies about 3 hours west of Jaipur; a deluxe bus here costs about Rs 75 ($1.70).

GETTING AROUND Pushkar is easily explored on foot. There is no public transport system (cycle- or auto-rickshaws) in town. If you prefer not to walk, the only option is to hire a private taxi, motorbike, or scooter (the latter costs Rs 250–Rs 300/$5.70–$6.85 per day).

WHERE TO STAY & DINE
You really want to get a room overlooking the sacred lake—despite the early-morning and evening chanting calls to *puja* and blaring temple music, it's by far the most atmospheric location in Pushkar. Of the surprisingly limited options that offer direct

Map labels:

New Delhi
Pushkar
India
Bay of Bengal

Pap Mochani Temple
Foot Hill Camp

Government Hospital
Marwar Bus Stand
Shyama Hospital

Heloj Road
Police Station

Mansar Rd.
EXHIBITION GROUND

Bari Basti

Maheshwari Dharamshala Temple

Baba Ramdeo Temple
Main Bazaar
Sadar Bazaar Rd.

Rajput Temple
Brahm Chowk

Gau Ghat
Pushkar Lake

Brahma Ghat
Jain Temple

Brahma Temple

Indra Ghat
Kotah Ghat

Savitri Temple
Hanuman Temple
Maha Prabhu Temple

Jagat Singh Palace
Raghunath (Vishnu) Temple
Hanuman Temple
Ajmer Bus Stand
Gurdwara
Ajmer Road

0   100 meters
0   100 yards

ACCOMMODATIONS ■
Bharatpur Palace **1**
Lake View **2**
Pushkar Palace **5**
Sai Baba Haveli **6**

DINING ◆
Baba Restaurant **4**
Sai Baba Restaurant **6**
Third Eye **3**

ⓘ Information
✉ Post Office

views onto the lake, Pushkar Palace is the only luxurious option; for the rest you'll have to rough it (we're talking basic furnishings—a plastic chair and bed and the possibility of sharing a bathroom and toilet). That said, the following two are well-situated heritage properties (once belonging to Rajput Maharajas) that overlook the lake and are acceptably clean. **Bharatpur Palace** (© 0145/277-2320; bharatpur_palace@yahoo.com) bears no obvious resemblance to a palace but overlooks the ghats and has some rooms with attached bathrooms; none of these have a view, though, so state your preference. The best views are had from the Maharaja's Room, which is literally just a room with a double bed (no attached bathroom), but every wall has double doors opening to views of the lake. Other rooms worth booking are nos. 1 and 5 (for the views but no en-suite bathroom), 6 (with tub), and 7 (with shower). Rooms range from Rs 450 to Rs 700 ($10–$16), going up to Rs 3,000 ($68) during the fair. **Lake View** (© 0145/277-2106) has a great rooftop terrace where meals are served, as well as a number of rooms. As at Bharatpur Palace, some come with tiny attached bathrooms but no views (Rs 250–Rs 300/$5.70–$6.85), and the rooms with lovely views have no attached bathrooms (Rs 150–Rs 200/$3.40–$4.55).

The best place to eat is one of the many vegetarian eateries that line the bazaar (note that you won't find meat, eggs, or alcohol served anywhere near the sacred lake of

(Finds) The Dargah Sharif & Other Ajmer Gems

Ajmer is not an attractive town, and most foreigners experience it only as a jumping-off point to the pilgrim town of Pushkar. However, it is worthwhile to plan your journey so that you can spend a few hours exploring Ajmer's fascinating sights (particularly the Dargah, one of the most spiritually reso- nant destinations in India) before you head the short 11km (7 miles) over a mountain pass to the laid-back atmosphere of Pushkar and its superior selection of accommodations.

Founded in the 7th century and strategically located within striking dis- tance of the Mewar (Udaipur) and Marwar (Jodhpur) dynasties, as well as encompassing most of the major trade routes, Ajmer has played a pivotal role in the affairs of Rajasthan over the years. The Mughal emperors real- ized that only by holding this city could they increase their power base in Rajasthan. This is principally why the great Mughal emperor Akbar courted the loyalty of the nearby Amber/Jaipur court, marrying one of its daughters. But Ajmer was important on an emotional and spiritual level too, for only by gaining a foothold in Ajmer could Akbar ensure a safe passage for Mus- lim pilgrims to **Dargah Sharif (Khwaja Moin-ud-Din Chisti's Dargah).** The great Sufi saint Khwaja Moin-ud-Din Chisti, "protector of the poor," was buried here in 1235.

Said to possess the ability to grant the wishes and desires of all those who visit it, the **Dargah Sharif** 🜲🜲 is the most sacred Islamic shrine in India, and a pilgrimage here is considered second in importance only to a visit to Mecca. After a living member of the Sufi sect, Sheikh Salim Chisti, blessed Akbar with the prophecy of a much-longed-for son (Emperor Jahangir, father of Shah Jahan, builder of the Taj), Emperor Akbar himself made the pilgrimage many times, traveling on foot from distant Fatehpur Sikri and presenting the shrine with cauldrons (near the entrance) large enough to cook food for 5,000 people. It was not only Akbar and his offspring who made the pilgrimage—even the Hindu Rajputs came to pay homage to "the divine soul" that lies within.

Today the shrine still attracts hundreds of pilgrims every day, swelling to thousands during special occasions such as Urs Mela (Oct/Nov), the anniver- sary of Akbar's death. Leaving your shoes at the entrance (Rs 10/25¢ at exit), you pass through imposing **Nizam Gate** and smaller **Shahjahani Gate;** to the right is **Akbar's mosque,** and opposite is the equally imposing **Buland Dar- waza.** Climb the steps to take a peek into the **two huge cauldrons** (3m/10 ft. round) that flank the gates—they come into their own at Urs when they are filled to the brim with a rice dish that is then distributed to the poor. To the right is **Mehfil Khana,** built in 1888 by the Nizam of Hyderabad. From here you enter another gateway into the courtyard, where you will find another mosque on the right, this one built by Shah Jahan in his character- istic white marble. You'll also see the great **Chisti's Tomb**—the small building topped by a marble dome and enclosed by marble lattice screens. In front of the tomb, the *qawwali* singers are seated, every day repeating the same beautiful haunting melodies (praising the saint) that have been sung for centuries. Everywhere, people abase themselves and sing, their eyes closed, hands spread wide on the floor or clutching their chests, while others feverishly pray and knot bits of fabrics to the latticework of the tomb or shower it with flowers. The scene is moving, the sense of faith palpable and, unlike the Dargah in Delhi, the atmosphere welcoming (though it's best to be discreet: no insensitive clicking of cameras or loud talking). Entry is free, but donations, paid to the office in the main courtyard, are welcome and are directly distributed to the poor. Entered off Dargah Bazaar, the Dargah is open daily, from 4 or 5am to 9 or 10pm (except during prayer times) depending on the season.

Having laid claim to Ajmer through a diplomatic marriage, Akbar built a red-sandstone fort he called **Daulat Khana (Abode of Riches)** in 1572. This was later renamed the Magazine by the British, who maintained a large garrison here, having also realized Ajmer's strategic importance. In 1908 it was again transformed, this time into the largely missable **Rajputana Museum** (Sat–Thurs 10am–4:30pm; Rs 3/6¢, Rs 10/25¢ camera). The fort is significant mostly from a historical perspective, for it is here in 1660 that the British got a toehold in India when Sir Thomas Roe, representative of the British East India Company, met Emperor Jahangir and gained his permission to establish the first British factory at Surat.

The British also established a number of first-rate educational institutions, particularly **Mayo College** ⌖, known as the Eton of the East. Originally designed to educate only the sons of the aristocracy, it opened its doors in 1875 to princes arriving on elephant-back, followed by retinues of 1,000 servants. The school is worth visiting, even just to view the building from the road; it's a superb example of Indo-Saracenic architecture, with much symbolic detailing. The sun and the moon, for instance (featured on the college hall roof and on the school coat of arms), signify the mythical descent of the maharajas (see "Once Were Warriors: The History of the Rajput," earlier in this chapter). To enter the school, you will need to get the principal's permission (with a bit of patience, this can be arranged through the gate attendant).

Another Ajmer attraction definitely worth seeing (it will only take about 10 min., and the entry fee is a negligible Rs 4/8¢) is **Svarna Nagari Hall** ⌖⌖ behind the Jain Nasiyan Temple in Anok Chowk. It's a totally unassuming building from the outside, but ascend the stairs to the second floor and you gaze down upon a fantasy world; a breathtaking display that fills the double-volume hall with tiny gilded figures celebrating scenes from Jain mythology. Sadly, no guide is available to explain what it all means, but the workmanship and sheer scale of the display are spellbinding.

> ## (Tips) Passport to Pushkar: Saying Your Prayers
>
> Proof of Pushkar's charm lies in the passport control as you enter the town—many foreigners (mostly Israeli hippies, hence the inclusion of falafels and pitas on the menu of even the most traditional Brahmin eatery) have come to experience its idyllic location and quaint laid-back vibe and have never left, marrying locals and starting small businesses. As a result, there is now a moratorium on the length of time you can stay—a maximum of 3 months—so have your passport on hand as you enter. For those who wish to walk onto the ghats lining the lake, you'll need an entirely different kind of passport: Brahmin priests will bully you into performing *puja*—prayers that involve a scattering of flowers into the lake—after which you will be expected to make a hefty donation (inquire at your hotel for the going rate or you will almost certainly be ripped off). The priest will then tie a thin red thread around your wrist, which you can brandish at the next Brahmin priest who will almost certainly approach you, but who will quickly retreat upon seeing your "passport." To experience Pushkar from a pilgrim's perspective, gain a closer insight into what makes this an important place for Hindu pilgrims, and gain your wrist thread without being ripped off, you may want to call on **Giriraj** (© 94143-00053; *puja* fee Rs 50/$1.15), a local priest who is also a licensed guide. His English isn't perfect, but he can throw some light on the history and background of the area as well as help out with practical information.

Pushkar), and as noted you will see menus in Hebrew and lately Korean as well. The usual rule applies: If it's full of customers, food will be freshly prepared and wonderful. **Prems Venkatesh,** a basic eatery overseen by a Brahmin who cooks his delicious chapatis with vegetables of the day and dal over a wood-burning fire, was widely considered the best in town for cheap Indian food; ask anyone to direct you there, but don't expect it to be sparkling clean. Then there are cuisines from around the world, all fairly Indianized: **Third Eye** serves decent Middle Eastern platters (some tables have nice lake views); **Sai Baba** (see below) has good (egg-less) croissants and a nice garden to sit in; and **Baba** (near the post office) serves everything from Lebanese to Indonesian. When the sun starts to set, you'll want to be seated at a table at the aptly named **Sunset Café** (on the same road as Pushkar Palace, just a little farther along, and overlooking the lake) with a cold milkshake. Average meals are also served here.

Note that if you haven't prebooked well in advance for the Pushkar *mela*, which takes place when the full moon appears in late October or early November, finding a decent bed anywhere in town can be hell. During the fair, the RTDC sets up additional accommodations in the **"Tourist Village Camp,"** which offers huts (Rs 2,500–Rs 5,000/ $57–$114), Swiss tents (Rs 5,500/$126), and standard tents (Rs 6,000–Rs 7,000/$137– $159). Rates vary depending on dates and include all (vegetarian) meals. (Note that these options, particularly the Swiss tents, are infinitely preferable to the "caravan dormitories" also on offer.) If you want a truly peaceful option, far from the madding crowd (and ideal if you're traveling with children), **Pushkar Resorts** (© 0145/277-2944 or -2945; www.pushkarresorts.com; pushkar@sancharnet.in) has 40 very pleasant cottages set on 6 hectares (15 acres) of palm-dotted lawns (room nos. 1, 2, and 14–16 are the most privately situated). Rooms have TVs and minibars with spruce bathrooms, but it is the verdant garden—a tranquil retreat from the town's noise—that is the main attraction. Besides the large pool, a number of activities are on offer (from playing pool to taking a caravan safari into the desert), designed to entertain the upmarket Indian families who frequent the resort. It's also a good option if you need a chilled beer to beat the heat; the resort is technically out of Pushkar, so alcohol is permitted here. The resort's location is also its primary drawback: It's 5km (3 miles) from town, so you're likely to feel very cut off from the place you've traveled so far to see. Another, slightly less upmarket but comfortable option, also on the town's outskirts but within walking distance of the center, is the 32-room **Hotel New Park** (© 0145/277-2464; fax 0145/277-2199). Each room has a TV and attached bathroom, and there's a pool.

If you're on a tight budget, **Chandra,** on Panchkund Road (© 0145/277-2366), is a real find: For Rs 250 ($5.70) per person you get to choose one of five very basic but sunny en-suite rooms, with windows overlooking a rose-and-vegetable garden, which in turn services the hippie-style restaurant (reggae music, tables in shack and garden, food "cooked with love by Sukha") run by the entrepreneurial Sukha just up the road. The center of town is an easy walk away. (Note that Chandra's full name is actually the rather delusional "Hotel Chandra Palace," no doubt bestowed by Sukha after imbibing one of his own *bhang* lassis.)

Two other budget options you may want to consider: **Sai Baba** restaurant and haveli (near Vara Ghat; © 0145/510-5161 or 98282-71025; lola_singh_modiano@hotmail. com; no credit cards) is run by Lola Modiano, a French woman who married locally. The guesthouse has nine very basic rooms with attached bathroom starting at Rs 300 ($6.85). Every Saturday night, festivities include a desert Gypsy (Kalbeliya dancers) dance program and party. The place is a favorite with young foreign tourists and hippies—it serves gratifying baked goods and has a liberal attitude toward smoking intoxicants. A fairly new entry is **Inn Seventh Heaven** (next to Mali ka Mandir; © 0145/510-5455; www.inn-seventh-heaven.com; Rs 300–Rs 750/$11–$17), located in a 100-year-old haveli with rooms around a beautiful courtyard and garden. Anoop, the enterprising young owner, has rather quickly made this inn popular with foreign tourists, in spite of its location (nowhere near the lake). It has a pleasant, informal, homey feel, and the charming rooftop restaurant does satisfying Indian food. *Note:* All accommodations have different tariffs for the period of the Pushkar Fair, anything from double to 10 times the normal rate.

Pushkar Palace *Value*   The pretty 400-year-old palace—its thick white walls reflected in the holy waters of the lake—is by far the best place to stay within Pushkar, not least due to the extensive renovations undertaken in 2002. The best rooms are the suites below the terrace (nos. 101–105)—these are the closest to the lake, with windows that provide serene (or surreal, depending on the time of day) views directly onto it. Room no. 102 is a particularly good option—it's a corner suite with additional windows. Alternatively, ask for a suite with a balcony. In the deluxe category, the corner rooms (nos. 209, 309, and 409), despite being significantly smaller but comfortably furnished, have the best views—you can literally lie in bed and watch the sunsets, which are stupendous. This is, in fact, one of the best reasons to stay here: the views of the lake, temples, and hills, behind which the sun sets, are both thrilling and exclusive to guests. Even if you don't have a room with the best of views (most are set behind the open-air corridors that link the rooms), you can enjoy it all from the terrace (effectively, the roof of the suites), where waiters are on hand to provide the necessary liquid refreshments (though be aware that, as elsewhere, no alcohol is allowed). Pushkar Palace also arranges a **Royal Desert Camp** during the *mela* ($150 double, including meals), which is the most luxurious temporary accommodations in town.

The Palace has a sister establishment, **Jagat Palace,** a relatively luxurious property built on the outskirts of town 4 years ago; the same rates apply. The design pays homage to Hindu elements, but it does not appear to have had an architect on board—the rooms really are lovely, but many of the interior spaces are gloomy, the atmosphere is soulless, and you have to exit the lobby and walk past the parking area to the back of the building to reach the pool (which, by the way, is fabulous). That said, it's probably the most luxurious option if Pushkar Palace is full, though you'll need a car or taxi to get to town.

Pushkar 305 022, Rajasthan. © **0145/277-2001** through -2402. Fax 0145/277-2226 or -2952. www.hotelpushkar palace.com. hppalace@datainfosys.net. 53 units. Rs 2,700 ($62) deluxe double; Rs 6,000 ($137) suite. Extra bed Rs 300–Rs 600 ($6.85–$14). AE, DC, MC, V. **Amenities:** Restaurant; bar and pool (in Jagat Palace); travel desk; camel/horse safaris; room service; laundry; doctor-on-call. *In room:* A/C, TV, minibar.

SHOPPING

The main thoroughfare, **Sadar Bazaar,** is just over 1km (a half-mile) long, and is lined with tiny shops selling ridiculously cheap (though usually low-quality) clothing, jewelry, leather sandals, excellent music (anything from Hindu temple to Hindi pop to global trance), and the best selection of books in Rajasthan. This is definitely the place to come with empty bags—its almost cheaper to stock up on a new wardrobe here than pay hotel laundry fees, and you can pick up a huge selection of Indian music to listen to back home and make you long to return.

7 Udaipur

405km (250 miles) SW of Jaipur; 260km (160 miles) S of Jodhpur

The "City of Sunrise," often described as the most romantic city in India, was built around four lakes, the placid blue waters reflecting ethereal white palaces and temples, beyond which shimmer the distant Aravalli Hills. Udaipur has a real sense of space and peace, and the city is mercifully free of the kind of intense capitalist hucksterism that so marks the Indian street experience. This may have something to do with its proud Hindu history, for the city is not only known for its gracious palaces, temperate climate, and beautiful views, but for maintaining a fierce independence from even the most powerful outside influences. It fought bloody wars to repel Turkish, Afghan, Tartar, and Mongol invaders and rejected allegiances with the Mughals, only to acquiesce in 1818, when the state grudgingly came under British political control.

Capital of the legendary Sisodias of Mewar, believed to be direct descendants of the Sun (an insignia you'll see everywhere), Udaipur was built on the shores of Lake Pichola by Udai Singh II in 1559, who returned here after the third and final sacking of the previous Mewar stronghold, Chittaurgarh (see "Top Excursions," later in this chapter). Udai Singh's son, Pratap, kept the Mughal invaders at bay for a further 25 years and is said to have been so disgusted by Man Singh and the Jaipur raja's obsequious relations with the Mughals that, after one historic meeting, he had the ground where Man Singh had walked washed with Ganges water in order to purify it. Maharana Fateh Singh was also the only Rajput prince who refused to attend the Delhi Durbar held for King George V in 1911, despite the fact that the British had acknowledged him as the head of the princely states of Rajputana.

Udaipur

Ambrai **11**
Amet Haveli **4**
Badi Haveli **3**
Fateh Prakash and
  Shiv Niwas Palace **9**
Hotel Hilltop Palace **1**
Jagat Niwas **8**
Kankarwa **8**
Lake Palace Hotel **7**
Lake Pichola Hotel **4**
Mahendra Prakash **10**
Trident Hilton **5**
Udai Kothi **2**
Udaivilas **6**

New Delhi
Udaipur
RAJASTHAN
India
Bay of Bengal

Sahelion-Ki-Bari

Sukadia Circle

Statue

MOTI MAGRI

Jetty

Entrance

Nehru Island Park

Fateh Sagar

Sagar Rd.

Lakshmi Vilas

Panchvati Rd.

Chetak Circle

Hospital Rd.

Hospital

Residency Rd.

Rani Rd.

Suaroop Sagar

Ashok Nagar Rd.

Rang Sagar

Silavat Van Rd.

Brahmpol Rd.

Heera Cycle Store

Clock Tower

Ganguar Ghat

Jagdish Temple St.

Jagdish Temple

Lal Ghat

Bhattiyani Chotta

Bapu Bazaar

To Airport (25 km)

Airport Rd.

City Palace & Museum

Udaipol Rd.

Lake Palace

Lake Palace Rd.

SAJJAN NIWAS GARDENS

Lake Pichola

Jagmandir Island

Sunset Point

City Railway Station

0   1/4 mi
0   0.25 km

N

421

Sadly, water—or the lack thereof—is proving to be the undoing of this proud and gracious city. A prolonged drought, combined with unbridled construction in the outlying catchment areas, has caused Udaipur's lakes to run bone-dry, and what was once the chief attraction of this city is—at least for the moment—absent. (At press time, however, there was hope: A 2005 monsoon filled the lake with about 3 feet of water!) Still, Udaipur's palaces, temples, and culture justify a visit, though you may choose to base yourself outside the city. It's worth checking with local authorities or the hotels before deciding where and how long to stay.

Much of Udaipur, particularly the old part located on the shores of Lake Pichola, is where you'll find the city's most striking landmarks—the towering **City Palace** and **Lake Palace**—and it still feels remarkably like a 16th-century Rajput stronghold, with the benevolent Maharana still treated like a reigning king by his devoted and loyal subjects. You can witness this firsthand by attending the temple at nearby Eklingji on a Monday evening, when the Maharana—the 76th ruler of one of the world's oldest surviving dynasties—often joins his subjects to pay his respects to Shiva.

Try to spend at least 3 to 4 days in Udaipur, whether you spend them aimlessly wandering its mazelike lanes, taking a slow cruise on Pichola Lake, exploring the giant medieval fortress and palaces that rise from its shores, or setting off to see the intricately carved Jain temples of Ranakpur and the ancient fort of Kumbhalgarh—or whether you do nothing but loll on a comfortable divan overlooking the lake. You'll find the City of Sunrise the most relaxing part of your sojourn in Rajasthan.

ESSENTIALS

VISITOR INFORMATION Rajasthan Tourist Development Corporation **(RTDC),** though inconveniently located in the Tourist Office at Fath Memorial in Suraj Pol (☎ **0294/241-1535;** Mon–Sat 10am–5pm), can arrange accommodations, licensed guides, maps, and brochures. Ask for the helpful young Yogesh Joshi in room no. 1, who can caution you about the latest scams to avoid. You can also call the RTDC Hotel Kajri at ☎ **0294/241-0501** through -0503 for tourist information and assistance. Satellite tourist offices can be found at the airport (☎ **0294/265-5433;** open at flight times) and at the railway station, which was scheduled to reopen once new train services begin (see "Getting There: By Train/Bus," below).

The most convenient place to draw money against your credit card/ATM card is near the Jagdish Temple (City Palace Rd.). There is also an ICICI Bank next to the Jet Airways office (Madhuban), an SBI ATM next to Indian Airlines (Delhi Gate), and several others near Town Hall, Bapu Bazaar. There are two convenient LKP foreign exchange offices on Lake Palace Road (next to Rang Niwas Palace Hotel) and near Jagdish Temple. The best private hospital, with 24-hour emergency rooms and pharmacy, is **Udaipur Hospital** on Suraj Pol Road near Sindhi Dharamsala (☎ **0294/510-1011** through -1013).

GETTING THERE **By Air** **Dabok Airport** is 25km (15 miles) from Udaipur. As always, **Jet Airways** is the preferable option (☎ **0294/256-1105-60**), connecting the city with Delhi, Mumbai (both 1 hr., 15 min.), and Jaipur (45 min.). **Indian Airlines** (☎ **0294/265-5453** airport, 0294/241-0999 Delhi Gate) covers the same routes, as well as Jodhpur. A regular non-air-conditioned taxi into town should cost about Rs 300 ($6.85). **Comfort Travels** offers comfortable air-conditioned taxis from their airport counter to the city for Rs 350 ($8).

By Train/Bus At press time Udaipur was not connected to the rest of India by train, though a new broad-gauge railway line was in the process of being built. It's expected to be up and running by 2006. Currently, your only other option into Udaipur is by bus; there are connections from Jaipur and Ahmedabad (roads are in fairly good condition). In the unlikely event that you've opted for a bus, you will most likely be dropped off just north of the City Railway Station.

GETTING AROUND   The best way to get around the main tourist sights (the area surrounding the City Palace) is on foot, but if you want to spend a rather satisfying day taking in all the sights in the city, consider renting a **moped** or **bicycle** from **Heera Cycle Store & Tours & Travels** (inside Hotel Badi Haveli, 86 Gangaur Ghat Rd., easy walking distance from Jagdish Temple; ☎ **0294/513-0625;** copy of passport and driver's license required; daily 7:30am–9pm; Rs 25–Rs 300/55¢–$6.85 per day).

For journeys farther afield, given the chaos on Indian roads, hiring a car with driver is probably the way to go; you will certainly need one for the recommended trips described below. To hire one for the day, or for a self-planned tour in Rajasthan, head for the RTDC at Surajpole (see "Visitor Information," above). This is also where to check out the range of half- or full-day government tours on offer, though note that organized tours can be too rushed or too slow, and can place you in close contact with odious fellow travelers; the quality of guides often leaves a lot to be desired as well. Should you wish to hire a car and driver from one of the many travel and tour agents that are more conveniently located in the Old City (see recommendations below), you might want to call the RTDC just to discern their going rate—at press time, between Rs 1,000 and Rs 1,400 ($23–$34) for a full day, or Rs 400 to Rs 600 ($9.10–$14) for 4 hours. Recommended travel and tour agents, all conveniently located within walking distance of the Old City sights, are the helpful **Comfort Travels and Tours,** near the City Palace (☎ **0294/242-1771,** main office ☎ **0294/241-1661** through -1663). They make all kinds of travel arrangements and also hire out cars at the going rate. The very efficient **Ramesh Dashora,** proprietor of Parul Tours and Travel, outside Jagat Niwas Hotel (☎ **0294/242-1697,** 0294/252-0363, or 94141-69597; parul_tour@ rediffmail.com), books packages and hotels and offers guides plus car for Rs 650 ($15) half-day and Rs 1,200 ($28) full day. Alternatively, call **Mohan Singh** (☎ **98293- 81935**), who drives an air-conditioned Ambassador. He understands enough English to take you sightseeing and is very well versed in routes and attractions. You can probably arrange a good deal with him for the duration of your stay.

FESTIVALS   Udaipur's biggest festivals are the **Mewar Festival,** held every March or April, and the **Holi Festival,** held every March. October's Ashwa Poojan is another celebration worth inquiring about (your hotel should be able to advise you on exact dates and where best to experience the festivities). The **Gangaur Festival** is celebrated with special zeal by the women of Udaipur (end of Mar to Apr). During this festival, unmarried women pray to the goddess Gauri (manifestation of Parvati, Shiva's wife) for a good husband, while the married pray for the well-being of their husbands and a happy married life. Women decorate their hands and feet with *mehendi* (tattoos of henna paste) and carry colorful images of Gauri and terra-cotta lamps on their heads as they dance and sing songs in street processions. At the end of the festival they break these lamp-pots and celebrate with a feast. Festivities last 18 days and include many colorful processions and a fireworks display.

WHAT TO SEE & DO

If your idea of a holiday is lying by a pool with a good book, only visits to the City and Lake palaces (see "Top Attractions," below) need top your list of things to do in

Udaipur proper. The city is the ideal base for a number of day trips, however. The most highly recommended is a round-trip through Kumbhalgarh Wildlife Sanctuary and Fort, taking in the temples of Ranakpur along the way, and possibly stopping at Eklingji on the way back (see "Top Excursions," below). The lovely, scenic drive passes picture-postcard rural hamlets and fields of mustard, scattered with boys tending cattle and women clad in bright saris tilling the soil.

For those who are interested in seeing more of the city, the following day tour—to be tailored to your needs—provides an overview of the top sights in and around Udaipur. Start your day by exploring the City Palace, which usually towers over the city's raison d'etre, Lake Pichola. Two more palaces can be seen on what would be the islands of Jag Niwas and Jag Mandir (see "Top Attractions," below). Exit through Tripolia Gate to explore the Old City of Udaipur, which sprawls north of the palace. **Jagdish Temple** ⚑, the largest in Udaipur, is its chief attraction. Despite some lovely exterior carvings (including hidden erotic pieces your guide will point out), the temple itself is rather ordinary (if you've seen a number of them elsewhere, that is), but its attraction lies in its massive popularity. The temple has seen a constant stream of people who come to worship Lord Jagannath, an aspect of Vishnu (the black stone image enshrined within), since it first opened its doors in 1652. *Arti* takes place at around 10am, 7:30pm, and 10pm—try to time your visit for when the *bhajans* (prayer-songs) make for a most atmospheric experience. (Remove your shoes before entering, and an attendant will look after them for a Rs 5/10¢ tip; no photography inside.) The bronze half-man, half-bird statue of Garuda outside is the vehicle of Vishnu. From Jagdish Temple you can wander the mazelike streets of old Udaipur, admiring the white-washed havelis and popping into tiny shops before reaching the clock tower that marks the northern edge. If you haven't picked up a bicycle from **Heera Cycle Store** (86 Gangaur Ghat Rd., near Jagdish Temple), catch a taxi from here (or have your driver waiting) to **Bharatiya Lok Kala Museum** (Panch Vati Rd.; daily 9am–6pm; entry Rs 35/65¢, Rs 10/25¢ camera, Rs 50/$1.15 video). This is unofficially known as Udaipur's "Puppet Museum" (Rajasthan being the birthplace of this favored Indian storytelling medium), where you can watch a good show, staged almost hourly throughout the day. The best is held each evening at 6pm (Rs 30/70¢) with traditional songs added on (though note that most hotels have a puppet show as part of their evening's entertainment). The folk museum also contains models, instruments, and photographs documenting other local traditions and crafts, but for this you're better off visiting **Shilpgram.** This rather faux rural arts-and-crafts "village" is located 5km (3 miles) out of town; follow the road that runs along the north of Fateh Sagar Lake (© **0294/243-1304;** daily 11am–7pm, folk dances 11am and 7pm; Rs 25/55¢, Rs 10/25¢ camera, Rs 50/$1.15 video; camel ride Rs 20/45¢). Created to "promote and preserve the traditional architecture, music, and crafts of the tribal village of western India," Shilpgram has a distinctly artificial feel but interesting cultural performances; you can also ride a camel and browse for tribal knickknacks that the "traditionally" attired craftspeople will be only too delighted to finally off-load. If you're in a particularly touristy mood, you can dress up in a traditional Rajasthani outfit and have your picture taken. Along the way, you can stop for a brief wander through **Saheliyon-ki-Bari (Garden of the Maids of Honour)** north of Bharatiya Lok Kala Museum—turn left at Sukadia Circle. Hours are daily 8am to 7:30pm; admission is Rs 5 (10¢). Created by Sangram Singh in the 18th century for the ladies of his household (some say to re-create the monsoon climate for his sickly daughter), this is billed as Udaipur's finest garden, but it suffers from neglect, with none of the fountains operating. Still, it's a peaceful place, and the array of established indigenous trees may interest keen botanists. If the monsoon has been good and lake levels in Udaipur have risen, from Saheliyon-ki-Bari make your way to nearby **Fateh Sagar Lake,** passing **Moti Magri** on your left, atop which is the statue of Maharana Pratap and his beloved horse, Chetak (largely missable, but the views from here are lovely). Fateh Sagar, the large lake that lies north of Lake Pichola, has a small island garden of its own: The rather neglected **Nehru Park,** though currently closed, is usually reached by ferry, but at press time the severe drought had decimated the park.

An excellent place to view the sunset is **Sajjan Garh (Monsoon Palace),** built by the Maharana Sajjan Singh as an observatory in the late 19th century. You can enter the palace building by tipping the guard (though it's a restricted security area). Head to one of the alcoves from where views of the surrounding mountains are breathtaking. If this sounds like one stop too many after a rather exhausting day, head straight for one of the rooftop or garden restaurants in the city; get a table on the **Sunset Terrace** (near the Dovecoat lobby of the Fateh Prakash hotel); or sit on the "deck" at the Lake Palace, where you can relax with a drink as the sun sinks behind the distant jagged outline of the Aravalli Hills.

TOP ATTRACTIONS

City Palace and Museum 𝕬𝕬𝕬   When the waters return to Lake Pichola, the palace's cream-colored stone walls tower some 30m (100 ft.) above its mirrorlike reflection in the lake, and stretch almost 250m (800 ft.) across its northwestern shore. Udaipur's 300-year-old City Palace actually comprises 11 palaces (or *mahals*) built by its successive maharanas, making it by far the largest palace complex in Rajasthan. Purchase the useful guidebook at the entrance (or hire the services of a guide through your hotel) to help you maneuver the sprawling museum, much of it connected by a maze of rather claustrophobic tunnel-like stairways designed to confuse and slow down potential invaders. (This is why it's essential to get here as soon as the palace doors open—finding yourself trapped between busloads of jeering families who mysteriously come to regular standstills in these airless passages is sheer purgatory.) The entire palace is a delight, but highlights include the large peacock mosaics in the 17th-century Mor (Peacock) Chowk; mirror-encrusted Moti Mahal; the glass and porcelain figures of Manak (Ruby) Mahal, which has a central garden; the collection of miniatures featuring Krishna legends in Krishna Vilas (dedicated to a 16-year-old princess who committed suicide here); exquisite Zenana Mahal (Palace of the Queens); and the Chinese and Dutch ceramics of Chini Mahal. When the lake levels are normal, the cusped windows provide superb views of the serene waters of Pichola Lake, on which white-marble Lake Palace appears to float. The last two palaces built, both now open to visitors wishing to overnight or dine, are the grand but rather staid **Shiv Niwas** and gorgeous **Fateh Prakash.** The latter is worth visiting for high tea to view the Durbar Hall's royal portrait gallery, with its massive chandeliers and Venetian mirrors, and to see the Crystal Gallery, which has a huge collection of rare cut-crystal furniture and ornaments imported by Maharana Sajjan Singh from England in 1877. (For more on these palaces, see "Where to Stay & Dine," later in this chapter.) Vintage-car lovers should ask about the tour of the Mewar family's Classic Car Collection. Set aside 3 hours to do the palace justice. *Tip:* As you may find it difficult to find postcards of the palace, this is one place it's worth paying to take in a camera.

City Palace Rs 50 ($1.15) Jagdish Temple end, Rs 75 ($1.70) via Hotel Fateh Prakash; Rs 200 ($4.55) any camera. Daily 9:30am–3:30pm. Crystal Gallery Rs 300 ($6.85); daily 10am–1pm and 3–8pm; no photography.

Fun Fact **Indian Solutions to a Global Problem**

The current Maharana Shri Arvind Singhji, 76th custodian of the house of Mewar, combines philanthropic interests with a keen capitalist eye—he owns some 12 heritage hotels throughout Rajasthan, from which a sizable part of the profits are funneled back into his **Maharana of Mewar Charitable Foundation.** Long concerned about the effects of global warming, particularly in Udaipur, which has seen a significant rise in average temperatures, the Maharana helped pioneer the world's first solar-powered water taxi and the world's first solar rickshaw, which have just completed pilot trials in Udaipur, with the ultimate aim of making Udaipur a solar-powered city. Because 86% of all the vehicles in India are two-stroke two-wheelers (motorcycles, mopeds, gas-powered scooters), which are responsible for a major percentage of the country's carbon dioxide emissions, this could go a long way toward solving India's pollution problems.

Lake Pichola & Lake Palace ✸✸✸   Hopefully, by the time you visit Udaipur, Lake Pichola will have returned to its former glorious state; in that spirit, we've retained a description of this Udaipur favorite. Most beautiful at sunrise and sunset, Lake Pichola reflects what seems to be a picture-perfect inversion of the many white-washed and cream buildings that rise majestically from its shores and islands, known locally as Jag Niwas and Jag Mandir. Jag Niwas island is entirely covered by the Lake Palace, built by the Maharana in 1740 as a summer idyll and today perhaps the most romantic—certainly the most photographed—hotel in India (see "Where to Stay & Dine," later in this chapter). What you will see if the lake remains parched is a magnificent palace that should be floating on water but instead sits on a vast, dry lake bed. A little farther south is the slightly larger Jag Mandir, upon which domed Gul Mahal stands. Famous as the star location in the movie *Octopussy*, it has also been a place of refuge: first for the young prince Shah Jahan who—in a typical Mughal ascension—was plotting to overthrow his father, Jahangir (incidentally, Udaipuris believe that Gul Mahal is what later inspired Jahan to build Taj Mahal); and later for European women and children, whom Maharana Swaroop Singh protected during the Mutiny. Usually you can catch a boat to Jag Mandir from the City Palace (Bansi Ghat) jetty, but once you have alighted, there's not much to do but purchase an overpriced refreshment; the trip around the lake includes a visit to Sunset Terrace (near Dovecoat Wing) or the Lake Palace Hotel. If you haven't booked a room at the hotel, make sure you come for dinner—the views alone are worth it, and the opulent and elegant setting is sublime (see "Where to Stay & Dine," later in this chapter).

To make a table reservation at Lake Palace, call © 0294/252-7961.

TOP EXCURSIONS

A number of recommended excursions from Udaipur can either be tackled as round-trips or as stopovers on your way elsewhere in the state. The first option is the easiest, a half-day excursion (at most) that takes in some of the most important temples in Udaipur. The second option—which you can combine with the first for a rather grueling but very satisfying round-trip—takes you to the awesome Jain temples at

Ranakpur through Kumbhalgarh Wildlife Sanctuary, past wonderful pastoral scenes that haven't changed since medieval times, to view magnificent Kumbhalgarh Fort. From here you can either head northwest for Jodhpur or double back to Udaipur, possibly taking in the temples at Nathdwara, Nagda, and Eklingji. (If you're pressed for time, leave out Nathdwara—beyond the superb examples of *pichhwai* paintings, there's not much to see, as non-Hindus may not enter the temple.) To plan this as a round-trip, you will need to hire a driver familiar with the distances and terrain, and overnight along the way (see the listing for Kumbhalgarh Fort, below).

The third option is another long full-day trip, this time with the sole purpose of viewing Chittaurgarh, site of the most legendary Mewar battles. From here you can return to Udaipur or push on east to the little town of Bundi (see earlier in this chapter), and from there proceed to Jaipur or Ranthambhore National Park. For those interested in an off-the-beaten-track experience to the south, the fourth option, relatively undiscovered Dungarpur Palace, is well worth the time, not least for Deco fans who will relish overnighting in the family manse—Udai Bilas Palace, a living Deco museum—before returning to Udaipur or pushing on to Gujarat. If Ranakpur's temples have whet your appetite for more, a fifth option, an excursion to the west ascending the Aravalli Hills to Mount Abu, the only hill station in Rajasthan and home to the most famous Dilwara Jain temples in India, can also be tackled from Udaipur, though the distances covered here will necessitate an overnight stay. For details on distances and all excursions, see a full description of the five day trips, below.

An excursion to an attraction that is not described in detail below, but which may interest birders or those in search of more peace, is **Jaisamand Lake,** the second-largest man-made lake in Asia, created in 1691 by Maharana Jai Singh and, thankfully, still containing water. Located a little over an hour away from Udaipur, it has a number of marble pavilions but is more famous for the many aquatic birds that have found a home in what is now **Jaisamand Wildlife Sanctuary.**

DAY TRIP 1: A HALF-DAY TEMPLE EXCURSION

Eklingji & Nagda Temples *★★*   Housing a manifestation of Shiva, the god who guards the fortunes of the rulers of Mewar, Eklingji is a lovely marble complex made up of 108 temples, the first of which was built in A.D. 734 by Bappa Rawal, legendary founder of the Sisodia clan, who ruled the Mewar kingdom for hundreds of years. The entire complex, most of it rebuilt in the 15th century, has a wonderfully uplifting atmosphere, particularly during prayer times (see below), and never more so than on the Monday evenings when the Maharana of Udaipur is in town and comes to pay his respects here, walking among his subjects as a mere mortal despite the attendant bowing and scraping. The four-faced black lingam (phallic symbol) apparently marks the spot where Bappa Rawal (that's him riding the peacock) was given the title Darwan ("servant") of Eklingji by his guru; outside, facing Shiva, is Nandi, Shiva's vehicle. Wander around the temple complex and you'll find a number of carvings from the *Kama Sutra;* your explorations won't exceed 30 minutes. Deserted **Nagda,** which lies 2km (1¼ miles) north, is a far cry from this vibrant place of worship. All that survives of the site of the ancient capital of Mewar, which dates back to A.D. 626, are the ruins of the Saas Bahu, a 10th-century Vaishnavite twin temple (*Saas* meaning "mother-in-law" and *Bahu* "daughter-in-law") and the remains of Adbhutji Temple. Regrettably, the temples have been vandalized over the years and look much the worse for wear—unless you're of the archaeological bent, skip them if you're pushed for time.

22km (14 miles) north of Udaipur (30–40-min. drive one-way). Eklingji daily 4:15–6:45am, 10:30am–1:30pm, and 5:15–7:45pm. Prayer times: 15-min. *artis* are performed at 5:30am, 8:15am, 9:15am, 3:30pm, 4:30pm, 5pm, and 6:30pm; a 45-min. *arti* is performed at 11:30am.

Nathdwara *⟨⟩* Said to be the second-richest temple in India, Nathdwara's Shri Nathji Temple, home to a 600-year-old black marble statue of Lord Krishna, is one of the most important pilgrimage sites in India, attracting thousands, particularly during the festivals of Diwali, Holi, and Janmashthami. According to legend, in 1669 as the statue was being carried from Mathura to protect it from the destructive blows of the pious Mughal emperor Aurangzeb, it fell off the wagon at this site; the carriers (no doubt pretty exhausted) took this as a sign and built the temple around the statue. That said, the interior is closed to non-Hindus, so many of you won't even get a glimpse of the statue. The main reason to visit is to view what many believe are the finest examples of *pichhwai* paintings that adorn the interior and exterior of the temple. Hand-spun cloth painted with vibrant scenes depicting Krishna's life, these were originally created to teach illiterate low castes (who in the past were also barred from entering the sacred inner sanctum). You can purchase your own *pichhwai* paintings in the local bazaar, or look for more examples in Udaipur. Note that this is also a center for traditional *meenakari* (enamel) work.

48km (30 miles) from Udaipur (1-hr. drive one-way).

DAY TRIP 2: A TEMPLE, A FORT & A WONDERFUL DRIVE

Ranakpur Temples *⟨⟩⟨⟩⟨⟩* If you visit only one temple complex in Rajasthan, it should be Jain. Those at Ranakpur offer the finest examples of the complex and sustained levels of craftsmanship the Jains are renowned for, comparable in every way to the more famous Dilwara Temples at Mount Abu. If anything, a visit here is preferable—despite being a great deal more accessible, the area is infinitely more peaceful, with less traffic. Known for their aestheticism and religious fervor (Jains are not only strict vegetarians, but the most orthodox among them walk with care to ensure no hapless insect should die underfoot due to their carelessness, and wear permanent masks to protect even the tiniest bug from the possibility of being ingested), the Jains put all their passion (and not inconsiderable wealth) into the creation of ornately carved temples. The Ranakpur Temples are jaw-droppingly beautiful, with exquisitely detailed relief carvings (and strangely, a few pieces of tinfoil) covering every inch of pillar, wall, and ceiling. The main triple-volume Chaumukha Temple, built from 1446 and dedicated to Adinatha Rishabdeva, the first Jain *tirthankara*, or "Enlightened One," is surrounded by 66 subsidiary shrines; inside are 1,444 intricately carved pillars—not one of them the same. (Incidentally, the land was donated to the Jains by Rana Kumbha, the warrior who built 32 forts, of which Kumbhalgarh is the most famous.) Note that no leather (not even a belt!) is allowed on the premises, no photography of the statues or enshrined deities is allowed (general temple pictures are permitted), and you are requested to dress conservatively (no showing of naked legs). The sign outside also states that menstruating women are strictly forbidden to enter. *Note:* There are no good accommodations in the immediate vicinity; best to push on to the **Aodhi Hotel,** near Kumbhalgarh Fort (see below) or, if you're on your way to Jodhpur, **Rawla Narlai** or **Deogarh Mahal** (see "Traveling between Udaipur & Jaipur/Jodhpur," later in this chapter). If you want to grab an early lunch of authentic Jain food, make your way to the canteen-style eatery near the main temple, which closes at 1:30pm; Rs 20 (45¢) buys you a good thali.

Tip: Two kilometers (1¼ miles) north (on the way to Jodphur or Kumbhalgarh), you will pass **Tribal Dhurrie Udyog,** a traditional *dhurrie* (carpet) "shop" (© **0294/ 241-7833**), where you can pick up a beautifully crafted 4×6m (13×20-ft.) carpet for Rs 3,000 ($68)—a great deal cheaper than what you'll pay in the cities.

65km (40 miles) from Udaipur (2½-hr. drive one-way). Rs 50 ($1.15) camera. 11:30am–5pm.

Kumbhalgarh Fort ✿✿✿ Built in the 15th century by Rana Kumbha, this mountain fortress is, together with Jodhpur's Mehrangarh Fort, one of the most impressive sights Rajasthan has to offer. Take one look at the impenetrable walls that snake for 36km (22 miles) along 13 mountain peaks, and you know that this is one of the most inaccessible fortifications ever built by humans. It was in fact only captured once, when the Mughal emperor Akbar had its water supply poisoned. This is also where the infant Udai Singh, who was spirited here by his nanny while Chittaurgarh (see below) was being sacked, spent his formative years. The wall, the second longest in the world, culminates in a fairy-tale fort within which lie the **Palace of Rana Kumbha** and **Badal Mahal** (or **Palace of Clouds,** so named because it literally is in the clouds during the monsoon months). The fort is situated deep within Kumbhalgarh Wildlife Sanctuary, and the drive there—through tiny villages and pastoral countryside—is one of the great highlights of a trip to Rajasthan and a great contrast to the crowded cities. Kumbhalgarh is considered the most important fort after Chittaurgarh, but its relative accessibility and the charm of the drive make this the preferable option.

To have adequate time to explore the fort, or to take in Eklingji on the return journey, it's worth overnighting near the fort. The closest and best choice is the **Aodhi Hotel,** owned by the HRH Group of Hotels (© **02954/24-2341** through -2346; www.hrhindia.com; Rs 4,000–Rs 5,000/$91–$114 double; see Fateh Prakash & Shiv Niwas Palaces, later in this chapter, for reservations details). It has spacious, comfortable rooms (each with TV and minibar, and bathroom fittings in a reasonable state) that cling to the hillside and overlook a large pool and a pretty alfresco dining area. Room nos. 4, 5, 10, 11, and 23 enjoy good views.

90km (56 miles) from Udaipur (2-hr. drive one-way; 1 hr. from Ranakpur Temples).

DAY TRIP 3: A HISTORY OF VALOR

Chittaurgarh (Chittor) ✿✿ Chittaurgarh is 3 hours from Udaipur and covers 280 hectares (700 acres), making it a rather long day trip, but it's well worth it if you're armed with information and a good imagination (both of which can be supplied by a good guide; ask your hotel for recommendations). Thrusting 180m (575 ft.) into the sky, the fort houses a number of monuments and memorials, but with much of it in ruins, its primary importance lies in its evocative history. The fort has witnessed some of the bloodiest battles in history, and songs recording the valor and sacrifice of its inhabitants are still sung today.

Built in the 7th century, it remained the capital of Mewar until 1568, when the capital was shifted to Udaipur. During this time Chittaurgarh was ravaged three times, but the story behind the first sacking that took place in 1303 during the reign of Rana Ratan Singh is perhaps the most romantic (see "Battling for a Glimpse of Beauty," below).

Chittaurgarh returned to Rajput rule in 1326 and the Mewar enjoyed 2 centuries of prosperity before it was again laid siege to, this time by Sultan Bahadur Shah of Gujarat. To save the life of the Rajput heir Udai Singh, his nursemaid Panna Dai sacrificed her own infant son, leaving him as a decoy for the murderous sultan and spiriting the tiny heir away to the safety of Kumbhalgarh Fort. The women and children

Battling for a Glimpse of Beauty

It is said that the rapacious sultan Allauddin Khilji laid siege to the fort because he had become obsessed with tales of the legendary beauty of the Maharana (or Rana) Ratan Singh's queen, Rani Padmini. He promised to withdraw, provided Singh allow him an opportunity to lay eyes on her—an outrageous demand considering that a strange man's gaze was tantamount to the defilement of a Rajput royal woman. But in the spirit of compromise, Singh reluctantly agreed to present him with her reflection in the lotus pond that lay below the palace's women's quarters. The sultan used this opportunity to betray the king, ambushing and capturing him on his departure. The next day a bereft Padmini sent word to the sultan that she would give herself to him in return for her husband and the withdrawal of his troops. She then descended through the seven *pols* (gates), surrounded by what appeared to be her maids-of-honor—Singh's troops, disguised as women. Singh was rescued from the sultan's camp, but the ensuing battle cost the lives of some 7,000 of Singh's men—a crippling loss. When it was clear that the Rajputs would be defeated, the funeral pyres were lit, and Padmini and 13,000 women and children committed *jauhar,* flinging themselves onto the flames, after which the last of Singh's men went to meet certain death below the ramparts.

of Chittaurgarh committed *jauhar* (mass ritual suicide) while their men died on the battlefields.

When, at the age of 13, Udai was reinstated at Chittaurgarh, he searched in earnest for a new site for the capital, building Udaipur on the shores of Lake Pichola. Eight years later, the Mughal emperor Akbar, trying to contain the arrogance of Udai Singh—who poured such contempt on Jai (of Jaipur) Singh's collaboration with the emperor—attacked Chittaurgarh. This time 30,000 Rajput lives were lost, and the women and children again flung themselves on the flames rather than be captured by the Muslims. Chittaurgarh was given back to the Rajputs in 1616, much of it in ruins, but by this time the royal family was comfortably ensconced in Udaipur, and the fort was never lived in again.

The fort is approached through seven massive **pols,** or gates—look for the *chhatri* (cenotaph) of the chivalrous Jaimal and his cousin Kala near Bhairon Pol. Jaimal was seriously wounded defending Chittaur against Emperor Akbar but he refused to give up and was carried back into battle on the shoulders of Kala, where both were slain. At Ram Pol is a **memorial to Phatta** who, at 16, having lost his father in battle and witnessed the deaths of his sword-wielding mother and young wife on the battlefield, led his saffron-robed men to certain death while the women of the fort yet again ended their lives by committing *jauhar.*

As you enter the final *pol,* you will see **Shingara Chauri Mandir,** a typically adorned Jain temple, and the crumbling **15th-century palace** built by Rana Kumbha up ahead. Under the palace lies a series of cellars where Padmini reputedly committed *jauhar* (see box). Rana Kumbha was one of the Mewar's most powerful rulers: In addition to the palace, he built nearby **Khumba Shyam Temple,** dedicated to Varah (an incarnation of Lord Vishnu), as well as **Meera Temple,** dedicated to the poet and princess Meera, whose devotion to Krishna reputedly saved her from being poisoned. (Incidentally, Krishna is usually depicted as blue as a result of the poison he consumed, thereby saving the world.) Note that inside the cenotaph in front of the temple is a **carved figure** of five human bodies with one head—in a rare overture to tolerance, this is supposed to demonstrate that all castes are ultimately equal. Farther south lies Kumbha's **Vijay Stambh (Tower of Victory)**—a lavishly ornamented tower built by Maharana Kumbha to commemorate his victory over the combined forces of Malwa and Gujarat.

Other sites of interest are **Padmini's Palace,** where the sultan Allauddin Khilji gazed upon Padmini's reflection in the lotus pond; **Kirti Stambh,** a 12th-century tower ornamented with figures, dedicated to the first Jain *tirthankara;* **Fateh Prakash Palace,** built for the Maharana during the 1920s and housing a dry archaeological museum (Sat–Thurs 10am–4:30pm; Rs 5/10¢); and **Kalika Mata Temple,** originally built as a Sun Temple by Bappa Rawal in the 8th century but rebuilt during the 14th century and dedicated to Kali, goddess of power and valor. Some of the best views are from **Gaumukh (Cow's Mouth) Reservoir,** so-called because the spring water trickles through a stone carving of a cow's mouth.

Accommodations in Chittor are limited, with no luxury options. If you *have* to overnight, the best options are **Meera** (© **01472/240-266;** Rs 550–Rs 990/$13–$22) and **Pratap Palace** (© **01472/240-099;** Rs 1,200–Rs 1,700/$28–$40).

115km (70 miles) northeast of Udaipur. A tour takes approximately 2 hr. **Note:** You can get here by train from Jaipur, but it's a long trip (16 hr.). Trains from Udaipur were not operational at press time, but were expected to resume by 2006. The railway station lies 4km (2½ miles) from the base of the fort; from here, you can catch a rickshaw to tour the fort—expect to pay at least Rs 120 ($3).

DAY TRIP 4: AN UNDISCOVERED PALACE & DECO DELIGHT

Dungarpur's Palaces ✶✶✶ *(Finds* It's hard for anyone flipping through Angelika Taschen's book, *Indian Style,* to refrain from gasping when you come to the pages recording the magnificent apartments of 13th-century **Juna Mahal.** A seven-story fortresslike structure that appears to spring forth from its rocky surrounds, the palace doesn't look like much from the outside, but inside, it houses one of the world's most interesting "art galleries": Every wall and column is covered with beautiful, intricate frescoes—tiny paintings; mosaics with glass, mirror, and tiles; or artfully used porcelain plates embedded into the walls. In one of the massive downstairs reception rooms, the entire floor is covered with huge decaying Persian carpets. Yet even though it houses a treasure trove of art and design, the palace is far from being a tourist attraction: There's no ticket office, no touts, no guides, no visitors—not even a single hawker in sight, only the toothless old retainer whose trembling hands hold the keys while he waits for you to drink it all in before he opens another, even more stunning room. Perhaps it is precisely this—viewing such beauty in absolute solitude—that makes the experience so special, but the artworks are considered to be of the very best in Rajasthan. Don't miss (you're unlikely to, as long as the old man is around to leer at your reaction) the collection of miniature paintings depicting scenes from the *Kama Sutra,* modestly hidden behind cupboard doors in the Maharaja's suite on the top floor.

To view the Juna Mahal, you will likely have to overnight at nearby **Udai Bilas Palace**—no hardship, as this, too, is a wonderful experience, particularly if you have any interest in the Deco period or relish a sense of nostalgia. Built on the shores of Gaibsagar Lake (great for birders, with 122 species recorded), it is both scenic and secluded and combines Rajput architecture and murals with original Art Deco furnishings and fittings—the work of Maharawal Laxman Singhji, who had three new wings built around lovely Ek Thambia Mahal (One-Pillared Palace) in 1940. Still the royal residence of the Maharawal and his family, the palace offers 20 old-fashioned rooms (old plumbing, beautiful Deco furniture in need of new springs, no in-room amenities—but simply charming, nonetheless) as well as a wonderful pool on the water's edge. If you can afford it, book a suite (our personal preference is no. 20, but really, it all depends on whether you fall in love with a particular lounge suite or carpet pattern or view). Ask whether you can wander around and take your pick; no. 7 is the best standard room.

120km (75 miles) south of Udaipur (2-hr. drive one-way); 175km (108 miles) from Ahmedabad, Gujarat. For reservations, contact Udai Bilas Palace, Dungarpur, Rajasthan 314 001 (© **02964/230-808;** fax 02964/231-008; www. udaibilaspalace.com). Rs 3,850–Rs 5,750 ($88–$131). Rs 1,000 ($23) extra bed. Taxes extra. Discounts May–Sept. MC, V.

DAY TRIP 5: ASCENDING MOUNT ABU

The Rajputs are said to have held the fire ceremony in which they were "reborn" as warriors on these lofty heights, but Mount Abu, so-called "Abode of the Gods," only became a destination for mere mortals a millennium later, when the British persuaded the Sirohi State to allow them to use it as a retreat from the searing heat of the plateaus that shimmer below. They were later joined by the Rajput princes, who built mini-palaces to show off and entertain the Britishers. At a cool 1,220m (390 ft.) above sea level, this is the only hill station in Rajasthan, and it's within easy striking distance of many of Gujarat's big cities, providing welcome relief for thousands of domestic visitors who come to paddle central **Nakki Lake** in giant swan boats and view the exquisite sunsets, all accompanied by the inevitable high-spirited carousing of friends and families.

Indeed, unless you put on your walking shoes and head for the hills, this is not the most peaceful of places; it's filled with a year-round festive spirit as families and honeymooners throng the streets, clutching ice creams or the manes of the ponies that clatter along, shaking their bells and feathered heads at passersby. Every evening at sunset, literally hundreds of people set off for **Sunset Point,** riding in large pramlike vehicles pushed by stringy men or mounting the ponies that congregate here in the hope of making their masters a few more rupees before the onset of night. The sun sinking into the plains that lie thousands of miles below is a truly wonderful sight, not least because you are sharing it with so many people, the smell of roasting peanuts permeating the air, and there is a rare sense of camaraderie as the crowd gives a roar of approval when the sun finally slips behind the horizon. If you have no anthropological bent, however, the real reason to venture so far off the beaten track (and unless you approach it from Gujarat, Mount Abu is a long and not altogether satisfactory detour) is to view the Dilwara Temples (not to be confused with Delwara, just north of Udaipur; see below), widely considered the best examples of Jain architecture in India, though we thought the temples at Ranakpur (see above) equally beautiful.

There is a plethora of hotels in town, most awful, but the following two are recommended. **The Jaipur House,** which the latest Jaipur Maharaja renovated and turned into an intimate hotel in 2002, is by far the best situated. Because of close family ties, the Jaipur Maharaja was given first choice of land by the then-ruler of Sirohi State, and in 1897 he built his Rajput-style mansion on the highest hilltop overlooking Nakki Lake. Guests have a choice of nine rooms in the heritage wing (avoid the 14 on offer in the new wing). All suites have views of the lake (for truly stupendous views, no. 201, "the Royal Suite," is fantastic); room no. 107 has no lake view but with two small balconies is the best standard room. Avoid no. 106, a horrid "junior suite." For bookings, contact ✆ **02974/235-176** or jaipurhouse@sancharnet.in. Doubles range from Rs 2,500 to Rs 3,995 ($57–$90). If you prefer a more old-fashioned, laid-back atmosphere and more personable service, **Palace Hotel (Bikaner House),** once the summer residence of the royal Bikaner family, was designed by that master of Indo-Saracenic style, Sir Swinton Jacob, in 1893. Enjoying a tranquil location near the Dilwara Temples, it is surrounded by sprawling grounds and forests. A million miles from the jovial madness that reigns in town, it will suit those who enjoy the timeless elegance of good design. Rooms in both wings have been given new leases on life with extensive renovations carried out in 2005, adding updated plumbing and bathroom fixtures and other modern comforts to the old-world charm. Make sure you have a room in the main house; the service (under the kind, professional Rajvirsinh) is faultless, and the genteel atmosphere very much captures the graciousness of a bygone era. For bookings, contact ✆ **02974/235-121** or 0297/238-673; bikhouse@sancharnet.in; www.palacehotel bikanerhouse.com. Rates are Rs 2,650 to Rs 3,500 ($61–$80). The hotels will happily arrange guides or transfers.

Dilwara Temples 🟊🟊🟊   Built between the 11th and 13th centuries, these "hymns in marble"—every interior wall and pillar is covered with the most intricate carvings, none of which are repeated—are worthy of inspiring great devotion, and are said to be unparalleled anywhere else in India (though Ranakpur comes pretty close). Of the five temples, **Vimala Vasahi** (1031), which took 1,500 artists and 1,200 laborers 14 years to complete; and **Luna Vasahi** (1231), are the most impressive. The full-color guidebook at the entrance is definitely worth purchasing (not least because photography is not allowed); it gives a breakdown of what you are looking at in each temple. Alternatively, hire the services of a guide through your hotel.

190km (118 miles) from Udaipur (a 5-hr. drive one-way). No entry fee. Dilwara Temples open noon–6pm. Note that no photography, leather, cameras, bare legs, food, recorders, or menstruating women are allowed on the premises, and no one is allowed to enter the cells or touch the sculptures.

WHERE TO STAY & DINE

The following reviews assume that—Vishnu willing—the waters have returned to a shimmering Lake Pichola. Call ahead and check about the status of the lake waters to make an informed lodging choice; we'd hate for you to fork out a load of cash for a special room, only to end up staring at a parched lake bed. For instance, without a view you can rule out the Fateh Prakash and Lake Palace and consider instead a room at the Kankarwa or one of the other more reasonably priced options, then head off to spend a night outside Udaipur, at Devi Garh, or stay at Deogarh Mahal or Rawla Narlai en route to Jaipur or Jodhpur. If, however, the monsoon has performed its miracle, make sure to book into a hotel or haveli with a view of the lake, preferably on the eastern shore so you face the sunset. The best accommodations are reviewed below, but the following also deserve a mention. The over-the-top Bhagwat Suite (room no. 209, Rs 4,000/$91 double), a large corner room in **Lake Pichola Hotel** on the western shore (✆ **0294/243-1197;** www.lakepicholahotel.com), has the most wonderful views of the lake and its palaces—you can literally see Lake Palace from your large brass four-poster bed or the glass alcove that juts over the lake. This is by far the best room; others range from livable (second floor) to awful (first floor). If you're literally counting your rupees, **Badi Haveli** (✆ **0294/241-2588;** hotelbadihaveli@yahoo.com; Rs 250–Rs 450/$5.70–$10) is the clean, well-run, well-located (near City Palace), 350-year-old home of Mr. Samant Bhatt, with monastic but scrupulously clean rooms. Some top-floor rooms have lovely views of the lake. Several notches higher but still in the budget category, the hotel **Mahendra Prakash** on Lake Palace Road is without lake views, but it does have a swimming pool and a cool garden; attractive decorative touches like colored window panes, wooden doors with ormolu mountings, and solid brass door knockers. Service is prompt and friendly. Make sure you get an air-conditioned room on the first floor; these have pretty carved balconies with cushioned seats (© **0294/24-19811;** udai99@hotmail. com; 1st-floor A/C double Rs 1,000/$23). Also see the review of Kankarwa, below. At the other end of the scale is the **Trident Hilton** (© **1-600-11-2122** or 0294/243-2200; udaipur@trident-hilton.com). A large, slick, purpose-built hotel—recently taken over by the Hilton—it has plenty of amenities and facilities but is set some way from the lake among the tranquil Aravalli Hills, about a 25-minute drive from town. At $100 to $200 per double (check online for daily rates and deals), this comfortable option offers relatively good value (pool-facing rooms dressed in indigo and gold are best) and will suit the less-adventurous traveler, but it's a bit soulless for our taste. Note that, as in our Jaipur listings, if a heritage property hasn't been included, it's because it hasn't made the grade.

When it comes to Udaipur's fine-dining experiences, you can spend an evening at the **Lake Palace Hotel,** where you can order a cocktail and settle on the "deck" to watch beautiful young Rajasthani women twirl to a hypnotic drumbeat (if your attention starts to wander, take in the sublime views of the City Palace turning pink) before retiring to the regal dining room for a sumptuous buffet, which we found a tad overpriced at Rs 1,500 ($35) per person. If the lake is still empty, a much better bet is Udaivilas's **Suryamahal** and **Udaimahal** (Udaimahal open for dinner only)—in fact, when it comes to quality of cuisine, the latter two win hands-down regardless of the status of the lake. See below for contact details.

A more casual dining experience is Fateh Prakash Palace's **Sunset Terrace** (see earlier in this chapter). This is indeed the perfect place to watch the sunset, and when the sun finally disappears behind the Aravalli Hills, the ambience just gets more romantic as candles are lit and the Lake Palace, which floats in the foreground, glows like a liner on the lake. That said, the food—which ranges from toasted sandwiches (adequate) to tandoori (overcooked)—is a bit of a letdown. Better fare, and more comfortable seating, are to be had at **Jagat Niwas** nearby (see below). Unlike almost everywhere else in town, this restaurant terrace is open to the cooling breezes but totally beneath a roof, which provides some escape from the midday heat. It has comfortable mattressed alcoves with bolsters where you can curl up with a book or appreciate the sublime views of the lake. This is the kind of place where you could spend an entire afternoon relaxing; in fact, one guest, who wasn't even staying in the hotel, did exactly that every day for the duration of his stay in Udaipur. Service is slow but friendly (some of the waiters have been here 10 years or more), and food is average to good. Stick to the Indian dishes, either the vegetarian (*paneer matar masala,* Indian ricotta-like cheese simmered in a thick gravy with peas and tomatoes; and *paneer do pyaja,* cheese cooked with onion, tomato, and chilies) or the local dishes like fish a la Jagat (slices of the local freshwater fish from Jaisamand Lake, caught daily, cooked in a lemon sauce, and served with chips) or Afghani *murgh malai tikka* (creamy chicken kebabs). Expect to pay Rs 60 to Rs 250 ($1.35–$5.70).

Two other dining options are worth considering, even without a lake to view. **Ambrai,** next door to the Amet Haveli, serves good standard tandoori fare (and some

Indo-Chinese and "Continental" as well). The place has a mellow ambience created by the warm light from candlelit tables, and wrought-iron chairs in the pleasant sprawling garden overlook the Lake Palace. **Udai Kothi's** rooftop restaurant is a lovely spot at night (especially with the terrace pool lit up), with excellent service. Choose a small alcove by the pool—with mirrored dome, cushions, candlelight, and a good butter chicken, this could be one of the most memorable meals you have in India.

A final note when it comes to dining experiences in Udaipur: Many guidebooks consider "high tea" at Fateh Prakash Palace a highlight, but personally we find it overrated. Yes, it has lovely views and a grand atmosphere, but the heavy curtains and carpets and general fuddy-duddy atmosphere make it the last place to experience the views and quality of light so particular to Udaipur. Do let us know if you differ.

Note: The prices for the accommodations below are sometimes given in rupees, with U.S. dollar conversions; others are stated in U.S. dollars only, which is how many hotels targeting foreign markets quote their rates.

LAKE PICHOLA

Lake Palace Hotel ✹✹✹   Just looking at a photograph of this 18th-century island palace is enough to make you want to start planning a trip to India, and when we first stayed here it certainly lived up to its promise. The standard rooms had enjoyed a much-needed upgrade (thank heavens for competition, in the shape of Udaivilas, which you can see glimmering on the other side of the lake). Both standard and deluxe rooms now feature opulent fabrics, walls with wood paneling and murals, lovely marble bathrooms, and well-crafted furniture; renovations also improved many of the public spaces. Best of all, everywhere you look—be it from the mango-shaded pool, your room, or the restaurant—you have picture-perfect views: the statuesque City Palace walls and crenelated rooftops to the east, the whitewashed havelis and temples of the Old City lining the shores of the lake to the north, the Aravalli Hills to the west, or Jag Mandir to the east. The best rooms (besides the suites) are the deluxe rooms facing east—the City Palace is lit up at night, giving you a 24-hour view. The huge and opulent suites were thankfully left as inherited from the royal family, and have a timeless grandeur that the City Palace hotels could only wish for—stained-glass windows, marble floors, crystal chandeliers, antique Rajasthani furniture, and old-fashioned pieces that wouldn't be out of place at Balmoral (Queen Elizabeth's favorite residence)—making them the epitome of 20th-century royal splendor. That said, the absence of a surrounding lake has had a very serious impact on the romance of staying here, with access (normally provided by 24-hr. water taxis) now by 4WD vehicles seen churning up the dry lake bed. Given that service and dining could do with improvement, you would—certainly as long as the drought endures—be far better off at Udaivilas.

P.O. Box 5, Udaipur 313 001. © **0294/252-8800.** Fax 0294/252-7975. www.tajhotels.com. 85 units. $475 deluxe lake-view double, $575 luxury double; $850–$2,000 suite. $50 extra person. AE, DC, MC, V. **Amenities:** 2 restaurants; bar; pool; mini-gym; travel desk (car hires, boat trips); 24-hr. water taxi; currency exchange; shopping; 24-hr. room service; babysitting; doctor-on-call; reading room. *In room:* A/C, TV, minibar, hair dryer.

EASTERN SHORES OF LAKE PICHOLA

Fateh Prakash & Shiv Niwas Palaces   The last two palaces built within the City Palace walls are now both hotels, but unless you want to overnight in what feels like a wealthy old aunt's large but stuffy apartment, there's only one section worth considering: the relatively new **Dovecoat Wing** ✹✹ in Fateh Prakash. After the Lake Palace, this is the next-best location in Udaipur: All the rooms in this wing, which stretches along the shoreline, have the most wonderful views of the lake and its palace, as well as views beyond the distant Aravalli Hills (perfect at both sunset and dawn); room nos. 511 and 617 even have little sitting rooms that jut over the water. Furnishings are elegant (predominantly salmon and white), bathrooms adequate (obviously done before bathrooms became a real focus in hotel design), and rates offer by far the best value in the palaces. By contrast, Fateh Prakash's much pricier "Regal Suites," while a great deal larger, are overdressed, overcarpeted, and old-fashioned—not always a bad thing, but these definitely need sprucing up; certainly those that don't even face the lake are a definite no-no. Management may try to persuade you to "upgrade" to these older apartments, but if you don't like the musty, almost claustrophobic atmosphere, insist that they honor your booked room in the lighter, breezier Dovecoat Wing. Crescent-shaped Shiv Niwas Palace, built around the pool courtyard, is positioned farther south, and without the lovely Lake Palace floating before you, its views are a great deal less magical. And that's *if* you get a lake view—again, don't bother staying here if you don't have one since it's hardly worth the price (rooms with lake views are listed with rates below). Service in both hotels is well-meaning but will almost certainly try your patience. The aptly named Sunset Terrace (see earlier in this chapter) is the best place to dine—the views are great, but don't expect much from the cuisine.

City Palace Complex, Udaipur 313 001. ✆ 0294/252-8016 or -8019. Fax 0294/252-8006. www.hrhindia.com. Fateh Prakash 28 units. Shiv Niwas 31 units. **Fateh Prakash:** $275 Dovecoat, $300 lake-facing Regal Suite, $250 Regal Suite. **Shiv Niwas:** $210 deluxe double (no views); $450 Terrace Suite (nos. 15 and 16 lake-facing), $600 Historic Suite (nos. 6 and 7 lake-facing), $750 Royal Suite (nos. 5 and 18 lake-facing), $900 Imperial Suite (no. 17 lake-facing). AE, MC, V. **Amenities** (shared by hotels): 3 restaurants; pool; squash; billiards; travel desk; doctor-on-call. *In room:* A/C, TV, minibar, hair dryer.

Jagat Niwas ℛ   Like its neighbor the Kankarwa, this 17th-century haveli literally rises from the waters of Lake Pichola. The difference is that Jag Niwas is more hotel than guesthouse, with a laid-back staff, a good travel desk/agent, and in-room amenities like air-conditioning, TVs, and telephones. Approached through a narrow street that runs into the entrance, it is essentially a cluster of buildings around a central courtyard. Rooms vary considerably, with only suites and deluxe rooms providing lake views—of these, nos. 110 and 116 (suites), and no. 102 (deluxe) are particularly pleasing options. Ceilings often feature colored glass baubles typical of Rajasthani havelis; walls have painted murals; fabrics are traditional Rajasthani block prints; and many rooms have alcoves with mattresses. In an irritating oversight, not a single room has a bedside reading lamp. Not all rooms have split air-conditioning—units with this are a great deal quieter than window units, so you might want to request it. The best part of the hotel is the wonderful covered terrace that overlooks the lake (see above) and hosts evening shows. Unless you prefer hotel-like amenities, choose the more stylish Kankarwa (see below), and come and relax on the terrace here as a visitor. If you want a pool, Udai Kothi (see below) is a better option.

23–25 Lal Ghat, Udaipur 313 001. ✆ 0294/242-0133 or -2860. Fax 0294/241-8512. www.jagatniwaspalace.com. mail@jagatniwaspalace.com. 29 units. Rs 1,250 ($30) standard A/C double, Rs 1,895 ($44) deluxe A/C double, Rs 2,650 ($61) super deluxe A/C double; Rs 3,300 ($75) A/C suite. AE, MC, V. **Amenities:** Lakeside terrace restaurant; travel desk/car hires; horseback riding and safaris arranged; laundry; doctor-on-call. *In room:* A/C (specify), TV (some rooms), hair dryer.

Kankarwa ℛℛ *Value*   A short stroll from the City Palace, this is by far the best budget option in town, if not the whole of Rajasthan. It's an elegant and professional family-run guesthouse in an ancient haveli right on the shores of Lake Pichola. We loved room no. 204; the simple whitewashed space has white bedding and traditional Rajasthani antiques; a single blood-red lamp perfectly offsets the cool white—this family has innate style. The compact bathrooms (most with shower only) are also whitewashed or tiled, only adding to the refreshing, clean atmosphere. Room no. 206 is a good twin-bed option with white-pillowed alcove (colored by stained-glass windows) and a great bathroom with a window. Other good options are nos. 217, 216, and 203—all with the same sense of cool fresh white offset with a touch of color. The Jag Niwas restaurant terrace is right next door, but if you want to enjoy what the family (who have, incidentally, been living here for 200 years) is having for dinner, they will put a lovely wrought-iron table (no plastic here!) on the rooftop terrace, where pink bougainvillea grows in pots, framing great views. A meal will set you back a mere Rs 200 ($4.55). The only possible drawback is the lack of amenities, but the family works hard at providing assistance. *Note:* Budget travelers may be interested to know that Kankarwa has two very small but comfortable rooms (no views) for Rs 750 ($17) that they don't usually advertise, having such high standards elsewhere.

26 Lal Ghat, Udaipur 313 001. © 0294/241-1457. Fax 0294/252-1403. www.indianheritagehotels.com. khaveli@ yahoo.com. 14 units. Rs 1,200–Rs 1,650 ($28–$38) double. MC, V. **Amenities:** Rooftop terrace; laundry.

WESTERN SHORES OF LAKE PICHOLA

Amet Haveli   Located on the shores of Lake Pichola, with views of Kankarwa and Jag Niwas directly opposite, this pretty 350-year-old haveli has enough charm to have found its way into glossy books on Indian style, but it's rather basic for anyone who wants a lot of amenities. Definitely book one of the suites—the hands-down winner is suite no. 7, which has a large mattressed *jarokha* that juts over the water, providing lovely views of the City Palace and Lake Palace; you can even see the City Palace from your king-size bed. Freshly whitewashed, with simple furnishings (no cupboards to speak of), the room is airy and light, and very good value. Suite no. 8 is slightly larger, but the views are not nearly as spectacular—again, this only matters if Lake Pichola's waters have returned. The adjacent restaurant, **Ambrai,** has a good reputation for its food (particularly tandoori dishes).

Outside Chandpole, Udaipur 313 001. © 0294/243-1085. regiudr@datainfosys.net. 7 units. Rs 1,850 ($42) double; Rs 2,150 ($50) suite. No credit cards. **Amenities:** Restaurant; laundry.

Udai Kothi   *Value* Not as well located (with regards to top attractions) as Jagat Niwas or Kankarwa, but still within walking distance of the Old City, this small hotel is a relatively authentic replica of a traditional haveli, albeit one with modern amenities (like Udaipur's only rooftop pool), standardized room features, and good value for money. There are three room categories—standard, deluxe, and suite—all with comfortable *jarokhas* (window seats) from which to enjoy the lake or garden view—ask for a room on the third floor for the best views. The rooftop terrace is where meals are served—the views at night, when the pool is lit up, are breathtaking, and service overall is generally efficient.

Udai Kothi, Udaipur 313 001. © 294/243-2810 or -2812. Fax 0294/243-0412. www.udaikothi.com. 25 units. Rs 2,000 ($46) standard garden-view double, Rs 2,500 ($57) deluxe double; Rs 3,000 ($68) suite. Rs 500 ($11) extra bed. Taxes extra. MC, V. **Amenities:** 2 restaurants; evening cultural shows; roof terrace; pool; health club; Jacuzzi; garden; travel desk; boating (when possible); bookshop; room service; laundry; doctor-on-call.

Udaivilas   After the deserved success of the Vilas properties in Jaipur, Agra, and Ranthambhore, Oberoi's superdeluxe Udaipur property, opened in 2002, has followed suit, and in the last 2 years has won awards too numerous to list. The palatial property features magnificent grounds (beautifully landscaped gardens as well as a wildlife conservatory where deer and peacock roam) and stunning interiors, including a massive central dome, lit up at night, that wouldn't look out of place on St. Peter's. Intricately crafted pieces and fabrics are artfully combined with Western decor to create the most elegantly dressed rooms and luxurious bathrooms in Udaipur. That said, there are a few conceptual flaws—primarily, the lack of access you have to the lake, despite the fact that the property is built on its shores. Almost none of the public spaces have views—you can see the lake from the spa pool, but the deck has been designed in such a way that all the lounge chairs face away from the lake waters. It seems a pity to travel all this way only to find yourself in a resort and room that could be anywhere (though as long as the lake remains dry, this is hardly an issue). Another seemingly good idea that ends up being impractical is the infinity pool that stretches the length of the superior deluxe wing—should you plunge straight in, you will disturb your neighbor's privacy and likewise, which kind of ruins the exclusivity of an otherwise absolutely gorgeous room. However, service standards at the Udaivilas are world-class, with well-trained staff ready to meet your every need. Dining is also superb, with executive chef Jean-François Pelaez there to ensure that the kitchen produces the most outstanding Western-Asian fusion meals—and the Indian food is hands-down the best in Udaipur.

Haridasji Ki Magri, Udaipur 313 001. ⓒ **0294/243-3300.** Oberoi hotels: ⓒ 800-562-3764. Fax 0294/243-3200. www. oberoihotels.com. 87 units. $530 deluxe double (no lake views or personal pool), $630 superior deluxe double with semi-private pool, some with lake-view; $2,500–$3,000 suite. AE, DC, MC, V. **Amenities:** 2 restaurants; lounge/bar; 9 pools (5 private); Banyan Spa (including Ayurvedic treatments); boating (when possible); adjacent wildlife conservatory; travel desk; limousine transfer from airport on request; Wi-Fi enabled; boutique; salon; 24-hr. room service; babysitting; laundry; doctor-on-call; butler service; CD/DVD library. In room: A/C, DVD/CD, TV, Internet connections, minibar, tea- and coffee-making facilities, fresh fruit and newspaper daily, hair dryer, iron on request, electronic safe, scale, magnifying shaving mirror.

AROUND UDAIPUR

Devi Garh ✸✸✸ "Went to see the City Palace this morning and couldn't wait to return to our very own," one guest remarked, and really, it *is* hard to tear yourself away from what is arguably the best hotel on the subcontinent. Devi Garh is more than beautiful, it is *inspiring*, particularly if you're a modern-design enthusiast. And with a staff-to-guest ratio of 4 to 1, all looking as if they've stepped out of an Armani ad for India, the service levels are unbeatable: extensive, personal, discreet, and intelligent. But what makes this an unparalleled masterpiece is the marriage of the towering exterior of an original 18th-century Rajput palace (which remains totally unchanged) with a reinvented minimalist interior. Utilizing the best young designers in India (which put a lie to the perception that design here reached its apotheosis with the Mughals), and financed by the latter-day patron Lekha Poddar, it took 15 years to transform the higgledy-piggledy rooms spread over 14 floors into 23 huge suites, with another 18 added in 2005. Within the almost stark, soothing space of each suite, there's none of the familiar Rajasthani accents, yet it remains uniquely Indian: Almost everything, from the bed and sofa bases to ashtrays and vases, is carved out of white marble, offset with flashes of color—flower motifs in semi-precious stones, bold swaths of gold inlay, or asymmetrical relief sculpture—designs that reinterpret India's centuries-old craftsmanship in dazzlingly modern ways. If that's not enough, the views of the majestic Aravalli Hills and tiny Delwara village, where life continues as it has for centuries, are perfectly framed by large sheets of squared-off glass—a modern element that is successfully hidden when viewing the pretty *jarokha* windows from the exterior. Below lies a heated green marble pool, tennis court, and spa (with great Ayurvedic treatments on offer), as well as the dining areas where more superb views (and wonderful cuisine) await. The hotel will arrange camel or horse safaris, jeep treks, or chauffeured tours: Udaipur, Eklingji, Nagda, Nathdwara, Kumbhalgarh Fort, and Ranakpur are all easily explored from here. Make every effort to include a night at this acclaimed *(Condé Nast Traveler, Vogue, Wallpaper)* hotel, though it will no doubt have you wishing you'd planned nothing other than to stay here for the duration of your trip.

26km (16 miles) or 45 min. from Udaipur. Devi Garh, Delwara Village, near Udaipur 313 001. ✆ **02953/28-9211,** Delhi 011/2335-4554, or 011/2375-5540. www.deviresorts.com. devigarh@deviresorts.com. 49 units. Apr 1–Sept 30/rest of the year $200/$350 garden suite, $350/$500 palace suite, $450/$700 Aravalli suite, $650/$900 Devi Garh suite. Oct 1–Mar: $150 tent. AE, DC, MC, V. **Amenities:** Restaurant; bar; pool; tennis court; health club/gym; spa; horse/camel riding; cycling; kite flying; pool table; table tennis; croquet; travel desk; salon; 24-hr. room service; babysitting; doctor-on-call; astrologer; library. *In room:* A/C, TV, DVD/CD, dataport, minibar.

TRAVELING BETWEEN UDAIPUR & JAIPUR/JODHPUR

Deogarh Mahal 🀫🀫   This is one of the best and most authentic heritage hotels in Rajasthan, though sadly a big hike in rates has meant it's not as good value as, say, Rawla Narlai. Then again, it is a far grander affair, comprising an ornate 17th-century fort-palace with domed turrets and balconies that tower over the little village below. Immaculately restored suites and deluxe rooms feature original frescoes and antiques. The palace is personally managed by the charming Thakur of Deogarh, who (like Kesri Singh in the Shekhawati region) makes you feel like a long-lost aristocrat. He is supported by a small, discreet professional staff (tipping, for instance, is only done via a central tipping box, reducing the irritating pressure that is part and parcel of traveling in India). Rooms vary considerably (you are welcome to look around when you arrive, and choose one), but all are beautifully furnished, with little done to change the authenticity of the architecture (right down to the slightly erratic plumbing). Book one of the six gorgeous suites (no. 235 is a particularly beautiful deluxe suite for 128€/$161; no. 211, the aptly named Royal Suite, goes for 220€/$273) and pretend that all you survey from your private balcony is yours. There's also a gorgeous pool, and the village is worth exploring. The traditional Rajasthani cuisine is delicious. Note that Deogarh is a good place to stop after you've visited the Ranakpur Temples and Kumbhalgarh Fort. From here you can proceed to Jodhpur (170km/105 miles away) or to Jaipur (280km/174 miles away).

Deogarh Madaria, District Rajsamand, Rajasthan 313 331. ✆ **02904/25-2777.** Fax 02904/25-2555. www.deogarh.com. info@deograhmahal.com. 50 units. 98€ ($123) deluxe double; 128€ ($161) deluxe suite, 220€ ($273) royal suite. Rates include breakfast. AE, DC, MC, V. **Amenities:** Restaurant; bar; coffee shop; pool; kids' pool; gym; Jacuzzi; in-house movies; lounge; library; Internet services; snooker; table tennis; travel desk; car hire; souvenir shop; Ayurvedic massage; babysitting; doctor-on-call. *In room:* A/C, TV, minibar, hair dryer, safe. Tea- and coffee-making facilities in suites.

Fort Chanwa 🀫   This red-sandstone fortress is an oasis of relative luxury at the end of a potholed road to Luni. Somehow this makes it feel a great deal more remotely situated than Rohet Garh, but logistically it's in fact a great deal closer to Jodhpur. Belonging to the present Jodhpur Maharaja's uncle, the 200-year-old property was renovated in 1998, and not always that sensitively. However, interiors (done by the Maharani) are very tasteful, and there's a pool, an Ayurvedic massage center, and a very sharp staff to oversee all your needs. The Maharaja Suite (no. 9)—a deluxe twin room, with a deep double bed–size alcove, is particularly lovely; a family or group should book nos. 12 and 14. Just a 40-minute drive from Jodhpur, this rural retreat will suit travelers who want to see Jodhpur's top attractions but who prefer to spend the night away from the city's chaos and pollution. Transfers from Jodhpur are easily arranged.

Luni village, 35km (22 miles) from Jodhpur. Bookings: 1 PWD Rd., Jodhpur 342 001. (℘ **0291/243-2460** or direct 02931/284-216. www.fortchanwa.com. 47 units. Rs 3,000–Rs 4,000 ($68–$91) double. AE, DC, MC, V. **Amenities:** Restaurant; evening entertainment; pool; Jacuzzi; steam and sauna; croquet; horse rides; travel desk; village safaris; excursions to Jodhpur; gift shop; room service; massage; babysitting; laundry. *In room:* A/C, hair dryer on request.

Rawla Narlai 🌟🌟 *Value*   A 17th-century hunting retreat of the Maharajah of Jodhpur, located in the heart of the arid Aravalli Hills halfway between Udaipur and Jodhpur, the lovely Rawla Narlai was only opened to paying guests in 1995 (and soon after was featured in numerous glossy magazines charmed by its pretty decor and low prices). The hotel was sensitively renovated to ensure that authenticity wasn't lost in the process of attaching bathrooms and enlarging the spaces. Rooms all differ but on the whole are really charming (we loved nos. 18 and 19), featuring touches like sepia photographs of the maharaja's ancestors, cusped window frames, frescoed walls, stained-glass windows, pretty alcoves, colored ceiling baubles, *jarokhas,* and views of the Shiva temple that rises from the rock "mountain" that can be seen for miles from the surrounding countryside. Well-lit deluxe tents with Western-style toilets are also a pleasant option and offer great value. Service is attentive, with plenty of warm touches (not least the hot-water bottle slipped between the sheets in winter). If you're on your way to Jodhpur, this makes an ideal and well-priced overnight stop after you visit the Jain temples of Ranakpur (less than an hour away) and/or Kumbhalgarh Fort. It's also a destination in its own right, one completely free of touts, shops, and pushers (though it has no pool). Enjoy a sunrise walk up to the Ganesh Rock or visits to local temples or the *baoli* (step well); or go horse riding on beautiful Marwari horses. Follow these activities with cocktails in the idyllic garden and a delectable rooftop dinner.

140km (86 miles) from Udaipur (via Ranakpur 125km/77 miles); 160km (100 miles) from Jodhpur. Reservations through Ajit Bhawan (see "Where to Stay & Dine" under "Jodhpur" below for central Delhi details). Near Circuit House, Jodhpur 342 006. (℘ **0291/251-0410,** 0291/251-1410, or 0291/251-0610. Fax 0291/251-0674. reservations@ajitbhawan.com. 25 units. Rs 3,800–Rs 4,500 ($86–$102), includes breakfast. AE, MC, V. **Amenities:** Restaurant; horse/camel safaris; rock climbing; excursions; laundry; doctor-on-call.

Rohet Garh 🌟 *Value*   It's not as pretty as Rawla Narlai, but the 300-year-old Rohet Garh is very professionally run, thanks to the fact that the aristocratic owner Sidharth Singh is still in residence, not only making guests comfortable but also struggling to help remedy local problems like the drought currently blighting the entire region. More important (for hydrohedonists at least), it has a lovely pool in the central courtyard, from which you can access the dining room, smartly attired with white linen tablecloths and napkins and serving good-quality Rajasthani food. The rural peace is intoxicating—the adjacent village is also not as poor as that at Rawla Narlai, inviting exploration without guilt. Rooms, as is always the case with heritage properties, vary (ask to see what's on offer when you arrive), but all are relatively spacious, featuring the usual frescoes and Rajasthani antiques. Book one of the most recently renovated rooms (nos. 6, 7) for the best bathrooms—however, these currently surround the pool, so they are not that private (for more privacy, ask for no. 15 or 30). A couple of the rooms have direct views into the stables—great for those kids who haven't outgrown the *Black Beauty* phase. Outings include visits to traditional Bishnoi villages and shepherds, with the possibility of witnessing a traditional ceremony.

Rohet Garh, Vill PO Rohet, District Pali, Rajasthan. (℘ **02936/268-231** or reservations in Jodhpur 0291/243-1161. Fax 0291/264-9368. www.rohetgarh.com. 33 units. Rs 3,500–Rs 5,000 ($80–$114). Extra bed Rs 500 ($11). AE, DC,

Eighteenth-Century Tree Huggers

Traveling on the road to or from Jodhpur, you will no doubt come across black buck, a delicate antelope with spiralling horns, and Khejri, the tough, desert-surviving trees that provide shelter and sustenance for the desert tribes and the black buck. Both animal and tree are sacred to the Bishnoi tribes, so much so that when an 18th-century Jodhpur ruler sent his army out to clear Khejri trees to make way for a new road, the Bishnoi women clung to the trees in protest—363 women died with their arms wrapped around their beloved Khejris before the Jodhpur king intervened. You can still visit the Bishnoi on "village safaris" offered by just about every hotel and guesthouse in town.

MC, V. **Amenities:** Restaurant; picnic lunch; pool; health club; jeep; horse and camel safaris; travel desk; bird-watching cycle trips; currency exchange; room service; laundry; doctor-on-call; cooking classes.

SHOPPING

Udaipur has a number of attractive handicrafts. You're probably best off purchasing them directly from small factories whose touts will beg you to visit, but do beware that the commission system can add significantly to the price, so don't buy the first beautiful thing you see. **Rajasthali** (Chetak Circle; beware similarly named stores elsewhere), the government-run handicraft shop, is a good place to both pick up basic handicrafts and gauge fair prices. **Mangalam** (Sukhadia Circle; ⓒ **0294/256-0259**) is best for textiles, handicrafts, *dhurries,* and a variety of products. The main shopping streets run from the City Palace along Jagdish Temple Street to the clock tower and beyond to Hathi Pol. Good areas are Suraj Pol, Bapu Bazaar, Chetak, and Ashwini markets. Udaipur is considered a good place to purchase miniature paintings (it has its unique style, but if you're looking for a bargain, you're better off purchasing in off-the-beaten-track towns, like Bundi) and *pichhwai* paintings—wall hangings painted on cloth or silk, often featuring scenes from Krishna's life, that originated in Nathdwara; see "Top Excursions," earlier in this chapter. Alternatively, you could pick up some of these at the City Palace Museum shop; their prices are higher but well worth the quality. Other goods worth keeping an eye out for are puppets and wooden folk toys, enamel or Meenakari work, *dhurries* (rugs), tie-dye and block-printed fabrics, embroidered bags and clothing, and silver jewelry. As is always the case, consider carefully before you buy (cheaper is not always better and often means the object is a poor imitation), and try to bargain. Plenty of places will try to sell you paintings, but if you're looking for top quality (or at least want to understand the difference), you'll need to visit the artist **Kamal Sharma** (ⓒ **0294/242-3451** or cell 98290-40851; 15A, New Colony, Kalaji-Goraji). A four-time national award winner; Sharma works on paper, marble, and silk. To view traditional Udaipur (and Gujarati) embroidery, visit **Jagdish Emporium** on City Palace Road. For beautiful beaded bags, head for Chandpole Road, where you will also find a number of jewelry stores.

8 Jodhpur

336km (208 miles) E of Jaipur; 260km (160 miles) NW of Udaipur

Founded in 1459 by Rao Jodhaji, chief of the Rathore Rajputs who ruled over Marwar, "land of death," Jodhpur was to become one of Rajputana's wealthiest cities, capitalizing on its central position on the Delhi–Gujarat trade route and protected by one of the most impenetrable forts in history. Today it is the state's second-largest city, much of it a sprawling, polluted metropolis, but within the old walls—where every building is painted the same light blue hue, earning Jodhpur the nickname "blue city"—you'll find a teeming maze of narrow medieval streets and bazaars, where life appears much as it has for centuries. Towering above is **Mehrangarh (Majestic) Fort,** its impenetrable walls rising like sheer cliffs from the rocky outcrop on which it is built. From its crenelated ramparts you enjoy postcard views of the ancient blue city below and, in the distance, the grand silhouette of **Umaid Bhawan Palace,** residence of the current Maharaja and heritage hotel. Within the fort is a typical Rajput palace that today houses one of the state's best-presented museums, artfully displaying the accumulated accouterments of the royal house of Rathore in the beautifully preserved royal apartments.

The labyrinthine Old City is a more visually exciting experience than Jaipur, but besides exploring these medieval streets and visiting Mehrangarh Fort and Umaid Bhawan Palace, there's not much to hold you here for more than a day or two—most people use Jodhpur as a jumping-off point to Jaisalmer or as an overnight stop before traveling on to Jaipur or Udaipur.

ESSENTIALS

VISITOR INFORMATION The tourist reception center is located in the **RTDC Ghoomar Tourist Bungalow,** on High Court Road (© 0291/254-5083; Mon–Sat 10am–5pm; closed second Sat of the month and Sun). Your own hotel's reception will assist with reservations for sightseeing and day tours (© 0291/254-8010 or -4010). The tourist **help line** number is © 1364 (Mon–Sat 9am–5pm). Convenient places to withdraw cash against your ATM card are the HDFC or ICICI ATM at Ratanada Chauraha, **UTI Bank** (near Kwality Inn, Chandra Hotel), or **Bank of Baroda** (Sojati Gate).

GETTING THERE Traveling by car from Udaipur takes approximately 5½ hours with no stops; the journey from Jaipur takes about 6½ to 7 hours. However, Jodhpur is very well connected by rail and air. As always, try to book flights with the more professional **Jet Airways** (© 0291/510-3333 or -2222 city office, 0291/251-5551 or -5552 airport), though you'll have to use **Indian Airlines** (© 0291/251-0757 or -0758 city office, 0291/251-2617 airport) if you want to fly to Udaipur. Jodhpur's **airport** (© 0291/251-2934) lies 4km (2½ miles) south of the city. Expect to pay about Rs 200 ($4.55) for a taxi into town, Rs 40 to Rs 50 (90¢–$1.15) for a rickshaw. Jodhpur's main **train station** (© 131 or 132) is on Station Road, just south of the Old City walls. The Mandor Express train links the city to Delhi in 12½ hours; the Jaipur Intercity Express gets you here from Jaipur in 5 hours. At press time, train services to/from Udaipur were suspended until the construction of the new railway line is completed sometime in 2006.

GETTING AROUND Rickshaws are the most useful way to get around the Old City (10- to 15-min. ride costs Rs 30–Rs 40/70¢–90¢), but you'll need to hire a taxi if you plan to visit the outlying attractions. To hire a car and driver for the day (or longer—for instance, for a round-trip to Jaisalmer or to Udaipur), contact **Rajasthan Tours** (© **0291/251-2428** or -2932; rajtoursjdh@sancharnet.com). **K. K. Holidays and Vacations** (33-B/34-A, opposite Custom House, Airport Rd.; © **0291/264-5767;** karnikripajodhpur@tantramail.com) is reliable, and arranges excursions, hotels, and transport at prevailing rates (at press time Rs 1,200/$28 for 8 hr./80km within Jodhpur).

FESTIVALS   Diwali, the Hindu New Year celebration that takes place in October/November, is celebrated all over India, but the "Festival of Lights" is particularly exciting when viewed from the lawns of Umaid Bhawan Palace. At the grand bash held by Maharaja Gaj Singh II, you can experience firsthand the deep reverence with which the former ruler of Jodhpur and Marwar is still treated—everyone wants to kiss the hem and touch the hand of their beloved father figure. The 2-day **Marwar Festival,** held during the full moon in October, is also worth attending, particularly to see the fire dance held on the Osian dunes. Celebrations include classical folk music concerts, puppet shows, camel polo, and even turban-tying contests. The end of the festivities is heralded with the **fire dance,** when men jump over burning wood to the rhythm of drums and chants. Sometimes dancers perform on top of red-hot coals, moving in an almost trancelike state to percussion beats.

WHAT TO SEE & DO

Having visited the fort and Umaid Bhawan Palace, there's no reason to overextend yourself, but some may opt to include a trip to **Mandore,** which lies 9km (6 miles) north of the Old City. The previous capital of Marwar (not to be confused with Mewar, the princely state of Udaipur), Mandore has as its principal attractions today gardens (in dire need of attention) in which lie the templelike cenotaphs built to honor the Rathore rulers before final rites were moved to Jaswant Thada (see Mehrangarh Fort & Museum, below). The largest and grandest of the red-sandstone structures was also the last to be built here; it commemorates the life of Maharaja Dhiraj Ajit Singh, who died in 1763. Beyond, in a totally separate section (pious to the end), is a group of smaller cenotaphs, built to commemorate the female counterparts. Opposite the weird but ultimately missable museum is the **Hall of Heroes,** a collection of 18th-century deities and Rajput heroes carved out of a rock wall. If you haven't tired of temples by now, you can move on to visit the Hindu and Jain temples at **Osian,** 65km (40 miles) north of Jodhpur. You first come across the **Vishnu** and **Harihara temples,** which were built between the 8th and 9th centuries, but more impressive (or at least still alive with worship) are **Sacchiya Mata** (12th c.) and **Mahavira Jain temples** (8th and 10th c.). See Ranakpur Temples, earlier in this chapter, for rules on entering a Jain temple. **Village safaris,** in which you are taken into the arid surrounds to get a taste of rural life, sample the food, and learn about traditional remedies and crafts, are also offered by a number of agents in Jodhpur—best to arrange this through the RTDC at the tourist office (see "Visitor Information," above) or Cosy Guest House (see "Where to Stay & Dine," below).

Mehrangarh Fort & Museum ���   "The work of angels, fairies and giants . . . he who walks through it loses sense of being among buildings; it as though he walked through mountain gorges . . ." wrote Rudyard Kipling in 1899. Little has changed since then, and for many this looming 15th-century edifice to Rajput valor is still Rajasthan's most impressive fort, with walls that soar like sheer cliffs 120m (400 ft.) high, literally dwarfing the city at its base, and a proud history of never having fallen to its many invaders. Before you start exploring the fort, get an audioguide (free with entry fee for foreigners; deposit of Rs 2,000/$46; passport or driver's license required). This is probably the best audioguide you will get at a tourist site in India, with sound effects and commentaries from former rulers of Jodhpur recorded on an MP3 player in seven languages. It also contains additional information on subjects like the caste system, the maharajas, miniature paintings, and more. If you prefer a more interactive tour, hire a local guide (Rs 100/$2.30) from your hotel or at the fort entrance, most of whom of course consider the audioguide useless. There is an elevator (Rs 15/35¢), but choose to walk past cannon-pockmarked and *sati*-daubed **Loha Gate** (the Maharajas' wives would traditionally immortalize their lives by leaving handprints on the fort walls before tossing themselves on the flames to join their deceased husbands). Once at the top, you enjoy not only the most spectacular view, but you enter one of India's finest museums: a rich collection of palanquins, royal cradles, miniature paintings, musical instruments, costumes, furniture, and armor. Every room is worth exploring (allow at least 2 hr.), but among the highlights are the gorgeous **royal chamber** where the Maharaja entertained his 30-plus wives (we're not even counting concubines); **Moti Mahal,** featuring the throne on which every Marwar Maharaja has been crowned; and **Phool Mahal,** the "dancing hall" with its pure gold ceiling. A massive **silk and velvet tent,** taken from Emperor Shah Jahan in Delhi, is a vivid illustration of the superlative wealth and decadent pomp with which the Rathore rulers lived. After visiting the courtyard of **Chamunda (Sun Goddess) Temple** (remember to remove your shoes), take the lane that leads to the left to view what is apparently among the rarest collections of cannons in India—again, the view alone is worth it. There is a very good museum shop (look out for the exquisite silk and chiffon fabrics made by Tyeb Khan, awarded the Master Craftsman award in 2001 by the president of India for his outstanding contribution to the nation) and restaurant where you can catch your breath.

On the road that leads to and from the fort, you will notice **Jaswant Thada,** a white marble cenotaph built to commemorate the life of Maharaja Jaswant Singh II, who died in 1899, and where the last rites of the Jodhpur rulers have been held since then. It's pretty enough, but after the magnificence of the fort's museum and forts, it can be a bit of a letdown. If you finish with the fort before sunset, descend to the cobbled streets of **Sadar Market,** where the sights and aromas of India's ancient and narrow streets—packed with cows, people, goats, carts, and chickens, and remarkably untouristed—may leave you wondering whether you've wandered onto the set of a movie about medieval times. If it all gets too claustrophobic, hire a rickshaw in which to sit in relative comfort and watch the passing parade. All in all, this will be one of your most satisfying outings in Rajasthan.

Admission Rs 250 ($5.70), camera and audioguide fee included; Rs 200 ($4.55) video. Lift Rs 15 (35¢). Jaswant Thada Rs 20 (45¢), Rs 25 (55¢) camera, Rs 50 ($1.15) video. Guide Rs 100 ($2.30). Museum daily 9am–5pm.

Umaid Bhawan Palace ⟨⟨⟨ Situated on another raised outcrop, with sprawling grounds creating an almost rural ambience, this splendid palace was built by Maharaja Umaid Singh (the current maharaja's father) as a poverty-relief exercise to aid his drought-stricken subjects. With 347 rooms, including a cinema, it was at the time the largest private residence in the world—a vivid reminder of the decadence the Rajput rulers enjoyed during the British Raj. Designed by Henry Lanchester, a great admirer of Lutyens (the man who designed New Delhi), it was commenced in 1929, took 3,000 laborers 13 years to complete, and remains one of the best examples of the Indo-Saracenic Art Deco style, topped with a massive dome which rises 56m (184 ft.) high, beyond which the buildings are perfectly symmetrical. If you don't choose to

Tips **The Future in the Palm of Your Hand**

Jodhpur is the home of a well-known astrologer and palmist, **Mr. Sharma,** who is in residence at the Mehrangarh Fort's Moti Mahal Chowk from 9am to 5pm daily. He will come if requested to the hotel Umaid Bhawan Palace between 7 and 9pm. To make an appointment, call the fort (© **0291/254-8790,** ext. 39), his cellphone (© **94141-30200**), or his residence (© **0291/2514614** or -1751). Remember to remove your nail polish.

overnight here, you should still visit—if only to sip coffee at The Pillars, from where you enjoy a spellbinding view of the fort in the distance (note that at press time there was some confusion as to whether non-staying guests could frequent The Pillars; to avoid disappointment, best to check beforehand, or act the part and say your keys are at reception). There is also a museum which features photographs of the construction and a model of the building (where you can see that the maharaja quite rightly has kept the best part, with outdoor pool, to himself), as well as items collected by his ancestors.

Entrance to the hotel and restaurants (unless you're overnighting) is Rs 350 ($8), payable at reception, and you can use this against whatever you eat or drink at either of the restaurants. Museum Rs 50 ($1.15). Daily 9am–5pm.

WHERE TO STAY & DINE

Within the Old City are a number of good budget options, including many family "paying guest" accommodations that are listed with the tourist office. If you don't want to take your chances, the following are worth noting. **Haveli Guest House** (© **0291/261-4615;** www.haveliguesthouse.net; bookings@haveliguesthouse.com; Rs 300–Rs 1,000/$6.85–$23) is a very hospitable and well-run establishment (more of an inn than a haveli) with simple en-suite rooms—make sure you book one that has a view of the fort (Rs 800/$18). You also get good fort views from the rooftop restaurant. For a more homey atmosphere, head for **Cosy Guest House** (© **0291/ 261-2066;** cosyguesthouse@yahoo.com; Rs 50–Rs 650/$1.15–$15). A Brahmin family–run 15th-century house with an array of basic, monastic rooms (ask for one with an attached bathroom, or one of the two new air-conditioned rooms) is aimed at the younger, more adventurous traveler. It's in the oldest, most beautiful part of the Blue City, and the views from the rooftop terrace are spectacular (mum cooks pretty good food, too). Because rickshaw drivers are not paid commission, you may struggle to find it: Ask to be dropped off at Novechokiya Road, then follow the signs. The walk is stiff but short—if you're arriving with heavy luggage, ask the owner, Mr. Joshi, to arrange a transfer. A new addition to Jodhpur's heritage scene, **Pal Haveli** is the only original haveli in the Old City, and *the* place to stay if you want to be in the real heart of the bustling (and admittedly noisy) town. Once you walk in, however, you can shut out the world and imagine you're living in a bygone era. Rooms are small with rickety plumbing, but the place makes up for its shortcomings with the ambience of an earlier era and a wonderful terrace view of Mehrangarh Fort and the town—perfect for alfresco dining (© **0291/243-9615** or 309-3328; info@pal-haveli.com; Rs 1,500–Rs 2,000/$35–$46).

If living in the Old City sounds a little rough, head for the outskirts of town (20 min. from the fort) to **Taj Hari Mahal** (© **0291/243-9700;** www.tajhotels.com; from $180), a very smart hotel built in the style of a Marwari palace. Aimed predominantly at the wealthy business market, this will suit those who have simply had enough of the chaos of India and want to be cocooned from it all in a modern hotel with professional service. Guest rooms are huge and elegantly dressed, with state-of-the-art conveniences and tiptop bathrooms. Public spaces are also luxurious and cool. The hotel's very modernity and mass-produced furnishings mean it is somewhat dull, with none of the charm of the palace or haveli hotels, but given the current neglected state of the Umaid Bhawan at press time, this was the only luxury five-star option with service and amenities to match.

Jodhpur is not renowned for its restaurants; you're pretty much limited to dining in hotels. Even if you're not overnighting at Umaid Bhawan, call and ask if renovations have been completed at **The Pillars,** the hotel's informal cafe-restaurant where you sit at the base of a cavernous colonnaded veranda that steps down to the palace lawns—get there before the sun goes down to watch the almost surreal changing hues of the sky over the fort, but don't expect miracles from the kitchen. Widely regarded as the best restaurant in town, with a great nighttime atmosphere (but do make sure they're serving in the garden), **On the Rocks** (next to Ajit Bhawan; ℭ 0291/510-2701 or -7880) is famous for its barbecue dishes—skewers of spicy vegetables, *paneer,* or meat tenderized in a yogurt-based marinade and cooked over an open fire. For a quieter, more leisurely dinner (but slow service) with good Indian food and lovely views, head to the Haveli Guest House's **rooftop restaurant.**

Ajit Bhawan ⟨ᴷⁱᵈˢ⟩
Built at the turn of the 20th century for Maharaj Ajit Singh (younger brother of the Maharaja Umaid Singh), this hotel incorporates crenelated castlelike walls and traditional Hindustani elements, resulting in a weird, rather kitschy mishmash. But it's a hugely popular place, and some prefer its more laid-back, down-home atmosphere (and, at press time, better service) to Umaid's plush palace. It's also significantly cheaper, and has a wonderful outdoor pool and a good restaurant. The kitsch continues inside as you wander through what appears to be a faux Rajasthani "village," with stone cottages leading off the central dining area and pool. Decor is generally very irreverent, which some may find amusing, but a few rooms have taken the kitsch theme a step too far (like no. 26, which has an indoor waterfall cascading over a rock, buck horns sprouting from its light fixtures, and a tiger skin behind the bed). That said, rooms are in mint condition (some bathrooms were being renovated at press time). If you can bag nos. 101 to 104, deluxe rooms each with a little balcony overlooking the pool (the best reason to book here), you'll have a better reason for smiling. Car enthusiasts may dig the fleet of 10 vintage cars on offer (Rs 10,000/$228 for 8 hr. sightseeing)—the oldest Buicks and Fords date back to 1928. Note that the palace was in fact split down the middle after a family feud. The adjacent **Ranbanka Hotel** is a more elegant version of Ajit Bhawan, but it is somehow soulless and a great deal less popular. Rates run between Rs 3,500 and Rs 4,500 ($80–$12) (ℭ **0291/251-2800** through -2803; www.ranbankahotels.com).

Ajit Bhawan, Jodhpur 342 006. ℭ **0291/251-0410** or -0610. Fax 0291/251-0674. www.ajitbhawan.com. 54 units. Rs 4,500 ($102) standard double; Rs 5,000 ($114) luxury double; Rs 5,500 ($125) luxury tent double; Rs 6,000 ($137) luxury suite. Rs 750 ($17) extra bed. All rates include breakfast. AE, DC, MC, V. **Amenities:** Restaurant; pool; health spa; travel desk; village safaris Rs 550 ($13); evening folk dancing; fleet of vintage cars for hire. *In room:* A/C, TV, minibar, hair dryer.

Bal Samand Lake Palace ⟨★★⟩
From the outset you need to know that what is being reviewed here are the Regal Suites in the actual Bal Samand palace, and not the relatively new wing with the standard "garden rooms" that lie somewhere behind the

palace in the huge gardens—if the Regal Suites aren't available, you may as well book into the Ajit Bhawan. A relatively tiny palace carved out of red sandstone, the Bal Samand appears to grow out of the dam-wall terrace that overlooks Bal Samand Lake. Surrounded by water, scrubland, and what once must have been beautifully land-scaped gardens, it's a grand rural oasis second to none, not least because you only share it with a maximum of 16 other guests. Book room no. 1 for the lake views, or the more private room no. 6, which is simply beautiful—a massive double-volume space with fabulous sandstone detailing, lots of lamps for atmospheric lighting, a gorgeous mix of Rajasthani and colonial furniture, a Jacuzzi-size bath, and an atmosphere fit for a king. Room nos. 2 and 3 are quite small by comparison, and room nos. 7, 8, and 9 are on the ground floor—which means they're a little closer to the large, not easily accessible outdoor pool. The biggest drawback is the thin service, which is well-mean-ing but certainly not up to scratch—most of the hotel staff are situated at the "garden room" wing, where the kitchen is, so room-service food (other than breakfast, which is cooked at the palace) will inevitably be cold. Not that it really matters, considering that the food is no reason to book here (avoid the European dishes)—this is such a romantic retreat that food may be the last thing on your mind.

7km (4½ miles) from Jodhpur. Mandore Rd., Jodhpur 342 026. ℂ **0291/257-1991** or 2572321 to -26. Fax 0291/257-240. balsamand_1@sify.com. 35 units. Rs 4,000 ($91) garden double; Rs 7,500 ($171) palace suite, Rs 9,500 ($216) regal suite. 20% discount off season. AE, MC, V. **Amenities:** Restaurant; pool; room service; laundry. *In room:* A/C, TV, minibar, tea- and coffee-making facilities, hair dryer and iron on request.

Devi Bhawan ⟨*Value*⟩ This low-slung sandstone residence is a great surprise—a bun-galow with free-standing cottages set within a lush, tranquil garden, and personally managed by a wonderful husband-and-wife team. The en-suite rooms (ask for an air-conditioned bungalow—no. 10 or suite no. 11, which has a large bathroom with tub) are clean and neat with simple furnishings, and there's not a hint of plastic anywhere. Bathroom fittings could be upgraded, however. The dining area spills onto a deep colonnaded veranda with garden views and tables prettily laid out with fabric table-cloths. Service is very personal, and a number of amenities are offered, including a new pool that should be completed at press time. All in all, this is a very comfortable, relaxing, good-value option, but not one to encourage you to extend your stay in Jodhpur.

Defence Lab. Rd., Ratanada Circle, Jodhpur 342 001. ℂ **0291/251-2215**, or -1067. devibhawan@sify.com. www.devibhawan.com. 13 units. Rs 800 ($18) garden double, Rs 950 ($22) bungalow double; Rs 1,200 ($28) suite. MC, V. **Amenities:** Restaurant; travel desk; jeep/horse-safaris; Internet access; laundry; doctor-on-call. *In room:* A/C (most rooms), TV.

Ratan Vilas ⟨⟨*Value*⟩⟩ Built in 1920 by current owner Brij Raj Singh's grandfather, this haveli has been painstakingly restored, preserving its traditional character while adding modern comforts—which makes it the best option by far in this price category (a great deal better than places like Karni Bhawan, which charges twice this, and supe-rior to Devi Bhawan, reviewed above.) It offers better value than anything you'll find inside the Old City. Air-conditioned rooms are immaculate and simple, tastefully styled with antique furniture (which Brij Raj collects) and traditional hand-block-printed curtains and bed sheets (book deluxe room no. 101, 102, or 104, or standard room no 3); the breezy, plant-filled central courtyard has a lovely swing where you can spend hours with a book. It's a homey place with old photographs and souvenirs adorning the walls—no five-star amenities, of course, but the food has home-cooked freshness, service is prompt and personalized, and you can even ask to step into the kitchen for a demonstration of traditional Rajasthani cooking. The only features the haveli lacks are a pool and a lush outdoor garden. Sun-worshippers can take advantage of the sun-deck chairs on the terrace and veranda, and Brij Raj (a keen polo player) maintains a stable of well-bred Marwari horses for residents to ride.

Ratan Vilas, Loco Shed Rd., Ratanada, Jodhpur 342 001. (©) **0291/261-4418.** Fax 0291/261-3011. ratanvilas_jod@ rediffmail.com or info@ratanvilas.com. 15 units. Rs 950–Rs 1,650 ($22–$38) double. Taxes extra. AE, MC, V. **Amenities:** Dining hall; bar; horse riding; jeep safari. *In room:* A/C, TV.

Umaid Bhawan Palace ⚅ Built on a rocky outcrop in the southeastern part of the city, with lovely views of the fort, this is not only one of Jodhpur's top attractions, but for years was regularly cited as one of the top heritage hotels in India. Its future has hung in the balance since 2003, with various hotel chains (including Aman) showing interest and then retreating—hardly surprising, perhaps, given the size of the palace alone. Thankfully, it was taken over by the Taj Group of Hotels in 2005, and after 2 years of neglect the hotel was undergoing serious renovations, with only a tiny fraction of the rooms open. Phase I of these renovations (30 rooms and a new outdoor pool) is expected to be completed by early 2006, but do call and check on the status of renovations before deciding whether to stay here. Be sure to ask for something with doors opening onto verandas that run the length of the palace. Many of the standard category do (or did pre-Taj); there are also units with private balconies featuring good views. Dining takes place in the grand **Marwar Hall** (often only open for breakfast), elegant **Risala** (again, expected to open at the end of 2005), or **The Pillars**—the latter your best bet by far, with spectacular views, especially from its extension, the plaza section. After dinner, catch the latest Bollywood blockbuster at the in-house cinema (on request).

Umaid Bhawan, Jodhpur. (©) **0291/251-0101.** Fax 0291/251-0100. 30 units. $275 deluxe double; $800 Regal Suite. $25 extra bed. AE, DC, MC, V. **Amenities:** 3 restaurants; lounge/reading room; indoor pool; tennis; squash; gym; billiards room; cinema; travel desk; palmist/astrologer on request. *In room:* A/C, TV, minibar.

SHOPPING

Jodhpur is famous for its antiques dealers, most lining the road that runs between Ajit Bhawan and Umaid Bhawan. These can be prohibitively pricey, however, particularly when you factor in freight prices. Jodhpur is also good for tie-dye fabrics. The best bazaars are around Sojati Gate, Tripolia, Khanda Falsa, and Lakhara—the latter specializes in colorful lac bangles, which make great gifts. If you're looking for more serious jewelry, head for Station Road. Traditional Jodhpur coats and riding breeches are now only made to order; ask your hotel to recommend a tailor.

9 Jaisalmer

285km (177 miles) W of Jodhpur; 333km (206 miles) SW of Bikaner

Jaisalmer was founded by Rao Jaisal in 1156, making it the oldest "living" fortified city in Rajasthan. For many, a visit here is the start of an enduring romance. Located in the heart of the Thar Desert on the far western border of India (55km/34 miles from Pakistan), it was strategically positioned on one of the central Asian trade routes, and fortunes were made by the Rajputs and Jain merchants who levied enormous taxes on caravans laden with silks and spices, particularly during the 14th and 16th centuries. In the 18th century, some merchants, wanting to expand their homes, moved out of the fort to settle on the plateau below. Much as in the Shekhawati region, the wealth generated by their taxes was used to decorate the havelis of these wealthy Jain businessmen. Where frescoes satisfied the Shekhawats, here power was expressed by the construction of mansions whose soft sandstone facades were embellished with intricate, almost lacelike carvings. These oft-photographed sandstone mansions are indeed breathtakingly beautiful, but it is Sonar Killa, literally "Golden Fort," that makes it worth traveling this far west. It may not be as impressive as Jodhpur's Mehrangarh Fort, but its charm lies in the fact that this is the world's only inhabited medieval fort, its families living in homes they have colonized for more than 800 years. Built entirely from yellow sandstone, the fort rises like a giant sandcastle from its desert surrounds, with great views from the tiny guesthouses that lie within its ramparts. Within you will find a place with no traffic, minimal pollution (watch out for the cow dung), and an awesome sense of timelessness. It takes no more than a few hours to tour the fort, including stops to visit the Jain and Hindu temples. And if you want to ride a camel into the sunset, Jaisalmer is probably the place to do it. So plan to spend 2 or more nights, not least because it takes so long to get here.

ESSENTIALS

VISITOR INFORMATION You'll find the **RTDC tourist office** near Gadi Sagar Pol (© 02922/25-2406; Mon–Sat 10am–6pm; closed second Sat of every month and Sun).

GETTING THERE At press time, there were no flights to Jaisalmer, and the nearest airport is at Jodhpur (a 5½-hr. drive, about 2 hr. longer in a bus—not recommended). *Tip:* The best place to stop for lunch or a snack on this route is **Manvar Desert Resort** (near Shergarh; © 02928/266-137), which serves a mean chicken *pakora*. It takes 6 to 7 hours to get from Bikaner to Jaisalmer by road. The train journey from Jodhpur takes 5½ hours (on the overnight Jodhpur–Jaisalmer Express), arriving at the station 2km (1¼ miles) east of town. Avoid the touts soliciting riders by asking your hotel to arrange a transfer. From Delhi, take the Delhi–Jaisalmer Express from Delhi's Sarai Rohilla Station; it departs Delhi at 5:25pm, and arrives in Jaisalmer at 1:30pm the next day.

GETTING AROUND Both inside and outside the fort, the town is small enough to explore on foot; for journeys farther afield you will need to hire an auto-rickshaw (at the station or Gadsisar Tank) or taxi (Sam Dunes). For the latter, you'll probably take an all-inclusive trip with your hotel, almost all of which offer safaris of various duration; or contact Harish Bhai at **K.K. Travels** (© 02992/253-087; kktravels_2000@yahoo.com). You'll also find taxis around Suraj Pol or within the fort.

FESTIVALS The **Desert Festival** held at the end of January or in February (incidentally, the best time of the year to visit Jaisalmer) is the highlight of the year, when dance shows, turban-tying competitions, and camel races are held below the fort, cheered on by colorful crowds who are as much a part of the spectacle as the entertainment. While its relative inaccessibility keeps tourist numbers down, during the festival the town is packed.

WHAT TO SEE & DO

Jaisalmer's main attraction is its yellow sandstone **fort,** whose 9m (29-ft.) walls grow in a roughly triangular shape, springing from Trikuta (Triangular) Hill, on which it is built, and buttressed by 99 bastions. Within you will find a number of elaborately carved havelis overlooking the narrow streets, but the best examples of Jaisalmer's unique **havelis** are situated in the town below. End the evening by taking a trip out to Sam Dunes to watch the **setting desert sun** from the back of a camel. If you're more sedentary, head for **Mirage,** the rooftop terrace at the Narayan Niwas Palace, for the best view of the Golden Fort; as the sky darkens, the fort starts to glow.

Other attractions are **Gadsisar Tank,** excavated by the Maharaja Gadsi Singh in 1367, which has a few temples and a *chhattri* (cenotaph) overlooking it but is principally worth visiting to access the nearby **Folklore Museum.** The private museum contains some interesting exhibits, particularly the handcrafted items (look for the mobile temple, and the depiction of the tragic love story of Princess Moomal and King Mahendra). Exhibits are not well labeled, however; if the proprietor, Mr. Sharma, is not on hand, a guide could prove useful here. Entrance (not always charged) is Rs 10 (25¢), or donations are welcome; hours are daily 8am to noon and 3 to 6pm. A shop at the end of the museum sells reasonably priced postcards (and overpriced books).

The best way to visit Jaisalmer's desert surrounds is on a **camel safari** (see below). Many include the following places of interest. **Amar Sagar** is a small settlement with a palace and a restored Jain temple built around the shores of a lake that lies 5km (3 miles) northwest of Jaisalmer. **Barra Bagh,** which lies 6km (3¾ miles) north of town, is a mini-oasis where you can view a collection of cenotaphs to Jaisalmer's Rajput rulers. Another 10km (6¼ miles) north lies **Lodurva,** once the capital of the Bhatti Rajputs before Jaisalmer was built. The main attractions here are more restored Jain temples, with the usual fine carvings. The entrance to **Thar Desert National Park** lies about an hour (45km/28 miles) from Jaisalmer, near Khuri. Wildlife you are likely to encounter include deer, desert fox, black buck, and the rare long-necked bird known as the Great Indian Bustard.

EXPLORING THE GOLDEN FORT

Some one thousand people still live in the tiny village inside **Sonar Killa,** or Golden Fort, which has twisting lanes so narrow they can be blocked by a single cow (be warned that these animals *know* that they have the right of way, so step aside). Exploring the fort is easily done in a morning—you access the fort through Gopa Chowk, ascending the battle-scarred ramparts to enter the main courtyard, overlooked by seven-story **Raja Mahal,** or Maharaja's Palace. Take a quick look around Raja Mahal (it's not one of the state's most impressive palaces), pausing in Juna Mahal. This is the palace's oldest part, dating back to the early 16th century, with additions and embellishments taking place over the next 200 years. The palace is open from 8am to 1pm and 3 to 5pm, and entry is Rs 50 ($1.15). Stop for a cup of *chai* on the rooftop of Hotel Paradise for sublime views, or head straight for the beautiful **Jain temples,** which lie west. The best among these (Rishabnath and Sambhavnath) are open only to non-Jains between 7am and noon. Entry is Rs 10 (25¢) and you will have to pay Rs 50 ($1.15) to take a camera in. No leather is allowed within the temple, and menstruating women are restricted from entering. Constructed between the 14th and 16th centuries, these temples are typical of Jain craftsmanship, with every wall and pillar as well as the ceiling covered with the most intricate relief carvings, and large statues representing the Jain *tirthankaras,* or "Enlightened Ones"—note that you cannot enter the caged sanctuaries in which these sculptures sit, or touch or photograph them. A small library has a collection of rare manuscripts, books, and miniature paintings. Take a breather at **Toap Khana (Place of Cannon)** for the views, then head north, turning right at some stage to find **Laxminath Temple** (if you're lost, ask for directions). Although the Jain temples are worth a visit to see the intricacy of the carvings, it is the Hindu temple that pulsates with energy, particularly if you get here when worshippers chant their *bhajans,* devotional songs (about 10:30am and at several other times during the day; check with your hotel). From here it's a short walk back to the main courtyard.

THE JAISALMER HAVELIS

Haveli refers to a traditional, ornate Rajasthani "mansion," with one or more internal courtyards. Steps lead up to an ornate door through which you enter a central courtyard, around which the family apartments are arranged. The facades of the Jaisalmer havelis, built as elsewhere by the town's wealthy merchants, are unsurpassed for the delicacy of their relief carvings, filigreed windows, and lacelike screens and *jarokhas* (small projecting balconies). A testament to the softness of the sandstone but even more to the skill of the *silavats,* Jaisalmer's community of stonemasons, these beautiful facades, some of which date back more than 300 years, have been perfectly preserved, thanks largely to the hot, dry climate. You will find them dotted all over town, but the most impressive are Patwon ki Haveli, Salim Singh ki Haveli, and Nathmalji ki Haveli. **Patwon ki Haveli** actually comprises five ornate houses built by the wealthy Patwon for his five sons between 1800 and 1860. The houses are connected from within (though some are privately owned and not open to the public) and have flat-topped roofs. Inside one of the houses is the Basant Art Emporium, where you can pick up truly exquisite handicrafts—but certainly not at bargain prices—collected by the owner from the desert tribes. The Patwon ki Haveli is open daily between 10am and 5pm; admission is Rs 10 (25¢). South of this, near the fort entrance, is **Salim Singh ki Haveli,** built by a particularly mean-spirited and greedy prime minister who extorted the hell out of the Rajput's kings' subjects, and even squeezed the royal family by providing huge loans and then charging exorbitant interest rates. It was apparently once two stories higher, but legend has it that the Rajput king blew away the top floors in a fit of pique, and Salim Singh was later stabbed to death. It's not necessary that you enter it, and it's not always open (though times advertised are 8am–6pm, up to 7pm in summer, with admission of Rs 15/35¢). You can't enter **Nathmalji ki Haveli,** but it's still worth swinging by to play "spot the difference" with the beautiful facade. The right and left wings look identical at first glance, but they were separately carved by two brothers—the numerous tiny differences can take hours to discover (this is where a guide comes in handy!). It's on the road to Malka Pol (just ask for directions). Note that many of the havelis now house overpriced handicraft shops. If you want to buy something, you'll have to bargain hard to get the prices down.

CAMEL SAFARI

Spending some time in the desert on camelback is touted as one of Jaisalmer's must-do activities, and although you can spend a night or even two "camping" out in the desert (some outfitters have semi-permanent camps, with en-suite tents), trekking to sites of interest during the day, most people choose to spend only a few hours in the desert, usually watching the sun set from **Sam Dunes.** Keep in mind that the popularity of these short trips means you will more than likely be surrounded by noisy travelers in areas that are looking increasingly degraded—with discarded bottles and cigarette packets, and kids cajoling you to buy warm colas and make "donations." If you can cope with staying "on board" a camel train for 2 to 3 hours every morning and afternoon, the best experience is to go on a trek that stops at various desert villages and temples, and lets you enjoy meals around bonfires under the stars and sleep in a temporary but comfortable camp—you will need to pack warm sleepwear for this, and you're pretty much at the mercy of fate when it comes to the group you land up with. It's not always a guarantee, but the pricier the safari, the better your chances. If this doesn't sound like too much of a commitment, and the idea of a communally enjoyed sunset doesn't ruin the romance for you, you can either take a camel ride at sunset from Sam Dunes, about an hour from town by car, or from Khuhri, which lies almost 2 hours away by car. The latter is obviously less popular, so it's not as busy, but it is no longer the unspoiled experience it was a decade ago. Almost every hotel and innumerable agents offer camel trips in various locations (you can opt for one just outside of town, where there are no dunes, but lovely fort views), or you can drive out yourself and negotiate directly with one of the camel drivers who line the road with camels—the state of the saddle is a good indication of which one to choose. Personally, we found the entire experience overrated, but then we like our luxuries, of which solitude is highly rated, and never more so than in India.

Should you wish to saddle up, the most reliable camel safari agent is **Royal Desert Safaris** (Nachana Haveli; ✆ 02992/252-538; rsafari@sancharnet.in). Expect an all-inclusive day trip to cost Rs 1,600 ($37) per head for a group of four or fewer people.

WHERE TO STAY

Jaisalmer offers two general choices: Stay inside the fort, or stay in the town that sprawls at its base. The ecologically sensitive make a strong argument for the latter: The increase in water usage, mostly due to tourist traffic, which relies on medieval drainage systems, has started to literally pulp the ancient sandstone fort, and clearly the best way to preserve it is to stay in town, which is also where the most luxurious accommodations are. But this means you'll miss out on the daily rituals of the people who live inside the fort's ramparts, and even if tourism is for most now the major source of income, it's still in many ways a very different and authentic experience. Note, however, that if you choose to stay inside the fort, no vehicles are allowed, so you may have to lug your luggage some way, lodgings can be claustrophobic, noise can be a problem, and in the midday heat you'll probably long for a pool. A surprising number of options are found within the fort, but none comes near the standard of **Killa Bhawan** (reviewed below). If you're watching your rupees, others worth mentioning are the artfully renovated **Simla** (✆ 02992/253-061; Rs 300–Rs 850/$6.85–$20)—the sandstone surfaces of every room and bathroom have been polished to reveal its gleaming, almost marblelike quality to good effect—and the popular **Hotel Paradise** (✆ 02992/252-674; hotel paradisejsm2001@yahoo.com; Rs 350–Rs 1,500/$8–$35). Aimed at budget travelers, Paradise offers very basic, cell-like rooms, but because it's situated right on the fort ramparts, it has awesome desert views (make sure you book a room with one); it also has a great rooftop terrace that draws a convivial crowd. Another well-known option is **Suraj**, in a beautiful haveli close to the Jain temples; ask for the front room (✆ 02992/251-623; hotelsurajjaisalmer@hotmail.com; Rs 450–Rs 1,200/$10–$28). **Hotel Jaisal Castle** is the first haveli-turned-hotel in the fort; no. 10 is the best room (✆ 02992/252-362; nnpjsm@sancharnet.in). Both have an atmospheric charm, but Suraj has no views and Jaisal has a very tired grandeur. From here on, the options get more basic.

Choices in town are a great deal blander but more comfortable. The well-known but disappointing **Narayan Niwas Palace** has some lovely public spaces, including a rooftop restaurant, Mirage, but a gloomy indoor pool and very second-rate rooms. Just out of town on Sam Road, **Rang Mahal, Gorbandh,** and **Heritage Inn** neighbor one another like three ugly sisters waiting for a miracle to revive their fortunes— all are relatively modern but incredibly dull. The only real alternative to Fort Rajwada (the most luxurious option in town; reviewed below) is **Jawahar Niwas Palace** (✆ 02992/25-2208 or -2288). Dating back to the 19th century, this small but lovely Rajput palace was built by the Maharwal Shalivahansinghji of Jaisalmer as a guesthouse, and four generations later the current head of the royal house of Jaisalmer opened it to paying guests. The original palace has large, elegant rooms (deluxe rooms are the ones to book), as well as some good-value rooms in a new wing with many amenities; it also has a great pool. Rates are Rs 3,440 to Rs 4,375 ($78–$100).

Fort Rajwada ☆☆ *Value*   The dapper and stylish entrepreneur Jitendra Rathore, who built Gorbandh, is the energy behind this latest and most luxurious option in Jaisalmer, and he's a mine of information about the town that he loves. Set on the outskirts, on 2 hectares (5½ acres) of land, the hotel has been built in the style of a palace but has all the comforts of the 21st century (barring the constant power failures that, thanks to generators, affect only the TV). Interiors were designed by the opera stage designer Stephanie Engeln, and the public spaces, particularly the double-volume bar, which could have been designed by Philippe Starck, feel like a grand set. Guest rooms are more standard but very comfortable and have great modern bathrooms; ask for one with a fort view. Cuisine at the Sonal and Roopal restaurants is superb (especially the tandoori dishes, which are fragrant and tender), and though service can be on the slow side, it is exceptionally friendly. The hotel is definitely the best choice in town if Killa Bhawan sounds like roughing it. Fort Rajwada also runs Royal Desert Safaris, where you can either dine or overnight after a camel ride at Sam Dune. However, you'll probably be lumped with a package tour that may or may not be the key to a memorable evening—a case of "if you can't beat them, join them."

Outside the fort. No 1 Hotel Complex, Jodhpur–Barmer Link Rd., Jaisalmer. ℂ **02992/25-3233**, –533, 02992/25-4608, or -4609. Fax 02992/25-3733. sales@fortrajwada.com. 91 units. $150 double; $250–$325 suite. $40 extra bed. AE, DC, MC, V. **Amenities:** 2 restaurants; bar; pool; health club; billiards room; travel desk; salon; 24-hr. room service; Ayurvedic massage; laundry; doctor-on-call. *In room:* A/C, TV, tea- and coffee-making facilities, hair dryer, safe.

Killa Bhawan ☆   This intimate and well-run little guesthouse is the most luxurious and stylish option in the fort. It really is a delightful choice given that it's been hewn out of a dwelling that's been around for 700-odd years. Only the lack of amenities, and the fact that most rooms share a communal shower and toilet, stop this lovely guesthouse, created by Swiss-Italian Luca Borella, from getting two stars. And bear in mind that the shared shower room is large and luxurious (and cleaned between showers), unlike the usual communal cupboard standard elsewhere. All rooms are beautifully furnished with lovely fabrics (and such thoughtful touches as gowns for guests to don before showering). The rooftop, which has stunning views, is comfortably furnished with mattresses and colorful cushions. Manager Manu and his brother Bharat are always on hand to arrange complimentary tea or coffee or to assist with anything from travel arrangements to dining choices.

Inside the fort. No. 445. ℂ **02992/25-1204** or 0299/25-0232. Fax 02992/25-4518. kbhawan@yahoo.com. www. killabhawan.com. 7 units. Rs 2,000 ($46) double with shared shower, Rs 2,700 ($62) double with attached bathroom and A/C. Rates include breakfast. MC, V. **Amenities:** Tea and coffee served all day; laundry.

WHERE TO DINE

If you prefer to eat within the Fort, **8 July Restaurant** and **Little Tibet** were recommended at press time for basics (lassis, milkshakes, sandwiches). It's best to ask around (though make sure the person you ask doesn't have a vested interest in the answer). You can also get a good meal at **Saffron** at the Nachana Haveli Hotel on Govardhan Chowk, or an inexpensive Rajasthani thali at **Bikaner** (off Hanuman Chowk). Alternatively, walk down into town to **Trio,** hands-down the best restaurant there (see below). Trio also caters for and is owned by the same folks who run Royal Desert

Safaris, a permanent tented camp with en-suite tents near Sam Dunes, and Fort Rajwada.

Trio ✦✦✦ RAJASTHANI   This unassuming eatery, with its open walls and thin cotton flaps providing a welcome through-breeze (not to mention views of the town and the Maharaja's palace), is Jaisalmer's top restaurant and one of the best in Rajasthan. It's not just that the food is delicious, but the chef brings a few interesting variations to signature Rajasthani dishes—a welcome relief to one who has exhausted the almost standardized North Indian menu. The *murgh-e-subz*—succulent, boneless strips of chicken stir-fried with shredded vegetables—is one not to miss. Alternatively, try the *ker sangri* (desert beans and capers), unique to a region that traditionally saw little meat. If you have a hearty appetite, the tandoor thali is tops: two chicken preparations (including the ubiquitous but delicious *tikka*), vegetable kebab, mint sauce, and *naan*. Sensitive stomachs can opt for the *kadhi pakora,* fried graham-flour dumplings dunked in yogurt sauce, or *bharwan aloo* (potatoes stuffed with mint paste and simmered in gravy). Wash down all of it with the coldest beers and Cokes in the state.

Near the Amar Sagar Gate, Gandhi Chowk. ✆ 02992/25-2733. Rs 45–Rs 215 ($1–$5). MC, V. Daily 11am–3:30pm and 6–10.30pm.

SHOPPING

Whatever you do, don't miss **Barmer Embroidery House** (near Patwon ki Haveli); it's owned by Abhimanyu Rathi, legendary for his fine eye for antique textiles. Designers have been known to cross the Thar just to plunder his exquisite selection. Jaisalmer is also famous for its wool products, particularly *dhurries* (rugs), as well as its fine hand embroidery, which turns average skirts and tops into real conversation pieces. Because the town is so easily explored, the best shopping experience is to set aside a morning and wander around, comparing prices before making your selection. Start by exploring the main **Bhatia Market** (begins at the entrance to the fort) and follow your nose. Note that **Rangoli** has a large collection of embroidered garments, particularly for children, and is a fixed-rate shop (you don't have to bargain), which can be quite a relief. You'll find it opposite the Bank of Baroda, in Gandhi Chowk. For more upmarket designer selections, stop at **Killa Boutique** (Gandhi Chowk), run by Luca Borella of Killa Bhawan, where you can pick up stylish fashion accessories, scarves, and Western outfits made of Indian fabrics and prints.

10 Gujarat

Gujaratis, known for their business acumen, have made their state one of the fastest-growing in India. Home to Hindus, Jains, Paris, and Muslims as well as the semi-nomadic tribes who inhabit the immense salt flats of Kutch, the state of Gujarat has seen its image tarnished by recent spates of politically fueled communal violence, and as a consequence its popularity as a travel destination has dropped off. But unlike the more volatile Kashmir, Gujarat's atmosphere remains essentially peaceful, and traveling through the state will expose you to a vast, varied, and dramatic Indian landscape, with some of the country's top architectural highlights. The experience is all the more pleasurable because it is so wonderfully free of the hucksters and beggars who plague the more popular tourist trails. Scattered around the state are modest palaces that have been converted into heritage hotels. Off the southern coast is the former Portuguese enclave of **Diu,** where you can laze on the beach and grab a beer far from the teeming crowds of Goa. Gujarat also has a number of excellent wildlife sanctuaries, including **Gir National**

Park, last refuge of the Asiatic lion. You can cover the state's top attractions in 5 days, but given the distances, we recommend you set aside at least a week. Either catch a train or plane to Ahmedabad from Mumbai, or combine the state with a driving tour of Rajasthan.

A DRIVING TOUR OF GUJARAT

You can drive to **Ahmedabad,** Gujarat's major city hub, from popular destinations in Rajasthan, including Mount Abu (215km/133 miles; 7 hr.) and Udaipur (251km/155 miles; 8 hr.). Should you choose to travel by road, two fine Solanki monuments await you in the remote region north of Ahmedabad: the millennium-old **Sun Temple** 👐👐👐 at Modhera is 100km (62 miles) short of Ahmedabad and close to beautiful **Rani-ni-Vav** 👐👐👐, a *baoli* (step well) at Patan. Representing the pinnacle of Solanki architecture, the magnificent Sun Temple predates the great Orissan Sun Temple in Konark. It is positioned in such a way that at dawn and during the equinoxes, the sun would have cast its rays on the deity within the inner sanctum. Built in 1026, it has survived Muslim iconoclasm and numerous natural disasters, but it lost many of its statues to the devastating earthquake of 2001. Considered the most impressive *baoli* in Gujarat, Rani-ka-Vav was built by a queen in the 11th century and is adorned with 800-odd sculptures that can be admired as you traverse the monumental carved steps leading down to the water's edge. You can make both of these stops en route from Rajasthan to Ahmedabad, after first overnighting at **Balaram Palace** (📞 **02742/28-4278** or 079/2657-8412; gopigroup@icenet.net; Rs 2,200–Rs 3,200/$51–$73 double), a pleasant heritage hotel close to the Rajasthani border. Completed in 1935, the palace overlooks a vast wildlife reserve and features Mughal domes, deep balconies, columned porticoes, and a vast rooftop where moonlit dinners can be arranged.

Established by the Muslim leader Ahmad Shah in 1411 on the banks of the Sabarmati River, the capital, Ahmedabad, has long been the center of a flourishing textile industry, earning it the nickname "Manchester of the East." An important commercial and industrial center, with trading houses and huge textile mills owned by some of India's wealthiest families, the city offers medieval mosques, colorful bazaars, and great modernist buildings designed by Le Corbusier. Full of combustible energy, the city is a fantastic jumble of old and new, where you'll regularly witness camel-drawn carts queuing up at traffic intersections alongside spluttering auto-rickshaws and Tata four-wheel-drives. While you're here, make time to visit the **Calico Museum** 👐👐👐 (📞 **079/2286-8172;** Thurs–Tues 10am–12:30pm and 2:30–5pm). Housed in a beautiful 200-year-old haveli made from carved Burma teak, this is possibly India's best-managed museum. Certainly it's the only one in which a knowledgeable and eloquent guide takes you through sumptuous textile galleries explaining each of the exhibits in detail. Gandhi's **Sabarmati Ashram** 👐👐👐 (📞 **079/2755-7277;** daily 8:30am–7pm) is another supremely peaceful diversion. Time allowing, the Jain **Hatheesing Temple** 👐👐, a beautiful edifice in gleaming marble with 52 cloistered shrines, each with its own marble *tirthankara* idol, is also worth exploring. Built in the 1420s by Ahmed Shah, **Jama Masjid** 👐👐 is the city's biggest mosque and in close proximity to many beautiful Muslim architectural highlights. Outside the east entrance is the **Tomb of Ahmed Shah,** always adorned with flowers and *chadars* (sacred cloths).

While you're in the city center, visit the 16th-century **Siddi Saiyad Mosque** 👐👐. Note the two wonderful yellow stone latticework screens *(jalis)* high on the western wall; the twirling Tree of Life designs have been carved with such intricate detail that you'll have trouble believing they're made from stone. Across the road from the mosque is a beautiful 1928 Art Deco haveli, **The House of Mangaldas Girdhardas** (© **079/2550-6946;** www.houseofmg.com; doubles from Rs 2,600/$63), which offers Ahmedabad's only heritage accommodations. Try to have lunch at the lovely rooftop restaurant, **Agashiye** 🌴🌴, where superb Gujarati *thalis* (multicourse meals) are served (thali Rs 245/$5.65). Last but not least (particularly if you're a fan of modern architecture), set aside time to visit Le Corbusier's award-winning **Sanskar Kendra** complex, with its galleries and museums.

Offering peace, quiet, great luxury, and a pool, the city's smartest (and most expensive) hotel is **Taj Residency Ummed** (© **079/5566-1234;** www.tajhotels.com; from $165 double), some distance from the city center.

Arguably the best restaurant in Gujarat, **Rajwadu** 🌴🌴🌴 (© **079/2664-3845;** www.rajwadu.com) is an excellent place for dinner. Reserve a table overlooking the water and arrive around 7pm, when the ingredients for the night are offered to the presiding deity, Ram. Then order the delicious vegetarian thali (a mere Rs 200/$4.55). **Vishalla** 🌴🌴 (© **079/2660-2422**) is another great spot to experience Gujarati dining, set in a re-created Gujarati village complete with old carts, buggies, clay pots, and objets d'art. At night, traditional puppet shows and folk-dance performances under lantern light accompany the meal, taken on the floor. Up to 32 different food items are piled onto your leaf platter.

Gujarat Tourism (© **079/2658-9683;** Mon–Sat 9:30am–6:30pm, closed Sun and second and fourth Sat of the month) and **Heritage Walking Tours** (© **079/ 2539-1811;** departures every 2 hr.; Rs 50/$1.15) are your best bets for excursions around the city.

If you want to escape Ahmedabad's heady vibe, a number of lovely, remote destinations are just hours away. **Utelia** 🌴🌴 (70km/43 miles away) is a charming village with natural hot sulphuric springs populated by traditional shepherds known as *Bharwads*. Consider spending a night here before continuing on to see the magnificent Jain temple city at Palitana, arguably Gujarat's top attraction. A gorgeous place to overnight is **Palace Utelia** 🌴🌴 (© **02714/26-2222;** utelia@icenet.net; Rs 2,500/$57), an Indo-Saracenic mansion built in 1895 by the Thakur of Utelia. Featuring lovely galleries and domes, it's beautifully restored and appealingly furnished—the en-suite guest rooms are enormous and overlook a pleasant courtyard, and even the bathrooms are massive. Book a room with air-conditioning and a private balcony. You can also book their heritage taxi, an air-conditioned 1956 Willy's station wagon driven by a chauffeur in traditional garb, for Rs 12 (30¢) per kilometer, to cover the sights. Outings to the excavated ruins of **Lothal** 🌴, an ancient city of the Indus Valley civilization (20 min. away), are also arranged in *charkas*, vehicles that are part-rickshaw, part-buggy, as are trips to the two nearby wildlife sanctuaries. February through March is foaling season at **Velavadar National Park** 🌴 (40km/25 miles from Utelia; open mid-Mar to mid-July), a haven for the once extensively hunted black buck, as well as endangered wolves. Birders should visit **Nal Sarovar Bird Sanctuary** (© **02715/24-5037**) between November and February, when around 250 species from as far away as Siberia arrive for the winter; it's a good opportunity to witness the intricate courtship dance of the Sarus crane.

A couple of hours south of Utelia is the fantastic hilltop Jain temple city at **Palitana** 🌴🌴🌴, an essential holy-pilgrimage destination for this nonviolent community. A city of gleaming marble monuments housing representations of the few human souls that have managed to be liberated from the cycle of life, Palitana has over 850 temples atop sacred **Mount Satrunjaya** (the "hill that conquers enemies"). The top is reached by climbing (or by being carried up) 3,572 steps—a stiff 2-hour ascent. Amid the massive warren of white marble shrines and temples, you'll encounter many devotees dressed in white, some wearing gauze masks to filter innocent microbes from the air that they breathe. Some of the devotees attain ecstatic heights, practicing their faith with devotional singing, clapping, and humming. Others create devotional patterns on the ground using rice and nuts, or are seen gently waving fly-whisks over the idols as a gesture of respect. Stay at the stately **Nilambag Palace Hotel** (✆ **0278/242-4241;** www.nilambagpalace.com; Rs 3,800–Rs 5,800/$86–$132 double) in Bhavnagar (50km/30 miles away), and have the staff make all arrangements for your Palitana excursion. Built in 1859, Nilambag is run by the Maharani of Bhavnagar, who still has servants quaking in her presence. Spacious palace rooms (no. 210 is the classiest) have high ceilings, antique writing desks and dressing tables, oversize canopied beds, traditional lacquered Gujarati armchairs *(sungeda)*, and lovely rugs on stone tile floors.

After the climb to Palitana's holy city, you'll have earned a break on the tiny island of **Diu** off the Gujarat mainland, officially the only place in this region allowed to sell liquor (it's a Union Territory, not part of Gujarat, which is a prohibition state). Here, it's quite common to overhear local sari-clad matriarchs gossiping in exuberant Portuguese—the colonial enclave only became part of India in 1961, when bombs were finally dropped to chase the Portuguese out. Diu remains lost in time, a mellow island appealing to exhausted travelers and Gujarati day-trippers; the latter are here because alcohol is cheap and plentiful. A sprawling fort, elegant Catholic churches, and old Portuguese mansions are on offer, but Diu is best appreciated for its unfettered beaches and languid atmosphere—perfect for a day or two of rejuvenation. Here, you arise from slumber to find the streets all but deserted, the bulk of the male population out at sea. Stay in a villa-style guest room at **Radhika Beach Resort** (✆ **02875/25-2553** through -2555; www.radhikaresort.com; doubles from Rs 1,750/$40) at Nagoa, a popular horseshoe-shaped beach that's safe for swimming.

From Diu, several hours by road take you through pleasant rural environs to **Gir Sanctuary** (400km/248 miles southwest of Ahmedabad), the only place outside Africa where you can spot lions in the wild. Although Asiatic lions were once found as far away as Bihar, only 300 remain today, and all live in this verdant region of Gujarat, also good for spotting king vultures, paradise flycatchers, pygmy woodpeckers, and crested serpent eagles. Along with around 200 panthers, you may also sight leopard, jungle cat, *chital,* rusty spotted cat, *nilgai,* hyena, *chinkara,* and *chowsingha.* Members of the Maldhari community, who rear cattle and live within the sanctuary, frequently lose livestock to the lions. The sanctuary is part of 1,412-sq.-km (545-sq.-mile) Gir National Park, which visitors can enter upon purchase of a permit; Sasan Gir, a one-street village, is the entry point. Note that in May temperatures can climb to a blistering 120°F (50°C), but this is also the best time to spot animals as they congregate at waterholes. **Taj Gir Lodge** (✆ **02877/28-5521** or -5501; www.tajhotels.com; doubles about $160) is the best lodging option (though at press time it was undergoing renovations and is expected to reopen late in 2005). The tariff includes one jungle safari and entry fees; staff here can assist with additional safari arrangements. For a more intimate and mid-range option, stay at **Maneland Jungle Lodge** (✆ **02877/28-5555;** www.maneland.com; Rs 2,000–Rs 5,000/$46–$114, includes breakfast). To see more temples, head to the coast to view beachfront **Somnath Temple** (45km/30 miles away), considered one of the 12 holiest Shaivite sites.

North of Gir, the **Great Rann of Kutch** 𝔊𝔊𝔊 is one of the most photogenic areas in India. Its strange, stark terrain conjures up a wonderfully haunting atmosphere, proving that deserts are not always wastelands of sand. Kutch, which was at the heart of the 2001 earthquake that shook Gujarat, is an 18,000-sq.-km (7,000-sq.-mile) salt flat that was once a navigable lake. For part of the year, the Great Rann becomes submerged in water; but when the floods recede and the clouds disappear, the sky turns a perfect blue and the earth is baked by the relentless sun, converting the vast expanse to a shimmering, hard crust of snow-white salt. This harsh, arid landscape is where the semi-nomadic Rabaris herd their sheep, goats, and camels, wending their way through Rajasthan and Gujarat on seasonal crossings. Kutch's pastoral communities live in mud-packed toadstool-shaped huts called *bhoongas*—featuring thick walls embellished with molded designs, whitewashed patterns, and brass appliqué (more settled communities will also use pieces of reflective metal or mirrors, making the surfaces sparkle like jewels). Excursions to view these strikingly decorated mud-hut villages inhabited by equally beautifully adorned people, known for their wonderful arts and crafts, are highly recommended. **Bhuj,** Kutch's principal town, is an ideal base from which to explore the region. Bhuj itself was virtually flattened during the earthquake in January 2001, so wherever you travel in this region, expect to see extensive construction and rebuilding taking place. When villages, handicrafts, and the urge to buy no longer excite you, visit the remote and serene Shaivite monastery at **Than,** where *bidi*-smoking *sadhus* (men who have renounced their worldly possessions) gather to drink *chai* and relax. During the winter the Rann hosts the largest colony of migratory flamingoes in the world as they arrive near **Khavda;** this is also one of the last habitats of the Asiatic wild ass. Near Bhuj is the ancient seaport of **Mandvi,** where you can visit fascinating **Vijay Vilas Palace** and watch *dhows* being built. In Bhuj you can stay at **Hotel Prince** (✆ **02832/22-0370** or -20371; princad1@sancharnet.in; book a deluxe, Rs 2,400/$55 double). However, better accommodations can be found 30 minutes from Bhuj at **Garha Safari Lodge** 𝔊 (Rs 2,450/$55 double), a far more personable place overlooking the Rudrani Dam. En-suite guest rooms are in thatched circular huts styled after Kutch village dwellings. The lodge organizes full-day outings to Banni villages as well as camel safaris. There's also a good trip to the 5,000-year-old Indus Valley city excavation site at Dholavira, which takes in extraordinary landscapes and shimmering salt-pan flats along the way. Kutchi meals are served in the garden restaurant, accompanied by traditional folk dancing. Book through www.garhatours. com or call ✆ **079/2657-9672.**

Returning to Ahmedabad from the Great Rann, it's possible to stop in the Little Rann where—coupled with experiencing the natural drama of a stark landscape powdered with salt crystals—you may encounter herds of Indian wild ass, or *onager,* India's last wild horses. Only around 1,000 survive, most in herds in **Little Rann of Kutch Wildlife Sanctuary.** You can also spot wolves, caracal, and *nilgai,* as well as migratory birds during the winter. Stay at **Rann Riders** (www.rannriders.com) in **Dasada,** which has quaint cottages equipped with air-conditioning and other amenities, from where you can take a jeep safari (best season Oct–Mar; Rs 5,080/$116 double, includes all meals, mineral water and cold drinks, and two safaris). You can arrange bookings through **North West Safaris** (91–92 Kamdhenu Complex, Ambawadi, Ahmedabad; ✆ **079/2630-2019** or -8031; ssibal@ad1.vsnl.net.in). The company also has a small lodge in Gir National Park and can organize itineraries.

Himachal Pradesh:
On Top of the World

Proclaimed by ancient Indian texts as *Devbhumi*—"Land of the Gods"—and believed to be the earthly home of the mighty Lord Shiva, this beautiful, far-flung region has an almost palpable presence of divinity. Bordered by Tibet to the east, Jammu and Kashmir to the north, and the Punjab to the west, the land-locked state is one of great topographic diversity, from vast bleak tracts of rust-colored high-altitude Trans-Himalayan desert to dense green deodar forests, apple orchards, cultivated terraces and, everywhere you look, sublime snow-capped mountains. This is also where you'll find the largest concentration of Buddhists, their atmospheric *gompas* (monasteries) a total contrast to the pageantry of Hindu temples.

Shimla, the state capital, is easily accessed from Delhi by train, preferably via the Punjabi town of Amritsar, where the shimmering **Golden Temple** of the Sikhs takes the honors as India's best cultural attraction. Shimla shouldn't hold you longer than it takes to get ready to tackle one of the greatest road adventures in Asia—negotiating the ledges, landslides, and hairpin bends of the **Hindustan-Tibet Road** through the remote valleys of Kinnaur, Lahaul, and Spiti. Hidden from the world for most of the year by a cloak of thick, impenetrable snow, these eastern-most districts emerge from their wintry slumber to reveal white-capped Himalayan mountains, lush green meadow-valleys dappled with flowers, and Tibetan

Buddhist *gompas,* of which **Tabo,** a World Heritage Site, is one of the most spiritual destinations in India. Due to limited accessibility (the region only opened to visitors in recent years and requires a special permit) and the impassability of the roads, the region remains the least visited and most exhilarating part of Himachal Pradesh. You should set aside at least 3 to 4 days to explore the area after arriving in Manali, a town somewhat enlivened (some say ruined) by its designated role as Himachal Pradesh's "hippie hot spot" and local honeymoon destination. You can either set off on a trek from this popular adventure center, or head west (via Mandi) to the tea-carpeted hills of the westernmost Kangra Valley and the hill station of **Dharamsala**—seat of the Tibetan government-in-exile and home to the Dalai Lama. Another option is to head north to the lunar landscapes of **Ladakh.**

Although Jammu and Kashmir, India's northernmost state, is a no-go area for most rational travelers, Ladakh, the western J&K province on the border of Tibet, is the fortunate exception. It sits astride the Ladakh and Zanskar mountains, surrounded by two of the world's highest ranges—the Greater Himalayas and the mighty Karako-ram—and nothing will prepare you for the breathtaking, stark beauty of the landscape. Jagged peaks, rocky uplands, and vast bar-ren plateaus are the dominant features of this harsh, dry land swept by dust devils and dotted with Buddhist *gompas,* large whitewashed *chortens* (commemorative cairns), and chest-high *mani* walls made from stacks of engraved stones. Aptly nick-named "Little Tibet," this is India at her remote best. Only visited for the few months of summer when the roads are passable, the world here has been frozen in time; the small Buddhist population continues to live as they have for centuries, totally untouched by outside influences. Spend at least 4 days here (adjusting to the high altitude takes time), then fly out to Delhi and rejoin the 21st century.

1 Staying Active

Himachal Pradesh and Ladakh are exceptional destinations for adventurous travelers. The area has a phenomenal array of trekking routes, and numerous tour operators offer anything from gentle strolls to walks lasting several days—including trips to serious rock faces for seasoned climbers. Besides the scenery, a visit here is an ideal opportunity to meet people totally untouched by the modern world—outside of a handful of towns, much of the population in this region is rural and dependent on agriculture. It is also home to some of the world's last nomadic people. **Manali** is a popular starting point for treks into the lush Kullu and Parvati valleys, while **Dharamsala** is a good base from which to explore the Dhauladhar mountain range. In Ladakh, expeditions out of **Leh** visit the many fascinating Buddhist monasteries, and the **Indus** and **Zanskar rivers** are excellent for white-water rafting. Note that most of the companies listed below are happy to arrange a variety of adventure activities almost anywhere in the Himalayas, including Sikkim (discussed in chapter 13).

IN MANALI   If you arrive in Manali with no prearranged outdoor activities, you can contact two places. **Himalayan Outdoor Centre** (en route to Rohtang Rd., 1.5km/1 mile from Manali; ⓒ 01902/25-2581 or 98160-03035) offers a wide range of adventure activities, including rafting on the Beas River, skiing (Apr to mid-May), snowboarding, treks, jeep safaris, and tandem paragliding. **Himalayan Quest Adventures** (above Chopsticks Restaurant, The Mall, Manali; ⓒ **01902/25-3139** or -2739; heaven_7_7@hotmail.com), a professional eco-friendly operation, offers trekking, jeep safaris, paragliding, and rafting trips throughout the region. Keeping up with the times, the company also offers snowboarding courses; a 5-day package will cost around $45 per day, including all equipment, lodging, and other fees. Besides organizing trekking in Himachal and Ladakh, **Himalayan Journeys The Adventure Company** (The Mall, Manali; ⓒ **01902/25-2365;** www.himalayanjourneysindia.com) arranges ski courses, jeep safaris, river-rafting expeditions, mountain-biking tours and, for well-heeled adventurers, luxury heli-skiing packages. This company is associated with the Australian outfit, Himachal Helicopter Skiing (see below).

IN LEH   For details on active vacations in Leh, see "Leh & Environs," later in this chapter.

JEEP SAFARI SPECIALISTS   **Banjara Camps & Retreats** ✶✶ (www.banjaracamps. com) operates a number of Trans-Himalayan jeep safaris, which generally start in Delhi and explore different parts of Himachal and Ladakh. Comfortable accommodations (some in beautifully situated deluxe campsites) and good meals accompany you along the way, and you can even customize your safari. Another outfitter that allows you to traverse the top of the world in comfort, **Wilderness Trekkers** (www.wilderness-trekkers.org), runs a weeklong adventure that takes in Himachal's Rohtang Pass, as well as some of Ladakh's most mesmerizing Buddhist *gompas*.

Himachal Pradesh

Moments **Chasing the World's Most Expensive White Powder**

Surrounded by soaring snowcapped peaks against a cerulean sky, you climb onto a pair of fat skis and tackle dry, calf-deep powder for heart-stopping, high-powered skiing. If you fancy the idea of being whisked onto pristine Himalayan slopes by helicopter to ski slopes with names like Nasty Nick and Powderbox, where good conditions mean runs of up to a kilometer or more, Manali, in central Himachal Pradesh, is where you should head. You'll need to fork out big bucks for this ultimate adrenaline rush adventure, but the helicopter ride saves you valuable time. From Manali, the snow-covered slopes are a mere 4 minutes away by chopper, a trip that otherwise would involve a grueling 4-day climb. Roddy McKenzie's **Himachal Helicopter Skiing** (© **00 61 3/9593-9853;** www.himachal.com) is an Australian outfit with over a decade's experience. Be warned, however: Avalanches are an ever-present risk, and general bad weather, or even low cloud cover, can undo any plans for a chopper's takeoff—and sorry, no refunds for ski time lost because of poor conditions. McKenzie's operation includes experienced guides who spend considerable time each morning testing the snow for safety prior to drops. Himachal Helicopter Skiing offers weeklong heli-skiing trips for upwards of $6,500 per person, based on two people sharing.

2 The Golden Temple in Amritsar

410km (254 miles) NW of Delhi

Amritsar (pronounced *Um-rit-sir*) has been the capital of the Sikh religion since the 16th century. Located in the northwestern state of Punjab, a wealthy and prosperous region and home to the majority of India's Sikhs, Amritsar is also home to India's most dazzling temple. A shimmering monument in marble, bronze, and gold leaf, and a vivid architectural celebration of Sikhism's devotion (a faith that actively preaches unity and equality among all religions), **The Golden Temple** is both fascinating and spiritually invigorating, combining sheer physical beauty with a truly sacred atmosphere. The way in which its devotees worship is enough to hold your attention—and your heart—completely captive.

ESSENTIALS

VISITOR INFORMATION The best place to get information about the Golden Temple and the Sikh faith is at the temple's own **Information Office** (© **0183/ 255-3954;** daily 7:30am–7:30pm Apr–June, 8am–7pm July–Mar). The **Punjab Government Tourist Office** (© **0183/240-2452;** Mon–Sat 9am–5pm) is at the Palace Hotel, opposite the railway station.

GETTING THERE & AWAY You can fly from Delhi or Chandigarh with **Indian Airlines** (39A Court Rd.; © **0183/221-3392,** -3393, or 141; Mon–Sat 10am–5pm), but the best way to get here is on the Shatabdi Express from Delhi (or you can travel from Mumbai on the Paschim Express). Taxis, auto-rickshaws, and bicycle-rickshaws are always available at the station to take you to your hotel. You'll want to avoid spending time tracking down tickets, so either book your return or onward journey in advance, or have your hotel handle your reservation. If you're stuck, there is a computerized train reservation facility located at the Golden Temple complex.

GETTING AROUND   Note that the highly recommended Mrs. Bhandari's Guest-house (below) will make all your transport and sightseeing arrangements for you. You can hire the services of a guide for Rs 550 to Rs 650 ($12.50–$14.75) half-day, or Rs 1,100 ($25) full day; car hire will be in addition to this. Cycle-rickshaws are popular, but if you're in a hurry, don't want to do battle with the glaring sun, or need to cover more than a few kilometers, opt for a car or auto-rickshaw instead.

FAST FACTS: Amritsar

Ambulance Dial (©) **0183/221-0964** for Kakkar Hospital's 24-hour ambulance service.

ATMs, Banks & Currency Exchange Several banks around The Golden Temple area provide necessary services.

Hospital Apollo Hospital ((©) **0183/254-5599**) at Bhushapura near Sultanwind Gate is one of the city's best. Excellent care is also available at **Kakkar Hospital** on Green Avenue ((©) **0183/250-6053** or -6015).

Post Office The **General Post Office** ((©) **0183/256-6032;** Mon–Sat 9am–5pm) is located on Court Road. There's also a post office with the same hours at The Golden Temple.

THE TOP ATTRACTIONS

The Golden Temple 𝒜𝒜𝒜 *Moments*   Prepare to be humbled by the most tangibly spiritual place in the country, one that, in its status as a living monument, even has the edge on the Taj Mahal. Arrive with a few good hours set aside and get lost in its magical beauty. Leave your shoes at the free facility near the entrance, cover your head (bandanas are provided, or you can purchase a "Golden Temple" souvenir bandana from a vendor), and wash your feet by wading through the shallow pool before entering. The most sacred part of the complex is **Hari Mandir Sahib (Divine Temple)** or **Darbar Sahib (Court of the Lord),** which you'll instantly recognize as the marble-and-gold sanctuary at the center of a large body of water within the temple complex. The name "Golden Temple" comes from this gold-plated building, which features

---

The Five "K's": How to Spot a Sikh

Most Sikh men wear turbans wrapped around their heads and sport full beards, making them highly visible in all parts of the world. However, there are five other symbols—known as the five K's (*kakkar* in Punjabi)—worn by Sikh men to indicate that they are part of Guru Gobind Singh's sacred Khalsa brotherhood, which unites all Sikhs. Traditionally, a Sikh man does not cut his hair or shave his beard. This hair is known as the *kesh,* and is kept neat with a comb known as the *kangha.* As a symbol of dignity and power, he carries a saber or sword, known as the *kirpan,* at all times. You won't see it, but a Sikh man wears loose underpants known as the *kaccha,* said to symbolize modesty. Finally, look on his right wrist: The *karra* is a traditional bangle of steel that indicates fearlessness and strength; pick one up as a reminder of your visit.

Bloody History of the Holy Temple

In 1984, the Sikh fundamentalist Sant Bhindranwale and his followers armed themselves and occupied The Golden Temple as part of a campaign for a separate Sikh state, which they wanted to call Khalistan. Acting on Prime Minister Indira Gandhi's orders, the Indian Army attacked, killing Bhindranwale and others and causing serious damage to the temple. Sikh honor was avenged when Indira Gandhi was later assassinated by two of her Sikh bodyguards, which in turn led to a massacre in which thousands of Sikhs lost their lives. The Sikh community refused to allow the central government to repair the damage to the temple, instead undertaking the work themselves. Although most of the cracks and crevices have been repaired, the incident has not been forgotten, and you will find many people in Amritsar keen to explain the Sikh side of the story.

---

copper cupolas and white marble walls encrusted with precious stones arranged in decorative floral patterns that show strong Islamic influence. Four *chattris* flank the structure, which is decorated inside and out with verses from the *Granth Sahib* (the Sikh Holy Book). Construction of the temple began in 1574, with ongoing restoration and embellishment over the years, including the addition in the 19th century of 100 kilograms (220 lb.) of gold to cover the inverted lotus-shaped dome.

To reach the temple, follow the *parikrama* (walkway), which circumscribes the sacred water tank—known as **Amrit Sarovar,** or the Pool of Nectar—in a clockwise direction. You'll need to cross a marble causeway, **Guru's Bridge,** which symbolizes the journey of the soul after death, in order to reach the *bangaldar* pavilion on which the temple stands. Access to the bridge is through marvelous **Darshani Deorhi,** a gateway marked by magnificent silver doors. Here, you will join the many devotees who, especially early and late in the day, pass through the temple to pay their respects (and give a donation) to their Holy Book. Within Hari Mandir, the scene—which is almost constantly being televised for Sikh viewers around India—is fascinating. Beneath a canopy studded with jewels, scriptures from the Holy Book are sung, while a crowd of fervent yet solemn devotees immerse themselves in the moment. A *chauri,* or whisk, is repeatedly waved dramatically in the air above the Book, while new musicians and singers continually join the ensemble after another participant has paid his respects. Like an organic human machine, lines of Sikhs pay their respects by touching their foreheads to the temple floor and walls, continuing in a clockwise direction at a moderate pace. Being among such gracious devotion will fill you with a sense of inner calm. Once you've passed through Hari Mandir, taking your time to drink in the atmosphere, head back along Guru's Bridge. It is along this bridge that the *Granth Sahib* is carried between Hari Mandir and **Akal Takht** (see "Spiritual Weightlifting," below), the seat of the Sikh parliament, built in 1609 and located directly across from Hari Mandir.

Don't miss **Guru-ka-Langar,** a community kitchen where each day around 35,000 people are fed by temple volunteers. In an act that symbolizes the Sikh belief in equality of all people, irrespective of caste or creed, anyone and everyone is welcomed and invited to join the communal breaking of bread. Guest quarters are also available for international Sikh visitors (for a nominal fee), and at least 400 simple rooms are provided free of charge to pilgrims. In the **Central Sikh Museum** at the main entrance, galleries display images and remembrances of Sikh gurus, warriors, and saints; note that it includes some graphic portraits of gurus being tortured and executed in terrifying ways.

Unlike in many other temples in India, here you feel genuinely welcome and not at all pressured to take out your wallet. In fact, so proud of their religion, culture, history, and temple are the local Sikhs that you will almost certainly be offered enthusiastic conversation and valuable information by one of the regular devotees—in return for nothing more than your attention. The welcoming information office to the left of the main gate gives helpful advice and information, as well as free guides and booklets on Sikhism (see the appendix for a brief précis).

For further information, contact the **Temple Manager** (© **0183/255-3953,** -3957, or -3958; fax 0183/255-3919), or call the **Information Office** (© **0183/255-3954**). Daily 7:30am–7:30pm in summer and 8am–7pm in winter. Activity at the temple goes on till late, and even when the last ceremonies of the evening have been concluded, volunteers get to work by cleaning or preparing for the next day. The main gate never closes, and Hari Mandir is open according to hours determined by the lunar cycle—some 20 hr. in summer and 18 hr. in winter. In summer, the closing ceremony takes place at 11pm and the sanctum is reopened at 2am. In winter, the times are 10pm and 3am, respectively.

Jallianwala Bagh   It was here, just a short walk from The Golden Temple, that one of the most dastardly events of British rule in India took place. On April 13, 1919, Brig.-Gen. Reginald Dwyer ordered the brutal massacre of hundreds of citizens who had gathered to protest the "imprisonment without trial" of two of their leaders under the newly passed Rowlatt Act. Now a leafy garden memorial, the park is surrounded by buildings on all sides; the British officers blocked the only access in and indiscriminately opened fire, gunning down many women and children. You can visit the martyr's gallery, and take a look at the bullet-pocked wall and the well where many, escaping bullets, jumped to their death.

Jallianwala Bagh. Daily 5am–7pm.

AN UNUSUAL OUTING
Flag Ceremony at Wagah Border *Moments*   One of the world's oddest spectator activities, this pompous display of military bravado is a major drawing card for Indian tourists who travel long distances to watch the "Retreat," a high-kicking, toe-stepping,

---

Moments Spiritual Weightlifting

The best time to visit The Golden Temple is during *Palki Sahib,* or the **night ceremony,** during which the *Granth Sahib* is carried from the main shrine in Hari Mandir to the sanctum, where it rests for a few hours until the opening ceremony the following morning. Any man can take part in this ceremony by joining one of the vibrant lines that form behind and ahead of the heavy palanquin on which the Holy Book is moved. Several devotees simultaneously help support each arm of the palanquin, giving each person a few seconds to take part in the auspicious event. As though it were being transported along a human conveyor belt, one person from each side moves away from the palanquin and is replaced by a new shoulder from each of the lines; in this way, everyone gets at least one chance to participate, and you can join the end of the line again and again until your shoulder no longer wishes to cooperate.

quick-marching ceremony wherein the Indian and Pakistani flags are lowered on either side of the only border that remains open between the two more-often-than-not hostile countries. A number of officers from each team puts on a raised-eyebrow performance to the satisfaction of the cheering, chanting crowds, seated on concrete grandstands on either side. The pointless exercise ends with the furious slamming of the border gates, at which time each side's flag is urgently carried to a room for overnight safekeeping. For anyone interested in unbridled nationalist pride, the Flag Ceremony is a memorable outing (only half an hour from Amritsar). Arrive well ahead of the crowds in order to get a close-up seat—the grimaces of the mighty military men in their rooster caps add to the fun, and you'll get a better look at the Pakistani delegation. Alternatively, find a way of organizing a VIP spot across the road from the crowd; a friendly call to a local politician might do the trick.

Wagah is at the border between India and Pakistan, 32km (20 miles) from Amritsar. Round-trip taxi around Rs 550 ($3) basic model car, Rs 1,000 ($23) four-wheel-drive.

WHERE TO STAY & DINE

That the people of Amritsar live to eat is obvious from the scores of *dhabas,* Punjabi-style "fast-food" joints serving tasty and filling *thalis* (multi-course platters), that showcase various traditional dishes everywhere. This is the land of *desi-ghee* (clarified butter) and butter, added to almost every dish: Those watching their weight or unable to consume rich, heavy food should take it easy on the Indian fare here. But if you're up for the adventure, this is a culinary exploration like few others in India, where for as little as Rs 50 ($1.15) you'll be served a sizeable spread that you eat with your fingers, dipping piping-hot *parathas* (fried flatbread) into *maa ki dal, channa,* and other concoctions arranged in little heaps on your platter.

For close to a hundred years, simple **Kesar da Dhaba** ✦✦ in Bazaar Passian has been serving superb vegetarian dishes. For Amritsari fish—here, fabulous batter-fried sole from the Beas River, flavored with *lovage* (a thyme-like spice)—you must go to **Makhan Dhaba** (Lawrence Rd.). **Kundan Dhaba** ✦✦, opposite Hall Gate, dishes out the yummiest *paratha* and *dal* in town, to be washed down with an utterly decadent *pedewalle lassi.* As far as *lassis* (yogurt drinks) go, Amritsar sets the standard; try **Ahuja Lassiwalla** (near Hindu Mahasabha College) or just about anywhere else you see a crowd. **Surjit Chicken** (Lawrence Rd.) is the spot if you're looking for a sit-down meal of delicious butter chicken and *kulchas* or *lachedar parathas.* If you're looking for a clean, glitzy restaurant that serves a wide range of dishes, head for **Crystal** (✆ **0183/ 222-5555** or -9999; Rs 90–Rs 200/$2.05–$4.55). It may not win any awards for atmosphere, but it's the most popular upmarket restaurant in town, and the food—an eclectic array of dishes (including Chinese and Continental) but with the emphasis on North Indian specialties—is excellent.

Amritsar has several fairly decent hotels, including the **Ritz Plaza Hotel** (45 Mall Rd.; ✆/fax **0183/256-2836** through -2839; www.sarovarparkplaza.com), which has comfortable rooms, a pool, and all the basic facilities for Rs 3,500 ($80) double (including breakfast). For personal service and a home-style stay, however, nothing comes close to the quintessentially Punjabi experience of Mrs. Bhandari's Guesthouse (reviewed below).

Mrs. Bhandari's Guesthouse ✦✦✦ *Value*   Mrs. Bhandari's is almost as much a reason to visit this corner of North India as The Golden Temple. Situated along a wide avenue in the peaceful, leafy Cantonment neighborhood, this is a very pleasant, comfortable and, above all, homey place in which to enjoy genuine Punjabi hospitality. The fabulously preserved late-Raj family estate packs in beautiful gardens, a welcoming pool, and its own team of curious water buffalo; these provide the essential ingredient (fresh dung) for homemade fire "briquettes." Accommodations vary in size and location, arranged in and around Mrs. Bhandari's charming home. Most rooms resemble "chummeries," the bachelor quarters assigned to Raj officials of junior rank with an attached room for their Indian servant. Interiors are modest but atmospheric, featuring high ceilings, Art Deco tiles, fine Indian throws over firm mattresses, and bathrooms with drench showers or old-fashioned tubs and original piping. Mrs. Bhandari has been living here since 1930, but the guesthouse is now run by her warm-spirited daughter, who will help you plan an enjoyable itinerary and organize all transport and temple visits. A one-way transfer from the railway station to the guesthouse is included in the room rate.

No. 10, Cantonment, Amritsar 143 001. ⓒ **0183/222-8509** or -2390. Fax 0183/222-2390. http://bhandari_ guesthouse.tripod.com. bgha10@gmail.com. 14 units. Rs 1,350 ($31) double, Rs 1,650 ($38) double with A/C and heater. Rs 300 ($6.85) extra bed. Camping Rs 165 ($3.75) per person with own equipment. MC, V. **Amenities:** Restaurant; pool open Mar–Nov; kids' play area; Internet; TV in lounge; tour guide, transport, and taxi arrangements; camping facilities; limited room service 8am–10pm; laundry. *In room:* A/C, heater, fireplace.

Ranjit's Svaasa 𝓚𝓚   Set in a 250-year-old redbrick mansion on Amritsar's Mall Road, Rama Mehra's retreat is not only a health-conscious one, it's also atmospheric: Rooms are furnished with old colonial furniture (including four-poster beds) and open onto a cool balcony overlooking a landscaped garden. Pleasant rooms aside, the focus here is on serving delicious, healthy, pesticide-free vegetarian food and providing healing therapies at the Spa Pavilion, where you can choose from an assortment of therapies ranging from bitter orange and cinnamon aromatherapy to Abhyanga Ayurvedic massage. A yoga hall and gymnasium round out the healthy living facilities of this friendly spa-hotel. You'll be happy to learn that the hot water in your room is heated by solar energy and rainwater saved during the monsoon.

47 A The Mall, Amritsar 143 001. ⓒ **0183/256-6618** or 0183/309-8840. Telefax 0183/500-3728. www.svaasa.com. spa@svaasa.com. 12 units. Rs 2,800 ($64) standard double; Rs 3,500 ($80) Regal Suite, Rs 5,000 ($114) Presidential Suite. Rs 750 ($17) extra bed. Rates include breakfast and taxes; ask about half- or full-moon spa packages. AE, MC, V. **Amenities:** Dining hall; pool; gym; small library; TV in lounge; limited room service; laundry; doctor-on call. *In room:* Tea- and coffee-making facilities, fridges in suites, hair dryer on request.

3 Shimla

107km (66 miles) NE of Chandigarh

In the days when Shimla inspired scenes from Rudyard Kipling's *Kim,* it was a popular pick-up center for lusty British officers and flirtatious maidens keen to create a stir among the scandal-mongerers who gathered along The Mall during the summers. Shimla enjoys a proud history as the preferred mountain escape retreat from the unbearable summer heat of the plains (or "downstairs," as many Himachalis refer to their low-altitude neighbors)—a cool spot in which to sink into a life of idle gossip, romantic conquests, and military brown-nosing. Today, this romantic image has been somewhat ruined by unchecked urbanization and reckless construction. Development has now been curbed, but the clogged roads and ugly concrete tenements that cling to the mountainsides beneath historic Shimla detract significantly from the town's former glory.

Visiting Le Corbusier's Chandigarh

Fans of the father of modernism, Le Corbusier, will appreciate the form and functionality of **Chandigarh**. When Punjab was divided after Partition, Lahore went to Pakistan, leaving the state without a capital; Chandigarh was envisioned as the new headquarters. When Punjab was once again divided into smaller states, the city became a Union Territory serving as the administrative capital for both Punjab and Haryana. Le Corbusier is largely responsible for designing the mesh of rectangular units, or "sectors," into which the city is divided. Characterized by exposed brickwork, boulder stone masonry, broad boulevards, large landscaped parks with abundant trees, and quadrants of tidy, self-sufficient neighborhoods made up of buildings with louvered screens *(brise-soleil)* and unfinished concrete surfaces, Le Corbusier's city doesn't quite function as the living organism it's intended to be. Urban decay and waste have crept in, but architecture buffs will find Le Corbusier's structural contributions intriguing. Architectural attractions in Chandigarh include the **Capitol Complex** ✦✦ (Sector 1), where the geometrical concrete buildings of the **Legislative Assembly, High Court,** and **Secretariat** represent structural innovation. At the southern end of the complex piazza, the **Vidhan Sabha (Legislative Assembly)** building is capped by a startling cupola, a pyramidal tower, and a cuboid tower, while within the portico is a bright **Cubist mural** by Le Corbusier himself. Also within the complex is the **Open Hand Monument,** a giant metal hand standing 26m (83 ft.) high that is able to rotate in the wind. Symbolizing the give-and-take of ideas, the hand has become the city's official emblem. Technically, tours of the complex start from the reception area, but these half-hourly episodes don't always materialize; check with someone from the **Chandigarh Industrial & Tourism Development Corporation (CITCO)** (✆ **0172/270-4761** or -4356) in advance. Locals go to walk, jog, and relax in the 8km-long (5-mile) linear park known as **Leisure Valley.** In Sector 16, the **Rose Garden** is the

Sprawling over seven hills fringed by dense forest and magnificent mountains, Shimla is a useful starting point from which to explore more untouched parts of Himachal, and the town's timbered cottages and wood-gabled buildings retain a degree of charm, but if you're expecting a quiet hill station, you may be disappointed. The Mall, a promenade on the southern slopes of the ridge, remains a pedestrian preserve, thronged by tourists and local Anglophiles who tend to echo the social mannerisms of the Raj at its most British. Below the ridge, however, an overwhelmingly Indian conglomeration of buildings constitutes the bazaar, and a sweep of modern dwellings has the distinctly untidy appearance of unplanned urban sprawl. Shimla is, however, in close proximity to a number of lesser-known hill resort getaways: Naldehra, Narkanda, Kufri, and Chadwick Falls are all destinations offering relative peace and quiet as well as scenic splendor guaranteed to capture your imagination. And for those seeking adventure and remote beauty, Shimla is a useful confluence of roads leading west to the Kangra Valley; north to Kullu, Lahaul, and Ladakh; and east into the valleys of Kinnaur and Spiti.

largest of its kind in Asia. In Sector 10, the **Sculpture Park** adjoining the Cultural Complex is worth exploring. Within the Complex, the **Art and Picture Gallery** (Tues–Sun 9.30am–5pm) includes Modernist works. If you'd like to deepen your knowledge of Chandigarh's planning and construction, visit the **City Museum** (Sector 10), where exhibits document the realization of the city.

Chandigarh's highlight is the **Rock Garden of Nek Chand** ***, a surreal fantasyland created by "outsider artist" Nek Chand—a road inspector—from rocks, concrete, and urban rubbish. Set on 8 hectares (20 acres) of wooded landscape, the "garden" comprises a series of mazelike archways, tunnels, pavilions, waterfalls, and bridges, with passages leading from one open-air gallery to another. Each gallery is occupied by unusual characters, figures, and creatures fashioned from an unbelievable array of materials Chand started collecting in 1958; almost half a century later, the garden continues to grow. If the artist is in residence when you visit, he'll be happy to chat with you about his project.

Chandigarh can be visited en route between Amritsar and Shimla, or directly from Delhi by train. The best connections between Delhi and Chandigarh are several daily Shatabdi Express trains or the Himalayan Queen. From Amritsar, choose the Paschim Express, a section of which also links Chandigarh with Kalka, starting point for the "toy train" to Shimla. The **railway station** (© 0172/265-3131, 0172/264-1651, -1131, or -1132) is in Sector 17, around 8km (5 miles) from the city center. For railway inquiries, call the **city reservation center** (© 0172/270-8573; Mon–Sat 8am–8pm, Sun 8am–2pm). **Chandigarh Tourism** (© 0172/270-3839 or 0172/505-5462) has offices at the airport and at the railway station. If you decide to spend the night, book at **Hotel Mount View** * (© 0172/274-0544 or -0444); insist on a guest room in the renovated section.

ESSENTIALS

GETTING THERE & AWAY   By Road   All of the more reputable hotels (see "Where to Stay & Dine," below) will arrange transfers from practically any starting point in India, should you wish to arrive in chauffeured style. From Delhi, you'll take National Highway 1 (Grand Trunk Rd.) north to Ambala (in Haryana) and then continue on a fierce and beautiful journey along a hillside road that snakes all the way up to Shimla. You can also drive directly from Chandigarh, following National Highway 21 south until you join the main Delhi–Shimla road.

By Air   Weather can interfere with flights in and out of Shimla's **Jubbarhatti Airport,** 23km (14 miles) from the city (taxi into town Rs 550/$13). Daily flights connect Shimla with Delhi (1 hr.). These also stop at Kullu's **Bhuntar Airport,** which serves northern Himachal Pradesh.

By Train   The most romantic way to get to Shimla, the **Himalayan Queen** runs from New Delhi to Kalka (640m/2,050 ft. above sea level), where the train switches

Tips **You Can't Eat the Plastic in your Wallet**

Obtaining cash against credit cards can be problematic in Himachal Pradesh and Ladakh. Only a select number of very upmarket hotels and several branches of the Bank of Baroda will advance cash against Visa and MasterCard, and only a handful of ATMs in the large tourist hubs are capable of handling international credit card cash advances. Easiest is to draw cash in Shimla. Certain shops in Dharamsala and Manali will give credit card advances for a 5% fee, but this is not official practice.

to a narrow-gauge track and continues on to Shimla (2,060m/6,500 ft.). Traveling at an average speed of 25 to 30kmph (15–48 mph), the "toy train" journey will consume nearly a full day of your itinerary. Its 96km (60 miles) travels through some 100 tunnels, numerous bridges, and sharp curves, taking in picturesque views of green forests and meadows, capsicum fields, and red-roofed chalets. The train back to Kalka departs Shimla at 10:35am, arriving in time for you to make the onward connection to Delhi, where you'll arrive before midnight. Check out the **Kalka-Shimla Railway website** (www.ksr100.com), set up in 2003 to commemorate the centenary of this railway line. *Note:* During the high season, it's difficult to secure tickets without at least several days' advance booking.

VISITOR INFORMATION   For friendly, helpful, and enthusiastic assistance on the entire Himachal region, pop into the **Himachal Pradesh Tourism Information Centre (HPTDC; © 0177/265-4589;** www.himachaltourism.nic.in), where Geeta Ram Ranote will provide you with everything from trekking tips to details of his favorite itineraries; beware, however, of taking his advice on accommodations—he, like many other government officials, is committed to sending you to HPTDC-run establishments, of which 99.9% are undesirable.

GETTING AROUND   On Foot   Central Shimla is free of traffic, which means that you'll spend much of your time exploring on foot. You'll need some degree of stamina to deal with the numerous steep inclines. A two-stage elevator, **The Lift,** operating between 8am and 10pm, connects The Mall with Cart Road; ticket prices are nominal.

By Car   Shimla has a number of restricted and sealed roads, and farther routes are no-go zones for heavier vehicles. Should you arrive in town by train, you can find a taxi (or even the odd auto-rickshaw), which will drop you at your hotel—although you may be surprised at the route necessary to get around "no traffic" zones. Day trips (see "Shimla Excursions," below) will generally require a taxi or jeep—but the prices can fluctuate wildly. Get advice from your hotel on hiring a car and driver at reasonable rates. For prepaid taxi trips, contact the government-run service at © 0177/265-8892, or **Vishal Himachal Taxi Operator Union** at © 0177/265-7645.

GUIDED TOURS & TRAVEL AGENTS   For intelligent, entertaining, and exclusive **tours of Shimla** itself, your best bet is to make contact with noted local writer Raaja Bhasin, author of *Simla—The Summer Capital of British India.* Raaja conducts interesting and tailormade walks around Shimla and will provide you with fond memories of the town and an acute understanding of its juicy history. E-mail or call Raaja in advance to make sure he's available (© 0177/265-3194; mail@raajabhasin.com;

www.raajabhasin.com). Tours normally start from your hotel and run from 10am to 5pm for a charge of $130 (for up to eight people; meals and transport, if required, cost extra). Additionally, he does shorter tours (2–3 hr.; cost varies) and all-day excursions outside Shimla ($150).

Government-operated tours are annoying, claustrophobic excursions, best avoided unless you're on a tight budget. The office of the **Himachal Pradesh Tourism Development Corporation** (**HPTDC**; ✆ **0177/265-2561** or -8302; www.hptdc.nic.in; Apr 15–July 15 and Sept 15–Jan 1 daily 9am–8pm, rest of year daily 9am–6pm) is along The Mall, near Scandal Point. The Mall has an abundance of travel agencies; use them to arrange transport, tours, and trekking around the state. For jeep safaris out of Shimla into Kinnaur and Spiti, see "Staying Active," earlier in this chapter.

FAST FACTS: Shimla

Ambulance Dial ✆ **0177/280-4648** or 0177/265-2102.

ATMs, Banks & Currency Exchange ICICI Bank has an ATM at Scandal Point, The Mall; and UTI Bank has one at 53 The Mall. You can change cash and traveler's checks, and organize cash advances on certain credit cards at ICICI Bank (address above; Mon–Sat 8am–8pm). In an emergency, guests at the Cecil and Wildflower Hall can also draw money against their credit cards for a small percentage.

Hospital For around-the-clock service, call **Tara Hospital** (✆ **0177/280-3275**).

Police There's a police office (✆ **0177/281-2344**) adjacent to the Town Hall, on The Mall. It's closed on Sunday.

Post Office The **General Post Office** (Mon–Sat 10am–6pm) is located just above Scandal Corner.

WHAT TO SEE & DO

Shimla's main promenade is **The Mall,** a pedestrian avenue stretching across the length of the city from Gopal Mandir in the west to the suburb of Chhota Shimla, roughly south of the town center. Along this stretch, crumbling remnants of the British Raj abound. Above The Mall is **The Ridge,** a wide-open esplanade watched over by a statue of Gandhi to the east, where the nearby Gothic **Christchurch** is one of Shimla's most imposing structures, situated adjacent the faux-Tudor half-timbered **library.** Note the fresco around the chancel window, designed by Lockwood Kipling, Rudyard's father.

Also on The Mall are the **Telegraph Office,** an interesting example of stone ashlar work completed in 1922 and, to its right, the old **Railway Booking Office,** a sadly decaying building frequently overrun by obnoxious monkeys. Marking the area where The Ridge joins up with The Mall, **Scandal Point** continues to be a popular social hangout, supposedly taking its name from an unconfirmed scandal involving the elopement of a handsome Patiala prince with the daughter of a British commander-in-chief. Beyond the fire station, after the dressed stone building housing the Municipal Offices, is the **Gaiety Theatre,** originally the Town Hall. Renowned for its excellent acoustics, the Gaiety continues to showcase local dramas on a stage where notable personalities, including Lord Robert Baden-Powell and novelist M. M. Kaye, once graced the planks—not all with great success; a fashionable piece of gossip tells how Rudyard Kipling was booed off the stage.

A short walk east of The Ridge will take you to the start of a rather strenuous but worthwhile hike to the summit of **Jakhu Hill** ☞ which, at an altitude of 2,445m (7,800 ft.), is Shimla's highest point and affords excellent views of the city and surrounding valleys. You need to trudge up a steep 1.5km (1-mile) path, commencing at The Ridge and culminating at Shimla's highest point, to get to the Hanuman Temple on Jakhu's summit. Try to make it to the top in time for sunrise or sunset, either of which is glorious. The little temple is dedicated to Hinduism's popular monkey god (who is said to have rested on Jakhu Hill on his return from a mission in the Himalayas). Today his brazen descendants continue to patrol the path, so beware of carrying food or doing *anything* likely to provoke them. After you sound the bell at the temple entrance, enter to discover a curious concoction of serious Hindu faith and jovial Christmas pomp suggested by the tinsel and streamer decorations; the priest will happily give you a blessing.

To the west of the city, beyond The Cecil Hotel, is the vast six-story Scottish baronial mansion formerly known as **Viceregal Lodge** ☞ (Observatory Hill; Tues–Sun 9am–1pm and 2–5pm). The admission fee of Rs 100 ($2.30) includes a guide. Built in 1888 at the behest of the British viceroy in an approximation of the Elizabethan style, the lodge is Shimla's single greatest architectural testament to the influence of the British Raj, and its luxuriant woodwork, handsome lawns, and lovely views attract numerous visitors. Even in 1888 it had electric light and an indoor tennis court, both rare for the times. The building was the summer residence of all viceroys until 1947, when India was granted independence and the building renamed Rashtrapati Niwas, a retreat for the president of India. The first president of India thought it should be put to better use, however, and in 1964 it was inhabited by the Indian Institute of Advanced Study, an academic foundation still housed here.

SHIMLA EXCURSIONS

A mere 12km (7½ miles) from Shimla, the forested village of **Mashobra** is great for scenic walks but is best visited as an excuse to step into one of India's loveliest hotels, **Wildflower Hall** (see "Where to Stay & Dine," below), for high tea or lunch. From the village, you can attempt a trek to the area's highest peak—Shali—which reaches 3,200m (10,000 ft.), or take the 2km (1¼-mile) pedestrian track to the "sacred grove" of Sipur, which is where you'll find the charming, indigenous-style temple dedicated to the local deity, Seep. Because they are considered the personal property of Seep, no trees may be cut here; so superstitious are the locals that they pat themselves down before leaving to ensure no fallen cedar needles have accidentally dropped on them. Beyond Mashobra is the popular picnicking resort of **Naldehra** (23km/14 miles from Shimla), which has an extraordinary 9-hole golf course designed by Lord Curzon (British viceroy of India, 1899–1905). Golfing on the world's highest course is best arranged through your hotel in Shimla, or you can opt to stay at one of the local "resorts"—**The Châlets Naldehra** (✆ **0177/274-7715** or 98160-62007; www.chaletsnaldehra.com; Rs 3,500–Rs 8,500/$80–$193) has a pleasing alpine feel, with clean, comfortable, Scandinavian prefab wood cabins. Staff will arrange golf, river rafting, horseback-riding, fishing, and a range of hikes. The hot sulphur springs of **Tattapani** lie a farther 28km (17 miles) away.

CHAIL

Chail (2,150m/7,000 ft.), 2 hours from Shimla, can be visited as a day trip out of the capital (or a relaxing, peaceful accommodations alternative; see below). Chail grew out of a romantic scandal, when Bhupinder Singh, the dashing Maharajah of Patiala, eloped with (or abducted, depending on who's telling the story) the daughter of Lord Kitchener. Predictably, the Maharajah was forced to return the daughter and was banned from ever again entering the Raj's summer capital. Enraged, the Raja combed the neighboring hills in search of a location from where he could literally look down on the town that had snubbed him. Chail was the answer to his ego-driven quest, and there he set about establishing his own "summer capital," building a lavish Georgian palace, as well as the highest cricket pitch in the world (2,444m/7,800 ft.). Sadly, the once-elegant palace has been converted into a poorly managed government-owned hotel.

WHERE TO STAY & DINE

A destination in its own right, the Oberoi's **Wildflower Hall** is by far your best option, but if the rates exceed your budget, nothing can beat the homey Raj-era experience of **Chapslee,** run by the aristocratic Kapurthalas. If neither of these or of the recommendations below suit you, you could try **Clarke's** (© **0177/265-1010;** clarkesreservations@sancharnet.in), a small, modest, Oberoi-owned hotel with dull but perfectly comfortable accommodations. The gray-and-white Tudor exterior is its best asset, though the dining room also has a good reputation. Alternatively, **Springfields** (© **0177/262-1297** or -1298; www.ushashriramhotels.com), a popular Bollywood film location, is a peaceful but slightly tattered alternative to Shimla's main center, with unobstructed mountain views. The better rooms (nos. 1, 5, and 6) have great charm—high ceilings, wooden floorboards, fireplace, large double beds, and generous bathrooms with huge shower areas. Doubles are Rs 4,400 to Rs 7,200 ($101–$164), which includes breakfast and one meal.

Finally, **high tea** at Wildflower Hall is legendary—sample the local infusions along with traditional Irish tea brack bread—a baked reminder of the Raj, speckled with raisins and sultanas, steeped in Darjeeling tea, and served with unsalted butter and lemon curd.

The Cecil 🐙🐙🐙   Originally built as a private residence back in 1884, the Cecil has hosted the likes of Mahatma Gandhi and continues to draw political figures and noted celebrities. It was rebuilt in the Gothic style of Shimla's most elegant Raj monuments, and the interiors are luxurious with plenty of wood paneling, leather, and opulent furniture. Guest rooms are sumptuous and tasteful, with wooden flooring, rich fabrics, and considerable attention to detail; each has a dressing room and a large bathroom with separate tub and shower. Opt for one of the south-facing rooms (nos. 411–415 are best) with spectacular views of the Shimla Valley foothills. Avoid the rooms in the older "Tudor Block," which feels a little claustrophobic and removed from the atmosphere of the main hotel. Facilities include a wonderful spa with a heated pool and a complete range of treatments to add a bit of decadence to your Himalayan sojourn. This is a less intimate, personal experience than Chapslee, but it will suit those who prefer the anonymity of luxury hotels and don't want to shell out for Wildflower Hall.

Chaura Maidan, Shimla 171 004. © **0177/280-4848.** Toll-free reservations in India: © **1600/11-2030.** Fax 0177/ 281-1024. www.oberoihotels.com. 79 units. $220 superior double, $235 premium double, $260 deluxe double; $400–$475 suite. $24 extra bed. Taxes extra. AE, DC, MC, V. **Amenities:** Restaurant; lounge bar; garden lounge; indoor pool; health center; spa w/Thai, Ayurvedic, and Balinese massage and aromatherapy; activity center w/billiards; children's activity center; 24-hr. room service; laundry; library. *In room:* A/C, TV, DVD player, minibar, tea-and coffee-making facilities, hair dryer, safe (except superior rooms).

Chapslee *finds* *Value* On the northeastern spur of the Shimla range, this charming home is the most authentically old-world lodging in town. Owned and lovingly managed by Ratanjit "Reggie" Singh, the regal grandson of Raja Charanjit Singh of Kapurthala, who bought the estate in 1938, Chapslee remains the quintessential creaky-floorboards Shimla homestead, its Raj-era aura hardly dented by modern conveniences or the slightly fraying Art Deco wallpaper. Originally built in 1835 as the summer residence of a British family, the house received an Edwardian face-lift in 1896 with teak paneling (part of the same consignment used for the Viceregal Lodge), wood parquet floors, and a dramatic staircase. Its current incarnation was undertaken when it became the summer residence of the Kapurthala royals. Be sure to request either of the two upstairs suites; the original master bedroom in each affords lovely valley views, a massive brass four-poster bed, and delicate ornamentation, as well as a vast bathroom with a raised tub, an enormous shower, a bidet, and its own fireplace. Chapslee's obvious aesthetic pleasures are a good match for the fairy-tale view of Shimla at twilight; with whiskey in hand, you can watch the city's lights come on from the garden terrace. Chapslee's excellent kitchen prepares British-influenced dishes, as well as delectable tandoori chicken and mouthwatering *shami* kebabs.

Chapslee, Shimla 171 001. © **0177/265-1577.** Fax 0177/265-8663. chapslee@vsnl.com. www.chapslee.com. 6 units. Rs 6,000–Rs 8,900 ($137–$202) double; inclusive of all meals, taxes, and service charges in lieu of tips; Rs 500–Rs 750 ($11–$17) winter surcharge Oct 15–Mar 31 includes heaters, fire. Foreigners may need to pay by international credit card; MC, V. **Amenities:** Dining room; bed tea and packed lunches; tennis court; croquet lawn; card room; library.

Wildflower Hall *finds* *Kids* Smack-dab in the middle of magnificent deodar cedar forests, atop its own hill a thousand feet above Shimla, surrounded by swirling mist and snowy peaks, this inspired remake of the fire-gutted mountain retreat of Lord Kitchener is the ideal setting for a beautifully eerie alpine fantasy. Affording showstopping views of some of the most spectacularly scenic mountains and valleys in India, this opulent yet surprisingly unpretentious Himalayan resort has all the seductive charms of a luxury hotel in a heritage property, with top-notch facilities and fine service. It's also dressed to perfection: Stately architecture is matched with tasteful reproduction furniture and carefully selected artworks and objets d'art. Guest rooms are well-appointed and spacious, with wood paneling, teak floors, walk-in closets, and exquisite bathrooms. Valley-view premium rooms are excellent (nos. 101, 201, 301, and 327 are most prized). Deluxe rooms have the added benefit of private balconies. Besides two outstanding restaurants, a spa restaurant (with movie screen) serves healthy meals; each dish comes with a card indicating the calories and food value. But the hotel's *pièce de résistance* is the magnificent spa, which offers an impressive range of services (including practically any massage you can imagine). For romantic hedonists, there are private spa suites for couples looking to share even the experience of pampering.

Mashobra, Chharabara, Shimla 171 012. © **0177/264-8585.** Toll-free reservations in India: © **1600/11-2030.** Fax 0177/264-8686. www.oberoihotels.com. reservations@wildflowerhall.com. 85 units. $355 deluxe double; $565 suite; $850 Lord Kitchener Suite. AE, DC, MC, V. **Amenities:** 2 restaurants; spa restaurant; bar; tennis court; heated indoor pool; spa w/gym, sauna, steam, Jacuzzi, and massage facilities, separate spa pavilion, and 2 private spa suites; outdoor Jacuzzi; horses and horse trail; trekking; bird-watching; archery; mountain biking; ice skating (winter); river-rafting; card room; billiards; travel arrangements; car hire; library; foreign exchange. *In room:* A/C, TV, dataport, DVD player, minibar, tea- and coffee-making facilities, electronic safe, butler.

SHOPPING

The cool nip in the evening air may well have you stocking up on colorful Kinnauri shawls, mufflers, and caps; Pangwali blankets from Chamba; and multicolored hand-knitted woolen socks from Lahaul. The best place to shop for these items and more is **Himachal Emporium** (3 The Mall; ℂ **0177/280-1234;** Mon–Sat 10am–7:30pm summer, 10am–7pm winter; closed 1–2:30pm). Try to speak to Mr. Yograj, who can help you choose good-quality woolen Kullu shawls, Pashminas, Kangra-school minia-ture paintings, or Buddhist *thangkas* (banners) from Kinnaur and Lahaul-Spiti.

4 Exploring Kinnaur & Spiti ✸✸✸

The arid, dust-covered, snowcapped slopes in the Indo-Tibetan regions of Kinnaur, Spiti, and Lahaul are the stuff adventurers' dreams are made of, offering sublime mountainscapes, twisting roads, and fascinating Tibetan Buddhist communities with atmospheric *gompas* (monasteries). Negotiating the rough, sandy, drop-off ledges of the **Hindustan-Tibet Road** (bizarrely enough, known as National Highway 22) is an action-packed art in itself. The impossible road is made all the more unnerving when buses, trucks, and jeeps headed in the opposite direction seem to appear out of nowhere, and landslides frequently disrupt routes entirely. Although the spectacular scenery is undoubtedly the highlight of any trip through Kinnaur and Spiti, there are also marvelous monuments, including some of the world's most intriguing Buddhist complexes (such as the World Heritage Site of **Tabo Monastery** in Spiti), as well as high-altitude villages that seem to cling to the sides of mountains or balance on the edges of sharp cliffs.

ESSENTIALS

VISITOR INFORMATION   Pick up information from the **tourism office in Shimla** (or Manali if you're doing the trip in reverse), and make detailed inquiries regarding accessibility and weather developments. Ajay Sud, an ex-army captain and adventurer who together with Rajesh Ojha founded **Banjara Camps,** is one of the best sources of information, tips, and assistance in the Kinnaur region. He's also a very experienced trekker and can give great advice and suggestions for treks throughout the Himalayas. He and the equally helpful Rajesh take turns manning the Sangla camp; best to reach either through the **head office** (1A Hauz Khas Village, New Delhi 110 016; ℂ **011/2686-1397;** fax 011/2685-5152; www.banjaracamps.com).

GETTING AROUND   Ultra-budget-conscious travelers undertake the journey in state buses that rely on luck as much as faith to reach their destination, while born-to-be-wild adventurers do it on the back of a motorbike. We highly recommend you rent a jeep and driver—the heftier the jeep (a sturdy TATA is your best bet), the bet-ter your chances of actually enjoying the adventure. Most of the villages can be explored on foot, and the region lends itself to trekking (see "Staying Active," earlier in this chapter). For one-stop shopping, we highly recommend you utilize the services of Banjara Camps (see "Visitor Information," above), which offers most of the best lodging options in the area and can arrange your entire jeep safari.

INNER LINE PERMITS   Foreigners may not travel through the zone closest to the Tibetan border without first obtaining an **Inner Line Permit** from one of several government offices in Himachal. It's a fairly easy, if laborious and frustrating, process (taking anywhere from 3 hr. to a whole day); you will need your passport, three passport-size photographs, and two copies of both the main page of your passport and your visa, before heading for the SDM (Sub-Divisional Magistrate) office where you complete an application form. The best place to apply is Recong Peo—the SDM's office is located in the Deputy Commissioner's Building near the town's bus stand, next door to the Hotel Snowview. One way of dealing with the slow pace is to apply and then collect your papers the following day after overnighting in beautiful Kalpa nearby. It's a good idea to phone ahead to ensure that the **SDM office** (© **01786/ 222253;** Mon–Sat 10am–5pm) is open on the day you plan to apply.

THE JOURNEY

Heading east out of Shimla, National Highway 22 takes you to **Narkanda** (2,708m/8,600 ft.), a ski resort (Jan–Mar) where you can take in excellent views from Hatu Peak. From Narkanda, a 16km (10-mile) detour off the main highway brings you to the vast apple orchards of Thanedar, heavy with fruit in summer. (Samuel Stokes, an American who settled here in the early 1900s, is credited with bringing over and planting the region's first apple trees.) Set in the midst of this sea of apple trees is the whitewashed **Banjara Camps' Orchard Retreat** ✿, its pleasant rooms decked with thick, colorful throws and attached bathrooms. It's a very comfortable place to kick back and relax and enjoy astonishingly beautiful sunsets. Prakash Thakur, host and owner of this lovely Himalayan getaway, is also the resident expert on local history and culture, and you can request a guide to take you for a fabulous 3-hour trek through the shady forest. Evenings are spent around a bonfire, where Prakash serves up anecdotes, *paneer*-on-a-toothpick, and spicy chicken snacks before an Indian buffet is laid out. Do taste the homemade apple juice, chutneys, and other concoctions Prakash makes from the orchard fruit (Rs 2,800/$64 double; see "Visitor Information," above).

From Thanedar you must backtrack to Narkanda, then continue north past the commercial town of **Rampur,** a former princely capital. The road descends towards the raging Sutlej River, following its contours until you come upon the dusty village of **Jeori.** From here, a twisting, hairpin-heavy climb leads to the charming village of **Sarahan** (2,165m/7,000 ft., 6 hr. from Shimla), which enjoys spectacular views of the snowcapped peaks across the river. Trapped in time, Sarahan is the site of the famous pagoda-style **Bhimakali Temple** ✿✿✿. You can overnight in Sarahan at the government-run **Hotel Shrikhand** (© **01782/27-4234;** www.hptdc.nic.in); although it's poorly maintained, the setting is out-of-this-world, rates are low (from Rs 1,000/$23), and you'll enjoy incredible views from your room. For the best room deal, book "half the cottage" (Rs 2,000/$46), which gets you a spacious, high-ceilinged room in a separate block with a fireplace, television, and enclosed porch/sitting room. The hotel has a small bar and a restaurant. Alternatively, try **Wildside: Off Beat Nature Retreat** (© **94180-00056** or 98153-57866). At press time there was talk of this becoming a Banjara-affiliated retreat, which would make these nine rooms (Rs 2,800/$64), located in an interesting teakwood building, your best option in Sarahan.

The next morning, follow the same road back down to Jeori. At Karchham (Baspa Junction), you'll take a sharp U-turn and follow the steep dirt tracks of the **Sangla Valley** ✿✿✿, through which the raging Baspa River flows. You won't find any flashy accommodations, but comfortable **Banjara Camp,** 8km (5 miles) beyond, is an excellent place to spend a night or two, and serves as the perfect base from which to explore the remote hamlet of **Chitkul** ✿✿ (3,450m/11,000 ft.). This Banjara Camp (see "Visitor Information" above; Rs 3,800/$86 double, includes all meals and taxes; open

Apr–Oct) comprises 17 comfortable tents with attached toilets and running water, in a gorgeous open meadow (wildflowers in full bloom July–Oct) alongside the Baspa River, beneath towering Khargala Peak. Make use of the opportunity to pick the brains of Banjara founders Ajay or Rajesh for details of the best treks in the area. Both are wonderful hosts, with plenty of ideas for what you can do (besides lying in one of the inviting hammocks overlooking the river). A selection of tasty Indian and Tibetan-inspired dishes is prepared at mealtimes and served in Makuti, the thatched dining area; but there's nothing stopping you from picking up fresh fish from a local farm (the area is known for trout fishing) and having the kitchen team cook it for you.

From Sangla, you will have to double back to National "Highway" 22 to continue east towards Kinnaur's main town of **Recong Peo** (2,670m/8,500 ft.), where you must complete the paperwork for your Inner Line Permit, which will permit you to enter the zone closest to the Tibetan border. While waiting for the bureaucratic wheels to turn, spend the night in the village of **Kalpa** 𝄞𝄞 (2,960m/9,400 ft.), well worth a visit for its crisp, clear air and view across the valley of the majestic Kinner-Kailash massif; it's a 30-minute drive into the mountain above Recong. **Hotel Kinner Villa** (𝒞 **01786/22-6006;** from Rs 1,100/$25 double) is the best place to stay, with simple, clean, and comfortable accommodations. Room no. 201 has the most exquisite view; nos. 101, 104, 202, and 207 aren't bad, either. When the hotel is quiet, you'll have to book meals in advance. Note, too, that Kalpa suffers from interminable power failures, so make sure the manager supplies you with candles.

Set out early the following day; once you pass the first Inner Line checkpoint at Jangi, you will notice dramatic changes in the landscape, as fir trees give way to rock and stone sloping up toward distant summits and down into the raging River Sutlej. The journey through Inner Line territory takes you past the off-limits turnoff for 5,500m-high (17,600-ft.) Shipki-La Pass, which heads into China. **Nako Lake** 𝄞 and its village lie farther along; beyond the turnoff for Nako, the road attains its most sinister aspect as you enter the notorious section known as the Maling Slide, heavily punctuated with precipitous drops—an ideal place to strengthen your faith in the divine. Upon reaching the final Inner Line checkpost at Sumdo—some 115km (71 miles) from Recong Peo and 363km (225 miles) from Shimla—the road heads north-west into the alien landscapes of Spiti.

The Buddhist town of **Tabo** 𝄞𝄞𝄞 (some 6 hr. from Recong) is the most frequented stop in Spiti, and for good reason (see "Top Attractions," below). We recommend you stay at **Banjara Camps' Tabo Retreat** (see "Visitor Information" above; doubles from Rs 2,800/$64; Apr–Oct). Architecturally, the building echoes Ladakhi style: simple, clean, comfortable, en-suite guest rooms have small, private balconies. Ask for an upper-level room facing the monastery. Omperkash Thakur is not only an efficient manager, but something of a culinary wizard, so there's plenty of carefully prepared food available. Many visitors traveling on a tight budget stay at the **rest house** in the monastery run by monks (𝒞 **01906/23-3313** or -3315; www.aarogya.com/tabo/location.html; Rs 300–Rs 550/$6.85–$13). It has simple guest rooms with attached bathrooms, all arranged around a peaceful central courtyard. You will most likely have to arrive here to arrange a room—phones in the area are notoriously unreliable.

Not far from Tabo is the village of **Dhankar** 𝄞𝄞𝄞, which hugs the side of a hill and offers breathtaking glimpses of the surrounding mountains and valley below—a visit to the precariously perched monastery makes for an excellent diversion. Visit Dhankar on your way from Tabo, and then continue on to the town of **Kaza.** As the administrative headquarters of Spiti, Kaza offers little excitement, but unless you really want to spend an entire day on the road, it's a useful base from which to visit the beautiful, fortresslike *gompa* of **Ki** 𝕉𝕉𝕉 and the high-altitude village of **Kibber** 𝕉𝕉. Plan on spending the night here at **Kaza Retreat,** another inn operated by the Banjara group (see "Visitor Information," above; doubles from Rs 2,800/$64). Guest rooms are simple but have attached Western bathrooms. If you're on a tighter budget, get a room at **Sakya's Abode** (© **01906/22256** or -22254). If you're traveling from Manali, make reservations through Ritesh Sood at the Himalayan Saga travel agency, near Club House, Manali (© **01902/25-1848** or 98161-46191). Doubles start at Rs 500 ($11).

From Kaza, either head for Manali to catch your breath, or travel directly to Leh. North of Spiti is **Lahaul** 𝕉𝕉𝕉. Linked to the rest of Himachal by the Rohtang Pass, dotted with villages of flat-roofed houses, fluttering prayer flags, and whitewashed *chortens,* Lahaul is cut off from the world by heavy snow for 8 months of the year. This mountainous region attracts adventurers to its Buddhist monasteries, mountain passes, spectacular glaciers, and high-altitude lakes. Visitors traveling by road to Leh in Ladakh, farther north, pass through Lahaul.

TOP ATTRACTIONS

Bhimakali Temple 𝕉𝕉   Chanting and music blast from the temple loudspeakers very early each morning and again in the evenings, transforming Sarahan village into a place that literally resonates with spirituality. Combining Hindu and Buddhist architectural elements, the main section of the temple comprises two pagoda-style pitched slate-roof towers. Built from layers of interlaced stone and timber, the towers rise from a courtyard around which are living quarters and a small museum with a collection of weapons and other unusual ritual objects and relics. Had you visited the temple 200 years ago, you might have witnessed one of the annual human sacrifices that kept the gods satisfied; today, animals suffice. The tower on the right was damaged in an earthquake a century ago, and the presiding deity was relocated to the tower on the left. Climb the stairs to get to the main shrine with its family of idols. Bhimakali is the main deity, while Durga, Ganesha, and even Buddha are all in attendance. The priests don't speak English, but it's worth taking part in the small *puja* (prayer) ceremony, so bring your rupees. Morning and evening prayers are scheduled but don't always take place.

Sarahan village center. No shoes, cameras, leather, or weapons. Daily 7am–8pm.

Tabo 𝕉𝕉𝕉   With a population of only 715, this Buddhist settlement situated at 3,050m (9,760 ft.) in lower Spiti is centered around its celebrated 2,000-year-old monastic complex, said to be the place where the present Dalai Lama will "retire." A serene village of flat-roofed houses topped by thatch packed with branches, mud, and grass, Tabo has as its focus its monastery—or "doctrinal enclave"—consisting of nine temple buildings, chambers for monks and nuns, 23 snow-white *chortens,* and piles of stones, each inscribed with scripture. The sanctity of this World Heritage Site is topped only by Tholing monastery in Tibet. Don't arrive expecting some cathedral-like masterpiece; Tabo Gompa is a rustic center that is more spiritually than architecturally engaging. A high mud wall surrounds the compound, and the pale mud-covered low-rise monastery buildings suggest nothing of the exquisite wall paintings and stucco statues within. You'll need a flashlight to properly appreciate many of the frescoes and other artworks that adorn the various dark, ancient spaces; only narrow shafts of natural light from small skylights illuminate the frescoed walls, saturated with rich colors and an incongruous variety of scenes. There's a distinctly surreal, often nightmarish quality to the work—gruesome torture scenes compete with images of meditative contemplation and spiritual discovery.

At the core of the complex is the **Temple of Enlightened Gods (Tsug Lha-khang)**, which includes the **Assembly Hall** (or *du-khang*) housing a 2m-high (6-ft.) white stucco image of Vairocana, one of the five spiritual sons of the primordial, self-creative Buddha, or Adibuddha. Below this are two images of the great translator and teacher Rin-Chan-Sang-Po, who is believed to have founded Tabo in A.D. 996. Thirty-three other life-size stucco deities surrounded by stylized flaming circles are bracketed along the walls. Directly behind the assembly hall is the **sanctum,** with five bodhisattvas of the Good Age and beautifully rendered Indian-style frescoes depicting the life of the Buddha. Monks are initiated in the smaller **Mystic Mandala Temple (dKyil-hKhor-khang),** situated behind the main temples. At the northern edge of the complex is the **Temple of Dromton (Brom-ston Lha-khang),** entered via a small portico and long passage. Only enter the **Mahakala Vajra-Bhairava Temple (Gon-Khang)** once you've performed a protective meditation—it's filled with fierce deities that inspire its nickname, "the temple of horrors." Just outside the complex are several contemporary monastic buildings, including an atmospheric guesthouse run by the monks. Above Tabo, across the highway, a group of caves on a sheer cliff-face was once used as monastic dwellings.

365km (226 miles) from Shimla, 295km (183 miles) from Kullu, 47km (29 miles) from Kaza. www.aarogya.com/tabo/index.html.

Dhankar Monastery ✦✦✦ *Dhankar* means "fort," and a glimpse of this monastery precariously perched on a hill jutting against a sharp mountainside certainly suggests its usefulness as a protective stronghold. Once the castle of the Nono, the ruler of Spiti, the building typifies the traditional architecture of the town. As if wedged between massive craggy outcrops, the rather dirty whitewashed flat-topped structures create a dramatic effect against stark fingers of hard rock. Entry to the temple is nerve-wracking; access steps and uppermost rooftops drop away to periously steep rocky slopes. Today, Dhankar is a repository of Bhoti-scripted Buddhist scriptures. You can visit this hilltop monastery as an excursion from Tabo, or en route to your next destination. It makes a sublime detour because it attracts considerably fewer visitors than relatively busy Tabo, and although the monastery interiors are rather small, the astonishing location and wonderful views more than make up for this.

Dhankar Tashi Choling Monastery, Spiti. Rs 25 (55¢) entry.

Kibber & Ki Gompa ✦✦✦ Just north of Kaza, a road veers off the main highway and zigzags its way up a steep mountainside. At the end of this stretch is Kibber, perched on a rocky spur at an altitude of 4,205m (13,450 ft.). Kibber enjoys a reputation as the highest permanent settlement with electricity and accessibility by motor road. Surrounded by limestone rocks and cliffs, the remote and isolated village offers stunning views of the barren valley below. There's even a handful of guesthouses should you require accommodations. Between Kibber and Kaza is Spiti's largest monastery, Ki Gompa, which is about 700 years old. Home to a large community of lamas (of the Gelugpa sect), Ki Gompa is well accustomed to receiving visitors; the monk on duty will brew you a welcoming cup of tea and show you around the different prayer rooms and assembly halls filled with holy relics. The most exciting time to visit is late June or early July, when a festival involving *chaam* dancing and the ceremonial burning of butter sculptures draws large numbers of pilgrims.

Ki Gompa is 12km (7½ miles) northwest of Kaza. Kibber is 4km (2½ miles) farther.

5 The Valley of the Gods: Central Himachal

Central Himachal's fertile valleys—centered around the towns of Mandi, Kullu, and Manali—are watered by the Beas River, and are famous for a variety of fruits, excellent treks, and what is considered—by the stoned hippies of Manali, at least—the finest marijuana in the world.

The drive from Shimla to Manali—starting point for the spectacular road journey to Leh and a number of adventure activities—is around 280km (174 miles) and can be done in a day. The route is scenic, especially in July and August, when the heavy monsoon rains cause the river to swell and waterfalls to cascade spectacularly. Time allowing, it's a good idea to spend the night en route in the scruffy town of Mandi, where you can use the atmospheric Raj Mahal palace hotel as a base for a visit to the nearby hill hamlet of **Rewalsar** ✔. The fascinating confluence of Buddhist, Sikh, and Hindu spirituality, centered around a small black lake teeming with fish (supposedly holy), beautifully reflects the soaring mountain ranges above. Sacred to all three religions, the lake's banks sport lively Buddhist *gompas,* an important Sikh *gurudwara* (place of worship), and a Hindu temple.

Farther north (about 70km/43 miles), in the heart of the Valley of the Gods, is the unattractive town of **Kullu,** famous for its sheer volume of Hindu temples and the Dussehra Festival (usually in Oct), which attracts substantial crowds and hundreds of valley gods to take part in the annual festivities: 7 days of jubilant processions, music, dancing, and markets. Unless you stop specifically to catch any festival action or want to visit the "first and biggest angora farm in Asia," there's no real reason to linger in Kullu.

Bhuntar, not too far south of Kullu, is the turnoff point for drives to Jari, Kasol, and the therapeutic hot springs of **Manikaran,** which is the main jumping-off point for a variety of treks to less-visited villages. **Khirganga,** farther east, is the site of even more thermal water springs, while isolated **Malana,** to the north, is an anthropologist's dream and home of the world's top-rated *ganja,* the famous Malana Gold, according to a recent competition held in Amsterdam. Adventures to any of these remote areas should not be undertaken without the help of a recognized guide—not only is getting lost a strong possibility, but there have been reports of what are believed to be drug-related crimes, including the assault and "disappearance'" of travelers.

ESSENTIALS

GETTING THERE & AROUND   It's possible to avoid Shimla entirely by flying directly to **Bhuntar Airport** 10km (6¼ miles) south of Kullu. In Manali, taxis and auto-rickshaws charge ridiculously inflated rates that fluctuate seasonally and according to the whim of the near-militant local taxi union. Hire a car for the duration of your stay; if you've used a car and driver to get to Manali, you might consider planning ahead to retain the service for any further travel, bearing in mind that a sturdy vehicle with off-road capabilities and a driver who knows the terrain will be essential if you plan on getting to Ladakh or the regions east of the Beas River.

VISITOR INFORMATION & TRAVEL AGENTS   For information about the Kullu and Parvati valleys, visit **Himachal Pradesh Tourism** (✆ **01902/22-2349**) in Kullu, near the maidan. In Manali, the **Tourist Information Centre** (The Mall, Manali; ✆ **01902/25-2175;** Mon–Sat 10am–1pm and 1:30–5pm) can give you a pile of booklets on destinations throughout the state (most of these are available from the far friendlier office in Shimla). An ad-saturated tourist map of Manali is available for Rs

> ## *Tips* Avoid the Rush
>
> The threat of war in the Kashmir has meant that Manali's popularity has soared over the last decade. Visitors who once would have gone to Kashmir for the snow and possibility of skiing now swamp Manali during the Indian high season, which stretches from April until the rains hit in early July, and then again from September to November. Manali's charms have been all but eroded by this perverse tourist explosion, which sets off a soulless cash-rally that seems to involve every proprietor, merchant, and taxi-tour operator in town; hotel tariffs also soar during this period. *Bottom line:* Try to avoid this usually peaceful town during these months.

15 (5¢), and more detailed books and booklets are available for purchase. **Matkon Travels** (© **01902/25-3738,** 98160-03738, or 98160-43738) can also help you with domestic flights and deluxe-bus bookings. Matkon works in conjunction with the **Himalayan Institute of Adventure Sports,** and offers sightseeing, trekking, rafting, paragliding, and skiing opportunities with reliable guides.

MANALI

Yes, it's set amid dense pine forests and shadowed by snowy peaks, but Manali's reputation as a spectacular Himalayan resort is much exaggerated. The primary reason to be here is to set off for Leh in Ladakh, a 2-day drive away, or to participate in the many treks or adventure sports, including heli-skiing.

Manali comprises several neighborhoods, each with a distinct personality. North of the Manalsu Nala River is **Old Manali,** with its historic stone buildings; to the west is the pleasant village of **Dhungri;** while messy **Model Town** is a motley collection of concrete buildings tucked behind the main bazaar area, concentrated around The Mall. East of the Beas River, a few kilometers north of Manali is **Vashisht,** a village known for its hot springs and laid-back atmosphere. Unfortunately, Vashisht has lost much of its charm thanks to an influx of long-stay budget tourists; a dunk in the communal hot-water bath of the local temple is hardly reason enough to visit.

The most peaceful area is **Dhungri Village** (around 2km/1¼ miles from the bazaar), where you can stroll through deodar forests or visit a 450-year-old temple where animal sacrifice is still practiced. On the outskirts of the neighborhood, the multi-tiered wooden pagoda-style **Hadimba Devi Temple** ❀, built in 1553, is Manali's oldest and most interesting shrine, dedicated to the demon goddess Hadimba (an incarnation of Kali). Look around for the sheltered sacrificial stone used for blood rituals during important ceremonies; the central hollow is where the blood from a slain buffalo or goat drains into Hadimba's mouth.

Another good walk takes you through Old Manali (center of cheap backpackers' accommodations), the temple dedicated to Manu, and beyond to silent hillside paths where you'll encounter village women passing the day over idle gossip while their men unhurriedly herd goats and cows toward greener pastures at higher altitudes. Most visitors pay a visit to Manali's two rather modern Buddhist *gompas* in the town's Tibetan quarter south of the bazaar. **Gadhan Thekchhokling gompa** was built in 1969, and is recognizable by its yellow, pagoda-style roof; memorial notices outside draw attention to the extermination of Tibetans in China.

Just 24km (15 miles) short of Manali is **Naggar,** which like Manali is slowly being wrecked by unchecked construction and tourism. Visit the **Nicholas Roerich Museum** ([tel **01902/24-8290** or -8590; Tues–Sun 10am–1pm and 2–6pm), where the famous Russian artist lived from 1923 until he died in 1947. In this small but well-maintained museum, paintings and books by the prolific artist and philosopher are on display. In this stunning location, it's easy to see why Roerich and his wife, Helena, were so inspired by their surroundings, though the same cannot be said of his artwork. Also part of the estate is the **Urusvati Himalayan Folk Art Museum** (Tues–Sun 10am–6pm), created for the preservation of folk art and craft.

WHERE TO STAY
MANDI & KULLU
If you're traveling by road from Shimla direct to either Manali or Dharamsala, it's a good idea to take a break en route. In Mandi, 70km (43 miles) south of Kullu, **Raj Mahal** (𝒸 **01905/22-2401** or -3434; fax 01905/22-5311), a creaky-floorboards "palace," is recommended for its serious time-warp character. Book one of the four enormous Royal Suites (Rs 1,500/$35 double), which showcase an assortment of kitsch furnishings and objets d'art (in one room a stuffed leopard grimaces on a table with rifles for legs!). Generally, the service at Raj Mahal is quite awful, and the ancient plumbing acts up at times, but as a place to lay your head for a night and as a base for visiting nearby Rewalsar, it's adequate. If you're after a more typical (and expensive) hotel experience, head on to **Apple Valley Resort** (𝒸 **01902/26-0001** or –0006), just short of Kullu town. Set on the banks of the Beas River, the luridly decorated country-style cabins with ivy-covered walls and stone chimneys will run you Rs 1,600 to Rs 3,200 ($37–$73) double, with meals; book no. 204, 205, or 206 for the best views.

MANALI
For the most atmospheric room in town, you're best off in an original lodge apartment at **Johnson's Lodge** or the privacy of **Leela Huts;** alternatively, stay at **Span Resorts** for its riverside location (see below for reviews of all). Manali's **Private Hoteliers' Information Centre** (The Mall, near the taxi stand) is well established and can assist you in finding suitably priced accommodations if you haven't prebooked. During the busy season (mid-Apr to early July) you will have difficulty finding any upmarket guest room in Manali at all.

Johnson's Lodge   Set among lovely lawns, this "lodge" was the first inhabited property in New Manali, and it offers a choice of vintage or modern accommodations not too far from the thick of things. Now run by Piya, the cosmopolitan granddaughter of the man who built the original stone lodge apartments, Johnson's may be relatively close to the bazaar, but it remains a tranquil spot with lovely views. If you opt for one of the newly constructed slate, stone, and wood guest rooms in the upper complex, ask for a corner unit—these are larger and have extra windows from which to enjoy the mountain scenes. If you'd prefer an old-fashioned experience, the three huge ivy-covered stone-walled balconied suites in the original building are atmospheric curiosities, with aging furnishings, original fittings, and loads of space. Wood-beam ceilings, screened windows, and small, homey kitchens add to the ambience. Ask for cottage no. 2, which is the neatest and quietest (and even has a TV). A pleasant, cafe-style restaurant offers all-day dining.

Circuit House Rd., Manali 175 131. 𝒸 **01902/25-3023** or 01902/25-3764. Fax 01902/24-5123. 18 units. New Wing: May 15–July 15 Rs 1,500 ($35) standard double, Rs 1,800 ($41) deluxe double. 50% discount rest of the year.

Original suites, for 4: Rs 4,500 ($102) May 15–July 15, 30% discount rest of the year. No credit cards. **Amenities:** Restaurant; laundry on request; doctor-on-call. *In room:* TV, heaters (in most).

Leela Huts 🍴 *Kids*   Popular with diplomats in need of a real break, this collection of five stone cottages is ideal if you're traveling with children or a group of friends. Set in a large garden of potted plants, fruit trees, and neatly hedged pathways, these rustic, comfortable, and rather large holiday cabins offer a pleasant respite from Manali's bustle, even during the height of the domestic tourist season. It's owned and run by the affable Mrs. Thakur and her family, and you are assured of friendly, helpful assistance throughout your stay. When the power goes down, as it tends to throughout Himachal, someone soon arrives to tend to your gas lanterns. Although the cottages are self-catering, you have the option of investing in a "cook-on-request" to tend to your culinary desires.

Sunshine Orchards, Club House Rd., Manali 175 131. ✆ **01902/25-2464.** Fax 01902/25-5035. www.leelahuts.com; info@leelahuts.com. 5 units. 3 3-bedroom cottages at Rs 4,500 ($102) Apr 15–June 30 and Sept 15–Jan 15, Rs 3,500 ($80) July 1–Sept 15; 2 2-bedroom cottages at Rs 3,500 ($80) Apr 15–June 30 and Sept 15–Jan 15, Rs 2,500 ($57) July 1–Sept 15. No credit cards. **Amenities:** Cook on request; badminton; basketball court; children's play area; tour and taxi arrangements; in-house doctor. *In room:* TV, kitchenette, fridge, gas cooker, fireplace.

Snowcrest Manor   Perched at the end of a very steep climb (Manali's highest point), and some distance above the sprawling bazaar, Snowcrest is a small, modest hotel with unimpeded views—the best in town. Guest rooms are simply furnished and showing their age somewhat, but they're clean and all you'll need for a night or two in this small town. Besides, the panoramic mountain views and small-town hospitality (staff will happily assist with any travel or sightseeing arrangements) is what you are here for. Ask for an upper-level deluxe room (the higher you go, the better the views), keep the floral-patterned curtains wide open, and enjoy the modest comforts of this unassuming but well-run inn.

Beyond Log Huts, Manali 175 131. ✆ **01902/25-3351.** Fax 01902/25-3188. Reservations in Delhi ✆ 011/2552-0914 or -0915. www.ushashriramhotels.com. 32 units. Rs 2,500 ($57) standard double, Rs 3,600 ($82) deluxe double; Rs 4,350 ($99) 3-person suite. Rs 600 ($14) extra bed. AE, DC, MC, V. **Amenities:** Restaurant; cybercafe; bar-cum-discotheque; fitness center; tours; sightseeing; adventure activities including fishing, river rafting, skiing, mountain biking, trekking, and paragliding; business facilities; room service (6am–midnight); laundry; doctor-on-call. *In room:* A/C, TV, central heating.

Span Resorts 🍴   A riverside location, 15km (9 miles) from the center of Manali, makes this resort a peaceful respite from the crowds, enhanced by the generous range of amenities and outdoor activities on offer. Accommodations are in stone-and-wood cottages shaped like stars and spread around well-maintained grounds; they're comfortable and offer a fair degree of privacy. Riverside units, with wooden floors, are the best. There isn't a heck of a lot of space, but each cottage has a fireplace and a covered porch from which to appreciate the relaxed setting and mountain views. There is plenty to keep you occupied during the snowy season, including the best-stocked bar in the state.

Kullu–Manali Hwy., P.O. Katrain 175 129. ✆ **01902/24-0138** or 01902/24-0538. Fax 01902/240140. www.span resorts.com. spanres@del3.vsnl.net.in. Reservations: Vijaya (1st Floor), 17 Barakhamba Rd., New Delhi 110 001. ✆ 011/2331-1434. Fax 011/2335-3148. 24 units. Rs 5,400 ($123) double, Rs 1,500 ($35) more for riverside double. Rs 775 ($18) children ages 6–12; Rs 1,550 ($36) extra bed for anyone 12 and above. 10% tax. Rates include all meals. AE, DC, MC, V. **Amenities:** Restaurant; bar; pool; mini-golf; tennis; basketball; gym; darts; croquet; card room; library; table tennis; children's park; billiards; badminton; travel assistance, taxis, tours, sightseeing; fishing, river rafting, skiing, horseback riding, trekking, and paragliding by arrangement; 24-hr. room service; laundry; doctor-on-call. *In room:* A/C, TV, minibar.

WHERE TO DINE

With Manali's tourism boom has come a flood of eating establishments, many of which indulge in unchecked fly-by-night copycat techniques; be sure to check details beyond the name of whichever establishment you choose. Bear in mind that none take credit cards, and most stay open from 9am to 11pm.

The best Indian restaurant, with typical Himachali cuisine, is **Mayur** (✆ **01902/25-2316;** Rs 40–Rs 200/90¢–$4.55). Kangra Valley–born Rajesh Sud has been in the restaurant business since 1970 and opened this Manali institution back in 1978. Fresh, locally caught wild trout, prepared in the tandoor oven with a subtle blend of yogurt and aromatic spices, is the highlight—ask for tandoori trout *machhli.* A good alternative is **Khyber** (✆ **01902/25-1972;** Rs 100–Rs 250/$2.30–$5.70), where longtime restaurateur Kawaljeet (he's also in charge of the popular nearby **Sher-e-Punjab** *dhaba,* open since 1972) serves up excellent Punjabi-style chicken, doused with exotic spices and cooked to perfection. Both are open from 11am to 11pm. With its first-story views over The Mall, Khyber's window tables are great for midafternoon people-watching— particularly when wet weather forces you indoors. For the best Tibetan cuisine, head for **Mount View** (✆ **01902/25-3617;** Rs 50–Rs 250/$1.15–$5.70), a laid-back diner where you can enjoy the best *momos* (dumplings) in town (try the ones with potato spinach filling). Any of the piping-hot Tibetan broths will pick you up when the cold gets too much, and there's an excellent range of vegetarian Chinese dishes. For Italian (including reasonably good coffee), **Il Forno,** housed in a century-old house in Dunghri en route to the Hadimba Temple, is your most authentic option, also with good views. Roberta Angelone, who is from Naples, creates outstanding fresh-made pastas (ask if the ravioli is available) and authentic pizzas (no phone; average meal Rs 300/$6.85). **Johnson's Café** ✪ (Johnson's Lodge, The Mall; ✆ **01902/24-5292;** Rs 70–Rs 200/$1.60–$4.55) is a cozy, informal venue that enjoys a lively atmosphere and has garden seating. It also has fresh trout—locally caught—on the menu, and it's a fine place to have coffee and breakfast while you plan the day's trek.

Up in Smoke

With the apple-market slump causing rising unemployment in recent years, the appeal of **marijuana,** Himachal Pradesh's naturally occurring crop, has become all too obvious. High on the knowledge of the availability of cheap and easy-to-come-by dope, backpackers and hippies have flocked to the region for decades. But over the last 3 years, some pockets of Himachal (such as Old Manali, Kasol, and Dharamsala) have become flooded with Israeli tourists, 20-somethings cutting loose after completing their mandatory 3-year stint in the army. The attraction here is of course drugs, with about 4,000 acres of Himachal reportedly under cannabis cultivation. The arrival of so many young Israelis has changed the tourism industry as well, with restaurants now serving falafel, baba ghanoush, and laban (yogurt), and a surprising number of signs and menus in Hebrew. There's serious smoke rising at full-moon rave parties where Boom Shiva (read: hashish) can be found in abundance and young Israelis inhale with "full power." Excessive indulgence has now motivated the Israeli government to sponsor a home in Old Manali to rescue drug-addicted youngsters, as well as Kfar Izum (Balance Village) on the Mediterranean coast to rehabilitate youth who are sending their futures up in smoke in Himachal.

6 Exploring Dharamsala & the Kangra Valley

Tenzin Gyatso, the 14th Dalai Lama, chose Dharamsala as the capital-in-exile of the Tibetan people after fleeing Chinese oppression in 1959, and whether it's the endless spinning of Buddhist prayer wheels or simply the divine presence of the Dalai Lama, the Tibetan enclave at Dharamsala draws seekers of spiritual enlightenment from all over the world.

Admittedly, a visit to Everyman's spiritual center of the universe seems like the ultimate New Age cliché, but the town and its environs have much more to recommend than the fervent chanting of *Om mani padme hum* ("Hail to the jewel in the lotus"). The natural beauty of the surrounding mountains and mist-soaked valleys compares favorably with that of any of Himachal's best-loved resort towns, and for those not single-mindedly wrapped up in a quest for spiritual fine-tuning with Buddhist lectures and meditation courses, this is an ideal base for walks and treks into the Dhauladhar range. It's also a good place to simply experience a toned-down India at a more leisurely pace.

The hillside town stretches along a spur of the Dhauladhar mountain range and is divided into two very distinct parts—**Lower Dharamsala** and **McLeod Ganj** (often called Little Lhasa). Only the latter is worth considering as a place to stay and explore; here you will encounter brightly robed Buddhist monks with umbrellas and Doc Marten boots, traditionally attired Tibetan women reciting holy mantras, and spiritual tourists in search of enlightenment. A former British hill station rocked by an earthquake in the early 1900s, McLeod Ganj today harbors several institutes and organizations dedicated to raising funds for the Tibetan people and promoting and preserving Buddhist culture. Among these is the Government-in-Exile's administration complex, or *Gangchen Kyishong*, where you'll find the fascinating **Library of Tibetan Works and Archives.** North of Dharamsala are spectacular mountain-hugging drives to the remote towns of Dalhousie and Chamba, while farther south you can visit the charming heritage village of **Pragpur** ✿✿ and explore the tea-covered valleys around historical **Taragarh Palace Hotel** ✿, not far from the town of Palampur.

ESSENTIALS

VISITOR INFORMATION   There's a **Tourist Information Office** (✆ **0189/222-1205;** Mon–Sat 10am–1:30pm and 2–5pm) in McLeod Ganj, but you'll be hard-pressed to squeeze anything worthwhile out of the lackluster staff; you'd do better to make enquiries at your hotel. *CONTACT* is a free monthly newsletter distributed in and around McLeod Ganj. Although its primary aim is to promote Buddhist issues, it also carries up-to-date information and advertisements regarding cultural events and activities likely to be of interest to foreign visitors. If you are here for massage, meditation, alternative healing, yoga, or Tibetan cooking classes, this publication will point you in the right direction. Also visit **www.dharamsalanet.com**.

GETTING THERE & AROUND   It's possible to drive from Shimla or Chandigarh to Dharamsala, and there are two great overnight options along the way—choose between **Taragarh Palace,** outside Palampur, or **The Judge's Court,** in Pragpur (see later in this chapter). The most pleasant way to get to the Kangra Valley directly from Delhi is by train (driving by car takes almost 12 hr.). The overnight Jammu Mail from Delhi allows you to rest up before hiring a car for the scenic 3-hour road trip from Panthankot to Dharamsala (80km/50 miles). At press time, no flights were operating to Kangra's Gaggal Airport, 15km (9 miles) from Dharamsala. In Dharamsala,

Enlightenment or Exploitation?

McLeod Ganj is probably the last place you'd expect to encounter any social tension, but if you want to get involved in the local politics, chat up the locals about the refugee situation. Thanks largely to the global popularity of the Dalai Lama and his ability to raise international interest—and massive funding—for the Tibetan cause, the Tibetan refugees in Dharamsala have managed to maintain their culture, and Tibetans argue that their people work harder and deserve the success they've achieved in the tourist-friendly enclave. On the other hand, Indians bemoan the internationally sponsored wealth that has accumulated around the disenfranchised Tibetans, and some take issue with Tibetan endeavors to rigorously preserve and promote their distinctive culture. It's a fascinating debate, one well worth discussing with the locals.

you will find it easy to get either a taxi or auto-rickshaw. (Auto-rickshaws are incredibly impractical, however, because of the engine-killing gradient of the town.) **Ways Tours & Travels** (Temple Rd., McLeod Ganj; © **01892/22-1910,** 01892/22-1355, or 01892/22-1988; waystour@vsnl.net) hires out cars with drivers for local sightseeing, and can help with all your travel arrangements as well as organize individually packaged tours throughout the region. You can also contact them in New Delhi, at House no. 18, New Tibetan Camp, Majnu-Ka-Tilla; call © **011/2381-3254** or 98112-89552.

THE TOP ATTRACTIONS

Thekchen Chöling Temple Complex 🏵🏵 Life in McLeod Ganj revolves around this Buddhist temple complex, linked to the off-limits private residence of the Dalai Lama. A good example of Buddhism's spiritual and artistic traditions, the complex comprises **Namgyal Monastery** and **Tsuglakhang Temple,** both worth a visit if you're keen to get a sense of active lamaistic practice. You'll often encounter monks debating in the courtyard or meditatively preparing colorful sand *mandalas,* diagrams that symbolize the universe and are used in the ritual of spiritual empowerment known as the *kalachakra* ceremony, after which the meticulous designs are destroyed. The *gompa* houses various cultural relics brought from Lhasa during the Cultural Revolution, including a 1,500-year-old idol of Guru Padmasambhav, and a life-size image of Avalokiteshvara, of whom the Dalai Lama is believed to be an incarnation. Public appearances by the Dalai Lama occur from time to time; consult the local authorities for information. The complex courtyard is the venue for an all-day festival of traditional dance held in honor of His Holiness's birthday on July 6, although the Dalai Lama is not always in attendance on this auspicious day. It's worthwhile to take a break from the prayer wheels and settle in at the tiny, laid-back cafe in the temple complex (which serves primarily as a vocational training opportunity for young Tibetans) to try out the international vegetarian dishes ranging from Indonesian *gado-gado* to Cuban *arro a la cubana.* This is a great place for a cup of pure South Indian coffee or Tibetan herbal tea. Snag the window-side table for beautiful views over the valley below.

Temple Rd. To obtain clearance for a public audience with the Dalai Lama, it's necessary to apply, with your passport, at the Security Office on Bhagsu Rd.

The Tibet Museum 🏵 If you'd like to learn more about the plight of the Tibetan people, then step into this sophisticated but rather depressing installation that provides a historical overview of the situation in Tibet. *A Long Look Homeward,* the main exhibition, consists of two parts. The downstairs display highlights the atrocities that have been carried out against millions of Tibetans during the Chinese occupation. Although events are detailed primarily through textual displays, the collection of data is emotionally challenging. Upstairs, the exhibition focuses more on Tibetan history. Particularly moving is the "testimony corner," where visitors can record the names of loved ones whose deaths are a result of the occupation. Lectures, presentations, and video screenings are presented in the small lecture hall; visit **www.thetibetmuseum.org** if you're interested in upcoming events.

Near the main temple and Namgyal Monastery Gate. Admission Rs 5 (10¢).Tues–Sun 10am–6pm.

Norbulingka Institute ✿✿✿ If you're interested in getting a firsthand understanding of the techniques (and unbelievable patience) required to produce authentic Tibetan arts and crafts, the institute is a good starting point. Set in well-tended grounds some 40 minutes from Dharamsala, it comprises workshops, training centers, a temple, a guesthouse, a cafe, and a doll museum. You can contact the management in advance to organize a tour through the facilities, where you can witness the creation of colorful tantric *thangkas* (embroidered wall hangings), paintings, metalware, furniture, and traditional garments. Tibetan language lessons are available for interested foreigners. The beautiful **Seat of Happiness Temple** ✿✿ features astounding murals, including impressions of all 14 Dalai Lamas and 1,173 images of the Buddha, which decorate the 13m-high (44-ft.) temple hall. The gilded copper Buddha Shakyamuni was crafted by Norbulingka's master statue-maker, Pemba Dorje, and is one of the largest of its kind outside Tibet; the arch behind the statue is decorated with sculpted clay images. Head for the richly ornamented temple rooftop for magnificent views of the surrounding landscape. The Institute's **Losel Doll Museum** ✿✿ features diorama-style displays of miniature figures (Tibetan dolls) in traditional costumes and historical regalia.

P.O. Sidhpur. ✆ **01892/24-6402** or 01892/46405. Fax 01892/246404. www.norbulingka.org. Admission Rs 20 (45¢). Daily 9am–6pm.

Tibetan Institute for Performing Arts (TIPA) One hour from McLeod Ganj is TIPA, one of the first institutes set up by the Dalai Lama when he settled in McLeod Ganj, for the study and preservation of traditional Tibetan opera, dance, and music. Tibetan opera *(Lhamo)* performances can be long (some last 6 hr.) and are best experienced during the annual 9-day-long Shoton Opera Festival held in February and March (usually in Dharamsala, but in 2005 at the Tibetan settlement of Bylakuppe, Karnataka). Many other performances are held throughout the year as well, and interested visitors are welcome to watch classes. Ask at your hotel, check bulletin boards in local cafes for announcements, or go to the website for details.

P.O. McLeod Ganj. ✆ **01892/22-0657**. www.tibetanarts.org.

Church Of St. John in the Wilderness ✿ Ten minutes of downhill walking from McLeod Ganj brings you to the Church of St. John in the Wilderness, surrounded by deodar cedars. It's a neo-Gothic stone construction, with its original Belgian stained glass intact in spite of a severe earthquake in 1905 that leveled the rest of town. Buried in the grassy adjoining graveyard is British Viceroy Lord Elgin (whose somewhat infamous father was responsible for the controversial Elgin Marbles).

Daily 10am–5pm.

WHERE TO STAY & DINE

The best place to stay is the Norbulingka Institute–run **Chonor House,** not least for its dining. If you have a yearning to live in a forest surrounded by nature's bounty, check out **Glenmoor Cottages.** (Both options are reviewed below.)

For a real budget option, consider peaceful **Cheryton Cottage** (Jogibara Rd.; *©* **01892/22-1993;** tcheryl_89@yahoo.com), where Alan and Cheryl Templeton rent out four rooms (Rs 450/$10 double) and an entire house (a steal at Rs 1,500/$35; rooms are often booked for long stays during the summer). The rooms are spartan 1970s throwbacks dressed in outrageous colors (of the four units, the aptly named "Blue" and "Pink" have views). Away from the noise of the central square and yet only a stone's throw from it, the very likable **Pema Thang** *©* guesthouse has spotless rooms with wood floors, an excellent restaurant, and a friendly, helpful manager, Mr. Lobsang Teshi. Ask for a room on one of the higher floors, though all overlook the valley (*©* **01892/22-1871;** doubles Rs 660–Rs 990/$15–$22). For those who prefer a more secluded stay, head out to **Dharamkot,** a small borough just outside McLeod Ganj with stupendous views of the Dhauladhar mountains and Kangra Valley. **Dev Cottages** (*©* **01892/22-1558**) has pleasant rooms with large windows, balconies, and lovely views, for Rs 1,200 ($28), including breakfast. Another option far from town but worth considering is **Norling Guesthouse** (at the Norbulingka Institute), which has six charming rooms from Rs 1,150 ($26).

As with many of the towns popular with tourists, McLeod Ganj is disproportionately restaurant-heavy. The best by far is Chonor House, which specializes in Tibetan cuisine (see below). Other Tibetan food restaurants worth highlighting are **Green Restaurant** (Bhagsunag Rd.; *©* **01892/22-1200**), which uses only organic produce; and **Namgyal Café** *©©* (at the Tsuglakhang or Main temple; *©* **01892/22-1040**), which serves what might be called Tibetan fusion. Try the tofu stroganoff or *tsampa* (roasted flour) crepes; if you're not feeling too experimental, stick to noodles, *momos,* or the brilliant thin-crust pizzas.

While Tibetan fare would appear to be the way to go, you'll pretty much find something for everyone—from falafels to focaccia, *momos* (dumplings) to tempura. At least four German bakeries and as many pizzerias also cater to the large number of foreigners who come to McLeod Ganj. There's even a nifty grub-'n'-pub style restaurant called **Mc'Llo** (at the top of Temple Rd.; *©* **01892/22-1280**), an extremely popular hangout for travelers that prides itself on having once entertained Pierce Brosnan (celebrity culture having few geographical boundaries). If you have a yen for Japanese, **Lung Ta,** an intimate diner with meat-free dishes from the land of the rising sun, includes a small floor-seating area with traditional low tables (Jogibara Rd.; *©* **01892/22-0689**). Daily set meals feature a curious mix of Japanese vegetarian dishes; on a typical day, you may be offered *kisetsu yasai no agebitashi* (stir-fried fresh seasonal vegetables), glass noodle (or other) salad, miso soup, and rice (on Tues and Thurs rice is replaced with a healthy number of assorted sushi rolls), all meals a real steal at Rs 100 ($23).

For Italian, head for **Nick's Italian Kitchen** (in the Kunga Guesthouse, Bhagsu Rd., McLeod Ganj; *©* **01892/22-1180**), which is something of a local institution. Tenzin, whose father worked as security officer for the Dalai Lama from the age of 18, is—like His Holiness—a proponent of vegetarianism, and his kitchen is therefore strictly non-meat. Gnocchi, cannelloni, and ravioli are prepared fresh every morning. The eggplant, spinach, and cheese lasagnas are star attractions, as is the aptly named "Pizza Everything."

The Dalai Lama Speaks Here & Richard Gere Slept There

Tenzin, from Nick's Italian Kitchen (above), is one of the best people to speak to if you're eager to organize an audience with His Holiness. A proud and committed follower of the Dalai Lama, he also organizes occasional talks on Tibet and Buddhism at the restaurant, and is overflowing with personal theories about the local community and the diplomatic situation with the Chinese government. Staunch Richard Gere fans traveling on a limited budget can try to get the Gere Suite of the **Kunga Guesthouse** upstairs from the restaurant; Richard was the first guest when it opened on January 24, 1996.

At the immaculate Norbulingka Institute, **Norling Café** ✦✦ (✆ **01892/246-402** or -6405; www.norbulingka.org) is great for healthy, wholesome dishes that can be taken on the patio, where you're likely to spot paradise flycatchers darting among the lush vegetation. You can also pre-order meals through the guesthouse. If it's too cold outside, sit in the cozy dining room, adorned with paintings done by the institute's artists.

Chonor House ✦✦✦ (Value)   One of the best reasons to spend any amount of time in Dharamsala is to sample each of the exquisitely decorated rooms that make up this charming Tibetan guesthouse at the toe-end of McLeod Ganj, a stone's throw away from the main *gompa*. Each room is uniquely themed according to aspects of Tibetan culture; the museum-standard murals created by different experts in conjunction with artists from the Norbulingka Institute (see above) neatly balance the beautifully crafted teak-and-rosewood furniture and hand-knotted carpets rendered by other Norbulingka teams. There are three categories of rooms, each offering different amenities: Some have balconies, some have tubs, and some (like the magnificent "Voyage at Sea" rooms) are simply enormous. "Nomad" features strikingly painted yaks, goats, and traveling tribespeople and also has a lovely balcony from which you have a direct view of the main *gompa*. The terrifically colorful Songsten Suite not only has a separate lounge and private balcony, but its own shrinelike cabinet showcasing statues of the three great kings of Tibet. There's a public homey sitting room furnished with plush sofas and a combination of parquet wood flooring and thick rugs. Indeed, you need hardly step outside the front door to get a good feel for Tibetan art and culture—this is a treasure chest of style and meticulous attention to details most Westerners probably don't think about. Dharamsala's best guesthouse also offers its most impressive dining opportunity. The menu is a veritable encyclopedia of Tibetan dishes—which have a way of becoming quite addictive. Share a plate of *momos* to start—these butter dumplings are steamed to perfection and filled with tasty fresh white cheese. Or experiment with the excellent *bobi,* which allows you to build your own Tibetan spring rolls, a fun alternative to the greasy version popular in Chinese takeout joints. You can build all night, using thinly grilled bread wraps, seasoned glass noodles, mixed vegetables, tofu, and Basmati rice. Or have the *bobi* as a starter, after which you can try the delicious fried *pishi* (wontons), deliciously seasoned *shabri* (meat or vegetable balls in garlic sauce), or steaming mutton-filled *shabalay* (bread pie). There's even a selection of scrumptious salads (try the cheese, carrot, apple, walnut, and spinach concoction). ***Note:*** Tibetan hospitality at its very best can, of course, do nothing to stop the chorus of barking hounds that seems to be the typical prelude—or interruption—to a good night's sleep.

Thekchen Choling Rd. (road ends at Pema Thang, walk the last 50m), P.O. McLeod Ganj, Dharamsala 176 219. ℂ **01892/22-1468** or -1006. Fax 01892/22-0815. chonorhs@norbulingka.org. www.norbulingka.org/site/visitors/ chonor.htm. 11 units. Rs 1,900–Rs 2,400 ($43–$55) double; Rs 2,800 ($64) suite. Rs 550 ($13) extra bed. MC, V. **Amenities:** Restaurant; boutique; room service 7am–10pm; laundry; TV room; cybercafe. *In room:* Heater, tea-making facility.

Glenmoor Cottages 🏵🏵   Located on a magnificent property in the midst of a hillside forest, 1km (½ mile) beyond McLeod Ganj, Glenmoor comprises five private cottages situated around an original colonial manor house, Om Bhawan, built by a Scotsman in the early 20th century. Dharamsala's most remote and peaceful lodging (you feel as if you're a thousand miles from anything), Glenmoor is owned and run by Ajai Singh, whose family bought the lovely, tree-covered property 6 decades back. The cottages are simple stone structures with pleasant pine interiors and private verandas from which to appreciate the infinite peace and quiet (save for the ceaseless chorus of cicadas) or to watch for exotic birds. The upper cottages are roomier and include both a dressing area and a larger split-level living room; there are only two of these, so book ahead. Guests can enjoy wholesome home-cooked Indian meals and simple continental breakfasts in the small restaurant at the manor house.

Mall Rd., Upper Dharamsala 176 219. ℂ **01892/22-1010.** Fax 01892/221021. www.glenmoorcottages.com. info@glenmoorcottages.com. 5 units. Rs 3,250 ($76) upper cottages, Rs 2,150 ($49) lower cottages. Rates exclude meals and taxes. MC, V. **Amenities:** Restaurant; room service 7am–9pm. *In room:* TV, heater, fridge.

SHOPPING

All manner of Tibetan handicrafts and faux antiques are sold just about everywhere in McLeod Ganj. Buy reasonably priced Tibetan rugs and handicrafts from the **Tibetan Handicraft Centre** (near Post Office, Jogibara Rd.; ℂ **01892/22-1415**) and the **Tibetan Children's Village Handicraft Centre** (ℂ **01892/22-1592**). **Stitches of Tibet** (Temple Rd.; ℂ **01892/22-1198** or -1527) is an enterprise that trains local women in handicraft production. Their shop stocks the completed handicrafts as well as Tibetan clothing. If you want to buy a traditional Tibetan *thangka* (painted or

---

A Taste of Tibet

Confused by what's on offer in the Tibetan restaurants of the Indian Himalayan region? Here's a guide: *Gyathuk* is a traditional egg noodle soup, typically prepared with tofu and black-and-white mushrooms. *Thenthuk* is a broth made with handmade noodles. *Pishi* is another name for wontons, often served in a vegetable broth with Tibetan tofu. You'll find Tibetan tofu and dumplings swimming in your *mothuk*, another traditional Tibetan broth. *Shabaklab* or *shabalay* is the Tibetan version of a pie, typically accompanied by broth. *Momos* are Tibetan dumplings, filled with cheese, vegetables, or meat. *Shabri* are seasoned meat or vegetable balls. *Bobi* are Tibetan spring rolls, filled with glass noodles, tofu, and mixed vegetables. Most Tibetan dishes can be served with vegetables, chicken, mutton, or even pork. *Bod-jha* is the staple Tibetan tea, copious quantities of which are consumed by Tibetans everywhere, and by almost no one else. It tastes nothing like any tea you've ever had—besides tea and milk, it contains salt and butter.

embroidered banner or wall decoration), the **Norbulingka Institute** is where this art is preserved and taught; they also take orders. Shop at the institute or at Chonor House, knowing that your purchase will actually contribute to the development of Tibetan craftsmanship. For books, visit **Namgyal Bookstore** in the temple complex; its excellent collection focuses primarily on Tibetan culture and Buddhism, but it has a good number of beautiful publications on Himachal Pradesh and other Himalayan regions as well. Also filled with an interesting assortment of books on the history, culture, and art of the region is **Youtse Book Shop** (Mount View Complex, Temple Rd.). Finally, don't miss stopping at **Nowrojee Store** (near the Bus Stand), run for six generations by a Parsi family, one of whom is said to have been the person who encouraged the Dalai Lama to settle here in 1959. This quaint place is worth a visit for its history alone, if not to pick up some interesting knickknacks.

NEAR DHARAMSALA

If you have the time and want to veer slightly off the beaten track, definitely head southeast of Dharamsala toward the gently undulating tea-covered hills of Kangra Valley. Although it lacks any particular charms of its own, **Palampur** is a popular starting point for Kangra Valley—but you'll be better off passing straight through and continuing for 14km (9 miles) to romantic **Taragarh Palace,** now run as a heritage hotel (reviewed below). Nearby is **Tashijong Monastery,** a colorful *gompa* established in the years after the Dalai Lama made his home in Dharamsala. The neighboring town of Baijnath is the site of the beautiful **Saivite Vaidyanath Temple complex** (Baijnath Main Rd.; daily 5am–9pm in summer and 6am–8pm in winter), one of the more interesting and best-preserved Hindu shrines in Himachal Pradesh, dating back to the early 13th century. Surrounded by a wall decorated by fine carvings, the main temple enshrines a squat Shiva lingam protected by a five-headed metallic cobra; devotees usually cover the lingam with flowers and other offerings.

Pragpur is a time-trapped village with mud-plastered, slate-roofed houses, elegant *havelis* (mansions), Italianate buildings, and narrow cobblestone roads. Designated India's first official "Heritage Village," this tiny hamlet was founded as a memorial to a brave warrior princess who led a resistance against invaders in the 17th century. Pragpur is wonderful to explore, a veritable warren of tiny lanes and old, atmospheric buildings. The surrounding landscape offers opportunities for nature walks, cycling, bird-watching, and fishing. Upper Pragpur is known for its home-weaving industry, so this is the place to look for good deals on local crafts. Spend the night in Pragpur's beautiful **Judge's Court,** one of Himachal's most enchanting hotels (reviewed below).

WHERE TO STAY

The Judge's Court This atmospheric Indo-European haveli, architecturally detailed with domes, galleries, terraces, and porticoes, is filled with the sort of tranquil charm that whisks guests straight back into a bygone age. Set on a magnificent property with orchards of mango, lychee, plum, persimmon, and citrus-fruit trees, the main manor house was built in 1918 by a descendant of Pragpur's founders as a gift for his son, a well-known judge of the Punjab High Court. Laboriously restored, the hotel offers a variety of accommodations. The very best guest room is the spookily romantic Judge's Suite, which has its own sitting room and two plush armchairs strategically placed in front of the fireplace. All of the rooms have their charms, however, including ancient bathrooms and original beds. Staff can assist you with exploring the village or finding adventure in Kangra Valley.

Note: If you want to stay in the heart of the medieval village, look into the availability of one of the two Judge's Court annexes: semi-detached 17th-century houses in Pragpur's highly atmospheric Kuthiala Courtyard. Visitors can rent these to experience life along the narrow lanes and cobbled walkways of the village—perfect for families, and ideal for romance. Marble floors are offset by mud-themed walls, an ancient gas-powered kitchen, and big bedrooms with tiny shuttered windows.

Heritage Village Pragpur, Tehsil Dehra, District Kangra 177 107. © **01970/24-5035** or 01970/24-5335. Reservations: 3/44, Shanti Niketan, New Delhi 110 021. © 011/2467-4135. Fax 011/2688-5970. www.judgescourt.com. 10 units. Rs 2,300 ($53) double; Rs 2,500 ($57) heritage cottage. Rs 700 ($16) extra bed. AE, MC, V. **Amenities:** Restaurant; cultural performances; local sightseeing, taxi, and travel arrangements; laundry. *In room:* A/C in some rooms, tea- and coffee-making facilities, heater, flashlight.

Taragarh Palace Hotel ⊛ A pleasant change from more commercial hill-station retreats such as Shimla and Mussourie, Kangra Valley attracts travelers seeking peace and tranquillity. At this 6-hectare (15-acre) forested estate, a touch of pre-independence class is thrown in for good measure. Once known as Al Hilal (The Land of the Crescent Moon), this Art Deco mansion (now described as the Heritage Wing) was built in the 1930s as the summer resort of the Nawab of Bahawalpur until he fled to Pakistan after Partition. One of the least-visited destinations in the heart of the scenic and serene Kangra Valley, Taragarh is surrounded by thick vegetation, moss-covered walls, and gorgeous grounds, making it particularly popular with meditation groups who come here for the clean air and idyllic environment. Reminiscent of the setting for a brooding Agatha Christie whodunit, the mansion is all high ceilings, broad staircases, chandeliers, and long passages. Book the characterful Maharajah, Maharani, or Rajmata suites—smart, spacious, and elegantly decorated with charming touches entirely absent from the rather dull double rooms, which are more reminiscent of English country-hotel rooms with musty carpets than royal retiring quarters (and which are also a tad on the small side). Better doubles are nos. 106 and 107 downstairs, which have larger bathrooms; and upstairs room nos. 210 and 211, which have small dressing room/studies. If you prefer your amenities brand new, check out the recently completed Palace Wing, with 14 units, as well as a business and fitness center. Traditional Indian, Kashmiri, and local dishes are served in the charming wood-paneled dining room dominated by a near-psychedelic red chandelier.

Taragarh Palace, Tehsil Baijnath, District Kangra 176 081. ©/fax **01894/242-034** or 01894/243-077. www.taragarh.com. www.welcomheritage.com. reservations@taragarh.com. Reservations: 15 Institutional Area, Lodhi Rd., New Delhi 110 003. © 011/2464-3046. Fax 011/2469-2317. 30 units. Rs 1,250 ($29) cabin double, Rs 2,750 ($62) standard double, Rs 3,500 ($80) deluxe double; Rs 3,950 ($90) suite. Extra bed 25% of room rent. AE, MC, V. **Amenities:** Restaurant; bar; pool; tennis court; badminton court; fitness center w/steam room; children's park; cybercafe; sightseeing, taxi, and travel arrangements; business center; room service (snacks and tea) 7am–10pm. *In room:* TV, heater, A/C in suites, minibar and tea- and coffee-making facilities in deluxe suites.

7 Leh & Environs ⊛⊛⊛

Leh is 475km (295 miles) from Manali

The region of Ladakh, in the state of Jammu and Kashmir, has often been described as a moonscape, a desolate high-altitude desert kingdom of mysticism and mystery. It is all of these, and more, a thoroughly awe-inspiring world of harsh reality, with few luxuries. Local lives are centered around Buddhism, yaks, and survival, and more recently on the small tourism industry that sprouts in the relatively warmer months of the year (July–Sept).

Leh, Ladakh's capital city, is little touched by rain, but the extreme cold during the long winter season means that this remote region remains isolated for much of the year. Come June, however, when the tourists begin to trickle into Leh, the sober, somber slumber of this remote high-altitude town lifts along with the temperatures. Situated in a fertile valley at the foot of Namgyal Tsemo peak, 8km (5 miles) north-east of the Indus River, Leh is deeply reliant on this short, intense tourist season. From June to September the surrounding barren mountains and distant snowcapped peaks are the perfect natural backdrop for the verdant fields and avenues of trees that cluster around the whitewashed, flat-roofed buildings.

Developed as a market for traders from across the North India belt, Leh was an important stop for travelers traversing the challenging caravan routes to Yarkand and Kashgar. The Silk Road brought Buddhist travelers, and today the population remains predominantly Buddhist. You can spend up to a week exploring the town and the numerous Buddhist monuments within a 2- or 3-hour drive of Leh. Adventure-seekers can get caught up in river-rafting on the Zanskar and Indus, high-level mountain-climbing, or treks into remote, barren wilderness regions, which can easily extend your stay by an additional week. The more laid-back traveler will be rewarded by awe-inspiring excursions to high-altitude lakes such as Pangong Tso and Tso Moriri.

ESSENTIALS

GETTING THERE   By Air   If you'd rather save time and get to Leh without the arduous cliff-hanging road journey, **Jet Airways** (Dreamland Complex, Main Bazaar; © **01982/25-0444;** Mon–Sat 10am–5pm, Sun 10am–3pm) now offers daily flights between New Delhi and Leh in the summer. The disadvantage of flying in is that you may need to spend up to 48 hours acclimatizing anyway, whereas the road journey gently puts you through your paces. Flying out of Leh is definitely a good idea; reserve a window seat. Indian Airlines also flies to Leh, but these flights are often booked up by military personnel.

By Road   Two rather tiring days are required to get from Manali to Leh. But for those seeking an adventurous road trip coupled with exquisite, endlessly changing scenery, the journey—by off-road vehicle or bus—is highly recommended. See "Negotiating the Manali–Leh Highway," below.

VISITOR INFORMATION   Leh has a Tourist Information Center, but you are advised not to waste your time there. Speak to your hotel manager or any of the many tour operators who offer various services throughout Ladakh.

GETTING AROUND   By Car   Thanks to a strong military presence in the region, Ladakh's roads are excellent and the network of accessible destinations extensive.

By Taxi   Although Leh has but one auto-rickshaw, it has as many as 1,500 taxis, but the fixed rates to practically any place in the state are high. Unless you've rented a vehicle outside Leh, you will have little choice but to cough up the dough. Your best bet is to share a jeep with fellow travelers interested in visiting similar destinations. For taxi rates and bookings, call the **Leh Taxi Stand** (© **01982/25-2723**). Note that if you travel from Leh to Zanskar or Kargil by taxi, you will have to hire a separate local taxi for internal travel in these districts. Inconvenient as it may be, it's a taxi union rule that is meant to protect the livelihood of the drivers in these less-visited districts.

Negotiating the Manali–Leh Highway

Nearly 500km (310 miles) of tricky roads, mountain passes, and exceptional roller-coaster scenery separates Leh from Manali. For most of the year, this spectacular stretch of road is closed to traffic, covered by thick snow. Even when the road is officially open in late June and early July, the danger of unexpected snowfall looms, bringing with it various risks associated with getting stuck in the middle of vast unpopulated areas with only freezing cold nights for company. Once summer has set in, a variety of makeshift *dhabas* and *chai* stalls are gathered in mini-colonies along the way. You'll need your passport for a string of checkpoints, the first of which is just beyond the Rohtang Pass at the head of the Kullu Valley. Beyond this, you enter **Lahaul,** a vast Trans-Himalayan landscape dotted with flat-roofed, whitewashed houses built from sun-dried bricks. **Sarchu,** a motley collection of tented camps, is where you'll probably bed down for the night; you'll be too cold to complain about the limited facilities. You reach the world's second-highest motorable road at the summit of the Taklang-La Pass (5,241m/17,469 ft.); here you will find a small multifaith shrine adorned by images of gurus, deities, and religious icons. Beyond the pass, exquisite mountains in a host of unbelievable colors compete with charming villages for your attention.

Your cheapest viable option is an ostensibly "luxury" bus operated by **HPTDC** (© **0177/265-2651;** www.hptdc.nic.in). For Rs 1,200 ($28) you get an ass-numbing 2-day trip with spartan tented accommodations and dinner en route near Sarchu. Occasional stops for *chai* and photographs are obligatory, but bring plenty of camera film and refreshments. Bottled water is particularly important because dehydration is one of the symptoms of altitude sickness. Jeeps and minivan taxis are pricier but represent relative luxury and the opportunity to explore villages and off-road sites along the way. Hiring your own vehicle and driver is an even better way to go, of course, if you don't mind paying between Rs 6,000 and Rs 12,000 ($137–$275). Bernard Lazarevitch is an adventurous European who offers "motorbike safaris" to fascinating destinations throughout northern India. When the Manali–Leh highway opens in late June, you can experience this legendary route by hopping onto the back of Bernard's bike or by joining one of his expeditions. For details, contact **AventureMoto** (www.AventureMoto.com; aventuremoto@yahoo.com).

GUIDED TOURS AND ADVENTURE & TREKKING COMPANIES   It's easy to plan your own outings and give the instructions to your jeep or taxi driver. If you want to deal with an outfitter, refer to the "Staying Active" section earlier in this chapter. If you are very keen on receiving expert information as you explore monasteries and other sights, then a licensed operator may be useful. Speak to Ghulam Mohiuddin at **Adventure North** (Hotel Dragon; © **01982/25-2139** or -2720; fax 01982/25-2720; advnorth@sancharnet.in) about organizing treks and adventures throughout Ladakh.

San Francisco–based **Geographic Expeditions** 𝕲𝕲𝕲 (www.geoex.com; ✆ 800/ 777-8183 in the U.S.) offers a 21-day Trans-Himalayan trek that passes through the old kingdom of Zanskar through Ladakh, hitting an altitude of 5,064m (16,880 ft.); though not for the fainthearted, it's an exhilarating way to experience one of India's most untouched regions. For more leisure-oriented travelers, the same company conducts jeep safaris of Ladakh. In Leh itself, **Rimo Expeditions** (Hotel Kanglhachen Complex, opposite the Police Station; ✆ 01982/25-3257; Gurgaon contact: 0124/ 2680-6027 through -6029; info@rimoexpeditions.com) is a very reliable outfit that undertakes various expeditions. The company also arranges less-hectic trekking expeditions, as well as jeep and yak safaris, and skiing, mountain biking, and challenging mountaineering packages for serious climbers. English-speaking mountain guides are provided, as well as all equipment, porters, cooks, and other staff. Another highly recommended operator is **Project Himalaya** 𝕲𝕲𝕲 (✆ 977/1436-0005 in Kathmandu; www.project-himalaya.com; info@project-himalaya.com), a Kathmandu-based company run by the professional, dynamic trio of Jamie McGuiness, Joel Schone, and Kim Bannister. Joel and Kim lead the Ladakh treks, which run 20 to 24 days; the adventurous should definitely consider taking their exploratory trek to uncommon regions that you won't find on a map. One of the best treks offered is the arduous 16-day **Chadar Trek** 𝕲𝕲𝕲 in winter along the semi-frozen Zanskar River. At night, outside temperatures plummet to a bone-chilling –22°F (–30°C), while all day long you defy the slippery ice that is thick enough to support your weight only 2 months a year, and perhaps meet local Zanskaris as they traverse this ancient route. Peruse their friendly, regularly updated website for more information. This is an outfit that does things differently, with small groups, highly personalized service, and a real concern for local support staff. Also operating along the Chadar route is **Aquaterra Adventures** 𝕲𝕲𝕲 (✆ 011/2921-2641 or -2760; www.treknraft.com), one of the best Indian adventure operators, which runs a wide range of tours and treks customized to suit your personal interests and abilities. Working with highly experienced and knowledgeable guides, Aquaterra is possibly the best choice for discerning travelers looking to raft the Indus or Zanskar rivers in Ladakh. You can also combine trekking and rafting trips or opt for a unique bicycle camping expedition.

WHAT TO SEE & DO

Leh's wide street **bazaar** runs east-west. Together with the labyrinth of adjoining side streets and alleys, the bazaar is the center of business and shopping—particularly for visitors who find the plethora of antiques shops irresistible. Locals tend to visit the alternative market nearer the Leh **polo ground,** east of the center. For a truly exotic and atmospheric experience, visit the **Old Village** 𝕲, a disorganized cluster of cobblestone lanes, ancient homes, and low-vaulted tunnels. It's well worth an exploratory jaunt, during which you should sample the freshly baked breads sold by local bakers. Walking northwest of the city (beyond the **Women's Alliance of Ladakh** headquarters, where you can shop for traditional Ladakhi handicrafts), you will quickly discover a **rural farmlike community.** Gone are the shops and eager sellers—here you'll find only fields of green sprinkled with bright yellow blossoms, gentle streams trickling past squat stone walls, and small Ladakhi houses with little vegetable gardens. To the west are the cobbled streets of the popular **Changspa** neighborhood, characterized by the number of guesthouses and laid-back marijuana-smoking travelers who come here for the pastoral atmosphere. To the west of

---

Tips **Altitude Sickness**

Arriving by air into Leh makes most people feel slightly knocked out, with headaches, loss of appetite, drowsiness, and disturbed sleep—all early signs of altitude sickness. It's necessary to stay put and drink lots of fluids for 48 hours to acclimatize before venturing higher into the mountains. Monitor your body and health, and don't ignore worsening symptoms, which could lead to a pulmonary or cerebral edema. In Leh you can get 24-hour medical help for altitude sickness at **Sonam Norbu Memorial (SNM) Hospital** (© 01982/253-629).

Changspa lies **Shanti Stupa,** a Buddhist monument most easily reached by motorable road. Inaugurated by the Dalai Lama in the 1980s, the large white *stupa* (commemorative cairn) was conceived as part of a Japanese-inspired peace movement to spread Buddhism throughout the world. From the vast courtyard at the base of the stupa you can enjoy matchless **panoramic views** ⚘⚘⚘ of Leh and the rugged beauty of the surrounding mountains, which seem to stretch on forever. Northeast of the main bazaar area is **Leh Palace,** which unfortunately is in a sorry state of disrepair. At press time reconstruction and repairs were ongoing, but until they are completed, the palace is best enjoyed from a distance.

WHERE TO STAY

With tourism the single most important industry in town, Leh is inundated with accommodations, but don't expect luxury. Hotels are priced according to unfathomable government regulations, so despite mediocre facilities, you may be paying unreasonable rates based on the fact that you, theoretically at least, have hot running water. **Shambha-La Hotel** is a little out of the center of things, but this is by far the most comfortable accommodations (reviewed below). Another worth considering is the spacious new suite (no. 15)—which includes a glassed-in deck with striking views of Leh Palace and the surrounding mountainscape—at the **Lotus Hotel** (© 01982/ 250265; fax 01982/252414; Rs 2,750/$63 double; all meals included).

Hotel Dragon   In its price range, the Dragon offers the best stay in Leh. Owned by Ghulam Mustafa and his brother Mohiuddin since 1974, this popular establishment has shown consistent improvement over the years. Each floor of the squat, traditionally styled building has its own terrace, and you can catch fantastic 360-degree views of Leh from the rooftop. The limited number of suites are well worth the extra $6— they're considerably better than the doubles with their kitschy shiny bedcovers. Also, the suites have tubs (although you should think twice before filling a bathtub in this water-strapped region). Upstairs, room nos. 131 through 133 are more spacious than the other, typically small—but neat and cozy—doubles. At night, when a campfire is lit, the small garden courtyard becomes an ideal spot at which to wind down the day. Delicious Ladakhi and Tibetan meals are served in the dining room, which is decorated with gorgeous paintings by Ghulam Mustafa, one of the owners.

Leh 194 101. © **01982/252139** or 01982/252720. Fax 01982/252720. www.travelladakh.com. 33 units. Rs 2,700 ($62) standard double, Rs 3,000 ($68) deluxe double; Rs 4,000 ($91) suite. Rates include all meals. No credit cards. **Amenities:** Dining hall; tours and sightseeing; conferencing; foreign exchange; shop; limited room service 4:30am–midnight; laundry; doctor-on-call.

Omasila   Built in the early 1980s, this intimate hotel occupying a pleasant Ladakhi-style building and offering an array of accommodations is adored by film crews. But Omasila enjoys a peaceful setting despite the occasional presence of an overbearing Bollywood director and its proximity to the backpackers' haven of Changspa. Fresh vegetables, apricots, and apples are grown in an adjoining garden, and the stream alongside is a natural aural tonic during laid-back afternoons on cane chairs on the terrace. In summer the mountains surrounding Leh provide the perfect backdrop for magnificent sweeps of colorful flora perfectly visible from each room in the hotel. The suites offer the most comfortable stay, with larger and better bathrooms (at least the showers are curtained) and a faint Tibetan-design aesthetic. For views to match the price, ask for suite no. 21, 23, or 26. Buffet meals are served in the relatively stylish "Ladakhi-Tibetan" restaurant, which features colorful murals.

Karzoo-Changspa, Leh 194 101. ⓒ **01982/252119**, 01982/251178, or 01982/250207. www.omasila.com. 33 units. Rs 2,700 ($62) standard double, Rs 3,000 ($68) deluxe double; Rs 4,000 ($91) suite. Rates include all meals. No credit cards. **Amenities:** Restaurant; tour and travel arrangements; room service; laundry; cybercafe; doctor-on-call; oxygen facilities. *In room:* TV, central heating.

Shambha-La Hotel ⓖ   This hotel was once a part of the excellent Oberoi chain; now only the bathroom towels suggest that former pedigree. Nevertheless, Shambha-La remains the best hotel in Leh, offering straightforward but dignified accommodations in a flat-roofed Ladakhi-style lodge with fluttering prayer flags and comfortable hammocks in the neat garden. Public areas—including a colorful Tibetan lounge area—are attractive, and the views from the upstairs terrace are mesmerizing. As with all of Leh's hotels, the bathroom facilities are merely adequate. Guest rooms are far from lavish, but you get a warm bed and you can book a stove-heated unit in the colder months. Power outages can be a serious problem this far from the town center, so have your hot shower early, just in case. A hotel jeep is on hand to drop you in town whenever you require a lift, and the helpful manager is a mine of useful information. The hotel also organizes tours to any destination in Ladakh; ask about their campsites in the Nubra Valley.

Note: Often considered in the same category as Shambha-La, the rather disappointing **Lha-Ri-Mo** (P.O. Leh 194 101; ⓒ **01982/25-2101** or -3345) is Ladakh's largest, slightly weathered hotel. Despite its relatively central location, beautiful views, and excellent Ladakhi building, service is stodgy, the public spaces are ugly, and the smallish rooms are musty.

South of the bazaar, Leh 194 101. ⓒ **01982/251100**, 01982/252607, or 01982/253500. Fax 01982/251100. www.welcomheritage.com. 26 units. Rs 3,000 ($68) double. Rs 1,200 ($28) extra bed. Rates include all meals. AE, MC, V. **Amenities:** Restaurant; TV lounge; billiards; travel assistance, tours, treks, sightseeing, and taxi arrangements; laundry; doctor-on-call; small library. *In room:* TV.

WHERE TO DINE

For the best Tibetan dishes in Leh, dinner at **The Tibetan Kitchen** (reviewed below) is highly recommended. In the Main Street Bazaar, you might be forgiven for not even noticing the very reliable **Himalaya Café** (ⓒ **01982/250144;** Rs 30–Rs 90/68¢–$2.05; no credit cards), where marvelous Tibetan and Chinese dishes are served in the Ladakhi version of a dimly lit bistro—one of the few eating establishments in Leh where you'll experience some sort of atmosphere. At first glance it would appear that the only real attraction at **Ibex Bar & Restaurant** (Fort Rd.; ⓒ **01982/25-2281;** everything under

Overnighting in a Ladakhi Yurt

If you don't mind being a short way out of Leh, reserve a yurt (a canvas-and-bamboo tentlike structure modeled on a Mongolian *akoi*) at **Ladakh Sarai,** 6km (4 miles) from Leh, in the peaceful hamlet of Sabu, and have all your treks and sightseeing outings expertly arranged for you. Each of the 14 circular tents is large and has twin beds, warm bedding, and an attached bathroom with hot water by the bucket and a Western toilet. Located among willow trees, the camp has a pleasant Ladakhi-style dining hall where traditional meals are served. During the day you can laze in a hammock and gaze at the surrounding mountains. **Tiger Mountain India** (www.tigermountainindia.com) runs Ladakh Sarai; reservations are through **Nature Safari** (① **011/2704-9446** or 011/2705-8833; www.naturesafariindia.com). Packages inclusive of meals and sightseeing start at $100 per person sharing.

$10) is the fact that you can order beer with your meal. While locals flock here to get loud and raucous, the extensive Indian menu is well worth perusing; the *seekh* kebabs are served with a delicious mint sauce *(pudina chutney),* and mutton and chicken curries are exceptional—perfect with steaming-hot *naan* bread.

For a Continental fix of filter coffee and croissants, a disproportionate number of German bakeries are scattered around the town. Main Street's upstairs eatery, **La Terrasse,** is a welcoming wannabe-Italian joint where you can order pizzas while enjoying views of Leh Palace from the alfresco terrace. In Main Street Bazaar, a cheerful Sikh Salvador Dalí look-alike mans the confectionery counter adjoining the popular **Café World Peace & Pumpernickel German Bakery.** He and his family sell delectable cakes, sweetmeats, and yummy apricot pie; if yak cheese is available, try it on freshly baked whole wheat bread. For a spacious, outdoorsy cafe experience, head to **Penguin Garden Restaurant & Bar & German Bakery** (Shamshu Complex, Fort Rd.; average meal Rs 200/$4.55), a laid-back hangout set in a large leafy courtyard with seating under a couple of apple trees decorated with speakers from which cool lounge tunes resonate. The confectionery is equally delicious and is a lovely place to chill out with the locals, who gather here to play cards and catch up on the latest Leh gossip; there's the added advantage of being able to order liquor with your meal. If you're looking for a great Indian lunch or dinner, be prepared to wait 30 minutes for the highly recommended *reshmi kebab,* a melt-in-the-mouth blend of minced chicken, mixed spices, and fresh herbs. While you wait, try a piece of delicious *kulcha,* which is similar to *naan* bread but comes filled with onions or a blend of spices. Penguin is also great for health food and salads and is the ideal spot to kick off your day with a filling breakfast. *Note:* On request, the Penguin staff will happily prepare special meals for road journeys or trekking trips. Their long-lasting trekking bread made from specially prepared sour dough lasts up to a week.

The Tibetan Kitchen *₭₭* *ⓥalue* TIBETAN   Tibetan fare is de rigueur in Leh, and after more than a decade, the town's best restaurant does not disappoint. Pre-order (one day ahead) the traditional Tibetan hot pot, or *gyako,* suitable for four fairly hungry diners: A brass pot with a communal broth is heated at the table, while salads, *papads,* fine noodles, rice, and mutton are served in abundance for you to cook at will.

Note that the restaurant has only one pot, so be sure to book well ahead. If you'd prefer to have your food cooked for you by skilled Tibetan and Nepalese chefs, there's plenty to choose from. Try wonton *pishi* soup, Tibetan salad (avocado, tomato, and mint), or delicious *shabalay* (a freshly baked meat- or vegetable-filled bun). The steamed mutton *momos* (dumplings), prepared with garlic and onion and served with a salad, are probably the best you'll find this side of the Indo-Tibetan border.

Hotel Tso-Kar, Fort Rd. ℂ **01982/25-3071.** Main courses Rs 60–Rs 230 ($1.35–$5.25); Tibetan hot pot for 4 Rs 1,600 ($37). No credit cards. Daily 8am–10pm.

DISCOVERING LADAKHI GOMPAS & OTHER DIVERSIONS
NORTH OF LEH

There are enough Buddhist *gompas* within easy reach of Leh to keep enthusiasts busy for several days. North along the road to Srinigar are **Phyang Gompa** ✸✸ (16km/10 miles from Leh), and 15th-century **Spituk Gompa** ✸✸ (8km/5 miles from Leh), which sits atop a lone rocky hill. If you're prepared to spend some time on the road (a scintillating journey), **Alchi** ✸✸✸ (along the left bank of the Indus around 70km/43 miles northwest of Leh, a short way off the Srinigar–Leh Rd.) is highly recommended. One of the oldest monasteries in the region, it dates back to the 11th century. Situated in a quiet hamlet with a handful of souvenir and snack stalls and some very modest budget accommodations, Alchi is centered around its inactive five-temple *gompa* complex, administered by the Yellow-Hat Gelugpa monks of Likir Monastery 30km (18 miles) across the river. You'll need a flashlight to explore the temple interiors, which are covered with vibrant, colorful, detailed murals. A courtyard leads to the *dukhang,* or assembly hall, where the statue of Avalokiteshvara is believed to be of pure gold.

On the way to Alchi, stop at **Basgo** ✸✸, where a hillside citadel consists of several Buddhist temples attached to a ruined castle. A two-story-high golden statue of the future Buddha is housed in the Maitreya Temple, which has fantastic murals of fierce divinities that were the guardian deities of the royal family once resident here.

SOUTH & EAST OF LEH

Venturing south of Leh along the same road that goes all the way to Manali, you can take in a number of monasteries, and one or two Ladakhi palaces. Located across from Choglamsar on the opposite side of the Indus, **Stok Palace** ✸✸ (May–Oct daily 8am–7pm; Rs 25/55¢) is the only inhabited palace in Ladakh, home to the 74th generation of the Namgyal dynasty. The land-holding rights of Stok were granted to the royal family by Gen. Zorawar Singh in 1834 when he deposed Tshe-spal-Namgyal, the *Gyalpo* (king) of Ladakh. It's an imposing complex, with around 80 rooms, only a few of which are still used by the current widowed *Gyalmo* (queen), who is sometimes in residence with her immediate family. Several rooms are taken up by the modest museum housed in one section. Museum highlights include a vast *thangka* collection, weapons, jewels and, of special note, the queen's *perak,* a turquoise-studded headdress. The ghostly Buddhist shrine is an experience not to be missed.

Fifteen kilometers (9 miles) from Leh, **Shey Palace and Monastery** ✸✸ (May–Oct, daily 8am–7pm; Rs 20/45¢) is worthwhile for the *gompa,* but the palace is little more than crumbling ruins. **Thikse Gompa** ✸✸✸ (daily 6am–6pm), 25km (16 miles) south of Leh, is a striking 12-story edifice with tapering walls that sits atop a craggy peak. From here you get magnificent views of the valley, strewn with whitewashed stupas.

Hidden from the world on a remote verdant hillock, **Hemis Gompa** &&& (45km/28 miles from Leh) is considered the wealthiest Ladakhi monastery, its atmospheric prayer and assembly halls rich with ancient relics and ritual symbols. During the summer season in June and July, the monastery comes alive for the annual **Hemis Tsechu** &&&, a festival commemorating Guru Padmasambhava's birth. Masked dancing by the lamas and ritual dramas are played out in the courtyard, and the locals sell Ladakhi handicrafts and jewelry. Every 12 years, a magnificent embroidered silk *thangka* (tantric wall hanging) is displayed to the public; the next such unveiling takes place in June 2016, when the Year of the Monkey comes around again. On your day-long trip into **Hemis National Park,** you may—with luck—come across brown bear, ibex, or (if the stars are truly aligned in your favor) the extremely elusive snow leopard. The popular Markha Valley trek also traverses this park.

East of Leh are two stunning high-altitude lakes that can be visited on a 2- to 3-day jeep safari. The only way to visit these lakes, close to the sensitive border with Tibet, is to book though an agent who can organize everything, including travel, guides, basic accommodations in tents or a village, and special permits. **Pangong Tso** && is a huge lake, a large chunk of which lies across the border; farther south is **Tso Moriri** &&&, where the colors of the water are as lovely as the birds you'll spot. The trip can include a visit to the **Chemdey** and **Tak-tok** monasteries. The trip for two costs about Rs 11,000 ($250) with Rimo Expeditions (see "Guided Tours and Adventure & Trekking Companies," earlier in this section).

NUBRA VALLEY

A 5-hour jeep drive over the world's highest motorable pass, **Khardung-La** (5,578m/18,000 ft.), now a veritable vehicle scrap dump, leads to northern Ladakh's lush **Nubra Valley** &&&, a fertile region with *gompas,* hot sulphur springs (at Panamik), and double-humped camels. Deep within the breathtaking Karakoram mountain range, the valley combines terrific desertscapes and fertile fields watered by the Siachen and Shayok rivers.

For centuries, the route into Nubra was part of the legendary Silk Route used by caravans of traders operating between the Punjab and various regions within central Asia. The valley is dotted with peaceful, pleasant, sparsely populated villages, but its

---

Rafting on the Indus & Zanskar &&

Without doubt, Zanskar offers one of the most exhilarating and challenging white-water rafting journeys in India. Beginning on the Doda River in deepest Zanskar, the multiday river adventure descends through rapids of grade IV and V, passes incredibly desolate, scenic gorges and stupendous cliffs down the Zanskar River, and ends at the Indus, near Alchi Monastery. The trips take a minimum of 12 days round-trip from Leh and are only for the truly energetic. If you're looking for something less hairy, there are tamer options close to Leh: a half-day rafting trip from Nimoo to Alchi that's got some adrenaline packed in, a 3-hour gentle rafting trip from Hemis to Choglamsar where your guide does most of the paddling work with well-practiced efficiency, or a 4-hour trip from Phey to Nimoo that packs in a bit of both. Trips cost about Rs 1,000 to Rs 1,500 ($23–$35) per head for the day.

little-explored landscape is the ultimate getaway for the traveler in search of escape; rent a bike and take time to explore. You need to arrange an Inner Line Permit in Leh (which can be done through any travel agent or through your hotel), and technically you must be traveling in a group of at least four people. Hire a jeep with driver (count on spending Rs 7,000/$160 for 3 days), and set off early in the day. **Shambha-La Hotel** (reviewed above) offers all-inclusive tours to the Nubra Valley, with accommodations at their own camping site. Otherwise, your best option for a comfortable night's stay is probably the village of Tegar, along the Nubra River, where **Hotel Yarab Tso** (reservations in Leh ✆ **01982/25-2480,** -2016, or -2095; doubles Rs 1,850/$43, including all meals) has clean accommodations with attached Western bathrooms.

12

Uttaranchal: Sacred Source of the Ganges

For devout Hindus, a trip into the Himalayan ranges of Uttaranchal—source of the sacred **Ganges**—is no mere journey, but a *yatra*, or spiritual pilgrimage. For the city-smothered traveler, it's balm for the soul, particularly the relatively untouched areas in Kumaon, which sees far less tourist traffic than the more hyped neighboring Himachal Pradesh, yet is in many ways more accessible, with plenty of wonderful places to stay. Comprising the territories of Garhwal (west) and Kumaon (east), tiny Uttaranchal is one of India's newest states, carved from Uttar Pradesh in 2000. Besides Hindu pilgrims and adventurous trekkers and river rafters, Garhwal attracts New Age Westerners who flock to the ashrams of **Rishikesh** on the banks of the holy river Ganges, and to nearby **Ananda-in-the-Himalayas,** one of the top spa destinations in the world. For visitors looking for a gentle road trip, the picturesque lower-altitude **hill stations of the Kumaon** offer glorious views of snowcapped mountains and a chance to spot tigers in one of the country's best-known wildlife sanctuaries, **Corbett National Park,** which vies with Rajasthan's Ranthambore National Park in terms of accessibility (264km/164 miles from Delhi; 6–7 hr. by road or rail).

1 Garhwal

Sacred source of the Ganges, the western part of Uttaranchal is where Hindu devotees come on mountain *yatras* (pilgrimages) to Badrinath, Kedarnath, Gangotri, and Yamunotri. Westerners tend to head for **Rishikesh,** said to be the "birthplace" of yoga. Today scores of garish concrete ashrams and temples draw visitors who seek out yogis and tantric enlightenment, as well as hippies and backpackers keen to contemplate life, the universe, and everything through an edifying cloud of hash smoke. Up in the hills, with staggering views of the vast Doon Valley and western Garhwal's Himalayan peaks, **Mussoorie** is the quintessential Raj-era hill station, but it gets crowded and detestable in summer (and on weekends), packed with honeymooning and vacationing domestic tourists who send the decibel level skyrocketing. In winter, however, much of its charm returns.

ESSENTIALS

GETTING THERE & AWAY **By Air** Dehra Dun's **Jolly Grant Airport** is a 50-minute flight from Delhi. From there, catch a taxi to either Mussoorie or Rishikesh, or have your hotel pick you up.

By Train Dehra Dun is the terminus of the Northern Railway, and is the jumping-off point for Mussoorie. For Rishikesh, Haridwar is the most convenient terminal,

Uttaranchal

30 minutes away by taxi. There are several good connections between the capital and both Dehra Dun and Haridwar, including the **Dehra Dun Shatabdi** and the **Dehra Dun Janshatabdi** (Mon–Sat), which stop at Haridwar. An overnight alternative is the **Mussoorie Express.**

By Road   The drive from Delhi to Rishikesh (250km/155 miles) takes between 5 and 6 hours. If you're at Corbett, the drive to Rishikesh takes around 4 hours. There are regular buses from Delhi to Haridwar and Rishikesh. Mussoorie is 280km (173 miles) from Delhi, including a final 33km (20 miles) from Dehra Dun, along a steeply ascending series of troublesome hairpin bends.

VISITOR INFORMATION   In Mussoorie, the **Uttaranchal Tourist Bureau** (© 0135/263-2863; Mon–Sat 10am–5pm, closed 2nd Sat of the month) is located near the ropeway, on the Mall. In Rishikesh, visit the **Garhwal Mandal Vikas Nigam (GMVN) Tourist Office** (Muni-ki Reti; © 0135/243-0799, -2648, or -5174; same hours as above; www.gmvnl.com). For rafting (Nov–May) and other adventure inquiries, call the GMVN office in Kaudiyala (© 01378-26-2911). Dehra Dun's GMVN office is at 74/1 Rajpur Rd. (© 0135/274-6817).

GETTING AROUND   Hire a car and driver for the duration of your visit, unless you plan on trekking. Note that in Mussoorie, the taxi union frowns upon outside taxis.

Trekking through the Land of the Gods

Below are some of the best treks in Uttaranchal. You should definitely engage the services of a guide for any of the routes, and don't skimp on equipment. Bring clothes and footwear to withstand extreme weather conditions. Note that certain treks in Garhwal require a **permit;** your trekking company can arrange this for you.

From Uttarkashi, a short drive takes you to Kalyani, which is the starting point for one of Garhwal's most popular treks—to fabulous **Dodital** ⟨, a striking lake surrounded by fantastic alpine forests. A relatively easy trek lasting 3 days, the 23km (14-mile) route takes you through the Asi Ganga River valley. Several treks of varying levels of difficulty start out from **Gangotri** (at an altitude of 3,000m/10,000 ft.), a small pilgrim town at the confluence of the rivers Bhagirathi and Kedar Ganga, in the shadow of Mount Sudarshan (6,500m/2,980 ft.), some 98km (60 miles) from Uttarkashi. From Gangotri, a beautiful 26km (16-mile) hike takes you along a gradual ascent along the Bhagirathi to **Gaumukh** ⟨⟨⟨, which is where the river has its source in the Gangotri Glacier—here the water gushes out from a small amphitheater carved out of the 15-to-20m (50–65-ft.) ice walls. En route, you pass through scenic alpine forests near Chirbasa, following an ancient pilgrimage route; a panorama of snowcapped peaks accompanies you throughout. At night, you camp on the banks of the embryonic Ganges, known here as the **Bhagirathi.** Beyond Gaumukh, you can cross the glacier to reach the high-altitude meadows of **Tapovan** and **Nandanvan,** although the route to Tapovan varies with the constant downward movement of the glacier. You can schedule the trek to last anywhere between 6 and 9 days, longer if you wish to explore the meadows and glaciers at the foot of Hinduism's center of the universe, **Mount Meru.** Another popular trek goes along **Kedar Ganga Valley,** from **Gangotri** to **Kedartal,** a gorgeous lake surrounded by mountain peaks.

One of the best-known routes in the Kumaon is the **Pindari Glacier Trek** ⟨, a fairly moderate trek that lasts up to 8 or 9 days and can be combined with a tour of Corbett National Park. A shorter trek takes you on a 20km (12-mile) climb through **Valley of Flowers National Park** ⟨, high up in the Himalayas. Between June and September, hundreds of species of flowers—many of them rare alpine varieties—fill the valley floor, through which the Pushpawati River flows. Nainital's **Parbat Tours** (✆ 05942/23-5656) organizes treks in the Kumaon. Operators that organize treks in Garhwal are **Garhwal Tours and Trekking** (✆ 0135/267-3607 or -7769; based in Dehra Dun) and **Garhwal Himalayan Explorations** (✆ 0135/243-3378 or -8728; www.the garhwalhimalayas.com; based in Rishikesh). For equipment rentals and other assistance, contact the local tourism office (see "Visitor Information," below).

MUSSOORIE

278km (172 miles) NE of Delhi; 35km (22 miles) N of Dehra Dun; 110km (68 miles) NW of Rishikesh

Smaller than Shimla and some 450m (1,500 ft.) lower, this hill station enjoys a more spectacular setting but has rather gone to seed, its regal colonial mansions all peeling plaster and overgrown hedges. It was once a favorite summer refuge of the Raj, but these days the strutting sahibs and memsahibs have been replaced by hordes of visitors escaping Delhi's blistering summer heat (which is when Mussoorie is best avoided). Until recently, Mussoorie's historical ambience was also overwhelmed by unchecked urban development; the government has now intervened (a little late, it must be said).

Unlike Shimla, Mussoorie in its glory days was pleasantly free of administrators, with plenty of nocturnal cavorting between young men and the wives of the hardworking bureaucrats who had remained back in the plains—it is said that a bell was rung just before dawn at the famous **Savoy Hotel** to encourage impious lovers to get back to their own beds. The quintessential crumbling relic, the Savoy has been visited by Indira Gandhi, the Dalai Lama, Jawaharlal Nehru, Haile Selassie, the king of Nepal, and Queen Mary, but it now tries to push barren, moldy rooms on unsuspecting travelers seeking Raj-era glory. Still, do ask the manager, Mr. Bhandari, to take you on a tour of the "best" rooms and of the melancholic **Writers' Bar,** which has hosted Rudyard Kipling, Pearl S. Buck, and Arthur Conan Doyle—but you'd better rush to pay your respects before the whole thing collapses.

The town's lifeline is the **Mall,** a stretch of pedestrian road that links its two centers, **Library Bazaar** and **Kulri Bazaar.** You can walk the entire length of the ridge, from the bandstand at the western end of the Mall to the old churches and cemeteries at the quieter end of Kulri. Above the town is **Gun Hill,** from where the British punctually fired their noonday guns. Today, visitors reach the summit by means of a ropeway, or rent horses for a 15-minute ride from the central police station. Along Mussoorie's upper ridge, **Camel's Back Road** is another fine place for a stroll. Farther east of Kulri Bazaar is **Landour,** which is quieter and better-preserved than touristy Mussoorie. Continue on foot for an hour beyond Kulri Bazaar and you'll reach **Lal Tibba,** where the lookout point provides sensational views of the Himalayas. Farther still is **Sisters' Bazaar,** a wooded area named for the nurses who attended to convalescing soldiers, and where you can explore an empty colonial mansion, said to be haunted.

WHERE TO STAY & DINE

The two best places to stay are **Kasmanda Palace Hotel** and **Claridges Nabha Retreat.** In the heart of town, Kasmanda is a stately, airy mansion where you can negotiate a 20% discount on a double room in low season. The well-preserved former holiday palace of the Maharajah of Kasmanda is packed with antiques, animal skins, and hunting trophies, including an elephant's-foot piano stool. Book a suite (Rs 2,500/$57), which has exceptional views of the Doon Valley even though it features stuffed animal heads mounted on the walls and a liberal use of gaudy floral fabrics (© **0135/263-0007** or -3949; www.heritagehotels.com/kasmanda; doubles from Rs 2,300/$54). Set on the outskirts of town, the Claridges Nabha is a serene and lovely estate (ca. 1845), once used by the Maharajah of Nabha for his summer escapades. In the surrounding cedar forest, langur monkeys perform acrobatic feats watched by visitors lounging on the terrace. The best accommodations are room nos. 110 through 115; these enjoy attractive forest views (no. 114 is the biggest). Disappointingly, guestroom fireplaces are no longer in use. The hotel conducts courtesy pick-ups from the Mall throughout the day (© **0135/263-1426,** -1427, or 011/2301-0211; fax 011/263-1425; www.claridges.com; doubles from Rs 5,000/$114, breakfast and dinner included; ask about special off-season discounts).

White-Water Adventures

If you'd like to raft the Ganges or the border-hugging Kali River, set aside several days for the adventure, allowing time for transfers and a variety of rapids, gorges, and the occasional shallow waterfall. Contact **Himalayan River Runners** ⭐ (N-8 Green Park, 1st Floor, New Delhi 110 016; ℂ **011/2696-6981** or -8169; fax 011/2686-5604; www.hrrindia.com), which provides overnight eco-friendly camping on the Ganges River beach. Or contact **Mercury Himalayan Explorations** ⭐ (ℂ **011/2334-0033** or -6209; www.himalayanadventure.com) for an all-inclusive experience that includes luxury tents and Western-style toilets. Also worth checking out are **Outdoor Adventures India** ⭐⭐ (T.G. 2A/3, Garden Estate, Mehrauli-Gurgaon Rd., Gurgaon; ℂ **0124-256-3649** or -3572; fax 0124/256-3648; www.outdooradventuresindia.com); and **Aquaterra Adventures India** ⭐⭐ (S-507, ground floor, Greater Kailash 2, New Delhi 110 048; ℂ **011/2921-2641** or -2760; www.treknraft.com). Both are good for light-hearted adventuring coupled with excellent food. Most importantly, the guides are adept at negotiating rivers.

RISHIKESH

It was The Beatles—who came here during the 1960s to visit the Maharishi (a visit that inspired much of *Sgt. Pepper*)—who put Rishikesh on the map, and today the town is full of ashrams and yoga schools catering to Westerners keen to fine-tune their spiritual tool kits. *Sadhus* (holy men) in ginger robes, hippies in tie-dyed cheesecloth, and backpackers with plenty of time (and plenty of First World credit) gather on the banks of the Ganga to talk about the evils of the West and the failure of communism. By day, it's a spiritual Disneyland, where the commercial excesses of packaged meditation hang heavily about the concrete ashrams, bedecked with gaudy statues of Vishnu and Shiva. But at night, to the accompaniment of hypnotic prayers and harmonious singing, Rishikesh undergoes a magical transformation. Thousands of golden marigolds and devotional candles mounted on banana leaves are set adrift upon the river, a gloriously simple spectacle, reminding all that this really is a spiritual retreat.

WHERE TO STAY & DINE

In a town full of ashrams and *sadhus,* you might very well expect Rishikesh luxury to involve a bed of sharpened nails. Fortunately, you can indulge in the unadulterated luxury of one of the country's finest spa resorts: **Ananda-in-the-Himalayas** (reviewed below). Of course, you won't be in Rishikesh itself (potentially a very good thing). But for a truly unusual place to stay, don't miss **The Glasshouse on the Ganges** (reviewed below), a work of remarkable design where you can hear the waters roaring by from the comfort of your four-poster bed; it gets our top recommendation. There are also several clean and convenient options that won't unsettle your budget (or your stomach). **High Banks Peasant Cottage** (Tapovan; ℂ **0135/243-1167;** fax 0135/243-1654; himalayas@vsnl.com) has four spartan guest rooms (none with views) and serves healthy vegetarian meals on request; its big claim to fame is that Kate Winslet reputedly stayed here. In the same cluster of guesthouses is **New Bhandari Swiss Cottage** (Shivananda Nagar, P.O. no. 12, Tapovan 249 192; ℂ **0135/243-5322**), which has a range of accommodations—opt for the rooftop suite (around Rs 1,500/$34) with air-conditioning, TV, and bathtub. About 19km (12 miles) from

Rishikesh is **Himalayan Hideaway** (© 011/2685-2602), a lodge owned by the couple who run the Himalayan River Runners outfit (their riverside camp is 2 km/1¼ miles away). Select a Ganga-view room (Rs 4,500/$102, breakfast and tea included), gorge on delicious meals, go rafting, or while away the hours watching the river.

Ananda-in-the-Himalayas ✦✦✦   At this destination spa, high-class pampering is the order of the day. The resort's immaculate, palatial reception rooms are in the restored Viceregal Palace, added to the palace of the Maharaja of Tehri Garhwal in 1910 to accommodate the likes of Lord Mountbatten. Now the grounds have been fabulously landscaped, enhanced with flower beds and water features, and primped to satisfy Western tastes. Some distance from the palace, in a dull five-story block (entirely out of synch with the historical appeal of the Viceregal Palace), guest accommodations are elegant, with chic-modern decor, teak parquet wood flooring, coir mats, ultra-comfortable beds, and balconies (the more expensive "valley view" is the category to go for). Yoga mats are placed in each room for personal use when attending the yoga and meditation classes. The comfortable, light-fitting *kurta* pajamas provided for you to wear throughout your stay are ideal if you're going to spend lots of time receiving treatments in the 1,951-sq.-m (21,000-sq.-ft.) Wellness Center. Choose between Thai, Ayurvedic, or Swedish massage, or lie back for an Ananda royal facial, seaweed body wrap, or Indian body mask. From the moment you wake (to a steaming cup of honey, lemon, and ginger tea) until you retire to a bath (for which a candle is lit to heat fragrant essential oils) and bed (warmed by a hot-water bottle), you'll feel extremely nurtured.

The Palace Estate, Narendra Nagar, Tehri Garhwal 249 175. © **01378/22-7500.** Fax 01378/22-7550 or 01378/22-7555. www.anandaspa.com. 75 units. $390 deluxe palace-view double, $450 deluxe valley-view double; $800–$1,550 suite. AE, MC, V. Amenities: Restaurant; pool; 6-hole golf course; squash court; jogging track; spa; daily health and relaxation program; limousine service; safaris; trekking; white-water rafting; room service; laundry and dry-cleaning service; in-house doctor; ashram; library. In room: A/C, TV, dataport, minibar, tea- and coffee-making facilities, hair dryer, magnifying shaving mirror, scale, electronic safe.

The Glasshouse on the Ganges ✦✦✦ (Value)   Spectacularly situated on the banks of the Ganges, 23km (16 miles) north of Rishikesh, this former garden-retreat of the Maharajahs of Tehri Garhwal is—quite correctly—billed as a "non-hotel." Extraordinary, design-conscious refurbishment has produced a series of individual accommodations, of which you have two general choices, either in the main block, fronted by a pillared veranda with relaxing planters' chairs; or in cottages in the lush gardens of hammock-strung mango, lychee, and citrus trees and tropical plants. The best of the lot (book well in advance!) is **Gangeshwari** ✦ (one of the cottages)—immaculately laid out and spacious, with its own lounge area and balcony, and a bathroom partially open to the elements where a sunken tub is carved from rock, and greenery spills down the walls. If it's not available, ask about the Jamuna Room, where simple antique furnishings (four-poster bed), a working fireplace, and soft white linen provide superb comfort. Of the cheaper rooms, which are much smaller, ask for the Gomti Room or the unit above it, and you'll enjoy views through large windows in a spacious environment. Ask for your breakfast or lunch to be served on the rock terrace perched over the Ganges.

23rd Milestone, Rishikesh-Badrinath Rd., Village and P.O. Gular-Dogi, Tehri-Garhwal District 249 303. © **01378/26-9224** or -9218. Reservations: Neemrana Hotels Pvt. Ltd., A-58 Nizamuddin E., New Delhi 110 013. © **011/2435-6145,** -8962, or -5214. Fax 011/2435-1112. www.neemranahotels.com. 16 units. Rs 2,200–Rs 3,000 ($51–$68) standard double; Rs 2,500–Rs 5,000 ($57–$114) double and deluxe suites; Rs 7,000 ($159) Gangeshwari triple suite. Rs 300 ($6.85) extra bed. AE, MC, V. Amenities: Restaurant; spa; travel assistance; laundry; doctor-on-call. In room: A/C, TV in some, phone in some.

2 Kumaon

It's not hard to fathom why the British Raj claimed this eastern pocket of Himalayan India from Nepal in 1815. Free of the hustle and bustle of urban India and blessed with a gentle, laid-back quality, the Kumaon, studded with gorgeous lakes, not all of which are overcrowded with construction, is great for viewing breathtaking scenery, breathing in restorative oxygen-rich air, taking wonderful walks, and seeing decaying reminders of the British preoccupation with transforming remote villages into proper English towns. Prominent among these are **Nainital** and **Ranikhet.** Both are surrounded by pine forests and are good spots for taking a break; the latter is prettier and arguably the most evocative former British hill station in India. A good route is to set off from Nainital, overnight at Mukteshwar, then set off for Binsar or Almora surrounds—this is untouched Kumaon, and we have listed two great accommodations. Next, either head east to Ranikhet or return back south to Naukuchiatal (or Jilling) for your next stop, ending your journey at Corbett National Park. Wherever you overnight, the road journeys between these destinations are the real joy of the Kumaon; when you're this close to gorgeous Himalayan mountain ranges, you simply cannot escape breathtaking views.

ESSENTIALS

GETTING THERE & AROUND   There are many trains heading out of both Delhi and Lucknow towards Kathgodam, 35km (28 miles) from Nainital. The overnight Ranikhet Express leaves Old Delhi at 10:45pm and arrives at 6:05am. There are always taxis (Rs 300–Rs 350/$6.85–$8) and share-taxis available (Rs 50–Rs 70/$1.15–$1.60 a seat), or you can have your hotel pick you up from the station. There are also overnight private deluxe buses (pick the Volvo) from Delhi to Nainital (Rs 300/$6.85). Ranikhet is an additional 60km (37 miles) from Nainital, or a 3½-hour journey from the Kathgodam railway station. Once you've found your bearings, hire a car (preferably a four-wheel-drive) and driver for the duration of your stay in Uttaranchal. You can expect to pay around Rs 8 (20¢) per kilometer, plus an additional fee per day and a reasonable contribution (Rs 200–Rs 250/$4.55–$5.70) towards the driver's overnight expenses.

VISITOR INFORMATION   While in Delhi, you can visit the **KMVN Tourist Information Office** (103 Indraprakash Building, 21 Barakhamba Rd.; ✆ **011/5151-9366;** fax 011/2331-9835; www.kmvn.org). In Nainital, the KMVN is at Oak Park House (✆ **05942/23-6356**).

A ROAD TRIP THROUGH KUMAON

Your first stop, Nainital, is set around the ebony-emerald **Naini Tal (Lake)**—according to Hindu mythology, one of the eyes of Shiva's wife, Sati. **Naina Devi Temple** is said to be the precise spot where Sati's eye fell when her body parts were scattered throughout the country in a bid to stop Shiva's "dance of cosmic destruction," which began when he discovered that Sati had immolated herself, an act provoked by her father's incessant insults of Shiva. High above the town, at 2,235m (7,450 ft.), is the aptly named **Snow View,** a hilltop area from where you can see Nanda Devi, India's second-highest peak. Make use of the Aerial Express ropeway; round-trips (daily 10am–5pm) cost Rs 65 ($1.45). You can overnight here, but Nainital is as ghastly as most of Himachal's towns, so we recommend you head just 26km (16 miles) east of Nainital to picturesque **Naukuchiatal (Nine-Cornered Lake).** According to local folklore, when you get to a

> ### *Tips* A Good Reason to Drive from Delhi
>
> Bypass extensions to National Highway 24 that link Delhi with popular weekend destinations mean that it's no longer a hellish struggle to drive from the capital to any of the popular resort areas in Uttaranchal's Kumaon region. Be sure to plan departure times carefully, in conjunction with your driver, in order to avoid the worst traffic. We highly recommend that you overnight en route to Corbett National Park or Nainital (320km/198 miles from Delhi), so you can stay at the **Mud Fort, Kuchesar** 🏠🏠 (Village Kuchesar, via B.B. Nagar, District Bulandshahr 245 402; ℂ **05736/27303**; www.neemranahotels.com; doubles Rs 1,800—Rs 2,000/$41–$46), less than 80km (50 miles) from Delhi. Built in the mid–18th century, the turreted, fortified citadel of the Kuchesar Jats overlooks fantastic gardens. Beautifully restored with tasteful, design-conscious interiors, the "hotel" is ideal for those with a yen for personal attention (there are only 10 guest rooms) and a setting devoid of phones and televisions. If the monsoon in the area has been heavy, the place may get a bit musty and damp between mid-July and mid-September. Avoid visiting during these months, unless there has been no rain. Besides exploring the historic fortress, you can spend time wandering through the local villages, far from tourist traps, touts, and civilization.

point where you can see all nine corners of the lake, make a wish and it will come true. This is certainly the case if you're looking for picture-perfect serenity, solitude, and enchanting trails, filled with wildflowers. Even if you don't opt to overnight here, make time for a day trip and take a leisurely ride or a swim in the lake. Alternatively, head north from Nainital to remote and lovely **Mukteshwar** some 50km (30 miles) away.

On a ridge some 2,254m (7,513 ft.) above sea level, where you are surrounded by little more than dramatic views of the Himalayas, conifer forests, fruit orchards, and fresh, clean air, Mukteshwar enjoys one of the most charming settings in the Kumaon. At the edge of town, atop a cliff, is century-old **Mukteshwar Temple,** dedicated to Lord Shiva. On the same hill is an ashram administered by a hermit whose disciples come from around the world. Behind the temple, a rocky cliff juts out of the hillside at Chauthi Jaali; take an early-morning walk here for stunning views.

Then, set off for Binsar, for the best view in motorable Kumaon. Here, in another of the region's most untouched areas, you can watch the sunrise over Nepal and the sunset on Garhwal. Time allowing, visit the **Jageshwar Temple** complex, and explore **Binsar Sanctuary** (Rs 100/$2.30 per head, Rs 50/$1.15 per car) to view Himalayan wildlife. Overnight at **Kalmatia Sangam,** near Almora (66km/41 miles from Nainital). If you haven't done so yet, head back to spend some time at Naukuchiatal, or set off east for Ranikhet.

Even more than Nainital, Ranikhet—surrounded by slopes draped with forests of thick pine and deodar and impeccable views of Nanda Devi—exudes the ambience of a haunted English Gothic township, forever waiting for a cloak of thick mist and the echoes of a long-lost era to descend.

Whether you arrive from Nainital (60km/37 miles away) or Binsar, you'll first encounter the typically Indian **Sadar Bazaar,** an unappealing town center that is entirely avoidable. Take the turnoff for the **Mall,** and head into the peaceful Cantonment area. Ranikhet is occupied by the army's Kumaon Regiment, which maintains a strict code that seems to have had a positive impact on the Sleepy Hollow serenity evident here. You'll encounter an abundance of flagstone colonial buildings topped by tin roofs, many used by the military and in fairly attractive condition, surrounded by hedges and greenery. **Lower Mall Road,** as you head farther south, is good for walks, with only ancient trees for company. Continue on, past 14th-century **Jhula Devi Temple,** and 10km (6¼ miles) south you'll come upon the state-run **Chaubatia Orchards,** a great place (though best avoided May–June) for a picnic (ask your hotel to pack one).

From here it's an easy drive to Corbett.

WHERE TO STAY & DINE

The Kumaon Hills are dotted with laid-back, atmospheric accommodations that offer guests the more intimate experience of a homestay and the opportunity to mingle with Indian families who live in the hills—a wonderful reprieve from overcrowded tourist hubs. Note, though, that because these are not hotels, hot water in the bathrooms often comes via a geyser, which must be switched on when required (or in buckets carried into your bathroom), Room service is limited, and food cannot be rustled up in minutes, on demand. If you'd prefer more conventional hotel-style accommodations, several of these are listed as well.

NAINITAL TO MUKTESHWAR

Besides Emily Lodge, reviewed below, a good place to stay in Nainital is the **Palace Belvedere** (© 05942/23-7434; www.welcomheritage.com). Built in 1897, this former summer palace offers a casual historic ambience with personal, attentive service. Book a lake-facing room (Rs 2,700/$60), which has an enclosed porch-cum-study (no. 19 is particularly large) from where the view of the sun rising over Nainital Lake is simply exquisite; even the bathrooms have views of the lake. Other than this, you can consider **The Naini Retreat** (© 05942/23-5105 or -5108; www.leisurehotels.co.in; doubles from Rs 5,000/$114, including breakfast and dinner). The gabled bluestone summer retreat of the Maharajah of Pilibhit, situated above Naini Lake, underwent a major overhaul early in 2003 but retains much of its charm. Standard rooms are neat but a tad cramped (book nos. 304–311), so it's best to reserve one of three garden suites, which share a common balcony. Another option worth considering is **Balrampur House** (© 05942/23-6236 or -9902; doubles Rs 2,500–Rs 4,500/$57–$102), once the summer home of the Maharaja of Balrampur and now a heritage hotel run by his descendant Jayendra Pratap Singh. Deluxe rooms are huge with big bathrooms but have shoebox cupboards and slightly worn carpets. Ask for one of the superior deluxe rooms (nos. 001, 004, 007), which are better furnished.

Nainital offers many accommodations, but a visit during peak season is likely to be accompanied by crowds, noise, and irritation. Duck the crowds by opting for one of the following fully reviewed options or for one of two recommendations at Naukuchiatal. **Déjà-vu** (© 011/2432-4426; samluthra@hotmail.com; Rs 3,500/$79 cottage) is a small, cozy, two-bedroom stand-alone overlooking the lake. It comes with cable TV and two housekeeping attendants who cook meals and cater to your needs. (However, be prepared for frequent power outages; there is a back-up generator but you may be expected to arrange and pay for fuel to run it.) For more hotel-style amenities, friendly staff, and good service, **The Lake Resort** (© 05942/24-7183 or -7184; lakeresort@sancharnet.in; from Rs 2,400/$55 double; Rs 3,000/$68 log hut) is a new hotel whose sprawling grounds hug Naukuchiatal Lake. Every room has a view of the lake; ask for the log hut with wooden floors and a bathtub for two. Room nos. 1, 5, and 12 have lounge areas and nice views, but bathrooms are small with no tubs.

The Cottage *Value* This 100-year-old house in an 3-hectare (8-acre) orchard has herringbone-patterned wood floors, ivy-covered stone walls, and a red tiled roof—all of which give it a distinctly English appearance and old-world charm, offset by the carved Kumaoni door and window frames. Owner Bhuvan Kumari loves to tell how she painstakingly created this dream house, a lovely, value-for-money homestay. Each room has a private patio with wonderful views of lush green mountains. The Middle Room (where floral drapes decorating the ceiling are a tad kitschy) is the best in the house; the Blue Room is great for more privacy and better views, but was a little too blue for our liking. The bed heights in the various guest rooms have been thoughtfully adjusted to give guests the best possible views. Tasty and simple food is served in the homey living/dining room.

Jeolikot, District Nainital. (C) **05942/22-4013**. Fax 05942/22-4182 www.jeolikot.com. 5 units. Rs 2,500 ($57) double. Rates include breakfast and dinner. Tea and coffee complimentary. No credit cards. **Amenities:** Dining hall; badminton; board games; transfers; driver lodging facility; room service for snacks (7am–10 pm); laundry; doctor-on-call. *In room:* Air–cooler.

Emily Lodge *⋆⋆* This colonial-era bungalow is the nicest homestay in Nainital. Gracious hosts Siddharth Singh and his family have a homey cottage well away from the main mall, done up in subdued floral drapes and country-home decor. Figures of elephants and birds stenciled on the walls give the place a lively ambience in spite of the hunting-lodge atmosphere created by the old teak wood furniture, deer horns, swords, and rifles adorning the walls. Warm and comfortable, the living room has an old fireplace that's lighted at mealtimes in cold weather; it's also where wholesome home-cooked meals are served. Rooms (of which there are only four) are clean and bathrooms spacious. Jim Corbett's house (Gurney House) is just a stone's throw away, and if you are lucky the caretaker might let you in.

Ayarpata Hill, near Sherwood College, Nainital. (C) **05942/23-5857** or 98373-73444. 4 units. Rs 2,500—Rs 3,000 ($57–$68) double. Rates include breakfast and dinner; tea and coffee complimentary. No credit cards. **Amenities:** Dining hall; board games; transfers; driver lodging facility; laundry facilities, doctor-on-call.

Jilling Estate *⋆* For a real outback experience in a magnificent setting, just 17km (11 miles) from Nainital, Jilling Estate is your best choice—though not for the faint-hearted or unfit. Access to this huge estate, where arch-conservationist Steve Lall, his wife Parvati, and daughter Nandini live a couple of kilometers from the nearest drivable road, is only by foot or horseback. All five rooms and cottages are completely private—you won't run into your neighbors even by chance. Facilities are rustic but extremely quaint; each room has an eclectic collection of books, and hot water for your bucket bath is heated on wooden fires by an attendant assigned to your room. Evenings are spent around a bonfire with the Lalls and their three friendly mutts. Steve may even encourage you to go for a completely private hike in the woods of his estate, in the buff. Or let Parvati teach you how to milk cows. The land phone here rarely works, but there is a mobile phone for emergencies.

P.O. Padampuri, District Nainital 263 136. (C) **05942/23-5493**. Reservations: Neelam Rai Singh, Beckon Tours Pvt. Ltd., G22 1st floor, Lajpat Nagar Part 1, New Delhi 110 024. (C) 011/2981-3546 or -0225. Fax 011/2981-4259. www.jilling.net. 5 units. Rs 2,500 ($57) double. Rate includes all meals. No credit cards. **Amenities:** Campfire; picnic baskets; trekking; camping; table-tennis, room service; laundry; mobile phone for emergencies.

Mountain Quail Camp ☆   The drive from Nainital to this out-of-the-way mountainside resort provides jaw-dropping views back down over the town and lake, as well as entrancing vistas of the Himalayan range—particularly gorgeous just after sunrise, when a striking color palette whips over mountain peaks. The hill-hugging half-hour journey brings you to a remote, exquisitely peaceful site with deluxe tents and a lodge in a clearing between forested hills and terraced farmland. Opt for the tented accommodations, which feature tiled attached bathrooms with basin, shower (with running hot water), and Western toilet. The bedroom interiors have patterned "walls," pitched roofs, carpets, and thick but uneven mattresses. The resort is ideal for scenic walks, bird-watching (aided by the resident birder), and easy treks, and even more perfect for doing nothing. There's a mobile phone for emergencies.

Pangot 263 001. ⓒ **05942/24-2126.** Reservations: Armaan Tours, Delhi, ⓒ 011/2433-6393, -2776, or 011/5155-1900. armaan@vsnl.com; blazertrail@hotmail.com. 10 tents, 3 lodge units. $90 tent double, $130 lodge double. Rates include all meals and 1 jungle walk. No credit cards. **Amenities:** Restaurant; trekking; fishing; camping; white-water rafting; doctor-on-call.

Mountain Trail   This is the best place to overnight if you want to stay in Mukteshwar itself. Mountain Trail is well-maintained and is on a terraced slope with a lovely rose garden and direct views of the Himalayas. Accommodations are large, neat, and simple. Ask for a deluxe double room; each has high-pitched ceilings, enclosed porch with exquisite views, large tiled shower, and fridge. All rooms are comfortable and spotless, and the pleasant restaurant has a working fireplace. There's no bar or room service, but most other facilities are available, and there's a game room with table tennis and a small library. The resort also runs a chocolaterie, where delicious center-filled chocolates are made with ingredients imported from Belgium.

P.O. Sargakhet, Mukteshwar 263 132. ⓒ **05942/28-6040** or -6240. www.mountaintrail.com. Reservations: Mountain Trail Holidays Pvt. Ltd., 224 Vardhaman Plaza, 9 Local Shopping Centre, I.P. Extension, Delhi 110 092. ⓒ 011/ 2765-2024, -4053, or -0008. 12 units. Rs 1,900 ($43) hill comfort double with veranda, Rs 2,300 ($53) deluxe double, Rs 2,600 ($60) superior double; Rs 3,000 ($68) 4-bed club deluxe family room, Rs 4,300 ($98) 2-bedroom combination for 4 adults. Rs 600 ($14) extra adult.. During high season (May–June) full-board packages only. AE, MC, V. **Amenities:** Restaurant; river rafting; adventure activities; game room; TV in lounge; room service; laundry; doctor-on-call; library; yoga and meditation in summer.

The Ramgarh Bungalows ☆☆   For a restful, soul-calming sojourn in atmospheric colonial accommodations that aren't quite hotels and are definitely not homestays, the Neemrana Hotels' Ramgarh Bungalows is hard to match. A great base from which to explore the Kumaon Hills, these 19th-century British bungalows feature deep verandas, bay windows, fireplaces, and dainty gardens bordered by chestnut trees. The Writers' Bungalow was built in 1860, while the Old Bungalow dates back to 1830; both have been given a bright, homey atmosphere with floral fabrics. Two additional bungalows, the Vista Bungalow and Rose Cottage, have recently been added, all dressed in the same 19th-century English ambience. All Old Bungalow rooms sleep three, while the Lemon Room in Vista Bungalow, and Rose Cottage's Magnolia Room, sleep four. Ramgarh is 24km (15 miles) from Mukteshwar; because of the remote location you must make travel arrangements and reservations in advance. There's no room service, but morning tea is brought to your room. Lawn tables, views, and the possibility of walks are all so alluring that even the laziest will be drawn outdoors.

Ramgarh (Malla), Kumaon Hills, Nainital District 263 137. ⓒ **05942/28-1156** or -1137. Reservations: Neemrana Hotels Pvt. Ltd., A-58 Nizamuddin E., New Delhi 110 013. ⓒ 011/2461-6145, -8962, or -5214. Fax 011/2462-1112. www.neemranahotels.com. 11 units. Rs 1,000–Rs 2,000 ($23–$46) Old Bungalow double, Rs 1,500–Rs 3,000

($34–$68) Writers' Bungalow double, Rs 1,750–Rs 3,000 ($41–$68) Vista Bungalow double; Rs 1,650–Rs 4,000 ($38–$91) Rose Cottage (sleeps 4). Rates include morning and evening tea and vary according to season. Taxes extra. AE, MC, V accepted at main office. **Amenities:** Restaurant; trekking; laundry; doctor-on-call.

Sitla Estate ⍟ *Kids*   This is a wonderful place to unwind, spot rare birds, and explore the Kumaon forests. Facilities are a bit rustic (hot water is available for only 2 hr. in the morning), but the stunning views of Himalayan peaks from your window more than make up for it. Deluxe rooms are lovely, with bay windows that allow you to sip tea and enjoy the sunrise from your bed. Vikram Maira, the genial owner-host, can suggest the best trails to take through dense forests, but just walking around the 16 hectares (39 acres) of orchards and organic gardens is a cleansing experience. Since Vikram is the head chef, spontaneous local counselor, and organizer of treks, river rafting, and jeep safaris, make sure you plan your next day with him the night before. And yes, he does cook up lip-smacking meals—his mulberry crumble is legendary. With farm animals and ponies around, there's plenty to keep kids occupied.

P.O. Mukteshwar, District Nainital 263 138. ✆ **05942/28-6330** or -6030. www.sitlaestate.com. 7 units. Rs 2,500 ($57) regular double, Rs 3,000 ($68) deluxe double; Rs 3,500 ($79) suite. No credit cards. Rates include all meals. **Amenities:** Dining hall; board games; river rafting; adventure activities; picnic lunch; transfers; laundry; doctor-on-call. *In room:* Tea- and coffee-making facilities, sawdust heater.

BINSAR & ALMORA SURROUNDS

High on the hill within Binsar Wildlife Sanctuary, the **Forest Resthouse** is characterized by long, musty rooms, high ceilings, old-fashioned furnishings, a lack of electricity, and ridiculously low room rates. The resthouse is looked after by a *chowkidar* (caretaker), who may even prepare meals for you if you bring your own supplies. Book a room through the **Almora Forest Office** (✆ **5962/23-1089;** http://almora.nic.in). Avoid the 500-year-old Almora town (34km/21 miles southwest of Binsar) entirely, but consider staying at wonderful **Kalmatia Sangam** (www.kalmatia-sangam.com) on the road to Kasardevi Temple. Also near Almora, within a forest, the **Deodars** (Papparsalle; ✆ **05962/23-3025;** rwheeler@rediffmail.com) is a family-run lodging with three guest rooms in an old stone cottage; solitude is guaranteed.

Club Mahindra Valley Resort Binsar ⍟   The 2002 appearance of this lovely luxury hideaway resort indicates the escalating interest in upmarket tourism in Uttaranchal. Stone pathways and slate stairways run between the studios and one-bedroom apartments spread across a terraced hillside. Each apartment (club suite) is huge, with

---

Tips **Flower Power**

En route from Nainital to Naukuchiatal, take a break at Bhowali, where you can buy the fresh produce of the region. Make sure you stop at **Fruitage,** which sells apple chutney and apricot halves and a refreshing rhododendron squash. Some species of rhododendron are believed to have medicinal qualities that cool you down (ideal on a hot day). In addition, The plant's extracts (or honey produced from its nectar) are thought to alleviate cardiac problems, high blood pressure, and asthma. Connoisseurs of honey should also stop at the sleepy state-run **apiary** in Jeolikot, 17km (11 miles) from Nainital, famous for its pure wildflower honey. Sample unique, naturally occurring honey varieties like mustard, lychee, and eucalyptus.

kitchenette, separate dining and sitting areas, Zen-style bedroom with rugs, and private balcony. Upbeat decor includes dark cream floor tiles, wood and cane furniture, and dark red rugs and ocher cushions offset by sandy-orange curtains and pale yellow fabrics. Bathrooms are large and have curtained drench showers. Deluxe accommodations are smaller but have the same well-considered, warm, contemporary decor. The management organizes a range of activities and excursions, primarily aimed at keeping well-heeled Indian guests busy. You can also chill out in the landscaped gardens. At night a bonfire warms guests in the icy air. The low season is from October until late December. Rates quoted below are first for low season, then for high season.

Bhainsori P.O., Binsar, Almora 263 684. (C) **05962/25-3028**, -3062, or -3174. Fax 05962/25-3035. www.clubmahindra. com. 37 units. Oct 1–Dec 20/rest of year: Rs 4,000/Rs 4,500 ($91/$102) deluxe suite, Rs 4,500/Rs 5,500 ($102/$125) club suite. Children under 12 stay free in parents' room. Rates include all meals, less $20 for room only. MC, V. **Amenities:** Restaurant; garden restaurant; cultural performances; table tennis; sightseeing excursions and adventure activities; camping; children's activity room; limited room service; laundry; doctor-on-call. *In room:* Heater, TV, minibar, microwave, tea- and coffee-making facilities.

Kalmatia Sangam ⭐⭐   Owners Geeta and Dieter Reeb believe in eco-conscious tourism, and the focus here is on nature and wellness. You won't find fancy amenities in any of the resort's nine cottage rooms, but each has a little balcony overlooking the valley and oozes charm. Eagle's Nest is the largest of the rooms, with the best views. Food is good and wholesome; alcohol is not available but you're free to bring your own. Though you can wander around endlessly on your own, the Reebs also conduct fascinating guided walks—including a village walk, which allows guests to observe the local architecture, walk through fields, and interact with locals. Everything about Kalmatia is geared toward de-stressing, so you can forget about walking if you don't want to, and instead get yourself a glass of rhododendron squash and retire to the library, or book a treatment or aromatherapy session with the resident reflexologist. For the higher price (compared with other Kumaon properties), you are assured utmost privacy, personalized attention, and serenity. The resort makes a point of employing people who live nearby, and also supports the local economy through a boutique (Kasa) that carries locally made linens, shawls, bamboo, and copper products.

Kalmat Estate, Post Bag 002, Almora 263 601. (C) **05962/23-3625.** Fax 05962/23-1572. www.kalmatia-sangam. com. Reservations: Kalmatia Sangam Travels Pvt. Ltd., c/o Triage Overseas, Mr. Basu or Mr. Khanduri, B-11, Gulmohar Park, New Delhi 110 049. 9 units. Rs 8,350 ($190) Eagles Nest double, Rs 5,100–Rs 6,850 ($116–$156) other doubles. Rates include all meals. MC, V (photocopy of passport required if paying by credit card). **Amenities:** Dining hall; transfers; resident reflexologist; aromatherapy; Ayurvedic diet advice; music library; book library; guided walks; picnic lunches; bonfire; room service only for snacks (6am–10:30pm); laundry; generator; doctor-on-call. *In room:* Wood-burning stove, fan.

Golf Anyone?

Play golf at what must be one of the most gorgeously scenic courses in India: The Kumaon Regiment's golf course at **Upat** near Ranikhet is set in pine forests and features a natural hazard—a 300m (1,000-ft.) cliff. Signboards threaten all non-military personnel who attempt to play here, but visitors are welcome (Mon, Tues, and Fri 7am–6pm; Wed, Thurs, and Sat 7am–12:30pm; 9 holes Rs 200/$4.60, clubs Rs 100/$2.30, caddy Rs 150–Rs 250/$3.40–$5.70).

Stinging Scarves

Hemp bags, shawls, and fabric, once all the rage, are now passé. The new products manufactured by local Kumaonis are stoles made from stinging nettle. The plant is converted into fiber, and the resulting hand-woven stoles are stylish, soft, and luxurious; they provide warmth as well and no, they don't itch. Buy a quality stole in Almora town (Rs 2,000–Rs 3,000/$46–$68).

RANIKHET

A charming alternative to the hotel reviewed below is **Chevron Rosemount** (© **05966/22-1391** or -0989; www.chevronhotels.com), a century-old, two-story colonial bungalow in a forest clearing that's showing its age in a charmingly dilapidated way. Reserve room no. 202, the Nirvana Suite (Rs 3,200/$73). Unwind on the armchairs, chaise longue, or large comfortable bed; the large bathroom has plenty of natural light. Another option worth considering is **Holm Farm** ⚜, the first bungalow in Ranikhet, with rooms from Rs 2,500 ($57). This is ideal for those looking for old-world charm—though when the place is full, you'll find tents pitched outside for guests (© **05966/22-0891** or -0831; www.holmfarmranikhet.com).

West View Hotel ⚜   This stone brick colonial mansion—an atmospheric relic of the Raj set in a lovely garden—offers spacious accommodations with carpeted bedrooms, old dark wooden furniture, upholstered armchairs, hard mattresses on big beds, and massive bathrooms with drench showers and natural light. Deluxe guest rooms have working stone fireplaces, half-canopied two-poster beds, and floral blinds and bed frills. Ask for the best room in the house, no. 21, which also has a view. Suites feature four-poster beds and separate lounges. Some of the rooms are only accessible via creaking wooden stairways. The public lounge is quaint and old-fashioned; the homey dining room with log fire has wallpapered walls decorated with blue-patterned porcelain plates. Note that hot water is only available mornings and evenings. The outdoor cafe is a pleasant spot at which to relax with a cappuccino and cake after traipsing around the hills nearby.

Mahatma Gandhi Rd., Ranikhet 263 645. © **05966/22-0261** or -1075. Fax 05966/22-0396. www.westviewhotel.com. Reservations: C-16 Greater Kailash 1, New Delhi 110 048. © 011/2648-5981. Fax 011/2648-5981. 18 units. Rs 2,400 ($55) double, Rs 2,900 ($67) deluxe double; Rs 3,900 ($89) luxury suite. Children 5–12 pay 25%. Rs 500 ($11) extra bed. Check online for special rates; up to 40% discount off season. Rates include breakfast and dinner. Taxes extra. No credit cards. **Amenities:** Restaurant; coffee shop; badminton; table tennis; horseback riding in season (May–June); indoor games; limited transport assistance; room service 7am–10pm; laundry; doctor-on-call. *In room:* TV.

3 Corbett National Park ⭐⭐⭐

264km (164 miles) NE of Delhi; 436km (279 miles) NW of Lucknow

Covering 1,319 sq. km (509 sq. miles), Corbett became India's first national park on August 8, 1936. When renowned conservationist Jim Corbett passed away in Kenya in 1955, it was renamed to honor the role he played in establishing the park.

The biggest draw of the park, of course, is the possibility of spotting a tiger in the wild. Project Tiger, a government undertaking aimed at saving India's dwindling tiger population, was launched here in 1973. Despite the fact that 140 or so tigers reside here,

The Hunter-Turned-Conservationist

Born in Nainital, Jim Corbett was a reformed hunter who, in his pre-conservationist years, hunted large animals for pleasure, killing his first leopard at the age of 8. During the 1920s, he gave up his bloody hobby but regularly shot man-eating tigers or cats believed to be threats to humans. To get yourself in the mood for your visit, pick up a collection of Corbett's fearsome hunting tales or a copy of his first book, *Man-Eaters of the Kumaon,* which recounts how he hunted and killed the Champawat tigress that was responsible for the death of 434 people.

sightings are not to be taken for granted, and your chances of an encounter are far better at Ranthambore (Rajasthan) and Bandavgarh (Madhya Pradesh). The advantage of Corbett, however, is that you can overnight in the park. The landscape consists of Sal forests and bamboo trees, with an abundance of other wildlife, including leopards, wild elephants, boars, black bears, sambar, spotted deer, four-horned antelope *(chausingha),* monkeys and, among the reptile population, pythons and the endangered gharial crocodile. Corbett's many water bodies are a birder's delight, with more than 400 species recorded. Inside the park, you can hole up in a watchtower near a waterhole for hours. Areas outside the park, especially along the Kosi River, are almost as good.

VISITING THE PARK

Seasons   Corbett is open from November 15 through June 15, closing when the monsoon causes rivers to flood their banks. Sightings are best between March and June.

Entering the Park   Access to the park is via the town of Ramnagar, where the **Park Office** (opposite the Ramnagar bus stand; ☎ **05947/25-1489;** daily: Dec–May 8:15am–noon and 1–4pm, June–Nov 10am–noon and 1–5pm) processes and issues the required permits, and handles all park accommodations as well as jeep safaris. There are direct trains from Delhi to Ramnagar; driving takes 6 to 8 hours (about 300km/186 miles). Corbett is divided into five mutually exclusive tourist zones, and you can visit only one zone at a time. If you do not have your own vehicle, hire one in Ramnagar or at Dhangari Gate. It's best to undertake jeep safaris early in the morning. You are not permitted to enter the park more than 30 minutes before the sun descends, and nighttime driving within Corbett is not allowed. Don't make the mistake of arriving in Ramnagar too late in the day; you will have to fill out forms, pay for permits and accommodations, and still get to the gate 30 minutes before sunset. Corbett is extremely popular and likely to be fully booked, so don't arrive unprepared.

Exploring the Park   Perhaps the most visually attractive area of the park is **Jhirna,** which is the only section that does not close during the monsoon season (June 15–Nov 15). Try to visit **Ramganga Reservoir,** where endangered gharial crocodiles bask on the banks and a sign warning against swimming proclaims that SURVIVORS WILL BE PROSECUTED. Surrounded by vast elephant grassland savannahs, **Dhikala** has the greatest selection of accommodations, and substitutes solitude for access to facilities like restaurants and film screenings. Dhikala is reached via **Dhangarhi Gate** (16km/10 miles north of Ramnagar); it's open daily 7am to 5pm in winter, and 6am to 6pm when the days are longer. **Elephant rides,** available from Dhikala and Bijrani, are the most promising and nature-friendly way of tracking tigers through the *chaur.* Departing at sunrise and sunset, each 2-hour ride through the forests and across the plains costs just Rs 300 ($6.85). You need to reserve well in advance (a full day is recommended), and reward your *mahout* (elephant handler) with a tip if you do, indeed, spot a tiger.

Tip: If you plan to go exploring by yourself for flexibility, you'll need your own vehicle from Delhi; otherwise all accommodations will arrange pick-ups from Ramnagar Station if you take the Ranikhet Express from Delhi or Kathgodam.

If you don't plan on staying in the park, it's far easier (particularly if you're staying at one of the resorts below) to have your hotel management make all your safari arrangements; the bureaucracy and form-filling that go with acquiring the necessary permits can be exasperating.

WHERE TO STAY & DINE
INSIDE THE PARK

We recommend that you stay outside the park—Corbett Ramganga and Solluna are some distance from the entrance, while Claridges Corbett Hideaway and Infinity are much closer. Although overnighting in the park has many advantages, comfort and service are not among them. The popular and often crowded **Dikhala** camp is the only place where you can get food in the park; it has two vegetarian restaurants. Dikhala's accommodations include cabins and three-bed "hutments" with attached bathrooms, and dorms that sleep 12 and are serviced by a separate washroom. **Forest bungalows (resthouses)** are scattered throughout the reserve and are best booked at least 1 month in advance; they offer seclusion and complete privacy, but—as with all of the resthouses outside Dikhala—you'll have to bring your own supplies. (Don't leave food lying around—there are reports of elephants ripping out the screen windows of forest resthouses in attempts to get to the provisions inside.) One of the best bungalows is at **Gairal,** near the Ramganga River and close to a hide bank. **Kandha Resthouse** is set on the highest point within the park. If you're up for a little more style, ask about **lodges** once used by British hunters; these have such unexpected luxuries as attached bathrooms, fireplaces, and carpets. For reservations for any of these camps, contact the Director, Corbett Reserve Reception Centre, Ramnagar 244 715 (© **05947/25-1489;** fax **05947/25-1376;** Dhikala tariffs: cabins Rs 1,300 ($30) per foreigner; log-hut dorms Rs 200 ($4.60) per foreigner; forest bungalows

---

Sightings from the Saddle

Saddle up for a 3-day (or 6-day) horse safari in the reserve forest bordering Corbett National Park. **Corbett Horse Safari** takes you out on thoroughbred horses retired from Mumbai's racetracks across the Kosi River, up and down ridges and mountains, through thick forests of *sal* and elephant and tiger country to Kaladungi, where Jim Corbett lived. Trips are led by Paramdeep Singh (Vicky), and horses have accompanying *syces* (stable-hands). Riders overnight in spartan 19th-century forest resthouses (or tents) along the way. The whole experience is a step back in time. Call © **011/2955-1191,** 011/5569-6444, or 98111-09596; or go to info@corbettriverside.com. Customized trips cost approximately Rs 5,000 to Rs 6,000 ($114–$137) per person, per day, all-inclusive.

Rs 1,300 ($30) per foreigner; no credit cards; ask about hiring guides and elephant and jeep safaris).

OUTSIDE THE PARK

There are dozens of accommodations from Ramnagar to Corbett and beyond. Nature lovers who don't necessarily require top-notch hotel amenities will love the rustic but terrific **Camp Forktail Creek** (⟨ℭ⟩ **05947/28-7804;** www.campforktailcreek.com). A double at Rs 3,800 ($86) includes all meals, cold drinks, and escorted walks; no credit cards. The place is run by a young, enthusiastic couple, Ritish Suri and Minakshi Pandey. Accommodations are in safari tents, with elevated wooden floors and attached toilets. Customized walks, safaris, and birding and angling trips include the services of a resident naturalist or tracker. Half- or full-day game drives cost Rs 1,500 to Rs 2,500 ($34–$57). In addition, they organize camping trips into the forest reserve and multiday elephant safaris. Delicious buffet-style meals are served in "The Thatch"; lit by lanterns at night (there is no electricity), it houses a collection of some 700 books for guests to peruse. For more conventional lodgings, book one of the following.

Claridges Corbett Hideaway   Pebbled pathways interweave with pretty gardens and cozy mustard-colored cottages in a mango orchard. The older, "jungle-themed" cottages have thatched pitched ceilings, stone-tile flooring, comfortable beds, and separate sitting areas with fireplaces. A lovely place to relax is the thatched-roof bar, with its distinguished air. There's a well-stocked library with a selection of Jim Corbett's books to get you in the mood for tiger-spotting safaris. If you don't feel like lazing, and you're not on the back of a pachyderm, you may wish to go river rafting on the Kosi River. Or check out the resort's herd of water buffalo. The evening's entertainment features Kumaoni folk dancing, a wildlife movie, or a slide show.

Zero Garjia, Dhikuli 224 715. ⟨ℭ⟩ **05947/28-4132** or -4134. Fax 05947/28-4133. www.corbetthideaway.com. 52 cottages. $210 standard double; $230 executive suite; $350 family suite for 2 adults and 2 kids. $75 extra person. Includes all meals and 1 jungle safari. AE, MC, V. **Amenities:** 2 restaurants; bar; pool; kids' pool; jeep, elephant, and coach safaris; river rafting; fishing; archery; table tennis; badminton; bird-watching; indoor games; billiards; nature shop; Ayurvedic massage; laundry; doctor-on-call. *In room:* A/C, tea- and coffee-making facilities.

Corbett Ramganga Resort   Tiger-spotting is not the only reason to venture into the lower Kumaon Mountains. Die-hard anglers head here in hope of bagging India's ultimate big-game fishing trophy: the mighty *mahseer.* This decade-old resort, on the banks of the Ramganga River, is not as attractive as its riverfront neighbor Solluna, but it draws an interesting mix of people, many here only to fish—the world record *mahseer* was bagged just 500m (1,600 ft.) from the Corbett Resort. Guest rooms are large and simple, in semicircular brick cabins with stone tile floors. We prefer the tented accommodations—each large, air-cooled, army-style structure is encased in a thatch shell, with a tiny dressing room and a small shower room attached; mattresses here are also more comfortable. At night, guests—mostly moneyed Indians and diplomats—gather around a bonfire and share rum-induced fishing tales; in the background, the gurgling Ramganga reminds you that you're miles away from the pollution, congestion, and ceaseless traffic of the cities. You might like to ask manager Surender Pal about a rainy night when he witnessed a standoff between a tiger and a boar outside his office. The resort organizes night safaris through the surrounding valleys, providing an opportunity for nocturnal tiger and leopard sightings. Buffet meals, served in a high-ceilinged, circular restaurant, are wonderful.

Village Jhamaria, P.O. Sankar, Marchula. ☎ **05966/28-1592** or -1692. Reservations: Surbhi Adventures, 5 Sainik Farms, New Delhi 110 062. ☎ 011/2955-1855 or -1417. Fax 011/2955-1428. www.ramganga.com. 20 units and 10 deluxe tents. Rs 4,350 ($99) tent double, Rs 4,950 ($112) deluxe double, Rs 5,450 ($124) superior double; Rs 6,500 ($148) suite. Rs 1,500 ($34) extra bed. Rates include all meals. AE, DC, MC, V. **Amenities:** Restaurant; bar service; pool; children's pool; snacks-only room service; tennis court; fishing; night safaris; river-rafting; rappelling and other adventure activities for groups only; badminton; cycling; indoor and outdoor games; day excursions; laundry; doctor-on-call. *In room:* A/C (tents are air-cooled only), heater. Suites have kitchenettes and tea- and coffee-making facilities.

Infinity Resorts ⍟ Activities at this pleasant riverside hotel center around a huge enclosed octagonal building with a terrace and indoor bonfire; this is where meals are served, wildlife movies are shown, and cultural performances are held. The deluxe guest rooms are worth paying a little more for; they lead off open corridors on the floor above the standard units. They're spacious (though not particularly tasteful), and each one has a large terrace with a river view. From your room, you can hear the river and enjoy great bird-watching. The setting is peaceful, perhaps more so than at Claridges Corbett Hideaway. There's a relaxing swimming pool, and a terraced rock embankment leads down to a riverside pond filled with *mahseer* and a nearby shrine to Ganesha. Hammocks are strung up between the mango trees and rhododendrons. The idyllic setting is wonderful for stretching out with a copy of Jim Corbett's memoirs.

P.O. Dhikuli, Ramnagar 244 715. ☎ **05947/25-1279** or -1280. Fax 05947/25-1880. www.tigercorbettindia.com. Reservations: 405, International Trade Tower, Nehru Place, New Delhi 110 017. ☎ 011/5160-8508 or -8510. Fax 011/5160-8509. 24 units. Oct 1–Jun 30/July 1-Sep 30: $190/$150 standard double, $200/$160 luxury double. $75 extra person. Rates include all meals and 1 safari per day. AE, DC, MC, V. **Amenities:** Restaurant; bar; cultural events; pool; health club; billiards and pool table; fishing; park jeep safaris; elephant safaris; nature walks; wildlife film shows; conference hall; souvenir shop; room service on request; laundry; medical center. *In room:* A/C, heater.

The Solluna Resort ⍟ Not as well-known as its older neighbor, Corbett Ramganga, this 10-hectare (25-acre) resort—named for the sun and the moon, and situated on the riverbank—has better rooms (gorgeous cottages, each with comfortable mattress, bay window seats, a skylight that allows you to watch the stars from your bed, a good tiled shower room, cupboard space, working surfaces, and two small private verandas with wicker chairs and a cane swing). However, it's not as popular as Corbett Ramganga, and not as convivial. Above the reception area (where there's a small dining area), a lovely viewing terrace with comfortable wicker chairs is great for lazing and drinking in the natural spectacle all around you. Expansive lawns surround the cottages, scattered with bougainvillea and mango and cherry trees. At night, pathways are lit up with storm lanterns, and a bonfire is lit for a communal chinwag. Alcohol isn't available, but you're welcome to bring your own.

Marchula 244 715. Reservations: ☎ **011/2354-0456** or 011/2331-0227. www.sollunaresort.com. 18 cottages and 5 tents. Rs 4,500 ($101) double. 2 children under 7 stay free in parents' room. Rs 1,800 ($41) extra person. Rates include all meals. Expect discounts of up to 50% during the off season mid-June to mid-Nov. No credit cards. **Amenities:** Restaurant; 24-hr. coffee shop; pool; mini-theater; safaris; fishing; bird-watching; sightseeing; limited room service; laundry; doctor-on-call. *In room:* A/C, heater, fridge, tea- and coffee-making facilities.

13

Kolkata (Calcutta) & East India

The image most people have of Calcutta is one of abject poverty and misery—mostly the result of media focus on Mother Teresa's good works. Despite this unfortunate perception, Kolkata (as the Communist-ruled West Bengal capital became known in 2001) attracts its fair share of visitors, many of whom are pleasantly surprised by the seductive charms of this intoxicating city.

Believed to be the ethereal abode of the goddess Kali, who embodies *shakti*—fortitude and strength—it is home to a joyous, cerebral, and sophisticated community; some of the best Raj-era architecture in India; many of the country's best artists; a thriving film and fashion industry; five-star hotels; and a host of superb restaurants.

Kolkata is also the natural starting point for a trip to the Himalayan mountains of the North, where you can drink in the crystal-clear air of **Darjeeling,** India's most famous hill station, imbibing the "champagne of teas" before picking up a permit to hike the tiny state of **Sikkim.** One of the least-explored regions of India, Sikkim is a world apart, surrounded by jagged peaks and home to snow-fed lakes, remote Buddhist monasteries, yak-herding Tibetans, high-altitude forests, and some 4,000 varieties of wildflowers (including 600 varieties of orchid).

South of West Bengal, in the coastal state of **Orissa**—often called the "soul of India"—you can join the pilgrims who gather by the thousands to pay homage to the Lord of the Universe, who resides at the seaside town of Puri. Within easy striking distance from here is Konark's **Sun Temple,** a World Heritage Site, a testament to the technical and artistic brilliance of Orissa in the 13th century, and unreservedly one of India's top attractions.

1 Kolkata

1,310km (812 miles) SE of Delhi

Once the proud capital of the British Raj, Kolkata is deeply evocative of an era and sensibility lost in time. Established as the trading post for the East India Company on the banks of the Hooghly River by Job Charnock in 1690, it grew to be the biggest colonial trade center in Asia, earning it the name "Jewel of the East." With its splendid Victorian buildings, ornamental pools, stone-paved footpaths, figured lampposts, and sweeping esplanade, it was entirely European in its architecture and sensibility, and the burgeoning city became the stomping ground of a new breed of sahibs and memsahibs who wore their white skins and British manners as though they were royal insignias. But Kolkata was effectively built on a disease-breeding swamp—the marshy delta of the Ganges and Brahmaputra rivers—and this, combined with the heat, humidity, and the Bengalis' prominence in the struggle for independence, finally persuaded the British to transfer the capital. In 1911 they left for Delhi, leaving Calcutta to rot.

East India

New Delhi

India

AREA OF
DETAIL

Bay of
Bengal

SIKKIM — Gangtok
Pelling
Kalimpong
Darjeeling
New Jalpaiguri — Siliguri
NEPAL
MEGHALAYA
BHUTAN
JALDAPARA
WILDLIFE
SANCTUARY
Cooch
Behar
Teesta River

Purnia
BIHAR
Raigànj
34
Ingraj Bazar
BANGLADESH
Ganga River
JHARKHAND
Baharampur
34
Dhanbad — Asansol
Durgapur
Navadwip
Jessore
Puruliya
Bankura
Barddhaman
2
Chandernagore
Bangaon
Bishnupur
35
33
Howrah — Dum Dum
Kolkata
(Calcutta)
Kharagpur
Haldia
SUNDARBANS
WILDLIFE
SANCTUARY
6   ORISSA
0   50 mi
0   50 km
N
Digha
SUNDARBANS

Kolkata (Calcutta)

DINING ◆

Ar-Han Thai **3**
Flury's **19**
The Hub **9**
Indian Coffee House **4**
Jong's **14**
Kewpie's **8**
Mainland China **7**
Mocambo **16**

Nizam's **13**
Peter Cat **18**
Royal Indian Hotel **1**
Saffron **17**
Shiraz **6**
Sonargaon **9**
Suruchi **5**
Taaja's **10**
Zaranj **14**

ACCOMMODATIONS ■

Fairlawn Hotel **15**
Hyatt Regency **2**
ITC Sonar Bangla **11**
Oberoi Grand **12**
The Park **17**
Taj Bengal **9**

CHOWRINGHEE & SUDDER ST.
(See inset top left)

South Park Street Cemetery
Park Circus
Park Circus Station

TANGRA

Science City

Eastern Metropolitan Bypass

Bantala Rd.

Kasba Rd.

Gol Park

Ballygunge Station

Ballygunge Cir. Rd.

Hazara Rd.

Rash Behari Ave.

Southern Ave.

Ganahat Rd.

Shakespeare Sarani

St. Paul's Cathedral

Chowringhee Rd.

Park St.

Sudder St.

Indian Museum

Rafi Ahmed Kidwai Rd.

Ripon St.

Padda Pukur Rd.

Ashutosh Mukherji Rd.

Kalighat Temple

Victoria Memorial

Ochterlony Monument

Fort William

MAIDAN

Hospital Rd.

Racecourse

Red Rd.

Kidderpore Rd.

St. George's Gate Rd.

Achacya Jagadish Chandra Bose Rd.

Goplanagar Rd.

National Library

Zoo

Canal Rd.

Ekbalpur Rd.

Diamond Harbour Rd.

Alipore Rd.

Station Rd.

N. R. Sarkar Ave.

Prince Anwar Shah Rd.

ROYAL GOLF CLUB

Tollygunge Club

Garden Reach Rd.

Circular Garden Reach Rd.

Hide Rd.

Taratal Rd.

Anoul Rd.

← To Botanical Gardens

0   1/2 mi
0   0.5 km

523

> ## *Tips* Exploring East India
>
> To cover all three eastern states, you will need a minimum of 9 days, ideally fly-ing directly to Bhubaneswar, capital of Orissa, to visit **Puri** and **Konark,** then heading northward to West Bengal to visit the capital, **Kolkata,** and the state's idyllic hill station, **Darjeeling.** End your tour in laid-back **Sikkim** before flying back to Delhi from nearby Bagdogra Airport. Set aside extra time for trekking in Sikkim or a tribal tour in Orissa.

Today, much of the city's architectural heritage stands crumbling and in ruins, its monumental colonial structures not nearly as well maintained as those of Mumbai. Moss and grime cover tattered buildings that should be celebrated as the city's finest—the collapsing masonry, peeling paint, and sun-scorched woodwork testaments to the indifference of time. Unable to stem the long-term industrial and commercial decline of the city, or the flood of refugees that have continually arrived from Bangladesh since the first days of Partition, the Communist ruling party (CPI) strug-gles to adequately provide for the city's 14 million inhabitants. The second-largest city on the subcontinent (after Mumbai), it is packed to capacity, politically beleaguered, and heavily polluted, an *entrêpote* of India's sorriest social woes.

Yet its proud citizens, who speak rapturously of its benefits over the other big Indian metropolises, fiercely tout the charms of Kolkata. In fact, meeting Bengalis is one of the best aspects of traveling here—Kolkata is the self-proclaimed capital of India's intellectuals, home to three Nobel Prize laureates (including the revered Rabindranath Tagore, who became Asia's first Nobel laureate in 1913) and an Oscar-winning film director (Satyajit Ray). Warm, helpful, and imbued with a great sense of humor (not to mention a famously keen appreciation for dining), the Bengalis live by the maxim that "what Bengal does today, India will do tomorrow." Engaging in lively discussion on the benefits or drawbacks of Communism, or on the original recipe for *sandesh* (milk-based sweets, a Bengali specialty), is likely to be one of your more mem-orable experiences in India.

In some ways, the city is as frightening as you might fear, a degraded mess where squalor, filth, and the ubiquitous *bustees* (slums) can overwhelm the senses. If you're in India to enjoy the country's softer side, don't tarry here. Head for the Himalayan mountainscapes of Sikkim or Darjeeling, or the temples and beaches of Orissa, farther south. But if you delight in eclectic city culture, spend at least 2 or 3 nights in this thrilling city.

ESSENTIALS

VISITOR INFORMATION   The **West Bengal Tourism Centre** (3/2 B.B.D. Bagh E.; ✆ **033/2248-8271,** -8272, or 033/2210-3199; Mon–Sat 10am–5:30pm) is good for up-to-date information (pick up a copy of *Kolkata This Fortnight,* a leaflet with information about current events). You can also arrange city tours here. Visit the **Government of India Regional Tourist Office** (MSE Building, 4 Shakespeare Sarani; ✆ **033/2282-5813,** -1475, or -7731) for (limited) information on the entire subcontinent. *Cal Calling* is a monthly catalog of events and general information.

GETTING THERE & AWAY   By Air   Kolkata is served by domestic flights from most major destinations in India. Netaji Subhash Chandra Bose International Airport, formerly Dum Dum Airport (℗ **033/2511-8787;** www.calcuttaairport.com) is 15km (9 miles) northeast. You can exchange currency and get tourist information from two separate booths here. Use the prepaid taxi stand (℗ **033/2511-1201**); the 40-minute trip into town should cost Rs 200 ($4.55).

By Train   Kolkata's **Howrah Junction** (℗ **033/26607410** or -7411), just south of Howrah Bridge, connects the city with most other parts of the country. It's made up of the adjoining Old and New Howrah stations. You should purchase tickets through your hotel or a travel agent, but there is a section specifically for foreigners in the main **reservations office** (daily 10am–5pm). For general inquiries, call ℗ **1310;** for prerecorded information, call ℗ **1331.** Trains to destinations farther east and to the northern areas of West Bengal often depart from **Sealdah Station** (Bepin Behari Ganguly St.; ℗ **033/2350-3535** or -3537); check your ticket to confirm which station you need to be at. Also arrive with time to spare so that you can navigate through the crowds and find out about any changes to the schedule.

By Road   Don't consider getting to or from Kolkata by motor vehicle (either driving yourself or by bus); otherwise you'll waste a great deal of your vacation time.

GETTING AROUND   By Taxi & Auto-Rickshaw   The full-to-capacity streets of Kolkata can be the very devil to get around, but a jaunt in a Morris Oxford is a good way to experience the city. Taxi drivers here are notoriously keen on ripping you off, even after you've negotiated a fare. Ask your hotel concierge for an approximate idea of the fare for your route, check that the meter is reset, and make sure that the driver knows where you're going (use a street map to ensure you aren't taken on a detour). You can hire a good car and driver through **Avis** (Oberoi Grand; ℗ **033/2249-2323,** ext. 6325 or 6335) or through **Hertz** (141 S.P. Mukherjee Rd.; ℗ **033/3095-2819** or -2820). See "Car Rentals" under "Fast Facts: Kolkata," below. Note that rickshaws are outlawed from entering many of the city's major streets. You may feel too guilty to engage the services of a hand-pulled rickshaw, but you're helping cut down on pollution and feed a family, so tip generously.

The Dance of Destruction

For Hindus, India is a Holy Land, with thousands of *tirthas*—celestial "crossover" points where mortals can access the world of the gods. Legend has it that these were created after Lord Shiva's wife, Sati, jumped into a fire in an act of shame because her father, Raja Daksha, had neglected to invite Shiva to an important ritual. Unable to bear the loss, the grief-struck Shiva—carrying Sati's body—began to pace India in a *tandava nritya,* or "dance of destruction." Terrified that his fury and pain would destroy the universe, Brahma, Vishnu, and Shani dispersed her body across the vast plains and peaks of India, and wherever a body part fell, this became a *tirtha.* Many of these are important pilgrimage sites Hindu believers must visit at least once in their lifetime, such as those at Varanasi (see chapter 9). One of Sati's toes also fell in a dense forest in southwest Bengal. Today, this site—now **Kalighat Temple**—is one of India's most important pilgrimage centers, where the goddess is worshipped as Kali. The toe is supposedly housed in a chamber of the temple. Every year in June, as part of a secretive ritual, the toe is bathed.

The Metro   India's first underground railway was started in Calcutta in 1984; it currently connects Tollygunge in the south with Dum Dum Station in the north. It's a reliable, clean, and surprisingly uncrowded transport option, and tickets are cheap (Rs 4–Rs 8/8¢–18¢). The Metro operates Monday through Saturday from 7am to 9:45pm, and on Sunday from 3 to 9:45pm. For information, contact the **Metro Rail Bhavan** (33/1 Jawaharlal Nehru Rd.; ℂ **033/2226-7280**).

By Bus or Tram   To experience India at its most confusing, claustrophobic, and unpredictable, by all means hop aboard one of Kolkata's battered buses or road-clogging trams. If you're looking for a joyride, take a tram around Victoria Memorial.

On Foot   Early morning is the best time to get out and stroll through the streets; it's still relatively quiet, and the air is cooler and less choked by pollution. Pick up a cup of tea from the *chai-wallas* who serve their sweet brew in tiny unfired clay cups—India's answer to the polystyrene cup, these are simply discarded after use.

GUIDED TOURS   The guide services of the following two men are worth booking before you arrive. **Shanti Bhattacharjee** is a retired history teacher with a profound knowledge of his city, who provides in-depth tours of Kolkata (ℂ **033/2350-1576**). He charges Rs 800 ($18) per day for a group of five people (all entrance and transport costs to be paid by tourists). Architect **Manish Chakrabovti** conducts **heritage walks** 𝄞𝄞 (usually on Sun) of northern Kolkata on behalf of Action Research in Conservation of Heritage (ℂ **033/2337-5757** or 033/2359-6303; archeritage@yahoo.co.uk). **The Tourism Centre** (3/2 B.B.D. Bagh E.; ℂ **033/2248-8271** or -8272) conducts two different daily sightseeing tours of the city; these inevitably involve a great deal of bus travel and little sightseeing. In the same center, the **West Bengal Tourist Development Corporation** (ℂ **033/2243-7260**) organizes short and long-distance tours of the state and selected destinations around the country.

FAST FACTS: Kolkata

Airlines **Jet Airways:** ℂ **033/2229-2227**, -2084, or 033/2256-1818. **Air Sahara:** ℂ **033/3030-2020** (toll-free). **Indian Airlines:** ℂ **033/2511-9720.**

Ambulance **Lifeline Diagnostic Centre and Nursing Home,** 4A Wood St. ℂ **033/ 2247-6301** or -8083. Has a 24-hour ambulance service.

American Express The office is located at 21 Old Court House St., near Raj Bhavan; ℂ **033/2222-3001** or -3026. Open Monday to Friday 10am to 2pm and Saturday 10am to noon.

Area Code The area code for **Kolkata** is **033.**

ATMs There are plenty of 24-hour ATMs: **Citibank** (Kanak Building, 41 J.L. Nehru [Chowringhee] Rd.; ℂ 033/2249-2095), **UTI Bank** (7 Shakespeare Sarani; ℂ 033/2282-2933), **HDFC Bank** (Stephen House, 4 B.B.D. Bagh E.; ℂ 033/ 2281-3838), **Standard Chartered Grindlays Bank** (41 J.L. Nehru [Chowringhee] Rd.; ℂ 033/22428888), and **HSBC Bank** (8 Netaji Subhash Rd., 31 B.B.D. Bagh; ℂ 033/2243-8585).

Banks Most banks are open Monday to Friday 10am to 2 or 3pm, and Saturday 10am to noon.

Car Rentals **Avis Rent-A-Car** is at the Oberoi Grand (15 Jawaharlal Nehru Rd.; ☎ **033/2249-2323**, ext. 6325 or 6335). Luxury cars are available from **Car-Cab** (2 Manook Lane, off Ezra St., Kolkata 1; ☎ **033/2235-3535**; vayuseva@cal. vsnl.net.in).

Consulates **United States:** 5/1 Ho Chi Minh Sarani; ☎ **033/2282-3611;** Monday to Friday 8am to 1pm and 2 to 5pm. **United Kingdom:** 1A Ho Chi Minh Sarani; ☎ **033/2288-5172;** Monday to Friday 8:30am–1pm and 1:30–4pm. **Canada:** Duncan House, 31 N.S. Rd.; ☎ **033/2230-8515;** Monday to Friday 9:30am–1pm.

Currency Exchange **Thomas Cook** is at 19B Shakespeare Sarani, 1st floor (☎ **033/2283-0473** or -0475); hours are Monday to Saturday 9:30am to 6pm.

Drugstores Twenty-four-hour chemists include **AMRI Apollo Hospital Pharmacy** (P4 Gariahat Rd., Block A-29; ☎ **033/2461-2626**, ext. 606), **Dhanwantary** (48A/1 Diamond Harbour Rd.; ☎ **033/2449-3204**), **Jeevan Deep** (1-14B Hazra Rd.; ☎ **033/2455-0926**), and **Life Care** (1/2A Hazra Rd.; ☎ **033/2475-4628**).

Emergencies For fire brigade, dial ☎ **101** or 033/2244-0101.

Hospitals **Belle Vue Clinic** (9 U.N. Brahmachari St.; ☎ **033/2247-2321**, -6921, -6925, or -7473) also has a blood bank. There are English-speaking doctors at the 24-hour **B.M. Birla Heart Research Center** (1/1A National Library Ave.; ☎ **033/2456-7001** to -7009).

Newspapers & Magazines Peruse the pages of *The Statesman,* one of India's oldest English dailies, for information about special events. Kolkata's other very popular paper is *The Telegraph,* which has a metro section that lists local events.

Police Dial ☎ **100** or **033/2214-5000** through -5004. Police headquarters are in Lal Bazaar (☎ **033/2214-3230** or -3024).

Post Office B.B.D. Bagh; Monday to Saturday 8am to 8:30pm and Sunday 8am to 3:30pm. There are also Western Union offices (☎ **1600/111-911** toll-free for a location near you) in several Kolkata post offices; open Monday to Saturday 8am to 8pm.

ORIENTATION

Kolkata is a huge, sprawling city, divided into **north** and **south,** both spread along the eastern bank of the Hooghly River, which divides it from the vast suburb of **Howrah,** located on the western bank. Howrah is where you'll be deposited if you arrive by train; the main station is close to the Howrah Bridge, which connects with the city proper. Just east and south of Howrah Bridge are Kolkata's commercial and tourist hubs, centered around **B.B.D. Bagh,** still known by its colonial name, Dalhousie Square, and the long stretch of road once known as **Chowringhee** (now Jawaharlal Nehru Rd.) that runs southward, alongside the Maidan, Kolkata's vast urban park. Many visitors base themselves around Chowringhee; nearby Sudder Street teems with budget accommodations, while Park Street has plenty of boutiques and fine restaurants.

To the northeast is the rapidly expanding business district of **Salt Lake City,** which has few historical sites but is steadily developing a reputation for its upscale business hotels and high-tech entertainment facilities. It's the closest district to the airport.

> **Tips** **Sorry, Wrong Number . . .**
>
> Dial (© 1952 for a recorded message (in English) if the number you're dialing has been changed.

WHAT TO SEE & DO

You need at least 2 full days to cover Kolkata. Spend the first day exploring central and south Kolkata, and the second visiting sites in the north, for which you should hire a car and driver.

DAY ONE (CENTRAL & SOUTH KOLKATA)

Start by catching a taxi south to the city's most famous temple, **Kalighat Kali** (p. 530). After this, visit Mother Teresa's **Nirmal Hriday** home for the destitute and dying, right next door (see "The Miracle of Mother Teresa & the 'Pure Hearts,'" on p. 530). Or, if you're a bookworm, check out the **National Library** in the 300-year-old former summer residence of Prince Azim-us-Shan, the grandson of Emperor Aurangzeb. The library has a catalog of over 2 million books. Our recommendation is to enjoy the relaxing, tranquil atmosphere of **South Park Street Cemetery** (p. 529) before you head into the chaos of central Kolkata. If you're hungry, nearby **Suruchi** (© 033/2229-1763; 89 Elliot Rd. near Mallik Bazaar; open Mon–Sat 10am–5:45pm, Sun 10am–3pm; no credit cards) is probably Kolkata's most authentic Bengali restaurant, with a no-frills, homegrown atmosphere.

You can save time by using a vehicle to move on to central Kolkata, or enjoy the walk along Park Street to **Chowringhee Road,** taking in the upmarket shops and boutiques and perhaps stopping at **Flury's** (© 033/2229-7664; daily 7:30am–10pm; credit cards accepted) for tea and a sandwich. Now officially known as "Jawaharlal Nehru Road," Chowringhee is Kolkata's main drag, with less human excrement along its sidewalks than almost anywhere else in the city. It is lined with colonial Victoriana—including the monumental **Indian Museum** (see below) and that pinnacle of Calcutta's society life, the **Oberoi Grand.** Continue north along Chowringhee into the heart of the city, where you can explore the roads around **B.B.D. Bagh** (see below).

When you've had your fill of life on the sidewalks, make your way south again, along Government Place East. You'll soon find yourself in the green expanse that is the **Maidan**—one of the largest city-center parks in the world—where the Ochterlony Monument, or **Shahid Minar (Martyr's Tower),** is worth noting. Walking west through the Maidan will bring you to **Eden Gardens,** India's most famous cricket stadium, while much farther south is the imperious **Victoria Memorial** (see below). Buy a ticket and venture in if you are keen to broaden your knowledge of the city's history. But don't feel guilty if you just want to lie on the lawn and watch Bengalis socializing. Otherwise, brave the traffic and catch a cab to Howrah to explore the 18th-century **Indian Botanical Gardens** (Shibpur; © 033/2668-0554; closes 1 hr. before sunset), said to house the largest banyan tree on earth. Scientists, when they are available (usually after 11:30am), will act as guides at no charge.

TOP ATTRACTIONS

B.B.D. Bagh ✦✦✦   For those interested in colonial architecture, this part of central Kolkata makes for very worthwhile exploration on foot. Once called Dalhousie Square, B.B.D. refers to the names of three Indian freedom fighters (Benoy, Badal, and Dinesh) who shot a British police inspector-general in 1930. At the center of the square *(bagh)* is Lal Dighi Tank, where locals wade and bathe in the dodgy-looking, spring-fed water. Most impressive of the surrounding monuments is the **Writers' Building,** the office of the West Bengal government, which stretches along B.B.D. Bagh North Road; it was built to house the British bachelors imported to serve the East India Company. Across the road is the early-19th-century **St. Andrew's Kirk,** recognizable by its tall white steeple. At the other end of B.B.D. Bagh North is the **General Post Office,** with a monumental rotunda; it's thought to be the site of the notorious Black Hole of Calcutta incident (see the appendix). Southwest of the tank is the St. Martin-in-the-Fields–inspired **St. John's Church** (© **033/2243-6098;** daily 9am–5pm; Rs 10/25¢) and, within the grounds, the tomb of Calcutta's founding father, Job Charnock. East of B.B.D. Bagh, to the south of Lal Bazaar, you'll find numerous tea merchants, where teas from Darjeeling, the Dooars, and Assam are packed and exported. **Nilhat House,** located behind the Old Mission Church, is the oldest tea auction house in India—join the action on Monday and Tuesday mornings.

Central Kolkata, south of Howrah Bridge, and north of Jawaharlal Nehru Rd.

Indian Museum 🞡🞡🞡

Containing things beautiful, unusual, and ancient, the museum is known to locals as *Jadu Ghar,* the House of Magic. The oldest institution of its kind in the Asia–Pacific region, it holds the country's largest repository of artifacts (over 100,000 exhibits). Among the dinosaur and mammoth skeletons and the 4,000-year-old Egyptian mummy are extraordinary Indian cultural items, including Shah Jahan's emerald goblet, and an urn said to contain the Buddha's ashes. Don't miss the cultural anthropology section—accompanied by good explanations—if you are interested in India's many tribal groups. The textiles-and-decorative-arts gallery is most impressive. It can be difficult to find, however—ask for assistance.

27 Jawaharlal Nehru Rd., at the corner of Sudder St. © **033/2249-5699.** Rs 150 ($3.45). Tues–Sun 10am–4pm.

South Park Street Cemetery 🞡🞡

This is Kolkata's most famous cemetery, where monumental gravestones and lichen- and moss-covered tombstones to large numbers of ill-fated Brits buried on Indian soil provide a tranquil retreat. A really atmospheric place to wander around, the cemetery contains headstones that bear unlikely epitaphs like MAJ. GEN. C. GREEN DIED 51TH OF JULY.

Park St. and southeast end of Cemetery Rd. Free admission. Daily 7:30am–4:30pm.

Victoria Memorial 🞡

Conceived of by Lord Curzon as a monument to his queen 4 years after her death, this domed structure is Kolkata's most recognizable landmark. It's billed as one of the city's top attractions, but with portraits of fairly boring-looking individuals filling many of the walls, it's more likely to excite Rajophiles. There are 25

The Tollywood Oscar Achiever

Kolkata has its own film industry, known throughout the Bengali world as Tollywood. In fact, it was this city that gave birth to India's finest filmmaker, **Satyajit Ray,** who died in 1992—the same year he received a Lifetime Achievement Oscar. While Bollywood was churning out dazzling choreographic daydreams, Ray made classic films that filled art-house cinemas around the world. For more on Ray, go to the appendix.

The Miracle of Mother Teresa & the "Pure Hearts"

Mother Teresa's **Missionaries of Charity (MOC)** is now headed by Sister Nirmala, a converted Brahmin. There are around 3,500 MOC sisters around the world, working in 569 centers in 120 countries, but their selfless efforts are not without controversy. Even during Mother Teresa's time, tales of pecuniary troubles and controversies over the way in which the poor and dying were being treated (and converted) beleaguered the MOC. There have always been plenty of cynics, despite the Vatican's confirmation of Mother Teresa's "miraculous" healing of a young woman's malignant tumor (the woman claims to have been cured after seeing Mother Teresa in her dreams), a move that has irritated rationalists and the medical profession. Still, in Kolkata alone, more than 50,000 destitute sick and dying are looked after by the blue-and-white sari-wearing nuns of the MOC, a demonstration of selflessness that you might deem miraculous in itself. Adjacent to the Kali Temple is "Pure Heart," or **Nirmal Hriday** (251 Kalighat Rd.; ✆ 033/2464-4223; Fri–Wed 8–11:30am and 3–5:30pm), the very first MOC center. **Mother House** (54 A.J.C. Bose Rd.; ✆ 033/2249-7115; same hours as Nirmal Hriday) is the MOC headquarters, where Mother Teresa is buried. Nearby is **Nirmal Shishu Bhawan** (78 A.J.C. Bose Rd.; same hours as Nirmal Hriday), where some 250 orphans are cared for.

galleries in the central hall, and about 3,500 articles relating to the Raj on display, including the queen's rosewood piano. Exhibits are not restricted to Raj-artifacts; the black marble throne that belonged to Siraj-ud-Daulah is impressive, as is a gigantic painting of a Jaipur royal procession, said to be one of the largest paintings in Asia.

Queen's Way. ✆ 033/2223-1889, -1890, or -1891. www.victoriamemorial-cal.org. Rs 150 ($3.45). Tues–Sun 10am–4:30pm. Sound-and-light show: Tues–Sun 7:15pm in English; Rs 20 (45¢).

Kalighat Kali Temple ✹✹   Violent, vengeful Kali is the patron goddess of Kolkata, and this temple complex—believed to be the site where the toe of Shiva's wife fell when her body was scattered across the earth by the gods anxious to stop Lord Shiva's dance of destruction (see "The Dance of Destruction," p. 525)—is a major pilgrimage center, drawing some 20,000 visitors each day. If you're a non-Hindu, you cannot enter the inner sanctum, sticky with the rotted remains of fresh flowers offered by devotees every day, but it's worth your while to explore the courtyards and the various stalls selling flowers, fruit, and religious paraphernalia. If you're uneasy about the idea of animal sacrifice, avoid the enclosure to the south of the temple where at least one goat is offered to Kali every day (a ritual that allegedly replaced the ancient practice of human sacrifice). Be equally wary of the so-called priests—temple "guides" who usher you into the complex and conduct a whirlwind tour of the facilities, only to present you with a donation book that records the radically generous donations of other foreigners.

Kalighat Rd., Kalighat. Daily 5am–1:30pm and 3–10pm (Tues, Sat, Sun, and festival days are terribly crowded with mile-long lines of devotees; Wed and Thurs are least congested.)

DAY TWO (NORTH KOLKATA)

Early in the morning, head toward **Howrah Bridge,** where you can witness people bathing at the *ghats* (steps leading down to the Hooghly River) or the pandemonium at the colorful **flower market** (you need to arrive before 7am). There you can sip *chai* and watch the stall holders deftly thread marigold garlands for the gods and bridal headgear from tuberoses and dahlias. Crossing over Howrah Bridge, head toward the **Belur Math Shrine** (see below). From here you can either incorporate a short stop at popular **Dakshineshwar Temple** (across Vivekananda Bridge; ℂ **033/2564-5222;** daily 6am–12:30pm and 3:30–8:30pm), or take a look at the potters' village at **Kumartuli** (N. Chitpur Rd.), a warren of alleys where clay deities and images of Mother Teresa are produced by the thousands. If you prefer to slow the pace, however, skip these and head south to beautiful **Paresnath Temple** (see below)—not as famous as the Kali temple, but certainly Kolkata's prettiest, and north Kolkata's star attraction. From here, you can head east to shop and eat at **Swabhumi Heritage Plaza,** a mall with 2.4 hectares (6 acres) of shopping, dining, and entertainment diversions; or head south to **Rabindra Bharati University Museum** (ℂ **033/2269-5241;** Tues–Sun 10:30am–4:30pm; Rs 50/$1.15; no photography) to visit the **Rabindranath Tagore House Museum.** Born to a wealthy entrepreneurial family in 1861, Tagore remains Bengal's best-loved artist and intellectual, and his home is filled with artworks and collectibles (closed Sun, and open only until 1:30pm on Sat). Move on to the nearby **Marble Palace** (see below).

By now, you may be in serious need of sustenance, which you'll find in the vicinity of the enormous **Nakhoda,** Calcutta's largest mosque (Rabindra Sarani and M.G. Rd.). The mosque is closed to non-Muslims during prayers, but is set within a busy bazaar area where Muslim tradespeople sell all sorts of goods, as well as a range of breads, sweetmeats, and snacks. Alternatively, enjoy a cheap, substantial Kolkata-Mughlai meal at the century-old **Royal Indian Hotel** (147 Rabindra Sarani; ℂ **033/ 2268-1073;** daily 10am–11:30pm). Browse through the thousands of bookstalls along **College Street,** and finish with coffee at the **Indian Coffee House** (see below).

Belur Math Shrine ⧆⧆   The headquarters of the international Ramakrishna Order, Belur Math combines the architectural elements of a church, a mosque, and a temple, symbolically embodying the teachings of the monk and seer Sri Ramakrishna Paramahansa. It was established in 1897, and the ashes of Sri Ramakrishna were placed here by his most prominent disciple, Swami Vivekananda, who also set up the Order. The location is lovely: Smaller shrines line the riverbank, and devotees and seekers of spiritual peace roam the grounds. Within the immaculate main shrine, activity is enlivened by evening *aarti* (musical prayers).

Belur Rd., Howrah. ℂ 033/2654-5700. Daily 6:30am–noon and 3:30–8pm.

College Street ⧆⧆   This stretch of road, deep in the heart of the university quarter, is famous for its 5,000 or so secondhand bookstalls, and for the renowned Presidency College, where India's greatest filmmaker, Satyajit Ray, studied. Many of the booksellers here are semi-literate, but remarkably, each is able to recall the titles and prices of thousands of academic and technical books, the volumes typically piled meters high. Look for the bust commemorating the father of Bengali prose literature, the reformer and philanthropist Pandit Iswar Chandra Vidyasagar, who also introduced a ban on forced marriages.

Bidhan Sarani, N. Kolkata.

Moments Meeting Bengalis

The **Indian Coffee House** (1st Floor, 15 Bankin Chatterjee St.; ℂ 033/2241-4869; Mon–Sat 9am–9pm, Sun 9am–12.30pm and 5–9pm), where the Young Bengal Movement started, is the quintessential College Street haunt. A lone photograph of Rabindranath Tagore looks across a vast former 1930s dance hall with sagging ceiling fans and scattered tables around which men, young and old, demonstratively argue the issues of the day. Surly waiters plod around rather aimlessly, so be patient while waiting for your greasy *pakora* and a strong Coorg. Meals are meager, but the coffee and conversation will get you buzzing. For an even more animated and authentic interaction with locals, head for the **Calcutta races** (www.rctconline.com); ask any waiter or at your hotel about the next event. All walks of life are to be seen here, many in their finest glad rags. As everyone celebrates the chance to escape their dharma, the atmosphere is electric.

Marble Palace 👁👁   Up a back street, in what was once known as Black Town, stands a vast mansion—a wonder to behold—sporting a plush Romanesque veneer that incorporates at least 90 different varieties of marble. Built in 1835 by the wealthy *zamindar* (landowner) Raja Rajendra Mullick Bahadur, this palatial family home has seen better days, and is now the center of a bitter feud between relatives, some of whom have been accused of sneaking off with the more valuable displays. But several works attributed to Titian and Renoir remain, while Venetian chandeliers; Ming vases; Egyptian statuary; and paintings, sculptures, furniture, and antique vases accumulated from 90 countries crowd the enormous, dimly lit rooms that open off deep verandas around an inner courtyard. Get there soon, since the feuding of the Mullicks makes it uncertain which prized item might next disappear. Admission is free, but you need a pass from the West Bengal Tourist Office; alternatively, offer the gate guard a bribe (Rs 50/$1.15) for instant access. You are expected to tip your guide.
46 Muktaram Basu St., off Chittaranjan Ave. ℂ 033/2269-3310. Tues–Wed and Fri–Sun 10am–4pm.

Paresnath Temple 👁👁👁   Jain temples are generally the most beautifully adorned in India, and Paresnath, dedicated to Sithalnath—one of the 24 perfect souls *(tirthankaras)* of the Jain religion—is no exception. Built in 1867 by a jeweler whose love of intricate designs, mirrors, and colored glass is evident everywhere, it boasts lavishly adorned patterned marble, beautiful European chandeliers, and stained-glass windows. A quiet garden is dotted with silver statues, and the temple houses an eternal flame that's apparently never gone out.
Badridas Temple St. Free admission. Daily 6am–noon and 3–7pm.

WHERE TO STAY

Decent budget rooms are all but nonexistent in Kolkata, and quality mid-range accommodations are also hard to find. For rooms under $50 you have two good options, both downtown in the busy Chowringhee area. The atmospheric **Fairlawn Hotel** (see below) should be your first choice. Or opt for **Middleton Inn,** a neat 21-room business hotel at 10 Middleton St. (ℂ 033/2216-0449 through -0452). The dull entrance belies the scrupulously clean deluxe air-conditioned doubles that go for just Rs 2,200 ($51), including breakfast. Service in general is crisp and courteous, and though there's no restaurant, they have 24-hour room service. If neither of these options is available, we highly recommend that you revise your budget to stay at one of the higher-end properties below.

Fairlawn Hotel ⊙ Hollywood's production of *City of Joy* made use of this small, popular heritage hotel and its neoclassical facade for several days of shooting, and it's also played host to British playwright Tom Stoppard, actress Felicity Kendal, and the musician Sting. Established by Armenian refugees who escaped Eastern Europe in 1917, the hotel remains a family enterprise run by the enthusiastic 84-year-old Mrs. Violet Smith and her hapless staff. News clippings, hotel awards, and copious family and celebrity photographs cover the walls, while old wicker chairs, vases, decorative plates, and even Buddhas and Ganeshas are used to create a homey atmosphere. Guest rooms (book nos. 16–21) are cozy, if simply furnished. Bathrooms are lovely, with polished red floors, old-fashioned bathtubs, and white wooden towel racks. In the kitchen, a wood- and coal-fire stove is used to prepare wholesome home-style meals from a menu that changes daily, but meal times are strict. The pleasant garden terrace has abundant greenery and is packed every night with Rajophiles and beer-swilling travelers.

13/A Sudder S., Kolkata 700 016. ⓒ 033/2252-1510 or -8767. Fax 033/2252-1835. www.fairlawnhotel.com. 18 units. $60 double with all meals, $50 double with breakfast. 20% discount Apr–Sept. AE, MC, V. **Amenities:** Restaurant; bar; travel assistance; limited room service; laundry; small library. *In room:* A/C, TV, tea-making facility. 1st-floor rooms have fridges.

Hyatt Regency ⊙⊙ *(Value)* If it's a design-conscious luxury hotel you're after, book yourself into the Hyatt, right next door to Swabhumi Heritage Park in the rapidly expanding business district of Salt Lake City. Stylish rooms (32 of which are nonsmoking) have wood floors, sunken baths, and walk-in closets. The large pool is backed by tall trees, while inside, a trendy cigar lounge appears suspended in mid-air. The hotel has added a new flavor to its dining line-up: an Italian restaurant, **La Cucina.**

JA-1, Sector III, Salt Lake City, Kolkata 700 098. ⓒ 033/2335-1234. Fax 033/2335-1235. www.hyatt.com. Toll-free reservations from within India: ⓒ 1-600-118-001. 235 units. Rs 4,000–Rs 5,000 ($91–$114) standard double; Rs 5,600–Rs 6,000 ($128–$137) Club Regency; Rs 10,000–Rs 14,000 ($230–$321) suite. Rates include breakfast. Club Regency rates include airport transfers. Taxes extra. Check the website for special offers. AE, DC, MC, V. **Amenities:** 2 restaurants; bar; pool; tennis; squash; fitness center and spa; concierge; salon; 24-hr. room service; babysitting; laundry and valet service; doctor-on-call. *In room:* A/C, TV, dataport, voice mail, tea- and coffee-making facilities, hair dryer, electronic safe.

ITC Sonar Bangla Sheraton Hotel and Towers ⊙⊙ If you want to stay far from the congested heart of Kolkata, you like large open spaces, and you want the pampering of a spa, this latest entry into Kolkata's luxury hotel market exudes luxury and comfort. If, however, you want to have the sights at your doorstep and prefer not to deal with endless taxi rip-offs, Oberoi Grand and The Park offer similar luxuries at the same price. Priding itself as a "business resort hotel," the ITC looks from the outside like the quintessential grotesque concrete structure rising from open marshland; once inside, you'll find a soporific escape from the intense reality of Kolkata. Courtyards and lily ponds separate accommodations blocks, each with its own lounge area and exclusive facilities. While some rooms in the Sheraton Tower overlook the pretty lily ponds, the rooms to ask for are the ITC One rooms that overlook the Sundarbans (littoral forests in the Ganges delta). Every room in the latter category (and above) also has a plush black leather massage lounger. Plus, the hotel's huge pool and spa are welcome respites after a day trudging Kolkata's streets. Schedule a meal at **Dum Pukht** or **Peshawari** to get a taste of Lucknowi or North West Frontier cuisine, respectively.

1 JBS Halden Ave., opposite Science City (Eastern Metropolitan Bypass), Kolkata 700 046. (C) 033/2345-4545. Fax 033/2345-4555. www.starwoodhotels.com. 239 units. $250 Executive Club double, $320 Sheraton Towers double, $350 ITC One double; $450 junior suite, $600 queen suite, $700 presidential suite. Rates include breakfast. Some rates include airport transfers and other privileges. Taxes extra. Check online for specials for stays of 2 nights or more. AE, DC, MC, V. **Amenities:** 5 restaurants; pastry shop; bar; lounges; nightclub; pool; chip and putt golf course; tennis courts; jogging track; health club; spa; travel desk; business services; hair salon; 24-hr. room service; babysitting; laundry; dry cleaning. *In room:* TV, dataport, minibar, tea- and coffee-making facilities, safe, weighing scale.

Oberoi Grand 🌟🌟🌟   This quintessential Kolkata monument is the city's top accommodations and one of the best hotels in India. Elegant, with regal old-world charm, its guest rooms draw ambassadors, diplomats, heads of state, and royalty (although the Hollywood crowd heads for The Park). Superior guest rooms (city or garden view) are marvelous; ask for room no. 432 if you want the biggest of the lot. If you want a private balcony, book a room on the third floor. In the central courtyard, you can sip gin and tonics around the best pool in town. And for inspiration about what to do when you run out of sights and restaurants, speak to the head concierge, Amitava Sarkar, whose knowledge and enthusiasm will deepen your appreciation of the city.

15 Jawaharlal Nehru Rd., Kolkata 700 013. (C) **033/2249-2323.** Fax 033/2249-1217. www.oberoihotels.com. 213 units. $270 superior city-view double, $285 premium garden-view double, $340 deluxe garden-view double; $500–$840 suite. Deluxe room and suite rates include breakfast and airport transfers. Check website for online discounts. AE, DC, MC, V. **Amenities:** 4 restaurants; 2 bars; pool; health club and spa; 24-hr. room service; babysitting; laundry and dry cleaning; doctor-on-call. *In room:* A/C, TV, DVD player, minibar, tea- and coffee-making facilities, hair dryer. Fax machines in deluxe rooms.

The Park 🌟🌟🌟   Space is something of a premium in Calcutta, and a stylish overhaul has transformed this tiny sliver of Park Street into a model of urban chic, the abode of choice for the likes of Penelope Cruz and Melanie Griffith. Guest rooms may be small, but they're neat, functional, and bright, with Art Deco elements, antique tribal artworks, and bold color combinations. Book a Residence Room and you get a private lounge, a slightly larger bedroom with walk-in dressing room, stylish furniture, a thick mattress on a queen-size bed, a floor butler, and a Jacuzzi in the bathroom. The Park also houses the city's hippest, most happening nightclub.

17 Park St., Kolkata 700 016. (C) **033/2249-3121,** -7336, or 033/2249-9000. Fax 033/2249-7343 or -4000. www.theparkhotels.com/calcutta_home.htm. 150 units. $225 superior double, $250 luxury double, $275 Residence/deluxe double; suite from $325. $25 extra bed. AE, DC, MC, V. **Amenities:** 3 restaurants; pub; disco; pool; golf on request; health club/fitness center; travel desk; doctor-on-call, 24-hr. currency exchange. *In room:* A/C, TV, DVD, dataport, minibar, hair dryer, safe, bowl of fruits.

Taj Bengal 🌟🌟   This smart hotel, popular with businesspeople, is a good choice if you want to stay south of the city, enjoy views of the Maidan, and dine in-house—Taj Bengal boasts some of Calcutta's most impressive restaurants. Besides **Sonargaon** and **The Hub,** both reviewed below, it houses one of India's best Chinese restaurants, **Chinoiserie.** Guest rooms on the third and fourth floors feature dark teakwood parquet floors, rugs, shimmering olive curtains, and paintings depicting Calcuttan city scenes. Club Rooms (top floor) have added space (thanks to a window alcove) and access to posh lounges and exclusive restaurants where the city's elite plot and play. The "gentlemen's club" ambience in the residents' lounge goes down well with a game of pool, a book from the small library, or time at the Internet bar.

34B Belvedere Rd., Alipore, Kolkata 700 027. (C) **033/2223-3939.** Fax 033/2223-1766. www.tajhotels.com. 229 units. $250 superior double, $265 deluxe double, $285 luxury double; $320 Taj Club; $350 executive suite. Rates include breakfast. Rates up to 50% lower Apr–Sept. AE, DC, MC, V. **Amenities:** 3 restaurants; bar; nightclub; tea lounge; patisserie; pool; health club; concierge; travel desk; salon; 24-hr. room service; laundry. *In room:* A/C, TV, Wi-Fi enabled, minibar, tea- and coffee-making facilities, hair dryer, electronic safe.

WHERE TO DINE

Bengalis are known for their fine palates and love of dining out, and a wide range of cuisines are theirs to choose from. Make sure to sample **Kolkata-Mughlai food**—blending the best of the Bengali *Nawabs'* cuisine with influences from the Deccan, Awadh, and North India—at least once. **Nizam's** (1 Corporation Place) claims to be the place where the *kathi* kebab roll (kebabs wrapped in a *paratha*—fried bread) was invented. The food is legendary, and the prices unbeatable. Another popular Bengali-Muslim joint is **Shiraz** (56 Park St., at the intersection of Park St. and A.J.C. Bose Rd.; © **033/2247-7702** or 033/2280-5006). Go to the first floor for air-conditioned comfort, or to the rooftop. The extensive menu includes numerous exotic-sounding Kolkata-Mughlai items, as well as a range of kebabs.

If you're in the vicinity of Nakhoda Mosque, try the **Royal Indian Hotel** (147 Rabindra Sarani; © **033/2268-1073**), which opened in 1905 and is the oldest restaurant of its kind. On Thursday or Sunday, you can order *murgh mussalam* (chicken), while the mutton *chanps tikiya* (chops) is legendary.

Chinese cuisine is popular with Kolkatans—**Mainland China** *(Uniworth House, 3A Gurusadary Rd.; © **033/2283-7964** through -7969) is currently considered the best place in town (vying with the Taj Bengal's in-house Chinese restaurant, **Chinoiserie**). Popular favorites include fish cooked in parsley sauce, Peking-style lamb cooked in black pepper sauce, Hunan-style prawns, and Szechuan chili crab. Be sure to reserve a table.

Park Street, one of the city's busiest hubs, is lined cheek-by-jowl with restaurants and stalls serving all kinds of interesting food. **Peter Cat** (18A Park St.; © **033/ 2229-8841** or 033/2217-2942), set in a pleasant colonial bungalow, serves an outstanding *chelo kebab* platter (Rs 116/$2.60), skewered meat kebabs on a bed of flavored rice. This is a popular after-work watering hole, though service is often shoddy. Avoid it at lunchtime on weekdays when it's packed with local office-goers. Also on Park Street is **Mocambo** (25B Park St.; © **033/2246-4300,** 033/2229-0095, or 2217-5372), which serves decent Western fare (try the tasty deviled crabs—Rs 120/$2.75) and sizzlers (steak or kebab and vegetable platters).

Anyone with a sweet tooth is headed for heaven: *Mishti doi* (yogurt with caramelized sugar) is a must-try, as are Bengali staples like *sandesh, chanar payesh, rossogolla,* and *khir kadom,* more delicately sweetened than the *gulab jamuns* and *halwas* of the north, and available all over the city. Shop where sweet gourmands do, at **Ganguram** (11 C.R. Ave.), **Gokul** (1 A.J.C. Bose Rd.), **Mithai** (48B Syed Amir Ali Ave.), and **Bhim Nag** (Bidhan Sarani).

Ar-Han Thai *(finds* THAI/ASIAN   Owner Prabhakar Singh has a long association with Thailand and, unable to live without the cuisine, he started this restaurant. Come for tasty portions of stir-fried chicken made with fresh chilies, garlic, and basil, or delicious broiled jumbo prawns in a tamarind sauce (call 24 hr. ahead to order this), cooked by Chef John Chen. The menu offers a range of noodle combinations; try yellow curry noodles with your choice of vegetables, chicken, prawns, or an eclectic combo. Come to this intimate restaurant hungry, because the portions are huge.

31 Bentick St. © **033/2243-7857** or 033/2243-6766. Reservations essential Fri–Sun. Main courses Rs 70–Rs 395 ($1.60–$9). AE, MC, V. Daily 11am–11:30pm.

Moments Fast Food, Kolkata Style

At almost any time of the day you'll see expectant customers standing outside the various *kathi* roll booths on Park St. They're waiting for one of Kolkata's favorite lunchtime snacks, a *paratha* (thick chapati, or fried bread) filled with spiced chicken, mutton, egg or *paneer* (Indian cheese) topped off with *chaat* masala, onion, and lemon juice—simply delicious. The hygiene at many of these places is often suspect, so look for a stall with lots of customers. (Try **Kusum** at 21 Park St., the one outside Oxford Book Store; or another stall next to Peter Cat.) Order the double-side egg mutton roll and avoid the accompanying green chutney.

The Hub ★★ ECLECTIC   Alex Bignotti, the Italian chef at this bright restaurant in the lobby of the Taj Bengal, likes to experiment. His highlight is the "food theater" experience, during which guests can watch a five-course meal being prepared, and then dig into the results. Definitely try the *ajwaini jhinga,* fresh Chilka prawns flavored with *ajwain* (thyme-like spice) and grilled in the tandoor oven; or the *gamberoni all' anice,* king prawns cooked in a heavenly Sambuca sauce. Or sample an Italian take on a local fish by ordering *beckti Mediterraneo.* The fare also includes burgers, pastas, thin-crusted pizzas (try the spicy *alla Indiana*), grills, and griddles.

Taj Bengal, 34B Belvedere Rd., Alipore. ✆ 033/2223-3939. Main courses Rs 220–Rs 620 ($3–$14). Food theater Rs 325–Rs 575 ($7.40–$13) per performance. AE, DC, MC, V. Open 24 hr.

Jong's ★★★ CHINESE/JAPANESE/THAI   Sharing an entrance with the equally excellent Indian restaurant **Zaranj** (see below), this stylish spot, with freshly renovated and expanded interiors, is our choice for top Asian restaurant in West Bengal. On offer is an eclectic and wildly exciting selection of well-considered dishes. Start with traditional *tom yam kai,* a spicy hot-and-sour chicken broth flavored with kafir lime leaves, lemon grass, and chili paste. Nonmeat-eaters should opt for *kaeng phak,* a Thai preparation of seasonal veggies cooked in a spicy curry with galangal, lemon grass, and kafir lime leaves, topped off with coconut milk. For your main course, favorites include ginger chicken, Shanghai-style tangerine chicken, coconut prawns with bamboo shoots, crab in a zesty Penang curry, and drunken fish made with Bay of Bengal *bekti* grilled in red wine.

26 J.L. Nehru Rd., Kolkata 700 087. ✆ 033/2249-5572, -9744, -0369, or -0370. Reservations highly recommended, essential at weekends. Main courses Rs 170–Rs 425 ($4.90–$9.70). AE, DC, MC, V. Wed–Mon 12:30–3pm and 7:30–11pm.

Kewpie's ★ BENGALI   Popular with local celebrities and bigwig visitors to the city, this tiny family kitchen has been well marketed but is not necessarily the most authentic (for that you're better off visiting **Suruchi,** ideally combined with a visit to South Park Cemetery). The menu changes daily, but the highlight is Kewpie's *thali* (multicourse platter)—various fish, vegetable, and meat items (or strictly vegetarian items), served with different breads. Talk to the helpful Purnima Dasgupta for explanations of the dishes or ingredients.

2 Elgin Lane, off Heysham Rd., behind Netaji Bhavan. ✆ 033/2475-9880 or 033/2476-9929. Minimum charge (thali) Rs 200 ($4.55) per person. MC, V. Tues–Sun 12:30–3pm and 7:30–11pm.

Saffron ★★★ CONTEMPORARY INDIAN/FUSION   Saffron's executive chef Abhijit Saha has transformed the menu to showcase local Bengali cuisine as well as a host of pan-Indian specialties, all cooked strictly using Indian methods, but often with ingredients from around the world. The flaming *daab chingri,* prawns simmered in coconut milk gravy and flambéed (in Malibu liqueur) in front of you, is a real treat, as is the Kerala masala duck. *Bhatti ka chanp,* a succulent piece of mutton marinated in balsamic vinegar and cooked in a tandoor, is one of the restaurant's signature dishes. Or try the more traditional saffron-infused *dum ghost biryani* or chicken Chettinad. Vegetarians are also well catered to. Leave space for *gulab jamun,* a dessert based on an old family recipe (topped with honey and stuffed with saffron and nuts). Note that The Park has a second restaurant, **Zen House** ⋆⋆, where Bangkok-born master chef Nut Kunlert serves Asian specialties like prawns, barbecued whole with a chili sauce; sweet-and-sour chicken prepared with a hint of ginger and jalapeño; or lemon-grass soufflé. Prices are similar to those at Saffron.

The Park hotel, 17 Park St. ⓒ 033/2249-3121. Main courses Rs 225–Rs 625 ($5.10–$14). AE, DC, MC, V. Daily 12:45–2:45pm and 7:30–11:45pm (last orders).

Sonargaon ⋆⋆⋆ BENGALI/INDIAN   Exposed stone masonry and Mediterranean-style whitewashed walls, wooden tables, tribal wall hangings, a separate fish-market kitchen (guests can watch their fish being cooked), and enormous storm lanterns set the right atmosphere for this upmarket take on village-style Bengali dining. Order a traditional Bengali *thali* (multicourse meal), served on a silver platter, and give yourself plenty of time to recover; diners tend to leave with full stomachs. Bengali specialties include a rich, spicy prawn curry *(chingri malai),* and *paturi maach*—sliced *bekti* fish coated with a paste of mustard and green chili, wrapped in a banana leaf, and steamed. For an excellent starter, get *kakori kebab* (minced lamb kebab) or, if you are looking for something milder, the *murgh* Wajid Ali (chicken breast pounded, marinated with saffron and other spices, and cooked in a mildly spiced sauce). Leave space for *rossogolla payesh,* a Bengali dessert made from *paneer* (cheese) and thickened sweet milk.

Taj Bengal, 34B Belvedere Rd., Alipore. ⓒ 033/2223-3939. Main courses Rs 295–Rs 695 ($6.70–$16). AE, DC, MC, V. Daily 12:30–2:45pm and 7:30–11:45pm.

Taaja's ⋆ ECLECTIC/INTERNATIONAL   For a wild variety of dishes from the world's kitchens and a dynamic, upbeat crowd, this charming, casual restaurant is a winner. Don't miss barbecued pork ribs, hot Singaporean prawns, Goan prawn *vindaloo,* Hungarian goulash, or the local *bekti* fish prepared with a Creole sauce. There are also dishes from Vietnam and Burma as well as Spanish paella, along with a selection of Indian specialties.

29/1A Ballygunge Circular Rd. ⓒ 033/2485-2915. Reservations for Sat and Sun evening essential. Main courses Rs 65–Rs 240 ($1.45–$5.45). AE, MC, V. Tues–Sun noon–4:30pm and 7–11pm.

Zaranj ⋆⋆⋆ NORTHWEST FRONTIER   Named for a hamlet in Afghanistan, this upmarket restaurant is one of the city's most opulent dining options, where miniature waterfalls and plush seating provide a warm, luxurious atmosphere. The **Raphael Lounge** is an ideal spot to kick off the evening in style, with its fine selection of imported wines and champagnes. Affable manager Dev Singh will help you pick fare to suit your taste buds, but if you like lamb, his hands-down recommendation is the Zaranj *raan.* Popular dishes include tandoori prawns *(jhinga)* and *dahi ka* kebab, prepared in the display kitchen behind a wall of glass. For dinner, be sure to reserve in advance, or you'll be watching the city's movers and groovers feasting while you wait.

26 Jawaharlal Nehru Rd. ⓒ 033/2249-5572, -9744, -0369, or -0370. Reservations essential. Main courses Rs 185–Rs 425 ($4.20–$9.65). AE, DC, MC, V. Daily 12:30–3pm and 7:30–11pm; closed at lunchtime on Tues.

SHOPPING

Kolkata is also renowned for its fashion designers. Look for garments by the promising local **Sabyasachi Mukherjee,** who is taking Kolkata's fashion industry to new heights (there's an outlet at 37/1C Hazra Rd.; ℂ **033/2454-3005**). Other names to be on the lookout for are **Kiran Uttan Ghosh** and **Shabari Datta.** For more contemporary Bengali fashion, pop into **Mithai** (433 Syed Amir Ali Ave.). For Bengali handicrafts, visit **Bengal Home Industries** (11 Camac St.; ℂ **033/2282-1562**) or **Sasha** (27 Mirza Ghalib St.; ℂ **033/2252-1586**). You can pick up a wide range of Indian curios, along with everything from saris to silk carpets, from the government-operated **Central Cottage Industries Emporium** in Chowringhee (7 Jawaharlal Nehru Rd.; ℂ **033/2228-4139** or -3205; Mon–Sat 10am–7pm).

Kolkata is also home to one of India's best bookstores, **Oxford Bookstore** (17 Park St., Kolkata 700 016; ℂ **033/2229-7662** or 033/2217-5266; oxfordkol@apeejaygroup.com; Mon–Sat 10am–9pm, Sun 11am–3pm), which carries a good range of local and imported periodicals, books on India and Calcutta, and fiction. Another shop worth investigating is **Family Book Shop** (1A Park St.; ℂ **033/2229-3486** or 033/3090-6003; Mon–Sat 10am–7:30pm); it's tiny but has an interesting upstairs section.

KOLKATA AFTER DARK

DRINKING & PARTYING

Kolkata is officially dry on Thursday, but this doesn't affect the upscale hotels. Local laws supposedly prohibit the sale of alcohol after 10:30pm, so if you're keen for an all-nighter, be sure to ask the exact time for last rounds at any bar you visit. In the budget-oriented Sudder Street precinct, the open-air bar at the **Fairlawn Hotel** (13/A Sudder St.; ℂ **033/2252-1510**) is wonderful for sundowners and early-evening drinks. It's not for nothing that **The Park** (ℂ **033/2249-3121** or -7336) is the place to hang out after hours—despite a postage stamp–size dance floor, **Someplace Else** rocks all night long. Together with **Tantra** ⍟ (also at The Park; 9pm–2am; Rs 3,000/$68 per couple), it attracts the city's hippest crowd.

LIVE PERFORMANCE

Theater, music, dance, and poetry recitals all thrive here. Check out the listings in *Kolkata This Fortnight* (free from tourist offices) or in the "Bulletin Board" section of *The Times of India.* Upscale hotels also carry the useful monthly booklet *Cal Calling.* **Rabindra Sadan** concert hall (A.J.C. Bose Rd. and Cathedral Rd.; ℂ **033/2223-9936** or -9917) hosts regular theater and musical events, as well as dance-drama performances and local-flavored Bengali poetry evenings. Cultural events also take place at the **Academy of Fine Arts** (2 Cathedral Rd.; ℂ **033/2223-4302**). The **British Council** (5 Shakespeare Sarani; ℂ **033/2242-5478**) often offers plays and performances in English. Bengali and English dramas are performed at **Kala Mandir** (48 Shakespeare Sarani; ℂ **033/2247-9086**). For musical programs, contact **Sisir Mancha** (1/1 A.J.C. Bose Rd.; ℂ **033/2223-5317**). Indo-German productions are occasionally held at **Max Mueller Bhavan** (8 Pramathesh Barua Sarani; ℂ **033/2475-9398**).

CINEMA, GALLERIES & EXHIBITIONS

Considered the art capital of India, Kolkata hosts an unimaginable number of art exhibitions. Scan the newspapers for information about what's on while you're in town. Or check out the **Birla Academy of Art and Culture** (108–109 Southern Ave.; ℂ **033/2466-2843**) or the **Centre for International Modern Art** (Sunny Towers, 43

Ashutosh Chowdhari Ave.; © **033/2485-8717;** Tues–Sat 11am–7pm, Mon 2–7pm, closed Sun). The **Academy of Fine Arts** (2 Cathedral Rd.; © **033/2223-4302**) has art galleries (daily 3–8pm) and a museum (Tues–Sun noon–6:30pm; admission Rs 5/10¢), where you can see works by Rabindranath Tagore.

The best cinema complex in the city is **Nandan** (1/1 A.J.C. Bose Rd.; © **033/ 2223-1210** or -0970), with excellent screens and a fantastic sound system. Nandan also regularly hosts art-film screenings and retrospectives. There are a number of cinemas in Chowringhee where you can watch movies in the company of feverishly excitable Indian audiences.

2 Orissa's Golden Temple Triangle

The tropical state that flourished during the 13th century on India's central eastern seaboard, Orissa is famous for its temples, which draw thousands of pilgrims here throughout the year, predominantly to **Jagannath Temple** in the coastal town of **Puri,** to worship Vishnu in his avatar as the Lord of the Universe. Architecturally, the **Sun Temple** at **Konark** is of even greater significance, with its massive stone-carved chariot adorned with sculptures, rising to carry Surya, the sun god, to the heavens. Even Orissa's capital, **Bhubaneswar** (the third point of Orissa's Golden Triangle), is more important for its enormous collection of Hindu temples—at one time 7,000—than it is as an administrative or industrial center.

Orissa remains largely tribal, with many villages still off-limits to outsiders, but the state is also well-known for its "Tribal Tourism." For the anthropologically inclined, this offers you a chance to get way off the beaten track and meet people who live almost completely on the fringes of civilization. The state is also a good place to pick up crafts, particularly textiles and paintings—even when tending to the rice paddies, the women of Orissa are dressed in glamorous saris. Cottage textile industries are the mainstays for entire villages, which produce beautiful *ikat* (patterned) textiles, palm-leaf paintings, and bright *patachitra* (cloth) paintings (the best-known of Orissa's handicrafts). *Note:* Although Orissa has long, golden beaches that curve around the Bay of Bengal, the infrastructure here is limited and the sea can be treacherous; beach lovers are best off heading for Kerala or Goa.

BHUBANESWAR
485km (300 miles) SW of Kolkata

Orissa's capital emerged in the 7th century as a center of prolific and accomplished temple building, and by the 11th century the city of Bhubaneswar (derived from Shiva's incarnation as Tribhubaneswar, Lord of the Three Worlds) had become a significant religious hub, with an estimated 7,000 temples. Of these, only several hundred remain, but those that survive reveal the evolution of the Nagara style into an architectural form unique to Orissa. You won't need to stay here more than a day—Konark's Sun Temple, one of India's top attractions, is just under an hour's drive away.

ESSENTIALS
VISITOR INFORMATION   If you're fortunate, the **Government of Orissa Tourist Office** (5 Jaydev Nagar; © **0674/243-1299;** Mon–Sat 10am–5pm, closed on the second Sat of each month) will be manned by Kamal Mohanty, who is passionate about his state and about improving the lot of tourism in the region.

GETTING THERE   By Air   Air Sahara (www.airsahara.net) and **Indian Airlines** (© **0674/253-0533** or –0544; http://indian-airlines.nic.in) have 55-minute daily flights from Kolkata. Indian Airlines also operates regular flights to and from Delhi (2 hr.), and Mumbai (3 hr.), and to and from several destinations in South India, including Chennai and Hyderabad. **Bhubaneswar's Biju Patnaik Airport** is about 4km (2½ miles) from the center, in the southwest. The airport has a tourist information counter, as well as a taxi service; though this is not a prepaid service, transfers into the city should cost no more than Rs 150 ($3.45).

By Train   The best train from Delhi is the **Rajdhani Express,** but the trip is lengthy—25 hours—and departures are only 2 days per week; other trains may take 30 to 42 hours. From Kolkata, the **Howrah-Puri Express** is the most convenient (it's overnight); however, the quickest is the **Faluknama Express** (under 7 hr.). Puri is 1½ hours from Bhubaneswar, and there is regular train service between the two cities. For inquiries and reservations, your best bet is to see a travel agent or to visit the train reservation office personally (see chapter 2).

By Road   If you want to drive or bus it here from Kolkata (500km/310 miles away), count on spending 13 hours propped up in your seat.

GETTING AROUND   By Taxi & Auto-Rickshaw   Auto-rickshaws in Bhubaneswar are unusually comfortable and well maintained. Drivers are genuinely helpful, if often unable to understand you. Taxis from Bhubaneswar to Puri or Konark are readily available; for taxi excursions, be clear about the duration of your journey, and the sights you wish to cover. Hiring a car and driver is a good way to save time. Try **Mercury Travels** at the Trident Hilton (Nayapalli; © **0674/230-1010,** ext. 49), or **Swosti Travels** (103 Janpath; © **0674/253-5773** or -5771)—each of which handles flights, car rentals, and tours of the state. Inexpensive full-day coach tours of the city and the entire Golden Triangle region are administered by the **O.T.D.C. Head Office** (© **0674/243-2382;** www.orissa-tourism.com/otdc.htm), but these are targeted at domestic visitors.

Tip: **Heritage Tours** is a reputable outfit with years of experience. Located at the entrance of the Mayfair Beach Resort in Puri, it specializes in "Lifestyle Tours" and tribal excursions. Besides organizing every aspect of trips lasting anything from 1 to 20 days, Heritage Tours also deals with ticketing and transportation matters.

BHUBANESWAR'S TOP ATTRACTIONS

In the heart of Bhubaneswar's Old Town, the most important temples—almost all Shaivite—are clustered around **Bindusagar Lake,** a holy reservoir believed to hold water from each and every holy river and lake in India. Of the 7,000 temples that are said to have once surrounded the tank, only around 500 remain. Traditionally, pilgrims perform their ablutions in the lake before heading into the temples to perform *puja* (a ritual of respect, such as prayer). The best are easily visited in a morning (more than three or four is overkill), leaving you time to explore some of the outlying sights during the afternoon.

The best of the city's Nagara-style temples (7th c. and 12th c. A.D.) are testament to both a radical resurgence of Hinduism and Buddhist defeat—frequently represented in temple sculptures by the image of a lion lunging for an elephant. With the exception of wonderful **Rajarani Temple** (see below), all of those worth visiting are living temples. The best are magnificently carved **Mukteshwar Temple**—the 10th-century "Gem of Orissan Architecture," where a squat, cobra-protected lingam stands in the sanctum sanctorum—and **Lingaraj Temple;** although the complex is off-limits to non-Hindus, you can admire it from a well-known vantage point, a raised platform built by the British, where you'll be harassed by a hood with a phony register of donations from other foreigners (ignore his advances and mention the police). If you have time, make a stop at the well-preserved 7th-century **Parasurameswar Temple (Brahmeswar),** for its lavish carvings, including a number of amorous couples. For something more "exotic," visit **Vaital Temple** ✦ and view its creepy tantric carvings; you'll need a flashlight to see the images of humans being put to death while the goddess Chamunda looks on.

Rajarani Temple ✦✦ Surrounded by open space and paddy fields, this 11th-century temple—maintained by the Archaeological Survey of India—glimmers in the light of day, built as it was using a superior-quality burgundy-gold sandstone. Unusual for Orissan temples, the tower *(shikhara)* features miniature versions of itself. Sculptural representations of lotus flowers with the guardians of the eight cardinal directions are a standout feature of the temple walls, which also feature delightful female figures engaged in mundane (but beautiful) daily activities.

Tankapani Rd. $5 equivalent to be paid in Indian rupees (Rs 220). Daily 6am–6pm.

Museum of Tribal Art and Artefacts ✦ Anything and everything connected with the life of Orissa's tribal people is on display in the exhibition rooms at this newly built museum decorated with primitive murals. Traditional costumes, jewelry, household appliances, and hunting equipment such as bows and arrows, axes, and traps for birds and fish indicate the ways of life of the tribal peoples of Orissa.

Near C.R.P. Sq., NH 5. ✆ 0674/256-1635 or -3649. Free admission. Mon–Sat 10am–5pm; closed 2nd Sat of each month.

Orissa State Museum ✦ This collection convincingly explains the religious context of Hindu sculptures, but you may be more fascinated by the erotic friezes that date back as far as the 7th century A.D. Upstairs, the **Manuscript Gallery** includes early examples of the type of work you'll encounter in some Orissan crafts villages. Along with a collection of musical instruments, a number of dioramas depict different Orissan tribes. Next door is a collection of *patachitra* (cloth) paintings dealing primarily with the Jagannath cult and tales from the *Ramayana.*

Lewis Rd., near Kalpana Sq. ✆ 0674/243-1597. Rs 50 ($1.15). Tues–Sun 10am–5pm.

Dhauli ✦ The glistening, white-domed **Shanti Stupa (Peace Pagoda)** at the top of Dhauli Hill is visible from the main road as you head toward this site where historic Ashokan rock edicts are carved. Guarded by pale yellow Ashokan lions, the Kalinga World Peace Pagoda is a celebration of Ashoka's decision, 2,300 years ago, to renounce violence and war and embrace Buddhism—a decision made in the wake of his massacre against the Kalinga people, then rulers of Orissa. A plaque here notes that Ashoka built 84,000 *stupas* (commemorative cairns), some as far away as Greece.

Free admission. Daily 5am–8pm.

WHERE TO STAY

Trident Hilton ✦✦ Situated some distance out of the city center, this classy low-rise hotel is surrounded by 5.6 hectares (14 acres) of exquisite lawns, mango groves, and rock gardens. Drawing businesspeople, travelers, and even the English cricket team, this is Bhubaneswar's most fabulous, and expensive, hotel. Stepping inside the lobby is like entering a temple, but sans the chaos brought by masses of worshippers.

The space has been carefully designed with stone columns, beautiful brickwork, and trellised railings enhanced by concealed lighting and spectacular brass-bell lighting features. Mythical lions perch above, looking down on guests as they arrive. In the evenings, live Indian music is played here. Guest rooms are smart, stylish, and well laid out, with pale parquet floors and sleek furniture, marble-topped surfaces, blue and beige fabrics, and scatter cushions. Individually lit gilt-framed color photographs of Orissan temple art and elegant stone reproductions of temple friezes decorate the walls. Suites have dressing rooms, marble chandeliers, and separate dining areas. Bird-watchers should ask for a room facing the rose garden. The kitchen will prepare a picnic hamper for you should you be heading out on a long day of temple-exploring.

C.B.-1, Nayapalli, Bhubaneswar 751 013. © 0674/230-1010. Fax 0674/230-1302. www.hilton.com. 62 units. $180 standard double; $190 superior double; $240 executive suite; $300 deluxe suite. AE, DC, MC, V. Check website for online specials. **Amenities:** Restaurant; bar; pool; 2 floodlit tennis courts; badminton court; jogging track; travel agency; business center; secretarial services; 24-hr. room service; babysitting; laundry, dry cleaning; doctor-on-call. *In room:* A/C, TV, Wi-Fi enabled, minibar, tea- and coffee-making facilities, hair dryer, safe, DVD player in suites.

WHERE TO DINE

Ignore the seedy neighborhood and dour look of the lodge where this upstairs eatery, **Venus Inn** (217 Bapuji Nagar; © **0674/253-1908;** daily 6:30am–10:30pm), is good for a quick South Indian *dosa* (savory pancake). Soft Hindi music fills the neat, clean interior as you dine on butter paper *masala dosa* (crepe-thin filled pancake), the onion *rawa masala dosa,* a *dosa* stuffed full of *potato,* or an *uttapam* (thicker pancake) with coconut. For the best chicken in town, **Cook's Kitchen** (260 Bapuji Nagar; © **0674/ 253-0025;** daily 10:30am–10:30pm) is the place to be—chicken *tikka* butter masala is for those who can handle their spices. Order an Orissan thali at Swosti Plaza's **Chandan** ⟨⟨ (© **0674/230-1936,** -1937, -1938, or 1939), where waiters in gold-trimmed red jackets (all part of the kitschy decor) can talk you through the evening's selection while old Hindi film music provides prerecorded entertainment. The menu changes daily, but a typical selection might include fragrant dry Oriya mutton *(mangsha kasha);* Rohu fish (beware of the fine bones) cooked in a mustard sauce *(sorisa machha);* traditionally prepared mixed vegetables *(santula);* and soft *paneer* (Indian cheese) cooked under charcoal and then caramelized *(chhena poda)*—all served with breads and condiments on a brass platter.

Hare Krishna ⟨⟨ PURE VEGETARIAN   You won't find garlic or onion (Hare Krishna culinary no-nos) in the vegetarian dishes served at this surreally decorated restaurant reached via a series of Art Deco linoleum steps. The food is rich and flavorful, so don't over-order. Lord Krishna's favorite is apparently Govinda's Pasanda, a *paneer* (Indian cheese) based dish that's heavy on the spices and includes cashew nuts, tomato, and fresh vegetables. Also spicy, but with an added hint of sour, is Chaitanya's Pasanda, made with *paneer* as well. We can heartily recommend Nanda Moharaja's *palak paneer,* which makes good use of mineral-rich spinach and is accompanied by thick, warm, fresh *naan.* The steaming-hot vegetable *biryani* is known as Bhaktivinod's Delight, and it's good.

1st floor, Lalchand Market, Jan Path. © **0674/253-4188.** Main courses Rs 50–Rs 85 ($1.15–$1.90). No credit cards. Daily 11am–3pm and 6:30–10:30pm.

SHOPPING

Sixteen kilometers (10 miles) north of Puri, **Raghurajpur Crafts Village,** a quaint rural village of thatched-roof houses, offers a variety of traditional Oriya crafts. Craftspeople will meet you as you emerge from your taxi or auto-rickshaw and lead you to their homes, which double as production centers for specific art forms. Along with a cup of *chai,* you'll be given a thorough account of the creative process. *Patachitra* paintings, the best-known of Orissa's handicrafts, fetch up to Rs 15,000 ($350) and are created on a cloth canvas, using a brush made from mouse hair. Vibrant colors are used to create extraordinarily detailed depictions of mythological events—most of these revolve around the life of Krishna. Also impressive are traditional palm-leaf drawings made with an iron pen. These are typically presented as a concertina-style fold-up poster made from palm fronds and featuring concealed erotic images and Sanskrit inscriptions. Those who want to watch artisans at work can spend time at the **Chitrakara** workshop (© **0675/ 227-4359;** daily 9am–7pm). *Note:* Although prices are reasonable, they are slightly inflated, and you shouldn't feel pressured to buy something you don't want.

EXPLORING PURI & THE SUN TEMPLE AT KONARK
Puri is 65km (40 miles) S of Bhubaneswar; Konark is 35km (28 miles) NE of Puri

Puri is considered one of the four holiest places in India, home to magnificent 15th-century **Sri Jagannath Temple,** where pilgrims throng to be absolved of past sins by the Lord of the Universe. But given that this is off-limits to non-Hindus, the real highlight lies farther up the coast, in the mellow town of Konark, site of the legendary 13th-century **Sun Temple.**

Sri Jagannath Temple ⋇   Topped by Vishnu's wheel and flag, the 64m (215-ft.) *shikhara* (spire) of Jagannath Temple dominates Puri's skyline, and it's possible to cir-cumambulate the entire complex by wandering through the market streets around the periphery walls. However, for non-Hindus, the best view of this mighty Kalinga tem-ple is from the balcony of **Raghunandan Library,** across the street. From here, you not only get a glimpse of the tremendously active temple life, but you'll be privy to the colorful activity around the souvenir stalls that spread around the temple in every direction. From this viewing point, both the size of the temple and the sheer numbers of swarming people are impressive; the temple buildings themselves are filthy with mildew. Incidentally, you will find images of Lord Jagannath and his siblings every-where in this part of India. Pitch-black with squat physiques and exaggerated features, they could well have been inspiration for the animation technique used by the creators of *South Park:* The crude, flat-featured, raccoon-eyed faces have thin red curling grins.
Raghunandan Library is open daily 7am–noon and 4–8pm. All rickshaw drivers can show you the way.

Sun Temple ⋇⋇⋇   Visualized as the gigantic chariot of Surya, the sun god, emerg-ing from the ocean, the Sun Temple at Konark was built (though not completed) at the zenith of Orissan architectural development, at the edge of a 483km (300-mile) beach. Guarded by stone elephants and mythical lions, the immense structure was carved from rock so as to look like an enormous war chariot (originally drawn by seven galloping horses), with detailed sculpted scenes of everyday facets of life. Even the spokes of the 24 giant wheels that adorn the base of the temple are intricately carved. The temple was at some point submerged by sand; when the ocean retreated just over a century ago, the temple that had been lost to the world was uncovered and excavated by the British. The entire complex is surrounded by a periphery wall. To first get an idea of the enormity of the project, circumnavigate the temple by slowly skirting this outer wall. The sanctum has collapsed inward, so it is no longer possible to enter the temple building, but you can clamber over most of the exterior for close-up views of the various scenes of love and war, trade and commerce, sports and mythical figures. Among the friezes are those depicting amorous dalliances between entwined couples—these provide stiff competition for the world-renowned sculpted erotica at Khajuraho—including spokes with miniature examples of the erotic carvings found all over the rest of the temple.

The earlier you arrive, the better your chances of enjoying this World Heritage Site in peace. Definitely avoid visiting the temple on the weekend, when day-tripping local visitors swarm to Konark as part of a high-paced pilgrimage around Orissa's golden circuit.

If you're here during the first week of December, you may be able to catch the 5-day **Konark Dance Festival** ✱✱✱ , which offers performances by some of the country's most sought-after dancers. The monument forms a remarkable backdrop to traditional dance styles accompanied by music played on classical Indian instruments.

Konark, 64km (40 miles) southeast of Bhubaneswar; 35km (21 miles) northeast of Puri. Rs 250 ($4.70). Sunrise–sunset. For information on the Konark Dance Festival, contact O.T.D.C. in Bhubaneswar (© 0674/243-2382).

WHERE TO STAY

Small, intimate, peaceful, and close to the beach, **Z Hotel**—the former seaside residence of the Raja of Serampore—is the best budget lodging in the state, offering huge, simply furnished guest rooms with sea views. Reserve room no. 25, 26, or 27 (© **06752/22-2554;** www.zhotelindia.com; Rs 500/$11; no credit cards) well in advance to secure an upstairs unit with attached bathroom (drench shower only). Don't miss the beach view from the rooftop which, unfortunately, also reveals Puri's unchecked development. Alternatively, try **Toshali Sands,** en route to Konark (© **06752/25-0571,** -0572, -0573, or -0574; www.toshalisands.com; doubles from Rs 2,550/$57). Though it's certainly never going to win any design awards, this is the closest acceptable accommodations to the Sun Temple. A beach lies nearby, and the restaurant's not bad. "Villa" units have been recently refurbished and are the best choices; they feature small sitting rooms, porches, shared kitchenettes, and big bathrooms with tubs.

Mayfair Beach Resort   This is the best place to stay in the vicinity of the Sun Temple by a long shot, popular with middle-class Indian families who come to strut their stuff on the wide expanse of beach, a short walk from the resort. However, service can be pretty surly. Disinterested staff members wear bright Hawaiian shirts, and the entrance and lobby areas are equally colorful, playing off the Jagannath Temple theme. The rough-hewn red-brick resort makes the most of its limited space, its gardens profuse with lovely trees, potted plants, and stone statues of various deities. Unless you can afford the presidential suite, book a garden cottage; it has a small sitting area, a semi-private veranda, and a small shower room. Beyond the crow-infested pool, which is neatly lined with white wood loungers, a nicely maintained stretch of beach is constantly watched by the resort's lifeguards, although hawkers still ply their trades. The major drawback here is an inconvenient 8am checkout, but if this doesn't suit you, say so, and the management may be able to accommodate you with a later checkout.

Chakratirtha Rd., Puri 752 002. © 06752/22-7800 through -7809. Fax 06752/22-4242. www.mayfairhotels.com. 34 units. Rs 3,600 ($82) deluxe double, Rs 3,800 ($86) cottage double; Rs 5,000 ($114) presidential suite. Rs 750 ($16) extra person. Ask about discounts. AE, MC, V. **Amenities:** 2 restaurants; 2 bars; pool; table tennis; pool table; health club; steam; Jacuzzi; indoor games; travel desk; currency exchange; boutique; 24-hr. room service; doctor-on-call. *In room:* A/C, TV, minibar.

WHERE TO DINE

Besides **Mayfair's Aquarium & Veranda** (© 06752/227-800), where you can sample Orissan seafood specialties (*chingudi tarkari*, prawns prepared in a traditional Orissan gravy, is delicious), you can dine at **Wild Grass** (V.I.P. Rd.; © 06752/ 22-9293; daily 11am–11pm; credit cards accepted for bills over Rs 2,000/$46; reasonably priced Ayurvedic spa), a self-consciously eco-friendly open-air restaurant set in a lush garden with stone and slate pathways and tables arranged in various nooks at different levels. Come for the delightful ambience, but don't expect the most spectacular food or service. One of the highlights here is an Orissan thali, but it must be ordered at least 6 hours in advance (well worth it). Grilled *brinjal* (eggplant, known as *baigan poda*) is another favorite; or try tandoori prawns, *nargisi* fish kebab, very affordable lobster, or prawn *malai* curry. For dessert, try the local cheesecake, *chhena poda*. **Restaurant Peace** is an utterly laid-back cafe-style eatery with plastic chairs under thatched roofing. Owner-manager Velu serves fresh locally caught fish and shellfish at ridiculously low prices: 10 grilled prawns cost around $2. Restaurant Peace opens early and serves the best bowl of muesli in India. A genuinely huge portion of fresh fruit, mixed nuts, curd, and honey is a perfect way to start the day (C.T. Rd.; © 06752/22-6642; daily 7am–11pm; no credit cards).

TRIBAL TOURS IN ORISSA

Venturing into Orissa's tribal heartland is a true off-the-beaten-track adventure, allowing you to meet people with social, cultural, and agricultural practices that have remained unchanged for centuries. Many of Orissa's tribal people are still hunter-gatherers, and are physically distinct from any other ethnic group on the subcontinent. Opportunities for travelers to interact with members of these unique societies are generally limited to weekly markets held at various tribal centers. Visitors with an especially strong interest in anthropology can arrange to spend a night or two in a traditional village, but expect plenty of walking—and forget any modern conveniences. You may, however, want to consider the fact that you will be visiting one of India's poorest regions. Also check whether any of the spoils of your tourist venture are actually reaching these village folk. Visitors have reported that some tribal tours are exploitative, making a freak-show/spectacle of the poor. In Puri, your best option for a responsibly organized tribal tour is **Heritage Tours** (p. 540); to ensure that a suitable trip is planned around your specific interests, e-mail the highly knowledgeable Bubu in advance (© 06752/22-3656; namaskar@heritagetours.org). A typical tribal tour for two persons will cost in the vicinity of $40 per person per day, for a minimum of 6 or 7 days. The fee factors in the services of a guide, an Ambassador car and driver, food, and (ultra-basic) accommodations.

3 Darjeeling

500km (310 miles) N of Kolkata

Darjeeling, "Land of the Celestial Thunderbolt," was given to the British as a "gift" from the once-independent kingdom of Sikkim. Lying in the Himalayan foothills and entirely surrounded by snowcapped vistas, Darjeeling soon became the favorite summer resort of the British Raj during the heyday of Calcutta—when Mark Twain visited, he exclaimed it was "the one land that all men desire to see, and having seen once by even a glimpse would not give that glimpse for the shows of the rest of the world combined." Today, the incredible view of the world's third-highest mountain, Mount Kanchenjunga (8,598m/27,400 ft.), is undoubtedly Darjeeling's best-loved attraction, though the town has also acquired a global reputation for producing the "champagne of teas," and retains some of its haunting Gothic Victorian ambience. Most visitors are here to pick up a permit and get acclimatized for hikes through the mountainous state of Sikkim. It's worth noting that if you want a sleepy colonial hill-station environment, with splendid flower-filled walks, this is not it. Head instead for nearby **Kalimpong,** which offers a number of charming old-world accommodations.

Two nights in Darjeeling should be more than enough, particularly if you're moving on to other Himalayan foothill towns. As with most hill stations, Darjeeling involves a considerable amount of climbing, and you'll do well to avoid the ugly mess of lower Darjeeling, which is typically congested, with suspicious odors, confusing back alleys, and a jumble of paths and stairways. Stick to The Mall and Chowrasta (crossroads) in upper Darjeeling, where life proceeds at a polite pace, and you can enjoy leisurely walks, stopping for a cup of tea or to browse shops stuffed full of trinkets and artifacts.

ESSENTIALS

VISITOR INFORMATION   Darjeeling's **Tourist Information Centre** (The Mall; ℂ **0354/225-5351** or -4214; Mon–Sat 10am–4:30pm June to mid-May; daily 9am–7pm mid-Mar to May) is helpful and will give you a free map of the area.

ACQUIRING YOUR SIKKIM PERMIT IN DARJEELING   Be warned: Getting your Sikkim permit is a laborious process that will last at least an hour. Take your passport to the **District Magistrate's Office** (off Hill Cart Rd.; Mon–Fri 10am–1pm and 2:30–4:30pm). Fill in a permit application form (remember to have it stamped), then go to the **Foreigners' Registration Office** (Laden La Rd.; ℂ **0354/225-4203;** daily 10am–7pm), where a policeman will endorse your form. Finally, head back to the District Magistrate's Office, making sure you arrive before closing time, and your passport will be stamped and the permit issued free of charge. Valid for 15 days, it states clearly which areas you may enter. (Permits also available from the Ministry of Home Affairs in New Delhi or from Indian consulates abroad.)

GETTING THERE   By Road   Darjeeling is 80km (50 miles) from Siliguri, which is the nearest main transit point. Buses from Darjeeling usually leave from the Bazaar bus stand on Hill Cart Road. Darjeeling is connected by road with Siliguri, Bagdogra, Gangtok, and Kathmandu across the Nepali border.

By Air   The nearest airport is at Bagdogra (near Siliguri), 90km (56 miles) away. **Jet Airways** and **Indian Airlines** (see chapter 2 for contact details) both have flights to Bagdogra from Kolkata (55 min.) and Delhi (via Guwahati). A taxi ride from Bagdogra to Darjeeling should take 3½ hours and cost about Rs 1,000 to Rs 1,500 ($23–$34). From Siliguri, catch the **toy train** (8 hr.; see below) or a **taxi** (2–3 hr.; Rs 800–Rs 1,000/$18–$23) to get to Darjeeling.

By Train   From Kolkata (Sealdah Station), the best option is the overnight Darjeeling Mail, which is supposed to arrive at the New Jalpaiguri railway station (scheduled arrival 8:40am) in time to connect with the Darjeeling Himalayan Railway's famous **toy train.** The toy train departs at 9am for the scenic 8-hour journey (see "The Most Spectacular Train Journey," below). Or you can hire a taxi or share a jeep (readily available), directly from the station, for the 3-hour, 88km (54-mile) journey to Darjeeling. Although the toy train runs daily, bad weather may disrupt services. If you intend to

Moments The Most Spectacular Train Journey

A polite voice at New Jalpaiguri railway station frequently announces that ". . . the train is running 30 minutes late, the inconvenience caused is deeply regretted. . . ." It's a small price to pay for what must be one of the slowest, most spectacular train journeys in the world. Since July 4, 1881, Darjeeling's aptly named **toy trains**—including the world's oldest functioning steam locomotive—have puffed and wheezed their ways between the hill station and the plains. In December 1999, the railway became India's 22nd World Heritage Site, only the second railway in the world to be so recognized on the list. The trip between New Jalpaiguri and Darjeeling covers a mere 87km (54 miles) but takes almost an entire day to transport passengers up 2,055m (6,850 ft.). En route, with rho-dodendron slopes, rolling hills, and Kanchenjunga in almost constant view, you pass through villages with names like Margaret's Hope, and puff right past the front doors of homes that range from shacks to quaint red-tiled cottages sur-rounded by potted flowers. You also traverse a total of 498 bridges and 153 unmanned level crossings. The final stop before Darjeeling is **Ghum (Ghoom)**, the second-highest railway station in the world. For details, see "Getting There by Train," above, or contact Mr. Sanjay, PRO Indian Railways (© **011/2338-5072**).

---

catch the toy train out of Darjeeling at the end of your stay, and wish to travel in first class (Rs 247/$5.65), you must book your ticket in advance at the counter at New Jalpaiguri Station. You can reserve other tickets for major trains out of New Jalpaiguri at the Darjeeling railway station daily between 8am and 2pm.

GETTING AROUND It's best to explore Darjeeling on foot, and if you need to haul luggage, ask for a porter and pay him well. Taxis are overpriced and unnecessary (with the exception of excursions to places some distance from the town). For local sightseeing tours or even jeep trips to Gangtok and other mid-distance destinations, contact the helpful **Darjeeling Transport Corporation** (30 Laden La Rd., opposite Apsara Hotel). It's open from 8am until 8pm and can advise you on alternatives if they're unable to accommodate you.

TREKKING & ADVENTURE ACTIVITIES Darjeeling is a good base for various "acclimatization treks" at lower altitudes than those you're going to come up against if you intend to trek in Sikkim. **Clubside Tours and Travels** (J.P. Sharma Rd.; © **0354/225-4646**, -4647, or -5123) offers sightseeing as well as trekking tours around Darjeeling and western Sikkim. For white-water rafting, contact **D.G.H.C. Tourism** (Silver Fir Building, The Mall; © **0354/225-5351**).

WHAT TO SEE & DO

Darjeeling is the type of place where you might easily find yourself wanting to do very little other than drink in the restorative climate and tea. There are over 70 different tea plantations in the area, and a typical tour (**Happy Valley Tea Estate** will usually accommodate visitors) demonstrates everything from harvesting to how different vari-eties of tea are sorted and prepared for export around the globe. For the finest selec-tion of organic and non-organic teas—20 to 30 plantations are represented—pay a visit to **Nathmulls** (© **0354/225-6437;** www.nathmulltea.com; Mon–Sat

9am–7pm), a family business that's been selling tea since 1931. For a good vantage point, climb **Observatory Hill,** held sacred by Hindus and Buddhists. A Kali shrine is guarded by foul-tempered monkeys that play on the colorful Buddhist prayer flags strung between the pine trees.

Darjeeling has a sizeable Tibetan presence and a number of Buddhist monasteries you can visit. Set against the backdrop of Kanchenjunga, colorful **Bhutia Busty Gompa,** near Chowrasta, is famous for the contents of its upstairs Buddhist library— one of the texts kept there is the original *Tibetan Book of the Dead.* On Tenzing Norgay Road, you may be able to buy Tibetan and Sikkimese handicrafts at **Aloobari Monastery.**

An hour's walk from town is **Padmaja Naidu Zoological Park,** where you can give the animals a miss and head straight for the secluded **Snow Leopard and Red Panda Breeding Programme,** the only successful breeding program of these endangered species in the world. Sit patiently and watch snow leopards in their cages or a red panda in the trees, or chat with Kiran Motane, the program's dedicated zoologist.

A GLORIOUS SUNRISE

Watching the sun rise from **Tiger Hill,** near the sleepy town of Ghoom, is one of the best things to do in the area (11km/7 miles from Darjeeling; private taxi costs Rs 450/$10 round-trip): The sight of the first rays of dawn carving a dramatic, golden silhouette around the not-too-distant eastern Himalayan peaks is brilliant. Occasionally, Mount Everest is also visible, just 225km (140 miles) away. Come armed with spare film and warm clothing—at an altitude of 2,550m (8,160 ft.), predawn Tiger Hill is bone-jarringly cold, and if you want to join the crowds who flock here each morning, you have to be up before dawn. The entry fee is Rs 5 (10¢), but you can pay a little extra for VIP treatment inside a special observation tower (Rs 40/90¢), where heating is accompanied by soothing Darjeeling tea. On the way back, visit **Ghoom (Liga Choling) Gompa;** possibly the best-known Buddhist monastery around Darjeeling, it was founded in the late 1800s and enshrines a 5m-high (16-ft.) clay statue of the Maitreya Buddha. In the early morning light, the colorfully painted figures over the facade and rooftops—intended to scare away evil spirits—are radiant. Along the exterior walls are prayer wheels that are spun in order to send countless prayers to the heavens, while inside, butter lamps are lit in offering to the deity.

WHERE TO STAY

Darjeeling is a great place to experience real colonial coziness, with several charming heritage hotels. In this category our preference is for **Mayfair Hill,** but **Windamere Hotel** (© **0354/225-4041** or -4042; www.windamerehotel.com; doubles from $132), originally a Victorian boardinghouse for English tea-planters on Observatory Hill, has atmospheric public spaces. (You can almost hear some wealthy memsahib tinkling away at one of the pianos, while guests celebrate another summer in the hills). Its huge heritage rooms come with immense charm. However, the hotel is showing signs of wear and tear (as you'd expect from a place built in 1889); sadly, this includes the service. Another good heritage property, the **New Elgin Hotel** (© **0354/ 225-7226** or -7227; www.elginhotels.com; doubles from $113) is one of Darjeeling's oldest hotels. With the air of a country manor, it is frequented by an upmarket foreign crowd looking to relive the splendor of the British Raj. Like Windamere, the public spaces are filled with old-world charm—old-fashioned sofas, deep armchairs, fireplaces, and beautiful rugs—but some of the rooms aren't quite as grand (some odd color combinations, too), and the bathrooms are small. The best views are from room nos. 21 to 23, 31 to 33, and 51 to 53.

Finally, if you want to be assured of absolute peace and quiet, head for the nearby hill station of Kalimpong (see "Looking for Orchids in Kalimpong," below).

Dekeling Hotel 🅵 *Value*   Some of the cedar-paneled guest rooms at this charming hotel (the best choice if you're on a tight budget) have the best views in town. Spotlessly clean and simple, this is the place to go for Tibetan hospitality (run by the wonderfully warm Norbu and Sangay Dekeva) rather than Raj-style sophistication. An old iron chimney heater keeps the lounge/library (stone tile floors, Tibetan sofas, *thangkas*, Tibetan paintings) cozy and warm; it's a wonderful place to kick back with a book, watched by the family dog, Doma. Guest rooms are basic, and although the bathrooms are a little small (with shower only), they're immaculately clean. On cold nights, a hot-water bottle is usually tucked into your bed. On the attic floor, room no. 3 has a 180-degree view that takes in Darjeeling town and Mount Kachenchunga in all its snowcapped magnificence. For security reasons, the hotel, located high above Dekevas Restaurant, is locked up at 10pm; inform the management by 9pm if you expect to be late, and a watchman will wait up for you.

51 Gandhi Rd., Darjeeling 734 101. © 0354/225-3298 or -4159. Fax 0354/225-3298. www.dekeling.com. 22 units. Rs 750 ($17) back-facing double, Rs 950 ($22) standard double, Rs 1,150 ($26) deluxe double, Rs 950 ($22) attic double. Rs 250 ($5.70) extra bed. Discounts of up to 50% off season (July 1–Sept 14 and Jan 15–Mar 14). AE, MC, V. **Amenities:** Restaurant; travel, sightseeing, and car rental assistance; limited room service; laundry; library. *In room:* Electric heater on request, TV.

Dekeling Resort 🅵 *Value*   This guesthouse (resort is an ill-chosen descriptor) is the best value-for-money deal in town. A stiff, athletic climb leads you to "Hawke's Nest," the colonial bungalow with a commanding location high above the town, now redubbed Dekeling Resort. Prayer flags flutter around this 120-year-old green-roofed, bay-windowed, two-leveled, all-suite cottage offering simple comfort, effortless charm, and complete privacy. There's a small, one-table dining room where breakfasts and home-cooked meals are served; or you can be served in bed, which the obliging

---

ᎢᎥᏗᎥ **Looking for Orchids in Kalimpong**

For even more peace and quiet, head for this nearby hill station. At an altitude of 1,250m (4,000 ft.), Kalimpong is a restorative destination, with magnificent views, relaxing walks, and an abundance of wild orchids. You'll find a variety of places to stay, including several charming hotels that will delight Raj-ophiles. **Silver Oaks** (Rinkingpong Rd.; © 03552/25-5296, -5766, or -5767; www.elginhotels. com) has excellent views and terrific old-world ambience; luxurious doubles go for Rs 3,800 ($86) including all meals. Representing real heritage, the **Himalayan Hotel** (Upper Cart Rd.; © 03552/25-5248; himhot@satyam.net.in) feels like the setting for a Sherlock Holmes mystery. Crammed full of history, it has a wonderful hilltop location (full-board doubles from Rs 4,600/$105).

staff of two will arrange. Ask for a double bed in an upstairs room; accommodations there are huge and charming, with wood floors, carved antique dressers, Tibetan rugs, pale floral fabrics, and lovely fireplaces. Bathrooms have large drench showers and plenty of natural light. This is a true haven if you don't mind the 20-minute walk to The Mall.

2 A.J.C. Bose Rd., Darjeeling 734 101. ℂ 0354/225-3092 or -3347. Fax 0354/225-3298 www.dekeling.com. 4 units. Rs 2,400 ($56) double without meals, Rs 3,700 ($86) double with meals. Up to 40% discount off season. AE, MC, V. **Amenities:** Dining room; lounge; assistance w/travel; sightseeing; car rental; room service; laundry. *In room:* TV, fireplace.

Mayfair Hill Resort 👉👉   Once the summer palace of the Maharajah of Nazargunj, this class act has warmer staff and better ambience than popular New Elgin, and the views are far superior. Two copper elephants guard the entrance of the main building, and a signboard informs guests of daily weather conditions. It's set in a lovely garden with potted plants, sculpted deities, and its own temple. The partially wood-paneled guest rooms—in ivy-covered buildings, which feel more like cozy cottages—are a tad feminine (floral fabrics, predominantly pink) but lovely, featuring Tibetan rugs, fireplaces, fine wooden furnishings, bay windows with seats, and entrance/dressing rooms. They receive plenty of natural light and enjoy superb views of the town, the mountains, and the valley below. The tiled, well-spaced bathrooms have good shelving and vintage-style free-standing wooden towel racks. Guests are allowed use of sports facilities at the Darjeeling Gymkhana Club.

Opposite Governor's House, The Mall, Darjeeling 734 101. ℂ 0354/225-6376 or -6476. Fax 0354/225-2674. www.mayfairhotels.com. 31 units. Rs 5,500 ($125) standard cottage double, Rs 6,500 ($148) heritage cottage double. Rs 2,000 ($46) extra bed. Rates include all meals. MC, V. **Amenities:** Restaurant; bar; health club and tennis privileges; pool table; billiards; squash; ice-skating; travel assistance; car rental; currency exchange; babysitting; laundry; doctor-on-call; library; tea-leaf shop. *In room:* Heater, TV, DVD player, tea- and coffee-making facilities, hair dryer, fireplace.

WHERE TO DINE

The following recommendations are all within walking distance of each other; ask for directions before you set out. For Tibetan food, **Dekevas Restaurant** (ℂ 0354/ 225-4159; no credit cards) has some delicious favorites, including *momos* (dumplings) and wonton soup, with a choice of chicken, pork, or vegetable as a base. Try a delicious *shabalay,* Tibetan pie filled with mince, onion, and spring onion; spice it up with a hint of chili sauce. Also sample the awesome *tsampa*—roasted barley served with cheese, butter, and a glass of milk. For those extra-cold days, it has a selection of soups. Also available are Chinese dishes, pizzas, and burgers. At **Lemon Grass** (also known as The Park) you can order from the Thai or Indian menu—the Indian tandoori chicken is a stand-out favorite (ℂ 0354/225-5270; no credit cards). Part of a three-floor food center, with a delicatessen and Internet cafe one floor below and an American diner at the basement level, **Glenary's** has been serving guests since 1935. Although staff may boast about the Continental cuisine, the best options are Indian— try *mahi tikka* (spicy fish tandoori) or *bhuna gosht,* a mutton curry cooked with ginger, garlic, and masala in its own juices (ℂ 0354/225-7554). Spectacular views of Mount Kachenjunga make **Keventer's Snack Bar** (1 Nehru Rd.; ℂ 0354/225-6542 or -4026) something of a Darjeeling institution, even if the food is nothing to write home about. Sit upstairs on the terrace for breakfast served by disaffected waiters in

Early to Bed, Early to Rise

Life kicks off early here, and fades early in the evening. By 8:30pm, you'd best be in your hotel, or perched at the bar at **Joey's Pub** (℘ **0354/225-8216;** 11am–10pm; no credit cards), which has an authentic British pub atmosphere and a well-stocked bar. Out of season, even restaurants close a touch earlier than seems appropriate, and darkness creeps quickly over the streets, sidewalks, and alleys. You'll need a flashlight to find your way back to your hotel at night.

maroon jackets. For more views that help mediocre food go down, **Windamere Hotel Restaurant** (Observatory Hill; ℘ **0354/225-4041** or -4042) is open for all meals and a good place to soak up Raj-era ambience.

4 Sikkim

Sikkim's original inhabitants are the Lepchas, also called Rongtub (literally "the dearest people of Mother Earth"), who call their land *Ney Mayal Lyang,* or "heaven." And how! Crammed in between Tibet, Nepal, Bhutan, and West Bengal, this tiny, mountainous state is as pristine a pocket of India as you are likely to encounter, with some 4,000 varieties of wildflowers (including 600 varieties of orchids), snow-fed lakes, high-altitude mountain forests, and hidden Buddhist monasteries. Some travelers come simply to enjoy the refreshing views and clean air, but most are here to tackle the fantastic treks through western Sikkim, exploring remote valleys and villages of yak-herding Tibetans. Ideally, you should spend a day or two in the state capital, **Gangtok,** to organize permits and transport/trekking arrangements, then head to **Pelling** before undertaking a demanding high-altitude trek for several days. Or you can skip Gangtok and either hire a jeep that goes directly from Siliguri (near the railway station at New Jalpaiguri) to Pelling, or travel from Bagdogra, the nearest airport; both are about 6 hours away by road.

ESSENTIALS

PERMITS   In addition to the standard visa, foreign visitors must be in possession of an **Inner Line Permit** (see "Acquiring your Sikkim Permit in Darjeeling," earlier in this chapter). This, together with your passport, must be carried at all times. If you wish to travel north of Gangtok or Pelling, you will require an additional endorsement or **Protected Area Permit** from Sikkim Tourism in Gangtok.

VISITOR INFORMATION   **Sikkim Tourism** (Mahatma Gandhi Marg; ℘ **03592/ 20-2634** or -2352; www.sikkimindia.com) is open Monday to Saturday, May through August, 10am to 4pm; March through April and September through October daily 9am to 7pm. The center has a computerized touch-screen kiosk that will provide more-or-less up-to-date tourist information (when it's working). This is where you can book highly recommended scenic helicopter rides. The office downstairs is where you must have your Sikkim permit endorsed if you intend to visit certain restricted areas in the state. There's also an **Information Counter** (℘ **0353/255-1036;** daily 10am–2:30pm) at Bagdogra Airport.

GETTING THERE   **Bagdogra** in neighboring West Bengal is the closest airport, and is served by flights from major cities like Kolkata and Delhi. From Bagdogra, Sikkim Helicopter Service runs daily 30-minute flights to Gangtok for around Rs 1,700 ($39), well worth it just for the views. Alternatively, taxis (4 hr.) and buses are available. Shared jeep services are also available from Darjeeling, Siliguri, and Kalimpong, all in West Bengal. These are highly affordable; book more than one seat for yourself, preferably the two front seats for the best views. If you're coming from Kathmandu, fly to **Bhadrapur** in east Nepal, and head to Gangtok via Kakarbhitta (on the Nepalese-Indian border) and Siliguri in West Bengal.

GETTING AROUND SIKKIM   Unless you pick up a helicopter from Bagdogra Airport, you will travel in Sikkim by road. Use either a private or shared jeep. Although roads are open throughout the year, bear in mind that all of Sikkim is mountainous and routes inevitably take far longer than they appear on maps. The shared taxi and jeep services from Gangtok to Pelling (Rs 130/$3) that depart twice a day at 7am and 12:30pm are served by **Nam Nam taxi stand;** book your seat in advance. Again, book both front seats, for the views, and also because drivers tend to pack way more people into the car than you'd have imagined possible. Sikkim's roads invariably traverse steep mountains and deep valleys, so travel can be exhausting (the journey to Pelling, via Ravangla, takes 5 hr.), but the scenery is spectacular. Within **Gangtok,** you're best off doing most of your wandering on foot; because of one-way roads, taxis are frequently required to skirt much of the city. To get to the Tibetology Institute and to Rumtek Monastery, you'll have to use a taxi.

GUIDED TOURS & TRAVEL AGENTS   **Blue Sky Tours & Travel** (Tourism Building, Mahatma Gandhi Marg; ✆ **03592/20-5113**) specializes in a jeep tour of northern Sikkim. They can also help you with local sightseeing, and offer a 2-day Monastery Tour that takes in several Buddhist monasteries in the state. Like all tour operators in Gangtok, their rates depend on the number of riders.

For trekking arrangements, try **Sikkim Tours & Travels** (Church Rd.; ✆ **03592/ 20-2188;** www.sikkimtours.com). **Tashila Tours & Travels** (✆ **03592/20-2978;** www.tashila.com) undertakes a range of services, including trekking, rafting, and specialist tours. **Modern Tours and Treks** (Mahatma Gandhi Rd., Gangtok; ✆ **03592/ 22-7319;** Wed–Mon 9am–9pm) organizes well-priced, all-inclusive treks and tours of Sikkim. **Siniolchu Tours and Travels** (✆ **03592/20-5569** or 94340-24572; slg_sinolchu@sancharnet.in; Mon–Sat 9am–1pm and 2–8pm) is reliable. Headquartered in Gangtok, it undertakes a wide range of spectacular treks and tours in various

---

View from the Sky

An alternative way to experience Sikkim is from the air. **Sikkim Helicopter Service** operates a five-seater throughout the year, closing only for repairs and maintenance. Bookings are taken at **Sikkim Tourism** in Gangtok (M.G. Marg; ✆ **03592/20-2352** or -2634). A 60-minute flight over western Sikkim costs Rs 3,750 ($85) per person (five people required), while the spectacular 90-minute Kanchenjunga flight costs Rs 7,500 ($170) per person (four people required). Flights must be confirmed the previous day. **Burtuk Helipad** (✆ **03592/20-5277** or 03592/22-1636) is 3km (2 miles) out of town.

⌒Fun Fact Who Will Rule the Black Hat Order?

In September 1992, an 8-year-old Tibetan boy named Ugen Thinley Dorjee was officially sanctified as the 17th Gyalwa Karmapa and new head of the "Black Hat" order, and recognized by the Dalai Lama as the true reincarnation of the 16th Karmapa. But controversy has surrounded Dorjee ever since his coronation at Tibet's Tshurpu monastery. Chinese authorities, welcoming him as a state guest, have been intent on using him as a political puppet, while a group of rival lamas have identified another candidate as the true reincarnation. In January 2000, Dorjee undertook a grueling 1,400km (858-mile) trek and escaped from Chinese-controlled Tibet in order to join the Dalai Lama in Dharamsala. There he waits for the dispute over his identity to be settled, hoping to take his place at Rumtek Monastery, which has been without a head since 1981.

---

regions of Sikkim and beyond. Most treks cost in the vicinity of $40 per person per day, and include tents, food, porters, yaks, and guides.

GANGTOK & ENVIRONS

Sikkim's capital sits at an altitude of 1,780m (5,800 ft.), straddling a high ridge where houses and concrete blocks spill down the hillside; below is the Ranipul River. With only 29,000 inhabitants, it's relatively laid-back and generally free from the malaise that stalks India's many overpopulated towns and cities. For visitors, the most noble of Gangtok's charms is its proximity to marvelous mountain vistas; the town itself is threatened by unchecked construction. A base for visitors who come to organize treks or wind down after a high-altitude experience, it's pleasant to roam around but certainly not packed with attractions. The town's most significant drawing card is the **Namgyal Institute of Tibetology** ⌐ (admission: Rs 10/25¢; Mon–Sat 10am–4pm), which houses a collection of Tibetan, Sanskrit, and Lepcha manuscripts, as well as statues, Buddhist icons, masks, scrolls, musical instruments, jewelry, ornaments, incense burners, and beautiful *thangkas* (painted or embroidered tapestry wall hangings). It's worth noting that at press time, some parts of Namgyal were under renovation.

Nearby, **Do-Drul Chorten** is a fine example of a whitewashed Buddhist stupa, encircled by prayer wheels. **Enchey Monastery** is a Tibetan Buddhist lamasery worth visiting, and the **Flower Exhibition Centre** (Rs 5/10¢ adults, Rs 5/10¢ camera), near White Hall, attracts orchid buffs. In the manner of traditional hill kingdom forts and castles, Sikkim's royalty once resided within the yellow tin-roofed palace in the uppermost reaches of the town. From here, the Chogyal and his family enjoyed the best views in Gangtok. Sadly, the Chogyal palace is off-limits to visitors. When the British turned up, they installed their very own "White Hall" alongside the palace and, despite initial bickering, soon got round to several decades of contented socializing.

Rumtek Monastery ⌐⌐ The region's top attraction lies 24km (15 miles) from Gangtok. Rigpe Dorjee, the "supreme head" of one of Tibetan Buddhism's four major sects—the Kagyu, or "Black Hat" order—revived it in 1959 after the Chinese invaded Tibet. Regarded as the richest Buddhist monastic center in India, Rumtek houses some of the world's rarest and most unique religious artifacts; its design is said to replicate that of the original Kagyu headquarters in Tibet. Try to get here during prayer times, when the red-carpeted benches are occupied by the Vajra chant and disciplinary master, who leads the chanting of prayers. The venerated part of the complex is the **Golden Stupa,** a 4m-high (13-ft.) *chorten* in which the mortal remains of the 16th Gyalwa Karmapa (founder of the Black Hat order; see box below) are enshrined. Gold-plated and embedded with jewels, turquoise, and coral, the stupa is kept in a locked shrine room, which must be specially unlocked for visitors. Ask a monk to help you track down the keeper of the key.

WHERE TO STAY & DINE

If you're traveling on a budget, **Mintokling Guest House** (© 03592/20-4226; mintokling@hotmail.com; doubles Rs 650–Rs 1,500 ($15–$34); all credit cards except American Express) is a Sikkimese home with fairly spacious, clean guest rooms; our favorite is no. 304. The owner is a fantastic source of information on Sikkimese history, especially if you're interested in the political lowdown; his mother was the niece of the last king of Sikkim.

Sikkim's smartest hotel, **Nor-Khill** (see below), also hosts its best restaurant, **Shangri-La** (© 03592/20-5637). Splurge on an all-inclusive full-course Sikkimese meal. Find out if stir-fried fiddlehead ferns or the popular *sisnu* (a dish made from stinging nettle) are available, and do try their juicy chicken *momos* (Tibetan dumplings). Book a table at the window. Nor-Khill also has the best pub in town, the cozy **Dragon Bar. Snowlion** (© 03592/20-2523 or -4962; all credit cards accepted) is equally good for Tibetan fare, including chicken *sha-dre* (rice noodles with a curry sauce) and *sumei,* or open *momos.* Adventurous diners can sample traditional *dre-thuk,* a thick, porridgelike rice soup topped with a mountain of finely grated cheese. They serve delicious, body-warming beverages—try the hot brandy toddy with brandy, rum, and cloves, or the hot whiskey lemonade.

Netuk House ★★ *Value* Buddhist prayer flags flutter above this gorgeously situated and well-run family guesthouse with real Sikkimese flavor. The warmly aristocratic Denzong family, who are always pleased to introduce guests to local culture, owns it. All accommodations are unique; four guest rooms are in the main house and six are in the colorful annex, with its traditional rainbow-hued Sikkimese-style facade. Guest rooms are simple but lovely, and have good, comfortable mattresses covered in crisp white linen. Carefully prepared traditional four-course Sikkimese meals are served in the dining room; just below is a charming Sikkimese-style living room with an old-fashioned wood-burning heater. There's also a lovely bar.

Tibet Rd., Gangtok 737 101. © 03592/20-2374 or 3592/22-6778. slg_netuk@sancharnet.in. 12 units. Rs 3,700 ($84) double. Rs 1,200 ($28) extra person. Rs 750 ($17) children 8–12, Rs 375 ($8.50) children 4–7, free for children under 4. Rates include all meals. No credit cards. **Amenities:** Restaurant; bar; TV lounge; travel assistance; sightseeing; car hire; laundry; doctor-on-call.

Nor-Khill ★★★ This stylish hotel offers the priciest and most luxurious accommodations in the state of Sikkim, fronted by a lovely lawn (sadly, overlooking Gangtok's new sports stadium). The newly renovated deluxe units resemble suites, with a large bedroom area extending off a comfortable and beautiful living area; views are excellent. Huge floral or dragon-motif rugs cover the wood tile floors, and the furnishings and fittings are carved and painted Sikkimese-style. Beds are a little narrow and slightly soft, but have lovely fabrics and scatter cushions. Bathrooms are spacious, with tubs and natural light. Standard doubles are spacious and equally beautiful; reserve room no. 43, which is large and well-positioned. The room rate includes all meals, served in the formal **Shangri-La Restaurant.**

Paljor Stadium Rd., Gangtok 737 101. ✆ **03592/20-5637** or 0359/22-0064. Fax 03592/20-5639. Reservations: 5 Park Row, 47 Park St., Kolkata 700 016. ✆ 033/2226-9878. Fax 033/2246-6388. www.elginhotels.com. 25 units. Rs 4,800 ($109) standard double. Rs 2,000 ($46) extra bed. Rates include all meals. AE, MC, V. **Amenities:** Restaurant; bar; travel assistance; currency exchange; gift shop; 24-hr. room service; babysitting; laundry; doctor-on-call. *In room:* Heater, TV.

NEAR RUMTEK
Where to Stay
Shambhala Mountain Resort ✦✦ *Value*   Occupying the side of a ridge, this pretty ivy-covered hotel is surrounded by rhododendrons in a peaceful setting. It has wonderful, good-value accommodations and a genuinely Sikkimese ambience, with smart, clean, bright public areas. Each deluxe room has a small private balcony overlooking a terraced valley slope, distant mountains, and the nearby Rumtek complex. For a good view, reserve room nos. 201 to 204. Alternatively, opt for one of two rather unique cottages—reached via a small footbridge. The all-wood bedrooms are filled with brightly painted Sikkimese tables, chairs, and cupboards, offset by pale-colored or white fabrics; the small, private patios have their own collections of fluttering prayer flags. Meals are taken in the beautiful wood-floor dining hall furnished with dark rattan chairs and decorated with Buddhist paintings, fans, and umbrellas.

Rumtek 737 135. ✆ **03592/25-2240** or -2275. Fax 03592/25-2240. shambhalamtnresorts@hotmail.com. 13 units. Room or cottage Rs 3,300 ($75) double with breakfast, Rs 3,900 ($88) double with breakfast and dinner, Rs 4,400 ($100) double with all meals. Children under 4 free, those ages 5–8 50%, 8–12 75%, and over 12, 90% of tariff. No credit cards. **Amenities:** Restaurant; bar; indoor games; local sightseeing; laundry; doctor-on-call. *In room:* Heater, TV.

PELLING & ENVIRONS
Traditionally a stopover for trekkers headed for Yoksum, Dzongri, and similar high-altitude spots in western Sikkim, Pelling has begun to establish itself as a tourist destination in its own right, and as a result, concrete lodges have sprung up indiscriminately to cash in on the passing trade. Nevertheless, the surrounding scenery is spectacular, and the sunrise behind snow-clad Khangchendzonga will leave you breathless. Besides hiking or rafting, the top attractions are the nearby monasteries. From Pelling, a pleasant 30-minute walk along the main road toward Geyzing will lead you to one of Sikkim's oldest and most revered monasteries, **Pemayangtse** ✦ (daily 7am–4pm), situated at 2,085m (6,672 ft.) in a cliff-top forest clearing. Set up as a monastery for *Ta-Sang,* or "pure monks" of the Nyingmapa order, Pemayangtse was established in 1705 by Lhatsun Chempo, one of the lamas who performed the consecration ritual of Sikkim's first king. Its prized treasure is a 7m-tall (22-ft.) wooden depiction of Guru

---

Himalayan Brew
Chang, made from fermented millet, is the brew of choice in Sikkim. It's usually served in a wooden tumbler (called a *tomba*) with a bamboo straw and should look like a small mountain of chestnut-colored caviar sprinkled with a few grains of rice. Believed to aid sleep, it supposedly never causes hangovers. Many Western travelers would disagree.

Husbands, Inc.

Part of Sikkim's unique high-altitude culture is the continued existence—typically in remote regions—of polyandrous communities, where one woman is married to a number of men. In some cases, a woman marries all the brothers from a single family. With the increasing modernization, however, such practices have now become rare.

Rinpoche's *Sang-tok-palri,* or "heavenly palace," encased in glass in the monastery's upper room. Note that it's worth trying to contact Yapo S. Yongda, who resides here—he's a fascinating source of information on Sikkimese history. Southeast of Pemayangtse (30-min. walk), on a lower hillock, are the ruins of the late-17th-century **Rabdentse Palace,** from where you can see **Tashiding Monastery** ⟨★★, one of the most idyllic, peaceful, and sublime monasteries in India. Hire a jeep from Pelling to get here (Rs 1,400/$32 round-trip). A mere glance at Tashiding's **Thongwa Rangdol,** Sikkim's most venerated *chorten,* will (if Buddhist legends are to be believed) absolve you of all your sins. Also of special significance is the *bhumpa,* a copper vase that contains the holy water used each year during the *Bhumchu* festival, when a sacred ritual reveals Sikkim's fate for the upcoming year. It's a somewhat stiff 50-minute hike in the opposite direction to hilltop **Sanga Choling Monastery** ⟨★—but it's worth it, for the most panoramic views around. Constructed in 1697, this is believed to be the second-oldest Buddhist monastery in Sikkim. Go when morning or evening prayers are held.

WHERE TO STAY & DINE

A cheaper option to Norbu Ghang, **Hotel Mount Pandim** is set atop a hill a 10-minute walk from Pemayangtse Monastery. Guest rooms and facilities are spartan, but they're generally clean, and the views over the surrounding valleys and expansive mountainside are awesome. Try to reserve deluxe room no. 203 (ⓒ **03595/25-0756** or -0573; www.sikkiminfo.com; doubles Rs 650–Rs 850/$15–$19). In Pelling itself, the best budget accommodations are at **Hotel Phamrong** (Upper Pelling; ⓒ **03595/ 25-8218** or -0660; mailphamrong@yahoo.com; doubles from Rs 950/$22), which has large en-suite rooms that generally come with fantastic views. Don't expect luxury, but the sunrises are brilliant. Pelling's best dining is at the Norbu Ghang Resort (see below), but the restaurant at tiny **Garuda** guest lodge (next door to Hotel Phamrong) serves a variety of dishes, including Tibetan and Sikkimese specialties.

Norbu Ghang Resort ⟨★   Norbu Ghang (which means "Jewel on the Hilltop") has the most tasteful accommodations in western Sikkim. It's built on four levels over a 2-hectare (5-acre) stretch of flower-speckled terraced hillside. The corrugated-roof cottages are fairly decent in size. All the best rooms and cottages have views of mighty Khangchendzonga (book cottage no. 601, 801, or 804). The resort also has Pelling's best restaurant, serving traditional Sikkimese cuisine.

Pelling 737 113. ⓒ **03595/25-8245,** -8272, or -0566. Fax 03595/25-8271. www.sikkiminfo.net/norbughang. 30 units. Rs 2,000 ($46) double, Rs 2,700 ($62) deluxe double; Rs 3,000 ($68) Denzong Suite. Rs 550 ($13) extra bed. MC. V. **Amenities:** Restaurant; bar; travel assistance; currency exchange; shop; room service; doctor-on-call. *In room:* Heater, TV.

TREKS THROUGH WESTERN SIKKIM 𝒜𝒜𝒜

Treks around western Sikkim are justifiably popular because of the spectacular views afforded throughout. If you want something relatively short and undemanding, the 4-day trek from Pelling to Tashiding and back is ideal, covering both cultural sights and majestic scenery. Far more challenging, and requiring more time and extra stamina, are the high-altitude treks to **Dzongri** (4,024m/12,870 ft.; 6 days) and **Goeche La** (4,940m/15,800 ft.; 9–10 days). There are also other treks to Singalila and Versay in the west, Greenlake in the north, and Kedi and Teenjure in the east. Trekking here is only allowed with a recognized trekking operator in Gangtok; a daily fee of $30 to $45 will include guides, porters, yaks, tents, and food. March through May, the fabulous—and less strenuous—5-day **Rhododendron Trek** through the exotic forests of the Singalila Range, near the border with Nepal, become possible. For trek operators, see "Essentials: Guided Tours & Travel Agents," above.

Appendix:
India in Depth

A great triangle of land thrusting out of Asia, past the Bay of Bengal and the Arabian Sea, and deep into the Indian Ocean, India is a vast country (similar in size to Europe) and home to an ancient culture with a host of historic and architectural treasures unparalleled in the world. But more than anything else, it is India's enigmatic "otherness" that so fascinates the first-time visitor, for perhaps no other country on earth can offer so much contrast—traveling within the subcontinent feels at times like traveling through time. From the snowy peaks of the Himalayas, where prayer flags flutter against an impossibly blue sky, to the golden deserts of Rajasthan and Gujarat, where women wear saris saturated with fuchsia and saffron; from the vast plains of Madhya Pradesh, dotted with ruins and tiger parks, to the lush tropical mountains and Paradisiacal beaches off the Malabar Coast, the spectrum of images and experiences is stupendous. Perhaps one of the most heterogeneous cultures in the world, with a mosaic of languages, dialects, religions, races, customs, and cuisines, India and its people cannot be defined, labeled, or pigeonholed—only experienced. Whether you're planning your trip to do a spiritual pilgrimage, view (or shop for) its myriad treasures, live like royalty in medieval palaces, unwind on unspoiled beaches, or simply indulge in the most holistic spa therapies known to man, India will leave an indelible impression on you. The following essays are merely a backdrop; to get to grips with the strange and fascinating world that is India, you will need to immerse yourself in some of the reading suggested at the end of this chapter. And travel to India again. And again. And again.

1 India Today

by Anita Pratap

Former CNN bureau chief for South Asia, freelance journalist, and columnist for *Outlook,* India's weekly newsmagazine

There are many ways to describe "modern" India, but perhaps the most fitting is "Land of Paradoxes." For whatever your understanding of India today, the exact opposite is probably equally true. Life has changed dramatically since India began to liberalize its economy in the 1990s, and yet it remains a land where several centuries exist simultaneously. If you visit one of its scientific centers, you could well believe you are at NASA, but walk to a village that still has no connection to a drivable road (and there are thousands of them), and you will find people living exactly as they did 2,000 years ago. More than 25% of the world's software engineers are Indian, but another 25% of the Indian population go to bed hungry every night. Women have risen to top positions of power and authority, yet millions struggle without the most basic human rights. India has the world's highest number of malnourished children, yet obesity in urban children is a new and menacing problem. The country has armed itself with nuclear weapons, but has difficulty providing drinking water to millions of its citizens. It ranks extremely low in the United Nations' Human Development Index, which measures quality of life (127th out of 177 countries), but in terms of purchasing parity, India is the fourth-biggest economy in the world after the United States, China, and Japan. No wonder India is confusing, confounding, incomprehensible. How can you make sense of this land? It's like emptying an ocean with a spoon.

All through the 1970s and even 1980s, Western diplomats and journalists predicted the "Balkanization" of India. It didn't happen. They predicted India would be a basket case. It didn't happen. In 1991, India's foreign exchange reserves plunged to a catastrophic $1 billion, barely sufficient to service 2 weeks of imports. India was forced to embark on a liberalization program, reducing aspects of government control such as high import tariffs and privatizing key sectors. Since then, India's economy has grown by an average of 6% annually, (in fact during 2004–05 India's $575-billion economy grew by a whopping 8.2%, a rate only rivaled by neighbor China), and today the reserves have reached a staggering $142 billion. According to statistics, the overall standard of living has improved since liberalization, but as rosy as all the numbers are, the truth is that the benefits of a booming economy have not reached farmers, who are a vast percentage of the population, and India still has the world's largest concentration of poor. Nearly 300 million people live without the basic necessities of life: water, food, roads, education, medical care, and jobs. These are the Indians living on the outer edges of the nation's consciousness, far away in remote tribal areas, barren wastelands, and dirty slums, totally outside the market economy. Their tragedy is that they lack the basic skills needed to gain entry into the marketplace. And no one is even trying to equip them.

This brings us to the inherent weakness of Indian politics. India is the world's largest democracy. Every national election is the biggest spectacle of fair and peaceful democracy that humankind has ever witnessed. And yet, increasingly you cannot deny that democracy is often a masquerade for a modern version of feudalism. Clan loyalties propel electoral victories. The victor rules his or her province like a medieval tribal chieftain, showing scant respect for merit or rule of law. Cronies are hand-picked for jobs, rivals are attacked or harassed, public funds are misused to promote personal agendas. Modern-day versions of Marie Antoinette abound in Indian democracy—during the acute summer water scarcity of 2003, the chief minister of Delhi, Sheila Dixit, actually urged her citizens not to bathe in tubs! Only a mere few thousand of Delhi's 12 million have access to tubs, and frequent water cuts are the real deterrent. And while the poor were dying of cold in January 2003 in nearby Uttar Pradesh, its chief minister, Mayawati, was strutting around in diamonds and celebrating her birthday with a cake the size of a minibus. One assumes that the withering media criticism that came her way would have wilted her arrogance but, far from being humbled, the lady turned her wrath on the media, countering that her low caste was the real reason for their criticism. Surprisingly, many low-caste people, whose cause she is supposed to champion, support her reasoning, marveling that she too can celebrate her birthday like India's rich. Never mind the waste of public funds that could have been used to buy blankets to save many people from freezing to death—Mayawati's outrageous behavior only filled them with pride and nationalistic fervor.

In fact, nationalism is one of the biggest growth industries in India, one that is guaranteed to stymie, if not wreck, genuine economic progress. In the last decade, the rise of Hindu nationalism has become a growing nightmare for India's Muslims and Christians. At the heart of this ideology is the belief that today's Muslims should be punished for historical wrongs perpetrated by medieval Muslim invaders and conquerors. The worst Hindu-Muslim rioting and looting happened in the western state of Gujarat in 2002, when Hindu mobs killed and maimed thousands of innocent Muslim civilians, including pregnant women and children, avenging another ghastly incident in which Muslim criminals roasted alive 58 Hindu pilgrims in a train. Nationalism also takes its toll in the dangerous Kashmir dispute that bedevils relations between the nuclear-capable neighbors India and Pakistan. The two countries have fought two of their three wars over Kashmir, engaged in another low-level conflict in 1998, and come to the brink of another in 2002, prevented mainly through diplomatic intervention by the U.S. Thankfully there has been a deep thawing in India-Pakistan relations since then, culminating in a joint statement issued by Prime Minister Vajpayee and President Musharraf at the SAARC Summit in Islamabad. Driven by popular enthusiasm and political initiatives on either side, the peace process has enjoyed a visible momentum with issues such as visa issuance, always a nightmare in either country, significantly improved. Though there is still a lack of progress in resolving many bilateral problems, at press time relations between the two countries were better than they had been in decades.

The problems of nationalism are often exacerbated by politicians who polarize Hindus and Muslims before elections in order to garner Hindu or Muslim votes— with Hindus constituting 80% of the population, Hindu nationalism clearly has a better chance of winning the electoral stakes. However, the general election of 2004 proved that the masses cannot be won over for long through this diabolical strategy of dividing communities, and in some subconscious way there seems to be a recognition that if divisive politics win, India will lose the opportunity to achieve her true destiny as a stable, prosperous giant in the 21st century. Deviating from the script, the Indian masses proved the media barons, opinion makers, psephologists (political scientists who study and even predict elections), exit-pollsters, and astrologers all wrong, and voted the Congress party back into power. The 2004 electoral upset for the BJP-led government was also in many ways a vote against the chauvinist, highly personalized campaign against Sonia Gandhi's foreign origins. In a country that is highly nationalistic and patriarchal, this was something of a surprise. But then India rarely follows a game plan, or delivers where expected.

Bill Clinton once said: "India remains a battleground for every single conflict the world has to win." Certainly India copes with massive problems—mounting corruption, joblessness, judicial bottlenecks with few convictions and delays of up to 20 years for delivering justice, AIDS, acute water shortages, poverty, disease, environmental degradation, unbearable overcrowding in metropolitan cities, crises of governance, sectarian violence, and terrorism. India adds one Australia to itself every year—*18 million people.* The rural poor (who form the majority) see children as an economic resource, the only security net for old age, and high child-mortality rates necessitate the need for more than one or two. Apart from India's huge natural growth rate, an estimated two million poor Bangladeshis slip into India every year in search of work.

It is really a miracle that India has not collapsed, but this is a country of remarkable stamina. The trouble is, India does not act until a crisis is full-blown. Indians are terrible at prevention, but terrific in crisis management. It is exasperating and frightening to see citizens and authorities insouciantly lurch towards the abyss. But once they reach the precipice, Indians are adept at pulling back quickly and effectively. They don't descend into chaos because they are adaptable and resilient. For if disparity is India's weakness, diversity and courage are her strengths. India has a strong network of grass-roots-level institutions, NGOs, and activists that form a kind of coral reef, erecting little barriers on which political and economic onslaughts falter, such as the recent attempts to build an industrial belt around the Taj Mahal that, once exposed in the media, were shelved. These onslaughts come from an array of "threats"—from local politicians to multinational corporations. Nobody can ride roughshod over India. Nobody can fool Indians. Foreigners may be smooth-talking, willing to bribe, have fancy degrees, and speak English with a beautiful accent. But they can neither arm-twist nor hoodwink Indians. The shenanigans of Enron were exposed first in India. India stood firm amid the Enron-orchestrated swirl of accusations of being difficult, corrupt, untrustworthy. All of which is true. But it was equally true of Enron. Eventually, it was Enron that went bust.

When they cannot do it their way and according to their schedule, politicians rail against the bureaucrats, trade unionists, judges, journalists, and NGOs. But this defensive "coral reef" is what has saved India from sliding precipitously to economic ruin. The pace of Indian economic reforms was widely attacked as too slow by the IMF and World Bank. And yet Joseph Stiglitz, winner of the Nobel Prize for Economics in 2001 and a former chief economist for the World Bank, now admits that India's caution and slow, deliberate steps are precisely what saved the nation from the catastrophic meltdowns and flights of capital that befell Asian and Latin American countries.

India has always been a giant and will continue to be a giant. But she will move at her own pace. She is not an Asian tiger. She is more like a stately Indian elephant. No one can whip or crack her into a run. If you try, the stubborn elephant will dig in her heels and refuse to budge. No power on earth can then force her to move. The desire for change and movement must come from within. India will move, but she will be slow, ponderous, circuitous. Progress will come, but it will come in measured steps, not necessarily in leaps and bounds. There is no point arguing whether this is good or bad. It is good and bad. And it is many things in between.

After all, this is India.

2 India Past to Present

by Nigel Worden
A professor of history specializing in Indian Ocean history

No visitor to India can fail to be overwhelmed by the combination of a bustling, modernizing nation and an ancient but omnipresent past. India's history is everywhere, in its temples and mosques, forts and palaces, tombs and monuments, but it has only recently become a single country, which makes its history a complex one. Successions of kingdoms and empires have controlled parts of the subcontinent, but none unified the whole—even the British Raj's "Jewel in the Crown of the Empire" excluded large swaths of territory ruled

Who is an authentic Indian and who isn't? Is India Indian? Does it matter?
Let's just say we're an ancient people learning to live in a recent nation . . .
                                        —Arundhati Roy, *The Algebra of Injustice*

by independent princes. Thus the accounts of history vary, and competing versions have often been the cause of bitter conflict. Given the tensions between Hindus and Muslims in South Asia, it is hardly surprising that the Islamic era in particular is highly controversial. Were the Muslims invaders and pillagers of an ancient Indian tradition, as Hindu nationalist historians claim? Or were they Indians who created a distinctive culture of architecture, painting, and literature by blending indigenous forms with Islamic influences? Is the Taj Mahal a uniquely Indian masterpiece, or a symbol of the Islamic oppressor? As is usually the case with history, it all depends on where you are, and who you're talking to.

ANCIENT INDIA   Historical accounts of India usually begin with the **Harappan civilization** of the Indus Valley, a sophisticated agricultural and urban society that flourished from 3000 to 1700 B.C. (about the same time as the earliest Egyptian civilization); although many of its sites are now located in latter-day Pakistan, you can view Harappan artifacts in places like the National Museum in New Delhi. Not much is known about the people, not least because their writing system has yet to be deciphered, but their active trade with the civilizations of the Euphrates (contemporary Iran and Iraq) show that northern India had links from very early on with the rest of Asia.

A more recognizably and distinctive "Indian" culture developed from around 1500 B.C in the northern part of the subcontinent, spreading steadily eastward in the 1st millennium B.C, although never penetrating to the far south. This is usually referred to as the **Vedic period.** The ancient written *Vedas* provide a rich record of this era, led by a Sanskrit-speaking elite, which embedded into India Hinduism the caste system (led by a Brahmin priesthood), and the dichotomy between a rural farming majority and an urbanized merchant class, all ruled by local kings and princes. A series of Vedic kingdoms rose and fell, each centered on a city, of which

Dateline

- **Circa 3000–1700 B.C.** Harappan civilization of the Indus Valley marks earliest farming communities in the region.
- **1500–600 B.C.** Vedic states in the north establish the basis of Hinduism and the caste system.
- **326 B.C.** Alexander the Great's army halts at the Indus.

- **322–185 B.C.** Mauryan state in North India; conversions to Buddhism under Asoka (reigned 272–232 B.C.).
- **A.D. 319–540** Gupta empire reunites northern India.
- **300–900** Pallava empire in Dravidian southern India.
- **900–1300** Chola empire in southern India.
- **1206–1400s** Islamic Delhi sultanates established in north.

- **1510** Portuguese establish first European coastal settlement in India.
- **1526** Mughal conquest of Delhi (returned permanently in 1555).
- **1556–1605** Akbar extends Mughal power.
- **1600** Founding of British East India Company.
- **1658–1707** Aurangzeb conquers south for Mughal empire.

Varanasi is today the oldest-living and best-known example. Much controversy surrounds the interpretation of the "Aryans," as the Vedic culture is known—some claim that they originated as invaders from the north who conquered and subjugated the local population, while Hindu nationalists today see them as the archetypal indigenous Indian—a controversy that makes Indian archaeology a tempestuous field of study. Whichever interpretation you buy into, the influence of the Vedic era is all-pervasive in modern Indian life, and the historical focus of a modern Hindu identity.

From the 6th century B.C., the Aryan states were themselves subject to invasions from the north, in a cycle of incursion and subsequent local adaptation that was to dominate much of India's history. Even Alexander the Great, hearing of the wealth and fertility of the area, tried to invade, but his army apparently refused to cross the Indus River and instead made their way back to Macedonia. Other invaders (or settlers, depending on your preference) of Greek, Persian, and central Asian origin moved in, challenging some of the indigenous states, such as Shakas of western India and the Magadha state of the northeast. In time, all of these newcomers were absorbed into the local population. It was during this period that

Siddhartha Gautama (Buddha) was born in latter-day Nepal; he later moved to India, where he sought—and found—enlightenment at Bodghaya, and starting teaching at Sarnath, just outside Varanasi.

The first large state to emerge in this region was under the **Mauryan rulers** (322–185 B.C.), who incorporated much of northern India, including the region west of the Indus; at its largest, it even reached south to Karnataka. The most famous of these rulers was **Asoka,** who converted to Buddhism after a particularly murderous episode of conquest pricked his conscience; he spread the Buddha's teachings throughout northern India, particularly at Sarnath and Sanchi, where you can still view the *stupas* (commemorative cairns) he built. Asoka's decrees, which were inscribed onto rock (literally), carved his reputation throughout the region, while his emblem of four back-to-back lion heads (which you can also view at Sarnath) has been adopted as the modern symbol of India.

Asoka's empire barely survived his death in 232 B.C., however, and in the subsequent centuries local states rose and fell in the north with alacrity. The **Gupta empire** emerged from A.D. 319 to 540 under Sumadra Gupta, who conquered the small kingdoms of much of northern India and Bengal, while his son extended

- **1739** Persian sacking of Delhi and removal of the Peacock Throne accelerates Mughal decline.
- **1757** Clive defeats *Nawab* of Bengal at Battle of Plassey, establishing British rule in Bengal.
- **1790s–1820s** British extend power in southern, western, and central India.
- **1856–57** Indian "Mutiny": uprising against British.

British sacking of Delhi and expulsion of Mughals.
- **1858** Dissolution of East India Company; India to be ruled directly from London.
- **1877** Queen Victoria declared Queen-Empress of India.
- **1885** Foundation of the Indian National Congress.
- **1890s** Bengal famine and plague epidemics.

- **1903** British capital moved from Calcutta to Delhi.
- **1905** Division of Bengal provokes boycott campaigns against British.
- **1906** Muslim League founded.
- **1915** Gandhi returns to India.
- **1919** Amritsar massacre galvanizes Indian nationalist opposition to British.

continues

its range to the west. This loose confederacy was marked by a reinvigoration of Hinduism and the power of the Brahmins, which reduced the influence of Buddhism in the subcontinent (though it had taken strong root in Sri Lanka and Southeast Asia). But Hun invasions from the north in turn destroyed Gupta power, and northern India was again split into numerous small kingdoms.

It should be noted that the southern part of India remained unaffected by these developments. With the exception of Asoka's Mauryan empire, none of the northern states extended their influence beyond the central plains, and South India developed its own economic systems, trading with Southeast Asia and across the western Indian Ocean as far afield as the Roman Empire. Dravidian kingdoms emerged, some of which established sizable empires such as the **Pallava** (A.D. 300–900) and **Chola** (A.D. 900–1300). Hinduism flourished, evident in the rich legacy of Dravidian temple architecture (notably at Thanjavur).

THE ISLAMIC ERA Even Indian historians refer to the period from the 10th to the 16th centuries as "medieval," but a more accurate characterization of it relates to the impact of Islam. Muslim influence from the northwest was evident in northern India from at least A.D. 1000, but it was only with the arrival of Islamic forces from the 13th century onward that its presence became dominant. A succession of fragmented and unstable Moslem states emerged around new centers such as Lahore (Pakistan), Delhi, and Agra, collectively known as the Delhi Sultanates. Conversions to Islam were made among the local population, mainly from the lower castes or where Hinduism was weaker, like in Bengal, but the majority of the population remained Hindu. In most areas the Muslim rulers and their administrators were but a thin layer, ruling societies that followed earlier traditions and practices.

In the south, Muslims made much less impact. Muslim raids in the 14th century instead led to unified Hindu resistance by the Vijayanagar empire centered in Hampi, which flourished in the south as one of the strongest Hindu states in Indian history, surviving until the 16th century.

By this stage a more vigorous wave of Islamization had emerged in the form of the **Mughals,** a dynasty that originated in the Persian borderlands (and was possibly driven south by the opposing might of Genghis Khan in central Asia). The Mughals established themselves initially in Kabul, then the Punjab, and in 1555 they finally conquered Delhi, which became their capital. Under **Akbar** (1556–1605) and **Aurangzeb** (1658–1707), the Mughals extended their empire south into the Deccan and, after defeating the Vijayanagar state, deep into the south, although their ambitions to conquer the entire subcontinent were stymied by the opposition of the Hindu Maratha states in the southwest.

Rulers such as Aurangzeb were not slow to show merciless terror against those who opposed them, but previous images of the Mughal empire's ruthless despotism have now been challenged by many historians, who point out that, other than Aurangzeb, the Mughal emperors were happy to allow local rulers to continue in power, provided they regularly sent tribute to Delhi and provided troops and cavalry when needed. Close to Delhi, the fiercely independent Hindu princes of Rajasthan retained their authority so long as they did not openly flout Mughal rule. Taxes were levied on landowners, but the levels were in general no higher than before. Trade and local textile production flourished in many regions, notably in Bengal and Gujarat. Muslim law, Persian language, and administrative structures were introduced, although in many outlying parts of the empire, local customs continued.

But by the 18th century, the Mughal empire was in decline. Some of this was the result of direct opposition, especially from the Marathas, who were consolidating their power in the southwest, but in other respects, decline might have been a product of the Mughal empire's own prosperity. Local regions such as Bengal, Oudh, and the Punjab began to benefit from economic growth and to assert their independence. When Delhi was attacked by yet more incursions from the north, culminating in the sacking of the city by Persians in 1739 and the hauling off of the fabulously valuable Peacock Throne, symbol of Mughal power, local regions went their own way. In Bengal, the local ruler made an agreement with foreign merchants who had appeared along the coast in the 17th century, allowing them to built a small settlement at the mouth of the Hooghly River (later to become Calcutta) and to trade in cotton and cloth in return for tribute. These foreign merchants were members of the British East India Company, formed in 1600, which had failed to establish a niche in the more lucrative spice trade of Southeast Asia, and was thus forced to settle for less-plum pickings along the Indian coastline: They obtained permission from locals to set up stations at Surat and what were to become the cities of Madras and Bombay. They were not the only Europeans to settle in India; the Portuguese had first established a base in Goa in 1510, and in the 17th century the Dutch made similar agreements with local rulers in Bengal, Nagapatnam, and the Malabar coast, while the French set up shop in Pondicherry. Even the Belgians, Danes, and Swedes formed trading companies, but unlike the others, they had little impact on the indigenous culture.

As was the case elsewhere, it was the British who moved from trade to empire in India. In part this was the outcome of inter-European rivalries: The English grabbed French ships and produce in India (along with French Canada) in the **Seven Years' War** (1756–63), then moved on Dutch posts in India and Sri Lanka after the Napoleonic wars. But the main impetus came from their dealings with Indian rulers. In Bengal, English traders were making a killing, often marrying local women and living the high life. Frustrated by their continued and unwelcome presence, the local *Nawab* attacked the English settlement at Calcutta in 1756, imprisoning a number of people in a cramped cell, where some suffocated. The "Black Hole of Calcutta" martyrs became a rallying cry to justify further incursions by the British: Troops were shipped to Calcutta, which defeated the *Nawab* at Plassey the following year and again in 1764. The British East India Company filled the local power vacuum—and although nominal vassals of the Mughals still lived in the Red Fort in Delhi, the East India Company was effectively the local government.

In the course of the late 18th and early 19th centuries, the Company's area of influence grew apace. Presenting itself as the "defenders of Bengal," it forged alliances and provided military support for local rulers in areas such as Bihar and the northwestern regions, then moved in when they defaulted on repayments. By the mid–19th century, English armies (manned overwhelmingly by Indian troops) overran Oudh and the Punjab. In the south the Company moved inland from Madras to the Carnatic and across to Malabar. It inherited the Mughals' rivalry with the Marathas (the region around latter-day Mumbai), which erupted into open warfare in 1810 and led to the Company's conquest of the western coast and its hinterland.

While extending their power base, the Company still claimed allegiance to the Mughals, whose emperor retained nominal control in Delhi. But this, too, was to end. In 1856 and 1857, following decades of resentment against British policies and their impact, an army mutiny (caused by the use of animal fat on bullet cartridges, which affronted the Hindus) triggered uprisings against the British across northern and central India. Despite claims by later nationalist historians that this was a united revolt against the foreign oppressor, most of the violence in the "Indian Mutiny" of 1856 to 1857 was by Indians against other Indians, in which old scores of class, religious, or regional rivalries were festering. Nonetheless, epic stories abounded of Indian valor or British heroism and martyrdom (depending, again, on which side told them). The British, taken by surprise, only regained control by the skin of their teeth—and by ruthless retaliation. Some of the resisters had appealed to the Mughal emperor to reassert control over India, which in an unwise moment he had agreed to do. The British army sacked Delhi, forced the emperor into exile, and declared the end of the Mughal empire. But London was unimpressed by the chaos that the East India Company rule and policies had brought, and moved to abolish the Company's charter, effectively establishing direct rule from London. The pretence was over. India was now to be ruled by a new foreign power.

THE RAJ The East India Company was replaced by a new system of government. The British Crown was represented in India by a viceroy sent out from London who presided over a professional class of British-born and (mainly) Oxbridge-educated administrators appointed through the Indian Civil Service. Most Indians never saw this relatively small body of men (never exceeding 5,000 at any one time), and they in turn were dependent on the military (still primarily composed of Indian troops, or *sepoys,* lorded over by a British officer class) and on another army of Indian lesser-ranking administrators, lawyers, and civil servants, who were prevented by race from rising to the upper ranks. For India, unlike British Africa and Australasia, was not to be a settler colony. The British initially played on the fiction that they were the legitimate successors to the Mughals, mounting spectacular *durbars* (receptions) to demonstrate their power and the loyalty of India's princes–in 1877 the occasion was used to declare an absent Victoria "Queen-Empress of India"; it was only in 1911 that the reigning British monarch finally attended a durbar. The British built a set of administrative buildings in "New Delhi," declared the capital in 1903, that today are considered the finest architectural achievements of the empire.

In many ways, British rule was a new experience for India. For one thing, the entire subcontinent was viewed as a single whole, despite the continuation of nominally independent princely states in many of its central regions. With a mania characteristic of the Victorian, the British mapped the landscape; surveyed the diverse systems of landholding; separated inhabitants by race, language, and caste (for census purposes); and built the huge railway network that connects the country today. Much of this had the practical purpose of raising revenues from trade and taxation, since the British were determined that the Raj should be self-financing. But it also created a body of knowledge that was to shape many of their political and social policies, and to solidify categories of race and caste that had earlier been somewhat more permeable.

The Indian economy in the era of the Raj became closely dependent on British and other imperial markets, with promotion of the export of raw materials rather than internal industrialization, although by the early 20th century, parts of Bengal and the region around Bombay were starting to manufacture for local purchasers. It was from the "new" Indian administrative and mercantile classes that the first stirrings of opposition to British rule came. The local modernizers demanded equal access to economic and political opportunities, rather than a return to India's precolonial past. Thus the first **Indian National Congress (INC)** was formed in 1885, with members primarily from Bengal, Bombay Presidency, and Madras. The INC carried out its proceedings in English, and called for access to the higher ranks of the civil service (with examinations for entry held in India, not in Britain) and for relief of the heavy levies on Indian-produced local textiles. By the turn of the 20th century, after the disastrous famine and plague epidemic that broke out in Bengal in the 1890s, more extremist members of the INC were demanding *swaraj,* or "self-rule," although what they had in mind was a degree of self-government akin to the British dominions in Canada, Australia, or South Africa, rather than total independence. An unpopular administrative division of Bengal in 1905 led to a boycott of British imports, and some Bengali intellectuals began to evoke Hindu notions of a free Indian nation. The British conceded limited electoral reform, granting a local franchise to a tiny percentage of the propertied, but they ominously listed voters in separate voter rolls according to whether they were Muslim or Hindu; a separate **Muslim League (ML)** was formed in 1906.

World War I, in which large numbers of Indian troops served the British cause, dampened anti-British protests and saw a pact between the ML and the INC, not least because of vague British promises of meaningful change once the war was won. But in 1919, British General Dwyer opened fire on a demonstration held in the enclosed space of the Jallianwala Bagh in Amritsar, killing and wounding over 2,000. This gave Indian nationalism its first clear martyrs, and the callousness with which Dwyer's actions were applauded by the British general public enflamed matters further.

The period between the two world wars saw a seismic transformation of Indian nationalism, growing from the protests of a small elite to a mass-based movement that overwhelmed the British. The figure with whom Indian nationalism is most associated is **Mohandas Karamchand Gandhi,** the "Mahatma." After an early career in law, he developed his concepts of *satyagraha* (nonviolent protest) and passive resistance in defending Indian interests in colonial South Africa before he returned to his native India in 1915. Gandhi persuaded the INC to embrace a concept of a united India that belonged to all Indians, irrespective of religion or caste. Mass support for Congress campaigns of non-cooperation with the colonial state was ensured by well-publicized and symbolic campaigns such as the 1930 march from Ahmedabad to the Gujarat coast to defy a salt tax by making salt from sea water. Membership of the INC soared to over two million. But not all of Gandhi's ideas were triumphs—he was much criticized by some for his failure to support the socialist leanings of Bombay factory workers, while others took little interest in his appeal for religious tolerance or equal acceptance of the outcast *dalits.* The British granted a degree of self-government to India in 1935, although only at the provincial level. Another group

that did not accept INC's call for unity was the Muslim League. Fearing Hindu domination in a united India (revealed by the 1935 elections), they began, under their leader Mohammed Ali Jinnah, to call for a separatist Islamic state named "Pakistan" (after the initials of areas they claimed: Punjab, the Afghan states, Kashmir, and Sind). At first, few took this seriously, although Gandhi was alarmed at the divisive trends.

World War II was to change everything. Gandhi and INC leaders called in 1942 for the British to "quit India" and were imprisoned. Although many Indian regiments in the British army supported the Allies, a number of other Indians joined the Japanese-trained Indian National Army under the INC leader Subhas Chandra Bose. After 1945, Muslim and Hindu violence broke out, with each side claiming power. The new Labor government in Britain was now anxious to divest itself of its troublesome Raj and sent Lord Mountbatten as a new viceroy to oversee the process. Mountbatten's decision that the British should cut their losses as quickly as possible by leaving in August 1947 took everyone by surprise. More seriously, he agreed to partition the country to appease Jinnah and the Muslim League rather than risk continuing civil war in the new state. In a frenzy of activity, "Partition" became official, and the boundaries of the new Pakistan were summarily drawn across the map, splitting the Punjab into two and dividing communities. Millions of refugees spent Independence Day desperately trying to get to the "right" side of the border, amid murderous attacks in which well over a million lost their lives. The trauma of these months still casts a deep shadow over the subcontinent. While the British Raj in India lasted less than a hundred years, the processes that led the British to divide the country into two states, India and Pakistan, have fundamentally shaped the modern nation state.

INDEPENDENT INDIA For almost 4 decades, independent India was to be governed by the INC, initially under its leader Jawaharlal Nehru, who had led Congress in the negotiations of 1946 and 1947. Gandhi was bitterly disillusioned by Partition, even proposing at one stage that Jinnah be made prime minister of India to restore unity. This was enough to alienate him from some Hindu nationalists, one of whom assassinated the Mahatma in 1948. Such rival visions of the Indian nation were to plague the new country.

The most pressing political issues centered around India's relations with Pakistan. The Indian government was (rightly) accused of fomenting dissent in East Pakistan in the late 1960s, leading to war in 1971. Continued conflict has centered around Kashmir, an independent princely state with a predominantly Muslim population but whose Hindu ruler, under threat from Muslim forces from Pakistan, placed it under Indian rule in 1948. Pakistani and Indian troops have tensely faced each other in the territory ever since. With the development of nuclear weapons by both states, and a militant Kashmiri independence movement, the area is a potential powder keg of international concern.

Under Nehru, internal stability was obtained, remarkable considering the circumstances of India's independence, and until his death in 1964, he established India as the world's leading postcolonial democracy, a key player (along with Sukarno's Indonesia) in the non-alignment movement that avoided Cold War conflicts. Communal rivalries were downplayed by a focus on India's secular status. Regional separatism continued to threaten unity, especially Tamil opposition to Hindi linguistic domination from Delhi, but this was resolved by a reorganization of local states along linguistic lines.

Nonetheless, Congress never obtained more than 45% of the national vote and only held power because of the division of its political opponents. After Nehru's death, its attraction weakened. In an attempt to restore its popularity, his daughter, Indira Gandhi (no relation to the Mahatma), became prime minister in 1966. From 1969, she implemented a more populist program of social change, including land reform and a planned economy—a program that was to alienate some of the richer landowners and regional party leaders. Economic restructuring led to strikes and civil opposition in the cities, and in 1975, a State of Emergency was declared that lasted 2 years. Believing that she had reasserted control, Indira Gandhi held elections in 1977. The result was the first defeat for Congress, although no party was able to form a united government to replace it, and by 1980 Gandhi was back in power.

The INC never regained its previous level of control, however. Resentment by Sikhs at their failure to secure autonomy in the Punjab culminated in 1984 with the Indian army's siege and capture of the main Sikh temple at Amritsar with thousands of casualties, and Indira Gandhi was assassinated by her Sikh bodyguards. Her son, Rajiv Gandhi, succeeded her, and instituted new programs of economic liberalization, but he also embroiled India unsuccessfully in the ongoing civil war in Sri Lanka, leading to his assassination in 1991 by a Tamil activist. Although his widow, the Italian-born Sonia Gandhi, inherited leadership of Congress, the era of the Nehru family's domination of Indian politics (which has been compared to the Kennedy family's political impact in the U.S.) was thought by many to be over.

In 1989, Congress was again defeated at the polls, this time led by the Hindu nationalist **Bharatiya Janata Party (BJP).** Although the BJP initially failed to hold

Impressions

'And do thy duty, even if it be humble,' says the Aryan Gita, 'rather than another's, even if it be great. To die in one's duty is life; to live in another's is death' . . . Indian poverty is more dehumanizing than any machine . . . men in India are units, locked up in the straitest obedience by their idea of their dharma. The blight of caste is not only untouchability; it is the overall obedience it imposes.

— V. S. Naipaul, *India: A Wounded Civilization*

together a coalition government, its strength grew. It accused Congress of allowing India to be dominated by outside interests, including globalized economic forces, but more specifically by Indian Muslims who it considered to be unduly tolerated under Congress's secular state policies. In 1992, a BJP-led campaign led to the destruction of the mosque at Ayodhya, believed to be the birthplace of the Hindu god Ram.

In the 1996 elections the BJP defeated a Congress government plagued by accusations of corruption and emerged as the leading group in the coalition governments that have ruled India since. Under the BJP Prime Minister Atal Behari Vajpayee, tensions with Muslim Pakistan increased, with both sides testing and threatening the use of nuclear weapons, especially in conflicts over Kashmir. Fortunately, 2003 saw a welcome cooling. In 2004 the confident BJP government called for early elections, hoping to cash in on a booming economy and developments in the India-Pakistan peace process.

Contrary to all expectations, however, the BJP did not win. Instead the Congress, which had been the opposition party for 8 years, took much of the vote, as did the Left (which unexpectedly won more than 60 seats in the 543-member house). Together with other parties, they formed a ruling coalition, the UPA (United Progressive Alliance). The next surprise came soon after, when the victorious Sonia Gandhi, leader of the Congress, declined to take on the job of prime minister, appointing instead Manmohan Singh, a former Indian finance minister, to the chair.

By mid-2005, the Congress had been in power for just one year; the opposition BJP was in disarray, its political plans to disrupt the functioning of the Congress-led government a mess, and its own dirty linen being washed in public view almost daily. Simultaneously, the normally tenuous relations between India and Pakistan had reached a new high—despite obstacles like unresolved disputes and cross-border terrorism—a strategic factor in the development of the region as a whole.

3 The Religions of India

The diversity of religious belief and practice in India is both unique and somewhat confounding. What follows is a very brief introduction to the religions that took root in India; this will hopefully provide some insight into the patterns and diversity that exist. Tribal religions, ostensibly pagan, often mixed with elements and practices of mainstream religions, still exist in isolated pockets, but are declining rapidly and are not covered here.

HINDUISM   To begin the unending journey of studying India, you need to take the first step toward understanding Hinduism, the religion of some 80% of India's population. It can only be a "first step" for, like India itself, Hinduism defies attempts to clearly define or categorize, and what may be described as universal Hindu religious practice in one place may very well be contradicted by others elsewhere.

Hinduism has no ecclesiastical order, nor is there a central religious book. (While many religious texts like the ancient *Upanishads* and *Bhagavad-Gita* exist, they are not the "word of god" like the Bible or the Koran.) It is not possible to convert to Hinduism; you are born Hindu, usually into one of the four main hierarchical castes (Brahmin, or "priest"; Kshatriya, or "warrior"; Vaisya, or "merchant"; Sudra, or "peasant") or—at the very bottom of the social order—you are born Dalit, better known as the "untouchables." Unlike organized religions such as Christianity or Islam where truth is specified, categorical, linear, and uni-dimensional, truth in Hinduism is in fact extremely multidimensional—contradictions are not bad, but inevitable. Unlike Christianity and Islam, which say there is one true path that leads to one God, Hinduism says there are many paths that lead to many gods (some say—probably hyperbolically—330 million gods, who epitomize a host of human qualities, from gluttony to vengefulness). This intrinsic Hindu acceptance of diversity and multiplicity has defined India's history, allowing it to successfully adapt by absorbing the beliefs of successive invaders. Even today it is not difficult for Hindus to look upon Allah or Jesus as deities worthy of veneration—more than half the devotees who flock to pray at the famous Muslim shrine in Ajmer in North India or at the fabled Velankanni Church in South India are Hindus.

Rather than a formal religion, Hinduism is considered a way of life, or *Sanatan Dharma* (an eternal path), in which the universe is part of an endless cycle of creation, preservation, and dissolution. The human soul is also part of this cycle, endlessly reincarnated, and seeking freedom. According to Hindu philosophy, we determine our destiny by our actions. *Karma* is the law of cause and effect through which individuals create their own destiny by virtuous thoughts, words, and deeds. Each of us can control the nature and experiences of the next life *(karma)* by "living right" or *dharma*—through *dharma* (a righteous pattern of conduct), individuals determine their *karma.* By resolving all *karmas,* the soul can finally attain *moksha,* an escape from the cycle of life.

There are many sects and denominations within Hinduism, and priests, *sadhus* (holy men), and other spiritually enlightened individuals are important parts of the religious process: *Bhakti* is devotion to and communication with the gods, which devotees express in the performance of *puja* (religious ritual-like prayer), *bhajan* (devotional singing), and meditation. *Puja* may be performed at home or in a temple in front of an idol(s) of god(s). It involves some kind of offering to the gods (flowers being the most common) and is an essential part of the practice of Hindu faith. For Hindus the physical symbol or idol of god is the material form through which god appears in this world. Hindu devotees may worship Shiva, Kali, Ganesha, or any one of thousands of gods and manifestations of gods in the Hindu pantheon, and may believe in a Supreme Being who is either their chosen deity or some unnamed force even higher than the gods. Hinduism believes in the existence of three worlds: The material universe we live in, the astral plane where angels and spirits live and, finally, the spiritual world of the gods.

BUDDHISM Though Buddhism originated in India around 500 B.C., when the Indian prince Siddhartha Gautama attained enlightenment and became the Buddha (Enlightened One) at Bodhgaya, only some eight million still practice the belief in India, the majority of them from Tibet or Nepal or converted during the mass conversion of lower castes by the anti-caste leader Dr. Ambedkar in 1956. (The Buddhist following is, of course, far higher outside India, particularly in the rest of Asia; even in the West, Buddhism appears to be on the rise.)

Unlike any other religion, Buddhism does not advocate belief in a godhead; it instead expects the individual to seek truth within his own experience and control his dharma and karma without relying on divine intervention. Buddhist philosophy is based on the idea that life is riddled with conflict and pain caused by desire (or craving) and ignorance, and to escape from this suffering you need to follow the Eight-Fold Path to gain Enlightenment, or *nirvana*. The Eight-Fold Path advocates Right Understanding, Right Thought, Right Speech, Right Action, Right Mode of Living, Right Endeavor, Right Mindfulness, and Right Concentration. As is the case in Hinduism, each of us carries our karma through a cycle of rebirths until the attainment of nirvana. Meditation, chanting, counting beads, and lighting lamps are some of the ways in which Buddhists pursue their spiritual goal of enlightenment.

JAINISM This began as a reform movement and became a religion under the 24th Jain *trithankara* (prophet) Vardhaman, later called Mahavira (incidentally, a contemporary of Buddha), in the 6th century B.C. Though it never spread beyond India, today some four million Jains live here, predominantly in Maharashtra and Gujarat. The principles of Jainism include strict vegetarianism and extreme reverence for all forms of life— even insects and plants are believed to have *jives,* or souls. Jains believe in reincarnation and salvation (or *moksha*), which can be achieved through respect for and consideration of all forms of life, and living a life of asceticism, meditation,

fasting, and pilgrimage to holy places. According to Jain philosophy, the soul journeys through 14 stages before the final burning up of all karma and freedom from bondage.

There are two sects of Jains—Svetambara and Digambara. Svetambara followers vow to avoid intentional injury to others and to lead a life of honesty and detachment from worldly passions. The Digambaras are even more strict in their beliefs and practices—as a symbol of their complete detachment from material possessions, the highest monks of this sect wear no clothes. In addition, unlike Svetambaras, Digambaras believe women cannot achieve *moksha.* Their temples are among the finest in India: Karnataka's famous Sravanbelagola Temple is a Digambara temple, while the celebrated Dilwara (Mount Abu, Rajasthan) and Shatrunjaya (Palitana, Gujarat) temples are important Svetambara places of pilgrimage.

SIKHISM This religion emerged in the 15th century out of a rejection of caste distinctions and idolatry under the founder, Guru Nanak, who wanted to bring together the best of Hinduism and Islam. Nine gurus, all of whom are equally revered by Sikhs, followed him, and today there are over 19 million Sikhs in India, mostly in Punjab. Like Hinduism, Sikhism accepts the doctrine of reincarnation, but worship is based on meditation and not ritual or asceticism. Like Muslims, Sikhs believe in one omnipresent universal God; worship takes place in *gurdwaras,* and the holy book is the *Granth Sahib.* The 16th-century Golden Temple at Amritsar is the holiest Sikh place of worship (and has a truly sacred atmosphere).

Charity is an important aspect of the religion, and the gurdwaras always run community kitchens where anyone can eat free. Sikhs are expected to never cut their hair—which makes Sikh men, who wind their long hair under large turbans and sport large beards, one of the most easily recognized male communities in India.

OTHER RELIGIONS Zoroastrianism, **Judaism, Islam,** and **Christianity** did not originate in India, but are all represented, with Islam and Christianity (which, incidentally, originated within 600 years of each other) the second- and third-largest religious groups, respectively, in India. Muslims comprise about 13% of the population, while Christians form just 2%. Every major Christian and Muslim sect and denomination is represented, and the beliefs and practices of each group vary accordingly, some with indigenous nuances. But overall they tend to follow the main tenets of these religions as practiced worldwide. It is estimated that only some 5,000 Jews still live in India, mostly in Mumbai, and these numbers continue to dwindle. Zoroastrianism, one of the world's oldest religions, dating back to the 7th or 6th century B.C., arrived in India in the 10th century A.D. with refugees fleeing religious persecution in Persia (latter-day Iran). Though numerically they are a tiny religious minority (70,000), the descendants of these refugees (called **Parsis**) have made a distinctive mark as a social and economic group in India. Followers believe in a single God, Ahura Mazda, whose prophet Zarathustra is their guide, and fire is considered sacred and symbolic of God. Parsis therefore worship in a Fire Temple (closed to non-Parsis), and Zoroastrian philosophy regards life as an eternal battle between the forces of good and evil. Again, the path to overcome evil is through good thoughts, words, and deeds. Where possible, their dead are placed in dry wells at a Tower of Silence to be consumed by vultures. This practice is based on the belief that since dead matter pollutes, cremation and burial would pollute the respective elements. Today's Parsis regard this unique method of disposing of the dead as being useful to the cycle of life even after death.

4 Indian Cuisine

by Niloufer Venkatraman
Anthropologist, writer, and dedicated foodie

Indian cooking is one of the great cuisines of the world. Like the country itself, however, it varies greatly from region to region, and you'll discover a great deal more to savor than the ubiquitous *kormas* and *tikka* masalas (known to the naive simply as "curry") with which most Westerners are familiar. Not only does each Indian community and ethnic and regional group have a distinct cuisine, but there is a great deal of fusion within the country—subtle variations and combinations you're only likely to pick up once you are familiar with the basics. A good way to sample a variety of dishes in a particular region is to order a *thali* (multicourse meal), in which an assortment of items is served. Basic staples that tend to be served with every meal throughout the subcontinent are rice, *dal* (lentils), and/or some form of *roti* (bread). The following is a brief summary of regional variations and general dining tips.

SOUTHERN STATES Food from the coastal areas of India almost always contains a generous quantity of coconut— besides using it in cooking, most Maharashtrian homes offer grated coconut as a garnish to every dish. Rice also dominates the food of southern India, as do their "breads," which are more like pancakes and made of a rice (and/or dal) batter—these *appams, idiapams,* and *dosas* are found throughout the south. *Dosas* are in fact a South Indian "breakfast" favorite (consumed anytime), as are *idlis* and *vadas,* all of which have become part of mainstream cooking in many parts of India. *Idli* is a steamed rice and lentil dumpling, *dosa* a pancake (similar batter), and *vada* a deep-fried doughnut-shaped snack. All should be eaten fresh and hot with a coconut chutney and *sambar,* which is a specially seasoned *dal* (lentils), also eaten with steamed rice. In Tamil Nadu a large number of people are vegetarian, but in Kerala, Goa, and Mumbai, you must sample the fresh fish! Delicious kebabs and slow-cooked meals are what you'll find in Hyderabadi cuisine; inspired by the courts of the *Nawabs* (nobles), it's similar to Mughlai cooking, but stronger in flavor.

NORTHERN STATES   India's great meat-eating tradition comes from the Mughals and Kashmiris, whose *rogan josh* and creamy *korma* dishes, along with kebabs and *biryanis,* have become the backbone of Indian restaurants overseas. The most popular tradition—tandoor (clay oven) cooking—is part of India's Mughal gastronomic heritage. Tandoor dishes are effectively "barbecued" vegetables, *paneer* (Indian cheese), or meat that has been marinated and tenderized in spiced yogurt, cooked over coals, and then either served "dry" as a kebab or in a rich spiced gravy like the *korma.* Recently revived is the tradition of *dum pukht,* enjoyed by the erstwhile *Nawabs* of Awadh in Lucknow and the surrounding area. All the ingredients are sealed and slow-cooked in a pot, around which coals are placed. Nothing escapes the sealed pot, preserving the flavors.

NORTHWEST (PUNJAB) SPECIALS Besides trying the various tandoor dishes, you should order *parathas:* A Punjabi specialty, this thick version of the traditional chapati is stuffed with potatoes, cabbage, radish, or a variety of other fillings. Be aware that many North Indians love their ghee (clarified butter); sensitive stomachs

(or those watching their weight) should simply specify that they would prefer their *paratha* without ghee. A general note of caution when dining in North India: If the menu specifies a choice between oil and ghee as a cooking method, you should probably specify the former. And keep in mind that if you exclusively eat oily, highly pungent, so-called Punjabi fare, you are bound to feel ill, so make sure you vary your meals by dining at South Indian restaurants, which combine a healthy balance of carbohydrate and protein (rice and dal); in northern states you will find *rotis* (breads) combined with *rajma* (kidney beans), *puris* (bread) with *chole* (chickpeas), and so on.

EASTERN STATES   Freshwater fish (such as *hilsa, bekti,* and *rohu*) take pride of place at the Bengali table, which incidentally considers itself to be the apotheosis of Indian cooking. In Bengal, mustard oil (which has its own powerful flavor) is the preferred cooking oil. Sweets are another Bengali gift to the world; these are made from milk that has been converted to *paneer* (Indian cheese) and that has names like *rosogolla* (or *rasgulla*) and *sandesh.*

SPICES   Literally hundreds of spices (masalas) and spice combinations form the culinary backdrop to India, but a few are used so often that they are considered indispensable. Turmeric *(haldi)*—in its common form a yellow powder with a slightly bitter flavor—is the foremost, not least for its antiseptic properties. Mustard seeds are also very important, particularly in the South. Cumin seeds and coriander seeds and their powders are widely used in different forms—whether you powder, roast, or fry a spice, and how you do so, makes a big difference in determining the flavors of a dish. Chili powder is another common ingredient, available in umpteen different varieties and potencies. Then there are the vital "sweet" spices—cardamom *(elaichi)*, clove *(lavang)*, cinnamon *(dalchini)*—which, along with black pepper *(kali miri)*, make up the key ingredients of the spice combination known as *garam masala*. Though tolerance to spicy food is extremely subjective, let your preference be known by asking whether the item is spicy-hot *(tikha hai?)* and indicating no-chili, medium-spicy, and so on. "Curry powder" as it is merchandised in the West is rarely found or used in India. "Curry" more or less defines the complex and very diverse combination of spices freshly ground together, often to create a spicy saucelike liquid that comes in varying degrees of pungency and varies in texture and consistency, from thin and smooth to thick and grainy, ideally accompanied by rice or breads.

STAPLES & ACCOMPANIMENTS

All over the country, Indian food is served with either the staple of rice or bread, or both—the most popular being unleavened (pan-roasted) breads (called *rotis*); tandoor-baked breads; deep-fried breads (*puris* and *bhaturas*) or pancake-style ones. Chapatis, thin whole-wheat breads roasted in a flat iron pan *(tava)*, are the most common bread eaten in Indian homes, though these are not as widely available as restaurant breads. The thicker version of chapatis are called *parathas*, which can be stuffed with an assortment of vegetables or even ground meat. Tandoor-roasted breads are made with a more refined flour and include *naans*, tandoori *rotis*, and the super-thin *roomali* (handkerchief) *rotis*. Tandoor breads turn a little leathery when cold and are best eaten fresh.

Dal, made of lentils (any of a huge variety) and seasoned with mustard, cumin, chilies, and/or other spices, is another Indian staple eaten throughout the country. *Khichdi*, a mixture of rice, lentils, and spices, is a great meal by itself and considered comfort food. In some parts it's served with *kadhi*—a savory sour yogurt–based stew to which chickpea flour dumplings may be added. You'll usually be served accompaniments in the form of onion and lime, chutneys, pickles, relishes, and a variety of yogurt-based salads called *raita*. *Papads* (roasted or fried lentil flour discs) are another favorite food accompaniment that arrive with your meal in a variety of shapes, sizes, and flavors.

MEAT A large number of Indians are vegetarian for religious reasons, with entire towns serving only vegetarian meals, but these are so delicious that meat lovers are unlikely to feel put out. Elsewhere, meat lovers should probably (unless you're dining in a top-end big-city restaurant) opt for the chicken and fish dishes—not only are these usually very tender and succulent, but the "mutton" or "lamb" promised on the menu is more often than not goat, while "beef" (seldom on the menu—beef is taboo for most Hindus, and the ban on cow slaughter continues to be a raging national debate) is usually water buffalo. Again, there are regional differences, like in "Portuguese" Goa, where pork is common.

SWEETS Indians love sweets (called *mithais, mishtaan*, or "sweet meats"), and they love them very sweet. In fact, Western palates often find Indian sweets *too* sweet; if this is the case, sample the dry-fruit-based sweets. Any occasion for celebration necessitates a round of sweets as a symbol of spreading sweetness (happiness). Every region of the country has a variety of specialty sweets made from an array of ingredients, but they are largely milk-based. This includes *pedas* and *laddus* (soft, circular), *barfis* (brownielike), *halwas* (sticky or wet), *kheer* (rice pudding–like), and so on. Whatever you do, don't miss the Indian *kulfi*, a creamy, rich ice cream flavored with saffron, nuts, or seasonal fruit.

FRUITS If the spiciness of the meals unsettles your stomach, try living on fruit for a day. You'll get a whole range of delicious tropical varieties (with any luck, in a basket in your hotel room) ranging from guavas and jackfruit to lychees and the most coveted fruit of them all, the mango. More than 200 varieties of mangoes are grown in India, but the most popular ones (Alphonso or *aphoos*) come from Maharashtra (Mar–June); try to taste one when you're in Mumbai.

BEVERAGES *Chai* (tea) is India's national drink. Normally served in small quantities, it is hot, made with milk usually flavored with ginger and/or cardamom, and rather sweet unless you request otherwise. Instant coffee is widely available (and may be mixed in your five-star hotel's "filter coffee" pot), but in South India you'll get excellent fresh brews. Another drink worth trying is *lassi*, liquefied sweetened yogurt. *Note:* The yogurt is sometimes thinned with water, so you're only safe consuming lassis in places where they can assure you no water was added at all, or where they will make it with bottled water (that you purchase separately). Lassi's close companion is *chaas,* a savory version that is very thin and served with Gujarati/Rajasthani meals. With southern food, it is served with a flavorful assortment of herbs and spices. In general, you should avoid ice in any beverage unless you are satisfied that it is made from boiled water.

EATING ETIQUETTE Eating with your hands: Indians generally eat with their hands, and although many don't do so in five-star Westernized restaurants, the majority will in most other places. Even the simplest restaurant will be able to provide a spoon as cutlery, but if you really want to experience your meal in an authentic manner, follow suit. Note that you should ideally only use your right hand (though in places where tourists go,

people are unlikely to be offended if you use your left). In the North, where the food is "drier," you are traditionally not supposed to dirty more than the first two digits of your fingers. In the South, where the food is much "wetter," you may use the whole hand to eat.

Sharing your food: It is typically Indian to share food or drinks, even if you don't really want to. On long train journeys, you're likely to meet Indian families carrying a lot of food, which they will invite you to share—do sample some, if only to get a taste of home cooking. In return, you can buy them a round of tea or cold drinks when the vendors come by.

Sharing food at a restaurant is another Indian norm; menus are set up to cater to this style of dining. So, for example, if two or more of you go to a Mughlai restaurant, you would order perhaps two kinds of kebabs, two kinds of meat/vegetable entrees, one rice, and several breads *(rotis).* It's a good way to try a range of items.

The hygiene of *jootha:* While sharing is good manners, *jootha* is considered offensive in many parts. This refers to drinking from the same glass, eating with the same spoon, taking a bite out of someone's sandwich, or "double dipping." To share a bread or snack, break off a piece; when sharing a bottle of water, don't put your mouth to it but tilt your head back and pour. Although there are no definite rules about what is permissible or not, just make sure that you use common courtesy when sharing a meal with others.

SALADS The practice of eating Western-style salads (except raw onion) is not very common, but most restaurants do have them on the menu. Beware that it is only advisable to eat these in top-end restaurants, and make sure that the vegetables have been freshly cut and washed in boiled water.

STREET FOOD   Even in smaller cities like Indore and Jaipur, street food has a fantastic tradition and following. *Samosas, vadas, bhelpuri, sev, bhajias,* and a host of deep-fried foods are all delicious, and you should try them on your trip. It's not easy for the first-time visitor to figure out which street foods are safe to eat, however—best to look for an outlet where loads of people are lined up; this means that neither the food nor the oil have been around long. Alternatively, ask your hotel for suggestions.

5 Reading India

by Jerry Pinto
Author, journalist, and poet

More than almost any other destination, India demands that you immerse yourself in the local culture to make sense of all you see and experience. And wherever you're headed in India, there's probably a novel you can read to explore the ways people are shaped by the landscape and history around them.

LITERATURE/FICTION   The late R. K. Narayan, one of the grand old men of Indian letters, offers a panoramic view of village life in India. He focuses on a gentle prelapsarian village in *Malgudi Days* (Penguin), a good introduction to his work. For a more politicized investigation of the caste system, you might want to read U. R. Ananthamurthy's *Samskara* (Oxford University Press, translated from Kannada), which deals with a dilemma that convulses a village after the death of an unclean Brahmin; or Raja Rao's *Kanthapura* (New Directions), set in a village in South India that has to face the storms of Mahatma Gandhi's civil disobedience movement.

Small-town India is well represented in Arundhati Roy's Booker Prize–winning novel, *The God of Small Things* (HarperCollins), which will make you want to travel the waterways of Kerala to see the village life she describes so vividly. Bhalchandra Nemade's *Cocoon* (National Book Trust) is often referred to as India's *Catcher in the Rye.*

Each of the big cities has at least one big novel. Mumbai's industrial past is presented in a charming story of two boys who grow up in a tenement in Kiran Nagarkar's *Raavan and Eddie* (Penguin India), while its underbelly has been graphically documented in the doorstop-size *Shantaram* (Penguin India) by Gregory David Roberts. Mumbai is also where Salman Rushdie grew up, and the city is one of the backdrops of his Booker of Bookers, *Midnight's Children* (Vintage), which tells of two babies swapped at birth, one Hindu and one Muslim, one rich and one poor, both born on the stroke of midnight at India's independence. Mumbai is also the backdrop for his more notorious *The Satanic Verses* (Viking). Rushdie's style of magic realism laced with Mumbai's street lingo was anticipated in G. V. Dessani's single brilliant novel, *All About H Hatterr* (Penguin India).

Kolkata has inspired a plethora of books, including Amit Chaudhuri's plangent tale of growing up in *A Strange and Sublime Address* (Vintage) and Amitav Ghosh's *The Hungry Tide* (Houghton Mifflin), which takes off from the 300-year-old city and stirs up sediment of language and memory in the distributaries of the Ganga, in the Sundarbans. Delhi has an eponymous novel, *Delhi* (Viking India), by one of India's most widely read writers, Khushwant Singh; the book deftly mixes history with contemporary life. (Singh's *Train to Pakistan* [Penguin India] should be read alongside Bhisham Sahni's *Tamas* [Penguin India] to understand the complicated ambivalence of India's relationship with its Islamic neighbor, Pakistan.) Chennai has been well-captured in C. S. Lakshmi's collection of short stories, *A Purple Sea* (University of Nebraska Press).

Another novel to sample is Vikram Seth's compendious look at arranged marriage, *A Suitable Boy* (HarperCollins). This enjoyable novel is set in several cities. If you drive from Varanasi to Agra, you will pass by the scene, described by Seth, of a disaster that befell pilgrims there in the 1980s. (You may also find yourself incorporating the phrase "a tight slap" into your speech; don't ask—just read.) Other novels of repute include Rohinton Mistry's charming stories of the minuscule Parsi community in *Such A Long Journey* (Random House) and *A Fine Balance* (Faber & Faber), with its unforgettable characters, set during 1975's State of Emergency; I. Allan Sealey's fictionalization of the life of the adventurer Claude Martin in *The Trotternama;* and Anita Desai's *Baumgartner's Bombay,* which takes a compassionate but clear-eyed look at German Jews, refugees from the Holocaust, who stayed on after the British left.

NONFICTION A good way to start a hot debate (as if an excuse were needed) is to be seen reading V. S. Naipaul's *India: A Million Mutinies Now* (Vintage). Many Western readers respond to the mixture of fear and fascination with which Naipaul considers the subcontinent. A far more contemporary and intriguing account of the nation-state that has remained a democracy for most of its 50-year history is offered by Sunil Khilnani's *The Idea of India* (Farrar, Straus & Giroux).

Journalist P. Sainath's *Everybody Loves A Good Drought* (Penguin India) has won 13 international awards at last count for his account of the country's poorest districts and the ways in which development schemes almost never help the ostensible beneficiaries. Suketu Mehta's *Maximum City* (Viking) captures the frenetic mood of Mumbai with its breathtaking scrutiny of the city's underbelly. Read it in association with *Bombay, Meri Jaan* (Penguin India; edited by Jerry Pinto and Naresh Fernandes), an anthology of writings about the city that includes names as varied as Andre Gidé and Duke Ellington. Gita Mehta's *Karma Cola* (Vintage) is an acerbic and witty investigation into the way in which unscrupulous gurus marketed Indian spirituality to credulous Westerners in search of "enlightenment."

Those interested in Indian spirituality will uncover a wealth of material. A good way to begin is to look at Kamala Subramaniam's *The Mahabharata* (Bharatiya Vidya Bhavan), the great epic tale of the war between two clans related by the ties of kinship. *The Mahabharata* also contains the *Bhagavad–Gita* or "The Celestial Song," which is often seen as the core of Hindu beliefs. *The Ramayana* (Penguin) by R. K. Narayan offers a good introduction to the epic of Rama, who is exiled and whose wife, Sita, is abducted by the demon king Ravana. Penguin India also does a compact series that includes *The Book of Krishna* by Pavan K. Varma, *The Book of the Buddha* by Arundhathi Subramaniam, and *The Book of the Devi* by Bulbul Sharma.

For a more academic approach to Indian history, try the somewhat pedantic *Modern South Asia: History, Culture, Political Economy,* by Sugata Bose and Ayesha Jalal (Routledge); *A History of*

India, by Peter Robb (Palgrave); or *A Concise History of India* by Barbara Metcalf and Thomas Metcalf (Cambridge University Press).

This is just a start. But be warned—the writing on India is as seductive as the place it describes. Once hooked, you'll want more.

6 Bollywood & Beyond: India on the Big Screen

by Jerry Pinto & Keith Bain

Mumbai's Hindi film industry, called Bollywood, is the biggest producer of films in the world, churning out hundreds of movies annually, all of which feature super-kitschy images of buxom, bee-stung-lipped heroines gyrating to high-pitched melodies while strapping studs thrust their groins in time to lip-synched banal-and-breezy lyrics. These are wonderful, predictable melodramas in which the hero is always valiant and virile, the woman always voluptuous and virtuous. The battle between good and evil (a bankable hero and a recognizably nasty villain) must be intense, long-winded, and ultimately unsurprising—audiences do not pay good money to be challenged, but to be entertained.

Before you choose to spend a hot sub-tropical afternoon watching a Hindi film, know that these films are long, averaging about 3 hours. This is because they are constructed more like Elizabethan plays or old operas. Their audiences do not come for tragedies or for comedies but for full-scale performances that give them everything: the chance to laugh and cry, to bemoan the violence done unto the hero, and the opportunity to cheer as justice is done. These films are also made in defiance of the Aristotelian requirements of unity in time and space, and require from you a willing suspension of disbelief. And though the genre film has just begun—a few historicals such as *Devdas* and *Parineeta* (The Espoused) (2005); some horror films like *Kaal* (Time) (2005) and *Darna Mana Hai* (Fear is Forbidden) (2003); and some war films, including *Lakshya* (Goal) (2004) and

Mission Kashmir (2000)—most Hindi films still work on this principle.

The top-bracket Bollywood stars, including the 65-year-old Amitabh Bachchan and the 40-something Shah Rukh Khan and Aamir Khan, are paid incredible sums by Indian standards, earning close to a million dollars for a film simply because they are the names that will bring in the audiences and the "repeat audiences." As it is all over the world, women get paid much less, often half of what the male stars are paid, but stars like Rani Mukherjee and Preity Zinta have their devoted followings.

To view Bollywood movies as the be-all and end-all of India's film industry would be akin to thinking that big-budget blockbusters are the only movies made by the U.S. film industry; in fact, Bollywood is only responsible for a small part of the huge number of films produced by India in several languages. The first Indian director to make international art audiences sit up and take notice was Kolkata-based Satyajit Ray. Although he made his films in the 1950s, he received a Lifetime Achievement Oscar for his prolific body of work in 1992. Operating out of West Bengal's "Tollywood," Ray made movies that were the antithesis of Bollywood's; he was the director who stated that "the man in the street is a more challenging subject for exploration than people in the heroic mold" and that he found "muted emotions more interesting and challenging." Ray directed some 40 feature films, documentaries, and short subjects, of which *Pather Panchali* (Song of the Little Road) in 1955, *Aparajito* (The Unvanquished) in

1956, *Apur Sansar* (The World of Apu) in 1959, and *Goopy Gyne Bagha Byne* (The Adventures of Goopy and Bagha) in 1968 were the most internationally acclaimed. There are, of course, other exceptions, like Guru Dutt, one of Bollywood's most successful directors of the 1950s, whose film **Pyaasa** (1957) was recently nominated one of the world's 100 best films by *Time* magazine.

Because India produces more than 700 films a year, it is in fact impossible to be monolithic about all products and speak of only a certain kind of film. Until recently, the government financed arthouse cinema, and there are signs of a growing "indie" movement in which young directors scrape together the finances and make the kind of films they want as opposed to the formulaic catch-all colorful song-and-dance extravaganzas that financiers are comfortable backing.

Be assured, however, that playing in a theater near you will be a film in which the rich hero meets the poor heroine and falls almost instantly in love. He will declare this in song, and the scene will change to New Zealand, Switzerland, or Southeast Asia, depending on which country is most eager to attract the new beneficiaries of India's globalization. The couple will find obstacles put in their path, some by their parents and others by the villain, who will at some point have cast his lecherous eyes on the heroine. Fairly standardized violence will follow—not as well-choreographed as that in Hong Kong movies, but about as believable in execution and scale. After this comes a misunderstanding that paves the way for another song expressing the grief of betrayal or the pain of parting or that sets up what the industry calls an "item number" (which may have derived from Mumbai slang for a pretty young thing, or an "item") in which a young dancer performs the equivalent of a pole dance for the audience. When the air is cleared, justice and peace have returned to the world, the good have been rewarded, and the villains are dead or rounded up. At the film's end, you will either be floored by the extravagant color, ravished by floods of emotion, and converted to another way of telling stories; or you will be repulsed by excess and sickened by melodrama and the way in which Caucasian extras are used to represent the decadent sexualized Other. But you will not be unmoved.

Index

A Guide for Every Type of Traveler

FROMMER'S® COMPLETE GUIDES

For independent leisure or business travelers who value complete coverage, candid advice, and lots of choices in all price ranges.

These are the most complete, up-to-date guides you can buy. Count on Frommer's for exact prices, savvy trip planning, sight-seeing advice, dozens of detailed maps, and candid reviews of hotels and restaurants in every price range. All Complete Guides offer special icons to point you to great finds, excellent values, and more. Every hotel, restaurant, and attraction is rated from zero to three stars to help you make the best choices.

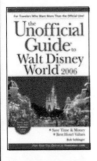

UNOFFICIAL GUIDES®

For honeymooners, families, business travelers, and anyone else who values no-nonsense, *Consumer Reports*–style advice.

Unofficial Guides are ideal for those who want to know the pros and cons of the places they are visiting and make informed decisions. The guides rank and rate every hotel, restaurant, and attraction, with evaluations based on reader surveys and critiques compiled by a team of unbiased inspectors.

FROMMER'S® IRREVERENT GUIDES

For experienced, sophisticated travelers looking for a fresh, candid perspective on a destination.

This unique series is perfect for anyone who wants a cutting-edge perspective on the hottest destinations. Covering all major cities around the globe, these guides are unabashedly honest and down-right hilarious. Decked out with a retro-savvy feel, each book features new photos, maps, and neighborhood references.

FROMMER'S® WITH KIDS GUIDES

For families traveling with children ages 2 to 14.

Here are the ultimate guides for a successful family vacation. Written by parents, they're packed with information on museums, outdoor activities, attractions, great drives and strolls, incredible parks, the liveliest places to stay and eat, and more.

Visit Frommers.com

WILEY
Now you know.

A Guide for Every Type of Traveler

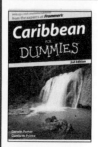

FOR DUMMIES® TRAVEL GUIDES

For curious, independent travelers.

The ultimate user-friendly trip planners, combining the broad appeal and time-tested features of the For Dummies guides with Frommer's accurate, up-to-date information and travel expertise. Written in a personal, conversational voice, For Dummies Travel Guides put the fun back into travel planning. They offer savvy, focused content on destinations and popular types of travel, with current and extensive coverage of hotels, restaurants, and attractions.

SUZY GERSHMAN'S BORN TO SHOP GUIDES

For avid shoppers seeking the best places to shop worldwide.

These savvy, opinionated guides, all personally researched and written by shopping guru Suzy Gershman, provide detailed descriptions of shopping neighborhoods, listings of conveniently located hotels and restaurants, easy-to-follow shopping tours, accurate maps, size conversion charts, and practical information about shipping, customs, VAT laws, and bargaining. The handy pocket size makes it easy to carry them in your purse while you shop 'til you drop.

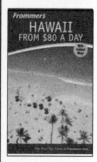

FROMMER'S® DOLLAR-A-DAY GUIDES

For independent travelers who want the very best for their money without sacrificing comfort or style.

The renowned series of guides that gave Frommer's its start is the only budget travel series for grown-ups—travelers with limited funds who still want to travel in comfort and style. The $-a-Day Guides are for travelers who want the very best values, but who also want to eat well and stay in comfortable hotels with modern amenities. Each guide is tailored to a specific daily budget and is filled with money-saving advice and detailed maps, plus comprehensive information on sightseeing, shopping, nightlife, and outdoor activities.

FROMMER'S® PORTABLE GUIDES

For short-term travelers who insist on value and a lightweight guide, including weekenders and convention-goers.

Frommer's inexpensive, pocket-sized Portable Guides offer travelers the very best of each destination so that they can make the best use of their limited time. The guides include all the detailed information and insider advice for which Frommer's is famous, but in a more concise, easy-to-carry format.

Visit Frommers.com

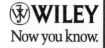

Now you know.

FROMMER'S® COMPLETE TRAVEL GUIDES

Alaska
Amalfi Coast
American Southwest
Amsterdam
Argentina & Chile
Arizona
Atlanta
Australia
Austria
Bahamas
Barcelona
Beijing
Belgium, Holland & Luxembourg
Belize
Bermuda
Boston
Brazil
British Columbia & the Canadian
  Rockies
Brussels & Bruges
Budapest & the Best of Hungary
Buenos Aires
Calgary
California
Canada
Cancún, Cozumel & the Yucatán
Cape Cod, Nantucket & Martha's
  Vineyard
Caribbean
Caribbean Ports of Call
Carolinas & Georgia
Chicago
China
Colorado
Costa Rica
Croatia
Cuba
Denmark
Denver, Boulder & Colorado Springs
Edinburgh & Glasgow
England
Europe
Europe by Rail

Florence, Tuscany & Umbria
Florida
France
Germany
Greece
Greek Islands
Hawaii
Hong Kong
Honolulu, Waikiki & Oahu
India
Ireland
Italy
Jamaica
Japan
Kauai
Las Vegas
London
Los Angeles
Los Cabos & Baja
Madrid
Maine Coast
Maryland & Delaware
Maui
Mexico
Montana & Wyoming
Montréal & Québec City
Moscow & St. Petersburg
Munich & the Bavarian Alps
Nashville & Memphis
New England
Newfoundland & Labrador
New Mexico
New Orleans
New York City
New York State
New Zealand
Northern Italy
Norway
Nova Scotia, New Brunswick &
  Prince Edward Island
Oregon
Paris
Peru

Philadelphia & the Amish Country
Portugal
Prague & the Best of the Czech
  Republic
Provence & the Riviera
Puerto Rico
Rome
San Antonio & Austin
San Diego
San Francisco
Santa Fe, Taos & Albuquerque
Scandinavia
Scotland
Seattle
Seville, Granada & the Best of
  Andalusia
Shanghai
Sicily
Singapore & Malaysia
South Africa
South America
South Florida
South Pacific
Southeast Asia
Spain
Sweden
Switzerland
Texas
Thailand
Tokyo
Toronto
Turkey
USA
Utah
Vancouver & Victoria
Vermont, New Hampshire & Maine
Vienna & the Danube Valley
Vietnam
Virgin Islands
Virginia
Walt Disney World® & Orlando
Washington, D.C.
Washington State

FROMMER'S® DOLLAR-A-DAY GUIDES

Australia from $60 a Day
California from $70 a Day
England from $75 a Day
Europe from $85 a Day
Florida from $70 a Day

Hawaii from $80 a Day
Ireland from $90 a Day
Italy from $90 a Day
London from $95 a Day

New York City from $90 a Day
Paris from $95 a Day
San Francisco from $70 a Day
Washington, D.C. from $80 a Day

FROMMER'S® PORTABLE GUIDES

Acapulco, Ixtapa & Zihuatanejo
Amsterdam
Aruba
Australia's Great Barrier Reef
Bahamas
Berlin
Big Island of Hawaii
Boston
California Wine Country
Cancún
Cayman Islands
Charleston
Chicago

Disneyland®
Dominican Republic
Dublin
Florence
Las Vegas
Las Vegas for Non-Gamblers
London
Los Angeles
Maui
Nantucket & Martha's Vineyard
New Orleans
New York City
Paris

Portland
Puerto Rico
Puerto Vallarta, Manzanillo &
  Guadalajara
Rio de Janeiro
San Diego
San Francisco
Savannah
Vancouver
Venice
Virgin Islands
Washington, D.C.
Whistler

FROMMER'S® CRUISE GUIDES

Alaska Cruises & Ports of Call

Cruises & Ports of Call

European Cruises & Ports of Call

FROMMER'S® DAY BY DAY GUIDES

Amsterdam	London	Rome
Chicago	New York City	San Francisco
Florence & Tuscany	Paris	Venice

FROMMER'S® NATIONAL PARK GUIDES

Algonquin Provincial Park	National Parks of the American West	Yosemite and Sequoia & Kings
Banff & Jasper	Rocky Mountain	Canyon
Grand Canyon	Yellowstone & Grand Teton	Zion & Bryce Canyon

FROMMER'S® MEMORABLE WALKS

Chicago	New York	Rome
London	Paris	San Francisco

FROMMER'S® WITH KIDS GUIDES

Chicago	National Parks	Toronto
Hawaii	New York City	Walt Disney World® & Orlando
Las Vegas	San Francisco	Washington, D.C.
London		

SUZY GERSHMAN'S BORN TO SHOP GUIDES

Born to Shop: France	Born to Shop: Italy	Born to Shop: New York
Born to Shop: Hong Kong, Shanghai & Beijing	Born to Shop: London	Born to Shop: Paris

FROMMER'S® IRREVERENT GUIDES

Amsterdam	Los Angeles	Rome
Boston	Manhattan	San Francisco
Chicago	New Orleans	Walt Disney World®
Las Vegas	Paris	Washington, D.C.
London		

FROMMER'S® BEST-LOVED DRIVING TOURS

Austria	Germany	Northern Italy
Britain	Ireland	Scotland
California	Italy	Spain
France	New England	Tuscany & Umbria

THE UNOFFICIAL GUIDES®

Adventure Travel in Alaska	Hawaii	Paris
Beyond Disney	Ireland	San Francisco
California with Kids	Las Vegas	South Florida including Miami &
Central Italy	London	the Keys
Chicago	Maui	Walt Disney World®
Cruises	Mexico's Best Beach Resorts	Walt Disney World® for
Disneyland®	Mini Las Vegas	Grown-ups
England	Mini Mickey	Walt Disney World® with Kids
Florida	New Orleans	Washington, D.C.
Florida with Kids	New York City	

SPECIAL-INTEREST TITLES

Athens Past & Present	Frommer's Exploring America by RV
Cities Ranked & Rated	Frommer's NYC Free & Dirt Cheap
Frommer's Best Day Trips from London	Frommer's Road Atlas Europe
Frommer's Best RV & Tent Campgrounds in the U.S.A.	Frommer's Road Atlas Ireland
	Retirement Places Rated

FROMMER'S® PHRASEFINDER DICTIONARY GUIDES

French	Italian	Spanish